Europe, 1789
W9-DGH-707
40°E
FINLAND
(Sweden)
Gulf of Bothnia
Torneälven
Umeälven
Åbo
Helsingfors
Vyborg
St. Petersburg
Stockholm
Saaremaa
Gotland
Öland
Baltic Sea
Lake Ladoga
Lake Onega
Volkhov
URAL MTS.
Volga
Moscow
RUSSIAN EMPIRE
Dvina
Neman
Danzig (Poland)
Minsk
POLAND
Vistula
Warsaw
Bug
Silesia
Kiev
Dnieper
Don
Donets
Galicia
Carpathian Mts.
HABSBURG POSSESSIONS
Southern Bug
Dniester
Prut
Moldavia
Buda
Pest
Tisza
Hungary
Transylvania
Siret
Maros (Mureș)
Drava
Belgrade
Wallachia
Bucharest
Danube
Kuban'
Caspian Sea
Black Sea
CAUCASUS MTS.
Morava
Balkan Mts.
MONTENEGRO
Maritsa
Vardar
OTTOMAN EMPIRE
Constantinople
Sea of Marmara
ASIA
Aegean Sea
Ionian Sea
Athens
N
0
200
400 mi.
400 km
Crete
(Ottoman Empire)
Cyprus

SCRIBNER LIBRARY OF MODERN EUROPE

EUROPE
1789 TO 1914

ENCYCLOPEDIA OF THE AGE OF INDUSTRY AND EMPIRE

EDITORIAL BOARD

SCRIBNER LIBRARY OF MODERN EUROPE

EUROPE 1789 TO 1914

ENCYCLOPEDIA OF THE AGE OF INDUSTRY AND EMPIRE

Volume 3

Ibsen to Owen

John Merriman and Jay Winter

EDITORS IN CHIEF

CHARLES SCRIBNER'S SONS

An imprint of Thomson Gale, a part of The Thomson Corporation

Detroit • New York • San Francisco • San Diego • New Haven, Conn. • Waterville, Maine • London • Munich

Europe 1789 to 1914: Encyclopedia of the Age of Industry and Empire

John Merriman
Jay Winter
Editors in Chief

For more information, contact
Thomson Gale
27500 Drake Rd.
Farmington Hills, MI 48331-3535
Or you can visit our Internet site at
http://www.gale.com

LIBRARY OF CONGRESS CATALOGING-IN-PUBLICATION DATA

Europe 1789 to 1914 : encyclopedia of the age of industry and empire / edited by John Merriman and Jay Winter.
p. cm. — (Scribner library of modern Europe)
Includes bibliographical references and index.
ISBN 0-684-31359-6 (set : alk. paper) — ISBN 0-684-31360-X (v. 1 : alk. paper) — ISBN 0-684-31361-8 (v. 2 : alk. paper) — ISBN 0-684-31362-6 (v. 3 : alk. paper) — ISBN 0-684-31363-4 (v. 4 : alk. paper) — ISBN 0-684-31364-2 (v. 5 : alk. paper) — ISBN 0-684-31496-7 (ebook)
1. Europe–History–1789-1900–Encyclopedias. 2. Europe–History–1871-1918–Encyclopedias. 3. Europe–Civilization–19th century–Encyclopedias. 4. Europe–Civilization–20th century–Encyclopedias. I. Merriman, John M. II. Winter, J. M.
D299.E735 2006
940.2'8–dc22 2006007335

This title is also available as an e-book and as a ten-volume set with Europe since 1914: Encyclopedia of the Age of War and Reconstruction.
E-book ISBN 0-684-31496-7
Ten-volume set ISBN 0-684-31530-0
Contact your Gale sales representative for ordering information.

Printed in the United States of America
10 9 8 7 6 5 4 3 2 1

CONTENTS OF THIS VOLUME

L

M

CONTENTS OF OTHER VOLUMES

VOLUME 1

C

VOLUME 2

C (CONTINUED)

D

E

F

G

H

VOLUME 4

P

Q

R

S

VOLUME 5

T

MAPS OF EUROPE, 1789 TO 1914

The maps on the following pages show the changes in European national boundaries from 1789 to 1914, including the unification of Italy and of Germany.

Europe, 1789
International border
City
N
0 100 200 mi.
0 100 200 km
Norwegian Sea
Faroe Islands
Shetland Islands
Orkney Islands
SWEDEN
Gulf of Bothnia
FINLAND (Sweden)
NORWAY (Denmark)
Helsingfors
Gulf of Finland
St. Petersburg
Christiania
Stockholm
Moscow
Scotland
Edinburgh
North Sea
Baltic Sea
RUSSIA
DENMARK
Copenhagen
Königsberg
Ireland
GREAT BRITAIN
Dublin
PRUSSIA
POLAND
Hanover
Berlin
Warsaw
Wales
England
Amsterdam
NETH.
London
Saxony
Brussels
Austrian Netherlands
HOLY ROMAN EMPIRE
Bohemia
Moravia
GALICIA
ATLANTIC OCEAN
HABSBURG POSSESSIONS
Paris
Austria
Vienna
Bavaria
Munich
Buda
Pest
Moldavia
TRANSYLVANIA
HUNGARY
SWISS CONFED.
Tyrol
FRANCE
Bay of Biscay
Wallachia
Black Sea
Milan
VENICE
PIEDMONT
Venice
Genoa
Florence
TUSCANY
PAPAL STATES
RAGUSA
MONTENEGRO
Constantinople
Adriatic Sea
ANDORRA
OTTOMAN EMPIRE
PORTUGAL
Corsica (France)
Rome
Madrid
NAPLES
Naples
Lisbon
SPAIN
Minorca (Great Britain)
SARDINIA
Athens
Tyrrhenian Sea
Majorca (Spain)
Iviza (Spain)
Ionian Sea
Sicily
Algiers
Tunis
Malta
Crete (Ottoman Empire)
OTTOMAN EMPIRE
Mediterranean Sea

France in 1789
International border
City
GREAT BRITAIN
English Channel
AUSTRIAN NETHERLANDS
GERMAN STATES
Flanders
Lille
Rouen
Île de France
Seine River
Normandy
Paris
Nancy
Lorraine
Alsace
Rhine River
Brittany
Loire River
Nantes
FRANCE
Franche Comté
NEUCHÂTEL
SWISS CONFEDERATION
ATLANTIC OCEAN
Poitou
La Rochelle
Burgundy
Geneva
Lyon
KINGDOM OF SARDINIA
Bay of Biscay
Bordeaux
Garonne River
Rhône River
AVIGNON
NICE
REPUBLIC OF GENOA
Guyenne and Gascony
Toulouse
Languedoc
Provence
Marseille
Corsica
ANDORRA
SPAIN
Mediterranean Sea
N
0 50 100 mi.
0 50 100 km

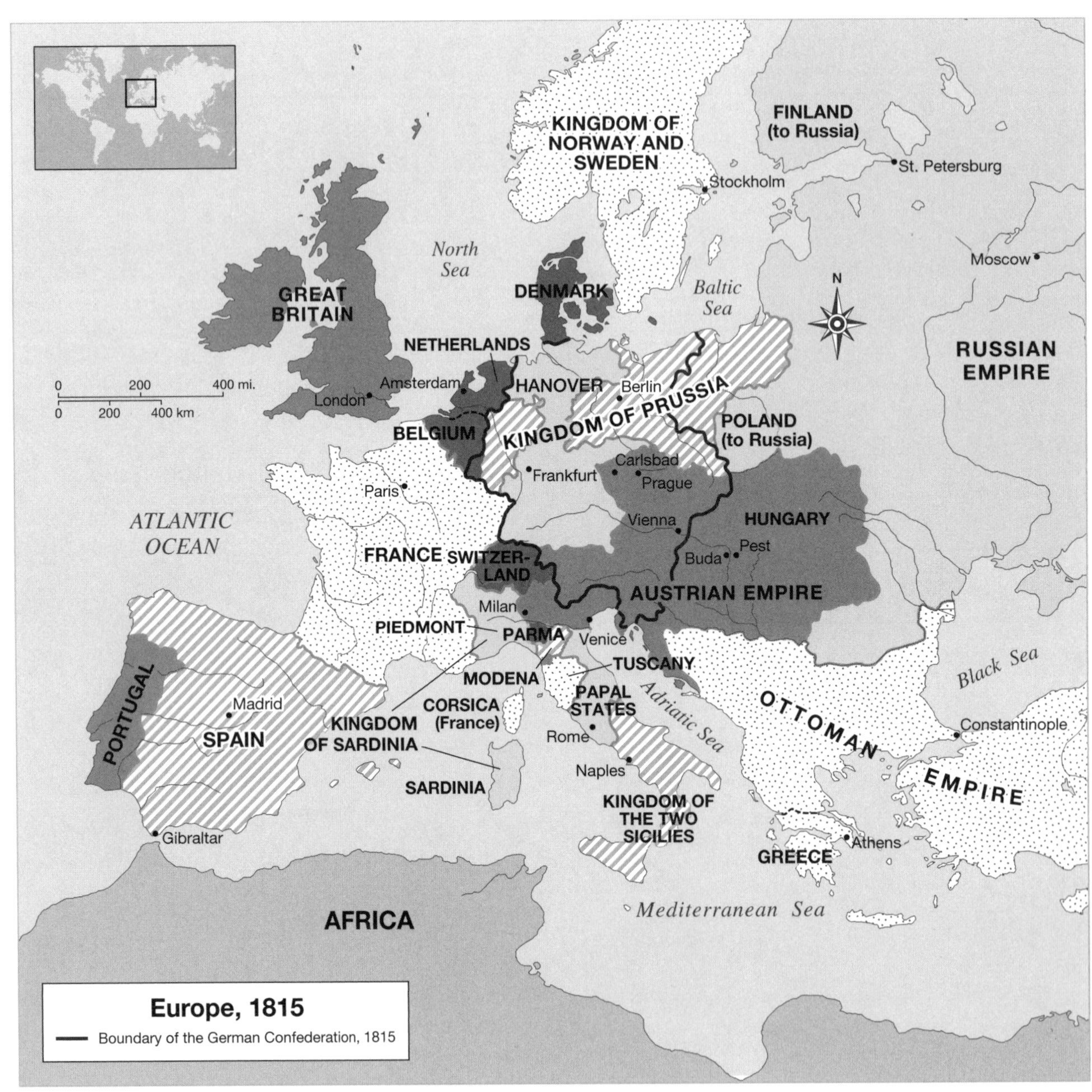
KINGDOM OF NORWAY AND SWEDEN
FINLAND (to Russia)
St. Petersburg
Stockholm
Moscow
North Sea
Baltic Sea
GREAT BRITAIN
DENMARK
NETHERLANDS
RUSSIAN EMPIRE
Amsterdam
London
HANOVER
Berlin
KINGDOM OF PRUSSIA
0 200 400 mi.
0 200 400 km
BELGIUM
POLAND (to Russia)
Carlsbad
Frankfurt
Prague
Paris
Vienna
HUNGARY
ATLANTIC OCEAN
FRANCE
SWITZERLAND
Buda
Pest
AUSTRIAN EMPIRE
Milan
PIEDMONT
PARMA
Venice
TUSCANY
MODENA
PAPAL STATES
Black Sea
Adriatic Sea
PORTUGAL
Madrid
CORSICA (France)
OTTOMAN EMPIRE
SPAIN
KINGDOM OF SARDINIA
Rome
Constantinople
Naples
SARDINIA
KINGDOM OF THE TWO SICILIES
Gibraltar
Athens
GREECE
Mediterranean Sea
AFRICA
Boundary of the German Confederation, 1815
Europe, 1815

Italian Unification
Kingdom of Sardinia, 1858
Added to Sardinia, 1859 and 1860
Added to Italy, 1866
Added to Italy, 1870
SWITZERLAND
AUSTRIA-HUNGARY
LOMBARDY
Milan
VENETIA
Venice
Turin
SAVOY
(to France)
PIEDMONT
PARMA
MODENA
Genoa
SAN MARINO
NICE
(to France)
LUCCA
Florence
Ligurian Sea
TUSCANY
PAPAL
STATES
Adriatic Sea
CORSICA
(France)
Rome
KINGDOM
OF THE
TWO SICILIES
Naples
SARDINIA
Tyrrhenian Sea
N
0
50
100 mi.
0
50
100 km
Mediterranean Sea
Palermo
SICILY
Ionian Sea

SWEDEN
DENMARK
North Sea
Baltic Sea
N
Schleswig
Holstein
Hamburg
Mecklenburg
Hanover
East Prussia
Pomerania
West Prussia
P
R
U
S
S
I
A
Brandenburg
Berlin
Posen
Vistula R.
NETHERLANDS
Westphalia
RUSSIA
BELGIUM
Rhine R.
Elbe R.
Oder R.
Ems
Thuringia
Saxony
Silesia
Sedan
LUX.
Frankfurt
Prague
Sadowa
To Paris
Metz
Main R.
Lorraine
Bavaria
Württemberg
AUSTRIA-HUNGARY
FRANCE
Alsace
Baden
Munich
Hohenzollern
Danube R.
Vienna
SWITZERLAND
0 50 100 mi.
0 50 100 km
German Unification
Prussia, 1865
Added to Prussia, 1866
Added to form North German Confederation, 1867
Added to form German empire, 1871
Boundary of German empire, 1871
Route of Prussian armies in Austro-Prussian War
Route of German armies in Franco-Prussian War
Battle sites

Europe, 1914
International border
N
0 250 500 mi.
0 250 500 km
ICELAND
ATLANTIC OCEAN
NORWAY
SWEDEN
North Sea
Baltic Sea
DENMARK
UNITED KINGDOM
RUSSIA
NETH.
GERMANY
BELG.
LUX.
Caspian Sea
FRANCE
SWITZ.
AUSTRIA-HUNGARY
ROMANIA
Black Sea
ANDORRA
ITALY
SERBIA
BULGARIA
PORTUGAL
SPAIN
MONT.
ALBANIA
GREECE
OTTOMAN EMPIRE
PERSIA
Spanish Morocco
Tunisia (Fr.)
Morocco (Fr.)
Mediterranean Sea
Algeria (Fr.)
Libya (It.)
Egypt (Br.)

IBSEN, HENRIK (1828–1906), Norwegian playwright.

Henrik Ibsen's ascendancy to the front rank of European writers in the second half of the nineteenth century was achieved against stupendous odds. He was born in 1828, in Skien, a small town in southern Norway. William Archer (1856–1924), his first major English translator, wrote: "his Dano-Norwegian language is spoken by some four and a half million people in all, and the number of foreigners who learn it is infinitesimal. The sheer force of his genius has broken this barrier of language" (Postlewait, p. 55). At the age of fifteen Ibsen left home for the coastal town of Grimstad as an apprentice to an apothecary and in 1850 left Grimstad for Christiania (now Oslo), having written verses in support of the European revolutionary events of 1848. In this year (1850) he published his first play, the tragedy *Catiline.*

Christiania (a raw, newly emerging "city" of about thirty thousand) was the capital of a country with no dramatic tradition. Its theater presented plays performed by Danish companies and imported from the current European repertoire that included no examples of major drama. Ibsen's early dramatic criticism in Christiania deplored the dismal state of the theater and of public taste. His first play to be staged, successfully by the Christiania theater in 1850, was the one-act *The Warrior's Barrow,* dramatizing a highly Romantic dialectic of pagan versus Christian, north versus south, and male versus female—polarities that continued, with much greater artistry, throughout his subsequent writing.

He abandoned a second career as a painter; but his plays display a heightened sense of the visual aspects of drama: the stage space a canvas for a thoroughly "composed" and powerful iconography. This became apparent after he abandoned the verse medium of *Peer Gynt* (1867). In his later realist cycle, the twelve plays from *Pillars of Society* (1877) to *When We Dead Awaken* (1899), the meticulously detailed stage set serves simultaneously as a vehicle of symbolic meaning and a determining element of the action, extending the overall metaphor of the play. The dynamic interplay between the stage space and the characters who occupy it generates much of the dramatic tension of Ibsen's realist dramaturgy.

In 1851 Ole Borneman Bull (1810–1880), a noted Norwegian violinist and theatrical manager, engaged Ibsen as "playwright in residence" for the newly created Norwegian Theatre in Bergen. Much of his responsibility consisted of staging what he termed "Scribe and Co.'s sugar-candy dramas"—well-made plays by the popular French dramatist Augustin-Eugène Scribe (1791–1861) and his followers. This involvement early in his career in the actual staging of plays, gave Ibsen a firm grounding in the technical aspects of the theater.

EARLY-NINETEENTH-CENTURY THEATER

The standing of the theater in Europe and the United States in the 1850s was at its lowest. In Britain, the last new play of any significance to

Henrik Ibsen, 1898. SNARK/ART RESOURCE, NY

appear before the arrival of *A Doll's House* in London in 1889 had been Richard Brinsley Sheridan's *The School for Scandal* (1777). During a century that saw the full flowering of the Romantic movement in poetry and the arts and the rise of the realistic novel as a major literary genre, with the exception of the German dramatists from Gotthold Ephraim Lessing (1729–1781) to Friedrich Hebbel (1813–1863), no drama of major significance appeared. No other period has been at once so fertile in literature and so barren in dramatic art.

The European stage, for most of the nineteenth century, was dominated by morally stereotypical melodramas whose audiences were dazzled by spectacular stage effects and the violent exercise of conventional emotions; or, for more refined tastes, technically adroit "well-made-plays" after the Scribean model, whose main themes were adultery and murder in the fashionable classes; or, a variant of these, "thesis plays," taking up some problem of topical social morality for a mildly controversial airing. Ibsen's plays, however, reflect stronger influences from such German dramatists as Johann Wolfgang von Goethe (1749–1832), Johann Christoph Friedrich von Schiller (1759–1805), Heinrich von Kleist (1777–1811), Friedrich Hebbel (1813–1863), and their Danish followers.

This was the cultural situation in the theater that Ibsen was so momentously to engage. Nineteenth-century society concealed a host of skeletons in the closets of its private and public life and maintained highly developed antennae for detecting any hint either of political subversion or, especially in Britain and the United States, "impropriety" in social mores. Ibsen's volatile confrontation with the theater of his time is one of the ironies of cultural history. His identity as a dramatist seemed programmed to repudiate, at every point, the medium he was intellectually to dominate. Although continually rejected and assailed by the public, reduced to poverty, in exile, he doggedly worked on the debased condition of the theater until he forged a modern drama for his own revolutionary artistic purpose. After his first major success, *Brand* (1866), at the age of thirty-eight he kept up his contentious stance toward the public, remaining a center of controversy until long after his death in 1906.

Like the composer Richard Wagner (1813–1883), Ibsen was determined that the medium he chose should be remade to conform to his artistic demands, setting the integrity of his art above all temptation to exploit a potentially very lucrative medium. Michael Meyer, in his biography of Ibsen, estimates that even at the height of his fame, in the more than a decade following *A Doll's House,* in which he created *Ghosts* (1881), *An Enemy of the People* (1882), *The Wild Duck* (1884), *Rosmersholm* (1886), *The Lady from the Sea* (1888), and *Hedda Gabler* (1890), Ibsen earned less from this total output than a fashionable playwright would make in a single year.

RECEPTION

It is not surprising that his plays were initially greeted with intense hostility by practitioners and defenders of the traditional drama. More surprising was the intensity, scale, and duration of that hostility across Europe and the United States. However, a minority public was evolving, hungry for a theater into which one could take one's intellect. This, in part, accounts for the success of Ibsen with the "thinking world" when, in the late 1880s, his plays began to appear on the European stage. Ibsen offered a drama that was in tune with the leading ideas and artistic achievements of the time. This minority was a highly critical, often rebellious intelligentsia variously at odds with the aesthetic, moral, political, and religious premises of conventional society. Ibsen's dramas addressed all levels of cultural alienation. Henry James, Thomas Hardy, George Augustus Moore, Oscar Wilde, George Bernard Shaw, and James Joyce were among the many who, with the progressive men and women of Europe, and later the United States, took up the cause of Ibsen and the new independent theater movement. This minority theater, the cradle of serious modern drama, came into being in Berlin (the Freie Bühne, 1889) and London (the Independent Theatre 1891) specifically to perform Ibsen's *Ghosts.* In Paris, André Antoine's recently created Théâtre Libre performed *Ghosts* in 1890. George Moore, sitting in the audience, was so moved by the play he became a founding member of a new Irish Literary Theatre—later to become Ireland's Abbey Theatre.

Drama now followed the other arts by splitting into mutually incompatible—and often hostile—mainstream and minority camps. Performing an Ibsen play was considered virtually an insurrectionary act (*Ghosts* was banned from public performance in England for twenty-three years), and Ibsen became the most vilified, championed, talked and written about individual in Europe. "It may be questioned," wrote James Joyce in his review of *When We Dead Awaken,* "whether any man has held so firm an empire over the thinking world in modern times." Within an astonishingly short time the theater, through Ibsen, had shaken off its insignificance and disrepute to became a major, and highly controversial, force in modern culture. His influence on modern drama is so great as to be almost incalculable.

George Bernard Shaw's *The Quintessence of Ibsenism* (1891, 1913) helped inaugurate an idea of Ibsen that stubbornly survives into the present as a writer of "problem plays" concerned with eradicating the social and ethical crises of middle-class culture. As early as 1907, Jennette Lee protested against this didactic interpretation. "The conception of a problem play as one in which some problem of modern life is discussed by the characters and worked out in the plot is foreign to Ibsen, as to all great artists" (Lee, p. 9).

An alternative tradition claims him as a consummate artist whose cycle of twelve plays in particular is one of the supreme achievements of modern literature. Ibsen interpretation and criticism continues to be as diverse and voluminous as that of any major writer.

See also **Chekhov, Anton; Shaw, George Bernard; Sweden and Norway.**

BIBLIOGRAPHY

Durbach, Errol. "A Century of Ibsen Criticism." In *The Cambridge Companion to Ibsen,* edited by James McFarlane. Cambridge, U.K., 1994.

Johnston, Brian. *The Ibsen Cycle.* Rev. ed. University Park, Pa., 1992.

Joyce, James. "Ibsen's New Drama." *Fortnightly Review* 73. April 1900.

Lee, Jennette. *The Ibsen Secret: A Key to the Prose Dramas of Henrik Ibsen.* New York, 1907. Reprint, Honolulu, Hawaii, 2001.

Meyer, Michael. *Ibsen: A Biography.* New York, 1971.

Postlewait, Thomas, ed. *William Archer on Ibsen.* Westport, Conn., 1984.

BRIAN JOHNSTON

IMMIGRATION AND INTERNAL MIGRATION.

The nineteenth century began with a rearrangement of European migration systems and with the population mobility, often involuntary, that was caused by first the revolution in France and then the imperial Napoleonic Wars. From the Congress of Vienna in 1815, which stabilized the old monarchical political regimes, to the 1880s, when industrialization reached its apogee in many societies, labor migrations increased within Europe. Another period of massive changes in patterns and intensity of migration began with the struggles for self-determination among people of the Habsburg-ruled Balkans in the 1880s. Every move by individual men and women or by families with children implied both an emigration from a region—rather than a state—of origin and an immigration to a region of destination. Many such moves were seasonal or lasted for only a few years—thus, in-migration was complemented by return migration. In German-speaking regions, in particular, journeymen artisans still pursued circular migrations: after years of practicing their craft away from their culture of socialization, they returned to where they had started, enriched by their experiences with distant or even foreign cultures. Young women in cultures in which marriage required a dowry often migrated to nearby towns or larger cities for several years of wage labor as domestic servants in middle-class families. Upon returning to their village of origin, they transferred urban middle-class styles of eating and dressing to the rural societies.

Mobility has often been associated with urbanization and the change from proto-industrial production in family homes to manufactured, centralized production by hand and, later, to machine-powered factories. In contrast, rural populations have been considered rooted in the soil, immobile, and ruled by tradition. However, any peasant family on a subsistence plot raising more than two children had to migrate to gain more land, send some sons and daughters off to wage labor elsewhere, or cut food consumption to below-subsistence levels in order to survive. Moreover, European agriculture was characterized by two peak time periods of work intensity, the sowing and the harvesting periods. In the latter, in particular, additional labor was needed, so migrant workers often joined harvesting crews. After each spring's seeding, the demand for labor decreased, and family members could be sent off to work for wages or, at least, to feed themselves elsewhere and thus relieve the tight family economy at home—a home that did not always provide sustenance. Even enserfed agrarian populations were not immobile. At various points, depending on changing social customs, economic productivity, and concepts of noble lifestyles, their owners might need either fewer or more serfs, so would release those who had become unnecessary or entice bound couples from neighboring estates. Marriage of serfs between estates also implied mobility. Thus, Europe's rural populations, even if tradition centered, had always been mobile; men and women had evaluated distant options and often changed their ways of life.

Historians accepting the nation-state paradigm with the corollary of fixed national identities and statewide institutions have often overlooked the interregional mobility within dynastic and other societies and have overestimated the cultural change involved in migration between states. Often, borderlands or whole regions were of a similar culture although ruled by different dynasties. A move from the Flemish- to the French-speaking region within Belgium involved a major cultural change, but a move from French-speaking southern Belgium to northern France involved little change and, before the late-nineteenth-century intensification of border controls, little paperwork. Yet Poles moving within their cultural region but between the segments ruled by the Romanov, the Hohenzollern, and the Habsburg empires faced major bureaucratic harassment. Furthermore, a move from the countryside into a larger city, or from rural labor regimes to industrial patterns of work and remuneration, even if within a region speaking the same language, involved major cultural changes in stages of economic development and patterns of everyday working life. Servant women's migrations between households of different class cultures similarly involved such cultural changes.

THE REVOLUTIONARY PERIOD, 1780S–1810S

In the second half of the eighteenth century, of the three major West European migration systems, only the North Sea system, centered on the urbanized Netherlands and their agrarian supply regions, retained its vitality; the Franco-Spanish system and that of the societies bordering the Baltic Sea had lost their dynamism. A migration system is defined as empirically verifiable migration by many individuals from a particular geographic and economic region over a sizable period of time toward a common region of destination connected by information flows. It may be of local extent (rural migration to the next city), of regional extent (the North Sea system), or of continental or transcontinental reach (migration in the Atlantic economies or in the Russo-Siberian system). The most important east European system, the migrations of agricultural settlers to the south Russian plains, also changed during this time period. Immigration from the densely populated south German regions, including members of religious groups, such as the Mennonites, intent on preserving their lifestyles, was declining while internal Russian north-south migrations as well as immigration from southeast European societies were increasing. From the southern German regions, from the late 1810s on, emigration destinations would be westward, transatlantic.

In place of the mid-eighteenth-century European systems, a considerable number of migration regions emerged around expanding cities, as documented by a Napoleonic census of 1811. These regions centered on the urban Netherlands, Paris, London, Madrid, and Rome, port towns along the shores of the Mediterranean, Vienna and Budapest, Lodz and Warsaw, St. Petersburg, Moscow, Kiev, and Odessa. "Immigrants" in the cities were usually rural populations denied "city-zenship," instead becoming urban inhabitants of lesser status. In addition, the increasing size of cities required a surrounding supply belt of intensive vegetable and dairy agriculture with a high demand for labor. Thus, in intra-agrarian migrations men and women moved from extensive grain growing and cattle raising to intensive vegetable gardening. Nearby towns were then often less than half a days' walk away.

Into this period of ongoing economic and social change with its migratory potential, the French Revolution introduced political democratization and, as a result, the flight of those whose position was threatened—aristocrats, nobles, priests—as well as the in-migration (temporary migration, in contrast to permanent *im*migration) of supporters of the new ideas who wanted to join the struggle for more equality. The loosely controlled inter-state borders temporarily became checkpoints: rulers wanted to keep revolutionaries out, and some encouraged fleeing nobles to join their society. Borders no longer merely separated the territories of one ruler from those of the next; they separated types of political regimes and hegemony of ideas about how societies should be ruled. Borders, formerly merely delineating dynastic ownership, came to separate political philosophies and types of institutional control. At the same time, religious identifications—Huguenot, Calvinist, Mennonite, Catholic, Orthodox, Anglican, or other—gave way to cultural identification: French, German-speaking, English, Russian, or Polish. Thus, the criteria for including or excluding people changed from religious to ethno-cultural and political. The religious refugee migrations of earlier centuries were replaced by small migrations of political exiles or large emigrations of men and women of disenfranchised classes or ethno-cultural groups.

During this period of massive change in political thought about categories of belonging, the "French" armies, consisting of men from many regions of mutually unintelligible dialects, moved across the former Bourbon, now the French state's borders. Napoleon's expansionism sent a many-cultured army of some six hundred thousand men, not counting the women and children following them, into culturally alien regions. The subsequent anti-Napoleonic wars to reassert dynastic rule again brought together soldiers from many different cultures and dialects. Wherever the mobile men of an army won or lost a battle, or wherever soldiers were immobilized due to illness or wounds or demobilized because they were no longer needed, some settled. Thus, in addition to creating refugees in occupied areas, involuntary wartime mobility, in the end, might have had the same outcome as voluntary migration. Backward information linkages to regions of origin often encouraged further mobility. By 1815, the politically unsettled times and resulting migrations came to an end, only to be followed by an unusually severe winter in 1816–1817, which caused famine migrations westward that established new patterns of mobility that were to last through the following decades of peace. Furthermore, the wartime cultural interactions established affinities and patterns of information flow that resulted in later migrations. For example, the presence of Russian troops in Paris led to a Francophilia that brought French teachers, artists, and other cultural, technical, and commercial personnel to Russia. The image of revolutionary Paris as a city of liberty made it the destination of Russian reformers and revolutionaries fleeing the tsarist regime.

MIGRATION IN THE PERIOD FROM 1815 TO THE 1880S

The societal, political, and economic factors that influenced patterns of migration in Europe involved the emergence of national consciousnesses among the middle classes—as opposed to the trans-European nobility, which married, migrated, and interacted across cultural and linguistic boundaries. This new self-awareness involved the struggle for constitutional, then republican, and finally democratic rule, with a high point in the revolutions of 1848–1849. Their repression sent a small number of highly influential and well-studied revolutionary intellectuals fleeing. Middle-class-driven economic changes involved the concentration of production in increasingly larger establishments that demanded in-migration of laboring men and women and, often, of whole families, as child labor was widespread. Serfdom was abolished in those European societies in which it still existed, for example, Prussia, through reforms in the wake of the French Revolution or as late as 1861, in the Tsarist Empire. There, a particular type of rural-turned-industrial serfdom had permitted serfs who were not needed on the estates to migrate to industries in return for a fee paid to their owners. Across Europe, hilly and mountainous regions, where agriculture was both labor intensive and unproductive, became regions of emigration toward cities in the plains. The Mediterranean Alpine ranges are the most frequently cited example.

In most of Europe, procreation resulted in more children than would ever be able to find jobs. Such young surplus populations became the temporary in-migrants and permanent immigrants in cities and industrializing regions—or, more precisely, in-migrants to segmented labor markets that provided sufficient income to survive and to form a family and raise children. Thus, migration was toward job-providing regions and to economic sectors commensurate with the migrants' qualifications, not to states or nations. In Britain, for example, migrant men and women followed the pull of English and Scottish lowland cities; in Russia and Italy, they selected industrializing cities; in the Germanies, port cities and the mining regions of Silesia and the Ruhr district. Throughout the century, migration was gendered, men and women often following different paths but searching each other out when ready for marriage. Community formation depended on family procreation—camps of transient male workers dissolved when particular job-providing infrastructural measures were completed.

Once mobility exceeded distances that could be traversed by walking, it required new kinds of transportation. Boat traffic, for example, along the Danube from the southern German region to the Balkans or South Russia, had been the major means of movement in the past. Transport, whether of migrants or of increasingly factory-produced goods, required ever-larger roads and, from the 1830s on, rail networks. The preparatory earthworks could easily be constructed by men from the respective local countryside, and such non-agricultural waged work served as a mobilizing factor: locally recruited laborers moved on with the extension of the roads and rails, and their families, sisters, or brides would follow. Europe's rail network expanded from 330 kilometers in 1831 to 300,000 kilometers in 1876. Thereafter, labor for infrastructural improvements and huge transportation projects was needed afar, for example, for the Panama Canal and railroad building on other continents. Intra-European migration became emigration from Europe.

The migration toward urban agglomerations, as a trans-European phenomenon, extended from Odessa and Moscow to Marseille, Glasgow, and Stockholm. While many migrants preferred to stay in a region in which they knew the language, they were still recognizable by their dialects and labeled "uncouth" or "unskilled" even if of the same ethnocultural group. Intercultural exchange resulted from migrations from economic peripheries to cores of investment. Governments and private entrepreneurs did not invest in regions they considered economically marginal. Thus, some cultural groups, the Slovaks in historic Hungary, for example, had to migrate out of their own cultural region to Budapest as one destination or to cities in North America. By the 1880s, the inhabitants of Budapest spoke four major languages, German, Magyar, Slovak, and Romanian; the city's labor movement was multilingual even though many working men and women were illiterate due to the Austro-Hungarian Empire's poorly developed educational system. Later, migrants to North America would transfer such rudimentary multilingualism of the illiterate to the U.S. labor movement. By the 1870s and 1880s, most European cities housed large numbers of immigrants; in many cities, as much as one-half of the population had not been born there. Quantitatively, the intra-European migration was far larger than the better-studied emigration to North America and, in smaller numbers, to other parts of the globe, but no precise figures are available. Many of the long-distance, transatlantic migrants first moved within Europe, temporarily stayed and earned money, and then moved on to transoceanic destinations.

At the end of this period, the national consciousness of the middle classes turned into nationalist hegemony of one sizable cultural group, still in the dynastic states. This group named itself "nation" and designated smaller cultural groups as "minorities." Thus, cultural hegemony was imposed internally over people of other cultures and, externally, borderlines become more culturally divisive. In consequence, patterns and directions of migration changed, as did patterns of acculturation and insertion after migration. Inter-regional migration increasingly became inter-state migration. Newcomers were labeled "aliens" or immigrants. Some states granted residence permits or even citizenship, while others admitted laborers only for a limited period of time. After 1871 the German Reich, for example, fearful that men and women of Polish culture would demand reestablishment of the independence of their state, forced Polish-cultured agricultural laborers from the Russian and the Austrian partition to leave the Reich each winter. Thus, they would be prevented from acculturating and organizing. Industrialists employing Polish and Ruthenian labor, however, invested in training, intending to recover cost and to produce with stable labor forces. They pressured the political authorities to permit such semi-skilled and skilled workers to stay. Across Europe, nationalization programs—Germanization, Austrianization, Russification, or other—led to cultural-economic emigrations and nationalized working classes who then often segregated immigrant workers into distinct organizations, such as Czech organizations in Vienna and east European Jewish ones in London.

The common juxtaposition of labor-exporting European (emigration) and labor-importing North American (immigration) countries is a simplification not supported by data. In the Europe of the 1880s, England, the Netherlands and Belgium, France, the west and central areas of Germany, Lower Austria, Bohemia, and Switzerland became labor-importing industrialized core countries. Societies and economies of the periphery—Ireland, Portugal and Spain, Italy and southeastern Europe, the Polish and Jewish territories, and the Scandinavian countries—were relegated to supplying labor. Great Britain and the Germanies exported settlers and workers while only a few left France, owing to an early stabilization of population levels. Belgium and sections of Austria also attracted large numbers of labor migrants while experiencing heavy out-migration at the same time. England drew workers mainly from its Irish colony, Switzerland from Italy (earlier from Germany), France from most of the neighboring countries as well as Poland, and Germany from Poland and Italy as well as from Sweden. Mass export of unskilled, mainly rural populations began early from Ireland to England. By the mid-nineteenth century, the Scandinavian countries exported labor; Italian and eastern European migration figures skyrocketed in the 1880s. In addition to local demand for immigrant labor, states with ports providing access to transatlantic shipping, the German Reich, the Habsburg's empire through Trieste, as well as Italy became the arenas of vast transit migrations destined for North America.

THE 1880S TO 1914

Toward the end of the long nineteenth century, the many-cultured, multiregional trans-European societies had divided themselves into bordered states with immigration, emigration, and internal migration, as well as with interactive borderlands and continued permeability of borders. Authoritarian regimes influenced patterns of politically motivated migration. Paris, London, and Swiss cities had become centers of political exiles. Increasing numbers of people fled from national-cultural as well as class and political oppression. Slovaks moved westward to Budapest, Czechs to Vienna, Poles to the Ruhr district and, often, in a second stage onward to North America. The political and the economic were closely related. Worst off were Russian Jews, a German-language (Yiddish) religiously defined group that came to be racialized. From their Lithuanian-Polish-Russian settlement region, mass flight from persecution and pogroms and mass migration to wage-providing jobs brought many to the German, French, and English cities as well as to those across the Atlantic. They came to stay as immigrants but faced heavy discrimination and exploitation.

The Romanov, Habsburg, and Hohenzollern empires, all encompassing many peoples, from the 1880s initiated processes of national homogenization—as the Bourbon and Windsor ones had done earlier. This sent members of "minorities" into emigration and outright flight and forced some immigrants to the national regimes to assimilate, to discard their culture of origin. Under dynastic rule, such newcomers could negotiate special protection for their ethnocultural ways of life as a ruler's new subjects. Some states' border controls attempted to keep immigrants out altogether. Differentiated gender roles induced women to leave societies with particularly constraining regulations. Daughters of educated Russian families migrated to Swiss universities for an academic education; many returned after completing their degree. Women from rural regions moved to less constraining urban life or on to the two North American societies of Canada and the United States. From the latter, women had a lower rate of return to their societies of origin than men; some female migrants had no intention of returning to face the more oppressive gender relations. In contrast, European states admitted men as return migrants from North America in relatively large percentages—between 10 and 20 percent of German-speaking and Jewish migrants returned, and 60 percent returned to the South Slav societies. They, in a way, were immigrants from the New World to the Old.

Others, who chose not to migrate, began to struggle for cultural, then national, self-determination, most prominently in the Habsburg-ruled multiple societies of the Balkans. Anti-imperial struggles had caused population displacement since the 1880s. The last three decades before 1914 became the initial stages of vast intra-European and transatlantic refugee movements. Europe's governments and nationalist chauvinism turned the societies from labor-migrant-attracting ones to refugee-generating staging areas for mass departures to new nation-states in Europe or to North America. This pre–World War I phenomenon was to last until the late 1940s.

See also **Demography; Emigration.**

BIBLIOGRAPHY

Anderson, Barbara A. *Internal Migration during Modernization in Late Nineteenth-Century Russia.* Princeton, N.J., 1980.

Bade, Klaus J. *Migration in European History.* Translated by Allison Brown. Malden, Mass., 2003.

Canny, Nicholas, ed. *Europeans on the Move: Studies on European Migration 1500–1800.* Oxford, U.K., 1994.

Hoerder, Dirk, and Leslie Page Moch, eds. *European Migrants: Global and Local Perspectives.* Boston, Mass., 1996.

Hoerder, Dirk, with Christiane Harzig and Adrian Shubert, eds. *The Historical Practice of Diversity: Transcultural Interactions from the Early Modern Mediterranean to the Postcolonial World.* New York, 2003.

Moch, Leslie Page. *Moving Europeans: Migration in Western Europe since 1650.* Bloomington, Ind., 1992.

Dirk Hoerder

IMPERIALISM. In the context of nineteenth-century Europe, imperialism—from the Latin root *imperium,* meaning power or rule—signifies domination or control by a strong nation over weaker ones. Its most dramatic manifestation between 1789 and 1914 was Napoleon I's conquest of much of Europe up until 1812. There is no logical reason why the term should not also embrace Russia and the United States' huge territorial expansions during the course of the nineteenth century. Before the 1870s however the word was nearly always used in the context of the Napoleonic Empire alone and then afterward to describe something else: the expansion of European states overseas, usually to found colonies in the world beyond the confines of their own continent. This is the most common use of the word in the twenty-first century. It can also be taken to mean the advocacy of such expansion. Thus, an imperialist is someone who believes that his or her nation should pursue imperial policies.

THE EARLY NINETEENTH CENTURY

Imperialism of this kind long predates the nineteenth century in effect if not in name. Since the seventeenth century at the latest, Spain, Portugal, France, Britain, the Netherlands, Denmark, and Sweden—the great seafaring nations—had all been grabbing overseas colonies, many of which still remained in their possession in 1789. By that time the most vigorous imperial nations were Britain and France, who had already clashed seriously over North America and India in the mid-eighteenth century, and were to continue this rivalry, mainly in the Caribbean, as a by-product of the Napoleonic Wars. The process continued thereafter, with Britain in particular—the major victor from the wars—extending its rule in western and southern Africa, India, and Australasia, and France in North and West Africa and southeast Asia. This was in spite of the fact that the rising ideology of the day in both countries, free market capitalism, painted imperialism as anachronistic and commercially unsound. Europeans at this time (before the 1870s) were not intentional imperialists. It happened, one could say, in spite of them.

The reasons were the expansion of Europe's trade under the impetus of industrialization; the self-confidence of European culture; and the material and technological gap that had opened up recently between European capacities and those of what was seen as the more "backward" world. Typically, the chain of events was this: a European trader sought a market in a "primitive" country; this created instability there; which in turn made force necessary to secure the market; which was then usually backed up with outside—that is, metropolitan—help. The same could occur with settlers seeking new lands to cultivate in the under-exploited parts of the world; with missionaries eager to enlighten those in darkness; and with humanitarians aiming to extirpate slavery (both European and indigenous) and also some of the less attractive forms of trade: drugs, arms, and alcohol. Usually in this period governments were reluctant to support their nationals more than was minimally necessary. This accounts for the very limited and scattered extent of most European overseas empires before the 1870s—usually just a few coastal stations—and their dependence on local collaboration to sustain them. The big exceptions were Britain's great colonies of settlement (British North America, Australia, New Zealand, Cape Colony in South Africa), where responsibility could be largely devolved to the emigrants, and British India, an inheritance from those eighteenth-century wars, which even at the time appeared anomalous to many.

As well as these, however, Europe also dominated other countries in ways that could be said to be at least quasi-imperialistic, through diplomacy, for example, ruling through puppets, or by virtue of the advantage that the free market invariably confers on powerful economies over weaker ones. The name given to this is informal imperialism; and it inevitably raises the question of how much domination, and of what kind, is required in order to qualify as imperialism. The mere spread of European trade and culture should almost certainly not be seen in this light. This is because some of it was also genuinely accepted—even demanded—by its recipients, and because many of the cultural values that are sometimes associated with Europe had a much wider provenance. (It is patronizing, even racist, to assume that every "progressive" idea could only have had a "Western" origin.) Two things were happening here. The first was the expansion of European institutions, people, and ideas—or ideas carried on the back of that expansion—into the wider world. The second was the mutation of that expansion into direct or informal imperial rule in some cases. The two were related, but not identical. The causes of each, also, were distinct: general and European in the first case, particular and local in the second. It is not always easy to see where the former shades into the latter, which is one reason why *imperialism* is so contentious a term. But the effort needs to be made. Otherwise we are left only with the choice of a narrow and misleading definition (formal empire), or a broad, vague, and analytically unhelpful one (Westernization).

THE "NEW IMPERIALISM"

From the 1870s onward this difficulty recedes a little, as many more areas of Western penetration in the world became hardened into colonies proper. The chief example of this is the scramble for Africa, which took place in the 1880s and 1890s. Before 1880 Africa was largely empty from a contemporary European perspective: that is, unfilled by what Europeans regarded as nations, and only significantly colonized at its northern and southern tips; or, from an alternative (African) viewpoint, free. By 1900 it was nearly all neatly parceled out among the imperial powers. In fact this exaggerates the changes that took place. Not only was European influence there greater before 1880 than those tiny enclaves on the

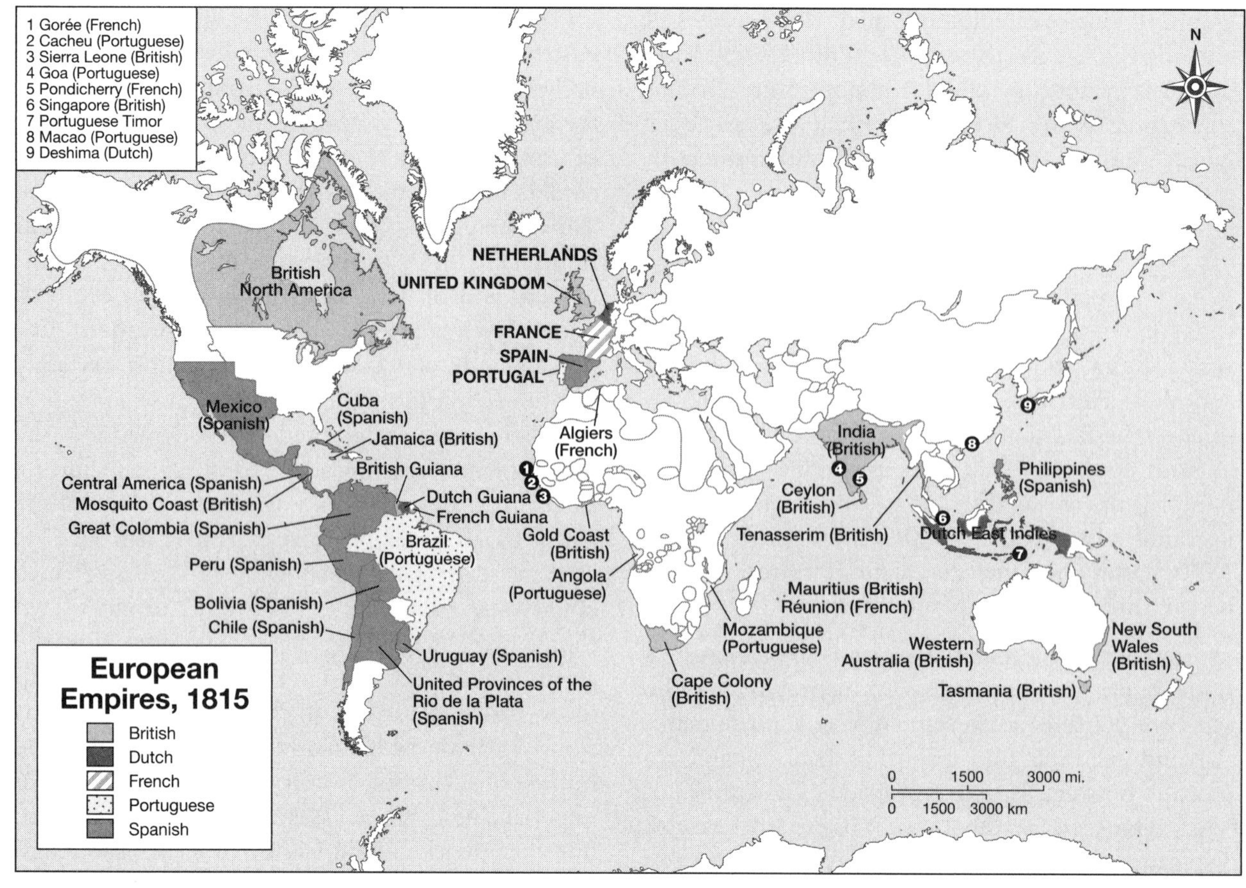

coasts indicate; it was also often less so after 1900 than all the solid imperial colorings imply. Some colonies were purely nominal. But this should not detract from the significance of what at the time was dubbed the "new" imperialism: new not in the sense of unprecedented, but fiercer, more deliberate, and competitive.

It also involved more European countries than before. Britain and France were still the leading imperial actors. Britain expanded its empire substantially in West, eastern, and southern Africa, and in the north of the continent too, albeit there (in Egypt) thinly disguised as a kind of protectorate, over a puppet khedive (ruler). Britain also picked up important colonial territories in southeast Asia and the Pacific. Most of these acquisitions were extensions of what earlier had been informal influence, exerted from coastal toeholds. France advanced south from Algeria and Tunisia, taking in most of the Sahara region; expanded its West African territories; and created a new empire—bordering Britain's—in Indochina. The other main expansionary power was Russia in central Asia. Of the remaining older imperial powers, Portugal and the Netherlands mainly consolidated what they already had; Spain lost ground, as it had been doing throughout the century; and Sweden sold its last remaining colony—Saint Barthélemy in the Caribbean—to France in 1878. In the 1880s these were joined by five other powers, for most of whom this was a novelty. The exception was the United States—no stranger at all to imperialism on the North American continent, of course—which first joined the overseas colonial game in the Caribbean, central America, and the Pacific (at the expense of the Spaniards, which made it a kind of anti-imperial imperialism) in the 1890s and 1900s. The others were Japan in the Far East; Germany in Africa and the Pacific; Italy in North Africa and Abyssinia; and, most surprisingly, King Leopold II of the Belgians (r. 1865–1909)—the person himself, not his nation—who took over the vast area of the Congo basin in Africa in 1884. It was the entry of these new players that turned the process into a competitive one, which it had not generally been before.

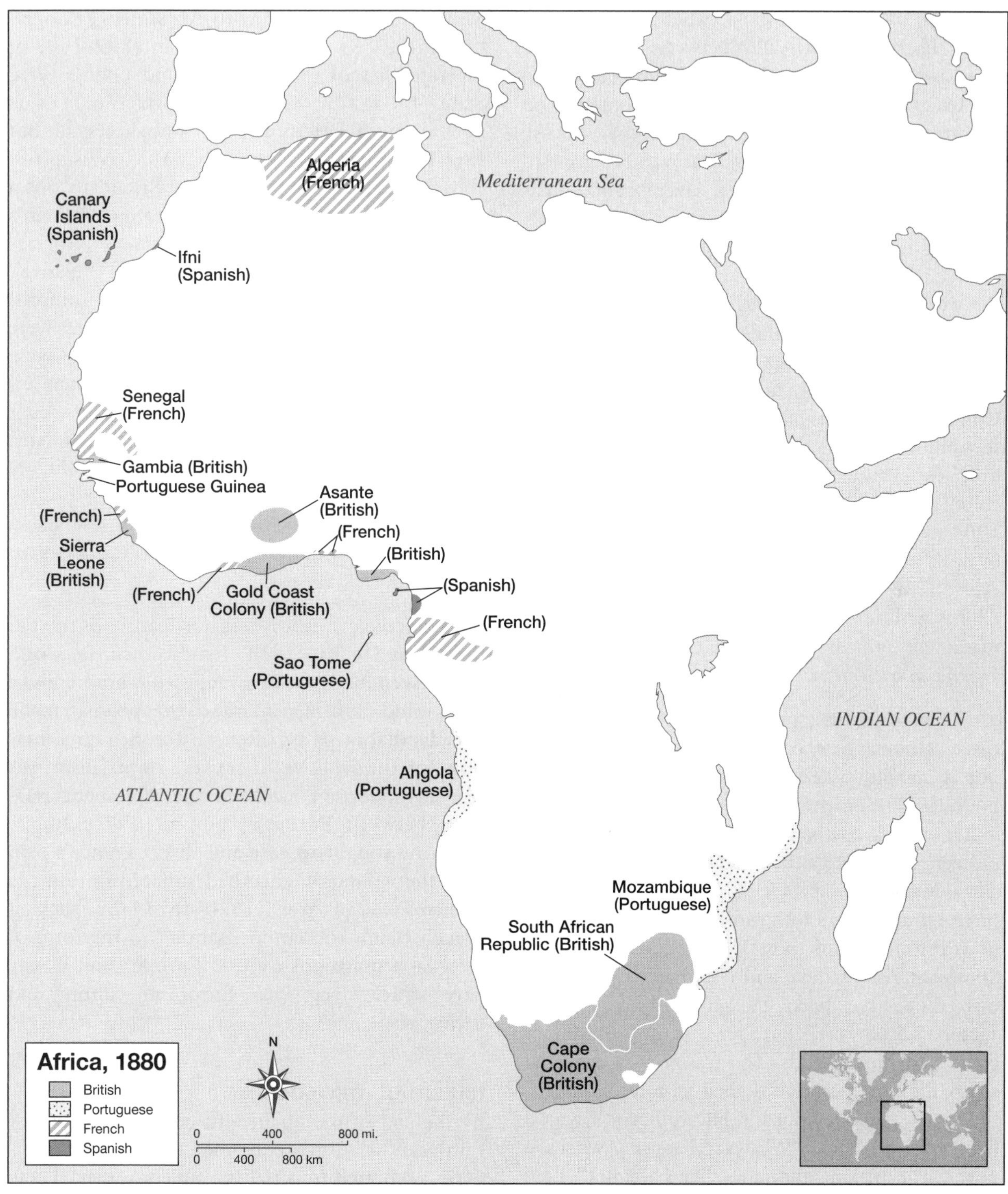

Again, however, the difference should not be exaggerated. The competition was rarely cutthroat. Many feared it would become so: with so many nations in the race now, and the "waste" places of the earth rapidly diminishing under their constant encroachment, the time must come when they would need to battle with one another to achieve their imperial ambitions. One interpretation of World War I sees it in this light. Before then, however, the partition of the wider world was done mainly cooperatively. Crises flared occasionally: between Britain and France at Fashoda in the

Sudan in 1898, for example (when France eventually backed down), and between Britain and Germany over southern Africa in 1896 (the "Kruger telegram" affair). There were also some minor skirmishes, especially in West Africa and Southeast Asia. The United States' colonial wars, of course, were with another—albeit decrepit—colonial power. More typical of this stage of Europe's imperial history, however, were the agreements between European governments that parceled out the world among them without needing to resort to war: the Berlin Conference of 1884–1885, which divided up western and central Africa with almost insulting ease, for example, and gave the Congo to King Leopold II partly to stop the others squabbling over it; the Anglo-German agreement over the eventual fate of the Portuguese African colonies in 1898; the Anglo-French Entente of 1904 over Egypt and North Africa; and the series of deals in the 1890s and 1900s that ensured that every alien power was given what it wanted in China without conflict. This may indicate the marginality of these colonial concerns to most European nations at this time.

This consensus, of course, did not embrace these nations' new colonial subjects. They were not generally asked for their views. Colonial boundary lines in Africa, for example, were notoriously drawn with little regard for what the indigenes regarded as national (that is, ethnic) divisions. Making good the Europeans' colonial claims often required wars with those indigenes: a continuous feature of this (post-1870) period, in Africa, Southeast Asia, China, and elsewhere. In Britain's case they have been characterized as "Queen Victoria's little wars," but they were not so little, of course, to their victims. The reason they appeared so to the conquerors was their vast technological superiority, well described in Hilaire Belloc's cynical (but satirical) lines: "Whatever happens, we have got / The maxim gun, and they have not" (*The Modern Traveller*, London, 1898, part 6). Even with that, however, things did not always go to plan militarily for the predators. The British were repeatedly repulsed from Afghanistan. A British squadron was overwhelmed by sheer numbers of Zulus at Isandlwana in South Africa in 1879. Italy suffered a humiliating defeat, at the hands of the "natives" at Adowa in 1896, that effectively put paid to its colonial claim to Abyssinia (Ethiopia) until the 1930s. Britain's seizure in 1899–1902 of the republics of the Transvaal and Orange Free State—the last pieces (before World War I) of its new southern African empire—was successful, but stretched Britain dangerously, which was probably the main factor persuading Britain to put a brake on colonial expansion thereafter. (Britain's adversaries there were the Afrikaners, or "Boers": of European—mainly Dutch—origin.) "Native" resistance was often vigorous, and could compromise the outcome even when the natives were defeated. (The Afrikaners, for example, were allowed to keep their racist electoral franchise.) Imperialism was not a simple matter of the West's imposing its power and wishes on its victims. Nor, incidentally, did it need to be enforced militarily in most instances, though the threat—or bluff—of force was nearly always there in the background. Empire-building often involved a degree of give and take.

Nonetheless, it was a major feature of the period from 1870 to 1914. Its effect on the world can be seen by comparing maps from both ends of the period, bearing in mind the proviso made already: that maps are often very crude representations of the realities of power. Imperialism was also an important factor in the diplomatic relations between European powers. For example, Germany sought to ease and divert France's pain over the wounds France had suffered during the Franco-Prussian War (1870–1871) by backing French claims to "compensation" in the form of colonial acquisitions outside Europe. And it may have struck deep into European culture and society also.

IMPERIAL IDEOLOGY

By the end of the nineteenth century most major European countries contained parties that positively advocated imperialism, unlike earlier. These parties were headed by prominent politicians like Joseph Chamberlain (1836–1914) in Britain and Jules Ferry (1832–1893) in France, supported in their turn by a number of publicists, economists, and historians, often organized into bodies like the (British) Royal Empire Society and the Deutsche Kolonialverein. Attempts were made to spread enthusiasm for empire more widely, through colo-

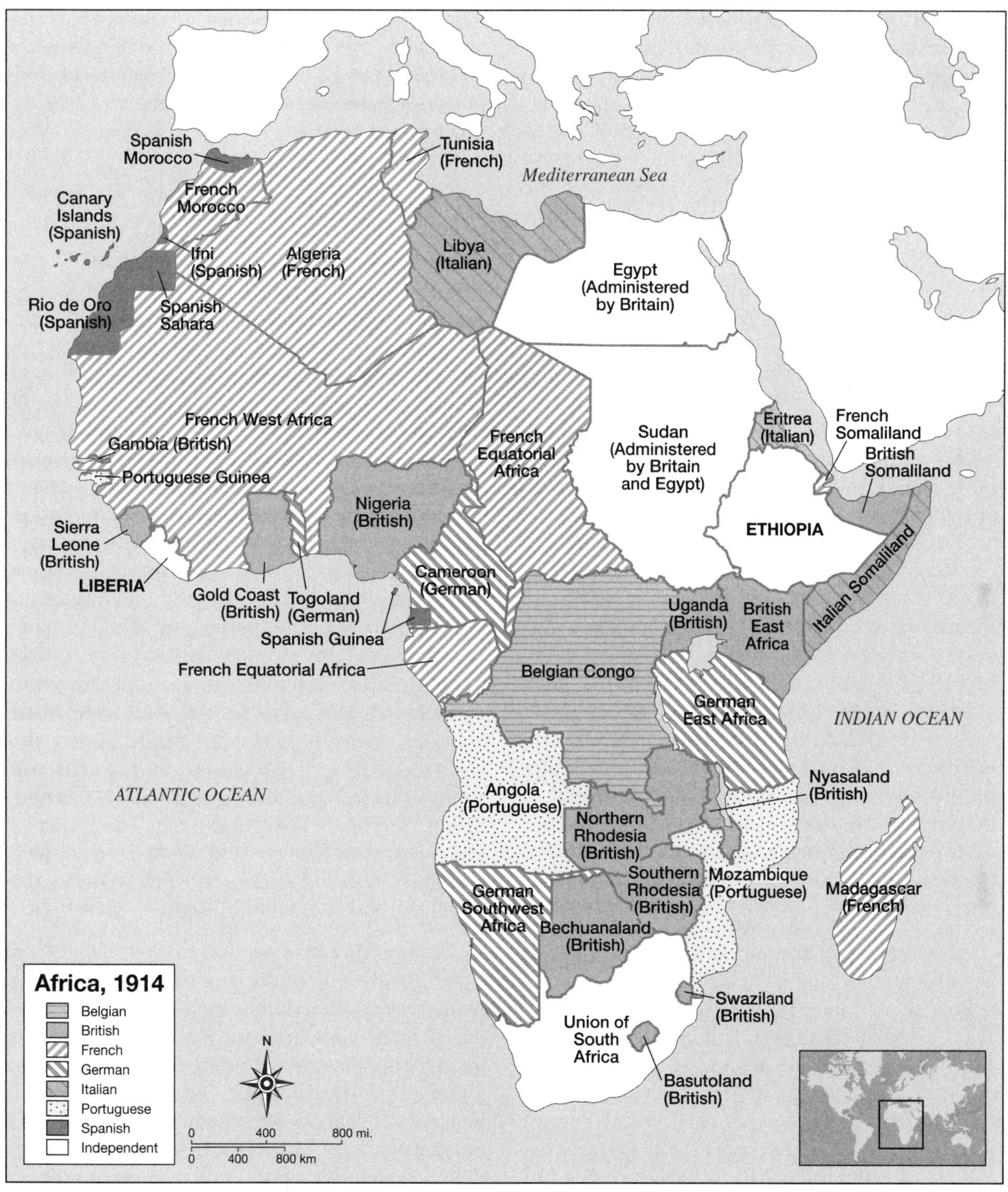

nial exhibitions, for example, and other forms of propaganda. The impact of this is controversial. There were various manifestations of popular imperialism, for example in the wild celebrations that gripped Britain after the relief of Mafeking during the second Boer War in March 1900, but these may have been superficial, not really indicating any great regard for or pride in the empire itself. The propagandists were certainly not satisfied. One of the great obstacles to popular imperialism, as they saw it, was the rise of socialism in Europe almost exactly contemporaneously. For their part many socialists believed that imperialism was intended mainly as a cynical device to counter the latter's appeal.

It also had, however, a rationale of its own; or rather, several, for "imperialism" was by no means a homogeneous or consistent ideology in the late nineteenth and early twentieth centuries. For example, imperialists could be nationalists or internationalists, authoritarians or liberals, capitalists or anticapitalists, and racists or egalitarians—in theory, at any rate. This goes far to explain the breadth of imperialism's appeal among intellectuals. But it had at least two common underlying characteristics. The first was a belief in the essential superiority of European civilization over other forms, usually seen in terms of "progress": that is, Europe (and America) represented the latest stage of humanity's "advance." This belief was natural for a continent that had itself self-evidently progressed or at least changed in so many ways in recent years, by contrast with what seemed to be the inertia of other cultures. It had two possible riders. One was to justify Europe's ruling other peoples, if those peoples were felt to be incapable of progressing to the same extent. That was if you were a racist. Alternatively, however, if you believed that Europe was merely "ahead" of other peoples along a road that was common to all of them, then it qualified Europe for showing those other peoples the way. Imperialism was justified as tutelage. That was its best, or at least its best-intentioned, side.

The other feature common to most imperialist ideologies arose out of a reading of the power politics of the time. Polities were getting bigger. The United States, Russia, and Germany were the chief contemporary examples. Many Europeans predicted these rising nations' domination of the world in the near future. (Some looked beyond that, and warned of the rise of Islam and China too.) Small states had no chance against powers like these; or, for some socialists, against the rising power of international capitalism, to which they were equally vulnerable. The only way to avoid being dominated was to become a dominating power yourself, with the proviso—which all empires at least claimed—that your domination would be better both for your own nation and for those you dominated than others' dominations might be. In the coming struggle for national survival in the world that many imperialists believed was inevitable—Social Darwinism had an obvious influence here—imperial expansion was the only way forward.

Imperialism was also commonly (but not universally) associated with other attitudes, most of them regarded as reactionary in the discourse of the time. Racism is one that has been mentioned already. There is no necessary and inevitable connection between these two ideologies: one could be an imperialist without being a strict racist, and obviously vice versa; but that connection could be difficult to avoid, especially in situations where the "native" subjects rejected the "enlightenment" offered them, as had happened during the Indian "Mutiny" (1857–1858), which was easier or more comfortable to explain in terms of racial inferiority. Another reactionary doctrine widely associated with imperialism was protectionism. This arose out of the defensive aspect of the "survival of the fittest" scenario. Nations and empires had to be self-sufficient. Most imperialists were therefore trade protectionists, and with some success so far as their nation's fiscal policies were concerned, although not in Britain's case before 1914. They were also notably "masculinist"—it required male strength to win and sustain an empire—and antiliberal, for much the same reason. Few leading imperialists, for example, were democrats. Imperialism therefore was usually, though not invariably, associated with the political Right.

It also however made some of the Right think again about their traditional conservative stances on domestic matters, and particularly social welfare, which became an issue for many of them in the light of the imperial struggles that seemed to be looming. "The Empire," wrote one (British) imperialist, "will not be maintained by a nation of outpatients." In Britain's case the problem was "physical deterioration" (as it was perceived); in France's the low birth rate; in Germany's the vulnerability of discontented workers to the sirens of socialism. Imperial nations needed healthy, vigorous, and loyal populaces to sustain themselves as such. It was this that turned many imperialists into social reformers, allying them with more progressive trends in their respective polities. For "genuine" socialists this merely confirmed their

British officers are carried across a shallow river by Africans. Engraving from *The Graphic,* 1890. MARY EVANS PICTURE LIBRARY

suspicions that the main object of imperialism was to take the wind out of their sails. For this and other reasons, anti-imperialism was probably as powerful an ideology throughout Europe as imperialism was, among those who were susceptible to any ideology at all.

EXPLANATIONS

That explanation—imperialism as a tool of domestic reaction—was one of a number that were around at the time and have proliferated since. It went hand in hand with another similarly critical one, which saw imperialism as a means of bypassing some of the difficulties the capitalist system seemed to be facing just then, so working to defuse socialism in another way. The argument was this: capitalism was overproducing—that is, turning out more products than could find markets domestically, which caused trade depressions, and might even lead it to collapse, to the advantage of the socialists, if additional markets could not be found elsewhere. An apocalyptic expression of this was the following alleged statement by Cecil Rhodes, the great British capitalist-imperialist, in the 1890s:

> In order to save the 40,000,000 inhabitants of the United Kingdom from a bloody civil war, we colonial statesmen must acquire new lands to settle the surplus population, to provide new markets for the goods produced by them in the factories and mines. The Empire, as I have always said, is a bread and butter question. If you want to avoid civil war, you must become imperialists. (quoted in Semmel, p. 16)

Others felt the same; for the French statesman Jules Ferry colonies were a "safety-valve" for the "superabundance of capital invested in industry" (quoted in Langer, p. 287); for the German economist Friedrich Fabri (1824–1891) they were "a matter of life and death," no less (quoted in Townsend, p. 80). There is no doubt that contemporaries conceived the colonies in this way. This was even before the argument became harnessed to a left-wing critique of empire at the hands of John Atkinson Hobson (1858–1940)—whose *Imperialism: A Study* (1902) attributed it to certain accidental malfunctions in the capitalist system: low wages, reducing the home market, and the disproportionate and malign influence of certain sectional interests—and of Vladimir Lenin (1870–1924), whose *Imperialism: The Highest Stage of Capitalism* (1917) saw the former as rooted in the essence of the latter, and especially in what he called "finance" (or investment) capitalism. For years the "capitalist theory of imperialism" held the stage so far as explanatory models for the phenomenon were concerned. It is what mainly contributed to imperialism's poor image for much of the later twentieth century, when a mere sniff of "mercenary motives" was sufficient to damn any enterprise.

In the later nineteenth century there was much less of this kind of prejudice against capitalist enterprise, even in colonial situations, where it was generally accepted as a means to benefit both sides. It is for this reason that economic motives were rarely hidden then, and indeed—it has often been suggested—may have been exaggerated in order to win over public opinion for colonial projects that had other motives behind them or that were economically highly unsound, as many of them turned out to be. There are a number of good arguments against the "capitalist theory," or at any rate a too rigid and deterministic version of it. One is that the colonies acquired by the European powers during their "capitalist imperialist" period were in fact nearly all marginal to the economies of the powers. (Of course this might not matter if Europeans expected otherwise.) Another is that it is difficult to link these motives directly with the details of most of the various acquisitions. Many of the latter are much more rationally explained on other—often local—grounds. A third is that most capitalists were in fact not particularly imperially minded: did not much care, that is, which country "ruled" their markets, so long as they were safe. A fourth may be that capitalism is still a going concern. Lenin predicted that it was only imperialism that was keeping it alive. Now that imperialism has gone, capitalism should have collapsed. That is, if imperialism is really regarded as a thing of the past, and not something that in fact survived formal "decolonization"—via U.S. foreign policy, for example, or what in the early-twenty-first century is called "globalization." It is considerations like this that make it impossible to dismiss "capitalist" explanations entirely. But there are alternative possibilities.

So far as personal "motives" are concerned, others certainly played a part. No one would claim that every humanitarian who lobbied for European annexation of a country in order to facilitate Christian missionary work, for example, or for the eradication of Arab slavery, was really a capitalist in disguise, or even necessarily the ally of one. In relation to France's north African acquisitions, individual military ambitions—often in defiance of metropolitan orders—were often crucial. We have seen how European diplomatic considerations could be important, in the case of Germany in the 1880s. One of the favorite explanations for Britain's concentration on Egypt and South Africa in the 1880s and 1890s is a "strategic" one: to safeguard Britain's naval routes (through the Suez Canal and around the Cape) to India and the further East. Several European statesmen saw colonies as a mark of prestige: "There has never been a great power without great colonies," as one Frenchman wrote (quoted in Brunschwig, *Mythes*, p. 24; author's translation). When France took Tunis in 1881, Léon-Michel Gambetta (1838–1882) is reputed to have run around Paris shouting, "France is becoming a great nation again!" (ibid., p. 55). Even in Britain, whose imperial status looked secure, Benjamin Disraeli (1804–1881) warned in 1872 of the damage that would be done to England's prestige if it ever let it go: "The issue . . . is whether you will be content to be a comfortable England, modelled and moulded upon Continental principles and meeting in due course an inevitable fate, or whether you will be a great country, an Imperial country, a country where your sons . . . command the respect of the world" (quoted in Faber, p. 64). Liberals of the time regarded that as highly reactionary. Perhaps it was; one other general theory of imperialism, associated with the Austrian sociologist Joseph Schumpeter (1883–1950), attributes it to an atavistic reversion to the "aristocratic" values of the past. Then there were those who felt Europe had a destiny to rule others, for the good of "civilization." "We happen to be the best people in the world," said Rhodes, again, "with the highest ideals of decency and justice, and the more of the world we inhabit, the better for humanity" (quoted in Faber, p. 64). Coming from Rhodes, these words may seem tainted by "mercenariness." But the same cannot necessarily be said of all these

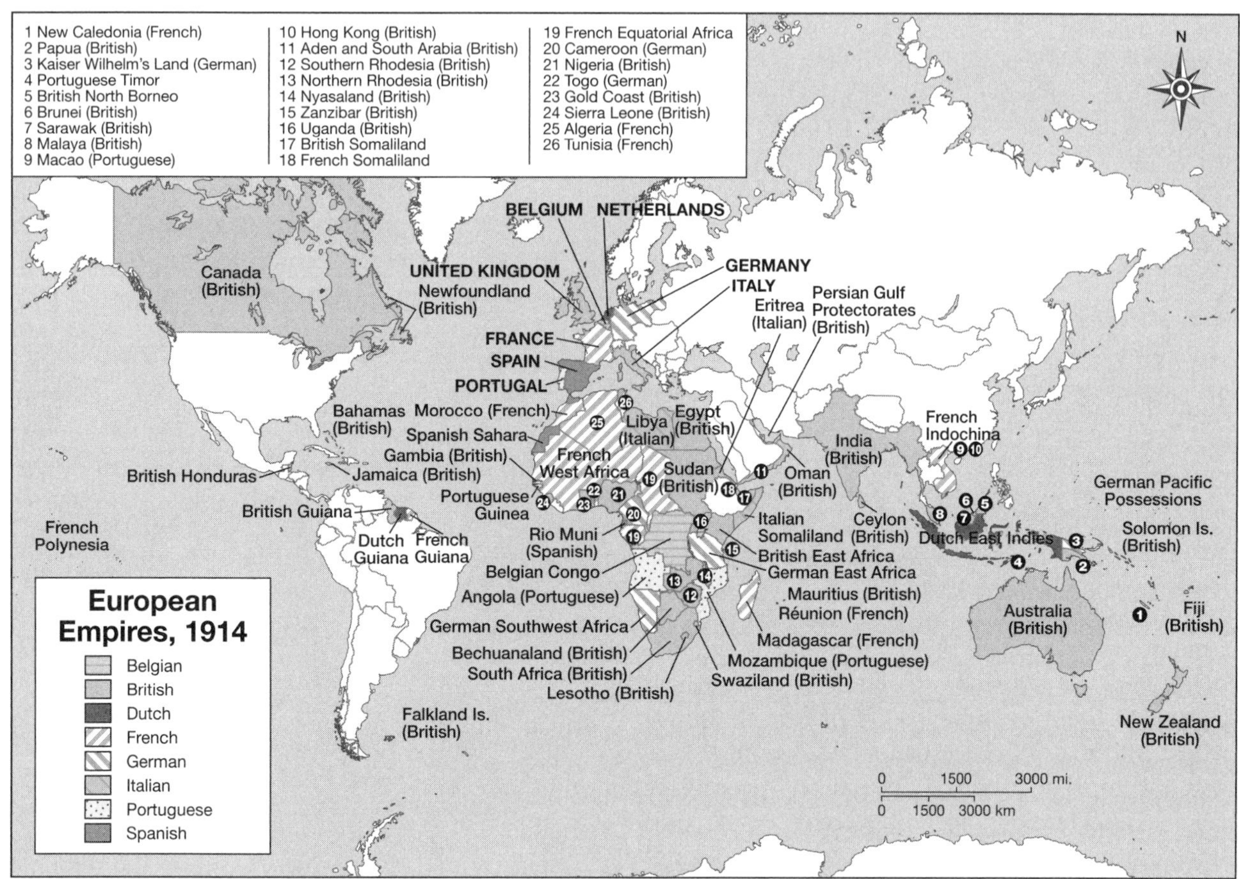

"idealistic" (as opposed to material) motives. Material considerations may have been the leading ones; or have set the invisible limits within which other factors might operate. That, however, is a question for theorists. The empirical evidence does not settle it on its own.

It may be that the true explanation for the distinctive imperialism of the late nineteenth and early twentieth centuries—not of the general dispersal of Europeans, their goods and ideas, that is, but of the shift from that to formal colonial annexation and rule—is both more accidental and more trivial than the grand theories of the Leninists and the Schumpeterians would suggest. Extraneous events happening around the 1870s had much to do with it. These included the trade depressions of the 1870s to 1890s, mild by later standards but a shock after the much sunnier 1850s and 1860s, when capitalism had seemed to have straightened out its initial systemic glitches; the unifications of Germany and Italy, raising them for the first time to positions where they could contemplate colonial expansion, and provoking France and Russia to redouble their own expansions; and the culmination of all those technological advances—especially in transport, weaponry, and medicine—that widened, to its maximum, the power differential between Europe and most of the rest of the world. That differential was vital. It meant that it was comparatively easy now for Europe to dominate other countries—though by no means certain, as has been shown—as well as even more likely than before that she should regard herself as "superior" to them. This in itself, however, did not guarantee an imperialist outcome. Even in the 1880s and 1890s most European governments and peoples were more wary of new overseas commitments than the actual events of this period would seem to imply. No one had ever proved that they were really worth the candle, certainly economically.

Three factors prompted the various "scrambles" of this period. The first was the new competition for territory, released by the political events of the 1860s and 1870s, and crowding the colonial scene for the older imperial powers. The second was the very apparent decline of the ideal of "free trade," which had been meant to make colonies irrelevant—if you could trade with a country anyway it should not matter whether you ruled it or not—but whose undermining by the new "protectionists" inevitably opened up the question again. At the very least countries might need to be taken in hand in order to ensure that they remained "free trade": which was why King Leopold II was given the Congo, on that very condition; and why it was named—in a way that came to seem somewhat incongruous later—the "Congo *Free* State." The third was the discovery by many of the more benevolent of the older established imperialists that their benevolence was not always welcomed by the natives as it should have been (in view of the self-evident benefits and truths that they were trying to disseminate), and was sometimes resisted forcibly; which persuaded them of the necessity of formal control where informal influence had sufficed earlier. This gave rise to what are called "peripheral" reasons for colonial intervention, different in each set of circumstances, which seems to make "general" theories of imperialism all the more implausible: at least, to explain this particular phase of the phenomenon.

The causes of imperialism are still controversial. It partly depends on one's definition of the term. There were general factors at work. The energies released by the Industrial Revolution contributed to the wide dispersal of Europeans overseas during the nineteenth century. The European Enlightenment nurtured attitudes of superiority. If dispersal and superiority are sufficient on their own to denote "imperialism," then its explanation can be sought there. That kind of "imperialism," however, did not need to transmute into more formal—or even "informal"—kinds. The reasons for that may be more vague, uncertain, particular, and mixed. They will also depend on one's ideological disposition: to rate material above "idealistic" factors, for example; or vice versa; or to rate "culture" ahead of either. The jury is still out on this.

IMPACT

The legacy of nineteenth- and early-twentieth-century imperialism is even more of an analytical minefield than the question of its causes. The reasons for this are threefold. The first is a general historical one: effects are always the most difficult things in history to divine. They involve considerations of alternative scenarios—what would India have been like without the raj? and so on—which can never be more than speculative. Second, on this particular issue: people have strong feelings about it, often unrelated—or only selectively related—to the "facts." *Imperialism* became a term of abuse on the political Left in the early twentieth century, and among Americans for different reasons (they would have to be, in view of the United States' own strong imperialist tradition), and remains so for probably the majority of people in the early twenty-first century. Third, there is the question of semantics, yet again. It depends what is meant by *imperialism.* In its broadest sense—Western expansion—it clearly had an immense impact: though it is difficult to be sure that some societies, at least, would not have "progressed" in roughly similar directions indigenously, and a matter of opinion whether those directions were on balance admirable or regrettable. There is also the question whether "Westernization" inevitably involves Western domination, which is surely the minimal prerequisite for a truly "imperialist" relationship.

Defenders of imperialism argued (some still do) that it was only through such domination that "civilized" institutions and practices could be introduced to "backward" societies. The answers to that are, firstly, that "imperialist" standards of "civilization," even at their best-intentioned, were often culture-based and ideologically driven (*vide* Christianity and the insistence of free markets); secondly, that imperial practice did not always meet the often exacting standards of the theories behind it; and thirdly, that imperial control might not be as effective a way of spreading these values as more subtle kinds of influence. "I know of no instance in history," wrote Alfred Lyall in 1882, "of a nation being educated by another nation into self-government and independence; every nation has fought its way up in the world as the English have done" (quoted in Owen, p. 169). In those cases where countries did emerge from periods of British rule into democracy—the United States and India are the greatest examples—it is debatable whether that was in obedience to or in reaction against their imperial masters. Most former colonies did not make that happy transition. Again, that may not necessarily have been the imperialists' fault, though they are often blamed for it, still.

The contingent evils of imperialism are well known. Wars against "natives" have been mentioned already. Some of those turned into bloody massacres: like the battle of Omdurman in the Sudan in 1898. Other atrocities included Britain's "Opium Wars" with China in the middle of the nineteenth century; Germany's massacre of the Hereros of South-West Africa in the early 1900s; Leopold II's cruel exploitation of his Congo State in the 1890s and 1900s, despite all his idealistic professions; and—among more "passive" outrages—the terrible Indian famines that Britain did little to prevent or relieve. For Europe itself imperialism may have been a source of profit—that is controversial, depending on what we wish to list in the "expenditure" column—and probably boosted political reaction, in particular militarism and racism, though to what extent is unclear.

On the other side of the equation were countless acts of self-sacrifice and paternalistic altruism by individual colonial rulers who were not mainly motivated by racial prejudice and greed. The problem here, however, was that their altruism could be misdirected. Benevolence does not always guarantee beneficent results. Even the best imperial intentions could be manipulated by special material interests and distorted by cultural prejudices. Imperialism also produces atrocities almost inevitably, and provokes resistance. The problem, of course, is that the absence of imperialism can also have unfortunate effects: leaving peoples vulnerable to their own tyrants, for example, or to the "informal" tyranny that it is arguable that the free market (or "globalization") represents. It was for this reason that many of the leading imperial critics of the early twentieth century, among them Hobson, advocated not its abolition, but its internationalization: a multinational body to share the responsibility of "raising" "uncivilized" peoples and protecting them from predators. Eventually that materialized in the post–World War I League of Nations "mandates" system, making new colonial rulers answerable to the international community, not just themselves. But in 1914 that was still just a dream.

See also **Africa; Boer War; Caribbean; Colonialism; Colonies; Egypt; Fashoda Affair; French Revolutionary Wars and Napoleonic Wars; Leopold II; Socialism.**

BIBLIOGRAPHY

Bayly, Christopher A. *Imperial Meridian: The British Empire and the World, 1780–1830.* New York, 1989.

Brunschwig, Henri. *Mythes et réalités de l'imperialisme colonial français, 1871–1914.* Paris, 1960. Translated by William Granville Brown as *French Colonialism, 1871–1914: Myths and Realities.* New York, 1966.

Cain, Peter, and Tony Hopkins. *British Imperialism, 1688–2000.* 2 vols. New York, 1993.

Etherington, Norman. *Theories of Imperialism: War, Conquest, and Capital.* Totowa, N.J., 1984.

Faber, Richard. *The Vision and the Need: Late Victorian Imperialist Aims.* London, 1966.

Fieldhouse, David K. *Economics and Empire, 1830–1914.* Ithaca, N.Y., 1973.

———. *Colonialism, 1870–1945: An Introduction.* New York, 1981.

Hobson, John Atkinson. *Imperialism: A Study.* London, 1902. The classic study.

Hyam, Ronald. *Britain's Imperial Century, 1815–1914: A Study of Empire and Expansion.* 3rd ed. New York, 2002.

Kiernan, Victor G. *European Empires from Conquest to Collapse, 1815–1960.* Leicester, U.K., 1982.

Langer, William L. *European Alliances and Alignments, 1871–1890.* New York, 1931. Still the best diplomatic history of imperialism.

MacKenzie, John. *Propaganda and Empire: The Manipulation of British Public Opinion, 1880–1960.* Dover, N.H., 1984.

Mommsen, Wolfgang J. *Theories of Imperialism.* Chicago, 1982.

Owen, Roger. *Lord Cromer: Victorian Imperialist, Edwardian Proconsul.* New York, 2004.

Porter, Andrew. *European Imperialism, 1860–1914.* London, 1994. The best short introduction.

Porter, Bernard. *The Lion's Share: A Short History of British Imperialism, 1850–2004.* 4th ed. New York, 2004.

Said, Edward. *Culture and Imperialism.* New York, 1993.

Semmel, Bernard. *Imperialism and Social Reform: English Social-Imperial Thought, 1895–1914.* Cambridge, Mass., 1960.

Townsend, Mary E. *The Rise and Fall of Germany's Colonial Empire, 1884–1918.* New York, 1930.

Wesseling, H. L. *Imperialism and Colonialism: Essays on the History of European Expansion.* Westport, Conn., 1997.

Bernard Porter

IMPRESSIONISM. Impressionism was an artistic movement that originated in France in the 1860s and 1870s. In 1874 painters including Claude Monet, Camille Pissarro, Pierre-Auguste Renoir, Alfred Sisley, Berthe Morisot, Edgar Degas, Armand Guillaumin, and Paul Cézanne participated in the first of eight independent impressionist exhibitions held until 1886. They had been friendly during the previous decade, when they encountered official resistance to their novel way of painting. Their independent exhibitions were their way of gaining exposure and of responding to traditions that had recently excluded them from the government-sponsored annual exhibitions called Salons. The core impressionists were eventually joined by Gustave Caillebotte and the American Mary Cassatt. Closely identified with the impressionists was Edouard Manet, whose controversial and ground-breaking works of the 1860s led the mostly younger painters to consider him their leader, even though he refused to exhibit in their shows. The older realist artist Gustave Courbet (1819–1877) had also inspired them—he became friendly with Monet while painting together on the Normandy beaches—and his challenges to the political and artistic establishment were notorious since the 1850s. Indeed, many critics saw impressionism as the natural consequence of Courbet's realism. Finally, the painter Jean-Frédéric Bazille had been a central figure in the group, but he was killed during the Franco-Prussian War (1870–1871), before he could join in the exhibitions he had helped conceive.

CHANGING CONCEPTS OF PAINTING

Impressionism transformed the Western conception of landscape painting from timeless and nostalgic idealizations of distant places to brightly colored, seemingly accurate representations of existing, often familiar sites seen at specific moments. Throughout the long history of landscape painting, nature was generally represented as a refuge and a place of freedom from the constraints of ordinary society. During the first half of the nineteenth century in France, the Swiss philosopher Jean-Jacques Rousseau's concept of a "return to nature" as a return to innocence and authenticity certainly underlay the moody and solitary landscapes of many painters of the Barbizon school, such as Théodore Rousseau, Jean-François Millet, and Jean-Baptiste-Camille Corot. The impressionists learned many lessons from these painters, especially Corot, who mentored both Pissarro and Morisot and who practiced *peinture claire,* that is, working on a light-colored ground as a way of enhancing luminosity. Yet, responding to calls for modernity and naturalism—to reflect the environments of contemporary (French) humanity—the impressionists were less interested in escape than in recording their peers at both work and play. Whether in landscapes or in paintings focused on the human figure, their settings and situations were always contemporary rather than historical or nostalgic. Thus, their works implied that history was constantly being made out of the ordinary visual facts and culture of everyday life, as well as that the times and places in which they were living were worthy of representation in art.

Although in the twenty-first century the practice of painting on the spot directly from observation is taken for granted, in the nineteenth century that commitment was controversial. It was inseparable from debates over the role of modern subjects in art (as opposed to classical traditions), and was accompanied by pejorative comparisons to photography, which was considered unselective and mechanical, hence noncreative. Impressionist practices were also fraught with political connotations, conditioned by the new prosperity and related democratic aspirations. With their views of specifically contemporary activities, whether in Parisian cafés, on beaches, or in flowery fields, or of the economic life on waterways, railways, and boulevards, the impressionists made their paintings sensitive and inclusive reflections of modernity.

The name *impressionism* was coined by a satirical critic named Louis Leroy following the first impressionist exhibition. Leroy made fun of Monet's *Impression: Sunrise* (1872), a sketch-like view of the harbor of the painter's native Le Havre: "*Impression*: I was sure of it. I was telling myself,

The first impressionist exhibition in Paris, 1874. Caricature by Amedée Charles Henri de Noe. The caption reads: "A revolution in painting! And a terrorizing beginning." BIBLIOTHÈQUE NATIONALE, PARIS, FRANCE/BRIDGEMAN ART LIBRARY/ARCHIVES CHARMET

since I'm so impressed, there must be an impression in it. And what freedom, what ease in handling! A sketch for wallpaper is more finished than that there seascape!" The same critic mockingly accused another painting by Monet of representing figures strolling along the Boulevard des Capucines as no better than "black tongue-lickings" and a painting by Pissarro of consisting of filthy "palette scrapings" (quoted in Berson, vol. 1, pp. 25–26). Such statements expressed disgust with a technique considered so shoddy that it failed to produce a realistic effect. Another name for the group, intransigents, although eventually abandoned, referred to a broader revolutionary significance, echoing as it did the name of a group of Spanish revolutionaries from the early 1870s. The impressionist exhibition followed by just a few years the Paris Commune (1871), a civil war that pitted leftists who had taken over the city against the more conservative government forces that controlled the French army. The result for the Communards was a predictable bloodbath, which consolidated the power of a right-wing coalition in a spirit of paranoia toward further challenges to authority. The impressionists elicited memories of radical politics because of their independent movement and their free and broken brushwork. They flouted the official art salons' monopoly on public exhibitions and their style of paint handling defied the traditional craft of academic art, which taught careful draftsmanship and polished finishing. In addition, they were seen as descendants of the realist Courbet, whose activism during the Commune landed him in jail following its defeat and then forced him into exile.

There are wide variations in the look of impressionist pictures, especially when comparing the relatively traditional handling and draftsmanship of Degas to the fragmented brushstrokes of pure color that Monet and Renoir developed side by side at La Grenouillère on the banks of the river Seine. It is sometimes said there were two factions within impressionism. Degas had an academic training that taught him respect for careful drawing and planning; and he hailed art as a carefully thought-through activity rather than a mere spontaneous response to external stimuli. Yet he and those impressionists in sympathy with him took pleasure in visual displays of their deliberate technical processes and decisions as much as Monet and other impressionists, for whom spontaneity and instantaneity were revealed by sketch-like open brushwork and the use of brilliant color.

For the latter, which also included Pissarro, Sisley, and Guillaumin, who painted primarily landscapes, working out of doors, or *en plein air,* was an important step away from the artifices and recipes of the studio. Their more urban colleagues Manet, Degas, and Caillebotte surveyed the dance halls and the Opéra, as well as shops and boulevards for scenes of pleasure and material consumption. The female impressionists, Morisot and Cassatt, given the limitations of their access to the primarily male public world, developed a flair for domestic scenes, although Morisot also painted some exquisite landscapes viewed from homes at the country or the seashore. Yet as different as all these artists appear or claimed to be, they shared a commitment to the representation of modern life based on direct observation of their own world, displayed through a variety of innovative technical approaches.

MODERNITY

For many, modernity was exemplified by countryside locations, leisure, and sporting activities. These are usually the most familiar and highly prized impressionist paintings. But Monet, Guillaumin, Pissarro, and Cézanne (in his early years) included as a counterpart to leisure scenes evidence of the productivity, infrastructure, and technologies that underlay French progress in the new industrial age. Indeed, the poet Charles Baudelaire (1821–1867), while lamenting the loss of taste occasioned by the rise of the bourgeoisie and photography, urged modern artists somehow to capture the essence of their world, which for him was one of constant change, including the flow of crowded commercial avenues and socializing at sidewalk cafés. In addition, the productive energies and speed associated with factories and train travel, as in Monet's Saint-Lazare train station series, were as much a part of the landscape of modern vision as were ladies on beaches and promenades among poppy fields. The liberal art critic Jules Castagnary actually called for a modern landscape that would reflect contemporary progress built on democratic change. And both critics urged a technique that would transcend the age-old opposition between line and color, which for centuries had been a staple of the academic discourse on art. They favored a method derived directly from actual experience. Baudelaire extolled the rapid sketching he found in the work of contemporary illustrators, especially Constantin Guys, who was known for watercolors depicting *flâneurs* strolling through the urban crowd. In his famous essay, *The Painter of Modern Life* (1863), Baudelaire made Guys's combination of the fleeting glance and analytic sharpness of vision an ideal for the painter of modernity. There is much evidence that Manet took these ideas seriously, and through his example they were echoed in the works of impressionism.

Implicit in the word *impression* are two ostensibly opposed concepts: that of the rapid look or instinctive judgment and that of the exact imprint, as in a photographic impression. Hence impressionism could appear to some a casual and imperfect practice, whereas to others the intuition that light is the basis of vision, and color its medium in art, was scientifically true and called forth comparisons to photography. Both points of view could result in praise or condemnation. An early impressionist masterpiece by Monet, the *Terrace at Sainte-Adresse* (1867) exemplifies these characteristics. It is one of those paintings that seems to express a moment in time so perfectly that one could judge the season and the time of day with almost expert accuracy. Yet at the same time as

The Terrace at Sainte-Adresse. Painting by Claude Monet, 1867. ©CHRISTIE'S IMAGES/CORBIS

it produces this effect of objectivity, the painting makes a generous display of pictorial gesture and technical artifice, as in its spots and dabs of red and yellow representing flowers and its squiggles and wavy lines of greens and blues imitating the constant movement of the harbor waters near Le Havre. The peculiar and pleasing stiffness of this composition typifies early impressionism, still under the thrall of Manet's confrontational flatness and broad areas of strong local color. Monet has clearly discarded the academic convention of perspective, which would structure his canvas as a window into deep space, in favor of a rigorous surface-based geometry, held together primarily by the vertical flag poles and strong horizontal fence-line, evoking the aesthetic of Japanese prints, which were popular at the time. Monet painted the picture from the window of the villa belonging to his aunt, whom he showed with his father, cousin, and a suitor enjoying fresh breezes credited in their time, as ours, with healthy effect. Yet even while the painting so easily exemplifies the themes of pleasure and open air associated with impressionist landscape, its background is the industrial shipping on which their booming native city of Le Havre and family business depended, and on which Monet focused in many other pictures devoted to his maritime home, including *Impression: Sunrise,* especially in the early 1870s when impressionism was emerging as a coherent movement.

Degas's *Musicians in the Orchestra* (c. 1870, reworked c. 1874–1876) is a representative masterpiece from the more urban and figure orientation within impressionism. The composition is divided boldly into close-up representations of musicians in the lower half with the ballerinas and stage-set above. In fact, the performance has come to an end. Stepping out of their roles as characters and chorus, the dancers are taking their bows; the musicians pause from their playing. Unlike the relatively precisely delineated portrait (though unidentified) heads of the musicians, the stage scenery is so sketchily painted, one could never mistake it for a genuine landscape. The glare of stage projectors on the prima ballerina's curtsy highlights the artifice underlying the performance and the diaphanous fabric of her costume. Whether Degas's compositional strategy has come from the close-range vision of opera glasses, the cropping effects of photography, the eye-grabbing strategies of Japanese prints, or the in-your-face aesthetics of caricature and popular illustrated newspapers does not matter; all such media evoke the modern age. Degas seems as interested in displaying his own performance as an artist as in revealing the strategies underlying the illusions produced by opera and the dance. He never allows the viewer to forget that he himself remains forever the stage manager, *metteur-en-scène* or choreographer of the realistic effects produced by his work.

Musicians in the Orchestra. Painting by Edgar Degas, 1870 and 1874–1876. ERICH LESSING/ART RESOURCE, NY

Although few impressionists were as self-conscious as Degas, they shared the commitment to develop a style that would embody their modernity as much as their subject matter. Renoir is another example of how impressionism is made up of special individuals sharing this common bond. In 1874 he exhibited *The Loge* as a kind of advertisement for the promise of his work. The female figure attending a theatrical or operatic performance is clearly a portrait—Renoir's forte and a means to earn his living through commissions. Yet the woman, a paid model, stands both for a general public of potential clients—of course, her male companion is the one likely to be paying—and a display of Renoir's special eye for women. Indeed, with her sumptuous garb and delicate features, she is as much an object of spectacle as is the painting itself. The viewer's erotic attraction to the woman's soft skin and seductive features coincides with materialistic appetite for the luxurious object created through generously applied paint and ravishing colors. The theme of vision and scopic consumption are not only implied by the theatrical setting but emphasized by the presence of opera glasses in the woman's hand. Moreover, her companion is preoccupied not with close-up viewing of the stage—his angle would be completely wrong—but by a sight we imagine as comparable to that presented by the painting itself. It is no accident to discover that Renoir believed in the inferiority of women except as objects to fulfill his manly and household needs, and whose ubiquity in his painting gave rise to his uniquely persuasive exercise of artistic potency.

Evoking the subtext of gender relations underlying much of Renoir's painting leads to considering other social meanings of impressionism. Pissarro was the most faithful of the impressionists, exhibiting in all eight of their exhibitions and often keeping the group together through persuasion as well as collaboration with members of both factions. Yet politically, Pissarro was the most extreme of the impressionists, accused by Renoir as "that Jew" who had tried to introduce anarchist painters into the group. In Pissarro's artwork, however, it is hard to find explicit political meanings. Rather, his choice of more rural than suburban settings suggested that his ideal world was a nostalgic precapitalist utopia in which community and privacy were in perfect balance, and in which labor was the redeeming virtue. In such primarily agricultural situations, Pissarro generally showed peasants at work, a far cry from the bourgeois pleasure-seekers of most impressionist landscape. He also made his brushwork appear more deliberately methodical and he attenuated his colors compared to most of his cohorts, in order to avoid the superficially pleasing decorative effects and ostentatious spontaneity he later dismissed as "romantic" impressionism.

An excellent example of such work is *Côte des Boeufs at L'Hermitage* (1877), in which studiously interlaced branches and the assemblage of houses they screen produce a tautly woven structure with the sort of rigor that Pissarro's younger companion at the time, Cézanne, much appreciated. A peasant woman and her son seem unexpectedly to have discovered the artist as they cross through the woods on their daily routine. Pissarro has so integrated them to his vision of rural stability that one hardly notices them at first. It was in such surroundings that Pissarro worked most comfortably, and given his large brood of children, he could not afford more sophisticated locations. Born on the Caribbean island of St. Thomas and a citizen of Denmark, Pissarro was an outsider to the Parisian and bourgeois world of most of his cohorts. Although Pissarro's social ideal of inclusion seems nostalgic for being based on a disappearing world, it was also progressive for its belief in the possibility of a harmonious future. Such motivations lay behind the investment of time and effort he made in the impressionist's collective movement, which embodied inclusive and democratic principles he hoped one day might extend to society as a whole.

The Côte des Boeufs at l'Hermitage Near Pontoise. Painting by Camille Pissarro, 1877. ©NATIONAL GALLERY COLLECTION; BY KIND PERMISSION OF THE TRUSTEES OF THE NATIONAL GALLERY, LONDON/ CORBIS

One of Mary Cassatt's masterpieces, *Little Girl in a Blue Armchair* (1878) shows how superb impressionist paintings could be made within the limitations of a bourgeois woman's life. Cassatt came from respectable society in Philadelphia, where she had studied at the famous Philadelphia Academy. A modern woman nonetheless, she came to Paris in order to pursue her artistic career. She knew that a proper lady could not go out without an escort, whether to the countryside or to observe modern life in cafés, museums, or the theater. Introduced to the impressionist circle by Degas, an artist who did many fascinating pictures of family and friends, Cassatt discovered that modern forms of beauty could be found in her immediate, if restricted, surroundings. A little girl just returned from school flops down on the soft armchair of her family's elegant and well-lit sitting room. Mother is still out shopping or visiting friends in the afternoon. Colorful slipcover patterns play vividly across the canvas in a space whose foreshortening is worthy of compositional strategies used by Cassatt's mentor, Degas. Like Degas and Manet, too, Cassatt makes reference to past art traditions through a device used by no less a master than Rembrandt to suggest an instant when privacy has been interrupted. The girl's pet terrier, probably Cassatt's own Yorkshire or a Griffon, lounges on the armchair next to her. Yet he faces the viewer in a way that acknowledges an outside presence and suggests the dog's readiness to pounce and yelp should there be any unseemly movement. With her petticoats showing, this is an intimate moment and the canine sentry must be equal to its duty. Like so much impressionist work, the picture looks casual and spontaneous—with its ostensibly unposed figure and broad brushwork. Yet the careful planning needed to produce such charming effects is driven by the ambition to make the greatest art from the most ordinary and insignificant circumstances.

IMPRESSIONISM AND POSITIVISM

Impressionism's commitment to direct observation and surface experience, along with its evocation of progressive change, are certainly associated with the spirit of positivism, a contemporary philosophy developed by Auguste Comte (1798–1857) and applied to art by his disciple and specialist in the psychology of perception, Hippolyte-Adolphe Taine. Comte's quasi-religion of progress based on scientific attitudes was followed by Taine's deterministic theories on the history of art. Their ideas might be stated as the relationship between art and its immediate physical and social environment, expressed through the empirical perceptions of the talented individual. Drawing on both Taine and Baudelaire, the novelist Émile Zola, a childhood friend of Cézanne through whom he met the impressionists, wrote famously that "art is no more nor less than a corner of nature seen through a temperament." This statement reminds us that whatever conception of nature one may have, each individual has a personal way of seeing it. Monet's concentration on the mutable elements of nature—the liquids and gases in water, clouds, and even the industrial vapors of locomotives—implies a concept of nature in which the only constant is its ever-changing flux and flow. The impressionists' concentration on the surface of forms evokes a sense that nature is a place unknowable other than by immediate and highly personal sensation, even when it is as ineffable as the interaction of light and form—what Monet at the time of his later paintings called "the envelope."

The association between these ideas and impressionism can be gauged by two developments from impressionism. The first is by the neo-impressionist critique of their achievement. Certain artists of the next generation, especially Georges Seurat (*Sunday Afternoon on the Island of La Grande Jatte*, 1886), according to the critic Félix Fénéon (1861–1944), sought to make impressionism more socially responsible and democratic by developing a collective technique accessible to all. Seurat exhibited his work along with others by him and a few followers in a separate room of the last impressionist exhibition in 1886. Hence, many saw his effort simply as the latest stage of impressionism. Seurat's dot-dash or pointillist method reduced the labor of painting to a repeatable formula, while at the same time creating the sensation of duration over time rather than a spontaneously grasped instant. On both grounds, neo-impressionism claimed greater objectivity, thus challenging the individualist basis of impressionist truth to nature in favor of a shared and more permanent, hence more classical, vision. Through Seurat's eyes, then, impressionism celebrated merely momentary, superficial pleasures and casual, intuitive craft rather than the mental and physical concentration derived from rational calculation and rigorous effort. This moralizing argument fit a political critique of bourgeois society that came to be associated with avant-garde painting of both the Right and the Left after impressionism.

Paul Cézanne also managed to transcend the impressionist sense of moment to produce what he called "a more lasting art, like that of the museums." In ways more fruitful than Seurat and more lasting for modern art, his increasing abstraction led toward future styles of the twentieth century, especially cubism. Yet Cézanne, who was of the same age group as the impressionists, and painted and exhibited with them in the 1870s, deserves to be classified among them because, unlike Seurat, he never abandoned their principle of working directly from the motif *en plein air* or of conceiving form in color. One of the classic paintings of Cézanne's mature style, *La Montagne Sainte-Victoire* (1886) was done at the same time as Seurat's *Grande Jatte,* and like the latter, it displays both a rigorous structure—note how the central tree focuses attention and flattens the composition—and a sense of temporal duration. Yet Cézanne's effects are produced by carefully applied patches of color, whose amazing economy lends an intellectual dignity associated with deep reflection to his labor rather than the impersonal mechanics of Seurat's dots or the spontaneous rapidity of earlier impressionism. Nor do Cézanne's paintings seem like visual fragments or slices of reality, as do many impressionist works. They come across as unified microcosms of both place and time, as exemplified by the absence of figures, the domineering presence of the greatest mountain in Cézanne's native Provence and the viaduct across the Arc River valley, which evokes Roman antiquity even though it was known to his countrymen as a recent railway construction. While incorporating lessons from neo-impressionism, then, Cézanne held fast to his impressionist roots.

IMPACT

In the other arts, impressionism's impact was limited. The sensitive, mobile surfaces of Auguste Rodin's bronze sculptures caught the light in ways associated with impressionism. Claude Debussy's music came to be called impressionist because its flowing, seemingly directionless style challenged past conventions and evoked certain motifs in nature associated with impressionist painting. In the literature of Henry James, the term refers to the literal naturalism of settings described in so much detail that it both overwhelms and yet concentrates one's anticipation of the narrative.

In painting, almost every country had its impressionist school; the British and the American, with their direct ties to Monet's circle, were the strongest. In later art, the abstract expressionism of artists like Jackson Pollock (1912–1956) has been traced to Claude Monet's late *Waterlilies,* and the contemporary painter Joan Mitchell (1926–1992), who spent much time near Monet's former residence in Giverny, has been called an "abstract impressionist." However, perhaps the greatest legacy of impressionism is that it is the most popular style for so many amateur art colonies and Sunday painters, who celebrate both nature and leisure while working hard to develop their personal techniques.

See also **Cézanne, Paul; Courbet, Gustave; Degas, Edgar; Monet, Claude; Morisot, Berthe; Painting; Pissarro, Camille; Realism and Naturalism; Renoir, Pierre-Auguste.**

BIBLIOGRAPHY

Berson, Ruth, ed. *The New Painting: Impressionism, 1874–1886: Documentation.* 2 vols. San Francisco, 1996.

Brettell, Richard. *Impression: Painting Quickly in France, 1860–1890.* New Haven, Conn., and London, 2001.

Callen, Anthea. *Techniques of the Impressionists.* London, 1982.

Clark, Timothy J. *The Painting of Modern Life: Paris in the Art of Manet and His Followers.* Princeton, N.J., 1984.

Herbert, Robert L. *Impressionism: Art, Leisure, and Parisian Society.* New Haven, Conn., and London, 1988.

Moffet, Charles S. *The New Painting: Impressionism, 1874–1886: An Exhibition.* The San Francisco Museum of Fine Arts, 1986. Exhibition catalog.

Rewald, John. *The History of Impressionsim.* 4th rev. edition. London and New York, 1973.

Rubin, James H. *Impressionism.* London, 1999.

Tinterow, Gary, and Henri Loyrette. *Origins of Impressionism.* The Metropolitan Museum of Art, New York, 1994. Exhibition catalog.

James H. Rubin

INDIA. The starting date for British rule in India is conventionally given as 1757, when East India Company forces commanded by Robert Clive (1725–1774) defeated the Nawab of Bengal, a vassal of the Mughal Empire, and asserted British military supremacy in the region. In 1765 the Mughal emperor presented the Company with the *diwani* of Bengal—the right to collect the tax revenues—making it the province's effective ruler. Under the administrations of Governor-Generals Warren Hastings (1732–1818) from 1772 to 1785 and Charles, Marquess Cornwallis (1738–1805) from 1786 to 1793, the East India Company spread its influence into independent kingdoms and Mughal provinces, notably Awadh and Arcot, backed with a growing army composed largely of Indian sepoys. The late eighteenth century also witnessed a flowering of cultural exchange between east and west, particularly in the Mughal centers of Lucknow and Hyderabad, where European officials adopted aspects of Indian court culture and often took Indian wives and consorts. The Asiatic Society of Bengal, founded in Calcutta in 1784, undertook sustained study of Indian culture, from religion to language to natural history; its first president, Sir William Jones (1746–1794), identified the kinship among Sanskrit, Greek, and Latin to discover the Indo-European language family.

The French Revolutionary and Napoleonic Wars had a major effect on the nature and scope of British rule in the subcontinent. Richard Colley Wellesley (1760–1842), governor-general from 1798 to 1805, used the threat of French expansion in the east (triggered by Napoleon Bonaparte's invasion of Egypt in 1798) as a pretext for consolidating and extending British power. One of Wellesley's preferred methods was the "subsidiary alliance system," whereby the East India Company assumed indirect control of provinces such as Awadh and Hyderabad by requiring regional rulers to garrison and pay for Company troops. In this manner the Company retained a regulating hand in the affairs of key states such as Awadh, Hyderabad, and Tanjore. Wellesley also waged war. By 1800 the East India Company army stood at two hundred thousand troops, with a European officer corps of about thirty thousand. In 1799 the British defeated and killed their most dangerous Indian enemy, Tipu Sultan (1750–1799) of Mysore, and placed his domains in the hands of a compliant puppet ruler. In 1803, after failing to impose a subsidiary alliance on the powerful Maratha confederacy, the Company went to war with the Marathas and succeeded in fracturing the union. The Company's Court of Directors in London objected to wars of expansion because of their high cost and recalled Wellesley in 1805. His successors pursued imperial consolidation, however, and by 1818, thanks to a series of subsidiary alliances and outright conquest, British suzerainty extended as far west as the River Sutlej in Punjab.

Purniya, Chief Minister of Mysore. Painting by Thomas Hickey c. 1801. Purniya played a major role in reconstituting the Kingdom of Mysore as a client state of the British East India Company. Although here his dress is Indian, the background features European symbols, including a Greek column. YALE CENTER FOR BRITISH ART, PAUL MELLON COLLECTION, USA/BRIDGEMAN ART LIBRARY

These conquests were accompanied by a wave of "Anglicist" administrative measures, which sought to reform Indian customs in keeping with British liberal ideals. Christian missionaries entered India after 1813, when the East India Company lost its monopoly on trade. In 1829 the Hindu practice of *sati,* or widow burning, was suppressed. British officials also aggressively hunted down practitioners of *thagi,* who supposedly performed ritual murder and robbery in the name of the goddess Kali. In 1835 Persian was replaced by English as an official language of East India Company business. Territorial expansion also continued, fueled by rising fears of Russian influence in India. The Afghan War of 1839–1842, in which a British force of 16,500 soldiers and camp-followers was virtually annihilated, led to the Company's last recall of a governor-general, in 1844; but the conquest of Sindh and Punjab in the 1840s extended British rule across modern-day Pakistan. The Company further enlarged its domains with the "doctrine of lapse," espoused by the governor-general, Lord Dalhousie (1812–1860; governor-general from 1848–1856), whereby if a regional prince died without a legitimate heir, the East India Company assumed control of his province. This proved especially controversial since the Company did not recognize adopted heirs, customary in Indian courts. In 1856 Dalhousie annexed the north Indian province of Awadh. The move was highly unpopular in South Asia, and helped fuel mounting opposition to Company rule.

The following winter, a new kind of rifle was distributed to the sepoys of the East India Company army. Rumor spread among the troops that the cartridges for the guns were greased with a combination of cow and pig fat, which meant that both Hindus and Muslims would be defiled when they bit the ends off the cartridges to load them. The rumor catalyzed long-standing discontent. On 10 May 1857 sepoys at Meerut shot their British officers and marched toward Delhi, the Mughal capital, thus beginning the Indian Mutiny-Rebellion. They called on the Mughal emperor, Bahadur Shah II (r. 1837–1858), to grant them his protection and set up a provisional government. Mutinies followed across the camps of the Bengal Army. British communities in Lucknow and Kanpur were besieged in horrific conditions, and hundreds of civilians massacred. Reprisals against the mutineers were equally savage, involving brutal degradation and summary executions. On 2 August 1858 the British Parliament formally assumed the reins of Indian government from the East India Company, thus commencing the "Raj." The East India Company was dissolved soon after, and the emperor exiled to Burma.

THE RAJ TO WORLD WAR I

By wiping out both the Mughal Empire and the East India Company, the British Raj ended two contradictions of earlier British rule: the paradox of a commercial company acting as a ruler; and the fiction that the East India Company governed as a vassal of the Mughal emperor. Much of India now belonged openly to the British Empire, was governed on behalf of the queen by a viceroy and his council, and was administered by the elite, tightly organized Indian Civil Service. The Indian army was restructured to maintain a ratio of one British soldier for every two sepoys, and recruitment efforts now focused on "martial races," believed to be more loyal. British communities withdrew into easily secured cantonments on the outskirts of Indian cities, and racial discrimination tended to replace the relative cultural tolerance of the Hastings era.

The British Raj also borrowed elements from the East India Company and Mughal government that had preceded it. The Raj pledged itself to nonintervention in matters of religion and to maintaining the integrity of the Indian princely states—which even at the time of independence covered approximately one-third of the subcontinent. Indian regional rulers were encouraged to associate themselves with Queen Victoria (r. 1837–1901), a relationship consolidated in 1876 when the queen was named Empress of India. The fusion of East and West found concrete form in the architecture of the period, much of it built in a new style called Indo-Saracenic, which mingled elements of Islamic and Hindu architecture with the gothic revivalism popular in Victorian Britain. Britain's symbolic appropriation of India reached its apogee under the viceroy from 1898 to 1905, Lord Curzon (1859–1925), who staged an elaborate coronation durbar (assembly of nobles) for Edward VII (r. 1901–1910) in 1903. Convergences and separations between British and Indian cultures were popularly captured by Rudyard Kipling (1865–1936) in his widely read poems, stories, and novels.

Britain's chief economic contribution to India is generally seen as the railroad network, which jumped from virtually nil in 1858 to twenty-five thousand miles of track by 1900. But the railroads also helped Britain turn India into a supplier of raw materials, such as cotton and jute, and a captive market for British manufactured goods. This had devastating effects on India's industrial development, both artisanal and factory-based. The trade imbalance, coupled with a steady depreciation of the rupee and burdensome "home charges"—by which India paid Britain for the cost of its administration—led Indian nationalists to characterize British rule as a drain of wealth. Politically and socially, British policies proved no less controversial. A prime example was the Ilbert Bill of 1883, a reforming measure that placed Indian and European justices on the same footing, thereby making it possible for Indians to judge European defendants. Members of the British-Indian community objected vehemently to the bill, formed leagues of protest, and forced the viceroy to back down.

The Ilbert Bill furor encouraged Indian nationalist sentiment to coalesce. In 1885 the Indian National Congress held its first meeting in Bombay. The body sought redress from the colonial government for injustices such as the hefty home charges and discrimination against Indian candidates who wished to enter the Indian Civil Service. Congress membership grew rapidly and the group soon became the leading organ of nationalist

Lord Curzon with the Maharaja of Rewa and Captain Wigram. Photograph from the British publication *The Sphere,* 13 June 1903. Viceroy Curzon (fourth from right) is shown with his aide de camp, Clive Wigram (third from right) and the Maharaja of Rewa (left of Curzon) and his retinue after a hunting expedition. Mary Evans Picture Library

opinion. Emerging calls for Indian self-government heightened dramatically in 1905 when the British government decided to partition Bengal into two provinces: one Hindu-majority province centered in Calcutta and one Muslim-majority province with its capital at Dhaka. The move appeared not only to violate Bengal's integrity as a region but also to promote a policy of "divide and rule" and foment communal hostility. Sponsored by Congress, Bengali Hindus boycotted British goods and made a point of using only Indian-made, or *swadeshi,* products instead (notably homespun fabrics). Meeting in Calcutta in 1906, Congress announced *swaraj,* or self-rule, as one of its central goals. The same year witnessed the founding of the Muslim League in Dhaka, designed to serve as the voice of Muslim nationalist opinion. More radical measures were favored by Bengali terrorists and supporters of the militant Marathi leader Bal Gangadar Tilak (1856–1920), who was jailed for sedition in 1908.

The newly elected British Liberal government of 1906 responded to protests in India with a series of limited reforms, known as the

Morley-Minto Reforms (1909). In 1911 Bengal was reunified, although the imperial capital was shifted from Calcutta to Delhi, where it would remain for the rest of the Raj. By the eve of World War I, key elements in the Indian nationalist movement were firmly in place. India had become the jewel in the crown of the British Empire, but how long it would remain so was open to debate.

See also **Colonialism; East India Company; Great Britain; Imperialism; Sepoy Mutiny.**

BIBLIOGRAPHY

Bayly, C. A. *Indian Society and the Making of the British Empire.* Cambridge, U.K., and New York, 1988.

Bose, Sugata, and Ayesha Jalal. *Modern South Asia: History, Culture, Political Economy.* New York, 1998.

Dirks, Nicholas B. *Castes of Mind: Colonialism and the Making of Modern India.* Princeton, N.J., 2001.

Mehta, Uday Singh. *Liberalism and Empire: A Study in Nineteenth-Century British Liberal Thought.* Chicago, 1999.

Metcalf, Thomas R. *Ideologies of the Raj.* Cambridge, U.K., and New York, 1994.

Sinha, Mrinalini. *Colonial Masculinitys: The "Manly Englishman" and the "Effeminate Bengali" in the Late Nineteenth Century.* Manchester, U.K., 1995.

MAYA JASANOFF

INDOCHINA. The word *Indo-China* appeared in English in 1810, and *Indo-Chine* in French a decade later. A linguist and a geographer coined the term for the peninsula between India and China. In the early twenty-first century it comprises Burma, Thailand, Cambodia, Laos, and Vietnam. In the early nineteenth century "Indochina" described no political boundary, but it bridged a cultural one. Theravada Buddhist realms using a variety of Indic alphabets occupied most of the peninsula, while a Confucian kingdom whose texts employed Chinese characters ruled the east coast. Yet the notion of a dichotomous zone of Indic and Sinic cultures was a European view. Mainland Southeast Asia's dozen kingdoms and principalities were ethnically diverse descendants of twenty-three fourteenth-century polities. Few of their inhabitants considered them local exemplars of distant centers of world civilizations. The early dissonance between indigenous and imperial geographies was mutual. In the eastern peninsula, terms for "Europeans" in Khmer (*barang*), Vietnamese (*phap*), and Lao (*falang*), derive from the Arabic for "Franks." Later, as subjects of French Indochina, speakers of those languages would rarely consider themselves "Indochinese."

In the early nineteenth century, political consolidation proceeded as dynamic new dynasties forged three dominant kingdoms. Those of Burma and Siam carved up the west and central peninsula. In the east, the new dynasty produced a new name. The vast Tay Son revolution launched in 1771 reunited the kingdom of Đai Viet ("Greater Viet") in 1786, after a century and a half of division. The Trinh and Nguyen families had ruled the country's "outer" north and "inner" south since 1627, maintaining the powerless Hanoi court of the Lê dynasty (1427–1788) as a symbol of unity. When the Lê monarch sought Chinese military aid in 1788, the Tay Son leader seized the throne. He drove out the invading Chinese to end the Lê era. Meanwhile, however, the surviving southern prince Nguyen Anh gathered a new army and took Saigon in 1788. Marching north, he overthrew the Tay Son in 1802. Assuming the regnal title Gia-Long and seeking Chinese recognition for his new Nguyen dynasty, he chose to give Đai Viet a new name, Nam Viet ("the Viet South"). The Chinese court, which had long termed it An Nam ("the pacified South"), amended this to Viet Nam. As "king of the Southern Viet Country" (*Viet Nam Quoc Vuong*), Gia-Long accepted China's suzerain ruling on his kingdom's name.

VIETNAM AND THE RISE OF GIA-LONG

"Viet Nam" made more than a nominal new start. Historian Alexander Woodside suggests that the Tay Son era "inaugurates modern Vietnamese history." The revolution reunified the country after growing successfully from its villages, "for the first time making the peasant world the crucial battle-ground for Vietnamese rulers and would-be rulers" (Woodside, pp. 3–4). Others, including Europeans, also entered Vietnamese politics. From the Siamese capital Bangkok, French bishop Pigneau de Behaine and four hundred French soldiers and sailors supported Gia-Long's rise to power. So did a Thai rebel and a Chinese pirate and their two fleets of junks, twenty thousand Siamese troops, and a former Cambodian palace slave with five thousand Khmer followers. Despite a history of sporadic ethnic violence, the region that became southern Indochina was a relatively open zone of diverse external and indigenous interaction. Ethnic and national divisions consolidated only slowly, under Nguyen and later French rule.

Vietnam's internal conflicts had forced closer contact with its Buddhist neighbors after centuries of uneven Confucian restrictions on commercial exchanges. Chinese merchants had monopolized much of the trade that mandarins permitted; a small Vietnamese trading class struggled to emerge. Tay Son rebels, seizing the port of Saigon in 1776, threw Chinese goods into the sea, and massacred ten thousand Chinese in 1782.

The upheaval also brought politico-cultural change. For three decades, bureaucratic appointments proceeded without the traditional triennial examinations in the Chinese Confucian classics. The Tay Son made Vietnamese the official language of government for the first time, and commissioned a new compilation of Đai Viet's history. Vietnam's *nom* script, employing Chinese characters to write sentences in Vietnamese, began to replace Chinese-language texts. Despite nine centuries of Chinese rule (42–939 C.E.), Confucianism had never dominated the diverse society of Đai Viet. Cults of indigenous spirits and female deities remained common. From the seventeenth century European missionaries converted tens of thousands of Vietnamese to Catholicism. The eighteenth century brought Đai Viet's incorporation of the largely Khmer, Theravada Buddhist region of the Mekong Delta, along with a revival of Vietnamese Mahayana Buddhism, a *nom* literary renaissance, and the rise of women writers such as Ho Xuan Huong (c. 1775–1820), and even a female Tay Son general, Bui Thi Xuan.

Faced with these challenges to the Confucian culture of government, in 1802 Gia-Long set about strengthening the "Chinese model." But pragmatism proved necessary. Gia-Long retained Europeans at his court and, while calling himself the "Son of Heaven," confided to a Frenchman that there was no such thing. Building his new capital at Hué in central Vietnam, Gia-Long replicated Beijing's "Forbidden City," referring to Vietnam as the "Middle Kingdom," yet he also recognized Siam as a peer: "Cambodia is a small country. . . . And we should maintain it as a child. We will be its mother; its father will be Siam" (Chandler 1983, p. 116). Gia-Long ordered "clear borders" between "the Vietnamese and the barbarians" (Choi, p. 34). In 1813, he restored the country's traditional name Đai Viet, and a thirteen-thousand-strong Vietnamese army installed a protectorate over Cambodia. Yet Gia-Long withdrew Vietnamese residents from there in 1815 to avoid "trouble with Cambodians in the future," and later ordered his officials to "prevent my people from intervening in their lives" (Choi, pp. 34–35).

Gia-Long's domestic rule was relentless. In 1804, he ordered the captive Tay Son woman general Bui Thi Xuan trampled to death by elephants. He adopted the legal code of China's Ching dynasty (1644–1911), subjecting mandarins whose wives or daughters visited Buddhist temples to forty strokes of a cane, and he banned construction of new temples. He reinstated Confucian classical examinations and had a fourteenth-century Chinese text, *Twenty-Four Stories of Filial Piety,* translated into *nom* as a primer for pupils. Wives had to obey their husbands, children parents, and subjects the ruler. Gia-Long compared his people to "a child who needs care. Now that the war is over people have been used to a hard life—so they are easily ordered about and work can be done. If one waits a few years they will be used to a peaceful life and won't obey easily." Confucian texts again guided government. The Vietnamese translator of *Twenty-Four Stories,* received in China as a "barbarian," quickly demonstrated Confucian scholarly accomplishment that the imperial court acknowledged.

As well as obedience from subjects, Confucianism required benevolence from rulers. Gia-Long urged the wealthy to donate food in hard times, and made land grants to the poor. His son and successor Minh-Mang (r. 1820–1841) followed suit, and built a "relief" system to meet food shortages in times of drought, flood, and fire. He ordered the rich to hand over two-thirds of their lands to the village communes, and forbade the sale of communal land for profit. In his view, "the relationship between a king and his people is like that of a good father with a young child who does not wait for the child to be cold to put clothes on him."

The stricter cultural controls both reflected and aggravated social unrest. Two hundred uprisings broke out during Minh-Mang's reign. He put down three major rebellions in the 1830s and a fourth in 1841. Minh-Mang tried unsuccessfully to ban the *nom* script in the first year of his reign. In 1840, he attempted to ban village theater performances, a venue for peasant gatherings. He complained that "a stupendous number of males and females, old people and young people, watch these plays. This must definitely be an evil custom" (Woodside, p. 27).

The Confucian restoration strengthened restrictions on trade. In the early 1820s American and English visitors considered Vietnamese "the ablest builders of ships," and "the best sailors in the Far East" (Chesneaux, p. 54). But in 1822, Đai Viet exported only seventeen thousand tonnes of goods to its main trading partner, China. A mandarin dismissed the merchant as one who "eats his meat in a big lump, very greedily" (Woodside, p. 35). British diplomat John Crawford reported of Gia-Long: "Some of the French officers who had been admitted into his confidence, and even familiarity, informed me that they had often ventured to recommend to him the encouragement of industry within his dominions, but that his constant reply was that he did not want rich subjects, as poor ones were more obedient." An English doctor lamented "the number of men engaged on work which is absolutely unproductive for the State, as well as being harmful to the practices of national industry. The lowliest mandarin is served by a multitude" (Chesneaux, p. 59).

Laos and Cambodia occupied the Mekong basin, separating Vietnam from Siam. Though well-watered, their soil infertility and low population density encouraged competition for labor rather than land. From 1824, officials of the new Siamese king, Rama III, carried out a population census on the west bank of the Mekong and began widespread tattooing of its Lao peasants to control their movement. In 1826, the hitherto loyal Lao monarch Anuvong (r. 1804–1828) rebelled against Siam. Crossing the Mekong from his capital, Viang Chan (Vientiane), his armies attempted to evacuate all the Lao to the east bank. When Siamese troops counterattacked, he appealed for Vietnamese support. The Siamese devastated Viang Chan; the French found only "huts among the ruins" four decades later. Siam's army forcibly deported the city's ten thousand families to the west bank along with much of the remaining population of central Laos and dispatched Anuvong to his death in Bangkok.

Siam's suppression of Laos preceded Vietnam's conquest of Cambodia. Partly to block the Siamese advances, Minh-Mang first seized much of east central and southern Laos, which he renamed Tran Ninh and Cam Lo. Yet with one-third of southern Vietnam still populated by non-Vietnamese, Đai Viet's greatest threat remained internal. The adopted son of the governor of Saigon, Lê Van Khoi, rebelled in 1833. With a French missionary by his side, Khoi won support from Mekong Delta Khmers, Chinese merchants in Saigon, and from Siam's Rama III, seeking access to the China trade. In 1834 Minh-Mang defeated the Siamese armies that had invaded through Cambodia, and he crushed Khoi the next year. Minh-Mang now had full control not only of Đai Viet, but also Cambodia, which became the protectorate province of Tran Tay Thanh. Now laying claim to more than the old Viet realm, in 1839 Minh-Mang renamed his kingdom Đai Nam, "the Great South."

At the height of its expansion, the Vietnamese kingdom had overreached. Cambodia's people had no wish to be "Vietnamized," but Minh-Mang instructed his commander there: "The barbarians have become my children now, and you should help them, and teach them our customs ... teach them to use oxen, teach them to grow more rice, teach them to raise mulberry trees, pigs and ducks. ... As for language, they should be taught to speak Vietnamese. [Our habits of] dress and table manners must also be followed. If there is any out-dated or barbarous custom that can be simplified or repressed, then do so. ... Let the good ideas seep in, turning the barbarians into civilized people" (Chandler, 1983, p. 126). Khmers had to grow their hair long, wear trousers instead of sarongs, eat with chopsticks, and perform unpaid labor for foreign mandarins.

Rebellions broke out every year from 1836. Minh-Mang wrote his viceroy in Phnom Penh: "Sometimes the Cambodians are loyal; at other times they betray us. We helped them when they were suffering, and lifted them out of the mud. ... Now they are rebellious: I am so angry that my hair stands upright. ... Hundreds of knives should be used against them, to chop them up, to dismember them." He added in another edict that Cambodian rebels must be "crushed to powder." Cambodian rebel leaders reciprocated: "We are happy killing Vietnamese. We no longer fear them; in all our battles, we are mindful of the three jewels [of Buddhist teaching]—the Buddha, the Law, and the monastic community" (Chandler 1973, pp. 153–154). Đai Nam slowly lost its hold on Cambodia by 1841, to the advantage of Siam.

Đai Nam now faced challenges from the West, in particular France, which called the country Annam, its former Chinese name. French bishops had developed a powerful interest there, home to about seventy thousand Catholics by 1820. Minh-Mang was less receptive to French influence than his father, and the last two Frenchmen left his court by 1824. The next year Minh-Mang attempted to ban Catholicism. He executed several Western missionaries in 1833, and Vietnamese Catholics in 1838–1839. Increasingly, French Catholics claimed the responsibility of protecting their co-religionists in Đai Nam.

The French also came for commerce, as did other Westerners. British missions reached Hué in 1803 and 1822. A French warship visited its port, Da Nang, in 1817. As France's first consul, in 1820 Louis XVIII appointed a Frenchman married to a Vietnamese. Even under Minh-Mang, Đai Nam was never closed to Western ideas. By 1836 it was buying British gunpowder. Troops in Western-style uniforms manned its cannons. Minh-Mang purchased steamships and set up a factory outside Hué to reproduce a steam engine while refusing Western expertise. The attempt failed. Vietnam would become the only Confucian country to be completely conquered by a European power.

Before he died, Minh-Mang sent an embassy to France to discuss a treaty and the question of Đai Nam's Catholics. Paris refused to negotiate. His successor Thieu-Tri (r. 1841–1847) imprisoned a French bishop in 1845. A U.S. ship briefly seized Da Nang in an unsuccessful attempt to have the bishop released. A mandarin wrote: "The barbarians from Europe have a very firm and very patient character. ... They never abandon an enterprise and are discouraged by no difficulty. For us this must be a matter of the greatest disquiet. These barbarians go into all kingdoms, and fear no fatigue. They bribe peoples, without any thought of cost" (Chesneaux, pp. 65–66).

In 1847, French vessels destroyed Vietnam's fleet at anchor in Da Nang harbor. Thieu-Tri wrote to his mistress: "Of old, the use of guns and of projectiles was unknown. But since [the Westerners] employed these engines of war, they have never lost a single battle and no fortress, however solid, has been able to withstand their assaults. At present everybody must agree that rifles and cannons are the Gods of Might." At least some Western powers agreed. In 1856 French ships bombarded Da Nang fort. In January 1857 a French missionary and lobbyist informed Napoleon III that "the easiest thing in the world" would be to occupy Cochin China, Đai Nam's southernmost region: "France has in the China seas ample forces for this task. ... The population, gentle, hardworking, very accessible to the preaching of the Christian faith, groans under a frightful tyranny. They would welcome us as liberators and benefactors. In a little time the entire population would become Catholic and devoted to France" (Hodgkin, p. 124).

REBELLION, OCCUPATION, AND SUBJUGATION OF ĐAI NAM

Đai Nam's peasants lived in misery. Rebellion erupted in 1854–1855. King Tu-Duc (r. 1847–1883) was presiding over repeated natural disasters. A Vietnamese historian has noted that "government supervision of hydraulic works was so inefficient that the Red River dyke at Van-giang was broken eighteen years in succession." A folk poem complained that "even a thousand years from now, people may still know of the hunger and sufferings in the reign of Tu Duc." Peasants began to believe the king had lost the "Mandate of Heaven." A revolt led by a Catholic Lê pretender wracked northern Đai Nam in the years 1861 to 1865.

Tu-Duc could not deal with both domestic unrest and foreign invasion. In late 1858, a

French expeditionary force landed near Da Nang, ordering the city to surrender. Strong Vietnamese resistance instead besieged the French positions. So the fleet sailed south and took Saigon on 18 February 1859. The French declared it a free port, open "to all friendly nations." When the Second Opium War ended, France turned to expansion. Tu-Duc had to surrender Cochin China's three eastern provinces, around Saigon, in 1862. French territory now separated the western three provinces from central and northern Đai Nam. The country was cut in two. Tu-Duc withdrew his mandarins from the French zone, which set up a new administration. In 1865 Saigon produced the first Vietnamese-language newspaper, *Gia Đinh Bao,* a monthly semiofficial newsletter using *quoc ngu,* a romanized script that missionaries had devised to write proselytizing texts in Vietnamese. *Gia Đinh Bao* was appearing three times per week by 1880. Viet Nam was on the verge of cultural transformation.

Siamese influence in Cambodia coexisted with dynastic and ethnic unrest. Colonial forces, steaming up the Mekong from Saigon, made Cambodia a French Protectorate in 1863. King Norodom (r. 1859–1904) hoped France would shield Cambodia from Siam and Đai Nam. But his main dangers were domestic. Though smaller and divided, they resembled the multiethnic forces fielded by Gia-long and Lê Van Khoi. Norodom's half-brother, Prince Si Votha, was already fomenting revolt against him, and two messianic Buddhist monks now launched their own rebellions. In 1865, one of them, Pou Kombo, a member of the small Kouy minority, recruited a thousand Khmers, three hundred Vietnamese, and a hundred Muslim Chams and tribal Stiengs. By late 1866, Pou Kombo fielded five thousand troops in a single battle, including seven to eight hundred Vietnamese. Royalist and colonial forces killed him the next year, but one of his lieutenants re-emerged five years later with four hundred followers "of every race in Indochina." Si Votha launched yet another rebellion in 1876–1877.

French forces slowly subjugated the rest of Đai Nam. They seized the three western provinces of Cochin China in 1867, and the country's center and north in 1882–1883. As the Romans had divided Gaul, the French partitioned Đai Nam into three parts—Cochin China (the south), Annam (the center), and Tonkin (the north). Some Vietnamese patriots saw collaboration as their only choice. In the 1860s, an anonymous "Letter from Cochin China" stated: "Alas, let us moderate our love for the fatherland; the wind of the West has blown lightly over us and made us shiver and tremble." Others would not submit, like the Cochin Chinese who told French forces in 1862: "If you wish for peace, give back his territory to our king. . . . Do you wish a ransom in exchange for our territory? We will pay it on condition that you will stop fighting and withdraw your troops to your possessions. We will even have gratitude for you, and your glory will be like the universe. Do you wish a concession to watch over your commercial interests ? We will consent to this. But if you refuse, we will not cease to fight in order to obey the wish of heaven."

Yet others saw only a third way out. Phan Thanh Gian, mandarin viceroy of Cochin China, committed suicide at the loss of his last three provinces. Gian had visited Europe in 1863, seen its industrial development, and written: "Under Heaven, everything is feasible to them, save only the matter of life and death." The French could not deny him suicide. The viceroy of Tonkin followed suit after the French successfully attacked Hanoi in April 1882.

STRUGGLE AGAINST FRENCH DOMINATION

Tu-Duc died the next year and turmoil wracked the court. Three boy-kings succeeded in turn, each quickly executed or deposed. The crown passed to fourteen-year-old Ham Nghi in 1885. The regent, Ton That Thuyet, spirited him into the hills and launched a royalist crusade against the French invaders. Under the royal name, Thuyet sent out an appeal for resistance, drawing a nationwide response from Confucian scholars. In Binh-Dinh, candidates taking classical examinations broke out of their enclosed camp and joined in the anti-French struggle. After three years of fighting in Annam and Tonkin, the French captured Ham Nghi. Until 1895, the mandarin Phan Dinh Phung led continued resistance, weighing the national plight over traditional obligations to ancestral tomb and village: "Now I have but one tomb, a very large one, that must be defended. . . . These events affected the whole country, the entire population."

A similar conflagration erupted in Cambodia. In June 1884, French governor Charles Thomson sailed three French gunboats up the Mekong and forcibly imposed France's right to introduce "all the administrative, judicial, financial and commercial reforms" it judged necessary, including the appointment of French *résidents* in provincial towns, the introduction of property in land, and outlawing slavery (Chandler, 1983, p. 143). As rebellion erupted in January 1885, Siam's King Chulalongkorn (r. 1868–1910) predicted that "the situation in Cambodia will deteriorate further," explaining: "Since the time the French assumed full administration of Cambodia, more taxes have been introduced and the tax collection procedure has been reorganized and tightened. People who have never been taxed or taxed very slightly naturally feel that the new taxes imposed on them by the French administration are unjust" (Natthawut, vol. 7, p. 91).

A two-year nationwide insurgency tied down thousands of colonial troops who took heavy casualties and caused significant destruction. In May 1885, for instance, after three hundred Khmers drove the French and their "Annamese" troops from the port of Kampot, escapees reported the retaliation: "The French sent two steamships and two Vietnamese ships to bombard the Khmer rebels. . . . The French then moved in and burned down the town" (*Chotmaihet Phraratkitraiwan*, pp. 63, 70). A French source estimated that deaths and an exodus to Siamese-controlled northwest Khmer provinces reduced the protectorate's population by 195,000. Colonial forces were able to quell the revolt in 1886 only with cooperation from King Norodom and the loss of 5,360 troops. Rebel Prince Si Votha fought on until 1889. His death in a remote jungle camp in 1892 ended three decades of dissidence.

China renounced its claim to suzerainty over Vietnam in June 1885. France built a new Indochinese empire by excluding Chinese and Siamese influence, and by exploiting divisions between Vietnamese, Cambodians, and Lao. Colonial official Jules Harmand wrote in 1885 that a person of Annamese "race" should accept that "our aid allows him to take vengeance for the humiliations and defeats that he has never forgiven his neighbours." Yet Annamese reluctance worried Paul Beau two decades later: "One must reawaken in them the expansionist instinct that seems to be flickering out" (Goscha, pp. 17, 19). Another French official took solace from what he called Cambodia's "strong national sentiment and traditional hatred for their former despoilers," as "a double immovable wall which must block all subversive projects" (Kiernan, p. 7).

The creation of "French Indochina" was completed in 1893 by seizure of the four northern and southern Lao kingdoms and principalities, after French gunboats forced Bangkok to surrender Siam's claim to the east bank of the Mekong. Luang Prabang, Viang Chan, Xieng Khouang, and Champassak, now comprising the Protectorate of Laos, were unified in 1899. Several hundred thousand Lao and various upland minorities were to become "Indochinese," along with the ten million Vietnamese and seven hundred thousand Khmers. Beginning in 1887, a French governor-general presided from Hanoi over French *résidents-supérieurs* in Tonkin, Annam, Cambodia, and Laos, the four territories subject to the French Foreign Ministry, and over the governor of Cochin China, which was constitutionally a colony run by Paris's colonial and naval ministries. The Radical politician Paul Doumer, governor-general of Indochina from 1897 to 1902, centralized its taxation, budget and government, which he ran with an advisory council of twenty French officials and five "indigenous high functionaries" chosen by the governor-general (Steinberg, p. 187). Finally, by further treaty with Siam in 1907, Indochina incorporated more Lao and Khmer territories west of the Mekong, including Battambang and Angkor Wat, which Bangkok had ruled since 1794.

"Indochina" gained little local resonance. In Vietnamese, *Dong-Duong* ("east of the ocean") had meant Japan, as its characters still did in Chinese. An 1898 *Dictionnaire Annamite-Français* published in Saigon fails to translate *Dong-Duong* as "Indo-Chine," a meaning that first appeared in a different *Dictionnaire Annamite-Français* published in Paris the next year. In 1920 French officials tried to substitute *Dong-Phap,* or "France d'Orient" (Goscha, pp. 15–16). Cambodians simply Khmerized the French as *indochen.*

Indochinese also pursued different paths to modernity. Vietnamese rebels had slaughtered many

Catholics, often mistakenly, for supposed collaboration with France. However, a leading Catholic *collaborateur*, Petrus Truong Vinh Ky, played a key role in disseminating the romanized *quoc ngu* alphabet, which facilitated Vietnamese absorption of Western ideas and technology. He wrote:

> Thanks to this writing, our poor disinherited country will be able to enter into the community of peoples and the great issues which the West has brought before the world; the sciences whose unexpected revelations strike the spirit and confound the intelligence will no longer be unfathomable mysteries to us, and these old errors, prejudices, absurd beliefs will disappear, giving way to true knowledge, to the high and serious inspiration of a wise philosophy. But for that one must have books, books, and still more books.

Eight centuries of bureaucratic examinations on Chinese classics would soon end, as Vietnam's Sino-Confucian heritage came under concerted attack. Yet the country's alternative cultural traditions of borrowing and adaptation also assisted Vietnamese modernization and international integration. As the romanized script spread, the country's first independent *quoc ngu* newspaper, *Nong Co Min Dam,* began publication in 1901. Cambodians and Lao continued to read and write in their Indic scripts. A Khmer-language newspaper, *Nagaravatta,* appeared in 1936, and a Lao counterpart in 1941, followed by short-lived romanization efforts in both countries and a Cambodian student's postwar invention, a Khmer-script typewriter.

LANDOWNING, ECONOMY, AND POLITICS

Indochina remained a constellation of peasant societies, but French rule brought partial economic revolution to Vietnam. Cochin China officials rewarded *collaborateurs* with huge tracts of land. Saigon developed an absentee landlord class, both French and Vietnamese, to whom peasants paid about half their crop in rent. French property law undercut the traditional power of village councils to redistribute land, while colonial officials and entrepreneurs drained large areas for new cultivation. Cochin China's ricelands quadrupled in area, its population tripling to 4.5 million. Vietnamese rice exports soared from 57,000 tonnes in 1860 to 1.55 million in 1937. Socioeconomic polarization escalated. Cochin China's wealthiest 2.5 percent of landholders owned more than fifty hectares each, totaling 45 percent of the riceland. In contrast, 72 percent of the peasants had less than five hectares, comprising only 15 percent of the land.

In the densely populated protectorate of Tonkin, 62 percent of farming families owned under two-fifths of a hectare, the poorest 90 percent owning only 37 percent of the land. However, northern landlords tended to be village residents rather than absentees. In sparsely populated Cambodia, peasants were more independent, and landlordism rarer. The poorest 43 percent of rural families owned less than one hectare, totaling 25 percent of the cultivated land, but a middle peasant majority owned 44 percent, leaving the wealthiest 6 percent, owning more than five hectares each, with 31 percent. Yet Cambodians paid the highest taxes in French Indochina. As rice production and exports increased, the world market penetrated both Vietnamese and Cambodian peasant life.

Vietnam also gained a working class, including up to fifty thousand workers in French-run coal and other mines in Tonkin. Conditions were poor, hours long, wages low, disease and death frequent. Workers labored on new coffee and tea plantations, railways, cotton mills, cement factories, and petroleum refineries. The French drafted another 100,000 northerners to labor on southern and Cambodian rubber plantations in the 1920s. For the first time, Vietnam was producing bulk exports. As the nation's culture became internationalized, so did its economy.

And its politics. In 1913, the French ended an era when they captured and beheaded the last rebel leader, De Tham, whose parents had fought the Nguyen dynasty in the 1840s. However, while holding out in the hills, De Tham had succeeded in passing on the torch of resistance by working with Vietnam's new generation of anticolonialists, who were led by Phan Boi Chau (1867–1940).

Son of a poor scholar family, Phan Boi Chau was sitting for his Confucian examinations in 1885 when word came of the young king's revolt. He and sixty fellow students tried to form a fighting force until a French patrol blasted the village. After passing the 1900 examinations, Chau followed the modernizing movements now developing in China. He read Liang Ch'i Ch'ao, who aimed to reform

China on the Western model. Chau visited China, and then Japan in 1905. Working secretly with De Tham until 1913, Chau ran Vietnam's anti-French underground for twenty years, sponsoring antitax riots in 1908 and leading the last Confucian-educated generation to modern nationalism. Chau's critique of "Mandarins" appeared in a text of that title, distributed in a Hanoi school set up under his inspiration in the early 1900s: "Not knowing about the existence of new books and periodicals is one thing. But knowing about them and yet sealing off, blocking out, insuring that the story is not heard or seen—that is building and preserving for oneself a fundamentally slave-like character. People of that type should really make us sick!" (Marr, 1971, p. 173).

A popular song of the era, "The haircutting chant," launched an anonymous call to Vietnamese men to avoid Chinese-style pigtails: "Study Western customs.... Don't lie, Today we clip, Tomorrow we shave!"

HO CHI MINH

Writing his autobiography in China in the 1930s, Chau recalled reciting poetry in 1899 in his native Nghe-An province, in central Vietnam. In his audience was a nine-year-old who would later take the name Ho Chi Minh. The region was the heartland of the 1885–1895 revolts; like Chau and their leader Phan Dinh Phung, Ho came from a Confucian scholar family. He studied Chinese and French, then taught *quoc ngu* and French for a year in southern Vietnam. In 1911, aged twenty-one, Ho took off to see the world. After a navigation course in Saigon, he worked for two years as a kitchen hand on a ship plying between France and Boston and New York. During World War I he washed dishes in a London hotel. The 1916 Easter Rising against British rule in Ireland caught his attention. Ho moved to Paris the next year, weeks before news arrived of the Russian Revolution.

France enlisted one hundred thousand Vietnamese to fight in World War I. Ho condemned their sacrifice in *The Trial of French Colonialism* (1923): "They perished in the poetic desert of the Balkans, wondering whether the mother country [France] intended to install herself as a favourite in the Turk's harem; why else should they have been sent here to be hacked up?" Ho joined the French Socialist Party because of its "sympathy for the struggle of the oppressed peoples."

At the 1919 Versailles Conference, Ho tried to present U.S. President Woodrow Wilson with a request for equal rights and freedoms for French and "Annamese." Expressing the continuing confusion of an emerging Vietnamese identity, Ho's petition alternated the terms "Annam" and "Indochina." Entitled *Revendications du peuple annamite,* it began: "the people of the former Annamese Empire, today French Indochina, submit to the honourable governments. ..." Later that year, Indochina's Governor-General Albert Sarraut proposed an "Indochinese Federation" to give Vietnamese a greater voice (Goscha, p. 46–47). The same year, 1919, saw the last Confucian examinations for appointments to the Vietnamese bureaucracy. *Quoc ngu* quickly replaced Chinese and *nom* as the national alphabet.

Modern Vietnamese literature emerged in the 1920s. In two decades ten thousand books and pamphlets appeared in *quoc ngu*—nearly fifteen million volumes circulated. One-tenth were "modernising essays and translations," mostly inspired by Western thought and technical achievements (Marr, 1981, p. 49). Readers of *quoc ngu* numbered more than two hundred thousand, and colonial schools enrolled one hundred thousand children each year. But the French built few schools in prewar Cambodia and Laos.

Ho Chi Minh's petition at Versailles made him well-known in France. In 1920 he became a founding member of the French Communist Party, as a "Representative of Indochina." He pricked the conscience of the French left by reminding it of the hardships France had imposed on Vietnam, Algeria, and Madagascar. In 1924 elections, Ho's newspaper *Le Paria* supported the Communist Party, "the only party to put up a coloured candidate in Paris."

Ho spent 1924 in the Soviet Union, meeting communists from around the world. He then moved to China, where he was based for the next twenty years. As a Comintern representative, he organized a Vietnamese communist movement, training its officers, and coordinating its activities with other Asian communists and anticolonialists. He launched the Vietnamese Communist Party in

February 1930, but the Comintern intervened to change its name to the Indochina Communist Party (ICP). As China's emperor had first imposed the name "Viet Nam" on Gia-Long's new dynasty in 1802, now the USSR insisted on Vietnamese communist responsibility for revolution throughout "Indochina." The former name outlived the latter.

If the French grip seemed strong to many "Indochinese," communist revolution was on the agenda. Nationalism emerged more slowly in Cambodia and Laos, and in all three countries it continued an uneasy coexistence with Vietnamese communist internationalism. In Hanoi on 2 September 1945, Ho Chi Minh, leading the Indochina Communist Party, proclaimed a new state, the Democratic Republic of Vietnam. Six years later, during a final war with France, the ICP began to dissolve itself into three national communist parties. After its victory at Dien Bien Phu in 1954, Cambodia, Laos, and a temporarily redivided Vietnam emerged as separate states. "French Indochina," as Hanoi later proclaimed, "passed into history" (Anon., p. 99). Vietnam was reunited in 1975, as it had been in 1786.

CONCLUSION

Indochina ultimately failed, not because a European term failed to bridge an Indic-Sinic cultural chasm, but because France had attempted to impose political unity by both external force and the simultaneous fostering of ethnic difference and antipathy. The imperial process of divide and rule undermined its own state-building. Centuries of consolidation of twenty-three medieval Southeast Asian kingdoms into several dominant powers favored the emergence of an Indochina polity. But Đai Nam's failure in Cambodia and Laos only prefigured that of France, whose dispatch of "Annamese" in Minh-Mang's footsteps exacerbated Khmer resentment at the dual colonial presence. If Minh-Mang provoked more virulent Cambodian reactions, French rule mobilized more concerted Vietnamese responses. Too few Annamese relished their new colonial assignment to a traditional external role, and within Vietnam colonial power and the internal divisions it imposed proved even less successful. French Indochina collapsed in multiple ironies. Its contradictory attempts to unify separate kingdoms by force and rule them by deepening divisions provoked not only ethnic nationalisms sufficiently distinct to preclude any postcolonial union, but also a muted resurgence of traditional interethnic collaboration in an anticolonial cause. France's occupation of a compact multinational territory only facilitated coordination of mounting resistance that doomed a complex colonial project.

See also **Colonialism; France; Imperialism.**

BIBLIOGRAPHY

Anonymous. *Kampuchea Dossier.* Vol. 1. Hanoi, 1978.

Chandler, David P. "Cambodia before the French: Politics in a Tributary Kingdom, 1794–1848." Ph.D. diss., University of Michigan, 1973.

———. *A History of Cambodia.* Boulder, Colo., 1983.

Chesneaux, Jean. *The Vietnamese Nation: Contribution to a History.* Translated by Malcolm Salmon. Sydney, 1966.

Choi Byung Wook. *Southern Vietnam under the Reign of Minh Mang (1820–1841): Central Policies and Local Response.* Ithaca, N.Y., 2004.

Chotmaihet Phraratkitraiwan Phraratniphon nai Phrarat Somdet Phrachulachomklaochaoyuhua. Translated by Chalong Soontravanich. Part 19. Bangkok, 1970.

Cook, Nola, and Li Tana, eds. *Water Frontier: Commerce and the Chinese in the Lower Mekong Region, 1750–1880.* Lanham, Md., 2004.

Dutton, George. *The Tay Son Uprising: Society and Rebellion in Eighteenth-Century Dai Viet.* Forthcoming.

Goscha, Christopher E. *Vietnam or Indochina? Contesting Concepts of Space in Vietnamese Nationalism, 1887–1954.* Copenhagen, 1995.

Hodgkin, Thomas L. *Vietnam: The Revolutionary Path.* New York and London, 1981.

Ho Xuan Huong. *Spring Essence: The Poetry of Ho Xuan Huong.* Edited and translated by John Balaban. Port Townsend, Wash., 2000.

Khin Sok. *Le Cambodge entre le Siam et le Vietnam (de 1775 à 1860).* Paris, 1991.

Kiernan, Ben. *How Pol Pot Came to Power: Colonialism, Nationalism and Communism in Cambodia, 1930–1975.* 2nd ed. New Haven, Conn., 2004.

Kiernan, Ben, and Chanthou Boua. *Peasants and Politics in Kampuchea, 1942–1981.* London 1982.

Lê Thành Khôi. *Histoire du Vietnam des origines à 1858.* Paris, 1982.

Li Tana. *Nguyen Cochinchina: Southern Vietnam in the Seventeenth and Eighteenth Centuries.* Ithaca, N.Y., 1998.

Lieberman, Victor. *Strange Parallels: Southeast Asia in Global Context, c.800–1830.* Vol. 1: *Integration on the Mainland.* New York, 2003.

Marr, David G. *Vietnamese Anticolonialism 1885–1925.* Berkeley, Calif., 1971.

———. *Vietnamese Tradition on Trial, 1920–1945.* Berkeley, Calif., 1981.

Moura, Jean. *Le royaume du Cambodge.* Paris, 1887.

Natthawut Sutthisonggram, ed. *Somdet Phrachaoborom-wongthoe Chao Fa Mahamala Krom Phya Bamrappar-apak: Phrarathathaleka Lae Kham Athibai.* 11 vols. Bangkok, 1973. Translated by Chalong Soontravanich.

Osborne, Milton E. *The French Presence in Cochinchina and Cambodia. Rule and Response (1859–1905).* Ithaca, N.Y., 1969.

Porter, D. Gareth. *The Myth of the Bloodbath: North Vietnam's Land Reform Reconsidered.* Interim Report No. 2. Ithaca, N.Y., 1972.

Rungswasdisab, Puangthong. *War and Trade: Siamese Interventions in Cambodia, 1767–1851.* Ph.D. diss., University of Wollongong (Australia), 1995.

Steinberg, David Joel, ed. *In Search of Southeast Asia: A Modern History.* Rev. ed. Honolulu, Hawaii, 1987.

Stuart-Fox, Martin. *The Lao Kingdom of Lan Xang: Rise and Decline.* Bangkok, 1998.

Weigersma, Nancy. *Vietnam: Peasant Land, Peasant Revolution: Patriarchy and Collectivity in the Rural Economy.* London, 1988.

Woodside, Alexander B. *Vietnam and the Chinese Model: A Comparative Study of Nguyên and Ch'ing Civil Government in the First Half of the Nineteenth Century.* Cambridge, Mass., 1971.

BEN KIERNAN

INDUSTRIALISM. *See* **Economic Growth and Industrialism.**

INDUSTRIAL REVOLUTION, FIRST.

British and European identities are historically based in the modernization and industrialization of the eighteenth and nineteenth centuries, which brought western dominion over the world for the nineteenth and much of the twentieth centuries. Was this achievement contingent on a prior superiority in environment, economy, mind, or culture, or was it mere accident? These questions demand comparative history and research into the connections between parts of the globe that before this were previously studied separately. A new history of Europe's—and especially Britain's—Industrial Revolution must be a history of comparisons, encounters, and connections between and among parts of Europe, Asia, Africa, and the Americas. This is a new approach to European industrialization, focusing on comparative environmental histories, on consumer cultures, on wider-world connections in trade and colonization, and investigating useful knowledge and institutional reform.

RECENT HISTORIES OF THE INDUSTRIAL REVOLUTION

Conceived of by historians writing between the 1950s and 1970s—the era of the Cold War—as the kick start to modern economic growth, the Industrial Revolution was about rapid economic change and social transformation. It was marked by the growth of factories and large-scale capital investment; it was caused by technology and capital formation led by industrialists and private investors. It was a British event, based on the underlying institutions of private property and liberal values, and its model provided a blueprint to post–World War II reconstruction and the development missions and plans made for third-world economies emerging from colonialism. Historians of that period saw the Industrial Revolution as a story of modernization, marked by key indicators in an economy and society. They looked for and debated their estimates on the growth of national output, capital formation, demographic growth, and changes in industrial structures.

A new story of the Industrial Revolution appeared in the 1970s and 1980s, however, matching the industrial restructuring and decline of that period. Historians began to call the industrial past to account, questioning the centrality to the Industrial Revolution of the sacred cows of the postwar boom—heavy capital investment, large-scale industry, regional concentration, and large, heavily capitalized factories. Britain's industrial decline during this period was reflected in its historians' challenges to the growth rates and industrial transformation claimed by earlier historians, including Phyllis Deane and William A. Cole, David Landes and Eric Hobsbawm. Estimates of economic growth and of the growth in real wages over the classic period of the Industrial Revolution, from 1760 to 1830, were successively scaled down. The Industrial Revolution as a concept seemed to have been rendered obsolete and it became clear that the kinds of economic change associated with the Industrial Revolution did not necessarily entail rapid increases in economic growth. The costs of warfare and population growth absorbed much of the improved productivity. Invention and its diffusion, furthermore, have very delayed effects on income per capita and standards of living. It should thus be no surprise that an intensive phase of mechanical invention in the 1760s and 1770s would not start to show results in macroeconomic indicators until the period after the Napoleonic Wars.

ECONOMIC INDICATORS AND COMPARATIVE ECONOMIC GROWTH

The way most economic historians perceived the Industrial Revolution both in the 1950s and 1960s and from the 1970s to the late 1990s was still relatively insular. The collection and analysis of new evidence on birth and death rates by the Cambridge Population Group and other evidence on grain yields endorsed theories of endogenous change in Britain, specifically economic growth caused by a combination of population growth and rising agricultural productivity. Macroeconomic indicators discounted a significant contribution from international trade, including colonial markets and the slave trade. One historiography of this period, investigating macroeconomic indicators, flattened the growth trends, confined what growth there was to a small though dynamic sector, the cotton industry, and turned the search for the sources of growth inward to national, regional, and even local factors. Others, however, turned to the productivity gains of small-scale farming and industry, to broad-based technological change based in skills and intermediate technologies, and to entrepreneurship and capital formation based in regional and community networks.

Some saw this scaled-down Industrial Revolution as a largely British affair; economic indicators showed a yawning gap between the British rates of population growth, agricultural productivity, urbanization, and real wages and those of the rest of Europe—especially those of Britain's great rival, France. Population growth was gradual in France, whereas in England it rose throughout the eighteenth century, and especially in its latter half. And although British real wages were relatively static through most of the eighteenth and early nineteenth centuries, they were still well above real wages in the rest of Europe. The proportion of British labor occupied in agriculture shrank continuously, while high proportions of the French labor force remained on the land; output per agricultural worker in France as late as 1840 was only 60 percent that of England. As late as the mid-nineteenth century, half the population of the United Kingdom lived in towns, whereas in France and Germany only one-quarter did. Britain achieved early ascendancy in cotton spinning to such a degree that France could not compete; French output per worker in cotton spinning was only 40 percent that of Britain in the 1830s and 1840s. And the British took over international markets in manufactured goods. By the mid-nineteenth century, 60 percent of British cotton output was exported, compared to only 10 percent in France, and Britain exported 25 percent of its total industrial output, compared to 10 to 12 percent in France.

PROTOINDUSTRIALIZATION

The traditions of comparative history that prevailed in the 1950s and 1960s posed the British Industrial Revolution as the yardstick by which to measure the performance of the rest of Europe. In contrast, the new economic history identified the sectoral and macroeconomic divide between Britain and Europe. In a comparative history of protoindustrialization, Franklin Mendels in an keynote article, and Peter Kriedte, Hans Medick, and Jürgen Schlumbohm in a jointly authored book, sought the seeds of change that generated industrial expansion and Europe's subsequently divergent paths.

View of Shrewsbury Across the Severn. Anonymous watercolor landscape shows air pollution created by English factories. VICTORIA & ALBERT MUSEUM, LONDON, UK/BRIDGEMAN ART LIBRARY

Protoindustrialization is a theory connecting the spread of rural industry, population growth, and social and institutional change. Its first proponents set out to explain socioeconomic change in Flanders and the German states. During the seventeenth century, agricultural, industrial, mercantile, and demographic change combined together to induce an unprecedented growth in decentralized manufacturing, most of which was located not in towns but in rural villages and drew on the labor of entire families, who organized their industrial work around the requirements of their agricultural holdings; much of the industrial work was, in fact, done by underemployed women. In the textile industry, this meant spinning and weaving, and entrepreneurs and artisans in the towns acquired and prepared the raw materials and carried out the final finishing processes under the supervision of merchants

Protoindustrialization was not just a descriptive category, it was a theory about why this kind of manufacturing arose and where it led. For Mendels, protoindustrialization was the first phase of industrialization. The rural labor force took up domestic industries, using their homes as workplaces, and produced for supra-regional markets. The population was thus liberated from the agrarian resource base; the labor force, which had previously been underutilized because of the seasonal nature of agrarian production, found employment, and eventually industry and agriculture specialized into specific regions.

The large numbers of regional case studies that followed this pioneering work, however, found no obvious link between protoindustrialization and later industrialization. In some regions, especially in Britain, a transition to the factory system ultimately took place. Examples include the Lancashire cotton industry, the west Yorkshire worsted woolen industry, the Belgian heavy metal and engineering industry, the woolen and cotton industries of northern France, the cotton industry of Saxony, and the Catalan and Swiss cotton and calico-printing industries. But in other regions, these protoindustries went into decline, notably in the south of Britain, which gradually converted back to agriculture over the course of the eighteenth century, or in the many parts of Europe that went into decline during and after the Napoleonic Wars.

The regional studies, however, underlined the ways that social, institutional, and political factors encouraged or inhibited regional industrial transformation. More significantly, the theory of protoindustrialization addressed the question of how work was organized and who did it. It also challenged those who argued that the rise of the factory system was the key signal of the Industrial Revolution. Historians discovered significant economic gains in the household and industrial division of labor as well as regional specialization arising from the spread of rural domestic industry during the protoindustrial phase, which led into and accompanied the factory system. Perhaps the alternative, smaller-scale units that coexisted with those factories were not as primitive as earlier historians believed. As historians often do, these historians were writing in tune with their times. New types of work organization were emerging in the 1970s and 1980s: network capitalism, just-in-time production systems, subcontracting, and franchises. There was a new skepticism over advantages offered by hierarchically organized management systems. The smokestack capitalism that was identified with the Victorians had had its day—its assembly lines and ramshackle sheds were abandoned for the airport and motorway flows of designer capitalism. In keeping with these new priorities, historians set about recovering the history and advantages of parallel forms of industrial organization in the Industrial Revolution itself.

This kind of protoindustry was infinitely flexible and complex. It was not just a stage on the way to the development of the factory system; it has lasted up to the early-twenty-first century, and indeed decentralized manufacture has reasserted itself in the subcontracting, franchises, science parks, silicon valleys, and especially third-world centers of child labor producing western luxury goods. The bulk of the labor force for the decentralized manufacture of the early industrial period was female; it was the mothers and teenage girls who carried forward the industrial expansion of the period, not male artisans. The new work opportunities for women and girls entailed profound gender divisions in the household economy, and were in many cases followed by increasing dependency on male earnings as these industries waned or gave way to the factory system's economies of scale. The work opportunities that might have brought earlier marriage, greater independence, and new consumer practices were frequently short-lived or episodic. They had the reverse effect of fixing people on the land and retaining family members to the household. They furthermore clustered women in low-wage, low-skill work that also so gendered the jobs they moved on to in workshops and factories.

Macroeconomic indicators and protoindustrialization pushed historians to look outward, not just to comparisons between their country or region and other parts of Europe, but to wider-world comparisons. This coincided with the profound economic, social, and cultural shift of the 1990s, globalization, and a renewed interest in the historical roots of worldwide connections.

DIVERGENCE BETWEEN EAST AND WEST

The Industrial Revolution is at the center of any investigation into the divergence between Europe and Asia. For a long time, studies of this divergence tended to ask why Europe was so rich and Asia so poor. In the late twentieth and early twenty-first centuries, the question shifted to why the Asian economies were growing so fast and whether Asian countries would become rich. Historians reopened debates on economic transition in Europe, but

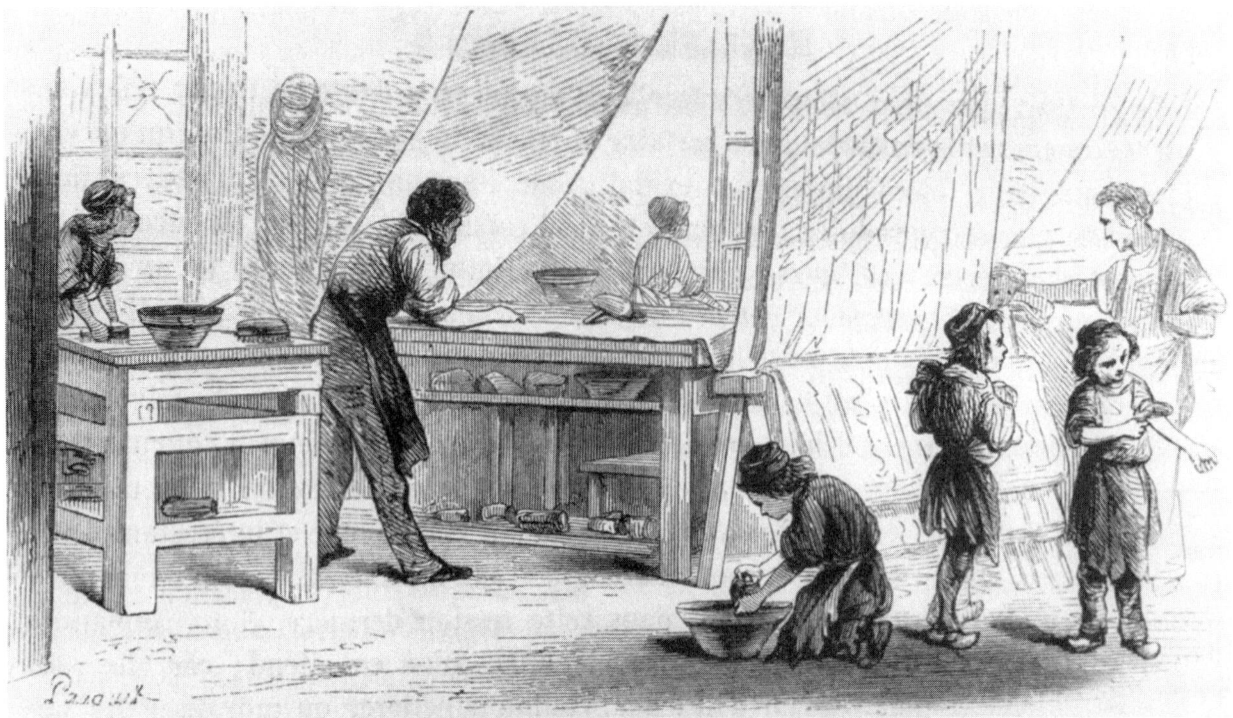

The Child of the Factory. Engraving c. 1842. Child labor was especially common in textile factories, where small hands could more easily repair broken threads in the looms. BIBLIOTHÈQUE DES ARTS DECORATIFS, PARIS, FRANCE/BRIDGEMAN ART LIBRARY/ARCHIVES CHARMET

from the perspective of developments in Asia, setting aside earlier arguments for European exceptionalism in favor of conjunctural features, which in the course of the eighteenth century set in motion a divergence in development between Europe and Asia. Kenneth Pomeranz has made a strong case that before the late eighteenth century more economic similarities than differences existed across Eurasia, and that divergence came afterward. Europe's lead over China, he argues, cannot be attributed to consumption and protoindustrialization, or to agricultural and labor productivity or market institutions. Instead, key imbalances emerged in the late eighteenth century, the period of the Industrial Revolution, and those imbalances were founded in natural resources. Europe's, and especially Britain's, access to coal and its development of technologies using coal, along with its access to the resources and land of New World colonies, gave it a crucial lead over Asia. Coal and colonies provided Europe with an advantageous "ghost acreage" not available to the Chinese.

This case for global divergence, so centered on developments in the eighteenth century, provides historians with ample opportunity to compare other elements of change in the same period. A comparison of European and Asian agricultural productivity, land organization, property relations, demography, and social institutions raises new questions about the Industrial Revolution. Was coal crucial? In its absence, would alternative low-energy, intensive industries not have developed, and water power, wind power, and peat burning provided for energy needs as they did in the Low Countries, Switzerland, parts of France, and New England? Perhaps the resulting Industrial Revolution would not have been so early or so revolutionary, but as Joel Mokyr argues, self-sustaining advances in Europe, which were in place by the eighteenth century, were enough to sustain the growing gap between Europe and the rest of the world.

A global history seeking the sources of divergence is still fundamentally a comparative history, and one of a very traditional kind. The questions it asks are set by older frameworks of debate, which sought to explain Britain's ascendancy over the rest of Europe. But a history of global encounters and connections over this period leads to explanations based in trade and cultural assimilation, in the transmission of knowledge, and in competitive responses to technology. Europe's Industrial Revolution grew from a conjuncture of wider-world discoveries, industrial expansion, new consumption practices, and new knowledge bases. But the core change that pushed this conjuncture into an Industrial Revolution was a capacity for self-sustaining technical progress. An account of the technological revolution led by Britain in the eighteenth century should not, however, be another account of British exceptionalism. Instead, it must be a European and a global story.

EARLY GLOBAL CONNECTIONS

How distinctive is globalization from earlier wider-world trade? Some historians (Kevin O'Rourke and Jeffrey Williamson) define the beginnings of globalization as the full integration of international commodity markets, with commodity price convergence as a key indicator, and date this from the late nineteenth century, although such an open world economy had not come into existence even in the early twenty-first century. Others (Dennis Flynn and Arturo Giraldez) define it as a condition whereby all important areas of the world exchange products continuously and on a scale large enough to have an effect on trading partners.

Was a global trading system one of the key factors contributing to industrialization? Christopher Bayly distinguishes globalization proper from an "archaic globalization" that focused on collecting charismatic goods and substances, on luxuries and honorific commodities from distant lands; examples include Kashmiri shawls, Chinese silks, Arabian horses, and precious stones. This, he argues, was very different from the market-driven uniformity of the early-twenty-first-century world. Too often historians look no further back than the seventeenth and eighteenth centuries for evidence of the wider-world trade that would sustain many of the features that they associate with industrialized communities: large scale production, standardized products, long-distance trade. But all of these conditions were present in Bronze Age societies, going back to the fourth millennium B.C.E.; they were significant and fully affected the wider society of the Roman Empire, then retreated for several hundred years. Such large-scale standardized production for long-distance trade marked China's Sung Dynasty, where ceramics were exported to Korea, Japan, Southeast Asia, India, Iraq, and Africa. A long prehistory of empires and societies engaged in advanced technologies, concentrated production processes, and standardized production serving large cities and long-distance trade was followed by periods of collapse or at least decline. But the period of early modern trade following the voyages of discovery from the sixteenth century set in motion the roots of an industrialization in Europe in which technological change and economic growth became a permanent condition.

EARLY MODERN GLOBAL TRADE AND THE INDUSTRIOUS REVOLUTION

In 1500 Asia held three-fifths of the world's population; China and India both had larger populations than Europe. Europe had only seven of the world's twenty-five largest cities in 1600, and only six in 1700. Before 1500 parts of the world other than Europe had wealth and knowledge far in advance of Europe's. This changed after the voyages of discovery. From this time on, Europe made an intense investment in trade and the Spanish, Portuguese, Dutch, French, and British invested in colonies and maritime bases. Ships and peoples moved in large numbers from Europe to other continents, and slaves were moved involuntarily from Africa. Europe's economies, and especially its Atlantic economies, became more trade intensive, and long-distance trade grew relative to per capita national income. Trade with Asia between 1500 and 1750 grew over 1 percent annually, and that with the Americas grew at over 2 percent annually. The reasons for this trade intensification lie in the rise of incomes of certain social classes and the part played by non-European and luxury goods in European consumer aspirations. The particular luxury goods brought back on the early voyages changed European diet, dress, and the social customs involved in eating and drinking, making a wide impact on all social classes. Addictive substances, stimulants, and sources of rapid energy—tea, coffee, sugar, and tobacco—changed diets. Chinese porcelain and its imitations provided the material culture underpinning new consumption rituals and the sociability associated with the new dietary supplements. Indian calicoes, followed by European imitations, underpinned a new fashion market. Plantation complexes and intensified trade drove down prices; imitations and technological innovation in ceramic, glass, and metal tableware, as well as textiles, changed material culture first for the middling classes and then for the laboring poor.

Jan de Vries explains how trade and consumption so changed the household behavior of ordinary people that they worked harder and shifted their labor from the household to the market economy. The attraction of commodities made outside the household, and especially those from distant places, induced many to buy commodities that were different from those they formerly made at home. They bought in packages—not just tea and coffee, but sugar, then easily replaceable and attractive plates, cups and saucers, and cutlery. Although fashion had long driven the markets for clothing, the varieties and price ranges made possible by Indian cottons created an altogether new level of textile consumption. Was northwestern Europe's consumption and industrious revolution bigger and more socially pervasive than those in China, Japan, and India? Certainly Europe learned this consumption from Asia. It responded to and absorbed some Asian consumer practices, such as drinking hot beverages in private and public social gatherings. It also adapted specific Asian goods, such as Chinese porcelain, to its own consumer practices. Although something is known about the expanding markets for luxury and fine consumer wares among merchants and urban middling groups in Ming China, Tokugawa Japan, and Mughal India, little is known yet about their connections to the wider dynamics of economic change. As Bayly argues, "It was European ships and commercial companies, not Asian and African producers of slaves, spices, calicoes or porcelains which were able to capture the greatest 'value added' as world trade expanded in the eighteenth century. . . . Europe connected, subjugated and made tributary other peoples' industrious revolutions" (p. 64).

But consumption and trade can only provide openings to increased productivity, not the means. Protoindustrialization created more industry and more goods; the industrious revolution created among ordinary people the desire and the capacity to consume these goods. Protoindustrialization and the Industrious Revolution did not offer alternatives to the Industrial Revolution but were, rather, preconditions. They underscored the broad base of economic and social change in the hundred years before the mid- to late eighteenth century. That change might have continued on its course—a framework, as set out by Adam Smith, of market expansion, specialization, and division of labor—had technology not provided the means to break through to an industrial revolution. Consuming is not as important as making and inventing; consuming, however, provides the incentives for both.

TECHNOLOGY AND USEFUL KNOWLEDGE

The foundations of a new economy, in which change became the normal condition, were laid down during the Industrial Revolution—1760 to 1830. They were made in production systems—in technology and the organization of work—and Britain led the transformation of both. For its manufacturers, entrepreneurs, and workforces, the key questions were "Does it work?" and "Can it make money?" In Mokyr's view, eighteenth-century Britain was a "technologically competent society." It had the engineers, mechanics, millwrights, and tinkerers. It had the fascination, projects, and knowledge that made up an "industrial Enlightenment." It developed "useful knowledge" as an engine of social progress. Such knowledge was not just about scientific theory; it was about practice, about bringing "the full force of human knowledge to bear on technology." It included artisanal knowledge as well as science, the knowledge of geography, plants, and animals as well as "knacks" and tacit knowledge passed on by practice, by doing, by transmission within families and work communities.

How can historians explain the technological momentum that seized Europe, and most notably Britain, in the years after 1750? There were the years of miracles, with their lead technologies and heroic inventors: Crompton's spinning mule, which was invented in 1769 and was soon connected first to the Newcomen then to the Watt steam engine to make possible the modern factory. Chlorine bleaching was introduced in 1774, Henry Cort's iron puddling in 1785, and Benjamin Huntsman's steel soon afterward. Some historians have seen these as macro inventions that shocked an economy into growth, the lucky breaks in small industries with elastic markets in an otherwise somnolent economy. Others have attributed the force of change to new energy sources: steam power released the environmental limits to growth. But these inventions were not exceptions to the rule. They were, as Mokyr argues, embedded in a pervasive inventiveness, T. S. Ashton's "wave of gadgets," Deirdre McCloskey's "age of improvement." It was not just cotton technology, steam power, and iron bridges that changed this world, but hot air balloons, smallpox inoculation, and gas lighting. Birmingham and the west Midlands, south Lancashire and southwest Scotland became technology hubs, centers for invention, attracting venture capital, if not yet significantly in the form of banks, then of projectors and speculators, merchants and other manufacturers.

The lead inventions are usually attributed to Britain, but close contacts in scientific and technological enquiry were forged across Europe, and especially between Britain and France. Inventors like John Kay immigrated to Paris; the French Jacquard loom was adopted in Britain. Matthew Boulton, James Watt, and Josiah Wedgwood all sent their sons to France for a period of study and work. France led in chemical innovation; Antoine Lavoisier's theory was complemented by Claude Berthollet's practice on chlorine bleaching, soaps, and dyes. Scientific investigators, inventors, projectors, and artisans traveled back and forth, establishing European-wide networks of knowledge. Other parts of Europe also had their high-technology regions. The Nord region of France had its cotton, linen, wool, and coal; Rouen on a much smaller scale was the Manchester of France. The Belgian-German region reaching down into the Rhine Valley produced textiles, minerals, metal wares, and engineering. Saxony rapidly expanded its production of minerals and textiles. And in southern Europe, Lyons, Lombardy, and Catalonia led the production of high-quality silks and printed cottons. Interaction among European producers, complementary production, and niche markets were not enough, however, to make the Industrial Revolution, in its classic years at least, a Europe-wide phenomenon. Technology, markets, and global power made this Britain's revolution.

Whatever factors fed into technological transition, the achievements—greatest in Britain—were such as to make economic growth a continuous and not just episodic condition. Those achievements were best summed up by David Landes in his seminal *Unbound Prometheus:* first, the substitution of machines—rapid, regular, precise, and tireless—for human skill and effort (Kay's flying shuttle, James Hargreave's jenny, Richard Arkwright's water frame, and Samuel Crompton's mule); second, the substitution of mechanically produced sources of power, notably steam power, for natural sources such as animal, wind, and water power; and third the use of new and far more abundant raw materials, marked especially by the substitution of mineral for vegetable or animal substances and the shift from a wood-fueled to a coal-fueled economy.

Innovation was not just in processes—in the tools, machines, materials, and energy that comprised and drove rapidly expanding industrial sectors. It was also in products, because invention was just as significantly about the invention of new products. Some were imitations of earlier European and Asian luxury goods, now made in hybrid materials and alloys and processed with coal not wood; others were restyled, or completely new. European manufacturers invented varieties and qualities of cotton textiles as rapidly as they adopted new spinning, weaving, and printing techniques. Innovations stretched beyond the range of material goods to gas lighting and smallpox vaccination. Product innovation was just as important to the British as it was to the French; the contrast between the standardized British products for mass markets and the French luxuries for the elites has been overdrawn. With Britain's technological leap forward came the ascendancy of certain goods: textiles, glassware and earthenware, metal goods, and machinery. The British invented and branded their consumer products as avidly as they did their tools and machinery. Cylinder-printed calicoes and Scottish and Irish linen appeared alongside the well-known broadcloth. Sheffield silver-plate and steel cutlery; Staffordshire and especially Wedgwood earthenware; Birmingham japanned tea trays; cut-steel chatelaines, buttons, and buckles; brass and silver-plate candlesticks and furniture handles; and silver-plated coffee pots and tea urns were the new

Jacquard power looms in an English textile factory. Jacquard's invention of a device for manufacturing patterned cloth was a watershed in the development of the textile industry. PRIVATE COLLECTION/BRIDGEMAN ART LIBRARY/THE STAPLETON COLLECTION

European consumer desirables. This British product and technological ascendancy, however, was set in the context of wider world and global developments.

WARS, COLONIES, AND MARKETS

Technology and markets became crucially bound up with empire in the late eighteenth century, and the British claimed all three. The late fifteenth- and sixteenth-century voyages of discovery, followed by long-distance trade and the establishment of colonies, provided immense riches and two centuries of economic growth to the Spanish and Portuguese; the Dutch drew even greater advantage from their wider-world encounter. But the Dutch, Spanish, and Portuguese engagement in European wars in the sixteenth and seventeenth centuries led to their relative decline; even so, Dutch per capita incomes exceeded British levels until the end of the eighteenth century. The Dutch Empire, however, remained limited in extent, if compared to the later French and British Empires—it failed to create large colonies in North America and Brazil, and it too went into relative decline after the French occupation of 1795 to 1815. The French and British competed for colonies and world trade, but the British took the high ground during the crucial years of the French and Haitian revolutions, years that also coincided with the most significant development of technology and new consumer products. Britain's effective fiscal system, based mainly on indirect taxation and the access this allowed to government loans, could provide the state the means to engage in an expansionist and mercantilist policy to extend trade and colonization. And British taxpayers and British and foreign investors funded the armies and navies needed to succeed in the many eighteenth-century wars in Europe and across global sea routes.

Britain's colonies and trading "factories" or merchant outposts, acquired across the east and west over the course of the eighteenth century, and its trade dominance nurtured by Navigation Acts and enormous investment in shipping and military defense, paid off by the last decades of the eighteenth century, and especially after the Napoleonic Wars. Losing its American colonies after the American Revolution did not make much difference after years of exporting British labor, entrepreneurship, and cultural identities to these territories. The United States, even without the political affiliation Britain still claimed of its Caribbean and Canadian colonies, provided a bulwark of food and raw materials, a safety valve for rapidly rising British populations, and the fastest growing markets for manufactured consumer goods to be found anywhere. British products were successful in American as well as home markets and went on from the early nineteenth century to become global products, desired across Europe as well as in Caribbean and Latin American markets and in colonial India, Australia, and Asia.

The European discovery of and trade with the wider world from the sixteenth century onward provided the heady germination for what would become the Industrial Revolution. Europeans sought out and then imitated exotic and luxury consumer goods. They applied technological ingenuity, indigenous resources, and eventually mechanization to produce a whole range of new consumer goods, making them accessible to wide parts of the population, not just to the elites. World trade first brought the inspiration of these products and new resources; later it brought markets, British global power, and empire to sustain a continuous process of industrialization and economic growth. The Industrial Revolution was a global phenomenon both in its inception and in its processes of economic transformation.

See also **Capitalism; Economic Growth and Industrialism; Industrial Revolution, Second; Science and Technology; Trade and Economic Growth.**

BIBLIOGRAPHY

Allen, Robert C. "The Great Divergence in European Wages and Prices from the Middle Ages to the First World War." *Explorations in Economic History* 3 (2001): 1–25

Bayly, Christopher Alan. *The Birth of the Modern World, 1780–1914: Global Connections and Comparisons.* Malden, Mass., 2004.

Berg, Maxine. *The Age of Manufactures: Industry, Innovation, and Work in Britain, 1770–1820.* London, 1994.

Crafts, Nicholas F. R. *British Economic Growth during the Industrial Revolution.* Oxford, U.K., 1985.

Crouzet, François. *Britain Ascendant: Comparative Studies in Franco-British Economic History.* Cambridge, U.K., 1990.

De Vries, Jan. "The Industrial Revolution and the Industrious Revolution." *Journal of Economic History* 54 (1994): 249–70.

Flynn, Dennis, and Giraldez, Arturo. "China and the Manila Galleons." In *World Silver and Monetary History in the Sixteenth and Seventeenth Centuries,* edited by Dennis Owen Flynn. Aldershot, U.K., 1996.

Gershenkron, Alexander. *Economic Backwardness in Historical Perspective: A Book of Essays.* Cambridge, Mass., 1962.

Kriedte, Peter, Hans Medick, and Jürgen Schlumbohm. *Industrialization before Industrialization: Rural Industry in the Genesis of Capitalism.* Translated by Beate Schempp. Cambridge, U.K., 1981.

Landes, David. *The Unbound Prometheus: Technological Change and Industrial Development in Western Europe from 1750 to the Present.* Cambridge, U.K., 1969.

———. *The Wealth and Poverty of Nations: Why Some Are So Rich and Some So Poor.* New York, 1998.

Mendels, Franklin. "Protoindustrialization: The First Phase of the Industrialization Process." *Journal of the Economic History* 32 (1972): 241–61.

Mokyr, Joel. "Accounting for the Industrial Revolution." In *The Cambridge Economic History of Modern Britain,* vol. 1, edited by Roderick Floud and Paul Johnson. Cambridge, U.K., 2004.

O'Brien, P. K., and S. L. Engerman. "The Industrial Revolution in Global Perspective." In *The Cambridge Economic History of Modern Britain,* vol. 1, edited by Roderick Floud and Paul Johnson. Cambridge, U.K., 2004.

O'Rourke, Kevin H., and Jeffrey G. Williamson. *Globalization and History: The Evolution of a Nineteenth-Century Atlantic Economy.* Cambridge, Mass., 1999.

Pomeranz, Kenneth. *The Great Divergence: China, Europe and the Making of the Modern World Economy.* Princeton, N.J., 2000.

Rostow, W. W. *The Stages of Economic Growth: A Non-Communist Manifesto.* Cambridge, U.K., 1960.

MAXINE BERG

INDUSTRIAL REVOLUTION, SECOND.

The term *Second Industrial Revolution* refers to a set of technological events that took place roughly between 1865 and 1914. Between the customary end of the First Industrial Revolution in the 1820s and the start of a new wave of spectacular inventions, technological progress had been anything but stagnant. The implicit notion that the periods of "Industrial Revolution" were more innovative than the half century in between is risky at best. Yet in some ways the innovations of the last third of the nineteenth century were not only spectacular and revolutionary, but they also set the technological trajectory of much of the twentieth century and made it into the period in which more economic growth took place than had in the entire history of the human race before.

Technology does not drive history. It is itself a function of cultural, social, and economic factors that have been a source of dispute and argument for generations. In the twenty-first century technology is widely seen as no less political and "socially constructed" than any other element of human culture. Such approaches are useful for certain purposes, but they tend at times to obscure that technology affects the human material condition irreversibly in directions that are notoriously difficult to predict. The years of the Second Industrial Revolution produced both the best and the worst that humankind could achieve in manipulating nature. Whatever one might think of the effects on the technological changes in this period, they ensured that human life in many dimensions would be transformed irrecognizably. Technology is knowledge. The artifacts and machines that often embody it are nothing without the underlying knowledge that makes it possible to design and construct them, and then to operate and repair them. The story of technology is therefore the story of the growth of useful knowledge, of the institutions and incentives that make it grow and disseminate it, and of the social capabilities that lead to its application.

The years from 1865 to 1914 witnessed an unprecedented growth in useful knowledge. Whether or not it was the most explosive period of growth in scientific knowledge ever is impossible to demonstrate. But it surely is the age in which science and technology became inextricably linked, in which the modern process of research and development itself was invented, and in which science indisputably established itself as indispensable to the process of economic growth. All the same, any facile generalizations about the connection between science and technology need to take account of the three basic facts of this period. First, science owed technology at least as much as technology owed science. Second, a great deal of technology still advanced with little or no scientific understanding of the processes involved. Third, many scientific advances took place that led to only few applications, and whose impact on technology, if any, was far in the future. What the experience of this age shows is that while "full understanding" was rarely a prerequisite for a technique to work and be implemented, a technique can be improved and adapted at a faster rate when it is better understood than when a technique has been discovered by accident or through trial-and-error. Many of the techniques that emerged in the post-1865 decades were based on a very partial understanding (or epistemic base) of the physical or chemical processes involved.

However, this base expanded during the period and eventually led to improvements and applications that would have amazed the original inventors. The relation between the epistemic base and the technique was at times subtle and involved, far beyond the standard "linear" model postulating that science leads to applied science and applied science to technology. Science played more of a role too in the new techniques of the post-1865 revolutions than it did in the First Industrial Revolution, but its role varied considerably between different economic activities.

The process of invention thus cannot be separated from "social knowledge." That such knowledge

Steam-powered loom in a woolen mill. From the *Catalan Illustrated,* 5 June 1888. PRIVATE COLLECTION/BRIDGEMAN ART LIBRARY/INDEX

was essential is illustrated by the frequent duplication of invention. Three of the best-known inventions of the Second Industrial Revolution, the Bessemer process of steelmaking, the red dye named alizarin, and the Bell telephone were made at practically the same time by different inventors. Far from demonstrating that "necessity is the mother of invention," this underlines that there was a common pool of underlying knowledge to which different people had access.

Inventions can be classified into *macroinventions,* major conceptual breakthroughs that occur fairly rarely and often are the result of individual genius and perseverance, and *microinventions,* which consist of small cumulative improvements and adaptations of existing technology. Many microinventions consisted of making small improvements in existing techniques or recombining them into new ones. Most productivity growth clearly occurred thanks to the cumulative effect of these small improvements. Without the great discontinuities, however, minor advances sooner or later were likely to have run into diminishing returns.

The new industries that the Second Industrial Revolution created often differed from the old ones in more than just the reliance on formal knowledge. The scale of production at the plant level increased: chemical and electrical plants were in general subject to economies of scale. The huge steel ships required much larger yards, and mass production, as we shall see, became the rule rather than the exception. As a result, the relation between industry and markets changed: new techniques required support from finance and capital markets, they needed workers with different skills and attitudes. If the modal worker in Europe in 1850 was still employed at home or in a small workshop, by 1914 most worked in large plants or offices.

Singling out technology as the prime player in the Second Industrial Revolution is to some extent arbitrary. The many subtle and complex ways in which technology interacted with the institutions of capitalism, changes in transportation and communications, political changes, urbanization, and imperialism, all created an economy that was far more "globalized" than anything that had come before or was to come after in the first half of the twentieth century. Yet without technology, none of these changes could have come about, and without better useful knowledge, technology would have eventually frozen in its tracks as it had done so often in previous centuries.

In what follows, this entry will outline the main technological developments of this era, noting in each case both the economic significance and the epistemic base that the techniques rested on. The entry will deal with the following general classes: materials, energy, engineering and communications, and biological technology (agriculture and medicine).

MATERIALS

Steel The material most associated with the Second Industrial Revolution is steel. By 1850 the age of iron had become fully established. But for many uses, wrought iron was inferior to steel. The wear and tear on wrought iron machine parts and rails made them expensive in use, and for many uses, especially in machines and construction, wrought iron was insufficiently tenacious and elastic. The problem was not making steel; the problem was making cheap steel. This problem was famously solved by Henry Bessemer (1813–1898) in 1856. The Bessemer converter used the fact that the impurities in cast iron consisted mostly of carbon, and that this carbon could be used as a fuel if air were blown through the molten metal. The interaction of the air's oxygen with the steel's carbon created intense heat, which kept the iron liquid. Thus, by adding the correct amount of carbon or by stopping the blowing at the right time, the desired mixture of iron and carbon could be created, the high temperature and turbulence of the molten mass ensuring an even mixture. At first, Bessemer steel was of very poor quality, but then a British steelmaker, Robert Mushet (1811–1891), discovered that the addition of *spiegeleisen,* an alloy of carbon, manganese, and iron, into the molten iron as a recarburizer solved the problem. The other drawback of Bessemer steel, as was soon discovered, was that phosphorus in the ores spoiled the quality of the steel, and thus the process was for a while confined to low-phosphorus Swedish and Spanish ores.

A different path was taken by Continental metallurgists, who jointly developed the Siemens-Martin open-hearth process, based on the idea of cofusion—melting together low-carbon wrought iron and high-carbon cast iron. The technique used hot waste gases to preheat incoming fuel and air, and mixed cast iron with wrought iron in the correct proportions to obtain steel. The hearths were lined with special brick linings to maintain the high temperatures. The process allowed the use of scrap iron and low grade fuels, and thus turned out to be more profitable than the Bessemer process in the long run. Open-hearth steel took longer to make than Bessemer steel, but as a result permitted better quality control. Bessemer steel also tended to fracture inexplicably under pressure, a problem that was eventually traced to small nitrogen impurities. In 1900 Andrew Carnegie, the American steel king, declared that the open-hearth process was the future of the industry.

Like the Bessemer process, the Siemens-Martin process was unable to use the phosphorus-rich iron ores found widely on the European Continent. Scientists and metallurgists did their best to resolve this bottleneck, but it fell to two British amateur inventors, Percy Gilchrist (1851–1935) and Sidney Thomas (1850–1885), to hit upon the solution in 1875. By adding to their firebricks limestone, which combined with the harmful phosphorus to create a basic slag, they neutralized the problem. It seems safe to say that the German steel industry could never have developed as it did without this invention. Not only were the cost advantages huge, but the Germans (who adopted the "basic" process immediately) also managed to convert the phosphoric slag into a useful fertilizer. While the Bessemer and Siemens-Martin processes produced bulk steel at rapidly falling prices, high-quality steel continued for a long time to be produced in Sheffield using the old crucible technique.

Cheap steel soon found many uses beyond its original spring and dagger demand; by 1880 buildings, ships, and railroad tracks were increasingly made out of steel. It became the fundamental material from which machines, weapons, and implements were made, as well as the tools that made them. Much of the technological development in other industries depended on the development of steel, from better tools and implements to

Krupp's Bessemer machine. Engraving by Robert Engels from the book *Krupp 1812–1912,* published for the Krupp centennial. The converter apparatus developed by Sir Henry Bessemer improved the process of steel manufacture in the mid-nineteenth century, and its adoption by the Krupp family at their factory in Essen, Germany, was a major step in the development of their industrial empire. MARY EVANS PICTURE LIBRARY

structures and locomotives it replaced other materials wherever possible. It created economic empires and legendary fortunes, from the great German magnates such as Krupp and Thyssen to the mammoth Carnegie steel corporation.

Steel was hardly an example of the science-leads-to-technology model. The Bessemer steel-making process of 1856 was made by a man who by his own admission had "very limited knowledge of iron metallurgy." Henry Bessemer's knowledge was so limited that the typical Bessemer blast, in his own words, was "a revelation to me, as I had in no way anticipated such results" (quoted in Carr and Taplin, p. 19). All the same, the growth of the epistemic base in the preceding half century was pivotal to the development of the process. Bessemer knew enough chemistry to realize that his process had succeeded and similar experiments by others had failed because the pig iron he had used was, by accident, singularly free of phosphorus. By adding carbon at the right time, he would get the correct mixture of carbon and iron—that is, steel. Subsequent improvements, too, were odd combinations of careful research and inspired guesswork. Steel was a paradigmatic "general purpose technology" because it combined with almost any area of production to increase productivity and capability.

Chemicals In chemicals, the story is a bit similar in that the first steps toward a new industry were made by a lucky if informed Briton. Sir William Henry Perkin (1838–1907), by a fortunate accident, made the first major discovery in what was to become the modern chemical industry. Perkin, however, was trained by August Wilhelm von Hofmann (1818–1892), who was teaching at the Royal College of Chemistry at the time, and his initial work was inspired and instigated by his German teacher. The eighteen-year-old Perkin searched for a chemical process to produce artificial quinine. While pursuing this work, he accidentally discovered in 1856 aniline purple, or as it became known, mauveine, which replaced the natural dye mauve. Three years later a French chemist, Emanuel Verguin (1814–1864), discovered aniline red, or magenta, as it came to be known. German chemists then began the search for other artificial dyes, and almost all additional successes in this area were scored by them. In the 1860s, Hofmann and Friedrich Kekulé von Stradonitz (1829–1896) formulated the structure of the dyestuff's molecules. In 1869, after years of hard work, a group of German chemists synthesized alizarin, the red dye previously produced from madder roots, beating Perkin to the patent office by one day. The discovery of alizarin in Britain marked the end of a series of brilliant but unsystematic inventions, whereas in Germany it marked the beginning of the process through which the Germans established their hegemony in chemical discovery.

Although Victorian Britain was still capable of achieving the lucky occasional masterstroke that opened a new area, the patient, systematic search for solutions by people with formal scientific and technical training better suited the German traditions. In 1840 Justus von Liebig (1803–1873), a chemistry professor at Giessen, published his *Organic Chemistry in Its Applications to Agriculture and Physiology,* which explained the importance of fertilizers and advocated the application of chemicals in agriculture. Other famed German chemists, such as Friedrich Wöhler, Robert Wilhelm Bunsen, Leopold Gmelin, Hofmann, and Kekulé von Stradonitz, jointly created modern organic chemistry, without which the chemical industry of the second half of the nineteenth century would not have been possible. It was one of the most prominent examples of how formal scientific knowledge came to affect production techniques. German chemists succeeded in developing indigotin (synthetic indigo, perfected in 1897) and sulphuric acid (1875). Soda-making had been revolutionized by the Belgian Ernest Solvay (1838–1922) in the 1860s. In explosives, dynamite, discovered by Alfred Nobel (1833–1896), was used in the construction of tunnels, roads, oil wells, and quarries. If ever there was a labor-saving invention, this was it. In the production of fertilizer, developments began to accelerate in the 1820s. Some of them were the result of resource discoveries, like Peruvian guano, which was imported in large quantities to fertilize the fields of England. Others were by-products of industrial processes. A Dublin physician, James Murray (1788–1871), showed in 1835 that superphosphates could be made by treating phosphate rocks with sulphuric acid. The big breakthrough came, however, in 1840 with the publication of von Liebig's work, commissioned by the British Association for the Advancement of Sciences. Research proceeded in England, where John Bennet Lawes (1814–1900) carried out path-breaking work in his famous experimental agricultural station at Rothamsted, where he put into practice the chemical insights provided by von Liebig. In 1843 he established a superphosphates factory that used mineral phosphates. In Germany, especially Saxony, state-supported institutions subsidized agricultural research and the results eventually led to vastly increased yields. Nitrogen fertilizers were produced from the caliche (natural sodium nitrate) mined in Chile.

The most striking macroinvention in chemistry came late in the Second Industrial Revolution. The Haber process to make ammonia—developed by Fritz Haber (1868–1934) and the chemists Carl Bosch (1874–1940) and Alwin Mittasch (1869–1953) of BASF (Baden Aniline and Soda Manufacturing)—and the discovery around 1908 of how to convert ammonia into nitric acid, made it possible for Germany to continue producing nitrates for fertilizers and explosives after its Chilean supplies were cut off during World War I. The ammonia-producing process must count as one of the most important inventions in the chemical industry ever and has been dubbed by Vaclav Smil as the most important invention of the modern age. It used two abundant substances, nitrogen and hydrogen, to produce the basis of the fertilizer and explosives industries for many years to come.

Chemistry also began its road toward the supply of new materials. Charles Goodyear (1800–1860), an American tinkerer, invented in 1839 the vulcanization process of rubber that made widespread industrial use of rubber possible. Another American, John Wesley Hyatt (1837–1920), succeeded in creating in 1869 the first synthetic plastic, which he called celluloid. Its economic importance was initially modest because of its inflammability, and it was primarily used for combs, knife handles, piano keys, and baby rattles, but it was a harbinger of things to come. The breakthrough in synthetic materials came only in 1907, when the Belgian-born American inventor Leo Hendrik Baekeland (1863–1944) discovered Bakelite. The reason for the long delay in the successful development of Bakelite was simply that neither chemical theory nor practice had been able to cope with such a substance before. Even Baekeland did not fully understand his own process, as the macromolecular chemical theories that explain synthetic materials were not developed until the 1920s. Once again, science and technology were moving ahead in leapfrogging fashion.

ENERGY

By 1850 energy production had reached a rather odd situation: steam power was spreading at an unprecedented rate through the adoption of locomotives, steamships, and stationary engines, yet the underlying physics was not well understood. This changed around 1850, when the work of Rudolf Clausius, James Prescott Joule, and others established what William Thomson (Lord Kelvin) called thermodynamics. Thermodynamics was rather quickly made accessible to engineers and designers by such men as William Rankine. The understanding of the principles governing the operation of devices that converted heat into work and their efficiency not only led to substantial improvement in the design of steam engines but also made people realize the limitations of steam. The Second Industrial Revolution thus led to the development of the internal combustion engine, an invention that like no other has determined the material culture of the twentieth century.

Internal combustion Harnessing energy efficiently was never a simple problem. During the nineteenth century dozens of inventors, realizing the advantages of internal combustion over steam, tried their hand at the problem. A working model of a gas engine was first constructed by the Belgian Étienne Lenoir (1822–1900) in 1859 and perfected in 1876, when a German traveling salesman, Nicolaus August Otto (1832–1891), built a gas engine using the eponymous four-stroke principle. Otto had worked on the problem since 1860, when he had read about Lenoir's machine in a newspaper. He was an inspired amateur without formal technical training. Otto initially saw the four-stroke engine as a makeshift solution to the problem of achieving a high enough compression and only later was his four-stroke principle, which is still the heart of most automobile engines, acclaimed as a brilliant breakthrough. The four-stroke principle was recognized as the only way in which a Lenoir-type engine could work efficiently. The "silent Otto," as it became known (to distinguish it from a noisier and less successful earlier version), was a huge financial success. The advantage of the gas engine was not its silence, but that, unlike the steam engine, it could be turned on and off at short notice. In 1885 two Germans, Gottlieb Wilhelm Daimler (1834–1900) and Carl Friedrich Benz (1844–1929), succeeded in building an Otto-type, four-stroke gasoline-burning engine, employing a primitive surface carburetor to mix the fuel with air. Benz's engine used an electrical induction coil powered by an accumulator, foreshadowing the modern spark plug. In 1893 Wilhelm Maybach (1846–1929), one of Daimler's employees, invented the modern float-feed carburetor.

The automobile became an economic reality after a lightning series of microinventions that solved many of the teething problems of the new technology: pneumatic tires, the radiator, the differential, the crank-starter, the steering wheel, and pedal-brake control. But the application of the four-stroke internal combustion engine and its cousin, the diesel engine, went far beyond the motor car: it made heavier-than-air flying machines possible, took a mobile source of energy to the fields in the form of tractors, and eventually replaced steam for all but the most specialized uses. Unlike the Otto engine, Rudolf Diesel's (1858–1913) machine was designed by a qualified engineer, trained in the modern physics of engines in search of an efficient thermodynamic cycle. Internal combustion marked a new age in energy sources. Until 1865 coal and peat had been the only sources of fossil fuel; by 1914 oil produced in Texas, Romania, and Russia was pointing to a new oil-driven energy age, now in its postmaturity.

Electricity The other development in energy technology associated with this age was electricity. Since the middle of the eighteenth century, electrical phenomena had fascinated inventors. Electrical power was used in scientific research, public displays, and from the late 1830s on in telegraphy. Other uses were believed to be possible, as Jules Verne's *20,000 Leagues under the Sea* (1870) illustrates. Between 1865 and 1890 most of the technical obstacles to Verne's dreams were overcome.

Among those were the problem of generation, resolved in the years 1866 to 1868 through the discovery of the principle of self-excitation, the need to transform high voltage current (the most efficient way to transport electricity) to low voltage (safe and effective in usage) through the Gaulard-Gibbs transformer, and the choice between alternating and direct current, decided in the late 1880s in favor of the former when Nikola Tesla (1856–1943) designed the polyphase electrical motor that could run on alternating current.

Electricity was of course not a form of energy but rather a mode of transporting and utilizing it; the real sources of power still had to come from traditional sources of energy such as water, steam, and later diesel engines. The steam turbine, another invention deeply indebted to thermodynamics, was developed by Charles Algernon Parsons (1859–1932) and Carl Gustaf Patrik de Laval (1845–1913) in 1884 and became central to electricity generation. The connection between science and the development of electricity is complex. In the decades before the Second Industrial Revolution scientists like Michael Faraday, André-Marie Ampère, and Georg Simon Ohm established empirical regularities such as the laws named after them.

Whether those insights constituted an epistemic base of sufficient width remains in dispute. The electron, the basic entity that makes electricity work was discovered only in 1897, and many of the major figures in the electricity revolution—above all, of course, Thomas Alva Edison (1847–1931)—had little or no command of the formal physics developed by James Clerk Maxwell (1831–1879), Hermann Ludwig Ferdinand von Helmholtz (1821–1894), and other pioneers of classical electrodynamics.

Yet the use of electricity transformed the age. It, too, was a general purpose technology if ever there was one. In lighting, heating, refrigeration, transportation, and production engineering, electricity lived up to the hopes that Faraday had maintained. It was clean, quiet, flexible, easy to control, and comparatively safe. Lights and motors could be turned on and off with the flip of a finger. On the shopfloor it was more efficient because it did not need shafting and belting, a major drain on energy space. Electrical power could be turned on when needed. But above all, electricity was divisible and democratic and could be provided to small producers and consumers with the same ease with which it was provided to large firms. In that sense, it went against the tide of the Second Industrial Revolution, which tended to favor large-scale production.

ENGINEERING, COMMUNICATIONS, AND TRANSPORTATION

The Second Industrial Revolution changed production engineering through a transformation so revolutionary and dramatic that while it was essentially unknown in 1850, by 1914 it was already becoming dominant, and by 1950 manufacturing was unimaginable without it. This process, often referred to as "mass production," actually consisted of a number of elements. One of those was *modularity* or the reliance on interchangeable parts, first introduced in firearms and clocks, and later applied to almost everything that had moving parts and to other components that could be produced in large batches and then assembled. For parts to be interchangeable, they needed to be produced with a tolerance sufficiently low to allow true interchangeability, which of course meant very high levels of accuracy in machine tools and cheap, high-quality materials, above all steel. The economies of scale that this permitted were only matched by the ease of repair that modularity implied. The development of *continuous flow* processes, often associated with assembly lines, were actually pioneered by meat packers engaged in *dis*assembly. The advantage of this system was that it rationalized a fine division of labor and yet imposed on the process a rate of speed determined by the employer. Henry Ford's (1863–1947) automobile assembly plant combined the concept of interchangeable parts with that of continuous flow processes, and allowed him to mass-produce a complex product and yet keep its price low enough that it could be sold as a people's vehicle. Europe saw that it worked and imitated: *Fordismus* became a buzzword in German manufacturing.

Mass production engineering was made possible by more than just precision engineering and clever redesign of plants. Success depended not only on the ingenuity and energy of the inventor but also on the willingness of contemporaries to accept the novelty, for workers to accept mind-numbingly monotonous work in which they surrendered any pretense of creativity, and for consumers to accept cookie-cutter identical products made in huge batches. Bicycles, sewing machines, agricultural equipment, clothes, and eventually Ford's model T provided the consumer with the option of cheap but nondistinctive products; those who wanted custom-made products had to pay for them. To be sure, not all manufacturing was of that nature, and there was always room for small, flexible firms who produced specialized products and used niche techniques.

The Second Industrial Revolution was also the age of the rise of technological "systems" an idea that was first enunciated in full by the historian Thomas Hughes. Again, some rudimentary "systems" of this nature were already in operation before 1870: railroad and telegraph networks and in large cities gas, water supply, and sewage systems were in existence. These systems expanded enormously after 1870, and a number of new ones were added: electrical power and telephone being the most important additions. Large technological systems turned from an exception to a commonplace.

Systems required a great deal of coordination that free markets did not always find easy to supply, and hence governments or other leading institutions ended up stepping in to determine technological standards such as railroad gauges, electricity voltages, the layout of typewriter keyboards, rules of the road, and other forms of standardization. The notion that technology consisted of separate components that could be optimized individually—never quite literally true—became less and less appropriate after 1870. This period was also the age in which communications technology changed pari passu with everything else. The most dramatic macroinvention had occurred before: the electric telegraph permitted transmission of information at a speed faster than people could move, previously limited to such devices as the semaphore and homing pigeons. After 1870 the telegraph continued to be improved and prices fell as the reach increased. Alexander Graham Bell's (1847–1922) and Elisha Gray's (1835–1901) telephone, supplemented by the switchboard (1878) and the loading coil (1899), made the telephone one of the most successful inventions of all time. Unlike the telegraph, it has had a remarkable capability of combining with other techniques such as satellites and cellular technology. The principle of wireless telegraphy, as yet unsuspected at that time, was implicit in the theory of electromagnetic waves proposed on purely theoretical grounds by James Clerk Maxwell (1831–1879) in 1865. The electromagnetic waves suggested by Maxwell were finally demonstrated to exist by a set of brilliant experiments conducted by Heinrich Rudolph Hertz in 1888. The Englishman Oliver Joseph Lodge (1851–1940) and the Italian Guglielmo Marconi (1874–1937) combined the theories of these ivory tower theorists into wireless telegraphy in the mid-1890s, and in 1906 the Americans Lee De Forest (1873–1961) and Reginald Aubrey Fessenden (1866–1932) showed how wireless radio could transmit not only Morse signals but sound waves as well through the miracle of amplitude modification.

The Le Creusot power hammer. Engraving c. 1880. Developed in 1876 by engineers working for the iron foundry at Le Creusot, France, the massive power hammer allowed the Le Creusot facility to dominate the industry. It was displayed at the Universal Exposition in Paris in 1878. PRIVATE COLLECTION/ BRIDGEMAN ART LIBRARY/ARCHIVES CHARMET

Transportation capabilities were shocked above all by the ability of people to conquer the air. For decades it was unclear whether or not that achievement would be attained through machines lighter than air, such as Zeppelins, and before Kitty Hawk (1903) many serious scientists doubted that machines heavier than air could ever fly. Here, then, was a classic case of practice outracing theory, though the Wright brothers (Wilbur [1867–1912] and Orville [1871–1948]) were well informed with the best-practice aeronautical engineering. Ocean shipping remained by far the most important form of transport, gaining in efficiency and frequency as ships were gaining in size, thanks to steel, turbines, and improvements in design. By 1914 sailing ships, for millennia the main source of long-distance mobility, were relegated to a rich person's toy, replaced by the giants such as the *Titanic*. On the other end of size scale stood that simple, obvious, person-sized mode of personal transportation, the bicycle—perfected by the Coventry mechanics James (1830–1881) and John K. Starley (1854–1901)—which, much like the mass transit systems that emerged in the 1880s, ensured poor people an alternative to walking.

BIOLOGICAL TECHNOLOGY

In an age when food was still the largest item in most household budgets, the standard of living of the population depended, above all, on food supply and nutrition. The new technologies of the nineteenth century affected food supplies through production, distribution, preservation, and eventually preparation. The fall in shipping prices meant that after 1870 Europe was the recipient of cheap agricultural products from the rest of the world. Agricultural productivity owed much to the extended use of fertilizers. Following the emergence of an epistemic base in organic chemistry in the 1840s, farmers learned to use nitrates, potassium, and phosphates. The productivity gains in European agriculture are hard to imagine without the gradual switch from natural fertilizer, produced mostly in loco by farm animals, to commercially produced chemical fertilizers.

Fertilizers were not the only scientific success in farming: the use of fungicides, such as the Bordeaux mixture, invented in 1885 by the French botanist Pierre-Marie Alexis Millardet (1838–1902) in 1885, helped conquer the dreaded potato blight that had devastated Ireland forty years earlier. Food supplies were also enhanced by better food preservation methods: refrigerated ships could carry fresh meat and dairy, but dehydration and canning were also continuously improved. Food consumption and human health were vastly enhanced by what remains the greatest discovery of the era: the germ theory of disease. Once it was understood that food putrefaction was caused by microorganisms, new processes like pasteurization could help preserve essential nutrients and drinking water could be purified (later chlorinated). The germ theory had an enormous impact on preventive medicine even if clinical technology advanced but little and helped bring about the sharp decline in mortality rates during the quarter century before World War I. While the pharmaceutical industry made little progress (Bayer's spectacularly successful aspirin in 1898 notwithstanding), the Second Industrial Revolution left people not only richer but also on average a lot healthier.

CONCLUSIONS

The Second Industrial Revolution was, in many ways, the continuation of the first. In many industries there was direct continuity. Yet it differed from its predecessor in a number of crucial aspects. First, it had a direct effect on real wages and standards of living, which rose significantly between 1870 and 1914. Its impact on economic growth and productivity was far more unequivocal than any technological advance associated with the First Industrial Revolution. It vastly augmented the direct effect of technological advances on daily life and household consumption. It contributed to the global integration of markets and information, a process that sadly came to an end in the fateful days of August 1914. Finally, by changing the relation between knowledge of nature and how it affected technological practices, it irreversibly changed the way technological change itself occurs. In so doing, what was learned and done in these years paved the way for many more industrial revolutions to come.

See also **Banks and Banking; Capitalism; Economic Growth and Industrialism; Industrial Revolution, First; Science and Technology.**

BIBLIOGRAPHY

Bryant, Lynwood. "The Beginnings of the Internal Combustion Engine." In *Technology in Western Civilization,* edited by Melvin Kranzberg and Carroll W. Pursell, Jr., vol. 1, 648–663. New York, 1967.

———. "The Role of Thermodynamics: The Evolution of the Heat Engine." *Technology and Culture* 14 (1973): 152–165.

Carr, James Cecil, and W. Taplin. *A History of the British Steel Industry.* Oxford, U.K., 1962.

Hounshell, David A. *From the American System to Mass Production, 1800–1932: The Development of Manufacturing Technology in the United States.* Baltimore, Md., 1984.

Hughes, Thomas P. *Networks of Power: Electrification in Western Society, 1880–1930.* Baltimore, Md., 1983.

Mokyr, Joel. *The Lever of Riches: Technological Creativity and Economic Progress.* New York, 1990.

———. *The Gifts of Athena: Historical Origins of the Knowledge Economy.* Princeton, N.J., 2002.

Smil, Vaclav. *Creating the Twentieth Century: Technical Innovations of 1867–1914 and Their Lasting Impact.* New York, 2005.

Smith, Crosbie, and M. Norton Wise. *Energy and Empire: A Biographical Study of Lord Kelvin.* Cambridge, U.K., 1989.

JOEL MOKYR

INGRES, JEAN-AUGUSTE-DOMINIQUE (1780–1867), French painter.

Jean-Auguste-Dominique Ingres inherited the mantle of Jacques Louis David (1748–1825) and remained the apostle of neoclassicism for half a century, despite fundamental antagonisms with the Academy and inconsistencies in his work and tastes. In the twentieth century, Ingres's linear forms, with their anatomical and spatial distortions, made him an acclaimed precursor of modernism.

Born in Montauban, a small town north of Toulouse, the son of an artisan and musician, Ingres came to Paris and entered David's studio in 1797. The linear surface patterns and flattened spaces of his early works owe much to the 1793 outline drawings for the *Iliad* by British artist John Flaxman (1755–1826) and to the broader interest among David's students in archaic periods considered primitive and anticlassical. At the Salon of 1806, critics decried the hard, cold light akin to "moonbeams" and the "Gothic" character of Ingres's exhibited works, including the monumental *Napoleon I on His Imperial Throne* and the three portraits of the *Rivière Family.* In 1819 the same invective was used for the *Grande Odalisque,* whose extra lumbar vertebrae, taken as a sign of the artist's prescient abstraction in the twentieth century, were then merely seen as evidence of faulty drawing. The more modeled, neo-Renaissance forms that define much of Ingres's later production first appear in his altarpiece *The Vow of Louis XIII.* Exhibited at the Salon of 1824, *The Vow* suited the political agenda of the restored Bourbon monarchy and, in the wake of the deaths of David and his most talented pupils—Anne-Louis Girodet de Roucy (1767–1824), Pierre-Narcisse Guérin (1774–1833), and Baron Antoine Jean Gros (1771–1835)—Ingres became the undisputed head of the neoclassical school and the symbol of a distinctly national art. Due in part to the uneven critical reception of his work in Paris, however, Ingres spent much of his life in Italy (1806–1820 in Rome, as a *pensionnaire* at the French Academy until 1811; 1820–1824 in Florence; 1834–1841 in Rome, as the Director of the French Academy). He married twice, to Madeleine Chapelle (1782–1849) in 1813 and to Delphine Ramel (1808–1887) in 1852.

A consummate draftsman, Ingres first supported himself in Italy by drawing portraits. But the process of drawing was integral to the conception, execution, and replication of his painted work. The range of his practice—from isolated motifs as small as an ear to compositional studies, from the most summary sketches to works of the utmost finish, from tracings after his own works to copies after engravings—and the sheer number of works produced—he bequeathed four thousand drawings alone to the museum in Montauban that bears his name—signals its importance. Yet during his lifetime the artist's insistence that he was a history painter was categorical.

The Apotheosis of Homer (1827), commissioned as a ceiling painting for the Louvre, is a zealous exercise in codifying Ingres's vision of history as it devolves from the blind poet at the center of the composition, the personifications of the *Iliad* and the *Odyssey* at his feet, and the throng of hierarchically arranged figures who pay homage, none of whom lived beyond the seventeenth century. A drawing of *Homer Deified* (1864–1865) updates the assembly to include David to the right of the outstretched arm of Nicholas Poussin (1594–1665) and a self-portrait—as a young servant peeking out from behind a new altar directly below the similar pedestal upon which Homer sits. Ingres's self-representation belies both his production and reputation as a painter of nudes and portraits, which, together with his drawings, secured his reputation as a modernist. Twentieth-century scholarship questioned the persistent myths about Ingres, illuminating the inconsistencies between his stated positions and his practice.

While the purity of his drawing and the finish of his oils are inconceivable without the training received in David's atelier, Ingres's incessant preoccupation with the individual motif worked against unified compositions; the parts are rarely, if ever, subordinated to the whole (see, for example, the unfinished commission for *The Golden Age,* 1839–1849). Interpretations of his preoccupation with repetition—reworking motifs and remaking entire compositions—extend from his avowed "pursuit of perfection" to an aesthetic of

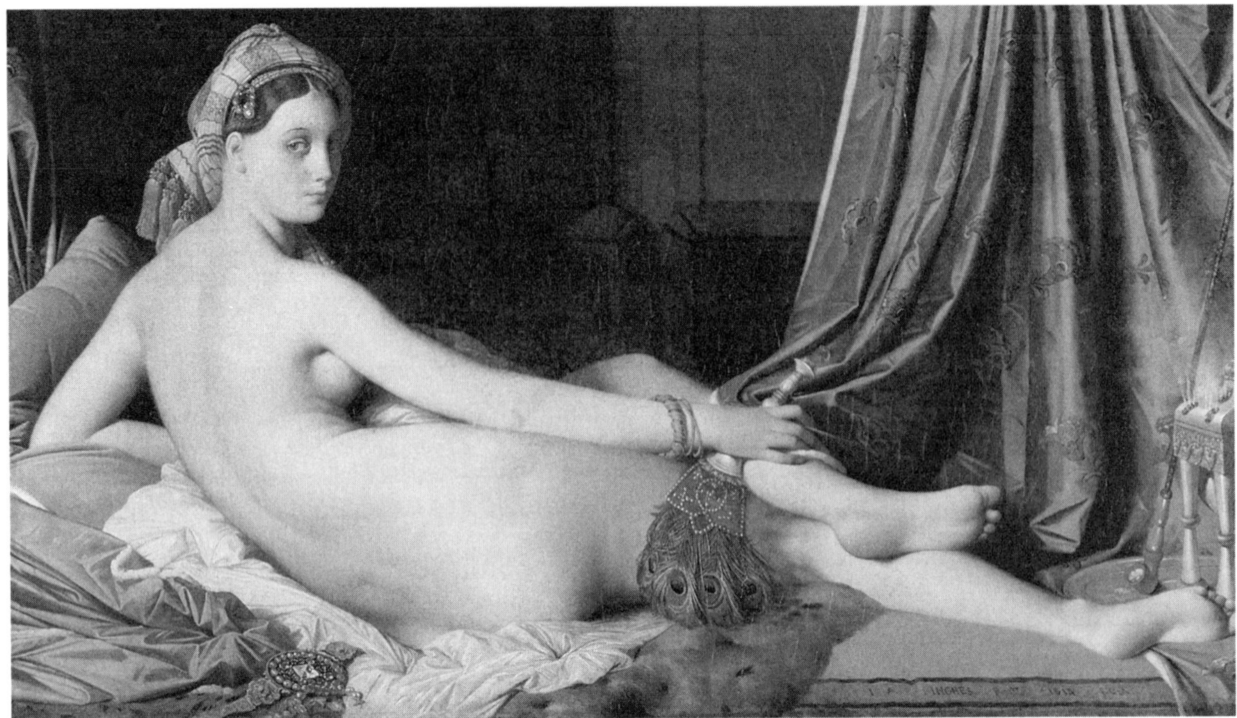

The Great Odalisque. Painting by Jean-Auguste-Dominique Ingres, 1814. ERICH LESSING/ART RESOURCE, NY

the shop window. If the emphasis on detail and the attention to historical accuracy that characterize his production lend support to this industrial model, it is the late work that best exemplifies it. The polychromed backgrounds (executed under the artist's direction by his students) of *Odalisque with Slave* (1839) and *Antiochus and Stratonice* (1840) recall both archaeological studies and pattern books; among his society portraits, *Madame Moitessier, Seated* (1856) is remarkable for its up-to-the-minute fashion augmented by a sumptuous display of luxury goods.

The wide range of sources, styles, and even spatial arrangements—ancient, medieval, Renaissance, and French history up to his own time—complicate Ingres's stated allegiances to Phidias (c. 500–432 B.C.E.) and to his beloved Raphael (1483–1520). The fresco-like *Romulus, Conqueror of Acron* (1812); the combination of Raphaelesque ideal and seventeenth-century costume in *The Vow*; the hierarchical arrangement of *homérides* as if in bas-relief against the Ionic hexastyle temple in *The Apotheosis*; or the High Renaissance figures and arching space in *Christ Among the Doctors* (1862) bespeak a concern for period style as much as for changing conditions of patronage. Ingres's practice also blurs distinctions between history and other genres. With its references to the Phidian colossus of Zeus at Olympia and to the figure of God the Father from Jan Van Eyck's late Gothic Ghent altarpiece (among the Napoleonic spoils on exhibition in Paris from 1799–1816), *Napoleon I on His Imperial Throne* is as much history painting as portraiture. So is *Madame Moitessier, Seated,* whose grandiose pose evokes Arcadia from the Roman fresco *Herakles Finding His Son Telephos.* The small scale and suggestive eroticism of *Antiochus and Stratonice* turn history into historical genre, in spite of Ingres's reliance on literary sources (Plutarch [46–120 C.E.]), classical statuary (the pose of Stratonice is that of the Roman statue *Pudicity*), and debates about ancient polychromy in the 1830s.

Perhaps the most influential legacy of Ingres's tendency to eroticize classicism is found in the female nude, whose serpentine forms lack skeletal structure, joints, and musculature. Ingres's anatomical and spatial distortions have come down to us most visibly in the work of Henri Matisse (1869–1954) and Pablo Picasso (1881–1973) but they have also engendered a critique of modernist production that deforms female bodies and naturalizes a male heterosexual maker and viewer. If *Achilles Receiving the Ambassadors of Agamemnon,* for which Ingres won the Prix de Rome in 1801, pictures the homosocial world so prominent in the work of David and his school in the 1790s, it is Ingres's subsequent, almost exclusively female nudes—*The Bather of Valpinçon* (1808), *The Great Odalisque* (1814), *Odalisque with Slave* (1839), *The Source* (1856), and *The Turkish Bath* (1862) among them—that transform conceptions of the genre for the next two centuries. Expanding the paradigms of connoisseurship, biography, and psychobiography, Ingres scholarship around the turn of the twenty-first century has turned its attention to patronage, identification, and desire in female as well as male viewers, and modernity and mass production, enriching our understanding of Ingres's complicated legacy in the process.

See also **David, Jacques-Louis; Painting.**

BIBLIOGRAPHY

Condon, Patricia, with Marjorie Cohn and Agnes Mongan. *Ingres In Pursuit of Perfection: The Art of J.-A.-D. Ingres.* Louisville, Ky., 1983.

Ockman, Carol. *Ingres's Eroticized Bodies: Retracing the Serpentine Line.* New Haven, Conn., 1995.

Rifkin, Adrian. *Ingres Then, and Now.* London, 2000.

Rosenblum, Robert. *Jean-Auguste-Dominique Ingres.* London, 1967. Reprint, New York, 1990.

Siegfried, Susan, and Adrian Rifkin, eds. *Fingering Ingres.* Oxford, U.K., 2001.

CAROL OCKMAN

INTELLECTUALS. The word *intellectual* used as a noun to describe a particular group of people has its origin in the early nineteenth century (around 1813), but as a description of how writers, philosophers, and scientists acted in the realm of politics it dates from the late nineteenth century in France. As Jürgen Habermas has argued, intellectuals were the representatives of an emergent public sphere. French *philosophes* in the *salons,* German philosophers in reading societies, and English writers in coffeehouses came together in a social space in order to participate, as independent critical thinkers, in the open and free discussion of issues of cultural and political interest. This rising group was the product of a new capitalist market economy that was progressively freeing the producers of ideas from the twin authorities of state and church. With the growth of the book trade and the expansion of the popular press, themselves the product of a growth of the reading public, writers and their like were able to establish a previously unknown level of autonomy.

From the seventeenth century onward a variety of different terms (including *les savants, les érudits, les gens de lettres,* as well as the hostile *les pédants*) were coined to describe this new group of people brought to the fore by a combination of technological revolution and the emergence of modern state power. As the locations in which knowledge was exchanged became increasingly diverse, the activity of producing knowledge became increasingly specialized, producing in its turn the newly defined vocation of the author. Perhaps no figure better represented this novel form than Voltaire (François-Marie Arouet, 1694–1778). Voltaire, the philosophe, committed himself to the battle for ideas and did so in opposition to those prepared to abuse power, be it secular or religious. He established the cause to which the intellectual was to be committed (the fight against injustice) as well as the methods that were to be used (argument, scorn, publicity) and did so in the belief that the philosophe had an overriding obligation to speak the truth, whatever the personal consequences. Moreover, it came to be believed that men such as Voltaire had the power to change the course of history and to bring governments to their knees. It was for this reason that many were later to conclude that the philosophes had *caused* the French Revolution. Although this is an exaggeration, it is possible to trace a line of descent that runs from Voltaire in the eighteenth century to Victor Hugo (1802–1885) and Émile Zola (1840–1902) in the nineteenth century and Albert Camus (1913–1960) and Jean-Paul Sartre (1905–1980) in the twentieth century. Each adopted the pose of what was later to be portrayed as that of the universal, committed intellectual.

Nevertheless, the role played by intellectuals and the extent of their autonomy varied considerably from country to country. In part this depended upon the formal liberties accorded by the state to forms of cultural expression. It reflected the extent to which intellectuals controlled their own publishing houses and magazines. Religion too played a part, with societies dominated by the Protestant, Catholic, or Muslim religions displaying markedly different levels of toleration toward the free expression of ideas. The relative prominence of one or more cultural centers within a society also had an impact, as did the importance and size of the university sector and the level of linguistic uniformity across a society.

If in Spain and Italy, for example, intellectuals have occupied a position similar to that of their French counterparts, there have been other countries (most notably Switzerland and the Scandinavian countries) where they have been relatively invisible. In England, by contrast, intellectuals have predominantly been absorbed into the ruling elite and have largely endorsed the dominant values of society. In America, intellectuals have struggled to be heard against a backdrop of anti-intellectualism and popular culture but even so there were those who managed to carve out a bohemian existence (most notably in New York). One characteristic however seems to be true in all cases: women were largely excluded from the category of intellectual.

Two specific examples might be examined in greater detail. It was in nineteenth-century Russia that the term *intelligentsia* came into common usage. Initially drawn almost exclusively from the nobility, its world was highly circumscribed, encompassing little more than the universities, aristocratic salons, and marginal reviews and periodicals. Alexander Herzen (1812–1870) spoke of an intelligentsia that enjoyed outer slavery and inner freedom. By midcentury the nature of the intelligentsia was changing as a consequence of a decline in aristocratic lifestyles and the growth of the modern professions. It was this new generation (the "sons" of Ivan Turgenev's [1818–1883] famous novel *Fathers and Sons* [1862]) who in the 1860s first started sporadic and mainly clandestine organizations designed to propagandize the vast masses of Russia's peasantry and to explain to them the nature of their exploitation. Idealizing the "people" and believing in their natural propensity toward socialism, this generation asserted the duty of intellectuals to bring about the extinction of the existing society. As Russia changed at the turn of the century, the next generation entered the world of revolutionary politics. Yet Vladimir Lenin's (1870–1924) Bolshevik Party was always suspicious of the intelligentsia and with the emergence of the Soviet regime set out to transform the intelligentsia into a salaried and integrated element of the state. In this it was largely successful.

It was however in the France of the Third Republic that the various factors favorable to the emergence of intellectuals as a distinct group produced the first full expression of what has come to be understood as the political intervention of intellectuals as autonomous actors. There the Republic had explicitly sought to produce a secular elite that could counterbalance the reactionary influence of the Catholic Church. In consequence, when the forces of reaction sought unjustly to imprison Alfred Dreyfus (1859–1935) on false charges of treason, writers including Zola, Anatole France (1844–1924), and Marcel Proust (1871–1922) intervened in the name of truth and justice in order to secure his release. They did so explicitly as *intellectuals*, speaking in the name of an authority that derived solely from their literary, cultural, and scientific activities, and it was in the name of that authority that they were listened to.

From the outset the term *intellectual* was deployed by political opponents as a term of abuse, indicating a group of uprooted and classless individuals who spoke about things they did not understand and with doleful consequences. "I have never called myself an intellectual," proclaimed the British philosopher Bertrand Russell (1872–1970), "and no one has ever dared call me one in my presence. I think that an intellectual may be defined as a person who pretends to have more intellect than he has, and I hope that this does not apply to me." These criticisms were often tinged with overt anti-Semitism. Yet the intervention at the turn of the twentieth century in defense of Dreyfus established an ideal type of what an intellectual should be and it has been an image that has had considerable currency until the present day (most notably in the writings of Edward Said [1935–2003]).

Yet the role of intellectuals was never a subject of agreement, especially so in the years of their emergence. The sociologist Karl Mannheim (1893–1947) conjured up the image of the "free-floating" intellectual, of someone who was "unanchored" and "unattached" and who therefore could be said to act independently of the claims of false ideology and self-interest. Julien Benda (1867–1956) gave this vision its clearest and best-known expression in his text *La Trahison des clercs* (1927; Treason of the intellectuals). Faced with the rise of both fascism and communism, Benda produced a passionate portrayal of the intellectual, locked in the ivory tower of reflection, who remained above the day-to-day world of political realities and compromise. The primary function of the intellectual was to place the values of knowledge before the values of action.

Several questions arose in relation to this picture of the autonomous intellectual. Was it an accurate portrayal of the role of intellectuals? Was autonomy the desirable goal it is taken to be? The Italian Marxist Antonio Gramsci (1891–1937) did not think so, preferring rather to praise the "organic" intellectual prepared to subordinate his or her efforts to the twin causes of the working class and the Communist Party. Paul Nizan (1905–1940) articulated the same theme in his blistering response to Benda's call for independence. To abstain from politics, Nizan countered, was to make a choice, and thus to side with the forces of capitalism and imperialism. After World War II this position attained almost the status of orthodoxy, receiving its clearest statement in the doctrine of commitment articulated by Sartre and Simone de Beauvoir (1908–1986). Max Weber (1864–1920) provided the most compelling reply to these arguments in two essays published in 1919. Weber argued that the vocation of politics demands a particular form of responsibility that is not appropriate in the world of scholarship. As such the scholar should aspire to maintain as high a level of impartiality as possible and to accept "value freedom" as a desirable and attainable goal. Later Raymond Aron (1905–1983), condemning what he termed "the opium of the intellectuals," reworked Max Weber's distinction between an "ethic of principled conviction" and an "ethic of responsibility" in order to expose the blindness of intellectuals toward the totalitarian regimes of the twentieth century and to argue that intellectuals should adopt a more modest function.

See also **Intelligentsia; Professions.**

BIBLIOGRAPHY

Aron, Raymond. *The Opium of the Intellectuals.* New Brunswick, N.J., 2001.

Carey, John. *The Intellectuals and the Masses: Pride and Prejudice among the Literary Intelligentsia, 1880–1939.* London, 1992.

Collini, Stefan. *Public Moralists: Political Thought and Intellectual Life in Britain 1850–1930.* Cambridge, U.K., 1991.

Fink, Leon, Stephen T. Leonard, and Donald M. Reid. *Intellectuals and Public Life: Between Radicalism and Reform.* Ithaca, N.Y., 1996.

Goldfarb, Jeffrey C. *Civility and Subversion: The Intellectual in Democratic Society.* Cambridge, U.K., 1998.

Gramsci, Antonio. *Selections from the Prison Notebooks of Antonio Gramsci.* Edited and translated by Quintin Hoare and Geoffrey Nowell Smith. London, 1971.

Jacoby, Russell. *The Last Intellectuals: American Culture in the Age of Academe.* New York, 1987.

Jennings, Jeremy, ed. *Intellectuals in Twentieth-Century France: Mandarins and Samurais.* London, 1993.

Jennings, Jeremy, and Anthony Kemp-Welch, eds. *Intellectuals in Politics: From the Dreyfus Affair to Salman Rushdie.* London, 1997.

Johnson, Paul. *Intellectuals.* London, 1988.

Maclean, Ian, Alan Montefiore, and Peter Winch. *The Political Responsibility of Intellectuals.* Cambridge, U.K., 1990.

Mannheim, Karl. *Ideology and Utopia.* 1936. London, 1960.

Michael, John. *Anxious Intellects: Academic Professionals, Public Intellectuals, and Enlightenment Values.* Durham, N.C., 2000.

Said, Edward. *Representations of the Intellectual.* London, 1994.

Small, Helen, ed. *The Public Intellectual.* Oxford, U.K., 2002.

Walzer, Michael. *The Company of Critics: Social Criticism and Political Commitment in the Twentieth Century.* London, 1989.

Weber, Max. *Political Writings.* Cambridge, U.K., and New York, 1994.

JEREMY JENNINGS

INTELLIGENTSIA. The concept of the intelligentsia was nurtured, challenged, and revitalized in Russia in the late nineteenth and early twentieth centuries. Used to describe a group of politically engaged intellectuals, the term spread from its east European origins and enjoyed a strong grip on the imagination and social science in much of the world for the next hundred years. Definitions of the intelligentsia, the imputed characteristics of its members, and the consequences of their actions inspired controversies from the start. The category has no fixed meaning in part because its founding assumption—that intellectuals have superior insight into the goals and means of politics—gives rise to conflicts, both about the claim itself and about the content of these goals and means. Nonetheless, intellectuals' own quarrels over who is in and who is out of the intelligentsia, as well as over its merits or demerits, have kept the concept alive as a proposition, if not a coherent social formation, for well more than a century.

The word *intelligentsia* was used in Polish political literature in the 1840s, although R. V. Ivanov-Razumnik, the author of an influential two-volume work, *The History of Russian Social Thought* (1906), claimed that the term had first been used in the 1860s by a minor Russian novelist. The rich medium of creativity and political disappointment of early-twentieth-century Russia produced compelling self-definitions and controversies around the concept. Ivanov-Razumnik's study, subtitled "Individualism and Philistinism in Russian Literature and Life of the Nineteenth Century," gave the Russian intelligentsia a definition and a history, linked to each other. His argument was that *intelligenty* (intellectuals) were "irreconcilably hostile" to the petty materialism of philistine life. The intelligentsia was an "ethically anti-Philistine, sociologically non-estate, non-class historically continuous group, characterized by the creation of new forms and ideals and putting these into practice in a tendency toward physical and mental, social and individual liberation of the personality" (Ivanov-Razumnik, vol. 1, p. 12). Values, creativity, activism, and membership in a group with a history—but not class or social estate—were postulated as core elements of an intelligentsia tradition.

What values? Not coincidentally, the word translated above as "Philistinism"—*meshchantsvo*—is related to merchants and small-scale marketing in Russian. Ivanov-Razumnik, and other Russian creators of the intelligentsia's mythology, regarded capitalism, commerce, and materialism as inimical to freedom, creativity, and social well-being. The association of the intelligentsia with an anticapitalist stance was one consequence of the group's self-definition at a time of rapid and, for some intellectuals, disturbing expansion of industrial production, commercial agriculture, and wage labor in Russia.

Anticapitalism was not the only, or even the necessary, condition of membership in the intelligentsia, however. Russian writers of different political and cultural perspectives—liberals, such as Pavel N. Milyukov, and Marxists, including Yuli Martov and Georgy Plekhanov—brought varieties of opposition to Russia's autocratic state in under the intelligentsia umbrella. For many commentators, the intelligentsia tradition began in the eighteenth century, when Alexander Radishchev and Nikolai Novikov published and were punished for their criticisms of Russian government and society. The genealogy continued through the middle of the nineteenth century, highlighted by the nobles associated with the failed Decembrist coup (1825), debates between Slavophiles and Westernizers, the literary commentaries of Vissarion Belinsky, the pessimistic reflections of Peter Chaadayev, and the eclectic writings of Alexander Herzen. The second half of the century added to the list critical publicists such as Nikolai Dobrolyubov and Nikolai Chernyshevsky, social theorists such as Peter Lavrov and Nikolai Mikhailovsky, and activists in the name of various causes—Mikhail Bakunin's anarchism, Plekhanov's Marxism. Writers and sometimes their literary creations were made part of this trajectory. Bazarov, the protagonist of Ivan Turgenev's novel *Fathers and Sons* (1862), was a controversial "nihilist" hero for the 1860s and later. What held this chain of many metals together were three qualities: opposition to the state, the claim to speak for the welfare of the polity, and persecution. The intelligentsia ideal—expressed by historical personalities or literary creations—was personal sacrifice for the cause of the general good, expressed in words or actions directed against the state.

From that time [the 1860s], the Russian intelligentsia becomes non-estate, non-class based, not only in its tasks, goals, ideals, but also in its composition, and, at the same time—of course a not accidental coincidence—the term intelligentsia itself appears in the present sense of the word. (R. V. Ivanov-Razumnik, 1906)

In the early twentieth century, three developments heightened controversies over who was in and who was out of the intelligentsia and simultaneously promoted the retrospective reconstruction of this "historically continuous group." One challenge was the growth of an educated society and the expansion of the liberal professions. The concerns of Russia's artists and journalists encompassed a wide array of interests, including fascinations that strayed far from the realist and positivist hegemonies of the previous century. A second challenge was the attraction of Russian intellectuals to neo-idealist and religious ideas, which eroded the earlier appeal of positivism and Marxism. A third challenge was fragmentation and contention within the political movements that had taken shape in the 1890s. The Social Democrats split into factions only a few years after their founding congress; later, even prominent Bolshevik intellectuals were attracted to antimaterialist philosophies.

Vladimir Lenin's 1902 pamphlet "What Is to Be Done?" can be read against this background as one of several assertions of the intelligentsia's importance. In Lenin's formulation, intellectuals, "educated representatives of the propertied classes," were essential to the formation of class consciousness among workers and thus to the triumph of socialism. Another then-obscure veteran of the Marxist labor movement of the 1890s, Jan Wacław Machajski, formulated a more sinister view of the intelligentsia as a class of "intellectual workers" who through their monopoly on education would manipulate socialism in their own interest. Once in power in a socialist regime, Machajski predicted, the intelligentsia would constitute a new ruling class.

The failure of the Revolution of 1905 to bring socialism, liberalism, or even representative government to life in an uncompromised manner, as well as the extensive liberalization of rules on the press, only abetted controversies over the intelligentsia. Was the intelligentsia a forceful and constructive element of Russian politics? This question roiled Russian society in 1909, when a group of prominent intellectuals, most of them ex-Marxist converts to neo-idealism, published *Vekhi* (Landmarks), a radical critique of the intelligentsia and a repudiation of its (presumed) traditions. The contributors to *Vekhi,* including the philosophers Nikolai Berdyayev, Sergei Bulgakov, and Semyon L. Frank, and the liberal nationalist Peter Struve, lambasted the intelligentsia for its narrow-minded positivism, its intolerant atheism, its fixation on revolutionary politics, and its disregard for moral principles, for law, and for personal responsibility. Bogdan Kistyakovsky castigated Plekhanov for his relativist slogan, "The success of the revolution is the highest law." Written in the bitter aftermath of 1905, during a rash of political assassinations, and in the face of the apparent incapacity of officials and elected representatives to work together in the Duma, the *Vekhi* group's harsh critique took the unusual step of placing a good share of the responsibility for Russia's troubles on the intelligentsia itself.

The intelligentsia—both radicals and reformists—struck back, with an outburst of publications that contradicted each other and simultaneously confirmed that, at least for its defenders, the intelligentsia was alive and kicking. But the *Vekhi* controversy clarified some aspects of intelligentsia myth-making. First, the myth was still powerful enough to inspire culture wars over the nature of the intelligentsia and its goals and principles, and second, it was a myth—not a socially definable reality, not an identifiable political program. Battles over what the intelligentsia was, combined with a relentless insistence that its values did matter, sustained the Russian intelligentsia as a cultural project into the years of war and revolution. But it was one cultural project among many, until the revolution of 1917 put the Russian intelligentsia on the world stage and up for reinterpretation once again.

Over the course of the twentieth century, the intelligentsia continued to accumulate meanings, both positive and negative. Within the Soviet

Union, the word was used at least three ways. One designation was simply "white-collar labor"; it employed Machajski's functionalist definition but not his critical stance to distinguish mental workers from physical ones. A second usage referred to the heroic tradition of the prerevolutionary past, now firmly fixed on a trajectory toward Bolshevik-led victory in 1917: who was in and who was out depended on officially defined linkages to the revolution. In yet another variant of the older term, some used it to describe dissident critics of the Soviet state.

Outside the Soviet Union, perspectives were similarly tied to politics. Reformers and revolutionaries attracted to the apparent victory of intellectuals and their progressive cause in Russia embraced the category for themselves, particularly the notion of political engagement. Others saw danger in intellectuals' applying their ideas to worldly politics: the French philosopher Julien Benda's *The Treason of the Clerks* (1927) was an early expression of a long line of cautionary critiques of intelligentsia activism and its outcomes. Two of the most influential social treatments of the intelligentsia were those of the German sociologist Karl Mannheim and the Italian politician Antonio Gramsci. Mannheim's *Ideology and Utopia* (1929) described intellectuals as floating "free" from their class position and as producers of a "scientific" politics. Gramsci split the intelligentsia into two camps: organic intellectuals who defended the interests of their own class and "traditional intellectuals" whose allegiance could be captured for the revolutionary cause.

By the 1950s, intellectuals who had direct experience of communist rule managed to reintroduce critical interpretations of the intelligentsia. The Yugoslav political leader and writer Milovan Djilas argued that the intelligentsia in Eastern Europe had become the managerial elite—the "new class"—of communism. Djilas, like Leon Trotsky (*The Revolution Betrayed,* 1937) and the Hungarian sociologists George Konrád and Ivan Szelenyi (*The Intellectuals on the Road to Class Power,* 1979), brought back to life Machajski's prerevolutionary warnings. Debates over the consequences of communist rule and intellectuals' responsibility for them continued after the collapse of the Soviet regimes in 1989 and 1991. In this post-Soviet context, theoretical interest in the "public sphere" or "civil society" eclipsed attention to the intelligentsia, perhaps only temporarily if one considers the circumstances of its origins.

See also **Anarchism; Civil Society; Intellectuals; Radicalism.**

BIBLIOGRAPHY

Primary Sources

Ivanov-Razumnik, R. V. *Istoriia russkoi obshchestvennoi mysli.* 2 vols. 3rd ed. St. Petersburg, 1911.

Miliukov, Pavel N. *Outlines of Russian Culture.* 3 vols. Edited by Michael Karpovich. Translated by Valentine Ughet and Eleanor Davis. Philadelphia, 1942. Reprint, New York, 1960. Abridged translation of *Ocherki po istorii russkoi kul'tury,* multiple editions, 1896–1918.

Secondary Sources

Berlin, Isaiah. *Russian Thinkers.* Edited by Henry Hardy and Aileen Kelly. New York, 1978.

Burbank, Jane. "Were the Russian *Intelligenty* Organic Intellectuals?" In *Intellectuals and Public Life: Between Radicalism and Reform,* edited by Leon Fink, Stephen T. Leonard, and Donald M. Reid, 97–120. Ithaca, N.Y., 1996.

Read, Christopher. *Religion, Revolution, and the Russian Intelligentsia, 1900–1912: The "Vekhi" Debate and Its Intellectual Background.* London, 1979.

Shatz, Marshall S. *Jan Wacław Machajski: A Radical Critic of the Russian Intelligentsia and Socialism.* Pittsburgh, Pa., 1989.

Walicki, Andrzej. *A History of Russian Thought from the Enlightenment to Marxism.* Translated by Hilda Andrews-Rusiecka. Stanford, Calif., 1979.

JANE BURBANK

INTERNATIONAL LAW. In 1795 the French National Convention received a proposal for a declaration on the law of nations. Although it was never formally adopted, the idea of national self-determination on which it was built had already been used in the Revolutionary Wars and became part of the official justification of the early Napoleonic campaigns in France's nearby territories. It is therefore no surprise that in legal terms, the post-Napoleonic restoration sought formally to reinstitute the *Droit public de l'Europe* (European public law) as the foundation of the diplomatic relations between European powers. Those principles had been articulated as part of the rationalistic natural law in the eighteenth century by the Swiss lawyer Emmerich (Emer) de Vattel in *Le droit des gens* (1758), but it was left for German public lawyers such as the Göttingen jurisconsult Georg Friedrich von Martens and the Heidelberg professor Johann Ludwig Klüber to link them to the 1815 settlement at Vienna.

A LAW BETWEEN EUROPEAN STATES

The system was founded on the sovereign independence of the European states existing in 1815 and states with populations of European origin (the United States and later the Latin American republics). Those states were assumed to enjoy independence and territorial inviolability, and the law that was binding on them was assumed to emerge from their sovereign will. Although legal theory was divided between adherents of rationalist natural law and the proponents of an emerging historical jurisprudence, neither put seriously to question the foundational nature of European statehood for the legal system. Irrespective of the doctrinal differences regarding the justification of the system, theory and practice agreed on two corollaries.

First, it followed from the independence of European states that they could only be bound by their consent. Thus there emerged a dense network of treaties—approximately sixteen thousand of them—in the period between 1815 and World War I. The treaties were no longer limited to military alliances but extended to the most varied aspects of technical and economic cooperation.

Although by far the largest number of treaties were still bilateral, toward the end of the century, an increasing amount of multilateral ("lawmaking") treaties laying out general rules of conduct and open for ratification by (European) states generally were adopted on matters such as maritime law (Paris Declaration, 1856), humanitarian rules of warfare (Geneva Convention, 1864; Hague Conventions, 1899, 1907), European behavior in Africa (Berlin Act, 1885), and the prohibition of slavery and the slave trade (Act of Brussels, 1890). The internationalization of navigable waterways such as the Rhine and the Scheldt was dealt with at the Vienna Congress and became the object of specific regulation later in the century. The Danube was opened for international navigation in the Peace of Paris, 1856, while the 1885 Berlin Act sought to do the same with the Congo and Niger Rivers. A convention of 1888 and treaties between the United States and Britain and Panama provided for the Panama Canal (1901, 1903). The establishment of the General Postal Union (Bern, 1874; later Universal Postal Union, UPU, 1878) began the move to regulating technical international cooperation within permanent organizations on matters such as the protection of industrial property and artistic works (1883, 1886), on rail transport (1890), radio and telegraphic communications (1906), as well as, for example, on the unification of weights and measures (1875) and health and hygiene (1903, 1907). The experience with the international unions and their secretariats was sometimes articulated in doctrine as "international administrative law" and gave significant support to the movement to permanent institutions and the League of Nations after World War I.

Second, whether the system was dated from the French Revolution or the Vienna settlement, it followed that those states that were in existence at that "year zero" received a special administrative function. Any changes in the system, including above all the admission of new members, would henceforth be controlled by the existing body of states. This lay the legal foundation for the predominant role of the Quadruple (later Quintuple) Alliance. Although the principle of legitimacy propagated by the Holy Alliance never dominated the *Droit public de l'Europe,* European affairs were regulated through Great Power consultation in formal congresses and conferences, of which the most notable after the Vienna Congress (1814–1815) were the Congresses of Verona (1822), Paris (1856), and Berlin (1878), the latter two dealing with the perennial "Eastern Question." The technique of collective recognition emerged as the means of entry for Greece (1821–1829) and Belgium (1830) into statehood. It was also used at Berlin (1878) to bring about the statehood of Bulgaria, Romania, and Serbia-Montenegro, and later in Berlin (1885) to lay the groundwork for the recognition of the "Independent State of the Congo" and to agree on some basic rules of European occupation of Africa. However, when the powers contemplated intervention to prevent Spain's South American colonies from attaining independence, the United States responded with the Monroe Doctrine (1823), which consolidated the formal independence of these new territorial units as well as American guardianship over them.

A PROCEDURAL LAW

The *Droit public de l'Europe* sought above all to regulate the interaction between European states both inside and beyond Europe. At its heart stood the formalization of the rules of European diplomacy. The ranking order of diplomatic representatives was regulated at Vienna and in the Aachen Protocol of 1818. The inviolability of diplomatic representatives was agreed on in bilateral treaties with non-European states. The intensification of commercial relations and foreign travel led to the reestablishment of the practice of consular relations after its decline in the Middle Ages. By 1910 the principal European powers had established about fifteen hundred professional consular offices. Instead of diplomatic immunities, the consuls enjoyed "functional" privileges relative to their position. Outside Europe, consular jurisdiction was set up by treaty as a means to extract criminal or civil disputes involving Europeans from local courts.

Scattered interstate arbitration had existed since the Jay Treaty (1794), but the successful 1872 settlement between Britain and the United States of the *Alabama* case, which had to do with the British violation of its neutrality duties during the U.S. Civil War, gave a great boost to the use of arbitration. The first step toward a permanent jurisdiction was taken at the 1899 Hague Peace Conference, as the Permanent Court of Arbitration was set up as a list of arbiters and a secretariat established in The Hague. The establishment of a real international court had to wait, however, until the setting up of the Permanent Court of International Justice as part of (though formally independent from) the League system in 1922.

NATIONALISM

The rules agreed to at Vienna aimed to reestablish great-power primacy in Europe. Later, and increasingly after 1848, the *Droit public de l'Europe* began to be read in view of the emerging principles of nationality and self-determination. The unification of Italy (1860) and Germany (1870–1871) called for a nationalist reading of international law. In Italy, liberal jurists such Pasquale Stanislao Mancini (1817–1888) articulated a "principle of nationalities" as the heart of the law, while German-speaking public lawyers developed complex theories of sovereignty sometimes to challenge (e.g., Adolf Lasson, 1837–1917) but more often to affirm a complex interdependence between domestic jurisdiction and international law (e.g., Georg Jellinek, 1851–1911).

EUROCENTRISM

The consolidation of nation-states in Europe supported the understanding of international law as a cultural achievement of European civilization. This is why the emphasis on sovereignty and consent never really undermined international law. On the contrary, liberal jurists and politicians such as the British prime minister William Ewart Gladstone (1809–1898), for example, integrated their nationalism within a cosmopolitan vision of the European nations' shared modernity. This was also visible in the strong support international law gave to the policy of formalizing European rule in the colonies after the 1870s and insisting on native treaties or effective occupation as a condition of formal title.

The scope of application of most international law, however, remained limited to relations between European states acting within Europe or the colonies. Although the "system" itself was not understood as applicable outside Europe, some parts of it were still extended to relations between Europeans and some of the more civilized "Oriental" states such as China, Japan, Siam, Egypt, and the Ottoman Empire. Although the Ottoman Empire was officially approved into the "European family of nations" in the Peace of Paris in 1856, this had little consequence to continuing European encroachments into its decaying realm. Colonial relations between Europeans and "half-civilized" countries were formalized in protectorate treaties and other unequal arrangements such as "capitulation regimes," which provided protection for European traders and travelers. Relations with "uncivilized" or "savage" communities of Africa and the Pacific islands were articulated by principles of natural law or acts (often of taking possession) with a more or less dubious international status.

RIGHT TO GO TO WAR

Although old theories of "just war" were formally incompatible with the view that the sovereignty of European states also included their unrestricted legal right to go to war, diplomats rarely treated warfare as a privilege and constantly invoked legal justifications such as a prior breach of treaty on the adversary's side. Toward the end of the century, lawyers became increasingly critical of "power politics," and formal doctrines such as "self-defense" and "self-help" were developed in order to regulate the right to wage war (*jus ad bellum*). Nevertheless, warfare involved the formal equality of the belligerent parties in a way that gave room to a highly developed law of neutrality whose rules were detailed in such instruments as the Declaration of Paris (1856) and especially the 1907 Conventions on rights and duties of neutrals in land and maritime warfare.

PACIFISM AND HUMANITARIANISM

After midcentury, unregulated warfare seemed scarcely compatible with European humanitarian and pacifist sentiments. The 1864 Geneva Convention set up procedures for the treatment of wounded soldiers and established the neutrality of the Red Cross. Repeated failures to observe the Convention in the Franco-Prussian War (1870–1871) led finally to the 1899 and 1907 Hague Peace Conferences, which adopted a series of conventions constituting the "Hague Law" on humanitarian rules of warfare. The Hague Conferences were intergovernmental conferences that sought to legislate general rules for the world and thus also provided a precedent to the diplomatic universalism that animated the work of the League of Nations. In addition to military and diplomatic experts, most delegations now for the first time included international lawyers, sometimes (as in the case of France), in key positions.

PROFESSIONALIZATION

During the Napoleonic Wars (1803–1815), international law, known as "law of nations," was taught at universities as part of natural law and was widely perceived either as a set of ethical principles providing an abstract justification for great-power diplomacy or simply a collection of the agreements that European states had concluded with each other. By midcentury, however, internationally minded liberal lawyers from Europe, the United States, and South America began to think of international law as part of the modernization of European societies. These lawyers organized themselves into a profession by the establishment of the first international law associations—the *Institut de droit international* and the Association for the Reform and Codification of International Law (later International Law Association) in 1873. They were instrumental in the launching of the first international law journals such as the *Revue de droit international et de législation comparée* (Brussels, 1869), *Zeitschrift für internationales Recht* (Berlin, 1891), the *Revue générale de droit international public* (Paris, 1894), and the *American Journal of International Law* (Washington, D.C., 1907). At the same time, the first chairs of international law proper were set up at European universities and the teaching of "the law of nature and of nations" was transformed into teaching of the rules and principles of the "international law of civilized nations." By the end of the century, Vattel's 1758 treatise was replaced by the often many-volumed textbooks, sometimes expressly written as "codes" of international law. These included works by Johann Kaspar Bluntschli (1872) and Franz von Holtzendorff (1885) in Germany; Henry Joseph François Xavier Bonfils (1898, later Bonfils-Fauchille) in France; Pasquale Fiore (1879–1884) in Italy; John George Phillimore (1854–1861), William Edward Hall (1880) and Lassa Francis Lawrence Oppenheim (1905) in Britain; Carlos Calvo (1868) in Argentina; and Fyodor Fyodorovich von Martens (1882) in Russia. Analogous formalization never took place in the United States, where the old overviews by James Kent (1826) and Henry Wheaton (1836) continued to appear in new editions.

See also **Berlin Conference; Brussels Declaration; Geneva Convention.**

BIBLIOGRAPHY

Anghie, Antony. *Imperialism, Sovereignty, and the Making of International Law*. Cambridge, U.K., 2005. See especially chapter 2.

Grewe, Wilhelm. *The Epochs of International Law*. Translated and revised by Michael Byers. Berlin, 2003. See part 4.

Kennedy, David. "International Law and the Nineteenth Century: History of an Illusion." *Nordic Journal of International Law* 65 (1996): 385–420.

Koskenniemi, Martti. *The Gentle Civilizer of Nations: The Rise and Fall of International Law, 1870–1960.* Cambridge, U.K., 2002. See chapters 1–2.

Nussbaum, Arthur. *A Concise History of International Law.* 2nd ed. New York, 1954. See chapter 6.

Ziegler, Karl-Heinz. *Völkerrechsgeschichte: Ein Studienbuch.* Munich, 1994. See chapter 9.

MARTTI KOSKENNIEMI

IRELAND. The gravitational force of the French Revolution reoriented the tides of Irish history, energizing its stagnant ponds. Theobald Wolfe Tone's famous *Argument on Behalf of the Catholics of Ireland* cogently demonstrated that if French Catholics could display such obvious political maturity, so could their Irish counterparts. The leading Catholic power in Europe had, astonishingly, produced a revolution more radical than the much vaunted Glorious (and Protestant) Revolution of 1688. The French Revolution was perceived in Ireland as a Catholic effort at liberty, and it rendered obsolete the old equation between Catholicism and despotism. It was in this sense that Tone described the revolution as "the morning star of liberty" in Ireland, ushering in the possibility of a novel alliance between Presbyterian and Catholic radicals. The Volunteers, with their enthusiastic Presbyterian backing, had acrimoniously disintegrated over the old bugbear of popery, but the French Revolution released this sectarian blockage, which had immobilized Irish political radicalism.

THE UNITED IRISHMEN AND THE 1798 REBELLION

In 1791 the United Irishmen were founded simultaneously in Belfast and Dublin to give cohesion and momentum to this new energy. It represented a novel attempt to breach the sectarian limits of England's Glorious Revolution (1688) by extending full citizenship rights to Catholics. The movement for the first time united in a single political organization a coalition of Presbyterian, Catholic, and Anglican radicals. By linking parliamentary reform and what was called the Catholic question, the United Irishmen offered the possibility of fundamentally altering the Williamite sectarian state that had been established in the 1690s and which excluded Catholics from citizenship rights through penal laws. The United Irishmen therefore created a moment of political optimism that lasted throughout the early 1790s. The moment passed, however, and the decade ended in a bloody uprising that cost thirty thousand lives.

By the early 1790s, it was becoming increasingly clear that the French Revolution would unleash a titanic European struggle between democracy and aristocracy, between republicanism and monarchy. As France and Great Britain moved inexorably toward conflict, it became apparent that the ensuing struggle would be a new kind of war, one based on principle and ideology and the clash of ideas, in contrast to earlier wars of tactical and dynastic advantage. The number of combatants and casualties escalated to unprecedented levels and the theater of war expanded to embrace all of Europe. The 1790s became the pivotal decade in modern European history as Britain and France locked horns in an international battle for domination and in the first war in which modernity confronted tradition. In Ireland, the United Irishmen, and with them political modernity, were among its casualties.

The success of the republican project in Ireland ultimately depended on the Franco-British struggle, and in the 1790s the outcome of that struggle was by no mean self-evident. Once war broke out, in 1793, the United Irishmen, which had been grudgingly tolerated in peacetime, was banned as a treasonable organization. An increasingly rigid conservative regime under William Pitt (1759–1806) took over in Britain, instinctively siding with the *ancien régime* in France and thereby demonstrating how shallow the democratic credentials of the Glorious Revolution were.

A severe crackdown on the United Irishmen followed. The founding of the Orange Order and the Armagh expulsions (the forcible removal of Catholics) in 1795 made sense in this context. The Orange Order was established in North Armagh, discreetly backed by local gentry and generals, to stiffen the loyalist backbone and to drive an Anglican loyalist wedge between Presbyterian/United Irish Antrim and Down, on one hand, and Catholic south Ulster, on the other. The nonsectarian appeal of the United Irishmen would now be met by a resoundingly sectarian Orange stance, which emphasized Englishness not Irishness, the past not the future, and disunited rather than united Irishmen. The United Irish project was derailed by the London and Dublin governments, which deliberately encouraged sectarianism to counter its influence. Ireland was to be returned, at a cost of thirty thousand lives in the 1798 rebellion, to the sectarian molds from which the United Irishmen had tried to rescue it.

THE ACT OF UNION

When news of the 1798 rebellion reached London, Pitt saw the opportunity to implement his plans for uniting England and Ireland, which had been frustrated until then. The Irish parliament would become a client parliament, existing solely to do England's bidding. The 1782 settlement, "Grattan's Parliament," which had strengthened the commercial and political autonomy of Ireland, had been a disaster for Britain, prized reluctantly from them at a moment of imperial vulnerability, and represented a fundamental loss of authority and of the assumption of Irish subordination. The Act of Union of 1800, however, which abolished the exclusively Protestant Irish parliament and created the United Kingdom of Great Britain and Ireland, immediately raised the issue of Catholic emancipation. Catholics had falsely assumed that their acquiescence in union would guarantee their emancipation, giving them the right to be elected as members of Parliament (MPs). The hypocrisy at the heart of the Union was that it was simultaneously sold to Catholics as a defense against the Protestants and to Protestants as a defense against the Catholics. The Act of Union was an imposed imperial solution to Irish problems. Its central failure was the inability to accompany it with Catholic emancipation, a failure determined by intense elite and popular British hostility to the idea of Catholics as fellow citizens.

The Union raised the stakes more for Britain than for Ireland. With London in the driver's seat, Ireland's problems could no longer be summarily dismissed as the result of Irish (Protestant and Papist) inability to rule themselves. Irish separatism threatened to break up Britain. Three short years after its passage, the Union itself was called into question by Robert Emmet's insurrection of 1803, which was fought on the streets of Dublin and shocked the complacent London elite, whose response was to safeguard the Union through a policy of coercive integration. By prioritizing Orangeism, Britishness, and the empire, while reinstating Protestant ascendancy (the position of Irish Protestants as a privileged minority within Ireland), the English ceded the concept of the Irish nation to the Catholics. In choosing an exclusively Protestant and coercive strategy, the British government ensured that Catholics would be turned from neutrality to hostility toward the Union. Once Catholic political activism revived, it would inevitably be pitted against the sectarian administration at home and a hostile or indifferent imperial parliament in London. In such circumstances, Catholic emancipation could only be taken, not granted, and the adversarial stance between Catholics and Protestants and between Catholics and the British state would be hardened and perpetuated.

Daniel O'Connell's political campaign for Catholic emancipation rocked British politics to its foundations. The Union had not delivered Ireland from sectarianism, poverty, or violence but rather deepened their insidious influence. Looked at in the long term, the Union also marked a decisive shift in the balance of power between Great Britain and Ireland. In 1800, when the Union passed, the ratio of population was two to one (ten million British to five million Irish). When the Union began to break up over a century later, the ratio was ten to one (forty million British to four million Irish).

CELTS AND SAXONS

It had been assumed by key British decision makers that Ireland's problems emanated from an Irish (Protestant and Catholic) inability to rule themselves and that the Westminster wand would magically metamorphose the Irish (like the Scots after their 1707 Union) into pliant British citizens. But Irish society under the Union became spectacularly more violent and poorer, posing a difficult question: Was it possible that British liberties were so narrowly conceived as to be incapable of making the short crossing to its nearest neighbor? Rather than conceive of such a devastating failure, they threw the blame for Irish problems back on Irish shoulders by blaming an old bugbear, Irish popery,

Irish peasants. A family of Irish peasants photographed in front of their home, 1880s. ©CORBIS

and a new one, Irish Celticism. Under the Union, Ireland became the Other within, whose poverty and violence became a curiously comforting antithesis to British prosperity and virtue. The first half of the nineteenth century witnessed the reorganization of the older European concept of national character, with its relatively sympathetic understanding of the interrelationship of geography, history, and culture, into a narrowly "racial" concept, which claimed that each country had a unique and unchanging racial destiny, genetically imprinting its national character. Ireland was Celtic, and that was a lower racial order, which accounted for the country's inferiority to Anglo-Saxon England. Celts were naturally lazy, feckless, and violent, lacking the integrity, individualism, and self-reliance of the Saxon.

According to the theory, these racial flaws, combined with popery, determined Ireland's endemic poverty and violence. Irish problems were not socioeconomic or political in character but genetically and religiously rooted. Irish crime and poverty were endemic, irrational, and natural, and were therefore impervious to moral or political persuasion. As a result, England could deny Irish Catholics democratic freedoms, run Ireland on British and essentially Orange lines, and to establish a lethal distance between Westminster and its Irish citizens—a distance so lethal as to kill over one million during the Irish famine barely a generation later.

THE FAMINE

By the first quarter of the nineteenth century, the Irish diet had become ever more potato-dependent. By the 1830s, one-third of the population (three million people) relied on potatoes for over 90 percent of their calorie intake. Only in the northeastern oatmeal zone did the potato not triumph utterly. The presence of cheap food in the form of the potato, fuel in the form of turf, and housing in the form of mud walls and thatch had permitted the population to expand prodigiously between 1760 and 1815, which in retrospect was the golden age of both the potato and the Irish poor. That golden age ended in the aftermath of the Napoleonic Wars, when a sharp depression bit into the area. Agricultural prices halved, the fickle

Attack on a Potato Store in Ireland. Engraving from the *Illustrated London News*, 25 June 1842. Although brought to a crisis by the blight and failure of the potato crop in 1845, the situation of Irish peasants had already become grave by the beginning of the decade, due in part to population pressures and partial crop failures. On 13 June 1842, starving peasants in Galway resorted to violence to obtain food from storehouses. Private Collection/Bridgeman Art Library

herring deserted the west coast (where they had been abundant between 1780 and 1810), the linen industry was dislocated by the advent of factory-based spinning and weaving—in all, a succession of hammer blows, accentuated by a series of wet summers and bad harvests.

In these circumstances, a crop failure would cause disaster; repeated failures would decimate the population. An unprecedented attack of *Phytopthora infestans,* the virus that caused potato blight, destroyed one-third of the crop in 1845, three-quarters in 1846 and 1847, and one-third in 1848. Massive mortality and emigration ensued: one million died and two million emigrated, largely to America, paralleling the three million people who had been almost totally dependent on the potato in the pre-famine period.

The Great Irish Famine (1845–1852) was the single most important event in Ireland in the modern period. Famine had become an increasingly remote event in Europe, and that Ireland should suffer a devastating episode was made all the more unusual because it was part of the richest, most powerful, and most centralized state in the world, the United Kingdom created by the Act of Union. The Great Famine disproportionately affected the three million potato-dependent people who comprised the notoriously poverty-stricken base of Irish society. These effects were compounded by doctrinaire government policies, designed as much to appease British opinion and to promote social engineering as to alleviate poverty or save lives. The population of the island had been halved by 1900, a change precipitated in part by a new social regime of endemic emigration by young people, delayed marriages, and abnormally high rates of celibacy.

How did the wealthy and powerful British state allow so many of its citizens to die of starvation? Its failure to shoulder the fiscal burden of the famine was clear. From 1845 to 1850, the British treasury spent £7 million on relief, less than half a percentage point of British gross national product over two years. It also expended millions on futile imperial wars in the same period. The culture of the pre-Darwinian mid-nineteenth century was still predominantly religious. The early nineteenth century witnessed numerous efforts to reconcile new sciences such as geology, botany, and economics to Christian doctrine, and it was in this hybrid form that they gained greater popular currency. The dynamics of religious enthusiasm and scientific advance combined to produce an interpretative framework for natural and social phenomena, and the British response to the famine was profoundly informed by the prevalent Protestant religious sensibility. The phenomenon of famine—saturated in biblical resonances—was understood in essentially religious terms as a form of providentialism—God's direct, personal intervention in the natural world.

From within this providentialist perspective, the evangelicals stressed the necessity of allowing the unrestricted operation of natural moral law, encouraging a minimalist response to the famine. This evangelical economics married Malthusian pessimism and a strident eschatological emphasis, both stressing the inevitability of the famine and its function as a retributive sign. The blight would allow the pernicious potato to be replaced as a food source by a better form such as grain, and this change in itself would force the feckless Irish up the ladder of civilization. The famine would thus present a short-term loss for a long-term gain. It would teach the Irish poor the immutable laws of political economy, encouraging them to exercise moral and religious restraint; by eliminating the potato that underpinned their monstrous overpopulation, it would give them room to become civilized.

CULTURAL IMPACT OF THE FAMINE

The Great Famine marked a watershed in many areas of Irish life, including demographics, economics, society, and culture. Yet the immediate response was sluggish. Ireland remained culturally comatose in the immediate post-famine period. The period beginning in the 1880s, however, when the post-famine generation took over, witnessed the creation of a series of radical responses to the famine legacy, including the Land League (1879), the Gaelic Athletic Association (1884), the Gaelic League (1893), and the Irish Literary Revival of the 1890s.

THE CATHOLIC CHURCH AND THE DEVOTIONAL REVOLUTION

Among the most significant impacts of the Great Famine was a shift in religious practice. The Devotional Revolution marks a startling transformation within Irish Catholicism, which occurred within a generation of the famine. It created an entirely revamped religious practice that hardened into a powerful and rigid cultural formation and remained essentially intact for over a century, only slowly dissolving from the 1960s onward.

In the pre-famine period, a vernacular style Catholicism had inserted deep roots among those social formations that the famine would decimate. This vernacular inheritance evolved organically out of the life of an intensely agrarian society, whose ritual rhythm was dominated by calendar custom and embedded in a numinous landscape of holy wells and pilgrimage sites. In this cultural matrix, behavior was regulated by custom and tradition: the central religious events were rites of passage and communal occasion like the pattern (annual commemorations at the local graveyard), the wake (ritualized mourning of the dead), and the station (community-based celebrations of the Mass). The trauma of the Great Famine, the associated decline of vernacular religion and popular culture, and the erosion of the Irish language created a cultural vacuum, which the Devotional Revolution filled. It institutionalized going to mass, new devotional practices such as novenas, forty-hour devotions, exposition of the host, and other ritualistic practices. The devastation wreaked by the famine strengthened the church's hand in the imposition of its modernizing moral crusade. Catholicism invaded the vacated cultural space and solved an identity crisis by offering a powerful surrogate language of symbolic identity in which Irishness and Catholicism were seen as reciprocal and congruent and religion articulated an artificial, symbolic language of identity to replace the living one being swept away by famine, emigration, and jolting sociocultural transformations. The institutional Catholic Church could also take advantage of the more homogenized post-famine social structure, which was receptive to bourgeois Roman Catholicism while the pre-famine potato people, the *bruscair an bhaile* (trash of the town), with their vigorous popular culture, were decimated and demoralized. The culture of poverty was supplanted by the culture of piety as the church injected a new social discipline of respectability. A growing political rapprochement with nationalists from these same bourgeois classes cemented an unusually cohesive and ideologically impregnable marriage of church and nation.

THE LAND LEAGUE

The founder of the Land League, Michael Davitt (1846–1906), was the son of evicted peasants who had emigrated from County Mayo to Lancashire as a result of the Great Famine, and he used his personal famine experiences as the spur to undermine Irish landlordism, which he blamed for his predicament. When Davitt returned to County Mayo in 1877, his goal was to organize "a war against landlordism for a root settlement of the land question." Remarkably, in a society that was still profoundly agrarian, Davitt's grassroots organization set in motion the legislative displacement of an entire landed class, predating the massive upheavals in Russia a few decades later. This achievement was predicated on his ability to fuse the agrarian and the political issues, bringing together under a common umbrella the Fenians' tradition of physical force and constitutional nationalism of the proponents of Home Rule. The Irish landed class had generally forfeited British sympathy during the famine, when they were blamed for having selfishly allowed huge pauper populations to build up on estates in order to swell their rentals. They were therefore seen as disposable, and this encouraged the British government in endorsing unusually broad state intervention in the rights of private property. This remorseless legislative euthanasia and the shift toward peasant proprietorship accelerated in the wake of the Land League and the novel and potent combination of agrarian and nationalist issues in Parnellite politics. The Gladstone (1881), Ashbourne (1885), Balfour (1891), and the generous Wyndham (1903) and Birrell (1909) Land Acts all encouraged or forced Irish landlords to divest themselves of their lands. By 1914, two-thirds of Irish tenants owned their land and a remarkably quiet social revolution had been effected.

CHARLES STUART PARNELL

In 1880 the political stage was set for a new development in Anglo-Irish relations with the election of William Ewart Gladstone (1809–1898) as British prime minister. Gladstone wooed the rising star of Irish Home Rule politics, Charles Stuart Parnell (1846–1891), who led a block of sixty-one Home Rule MPs at Westminster. The aloof and patrician Parnell, who disdained theory for political practice, ran a disciplined party machine. The Irish nationalist Patrick Pearse (1879–1916) described him as "an embodied conviction," and his single-minded pursuit of Home Rule generated messianic fervor. In the 1880s, Parnell launched the New Departure, with its three defining elements: (1) link the land and the national questions, identifying land agitation as the engine that would pull the Home Rule train; (2) bring together under Parnell's leadership the hitherto bitterly opposed traditions of constitutional and physical-force nationalism; and (3) hammer out an alliance between the Catholic Church and nationalist politics. These innovations united Irish politics around him and allowed Parnell to position Home Rule at the heart of the British political agenda. The downside was that the issue polarized British politics. Gladstone's Liberals traded Parnell's votes in Westminster for Liberal support for Home Rule, but the rival Conservatives supported the Ulster Unionists (playing the Orange card). Home Rule eventually became a casualty of internal British political divisions.

In 1890, just when it seemed that Parnell had generated irresistible momentum behind home rule, a sensational sex scandal involving his married mistress, Kitty O'Shea, erupted and overnight

Land League protestors, Kildare, Ireland, January 1881. Violence and protests against the 1870 Land Act escalated throughout the following decade, forcing the passage of the second Land Act in 1881. This engraving depicts the burning of leases held by the Duke of Leinster; the burning of a lease held by such a prominent landowner was a particularly provocative form of protest. ©CORBIS

destroyed Parnell's carefully constructed alliances. The fallout poisoned Irish politics for a generation. A broken Parnell died soon after.

THE RISE OF SINN FÉIN

On 11 October 1899, the Boer War broke out. When it was revealed that the British had maintained concentration camps for Boer women and children, where at least 16,000 died in a single year, the brutality of the British imperial mission was exposed and sympathy was created for the Boers. A pro-Boer Transvaal Committee was established in 1899, which provided the nucleus of the deeply anti-imperial Sinn Féin. By contrast, the Irish Parliamentary Party, under the leadership of John Redmond (1856–1918), espoused Home Rule within the empire and supported the Boer War. A growing divide between radical separatists and conservative parliamentarians was emerging.

Cultural energies were also flooding into the political arena. The Parnell scandal poisoned young people's attitude to Home Rule infighting, and an entire generation turned instead toward cultural activities. Building on the cultural separatism of the Gaelic Athletic Association (promoting the games of hurling and Gaelic football in place of soccer and rugby) established by Michael Cusack in 1884, other organizations were created, notably the Gaelic League, founded by Douglas Hyde in 1893 (with the aim of reviving the Irish language), and the Irish Literary Theatre of 1899, which evolved into the Abbey Theatre in 1904. A positive emphasis on the Celtic nature of Ireland also emerged. By a strategic inversion, the attributes that were previously ascribed to the Celts and despised as vices—non-materialism, dreaminess, instability—were reinvented as virtues, with Celtic charm rebuking the Saxon culture, which was

The Riots in Belfast: The Police Charging the Mob in the Brickfields. Engraving from *The Illustrated London News*, 19 June 1886. Protestants in Ulster demonstrate in opposition to Gladstone's 1886 proposal for Home Rule. PRIVATE COLLECTION/BRIDGEMAN ART LIBRARY

recast as stolid and slavish, bringing with it a "filthy modern tide" (Yeats). Ironically, that inversion began at the metropolitan center with the English critic Matthew Arnold, but it was quickly championed by the poet William Butler Yeats and appropriated by the Irish Literary Revival. The belief grew that a Home Rule parliament in Dublin meant little if no distinctive Irish nationality existed to be guarded and developed.

The Irish Revival was not some dreamy Celtic literary movement of writers and mystics looking nostalgically backward to a romantic past. It was a progressive movement, featuring a series of self-help groups that focused on local modes of production both cultural and economic: Irish literature, Irish theater, Irish games, Irish economic development. A considerable overlap in membership existed in these cultural organizations at both executive and grassroots levels, and their activities crossed class, party, and sectarian divisions. These networks shaped the emerging nationalist political movement. They did not involve a clear-cut severance of (high-minded) culture from (grubby) politics. No conflict between Protestant Anglo-Ireland, representing high culture, and a philistine Catholic/Gaelic middle class or peasant culture was involved. Cultural self-belief was the bedrock of the struggle for national independence, for economic advances, for cultural autonomy. These ostensibly different activities shared a common goal: to generate a new public sphere in Ireland, which would form the basis of a revitalized citizenship and a new civic nationalism based on republicanism.

The spirit of self-reliance was the spirit of Sinn Féin (Ourselves), the separatist party founded in 1907 to harness these energies in the political sphere. Sinn Féin saw culture as instrumental: "The language itself is not an end but a means to an end." The party was viciously anti-Redmondite, espoused abstention from the Westminster parliament, and claimed the right to use physical force if necessary to win Ireland's freedom. The split

Evictions in County Donegal c. 1889. Carts stand ready to transport the possessions of families being evicted from their homes in the town of Falcarragh. ©SEAN SEXTON COLLECTION/CORBIS

between the constitutional and the militant versions of Irish nationalism was widening dramatically, and tensions rose.

HOME RULE

The British Liberals under Gladstone initially aligned themselves with the Irish Parliamentary Party to secure party political advantage over the British Tories. After the 1910 election, Redmond's Irish Parliamentary Party held the balance of power at Westminster. The Liberal Party had to turn to Redmond to shore it up, and his price was the passage of the Third Home Rule Bill, which gained royal assent in May 1914. This created a massive Ulster Unionist backlash. In July 1912, thirteen thousand people attended an anti–Home Rule rally in London, which was addressed by Andrew Bonar Law, leader of the Tory-Orange Alliance, who ratcheted up the tension by proclaiming that "I can imagine no length of resistance to which Ulster will go in which I should not be prepared to support them."

The Ulster Unionists were led by the talented and aggressive lawyer Edward Carson (1854–1935), who had achieved notoriety through his brutal prosecution of Oscar Wilde in the celebrated 1895 law case. In 1912 Carson organized the Solemn League and Covenant—a potent brew of history, religion, and imperialism that cemented the diversities of Ulster Protestantism into a common political cause—to resist Home Rule on the grounds that it would be Rome rule. Two hundred thousand people signed the covenant. Belfast was then at its zenith as a British industrial giant and saw no advantages in being yoked to the agrarian south. The idea of partition began to be floated in British political circles. The paramilitarization of Irish society started with the Ulster Volunteer Force, established by Carson in 1913 with the aim of defending Ulster militarily against Home

Rule, by force if necessary. It quickly organized the Larne gunrunning, illegally importing twenty-four thousand German rifles.

Nationalists were provoked to respond in kind. Redmond established the Irish Volunteers to match Carson's. The Fenians regrouped as the Irish Republican Brotherhood and the workers movement had its Irish Citizen Army. As all these paramilitary bodies mobilized in a massive militarization north and south, many felt that a civil war was looming.

THE FIRST WORLD WAR AND THE 1916 RISING

When the First World War unexpectedly broke out in 1914, Redmond offered unconditional support for the British war effort, and with his assent the Home Rule bill was shelved until the end of war. Sinn Féin, adept at propaganda, now broke with Redmond over Irish involvement in what it portrayed as a futile imperial war and organized vigorously against recruitment and the threat of conscription. This aligned Sinn Féin for the first time with the hitherto Redmondite Catholic Church, which also opposed conscription. Between 140,000 and 200,000 Irish enlisted in the war, and a minimum of 27,000 died. The Ulster regiments were decimated at the Battle of Somme in 1916.

Physical-force nationalists saw the war as offering the possibility of achieving independence though insurrection on the ground that "England's difficulty is Ireland's opportunity." Others, notably Patrick Pearse, believed that the Irish cause needed to be redeemed through a blood sacrifice. At Easter 1916, Pearse led an insurrection, seizing the General Post Office (GPO) and proclaiming an Irish Republic. The rebels fought against overwhelming odds and Pearse surrendered to prevent bloodshed.

The Irish public, aghast at the center of Dublin being reduced to rubble, were initially hostile to the rebels. However, the British shot sixteen leaders at Kilmainham Gaol following peremptory courts-martial. Public sympathy then swung back behind the rebels as the executed men were seen as martyrs. Sinn Féin unexpectedly benefited from the 1916 Rising partly because they were credited for organizing it (the British insisted on calling it "the Sinn Féin rising"). As a result, Sinn Féin grew in authority and used 1916 as an effective propaganda and recruiting device. Support leached away from Redmond as the carnage of the unpopular world war deluged Europe in blood.

THE AFTERMATH

Eamon de Valera (1882–1975), the senior survivor of 1916, was elected president of Sinn Féin and soon eclipsed Redmond as the principal Irish leader. In 1918, the recruit-starved British decided to extend conscription to Ireland. Sinn Féin could now legitimately present itself as a peace party that alone could save the country from the horrors of war into which Redmond had so recklessly plunged Ireland. In the general election of 1918, two million voted, delivering a Sinn Féin landslide. They stood on an abstentionist platform and claimed that they had now been given an overwhelming democratic mandate to withdraw from Westminster. On 21 January 1919, they unilaterally set up their own parliament, Dáil Éireann, in the Mansion House in Dublin with de Valera as the first president. The seeds were now sown for a war of independence, a divisive treaty, a bloody civil war, and partition. As the critic Edward Said put it: "Imperial powers begin by divide and rule: they end by divide and quit."

See also **Colonies; Dublin; Great Britain; O'Connell, Daniel; O'Connor, Feargus; Peasants; Scotland.**

BIBLIOGRAPHY

Donnelly, James S. *The Great Irish Potato Famine.* Thrupp, Stroud, Gloucestershire, U.K., 2001.

Larkin, Emmet J. *The Historical Dimensions of Irish Catholicism.* Washington, D.C., 1984.

Mathews, P. J. *Revival: The Abbey Theatre, Sinn Féin, the Gaelic League, and the Co-Operative Movement.* Cork, Ireland, 2003.

O'Grada, Cormac. *Ireland: A New Economic History, 1780–1939.* Oxford, U.K., 1994.

O'Tuathaigh, Gearoid. *Ireland before the Famine, 1798–1848.* Dublin, 1990.

Vaughan, W. E., ed. *Ireland under the Union, 1801–1870.* Vol. 5 of *A New History of Ireland.* Oxford, U.K., 1989.

———. *Ireland under the Union, 1870–1921.* Vol. 6 of *A New History of Ireland* Oxford, U.K., 1996.

Whelan, Kevin. "The Post-Famine Period." In *The Cambridge Companion to Modern Irish Culture,* edited by Joe Cleary and Claire Connolly. Cambridge, U.K., 2005.

KEVIN WHELAN

ISTANBUL. Istanbul, also known as Constantinople/Kostantiniyye, was the capital of the Ottoman Empire from 1453 to the founding of the Turkish Republic in 1923. In Ottoman usage, the name Istanbul refers to the traditional core of the city, a triangular peninsula on the European side of the Bosphorus surrounded by medieval Byzantine walls and bounded by the Marmara Sea to the south and the Golden Horn to the north. Occasionally, Istanbul was also used to denote the broader urban area including the townships of Eyüp and Galata on the European coast and Üsküdar (Scutari) in Asia.

PREMODERN ISTANBUL: THE SEGREGATED CITY

Istanbul was the commercial, financial, and political hub of a multi-ethnic and multi-confessional empire whose center of gravity was western Anatolia and the Balkans. Prior to its drastic social and morphological transformation in the nineteenth century, the dense imperial capital functioned as the microcosm of the traditional Ottoman order. For centuries, the diverse populations inhabiting the city coexisted relatively peacefully due to a complex system of ethno-religious segregation whereby the major non-Muslim groups (namely, the Greeks, Armenians, and Jews) were recognized by the dominant Muslim polity as separate communities and enjoyed autonomy in their internal affairs. The rich social and cultural ferment of Istanbul that was to astound generations of foreign travelers should not, however, be taken anachronistically as a sign of cosmopolitan harmony and unity. The Ottoman modus vivendi that had nourished the city throughout the centuries depended upon a pre-modern and patriarchal system of controls and restrictions geared toward avoiding conflict between communities and reaping the maximum political and economic benefit for the state.

Istanbul's traditional urban configuration was mainly shaped along the prescribed ethno-religious criteria of segregation. The city was made up of largely self-sufficient neighborhoods called *mahalles,* usually formed around a mosque, a church, or a synagogue. Although not walled-in like ghettos, the neighborhoods constituted organically unified urban entities whose inhabitants were mostly (but seldom exclusively) members of the same community. Characterized by narrow winding streets and cul-de-sacs, each *mahalle* unit demarcated a semi-private domain that engendered a high level of solidarity among its inhabitants who had to share responsibility in their dealings with the state.

By the eighteenth century, most non-Muslims lived in the fringes of the walled city and beyond in order to diminish the restrictive sway of central authority and the additional weight of communal pressures. While the center of the peninsula contained predominantly Muslim neighborhoods, the Armenians chose to settle along the southern walls of the city, and the Jews along sections of the Golden Horn, while the Greeks inhabited the Golden Horn, Marmara, and Bosphorus shores. Once a Genoese trade colony, the walled suburb of Galata maintained its "Frankish" character throughout the Ottoman centuries, as it remained the primary locus of European diplomatic and commercial presence in Istanbul.

MODERNIZATION: THE CHALLENGE OF URBAN INTEGRATION

The Ottoman nineteenth century began with the reign of Sultan Mahmud II (r. 1808–1839), the first "modernizer" who had the political clout to topple the traditional balances of power. Following the eighteenth century, when central power was at a low ebb in the Ottoman domain, Mahmud II laid out the foundations of a modern and centralized governmental system based on Western models. In order to obtain a clear slate upon which he could base his modern state apparatus, Mahmud eliminated all peripheral power groups—the Janissary corps, a major public agent in the urban arena, was brutally eradicated in 1826, and the significant influence of provincial notables was drastically curbed. Mahmud's judicial, military, administrative, and educational reforms were coupled by a conscious policy to Westernize the cultural image of the Ottoman state. Starting with the time of

Istanbul, photographed in the 1870s. ©MICHAEL MASLAN HISTORIC PHOTOGRAPHS/CORBIS

Mahmud II, replanning Istanbul as a European capital, a well-structured and efficiently controlled city with modern public amenities and sanitary standards, was among the ultimate dreams of generations of Ottoman reformers. Mahmud not only launched a centralized administrative body to coordinate various disconnected municipal services, but also commissioned a German engineer, Helmuth von Moltke, to draw a detailed map of the city and propose a plan for the regularization of the urban fabric. Although unimplemented, the proposal delineated the essential tenets of a long-term urban reform agenda for modernizing the late Ottoman capital: the enlargement of the main arteries and the creation of public squares, the regularization of the organic street network and the quays, and the replacement of typical wooden construction (implying almost all residential units) with fireproof structures of stone or brick.

The late Ottoman plans to transform Istanbul on the model of prominent European capitals were consistently hampered by the grim social and economic realities of a feverishly reshaping "ramshackle empire." In most cases, the state's efforts for wide-scale urban intervention were to remain fragmentary or simply ineffectual. Nevertheless, as the primary site of the nineteenth-century Westernizing experiment, Istanbul was to undergo its most radical phase of morphological, demographic, social, and cultural transformation since its reconstruction after the initial Ottoman takeover.

A crucial turning point in this transformative phase was the declaration of the edict of *Gülhane* (rose chamber) in 1839, at the onset of the reign of Abdülmecid (r. 1839–1861), marking the emergence of a radically new vision of state and society in the Ottoman realm. The edict was a formal manifestation of the state's commitment to create a more secularized and egalitarian political entity based on European concepts of administration. As such, it initiated a period of intense modernizing reforms known in Turkish historiography as the *Tanzimat* (reordering) era (beginning in 1839 and ending in 1876, with the inauguration of the first Ottoman constitution). Coordinated by the potent bureaucratic elite, the extensive measures of the Tanzimat were destined to penetrate, regulate, and restructure many areas of social and political life hitherto untouched by the state.

In reinstalling central authority by means of a modern and secular administrative apparatus, the Ottoman state had to abandon its traditional role as the "magnanimous arbiter" between separate communities and extend its services uniformly to all citizens, regardless of ethnicity or faith. In terms of urban administration, this entailed the implementation of a series of reforms, starting with the Tanzimat, geared toward homogenizing the fragmented urban layout of Istanbul and integrating the entire city into a metropolitan whole. The decisive Building Regulation of 1848 was the first in a series of municipal laws and institutional rearrangements that abolished the restrictive, community-based categories of pre-Tanzimat administration and sought to overcome the rigidly compartmentalized network of the self-enclosed *mahalles.* Particularly in the latter half of the nineteenth century, after two major fires that devastated entire neighborhoods in the residential heart of the city, the historical peninsula became the focus of a rigorous planning and rebuilding program. Among the most urgent items on the urban reform agenda was the standardization of the intricate street network, essential for the efficient access of goods, services, and police forces. The implementation of the new model remained piecemeal and incremental, however, since expropriation was largely limited to fragmentary areas cleared by fires.

Nevertheless, under the supervision of a new municipal organ, the Commission for Road Improvement (established in 1865), some major arteries were widened, such as the major Byzantine/Ottoman ceremonial route (*Mese/Divanyolu*) constituting the backbone of the old city. Inspired by Georges-Eugène Haussmann's Paris, the commission also introduced new standards of urban monumentality in the Ottoman realm. Major Ottoman and Byzantine landmarks were restored (such as the Hagia Sophia, Constantine's column) and their dense surroundings were cleared to make room for spacious urban squares along the central route. Until the first decades of the new century, the historical peninsula was embellished with imposing official buildings in the European classical or the newfangled "neo-Ottoman" style (such as the university, the Imperial Museum of Antiquities, and the Ministry of War complex) in order to project the image of a modernized imperial capital occupying the imaginary boundaries between the east and the west.

On a broader scale, Istanbul's traditional core was connected to its rapidly expanding hinterland through a complex transport network developed by private investors throughout the nineteenth century. A major step in delineating a broad and integrated metropolitan area in Istanbul was the building of two bridges on the Golden Horn (in 1836 and 1845) that linked the historical peninsula to the Galata area. Starting in 1851, rowboats were replaced by regular commuter ferry lines that provided fast access to settlements on the Bosphorus and Marmara coast. By the 1860s, a growing network of tram lines followed the street-widening program in Istanbul and Galata, while distant Marmara suburbs were linked to the center by a railroad that extended first to Sofia (1874), and later to Vienna (1888). These major interventions by the state were destined to alter the rigid urban configuration of the traditional city core and to control the rapid growth of new settlements. Yet, above anything else, and beyond the power of central authority, it was the overwhelming weight of economic and demographic forces that determined the actual course of change for the Ottoman capital.

COSMOPOLITANISM AND BIFURCATION

Istanbul's population more than doubled in the second half of the nineteenth century. Totaling 391,000 in 1844, the population of the metropolitan area exceeded 850,000 by 1886. A major reason for the sudden upsurge was the intensifying rate of the empire's territorial disintegration. In the wake of violent clashes and tremendous losses in the Balkans (as in the case of the 1878 Russo-Turkish War, or

The Yeni Camii, or New Mosque, in Istanbul, as seen from the harbor, c. 1895. ©HISTORICAL PICTURE ARCHIVE/CORBIS the decisive Balkan Wars of 1912), the social topography of late Ottoman Istanbul was altered by a steady influx of Muslim refugees.

Beyond the human toll of the Balkan struggles, a major factor in the reshaping of nineteenth-century Istanbul was the radical increase in the number of its European dwellers. The rationalized administrative structure and the liberal trade policies prompted by the Tanzimat regime turned the empire into a lucrative center for foreign investment. While the Ottoman Empire was rapidly integrated into the capitalist world economy, the Galata area gained prominence as the commercial, financial, and diplomatic center of western presence. Crowded with multi-story office buildings, modern schools, hospitals, banks, and a bustling stock exchange, Galata emerged as the unrivalled locus of power in the Ottoman capital, briskly marginalizing the traditional core of the city.

The soaring Levantine population of Istanbul, alongside members of the predominantly non-Muslim bourgeoisie, formed a dense residential sprawl beyond the northern walls of Galata, along the main axis of the Grande Rue de Pera. Adorned with Parisian-style apartment buildings, public parks, cafes, bars, hotels, shops, and passages, Pera (now Beyoglu) developed as a peripheral European microcosm that drew into its orbit all Stambouliots of Westernized proclivities. The growing weight of western political, economic, and cultural presence made the Galata area the privileged showground of modern public amenities in Istanbul. In 1855, when the Istanbul peninsula still largely maintained its traditional character, the model Sixth District of Galata was the first to enjoy modern municipal services such as street lighting, garbage collection, and water and sewage systems. A systematic and comprehensive provision of such services to the entire Istanbul area was to be fully realized only during the Young Turk regime at the turn of the following century.

Nineteenth-century Istanbul was a bifurcated city, with a diminishing traditional center to the south of the Golden Horn and a thriving modern one to the north. The ascendancy of the latter was further enhanced by the definitive move of the imperial seat of residence in 1855 from the Topkapi Palace within the city walls to Dolmabahçe on the European shore of the Bosphorus. The new imperial complex at Dolmabahçe, comprising an extravagant Europeanized palace, a public square, a royal mosque, and an opera building, was closely linked to the Pera neighborhood up the hill, where the Tanzimat sultans frequented tea parties and theater performances. The relocation of the palace provided further impetus for members of the predominantly Muslim bureaucratic elite to move out of the old city and settle in modern districts in the vicinity of the new center. In the last decades of the nineteenth century, Stambouliots of diverse ethnic and religious origins intermingled in the developing neighborhoods north of Pera, such as Nişantaşı, Teşvikiye, and Şişli, where they shared an urban cosmopolitan culture defined markedly along European values and lifestyle.

Still, the worldly cosmopolitanism of new Istanbul was a highly fragile construction, since the social networks and cultural allegiances that held it together were largely predicated upon western economic and political hegemony. When Istanbul was occupied by the Allied powers at the end of World War I, the Grande Rue de Pera was entirely adorned with the flags of the vanquishers. For members of the nationalist resistance movement based in Ankara, the cosmopolitan ambience of Istanbul was distinctly redolent of the corruption and duplicity of the old regime. That Istanbul was to be inscribed in Turkish nationalist mythology as the "Ottoman Gomorrah," whose bitter memory was to be maintained in order to cherish the purity of the new nation.

See also **Cities and Towns; Ottoman Empire.**

BIBLIOGRAPHY

Amicis, Edmondo de. *Constantinople.* 2 vols. Translated by Maria H. Lansdale. Philadelphia, 1896. Translation of *Costantinopoli* (1878).

Çelik, Zeynep. *The Remaking of Istanbul: Portrait of an Ottoman City in the Nineteenth Century.* Berkeley, Calif., 1986.

Eldem, Edhem, Daniel Goffman, and Bruce Masters, eds. *The Ottoman City between East and West: Aleppo, Izmir and Istanbul.* New York, 1999.

Kuban, Doğan. *Istanbul, an Urban History: Byzantion, Constantinopolis, Istanbul.* Istanbul, 1996.

Lewis, Bernard. *Istanbul and the Civilization of the Ottoman Empire.* Norman, Okla., 1963.

Mansel, Philip. *Constantinople: City of the World's Desire, 1453–1924.* London, 1995.

Mardin, Şerif. "Super Westernization in Urban Life in the Ottoman Empire in the Last Quarter of the Nineteenth Century." In *Turkey: Geographic and Social Perspectives,* edited by P. Benedict, E. Tümertekin, and F. Mansur, 403–446. Leiden, 1974.

Zürcher, Erik, J. *Turkey: A Modern History.* London, 1993.

AHMET ERSOY

ITALY. News of the 1789 agitations in France elicited predictably mixed reactions in Italy. Governments feared that the French example might be infectious, but there was considerable sympathy for the insurgents outside government circles. The demands of French insurgents in 1789 sounded familiar to many Italians. Reformers in the peninsula had also called for constitutions and representative assemblies and the abolition of feudal and clerical privileges. Sympathizers and opponents of reform were present at all social levels. Members of the nobility wanted to check the power of monarchs who attacked the "liberties" of their estate, the clergy was divided over questions of religious reform, the middle classes wanted easier access to careers and public offices, artisans and peasants chafed under the weight of high taxes, rising prices, and food shortages. It did not pass unnoticed that food rioters in Piedmont rallied to the cry of "Long live Paris, long live France." Revolution could not break out in Italy, which was divided into many states and under the control of Austria since the end of the War of the Spanish Succession (1701–1714), but it was possible for revolution to occur in Italy if brought there by a power strong enough to challenge Austrian hegemony.

ITALY IN 1789

Absolute monarchs had led the reform movement before 1789, with the more absolute leading the way. The Habsburgs were at the forefront as direct rulers of Lombardy, which as a family possession was an integral part of their empire. Empress Maria Theresa (r. 1740–1780) and her son Joseph II (r. 1780–1790) centralized the administration, carried out land censuses, improved the collection of taxes, curbed the privileges of clergy and nobility, and established a state bureaucracy based on merit and competence. The Grand Duchy of Tuscany ruled by Joseph's brother Peter Leopold (r. 1765–1790) carried out similar reforms, moved in the direction of free trade, and went so far as to dissolve the Tuscan army in order to devote more resources to domestic improvements.

The picture was mixed elsewhere in the peninsula. A branch of the Spanish Bourbons governed the Kingdom of Naples (renamed Kingdom of the Two Sicilies in 1816), the largest and most populous of the Italian states. Under Don Carlos (later Charles III of Spain, ruled Naples 1735–1759) and in the early years of the reign of his son Ferdinand I (r. 1759–1825), the southern kingdom enacted far-reaching reforms to rein in clergy and nobility and stimulate the economy. Bourbons also carried out reforms in the small Duchy of Parma in the north. The neighboring Duchy of Modena, ruled by the Este family, was cautious in matters of reform. In the Papal States, attempts at reform were halfhearted and ineffectual, but eighteenth-century Rome was notable for the artistic and literary works that it produced. The states least interested in reform were the republics of Venice, Genoa, and Lucca, which were dominated by their respective aristocracies. Progressive thinkers did not think much of republics before the French Revolution.

The Kingdom of Sardinia was a special case. It is often referred to as Piedmont-Sardinia because economically and politically it was centered on the mainland region of Piedmont. It also included the region of Savoy that was the birthplace of its ruling dynasty (House of Savoy), on the French side of the Alps. The reforms implemented by the House of Savoy improved the administration and the army. Piedmont-Sardinia was poised to take advantage of opportunities for territorial expansion in Italy. Its pursuit of territorial gains merged with the movement for national unification in the nineteenth century.

THE FRENCH REVOLUTION AND THE NAPOLEONIC INVASIONS

The French Revolution came to Italy in 1796 at the point of French bayonets. The delay and the manner of appearance are important. By 1796, the revolution had gone through several phases. During the Jacobin phase from 1792 to 1794, the monarchy was abolished, the king and queen of France executed, real and suspected enemies of the Revolution liquidated on a grand scale, and war had broken out. It was harder for many Italians to like the Revolution after it had revealed its more radical nature, and harder still in 1796 when it was brought to Italy by the half-starved soldiers of Napoleon I (r. 1804–1814/15), who motivated them with promises of glory and booty to be won in the rich plains of Lombardy. Still, in spite of the large-scale robberies and depredations, a significant number of Italians supported the French occupation. The most enthusiastic supporters were dubbed Jacobins. A minority of true believers, Italian Jacobins believed in the revolutionary ideals of liberty, equality, and fraternity, and greeted the French as liberators. In the years 1796 to 1799, borders changed, republics replaced monarchies, privileges were abolished. Napoleon was not held back by religious scruples or reverence for history. The uncooperative Pope Pius VI (r. 1775–1799) was arrested and carted off to France, where he died. France annexed Savoy and Piedmont. The venerable Republic of Venice ceased to exist when Napoleon ceded it to Austria with the Treaty of Campo Formio (October 1797). That same year, Napoleon established the Cisalpine Republic in the Po Valley as a French client state. Renamed the Italian Republic in 1802, it was a concession to Italian pride. So was the adoption of the green, white, and red Italian tricolor as the flag of the republic, patterned on the flag of Revolutionary France. In 1797, Melchiorre Gioia (1767–1829) won a prize for an essay arguing that Italians would be happiest if united under a republican form of government.

The French presence in the north emboldened Italian Jacobins in Rome and Naples. The Roman Republic set up in 1798 proclaimed the end of the pope's temporal rule. Radical leaders formed the Parthenopean Republic in January 1799. During the six months of its existence, the Parthenopean Republic attacked feudal privileges, opposed the clergy, and favored secular education. It claimed to speak for the people, but the majority did not support it. Vincenzo Cuoco (1770–1823), in his essay *Saggio storico sulla rivoluzione napoletana* (1801), described the Jacobin revolution as "passive" because it disregarded the needs of the masses and attacked the traditional institutions of the kingdom to which the peasantry and urban poor were loyal. His criticism underscored the isolation of Jacobins. The revolutionary *triennio* of 1796–1799 ended when Napoleon's enemies took advantage of his absence in Egypt to overturn the French-inspired republics, and peasants and the urban poor turned against the Jacobins.

French power was restored when Napoleon staged another invasion and defeated the Austrians at the Battle of Marengo (14 June 1800). That date marks the beginning of the Napoleonic age, for by that time Napoleon's personal power was secure. The period of revolutionary experimentation was over. Napoleon was crowned emperor in 1804; a year later he assumed the title of king of Italy. The Italian Republic became the Kingdom of Italy, governed by Napoleon's adopted son Eugéne de Beauharnais (1781–1824). In 1805, about one-third of the Italian peninsula, including the regions of Piedmont, Liguria, and Tuscany, became part of France. In 1806, Napoleon's older brother Joseph Bonaparte (1768–1844) became king of Naples. Joachim Murat (1767–1815), Napoleon's swashbuckling brother-in-law, replaced Joseph in 1808. Murat's resistance to Napoleon's demands, his personal magnetism, and love of display won him considerable popularity in Naples, and a posthumous reputation, probably undeserved, as a champion of Italian independence. France annexed the Papal States in 1809, and in 1811 Napoleon conferred the title of king of Rome on his newborn son and heir to the imperial throne.

Italy contributed revenue and manpower to the French Empire. Taxation was heavy, and conscription in the Kingdom of Italy raised more than 200,000 soldiers for Napoleon's armies, more than any other satellite state. Napoleon regarded the southern provinces of the peninsula as more valuable for the revenue they could provide than as a source of cannon fodder, for he had a low opinion of the martial qualities of southerners. Sicily and Sardinia, protected by the British navy, were never part of Napoleon's empire. Napoleonic legislation abolished feudal obligations and restrictions on the sale and purchase of land, and introduced centralized administration on the French model; uniform civil, commercial, and penal codes; and uniform weights and measures. Military conquest simplified political borders. There were now three main territorial divisions in Italy. Piedmont, Liguria, Tuscany, Parma and Piacenza, Umbria, Latium, and the Illyrian provinces on the eastern shore of the Adriatic Sea were integral parts of the French Empire. The Kingdom of Italy in the north and the Kingdom of Naples in the south were client states with limited autonomy.

The simplification of internal borders, adoption of uniform law codes, and military conscription are credited with preparing the ground for the Risorgimento, the movement for Italian independence and unity that developed in the nineteenth century. Uniform weights and measures, abolition of internal tariffs, land reform, secular education, and the revolutionary principle of the "career open to talent" were certainly part of the process of modernization that was also an aim of the Risorgimento. But the benefits were unevenly distributed. Careers benefited those who possessed the educational qualifications required to pursue them. Manufacturing gained in those regions that were part of France, but suffered where they were impeded by the protectionist provisions of Napoleon's Continental System. Taxes, military conscription, and anticlerical policies generated popular resistance and atrocities committed by both sides, especially in the south. The secret association of the Carboneria, destined to play a significant role in the early stages of the Risorgimento, was founded in Naples in 1807–1810, probably by Neapolitan officers disenchanted with Napoleonic rule.

THE CONGRESS OF VIENNA AND THE RESTORATION (1815–1848)

The principal aim of the Congress of Vienna (1814–1815) that ended the Napoleonic Wars was to prevent the recurrence of war and revolution, which were blamed on the spirit of revolution emanating from France. Political boundaries were redesigned to surround France with larger border-states as a first line of defense against a recurrence of French expansionism. That was the function of the newly established Kingdom of the Netherlands on France's northern border and of an enlarged Piedmont-Sardinia on the southern. Piedmont-Sardinia received the territory of the former Republic of Genoa, gaining an important port city and better access to the sea. King Victor Emmanuel I (r. 1802–1821) returned to the capital city of Turin eager to wipe out the vestiges of Jacobin rule, but he kept the centralized administration, improved collection of taxes, and better management of government finances that the French had introduced in his absence.

The Congress of Vienna acknowledged that policing Italy was Austria's responsibility. Austria added Venetia to Lombardy, the two regions forming the kingdom of Lombardy-Venetia within the Austrian Empire. To its credit, Austria sought to gain favor by encouraging its Italian client states to set an example of correct administration, be conciliatory toward former enemies, and win their cooperation. Pragmatic functionaries like Luigi de' Medici (1759–1830), chief adviser to King Ferdinand I of Naples, and Cardinal Ercole Consalvi (1757–1824), papal adviser and diplomat, followed the advice. Their efforts were stymied by the opposition of *zelanti,* die-hard conservatives opposed to all concessions. Ferdinand I of Naples and Pope Pius VII (r. 1800–1823) supported reform, but were ultimately held back by reliance on conservative support and by fear of revolution. Conciliatory policies worked best in Lombardy-Venetia, Parma, and Tuscany, the states with the closest ties to the Habsburg dynasty.

Few could blame Austrian Chancellor Prince Clemens von Metternich (1773–1859) for ignoring demands for Italian independence in 1815. But the sense of Italian nationality did exist in the minds of educated Italians brought up on the works of Dante (1265–1321) and Niccolò Machiavelli (1469–1527), and on memories of past Italian greatness and power. The poet Vittorio Alfieri (1749–1803) called on fellow Italians to reject all forms of servility and assert their national dignity. His hatred of Napoleonic France expressed the primitive form of patriotism that thrives on resentment of things foreign. The tradition of literary patriotism lived on in the writings of Ugo Foscolo (1778–1827), who directed his barbs against both Napoleon and Austria. Literature became a weapon in the hands of Romantic writers of the next generation. Alessandro Manzoni's novel *I promessi sposi* (1827; *The Betrothed*) expressed faith in the redeeming power of religion and the common people. Its popularity helped to establish Tuscan

Young men play the game of cappelletto on the streets of Naples. Photograph by Fratelli Alinari, 1897. At the end of the nineteenth century, Naples became a center for genre photographers who capitalized on the city's reputation as a lively and picturesque travel destination. ©ALINARI ARCHIVES/CORBIS

as the literary language of educated Italians. The novels of Massimo d'Azeglio (1798–1866), a future prime minister of Piedmont, catered to national pride by portraying the military valor of Italians in earlier times.

When revolution spread across the Mediterranean region in the years 1820 and 1821, insurgents in Naples and Piedmont demanded Italian independence and constitutional government. Secret societies carried revolution across political borders, relying on a network of cells that drew in military officers, public servants, students, journalists, lawyers, and artisans. Greece won its independence from the Ottoman Empire after a protracted struggle with English help. No such help was available to the Italian insurgents, who after winning some preliminary concessions were put down by Austrian intervention. Besides Austrian intervention, the failure was also attributed to popular apathy, the secret nature of the societies that limited their reach to the initiated few, and the insurgents' naive trust in the willingness of monarchs to grant reforms.

The limitations of secret societies were well understood by Giuseppe Mazzini (1805–1872), a young Genoese patriot who joined the Carboneria in 1827. Impatient with the hocus-pocus rituals of the society and eager for action, he struck out in a new direction. Young Italy, the association that he founded in 1831, did not keep its program secret and recruited far and wide. It declared open war on monarchy, proclaimed its republicanism, called for national independence and unity, armed insurrection, and claimed to speak for the Italian people. Mazzini believed in the power of the printed word and used it effectively to spread his message among educated Italians.

Young Italy could not deliver a successful revolution. It was penetrated by spies, wracked by internal dissent, and crippled by police surveillance. But failure did not discourage Mazzini. When Young Italy's attempts at revolution in Italy failed in 1833 and 1834, Mazzini raised the stakes by founding Young Europe, which was intended to create a united revolutionary front across Europe. Italians, Germans, Hungarians, Poles, and southern Slavs were to unite in an alliance of the people against Metternich's alliance of monarchs. Internal dissent hampered Young Europe without diminishing its appeal. Its call was heard by a young Sardinian naval officer named Giuseppe Garibaldi (1807–1882) in political exile in South America. The future liberator of southern Italy honed his military skills in obscure South American conflicts, in which he fought with youthful self-confidence in the name of liberty.

Governments breathed a sigh of relief after the failure of Young Italy. Now that the danger of revolution was over, some thought that they could try their hand at cautious reform. Piedmont-Sardinia had a new monarch in the person of Charles Albert (r. 1831–1849). As enigmatic a figure as any that was ever in the public eye, Charles Albert had connived with insurgents in 1821 when he was in line to occupy the throne, then had made amends by leading conservative forces against liberal insurgents in Spain. His ambiguous conduct earned him the nicknames of the Sphinx and King Waffle. He thought that he could fight the revolution with reforms compatible with the principle of absolute monarchy. In the late 1830s he instituted an advisory council of state, abolished internal tolls and feudal obligations, adopted uniform law codes, negotiated trade treaties, promoted maritime trade, and built up the navy and merchant marine. Charles Albert was no liberal, but he set the kingdom on the path of cautious reform that would later make the Kingdom of Sardinia the darling of Italian liberals. He was also a thorn in Austria's side, for he was as interested as any of his forebears in enlarging his domain at Austria's expense by pursuing the "policy of the artichoke," whereby Piedmont-Sardinia was to gobble up the rest of Italy one leaf at a time.

Italian society did not stand still during the Restoration period (1815–1848). Governments built roads and ports, encouraged trade, subsidized industries, and encouraged the pursuit of "useful knowledge." The first Italian railroad was inaugurated in Naples in 1839. The Rothschilds made Naples the center of their Mediterranean operations. The Papal States under Gregory XVI (r. 1831–1846) discouraged secular education, rejected freedom of expression, laissez-faire economics, and industrialization. Uneven development, rather than stagnation, best characterizes Italy during the Restoration.

Most cities were stagnant, but there were exceptions. Milan, Turin, and seaports like Trieste and Livorno were thriving centers of commerce and manufacturing. Agriculture was by far the most important sector of the economy. The well-irrigated lands of the Po Valley moved toward specialized, market-oriented production and use of wage labor. Growing dependence on maize caused outbreaks of pellagra due to spoiled supplies. In central Italy, the form of sharecropping known as *mezzadria* prevailed. It was labor intensive, aimed at maximum self-sufficiency, and discouraged recourse to markets. But it provided security of income for landlords and of tenure for tenants, as land contracts were of long duration. Absentee-owned latifundia estates provided precarious employment for a growing rural population in the south, setting the stage for mass emigration. Vagabondage and brigandage were recurring problems in many parts of Italy. Recent historical interpretations stress that it was the inability of papal and Bourbon governments to provide security that aroused discontent with their rule and sustained the movement for national unification under the energetic leadership of Piedmont-Sardinia.

The struggle for national unification developed in new directions in the 1840s. The publication in 1843 of Vincenzo Gioberti's *Del primato morale e civile degli italiani* (On the moral and civil primacy of the Italian people) inspired the Neo-Guelph movement that called on Rome and the papacy to take up the cause of Italian independence. The Neo-Guelphs aimed at a loose confederation of states under the presidency of the pope, and believed that such an outcome could be attained without recourse to violence and revolution. It seemed highly unlikely

Street vendor selling water, Palermo, c. 1900. © ALINARI ARCHIVES/CORBIS

that the ultraconservative Gregory XVI would lead a national crusade, but history played one of its curious tricks when the College of Cardinals elected a pope with liberal credentials in 1846. The election of Pius IX (r. 1846–1878) was the bolt of lightening that stunned Metternich and electrified liberals. To the liberals' acclaim, the new pope announced reforms that included amnesty for political prisoners, institution of a civic guard, a council of ministers, and a free press.

THE REVOLUTIONS OF 1848

Revolution came to Italy and the rest of Europe in 1848. Poor harvests, heavy taxation, anti-Austrian sentiments, and expectations that the pope would lead the fight for independence proved to be an explosive mixture. In January 1848 there were popular protests in Lombardy, Tuscany, and Sicily. Sicilian insurgents seized control of the capital city of Palermo, called for a regional parliament, decreed an end to Bourbon rule over the island, adopted the Italian tricolor, and sought to gain autonomous status for the island under the Piedmontese rule. With unrest spreading to the rest of the realm, Ferdinand II of Naples (r. 1830–1859) promised a constitution. Within a month, Leopold II of Tuscany (r. 1824–1859), Pius IX, and Charles Albert followed suit.

Lombardy became the epicenter of revolution when insurgents took to the streets of Milan and compelled Austrian troops to evacuate the city after five days of fighting. The Five Days of Milan entered the history books as a victory for the people. Charles Albert took advantage of Austria's disarray after Metternich was removed from office to declare war on Austria. His proclamation of 23 March 1848 promised that he would bring Italians under Austrian rule "the help that a brother expects from a brother, a friend from a friend." In the euphoria of the moment and under pressure from liberals, the governments of Naples and Rome also dispatched troops to fight the Austrians. They soon recalled them because neither Ferdinand II nor Pius IX was eager to fight Austria, and both realized that it was not in their interest to have a larger and more powerful Piedmont as their neighbor. They need not have worried, for the Austrians recovered and defeated the Piedmontese, compelling Charles Albert to sue for an armistice on 8 August 1848. The conflict remembered as Italy's first war of national independence would end for good on 23 March 1849 at the Battle of Novara, when the Austrians inflicted a second and decisive defeat on the Piedmontese.

Insurgencies were still under way in Venice, Florence, Rome, and Naples. The most dramatic was the one in Rome, where insurgents assassinated the pope's prime minister. Pius IX had tried to cope with the forces he had helped unleash by appointing a prime minister. Pellegrino Rossi (1787–1848), a political exile of 1820, was a law expert, university professor, economist, and diplomat. He believed in reform, but not in revolution, and wanted nothing to do with popular assemblies and the mob. Pius IX left Rome in disguise a few days after Rossi's murder on 15 November 1848, leaving the city in the hands of radical elements who called for popular elections, proclaimed a republic, and declared the pope deposed as a temporal ruler.

Mazzini and Garibaldi were the dominant figures of the Roman Republic of 1849. Both had returned from exile to participate in the revolution, Garibaldi sailing from South America with a small retinue of followers. Mazzini saw the Roman Republic as the starting point of worldwide revolution. As the Rome of the Caesars had given the world the *Pax Romana,* and the Rome of the Popes had brought Christianity, the Rome of the People would inaugurate the age of democratic government. Pius IX regarded what was happening in Rome as the usurpation of legitimate papal power and called on the governments of Europe to protect the church. Austria, France, Spain, and Naples responded with troops. Garibaldi took charge of defending the city and the republic. His volunteer troops conducted a gallant defense, but eventually had to yield to superior numbers, equipment, and training. Garibaldi's defense of the Roman Republic became the stuff of legend. Mazzini boasted that republicans had shown the greatest resolve and given the cause of Italian unity a roster of martyrs that would inspire patriots for generations to come. Ordinary people participated for the first time in elections, joined political circles, and took a stand on public issues. The memory of grassroots participation may have been the most important legacy of the Roman Republic.

THE POLITICS OF NATIONAL INDEPENDENCE (1849–1859)

It was not understood right away that there would be no repeat of revolution after 1848. Mazzini continued to plan unsuccessful insurgencies that alienated many sympathizers. By the mid-1850s, the political initiative that he craved passed to public figures that had their hands on the levers of power, controlled the resources of government, and approached the question of Italian independence with fewer preconceptions. Moderate liberals looked to Piedmont-Sardinia and its young king Victor Emmanuel II (r. 1849–1878), who succeeded to the throne following the resignation of his father Charles Albert. Piedmont-Sardinia was the only Italian state that retained the constitution granted in 1848, which provided for an elective lower house of parliament and protected civil liberties and freedom of association. It would pass on this constitution to the Kingdom of Italy formed in 1861, and it would remain the fundamental law of the land until 1946 when Italians voted the monarchy out of existence.

Victor Emmanuel II gave an impression of bluntness and sincerity that contrasted favorably with his father's ambiguous image. His followers seized upon these genuine qualities to portray him as *Re Galantuomo* (Trustworthy King), a monarch who could relate to simple folks. But the man of the hour was Count Cavour (Camillo Benso, 1810–1861), who served as Victor Emmanuel II's prime minister from November 1852 until his death with only one brief interruption. Cavour believed in constitutional monarchy, parliamentary government, civil liberties, limited voting rights, and free trade, the distinctive traits of nineteenth-century liberals who trusted neither absolute monarchs nor the people at large. His admirers insisted on his fundamental liberalism; his detractors insisted on its limitations and his propensity to sacrifice liberal principles to political expediency. Another image, entirely posthumous, portrayed him as a patient weaver (*il tessitore*) working on a secret plan to unify Italy. That last image was the least credible of all.

Cavour was far from being universally popular. In the democratic camp where republican sentiments prevailed, many regarded him as a mere servant of a royal dynasty, and therefore not a true patriot. But not all democrats were intransigent republicans. After the experiences of 1848 and more years of exile, Garibaldi was willing to come to terms with the Piedmontese monarchy if it would put its army and resources in the service of the national cause. He distrusted Cavour, but believed in Victor Emmanuel II—like a peasant in awe of authority, acidly said Mazzini, whose unrequited wish was to have Garibaldi on his side against the king. Unlike Mazzini who still believed that small-scale uprisings could trigger a general revolution, Garibaldi understood that untrained fighters were no match for regular troops. He would fight with his volunteer troops, which he trained to maneuver quickly and use shock tactics, but the Piedmontese army would have to be involved if Italy was to be unified, and that army was loyal to the king. The Italian National Society, founded in August 1857, served as a bridge between Garibaldi and Cavour, republicans and monarchists, liberals and democrats. It announced its commitment to "Italy and Victor Emmanuel," operated openly in Piedmont-Sardinia and secretly elsewhere in Italy, engaged in political propaganda, and stashed weapons for a showdown with Austria. It served the monarchy, but also pressured the monarchy to work with the volunteer movement that represented the spontaneous and democratic element of the national movement.

It was Cavour's task to prepare for war. He is often compared to Otto von Bismarck (1815–1898), for they were the principal architects of political unification in Italy and Germany respectively. They were *Realpolitik* figures, meaning that they relied on military power and diplomacy to pursue their objectives, distrusted popular initiatives, and put ideals in the service of politics rather than vice versa. Both relied on diplomacy and war, but Cavour had the difficult task of finding a partner or partners that would lend military help against Austria, for the Piedmontese army was not strong enough to go at it alone. Bismarck, who had at his disposal the far more powerful Prussian army, used diplomacy to isolate his enemies one at a time. Cavour admired England, but England was an unlikely military partner. He therefore set his eyes on France and its new emperor Napoleon III (r. 1852–1871), who had joined the Carboneria in his youth, favored Italian independence, was eager to emulate the military feats of his uncle Napoleon I, challenge Austrian hegemony, and return Italy to France's sphere of influence. Piedmont's participation in the Crimean War (1853–1856) on the side of England and France was intended to end Piedmont's diplomatic isolation and embarrass the Austrian government, which opted out of that conflict. The payoff came in the form of a secret deal that Cavour and the French emperor worked out near the French resort town of Plombières in July 1858. The agreement of Plombières promised France the territories of Nice and Savoy in return for French military intervention in a war against Austria and a rearrangement of borders and dynasties within Italy that would be advantageous for both France and Piedmont-Sardinia. An enlarged Piedmont-Sardinia would be the strongest power in Italy, but not strong enough to pose a threat to France, which with its victory would replace Austria as the hegemonic Continental power.

THE WAR OF 1859, GARIBALDI'S THOUSAND, AND UNIFICATION

Cavour's diplomacy made possible the War of 1859, which Italians remember as their second war of independence. The war was decided by the two bloody battles of Magenta and Solferino fought in June 1859. They were Austrian losses, but the Austrian army was still in Lombardy when Napoleon III and Austrian Emperor Francis Joseph I (r. 1848–1916) signed a surprise armistice on 5 July. The conflict was supposed to continue until the Austrians were evicted from Lombardy and Venetia, which were then to go to Piedmont. Piedmont would then cede Nice and Savoy to France.

In the event, Piedmont had to be satisfied with Lombardy, and France did not get Nice and Savoy. The outcome was disappointing for Cavour, who resigned as prime minister and was out of office for six months, but Austria's defeat set in motion a chain of unforeseen events that eventually gave Piedmont-Sardinia much more than Cavour had bargained for. Emboldened patriots in Tuscany, Parma, Modena, and the northern provinces of the papal Romagna staged coups, set up provisional governments, and demanded annexation to Piedmont-Sardinia. An uprising in Sicily enticed Garibaldi to launch an expedition to the island with volunteers. The legendary Expedition of the Thousand sailed from the town of Quarto near Genoa in May 1860 officially ignored by the Piedmontese government. Cavour did not approve, but did not dare stop the enormously popular Garibaldi, who had the king's secret blessing. Stopping Garibaldi might have given Cavour's political rivals enough leverage to bring down his government.

Garibaldi's victories in the south brought the national unification movement to near completion. Sicily, the entire southern mainland, and a large swath of papal territory fell into the hands of Piedmont-Sardinia, which intervened militarily in the final stages of the operation to mop up the last vestiges of resistance. The Kingdom of Italy was officially proclaimed on 17 March 1861. Excluded from its territory were Rome and its surrounding territory, which were what was left of the Papal States, and the Austrian possessions in the north. Venetia, the provinces of Trent and Trieste, and the Istrian peninsula remained under Austrian control. Italy gained Venetia in 1866 after fighting another war against Austria, this time as Prussia's ally (the third war of national independence to Italians, Seven Weeks' War to the rest of the world). Rome became the capital of Italy in September 1870 when Italian troops moved in over the token resistance of the papal army. Italy gained Trent, Trieste, and Istria when the Austrian Empire disintegrated at the end of World War I. Italy's final confrontation with Austria was a fourth war of national independence.

Italy faced a new set of problems after unification. It was a country of 21.8 million people, which grew to 26.8 million in 1871 with the acquisition of Rome and Venice. Most of its population was illiterate and poor. The economy was agricultural, with a weak manufacturing sector and enormous regional disparities, the most glaring being the gap between north and south. Only about 2 percent of the people spoke the Tuscan national language; the use of regional dialects and local vernaculars was the norm everywhere. Seven previously separate states, each with its own government, laws, budgets, police, and army had to be merged into a single national entity. How to integrate these diverse populations and institutions was the pressing issue of the moment. Democrats urged that it be done by summoning a representative national assembly to discuss and legislate. The government chose instead the speedier, more direct approach of extending the laws and administrative practices of Piedmont-Sardinia to the rest of the country. It was perhaps a sensible decision given the uncertainties of the moment and the fear that a unity so quickly achieved could be undone by protracted political wrangling. Sensible or not, it altered the perception of the national movement. The decision to "Piedmontize" the entire country, the first of many controversial government decisions, smacked of conquest rather than liberation.

Popular discontent was most pronounced in the southern regions, where bands of irregular fighters, promptly dubbed "brigands" by the government, took up arms against the state. Southern "brigandage" persisted for nearly a decade, required the deployment of some 120,000 troops, placing parts of the south under martial law, and cost the army more casualties than all the wars of independence combined. Brigandage was the first manifestation of the Southern Question, a question that still troubles national politics at the start of the twenty-first century. Mass emigration developed on a large scale in the 1880s and 1890s. It was heavily southern and had many causes, including the attraction of new economic opportunities in the Americas. That was the pull. On the push side were developments attributable directly or indirectly to national unification. Southern manufacturing could not compete with manufacturing in the north when deprived of the protective tariffs that sustained it before unification. Southern agriculture experienced a similar crisis, although its crisis was due more to competition from foreign producers and to unwise tariff policies adopted by the national government. Compensating shifts of production toward crop specialization occurred but did not improve the conditions of most land workers. Political repression also played a role, as indicated by the upsurge in Sicilian emigration after the island experienced the imposition of martial law in 1893–1894 to quell the disturbances of the *fasci siciliani,* triggered by economic and political grievances.

Troubled relations of church and state were also a persistent problem. The loss of Rome in 1870 put an end to papal temporal rule. Locked in the tiny enclave of the Vatican, Pius IX proclaimed himself a prisoner, denounced the loss of territory as an act of thievery, refused to recognize the Italian state, and urged Catholics to boycott it. The confrontation with the Italian state set papal policy against the sins of modern civilization that Pius IX denounced in the Syllabus of Errors (1864). These included rationalism, free thought, religious freedom, secular education, socialism, Protestantism, and the separation of church and state. Generations of Italian Catholics faced the dilemma of choosing between the authority of the church, which exhorted them to boycott national politics, and the state that demanded primary allegiance. The conflict of church and state ended with the signing of the Concordat and Lateran Pact in 1929. Benito Mussolini (1883–1945) and the Fascist regime in power at that time touted the settlement as one of their great achievements, one that certainly contributed to the overwhelming endorsement of the regime by the vast majority of Italians in the national plebiscite that was held later that year.

ITALY AFTER CAVOUR (1861–1876)

Cavour died prematurely and unexpectedly in June 1861. His death left a huge political void, for there was no obvious successor of comparable political skill and prestige to take on the challenge of governing the country so recently unified. His political heirs made up a loose political formation called the Historical Right. They were mostly northern politicians, sincere patriots, and competent administrators who wanted to govern responsibly and did not fear unpopularity. They saw it as their duty to put government finances on a sound footing, enforce the law, and promote economic growth. They wanted a balanced budget, financial stability, and investor confidence. They spent carefully and taxed reluctantly, but spend and tax they did because the needs were many. Building railroads to bind together the different regions, improving public education, fighting the second war of independence (1866), and repressing brigandage were top priorities. They believed that spreading the tax burden around so that it affected even the poorest was a good thing, because paying taxes gave everyone a stake in the system and made for responsible citizens. The most unpopular tax of all was the grist tax (*macinato*) levied on milling operations. When that tax went into effect in 1869, large-scale riots broke out and the army had to be called out to restore order. The most typical figure of the Historical Right was Quintino Sella (1827–1884), who held the post of finance minister off and on during the period when the Historical Right controlled parliament. He embodied the *politica della lesina* (policy of tight spending) that brought about the Historical Right's crowning achievement. On 16 March 1876, the government announced its first budget surplus; two days later it lost a key vote and had to resign. The heirs of Cavour would never regain power.

Their successors are known collectively as the Liberal Left, to distinguish them from the socialist left that developed during their watch. Many were former Mazzinians who had made their peace with the monarchy. They saw themselves as a progressive force, promised to reduce taxes, broaden the suffrage, take a strong stand against clerical power, and pursue a more active foreign policy. Unlike the Historical Right, the Liberal Left had a strong constituency in the south. They abolished the hated grist tax (1880), expanded the suffrage from 2 percent to 7 percent of the population (1882), ratcheted up the anticlerical campaign, and ended Italy's diplomatic isolation by concluding the Triple Alliance with Germany and Austria (1882). The first decisive step toward colonial expansion occurred that same year when the government established the colony of Eritrea on the coast of the Red Sea. Not particularly concerned with balancing the budget, the Liberal Left spent merrily, particularly to build up a large navy, which they deemed indispensable if Italy was to be a great power.

THE CRISIS OF LIBERALISM (1876–1901)

The dominant figures of the Liberal Left were Agostino Depretis (1813–1887), who served three times as prime minister from 1876 until his death in office in 1887, and Francesco Crispi (1818–1901), a Sicilian and the first southerner to hold the office of prime minister, which he did in 1887–1891 and 1893–1896. Depretis, an adroit politician, conjured up parliamentary majorities by bargaining with anyone willing to deal. He practiced the art of *trasformismo* (transformism), which according to his critics sacrificed principles to political expediency. Such accommodating politics stirred opposition within the Liberal Left, which was a loose and fractious grouping rather than a real political party. Crispi posed as the "man of destiny" who would restore integrity to the political process and win for Italy the international status to which it was entitled. He enacted many timely reforms in his first years in office, improving the functioning of the courts, extending the right to vote in local elections, introducing programs of public sanitation, and laws for the protection of emigrants. Foreign policy proved to be Crispi's undoing. His career ended in humiliation and disaster when an Italian expeditionary force, marching from Eritrea into Ethiopia to enforce a territorial claim, was surrounded and destroyed at the battle of Adwa (March 1896). The ensuing furor at home forced Crispi to resign as prime minister and injected into Italian politics the explosive issue of revenge, which ultranationalists used to inflame public opinion against weak liberal government and fascists raised to justify other colonial ventures.

In the five years of political and social turmoil that followed Crispi's resignation, the country experienced frequent changes of government, widespread popular tumults, an attempt by conservatives to expand the powers of the crown at the expense of parliament, and a parliamentary revolt to protect parliament's prerogatives. The 1890s saw the growth of a militant socialist movement that championed the rights of workers and peasants. The Italian Socialist Party, founded in stages from 1892 to 1895, was the first real political party on the Italian scene, but party discipline was constantly tested by internal tensions. It tried to accommodate both reformists who believed in the power of the ballot, working with parliament, and gradual evolution toward a socialist society, and revolutionaries who preached the violent overthrow of capitalism and the government.

Conservatives of all stripes regarded socialism as a major threat, and their fear of revolution intensified when the country experienced protests and mass demonstrations on an unprecedented scale. During the *fatti di maggio* of May 1898, tens of thousands of demonstrators took to the streets, riots ensued, martial law was declared, and the government arrested leaders of the opposition. The army opened up with artillery on demonstrators in Milan, inflicting hundreds of casualties. A self-appointed avenger of the people emerged in the person of one Gaetano Bresci (1869–1901). A Tuscan anarchist and worker in the textile mills of Paterson, New Jersey, Bresci held the king responsible for the massacre, returned to Italy, and shot King Umberto I (r. 1878–1900), son and successor to Victor Emmanuel II, dead on 29 July 1900.

The impression was enormous; many feared that the country was slipping into anarchy. That it did not do so was largely due to the parliamentary majority, which beat back the efforts of strict constitutionalists to curtail its powers, and then managed to produce liberal coalitions that steered the country away from the brink of all-out crisis. The reign of the new king began auspiciously. Victor Emmanuel III (r. 1900–1946), later fatally compromised by his association with the Fascist regime, was eager to disassociate himself from the repressive measures of previous governments and disinclined to interfere with the workings of parliament. He was willing to work with a new leadership that transcended the passions and diatribes rooted in the history of the Risorgimento.

THE LIBERALISM OF GIOVANNI GIOLITTI (1901–1914)

Thus began the era of Giovanni Giolitti (1842–1928), a new-generation politician who had risen through the public administration, had a thorough understanding of the machinery of government, and was willing to deal with liberals, socialists, and Catholic members of parliament. It helped that he had no personal connection with partisan passions of Risorgimento politics. Giolitti, a liberal, won the support of socialists by playing on their fears of conservatives and of conservatives by playing on their fears of socialists. He could exploit the freedom of action that comes from occupying the political middle ground.

The "age of Giolittian democracy" extends from 1901, when Giolitti was minister of the interior in a government headed by the liberal Giuseppe Zanardelli (1826–1903), who was old and ailing, to 1914 when he stepped out of office. Between those two dates Giolitti was prime minister three times, in 1903–1905, 1906–1909, and 1911–1914. But in or out of office, few doubted that he was the real political power that could get things done. Observers opined that he stepped out of power tactically to avoid bearing the brunt of some particularly odious measures, putting that onus on the victims of his political realism. Critics called him a corruptor of the political process. Giolitti respected parliament, but getting cooperative parliamentary majorities required influencing the vote in ways that were not above board. Electoral fraud or sleight-of-hand was not unusual, especially in the south, where Giolitti's lieutenants felt that they could operate without close scrutiny by the press. The south was a huge reservoir of votes for Giolittian candidates, to the chagrin of his enemies who dubbed him *il ministro della mala vita* (minister of the racketeers). Giolitti's defense was that government had to deal with people as they are: a hunchback requires a crooked coat.

Giolitti's parliaments spanned the spectrum from Catholics (who now had a special papal dispensation to vote against anticlerical and socialist candidates), to liberals, and socialists. His policies were flexible enough to encompass the whole spectrum and offer something to everyone who was willing to cooperate. As difficult as it is to assess the principles and motivations of this slippery

Women spinning glass thread, 1905. The island of Murano, in Venice, has been the site of glassmaking since the thirteenth century. ©CORBIS

figure, there is no doubt that his politics produced fundamental breakthroughs that took Italy into the age of popular participation in government and public life. He established the practice of government neutrality in labor conflict and recognized the right of workers to organize for purposes of collective bargaining (a law long on the books, but frequently disregarded) as long as their activities did not threaten the public order. The country's most powerful labor union, the General Confederation of Labor, was founded in 1906. He steered through parliament the electoral reform bill of 1912 that gave the vote to most males (women could vote in local elections, but had to wait until 1946 to vote in national elections). That measure expanded the electorate from 3 million to 8.5 million voters and marked the beginning of the era of mass politics. Giolitti regarded the new electoral law as his political masterpiece and crowning achievement.

Giolitti had a low opinion of the military (he once remarked that Italy had won in World War I because the other side also had generals) and did not approve of military ventures. Nevertheless, he did bring the country to war in 1911. His reasons for doing so are still the subject of debate, but certainly the acquiescence of the Great Powers, pressure of special interests at home, weakness of the opponent, and desire to appease nationalist sentiments played a role. The enemy was the Ottoman Empire, long considered the "sick man of Europe," and therefore ripe for the plucking. There was Catholic support for war against a Muslim power. Middle-class Italians, appalled and humiliated by the emigration of millions of their poor compatriots, welcomed a place where Italy's surplus population could settle under the national flag. A small but vehement nationalist movement called for an act of force to erase the humiliating memory of 1896.

The Italian-Turkish War, fought from September 1911 to October 1912, gained Italy the colony of Libya and a foothold in North Africa. Nationalists called it Italy's "Fourth Shore" because of Libya's closeness to Sicily, and envisaged further expansion. Giolitti had no desire to go further, but the elections of 1913, the first held on the basis of the greatly expanded suffrage, yielded such a slight government majority that in March 1914 he stepped down to wait for a better day. It seemed a wise move at the time. His successor, the conservative southerner Antonio Salandra (1853–1931), had to quell outbreaks of domestic violence in June 1914 even more disruptive than those of 1898. During Red Week (7–14 June 1914), anarchist, republican, and socialist agitators took over local administrations in central and northern Italy, declared independent republics in the seized territories, issued currencies, abolished taxes, interrupted railway traffic, and ransacked wealthy homes. Once again, the country appeared to be on the brink of revolution or civil war. Among the ringleaders were the socialists Mussolini and Pietro Nenni (1891–1980), whose paths would later diverge in very different directions.

THE DECISION TO GO TO WAR (1914–1915)

The outbreak of war in Europe in August 1914 kept Salandra's government in power far longer than expected. Salandra and his foreign minister Antonino Paternò Castello, marquis di San Giuliano (1852–1914) adopted a policy of watchful neutrality. Claiming that the Triple Alliance with Germany and Austria-Hungary was defensive in nature and that its partners had ignored the obligation to consult adequately with Italy before going to war, the government demanded assurances of territorial compensations before making a decision. But Italy's territorial demands centered on the cities of Trento and Trieste, which the Austrians were understandably reluctant to give up. France and Great Britain (less so Russia) had no such qualms and promised them freely. Salandra's government actually negotiated with both sides, but in a lopsided fashion, for while it promised Austria no more than continued Italian neutrality for the territories it wanted, it promised the Triple Entente powers intervention on their side in return for the territories of Trent and the Trentino region, Trieste and the Istrian peninsula, Dalmatia, a sphere of influence in the Balkans, and colonial compensations. Salandra invoked "sacred egoism" as the patriotic rationale for the hard bargain that he and Sidney Sonnino (1847–1922), San Giuliano's successor at the foreign ministry, sealed in the secret Pact of London, signed on 26 April 1915.

A contentious domestic debate developed. While the government negotiated with both sides, Italians lined up in opposing camps for or against intervention. Most Catholics, socialists, and liberals favored neutrality, particularly because the Austrian government seemed willing to make territorial concessions just to keep Italy out of the war. Giolitti expressed the view that Italy could gain much by remaining neutral. Pope Benedict XV (r. 1914–1922) favored nonintervention and condemned the secret negotiations with the Entente powers. Socialists denounced the war as a capitalist plot, but a dissenting minority led by Mussolini called for intervention on the grounds that war would hasten the outbreak of proletarian revolution. That happened in Russia, but not in Italy. Mussolini's prediction came true, however, in an unexpected way, when he worked on the resentments and hopes aroused by the war to bring on a fascist revolution in 1919–1922.

Italy declared war on Austria-Hungary on 23 May 1915. The Pact of London did not oblige Italy to declare war on Germany, but it did so on 28 August 1916 to fall in line with its partners. Parliament was not consulted in either case, for the constitution gave the crown the exclusive right to make war and peace. Although excluded from the decision, parliament rallied behind the government and the war effort in the spirit of patriotism. The Socialist Party did not, but its formula to "neither support nor sabotage" the war satisfied neither neutralists nor interventionists, the latter accusing it of obstructing the war effort and undermining troop morale. The divide between neutralists and interventionists that formed in 1914 and 1915 and hardened during the war was never bridged. It surfaced in the immediate postwar years as the basic point of contention between socialists and fascists, the latter claiming to speak for what Mussolini called the *trincerocrazia* (aristocracy of the trenches) and for all patriotic Italians. Intervention and war thus cast a long and tragic shadow over the course of Italian history.

See also **Carbonari; Cavour, Count (Camillo Benso); Charles Albert; Crispi, Francesco; Garibaldi, Giuseppe; Giolitti, Giovanni; Kingdom of the Two Sicilies; Papal State; Piedmont-Savoy; Pius IX; Umberto I; Victor Emmanuel II.**

BIBLIOGRAPHY

Askew, William C. *Europe and Italy's Acquisition of Libya, 1911–1912.* Durham, N.C., 1942.

Beales, Derek, and Eugenio F. Biagini. *The Risorgimento and the Unification of Italy.* 2nd ed. London, 2002.

Bosworth, Richard J. B. *Italy, the Least of the Great Powers; Italian Foreign Policy Before the First World War.* Cambridge, U.K., 1979.

Broers, Michael. *Politics and Religion in Napoleonic Italy: The War against God, 1801–1814.* London, 2002.

Coppa, Frank J. *The Origins of the Italian Wars of Independence.* London, 1992.

Davis, John A. *Conflict and Control: Law and Order in Nineteenth-Century Italy.* Atlantic Highlands, N.J., 1988.

Davis, John A., ed. *Italy in the Nineteenth Century, 1796–1900.* Oxford, U.K., 2000.

De Grand, Alexander J. *The Hunchback's Tailor: Giovanni Giolitti and Liberal Italy from the Challenge of Mass Politics to the Rise of Fascism, 1882–1922.* Westport, Conn., 2001.

Duggan, Christopher. *Francesco Crispi, 1818–1901: From Nation to Nationalism.* Oxford, U.K., 2002.

Foerster, Robert F. *The Italian Emigration of Our Times.* Cambridge, Mass., 1919.

Gabaccia, Donna R. *Italy's Many Diasporas.* London, 2000.

Greenfield, Kent Roberts. *Economics and Liberalism in the Risorgimento: A Study of Nationalism in Lombardy, 1814–1848.* Rev. ed. Baltimore, Md., 1965.

Grew, Raymond. *A Sterner Plan for Italian Unity: The Italian National Society in the Risorgimento.* Princeton, N.J., 1963.

Hearder, Harry. *Italy in the Age of the Risorgimento, 1790–1870.* London, 1983.

Hess, Robert L. *Italian Colonialism in Somalia.* Chicago, 1966.

Hostetter, Richard. *The Italian Socialist Movement: Origins (1860–1882).* Princeton, N.J., 1958.

Jemolo, Arturo Carlo. *Church and State in Italy, 1850–1960.* Oxford, U.K., 1960.

Laven, David. *Venice and Venetia under the Habsburgs, 1815–1835.* Oxford, U.K., 2002.

Lovett, Clara M. *The Democratic Movement in Italy, 1830–1876.* Cambridge, Mass., 1982.

Mack Smith, Denis. *Cavour and Garibaldi, 1860: A Study in Political Conflict.* Cambridge, U.K., 1954.

Mack Smith, Denis, ed. *The Making of Italy, 1796–1866.* New York, 1988.

Miller, James Edward. *From Elite to Mass Politics: Italian Socialism in the Giolittian Era, 1900–1914.* Kent, Ohio, 1990.

Pernicone, Nunzio. *Italian Anarchism, 1864–1892.* Princeton, N.J., 1993.

Riall, Lucy. *Sicily and the Unification of Italy: Liberal Policy and Local Power.* Oxford, U.K., 1998.

Salomone, A. William. *Italy in the Giolittian Era: Italian Democracy in the Making, 1900–1914.* 2nd ed. Philadelphia, 1960.

Sarti, Roland. *Mazzini: A Life for the Religion of Politics.* Westport, Conn., 1997.

Seton-Watson, Christopher. *Italy from Liberalism to Fascism, 1870–1925.* London, 1967.

Thayer, John A. *Italy and the Great War: Politics and Culture, 1870–1915.* Madison, Wis., 1964.

Whittam, John. *The Politics of the Italian Army, 1861–1918.* London, 1977.

Roland Sarti

JACOBINS. The name *Jacobin* derives from the Jacobin convent situated near the National Assembly where the radical Breton deputies who had founded a political club at Versailles reestablished themselves after their move to Paris in October 1789. The term *Jacobin* is generally applied to those militant French revolutionaries who supported the draconian measures taken by the National Convention during the prolonged crisis of the period 1792 to 1794. More broadly, however, it may be applied to the dominant political tendency of the Revolution from 1789 until the closure of the Jacobin Club of Paris on 12 November 1794.

There were four broad phases in the life of this key political organization. The first coincided with the period of the constitutional monarchy, when the club was known as the Societies of the Friends of the Constitution. Fees were high and membership was limited to "patriotic" deputies until the club spread to the provinces: there would be 150 provincial affiliates by the end of 1790.

The second phase was precipitated by the abortive flight of Louis XVI in June 1791. Prominent Jacobins joined more radical clubs in calling for Louis's forced abdication, but most of the members of the National Assembly were concerned with consolidating the state of the Revolution as expressed in the new constitution, and deserted the Jacobin Club for the Feuillants, similarly named after its meeting place in a former convent. The issue of Louis's loyalty, however, was far from resolved.

The outbreak of war in April 1792 made Louis's position untenable, because repeated military defeats and the defection of thousands of noble army officers further convinced public opinion that the king was in league with the enemy through the maleficent influence of the Austrian queen, Marie-Antoinette. Louis was overthrown on 10 August and the republic proclaimed by a new, more democratic National Convention in September. Despite the considerable consensus in the Convention, in the autumn and winter of 1792–1793 it tended to divide between Jacobins and their antagonists, the "Girondins." In social and political terms, Jacobins such as Maximilien Robespierre, Georges Danton, Camille Desmoulins, and Jean-Paul Marat were somewhat closer to the popular movement, and the Jacobins' habit of sitting together on the upper-left-hand benches in the Convention quickly earned them the epithet of "Mountain" and an image of uncompromising republicanism, for example, over the fate of Louis XVI.

In the context of the deteriorating military situation in the winter and spring of 1793, most of the uncommitted deputies in the Convention swung behind the Jacobins' emergency proposals. This was the dominant, third phase of the Jacobins' existence. Between March and May 1793 the Convention placed executive powers in a Committee of Public Safety with policing powers vested in a Committee of General Security, and it acted to supervise the army through "deputies on mission." It passed decrees declaring émigrés "civilly dead," providing for public relief, and placing controls on grain and bread prices.

The central objective of the Jacobin Committee of Public Safety, to which Robespierre was elected on 27 July, was to take the emergency measures necessary to defeat internal counterrevolutionaries and the foreign armies on French soil. Only then would the implementation of the Jacobins' democratic constitution of June 1793 be possible. Jacobinism was an ideology in which the language of patriotism, sacrifice, and citizenship—the rule of virtue—was melded with the exigencies of requisitioning and conscription. It had supporters across the country: there were perhaps six thousand Jacobin clubs and popular societies created during the Terror, although many of them were short-lived. From 1793 to 1794 the membership of these clubs came to be dominated by artisans and shopkeepers. The social content of Jacobinism during this most radical phase placed primacy on republican education, social welfare, and an equality of social rights and obligations; above all, however, this heterogeneous group was held together by its commitment to national unity and the survival of the republic.

For the majority of the Convention, however, the goal of the Terror was the attainment of peace, and economic and political controls were accepted as temporary and regrettable impositions to that end rather than for the realization of the Jacobins' sweeping proposals to regenerate society. Once the military crisis had lessened by June, the dominant Jacobins in the Committee of Public Safety found themselves increasingly unable to appeal to the crisis as impelling a continuation of martial law. Robespierre and his associates were removed from power and executed on 9–10 Thermidor Year II (27–28 July 1794). Within a month, about two hundred provincial Jacobin clubs had complained angrily about the unexpected repercussions against all those associated with the Jacobin dominance of the Year II. They were silenced by a bitter social reaction. Active Jacobins were arrested in Paris, Jacobins in provincial towns were assassinated, and the Jacobin Club itself was closed down in November.

The final phase of the Jacobin tendency during the French Revolution was its afterlife, as former Jacobins sought both to avoid reprisals and to keep alive the hopes that the republic would again become democratic and socially radical. In the south and west, up to two thousand Jacobins were killed by "white Terror" gangs: the victims were often purchasers of nationalized property, and many of them were Protestants. Only sporadically, as in the national elections of 1798, was there a resurgence in support for the Jacobin project; it was rather in the militant republicanism of the nineteenth century that Jacobinism was to find louder echoes.

See also **Committee of Public Safety; Danton, Georges-Jacques; French Revolution; Girondins; Marat, Jean-Paul; Robespierre, Maximilien.**

BIBLIOGRAPHY

Desan, Suzanne. "'Constitutional Amazons': Jacobin Women's Clubs in the French Revolution." In *Re-creating Authority in Revolutionary France,* edited by Bryant T. Ragan Jr. and Elizabeth A. Williams, 11–35. New Brunswick, N.J., 1992.

Furet, François, and Mona Ozouf, eds. *A Critical Dictionary of the French Revolution.* Translated by Arthur Goldhammer. Cambridge, Mass., 1989.

Gough, Hugh. *The Terror in the French Revolution.* Basingstoke, U.K., 1998.

Gross, Jean-Pierre. *Fair Shares for All: Jacobin Egalitarianism in Practice.* Cambridge, U.K., 1997.

Jones, Colin. *The Longman Companion to the French Revolution.* London, 1988.

Kennedy, Michael L. *The Jacobin Club of Marseilles, 1790–1794.* Ithaca, N.Y., 1973.

———. *The Jacobin Clubs in the French Revolution: The First Years.* Princeton, N.J., 1982.

———. *The Jacobin Clubs in the French Revolution: The Middle Years.* Princeton, N.J., 1988.

———. *The Jacobin Clubs in the French Revolution, 1793–1795.* New York, 2000.

Palmer, R. R. *Twelve Who Ruled: The Year of the Terror in the French Revolution.* 1941. Reprint, with a new preface by the author, Princeton, N.J., 1989.

Patrick, Alison. *The Men of the First French Republic: Political Alignments in the National Convention of 1792.* Baltimore, Md. 1972.

PETER MCPHEE

JADIDS. Jadidism (a word meaning modernism, from the Arabic *Jadid,* meaning new) was a late-nineteenth-century movement of intellectual and political self-renewal and resistance among the Muslim subjects of the Russian Empire.

ORIGINS OF JADIDISM

Russian annexation of the Crimea in 1783, the definitive conquest of the Caucasus in the 1850s, and expansion into the Islamic heartlands of Central Asia meant that by the turn of the twentieth century some thirteen million Muslims, 10 percent of the Russian Empire's population according to the 1897 census, lived under Russian rule. Russian colonialism used different methods to control these populations, ranging from outright Russification and attempted conversion to Orthodoxy, to cooperation and cajoling. Jadidism was born as a cultural movement stressing the education of children, economic development, emancipation of women, language reform, new forms of media such as newspapers and magazines, and the voicing of public opinion.

İsmail Bey Gasprinski (1851–1914), Crimean Tatar reformer, educator, and publicist, is seen as the intellectual founder of jadidism. Born in a small Crimean village to a family that had served in the Russian armed forces for two generations, Gasprinski became the most influential figure in the jadidist movement. Straddling two cultures, Russian and Turkic, Gasprinski (or Gaspirali as he is called in Turkish) served four years as the mayor of Bakhchisaray (Bahçesaray), the administrative center of the Crimea, from 1878 to 1882. In this period he published a seminal essay on Russian Muslims, *Russkoe musulmantsvo* (The Russian Islamic world). He was also given permission by the Russian censor to publish his newspaper, *Perevodchik/Tercüman* (The interpreter), in Russian and Turkish. During a career that spanned thirty years, Gasprinski appealed to Russian Muslims to abandon misdirected Islamic zeal and seize the tools of modernity such as modern schooling and technology. Modernity was not only compatible with Islam, he argued, but also indispensable if Muslims worldwide were to resist the intellectual assault of colonialism. His ideas found a broad audience not only in the Russian Empire but also in India, Egypt, and the rest of the Muslim world. In fact, the cultural program of modern republican Turkey, established after 1923, owed much to the jadidists. Gasprinski always remained a controversial figure because he wrote that Muslims should actually collaborate with the Russian authorities if they wanted to modernize themselves. He took the "civilizing mission" of Russian liberals at its word and appealed to the Russian authorities to stop seeing Muslims only as potentially seditious subjects but to give them the opportunity to show their loyalty. This attitude was seen by some of the more militant Russian Muslims as toadying, and the Russian authorities never really trusted Gasprinski.

OTHER PROMINENT JADDISTS

Another major figure of the jadidist movement was Yusuf Akçura (Akchurin; 1876–1935). Born in Kazan, Akçura's family moved to Istanbul where he attended the Imperial Military Academy. Exiled in 1898 to Ottoman North Africa, he escaped to Paris in 1899 where he attended the École Libre des Sciences Politique. In 1903 he went back to Kazan where he published his seminal work, *Üç Tarzı Siyaset* (Three types of politics), in which he argued for the union of all Turkic peoples of Russia. This would earn him the title "Father of Pan-Turkism." He published the newspaper *Kazan Muhbiri* (The Kazan informer) in 1904 and was among the leading organizers of the party known as the Alliance of Russian Muslims (1905). In 1920 he joined the Turkish nationalist movement in Ankara where he was a major influence on the government's program of Turkish nationalism. Akçura died in Ankara.

Ahmet Ağaoğlu (Aghayef; 1869–1939), a jadidist of the same generation, was born in Karabakh, Azerbaijan. At the insistence of his mother, he attended the local Russian gymnasium where he was introduced to Western influences. He later went to Paris where he studied under the philosopher Ernest Renan and became greatly influenced by his ideas. Another influence on the young Ağaoğlu was the Islamist militant Jamāl ad-Dīn al-Afghānī who promoted Islamist views. In 1894 Ağaoğlu returned to Azerbaijan where he struggled for the unity of Russian Muslims and founded the Difai, a secret society. In 1909, under pressure from tsarist authorities, he immigrated to the Ottoman Empire, where he joined the Young Turk movement. In this period he became a fervent advocate of Turkism, which he combined with liberal democracy. In 1921 Ağaoğlu joined the nationalists in Ankara. Yet, in his later years he adopted a critical position toward the single-party rule of Kemal Atatürk. By the time of his death he was somewhat marginalized.

Perhaps the most striking figure of all the jadidists was Sultan Galiyev (1882–c.1940). Born in a small village in Bashkortostan, Galiyev received his early education in the Tatar institute in Kazan. By the early twentieth century he came under Bolshevik influences and after the October Revolution in 1917 he was invited to join the All-Russian Islamic Congress meeting in Moscow, where he was elected to the post of general secretary. He later joined the Committee of Muslim Socialists in Kazan, which aimed to create a Muslim-Turkic state under the protection of the Soviet Union. At this point he fell out with the jadidists as his position became more socialist, and he grew more estranged from Islam. He was the primary organizer of the Islamic Red Army. By the early 1920s Galiyev had become a close associate of Vladimir Lenin and Leon Trotsky. In 1920 he was the name behind the Congress of Eastern Peoples, held in Baku. The congress appealed to all the colonized peoples to rise up against imperialism. Galiyev was later arrested by Joseph Stalin for counterrevolutionary activities and died in mysterious circumstances.

There were many other jadidists from a wide variety of political persuasions. What united them all was a solid basic education in Russian schools; being imbued with the ideals of modernity, although they interpreted them in many ways; and a feeling of belonging to an Islamic-Turkic world.

See also **Education; Young Turks.**

BIBLIOGRAPHY

Georgeon, François. *Aux origines du nationalisme turc: Yusuf Akçura, 1876-1935.* Paris, 1980.

———. "Yusuf Akura: Deuxieme Partie—Le Mouvement National des Musulmans de Russie (1905–1908)." *Central Asian Survey* 5, no. 2 (1986).

Lazzerini, Edward J. "Local Accommodation and Resistance to Colonialism in Nineteenth Century Crimea." In *Russia's Orient: Imperial Borderlands and Peoples, 1700–1917,* edited by Daniel R. Brower and Edward J. Lazzerini, 169–187. Bloomington, Ind., 1997.

Rorlich, Azade-Ayse. *The Volga Tatars: A Profile in National Resilience.* Stanford, Calif., 1986.

Zenkovsky, Serge A. *Pan-Turkism and Islam in Russia.* Cambridge, Mass., 1960.

SELIM DERINGIL

JAPAN. Europe's "long nineteenth century" coincided with a fundamental transformation in Japanese society, politics, and economics, ending seven centuries of samurai rule and bringing the country into its modern era. A chief cause of this revolution was Japan's encounter with Western, primarily European, imperialism.

BACKGROUND

By 1800, political equilibrium had been maintained in Japan for two centuries. The country had a population of roughly thirty million people and was divided into landed domains held by samurai lords (daimyo). More than 250 such domains existed in 1800, ranging from district-sized parcels to regional territories. At the apex of this political system sat the Tokugawa family, which held approximately one-quarter of all Japanese land either directly or indirectly through house vassals. The head of the Tokugawa held the position of shogun, an investiture by the emperor that made him chief of the military estate. Although in theory subordinate to the emperor, the shogun controlled foreign affairs and kept watch over the daimyo, most of whom were not allied politically with the Tokugawa.

Within his domain, each daimyo was supreme, controlling all human and material resources. Each domain contained one castle town, which served as a political and economic center for the realm. Samurai vassals of the daimyo filled administrative and military functions. Edo (now Tokyo), the castle town of the shogun and de facto capital of Japan, had a population of roughly one million persons in the nineteenth century. Since the late sixteenth century, social order had been kept by dividing the population into a four-tiered system of status groups. At the top were the samurai, the hereditary warrior caste; next were the farmers, who made up around ninety percent of the population; third in rank came artisans; and finally merchants. This Confucian-inspired system was in theory absolute, but the gradual impoverishment of many samurai and the enrichment of artisans and merchants during the eighteenth and nineteenth centuries, combined with a fair degree of mobility for peasants, made the arrangement more fluid than official ideology acknowledged.

Customs house in Yokohama, 1861. The port of Yokahama was opened to Western trade in 1859. ©CORBIS

An urbanized, literate society by 1800, Japan had tightly regulated contact with the outer world, a policy imposed by the first Tokugawa shoguns back in the early seventeenth century. For nearly two hundred years, the only Westerners allowed legally in Japan were the Dutch, who were restricted to a small manmade island in the southern port city of Nagasaki. Fear of Christian missionaries allying with anti-Tokugawa daimyo had pushed the early shoguns to prohibit both Christianity and Westerners, except for the Dutch traders. Even during the 1700s, however, Western sciences such as medicine and astronomy, and European styles of painting, were introduced into Japan, usually with official patronage.

THE CHALLENGE TO SECLUSION

In the last decade of the eighteenth century, this tightly controlled world was challenged by Western maritime powers seeking access to Japanese land and markets. The first threat came from Russian probing from the north down the Kuril Island chain. From the early 1790s, various Russian expeditions sought trading privileges, but were all rebuffed, leading to Russian pillaging of northern Japanese villages in 1806–1807 and the capture of a Russian officer, Vasili Golovnin, in 1811. In addition to these Russian threats, the appearance of both British warships in Japanese waters during the Napoleonic Wars and American whalers led to the promulgation of an 1825 edict to drive foreign ships off Japan's shores. British victory over China in the 1839–1842 Opium Wars further worried Japanese leaders about the growing threat of Western imperialism.

The first treaty signed with a Western nation, however, was with the Americans. Commodore Matthew Calbraith Perry (1794–1858) presented U.S. demands for landing rights in July 1853, and returned in March 1854 to complete a treaty. Four years later, Townsend Harris (1804–1878), acting as U.S. consul, signed the first full-fledged commercial treaty with Japan, in July 1858. Great Britain, Holland, Russia, and France quickly followed suit, inaugurating the era of the so-called unequal treaties, which included a provision of extraterritoriality, lack of tariff autonomy, and one-sided most-favored-nation (MFN) status. Domestic opposition to the presence of Western merchants in port cities such as Yokohama, which opened for trade in July 1859, led to anti-Western samurai assassinating foreigners and attacking Western targets. In response, the capitals of the most anti-Western (and anti-Tokugawa) domains were bombarded by Britain and the other treaty powers in 1863 and 1864. The resulting political crisis led to conflict between the Tokugawa *bakufu* (military government) and the two domains of Satsuma and Chôshû, which ended in the military defeat and collapse of Tokugawa power in January 1868.

ENGAGING THE WORLD

The victorious domains, led by mid-rank samurai such as Ôkubo Toshimichi (1831–1878), Kido Kôin (1833–1877), and Saigô Takamori (1828–1877), dismantled the Tokugawa *bakufu* and slowly developed a more centralized government headed by the young Meiji emperor. With the abolishment of the domains in August 1871, attention could be turned to foreign affairs. The first concerted diplomatic effort by the Meiji government was an attempt to revise the 1858 commercial treaties, in the hopes of ending extraterritoriality, regaining tariff autonomy, and extending MFN privileges to Japan. In 1871, a high-level embassy headed by Iwakura Tomomi (1825–1883) left for America and Europe to begin renegotiation. Rebuffed by U.S. Secretary of State Hamilton Fish (1808–1893) and British Foreign Secretary Granville George Leveson-Gower (Lord Granville, 1815–1891), the embassy members spent most of their time abroad until 1873 studying American and European political, economic, and social systems. A radical modernization program was adopted on their return, which was designed to strengthen Japan vis-à-vis the West and eventually achieve revision.

The early 1870s and 1880s were a period of great importation from the West, though it was done selectively. Scottish engineers such as Richard Brunton (1841–1901) built railways and bridges, and installed urban infrastructure; architects such as Josiah Condo (1852–1920) reshaped Tokyo; naval expertise was provided by Great Britain; France and, after 1870, Germany served as the model for the new conscript army; the French legal theorist Gustave Boissonade (1825–1910) helped draft Japan's new civil codes; and Germany's centralized constitution heavily influenced Itô Hirobumi (1841–1909) in the drafting of Japan's, which was promulgated in a European-style ceremony in 1889, followed a year later by the opening of the parliamentary Diet.

This importation of foreign, primarily European, expertise was accompanied by a fertile cultural exchange during the Meiji era. Until 1899, Westerners were restricted to a few foreign settlements in ports and major cities. In some of these, such as Yokohama, Kobe, and Tokyo, Japanese and Westerners readily mixed. Urban Japanese adopted the manners and customs of European daily life in dress, dining, and social activities. Tokyo was transformed in the latter nineteenth century from a small castle town of wooden houses and canals into a modern city of brick buildings and open thoroughfares, symbolized by the European-style balls given by Japan's political and social elite at Condon's architectural masterpiece, the Rokumeikan (Deer Cry Pavilion). Intellectual exchange was fostered by the British-founded Asiatic Society of Japan (1872) and cultural relations developed through bilateral groups such as the Japan Society of London (1890). Japanese art forms also greatly influenced European painters such as Vincent van Gogh (1853–1890) and Claude Monet (1840–1926).

NATIONALISM AND IMPERIALISM

Despite a flourishing trade in tea, silks, and art, Japanese-European relations were strained by the continued existence of the unequal treaties. Revision of the treaties remained the prime diplomatic goal of the Meiji government. Due in part to the Iwakura mission's failure to renegotiate, Tokyo embarked on a gradual policy of building up its regional power along with its modernization programs.

In 1874, Japanese troops invaded Formosa (Taiwan) to avenge the killing of Ryûkyûan fishermen by Formosan aborigines, thus directly asserting

Japanese officers in Western dress, 1866. The rapid westernization of Japanese society after 1854 is addressed in this engraving. A Japanese military officer in traditional dress, far right, is horrified by the Western dress of his fellow officers. ©CORBIS

Japan's interests over territory traditionally identified with China. Tokyo also incorporated the Ryûkyûan kingdom as the prefecture of Okinawa in 1879, giving Japan a presence in southern waters closer to China. Korea, however, remained Japan's key strategic concern throughout the nineteenth and early twentieth centuries. The 1876 Treaty of Kanghwa was Tokyo's first unequal treaty imposed on another country, raising tensions between Japan and China over influence on the peninsula. An 1884 Japanese-supported coup in Seoul was suppressed but resulted in the dispatch of both Japanese and Chinese troops to the kingdom.

Japan's growing regional strength and widespread domestic modernization pushed the Western powers into renegotiating the 1858 commercial treaties, though Western reluctance to surrender extraterritoriality without a comprehensive Japanese penal code, and the lack of desire to grant Tokyo tariff autonomy, made progress difficult. An 1878 tariff agreement with the United States was scuttled by Great Britain, and both bilateral and multilateral negotiations continued fitfully during the 1880s. By 1887, a draft treaty was reached, but when details of Tokyo's acquiescence in setting up courts including foreign judges were leaked, public outrage caused the resignation of Foreign Minister Inoue Kaoru (1835–1915). Two years later, nationalist fanatics attempted to assassinate Foreign Minister Marquis Okuma Shigenobu (1838–1922) over his role in revision, and negotiations again came to a temporary halt. A renewed effort in the early 1890s under the leadership of Foreign Minister Mutsu Munemitsu (1844–1897) finally resulted in a new commercial treaty with Great Britain in July 1894, followed by agreement with all remaining treaty powers. By the terms of the Aoki-Kimberley Treaty, extraterritoriality would end in 1899 and tariff autonomy would be regained in 1911, thus making Japan the first non-Western country to negotiate a position of equality with the leading European powers.

During these years, however, tensions with China over Korea had intensified. Just two weeks after signing the Aoki-Kimberley Treaty, Japan attacked Chinese naval forces in August 1894. Full-fledged war in northern China broke out, and in 1895, the Ch'ing court sued for peace, acknowledging Japan's predominant position in Korea, agreeing to pay a massive indemnity, and ceding Tokyo control over Formosa and the strategically important Liaotung Peninsula. Despite its position as the new leading East Asian hegemon, however, Tokyo was forced by Russia, France, and Germany to return Liaotung. This Triple Intervention poisoned relations with Russia and raised Japanese fears over St. Petersburg's interests in Korea and northern China.

Various attempts to reach a modus vivendi with Russia failed in the latter 1890s, and Tokyo again began to consider military force as the only guarantor of Japan's national interests. In part to assert its position in Asia, Japan sent the largest contingent of Allied troops to Peking (Beijing) in 1900 to protect the foreign settlement from the Boxer uprising. Tokyo's diplomatic masterstroke was the 1902 Anglo-Japanese Alliance, which made Japan the principal partner of Great Britain in East Asia, isolated Russia, and blocked French support for St. Petersburg (under the Franco-Russian alliance) in case of a Russo-Japanese conflict, since that would draw London in on Japan's side.

With the alliance in hand, Tokyo attempted once more to reach agreement with Russia over spheres of influence in Northeast Asia. When St. Petersburg refused to recognize Japan's special interests over Korea, and in light of Russian control over the building of the South Manchurian Railway, Tokyo launched a surprise attack in March 1904 on the Russian Pacific Fleet anchored at Port Arthur.

The Russo-Japanese War for the first time pitted an industrialized Asian nation against a European Great Power. By 1905, both sides were exhausted by the fighting and welcomed the peace mediation of U.S. President Theodore Roosevelt (1858–1919). By the terms of the Treaty of Portsmouth (1905), Japan received unfettered influence in Korea, a large indemnity, and general recognition that it was now a great power. Tokyo annexed Korea in 1905 and formally colonized it in 1910 after the assassination of governor general Itô Hirobumi, the former Japanese premier, by a Korean nationalist.

In 1912, the Meiji emperor died, ending a remarkable four-decade period of modernization, deepened cultural contact, and increased political and military conflict with Europe, and Japan's emergence as a world power. Having absorbed the lessons of European industrialization, state centralization, and imperialism, Japan was poised on the eve of World War I to expand its influence further in Asia, leading ultimately to global conflict with the West.

See also **Mukden, Battle of; Portsmouth, Treaty of; Russo-Japanese War.**

BIBLIOGRAPHY

Auslin, Michael R. *Negotiating with Imperialism: The Unequal Treaties and the Culture of Japanese Diplomacy.* Cambridge, Mass., 2004.

Beasley, William G. *Japanese Imperialism, 1894–1945.* Oxford, U.K., 1987.

Fox, Grace. *Britain and Japan, 1858–1883.* Oxford, U.K., 1969.

Iriye, Akira. "Japan's Drive to Great Power Status." In *The Cambridge History of Japan.* Vol. 5, edited by John W. Hall, et al. Cambridge, U.K., 1991.

Keene, Donald. *The Japanese Discovery of Europe, 1720–1830.* Stanford, Calif., 1969.

Lensen, George Alexander. *The Russian Push toward Japan: Russo-Japanese Relations, 1697–1875.* Princeton, N.J., 1959.

Sims, Richard. *French Policy towards the Bakufu and Meiji Japan, 1854–1895.* Kent, U.K., 1996.

MICHAEL R. AUSLIN

JARRY, ALFRED (1873–1907), French playwright, journalist, and poet.

Alfred Jarry was born on 8 September 1873 in Laval and died on 1 November 1907 in Paris. His childhood was spent in the countryside with his mother and his sister, Charlotte; his father, a tradesman, was an absent figure. Jarry was a highly able pupil who wrote poems and plays from the time he was twelve years old (preserved under the title *Ontogenie*). In 1889, at the lycée in Rennes, he encountered M. Hébert, a physics teacher whom Jarry and his classmates found ridiculous and satirized in plays and poems. This provided Jarry with the inspiration for his play *Ubu roi*.

Having settled in Paris, Jarry did not gain entry to the École Normale Supérieure, but in 1894 he joined the group associated with the journal *Mercure de France,* whose founder, Alfred Vallette, and his wife, Rachilde, became Jarry's closest friends. With Rémy de Gourmont (1858–1915), he published *L'ymagier*, an art journal dedicated to modern and ancient engravings, such as prints from Épinal, in northeastern France, and woodcuts by Albrecht Dürer (1471–1528). He traveled to Pont-Aven to meet Paul Gauguin (1848–1903) and Charles Filiger (1863–1928), about whom he wrote articles, and in Paris he associated with Henri Rousseau (1844–1910), who painted his portrait.

Alfred Jarry. Drawing by F. A. Cazals, 1897. ©BETTMANN/CORBIS

Jarry published a collection of poetry (*Les minutes de sable mémorial,* 1894), followed by a symbolist drama (*César-Antéchrist,* 1895), which brought him to the attention of the public and in particular of Stéphane Mallarmé (1842–1898). He was a close friend of Paul Valéry (1871–1945) for a time. His major achievement came in 1896, with the performance of his play *Ubu roi* at the Théâtre de l'Oeuvre; deliberately crude and primitive, this farce was shocking in a venue dedicated to the Norwegian poet and dramatist Henrik Johan Ibsen (1828–1906) and the Belgian poet, dramatist, and essayist Maurice Maeterlinck (1862–1949), not least because Jarry invented a stage set that broke with the established conventions. The huge scandal of the opening (10 December 1896) brought him fame; from then on he constantly played the character Père Ubu in his daily life, adopting the tone and figures of speech of the cowardly and grotesque buffoon—so much so that the character became a monster that devoured his personality. Jarry nevertheless produced some learned and subtle works, including *Les jours et les nuits* (1897; Days and nights), an extraordinary sequence of escapes into dreams, memories, or drugs, and *L'amour absolu* (1899; Absolute love), a still deeper exploration of early childhood that was relived through hypnotism. From 1898, Jarry adopted a bohemian life, living on the banks of the Seine, where his greatest pleasures were fishing, canoeing, and cycling, as well as drinking, which assumed an increasingly important role.

From 1901 to 1903, for the *Revue blanche,* founded by the Natanson brothers (Thadée, Alexandre, and Alfred), Jarry wrote some brilliant columns, which he called "speculations," in which he developed the absurdist idea of *pataphysics*—a snippet of news, a show, or a minuscule anecdote would pave the way for simultaneously dizzying and logical conclusions. *Pataphysics* (a term that came from *Ubu roi*) was the "science of imaginary solutions," the "science of exceptions." An absurdist concept that attempts to examine what lies beyond metaphyics, *pataphysics* parodies modern science. Jarry also wrote two novels: *Messaline*

(1901; Messalina), a set of variations on themes from antiquity; and *Le surmâle* (1902; The supermale), "a modern novel," which addresses the fascination with science and "celibate machines" that take humankind beyond its natural forces both in the realm of sexuality and in sporting records.

When publication of the *Revue blanche* ceased in April 1903, Jarry lost his main source of income and began to live in increasingly impoverished conditions. The theater continued to be a source of work: with the composer Claude Terrasse he worked on many operetta libretti and a major opéra bouffe project, based on François Rabelais's *Pantagruel* (1532), that reached a few thousand pages but never saw the light of day.

His final years were dominated by poverty. His friends were generous in their help, but his health was deteriorating; Jarry began to spend more and more time in Laval with his sister. He managed to publish three plays—*Ubu sur la butte* (1901), a new version of *Ubu roi* for puppets; *Par la taille* (1906), a protofuturist operetta; and *Le moutardier du pape* (1907). He mainly worked on two large projects: a collection of his columns entitled *La chandelle verte* and a novel, *La dragonne,* that remained unfinished despite all his efforts—the astounding extant fragments are simultaneously a genealogical reverie, a treaty on strategy, a descent into hell, and a journey in time (Jarry was an assiduous reader of H. G. Wells).

Jarry emerged from the postsymbolist crisis by inventing modern myths such as *Ubu roi* and *Le surmâle.* These figures brought Jarry the friendly curiosity of Guillaume Apollinaire (1880–1918) and Emilio Filippo Tommaso Marinetti (1876–1944), both of whom published his work in their early journals. Through them, Jarry became a tutelary figure of the avant-garde, admired by the dadaists and the surrealists, particularly the poet André Breton (1896–1966) and the artist Marcel Duchamp (1887–1968).

See also **Avant-Garde; Fin de Siècle; France.**

BIBLIOGRAPHY

Primary Sources

Jarry, Alfred. *Oeuvres completes: Textes établis, présentés, et annotés par Michel Arrivé.* 3 vols. Paris, 1972–1988.

Secondary Sources

Arnaud, Noël. *Alfred Jarry: d'Ubu roi au Docteur Faustroll.* Paris, 1974.

Besnier, Patrick. *Alfred Jarry.* Paris, 2005.

Fell, Jill. *Alfred Jarry: An Imagination in Revolt.* Madison, N.J., 2005.

PATRICK BESNIER

JAURÈS, JEAN (1859–1914), French politician.

In the collective memory of the French, there are few who embody, as did Jean-Joseph-Marie-Auguste Jaurès, the faculty for being in politics and still considering political action as an ethical priority. For nearly twenty years, with an interruption in the legislature from 1898 to 1902, he was one of the prominent figures in parliamentary life, though he never participated in any government. Even his adversaries recognized his exceptional skill as an orator. He could not only sway the course of an assembly deliberation, but also speak to the people in a language that revealed to them the better world they each had within them. The father of the unification of the various French socialist movements into one single party, and a staunch opponent of war, he was murdered on 31 July 1914, making him more than just the "hero killed ahead of the armies" as Anna-Élisabeth Mathieu de Noailles (1876–1933) sang, but the sacrificed prophet of peace.

THE SHAPING OF AN INTELLECTUAL

Jean Jaurès did not emerge from the laboring classes. His father, Jules Jaurès, was an unsuccessful businessman, but by the time of his death, in 1882, Jules was the landlord of a seven-hectare farm, the Fedial, near Castres, the county seat of the Tarn. It was in Castres where Jean, on 3 September 1859, and his younger brother Louis were born. Their mother, Marie-Adélaide Barbaza, from a Catholic family, was a good example of the middle bourgeoisie of Castres.

They lived in relative ease: Jean entered his native town's secondary public school at age ten on a scholarship. His ascension was exemplary in that it was first and foremost due to his excellent school results. In 1876 he received a scholarship to attend prep school in Paris for the entrance exam to the École Normale Supérieure of Ulm Street (ENS). Two years later, he was placed first at the ENS, ahead of Henri-Louis Bergson (1859–1941). Like Bergson, Jaurès leaned toward philosophy; in 1881 he was placed third on the certification exam (*agrégation*), this time behind Bergson. Among the most important people he met at the ENS was Lucien Herr, who was named ENS librarian in 1889, and who had exercised his influence on a number of students, making him an eminent figure in "intellectual socialism."

Appointed at his request to the Albi high school, in 1883 Jaurès began teaching an undergraduate seminar and a class on moral philosophy at the University of Toulouse. He remained a professor in his ways and was always conscious of a teacher's social role, be it as the Toulouse mayor's adjunct in 1890, or as a collaborator, from 1905 to his death, in the *Revue de l'enseignement primaire et primaire supérieur* (Review of primary and middle school education). He was also always an astonishing "reader," a name he adopted when signing the literary chronicles he contributed to *La dépêche de Toulouse* as of 1893. When he came to Toulouse to give a lecture in support of the railway workers who had been dismissed after their strike of 1910, he spoke of the Russian novelist and moral philosopher Leo Tolstoy. This choice is perhaps enough to measure the cultural contrast between that era and the early twenty-first century.

A YOUNG REPUBLICAN DEPUTY

Jaurès's parliamentary career began before his studies ended. He was twenty-six years old when he entered the Palais-Bourbon in 1885, elected on the republican list of his département of the Tarn. His young age may alone explain the discretion of his first mandate, which was not renewed in 1889. He returned to his teaching and his studies, but especially to his loved ones—that same year, he and his wife, Louise, whom he had married in 1886, had a daughter named Madeleine. He wrote his two theses, the French and the Latin, *De la réalité du monde* sensible (Of the reality of the world), and defended them at the Sorbonne in the beginning of 1892.

This initial relationship between metaphysical reflection and political commitment is essential in understanding how Jaurès subsequently made sure that words and action went hand in hand. First, his metaphysics amounted to total trust in mankind, but without completely negating God, an idea that had a place in his quest for moral perfection and social harmony. His ideas, therefore, distanced him from the "secularism" of his comrades. Second, he understood that he was on the wrong path in thinking, as he wrote in 1897, "that by logical and interior evolution, the entire governmental Republic must be bent on the idea of social equality, and on the fraternal organization of work and property." As of 1886, when defending his proposal for a law on worker pensions, he had declared himself a partisan of the "socialist idea."

Strengthened by this ascension and the experience he gained as a member of the Toulouse municipal council, and upon the request of the Socialists in the small industrial town of Carmaux, Jaurès ran for election in the fall of 1892, and won by a small margin on the French Labor Party program of Jules Guesde (1845–1922). He remained loyal to a constituency still strongly influenced by the notables of old, such as the Solages and Reille families, and within which the indecisive balance between labor votes and farmer votes made any majority doubtful. He was devoted both to the Carmaux miners, who ran a difficult strike in 1892, and also to the glass workers engaged in a struggle with their employer, Rességuier, both on location and in the National Assembly. Workers found in him not only a representative eager to plead for conciliation and arbitration, but, more importantly, the organizer of a mobilization that resulted in the creation of a Workers' Cooperative inaugurated on 25 October 1896.

THE ORATOR

On 21 November 1893, Jaurès engineered the fall of the government, achieving immediate celebrity. He criticized the prime minister (president of the council) Charles Alexandre Dupuy (1851–1923), a longtime academy inspector, for holding to the narrow rationalism of new popular education, and disguising it as social policy: "You've interrupted the old song that was human misery's lullaby... and human misery has woken up screaming, it has stood up before you and today it demands its rightful place, its great place in the sun of the natural world, the only one you have not yet eclipsed."

Jaurès's eloquence moved from his teacher's lectern to the podium of the National Assembly and to the stage of the political meeting, from the struggle for socialist unity to the "war on war" campaign. The election of some forty socialist deputies in the summer of 1893 stimulated him. Discreet, reserved, as a young republican deputy, Jaurès was now in the foreground as a socialist orator. When Alexandre-Félix-Joseph Ribot (1842–1923) asked him the explanation for this change, noted by all who remembered him when he first got to the National Assembly, Jaurès made this answer, which sheds light on his progression toward socialism: "I was like a volcano spewing out ice." For the author Jean Guéhenno, who as a child saw Jaurès speak in 1906 at Fougères, in Brittany, during the great strike of the shoe industry workers,

> he had became the Orator, in the deepest sense that word could have meant in ancient republics. *Orator*. The man who speaks and thus defines the world, gives it life for us men, and cleans it up, corrects its mistakes, if need be, the man who pleads and persuades and convinces and who begs, and who slowly changes us and converts us to justice and truth. (p. 44)

THE *DREYFUSARD*

The Dreyfus affair was one of the great battles of Jaurès's life. He was not an early *dreyfusard*, or supporter of Alfred Dreyfus (1859–1935), but he was certainly one of the most persevering. In his case it was not, as it was for Émile Zola (1840–1902), out of an aversion to anti-Semitism that he embraced the cause of Captain Dreyfus. Militarism was his true enemy, that is, the caste spirit that continued to permeate an army that successive governments, in his mind, had not dared, or did not know how, to turn into a truly republican institution. So he first attacked the military court system, this special tribunal, free to condemn on the basis of "evidence" that it had itself fabricated.

Les Preuves (Proof) was precisely the title he gave his articles in *La petite république socialiste* in August 1898. To the comrades of the French Labor Party, for whom "only class struggle and social revolution matter," he answered straightaway: "If Dreyfus ... is innocent, then he is stripped of all class characteristics by the very extent of the disaster.... In revolutionary combat, we can still keep human guts; to remain socialist, we are not obligated to flee outside of humanity." His political commitment, cemented with the publication of *J'accuse* by Zola, on 13 January—he testified at Zola's trial on 12 February—cost him his seat as a deputy on 8 May, in favor of the Marquis de Solages. Jaurès refused a second-round sure election in Paris.

He therefore had more time on his hands. He used it first to advocate for Dreyfus, particularly in his own region in the south of France. After the incoherent verdict pronounced by the court of appeals in Rennes—Dreyfus was found guilty again but this time with extenuating circumstances—the issue of presidential pardon came up, which Jaurès, against Georges Clemenceau (1841–1929), advised that Dreyfus should accept. But he urged Dreyfus to pursue the struggle until fully rehabilitated. And it was Jaurès who, upon returning to the National Assembly in 1902, relaunched the case in order to get the appeals court to definitively repair the injustice, which it did in 1906. The greater freedom that his electoral defeat in 1898 brought him also enabled him to begin writing his *Histoire socialiste de la Révolution francaise* (1901–1907; Socialist history of the French Revolution). Then he participated in the debate triggered among socialists by the entrance of their parliamentary leader, Alexandre Millerand (1859–1943), into the government of "republican defense" formed by Pierre-Marie-René Waldeck-Rousseau (1846–1904) on 22 June 1899. Millerand worked alongside General Gaston-Alexandre-Auguste de Galliffet (1830–1909), one of those responsible for the repression of the Commune of Paris in 1871.

FROM THE "LEFTIST BLOC" TO SOCIALIST UNITY

Jaurès approved of socialists participating in the government, and therefore of the choice of partial reform, even though this was difficult to reconcile with the socialist project of immediate and integral revolution. In his eyes, action in service of the working class did not exclude putting republican institutions to good use—or better still, reforming those institutions, subject to democratic consent. To put this kind of reform into effect, two kinds of organization had to be created: the trade union and the party. Jaurès therefore opted for a model of "social democracy" that fell far short of winning consensus in his own party. He took as priorities the strengthening of trade unions, both in organizing labor and in labor disputes, as well as the need for unity between various socialist groups, such as supporters of Guesde, Paul Brousse (1844–1912), Édouard-Marie Vaillant (1840–1915), or the supporters of Jean Allemane (1843–1935) or the independents.

Unity took a long time coming because this diversity was the product of the very history of the French labor movement. In 1899–1900, Jaurès failed in his attempt to have a Belgian-style formula adopted, in which the party would gather together professional, union, and political organizations. The General Confederation of Labor (CGT), created in 1895, mistrusted parliamentary action and leaned toward revolutionary syndicalism. As of 1902, competition intensified between the Socialist Party of France of Guesde and Vaillant and Jaurès's own French Socialist Party. Jaurès was one of the principal supporters of the government of Emile Combes (1835–1921). From January 1903 to January 1904, he was vice-president of the National Assembly and one of the most active members of the leftist delegation, on whom the prime minister relied. Once Combes was overthrown, Jaurès played a determining role in the process that resulted in the separation of church and state on 9 December 1905. He and Aristide Briand, deputy of Saint-Étienne, and reporter of the law, devised a formula for "religious associations" formed according to the "rules for the overall organization of religion" that was acceptable to Catholics.

The French Section of the Workers' International (Section Française de l'Internationale Ouvrière or SFIO) emerged during a 23–26 April meeting held in Paris, at the Globe Hall. But this had required the intervention of the International at its congress in Amsterdam (August 1904). In appearance at least, Guesde's views were preferred to those of Jaurès. But other struggles would allow Jaurès to consolidate his political rise, particularly the actions of the wine makers of the south in 1907. As a man who was introduced early on to the condition of farmers, especially in the south, he could hardly be indifferent to their struggles. At the congress of Toulouse of 1908, his motion, adopted almost unanimously, enabled the SFIO, until then a minimal association between rival organizations, to become a full-fledged modern party.

THE CAUSE FOR PEACE

"The Party is making me who I am," Jaurès said and why not believe it? But the party did not absorb all of his energy. Man of the verb, he was naturally a man of the press. He contributed regularly to the *Dépêche de Toulouse* from 1887 to 1914, and was the political director of *La petite république* from 1898 to 1903. He also created and ran his own periodical, *L'humanité,* beginning in 1904. This was certainly a "socialist paper," but was not the paper of the Socialist Party. An "open Tribune" was added to it in August 1906, open to the CGT. The paper experienced financial problems in 1906–1907, but by 1912 a print run of eighty thousand copies was achieved. Changing the format to a six-page daily in January 1913 proved to be a lucrative decision, as the number of copies printed reached 150,000 in 1914.

In *L'humanité,* young intellectuals such as Jean-Richard Bloch joined with the older Dreyfus supporters such as Anatole France to support Jaurès in his fight for peace. This fight was not only inspired by the rise of nationalism that followed the Franco-German crisis of 1905. Jaurès was also worried about the turn that the French colonial venture was taking in both Algeria and Tunisia. For Jaurès, the effects of nationalism were threatening for more reasons than their continued nurturing of the possibility of war between France and Germany. It seemed to him that the weakening of the Ottoman Empire was the greatest factor in the instability of a Europe where, as he foresaw in 1895, the rivalry between the "imperial societies" bore "war within them as rain clouds bear a storm." As early as 1896 he had interceded in support of the persecuted Armenians, and in 1908 he put all his hope in the "Young Turks" revolution. The Balkan Wars (1912–1913) cemented his conviction that modern war could only be a horrific massacre. But he had not waited for that moment, he had already begun unrelentingly spreading what the French politician Vincent Auriol (1884–1966) called his "apostle's faith" at the service of peace.

Already in 1907 at the SFIO congress in Nancy (France) and at the congress of the International in Stuttgart (Germany), he had asked that the struggle against war become a priority, even if that meant calling a labor strike. In his *Armée nouvelle* (New army) project, in 1911, he elaborated on his conception of national defense, based on popular mobilization when democratic principles were threatened. He won a decision from the International's political bureau to hold a special congress at Bâle, on 24 and 25 November 1912. In France he participated in the campaign against the lengthening of military service to three years, which culminated in the meeting at Pré-Saint-Gervais on 25 May 1913. When the military law was passed in July, Jaurès became the target of harsh attacks. Some, such as the writer Charles-Pierre Péguy (1873–1914), his former admirer, accused him of weakening a preparation for war that had now become necessary. Others reproached him for his blind trust in German social-democrats.

Le Petit Parisien

5 centimes Le plus fort tirage des journaux du monde entier 5 centimes

HEURES TRAGIQUES

La situation internationale s'aggrave :

A la mobilisation partielle russe répond la mobilisation générale autrichienne

A l'état de siège déclaré en Allemagne répondent de sérieuses mesures militaires françaises

ON A ASSASSINÉ JAURÈS

La situation

L'effort militaire est activé partout

Une proclamation du gouvernement

L'action diplomatique n'est pas arrêtée

L'assassinat

JEAN JAURÈS

L'ARRESTATION DE L'ASSASSIN

Newspaper report of the assassination of Jaurès, 1 August 1914. Bibliothèque Historique de la Ville de Paris, Paris, France/Bridgeman Art Library/Archives Charmet

THE FIRST CASUALTY OF THE WAR

The results of the polls of April–May 1914 showed that his arguments had weight: for the first time, 103 Socialists would sit in the National Assembly. But he would only be hated more for it. After the assassination of the Austrian archduke Francis Ferdinand in Sarajevo on 28 June, he doubled his efforts to save the peace. On 14 July at the SFIO congress in Paris, he passed a vote for "a simultaneously and internationally organized labor strike." On 18 July, in *L'humanité,* he stated that "whatever our adversaries may say, there is no contradiction in making the maximum effort to ensure peace and, if this war breaks out in spite of us, in making the maximum effort to ensure the independence and integrity of the Nation."

On the morning of 31 July, Jaurès's last article for *L'humanité* appeared, entitled "Keeping Calm Is Necessary." The German ultimatum was given to the French government during the day. On that last night of peace, Jaurès was dining at the Café du Croissant, only a stone's throw away from the paper's offices, at 142 Monmartre Street when a stranger, Raoul Villain, shot him at point-blank range. The announcement of his death on 1 August, the day of general mobilization, was the first act of the "sacred union" to which the president of the republic Raymond Poincaré called the French in his address to Parliament on 4 August. Also on 4 August, the day of Jaurès's funeral, Paul-Eugène-Louis Deschanel, president of the National Assembly, saluted Jaurès as a "martyr to his ideas," and the secretary general of the CGT, Léon Jouhaux, vowed before the coffin to rally labor to this "sacred union," which the German war declaration justified, and to endorse the duty of defending their "homeland in danger."

THE LEFT GRATEFUL TO A GREAT MAN

The cult of Jaurès began the very day following the assassination. But after so many hateful attacks, and such a complete failure of the international strike-to-save-the-peace project, consensus would not be without ambiguities. Once dead, Jaurès took his place in the arsenal of symbols used by the Left. The symbol was both unifying and pacifist. But this unity—forged in the anger triggered by the acquittal of his murderer on 29 March 1919, which brought out 100,000 to 150,000 people to protest in Paris on 6 April—was followed by a split between socialists and communists at the congress of Tours in December 1920, and by the problematic union of the leftist cartel, which, in 1924, having won a majority in the elections, decided to transfer Jaurès's ashes to the Pantheon. While Carmaux miners stood by the catafalque on 23 November, communist activists protested outside the official funeral procession. "We keep him for ourselves," declared Léon Blum (1872–1950) in the name of socialists, "but in keeping him we also give him to the Nation and to history."

At the end of February 1895, Theodor Herzl, a correspondent in Paris for the big Austrian daily newspaper *Neue freie Presse,* both an admiring and railing witness of French political mores, wanted to record a speech by Jaurès on a cylinder. On this cylinder, he suggested, future generations could find the magic of a "rhapsodist," a worthy heir to Léon Gambetta, and "all the resonance of the insane agitation that has marked the public life of a great nation." He still asked himself: "will they be moved, or will they rail us and wonder what the reason was for all this noise?" Barring any unforeseen discovery, there is no reason to believe Jaurès's voice was ever recorded. But his word lives on. This is undoubtedly because, being a utopian thinker rather than a realist politician, he posed questions about property, justice, science and faith, defense and peace that are all essential for the future of democratic societies. And these questions have not lost any of their pertinence, because they cannot be given any definitive answers. The ultimate lesson Jaurès taught us is found in his untiring efforts to overcome a contradiction: too sincere a republican to believe in the imminence of the revolution but too passionate a socialist to be satisfied with the Republic as it was, he saw politics as the means to "bring all men to enjoy the fullness of humanity." Who would want to renounce that ambition today?

See also **Dreyfus Affair; First International; France; Pacifism; Socialism.**

BIBLIOGRAPHY

Goldberg, Harvey. *The Life of Jean Jaurès.* Madison, Wis., 1962.

Guéhenno, Jean. *La mort des autres.* Paris, 1968.

Jaurès, Jean. *Œuvres.* 4 vols. Paris, 2000–2001.

Launay, Michel. *Jaurès orateur ou l'oiseau rare.* Paris, 2000.

Levy-Bruhl, Lucien. *Jean Jaurès: Esquisse biographique.* Paris, 1924.

Rabaut, Jean. *Jean Jaurès.* Paris, 1981.

Rappoport, Charles. *Jean Jaurès: L'homme, le penseur, le socialiste.* Paris, 1915. Rev. ed, edited by Claudie Weill and Daniel Lindenberg. Paris, 1984.

Rebérioux, Madeleine. *Jaurès: La parole et l'acte.* Paris, 1994.

Rioux, Jean-Pierre. *Jean Jaurès.* Paris, 2005.

JEAN-FRANÇOIS CHANET

JELAČIĆ, JOSIP (1801–1859), Croatian military leader.

Josip Jelačić served as Ban (governor) of Croatia and head of the armies of Croatia and the Croatian-Slavonian sections of the Habsburg military frontier during the Hungarian Revolution of 1848–1849. In his military capacity, he led Habsburg forces against the revolutionary Hungarian government. He enjoys a mixed legacy as a Croatian patriot, archconservative, and rabid Hungarophobe.

Jelačić was born on 16 October 1801, in the town of Petrovaradin. He was educated in Vienna at the Theresianum. In 1819 he was commissioned an officer in the Habsburg army. In 1830 he was named commander of the 7th Regiment in Ogulin (in the military frontier). He later served under Joseph Radetzky in northern Italy, in Dalmatia, and finally as the commander of the 1st Banal Regiment in Glina. He is said to have only been truly at home among his frontiersmen. During the years before 1848, he developed a profound Croatian patriotism and a no less profound loyalty to his Habsburg emperors. Jelačić was an enthusiastic supporter of the Illyrian movement, which had many adherents among the frontier military class.

Jelačić was named Ban of Croatia by the Croatian Sabor (diet) on 23 March 1848. He was confirmed in this position by the Habsburg emperor Ferdinand a week later. The Sabor and the emperor (more likely, his advisers) supported Jelačić for different reasons. The Illyrians in Zagreb saw him as a person whose loyalty to the monarch could not be questioned, but whose Croatian patriotism might allow Croatia to emerge from the revolutionary period with some gains. Vienna saw Jelačić as a popular but conservative Croat whose appointment would satisfy Croatian nationalism and serve to nip in the bud any Croatian independence movement, should one develop. Jelačić's appointment served to heighten antagonism between Croatia and Hungary. Ultimately, Vienna was more right than Zagreb.

The Hungarian government was displeased by the appointment of Jelačić as ban, not least because it was ignored in the process. As a constituent part of the kingdom of Hungary, it was normal practice for the Hungarian government to appoint and confirm bans of Croatia. On 12 April 1848, Jelačić was called to Buda by the palatine (emperor's representative) of Hungary, but Jelačić, exhibiting a tendency that he would develop further, simply refused to go. At this point, he took the position that he understood the needs of the empire better than the imperial government. The new Hungarian government continued to insist that Jelačić was an unconstitutional ban whose behavior was treasonous; Vienna's position would waver over time.

One of Jelačić's first acts as ban of Croatia was to deny Hungarian sovereignty over Croatia/Slavonia. He also enacted some of the changes that the Illyrians had demanded earlier, including incrementally expanding the franchise. On 5 June 1848, he was installed as ban with the oath given by Josip Rajačić, the metropolitan of the Serbian Orthodox church. This event had mixed meanings. Rajačić had come to Zagreb at the head of a delegation that demanded an end to Hungarian control of Serbian regions of southern Hungary and the elevation of the metropolitan of the Serbian Orthodox church to the position of patriarch. He also hoped to forge a Croato-Serbian alliance against revolutionary Hungary. The bishop of Zagreb had left the city, which left Rajačić to administer the oath of office (to preserve their emperor and the triune kingdom) to Jelačić. The event has thus been described as an example of Yugoslavism in action. Jelačić, who probably felt the pull of brotherhood with the Serbs, was primarily interested in freeing Croatia from Hungarian tutelage, while Rajačić's own goals were more determinedly Serbian. As long as the goals demanded united action, united the Croats and Serbs could be.

Jelačić's most memorable and lasting acts came as a military leader. In June, the revolutionary Hungarian government of Lajos Kossuth and Lajos Batthyány demanded once again that the imperial government remove Jelačić from his positions; Emperor Ferdinand signed off on this proposal, but Jelačić simply ignored him. On 11 September 1848, Jelačić led his troops into Hungary, where they discovered that Hungarian troops wished to avoid any real fight. Jelačić's troops acted in accord with frontier tradition, which, in battle with the Ottomans, called for looting and generally bad behavior. Jelačić thus contributed to the radicalization of the Hungarian peasantry and the loss of the propaganda war between Austria and Hungary. On 29 September, Croatian troops lost the Battle of Pakozd, southwest of Budapest, to Hungarian forces. A day before that battle, the imperial commissioner to Hungary, Ferenc Lamberg, was murdered in Budapest. The murder served to fully sever relations between Hungary's revolutionary government and Vienna. From that point, Vienna backed Jelačić. On 3 October Jelačić was named commander in chief of imperial forces in Hungary.

During action in Hungary, revolution broke out in Vienna. Jelačić decided at that point to split his forces and take the main body to Vienna in support of the emperor. This he did in late October 1848, his forces contributing to the bombardment of Vienna and the collapse of the revolution there. In April 1849, Jelačić's forces were back in the field in Hungary, but they were exhausted and ineffective. When the Hungarian revolution was crushed, it was crushed by Russian intervention, not a crusading Croatian frontiersman and ban. By the time Jelačić could return to Vienna and then Zagreb, the absolutist regime of Alexander von Bach had tightened its grip on imperial political life. The Croatian Sabor was suspended. Jelačić's dream of an autonomous Croatia within a restructured federal empire died. Jelačić himself died an unhappy man in 1859.

See also **Austria-Hungary; Gaj, Ljudevit; Kossuth, Lajos; Nationalism; Revolutions of 1848.**

BIBLIOGRAPHY

Deák, Istvan. *The Lawful Revolution: Luis Kossuth and the Hungarians, 1848–1849.* New York, 1979.

Tanner, Marcus. *Croatia: A Nation Forged in War.* New Haven, Conn., 1997.

NICHOLAS MILLER

JENA, BATTLE OF. On the morning of 14 October 1806, Napoleon I attacked the Prussian army under Prince Friedrich Ludwig Hohenlohe west of Jena. Napoleon did not realize, and later tried to minimize, the fact that his troops outnumbered the Prussians by more than two to one (96,000 to 38,000). Although French tactics were more flexible, the Prussians fought well on the whole. Indeed, according to French accounts, the Prussian infantry attacked and counterattacked on several occasions, splitting the French forces and driving them back. But the Prussians were too few, never pushed their advantages, and permitted the French to grow in strength throughout the fight. After six hours of intense combat, the French attacked in force. Two hours later the Prussian army broke and fled in disarray. The French sustained 5,000 casualties; the Prussians 11,000 plus 15,000 captured.

Meanwhile, 19 kilometers (12 miles) north of Jena at Auerstedt, an epic defensive battle took place. Marshal Louis-Nicolas Davout, with a single corps, met and defeated the main Prussian army under the Duke of Brunswick (63,000 men), a force more than twice the size of Davout's corps (26,000 men). At approximately the same time Napoleon attacked Hohenlohe at Jena, Davout encountered the Prussians at Auerstedt. Although the Prussian cavalry attacked at will, it accomplished little against the French squares. When the Duke of Brunswick was mortally wounded early in the fight, King Frederick William III personally assumed command, and the situation for the Prussians improved. But after five hours of battle, just when the Prussians were about to turn the French flank, Davout's last division arrived, threw the Prussians back, and turned their flank instead. Shortly after noon, the Prussian army broke completely. The victory was Davout's, and it was complete, but the cost had been high. French casualties were more than 25 percent killed and wounded. Few French units of any size escaped unharmed. The Prussians suffered more, with 12,000 killed or wounded and 3,000 captured.

IMMEDIATE AFTERMATH

Following this double disaster, the Prussian army disintegrated before the rapid and ruthless French pursuit. The retreat was poorly planned and directed. Supply and transport broke down completely. Too many units dissolved into undisciplined masses intent only on escaping the pursuing French. Fortresses and depots, where troops might have been reorganized and reequipped to fight another day, were surrendered by their commanders, most without a fight. A year earlier Napoleon had destroyed the Austro-Russian coalition in three months. Now he overran Prussia in as many weeks.

ANALYSIS OF THE BATTLES

Major credit for destroying the Prussian army must go to Davout. Without question, the major battle was fought at Auerstedt, not at Jena. Had Davout been overrun on 14 October, the Prussians might have escaped to join the Russians, making a final French victory over the coalition more difficult. Considering another alternative, had the Prussians defeated Davout at Auerstedt, they might have concentrated against Napoleon at Jena and handed Napoleon his first major defeat. Indeed, this is what Napoleon feared the most. That is why when Napoleon heard of the extent of Davout's victory at Auerstedt, he refused to believe it. After two days of pouting, Napoleon finally accepted the facts and wrote Davout a letter of congratulations, but he stated that it was for Davout's subordinate generals and men. Even on the battle streamers of the French regiments that fought at either battle, Napoleon had *Jena*, not *Auerstedt*, emblazoned.

Napoleon had misjudged where the major Prussian army lay and thus gave his full attention to the action at Jena and none to that at Auerstedt. When he moved on the false assumption that the main Prussian army lay before him, Napoleon's imagination took over. By late afternoon, he had convinced himself he had 60,000 or more Prussians before him, when he actually had less than half that number. Napoleon also benefited at Jena from the actions of good subordinates, most notably Marshal Jean

Lannes. But he also had an obliging enemy. The Prussians went far toward defeating themselves, both at Jena and Auerstedt. They had grossly overestimated the strength and effectiveness of their own army. They had advanced without waiting for the Russians, extended their forces westward, and made themselves vulnerable to a French counterstroke. They had no effective central command, the armies of Brunswick and Hohenlohe were separated, and there was little coordination between the two.

THE LARGER PICTURE

Many contemporaries at the time, and many historians since, have seen these battles as a confrontation between the old and the new, in which the traditional was measured against the modern and found wanting. But the Prussian army in 1806 was not the museum piece so widely accepted among historians and critics over the past two centuries. On the contrary, the Prussian army was among the most enlightened military establishments of the Napoleonic era. It had the Militärische Gesellschaft (Military Society), an academic society where officers gathered weekly to discuss the changing art of war. This was the first and only military study group of its time, and had members from practically every garrison in Prussia. Their discussions covered the entire spectrum of war and laid the foundation for the later reform of the Prussian army after its defeat at Jena and Auerstedt. Prussia also had the first true general staff in the modern sense, as well as educational institutions designed specifically to develop leaders. In theory, Prussia had both the organization and intellect that would enable it to meet the challenge of the French. All that remained was the test of battle. And there Prussia failed.

In the final analysis, the inexperienced Prussian army fought the most seasoned and experienced army in the world. In the decade before Jena and Auerstedt, while the Prussians were at peace, the French army had been waging war almost unceasingly. Additionally, Prussian senior leaders were not motivated by a dominant strategic vision, nor did they possess Napoleon's energy and ruthlessness. Before any shot was fired, the Prussians had allowed Napoleon to concentrate an enormous amount of combat power in an area from which he threatened the very existence of the Prussian state. What made the difference at Jena and Auerstedt was the lack of personal initiative among Prussian commanders; poor coordination among their forces and within each command; a lack of a combined arms doctrine between infantry, cavalry, and artillery; and a weak, almost nonexistent, central control. And yet, seven years after Jena and Auerstedt, Prussia fielded one of the finest armies of the Napoleonic era. The rapid rejuvenation of the Prussian army in this short span demonstrated that the old system was by no means totally decrepit, as so many people then and now still believe.

See also **French Revolutionary Wars and Napoleonic Wars; Napoleon; Prussia.**

BIBLIOGRAPHY

Chandler, David G. *Jena, 1806: Napoleon Destroys Prussia.* London, 1993.

Gates, David. *The Napoleonic Wars, 1803–1815.* London, 1997.

Lettow-Vorbeck, Oscar von. *Der Krieg von 1806 und 1807.* Vol. 1: *Jena und Auerstedt.* Berlin, 1899.

Maude, F. N. *The Jena Campaign, 1806.* 1909. Reprint, London, 1998.

Paret, Peter. "Jena and Auerstedt." In his *Understanding War: Essays on Clausewitz and the History of Military Power,* 85–92. Princeton, N.J., 1992.

Petre, F. Loraine. *Napoleon's Conquest of Prussia, 1806.* 1907. Reprint, London, 1993.

Showalter, Dennis E. "Hubertusberg to Auerstädt: The Prussian Army in Decline." *German History* 12, no. 3 (1994): 308–333.

CHARLES E. WHITE

JENNER, EDWARD (1749–1823), English physician.

Edward Jenner is commonly regarded as the simple country doctor who, by recognizing the value of prudential folk-knowledge, and by acting with selfless determination to promote his "discovery" of vaccination, started the long march toward the ultimate eradication of smallpox, as yet the only disease to have been effectively eliminated through human endeavor. However, since the 1980s some historical scholarship has sought to explode this myth of heroic individualism by emphasizing the broader medical context in which Jenner operated and by demonstrating how the ultimate acceptance of vaccination was due as much to the effectiveness of his social networks and the efforts of his supporters as to any intrinsic "scientific" superiority over alternative practices.

EARLY LIFE AND EDUCATION

Edward Jenner was born in Berkeley, Gloucestershire, on 17 May 1749 to Sarah Jenner (née Head) and her husband, Stephen, the local vicar. He was the eighth of nine children, and one of six to survive childhood. In October 1754, when Edward was just nine years old, his mother died during childbirth; his father followed just two months later. Orphaned, Edward was cared for by his sisters.

In 1764 Jenner was apprenticed to an apothecary in Chipping Sodbury. Six years later he traveled to London to perfect his knowledge of anatomy and surgery. In the metropolis, the simple country surgeon of legend assimilated himself into a social network that encompassed some of the most influential natural philosophers of the late Enlightenment, including the surgeons John Hunter (1728–1793), Everard Home (1756–1832), and Henry Cline (1750–1827), and the botanist Joseph Banks (1743–1820).

In 1772 Jenner returned to Berkeley to practice as a surgeon-apothecary, remaining there for much of the rest of his life. In March 1788, at the age of thirty-eight, he married Catherine Kingscote (1760/1–1815), the daughter of a wealthy local gentry family. During their relatively short life together they had three children, Edward (1789–1810), Catherine (1794–1833), and Robert Fitzharding (1797–1854).

Jenner entertained a wide range of intellectual interests in poetry, botany, and natural history and was elected to the Royal Society in 1789. The importance of sociability to the practice of medicine in this period is evident in his reputation as a fine host and in the names of two local bodies of which he was a member, the Convivio-Medical Society of Alveston and the Medico-Convivial Society, which he helped to establish at Rodborough in 1788.

VACCINATION

Smallpox, a disfiguring and potentially lethal disease, was virtually endemic in eighteenth-century Britain and was the subject of considerable medical and public debate. The practice of inoculation, by which matter from the pustule of a smallpox victim was introduced into the skin of a healthy person to produce a mild immunizing infection, had been introduced into Britain by Lady Mary Wortley Montagu in 1721. Inoculation had received the support of the Royal College of Physicians in 1754 and was a fairly widespread practice by the end of the eighteenth century. Inoculation had its problems, however. Although rare, it was not unknown for inoculated persons to develop full-blown smallpox. Fears were also expressed that it could lead to the outbreak of an epidemic among the uninoculated population.

Jenner seems to have long been aware of the idea, prevalent in the rural areas of western England, that those who contracted cowpox, a similar, but much milder and more localized disease present in cattle, never caught smallpox. He had discussed the matter with friends and colleagues in the early 1770s but it was not until the 1790s that he undertook preliminary investigations. In 1796 Jenner (now a physician, courtesy of the University of St. Andrew's) recorded his first attempt to inoculate using cowpox matter, which was taken from the pustule of a milkmaid, Sarah Nelmes (who had allegedly contracted it from a cow called Blossom), and given to a boy named James Phipps. Jenner subsequently inoculated Phipps with smallpox, but the boy remained unaffected, suggesting that cowpox had indeed conferred immunity to the disease. Jenner intended to publish his findings in the *Philosophical Transactions* but was discouraged from doing so by Home and Banks. He thus undertook further investigations before publishing his *Inquiry into … Cowpox* (1798). In this and subsequent publications he asserted that cowpox could offer lifelong immunity to smallpox and could be serially transferred from arm to arm.

Vaccination (a term deriving from the Latin *vacca* for "cow"), excited much interest, but also aroused a great deal of controversy among those who were attached to the existing practice of inoculation and those who were opposed, morally and/or intellectually, to the introduction of pathological animal matter into the human body. Despite this, however, Jenner's theories gained ground, not least because of his social connections.

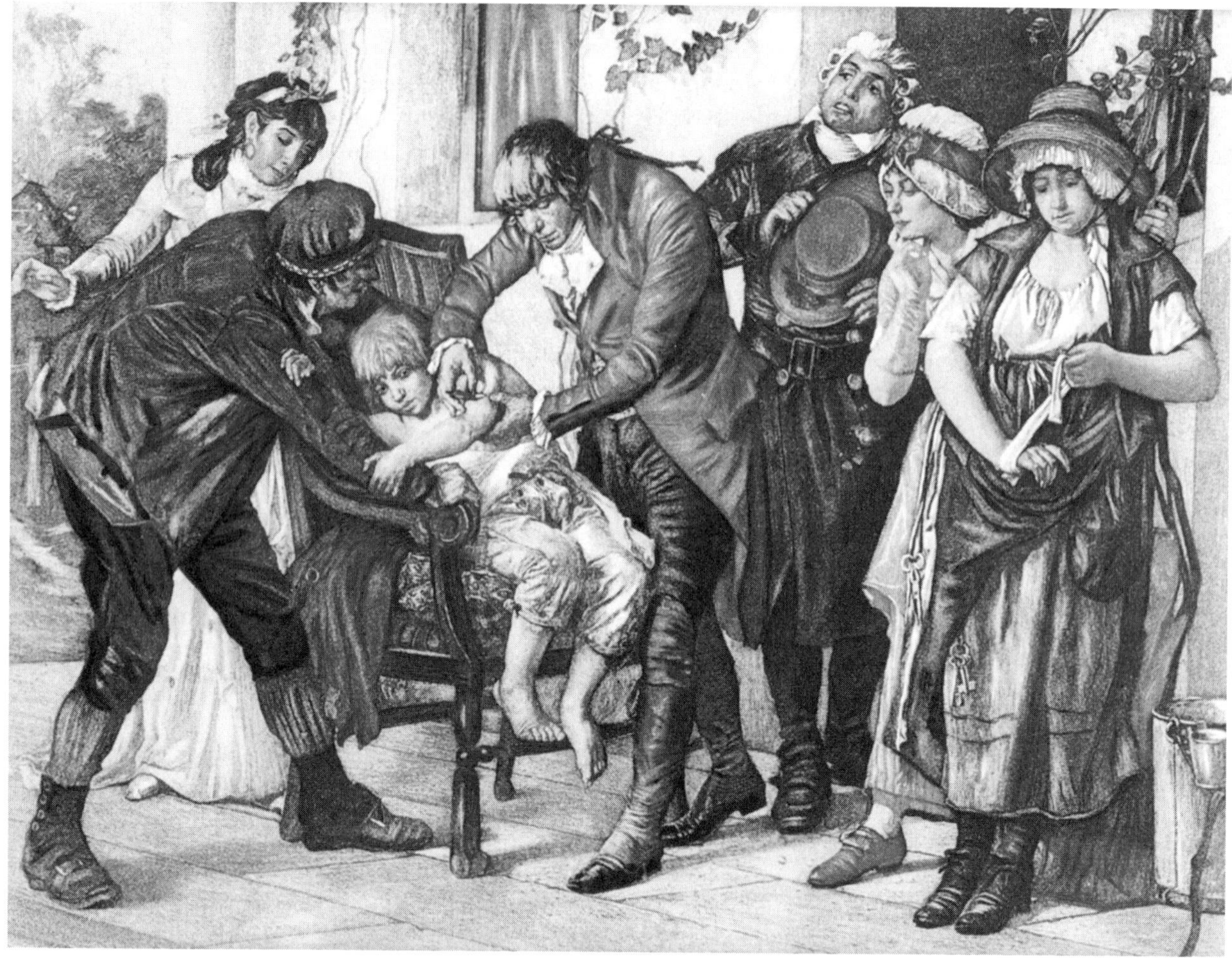

Edward Jenner administers the first smallpox vaccination. Engraving after a painting by G. G. Melingue, 1796. ©BETTMANN/CORBIS

He enjoyed the support of many influential metropolitan practitioners and secured the patronage of George III (r. 1760–1820), Queen Charlotte, and the Prince of Wales (who, as George IV, made him physician-extraordinary in 1821). Vaccination was officially adopted by the army and navy, and in 1802 Jenner received a parliamentary grant of £10,000, followed in 1807 by a further award of £20,000, to compensate him for the fact that he had made no direct profit from his researches.

Jenner's fame was in part a combination of his own talent for self-promotion and the mythologizing activities of his supporters, both during his life and after his death. In 1803 they founded the Royal Jennerian Society (reformed as the National Vaccine Establishment in 1809) to promote the practice of vaccination. In addition, paintings were commissioned, medals struck, and statues built, all of which contributed to the image of Jenner as a man of singular genius.

Edward Jenner died from a stroke at his house in Berkeley on 26 January 1823. By this time vaccination was an established practice in Britain, and in 1840 it was made freely available to all by law. This was followed in 1853 by legislation making it compulsory for all infants. Nonetheless, it continued to arouse controversy well into the twentieth century and was opposed by those who objected to it on moral or religious grounds ("conscientious objection" was permitted by an act of 1898), those who objected to the legislative establishment of medical professional authority, and others who saw it as an infringement of the rights of the individual.

See also **Disease; Public Health; Science and Technology; Smallpox.**

BIBLIOGRAPHY

Baxby, Derrick. *Jenner's Smallpox Vaccine: The Riddle of Vaccinia Virus and Its Origin.* London, 1981.

Bazin, Hervé. *The Eradication of Smallpox: Edward Jenner and the First and Only Eradication of a Human Infectious Disease.* Translated by Andrew and Glenise Morgan. London, 2000.

Fisher, Richard B. *Edward Jenner, 1749–1823.* London, 1991. A good general biography.

Le Fanu, William. *A Bibliography of Edward Jenner.* 2nd rev. ed. Winchester, U.K., 1985. A thorough bibliography of Jenner' writings.

Razzell, Peter E. *Edward Jenner's Cowpox Vaccine: The History of a Medical Myth.* 2nd ed. Firle, 1980. An interesting revisionist account.

Saunders, Paul. *Edward Jenner, the Cheltenham Years, 1795–1823: Being a Chronicle of the Vaccination Campaign.* Hanover, N.H., 1982.

MICHAEL BROWN

JEWISH EMANCIPATION. At the turn of the nineteenth century Heinrich Heine (1797–1856), asking rhetorically what the great task of the day was, stated: "It is emancipation. Not simply the emancipation of the Irish, the Greeks, Frankfort Jews, West Indian blacks, and all such oppressed peoples, but the emancipation of the whole world, and especially of Europe" (quoted in Sachar, p. 106). Heine may have conflated religious, ethnic, racial, geographic, and national distinctions. There was prescience, however, in his implication that the granting of equal rights to the Jews would be inextricably linked to the emancipation of oppressed groups, the socioeconomic transformation of Europe, and the emergence of newly created nation-states.

Jewish emancipation in western, central, and eastern Europe spanned more than one hundred years (France, 1791; Belgium, 1831; Great Britain, 1858; Italy, 1861; Austria-Hungary, 1867; Germany, 1871; Switzerland, 1874; Serbia and Bulgaria, 1878). The decrees and public debates of revolutionary and Napoleonic France consistently provided the paradigm for this often tortuous process.

By the end of the eighteenth century, except for the Iberian peninsula, Jews had returned to Europe west of the Russian Empire. Although subject to numerous and oppressive geographic and financial restrictions, which often confined them to cramped quarters and ghettos, to lending money and dealing in used clothing, and to a dress code designed to call attention to their status and identity, they were almost universally granted the privilege of juridical autonomy. They numbered 175,000 in Germany, 70,000 in the Austrian Empire, 100,000 in Hungary, 40,000 in France, 50,000 in Holland, and 25,000 in Great Britain.

By the end of the eighteenth century, among "enlightened" Jews and non-Jews, there had also evolved an image of the future in which everything pertaining to the Jews—their education, economic diversification, language, and civil status—was to be radically altered. Some, of course, challenged this image, arguing that it was predicated on a diminution of the Christian character of society and of the Jews' theological significance for Christianity. Others argued that the religion, traditions, and messianic expectations of the Jews made their integration neither possible nor desirable. Among the Jews as well there was much debate concerning the cost of their integration. Although welcoming an end to oppressive regulations that constrained their life, the rabbis and leadership struggled to retain the autonomy of their communities and the validity of Jewish tradition.

In 1782 Holy Roman Emperor Joseph II passed an Edict of Tolerance, which, along with other decrees specific to the Jews, denied them rabbincal jurisdiction, made them liable for military service, and permitted them to discard special emblems and dress; learn handicrafts, arts, and sciences; and enter universities and academics. In 1784 French king Louis XVI issued his Lettres Patentes, which denied the right of local authorities to expel Jews legitimately resident in Alsace, provided formal recognition of the authority of the lay leaders and rabbis, and modestly expended their range of economic activities. The motivations behind these decrees differed significantly. Joseph had in mind an ambitious overhaul of his empire, which included ensuring that all his subjects become equally productive regardless of religious opinions or influential status. Louis XVI was merely responding to an increasingly volatile situation in Alsace. Significantly for future events, they both gave voice to a contingency of toleration and fueled ambivalence.

Although the Jewish leadership, whose authority remained intact, generally reacted positively to the reforms in France, reaction to the far more radical reforms proposed by Joseph II was intense and heated. For some, primarily the *maskilim* (religious enlighteners), the edict represented the opportunity for Jews to embrace the educational and linguistic reforms of a "great man, a savior to mankind, an exalted emperor." For others, rabbis and traditionalists, the reforms challenged the primacy of Torah and threatened acculturation to the non-Jewish world.

Reforms, edicts, and enlightened despotism belonged to the *ancien régime*. By the summer of 1789, with the Declaration of the Rights of Man and the Citizen, France posed a new ideal of citizenship—democratic, noncorporatist, and inclusive. It was only a matter of months before the debates in the National Assembly focused on whether Jews, too, were to be included in the newly emerging state. "To call the Jews citizens," the Abbé Maury proclaimed, "would be as if one would say that, without letters of naturalization and without ceasing to be English and Danish, the English and Danes could become French" (*Archives Parlementaires* [Paris, 1878], vol. X, p. 757). While some deputies argued that the Jews should be excluded altogether, others suggested "tolerating" them or even giving them "hospitality," "protection," and "security." To this another deputy, Clermont-Tonnerre, countered with what would soon become the model for integration of the Jews as well as the leitmotif of future debate on the terms of their emancipation: "We must refuse everything to the Jews as a nation. We must grant everything to them as individuals."

Although the revolutionaries welcomed non-Catholics as full members of the body politic in December 1789, they could resolve nothing concerning the Jews. As a result, the disparate communities of France—Sephardim (Spanish and Portuguese Jews) in the Southwest, Ashkenazim (eastern European Jews) in the Northeast, and a small and illegal community in Paris—were for the first time identified as one—if only in their exclusion. Within a month the acculturated Jews of Bordeaux and Bayonne had lobbied and received particular attention from the National Assembly, which decreed on 28 January 1790 that they were to continue to enjoy the rights they had previously enjoyed, including active citizenship. This recognition was not to presume any decision concerning the Ashkenazim of the northeast.

The enfranchisement of the Sephardim was a vindication less of the principles of the Revolution than of the privileged position these few thousand Jews had consistently enjoyed in the *ancien régime*. Yet the decree of 1790 was significant. It not only communicated to the rest of the Jews the necessary terms for their citizenship (most importantly that juridical autonomy would be unacceptable) but also empowered them in their response to its postponement.

When emancipation finally came, in contrast to the debates of December 1789 as well as those of January–February 1790, the vote had little to do with the Jews, their patriotism, or their equality. On the contrary, a commitment to France, the ideals of the Revolution, and the constitution had led the revolutionaries to acknowledge the Jews as fellow citizens. They had done so, moreover, by granting citizenship to "individuals of the Jewish persuasion," thus ending the autonomy of the Jewish communities and begging the question of Judaism as more than a set of religious beliefs.

The Jews of France continued their economic practices and bore the brunt of traditional enmities; they also took the civil oaths required of them, entered the army, and actively participated in the national guard. In an eloquent *Lettre d'un citoyen* (Letter of a citizen), signed Juif, citoyen actif (Jew, active citizen), Berr Isaac Berr of Nancy assured the religiously observant among his coreligionists that with their oath they renounced only their servitude. He placed citizenship in traditional terms, suggesting that God had chosen the French to effect the regeneration of the Jews. With the Berlin *maskilim* as his guide, he also outlined the educational, linguistic, and professional changes he believed necessary to transform Jews into respected citizens and their communities into voluntary associations.

The French armies extended the emancipation of 1791 to Italy, Holland, Belgium, and southern Germany. Since Prussia had included among its reforms a decree emancipating its Jews, and Great Britain had quietly permitted significant social and economic integration, only the status of those Jews residing in the Austrian Empire remained unchanged.

Napoleon raised anew the question of citizenship for the Jews when he convened an Assembly of Jewish Notables (1806) and a Grand Sanhedrin (1807). Requiring from these bodies concrete guarantees "converted into religious doctrines," he both redefined the terms of Jewish emancipation and permanently linked it to the ambiguities and contingencies articulated throughout the eighteenth century.

With Napoleon's defeat, restrictions were restored and Jewish disabilities revived. Rome, for example, returned its Jews to the ghetto. Although the Treaty of Vienna (1815) assured the Jews enjoyment of all rights accorded to them "in" the several German states, a last-minute shift to "by" left only the Jews of Prussia with rights. Hostility to the enlightenment, to Napoleon, and to religious skepticism fed traditional enmities and provided additional justification for excluding the Jews.

The decisions of the Napoleonic Sanhedrin, and their preamble that "Israel no longer forms a nation" provided a template of political emancipation and acculturation for the Jews of Europe and later the United States. Conferences, convened in Brunswick, Frankfurt, and Breslau (1844–1846), set an agenda of reforming Judaism to insure compatibility with "the spirit of the age." From these often-heated rabbinic debates emerged Reform, Conservative, and Neo-Orthodox Judaism. All welcomed emancipation, which by 1914 was denied only to the Jews of Romania and the Russian Empire.

Historians continue to debate the motives behind emancipating the Jews and the price the Jews paid, the extent to which modernization was linked to emancipation, and the halakhic (Jewish legal) significance of the decisions promulgated by the Napoleonic Sanhedrin. The Zionist movement, moreover, founded at the end of the nineteenth century, rejected the premises of the debates of 1790, questioned emancipation itself, and asserted in its stead a paradigm of Jewish nationhood.

See also **Anti-Semitism; Jews and Judaism; Minorities; Nationalism; Religion.**

BIBLIOGRAPHY

Brenner, Michael, Vicki Caron, and Uri Kaufmann, eds. *Jewish Emancipation Reconsidered: The French and German Models.* London and Tübingen, 2003.

Liedtke, Rainer, and Stephan Wendehorst, eds. *The Emancipation of Catholics, Jews and Protestants: Minorities and the Nation State in Nineteenth-Century Europe.* Manchester, U.K., and New York, 1999.

Kieval, Hillel J. *The Making of Czech Jewry: National Conflict and Jewish Society in Bohemia, 1870–1918.* New York and Oxford, U.K., 1988.

Malino, Frances. *A Jew in the French Revolution: The Life of Zalkind Hourwitz.* Oxford, U.K., and New York, 1996.

Rozenblit, Marsha. *The Jews of Vienna, 1867–1914: Assimilation and Identity.* Albany, N.Y., 1983.

Sachar, Howard M. *The Course of Modern Jewish History.* New York, 1990.

Frances Malino

JEWS AND JUDAISM. On the eve of the French Revolution there were some two million Jews unevenly distributed throughout Europe. By 1914 their numbers had grown to 9.1 million. Although there were communities of Jews in England, France, the Netherlands, Germany, and Italy, most Jews lived in east central and eastern Europe. At the turn of the twentieth century the largest Jewish population was found in the Russian Empire (more than five million), followed by the Habsburg Empire (more than two million). The large Jewish communities in the east were a legacy of the medieval experience of European Jews who had migrated eastward with their expulsion from England, France, Spain, and some German localities. Poland, which was dismembered and incorporated into the Russian and Habsburg Empires and Prussia at the end of the eighteenth century, in particular welcomed their settlement because of their commercial and managerial skills.

European Jews began the nineteenth century as a distinctive group, characterized not only by their dissent from Christianity, the religion that most Europeans then believed was essential for belonging in all European societies, but also by their civic status and their economic profile. Because of the nature of their "otherness" and the Christian theological view of Jews as deicides, Jews and Judaism were almost universally stigmatized throughout Europe. Jews lived in governmentally recognized, compulsory corporate communities, many of them located in rural areas. Although the state had begun to erode the right of Jews to govern themselves according to halakah (Jewish law), Jewish communities retained the power to tax their members.

In the course of the long nineteenth century Jews, especially in western and central Europe, experienced far-reaching changes in their civic and economic status. In both east and west, European Jews responded to new political, intellectual, and economic challenges by reconstructing their identities and transforming their religious and cultural expressions. The pace and trajectory of change was influenced by class, gender, level of urbanization, and especially national and local political and cultural factors.

A kosher bakery in the Jewish quarter of Paris, c. 1900.
©HULTON-DEUTSCH COLLECTION/CORBIS

ENLIGHTENMENT AND EMANCIPATION

The anomaly of the Jewish community's status, and the concern among both politicians and intellectuals in the west with the question of individual rights, made the "Jewish Question" among the most hotly debated issues at the end of the eighteenth century in the west, even though Jews composed no more than 1 percent of the total population in any country of western or central Europe. The situation of the Jews raised questions about the nature of citizenship and the capacity of human beings to change. Both those who supported extending civic and economic rights to Jews—a process later called emancipation—and those who opposed that step agreed that Jewish behavior was reprehensible. Where they disagreed was whether Jews' changing their behavior was a prerequisite for emancipation or would follow inexorably after the lifting of restrictions upon them. They also disputed whether Judaism itself was an impediment to appropriate civil behavior. Emancipation presumed that Jews would become like their neighbors, though Enlightenment thinkers accepted religious affiliation as a legitimate form of difference. The debates about the Jewish Question laid the groundwork for the first act of emancipation of Jews in Europe. As they sought to create a new, modern state, the activists of the French Revolution conferred citizenship on Jews in 1790 and 1791.

The late eighteenth century witnessed not only new ideas about the status of Jews but also new economic possibilities that had far-reaching implications for European Jewry. A small number of Jews in the west, primarily in the German lands, parlayed their experience in commerce and finance to accumulate great wealth by the last few decades of the century. They recognized the attractiveness of the larger society as well as the new approaches toward Jews that Enlightenment thinkers were promulgating. It was from their ranks that support for a new set of values and standards for Jews emerged; the wealthy financed the publications and the educational institutions that disseminated those ideas.

Within the Jewish community that new approach became known as *Haskalah,* from the Hebrew term for Enlightenment. Addressing themselves primarily to a male audience, Haskalah activists argued that Jews were obliged to acquire secular learning and to participate in the larger societies in which they lived. In sociological terms they were to consider the respectable burgher class as their reference group, rather than the learned elites of the traditional Jewish community. Beginning with the Habsburg emperor Joseph II's 1781 Edict of Toleration, they supported governmental legislation that extended rights to Jews while also demanding their acculturation, in terms of language, education, and public behavior, to the general polity. The Haskalah was an elite, rather than a mass movement, but it provided an alternate leadership within the Jewish community and a new vision of how Jews should think about their identities and their relations to their neighbors. Laypeople whose authority derived from their success in the general society or from their attainment of a high degree of secular culture became the leaders, and they challenged the traditional rabbinic authorities. The Haskalah began in Germany but its very success led to its loss of specific identity by the first decade of the nineteenth century. In eastern Europe the Haskalah movement, despite its lack of unity, was an influential voice for modernization from the 1820s through the 1870s. The books and articles, newspapers, and schools created by *maskilim* (proponents of Haskalah) spearheaded a Kulturkampf between traditionalists and modernizers in eastern Europe.

From the 1780s on, a revolution occurred in the type of education Jews received. Increasingly a modernizing Jewish leadership, in collaboration with governmental authorities, ensured that Jewish youth acquired a secular elementary education. Jewish lay leaders promoted a change in the very concept of what a (male) Jew needed to know to make his way in the world and to become recognized as educated. Secular education, offered in different institutional settings, replaced the study of Hebrew and traditional rabbinic texts. Jews gradually acquired facility in German, French, or English. The heder, the traditional private Jewish school, succumbed to the lure of secular learning and to the introduction of laws of compulsory education throughout the west in the early nineteenth century. Wealthy parents provided private tutoring for their children, but increasingly Jews enrolled their children in modern Jewish schools, which emphasized secular subjects, or later in public schools. By the second half of the nineteenth century Jews were disproportionately represented in high schools and universities in Germany, Austria, and France.

In the Russian Empire and Galicia many Jews continued to provide a traditional Jewish education for their children, but new opportunities emerged in the nineteenth century. Galician Jews had access to state schools as early as the end of the eighteenth century, while the tsarist regime established secular Jewish schools for males beginning in the 1840s as a way to Russify its Jewish population. Teacher training seminaries and state rabbinical schools offered opportunities for youth of impoverished families to escape the difficult life to which they seemed destined. The Haskalah movement pioneered at midcentury in the establishment of Jewish girls' schools, realizing that traditional elites would pay them much less attention than schools for males. The small minority of wealthy Jewish families also had access to secondary and university education for their sons and to a lesser extent their daughters.

The promise of full political equality was realized slowly in Europe. Only the forty thousand or so Jews of France became citizens in the egalitarian fervor of the early years of the French Revolution. In central Europe political equality was achieved in fits and starts. Napoleon I's army brought temporary emancipation to Jews in the Netherlands, Italy, and parts of Germany, but his defeat led to reversals in Jewish status. Jews achieved equal citizenship in the Austro-Hungarian Empire in 1867, in unified Italy in 1870 (the process having begun in 1848), and in the new state of Germany in 1871. Emancipation of the Jews in England is often dated to 1858 when a Jew was allowed to take his seat in Parliament without swearing "on the true faith of a Christian." Most Jews, however, were already fully assimilated to English culture and enjoyed economic rights. In the Russian Empire, the western concept of the equality of all citizens became a reality only with the downfall of the tsarist regime in the first Russian Revolution of March 1917. A survey of the Jewish situation throughout Europe makes it

A Jewish boy studies the Talmud, Piaseczno, Poland, c. 1900. ©BETTMANN/CORBIS

clear that political change did not play *the* decisive role in the social change that Jews experienced in the modern period.

THE CHANGING ECONOMIC ROLE OF EUROPEAN JEWRY

The lay communal leaders of the Jewish community, along with most Jews, considered the lifting of restrictions on their economic activity as the most important aspect of the changes in Jewish political status in the late eighteenth and early nineteenth century. In central Europe, while intellectuals and activists continued to lobby for Jewish emancipation, the growth in economic opportunities provided Jews with considerable compensation for their second-class political status. In the Russian Empire, too, governmental Jewish policy was evaluated not in terms of theoretical ideals but whether it permitted Jews living within the Pale of Settlement, the ten provinces in the western part of Russia to which they were largely confined, to maintain or expand their economic activities and pursue their lives unhampered by governmental interference. For the most ambitious and wealthiest Jews, the ability to move outside the Pale in search of education or professional advancement was the key measure of state policy.

In the west, at the beginning of the modern period, the vast majority of Jews eked out a modest living, in some form of petty commerce. Many of the men were peddlers, who were often away for much of the week, and sometimes longer, as they traveled through their territory. As in most preindustrial societies, women contributed to the family economy by assisting in the family business as well as managing the household. Jews who lived in rural areas also were heavily involved in the cattle trade and to a lesser extent in the more lucrative horse trade and in commerce in other agricultural

The Great Jew and Tartar Market, Moscow. Photograph c. 1900. ©CORBIS

products. Some peddlers and traders in animals combined money lending with their commerce, often serving as the only sources of credit for their peasant customers. A smaller percentage of the Jewish population was composed of artisans—tailors, shoemakers, and tinsmiths.

Peddling continued as a major occupation for Jews into the middle of the nineteenth century in western and central Europe, even as Jews urbanized. Many Jews, however, accumulated sufficient wealth to open small retail shops, and some built large businesses in retail and wholesale trade. Jews were well suited to take advantage of early capitalist conditions: they were not tied to the land or to restrictive artisan guild codes; they understood the workings of a money economy; and they were willing to take risks. By the last quarter of the century, in Germany for example, Jews, who had paid fewer taxes than their gentile neighbors at the beginning of the century because of their relative poverty, were paying more taxes than the surrounding population. Some Jews—the international banking family of the Rothschilds merely the most notable—became major players in the financial world and key investors in such capitalist ventures as the building of railroads. The social mobility and urbanization of nineteenth-century European Jews enabled them to become professionals and to participate in urban culture as consumers, creators, and entrepreneurs. Jewish writers, journalists, and artists were prominent in the bourgeois and avant-garde culture of such cities as Berlin and Vienna.

Jews in western and central Europe aspired to the bourgeoisie, with its respectability and its sharp gender division of the public (male) and private (female) spheres. Their economic success enabled growing numbers of Jews in France, England, Germany, and the Habsburg Empire to achieve a bourgeois style of life by the last quarter of the nineteenth century. The very economic success of central and west European Jews throughout the nineteenth century ironically contributed to Jews' difference from the larger population. If the assimilation of Jews was the goal of their emancipation, their concentration in commerce, as well as their high level of urbanization and education, contributed to their difference from their neighbors. Although they adopted the culture of their bourgeois neighbors, speaking the language of the larger society and participating in general public life, they maintained, in the words of one historian, a "distinctive subculture."

The Russian Empire came late to the capitalist developments of modern Europe. Within the Pale of Settlement until the emancipation of the serfs in 1861, Jews served as the intermediaries between the serfs and the urban consumer, bringing the serfs' agricultural products to market and selling them manufactured goods. Indeed, the emancipation of the serfs worsened economic conditions for Jews. In the villages for much of the nineteenth century Jews also functioned as innkeepers who purveyed alcohol. Petty commerce and artisanry predominated among the occupations of Jews in the Russian Empire and also in Galicia. Governmental restrictions contributed to economic stagnation. Although Jews urbanized during this period, becoming the dominant group in many cities of the Pale, they did not experience the economic mobility that characterized Jewish life in western Europe. The bourgeois model affected only a small proportion of Jews because economic conditions did not permit it to flourish; women had to contribute to the economic support of their families. Only a tiny percentage of Jews in Russia, the beneficiaries of what one historian has called the policy of "selective integration," succeeded in achieving special status, including the right to live outside the Pale, as merchants of the first degree or professionals.

CONSTRUCTING A EUROPEAN IDENTITY

As they prospered in their new economic endeavors and responded to the new ideas that promoted the importance of acquiring secular culture, Jews developed a public identity. In all countries of the west, Jewish spokesmen declared the consonance of Judaism with the particular values of the country in which they lived. Being a good Jew made one a good German or Frenchman, and vice versa. Although Jews maintained, and expressed, a sense of mutual obligations, a common past, and a linked fate that transcended national borders, they described themselves as sharing a religious tradition rather than as members of a "nation."

The acquisition of secular culture, combined with their bourgeois aspirations, led many Jews to seek ways to construct a Judaism consonant with their values and likely to meet with public approval. As they acculturated, their observance of Jewish ritual declined and was relegated to the home. They also sought aesthetic changes in public ritual that met their newly adopted bourgeois standards. New forms of Judaism emerged throughout western and central Europe, but the pressure for ideological as well as practical change was strongest in Germany, where Jews felt that their civic equality depended on demonstrating the appropriateness of modern Judaism within European culture. By the 1840s Reform Judaism in Germany had developed its own university-trained rabbis, synagogues, and theology. The official Judaism of British and French Jewry remained ideologically traditional, but both became aesthetically modern. It has been estimated that Jews who observed traditional Judaism constituted only 10 to 15 percent of the Jewish population in western and central Europe by the end of the century.

Jews in eastern European societies abandoned Jewish practice more slowly than in the west, and traditional Jews composed at least half of the local Jewish population in 1914. The modern currents that emerged in eastern European Jewish communities were not religious but rather secular and political. Jewish youth in the Russian Empire in particular were greatly affected by radical political movements that envisioned the overthrow of autocracy and the establishment of a just society. They affiliated with general revolutionary political groups and established their own Jewish socialist

The Jewish quarter of Frankfurt, Germany, photographed in the nineteenth century. ©HULTON-DEUTSCH COLLECTION/CORBIS

party, familiarly known as the Bund. Zionism, the Jewish nationalist movement that emerged at the end of the century, was even more popular.

ANTI-SEMITISM

Until the last quarter of the nineteenth century, anti-Semitism was a minor annoyance to most European Jews. In the west, Jews viewed the sporadic instances of anti-Semitic invective or violence as a sign that the new rationalist ideas of the Enlightenment had not yet fully triumphed. In the east, Jews felt that the harsh policies of Tsar Nicholas I had been abandoned for a gentler governmental policy when he was succeeded by Alexander II in 1855.

The anti-Semitism that emerged in western and central Europe was different from earlier forms of Jew-hatred. Although it drew on traditional religious tropes, it was highly politicized and was directed primarily at Jews who had entered into, and succeeded in, the larger society. Assimilated Jews symbolized the destructive power of capitalism and the evils of a modern urbanized society. Modern anti-Semitism, rooted in a Romantic, and in some places increasingly racist nationalism, was a transnational European phenomenon, with different local manifestations. It emerged first in Germany, reaching its peak in the early 1890s, when one of Germany's major political parties, the Conservative Party, adopted an anti-Semitic plank in its platform. Anti-Semitism was a central component of the Dreyfus affair, which absorbed large segments of French society at the turn of the twentieth century and resulted, at its height in 1898, in sporadic physical attacks against Jews. In Austria anti-Semitism was rampant, and an anti-Semite, Karl Lueger, served as mayor of Vienna from 1897 to 1910. Although anti-Semitism disturbed Jews and interfered with the careers of some, they did not see it as a threat, and by the time of World War I it had declined as a political phenomenon.

In the Russian Empire, on the other hand, anti-Semitism became a violent expression of popular resentment. Beginning with the pogroms of 1881 and 1882, Jews became victims in periodic outbursts that often accompanied revolutionary fervor, as in the years from 1903 to 1905. The government's policy toward the Jews became more discriminatory, and hopes for increasing rights under a tsarist regime withered. A combination of poverty and anti-Semitism spurred the emigration westward of at least a third of the Jews of the Russian Empire.

CONCLUSIONS

Looking back at the long nineteenth century, most Jews in the west were cognizant of their long trajectory of civic emancipation, acculturation, and reconstructed identities. Although they recognized their social marginality, they did not shy away from participating in the cultures of their respective societies. Indeed, Jews played a prominent role in the artistic, literary, and theatrical cultures of Vienna and Berlin, in particular. Although most Jews in the east saw emigration as a preferred solution to their economic and political problems, some still saw a better future for themselves where they were, through a reform of tsarist autocracy or its overthrow. The Jewish Question, so hotly debated a century earlier, had not disappeared but did not seem an insurmountable problem to most European Jews.

See also **Anti-Semitism; Catholicism; Citizenship; Minorities; Nationalism; Pogroms; Protestantism; Zionism.**

BIBLIOGRAPHY

Birnbaum, Pierre, and Ira Katznelson, eds. *Paths of Emancipation: Jews, States, and Citizenship.* Princeton, N.J., 1995.

Feiner, Shmuel. *The Jewish Enlightenment.* Translated by Chaya Naor. Philadelphia, 2003.

Freeze, ChaeRan Y. *Jewish Marriage and Divorce in Imperial Russia.* Hanover, N.H., 2002.

Hyman, Paula E. *The Jews of Modern France.* Berkeley, Calif., 1998.

Kaplan, Marion A. *The Making of the Jewish Middle Class: Women, Family, and Identity in Imperial Germany.* New York, 1991.

Katz, Jacob. *Out of the Ghetto: The Social Background of Jewish Emancipation, 1770–1870.* Cambridge, Mass., 1973.

Klier, John Doyle. *Imperial Russia's Jewish Question, 1855–1881.* Cambridge, U.K., 1995.

Meyer, Michael A. *Response to Modernity: A History of the Reform Movement in Judaism.* New York, 1988.

Nathans, Benjamin. *Beyond the Pale: The Jewish Encounter with Late Imperial Russia.* Berkeley, Calif., 2002.

Rozenblit, Marsha L. *The Jews of Vienna, 1867–1914: Assimilation and Identity.* Albany, N.Y., 1983.

Sorkin, David. *The Transformation of German Jewry, 1780–1840.* New York, 1987.

Stanislawski, Michael. *Tsar Nicholas I and the Jews: The Transformations of Jewish Society in Russia, 1825–1855.* Philadelphia, 1983.

Paula E. Hyman

JINGOISM. The word *jingoism,* signifying the assertive expression of nationalist feelings, comes from a London music hall song of 1877. The occasion was the Russo-Turkish War that had broken out in April and which, if the Russians were victorious, seemed to threaten British interests in the region. The song's chorus went: "We don't want to fight, / But by Jingo if we do / We've got the ships, we've got the men, we've got the money too. / We won't let the Russians get to Constantinople." In late 1877 and early 1878, there was a strong movement with many public meetings in Britain against involvement in the war, but at the end of January these meetings began to be broken up by supporters of a more assertive policy. The peace party was thoroughly alarmed at the violence and the apparent turn of public opinion, and one of them, aware of the popularity of the song, labeled their opponents "Jingoes." The term took hold, and soon extended to *jingoism* to describe the kind of policy associated with the Conservative government under Benjamin Disraeli (1804–1881), first on the Eastern Question, and then in its involvement in Afghanistan and South Africa.

Although some so-called Jingoes were happy to accept the label, the term throughout the period up to 1914 was mainly used by their opponents who, in an age of widening democracy, were alarmed at the attraction of so many potential voters to what seemed to them to be irrational and dangerous policies. In *The Psychology of Jingoism* (1901), published in the midst of the South African, or Boer, War (1899–1902) when peace meetings were again broken up, the Liberal publicist J. A. Hobson explained jingoism as a coming together of the survival of brutality and credulity from "savage nature" and certain conditions of modern civilization, especially the power of the media and the rootlessness of town life.

It is difficult to be certain of the appeal of jingoism, particularly as it carried no obviously definable meaning. Over time jingoism ceased to be associated exclusively with those who broke up public meetings and came to signify anyone who supported a patriotic policy. Within Britain, jingoism was particularly associated with London, though it was by no means confined to it. Contemporary critics argued that Jingoes were to be found in all classes, but gave special prominence to the presence in Jingo crowds of medical students, members of the stock exchange, and workers spilling out of pubs and music halls. Modern historians have argued that jingoism's appeal was primarily to the lower middle classes, particularly clerks, who overcame status anxieties by affirming their loyalty to nation.

Jingoism needs to be seen as the British expression of an assertive nationalism to be found all over Europe. In France, similar types of action and thought were known as *chauvinism*. Although by 1914 *militarism* had partially replaced *jingoism* as the word peace-loving liberals and socialists were most likely to use to describe their opponents, it was still useful in stirring up fears of the threat posed by right-wing nationalism to the prospects for both peace and democracy.

See also **Boer War; Disraeli, Benjamin; Eastern Question; Nationalism; Russo-Turkish War.**

BIBLIOGRAPHY

Cunningham, Hugh. "Jingoism in 1877–78." *Victorian Studies* 14 (1971): 429–453.

Price, Richard. *An Imperial War and the British Working Class: Attitudes and Reactions to the Boer War, 1899–1902.* London, 1972.

Taylor, Miles. "Patriotism, History, and the Left in Twentieth-Century Britain." *Historical Journal* 33 (1990): 971–987.

Ward, Paul. *Red Flag and Union Jack: Englishness, Patriotism and the British Left, 1881–1924.* Woodbridge, U.K., 1998.

Hugh Cunningham

JOHN, ARCHDUKE OF AUSTRIA

(1782–1859), and imperial regent of Germany.

John was born 20 January 1782 in Florence and died 10 May 1859 in Graz. An enthusiastic supporter of Enlightenment, progress, civil society, and national self-determination, John has the reputation of being the "liberal Habsburg." John was often at odds with the rest of the Habsburg family, as became particularly clear in the 1848 revolution, but he was not prepared to break with it. His career was seen at the time as ending in failure, but it represents an intriguing alternative perspective in Austrian—and German—history.

Raised in his first years in Florence, under the Enlightened spirit of his father, Grand Duke Leopold, brother of Holy Roman Emperor Joseph II, John came to Vienna in 1790, when his father became Emperor Leopold II. His parents' death in 1792 led to John becoming the ward of his eldest brother, Holy Roman Emperor Francis II (who also became Francis I, emperor of Austria), who set him on the path of a military career. John retained, however, a strong attachment to Enlightenment principles, especially a faith in the natural right of peoples to self-determination. In 1800 he was sent to the Tyrol as the representative of his brother, the emperor, and invested his considerable energies into setting up a *Landwehr* (militia) and rallying the Tyroleans in the battle against the French, but also in involving himself in many aspects of Tyrolean life, in a way quite different from most archdukes. In 1805 Tyrol was ceded to Bavaria, and John was forced to move to Inner Austria (Carinthia, Carniola, and Styria), where he also organized a *Landwehr*, which, he hoped, would prove the focus of a new "national spirit," in the manner of the French *levée en masse*. In 1809 he led this militia as part of the Austrian effort against the French, and he was also a main instigator of the Tyrolean Revolt of the same year, led by Andreas Hofer. Defeat of both by the

French led to the humiliating Treaty of Schönbrunn, and Emperor Francis I banned his brother John from ever setting foot in Tyrol again.

From 1811 John employed his policy of direct involvement with the "people" in another Austrian province, Styria. Although he had no official role or title, he became the leading light of the province's society. He dedicated himself to improvement in all its forms, much like an English gentleman of the period, providing a model in agriculture, industry, and science. His collections and library, the "Joanneum," were brought to Graz and opened to the public in 1809, finding permanent housing in1811. He also was active as a founder and protector of many associations (*Vereine*), thus creating a network of civil society to mitigate, or even counter, the reactionary absolutism of the post-1815 Habsburg regime. He was even involved in having the railway to Trieste come through Graz and Styria and not western Hungary. His status as the "great commoner" was confirmed by his love affair and marriage, in 1829, with Anna Plochl, the daughter of the postmaster in Aussee.

John's reputation as a hero of the people, both in Tyrol and Styria, stood him in good stead in the events of the spring of 1848. A strong critic of the policies of Clemens von Metternich, John was instrumental in getting the Habsburg family to sack the aging chancellor on 13 March 1848, and in the ensuing revolutionary events was often a mediator between the court and the revolutionaries. When the court fled Vienna for Innsbruck in May, it was John who was sent back to Vienna in June as the emperor's deputy, and who on July 22 opened the *Reichstag* (constituent assembly). In the interim, John, who had espoused a form of German nationalism since his days in Tyrol, had also been in Frankfurt am Main, where the newly elected, All-German Parliament in the Paulskirche had on 26 June elected him as *Reichsverweser* (imperial regent or administrator). John, however, was unable to use his new position to shape German (or Austrian) politics so as to realize his goal of a united and liberal Germany. Instead, with John now mainly in Frankfurt, the Habsburg court took an increasingly reactionary trajectory, and John's dynastic loyalty did not allow him to make the sort of decisive break that could have rescued the revolution from the onset of reaction. John's role, like the revolution, thus ended ignominiously with his resignation as *Reichsverweser* on 20 December 1849 and his return to Styria.

John remained active in Styrian life until his death in 1859, serving, among other things, as elected mayor of the village of Stainz. His descendants were given the title Counts of Meran. John was buried on the family property at Schenna, near Meran (Merano) in South Tyrol.

See also **Austria-Hungary; Francis I; Revolutions of 1848.**

BIBLIOGRAPHY

Klingenstein, Grete, ed. *Erzherzog Johann von Österreich: Beiträge zur Geschichte seiner Zeit.* Graz, 1982.

Magenschab, Hans. *Erzherzog Johann: Habsburgs grüner Rebell.* Munich, 1995.

Theiss, Viktor. *Erzherzog Johann, der steirische Prinz.* Edited by G. Klingenstein. Vienna, 1981.

Wheatcroft, Andrew. *The Habsburgs: Embodying Empire.* Harmondsworth, U.K., 1995.

STEVEN BELLER

JOMINI, ANTOINE-HENRI DE

(1779– 1869), French and Russian soldier and strategic theorist.

Antoine-Henri Jomini was the most influential military writer of the nineteenth century and an outstanding proponent of the idea that war could be conducted on the basis of a small number of permanently valid principles. He was born in Switzerland in 1779 and served as a staff officer in the armies of the Revolution and Napoleon. He abandoned the French cause in 1813, however, and went to serve in Russia, where he later rose to the rank of general. He was enormously prolific and wrote dozens of books, of which the best remembered is *Précis de l'art de la guerre* (Summary of the art of war, 1838). All of Jomini's works were suffused by the spirit of scientific rationality that had become characteristic of military writing in the previous century. He is best understood as the culminating figure of Enlightenment military theory, whose central achievement was to assimilate the destabilizing dynamism of Napoleonic warfare to the risk-averse analytic traditions of the Old Regime.

Those traditions described the art of war in terms that could best be portrayed on a map. Jomini agreed, though he was less willing than his predecessors to assign decisive significance to permanent terrain features or man-made fortifications. Instead he emphasized the relational maneuver of opposing armies, whose dynamic relationship in time and space defined the strategic possibilities of a military campaign. At bottom, the general's task was always the same: to concentrate superior forces at what Jomini called "the decisive point," a point that was defined by the interactive decisions of the opposing commanders themselves. As a matter of principle, Jomini insisted, every army should seek to divide the enemy's forces while concentrating its own, and should always maneuver so as to threaten the enemy's communications while keeping its own base secure. Doing so was by no means a mechanical process. Like his great contemporary, Carl von Clausewitz (1780–1831), Jomini was aware of the intellectual and emotional demands that war made upon its participants. He accepted that the object of military maneuver was to bring about combat, and not to substitute for it. Yet he was also convinced that a firm grasp of war's scientific basis insured that such fighting as was required would always take place on the most favorable terms. If his work did not quite amount to a recipe for victory, it nevertheless afforded significant assurance that war could be mastered intellectually, if only it were approached in the same spirit of progressive rationality that characterized so much of European public life in the nineteenth century.

It is not always easy to recognize Jomini's work for the conservative synthesis that it was. His writings stress the superiority of the offensive and the importance of seizing the initiative and dominating the enemy—all paradigmatic virtues exemplified by Napoleon I (r. 1804–1814/15) himself. Yet Jomini missed the fierce improvisational spirit that made Napoleon such a fearsome opponent. Instead, he argued that the same kinds of results could be achieved by methodical planning, massed forces, and secure lines of communications, all of which had the practical effect of making the other things he admired—aggressiveness, cunning, surprise, vigorous pursuit—impossible to achieve. His ideas, as he recognized, were best suited to small, professional armies fighting for limited stakes, precisely the kinds of armed forces that dominated Europe in the wake of Napoleon's defeat. The future, however, belonged to enormous armies employing profoundly destructive new technologies. In that less constrained tactical environment, military decisions were seen to depend not upon the careful application of scientific methods, but on a remorseless willingness to inflict and endure suffering on a mass scale. Jomini's personal reputation thus fell into eclipse. Yet his achievement should not be underestimated. Jomini rescued the scientific spirit of the Enlightenment from the mechanical rigidity that always threatened to render it ridiculous, and he instilled the study of war with a determined but flexible rationalism that persists to this day. All good armies of the early twenty-first century purport to base their doctrine and operational methods on the flexible application of general principles recognizably similar to those Jomini identified.

See also **Armies; Clausewitz, Carl von; French Revolutionary Wars and Napoleonic Wars; Military Tactics.**

BIBLIOGRAPHY

Brinton, Crane, Gordon A. Craig, and Felix Gilbert. "Jomini." In *Makers of Modern Strategy*, edited by Edward Mead Earle, 77–92. Princeton, N.J., 1943.

Howard, Michael. "Jomini and the Classical Tradition." In *The Theory and Practice of War*, 3–20. Bloomington, Ind., 1965.

Shy, John. "Jomini." In *Makers of Modern Strategy*, edited by Peter Paret, 143–185. Princeton, N.J., 1986.

Daniel Moran

JUNG, CARL GUSTAV (1875–1961),

Swiss psychiatrist and founder of analytic psychology.

Carl Gustav Jung was born in Kesswil on Lake Constance, in 1875. His family moved to Laufen by the Rhine falls when he was six months old. He was the oldest child and had one sister, Gertrud. His father, Paul Jung, was a pastor in the Swiss Reformed Church. His youth was marked by vivid dreams, intense religious questioning, and extensive reading. He was particularly struck with the works of Johann Wolfgang von Goethe (1749–1832), Arthur Schopenhauer (1788–1860), Friedrich Wilhelm Nietzsche (1844–1900), Meister Johannes Eckhart (c. 1260–?1327), and Emanuel Swedenborg (1688–1772). From 1895 he studied medicine at the University of Basel and participated in a student debating society, the Zofingia society. Spiritualism, which spread across Europe in the latter half of the nineteenth century, particularly interested him, as the spiritualists appeared to be attempting to use scientific means to explore the supernatural, and prove the immortality of the soul. In 1896 Jung and his fellow students engaged in a long series of seances with his cousin Hélène Preiswerk, who appeared to have mediumistic abilities. These sittings were discontinued when she was caught cheating.

PSYCHIATRY

On reading Richard von Krafft-Ebing's *Text-Book of Psychiatry* in 1899, Jung realized that his vocation lay in psychiatry. After his medical studies, he took up a post as an assistant physician at Burghölzli Hospital at the end of 1900. The Burghölzli was a progressive university clinic, under the directorship of Eugen Bleuler. At the end of the nineteenth century, numerous figures attempted to found a new scientific psychology. It was held that by turning psychology into a science through introducing scientific methods, all prior forms of human understanding would be revolutionized. Thanks to Bleuler and his predecessor Auguste Henri Forel (1848–1931), psychological research and hypnosis played prominent roles at the Burghölzli. It was hoped that the new psychology would transform psychiatry.

In 1902 Jung presented his medical dissertation, which focused on the psychogenesis of spiritualistic phenomena, in the form of an analysis of his seances with Hélène Preiswerk. This work was strongly marked by the impact of the psychological approach to mediumship developed by Frederic William Henry Myers (1843–1901), William James (1842–1910), and in particular Théodore Flournoy (1854–1921). In the same year, Jung became engaged to Emma Rauschenbach, whom he married and with whom he had five children. In 1902 and 1903, he went to Paris to study with the leading French psychologist, Pierre-Marie-Félix Janet, who was lecturing at the Collège de France. On his return, he devoted his work to the analysis of linguistic associations, in collaboration with Franz Riklin.

The conceptual basis of Jung's early work lay in the dynamic psychologies of the subconscious developed by Flournoy and Janet; he attempted to fuse these psychologies with the research methodology of Wilhelm Wundt (1832–1920) and Emil Kraepelin (1856–1926). Jung and Riklin attempted to utilize the associations experiment, in which a subject was read a list of words and asked to respond with the first word that came to mind, as a quick and reliable means for differential diagnosis. They failed in this regard, but were struck by the significance of disturbances of reaction and prolonged response times. They argued that these disturbed reactions were due to the presence of emotionally stressed complexes, and used their experiments to develop a general psychology of complexes.

This work established Jung's reputation as one of the rising stars of European psychiatry. In 1906, he applied his new theory of complexes to study the psychogenesis of dementia praecox (later called schizophrenia), and to demonstrate the intelligibility of delusional formations. For Jung, along with a number of other psychiatrists and psychologists at this time, such as Adolf Meyer and Pierre Janet, insanity was not regarded as something completely set apart from sanity, but rather, as lying on the extreme end of a spectrum.

PSYCHOANALYSIS

By 1907 Jung became increasingly disenchanted by the limitations of experimental and statistical methods in psychiatry and psychology. In the outpatient clinic that Forel had established at the Burghölzli, he presented hypnotic demonstrations. This led to his interest in therapeutics and to the use of the clinical encounter as a method of research. Bleuler had introduced psychoanalysis into the Burghölzli and initiated a correspondence with Sigmund Freud (1856–1939). In 1906 Jung entered into communication with Freud. Their relationship has been much mythologized. A Freudocentric legend arose, which viewed Freud and psychoanalysis as the principal source for Jung's work. This has led to the complete mislocation of Jung's work in the intellectual history of the twentieth century. On numerous occasions, Jung protested against this, and insisted that his real teachers were Eugen Bleuler, Théodore Flournoy, and Pierre Janet. It is clear that Freud and Jung came from quite different intellectual traditions and were drawn together by shared interests in the psychogenesis of mental disorders and psychotherapy. Their intention was to form a scientific psychotherapy based on the new psychology, and, in turn, to ground psychology on the in-depth clinical investigation of individual lives.

With the lead of Bleuler and Jung, the Burghölzli became the center of the psychoanalytic movement. Because of their advocacy, psychoanalysis gained a hearing in the German psychiatric world. In 1908 a journal was founded, the *Jahrbuch für psychoanalytische und psychopathologische Forschungen,* with Bleuler and Jung as the editors. In 1909 Jung received an honorary degree from Clark University for his association researches. The following year, an international psychoanalytic association was formed with Jung as the president. During the period of his collaboration with Freud, he was a principal architect of the psychoanalytic movement. From the start, the movement was riven by dissensions and acrimonious disagreements.

MYTHOLOGY, FOLKLORE, AND RELIGION

In 1908 Jung bought some land by the shore of Lake Zürich in Küsnacht and had a house built, where he resided for the rest of his life. In 1909 he resigned from the Burghölzli to devote himself to his private practice and research. This coincided with a shift in his research interests to the study of mythology, folklore, and religion, and he assembled a vast private library of scholarly works. These researches culminated in *Wandlungen und Symbole der Libido* (1911–1912; *Transformations and Symbols of the Libido*). Taking his cue from William James, Jung contrasted directed thinking and fantasy thinking. The former was verbal and logical. The latter was passive, associative, and imagistic. The former was exemplified by science and the latter by mythology. Reiterating the anthropological equation between the prehistoric, the primitive, and the child, he held that the elucidation of current-day fantasy thinking in adults would concurrently shed light on the thought of children, savages, and prehistoric peoples.

The end of the nineteenth century saw an explosion of scholarship in the newly founded disciplines of comparative religion and *Völkerpsychologie.* Primary texts were collected and translated for the first time and subjected to historical scholarship in collections such as Max Müller's *Sacred Books of the East* (1879–1910). Drawing on this large body of work, Jung synthesized nineteenth-century theories of memory, heredity, and the unconscious and posited a phylogenetic layer to the unconscious that was still present in everyone, consisting of mythological images. For Jung, myths were symbols of the libido and they depicted its typical movements. He used the comparative method of anthropology to assemble a vast panoply of myths, and then subjected them to analytic interpretation. He later termed his use of the comparative method "amplification." One particular myth was given a central role: that of the hero. For Jung, this represented the life of the individual, attempting to become independent and to free himself from the mother. He interpreted the incest motif as an attempt to return to the mother to be reborn. He later heralded this work as marking the discovery of the collective unconscious, though the term itself was of a later date.

In a series of articles from 1912, Jung's colleague Alphonse Maeder, taking his cue from Flournoy, argued that dreams had a function other than that of wish fulfillment, which was a balancing or compensatory function. Dreams were attempts to solve the individual's moral conflicts. As such, they did not merely point to the past, but prepared the way for the future. Jung was working along similar lines and adopted Maeder's positions. For Jung and Maeder, the alteration of the conception of the dream brought with it an alteration of all other phenomena associated with the unconscious.

In 1913 Jung developed his conception of personality types, a subject which had been much debated in individual psychology. He argued that corresponding to the differences between hysteria and schizophrenia, there existed two general classes of person, who could be characterized by whether their libido tended to move toward the world (extraverts) or toward themselves (introverts). Through developing type theory, Jung shifted his concerns from psychopathology to a general psychology of normal functioning.

By the outbreak of war, Jung had made critical interlinked contributions to the development of psychical research, dynamic psychiatry, psychological testing, psychotherapy, psychoanalysis, cultural psychology, and the psychology of personality, hence playing an important role in the rise of modern psychological culture. In the summer of 1914, Jung and the Zurich Psychoanalytic Association ceded from the International Psychoanalytic Association, and formed the Association for Analytical Psychology, citing Freud's attempt to assert absolute authority over theoretical developments in psychoanalysis as the reason for their secession. Jung was now the head of his own school of psychology, which he called analytical psychology, synthesizing his earlier work to form its theoretical underpinnings. As a "popular" psychology and as a psychotherapy, this was to have significant and long-standing ramifications in the twentieth century.

See also **Freud, Sigmund; Psychoanalysis; Psychology.**

BIBLIOGRAPHY

Bennet, Edward Armstrong. *Meetings with Jung: Conversations Recorded by E. A. Bennet during the Years 1946–1961.* Einsiedeln, 1982.

Ellenberger, Henri. *The Discovery of the Unconscious: The History and Evolution of Dynamic Psychiatry.* New York, 1970.

Hannah, Barbara. *Jung: His Life and Work, A Biographical Memoir.* New York, 1976.

Heisig, James. *Imago Dei: A Study of C. G. Jung's Psychology of Religion.* Lewisburg, 1979.

Jung, C. G. *Collected Works.* Edited by Sir Herbert Read, Michael Fordham, and Gerhard Adler; executive editor, William McGuire; translated by Richard Hull. London and Princeton, N.J., 1944–.

———. *Analytical Psychology: Notes of the Seminar Given in 1925.* Edited by William McGuire. London and Princeton, N.J., 1989.

McGuire, William, ed. *The Freud/Jung Letters: The Correspondence between Sigmund Freud and C. G. Jung.* Translated by Ralph Mannheim and R. F. C. Hull. London and Princeton, N.J., 1974.

Shamdasani, Sonu. *Jung and the Making of Modern Psychology: The Dream of a Science.* Cambridge, U.K., 2003.

Sonu Shamdasani

KADETS. The Kadets was the nickname for the liberal Constitutional Democratic Party, or Party of People's Freedom (the nickname deriving from the initials of the party's name in Russian). Founded in October 1905, the Kadets comprised Russia's largest nonrevolutionary party prior to 1917.

The party's name reflected its fundamental goals: transformation of Russia into a constitutional state based upon law, and democratization of its political and social order. Its program called for civil rights for all citizens, including freedom of speech, assembly, and religion; equality before the law; creation of a legislative body elected by universal suffrage (female as well as male); separation of church and state; an independent judiciary; and greater rights of local self-government. The program also contained important social provisions, such as the right to unionize and strike, mandatory health insurance and state-funded old-age pensions, a progressive income tax, and the creation of a state land fund to benefit the peasantry. These social reforms, which put the Kadets to the left of other European liberal parties of the time, reflected both the party's bid for mass support, and its belief that individual freedom could not be fully realized without broader opportunity and social protections.

The Constitutional Democrats enjoyed their greatest influence in the tumultuous period from 1905 to 1907, with approximately one hundred thousand dues-paying members and 346 local party organizations. The historian Pavel Milyukov headed the party for most of its existence; other prominent leaders included Peter Struve, Ivan Petrunkevich, Vasily Maklakov, Prince Dmitri Shakhovskoi, Vladimir Nabokov (father of the novelist), Maxim Vinaver, Andrei Shingarev, and Ariadna Tyrkova. The Kadets' makeup was diverse, including large numbers of educated professionals (professors, lawyers, doctors); low-level white-collar workers and teachers; small traders, artisans, and shop clerks; and some workers and peasants, though not as many as hoped for. The party's commitment to equal rights and cultural self-determination for minorities attracted many non-Russian subjects of the empire, especially Ukrainians, Armenians, and Jews, while its relative indifference to issues of economic development limited its attraction for the so-called big bourgeoisie. This social diversity corresponded to the liberals' self-image of their party as representing the whole nation by standing above the interests of any single class (*nadklassnost*); nonetheless, critics on the Left derogated the Kadets as bourgeois.

In April 1906, in Russia's first-ever national elections, the Constitutional Democrats won almost one-third of the seats to the Duma, becoming the largest single party in the lower house. A mutual lack of trust between government and Duma resulted in a speedy dissolution, in July 1906, with the Kadets criticized in many quarters for intransigence. The Kadets again won the largest number of seats in elections to the Second Duma, in early 1907, although fiercer competition from socialists reduced their deputies to one hundred. Despite liberals' efforts to make the Second Duma a more productive and cooperative body, the government considered it too radical and dissolved the legislature after just three months, simultaneously promulgating a restrictive electoral law that disenfranchised many liberal constituents. In consequence, in the Third and Fourth Dumas the Kadets' seats shrank to roughly 55 out of 449.

In the more repressive period of 1907 to 1914, the party experienced a marked decline in its membership and political influence. It helped pass important educational reforms, but its unsuccessful efforts to block chauvinistic nationalist legislation and to curb military spending reinforced conservatives' belief that the liberals were deficient in patriotism. World War I, however, helped restore the party's fortunes, as the Kadets wholeheartedly supported the war effort and played a leading role in nationwide relief organizations, such as the Union of Cities. In summer 1915 the Kadets were instrumental in organizing the Progressive Bloc, a broad, reformist Duma coalition seeking to restore public confidence in the conduct of the war.

When revolution occurred in February (March, new style) 1917, the Kadets seemed well positioned to become the most influential party in "new, free Russia," helping to organize the first provisional government and taking five of twelve cabinet-level posts. But the party's support for keeping Russia in the war, and related insistence on restoring military discipline and postponing social reforms, speedily eroded its popularity. The liberal Kadets condemned the Bolshevik seizure of power in October (November, N.S.) and were the first party outlawed by the new Soviet government, in December 1917; many Kadets joined the anti-Bolshevik forces in the Russian civil war (1918–1920).

See also **Milyukov, Pavel; Octobrists; Revolution of 1905 (Russia).**

BIBLIOGRAPHY

Rosenberg, William G. *Liberals in the Russian Revolution: The Constitutional Democratic Party, 1917–1921.* Princeton, N.J., 1974.

Shelokhaev, V. V. *Ideologiia i politicheskaia organizatsiia rossiiskoi liberalnoi burzhuazii, 1907–1914 gg.* Moscow, 1991.

Stockdale, Melissa. "Liberalism and Democracy: The Constitutional Democratic Party." In *Russia under the Last Tsar: Opposition and Subversion, 1894–1917,* edited by Anna Geifman, 153–178. Oxford, U.K., 1999.

MELISSA K. STOCKDALE

KAFKA, FRANZ (1883–1924), Austrian German author.

Franz Kafka was born in Prague, Bohemia, at that time one of the major population centers of the Austrian-Hungarian Empire. The German enclave in Prague developed a literary German that reflected its hyperawareness of its isolation within the Czech majority. Kafka's German prose is considered among the cleanest, strongest expressions of the German language throughout its literary history. Kafka considered himself a graphic artist, and his drawings accompanied his manuscripts throughout his life. He turned gradually to prose while studying law, publishing his first book of eight short stories in 1908.

Upon graduating law school, Kafka worked for the Austrian government in the seminationalized Workers' Accident Insurance Institute in Prague from 1908 until a year before his death in 1923. His experience in the law informed his stories and novels: His posthumous novels *Der Prozess* (1925; *The Trial*) and *Das Schloss* (1926; *The Castle*) deal with criminal and civil litigation as symbols and processes of human existence in culture. *Kafkaesque* is the adjective that expresses the absurdity, indeed surreal horror of plunging into these processes in the conduct of a life. Kafka's vision of the individual caught in the mazes of the twentieth-century state resonated in his time, as well as in the light of the totalitarian state that arose shortly after his death, and early critical appreciation of him highlighted this existential plight.

Kafka's visual intelligence, attested to by his lifelong friend and first biographer Max Brod, was enhanced by his studies of the descriptive psychology of Franz Brentano (1838–1917) and Anton Marty (1847–1914), and his familiarity with Sigmund Freud's understanding of the expressions of mind in human gesture. His prose has been described as that of the exact human gesture by the Weimar German critic Walter Benjamin and his own Austrian German contemporary Robert von Musil.

Kafka's prose was directed at two audiences, the average reader and the writer. His appeal to the ordinary reader is achieved by his clean, disarmingly simple prose. Kafka is said to have read children's stories before he wrote, taking a preparatory cue from one of his own favorite authors, Gustave Flaubert (1821–1880). Kafka directed his publisher, Kurt Wolff, to issue his 1919 collection of stories *Ein Landarzt* (*A Country Doctor*) with the larger type face of a primer. Kafka increasingly brought myths and legends into his stories to broaden the appeal to an ordinary audience. The mythic material is given interesting twists to provoke reader deliberation of meaning.

The narrative level that is directed to his contemporary writers is an encoded one, wordplay and imagery that even in its simple prose is designed to evoke reflection on past literary as well as pictorial methods of comprehending reality. Kafka saw himself as a writer in a tradition of the written story that stretched back into the earliest modern prose experiments of the seventeenth century. He believed that only through an aesthetic perspective could people guide themselves toward an authentic, that is, truthful life, and that his generation of artists had a mission to augment the aesthetic understandings of their predecessors. Kafka agreed with Friedrich Wilhelm Nietzsche (1844–1900) and his contemporaries that aesthetics could engender a more rigorous knowing and living. As he wrote in his journals of 1918: "Art flies towards the truth, but with the decisive intent not to be burnt. Its gift lies in its ability to find the saving beam of light in the dark emptiness, without previously knowing of its existence" (1953, p. 104). The best criticism of the late twentieth century took up Kafka's concern with aesthetics, both visual and verbal. While controversy still occurs over the chapter sequences of his three major novels, still unpublished in his lifetime, *Amerika, The Trial,* and *The Castle,* there is a consensus among scores of scholars that Kafka's own aesthetic concerns justify a critical focus on literary theory, linguistics, and semiotics as the major avenues for comprehending the intent and meaning of his prose.

Kafka's engagement to Felice Bauer before World War I and his later romance with Milena Polak, née Jesenská, were the most intense dramas of his life, generating two collections of love letters that are as humanly instructive as his fiction. The women of his novels have the strength and sexual aliveness that he retreated from in his actual relations, which he justified by an unwillingness to commit to a relationship that might compromise his artistry.

See also **Nietzsche, Friedrich.**

BIBLIOGRAPHY

Primary Sources

Kafka, Franz. *The Complete Stories.* Edited by Nahum N. Glatzer; with a foreword by John Updike. New York, 1995. Translation of short stories published during Kafka's lifetime, 1908–1924.

———. *Hochzeitsvorbereitungen auf dem Lande.* Frankfurt am Main, 1953. Journal. Translated as *Wedding Preparations in the Country, and Other Posthumous Prose Writings,* with notes by Max Brod. Translated from the German by Ernst Kaiser and Eithne Wilkins. London, 1973.

Secondary Sources

Gray, Richard T., ed. *Approaches to Teaching Kafka's Short Fiction.* New York, 1995. A collection of criticism, selected by the Modern Language Association of America.

Preece, Julian, ed. *The Cambridge Companion to Kafka.* Cambridge, U.K., 2002. Includes sociological and gender studies, alongside the aesthetic analyses.

Rolleston, James, ed. *A Companion to the Works of Franz Kafka.* Rochester, N.Y., 2002. A range of critical perspectives that includes the social-historical as well as linguistic and semiotic.

MARK E. BLUM

KANDINSKY, VASILY (1866–1944), Russian painter.

It was only years after he began painting in an abstract style that Vasily Kandinsky claimed priority as that style's originator. In an autobiographical sketch of 1919, he referred to himself as "the first painter to base painting upon purely pictorial means of expression and abandon objects in his pictures" (Kandinsky, p. 431), dating his first such painting to 1911. By then Kazimir Malevich and Piet Mondrian were achieving notice for their abstract work. In the 1930s, when abstraction seemed to have established itself as the climax, if not the very definition, of modernist painting, Kandinsky renewed his claim even more emphatically: his *Picture with a Circle* of 1911, he wrote, was "actually the first abstract picture in the world, because no other painter was painting in the abstract at the time. So it is a 'historic picture'" (quoted in Hahl-Koch, p. 184).

Whether or not Kandinsky was literally correct, he was philosophically justified; *Picture* was the first work to be painted according to an explicitly abstract aesthetic, worked out even before he had painted a single work in that style. "On the Spiritual in Art" (1912; completed 1909) was a manifesto that cast the idea of abstraction not just as a style of painting but as a philosophical-aesthetic challenge to the contemporary European bourgeois worldview. It became one of the defining documents of modernism.

AESTHETIC LIBERALISM

Kandinsky was born in Moscow on 16 December (4 December, old style) 1866 into a well-off, progressive, middle-class merchant family. His parents divorced, at his mother's initiative, when he was four, and he was brought up by his father and maternal aunt. He remained close to his mother, however, whose strong personality he identified with "Mother Moscow," the city he once described in an ideal visual moment in the late afternoon sun as a totality that unified all opposites in a symphonic harmony of color and served as the inspiration for all his work. Though drawn early to art, Kandinsky pursued training in law and economics as a member of the liberal Russian intelligentsia intent on bringing backward Russia into the modern world. At age thirty, disillusioned with the reformist potential of the social sciences, he abruptly decided to study painting and left Russia for Munich, a favored destination for expatriate Russian artists. But the idealism of Russian liberal reform would forever inform the purpose of his painting.

Kandinsky's aesthetic liberalism was a peculiarly Russian blend of nativist populism, Orthodox religiosity, and artistic symbolism. While desiring liberal political institutions, he rejected the selfish, materialistic individualism of the West. The communalism of "Old Russia," its classes united by common spiritual values, was to be the model of the new. In Russian symbolist doctrine, the artist had a special role in its creation. The purpose of art was to create images of harmony out of conflict, which could inspire in its audiences the spiritual transformation necessary for social and political change. But to produce these the artist must first realize harmony within himself; because of the egoism of modern man, this could be achieved only through the transformative love of woman. In this conception the feminine was understood as both a higher spiritual form inspiring man and the equal "other" of the masculine, the recognition of whose individuality through love could overcome the selfishness of contemporary life. Kandinsky was committed to both feminine idealization and sexual equality in life and in art, which for the symbolists were one.

After a brief period of apprenticeship, Kandinsky started his own art association and school, the Phalanx, which admitted women equally with men. The love affair he began with one of his young students, Gabriele Münter, profoundly influenced the next phase of his work. His confessedly "scrappy" production of land- and townscapes, symbolist fairy tales, and Jugendstil (art nouveau) graphic works increased dramatically to include new themes of life in Old Russia, period images of elegant women, and loving couples in medieval settings. These genres reached their climax in two Paris paintings of 1907, *Riding Couple,* a pointillist-inspired, gorgeously colored scene of courtly lovers on a steed against the background of medieval Moscow; and *Motley Life,* a larger canvas crowded with figures representing the spectrum of occupations and classes in Old Russia, the social context of romantic love.

TOWARD ABSTRACTION

These paintings, however, marked the end of a phase. Aesthetic and romantic crises pushed Kandinsky in radically new directions. In Paris he had encountered the fauvist color innovations of Henri Matisse, a major step in the emancipation of painting from representation. That emancipation was something Kandinsky had been groping for, for he had long felt his veneration for nature's creativity to be self-defeating: attempting to reproduce nature's colors left the painter a mere imitator, not an original creator. But he had been stymied because he also believed that it was only under the aegis of (feminine) nature, and its human counterpart feminine love, that he could produce great work. Disappointment in the creative potential of his relationship with Münter, along with the new technical means suggested by Matisse, opened a period of brilliant color experimentation in Kandinsky's work around 1908. These "fauvist" images, however, rapidly moved ever closer to pure abstraction.

Before they reached it, Kandinsky announced the goal of his journey. In "On the Spiritual in Art," he proclaimed the bankruptcy of the modern spirit of materialism in politics, economics, philosophy, and art. The competition for wealth had "turned the life of the universe into an evil, purposeless game"; scientific positivism and naturalism in art had produced in the soul seeds of "desperation, unbelief, lack of purpose" (Kandinsky, p. 128). Painting had to be revolutionized in order to rescue the human spirit by returning art to its "objective element," the "pure and eternal" vision of harmony. But to be persuasive to contemporaries, harmony could be achieved only by going *through* the "temporal-subjective" strife of modernity, not avoiding it. "Clashing discords ... great questionings, apparently purposeless strivings, stress and longing ... opposites and contradictions—this is our harmony," Kandinsky asserted programmatically (p. 193). The technical means of realizing it involved above all synthesizing colors representing conflicting emotions and mental states, "each with its separate existence, but each blended into a common life, which is called a picture by the force of inner necessity" (p. 193).

Among the current inspirations for his ideas about abstraction was Mme. Blavatsky's theosophical movement, whose claim to hold a set of beliefs about the divine origin of the universe that was at the root of all existing religions evoked spirituality without specific imagery. But it was his encounter with Arnold Schoenberg's "atonal" music, with its "emancipation of dissonance" from the established, "natural" tonal system, which enabled Kandinsky to make the final break with representation. The sudden revelation that colors did not necessarily have fixed meanings but could be infinitely redefined by their different uses and contexts "tore open ... the gates of the realm of absolute art" (Kandinsky, p. 398). At last the painter could, like nature, create ex nihilo, and be nature's equal in originality and power.

Between 1911 and 1914, Kandinsky produced an enormous output of both abstract and thematic works. The line between them is not sharp; many paintings with nonthematic titles, particularly the two numbered series called "Improvisations" and the more ambitious, larger-scale "Compositions," abound with discernible objects. In general the paintings of this period represent two main themes, recapitulating in Kandinsky's new aesthetic language his constant concerns: on the one hand representations of conflict, battle, and destruction, prominently including biblical images of Noah's flood and the Apocalypse, and on the other representations of paradise as a Garden of Love strewn with sexually united couples (e.g., *Improvisation 27,* 1912). Dualistic structures contrasting and balancing the two themes, as in *Composition IV* (1911), give way approaching 1914 to denser, more apparently chaotic biomorphic canvases working to create harmony out of fragmentation rather than polarities, culminating in the prewar *Composition VII* (1913).

Kandinsky also worked to educate potential audiences in his new ideas, and create a market for his work, by organizing groups of like-minded colleagues who drew up manifestos, published almanacs, and organized exhibitions. He formed the New Artists' Association of Munich with Alexei von Jawlensky, Marianne von Werefkin, and others in 1909. When his work became too radical for some of his colleagues, Kandinsky broke with them and established another group, the Blue Rider (Blaue Reiter), with Franz Marc and August Macke. The *Blue Rider Almanac* (1912), a heterogeneous collection of materials including theoretical prose pieces, illustrations, and Kandinsky's own drama, *Yellow Sound,* did much, along with the Blue Rider exhibitions, to bring modernist work into the cultural consciousness of Germany. The *Almanac* too became one of the landmarks of European modernism.

THE BAUHAUS PHASE AND AFTER

The outbreak of war in 1914 forced Kandinsky to leave Germany as an enemy alien. His departure led to the final break with Münter. Under the new Soviet regime, Kandinsky served for a time in the Ministry of Culture, seeding provincial museums with modernist paintings in an effort to bring

Composition 4. Painting by Vasily Kandinsky, 1911. ERICH LESSING/ART RESOURCE, NY.

contemporary art to broader masses of people. His sense that the regime was increasingly critical of his formalism, however, took him back to Germany in 1921, where he soon became one of the leading artists at the new Bauhaus school, teaching principles of form. His work by then had undergone another dramatic change, from biomorphism to much more rigid geometrical forms. Malevich's suprematism may have partly influenced the change, but the change was also connected with Kandinsky's sense that his previous methods did not, and perhaps could not, create the harmonious order he sought. After the Nazis rose to power, Kandinsky's work, along with that of other modernists, was condemned as "degenerate art." When the Nazis closed the Bauhaus in 1933, Kandinsky was forced into exile in Paris, where his work underwent yet another stylistic change under the impact of surrealism. He died near Paris, in Neuilly-sur-Seine, France, on 13 December 1944.

See also **Avant-Garde; Matisse, Henri; Modernism; Painting; Russia; Symbolism.**

BIBLIOGRAPHY

Grohmann, Will. *Wassily Kandinsky: Life and Work.* Translated by Norbert Guterman. New York, 1958.

Hahl-Koch, Jelena. *Kandinsky.* Translated by Karin Brown, Ralph Harratz, and Katharine Harrison. New York, 1993.

Izenberg, Gerald N. *Modernism and Masculinity: Mann, Wedekind, Kandinsky through World War I.* Chicago, 2000.

Kandinsky, Vasily. *Kandinsky: Complete Writings on Art.* Edited by Kenneth C. Lindsay and Peter Vergo. Boston, 1982.

Long, Rose-Carol Washton. *Kandinsky: The Development of an Abstract Style.* Oxford, 1980.

Ringbom, Sixten. *The Sounding Cosmos: A Study in the Spiritualism of Kandinsky and the Genesis of Abstract Painting.* Åbo, Finland, 1970.

Weiss, Peg. *Kandinsky in Munich: The Formative Jugendstil Years.* Princeton, N.J., 1979.

———. *Kandinsky and Old Russia: The Artist as Ethnographer and Shaman.* New Haven, Conn., 1995.

GERALD N. IZENBERG

KARADJORDJE (Djordje Petrović; 1768–1817), Serbian revolutionary leader.

Djordje Petrović, known as "Karadjordje" (*kara* is a Turkish prefix meaning *black*), led the Serbian revolution of 1804–1813. In the process, he created one of two rival Serbian royal dynasties (the Obrenovićes being the other) and contributed to the birth of one of Serbia's lasting political tensions, between centralized personal leadership and oligarchic rule. He is the most famous and the most mythologized figure to emerge from the first Serbian revolution.

Karadjordje was born in 1768, in Topola, central Serbia. His family was not of influential social status—he was neither a *knez* (priest) nor a merchant of note. In adulthood he pursued the pig trade. During the Austro-Turkish War of 1788–1791, he fought in a special Serbian formation, the Freicorps, which was created by the Habsburgs to take advantage of Serbian hostility to Ottoman administration. When that war ended unfavorably for the Serbs, he became involved in various attempts to raise a Serbian rebellion in the region known as the Šumadija, then formally known as the *pashalik* of Belgrade. At the turn of the nineteenth century, Serbs suffered from the disorder then endemic in the Ottoman borderlands. In particular, Belgrade had come under the control of "the four *dayis*," four janissaries who treated the city and its environs as their personal fiefdom.

The first Serbian uprising began in February 1804; Karadjordje was not its original leader, nor was he expected to be one. In early February, though, when the *dayis* began a slaughter of Serbian notables, he may (legend has it, anyway) have killed Turks who were sent to kill him. In any case, he took to the hills to fight. Later that month, as Serbian insurrectionaries sought a leader, he was elected when other candidates refused. He is alleged to have said before his election that he would rule mercilessly and violently, but fairly.

When the initial insurrection succeeded with the help of Ottoman forces in killing the *dayis*, Karadjordje left his first real mark on Serbian history, for he demanded that the Serbs fight on instead of remaining satisfied with their limited gains. The peasant rebellion became a national revolution. In 1805 the Ottomans attacked. The Serbs defeated the Ottoman army sent to pacify them, and the revolution was on. By late 1806 the Ottomans granted Serbs the autonomy they had sought earlier, but with the outbreak of war between Russia and the Turks in December 1806, the Serbian leadership opted to join Russia in the hope of attaining independence. Having achieved control over the *pashalik* of Belgrade, the Serbs might have solidified their position had Russia not abandoned them to the Ottomans in the Treaty of Bucharest of 1812. In 1813 the Ottomans were able to thoroughly crush the revolutionaries, now without their Russian supporters. As a result, Karadjordje and most of the other surviving participants in nine years of revolution fled across the Sava River to Zemun, in the Habsburg Monarchy.

Karadjordje was a stark figure, violent and ruthless, who demanded absolute power in his position at the head of the revolution. This desire brought him into conflict with the dominant forces in Serbia's peasant society, the local notables who ruled as warlords over their local lands. Emerging victorious among the Serbian notables required political cunning and violence. He was more violent than cunning. In December 1807, Karadjordje rigged a local assembly to declare him "hereditary ruler"; in 1811 he had himself declared "Supreme Leader" of the Serbs. In neither case did the appellation hold—instead, he maintained his position of power because he had a general rather than provincial vision of a future Serbia, and because he fought while many others pondered.

Karadjordje died violently at the hands of other Serbs. In 1815 another insurrection broke out against Ottoman control of Serbia, this one led by a new generation headed by Miloš Obrenović. Miloš was less capricious and more calculating than Karadjordje had been and believed it would be wise to try to maintain the gains of the second insurrection via diplomacy. When Karadjordje returned to Serbia in 1817, Miloš immediately had him murdered. To Miloš, Karadjordje was nothing more than a promise of more violence. The murder launched Miloš's career as leader of autonomous Serbia just as it launched the rivalry between the houses of Karadjordjević and Obrenović. It also bore a dual metaphor that would resonate in Serbian politics thereafter: Karadjordje became the symbol of the man of action, while Miloš became the symbol of deceit and cunning. On balance, history and popular opinion in Serbia have been kinder to Karadjordje.

See also **Nationalism; Ottoman Empire.**

BIBLIOGRAPHY

Pavlowitch, Stevan K. *Serbia: The History of an Idea.* New York, 2002.

Petrovich, Michael Boro. *A History of Modern Serbia, 1804–1918.* 2 vols. New York, 1976.

Nicholas Miller

KAUTSKY, KARL (1854–1938), Marxist theoretician.

Karl Kautsky was the most important Marxist theoretician from the death of Engels in 1895 to the outbreak of World War I in 1914. Born to an artistic, German-speaking, middle-class family in Prague, Kautsky grew up and was educated in Vienna. As a young man he participated in the nascent worker-socialist movement in Austria, but then moved on to richer grounds. After a period of exile in London, where he briefly met Karl Marx (1818–1883) and established a much closer relationship with Friedrich Engels (1820–1895), Kautsky became one of the leading intellectuals of the German and international socialist movements. In addition to being the principal author of the German Social Democratic Party's (Sozialdemokratische Partei Deutschland, SPD) Erfurt program (1891), which announced the party's putative basis in Marxian theory, Kautsky was for nearly thirty years editor of the leading Marxist journal, *Die Neue Zeit*. In this latter capacity, he dealt with all the most important Marxist theoreticians of his time, not only Europeans, but also those in Asia, Australia, North and South America, and elsewhere, who saw themselves as part of the worldwide upswelling of Marxist theory, history, and contemporary political analysis. Kautsky's significance as a theoretician and popularizer of Marxism corresponded to the rise and impressive growth of socialist, working-class parties in Europe and much of the rest of the world.

Kautsky was primarily important in two capacities—as a popularizer of Marxism and as the theoretician of the Marxist mainstream of the SPD. In the first capacity, his works like *The Economic Doctrines of Karl Marx* (1883) and *The Erfurt Program* (1892) (both of which went through innumerable editions and translations), played a significant role in establishing Marx's critique of modern capitalism as legitimate and useful to the emerging workers' movements. Vladimir Lenin (1870–1924) frequently identified Kautsky as one of the major influences that led him to Marxism, and *Economic Doctrines* was the first full-length Marxian work translated into Chinese. In the second capacity, as theoretician of the SPD, Kautsky served to reinforce the positions of the long-time party leader, August Bebel (1840–1913), and to counterattacks from the right, especially Eduard Bernstein's (1850–1932) revisionism, and the left, especially Rosa Luxemburg's (1870–1919) radical calls for violent action in the streets to bring about the socialist revolution. Time and again, Bebel called on Kautsky to criticize on the theoretical level those elements of the party who would move it to the right, in the direction of pure reformism, or to the left, in the direction of pressing for revolution at every opportunity, which might well have cost the movement dearly in terms of loss of life and legitimacy. The clearest statement of this centrist position came in *Der Weg zur Macht* (1909; *The Road to Power*), in which he urged the party to stay the course between outright reformism and reckless activism in the streets.

While not an innovator in Marxian theory, Kautsky did popularize the worldview and language of Marxism. He was heavily influenced both by Charles Darwin's (1809–1882) evolutionary theory and by Engels's inclination to expand Marx's philosophical analysis of modern capitalism into a comprehensive natural-scientific based view that encompassed the whole of natural history and human society. Kautsky would not have been nearly as important as he was if he had not been backed, largely in the person of August Bebel, by the enormous prestige of the German Social Democratic Party. Although no longer held in high esteem, Kautsky should be recognized for what he was, namely, a popularizer of a seductive and alluring theory of modern society.

See also **Bebel, August; Bernstein, Eduard; Engels, Friedrich; Jaurès, Jean; Lenin, Vladimir; Marx, Karl; Second International; Socialism.**

BIBLIOGRAPHY

Gilcher-Holtey, Ingrid. *Das Mandat des Intellecktuellen: Karl Kautsky und die Sozialdemokratie.* Berlin, 1986.

Salvadori, Massimo L. *Karl Kautsky and the Socialist Revolution, 1880–1938.* Translated by Jon Rothschild. London, 1979.

Steenson, Gary P. *Karl Kautsky, 1854–1938: Marxism in the Classical Years.* Pittsburgh, 1978.

Gary P. Steenson

KELVIN, LORD (WILLIAM THOMSON) (1824–1907), British scientist.

The fourth child of James and Margaret Thomson, William Thomson was born in Belfast. His mathematician father taught at the Belfast Academical Institution, well known for its political and religious radicalism. His mother, who came from a Glasgow commercial family, died when William was six. In 1832 his father was offered the chair of mathematics at the University of Glasgow and there continued to exert a profound influence on the education of his children. William enjoyed a broad philosophical curriculum at Glasgow but left without taking a degree in order to enter Peterhouse, Cambridge, as an undergraduate. Following several years of intensive mathematical study he emerged second in the 1845 "Mathematics Tripos," the intensely competitive examinations that ranked final-year students in order of mathematical merit. Enhancing his experimental skills in Paris, he was elected in 1846 as Glasgow University professor of natural philosophy, a post from which he retired in 1899.

In a scientific paper written when he was seventeen, Thomson used Jean-Baptiste-Joseph Fourier's (1768–1830) mathematical treatment of heat flow to replace action-at-a-distance forces in electrostatics with continuous-flow models. His radical approach later inspired James Clerk Maxwell's electromagnetic field theory, which found expression in the celebrated *Treatise on Electricity and Magnetism* (1873). Thomson himself extended Fourier's techniques to analyze electric signals transmitted through long-distance telegraph wires. Retardation of such signals had raised concerns among telegraph projectors, especially in relation to the economic viability of undersea cables. Thomson's analysis enabled him to advise on the optimum dimensions for projected transatlantic and imperial telegraphs. He also constructed extremely delicate measuring instruments, most notably a "marine mirror galvanometer," for use in telegraphic engineering. For these services to the empire, he was knighted by Queen Victoria in 1866, following completion of the first successful Atlantic telegraph.

Just two years into his professorship at Glasgow, Thomson formulated an "absolute" scale of temperature (later named the Kelvin Scale in his honor) which differed from traditional scales in being independent of any specific substance such as mercury. It depended on Thomson's recent commitment to Sadi Carnot's theory of the motive power of heat in which the "fall" of heat between a high temperature (the boiler) and a low temperature (the condenser) *drove* a heat engine just as the fall of water drove a waterwheel. Thomson's insight was to correlate temperature difference—the "fall"—with work done rather than with a particular working substance.

These researches took place within a larger context that generated, over the next decade, the new sciences of thermodynamics and energy. In the 1840s the Manchester experimentalist James Joule had been conducting laboratory investigations to determine the quantitative relationship between work done and heat produced. Thomson initially accepted Joule's findings that work could be converted into heat, as in friction, according to an exact equivalent. Committed to Carnot's theory, however, he could not accept the converse that work, once converted into heat, could then simply be recovered as useful work. Aided by similar investigations recently undertaken by the Scottish engineer William John Macquorn Rankine and the German physicist Rudolf Clausius, Thomson produced a reconciliation of Joule and Carnot in 1850–1851. For the production of work or motive power, a "thermo-dynamic engine" (Thomson's name for a heat engine) required two principles, the conversion of an exact amount of heat into the work done and the transfer of a certain amount of heat from high to low temperature. These principles formed the basis for the two laws of thermodynamics. The new science offered the empire's marine engineers—many located in Glasgow—an incentive to design steam engines of much higher pressures, which in accordance with thermodynamic laws would offer greater economy of fuel consumption.

Thomson and Rankine then introduced the terms *actual* (later *kinetic*) and *potential* energy. The laws of energy conservation and dissipation became the foundation of a new "science of energy," and the physics discipline quickly became redefined as the study of energy and its transformations. Thomson and his Edinburgh University colleague Peter Guthrie Tait initiated, but never completed, a vast project to develop an energy perspective in all branches of physical science, which would find embodiment in their *Treatise on Natural Philosophy* (1867).

Using these energy laws, Thomson arrived at ages for the earth and sun (20–100 million years). He explicitly challenged the geological timescales and assumptions on which Charles Darwin had built his controversial theory of evolution by means of natural selection (1859). The famous evolutionist later admitted that of the many objections raised to his theory, Thomson's proved the most difficult to counter.

Thomson developed his private laboratory into the first university physical laboratory in Britain. The work extended beyond telegraphic testing and invention to the patenting and manufacture of a large range of scientific, industrial, and navigational instruments. The wealth generated enabled him to purchase in 1870 a 126-ton schooner yacht, *Lalla Rookh,* which served as a laboratory afloat, especially for testing his mariner's compass and mechanical sounding machine. When in 1892 he was elevated to the peerage, he became the first British scientist to be so honored. Taking the title Baron Kelvin from the tributary of the River Clyde that flowed close to the University, Lord Kelvin continued to publish scientific papers until he found a last resting place in Westminster Abbey, not far from the tomb of Sir Isaac Newton.

See also **Science and Technology.**

BIBLIOGRAPHY

Smith, Crosbie. *The Science of Energy: A Cultural History of Energy Physics in Victorian Britain.* Chicago and London, 1998.

Smith, Crosbie, and M. Norton Wise. *Energy and Empire: A Biographical Study of Lord Kelvin.* Cambridge, U.K., 1989.

CROSBIE SMITH

KIERKEGAARD, SØREN (1813–1855), Danish philosopher.

Søren Aabye Kierkegaard is often referred to as the father of twentieth-century existentialism, though his reputation in his own time was that of a writer and culture critic. The legacy of Kierkegaard's writing took time to expand beyond its local origins, for while most of his illustrious contemporaries in the "golden age" of Danish art, letters, and science sought a response in German culture, he himself, like his contemporary Hans Christian Andersen (1805–1875) addressed a native readership, writing exclusively in Danish, a language he claimed was particularly well suited to his creative powers. Presenting himself as a "poet" or writer rather than a scholar, Kierkegaard combines many authorial categories, defying conventional boundaries between philosophy, theology, psychology, literary criticism, and fiction. His writings display considerable erudition as well as a wealth of original psychological insight.

Born in Copenhagen, Kierkegaard was the youngest of seven children, five of whom, along with their mother, died before he was twenty-one. Kierkegaard was brought up strictly both at school and at home, where his father, once in feudal bondage but having at the age of forty-one retired as a highly successful tradesman, attended personally to his family's upbringing. After his father's death in 1838, Kierkegaard and his surviving elder brother inherited a considerable fortune. Kierkegaard completed his long-delayed theological studies, became engaged, and received his doctorate with a dissertation *On the Concept of Irony with Continual Reference to Socrates* (1841). Immediately afterward he broke off his engagement and, renouncing an academic career, left for Berlin where, on the first of four visits to that city, he began the pseudonymous authorship on which his international fame chiefly rests.

Apart from a first publication, *From the Papers of One Still Living* (1838), in which he criticizes a novel by Hans Christian Andersen, and the doctoral dissertation three years later, Kierkegaard's main authorship is divided into two series: the pseudonymous works and the signed religious discourses, which he entitled "edifying" (or "up-building") and, later, "Christian." The two series were written in parallel, at times works from both being published simultaneously. Kierkegaard's first pseudonymous work, *Either/Or,* published in 1843, was an immediate success. It was quickly followed by *Repetition* and *Fear and Trembling,* both published in that same year. In 1844 there followed *Philosophical Fragments* and *The Concept of Anxiety,* and in 1845 *Stages on Life's Way.* Kierkegaard intended to bring the pseudonymous series to a close with the lengthy *Concluding Unscientific Postscript to the Philosophical Fragments* (1846).

Following a famous self-provoked feud with a satirical weekly, and dropping vague plans of retirement to a country pastorate, Kierkegaard took up his pen once more. Notable among the several publications that ensued were the signed *Works of Love* (1847) and two further pseudonymous works. The former expounds an ideal of unselfish, Christian love, while the first of the latter two, *The Sickness unto Death* (1849), offers a systematic analysis of progressively deliberate renunciations of a Christian form of human fulfilment, all of them characterized as forms first of despair and then of sin. *Practice in Christianity* (1850) resumes the theme of the paradox of the Incarnation (that the eternal should have become historical), central in the earlier *Philosophical Fragments.* Through its emphasis on the degradation suffered by Christ, and against the background of what Kierkegaard saw as an absence of any corresponding self-denial in the Danish clergy, this reworking of the paradox theme paved the way for an open attack on the Danish state church, provoking a conflict that was at its peak at the time of Kierkegaard's death, in 1855, at the age of forty-two.

Søren Kierkegaard. Undated drawing by his brother. ©Bettmann/Corbis

WORKS

The lengthy *Postscript* (whose pseudonymous author, Johannes Climacus, is also the author of the much shorter *Philosophical Fragments*) is the most explicitly philosophical of the pseudonymous works. Often regarded as a locus classicus of anti-Hegelianism, *Concluding Unscientific Postscript* can also be read as a polemic against the German Romantics. Protagonists of the Romantic movement opposed a tradition based on a belief in the superiority of reason as a guide to all knowledge as too abstract and formal to fully capture reality. They sought a richer experience of reality through artistically creative but also religious experience, with an emphasis on subjectivity. Focused on Christianity, *Postscript* aims to demolish any belief in the possibility of arriving at a saving truth, whether achieved through objective means (history, idealist philosophy, or the mere test of time) or in the form of some truth-guaranteeing quality of experience (subjectivity). Although Christian truth is indeed available only to the individual as such, or to someone who can think subjectively (the person who, in philosophical reflection, does not forget or abstract from the fact that he or she is an existing individual confined to time and facing an open future), grasping that truth requires an act of faith that has no support in any form of evidence or authority, objective or subjective. The true believer is one who, willingly and passionately embracing the paradox of the Incarnation, personally bears the burden of responsibility for acknowledging its revelation.

The pseudonymous works from *Either/Or* to *Postscript* appear to be measuring out the steps that need to be taken, and the distance in self-understanding traversed, before a person arrives at a point where his or her situation calls genuinely for a religious solution and thus for the faith outlined in *Postscript.* Readers familiar with the facts of Kierkegaard's own life will readily detect the relevance of these for the themes that emerge in these works, among them *Either/Or*'s "choice of oneself" and *Fear and Trembling*'s "suspension of the ethical." The notion of a life-view is central. It is to be found in Kierkegaard's earliest publication and later developed into that of the three stages, presented in *Stages on Life's Way* and defined in later sections of *Postscript.* The aesthetic and ethical stages are first presented in *Either/Or* and offered as alternative life-views for the reader to choose between. These are gradually supplemented in the later works by the religious stage (in fact two stages, referred to as A and B).

Postscript indicates for the subjective thinker where one must stand to find the object of a faith that is specifically Christian (the paradoxical religiousness B), but at the same time makes it clear that someone truthfully adopting a Christian point of view can no longer use a shared language to convey what it means to adopt it. This might indicate that little or nothing can be said from the point of view of religiousness B itself. The requirements of a religious and of a Christian life-view are nevertheless cogently and movingly expressed in the edifying and Christian discourses published in parallel with the pseudonyms. By conveying the distance between shallow and conciliatory readings of scripture and the hardness of their teaching when literally interpreted, these, too, bear witness to a dialectical aspect in Kierkegaard's writings. Thus, in its more than three hundred and fifty pages, *Works of Love* presents a paradigm of unselfish love that makes ordinary human attachments appear self-serving and therefore not properly forms of love at all.

Kierkegaard's reputation as one of Georg Wilhelm Friedrich Hegel's (1770–1831) most devastating critics rests on certain isolated but crucial passages including that, in the early part of *Postscript,* where the author rejects the possibility of an "existential system" on the grounds that it cannot capture the forward movement of existence (*Tilværelse*—a Danish near-equivalent of the German *Dasein,* made famous in the early work of Martin Heidegger). Kierkegaard is said to have had Hegelian sympathies in his student days and his later thought owes much both in structure and substance to Hegel. In this he resembles that other reputed archcritic of Hegel, Karl Marx (1818–1883), who also had a Hegelian past, and whose covertly Hegelian background of his later thought first came clearly to light with the late discovery of his early writings. In broad philosophical terms Hegel, Kierkegaard, and Marx can all be labeled "dialectical" thinkers. For them, reality reveals itself most cogently and truthfully in the form of opposites, or "contradictions," whose resolution it is then the task of such a thinker to formulate and help us to envisage as humankind's proper goal. For Hegel such resolutions occur in our understanding as it converges ideally on a vision of absolute knowledge as reason. For Marx the tensions are to be found in the working arrangements of society, and the corresponding resolutions require political action on the part of those collectives best placed to bring them about. The tensions that Kierkegaard brings to mind concern dilemmas faced by individuals in their confrontation with life, independently of the political situation (though it may be argued that they become salient only under certain political conditions).

Kierkegaard's influence on European thought came late. Where Marx's writings led quickly to revolutionary politics and to an explosive development in the field of social economics, the impact of Kierkegaard's writings was first felt in the comparatively esoteric circles of "dialectical theology," in which Karl Barth (1886–1968) and others stressed human isolation from God and the need for grace.

In the early 1920s Kierkegaard was translated into several languages, including Russian, and was widely read in both academic and literary circles in Germany, where as a student the Hungarian and later communist apologist György Lukács (1885–1971) was an admirer (and later critic). But it was not until the 1920s and 1930s, through the intermediaries of Karl Jaspers (1883–1969), Martin Heidegger (1889–1976), and Jean-Paul Sartre (1905–1980), the second of whom is heavily indebted to the Danish thinker, that Kierkegaard became a familiar point of reference among intellectuals and was heralded as the "father of existentialism."

By the end of the twentieth century, having long been cultivated on the American side of the Atlantic, not least by Lutheran academics in the Midwest, Kierkegaard had attracted a new audience, more perceptive to his focus on and deployment of irony. Some commentators have been inclined to read Kierkegaard as a prophet of postmodernism, though others will claim that his authorship is modernist at core. In his campaigning for what he called "Christianity within Christendom," the latter read Kierkegaard as replacing the Hegelian absolute with another (kind of) single truth upon which all understandings converge. Yet it cannot be denied that, with their diverse vantage points and differently shaded vantage-points and "life-views," Kierkegaard's pseudonymous writings show considerable affinity with postmodern styles and attitudes.

INFLUENCE

In a posthumously published work (*The Point of View for My Activity as an Author*; 1859) Kierkegaard claimed to have been "from first to last" a religious writer. Although the claim can be (and has been) questioned as an attempt to stage-manage his own future reputation, given a generous interpretation it is one that finds corroboration in the journals as well as in the texts themselves. If to some present-day admirers Kierkegaard's declared religious intention reduces the general relevance of the content of the writings themselves, others may see in him a resource for a regeneration of religiosity beyond postmodernism. Thus recourse to the "dialectic" that inspired Barthian theology, with its emphasis on God's "otherness," can help to break anthropomorphic habits of thought, such as incline us to believe that God must have a "cause" that we can serve, and that since (as many have claimed) human reason is inherently goal-directed, then any idea we have of being in God's service must be one of fulfilling a divine "purpose," rather than, say, that of performing daily tasks and fulfilling normal obligations in God's spirit and presence. The question of whether or how far such suggestions are in Kierkegaard's spirit must remain a matter of textual interpretation, but its doing so would testify to the continuing power of the thought of a writer whom the twentieth-century philosopher Ludwig Wittgenstein once described as the nineteenth century's "most profound thinker."

See also **Denmark; Hegel, Georg Wilhelm Friedrich; Marx, Karl.**

BIBLIOGRAPHY

Primary Sources

Kierkegaard, Søren. *Kierkegaard's Writings.* Edited and translated by Howard V. Hong, Edna H. Hong, Henrik Rosenmeier, Reidar Thomte, et al. Projected 26 volumes. Princeton, N.J., 1978–1997.

———. *Fear and Trembling.* Translated by Alastair Hannay. New York, 1985.

———. *The Sickness unto Death.* Translated by Alastair Hannay. New York, 1989.

———. *Either/Or: A Fragment of Life.* Translated by Alastair Hannay. New York, 1992.

———. *Papers and Journals: A Selection.* Translated by Alastair Hannay. New York, 1996.

———. *A Literary Review.* Translated by Alastair Hannay. New York, 2001.

———. *Kierkegaard's Journals and Notebooks.* 11 vols. Edited by Alastair Hannay et al. Princeton, N.J., 2005–.

Secondary Sources

Garff, Joakim. *Søren Kierkegaard: A Biography.* Translated by Bruce M. Kirmmse. Princeton, N.J., 2005.

Hannay, Alastair. *Kierkegaard: A Biography.* New York, 2001.

Hannay, Alastair, and Gordon D. Marino, eds. *The Cambridge Companion to Kierkegaard.* New York, 1998.

Kirmmse, Bruce H. *Kierkegaard in Golden Age Denmark.* Bloomington, Ind., 1990.

Kirmmse, Bruce H., ed. *Encounters with Kierkegaard: A Life as Seen by His Contemporaries.* Translated by Bruce H. Kirmmse and Virginia R. Laursen. Princeton, N.J., 1996.

Matustík, Martin J., and Merold Westphal, eds. *Kierkegaard in Post/Modernity.* Bloomington, Ind., 1995.

Rée, Jonathan, and Jane Chamberlain, eds. *Kierkegaard: A Critical Reader.* Malden, Mass., 1998.

Stewart, Jon. *Kierkegaard's Relations to Hegel Reconsidered.* New York, 2003.

ALASTAIR HANNAY

KINGDOM OF THE TWO SICILIES.

The Kingdom of the Two Sicilies (1734–1860) was the oldest and largest of the Italian states in the nineteenth century, and its collapse in 1860 unexpectedly ensured Italy's political unification. After two centuries of Spanish rule and then a brief Austrian occupation, the kingdom became an independent dynastic state ruled by a cadet branch of the Spanish Bourbons in 1734. Until 1816 Naples and Sicily were separate kingdoms, each with their own laws, customs, and constitutions. The mainland's population was five million in 1800, with nearly a million in Sicily. With a half-million souls Naples was the biggest city in Italy and the third largest in Europe after London and Paris, while Palermo, with 200,000 inhabitants, was slightly bigger than Rome at the close of the eighteenth century. But the size of these cities was a consequence of privileges that eighteenth-century critics believed contributed to the poverty of much of the rest of the kingdom. The privileges of the lay and ecclesiastical feudatories were more extensive than in any other western European monarchy, but the attempts by the Bourbon rulers to reform the *ancien régime* monarchy met with fierce resistance.

In 1794 the Kingdom of the Two Sicilies joined the coalition against Revolutionary France, but the preparations for war placed huge strains on the monarchy, which collapsed in November 1798 when King Ferdinand IV was defeated while trying to dislodge a French army that had set up a republican government in Rome earlier in the year. The king and his court fled to Sicily on Admiral Horatio Nelson's warship, while a French army established a republic in Naples in January 1799.

The Neapolitan Republic is best known for the manner of its fall in June 1799 when its supporters were massacred by a fanatical popular counterrevolution—the Most Christian Army of the Holy Faith (the Santafede)—led by Cardinal Fabrizio Ruffo. In fact, like its sister republics, the Neapolitan Republic fell because the Directory pulled its armies out of Italy and because the city was blockaded by Nelson's ships. But the savagery of the Royal Terror that followed caused revulsion throughout Europe, and Nelson's involvement was later described as a "stain on England's honor."

In 1806 the mainland was again invaded by a French army, and the Bourbons again fled to Sicily. Napoleon's brother Joseph ruled in Naples until 1808, when he was transferred to Spain and replaced by the emperor's brother-in-law Joachim Murat. Relations between Naples and Paris became strained after Murat's arrival and exposed the rapacious colonial foundations of Napoleon's empire. Although Murat did not share the fate of Louis Bonaparte, who had been removed from the throne of Holland in 1810, in 1814 he defected to the Allies in the hope of saving his kingdom. But the Allies refused to make guarantees, so Murat again rallied to Napoleon after the flight from Elba in 1815. The Napoleonic episode in southern Italy came to a close when Murat was defeated by the Austrians at Tolentino in May.

During the brief period of French rule the Neapolitan monarchy was completely reorganized. Feudalism was abolished, central and local government was reorganized along French lines, the Napoleonic Code was introduced, and the debts of the old monarchy were redeemed through the suppression of over 1,300 religious houses. But hostility to French imperialism also gave rise to demands for constitutional government in the final years of Murat's reign, which found an organizational base in the secret societies, especially the Carbonari.

When the Bourbons returned to Naples in 1815 they not only retained all the reforms introduced by the French (except only for civil divorce) but in 1816 also extended them to Sicily, which lost its centuries-old autonomy. To acknowledge the union the king changed his title to Ferdinand I, but the resentment of the Sicilians and the continuing pressure for a constitution were the main causes of the revolutions that started in the Bourbon army in July 1820. The principal demands were for greater local autonomy and political freedom, but after nine months of constitutional government the Kingdom of the Two Sicilies was again invaded by an Austrian army in March 1821. A systematic purge of all suspected liberals followed, as well as measures to protect the kingdom's economy. Its finances had been bankrupted by the revolution and in 1822 its debts were acquired by the Rothschild bank. High protective tariffs were adopted to reduce dependence on foreign imports, but this led to a trade war with Britain that culminated in 1840 when British gunboats entered the Bay of Naples and forced the government to submit.

After the reactionary reign of Francis I (1825–1830), the accession of Ferdinand II (the nephew of Louis-Philippe, France's constitutional monarch) in 1830 raised hopes of political change that never materialized. As economic conditions deteriorated in the early 1840s popular discontent grew, especially in the rural areas, but an attempt by the Venetian brothers Attilio and Emilio Bandiera to start a revolt in Calabria was quickly suppressed. Four years later, however, in January 1848, the European revolutions began in Palermo. In an attempt to contain the protests Ferdinand II of Naples was the first Italian ruler to concede constitutional government, but on May 15 he was also the first to stage a successful counterrevolution.

As in 1820, Palermo adopted the separatist cause that brought it into collision with liberals in Naples and with many other Sicilian towns. But unlike in 1820, the army remained loyal to the monarchy. Order was quickly restored in the mainland provinces, and in October the Bourbon navy shelled Messina, which earned King Ferdinand the title of "King Bomba"; Palermo held out until May 1849.

The Neapolitan Bourbons were the only Italian rulers to overthrow the revolutions without external assistance, but their victory left them isolated diplomatically. Piedmont was now a constitutional monarchy while throughout Europe, King Bomba was the personification of reaction—a reputation that was reinforced when the English liberal politician William Gladstone protested the treatment of Neapolitan political prisoners and denounced the Bourbon monarchy as "the negation of God set up as a system of government."

The greatest danger to the Neapolitan Bourbons was posed by the decline of Austrian power, and Austria's defeat in 1859 left the kingdom without allies. The consequences became evident when Garibaldi's landing at Marsala in May 1860 triggered the third and finally successful Sicilian separatist revolt. By now the monarchy also had lost the support of the landowners on the mainland, and although the army remained loyal, it was unable to face both Garibaldi's Redshirts and the Piedmontese army that illegally invaded the kingdom in October 1860 on the pretext of protecting the pope. After narrowly escaping an artillery bombardment at Gaeta in flagrant violation of the armistice, the last king of the Two Sicilies, Francis II, who had succeeded his father barely a year earlier, was carried to Rome and exile on a British warship.

Hurriedly organized plebiscites on the mainland and in Sicily in October and November endorsed annexation to Piedmont and hence the end of the kingdom. In many parts of the south, however, unification was experienced as military occupation. Large numbers of former Bourbon soldiers died of disease and mistreatment in concentration camps, while opponents of the Piedmontese monarchy were excluded from public office. Within a year much of the south and Sicily was in open revolt, a situation the government deliberately disguised as "brigandage." But between 1861 and 1864 more men were engaged in the operations against supposed brigands and more lives were lost than in all the previous wars of independence, and in 1866 the navy had to be used to repress another separatist revolt in Palermo.

At the time of unification the differences between north and south were much less than they would be by the end of the century. But the extension of Piedmont's free trade measures in 1861 caused the collapse of the southern industries, which included the biggest engineering and shipbuilding factories in Italy. The most advanced sectors of the southern economies would be devastated by the agricultural crisis that struck the whole of Europe in the 1880s, but the south suffered more generally from neglect, overtaxation, and lack of investment. In the closing decade of the century renewed popular unrest and the beginnings of the great transoceanic emigration indicated that once it had ceased to be a kingdom the south had simply become a problem: "the southern problem."

See also **Carbonari; Garibaldi, Giuseppe; Italy; Naples; Sicily.**

BIBLIOGRAPHY

Astarita, Tommaso. *Between the Salt Water and the Holy Water: A History of Southern Italy.* New York and London, 2005.

Davis, John A., ed. *Italy in the Nineteenth Century.* Oxford, U.K., 2000.

JOHN A. DAVIS

KIPLING, RUDYARD (1865–1936), English writer.

Arguably the dominant figure in English literature of the 1890s, when he published more than two hundred works of poetry and prose to almost unbroken acclaim, Rudyard Kipling's unswerving imperialism, and apparent indifference to literary modernism, caused a downturn in his reputation in the years following World War I; Kipling is one of the few English writers to have aligned himself with the politico-military establishment rather than against it. Yet Kipling has always attracted admirers—among them T. S. Eliot (1888–1965), W. H. Auden (1907–1973), Randall Jarrell (1914–1965), and Jorge Luis Borges (1899–1986)—and his status as one of the greatest English writers of the short story is by now widely acknowledged.

EARLY YEARS

Kipling was born in Bombay in 1865, the son of Lockwood Kipling, who was in India to teach architectural sculpture, and Alice Macdonald, through whose sisters he was connected by marriage to the worlds of art and politics; the painter Edward Burne-Jones was his uncle, and Stanley Baldwin, the future prime minister, a cousin. His childhood was idyllic until in 1871 he and his younger sister Trix were taken "home" to England and left as the boarders of a Mrs. Holloway. Here, withdrawn and unhappy, he learned to observe moods and tempers, and consoled himself by reading; his story "Baa Baa, Black Sheep" (1888) is a fictional record of his experiences. In January 1878 he was sent to the United Services College, an impoverished public school for the sons of army officers, and the setting for the stories in *Stalky & Co.* (1899). Excused from games because of his poor eyesight, he was given the run of the library and encouraged to write. In 1882 he left school to work as a journalist in India, at first in Lahore, and later in Allahabad, where his duties shifted gradually from journalism proper to the supply of poems and stories. In 1889 he returned to England, to take literary London by storm.

To his contemporaries, the early stories, beginning with the collections *Plain Tales from the Hills* (1888) and *Soldiers Three* (1890), seemed to derive from journalism: smart, knowing accounts of Anglo-Indian intrigues, the pleasures and hardships of barracks life, the exotic but threatening world of the native population. That much of this material was new to a London audience no doubt contributed to its popularity. What strikes the twenty-first-century reader is rather the instability of the stories, figured in the way so many of them turn on lost or mistaken identities. "India" in Kipling's work is both a land to be governed for the sake of the empire and a testing ground in which white men can discover what strength, or weakness, is in them.

EARLY WRITING

Kipling continued to produce stories and poems at an astonishing rate, including his first (not very successful) novel, *The Light that Failed* (1890), and the highly successful collection *Barrack-Room Ballads* (1892). In 1892, following what seems to have been a breakdown, he married an American, Caroline Balestier, and moved with her to Vermont. Here they had two children, Josephine (b. 1893), and Elsie (b. 1896). Kipling made a number of American friends, among them Theodore Roosevelt, and as well as the two *Jungle Books* (1894) wrote a novel with an American subject, *Captains Courageous* (1897), but in 1896 a quarrel with his brother-in-law persuaded him to return to England. In 1899, on a visit to New York with his family, now including a third child, John (b. 1897), Kipling fell seriously ill and his daughter Josephine died. He never visited the United States again.

SOUTH AFRICA AND ENGLAND

Kipling's interests turned to South Africa, prompted partly by the need to winter abroad, partly by his commitment to the British cause during and after the Boer War (1899–1902). Despite the success of the novel *Kim* (1901), the most generous of his books, and of the *Just So Stories* (begun as stories for Josephine), his reputation was on the wane. To many of his contemporaries, his imperialism seemed unduly harsh, and his anxiety over Britain's military unpreparedness seemed overstated. Increasingly, and with increasing bitterness, as in the poems in *The Five Nations* (1903), Kipling found himself writing in opposition to the dominant mood of the times.

The purchase in 1902 of Bateman's, a house in the Sussex countryside, helped to soften his temper. His political conservatism and his new status as one of the gentry were brought together in the stories and poems of *Puck of Pook's Hill* (1906) and *Rewards and Fairies* (1910), a series of fictional excavations into the history of the English countryside reading back through the sweetness of the landscape to the bitter and violent deeds by which it had been won and by which it must now be defended: henceforth a constant theme in his life and writing. At the same time, *Traffics and Discoveries* (1904) included two stories, "They" and "Mrs Bathurst," that exhibit a delicacy, a compassion, and an interest in the supernatural, which were to mark the more tolerant stories of his last decade. That Kipling's politics were frequently strident—anti-Irish, anti-German, anti-Jewish—has too often, wrongly, been taken to suggest that his stories must be similarly limited.

LATER YEARS

In 1907 Kipling was awarded the Nobel prize for literature, the first Englishman to receive the award. But the chief event of the second half of his life was the death in battle of his son, John, at Loos in 1915. Nothing could compensate him for the loss, nor could he ever forgive Germany. Yet while his war stories include the ferocious "Swept and Garnished" and "Mary Postgate" (1915), he wrote others that deal sympathetically with war neurosis ("shell-shock"), healing, and forgiveness, including "The Gardener" and "The Wish House" (*Debits and Credits,* 1926), and "Dayspring Mishandled," in *Limits and Renewals* (1932). Many of these later stories are allusive, elliptical, and self-reflexive, crosscutting between high and popular culture: not modernist, but with affinities to modernism, as Edmund Wilson (1895–1972) recognized in a review of *Debits and Credits.* But Kipling had no interest in literary movements and cliques; in any case, his health was poor, as was that of his wife, and he divided his time between writing, traveling, often for the sake of his health or hers, and campaigning for such causes as compulsory national service and rearmament, in the face of what he saw as the imminent threat from German militarism. In 1935 he began work on an autobiography, *Something of Myself,* a text as cunning and elliptical as any of the stories. In January 1936 he was taken into the hospital with a burst ulcer; he died there on 18 January and was buried five days later in Westminster Abbey.

See also **Great Britain; Imperialism; India.**

BIBLIOGRAPHY

Carrington, Charles. *Rudyard Kipling: His Life and Work.* Harmondsworth, U.K., 1955; 1970.

Gilbert, Elliot, ed. *Kipling and the Critics.* New York, 1965.

Lycett, Andrew. *Rudyard Kipling.* London, 1999.

Mallett, Phillip. *Rudyard Kipling: A Literary Life.* London, 2004.

Mallett, Phillip, ed. *Kipling Considered.* London, 1989.

Ricketts, Harry. *The Unforgiving Minute: A Life of Rudyard Kipling.* London, 1999.

Rutherford, Andrew, ed. *Kipling's Mind and Art.* Edinburgh and London, 1964.

Phillip Mallett

KITCHENER, HORATIO HERBERT

(1850–1916), 1st Earl Kitchener of Khartoum, British Field Marshal, and imperial statesman.

Horatio Herbert Kitchener was born in Ireland in 1850. Trained at the Royal Military Academy at Woolwich and commissioned in the Royal Engineers, Kitchener served in Palestine and Cyprus before being posted to the Egyptian army.

As its commander-in-chief in the 1890s, Kitchener led the British reconquest of Sudan before being appointed chief of staff to Field Marshal Lord Frederick Sleigh Roberts (1832–1914) in the Boer War. After succeeding Roberts as South African campaign commander, Kitchener ran the imperial army in India until 1909, when he was elevated to field marshal. In 1914 he became secretary of state for war, massively expanding the army in anticipation of lengthy hostilities. He was drowned in 1916 when his ship sank on a mission to Russia.

A severe and aloof martial figure, Kitchener acquired an early reputation as a proficient engineer, colonial expeditionary surveyor, and linguist, and went on to become known for obsessively personal control of campaigns, defined by an unwillingness to delegate command authority and a supreme indifference to human casualties, including those on his own side.

Kitchener's career as a commander peaked in the conduct of rural colonial warfare, where large-scale field operations across African territories confirmed his quintessential organizational spadework and characteristic brutality. This was seen first in the Anglo-Egyptian invasion of Sudan in 1896. In a deliberately slow and methodical advance from Cairo, Kitchener buttressed his technological superiority in firepower and equipment with elaborate desert cartography and a thick flow of local intelligence. His solution to one of the great problems of protracted colonial campaigns, that of transport and supply, was a staged penetration of the Sudan in which his forces advanced more than a thousand miles inland from the Mediterranean. As his expeditionary force marched up the Nile, laborers laid hundreds of miles of railway track and constructed fortified depots, establishing a communications spine back to base. In effect, the pace of conquest was set by the rate of railway building up the main Nile and across the desert, proceeding through a series of spurts and pauses to allow track to be pushed up.

Kitchener was also adroit in exploiting the riverine potential of his route, hauling in gunboats to assist bombardment of the riverbank positions of his Mahdist enemy. This, too, entailed laborious adaptation to local terrain. At times, floodwaters

Lord Kitchener. Undated photograph. © HULTON-DEUTSCH COLLECTION/CORBIS

lifted Kitchener's gunboats over cataracts, but mostly they had to be dismantled at each cataract and completely reassembled after crossing. Exploiting the advantages of industrialization, Kitchener's rail and river movement provided an imposing concentration of logistical and combat power for a thrust deep into the heart of the Sudan.

Kitchener revealed himself as no great tactician in combat with defending Mahdist forces. Although his army was consistently on top, its victories during 1896–1898, even at the decisive Omdurman, were not achieved without difficulties. British organization, British discipline, and British command of technology nevertheless always ultimately tipped the scales against peasant warriors. Constantly hugging the Nile, Kitchener's infantry had the close protection of lethal, high-angle gunboat fire. When his troops could mow down attack formations with magazine rifle and machine gun fire before unleashing cavalry on fleeing survivors, there was little need to move beyond their protective screen.

Britain's Sudanese opponents repeatedly underestimated the invaders' firepower, a misjudgment made worse by traditional tactics of trying to engage at close quarters. Kitchener inflicted huge losses in several encounters that were more massacres than battles. He also sanctioned controversial conduct by his army, including summary executions, looting, and the desecration of religious sites. These were termed politically necessary acts to destroy "the fanatical feeling" of Mahdist Islam.

Kitchener's pulverizing of Sudan provided an indication of his approach to making war upon the republican Boers of South Africa, opponents who, although small in number, were tactically astute, highly mobile horsemen, and well-armed. As Britain's commander during the extended 1900–1902 guerrilla war phase of the South African conflict, Kitchener assumed authority at a time when the war was not going particularly well for the British. His main challenge was devising a strategy to choke roving Boer commandos into submission.

Under Kitchener's familiar iron will, high-level core staff planning became more rigorous, improving coordination between military command and political imperatives. Kitchener boosted the capability of the Field Intelligence Department, stocking it with thousands of local pro-British white agents and loyalist black scouts and spies who monitored the countryside. He drew on his Sudanese experience in engineering and used conscripted African labor to extend river bridging and maintain essential rail communications. Working from a north-south intelligence grid of the South African interior, he completed as well another large feat of military engineering. Thousands of blockhouses were erected; lines of barbed wire were laid down; and telegraph, telephone, and carrier pigeon connections were established to integrate these new fortified positions. The Royal Engineers furnished power and lighting to the network, enabling continuous surveillance. As these gridlike catchment zones were established, Kitchener organized fast-moving flying columns to conduct mounted sweeps between them, systematically clearing areas of guerrilla resistance.

Kitchener also hit at republican morale by fostering Boer collaboration with the imperialist cause, placing several thousand surrendered insurgents under the British flag as turncoat National Scouts. This measure fractured the Boers' anti-imperialist war effort and sowed bitter divisions in postwar South Africa between "hands-uppers" and "bitter-enders."

The most fearsome element of Kitchener's counterinsurgency campaign, however, was an intensification of the scorched-earth strategy initiated by his predecessor, Lord Roberts, as a reprisal for resistance to British conquest and occupation. To deny Boer forces supplies and the moral sustenance of civilian support, Kitchener carried the war to thousands of rural homesteads. In an incendiary swathe of destruction, crops were fired, cattle driven off, and houses burnt or dynamited. Women, children, old men, and African tenant cultivators and servants were corralled into white and black concentration camps as refugees or "undesirables" (those with kinsmen on commando). In Kitchener's colonial war of attrition, the chief purpose of internment was to hold an enemy society hostage to force its belligerents into giving up their stubborn fight. Soaring mortality rates in unsanitary camps by 1901 contributed to a rising despair in republican ranks that was decisive in forcing the Boers to capitulate in 1902. Only then, with Boer republicanism crushed militarily, did Kitchener throw his support behind a conciliatory and lenient Anglo-Boer peace to rebuild a white settler order.

See also **Boer War; Imperialism; Military Tactics; Omdurman; South Africa.**

BIBLIOGRAPHY

Coetzer, Owen. *Fire in the Sky: The Destruction of the Orange Free State, 1899–1902.* Johannesburg, 2000.

Holt, P. M. *The Mahdist State in the Sudan: 1881–1898.* 2nd ed. Oxford, U.K., 1970.

Pollock, John Charles. *Kitchener: The Road to Omdurman.* London, 1999.

Pretorius, Fransjohan, ed. *Scorched Earth.* Cape Town, 2001.

Spies, S. B. *Methods of Barbarism?: Roberts and Kitchener and Civilians in the Boer Republics, January 1900–May 1902.* Johannesburg, 2001.

Vandervort, Bruce. *Wars of Imperial Conquest in Africa, 1830–1914.* Bloomington, Ind., 1998.

Bill Nasson

KLIMT, GUSTAV (1862–1918), Austrian painter and founding member of the Viennese Secession.

Gustav Klimt was a galvanizing figure in fin-de-siècle Vienna, which in no small measure due to him turned into an alternative center of the European art world alongside Paris. Born in Vienna, he studied from 1876 to 1883 at the Kunstgewerbeschule of the Österreichisches Museum für Kunst und Industrie. His initial reputation as an academic painter culminated in well-received commissions for ceiling paintings in the staircases of Vienna's Burgtheater (1886–1888) and Kunsthistorisches Museum (1890–1891). Executed in collaboration with his brother Ernst and their colleague Franz Matsch, Klimt contributed mythological and historical scenes relating to the theater at the former, and spandrels—the space between the arches and their frames—representing Egyptian art, Greek art, and early Italian art at the latter. A decisive turning point in Klimt's career came with the 1892 commission by the Austrian Ministry of Education to collaborate with Matsch on the ceiling paintings in the Great Hall of the University of Vienna. In the course of his work on these canvases, the academic painter steeped in neoclassical tradition transformed himself into a modern artist.

Klimt was placed in charge of three of four paintings representing the faculties—philosophy, medicine, and jurisprudence, with theology to be painted by Matsch—and several related spandrels. While Klimt's first sketches were still in keeping with his early academic manner, the compositions gradually evolved to embody his mature, modern style: allegories in the form of eroticized, primarily female bodies and hauntingly isolated faces embedded in large-scale, nonrepresentational areas. The latter were filled with an amorphous haze or manifold ornamental patterns derived from Mycenaean, Egyptian, and Byzantine art. If his patrons, a university commission reporting to the Ministry of Education, were skeptical and in effect rejected the results Klimt presented, this was due to dramatic changes in conception and style. These changes clashed with the work of his collaborator and made the paintings unsuitable for viewing from far below. Klimt worked on the paintings until 1907, long after any hope of their installation was lost, but they remained unfinished and ultimately perished in a fire in 1945 at Schloss Immendorf, where they had been brought for protection from the war.

Versions of Klimt's university paintings were on view in exhibitions of the Vereinigung bildender Künstler Österreichs (Sezession)—commonly known as the Vienna Secession—in 1900, 1901, 1902, and 1903. The organization was founded in 1897 by a group of artists, designers, and architects that broke away from the established local society of artists, the Künstlerhausgenossenschaft (Artists' house society), in order to promote modern, international trends in the visual arts through its journal, *Ver Sacrum,* and through regular exhibitions in its own building designed by its architect member Joseph Maria Olbrich. As one of its oldest and best-known members, Klimt exerted great influence over the new organization: he served as its first president, designed the poster and catalog cover for the inaugural exhibition, and received his own one-man exhibition, *Klimt-Kollektive,* in 1903, displaying seventy-eight paintings and drawings. His contribution featured prominently in the Secession's legendary fourteenth exhibition of 1902, which involved a large-scale collaborative *Gesamtkunstwerk* (total work of art) of frescoes, sculptures, reliefs, and interior designs centered around a Beethoven statue by the German artist Max Klinger. Klimt's *Beethoven Frieze,* restored in 1985, stretched over three walls of a room framing the view into the main room. Its underlying program was humanity's progress from desire to fulfillment, which has been read as a representation of the "Ode to Joy" in Beethoven's Ninth Symphony. Abstract elements and areas now became even more prominent than in the university paintings. Ornamental patterns proliferate independently and far beyond the clothes and decorative objects worn by the allegorical figures. Their meanings shift, alternately suggesting material luxury, sensual excess, and spiritual transcendence.

The Vienna Secession is best known in the early twenty-first century for the kind of integration of visual and applied arts exemplified by the Beethoven exhibition. That shared interest prevailed until 1905. Klimt and especially his peers had already shifted their efforts to a new workshop-like organization known as the Wiener Werkstätte (Vienna workshop) and left the Secession following internal

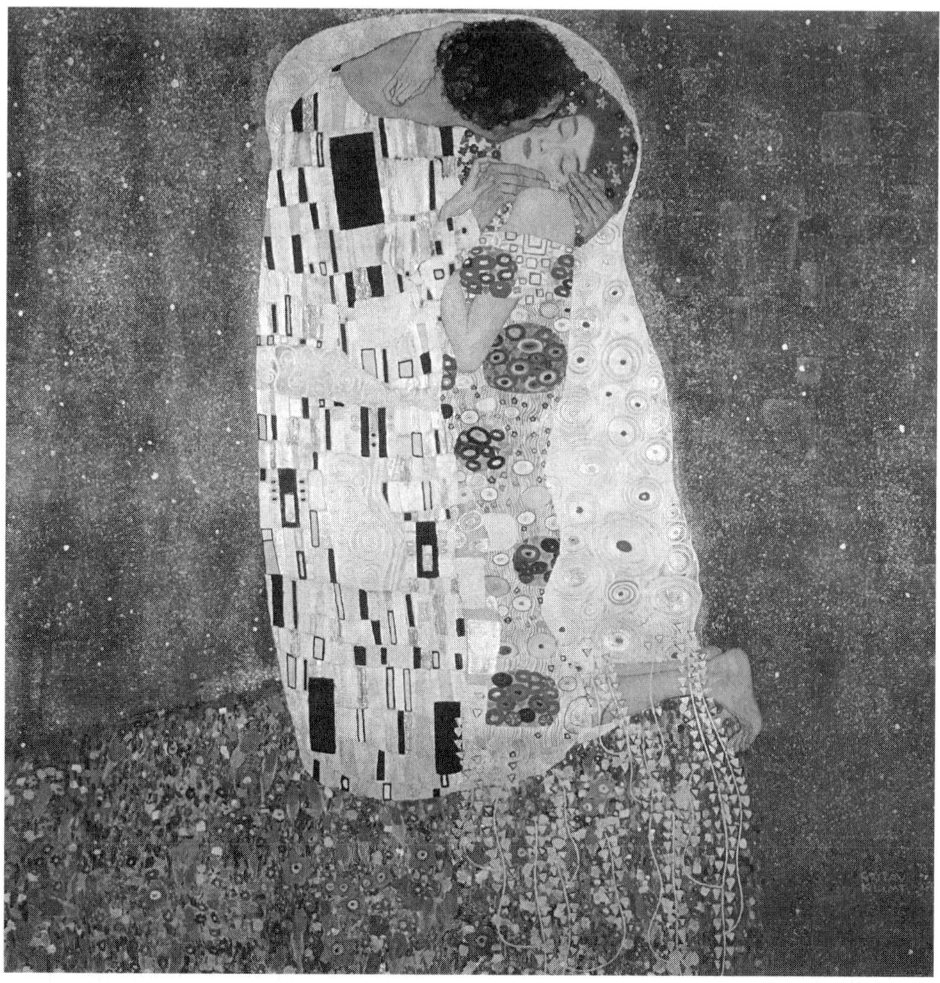

The Kiss. Painting by Gustave Klimt, 1907–1908. ©CORBIS

splits with artists favoring easel painting. Decorative techniques, materials, and motifs played an increasingly important role in Klimt's work. The *Stoclet Frieze*—the painter's contribution to the Wiener Werkstätte's magnum opus, the design of the palace of the Belgian millionaire Adolphe Stoclet in Brussels—eclectically applied materials such as gold, silver, enamel, coral, and semiprecious stones in techniques such as inlay and mosaic. Likewise Klimt's paintings on canvas entered the so-called golden period, exemplified famously by allegories like *The Kiss* of 1907–1908 and female portraits like *Adele Bloch-Bauer I.* Human faces seem mere excuses for ornamental patterns in different tones of gold, amounting both to perceptual onslaught and fetishistic displacement, that is, a transfer of erotic desire for a person onto a substitute. Klimt was often accused for producing pornography while his sitters were suspected of having affairs with the artist. However, the eroticism is greatly tamed in Klimt's paintings by the proliferation of the decorative, especially in comparison to Klimt's drawings, which count among the most erotically evocative and elegantly sensuous works of modern art.

Klimt is broadly associated with late-nineteenth-century symbolist art, which also combined figurative motifs and abstract means to represent personifications of emotional and spiritual states. Leading contemporary painters such as Paul Cézanne and Paul Gauguin, sometimes categorized as symbolist, would prove influential to the beginnings of purely abstract art in the early twentieth century. Klimt never had the same impact, perhaps because his understanding of the signifying capacity of pure forms and colors was more limited, and certainly more playful, than the systematic investigations of his contemporaries.

See also **Fin de Siècle; Modernism; Symbolism; Vienna.**

BIBLIOGRAPHY

Primary Sources

Bahr, Hermann. *Gegen Klimt.* Vienna and Leipzig, 1903.

Nebehay, Christian M., ed. *Gustav Klimt: Eine Dokumentation.* Vienna, 1969.

Novotny, Fritz, and Johannes Dobai. *Gustav Klimt, with a Catalogue Raisonné of His Paintings.* Translated by Karen Olga Philippson. London and New York, 1968.

Secondary Sources

Goldwater, Robert. *Symbolism.* New York, 1979.

Natter, Tobias G., and Gerbert Frodl. *Klimt's Women.* Exhibition catalog. Cologne and New Haven, Conn., 2000.

Vergo, Peter. *Art in Vienna 1898–1918: Klimt, Kokoschka, Schiele, and Their Contemporaries.* Oxford, U.K., 1975.

CHRISTINE MEHRING

KOCH, ROBERT (1843–1910), German bacteriologist.

Heinrich Hermann Robert Koch was one of the founding fathers of medical bacteriology, a discipline that established the association of bacteria with disease. He identified a number of bacterial pathogens, devised or improved essential laboratory technologies within the field, reflected on the methodology of establishing bacterial etiologies of infectious diseases, and developed a number of practical applications.

EDUCATION AND EARLY CAREER

Koch was born 11 December 1843 into the family of a senior mining official in Clausthal, a northern German town. Six of his eight brothers emigrated from Germany, but Koch—who dreamed of emigration himself—stayed and attended the nearby University of Göttingen in 1862. What remained from his youthful dreams was a passion for travel that played an important role in the later stages of his career. Koch initially studied natural sciences, but decided on medicine in 1863 and turned out to be a gifted student. Even though Friedrich Gustav Jacob Henle (1809–1885), who had written an influential treatise on infectious diseases and their causation in 1840, was one of his teachers, it is unlikely that Koch received any inspiration for his future career during his years in Göttingen.

In 1866 he left the university, married Emmy Fraatz, and tried to establish himself as a general practitioner. After several failed attempts to find a position that satisfied his financial needs, Koch finally settled in 1872 as district physician in Pomeranian Wollstein (today Wolstyn, Poland). It seems that he started to work as a bacteriologist in 1873; the chosen object of study was anthrax, a common veterinary disease that was well researched. That this condition could be transmitted by rod-shaped structures found in the blood of infected animals was widely assumed. Koch based his experiments on the microbiology of Ferdinand Julius Cohn (1828–1898), a botanist from Breslau (today Wrocław, Poland), and was able to identify these structures as *Bacillus anthracis.* He established its full life cycle and demonstrated its pathogenicity in animal experiments.

It is not surprising that Koch then turned to Cohn. The latter gave him an enthusiastic welcome and published Koch's paper in a journal that he edited. He also freed him intellectually from the solitude of his countryside practice and brought him into contact with the Breslau pathologist Julius Friedrich Cohnheim (1839–1884) and Carl Weigert (1845–1904), his prosector (one who performs dissections for anatomic demonstration). This opened contacts into the medical world and enabled Koch to complete his education as a medical researcher by learning up-to-date methods of experimental pathology such as the use of the microtome or staining preparations with aniline dyes.

It was on this basis that Koch from 1877 made his own contributions to methodology and technology, most notably the microphotography of bacteria. This improved technology was then tried on the pièce de résistance of pathology of the time, the etiology of septic infections, on which Koch published in 1878. He showed himself to be an ingenious animal experimenter who succeeded in taking the study of human infectious diseases away from the sickbed and into the laboratory. It was also in this context that Koch for the first time made systematic arguments about how to establish bacterial etiologies. These later became known as *Koch's postulates* and included the three steps of isolation, cultivation, and inoculation. However, methodology differed widely over the years, and the phrase *Koch's postulates* was coined by others.

In 1880 Koch took up an academic position. With Cohnheim's help he became head of the imperial health offices bacteriological laboratory and moved to Berlin. The following years were his most productive. He published on laboratory technique in "Zur Untersuchung pathogener Mikroorganismen" ("On the Study of Pathogenic Organisms"), which described his own method of producing mass pure cultures and other important work such as methods for sterilization. In the same period Koch increased the cohesiveness of his group by launching an attack on the French bacteriologist Louis Pasteur (1822–1895).

World fame came in two steps. First, on 24 March 1882 Koch presented the tubercle bacillus *Mycobacterium tuberculosis* as the pathogen of that condition. Even though Koch was by no means the first to advocate the idea of tuberculosis as an infectious disease, it was his bacillus that firmly established the connection of the various clinical forms of that disease and paved the way to an easy and plausible understanding of its etiology. His identification of the *Vibrio cholera* as the pathogen of cholera in 1884 was much less satisfying on the scientific side—it did not fulfill the standards of the postulates, and the bacterium as such had been known for decades. However, because part of the research was carried out during an expedition to Egypt and India and because the work itself represented sharp competition with a French group, it raised enormous public interest and shaped Koch's image as a crusader against plagues.

CRISES

The years after 1885 brought a series of crises to Koch's life and work. After a failed attempt to found and head an imperial institute for bacteriology, Koch was promoted to a professorship at Berlin University in 1885. However, this appointment had been forced on the university by the state administration and was met with stiff resistance from inside the faculty of medicine. Koch had little experience and liking for professorial obligations. Moreover, Koch had problems with his research strategies. While his early successes had largely depended on microbe hunting, it was clear that this could hardly be prolonged. Furthermore, the popular embodiment of diseases as bacteria had raised hopes of specific therapies. These hopes had remained unfulfilled, while—to make things worse—Koch's rival Pasteur had achieved a public triumph with his rabies vaccine in 1885.

Koch attempted to find a way out of this crisis by developing a remedy for tuberculosis, which became known as tuberculin. When tuberculin became available in late 1890, it produced an unprecedented euphoria, even though its composition was kept secret. Public pressure led Koch to publish a description of tuberculin, which turned out to be an extract of tuberculosis pure cultures dissolved in glycerine. It turned out that his secrecy had blocked from view his fantastic commercial plans and the fact that his views on the medicine's therapeutic qualities were highly speculative. Separation from his wife and an affair with the seventeen-year-old student of fine arts Hedwig Freiberg, who later became his second wife, damaged his reputation further, and in early summer 1891 Koch found himself in public disgrace.

Still, Prussian government officials had used the short-lived euphoria following the release of tuberculin to get a parliament decision to found a new institute for research on infectious diseases. In 1891 Koch was appointed director of what today is the Robert-Koch-Institute in Berlin, but he had to accept harsh conditions: he effectively lost the right to hold patents since he had to assign all rights to his future inventions to the Prussian state in advance.

Koch's reputation was restored by the 1892 cholera epidemic that hit Hamburg, where the municipal sanitary administration had produced a disaster. A team of hygienists headed by Koch was sent in by the imperial government to combat the epidemic. On the scientific side the cholera epidemic was a turning point for Koch, who now abandoned the rather simple models of infection that he had employed so far. Epidemiology became important for him; he began to take note of phenomena such as aclinical or subclinical infections, and a few years later put forward the concept of healthy carriers (individuals who carried a disease without showing any symptoms of it themselves), which greatly influenced infectiology and epidemiology.

Beginning in the mid-1890s, Koch focused on tropical infections of humans and animals. Such research enabled him to combine his interest in epidemiology with his lifelong passion for travel and to relaunch his old interest in etiology in research on vector-borne tropical diseases. Long periods of absence from Berlin followed, during which the directorship of his institute was effectively left to others. Koch frequently worked for the British colonial office on cattle diseases, and his research on human diseases centered on the two paradigmatic diseases of tropical medicine, malaria and sleeping sickness. In the first case he focused on the developmental cycle of the pathogen, *Plasmodium falciparum*. In the latter case his work took a more therapeutic direction. This culminated in a large expedition from 1906 to 1907, which occurred after his early retirement in 1904. Because Koch failed to openly reveal the poor efficacy and severe side effects of atoxyl in treating sleeping sickness, this medicine became the basis of a large eradication campaign in the German colonies.

Koch received numerous honors, such as the the Nobel prize in 1905 as well as Prussia's most prestigious medal, awarded the following year. Koch died on 27 May 1910 during a stay at the south German spa of Baden-Baden.

See also **Cholera; Disease; Pasteur, Louis; Public Health; Tuberculosis.**

BIBLIOGRAPHY

Primary Sources

Essays of Robert Koch. Translated by K. Codell Carter. New York, 1987.

Gesammelte Werke von Robert Koch. 2 vols. Edited by Julius Schwalbe. Leipzig, Germany, 1912.

Secondary Sources

Brock, Thomas D. *Robert Koch: A Life in Medicine and Bacteriology.* Madison, Wis., 1988.

Gradmann, Christoph. *Krankheit im Labor: Robert Koch und die medizinische Bakteriologie.* Göttingen, Germany, 2005.

CHRISTOPH GRADMANN

KOŚCIUSZKO, TADEUSZ (1746–1817),

Polish patriot.

Born on 4 February 1746, Tadeusz Andrzej Bonawentura Kościuszko came from a middling noble family in eastern Poland. His fight for national independence, his support for social justice, and his selflessness earned him acclaim in his lifetime and veneration from later generations of both nationalists and social radicals.

Kościuszko studied military engineering in Warsaw and Paris and fought in the American Revolutionary army as colonel of engineers. He constructed fortifications for Philadelphia (1776–1777), Fort Ticonderoga (1777), and West Point (1778–1780). His field fortifications at the Battle of Saratoga (1777) and his service as engineer, logistics expert, and battlefield captain in the southern campaigns (1780–1782) were highly regarded. After the war, Kościuszko was promoted to brevet brigadier general, was one of the founders of the Society of the Cincinnati, and was given his substantial back pay. In America, Kościuszko crystallized his philosophical support for social and political democracy and learned specific techniques for organizing armies based on commitment and enthusiasm rather than rigorous training.

Returning to Poland, Kościuszko settled on his estates until 1789 when he was commissioned general. Service in the 1792 Russo-Polish War earned him promotion and honorary French citizenship. He resigned and went into exile when the war ended prematurely. As an émigré leader, Kościuszko went in January 1793 on an unsuccessful mission to gain French support for an uprising. After his return, he was chosen commander of the future uprising and traveled to the Austrian-Polish border to check on preparations, which he judged insufficient.

Impelled by Russian-ordered cuts to the Polish army, Kościuszko launched the insurrection in Kraków (Cracow) on 23 March 1794, making a dramatic appearance on the Market Square and taking command of the garrison. He was appointed "dictator" with full military and civil powers, although in practice he shared civil power with experienced political leaders. Other units of the Polish Army joined him, and he declared a *levée en masse* of nobles, burghers, and peasants. He had at his disposal fifty-five thousand regular troops plus twenty-eight thousand militia, and thousands more enlisted for local defense. The Russians and Prussians opposed him with twice the force and much better equipment.

Kościuszko marched toward Warsaw with four thousand regular soldiers and two thousand peasant recruits and defeated the Russians at Racławice, near Cracow, on 4 April when he personally led a charge by peasants armed with scythes. The arrival of fresh Russian units forced him to retreat, however. A successful uprising in Warsaw on 24 April allowed Kościuszko to move north. Prussian and Russian forces defeated him at Szczekociny (10 June), but he got through and defended the capital until a revolt in western Poland forced the Prussian and Russian armies to retreat in early September. The dispatch of Russian reinforcements forced him to take the offensive. Losing the battle of Maciejowice (10 October), Kościuszko was badly wounded, captured, and sent to St. Petersburg.

Throughout the insurrection, Kościuszko mediated between left and right. Radicals approved his Połaniec Manifesto, which granted peasants personal freedom and reduced their labor obligations, and his efforts to recruit peasants. Yet Kościuszko supported conservatives by relieving a leading radical of command in Wilno (Vilnius) and suppressing radical mobs in Warsaw. He restricted but protected the unpopular Polish king, Stanisław II August Poniatowski (r. 1764–1795).

Freed by Russian Emperor Paul I, Kościuszko came to America in August 1797 but left for France in May 1798. Personal friendship led Vice President Thomas Jefferson to serve as the executor of Kościuszko's will, which provided funds to emancipate and educate African American slaves. In France, Kościuszko helped organize the Polish legions to support the French armies in Italy but became increasingly suspicious of French motives, particularly when Napoleon took power. Despite joining the Polish Republican Society, his growing conviction that Poland had to win independence without foreign assistance by emancipating the serfs and creating a strong national government isolated him politically. He withdrew from politics.

Both Napoleon (1807) and Alexander I (1815) unsuccessfully attempted to recruit Kościuszko to lead their versions of Polish statehood. He rebuffed them, posing unacceptable demands for a parliamentary government and eastern borders that extended well beyond pre-partition levels, and moved in 1815 to Solothurn, Switzerland, where he died on 15 October 1817. Kościuszko was buried in Wawel Castle (Cracow) while his heart was buried in Solothurn; it was returned to Poland in 1927.

After his death, Kościuszko's reputation solidified into inviolable legend. Poles celebrated him by building a large memorial hill near Kraków (completed in 1823), and in numerous paintings (notably by Jan Matejko, 1888) and literary portraits (notably by Nobel laureate Władysław Reymont). His death was often commemorated through illegal political demonstrations, and Polish emigrants also celebrate the Kościuszko cult, notably through museums in Rapperswil and Solothurn, Switzerland, and the Kościuszko Foundation (New York). The highest peak in Australia, a county in Indiana, an island in Alaska, and towns in Mississippi and Texas have been named after him.

See also **Nationalism; Poland; Russia.**

BIBLIOGRAPHY

Korzon, Tadeusz. *Kościuszko: Biografia z dokumentów wysnuta.* Cracow, Poland, 1894. The most complete biography. In Polish.

Pula, James S. *Thaddeus Kościuszko: The Purest Son of Liberty.* New York, 1999. Emphasizes Kościuszko's American activities.

Szyndler, Bartłomiej. *Tadeusz Kościuszko.* Warsaw, 1991. Includes historiographical references. In Polish.

DANIEL STONE

KOSSUTH, LAJOS (1802–1894), Hungarian politician and statesman.

Lajos (Louis) Kossuth is perhaps the most esteemed leader in Hungarian history and one of the least respected in the neighboring countries of Europe. This was because he attempted to combine a liberal, reformist program with activist nationalism.

Kossuth was born a Lutheran on 19 September 1802, at Monok, in Zemplén County, which lies in the northeastern corner of post-1918, diminished Hungary. His ancient but by no-means-wealthy noble family originated from Túróc County in modern northern Slovakia. Like all nobles, the Kossuths belonged to the exclusive *Natio Hungarica,* which denoted status and privilege more than nationality. Kossuth later found his life mission in elevating the rest of the country's inhabitants, some 90 percent of the total population, to the legal and political status of the *Natio Hungarica.* He also hoped to turn them into Hungarian patriots and, if possible, Hungarian speakers. Yet even his own mother was a German speaker from the neighboring Zipser German settlement.

A lawyer in the service of one of Hungary's great landowning families, Kossuth's father became impoverished and unemployed, yet Lajos received an education befitting a member of the nobility: Latin—then still the language of administration, politics, as well as education in Hungary—and law, which, among other things, qualified one for office in the fifty-odd noble-run county administrations. Kossuth assumed his first official role in 1827 in his native Zemplén County, efficiently fighting a cholera epidemic, among other things, but in 1832 he had to leave his position because of a scandal involving the misappropriation of funds. Ironically, it was this incident—in which he seems to have been guilty at least of negligence—that catapulted him into national politics, his liberal patrons having sent him to represent an absentee aristocrat in the National Diet. Once there, Kossuth defied censorship by writing his own dietal or parliamentary reports, which students copied by hand and which were widely distributed. He thus became one of the first noblemen to earn a living as a journalist, an endeavor made possible by his talent and the political ferment in the country.

Gentlemen,—In ascending the tribune to demand of you to save our country, the awful magnificence of the moment weighs oppressively on my bosom. I feel as if God had placed into my hands the trumpet to arouse the dead, that—if still sinners and weak—they may not relapse into eternal death, but that they may wake for eternity, if any vigor of life be yet in them. Thus, at this moment, stands the fate of the nation. . . .[Some six thousand words later] . . . Gentlemen, what I meant to say is, that this request on the part of the government ought not to be considered as a vote of confidence. No; we ask for your vote for the preservation of the country! And I would ask you, gentlemen, if anywhere in the country a breast sighs for liberation, or a wish waits for its fulfillment, let the breast suffer for a while, let that wish have a little patience, until we have saved the country. (Cheers.) This is my request! You all have risen to a man, and I bow before the nation's greatness! If your energy equals your patriotism, I will make bold to say, that even the gates of hell shall not prevail against Hungary!

The above are the beginning and the end of Louis Kossuth's great speech in parliament on 11 July 1848, where he asked for forty thousand forints for the defense of the country. It is quoted as note 9 in the appendix of William H. Stiles's *Austria in 1848–49* (2 vols. New York, 1852. Reprint, New York, 1971, vol. II, pp. 384 and 394). Stiles was the U.S. chargé in Vienna at that time and sympathetic to the cause of Kossuth. The text contains a few corrections by István Deák, based on the original Hungarian.

JOURNALIST AND POLITICIAN

Nominally, Hungary was a sovereign country at that time, to be governed according to its own laws by the king in concert with the nobility. The trouble was that the king was also emperor of Austria, with manifold interests in Europe, and that the *Natio Hungarica* preferred the politics of grievances to much-needed economic, social, and administrative reforms. The diet, meeting in Pozsony (Pressburg, Bratislava), close to Vienna, served mainly as an intermediary between the absolutist court and the restive county administrations that felt entitled not to execute laws and decrees that, in their opinion, violated the nation's ancient constitution. It was the stalemate between king and nobility that prompted members of the famous "reform generation" to devise diverse modernization programs, such as Count István Széchenyi's call for economic and technological progress; Baron Miklós Wesselényi's—and later Kossuth's—preference for creating first a sense of nationality in the population; Baron József Eötvös's advocacy of educational reform as well as administrative centralization; and Ferenc Deák's insistence on the overhauling of the country's archaic judicial practices.

First a very junior partner among the greats, Kossuth gradually assumed more importance by controlling a part of public opinion. When the session of the diet ended in 1836, he turned to writing and editing the municipal reports, which dealt with the work of the county assemblies. In 1837 he was arrested and charged with disloyalty and sedition; he spent three years in jail, which not only allowed him to learn the basis of his later magnificent English but also made him a national martyr. Hoping to tame the fierce agitator, Chancellor Prince Clemens von Metternich (1773–1859) now allowed Kossuth to edit the newspaper *Pesti Hírlap*. Yet by 1844, when he was finally removed from his post, Kossuth had brought the country closer to revolution and had, incidentally, also done much for the rejuvenation of the Hungarian language.

In 1841, Kossuth married Teréz Meszlényi, a Catholic gentlewoman whom Kossuth's admirers tended to dislike but who remained loyal to her husband until her death in Italian exile in 1865. They had a daughter and two sons; of the two, Ferenc would become an influential politician, less because of his talent than because of his name. Of Kossuth's relations with his wife next to nothing is known, just as little is known of the friendships and private passions of this eminently political person.

As political life heated up and politicians chose between calling themselves liberals or conservatives, personal differences also came to the fore. The most famous of these differences was that between Széchenyi and Kossuth: the first a titled aristocrat, wealthy, well traveled, moody, and darkly pessimistic; the second without any land to his name, with no personal knowledge of the world, but supremely self-confident. Széchenyi wanted Hungary to be rich and its society cultured (he did much to improve banking, transportation, and culture) and only then truly sovereign, but still under the aegis of the beneficial Austrian connection; Kossuth recognized the importance of all this but felt that, without genuine sovereignty, nothing could be achieved. This, especially, because he felt the need to control and to convert the ethnic minorities: Germans, Slovaks, Ruthenes, Romanians, and Serbs, who together made up about 60 percent of the population.

No longer an editor, Kossuth sought success—and livelihood—in heading various voluntary associations, such as those concerning maritime development and the defense of trade and industry. Once a passionate free-trader, he now advocated tariff barriers even against Austria so as to enable Hungary to develop its own industry. In 1847 Kossuth became the leader of the lower house's main opposition party.

"I have just signed my death sentence! My head will certainly land on the block! . . . I shall be hanged with Kossuth."

Diary entry by Count István Széchenyi on 23 March 1848, upon accepting the post of minister of public works and transport in the newly formed constitutional government of which Count Lajos Batthyányi was the head and Kossuth minister of finance. Even though Kossuth called Széchenyi "the greatest Hungarian," the two were bitter political opponents. Quoted in György Spira, *A Hungarian Count in the Revolution of 1848.* Translated by Thomas Land, translation revised by Richard E. Allen. Budapest, 1974, p. 67.

Early in 1848, the news of revolutionary agitation in Italy and Paris threatened to ruin the monarchy's shaky finances; this alerted Kossuth to the possibility of wresting concessions from the advisers in the court of Ferdinand I (r. 1835–1848), the retarded king-emperor. On March 3, Kossuth proposed in the diet the emancipation of the serfs and the appointment of a government responsible to the parliament. The speech inspired the Viennese to make their revolution on 13 March and young intellectuals in Budapest to proceed to their bloodless revolution on 15 March. Besieged by his own subjects, who all wanted change while professing loyalty to his person, and under attack by the king of Piedmont-Sardinia in northern Italy, Ferdinand was ready to surrender to all. On 7 April 1848, Hungary was granted its own government with Kossuth as finance minister and Széchenyi as minister of public works and transport. The new constitution transformed the country—at least in theory—into a modern, liberal state with even a degree of control over the monarchy's military and foreign affairs. In all this and more, Kossuth had been the driving force.

FROM MINISTER TO DICTATOR TO CONSTITUTIONAL GOVERNOR-PRESIDENT

All would have been well had Croatia, a subordinate kingdom, not asked for the same rights that Hungary had achieved, and had the self-appointed leaders of the different ethnic minorities not demanded recognition of their national groups. While willing to grant Croatia complete autonomy on the basis of its historic privileges, Kossuth and his colleagues rejected the demands of the ethnic minorities by arguing that Hungary, which had just recently replaced corporate and territorial privilege with the rights of the individual, could not possibly grant new territorial and group autonomies.

In June, Serbs revolted in southern Hungary; in July, Kossuth as minister of finance announced in one of his most memorable speeches that Hungary would raise funds to finance its own army while denying funds to the king for the defense of his possessions in Italy. On 6 September, Kossuth issued the first—illegal—Hungarian banknotes. Five days later, the Vienna-appointed governor of Croatia invaded Hungary with his troops, whether or not at the orders of the court remains unclear. In order to avoid open confrontation with the king and the new, liberal Austrian cabinet, the government of Count Lajos Batthyány (1806–1849) resigned, but Kossuth and one other minister remained at their posts. A few days later, the recently constituted parliament appointed Kossuth head of the so-called National Defense Committee with extensive wartime rights.

Lajos Kossuth. Colored engraving, 1849. Hadtorteneti Muzeum, Budapest, Hungary/Bridgeman Art Library/Archives Charmet

Kossuth used his extraordinary oratorical abilities and his talent as an administrator to create an army, which was badly needed because, following the attack by Serbs and Croats, many Romanians also revolted and, in December, the imperial army itself invaded Hungary. At first, defeat after defeat plagued the motley Hungarian army of ex-regulars and unreliable volunteers, forcing Kossuth and the parliament to flee from Budapest to eastern Hungary. But then the Hungarians used their administrative experience to raise and equip an army of conscripts that, in the spring of 1849, beat back the Austrians. On 14 April 1849, a triumphant parliament in Debrecen proclaimed the dethronement of the House of Habsburg-Lorraine and elected Kossuth governor-president. The Declaration of Independence, drafted by Kossuth, dealt mainly with Hungary's historic grievances, proving again that he was no revolutionary.

Making Kossuth governor-president must be judged a mistake, in part because the virtual dictator thereby became a sort of a constitutional monarch, and in part because the Declaration forced the European governments to take a stand. None recognized the new state, and the British especially made clear that a strong Habsburg monarchy was a European necessity. General Artúr Görgey (1818–1916), who was Kossuth's brilliant young military commander, had not even completed the reconquest of Budapest when Tsar Nicholas I (r. 1825–1855) announced his decision to rush to the aid of Emperor Francis Joseph I (r. 1848–1916) against what Nicholas insisted on seeing as a bunch of near-communist rebels.

The Hungarians proved powerless against a resurgent Austrian army, which was supported by most of the nationalities in the Habsburg monarchy, and against a huge Russian invasion force. No sooner had Kossuth made his triumphant entry to the Hungarian capital than he was forced to flee to southeastern Hungary where the last battles of the War of Independence were to be fought. As a final noble gesture, at the end of July parliament adopted a law giving more rights to the ethnic minorities and another guaranteeing the Jews complete legal equality.

Following a last devastating defeat, Kossuth resigned as governor-president and appointed Görgey dictator of Hungary; on 11 August, the general surrendered his troops to the Russians; a few days later Kossuth and his entourage fled to Turkish territory. As soon as he was abroad, however, he again began using the title of governor-president and accused Görgey of treason.

IN EXILE

The Ottoman government, no matter how sympathetic, was forced by Russian and Austrian pressure to assign Kossuth an involuntary residence in Kiutahia, Asia Minor. While most of the refugees returned to Hungary, Kossuth benefited from multiple invitations to visit the United Kingdom and the United States. He was feted as the champion of liberty and the great emancipator. His visit to the United States in 1851 and 1852 resembled a triumphant march, while orators, including the future president Abraham Lincoln (1809–1865), called him the Hungarian George Washington. Everywhere he went, including an appearance at the joint session of the U.S. Congress, he delivered dazzling speeches in English that were to serve as teaching material in the field of rhetorics for many years to come, but he was unable either to raise funds for an army of liberation or to persuade the United States to intervene in the affairs of Europe.

Back in England, he was feted again and negotiated with heads of state but his only opportunity to return to Hungary, in 1859 on the coattails of the French army, ended abruptly when Napoleon III (1808–1873) concluded an armistice with the defeated Austrian emperor. What put a complete end to his dreams was, however, the compromise agreement of 1867 in which Hungarians decided to share power with the German Austrians in the multinational, so-called dual monarchy.

Kossuth had warned against an agreement that would tie Hungary to the fate of the Habsburg dynasty, but the Hungarians no longer listened to him, least of all the leaders of the Kossuth Party who became more and more expansionist and chauvinistic. While in exile, Kossuth devised various plans for a Central European federation, but such ideas could have no chance of success in an age of heightened nationalism. In old age, Kossuth spoke up repeatedly against illiberal politics and especially against anti-Semitism; his main occupation in Torino, Italy, was, however, to receive delegations of admirers, to write his voluminous memoirs, and to edit his invaluable papers, which fill dozens of volumes. He would not return to Hungary while his archenemy, Francis Joseph I, was king. He died in Torino on 20 March 1894 at the age of ninety-two and was buried in Budapest in the presence of millions. Today, there is no settlement in Hungary without a Kossuth Square or a Kossuth Street.

The Kossuth cult has never abated; his name is on the lips of every politician, although the left, especially the Communists, had tried to monopolize his historic heritage. No doubt, he gave hope to the poor, especially peasants, and he opened the way to the modernization of his country, but he also burdened the shoulders of his compatriots with the dilemma of unrealizable national ambitions.

See also **Austria-Hungary; Deák, Ferenc; Francis Joseph; Jelačić, Josip; Nationalism; Revolutions of 1848.**

BIBLIOGRAPHY

Primary Sources

Haraszti, Éva H. *Kossuth as an English Journalist.* Translated by Brian McLean. Boulder, Colo., 1990. Contains 110 articles and letters published by Kossuth in English in the year 1855.

The Life of Governor Louis Kossuth with his Public Speeches in the United States and a Brief History of the Hungarian War of Independence. New York, 1852. Reprint, Budapest, 2001.

Pulszky, Francis, and Theresa Pulszky. *White, Red, Black.* Kassel, 1853. Reprint, New York, 1970. Fascinating memoirs by one of Kossuth's main political associates and the latter's Austrian wife.

Secondary Sources

Deák, István. *The Lawful Revolution: Louis Kossuth and the Hungarians, 1848–1849.* New York, 1979. The only comprehensive, relatively recent publication on Hungary's greatest statesman and the revolution of which he was the leader.

Komlos, John H. *Louis Kossuth in America, 1851–1852.* Buffalo, N.Y., 1973.

Spencer, Donald S. *Louis Kossuth and Young America: A Study of Sectionalism and Foreign Policy, 1848–1852.*

Columbia, Mo., 1977. How Kossuth's presence upset American party politics.

Szabad, György. *Kossuth on the Political System of the United States of America.* Budapest, 1975.

István Deák

KRAFFT-EBING, RICHARD VON

(1840–1902), German psychiatrist.

One of the most prominent psychiatrists in Central Europe prior to Freud, Richard von Krafft-Ebing started his career working in asylums, but the desire to escape the constraints of institutional psychiatry, which had become more akin to routine custodial care than to a gratifying scientific calling, drove him to broaden his professional territory. As a professor of psychiatry at the Universities of Strassburg (1871–1872), Graz (1872–1889), and Vienna (1889–1902), he became actively engaged in the process in which the main institutional locus of this medical specialty shifted from the asylum to the university. Also, he transcended the institutional confines of psychiatry by developing a private practice, founding a private sanatorium, and advancing its moral role in society. Krafft-Ebing's general theories of psychopathology were rather incoherent: his work embraced biological models of mental illness, including degeneration theory, as well as a psychological understanding of mental disorders. His ideas about the proper explanation and treatment of mental disorders were more or less geared to the changing institutional contexts in which he worked and the shifting social background of his patients. Moving from the public asylum to the university clinic, and founding a sanatorium and a private practice, he tried to enlarge psychiatry's domain as well as to attract a new clientele. Whereas the somatic model of mental disease and degeneration theory promoted the scientific status of psychiatry, a psychological approach was more fruitful to attract middle and upper class patients suffering from rather mild disorders like nervousness, neurasthenia, or sexual perversion.

Krafft-Ebing worked in many fields of psychiatry, but he is remembered chiefly as the author of *Psychopathia sexualis.* This book made him one of the founding fathers of medical sexology. The first edition of this best-seller appeared in 1886, followed soon by several new and elaborated editions and translations in several languages. Krafft-Ebing revised it several times, especially by adding new categories of sexual deviance and more and more case histories. By naming and classifying virtually all nonprocreative sexuality, he synthesized medical knowledge of what then was labeled as perversion. Although he also paid attention to voyeurism, exhibitionism, pedophilia, bestiality, and other sexual behaviors, Krafft-Ebing distinguished four fundamental forms of perversion: (1) contrary sexual feeling or inversion, including various mixtures of manliness and femininity that in the twentieth century would gradually be differentiated into homosexuality, androgyny, and transvestitism; (2) fetishism, the erotic obsession with certain parts of the body or objects; (3) sadism and (4) masochism, neologisms actually coined by him, the first inspired by the Marquis de Sade (1740–1814) and the second by the writer Leopold von Sacher-Masoch (1836–1895).

Krafft-Ebing's interest in sexual deviance was linked to forensic psychiatry, in which he was a leading expert. *Psychopathia sexualis* was written for lawyers and doctors discussing sexual crimes in court. His main thrust was that in many cases sexual deviance should no longer be regarded as simply sin and crime, but as symptoms of pathology. Since mental and nervous disorders often diminished responsibility, he pointed out, most sex offenders should not be punished, but treated as patients. Like other psychiatrists in the late nineteenth century, Krafft-Ebing shifted the focus from immoral acts, a temporary deviation of the norm, to a pathological condition. Influenced by the natural-scientific approach in German psychiatry as well as by degeneration theory, he explained perversions as inborn instincts, as deviations of normal biological evolution.

Krafft-Ebing's work appears to be typical of what Michel Foucault (1926–1984), in his influential *The History of Sexuality* (1978), designates as the medical construction of sexuality. Under the influence of Foucault, it has become a truism that physicians, by describing and categorizing nonprocreative sexualities, were very influential in effecting a fundamental transformation of the social and psychological reality of sexual deviance from a form of immoral behavior to a pathological way of being. The argument runs thus: by differentiating between the normal and the abnormal and by stigmatizing deviance as illness, the medical profession, as the exponent of a "bio-power," was not only constructing the modern idea of sexual identity but also controlling the pleasures of the body. Following Foucault, several scholars have associated the emergence of sexology with a deplorable medical colonization, replacing religious and judicial authority with scientific control. However, some late-twentieth- and early-twenty-first-century historical studies suggest that medical labeling and its disciplining effects have been overemphasized as the major determinants in the process creating sexual identities. Too readily the conclusion has been drawn that the individuals labeled as perverts were passive victims, trapped in the medical discourse.

To be sure, like other psychiatrists, Krafft-Ebing surrounded sexual deviance with an aura of pathology and he echoed nineteenth-century stereotypical thinking on sexual issues. However, his views were all but static or coherent and there were many contradictions and ambiguities in his work. It was open to divergent meanings, and contemporaries—among them many of Krafft-Ebing's patients, correspondents, and informants—have indeed read it in different ways. *Psychopathia sexualis* did not only gratify one's curiosity about sexuality and make sexual variance imaginable, but individuals concerned viewed it also as an endorsement of their desires and behavior. Its numerous case histories revealed to them that they were not unique in their sexual desire. Krafft-Ebing's work was the impetus to self-awareness and self-expression, and many suggested that it had brought them relief. What is striking is not only that life histories were so prominent in *Psychopathia sexualis* and his other publications, but that the autobiographical accounts were not forced into the straitjacket of his sexual pathology. Many of the life histories were submitted voluntarily and although their authors demonstrated a considerable degree of suffering, this did not necessarily mean that they considered themselves to be immoral or ill. The medical model was employed by many of them for their own purposes to mitigate feelings of guilt, to give perversion the stamp of naturalness, and to part with the charge of immorality and illegality. Several went to the psychiatrist not so much seeking a cure but to develop a dialogue about their nature and social situation. In fact, Krafft-Ebing responded to these "stepchildren of nature," as he characterized them. Even if they criticized medical thinking and the social suppression of their sexual desires, he still published their letters and autobiographies uncensored, and he also acknowledged that some of them had influenced him. Lay views and medical views of sexuality overlapped.

As more and more private patients and correspondents came up with life histories that did not fit the established perception of psychiatry and bourgeois morality, Krafft-Ebing's approach became more enmeshed in contradictory views and interests. The psychiatric understanding of perversions moved between scientific control and the realization of the liberal ideals of individual self-expression, self-realization, and emancipation. Whether the scale tipped to one side or the other depended to a large extent on the social position and gender of the psychiatrist's clients. Upper and middle class men capitalized on psychiatric models in order to explain and to justify themselves. But lower class men, prosecuted sexual offenders, and most female patients were generally not in a position to escape the coercion that undeniably was part of psychiatric practice as well.

See also **Psychoanalysis; Psychology; Sexuality.**

BIBLIOGRAPHY

Foucault, Michel. *The History of Sexuality.* Vol.1: *An Introduction.* Translated by Robert Hurley. New York, 1978.

Krafft-Ebing, Richard von. *Psychopathia sexualis: Eine klinisch-forensische Studie.* Stuttgart, 1886. Between 1886 and 1903 Krafft-Ebing published twelve editions of *Psychopathia sexualis.* Reprint, edited by Brian King, Burbank, Calif., 1999.

Müller, Klaus. *Aber in meinem Herzen sprach eine Stimme so laut: Homosexuelle Autobiographien und medizinische Pathographien im neunzehnten Jahrhundert.* Berlin, 1991.

Oosterhuis, Harry. *Stepchildren of Nature: Krafft-Ebing, Psychiatry, and the Making of Sexual Identity.* Chicago, 2000.

HARRY OOSTERHUIS

KROPOTKIN, PETER (1842–1921), Russian geographer, author, revolutionary, anarchist theorist.

In the years before World War I, Peter Kropotkin was the Western world's foremost theoretician of the philosophy and politics of anarchism. During the course of his long life, he achieved fame in a number of diverse fields of knowledge. While still in his twenties, Kropotkin was elected to the Russian Imperial Geographical Society as a result of his pioneering explorations in Finland and Siberia. Later, he became a well-known journalist, editor, and author of a number of books, including his inspiring autobiography, *Memoirs of a Revolutionary,* and his scientific alternative to Herbert Spencer's social Darwinian evolutionary theory, *Mutual Aid.*

Kropotkin was born in 1842 into extraordinary privilege, inheriting the title of prince from his father. His formative years were spent on the family's primary country estate as well in a Moscow mansion surrounded by the culture of serfdom. He attended the empire's most elite school and served in the military before becoming disenchanted with the possibilities of reform under Tsar Alexander II. In 1872, searching for a new path, he underwent a transformative experience in the Swiss Jura Mountains, where he discovered survivors of the Paris Commune carnage who had established an independent society without allegiance to any government.

Returning to Russia, Kropotkin joined the leading underground revolutionary organization, the Chaikovsky Circle, where he wrote his first anarchist treatise, "Must We Occupy Ourselves with an Examination of the Ideal of a Future System?" He was arrested and imprisoned by the tsarist police for his activities, but made one of the rare escapes from the infamous Peter and Paul Fortress with help from his comrades still at large in 1876. He fled to Paris, where he immediately established himself as the successor to the deceased founders of modern anarchism, Pierre-Joseph Proudhon and Mikhail Bakunin. He was arrested by the French authorities for condoning the violent protests of miners in Lyon in his newspaper, *La Révolté,* and imprisoned for three years, but took his revenge by writing the first comparative history of conditions of penal servitude, *In Russian and French Prisons* (1887).

Unable to remain in France after his release from prison, Kropotkin moved to London, where he spent the next two very productive decades. He created the English-speaking world's most influential anarchist newspaper, *Freedom,* which is still published, and lobbied successfully, with the help of several sympathetic British members of Parliament, against the evils of the tsarist regime in the House of Commons, where his brief was introduced prior to its publication as a pamphlet, *The Terror in Russia* (1909). One measure of his renown was the invitation he received to write the article on anarchism for the celebrated eleventh edition of the *Encyclopaedia Britannica.* Equally significant was Kropotkin's shock when he learned that the editors, without his consent, had added a long note to the article listing the acts of political violence associated with the widespread anarchist movement of the time, a subject Kropotkin had deliberately not included.

Kropotkin's main contribution to political theory remains his critique of authority and his radical concept of a future stateless society in which both freedom and equality would be realized. His argument was grounded in a comprehensive assault on both the liberal and conservative interpretations of the theory of the social contract as conceptualized in Hobbes's *Leviathan* (and refined by John Locke and Jean-Jacques Rousseau) as well as the schools of thought and movements oriented around species (Charles Darwin) or class (Karl Marx) conflict. He located numerous examples in ancient, medieval, and modern history of independent and cooperative activities that resulted from collective efforts to overthrow or transcend the abusive power of kings, landowners, armies, and clerics and their justifying legal codes.

Although Kropotkin agonized over the ethics of employing violence in the name of genuine liberty, he consistently supported his colleague Paul Brousse's formulation of "propaganda by the deed." By this, Kropotkin meant that the assassinations of major political leaders, which had spread like an epidemic in the 1890s across Europe, had to be understood in their proper social context. The "terrorists" who threw their bombs in Naples, Paris, Madrid, Berlin, and London as they cried "long live anarchy!" were motivated by the horrendous conditions of inequality that had become intolerable for the majority of society. In his view, the assassins of terror were representatives of popular rebellion against the immoral authority of state, church, and ruling classes. Left to their own devices, without those institutions of control and oppression, ordinary people would find cooperative methods of production and exchange to replace the vicious competition of capitalism. Kropotkin believed that he was already witnessing the birth pangs of that future society, as municipalities at the federal level (rather than central authorities) in many European towns and cities had created free parks, public entertainment, and cooperative shops operating without profit or managerial hierarchies.

Kropotkin's influence spread as his followers expanded around the globe. However, his decision to support the anti-German allies in World War I split and seriously weakened the anarchist movement. Nevertheless, he lived long enough to enjoy the consequences of the fall of the Romanov dynasty in 1917. As part of the general amnesty offered by the Russian Provisional Government to all exiles and political prisoners, Kropotkin returned to his native land at the age of seventy-five. His last years were spent encouraging anarchist parties and organizations in Russia despite Vladimir Lenin's efforts to isolate him and limit his influence. One of his most dedicated disciples, the deported American anarchist Emma Goldman, visited him just before he died in 1921. His funeral was the last public anarchist demonstration permitted in the Soviet Union.

See also **Anarchism; Bakunin, Mikhail; Proudhon, Pierre-Joseph.**

BIBLIOGRAPHY

Cahm, Caroline. *Kropotkin and the Rise of Revolutionary Anarchism, 1872–1886.* Cambridge, U.K., 1989.

Joll, James. *The Anarchists.* Boston, 1965.

Kropotkin, Peter. *Memoirs of a Revolutionist.* Boston, 1899.

———. *Mutual Aid: A Factor in Evolution.* London, 1904.

———. *Selected Writings on Anarchism and Revolution.* Edited by Martin A. Miller. Cambridge, Mass., 1970.

Miller, Martin A. *Kropotkin.* Chicago, 1976.

Woodcock, George. *Anarchism: A History of Libertarian Ideas and Movements.* Cleveland, Ohio, 1962.

MARTIN A. MILLER

KRUPP. Steel, the key material of the Industrial Revolution on which the Krupp family founded its industrial empire in Germany, offers higher strength, hardness, and elasticity than other ferrous metals. In 1811, Friedrich Krupp (1787–1826), an offspring of a prosperous trading family from Essen, founded a workshop for the production of cast steel on a plot of land bought from his grandmother. He hoped to profit from the high demand for steel in a Napoleonic Europe that was deprived of English steel exports as Great Britain sought to weaken France's supremacy through restrictive trade policies. Technical difficulties, as well as, after Napoleon's defeat in 1815, the renewed influx of English steel, whose manufacturers dominated European markets until well into the second half of the nineteenth century, led to persistent, severe losses in Krupp's workshop. On the verge of personal bankruptcy, Friedrich Krupp died an exhausted, frustrated man at the early age of thirty-nine.

EXPANSION UNDER ALFRED KRUPP (1812–1887)

When Alfred Krupp, Friedrich's fourteen-year-old son, assumed managerial responsibility for the heavily indebted workshop with four employees in 1826, he devoted himself to the business with the monomaniacal energy that was to characterize his career. At the heart of the company's long-term success lay a reputation for high quality that allowed it to emerge as a competitor of English manufacturers. Alfred Krupp immersed himself in the technical details of steel production, personally supervising production processes on the shop floor throughout his entire professional life. Once the workshop had overcome initial technical problems, it widened its product range to enter new markets during the 1830s. In addition to craft tools and minting stamps for coin production, Krupp began to produce springs, axles, railway wheels, crankshafts, gun barrels and—starting in the 1850s—cannons. Product diversification combined with a rapidly growing workforce. Having gradually expanded to employ 240 people by 1850, in the next two decades the company benefited from dynamic industrialization processes that transformed the Ruhr area around Essen into the core region of the German industrial landscape.

The Krupp industrial complex on the Ruhr River, Essen, Germany. Postcard c. 1900. MARY EVANS PICTURE LIBRARY

The company took advantage of expanding steel markets in the manufacturing and railway sectors. During the 1860s, it also developed into a leading military supplier, the Prussian army being its most important customer. Armaments accounted for 56 percent of the company's turnover in 1876, which led to Alfred Krupp being nicknamed the "cannon king." By 1873, the steelworks in Essen employed nearly 12,000 people and a further 4,100 workers in subsidiary enterprises.

INDUSTRIAL MANAGEMENT UNDER ALFRED KRUPP

Much of this expansion was predicated on high-risk investment strategies. Until the 1870s, Krupp invariably reinvested profits in new production facilities, subsidiary companies, and large stockpiles. This dynamic expansion, however, came at the price of low reserves, and the policy of immediate re-investment repeatedly subjected the company to major perils during recessions. The steelworks that had impressed domestic and foreign observers as evidence of the industrial power fuelling the German Empire only narrowly averted bankruptcy by laying off more than two thousand laborers in the mid-1870s. Thereafter, Alfred Krupp focused more strongly on the financial consolidation of his company.

An acute sense for self-promotion complemented Alfred Krupp's business acumen and technical skill. He personally lobbied crowned heads and enjoyed a particularly good relationship with the Prussian monarch and subsequent German emperor William I (1797–1888). This connection led to armaments contracts and lucrative orders for railway equipment. Krupp also wooed potential customers, including heads of state, during spectacular tours of his gigantic production facilities. In 1861, the Prussian king left Essen profoundly impressed after a demonstration of steam hammer "Fritz," a legendary "monster" weighing fifty tons. Moreover, Alfred Krupp devoted considerable attention to public relations efforts to secure and maintain an international reputation. The company was a regular participant at world fairs on both sides of the Atlantic; its displays usually included superlative exhibits such as the largest steel block or the biggest gun on show.

Armored gun emplacements at the Grusonwerk factory. Engraving by Robert Engels from the book *Krupp 1812–1912*, published for the Krupp centennial. MARY EVANS PICTURE LIBRARY

By his own account a man with an impatient and brash disposition, Alfred Krupp practiced a direct leadership style to assert his authority over all areas within his works. Personal control, however, was increasingly difficult to achieve as the enterprise grew, a process that required the development of formal management routines within growing hierarchical administrative structures. Although Alfred Krupp was forced to tolerate frictions with his managers, he demanded unqualified loyalty from his manual workers. He was the prototypical example of an entrepreneur who conceived of himself as a stern yet benevolent patriarch. In keeping with this authoritarian understanding of business leadership, the company strictly monitored its employees' private sphere. Workers with socialist sympathies were fired, as were those pursuing "immoral" lifestyles. This high-handed approach to industrial relations went hand-in-hand with Krupp's sense of responsibility for the well-being of "his" workers that led him to offer social provisions that were exceptionally generous by contemporary standards. The company sponsored consumer associations offering foodstuffs at subsidized prices, health insurance, and pension schemes, as well as housing programs. As a result of these welfare programs, Krupp's factory succeeded in attracting and retaining a skilled labor force with low fluctuation rates.

THE STEELWORKS FROM ALFRED KRUPP'S DEATH TO WORLD WAR I

By the time Alfred Krupp died of a heart attack in 1887, his steelworks had become a European industrial giant with excellent connections to the political establishment of the German Empire, and beyond. Krupp was succeeded by his son Friedrich Alfred Krupp (1854–1902), who, while continuing the firm's social policies, further expanded the business, not least through mergers with competitors. Friedrich Alfred Krupp died under mysterious circumstances amid rumors of suicide on the Italian island of Capri after press allegations of a sexual scandal involving young men. After the turn of the century, Gustav Krupp von Bohlen und Halbach (1870–1950), who had married into the family, took over the directorship of the company, which profited from the booming international economy as well as the arms race before World War I. By 1914, the company had become Germany's largest private employer, with a workforce of eighty-one thousand employees.

See also **Germany; Industrial Revolution, First; Industrial Revolution, Second.**

BIBLIOGRAPHY

Berdrow, Wilhelm. *The Krupps.* Translated by Fritz Homann. Berlin, 1937.

Epkenhans, Michael. "Krupp and the Imperial German Navy 1898–1914: A Reassessment." *Journal of Military History* 64 (2000): 355–370.

Köhne-Lindenlaub, Renate. "Friedrich Krupp GmbH." In *International Directory of Company Histories,* vol. 5, 85–89. Chicago, 1992.

BERNHARD RIEGER

KULISCIOFF, ANNA (1854–1925), Italian socialist.

Born into a Russian Jewish merchant family, Anna Kuliscioff was sent to Switzerland to complete her studies in 1871 but gravitated to a group of politically active Russian students. On her return home in 1873, she joined the populist "go to the people" movement. She left Russia definitively in 1877 for Switzerland, where she met the Italian anarchist Andrea Costa. The years between 1879 and 1881 were decisive in Kuliscioff's and Costa's transformation from anarchism to socialism. Her own statement at her trial in Florence in 1879 for membership in a subversive organization pointed to her future political evolution: "Revolutions cannot be made by [Socialist] Internationals out of thin air because it is not for individuals to make them nor to provoke them; it is the people who do it. Therefore it makes no sense to rise up in armed bands but to wait until these bands form naturally and then direct them along socialist principles" (Riosa, p. 5).

After moving between France and Italy, Kuliscioff resumed her studies at the medical faculty in Switzerland from 1882 to 1884 and then at the University of Naples, where she received her medical degree in 1886. The move to Naples ended her relationship with Costa. In 1885 she met Filippo Turati, with whom she established a personal and intellectual relationship that shaped the Italian Socialist Party from its foundation in 1892 to the post–World War I period. In 1891 they began to edit the socialist journal *Critica sociale.* In *Critica sociale* Kuliscioff turned her attention to the problems of women workers, which she integrated into but did not equate with the larger social problem of proletarian emancipation. Kuliscioff opposed autonomous feminist organzations and was instrumental in distinguishing socialist from bourgeois feminism. For instance, she did not involve herself in the largely middle-class campaign for legalization of divorce. She was one of the founders of the women's section of the Milanese Labor Chamber in 1891. Kuliscioff supported the right to vote for women and the eight-hour day, and at the turn of the century she drafted a proposed law to offer women maternity leave with pay, restrictions on night labor, and a guaranteed day of rest. In contrast to many socialists, she understood that legislation for women was not a step to returning them to the home but was essential to their integration in modern society.

Kuliscioff was one of the organizers of the 1892 Genoa congress that formed the Italian Socialist Party. During the 1890s she urged the new party to engage itself in the political life of the country. Like Turati she was convinced that a necessary step to the socialist revolution was the democratization of Italy. During the repression after the riots of May 1898 Kuliscioff was arrested along with other leading socialists. On her release after seven months in jail she supported the alliance between the Italian Socialist Party and middle-class liberals for a return to constitutional legality. Kuliscioff joined Turati in urging Socialist support for the Zanardelli-Giolitti government from 1901 to 1903. Giovanni Giolitti, as interior minister, proclaimed government neutrality in labor disputes between private parties, although he was hostile to strikes in the public sector. Giolitti's failure to deliver substantial reform from 1904 to 1909 disappointed

Kuliscioff, but she never entirely lost faith in the Piedmontese statesman. However, she was aware that concrete achievements were essential if the reformists were to keep control of the Socialist Party. At the party congress in 1908 Kuliscioff joined Gaetano Salvemini in pressing for a program of fundamental reforms, including universal suffrage. In 1910 she broke with Turati by calling for the right to vote for women, which her companion did not favor. She also criticized the Socialist Party's willingness to accept limited voting reform from the government of Luigi Luzzatti in 1910. When the Giolitti goverment of 1911 accepted almost universal male suffrage, Kuliscioff continued to press for the vote for women on the pages of *La difesa delle lavoratrici,* the Socialist newspaper for women workers that she directed.

Kuliscioff also broke with the official party position during World War I, when she favored support for the Entente, the alliance of Britain, France, and Russia, over the party stand in favor of neutrality between the contending parties. She supported the first Russian Revolution of February 1917 but was instinctively hostile to the Bolshevik Revolution. Both Kuliscioff and Turati became increasingly isolated in the radicalized politics of 1919 to 1922 and both watched impotently as the Fascists stormed to power.

See also **Feminism; Italy; Socialism; Suffragism; Turati, Filippo.**

BIBLIOGRAPHY

Casalini, Maria. *La signora del socialismo italiano: Vita di Anna Kuliscioff.* Rome, 1987.

Riosa, Alceo, ed. *Anna Kuliscioff e l'età del riformismo: Atti del Convegno di Milano, dicembre 1976.* Rome, 1978.

Slaughter, Jane, and Robert Kern, eds. *European Women on the Left: Socialism, Feminism, and the Problems Faced by Political Women, 1880 to the Present.* Westport, Conn., 1981.

ALEXANDER DE GRAND

KULTURKAMPF. The Kulturkampf, or "struggle for civilization," was an episode of first-rate importance in modern German history in which Otto von Bismarck (Germany's chancellor and Prussia's minister-president; 1815–1898) and his political allies attempted to weaken the German Catholic church's ties to the papacy, to bring that church under stricter state control, and to forge a common culture across Germany's confessional divide. Fought chiefly in the Hohenzollern kingdom of Prussia and to a lesser extent in Germany as a whole, the Kulturkampf began in 1871, escalated sharply until 1878, and then gradually wound down until its end in 1887. This dispute took its grandiloquent name following a speech in January 1873 in which Rudolf Virchow (1821–1902), a prominent scientist and liberal politician, described the intensifying church–state disagreement as nothing less than a monumental struggle between two competing cultural viewpoints. The term embodied all the confidence, optimism, and belief in progress so characteristic of liberal thinking during the 1860s and 1870s.

The Kulturkampf owed its origins to complex elements and motives, including the existence of a post-Reformation religious, regional, and cultural divide that separated Germany's Catholic and Protestant worlds. Even with national unification in 1870–1871, Germany's confessional division meant that a profound religious rift ran straight through the empire, a rift that shaped and molded the way in which Germans imagined their nation and attempted to construct a national identity. More immediate causes for the Kulturkampf ranged from widespread dismay regarding papal denunciations of progress, liberalism, and modern culture vehemently expressed by the Syllabus of Errors in 1864 to the sweeping claims of papal infallibility promulgated by the Vatican Council in 1870, and from the fears and frustrations among Germany's Liberals regarding a post-1848 Catholic religious revival to the challenge a rejuvenated Catholicism represented to liberal claims of cultural, social, political, and economic superiority. Without the encouragement and aid of these Liberals, other interest groups, and constituencies, which in turn were energized and emboldened by Bismarck's endorsement of their cause, it is difficult to see how the Kulturkampf could have descended to the levels of loathing it did, dividing the country into two mutually uncompromising universes. But the Kulturkampf's beginnings also owed much to Bismarck's fears regarding Polish political unrest and unfavorable demographic shifts that threatened

German control in Prussia's eastern districts, his desire to exploit the schism caused by the new doctrine of infallibility within the Roman church and spearheaded by the so-called Old Catholic sect, and his alarm at the reappearance of a Catholic political movement—the Center Party—in 1870–1871 that stood against Germany's new political arrangements. His principle aims in the Kulturkampf, therefore, were to limit the scope of the damage that might be caused by the infallibility dogma and to consolidate German unity against both Catholics and Poles, who, he repeatedly said, pursued religious objectives and ethnic goals to the detriment of the newly fashioned German Reich.

RESTRICTIONS AND CONTROLS

Although Pope Pius IX (r. 1846–1878) and others portrayed the plight of the church and its adherents as a massive persecution not unlike that of ancient Rome, the Kulturkampf's regulations avoided a direct confrontation with religious belief per se, emphasizing instead specific limitations and controls on its practice. To this end, Bismarck's government in 1871 abolished the "Catholic department" in Prussia's Ministry of Ecclesiastical Affairs and prohibited all expression of political opinion from the pulpit. Additional legislation in 1872 eliminated ecclesiastical influence in curricular matters and the supervision of schools, prohibited members of religious orders from teaching in the public educational system, and expelled the Jesuit order from German territory. To undercut papal authority, the Prussian government in that same year also severed diplomatic relations with the Holy See. The so-called May Laws, adopted by Parliament in 1873, placed the training and appointment of clergy in Prussia under state supervision or jurisdiction. Still another statute adopted in 1874 permitted the government to intern, strip of citizenship, and/or deport clergy found in noncompliance with the May Laws of the previous year. The Prussian government also introduced compulsory civil marriage in 1874, a step extended to the entire Reich a year later. Legislation accepted in 1875 abolished religious orders and congregations (with the exception of those involved in nursing the sick), terminated state subsidies to the Catholic Church, deleted religious guarantees from the Prussian constitution, and permitted Old Catholics to share church property and endowments with their former coreligionists. In 1874 and 1875, furthermore, Prussian authorities pushed through statutes permitting state agents to take charge of bishoprics where the incumbent was in prison or exile and allowed laymen to assume administrative responsibilities at the parish level. Each of these statutes represented not the next item in a preconceived or comprehensive repressive agenda, but a necessary step to cope with developments that were neither coherently planned nor accurately foreseen.

As a consequence of the Kulturkampf's legislation, the Roman Church paid a heavy price in terms of decimated clergy, alienated revenues, and widespread hardship for the laity. Bishops, the parochial clergy, and the members of monastic houses paid the heaviest toll. More than half of Prussia's episcopate went into exile or prison, nearly a quarter of all parish priests lost their pastoral appointments, and a third or more of all religious orders suffered the loss of home and function. Before the Kulturkampf came to an end, the church as an institution lost fifteen to sixteen million marks in state subsidies.

Ordinary Catholics also suffered grievously. Thousands found themselves without spiritual ministration, and for that reason regularity of sacramental observance became increasingly difficult. Others were jailed or fined for participating in demonstrations in support of their church leaders. Still others were the casualties of slander and malice or simply felt the strain of isolation. A purge of the state bureaucracy cost dozens of Catholic civil servants their careers and livelihoods. The Kulturkampf also subjected the confessional press and its representatives to stricter controls. Police officials harassed, intimidated, censored, or even fined and imprisoned Catholic editors and journalists to silence the news they reported and the opinions they expressed.

CATHOLIC RESISTANCE

Despite the ordeal to which they were subjected, Catholics continued to resist the Kulturkampf's new church regulations and to disobey the measures designed to intimidate them. The most important forums for the expression of that resistance were the Reichstag and the Prussian Parliament, in which the Center Party dramatically increased its representation between 1870–1871 and 1874. No Catholic political leader better personified that opposition than Ludwig Windthorst (1812–1891), a superb orator and gifted tactician widely acknowledged by friend and foe alike as Bismarck's most abrasive and formidable parliamentary critic. He organized the Centrist deputies into an obstructionist bloc that kept attention focused on the grievances of their coreligionists.

In addition to the trouble caused by the Center Party and its leader, the government and its supporters also had to contend with widespread and open resistance. This extraparliamentary opposition was expressed through the organization of mass meetings, boycotts, civil disobedience, and petitions, even open defiance and public disturbance on a massive, chaotic scale. Bismarck himself narrowly escaped an assassination attempt in July 1874, and many of his associates received death threats. Imperial Germany, it is said, did not again witness collective action on such a scale until the revolutions that engulfed the country at the end of World War I.

LIQUIDATING THE KULTURKAMPF

This expanding opposition with its promise of interminable conflict, together with his own inability to find a formula for victory within the boundaries of accepted political action and without changing the size and shape of his government, prompted Bismarck by the late 1870s to normalize relations with the Roman Church. He also found himself increasingly distracted from the Kulturkampf by the rapid growth of the Social Democratic Party and the threat he believed this movement represented to Germany's internal political and social arrangements. But Bismarck's desire to find a *modus vivendi* with the Roman Church and its German adherents was also prompted by the accession of a more moderate pontiff following the death of the intransigent Pius IX in 1878. Although the Prussian government initiated contacts between Berlin and Rome, early negotiations proved disappointing. Unable to reach an acceptable compromise with Leo XIII (r. 1878–1903), the new pope, Bismarck chose instead unilaterally to ease the Kulturkampf by legislative and administrative action. Major steps in this direction included the Relief Law of 1880, which relaxed key features of the May Laws, permitted parishes with pastors to aid those without, and paved the way for the return of deposed clergy to vacant parishes and episcopal sees. In addition, Berlin restored diplomatic ties with the Holy See in 1882. These steps, however, including a visit of the Prussian Crown Prince Frederick William (1831–1888) in 1883 to the Roman pontiff, did little to assuage the misgivings of the Center Party and the Roman Curia. What did make the pope more tractable, on the other hand, was Bismarck's request to Leo in 1885 to arbitrate a colonial dispute between Germany and Spain over competing claims to the Caroline Islands and the Palua Island group in Micronesia. This request produced a more favorable climate for direct church–state negotiations, outflanked Windthorst and the obstreperous Center Party, and led to acceptance of the Peace Law of 1886. This accord required the Prussian government to repeal, reduce in severity, or simply allow to fall into disuse much of the Kulturkampf legislation. To this end, Prussian authorities abolished the special examinations in philosophy, history, and German literature demanded of ordinands by the May Laws, recognized the pope's disciplinary power over the clergy, did away with the special tribunal that had acted on appeals against episcopal decisions, and reopened diocesan seminaries. The agreement also called for Prussia to resume financial aid to the church and to permit religious orders and congregations—at the discretion of the government—to reestablish chapter houses and to resume their previous activities.

Although both sides acknowledged the end of the Kulturkampf by mid-1887, not all restrictions and controls disappeared or even fell into disuse. The guarantees of religious freedom, abolished from the Prussian constitution at the height of the Kulturkampf, were not reinstated. Civil marriage was retained, as was state supervision of schools, the right of Prussian subjects to disassociate themselves from formal church affiliation, and the state's power to veto ecclesiastical appointments. The separate department for Catholic affairs in the Ministry of Ecclesiastical Affairs was not revived. Prussia's authority to deprive recalcitrant clergy of their citizenship and to deport them physically was not lifted until 1890. The Jesuit Law, despite a partial repeal in 1904, was not abandoned until 1917. And restrictions against political use of the pulpit remained in force until 1953. While the final settlement brought a close to the Kulturkampf as a formal conflict, it did little or nothing at all to end less-overt forms of discrimination or what Catholics derisively called a "silent" Kulturkampf.

AFTERMATH AND LEGACY

The Kulturkampf left permanent scars, both for the Catholic populace and for Prussian and German society as a whole. Although Catholics suffered grievously during the Kulturkampf, when assessed in terms of its larger purpose—as a means to eradicate Catholicism as a major factor in Germany's political life, to break Catholic opposition to governmental policy, or to consolidate national unity—the Kulturkampf was a conspicuous failure and a disappointment to its proponents. Despite Bismarck's best efforts, the Center Party remained unbroken and even established itself as a potent political force that he could not ignore. Catholic morale did not disintegrate, and Catholics remained a coherent bloc within German society. The Polish-speaking inhabitants of Prussia's eastern provinces also continued to resist demands for conformity. Even the intention to forge national unity across Germany's religious divide only served to create more dissension because the Kulturkampf left Germany more divided than ever, divided by suspicion, fear, and mutual misunderstanding. As the defining experience of their lives, the Kulturkampf entered deeply into the collective memory of countless Catholics and influenced the attitudes and behavior of their community well into the twentieth century.

It is good to remember, of course, that the Prussian Kulturkampf as a "culture war" did not stand alone. Similar conflicts, less well known and on a smaller scale, occurred elsewhere in Europe and even in Germany itself. Following Europe's mid-century revolutions, Catholic areas witnessed a vigorous religious renewal. Fashioned and dominated by the clergy and sustained within an institutional framework of new associations and organizations, this revival introduced a new, popular morality encouraged by missions, revival meetings, pilgrimages, and other forms of religious expression and practice. This reshaped Catholicism, like the secular, liberal, and anticlerical political culture with which it often collided, was a transnational phenomenon. It is not surprising, therefore, that from the mid- to later nineteenth century lesser German states such as Baden or Hesse-Darmstadt, or Switzerland, France, Belgium, and countries elsewhere in Europe experienced cultural clashes similar to Prussia's Kulturkampf.

See also **Bismarck, Otto von; Catholicism; Catholicism, Political; Center Party; Germany; Liberalism; Pius IX; Prussia; Windthorst, Ludwig.**

BIBLIOGRAPHY

Anderson, Margaret Lavinia. *Windthorst: A Political Biography.* Oxford, U.K., 1981.

Blackbourn, David. *Marpingen: Apparitions of the Virgin Mary in Nineteenth-Century Germany.* New York, 1994.

Clark, Christopher, and Wolfram Kaiser, eds. *Culture Wars: Secular-Catholic Conflict in Nineteenth-Century Europe.* Cambridge, U.K., 2003.

Gross, Michael B. *The War against Catholicism: Liberalism and the Anti-Catholic Imagination in Nineteenth-Century Germany.* Ann Arbor, Mich., 2004.

Mergel, Thomas. *Zwischen Klasse und Konfession. Katholisches Bürgertum im Rheinland 1794–1914.* Göttingen, 1994.

Ross, Ronald J. *The Failure of Bismarck's Kulturkampf: Catholicism and State Power in Imperial Germany, 1871–1887.* Washington, D.C., 1998.

Schmidt-Volkmar, Erich. *Der Kulturkampf in Deutschland 1871–1890.* Göttingen, Germany, 1962.

Smith, Helmut Walser. *German Nationalism and Religious Conflict: Culture, Ideology, Politics, 1870–1914.* Princeton, N.J., 1995.

Sperber, Jonathan. *Popular Catholicism in Nineteenth-Century Germany.* Princeton, N.J., 1984.

Weber, Christoph. *Kirchliche Politik zwischen Rom, Berlin und Trier 1876–1888. Die Beilegung des preußischen Kulturkampfes.* Mainz, Germany, 1970.

Ronald J. Ross

KUTUZOV, MIKHAIL (1745–1813),

Russian field marshal.

Field Marshal Kutuzov's career is emblematic of the evolution of a uniquely Russian military institution following the reign of Peter the Great in the early eighteenth century. It was Peter who had thoroughly reformed the kingdom of Muscovy's armed forces by establishing a standing conscript army and professional officer corps, modeled on Western standards, to defend and expand his newly proclaimed Russian Empire. He also decreed a lifetime obligation of state service for the nobility, preferably in the army, to staff his new state edifice. At a moment of crisis almost a century later, Kutuzov, a native Russian, would defeat a foreign invader, preserve the ruling dynasty, and project the empire to its apogee of power.

Born in 1745 into a noble family, the son of a career officer and general, Mikhail Kutuzov began his military career as a cadet at the Artillery-Engineer School. He entered formal service at the age of nineteen, in the context of a remarkably successful series of wars that established Russia as a Great Power and its army as a formidable force. After service in campaigns against Poland in the 1760s, Kutuzov was transferred south, where during wars with the Ottoman Empire he served intermittently for the next twenty-five years, being wounded twice and losing sight in his right eye. Rising in the ranks, a protégé of the legendary Marshal Alexander Suvorov, Kutuzov exhibited the strategy, tactics, and leadership that distinguished the evolving Russian military "school," emphasizing speed, mobility, tactical flexibility, shock action, and the bonds of morale between officer and soldier.

Following a brief period in government service and retirement, Kutuzov reached the peak of his career during the wars of the French Revolution and Napoleon. His fortunes would suffer, however, because of his unhappy relationship with Tsar Alexander I (r. 1801–1825). At the battle of Austerlitz in 1805 it was Kutuzov who correctly discerned Napoleon's intentions and thus counseled withdrawal, yet was personally overruled by Alexander, who ordered attack. Alexander never forgave Kutuzov for the ensuing debacle, and the general would never again enjoy the full trust of the tsar. Kutuzov went off to war successfully with the Turks, but at the height of Napoleon's invasion of Russia in summer 1812, he was languishing as commander of the St. Petersburg militia. Yet in the face of continuing retreat, mounting political pressure, and Kutuzov's own notable reputation, the tsar reluctantly appointed him to overall command.

Contending with an acclaimed adversary, scheming comrades, a resentful sovereign, and a volatile populace, Kutuzov first ordered the army to halt its retreat and fight, which it did at terrible cost at Borodino on 7 September. The battle was a tactical victory for Napoleon, but was strategically indecisive. Kutuzov then decided to continue his predecessor's strategy of deliberate withdrawal, culminating in the fateful decision to abandon Moscow itself, while skillfully maneuvering his forces out of the Grande Armée's reach. He thereby sought to present Napoleon with a strategic vacuum that would frustrate his desire for a decisive battle leading to a negotiated peace. In belated recognition of Kutuzov's checkmate, Napoleon ultimately made his decision to retreat from Russia in late October. Kutuzov had his forces shadow the Grande Armée along its path over the next two months, yet again sought mostly to avoid decisive battle. He instead allowed attacks by peasant militia, guerrilla bands, and detachments of Cossacks to bleed Napoleon's forces and later let the even more brutal adversaries of bitter cold and desperate famine do their work for him.

However Kutuzov's strategic vision and tactical shrewdness employed first in deliberate retreat and then cautious pursuit, not decisive attack, won him only the disgust of many of his fellow generals, as well as of the tsar himself. Further, with regard to the military campaign beyond the empire's borders, Kutuzov saw the defense of the Russian state as the army's primary duty. He thus found himself at odds with Alexander's increasingly messianic vision of himself as the crusading protector of dynastic legitimacy and European law and order. Appointed to nominal command of the coalition armies nonetheless, Kutuzov would not see the final campaign against Napoleon. He fell sick and died in April 1813.

The historical memory of Kutuzov contrasts sharply with official distrust of him. While scholars continue to debate the character of the conflict as a "national" struggle, it is undeniable that in the face of a brutal invasion and occupation, the Russian people perceived the war not as one of defense, but survival. Kutuzov became emblematic of the sacrifice, determination, and sense of unity demonstrated in the Russians' resistance. He embodied the popular, as opposed to the dynastic, interpretation of the victory, a status immortalized by Leo Tolstoy's literary portrait of Kutuzov in the novel *War and Peace.*

See also **Austerlitz; Borodino; French Revolutionary Wars and Napoleonic Wars; Military Tactics; Napoleon; Russia.**

BIBLIOGRAPHY

Fuller, William C., Jr. *Strategy and Power in Russia, 1600–1914.* New York, 1992.

Kagan, Frederick W., and Robin Higham, eds. *The Military History of Tsarist Russia.* New York, 2002.

Pinter, Walter. "Russian Military Thought: The Western Model and the Shadow of Suvorov." In *Makers of Modern Strategy: From Machiavelli to the Nuclear Age,* edited by Peter Paret, 354–375. Princeton, N.J., 1986.

Riley, J. P. *Napoleon and the World War of 1813: Lessons in Coalition Warfighting.* Portland, Ore., 2000.

Tarle, Eugene. *Napoleon's Invasion of Russia, 1812.* Translated by Norbert Guterman and Ralph Manheim. 1942. Reprint, New York, 1971.

GREGORY VITARBO

LABOR MOVEMENTS.

LABOR MOVEMENTS. Labor movements emerged from the momentous social and political transformations of nineteenth-century Europe. The transition from state-chartered guilds and customary practices of manufacturing to capitalist forms of property and industrial organization introduced "free" markets for labor as a saleable commodity by the early decades of the nineteenth century. In this context, wage earners began to embrace new social identities as workers and members of the working classes and to create voluntary associations, trade unions, and political parties, which adopted strategies of collective interest representation and forms of work-based protest in order to pursue a variety of aims. Over the course of the nineteenth century, European labor movements provided the necessary resources for workers to improve their wages and conditions of employment, to demand social rights, and to enter into the formal arenas of party and parliamentary politics as independent political actors. As active participants in public life, European workers and their allies developed new political languages, ranging from socialism to anarchism. The latter called for the emancipation of wage earners from their subordination to employers and the structural inequalities of market relations and capitalist industrialization. They articulated new visions of democracy that challenged many of the prevailing social and political hierarchies of nineteenth-century Europe.

THE NEW LABOR ORGANIZATIONS AND THE LANGUAGES OF CLASS

Labor movements are complex formations composed of strategies, organizations, and actions that link wage earners across trades and industries through issues related to work and social need. Their origins can be traced to the wider economic and political revolutions that occurred in Europe in the late eighteenth and early nineteenth centuries. In the wake of political revolution in England in 1688 and France in 1789, parliaments or national assemblies introduced legislation redefining the right to property, previously constrained by collective social custom and royal decrees and divided into many partial rights, as an absolute right to property, giving owners the full power to dispose of their assets or capital as they wished. This process took place gradually in England, where common lands were enclosed and statutory regulation of wages and prices was rescinded over the course of the eighteenth century. It happened more suddenly on the Continent, beginning with the abolition of feudal privileges and social relations in France in August 1789. In order to ensure that individual property rights remained unfettered by collective or community claims, workers' corporations or combinations were also banned in France in 1791, in England in 1799 and 1800, and later in the German states, beginning for the most part in Prussia in 1810. These legal measures combined with already evolving capitalist methods of production and subcontracting outside of existing statutes and trade regulations to transform the world of preindustrial manufacturing in two principal ways. First, they abolished or rendered obsolete the guilds, which were royally chartered communities of artisans who maintained collective control over all aspects of individual trades, and the masters' and journeymen's corporations, brotherhoods, and religious confraternities, which were organized by individual trade, enforced the elaborate rules and rituals of preindustrial work life, and maintained the skilled status of their members. Second, the new laws and measures dismantled the legal apparatus of preindustrial wage negotiations, which involved royal courts and magistracies in the arbitration of labor disputes between masters and journeymen. In their wake, workers who had been classified as skilled artisans and legally empowered to regulate their own trade collectively now became individual wage earners, whose labor was a commodity to be negotiated and sold freely to individual employers in labor markets.

In this new context, the most important workers' associations were the friendly, benefit, or mutual aid societies that proliferated after 1800 in reaction to the expansion of wage labor and level of industrialization throughout Europe. In England, the number of benefit societies grew after the 1760s but expanded exponentially after 1800; by 1815, the friendly societies in Britain already claimed some 925,000 members. In France, there were over two thousand mutual aid societies in the 1840s; in the German states, they were established during the first decades of the nineteenth century; in southern countries like Spain they appeared after 1840; and in Russia, mutual aid societies were first created in the 1860s and 1870s. These societies were legal voluntary associations that provided their members with financial support in case of illness, retirement, and death. Though not allowed to engage in labor actions or political activity, in certain contexts these associations did evolve into militant strike organizations with connections to other organizations and movements. For example, benefit societies in England, which were often barely concealed strike organizations, were involved in the general wage agitations of the cotton spinners in Manchester in 1818 and the demonstrations to secure constitutional liberties during the Queen Caroline affair in 1820 and 1821; still others transformed themselves into cooperatives and became part of the Owenite socialist movement of the 1830s; and many, like the London shipwrights' Provident Union, were active in efforts to form trade unions and support strikers in the 1820s and 1830s. In France, mutual aid societies formed the basis of strikes launched by the hatters of Paris in 1830 and the shoemakers and tanners of Marseilles in 1833 and 1834; the strikes throughout France in 1933; and the massive silk weavers' uprising in Lyon in 1834.

Nevertheless, the most novel departure in worker self-organization came with the trade unions, which developed into wider workers' movements before 1848. Many scholars argue that trade unions existed as far back as the seventeenth century in Britain, but the term *trade union* and its distinctive strategies and forms of organization emerged in the nineteenth century. Trade unions generally favored planned and procedural forms of collective interest representation—negotiations with employers or the withholding of labor in a calculated manner—rather than spontaneous or temporary forms of individual and collective direct action, including machine-breaking, sudden work stoppages, and festival-like street demonstrations. Unlike the mainly local activities of artisans' corporations, trade unions often attempted to build wider solidarities among workers across industries and sometimes across trades. Finally, trade unions gradually adopted a new strategic orientation: they sought first to negotiate with employers rather than state officials as the forces of the market and industrial discipline replaced the preindustrial framework of corporate law and economic regulation that had once mediated disputes between masters and journeymen. Before 1848, the first trade unions emerged in Britain, where workers' combinations were legalized in 1824. From 1825 to 1834, Britain witnessed the rise of labor militancy and the formation of short-lived trade unions, ranging from the General Union of Carpenters and Joiners in 1827 to the General Union of Spinners in 1829 to the Grand National Consolidated Trades Union in 1834. The latter, the first significant attempt to form a nationwide trade-union federation, temporarily claimed some sixteen thousand members. In addition, Britain witnessed the first planned general strike, involving some five hundred thousand workers and their associated trade unions and trade conferences, which extended across the industrial districts of the country from Scotland to Wales in 1842.

Corrupt trade union leaders. Nineteenth-century cartoon from *McClean's Monthly Sheet of Caricatures.* The growth and consolidation of trade unions in England led to skepticism about the real goals of labor leaders as well as concerns about abuses of power.

In this context of attempted cross-trade alliances and negotiations with employers, European workers began to establish labor movements on the basis of class identities: they came to define their own interests against the interests of employers and they increasingly came to see themselves as members of the working classes in opposition to other classes, rather than just in terms of their specific occupational identities or in relation to wider preindustrial social identities of estates, orders, and ranks. During the 1820s and 1830s in Britain, the political languages of artisans, tradesmen, union leaders, and radicals—as well as self-defined members of the "middle class"—became saturated with references to "working men," the "laboring classes," or the "working classes" in the context of the new labor militancy and trade union formation. Moreover, major political conflicts, like the Peterloo massacre in 1819 (in which government troops shot at working-class protestors in Manchester who were calling for political freedoms) or the Reform Bill of 1832 (which failed to enfranchise those without property) gave political definition to the working classes. In France, artisans began to define themselves as workers by 1830 in similar contexts of labor mobilization and political protest. In the wake of the July Revolution of 1830, which established a liberal constitutional monarchy in France, new organizations like the Society of the Rights of Man and Friends of the People emerged and three new workers' journals—*The Artisan: Journal of the Working Class; The Workers' Journal;* and *The People: General Workers' Journal, Edited by Themselves*—had appeared, all of which spoke to workers and workers' interests. In the German states, the term *worker* came into use slightly later, in the 1830s and 1840s, in debates over the "social question" or the "worker question," and was embraced by workers themselves during this period, especially in the radical and socialist clubs of journeymen and political émigrés in Zurich, Paris, Brussels, and London.

SKILLED MALE ARTISANS, POLITICAL RADICALISM, AND EARLY SOCIALISM

Nineteenth-century labor movements were led not by unskilled factory hands or classic proletarians, as scholarly interpretations once suggested, but by male artisans or craftsmen. Historians generally explain the preeminence of artisans in terms of the general process of proletarianization, which involved the increasing division of labor and subcontracting schemes rather than the creation of factories and mechanization. This process increasingly de-skilled workers or degraded various trades and provoked craftsmen into defending their skilled status, maintaining their shop floor autonomy, and reversing a situation of increasingly overcrowded trades, rising unemployment, and declining wages. The early labor leaders and working-class militants in England were mostly male printers, tailors, and hand-loom weavers experiencing the transition to new manufacturing processes and divisions of labor. In France, the most organized and militant workers in the 1830s were the tailors and shoemakers and the more highly skilled typographers and silk weavers, but by the 1840s the leading militants came from the ranks of skilled metal workers, leather workers, and construction workers. Similarly, in the German states, the early labor militants were mostly male printers, cigar makers, tailors, shoemakers, joiners, carpenters, and masons—urban artisans, often with long guild traditions, who were experiencing the full impact of market reforms. Leaders and members of the early labor organizations came from these trades and expressed their political interests variously in movements for parliamentary-democratic reform and socialism.

In Britain, the most consequential organized political activity of workers before 1848 took place within Chartism, a national movement for constitutional reform during the 1830s and 1840s. Chartism was based on the People's Charter, a six-point program calling for universal male suffrage, the secret ballot, salaries and the abolition of property qualifications for members of Parliament, equal electoral districts, and annual parliaments. Authored in 1838 by William Lovell, a cabinetmaker and leader of the London Working Men's Association, and Frances Place, a radical tailor from London, the Charter galvanized a mass movement throughout England, encompassing demonstrations and petitions with millions of signatures. Historians have debated the class character of Chartism, and most have acknowledged the varied sociology of the movement, which included artisans, factory workers, miners, small shopkeepers, independent tradesmen, and middle-class radicals. Some historians even question whether Chartism was a workers' movement at all in light of its overtly political-constitutional aims. But this perspective considerably obscures the movement's class accents—the articulation of the word *people* with the terms *laboring class* or *working class* in its discourse; the general preoccupation with economic and social problems, including concerns about the social and moral consequences of working conditions in large enterprises expressed in debates over the "factory question," in Chartist speeches and publications like the *Northern Star;* and the involvement of trade unions, working men's associations, and friendly societies from London and the northern industrial districts in Chartist agitation. Indeed, the People's Charter focused on matters that were intrinsically economic and social: the property qualifications that upheld the existing political order.

If Chartism drew its energies from a wider social coalition, the more overtly working-class political movements of the early nineteenth century emerged from the activities and agitations of the socialists during the 1830s. In Britain, Owenite socialism, which was based on the ideas of the Welsh entrepreneur Robert Owen, emerged as a diverse movement that criticized the new social inequality associated with unrestrained economic competition and established seven rural utopian communities or "villages of cooperation." But in the late 1820s, the movement became oriented more directly toward the needs of workers, and by 1832 Owenite socialists had established over five hundred cooperative societies, workshops, and labor exchanges before they became involved in more militant trade union activity, including the efforts to form the Grand National Consolidated Trades Union. Far more significant were the socialist movements in France, where most of the major early theorists of socialism, including Charles Fourier, Henri de Saint-Simon, Étienne Cabet,

Philippe Buchez, and Pierre-Joseph Proudhon, were active from the 1820s to the 1840s. French workers and political radicals drew eclectically on the ideas of these figures and developed a widely shared federalist trade socialism, which sought to bring about the collective ownership of production by means of the organization of workers into a democratic federation of self-governing producers' associations and cooperatives. In the 1830s and 1840s they articulated these ideas in the language of republican socialism, which brought calls for the workers' rights to association and to property in their own labor in line with demands for civil rights and a political order based on direct democracy and the republican tradition of the French Revolution.

These socialist ideas became central to the labor ferment of the 1840s and the dramatic events during the Revolution of 1848, which involved the first uprising explicitly of workers. After King Louis-Philippe was driven from the throne by the Paris insurrection of February, workers attempted to create a democratic and social republic that guaranteed both political rights and the right to labor. With the aid of the socialist Louis Blanc, a member of the provisional government, the right to labor was decreed on 25 February and by March workers were told that they would be guaranteed the "legitimate fruits of their labor." For workers, the right to labor was embodied in the new National Workshops, which were government-sponsored public works establishments set up to provide jobs for the unemployed, and the Luxembourg Commission, a government advisory body assigned the task of finding a solution to the labor problem. Parisian workers, who began organizing into democratic-republican trade corporations, viewed these institutions as the beginning of a new social republic, in which the conditions of work and production were to be governed by free associations of democratically organized producer cooperatives. When a new government abolished the National Workshops on 21 June, workers interpreted the action as a violation of their right to associate and an attack on the basic principles of the social republic. Immediately, their protests turned into full-scale insurrection in Paris; after four days of bloody fighting known as the June Days, government troops crushed the uprising, killing between fifteen hundred and three thousand insurgents and arresting or sending into exile some twelve thousand others.

In the German states, events were also driven, at least in part, by the protests and organizations of workers. Before 1848, labor militancy was largely confined to machine breaking and rioting in industrializing regions, most dramatically illustrated by the 1844 Silesian weavers' rebellion—a series of violent protests against low wages and the introduction of machines in the textile industry. But in March 1848, mass demonstrations forced the ruling monarchs in several German states, including Prussia and Austria, to permit independent political activity, including the middle-class Frankfurt parliament and workers' congresses. As master artisans held meetings to call for the restoration of guild privileges, journeymen met in Frankfurt, Berlin, and Mainz to build trade organizations among printers, tailors, and shoemakers, and to improve the lot of workers generally. The most significant departures from preindustrial economic understandings and guild exclusivity of the masters' organizations included the General German Workers' Congress, organized by journeymen excluded from the artisans' congress and held in Frankfurt from July to September 1848, and the Berlin Workers' Congress, led by the socialist printer Stephan Born in August. Referring to their assembly as a "general workers' parliament," delegates at the Berlin congress pushed for a range of measures that, despite their reformist character, bore the unmistakable traces of socialism, including demands for a right to work, social welfare, public education, progressive income taxes, the regulation of working hours, and the creation of ministries of labor, whose ministers would be elected by workers themselves. Born also helped to found the Workers' Brotherhood, a self-help organization that promoted workers' associations, cooperative production, and democratic change. Before its dissolution in 1850, the Brotherhood claimed some eighteen thousand members throughout the German states.

Perhaps most striking about these early socialist movements was their appeal to women and their often unconventional gender politics. If working-class Chartist men based their claims for political rights and honorable labor on the active exclusion of women from work and politics and Proudhon offered a sternly patriarchal vision of a new social order, Owenite socialists and followers of Fourier openly called for equality between the sexes. Many Owenite societies and cooperatives actively recruited women and defended their rights as workers in the 1820s and 1830s; and they were often led by female speakers and organizers, including the feminist socialists Anna Wheeler, Frances Wright, Eliza Macauley, and Frances Morrison, who spoke on a wide range of issues related to women's rights. In France, socialist feminists like Flora Tristan and Jenny d'Héricourt developed versions of republican socialism that included women's right to work and equality with men. During the Revolution of 1848, the provisional government set up a Commission of Women's National Workshops and women began to organize their own trade organizations to represent themselves as workers. Jeanne Deroin and Eugénie Niboyet established a socialist-feminist newspaper, *The Voice of Women,* which called for a social republic in which women could obtain a divorce, remain independent from their husbands, care for their children, control their wages, and be guaranteed the right to work.

CRAFT UNIONS, SOCIALISM, AND THE ORIGINS OF LABOR INTERNATIONALISM

A new era of labor organization and political activity began in the 1860s and 1870s, in the wake of a series of major political-constitutional changes and an economic boom throughout Europe. Despite state repression in 1848 and 1849 and the conservative restoration of the 1850s, European monarchs and rulers, often prompted by modernizing liberals, approved formal constitutions and introduced new political rights and legal codes enhancing or introducing capitalist financial and market reforms. This general reforming activity was most dramatic in the cases of Italy and Germany, where new nation-states, legal systems, and economies were forged in the 1860s, but it was also reflected to varying degrees in constitutional changes and labor reforms in France, Belgium, Sweden, Austria-Hungary, Spain, and Russia from the 1860s to the 1870s. The reforms introduced the commercial and labor laws necessary for the operations of "free" markets for commodities and labor. In particular, they rescinded remaining guild restrictions and forms of bonded labor and introduced constitutional and legal rights to association that allowed trade unions and socialist parties to organize. The reforms were accompanied by a period of general economic growth (with brief downturns in 1857–1858 and 1866–1868) that resulted in unprecedented rates of industrial production in capital goods industries, the rapid expansion of financial credit and joint-stock companies, and rising levels of industrial employment. These changes affected the early industrializers, Britain and Belgium, but they also began to transform the accelerating capitalist economies of Germany and France as well as previously nonindustrialized regions in Switzerland, Sweden, Italy, Spain, and Russia.

Consequently, this era witnessed the formation of trade unions across the Continent—primarily craft unions, which were restricted to a particular trade and skill level. Britain led the way in this regard, with the creation of organizations like the Amalgamated Society of Engineers in 1851, the Amalgamated Society of Cotton Spinners in 1853, and the Yorkshire Miners' Associations in 1858. Union membership increased from roughly two hundred thousand in 1850 to some 1.6 million by 1876. In Germany, trade union organization began with the cigar workers and printers in 1865 and continued with the creation of unions for tailors, shoemakers, masons, carpenters, woodworkers, and metalworkers in 1867–1868. France also witnessed the proliferation of its first trade unions, or *syndicats,* which were mainly composed of craft workers in small enterprises during this period. In previously nonindustrialized regions of the Habsburg Empire, the numbers of trade union members increased exponentially from 1869 to 1872: in Vienna from ten thousand to thirty-five thousand and in the Czech lands from five thousand to seventeen thousand. In Russia, workers formed their first circles in the 1860s and the first trade union, the Northern Union of Russian Workers, in St. Petersburg in 1878. The most important cause and consequence of this early phase of trade unionism was the first European-wide strike wave, which from 1868 to 1873 extended at various times from the more industrialized countries of Britain, Belgium, France, and Germany to less industrialized countries like Italy, Spain, and Russia.

This activity was often linked to the formation of workers' political parties and the first transnational organization of European labor movements. The first workers' parties were created in Germany during this period: Ferdinand Lassalle's General Association of German Workers (1863) and the Social Democratic Labor Party (1869), led by August Bebel and Wilhelm Liebknecht, which were merged in 1875 to form the German Social Democratic Party (SPD). But the center of political activity during this period was the International Workingmen's Association, commonly known as the First International, an ideologically diverse organization composed of members from Britain, Belgium, the Netherlands, France, Germany, Switzerland, Austria, the Czech lands, Italy, Spain, Ireland, the United States, and the Scandinavian countries. Founded in 1864, the First International sought the "emancipation of the working class" and the "abolition of all class rule"; "without regard to color, creed, or nationality," it engaged in campaigns of support for labor organizations and striking workers across Europe. But the organization was divided between the social democratic program of Karl Marx and the anarchist views of Mikhail Bakunin. Marx combined a materialist analysis of productive relations under capitalism and the rise of class conflict between bourgeoisie and proletariat with a political practice that focused on organizing workers into centralized and legal political parties in preparation for the ultimate seizure of state power. By contrast, Bakunin rejected political parties and state power and emphasized the role of insurrectionary direct action as the catalyst of revolution. He called for the eventual formation of self-governing local communes, which would ultimately be linked loosely together in a "universal people's federation." Although Marx outmaneuvered Bakunin and the anarchists, his tactical victory effectively brought an end to the International by 1872. Support for the First International had also been weakened by another event: the violent suppression of the Paris Commune in the spring of 1871. In the midst of civil war in France, republicans in the capital city elected a new revolutionary government, the Paris Commune, which included many socialists and anarchists and was supported by the First International, in opposition to the monarchist regime based in Versailles. The Commune explicitly identified with the cause of workers and introduced a series of labor and social reforms, including the establishment of public contracts for unions, worker control over abandoned workshops, women's trade unions, and workshops for unemployed women. This experiment in a limited "cooperative socialism," however, was crushed after monarchist troops entered Paris and retook the city during the week of May 21–28, known as Bloody Week. At least twenty-five thousand Parisians were killed, many by means of summary execution, and another forty thousand, mostly workers, were arrested.

MASS UNIONISM, THE ORGANIZATION OF INDUSTRIAL RELATIONS, AND THE STATE

This early period of national craft unions was followed by a phase of mass unionism from the 1880s to 1914, involving the creation of general or industrial unions with much larger and more inclusive memberships. In Britain, "new unionism" emerged in the wake of the successful dockworkers strike of 1889, when general unions, which organized workers outside of the craft unions and across a variety of skill levels and trades, were formed among dockworkers, gas workers, and general laborers. In Germany, metalworkers and woodworkers created the first industrial unions after the mass miners' strikes in 1889; these unions recruited all workers from a single industry regardless of specific occupation or levels of skill. They were followed by the construction workers, miners, textile workers, and transport workers. Industrial unions also took hold in other industrializing countries of northern and central Europe, including the Netherlands, Norway, Sweden, and Austria. In France, Italy, and Spain, a different model of union activity and organization was predominant. Here trade unions were primarily local, organized through the local chamber of labor (*bourse du travail, camera del lavoro,* or *centro*), which drew on the support of workers from different occupations and skill levels. In addition, the north-central European model of national trade union organization brought the unions into close alliance with socialist parties, while the trade union federations in southern Europe—the General Confederation of Labor (CGT) in France, the General Confederation of Labor (CGL) in Italy, and the General Union of Workers (UGT) in Spain—maintained

Trade union conference, London, 1900. Delegates are gathered to debate whether or not railway and other transport workers will support striking miners. ©BETTMANN/CORBIS

their distance from the workers' parties. Despite this organizational diversity, however, workers established national trade union federations and commissions in nearly all European countries during this period. With the exception of the Trades Union Congress in Britain, which was founded in 1868, federations or national councils were formed after the late 1880s in Spain, Germany, Hungary, Austria, France, Belgium, Denmark, Sweden, Norway, Bulgaria, the Netherlands, and Italy. The result of this organizational activity was the exponential growth of union membership everywhere. From 1887 to 1913, the number of trade unionist members rose from 674,000 to 4,107,000 in Britain, from 146,361 to 3,928,900 in Germany; and from 140,000 to 1,027,000 in France. Perhaps more striking, after 1904, the size of trade union movements tripled in Austria and doubled in Norway, Sweden, and Hungary. This activity translated into dramatic increases in labor militancy, larger and even nationwide labor disputes, and the definition of national labor issues like the eight-hour day, factory mechanization, and industrial rationalization, the comprehensive bureaucratic reorganization of the manufacturing process and work tasks according to scientific and technocratic measures of efficiency after the 1890s.

It was once customary to explain this expansion of European labor movements in terms of structural economic transformations associated with the Second Industrial Revolution—the growing size and scope of manufacturing concerns, the increasing mechanization and division of labor in heavy manufacturing, and the attendant increase in the number of "semi-skilled" laborers, who became the main recruits for the new trade unions and socialist parties. But numerous scholars point out that these changes were not universal, even in the most advanced industrial economies, and that the formation of national labor movements and mass unions was also related to political factors, including competition within and between labor movements, the response of employers to trade unions, and the legal frameworks and forms of state regulation that shaped labor relations and disputes throughout Europe during this period. The formation of industry-wide and national unions and union federations emerged out of struggles between advocates of general or industrial unions and advocates of local and craft unions, conflicts that often overlapped with the socialist or anarchist sympathies of union leaders and members. Efforts to build general unions in Britain, for example, proceeded outside of the craft unions, whose leaders resisted the threats to the privileges of skill implied by general unionism. In Germany, the model of the industrial union was actively imposed on traditions of craft and local autonomy. This conflict came to a head in 1907–1908, when SPD leaders prevented their members from becoming members of the Free Alliance, an umbrella organization of craft and local unions in Berlin with diverse ideological affiliations, including anarchism and anarchosyndicalism. This measure imposed centralized control over the Berlin labor movement, sacrificing grassroots and local democracy to the imperatives of bureaucratic organization in the struggle against employers. In addition to this internal opposition, the new mass unions faced opponents in the form of confessional labor organizations, which were established by Catholics or Protestants in countries like Belgium, the Netherlands, and Germany after 1890 in order to combat socialist trade unions. They attempted to promote "social peace" by means of limited measures of social reform, worker self-help, and religious-moral instruction. Finally, after 1899 many industrialists in France, Switzerland, and Germany began to create their own company-loyal or "yellow" unions, with nonstrike clauses and special privileges, in order to win supporters away from the trade unions.

In addition, the mass union movements evolved in relation to employer organizations and new forms of state intervention in industrial relations and disputes after 1890. In Britain, one model of industrial bargaining emerged as employers' responded to the rise of labor militancy after 1889 with their own organizations, such as the Shipping Federation and the Engineering Employer's Federation, which ultimately recognized the unions and accepted the principle of collective bargaining. The latter took place in conjunction with a less repressive state, which gave new powers of mediation to the Labour Department of the Board of Trade, especially in the wake of the Conciliation Act of 1896, and contributed to a framework of industrial relations that curbed the political radicalism of the unions. This model to a certain extent also characterized labor relations in Denmark, Sweden, and the Netherlands after 1899. A different pattern emerged in Germany, where employers in heavy industry built powerful regional and national organizations, implemented an extensive array of anti-union initiatives (labor exchanges, blacklists, company-loyal unions), and refused to recognize the trade unions. The state conferred legality on the workers' organizations, and even introduced industrial courts for the resolution of labor disputes in 1891, but it resorted to routine surveillance and arrests of labor and social democratic leaders. This combination of formal legality and abiding repression confirmed both a practical reformism and rhetorical radicalism within the leadership of the socialist trade union movement. In France and Italy, yet another model obtained: here employers were generally hostile toward trade unions and the state only belatedly allowed for labor organization. Despite attempts to introduce new mechanisms for industrial arbitration in France in 1892 and in Italy in 1902, laws in these countries had long forced labor movements to remain decentralized, and the state routinely repressed, often quite violently, labor actions and protests. In France, rights to assemble and to a free press were only guaranteed in 1881, unions were re-legalized in 1884, and not until 1901 was the full right to association guaranteed in law. Until this time, national trade union federations were forbidden and the syndicates were only allowed to engage in "the study and defense of economic, industrial, commercial, and agricultural interests." The 1901 Law on Associations militated against national, organizational, or ideological unity within the French labor movement, but it failed to curb the comparatively high levels of industrial and political militancy among French workers.

THE VARIETIES OF WORKER POLITICS AND THE EXTENSION OF DEMOCRACY

In light of these differences, it is no surprise that labor movements were associated with varied political ideologies and workers' parties, but all of them contributed to rising civic participation, the emergence of mass politics, and democratic transformations across Europe during the two decades before 1914. After 1900, social democratic parties were dominant in northern and central Europe, from Scandinavia and the Low Countries to Germany, Austria, and the Czech lands. Most of these parties embraced the socialism of Marx; they were committed both to the aim of proletarian revolution and the necessity of working for political and social democracy within the framework of existing parliamentary-constitutional states. The principal exception in this regard was Britain, where socialism and syndicalism were comparatively weak and the labor movements found political representation primarily within the Liberal Party until the establishment of an independent Labour Party in 1906. By contrast, the labor movements in southern Europe, France, Italy, and Spain largely remained under the influence of syndicalism and anarchism. In France, for example, the divisions between the Marxist Socialist Party of France and the reformist French Socialist Party were overcome with the formation of the French section of the Working-Class International (SFIO) in 1905, but the SFIO never managed to win over the General Confederation of Labor (CGT). The latter maintained its commitment to syndicalism, which combined the insurrectionary revolutionism and direct action of previous anarchist thought with the mass organization of workers in unions or *syndicats*. It rejected political parties and all forms of state organization in favor of the self-organization of free producers and saw the strike as the most effective means of worker self-assertion.

The new workers' parties, and their trade union allies, expanded definitions of democracy and fought for important democratic changes across Europe during the prewar decade. Most socialists, like Marx, sought to extend democracy beyond the formal legal conditions of political "freedom" into domains of civil society, especially the economy. In this sense, European labor movements not only established a vast array of social welfare institutions, including producers and consumers' cooperatives, and sought to establish social assistance or welfare as a right; they also created these institutions according to principles of democratic self-administration. This applied as much to the activities of the social democratic parties of northern and central Europe in the domains of the workplace and municipal politics, where they sought representation for workers in labor exchanges and sickness insurance institutions, as it did to the impressive local activities of the French, Italian, and Spanish syndicalist and anarchist movements. In the case of the syndicalists of France and Italy, much of this activity was organized through the chambers of labor, which proliferated after 1887 in France (and formed their own national federation in 1892) and after 1890 in Italy. The chambers began as labor exchanges but quickly turned into self-governing coordinating instances for trade unions and workers' organizations and, especially in Italy, venues for the organization of popular leisure and recreational activities. Indeed, in this latter sense the labor movements attempted to democratize the domain of culture. The German social democratic movement, for example, sponsored a large network of cultural institutions and activities, ranging from theater associations and libraries to bicycling and sports clubs, that were designed to provide access to literature, classical music, and leisure activities unavailable to most wage earners.

The labor movements were the most consistent advocates of women's emancipation and suffrage outside of the feminist organizations, whose numbers were limited on the Continent. The most notable party in this regard was the SPD, which was committed to sexual equality and the "abolition of all laws which place women at a disadvantage to men in public and civic law" by its program of 1891. The SPD put forward proposals related to the needs of women, including equal pay, socialized child-care, and the right to

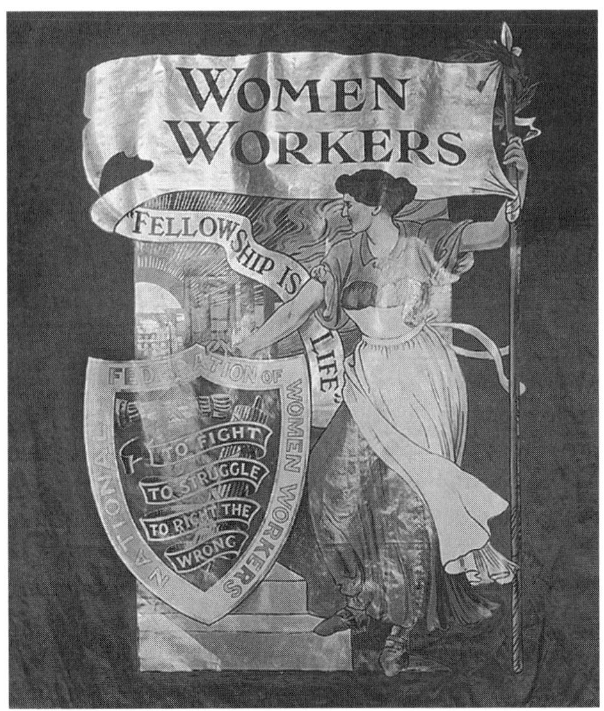

The banner of the National Federation of Women Workers. Photograph, 1914. Founded in 1906 by British activist Mary MacArthur, the National Federation of Women Workers amalgamated a number of disparate women's labor groups, providing greater negotiating power and more support for striking workers. ©HULTON-DEUTSCH COLLECTION/CORBIS

equal education, abortion, and contraception. By 1914, the number of women in the party, which included the prominent leader Clara Zetkin, had risen to just under 175,000. In several other countries, including Austria, Denmark, Finland, Sweden, Norway, the Netherlands, Belgium, France, Italy, and Britain, socialists also supported women's right to vote and were largely responsible for the eventual attainment of female suffrage after World War I. After 1900 women became increasingly active in unions across the Continent, primarily in the textile and garment industries. In Britain, for example, women made up over half of the union membership in the cotton industry by 1910; and in Germany, women made up some 36 percent of the socialist textile union membership by 1907. These commitments ran parallel to the gender politics of the anarchist movements in places like Spain, where criticism of the bourgeois family as the site of patriarchal tyranny, in part drawn on the theories of Bakunin, prompted the formation of women's labor organizations (syndicates) in regions like Catalonia and Andalusia.

The labor movements and workers' parties were also the most consistent advocates of democracy in a more conventional political sense, winning large constituencies of workers and socialist sympathizers in parliamentary elections. By 1914, the socialist parties of Finland, Sweden, Norway, Denmark, Germany, Austria, and the Czech lands were winning at least one quarter of all votes cast in national elections. In the cases of Germany, Sweden, Norway, and Finland, they surpassed all other parties in electoral strength, with over 30 percent of the popular vote. Indeed, the popularity of the socialist parties and labor movements in part rested precisely on their consistent support for democratic suffrage. In Belgium, workers launched general strikes in 1886, 1893, 1902, and 1913 in favor of universal and equal suffrage; in Sweden, socialists allied with liberals in a fifteen-year campaign that secured universal male suffrage in 1907, after a threatened general strike; in Norway, the labor agitations of the 1890s finally persuaded liberals to accept universal male suffrage by 1898; in Finland, a new constitution with universal suffrage rights was secured in the general strike of 1905; in the Austrian half of the Habsburg empire, workers' demonstrations brought about universal male suffrage in 1907; and in Russia, the extraordinary mass unrest of 1905, begun when government troops shot on a peaceful protest by workers in St. Petersburg in January, forced Tsar Nicholas II to promulgate a constitution with a full catalog of civil liberties and new labor legislation, which led to mass unionization in the industrial centers of St. Petersburg and Moscow and the temporary opening up of civil society from 1906 to 1907.

Yet there were important limitations to these democratic visions and actions, especially in relation to women and other categories of workers. Socialist commitments to sexual equality were routinely undermined by their emphasis on class over gender concerns and what some scholars refer to as the abiding "proletarian antifeminism" of many socialist leaders and trade unionists. Women, who formed roughly a third of the paid labor force in Britain, Germany, France, and Italy and about 30 percent of the industrial labor force in Russia by 1914, were routinely marginalized or excluded by male trade union leaders, who often demanded "family wages" on the basis of the male breadwinner norm, viewed women as cheap union-busting labor, or assumed women had little interest in union matters. Moreover, socialists and labor movement leaders generally appealed to the so-called respectable working class and failed to recruit significant numbers of casual laborers and domestic workers. And despite the rural backing of the Swedish and Finnish socialist parties and the remarkable success of the Italian Socialist Party in winning the support of the Federation of Land Workers' Leagues, socialist definitions of the worker or "proletarian" in terms of the industrial wage earner resulted in a general neglect of agricultural workers. Finally, ethnonational tensions militated against labor solidarity and democratic principles; this was the case, for example, in Belgium, where Francophone workers confronted Flemish-speaking workers, and in Germany, where the labor movement largely failed to win the support of Polish-speaking workers in the Ruhr.

Despite these failures, the European labor movements developed a program of working-class emancipation and labor internationalism that far surpassed the democratic commitments of other social and political movements by the beginning of the twentieth century. In the spirit of the First International, a Second International was founded in July 1889 by labor delegates from France, Germany, Britain, Belgium, Italy, Austria, the Netherlands, Denmark, Sweden, Norway, Switzerland, Hungary, Bohemia, Poland, Russian, Romania, Bulgaria, Spain, Portugal, the United States, and Argentina. Based in Brussels, the Second International organized opposition to capitalism across national borders and called for the revolutionary transformation of the social order. It offered practical support to trade unions and striking workers as well as assistance to workers' parties and their political campaigns. In this sense, the Second International, anchored by the SPD, embraced the social-democratic strategies of the late Karl Marx, especially after the anarchists were formally expelled from the organization at the London congress in 1896. This meant that leaders of the Second International were also the most determined advocates of basic democratic aims, including universal suffrage and sexual and racial equality. In their insistence that all workers had more in common with each other than with the middle and upper classes in their own countries, they rejected national chauvinism—perhaps their most striking departure from conventional politics in a Europe rife with ethnic tensions and national rivalries on the eve of World War I. If they failed in many ways, most fatefully in their inability to overcome national hostilities and prevent the outbreak of war in August 1914, a number of their goals, from the introduction of the eight-hour day and the recognition of trade unions to the establishment of public welfare and universal suffrage, were variously realized largely in response to the wartime and postwar insurgencies and labor mobilizations throughout Europe from 1917 to 1920.

See also **Anarchosyndicalism; Artisans and Guilds; Captain Swing; Class and Social Relations; Factories; Industrial Revolution, First; Industrial Revolution, Second; Machine Breaking; Socialism; Strikes; Syndicalism.**

BIBLIOGRAPHY

Bezucha, Robert J. *The Lyon Uprising of 1934: Social and Political Conflict in the Early July Monarchy.* Cambridge, Mass., 1974.

Bonnell, Victoria E. *Roots of Rebellion: Workers' Politics and Organizations in St. Petersburg and Moscow, 1900–1914.* Berkeley, Calif., 1983.

Braunthal, Julius. *History of the International.* Vol. 1: *1864–1914.* Translated by Henry Collins and Kenneth Mitchell. London, 1966. Translation of *Geschichte der Internationale.*

Canning, Kathleen. *Languages of Labor and Gender: Female Factory Work in Germany, 1850–1914.* Ithaca, N.Y., 1996.

Clark, Anna. *The Struggle for the Breeches: Gender and the Making of the British Working Class.* Berkeley, Calif., 1995.

Eley, Geoff. *Forging Democracy: The History of the Left in Europe, 1850–2000.* New York, 2002.

Geary, Dick, ed. *Labour and Socialist Movements in Europe before 1914.* Oxford, U.K., 1989.

Hobsbawm, Eric. *Workers: Worlds of Labor.* New York, 1984.

Joll, James. *The Second International 1889–1914.* Rev. ed., London, 1974.

———. *The Anarchists.* Cambridge, Mass., 1979.

Jones, Gareth Stedman. *Languages of Class: Studies in English Working Class History, 1832–1982.* Cambridge, U.K., 1983.

Kaplan, Temma. *Anarchists of Andalusia, 1868–1903.* Princeton, N.J., 1977.

Merriman, John M. *The Red City: Limoges and the French Nineteenth Century.* New York, 1985.

Mommsen, Wolfgang J., and Hans-Gerhard Husung, eds. *The Development of Trade Unionism in Great Britain and Germany, 1880–1914.* London, 1985.

Moss, Bernard H. *The Origins of the French Labor Movement 1830–1914: The Socialism of Skilled Workers.* Berkeley, Calif., 1976.

Prothero, I. J. *Artisans and Politics in Early Nineteenth-Century London: John Gast and His Times.* Folkestone, U.K., 1979.

Quataert, Jean H. *Reluctant Feminists in German Social Democracy, 1885–1917.* Princeton, N.J., 1979.

Scott, Joan Wallach. *Gender and the Politics of History.* Rev. ed., New York, 1999.

Sewell, William H. *Work and Revolution in France: The Language of Labor from the Old Regime to 1848.* Cambridge, U.K., 1980.

Strikwerda, Carl. *A House Divided: Catholics, Socialists, and Flemish Nationalists in Nineteenth-Century Belgium.* Lanham, Md., 1997.

Taylor, Barbara. *Eve and the New Jerusalem: Socialism and Feminism in the Nineteenth Century.* New York, 1983.

Thompson, Dorothy. *The Chartists: Popular Politics in the Industrial Revolution.* New York, 1984.

Thompson, E. P. *The Making of the English Working Class.* New York, 1963.

DENNIS SWEENEY

LABOUR PARTY. The Labour Party came into existence on 27 February 1900 as the Labour Representation Committee (LRC), an alliance of trade unions and socialist organizations—the Social Democratic Federation (SDF), the Independent Labour Party (ILP), and the Fabian Society. It resolved to work as an independent group in Parliament, distinct from the Liberals. Its growth was spectacular and within twenty-four years it had formed its first government, although it was a minority one, and had replaced the Liberal Party as the progressive party of British politics.

ALLIANCE

The Labour Party had emerged from the political and economic conditions of the 1880s and 1890s, which had seen the emergence of socialist groups and most obviously the ILP, which had been formed as a national organization in Bradford in January 1893. Although organizations such as the SDF and the Socialist League had worked with trade unions in the early years of their existence, it was the ILP, perhaps more than other socialist organizations, that favored and developed the trade union alliance. The ILP was dominated by leaders who had been, or were, active trade unionists. James Keir Hardie (1856–1915) had been a miner and Tom Mann (1856–1941), an early member, was a skilled engineer who focused his efforts on organizing general trade unionism among the unskilled and semi-skilled workers.

Hardie, who became member of Parliament (MP) for West Ham South in 1892, was a keen advocate of the "Labour Alliance" between trade unionist and socialists. Once he and twenty-seven other ILP candidates were defeated in their parliamentary candidatures during the general election of 1895 he resolved to create that alliance just as much as he rejected the idea of socialist unity with the SDF. As a result of his pressure, and that of socialist trade unionists, the Trades Union Congress, the representative body of British trade unionism, discussed the resolution to hold a joint conference at its TUC meeting at Doncaster in 1899. The motion was passed, the meeting was held in London on 27 February 1900, and an executive of twelve trade unionists and six socialists was formed, although it was soon amended to seven and five, respectively. It was the trade unions that dominated this organization and it became a party demanding purely political independence for the working classes. It did not attach itself to the idea of a class war nor, indeed, to socialism until 1918.

At first the LRC was a small and relatively limited organization, with forty-one trade unions affiliated to it and 353,700 members led by James Ramsay MacDonald (1866–1937), a young socialist from Scotland, who became its secretary. Indeed, during its early years it was effectively run from MacDonald's flat at 3 Lincoln's Inn Fields, London. Immediately faced with a general election, it stood fifteen candidates who gained just short of sixty-three thousand votes and secured the return of Hardie, for Merthyr Tydfil, and Richard Bell, of the Amalgamated Society of Railway Servants, for

Derby. This was rather disappointing reward for its efforts, but the fortunes of the LRC soon changed when, in September 1900, the High Court ruled that the Amalgamated Society of Railway Servants (ASRS) was liable to pay the company costs of its dispute with the Taff Vale Railway Company in South Wales. Although this decision was turned over on appeal it was, in July 1901, upheld again by the House of Lords. This cost the ASRS £23,000 in January 1903. This action, and other industrial disputes, encouraged trade unions to affiliate to the LRC, since it was clear that they needed political power to overthrow the economic judgment. By February 1902 it had 455,000 members, and its membership increased quickly thereafter. Also at this time, MacDonald organized a number of secret meetings with the Liberals and concluded the secret Lib-Lab (Gladstone-MacDonald) pact in 1903, whereby the Liberals and LRC agreed to allow the other a free run against the Conservatives in about thirty seats each. Soon afterward, Will Crook and Arthur Henderson (1863–1935) both won parliamentary by-elections. The LRC was growing fast.

The LRC's big breakthrough, however, occurred in the January and February 1906 general election, when twenty-nine LRC candidates, soon to be increased to thirty, won their parliamentary contests. Of these, twenty-three were trade unionists and eighteen described themselves as active socialists. Shortly afterward the LRC changed its name to the Labour Party.

Although it associated with the new Liberal government, the Labour Party initiated a number of its own campaigns, the most obvious being the "Right to Work" campaign of 1907 and 1908. Yet that campaign and others failed, and frustrations at the perceived failings of the Parliamentary Labour Party (its MPs in Parliament) developed, even though the liability of trade unions to pay the employer's costs in strikes, the Taff Vale Judgement, was removed in 1906. Indeed, the Labour Party's slow development led Ben Tillett (1860–1943) in 1908 to produce his critical pamphlet *Is the Parliamentary Labour Party a Failure?*

PARTY GROWTH

Despite this frustration, the trade union movement began to join the Labour Party in ever greater numbers. The half a million members of the Miners' Federation of Great Britain affiliated on 1 January 1909. Yet many trade unionists whose union joined the Labour Party were Liberals and Tories and objected to the trade unions paying a political levy to the Labour Party. The railwayman W. V. Osborne made such an objection in 1909 and the House of Lords concurred that the enforced payment of a political levy was illegal. This seriously damaged the Labour Party finances. Shortly afterward Labour was faced with contesting two general elections in 1910, as a result of the Chancellor of the Exchequer David Lloyd George's attempt to get his Liberal budget measures forced through the House of Lords. Labour returned a mere forty MPs in the January general election and forty-two MPs in 1910, which, given its progress among the unions, represented something of a failure.

Nevertheless, Labour Party fortunes began to improve. MacDonald gave up his role as secretary, to Arthur Henderson (1863–1935), and assumed the responsibility of chairman of the Parliamentary Labour Party bringing to that position his charisma, oratorical powers, and, above all, immense organizational skills. Under his leadership regional Labour Party organizations were set up, and two national agents were appointed. In addition, legislation in 1911 gave MPs an income of £400 a year, thus reducing the burden on Labour Party finances, and the Trade Union Act of 1913 confirmed that trade unions could not automatically pay funds into the Labour Party coffers but did allow trade unions to do so subject to the approval of a ballot from which individuals could "contract out" if they so wished. The Labour Party also prospered with the growth of trade unionism after 1910, and its affiliated trade union membership rose from about 1.2 million in 1910 to 1.86 million in 1912, before falling to about 1.5 million in 1914, as a result of the "contracting out" clause. In other words, by 1914 its affiliated membership amounted to just under 60 percent of the 2.7 million members affiliated to the Trades Union Congress, and about 40 percent of the trade unionists in the country.

In the years immediately before World War I (1914–1918) the Labour Party was being challenged on all sides in its claim to be the party of the working classes. The Liberals hoped to revive their claims to that title as the Liberal governments pressed forward with social reforms, including old-age pensions and national insurance to deal with unemployment and ill-health. Indeed, some historians, such as P. F. Clarke, have maintained that the Liberal Party was successful in attracting the working classes to their cause. However, other historians have maintained that the Labour Party was progressing and that from about 1909 onward was winning municipal and local election results more readily than its parliamentary successes would suggest, largely because more working-class voters had a municipal or local vote than held the parliamentary franchise.

On the eve of World War I the Labour Party was also faced by challenges from within the labor movements. Marxist groups came together to form the British Socialist Party in 1911–1912, guild socialism emerged, and industrial syndicalist groups emerged under the leadership of Tom Mann and played a part in the strikes and industrial unrest of prewar years. However, none of them seriously challenged the authority of the Labour Party to act as the legitimate representative of the British working classes. In the final analysis the Labour Party was clearly the representative body of working-class opinion in Britain and even the efforts of the Liberal Party to reexert its influence were faltering on the eve of the Great War.

See also **Great Britain; Socialism; Working Class.**

BIBLIOGRAPHY

Clarke, P. F. *Lancashire and the New Liberalism.* Cambridge, U.K., 1971.

Laybourn, Keith. *The Rise of the Labour Party, 1890–1979.* London, 1988.

———. *A Century of Labour: A History of the Labour Party, 1900–2000.* Stroud, U.K., 2000.

McKibbin, Ross. *The Evolution of the Labour Party, 1910–1924.* Oxford, U.K., 1974.

Morgan, Kenneth O. *Labour People: Leaders and Lieutenants, Hardie to Kinnock.* London, 1987.

Thorpe, Andrew. *A History of the British Labour Party.* 2nd ed. Basingstoke, U.K., 2001.

KEITH LAYBOURN

LAENNEC, RENÉ (1781–1826), French physician.

Born in Quimper, Brittany, on 17 February 1781, René Théophile Hyacinthe Laennec was the eldest child of three. Their mother died in 1786 and their father, a magistrate and poet, was incapable of caring for his family. Laennec and his brother went to live with their uncle, Guillaume Laennec, a physician at Nantes. As an adolescent, Laennec began the study of medicine under the tutelage of his uncle. The Revolution disrupted his home and education, leaving a deep impression on his spiritual and political views. He thereafter opposed the atheism and republicanism of the new intelligentsia, and later joined the Congrégation, a clandestine group of Catholics. In 1801, he began his studies at the newly reopened medical school in Paris, where he studied with Jean Noël Hallé and Baron Jean-Nicolas Corvisart des Marets, physician to Napoleon Bonaparte. Corvisart had developed Leopold Auenbrugger's examination technique of percussion, which involved tapping on the chest to determine the state of the organs inside. Corvisart correlated sounds emanating from the chests of living patients with later findings at autopsy, and after twenty years of experimentation published a treatise on heart disease (1806) and an amplified translation of Auenbrugger's work (1808).

A witness to Corvisart's research, Laennec excelled in the new science of pathological anatomy. Conducted by dissection of cadavers, abnormal (or pathological) anatomy was increasingly thought to be of importance to medicine; however, its utility at the bedside, before the patient died, was obscure. Laennec taught private courses and penned a treatise on the subject. He wrote and edited scientific articles for Corvisart's *Journal de Médecine;* his special interests were parasitology, ancient medicine, music, and Greek, Latin, and Breton languages. Laennec's 1804 thesis was an original interpretation of Hippocratic passages that reconciled the father of medicine with the new anatomoclinical ideals.

At his graduation in 1804, Laennec won several prizes and hoped to join the Paris faculty, but he was repeatedly passed over for academic jobs, probably because of his political and religious conservatism. He entered clinical practice in Paris in order to sustain his research in pathological anatomy and provide for his family. Clerics, Bretons, and returning émigrés made up his clientele, which included Cardinal Joseph Fesch, François-René de Chateaubriand, Hughes-Félicité-Robert de Lamennais, and Victor Cousin.

Following the restoration of the French throne, Laennec was rewarded for his long-standing royalism with a position at Necker Hospital. This 1816 appointment coincided closely with his discovery of mediate auscultation, the idea that breath and voice sounds from the chest could be heard more clearly with the aid of a mediator. This led to the invention for which he is most famous, the stethoscope, the name derived from the Greek words for *chest* and *exploration*. The device was initially a rolled paper notebook that he later replaced with a wooden cylinder. Like his teacher Corvisart, Laennec correlated the sounds heard in his hospital patients with the morbid findings at their autopsies. This research resulted in a new vocabulary of the organic changes that occurred inside a patient's body before death, and helped to make abnormal anatomy useful in the clinical setting. The new method was described in Laennec's treatise, *De l'auscultation mediate* (On mediate auscultation), which appeared in 1819. In 1821, British physician John Forbes published a partial translation in English, and within five years auscultation was widely practiced in Europe and North America. A second edition appeared in 1826 and was translated into English by Forbes the following year.

In 1822, Laennec took up the chair of clinical medicine at the Collège de France, and he also accepted a position as court physician to the duchesse Marie-Caroline de Berry. In 1823 he succeeded his teacher Corvisart as physician at the Hôpital de la Charité in Paris. In his teaching, Laennec often criticized a too-rigid application of anatomy to bedside medicine, and he emphasized the importance of psychic well-being to bodily health. For some critics, this stance was baffling, as the inventor appeared to reject the significance of his own achievements. Laennec's stethoscope had increased the relevance of pathological anatomy to bedside medicine. It also encouraged a reconceptualization of diseases as products of organic change rather than clusters of subjective symptoms. As a result, auscultation supported a paradigm shift in medical epistemology—not only for chest diseases, but for all diseases: from patient-based diagnosis based on descriptions of symptoms to physician-based diagnosis based on the status of body organs. The stethoscope has been credited with the triumph of anatomical medicine, but it also has been described as the first instrument of medical technology to distance and diminish the role of the patient in his or her own illness experience.

Laennec lived to see his stethoscope widely accepted in Europe and America. Laboring through bouts of tuberculosis, he completed the second edition of his treatise in spring 1826, and immediately embarked on the arduous journey to his home in Brittany, where he died just a few weeks later on 13 August.

See also **Disease; Science and Technology; Tuberculosis.**

BIBLIOGRAPHY

Duffin, Jacalyn. *To See with a Better Eye: A Life of R. T. H. Laennec*. Princeton, N.J., 1998.

Laennec, R. T. H. *De l'auscultation médiate, ou traité du diagnostique des maladies des poumons et du coeur*. 2 vols. Paris, 1819. 2nd ed., Paris, 1826. Translated as *A Treatise of Diseases of the Chest and on Mediate Auscultation* by John Forbes. London, 1827.

JACALYN DUFFIN

LAFAYETTE, MARQUIS DE (1757–1834), French statesman and officer.

Marie-Joseph-Paul-Yves-Roch-Gilbert du Motier, the marquis de Lafayette, was an influential leader and symbol of early French liberalism. He became the best-known European supporter of the American Revolution, a staunch advocate of the revolutionary "rights of man," and a prominent defender of national independence movements throughout Europe and the Americas. His long political career symbolized many of the ideas as well as the optimism of a revolutionary era that extended from the American War for Independence in 1776 to the French Revolution of 1830. He had an exceptional ability to mediate among political leaders and political movements on both sides of the Atlantic, though he never reached his political goals in Europe with the same clarity or success that he achieved in the final military victory of the American Revolution.

Lafayette was born into a noble family in the central French province of Auvergne. His parents both died while he was still a child, but his wealth and noble status led to an advantageous marriage with Adrienne de Noailles (1759–1807), who belonged to one of the most powerful families in eighteenth-century France. Lafayette thus gained a position in the prestigious Noailles Dragoons and began the typical career of a noble officer in the French army.

THE AMERICAN REVOLUTION

In contrast to most of his peers, however, he developed an early political interest in America's struggle for independence from Britain. He therefore decided for both personal and political reasons (but without royal permission) to set off in April 1777 for America. The Continental Congress, recognizing the possible value of his connections in France, commissioned Lafayette to the rank of unpaid major general in the Continental army. He soon demonstrated his courage in battle, gained the trust of George Washington, and later served as a cross-cultural mediator in the French-American alliance.

Lafayette's military leadership contributed significantly to the American cause, especially in the Virginia campaign that led to the decisive American victory at Yorktown in 1781. But Lafayette's political education and support for the new nation's political identity ultimately became the most important aspects of his experience in the American Revolution. He learned that military victories depended on political will as well as a strategic military plan and that modern campaigns for national independence required a political narrative about collective and individual rights.

Lafayette's prominent role in the American Revolution provided a foundation for his later leadership in the emerging political movement for new rights and reforms in late-eighteenth-century France. He strongly supported efforts to abolish slavery in the French colonies and also joined a campaign that succeeded in gaining new civil rights for French Protestants. Lafayette was thus already an influential liberal leader before the French Revolution began in 1789, but the upheaval of that year carried him to the center of political events.

Marquis de Lafayette. Portrait engraving, 1789. Snark/Art Resource, NY

THE EARLY YEARS OF THE FRENCH REVOLUTION

Elected to the Estates-General as a representative of the nobility, he quickly entered the National Assembly after it proclaimed itself the sovereign legislative body of the French nation. Lafayette's political objectives in the Revolution always focused on two themes—liberty and order—both of which he sought to promote through the institutions of the rapidly evolving new regime.

Lafayette introduced his conception of liberty into the proceedings of the National Assembly on 11 July 1789, when he put forward his proposal for a French declaration of the "rights of man." This declaration, modeled on earlier statements of "rights" in various American state constitutions and in the new American Bill of Rights, launched a debate that led finally (27 August 1789) to the assembly's adoption of the much-revised Declaration of the Rights of Man and of the Citizen, which would become the most famous and influential document of the French Revolution.

Lafayette's desire to establish the broadest political principles of human rights and liberty was always linked to a deep concern about the dangers of social disorder and violence. He therefore strongly endorsed the creation of a new National Guard immediately after the Parisian crowd's violent assault on the Bastille prison (14 July 1789). The National Assembly voted to make Lafayette the guard's first commander, thereby giving him a major military and political role in the following two years of revolutionary change. He sought to protect the deliberations of the National Assembly and the security of the royal family as well as public order on the streets of Paris, but both the royalists and the emerging republicans gradually turned against him.

Favoring a moderate constitutional monarchy, Lafayette was condemned by royalists for tolerating unruly crowds and by revolutionaries for protecting nobles, arresting radicals, and supporting King Louis XVI. He resigned from his command of the National Guard in the fall of 1791 and withdrew to his ancestral home in Auvergne. This brief retirement lasted only until he was appointed to command an army that was reorganized during the months before France declared war on Prussia and Austria in April 1792; and he also commanded another French army after the war began.

YEARS OF IMPRISONMENT, EXILE, AND RETIREMENT

As the Jacobins and other radical republicans rose to power in the summer of 1792, however, Lafayette lost all political support and fled the country. He tried to reach Holland in order to find passage to America, but he was captured by the Austrian army and imprisoned for five years. Although his release was eventually negotiated in a treaty with the Austrian government, Lafayette could not return to France until Napoleon Bonaparte seized political power at the end of 1799.

Lafayette gradually settled into the quiet life of a gentleman farmer at a family château called La Grange, in the countryside southeast of Paris, and he played no part in public affairs over the next fifteen years. Lafayette refused to cooperate with Napoleon's authoritarian regime and referred constantly to Jeffersonian America as the main refuge of liberty in the modern world. His political activities during this period took the form of private correspondence with liberal critics of the Napoleonic empire. He sought to sustain a liberal political alternative to the imperial system by praising the American Revolution, the new American republic, and the ideals of the early French Revolution.

RETURN TO POLITICAL LIFE IN LATER YEARS

The Bourbon Restoration in 1815 and the creation of the new Chamber of Deputies gave Lafayette the opportunity to regain a place in French political culture. Elected to the Chamber in 1818, he worked closely with other liberals such as Benjamin Constant to defend freedom of the press, an independent judiciary, electoral reforms, and the political rights of liberal movements throughout Europe.

The French police kept Lafayette under permanent surveillance, in part because he often hosted foreign radicals at La Grange and corresponded with secret, antigovernment groups within France itself. He also developed close friendships with a diverse group of women writers and political activists, firmly supporting the controversial books and political actions of liberal women such as Germaine de Staël, the Scottish-born American abolitionist Fanny Wright, the Irish novelist Lady Sydney Morgan, and the Italian nationalist Cristina Belgioioso. His international political correspondence during the 1820s provided ideological support for liberal national movements in Latin America, Spain, and Greece. He compared such political struggles to the earlier American war for national independence, and he remained optimistic about the eventual triumph of liberal nationalisms and constitutional reforms in most of Europe.

Meanwhile, he lost an election in 1824 and found his desire for political change stymied by the conservative ascendancy in France. He therefore accepted an official invitation for a national tour of the United States, where he was universally praised as the esteemed defender of liberty, order, and the achievements of the new American nation.

Lafayette later regained his seat in the Chamber of Deputies and moved again to the center of French political culture in the Revolution of 1830. When Parisian crowds took up arms and forced King Charles X to abandon his throne, the aging general returned to his old position as commander of the French National Guard. Although he embraced the new French king, Louis-Philippe, he also called repeatedly for a "throne surrounded by republican institutions," by which he meant that France should have a constitutional monarchy and that the government should protect all of the fundamental "rights of man." Reiterating his perennial defense of liberty and order, Lafayette lost favor again with both the conservative monarchists and the radical republicans.

He was thus forced to resign his command of the National Guard, whereupon he went back to the Chamber of Deputies and spoke often about the dangers of internal government repression and reactionary policies abroad. He also continued to support national independence movements in Poland, Italy, and Greece, all of which he saw as necessary preludes for the free and orderly political systems that he envisioned as the European political culture of the future.

LEGACY

By the time of Lafayette's death in 1834, the more radical European political movements were turning toward socialism, and the reigning powers were still resisting most of the liberal national movements he had promoted. The European campaign to create liberal institutions would nevertheless ultimately manage to establish the kind of widespread constitutional government and human rights that Lafayette had advocated. But his life and famous actions always elicited the highest praise from Americans, whose national revolution he had joined in 1777 and whose liberal conceptions of national sovereignty and human rights he had defended and adapted during a long, controversial political career in Europe.

See also **Charles X; France; French Revolution; Louis XVIII; Revolutions of 1820; Revolutions of 1830.**

BIBLIOGRAPHY

Gottschalk, Louis, and Margaret Maddox. *Lafayette in the French Revolution: From the October Days through the Federation.* Chicago, 1973.

———. *Lafayette in the French Revolution: Through the October Days.* Chicago, 1969.

Kramer, Lloyd. *Lafayette in Two Worlds: Public Cultures and Personal Identities in an Age of Revolutions.* Chapel Hill, N.C., 1996.

Neely, Sylvia. *Lafayette and the Liberal Ideal, 1814–1824: Politics and Conspiracy in an Age of Reaction.* Carbondale, Ill., 1991.

Unger, Harlow Giles. *Lafayette.* New York, 2002.

LLOYD KRAMER

LAMARCK, JEAN-BAPTISTE (1744–1829), one of the world's leading zoologists and also the first biologist to offer a full-scale theory of organic evolution.

Jean-Baptiste Lamarck was born in the small village of Bazentin in the Picardie region of France. The youngest child in a large family of the French lesser nobility, he was destined by his parents to be a priest. After his father died, he decided to pursue a military career instead. He served in the army from 1761 until an injury in 1768 forced him to resign. He subsequently made his way to Paris, where he successively worked in a bank, attended medical school, and finally concluded that what he wanted to do most was be a botanist.

Lamarck first gained visibility as a botanist by announcing to the botanists of the Jardin du Roi (the King's garden) that he could produce a guide to the plants of France superior to any guide then in existence. His project attracted the attention of the institution's director, Georges Louis Leclerc de Buffon (1707–1788), who arranged to have Lamarck's *Flore française* (Flora of France) published in 1778 at government expense. Buffon also championed Lamarck's election to the Academy of Sciences and gave him the official title of "correspondent" of the Jardin du Roi.

Lamarck worked productively as a botanist through the 1780s. In 1789, the year after Buffon's death, he secured from Buffon's successor at the Jardin du Roi a salaried position, that of "botanist of the king and keeper of the king's herbaria." During the French Revolution, however, royal associations became liabilities. In 1793 the Jardin du Roi was reconstituted as the National Museum of Natural History. In the reshuffling of staff at the institution, Lamarck lost his position as a botanist but received a whole new responsibility, the professorship of "worms, insects, and microscopic animals." His expertise in this area at the time was limited to what he knew as the result of being a collector of shells. Nevertheless, as he worked over the next two decades with the museum's burgeoning collections, he became the leading authority on that part of the animal kingdom he himself designated as the "invertebrates."

Lamarck was not content, however, to restrict his attention to the classification of the invertebrates. From the mid-1770s onward he nursed broad speculative notions about chemistry and meteorology, and in the 1790s he began publishing on these subjects, generally to the detriment of his reputation, since leaders in the scientific community were inclined to dismiss his formulations as examples of uncritical "system-building."

Lamarck first endorsed the idea of species mutability in 1800 in a lecture he delivered to his class on invertebrate zoology at the museum. Precisely what inspired his belief in organic mutability is uncertain, but one issue that concerned him at this time was the relation between fossil and living forms of shellfish. Confronted with the idea of species extinction, but reluctant to believe that extinction had occurred on a broad scale, he chose to think that living creatures had been gradually transformed over time in response to climatic changes on the earth's surface. He thereby took a position directly contrary to that of his colleague, Georges Cuvier (1769–1832), who opposed the idea of organic transformation while arguing that great catastrophes in the earth's past had wiped out entire assemblages of large land animals. Lamarck advanced his transformist theory at length in his 1809 *Philosophie zoologique* (Zoological Philosophy) and again in 1815 in his great treatise on invertebrate classification, *Histoire naturelle des animaux sans vertèbres* (Natural history of the invertebrates).

Lamarck's zoological theorizing encompassed much more than an explanation of how species change. He sought to account for the nature and origin of life, the production of the different forms of animal organization, and the diverse faculties to which these different forms of organization give rise. His explanation of the successive production of living forms began with the claim that the simplest forms of plant and animal life were produced by spontaneous generation. He believed these forms were then successively modified by two very different causes. The first, which he named "the power of life," was responsible for the general tendency toward increased complexity seen in the plant and animal classes alike. The second was the modifying influence of the environment, which tended to interfere with the general tendency toward increased complexity.

Lamarck's explanation of the influence of the environment on animal forms depended on the idea with which his name is now most frequently associated, "the inheritance of acquired characteristics." Changes in the environment, he claimed, led animals to develop new habits, causing them to use some organs more and other organs less. The more frequent use of an organ tended to strengthen and develop it, the less frequent use of an organ tended to weaken it and cause it to atrophy. Bodily changes thus acquired were then passed on to the next generation (provided, in the case of sexually reproducing organisms, that both parents had undergone the same changes). Habits maintained over many generations, together with the inheritance of acquired characteristics, thereby led to such diverse structural features as the long neck and forelegs of the giraffe and the rudimentary eyes of the mole.

The belief that acquired characteristics could be inherited was a commonplace in Lamarck's day. What was not accepted, however, was Lamarck's claim that such modifications could go so far as to result in new species. It was only after the 1859 publication of *Origin of Species* by Charles Darwin (1809–1882) that the idea of organic evolution gained widespread acceptance in the scientific community. It was only then, furthermore, that the inheritance of acquired characteristics came to be identified as a distinctively "Lamarckian" idea, in contrast to the Darwinian theory of natural selection. The reality of the inheritance of acquired characteristics was not seriously challenged until the 1880s. It continued to have adherents among biologists well into the twentieth century, but support for it waned as the experimental and other evidence advanced on its behalf was shown to be susceptible to other interpretations.

Lamarck died in 1829, blind and impoverished. In the twenty-first century his name is associated primarily with the now-discredited idea of the inheritance of acquired characteristics, but he deserves to be remembered more generally for his contributions to botanical and zoological systematics and for having been the first writer to set forth a detailed, comprehensive theory of organic evolution.

See also **Cuvier, Georges; Darwin, Charles; Evolution; Science and Technology.**

BIBLIOGRAPHY

Burkhardt, Richard W., Jr. *The Spirit of System: Lamarck and Evolutionary Biology.* Cambridge, Mass., 1995.

Corsi, Pietro. *The Age of Lamarck: Evolutionary Theories in France, 1790–1830.* Translated by Jonathon Mandelbaum. Berkeley, Calif., 1988.

Lamarck, Jean Baptiste. *Zoological Philosophy: An Exposition with Regard to the Natural History of Animals.* Translated by Hugh Elliot. Chicago, 1984.

Richard W. Burkhardt Jr.

LAMARTINE, ALPHONSE

LAMARTINE, ALPHONSE (1790–1869), a major literary and political figure in France.

Alphonse Marie Louis de Lamartine was born in Mâcon, the only son of aristocratic, landowning parents, on 21 October 1790. After attending a Jesuit college at Belley in Savoy, Lamartine led a rather aimless existence, because the royalist traditions of his family prevented him from serving Napoleonic France. He did, however, make a prolonged visit to Italy (July 1811–April 1812), during which he had a love affair that later became a source of poetic inspiration.

The fall of Napoleon's empire interrupted Lamartine's idle and dissipated life. In July 1814 he was commissioned into the royal bodyguard and helped to escort Louis XVIII (r. 1814–1824) out of France in March 1815. After the second abdication (22 June 1815) of Napoleon I (r. 1804–1814/15), Lamartine resigned his army commission. Unsuccessful in his attempts to become a subprefect, he wrote poetry, had affairs with married women, and gained an entry into aristocratic and royalist Paris society. His influential friends and his reputation as a poet helped to secure his appointment in March 1820 as an attaché at the French embassy in Naples. The same month a collection of twenty-four of his poems was published anonymously, entitled *Méditations Poétiques.* A sensational success, the *Méditations Poétiques* rapidly made Lamartine one of France's most famous Romantic poets. Shortly afterward, on 6 June 1820, Lamartine married an Anglo-Dutch heiress, Marianne Birch. As a diplomat, Lamartine served in Naples and from 1825 in Florence, while continuing to write poetry and beginning to develop political interests and ambitions. He published two further collections of poems, *Nouvelles méditations poétiques* (September 1823) and *Harmonies poétiques et religieuses* (June 1830), as well as individual poems such as *La Mort de Socrate* (September 1823) and *Le Dernier chant du pèlerinage d'Harold* (May 1825). These literary achievements were officially recognized by his admission to membership of the French Academy (1 April 1830).

Meanwhile, Lamartine was moving politically from royalism toward liberalism and indicating an interest in becoming a member of the Chamber of Deputies. In October 1829 he politely refused to serve the reactionary Polignac government, though he did not participate in the July 1830 Revolution, which replaced the Restoration monarchy of Charles X (r. 1824–1830) with the initially more liberal July Monarchy of Louis-Philippe (r. 1830–1848). After the Revolution of July 1830, Lamartine resigned from the diplomatic corps but at the same time swore an oath of allegiance to Louis-Philippe. Following unsuccessful attempts to gain election to the Chamber of Deputies in three constituencies (July 1831 and June 1832), Lamartine with his wife and daughter Julia made a long journey to the Middle East (July 1832–October 1833). Julia died in Beirut on 7 December 1832, leaving the Lamartines grief-stricken and childless (a son had died in November 1822). However, on 7 January 1833 a constituency in the Nord elected Lamartine to the Chamber of Deputies; and his Middle East journey led to a new publication, the *Voyage en Orient* (1835).

Consistently reelected to parliament, first in the Nord and from 1837 in his home constituency of Saône-et-Loire in Burgundy, Lamartine became a prominent liberal deputy who maintained his independence from successive governments. In a parliamentary speech of 27 January 1843, he announced that he was joining the left-wing opposition to the ministry of François-Pierre-Guillaume Guizot (1787–1874). He also began writing a *Histoire des*

Girondins (1847), controversially sympathetic toward the Revolution and even toward Maximilien Robespierre (1758–1794). Lamartine's increasing reputation as a radical, and his parliamentary speech on 24 February 1848 rejecting a regency and demanding a provisional government, led to his inclusion in the republican government formed after the abdication of Louis-Philippe.

In the National Assembly elections of 23 April 1848, Lamartine was elected in ten departments with 1,283,501 votes, but he rapidly lost his popularity by insisting on the inclusion of Alexandre-Auguste Ledru-Rollin (1807–1874), a left-wing republican, in the government known as the Executive Commission formed on 10 May. The outbreak in Paris of a working-class insurrection—the June Days—on 24 June forced the resignation of Lamartine and the other members of the Executive Commission. The presidential election of 10 December 1848 demonstrated Lamartine's political marginalization—he received just 20,938 votes. Although elected a member of the National Assembly from July 1849 to Louis-Napoleon Bonaparte's (1808–1873) coup d'état of 2 December 1851, Lamartine's political career was effectively over. Financial problems, however, forced him to continue writing a series of historical and literary works almost until his death (28 February 1869).

See also **France; Revolutions of 1848; Romanticism.**

BIBLIOGRAPHY

Primary Sources

Lamartine, Alphonse de. *Oeuvres poétiques completes.* Edited by Marius-François Guyard. Paris, 1963.

———. *Correspondance Lamartine-Virieu, 1808–1841.* Edited by Marie-Renée Morin. 4 vols. Paris, 1987–1998.

Secondary Sources

Fortescue, William. *Alphonse de Lamartine: A Political Biography.* London, 1983.

WILLIAM FORTESCUE

LANDED ELITES. The relationship of elites to landownership in Europe from 1789 to 1914 was very diverse, complicated by the variety of geographical regions, the multiplicity of systems of landownership from large estates of more than 1,000 hectares to small farms, the existence of tracts of common lands and forests, the wide variety of forms of tenancy of arable land at the lower levels of rural society, and political changes in states. Throughout the nineteenth century agriculture was the leading economic activity of Europeans save in the United Kingdom where 8 percent of the employed male population was in agriculture in 1911. After 1914 it was approximately 24 percent for the German Empire, 30 percent in France, and 52 percent in Russia. Historians and geographers have produced a variety of local studies of particular regions but they are so disparate that it is not possible to extrapolate continuous series of statistics about the social origins of landowners and estate size and values throughout Europe.

Landownership remained an important element of the definition of elite status in society during the nineteenth century, especially for aristocrats and nobles but also for rich commoners. Landownership was attractive to the elite—meaning the wealthiest 5 percent of families within their nations or territories—because of the ongoing prestige of the feudal origins of European nobilities in the Middle Ages. Many nobles claimed a feudal origin from a title bestowed by a king or emperor but others claimed to be immemorial nobility, meaning that it was so old that there was no record of its origin. The family seat was either passed down by primogeniture or acquired through a dowry of a new spouse. In Poland before the nineteenth century the monarchy was elected by the nobility and the descendants of those noble families, the *szlachta,* continued to avoid intermarriage with plebians and to claim hereditary military prowess for the males.

The European understanding of the desirability of keeping at least part of family wealth in the form of landownership had been affected by the eighteenth-century French economists known as physiocrats (especially François Quesnay, 1694–1774) who taught that agriculture yielded a net surplus while manufacturing did not. It was better to invest in land at a time of rising population than to search for the monetary rewards invoked by mercantilism. A corollary was that large landowners should interest themselves in agricultural improvement.

In the post-Napoleonic constitutional monarchy in France that was organized according to the Constitutional Charter of 1814, franchise was given to adult males on the basis of their declared levels of taxation paid. The land tax was at a higher rate than that on commercial premises. Political theorists of the time identified landowners as being particularly responsible for safeguarding the public good. Large landowners were thought to influence the politics of their tenants and laborers.

Europe in the nineteenth century was to undergo aspects of the industrial revolution brought about by use of steam power, improved metallurgical techniques for the production of iron and steel, and above all the introduction of a complex railway system that crisscrossed the Continent by 1914 and the invention of the automobile. The effects of these innovations and the developments of the banking system and that of stock exchanges provided large rewards to individuals and families who participated in new opportunities. Many of those individuals and their families were able to buy urban real estate and also country estates that permitted them to mimic the lifestyle of the landed nobility. One of the major trends of the social history of nineteenth-century Europe was the rise in urbanization and the growing proportion of the population that lived in towns of more than five thousand inhabitants.

Elite members bought land for recreational use, especially hunting, shooting, and horseback riding, and constructed large country houses set in parkland and gardens for their families and visitors. They also provided lodgings and work space for servants and laborers. Ownership of a country house where guests could be housed in gracious surroundings for days was one sign of membership in the elite.

Feudal dues were one of the forms of property ended by the Revolution in France in the session of the National Assembly through the night of 4 August 1789. Abolition of such payments and services and the emancipation of rural workers from forms of serfdom that restricted their economic independence took place in many other parts of Europe during the nineteenth century. The confiscations of some noble and clerical properties in France during the Revolution of 1789 meant that many townspeople were able to purchase land. The property transfers mainly benefited the legal profession and the middle classes. In other parts of Europe conditions were slower to change. Confiscations of monastic and some aristocratic land and its subsequent sale took place in Portugal in 1834 and in Spain in 1836.

In eastern Europe members of the Prussian Junker class were more successful in retaining their rural authority. Baron Karl vom Stein's (1757–1831) 1807 October Edict abolished the Brandenburg-Prussian villagers' personal legal liabilities without compensating the former overlords. This opened up a free land market so that estate owners might now emerge from any social class if they had the requisite cash. Elsewhere, further land-reform measures led to the emancipation of farmers and peasants from restraints on their economic independence and also enclosed formerly village-controlled common lands and forest. This produced large estates worked by laborers resident in small villages and also created village-based family farms. The nineteenth century saw the shift from unpaid manorial service to modern wage labor for rural workers. However serfdom, meaning that peasants were legally linked to work on the estates where they lived, continued until 1861 in Russia. Although direct legal authority over the peasantry by noble landowners was everywhere diminishing during the nineteenth century there was a residual prestige for a style of life which involved a stately home, considered to be a family seat, set in a rural estate.

In many parts of Europe large country houses were repaired or rebuilt in the nineteenth century to sustain a symbolism of the aristocratic lifestyle. Noblewomen projected a powerful image of family life, social roles, and interclass attitudes. Members of the elite kept significant amounts of family capital in landownership. Some of the elite interested themselves in improving the agricultural yields of their properties by studying new techniques of seeding, plowing, and applying chemical fertilizers and pesticides. England, the Low Countries, and northern France were the first regions to undergo an agricultural revolution efficient enough to generate surplus capital linked to the Industrial Revolution.

It can be argued that as a general rule in Europe effective landowner power depended on a residence in the country seat for at least part of the year. Thousands of wealthy titled families would

Shooting party at Kinnaird House, Scotland, 1869. Hunting parties held on country estates remained a primary feature of British upper-class social life throughout the nineteenth century. The possession of such an estate carried great prestige and was the privilege of only the wealthiest citizens. ©HULTON-DEUTSCH COLLECTION/CORBIS

leave Moscow to spend the summer on their country estates and the same could be said of cities like Vienna and Berlin. Families that laid no historical claim to noble titles, as well as those who received distinctions from rulers who still dispensed them, like the British, French, Portuguese, Spanish, Italian, German, Austro-Hungarian, Russian, and other monarchs, typically sought to purchase country houses. These were often called a *Schloss,* chateau, or manor house and had an estate farmed either by laborers under the direction of the chatelain or his agents. Parts of it could be rented out to tenant farmers.

Europe in 1914 had lost some title-granting crowns, as in France, and had gained others, as in the Kingdom of Italy and the German Reich. In some countries legislation had stripped aristocrats of privileges. Changes in inheritance laws in many countries undermined the system of primogeniture, in which the eldest male child received a disproportunate amount of the estate at the expense of an equal share for his siblings. In Britain this system was called the strict settlement. The abolition in Spain during the 1820s of entailed properties that passed to the eldest son in each generation caused a breakup of noble estates.

In almost all of Europe there were those who claimed nobility even if some republics were indifferent. In fact the continuities of old elites into the nineteenth century remained a crucial element of the European past. Nobles found a place in understanding the European century of world domination, the nineteenth. Karl Marx (1818–1883) had restated the inevitability of class conflict between a bourgeoisie enriched by modernity and factories and the enfeebled old aristocracy whose wealth was primarily in land. The workers who were exploited to provide the wealth of the bourgeoisie would, when they were conscious of their exploitation, revolt against their oppressors. In the perspective of those who saw agriculture as the basis of the state the harmonious relationship of large landowners, who were often aristocrats, with the peasants who worked the land for them was seen as the core value.

An argument has been sustained regarding the abiding influence of aristocrats in politics and war in Europe. The world of nobles as models of good living was gradually divorced from a political language of royalism or legitimism or Bonapartism. Quite soon after the French Revolution various social theorists addressed the issue of the existence of nobilities in society. At least some nobles tried to introduce divine purpose into their existence. One example was published in London in French by an unidentified *émigré* in 1812: *Letter on the nobility, or Emile corrected on the nature, rank, dignity and the necessuty of the nobility in every country; the origin of its lands, titles, estates and possessions. Deplorable blindness about this order. Frenzy of the factious who seek to destroy it. Destructive system which upsets the world. Fertile source of calamities for peoples, etc. etc.* in which the author points out what was happening to the Spanish nobility at the time of his publication and that French revolutionary hostility to nobility made plain to nobles in other lands the "grievous fate that would engulf them unless they hastened to recognize the danger." By the end of the nineteenth century nobody published books claiming divine protection for nobility. Instead the argument would be one in favor of a service nobility that passed on particularly valuable traditions in its family formations. This might show itself in diplomacy or banking; in due course the nobility would show interest in the arts, science, and high technology. It can be argued that the elite was more open to new recruits with new ways of making a living before World War I than it had been at the onset of the French Revolution.

The Cavazza family of Bologna, Italy, showed the place of landownership in aristocratic assimilation into the local elite by a successful banker ennobled in the 1880s for public service and charity. His son, Count Francesco Cavazza (1860–1942), invested extensively in rural properties and was the second biggest landowner in the province by 1914. He married a countess from an older lineage and he purchased and renovated a fifteenth-century walled castle outside Bologna. His activities were now those of an aristocratic landowner who was noted for charity, a patron of the arts, and a parliamentary deputy first elected in 1913. With modifications caused by local circumstances elsewhere in Europe similar examples can be found of the linkage of elites and land.

See also **Aristocracy; Bourgeoisie; Class and Social Relations; Peasants.**

BIBLIOGRAPHY

Gibson, Ralph, and Martin Blinkhorn, eds. *Landownership and Power in Modern Europe.* London, 1991.

Girouard, Mark. *Life in the French Country House.* New York, 2000.

Godsey, William D., Jr. *Nobles and Nation in Central Europe: Free Imperial Knights in the Age of Revolution, 1750–1850.* Cambridge, U.K., and New York, 2004.

Hagen, William W. *Ordinary Prussians: Brandenburg Junkers and Villagers, 1500–1840.* Cambridge, U.K., and New York, 2002.

DAVID HIGGS

LARREY, DOMINIQUE-JEAN (1766–1842), French surgeon.

Soldiers in the Revolutionary and Napoleonic era encountered the same perils that had governed the battlefield since the gunpowder revolution began three centuries earlier. Bullets shattered bone, shredded soft tissue, and usually remained embedded in the wounded man, thus creating the conditions for infection, particularly if foreign objects such as pieces of the uniform entered the wound. Saber cuts ripped flesh from bone, while lance thrusts lacerated organs and arteries. Round shot and grape often tore limbs from bodies and decapitated men where they stood. Disease, malnutrition, poor sanitation, and physical exhaustion usually claimed more lives on campaign than actual combat; a typical army lost over 10 percent of its combat effectiveness to the sick list.

The French Revolution and Napoleonic era ushered in a new age of warfare. The massed batteries, deep attack columns, and massive frontal assaults that became common in Napoleonic battles claimed unprecedented numbers of casualties.

Military medical services, which had stagnated for much of the eighteenth century, needed revolutionary innovations to keep pace. Unfortunately, improvements in the medical services lagged far behind changes in warfare.

Most armies campaigned with an accompanying hospital that stood far behind the front lines. The wounded either depended on comrades to help them get to the rear or had to make their way to the hospital, often bloodied, disoriented, and in excruciating pain. Severely wounded soldiers had to remain on the field until combat ceased, sometimes waiting days before they received aid. If the wounded managed to reach the hospital, available medical services afforded little comfort. Surgeons often used their fingers to probe a wound for bullets and shell fragments. Primitive instruments and unclean conditions made attempts at extraction risky. Amputation remained the primary method of treating limb trauma. Gangrene, an ever-present concern, could develop if the surgeon failed to remove all of the dead flesh from around the wound. Shock and infection, the usual consequences of surgery, had to be treated in hospitals rife with contagions that claimed more lives than the enemy.

Most associated with the improvement of medical services during the Revolutionary and Napoleonic era is the French surgeon Dominique-Jean Larrey. The young Larrey began his medical studies in Toulouse. After completing his formal training in Paris, he secured his first position in the medical field in 1787 as a surgeon on the French frigate *La Vigilante*. When the Revolutionary Wars began in 1792, Larrey volunteered as an assistant surgeon in the Army of the Rhine. He saw firsthand the need to reform the method of evacuating the wounded from the battlefield. Under Larrey's direction, the French established a system of "flying ambulances" that carried wounded in light, horse-drawn carts from the battlefield to mobile field hospitals, where surgeons could begin treatment immediately. Such a system proved invaluable because the speed of treatment often determined if a wounded soldier would recover. Larrey's ambulance corps launched his career. After Larrey received a professorship at Paris's new school of military medicine at Val-de-Grâce in 1796, young General Napoleon Bonaparte summoned him to implement his ambulance system in the French Army of Italy. Two years later, Larrey accompanied the French Army of the Orient to Egypt, Palestine, and Syria, where he and his assistants refined the technique of evacuating the wounded and performing lifesaving procedures on the field of battle. In 1805, now Emperor Napoleon I promoted Larrey to inspector general of the Service de Santé (Office of Army Health), and later, in 1812, chief surgeon of the Grande Armée.

Although he showered Larrey with gifts, Napoleon refused to sanction the existence of a permanent medical corps and actually mistrusted doctors in general, claiming that their inexperience did more harm to his army than the enemy's artillery. Larrey and others struggled to create a permanent medical corps, but could not overcome the low priority that Napoleon placed on medical needs. Prior to the war against Prussia in 1806, Larrey assigned a flying ambulance detachment to each of the six corps that made up Napoleon's army. Because of Napoleon's refusal to acknowledge the importance of medical officers by granting them full equality with other officers, Larrey could not field a full complement of surgeons. In 1812 Larrey formed eleven flying ambulance detachments to accompany the French army into Russia. This number, however, proved woefully inadequate to support the 500,000 men who crossed the Russian frontier. Although the emperor made sure that his elite Imperial Guard had the very best medical services, the rest of the French army suffered from Napoleon's detached regard for life. This can be especially seen in the 1813 and 1814 campaigns, when poor supply, health care, and sanitation contributed just as much to the defeat of French forces as the enemy coalition.

See also **Armies; Disease; French Revolutionary Wars and Napoleonic Wars; Napoleon; Nightingale, Florence.**

BIBLIOGRAPHY

Primary Sources

Larrey, Dominique-Jean. *Mémoires de chirurgie militaire, et campagnes.* 4 vols. Paris, 1812–1817.

Secondary Sources

Elting, John R. *Swords around a Throne: Napoleon's Grande Armée.* New York, 1988.

Vess, David M. *Medical Revolution in France, 1789–1796.* Gainesville, Fla., 1975.

MICHAEL V. LEGGIERE

LASKER-SCHÜLER, ELSE (1869–1945), German Jewish writer.

Born 11 February 1869 in Elberfeld, the Rhineland, Else Lasker-Schüler grew up in a well-to-do assimilated Jewish family, the youngest of six children. Her father was a banker and builder. She attended a progressive girls' school until she was about thirteen when, due to illness, she was educated at home. In 1894 she married the physician Berthold Lasker and moved to Berlin. There she took lessons in art and entered the literary circles of the burgeoning avant-garde that was very much under the influence of Friedrich Nietzsche (1844–1900). Artists' communities sprung up around Berlin, advocating a radical renewal of life and art, and Lasker-Schüler was their frequent guest. The growing estrangement from her husband, her insistence that he was not the father of her son Paul, born in 1899, give proof of her determination to free herself from bourgeois constraints. In the same year she published her first poems.

After her divorce in 1903, Lasker-Schüler married the musician Georg Levin, whom she renamed Herwarth Walden (1878–1941). Always in precarious financial situations, the couple nevertheless fought without compromise for an aesthetic renewal with publications, readings, and concerts in Walden's Verein für Kunst (Association for Art) by far the most prestigious of the many artistic organizations of the time in Berlin. In 1910 Walden, in close collaboration with Karl Kraus (1874–1936) in Vienna, founded the periodical *Der Sturm* (The storm). It became the mouthpiece for expressionist art and literature in which Lasker-Schüler published widely. The marriage ended in 1912.

Lasker-Schüler continued to live in Berlin, adding to her meager honoraria by selling her exquisite drawings. Her son, a gifted artist himself, died of tuberculosis in 1927. During the Weimar Republic (1919–1933) she was recognized as the greatest living German woman poet. In April 1933 she fled to Switzerland, which she was forced to leave in 1939. She died in Jerusalem in January 1945.

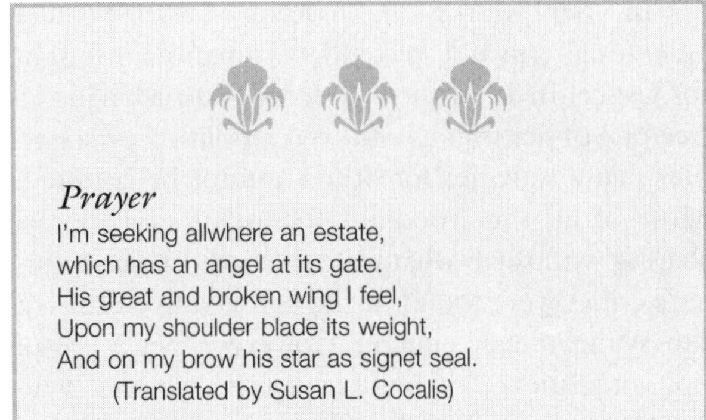

Prayer

I'm seeking allwhere an estate,
which has an angel at its gate.
His great and broken wing I feel,
Upon my shoulder blade its weight,
And on my brow his star as signet seal.

(Translated by Susan L. Cocalis)

Lasker-Schüler became most famous for her poetry: passionate early poems that employ art nouveau imagery written around 1900; the strong *Hebräische Balladen* (1913; Hebrew ballads), glorifying Biblical figures; poems in praise of young painters like Franz Marc (1880–1916), and poets like Gottfried Benn (1886–1956) and Georg Trakl (1887–1914), whose genius she was among the first to recognize. Like many artists and poets of her time, Lasker-Schüler was inspired by Asian art, including dance. She had created a realm within her artwork that she called *Theben* (Thebes), and ruled as "Prince Jussuf." Her alterego also appeared in fantastic Oriental stories and in her drawings surrounded by her artist friends. Her *Briefe nach Norwegen* (1912–1913; Letters to Norway) depict the Berlin bohemia that congregated in the famous Café des Westens. Lasker-Schüler was also a great essayist. Her love for nature and her deep religiosity are evident in many of her prose texts. In the first of her three plays, *Die Wupper* (1909), named for the river of her hometown, she creates a magically realistic picture of an industrial city.

World War I took the lives of many poets and painters she had praised in her writings. She opposed the war from the beginning, knowing that it would destroy the hopes for a truly modern Europe not divided by nationalistic strife but united by the common goals of its artists. She poured out her utter despair in the fictitious letters to her Blue Rider, the painter Franz Marc, which she published as "Briefe und Bilder" (1913–1917; Letters and pictures) in various journals and later the volume *Der Malik. Eine Kaisergeschichte* (1919; The Malik: The story of an emperor).

In her works and deeds Lasker-Schüler emerges as a proud Jew and a woman who fought for justice. In 1914 she traveled to Russia, trying to free one of her friends who was a political prisoner. Her many activities for others cannot be counted. Most of all she stood up for artists and writers sharing with them what little she had. Lasker-Schüler's critics were found in the conservative camp of the Wilhelminian empire. However, they were of no consequence. Considering the writers who wrote about and dedicated their poems to her (Gottfried Benn, Georg Trakl), the painters who painted her (Karl Schmidt-Rottluff [1884–1976], Jankel Adler [1895–1949]), and the composers who set her poems to music (Paul Hindemith [1895–1963], Ernst Krenek [1900–1991]), it is evident that the truly great were always on her side.

See also **Avant-Garde.**

BIBLIOGRAPHY

Primary Sources

Lasker-Schüler, Else. *Hebrew Ballads and Other Poems.* Translated, edited, and with an introduction by Audri Durchslag and Jeanette Litman-Demeestère. Philadelphia, 1980.

———. *"Your Diamond Dreams Cut Open My Arteries." Poems by Else Lasker-Schüler.* Translated and with an introduction by Robert P. Newton. Chapel Hill, N.C., 1982.

———. *Concert.* Translated by Jean M. Snook. Lincoln, Nebr., 1994.

———. *Werke und Briefe.* Frankfurt am Main, 1996–.

Secondary Sources

Bauschinger, Sigrid. *Else Lasker-Schüler: Biographie.* Göttingen, 2004.

Falkenberg, Betty. *Else Lasker-Schüler: A Life.* Jefferson, N.C., 2003.

Jones, Calvin N. *The Literary Reputation of Else Lasker-Schüler: Criticism 1901–1993.* Columbia, S.C., 1994.

SIGRID BAUSCHINGER

LASSALLE, FERDINAND (1825–1864),

German socialist leader.

Ferdinand Lassalle was a nearly legendary figure in the history of the German working-class movement; his influence went far beyond his theoretical, organizational, programmatic, or practical contributions, none of which was either significant or long lasting. His less than two-year association with one of the earliest worker associations in the post-1848 era, the *Allgemeiner deutscher Arbeiterverein* (ADAV), from 1863 to 1864, left little organizational or programmatic legacy, but he continued for decades to be heralded by much of the rank and file as one of the founders of the movement.

Although he never trained in law, Lassalle first made a name for himself in the German courts. In the 1840s, he successfully defended the great poet Heinrich Heine (1797–1856) in an inheritance case and later won even more renown for his part in a long, complicated, and embarrassing divorce case involving Countess Sophie von Hatzfeldt (1801–1885). Thus when in the late 1850s Lassalle began taking public positions with regard to the workers, he was already a well-known figure. What appealed most to the emerging working-class movement in Lassalle's writings was his opposition to an alliance between the liberals and the workers and his call for universal male suffrage. Thus in 1863 when a group of Leipzig workers established the ADAV independent workers organization, they issued an invitation to Lassalle to attend the founding congress, hoping that his presence would counter the influence of liberals who sought to keep the workers politically dependent.

Even with the flamboyant and famous Lassalle as president, the ADAV never met with great success; by 1868, it had fewer than 8,000 members, less than a quarter of the number Lassalle had originally predicted. Furthermore, he seems to have advocated universal male suffrage largely as a tactical move, hoping to promote civil war when the bourgeoisie reacted to the loss of its special status. His conception of democracy had more in common with the Jacobin notion of some vague collective will than with representative democracy in a parliamentary sense. Furthermore, late in his life, Lassalle made overtures to the Prussian government about the possibility of having the state finance workers' cooperatives as a means of overcoming what he saw as the "iron law of wages," which kept workers permanently poor under the reign of capitalism. He even met personally with

Otto von Bismarck (1815–1898) in hopes of convincing the Iron Chancellor that he could win the support of the workers against the liberals by pledging such support for cooperatives. However, Bismarck soon realized that he did not need, nor could Lassalle deliver, the support of the workers, so nothing came of the negotiations.

Eventually, the party that grew out of the 1869 merger of the ADAV and its rival organization, the *Verband deutscher Arbeitervereine* (VDAV), drew much more heavily in doctrinal and organizational terms from the latter than the former. The *Sozialdemokratische Arbeiterpartei* (SDAP) was much more heavily influenced by August Bebel (1840–1913) and Wilhelm Liebknecht (1826–1900) and their form of Marxism than by Lassalle. In 1891, this party adopted the name *Sozialdemokratische Partei Deutschlands* (SPD). It was a parliamentary party that soon became the largest party in Germany, having moved far away from Lassalle's notion of Jacobin democracy and state-financed workers' cooperatives. The workers' movement of which the SPD was the central element eventually also encompassed workers' cooperatives, a massive system of newspapers and journals, and a vast array of workers' social, athletic, and cultural clubs, and had very close ties with the so-called free trade unions.

Ironically, Lassalle's single significant theoretical contribution to the German movement, *Herr Bastiat-Schulze von Delitzsch, der ökonomische Julian, order: Capital und Arbeit* (1864), while ostensibly an attack on the liberal-worker alliance Lassalle so opposed, was probably more important for its popularization of Marxian concepts, albeit in somewhat distorted form. In this work, Lassalle dealt with the historical developmental tendencies of capitalism in a way that helped open the door to reception of works by Karl Marx (1818–1883) and Friedrich Engels (1820–1885). However, Marx and Engels were never grateful for this and consistently saw Lassalle as an ideological opponent.

Lassalle died young, killed in a silly, if romantic, duel over a woman. His reputation benefited, perhaps, from his dying young, as have those of so many other legendary figures; had he lived longer, the inadequacies of his positions would have been revealed. However, his call in 1863 for workers to break with their former liberal allies touched a sympathetic chord among the many increasingly class-conscious workers. He also impressed many of the same people with his flamboyance, his fashionable dress, and his hobnobbing with the famous and powerful. Such style was generally lacking among other leaders of the emerging workers' movement, which probably helps explain why Lassalle, despite having contributed so little of substance, was so fondly remembered for so long by so many in the movement.

See also **Bismarck, Otto von; Germany; Labor Movements; Marx, Karl; Prussia; Revolutions of 1848; Socialism.**

BIBLIOGRAPHY

Hubbard, Elbert. *Ferdinand Lassalle and Helene von Donniges.* East Aurora, N.Y., 1906. (Little Journeys to the Homes of Great Lovers series, v. 19, no. 4).

Lassalle, Ferdinand. *Herr Bastiat-Schulze von Delitzsch, der ökonomische Julian, oder: Capital und Arbeit.* Berlin, 1864.

Na'aman, Shlomo. *Lassalle.* Hannover, 1970.

GARY P. STEENSON

LAVOISIER, ANTOINE (1743–1794),

French scientist, commonly considered the founder of modern chemistry.

Antoine Laurent Lavoisier was born in Paris, France on 26 August 1743. A child of privilege (his father was a wealthy lawyer and his mother was the daughter of a well-to-do attorney), Antoine was educated, from the age of eleven, at the Collège Mazarin, from which he received a baccalaureate in law in 1763. By this time his passion for science had already eclipsed his interest in law, and he participated in the expeditions of geologist Jean-Étienne Guettard (1715–1786) to prepare the first mineralogical atlas of France. To enhance his knowledge of the chemical nature of minerals, Lavoisier attended the lectures of the chemist Guillaume-François Rouelle (1703–1770) and began doing research on gypsum in a laboratory that he set up in his Parisian home. To support his scientific activities, Lavoisier supplemented the inheritance he received from his father with a 1768 investment in the Ferme générale, a private agency used by the French government to collect taxes on tobacco, salt, and imported goods. During this period Lavoisier was elected to the Academy of Sciences on the basis of some work he had done with Guettard.

Through his participation in the Ferme générale, Lavoisier met Marie Anne Paulze, the thirteen-year-old daughter of a fellow member, and married her in 1771. A talented linguist and artist, she translated English scientific publications into French for her husband and drew the illustrations for his papers and books. During the 1770s this research centered on combustion and calcination (the formation of a powdery substance, or calx, from roasting a metal or mineral). In the spring of 1772, Lavoisier served as a member of a committee formed by the Academy of Sciences to study the disappearance of diamonds when they were intensely heated. He was eventually able to establish that the diamonds' destruction was due to combustion, with fixed air (which he would later name "carbon dioxide") as the product.

Some scholars have proposed that Lavoisier's important work on combustion originated in his research on chemical effervescence, a process in which certain substances, when heated, release a gas. In the summer of 1772 he found that litharge, a lead ore, when heated with charcoal produced both lead and a gas. He also knew that metals absorbed air to form calxes. Further studies in the fall showed that phosphorus combined with a large quantity of air when it burned, as did sulfur. At this time Lavoisier mistakenly believed that this weight gain accompanying combustion and calcination was due to fixed air. His confusion was not resolved until the English chemist Joseph Priestley (1733–1804), on his 1774 visit to Paris, informed him of his discovery of a new gas that he had called "dephlogisticated air." Though Lavoisier, in his writings, downplayed the significance of Priestley's influence, many modern scholars see this discovery of an "air" that facilitated burning as crucial in the evolution of his understanding of chemistry.

With apparatus and techniques superior to Priestley's, Lavoisier was able to confirm and extend the English chemist's work on this "eminently respirable air." By 1777 he was convinced that the elemental atmospheric air of past natural philosophers was actually a mixture of two gases, one aiding combustion, the other frustrating it. Because the vital air aiding combustion formed acids when it combined with such nonmetals as sulfur and phosphorus, Lavoisier called it *oxygen* from the Greek roots signifying "acid producer." Eventually he became convinced of the elemental nature of oxygen, and he used it in his new theory of combustion: burning was simply oxidation. He also criticized the phlogiston theory, which interpreted combustion as the liberation of a constituent (called *phlogiston*) from burnable substances.

During the 1780s, Lavoisier extended his oxygen theory to include respiration and the composition of water. He and Pierre-Simon de Laplace (1749–1827) did a series of experiments on living things in which they found that a guinea pig, like a candle flame, generated both heat and carbon dioxide. Influenced by the experiments of English chemist Henry Cavendish (1731–1810) on "inflammable air," whose combustion produced water, Lavoisier argued that water is actually a compound of two gases, hydrogen (his name for "inflammable air") and oxygen. Although Lavoisier denigrated Cavendish's interpretation of his discovery in terms of the phlogiston theory, modern scholars, while admitting the superiority of Lavoisier's explanation, think that he went too far in claiming that he should be credited with the discovery of water's compound nature.

To help establish his new oxygen theory, Lavoisier and his principal French followers published a book on chemical nomenclature that helped establish a new and clearer language for chemistry. Lavoisier used this new terminology in his most important work, *Traité élémentaire de chimie* (Elementary treatise of chemistry, 1789). Like Isaac Newton's (1642–1727) *Principia,* Lavoisier's *Traité* marked the origin of an important modern science. This first textbook of the new chemistry contained a table of elements and the first clear statement of the law of the conservation of matter.

During the final five years of his life, Lavoisier participated in the development and implementation of the metric system, improved French gunpowder, suggested hospital and prison reforms, and published influential papers on experimental farming and economics. Despite his services to science and the state, he was unfortunate in being a political moderate at a time of extremists. In 1794, during the Reign of Terror, he and many other tax farmers were guillotined. Neither his head nor his body has ever been found.

See also **Chemistry; France; French Revolution; Reign of Terror; Science and Technology.**

BIBLIOGRAPHY

Primary Sources

Duveen, Denis I., and Herbert S. Klickstein. *A Bibliography of the Works of Antoine Laurent Lavoisier, 1743–1794.* London, 1954. This book, whose goal was to gather information on all Lavoisier's publications, had to be supplemented with another work published in 1965, which also included items written about Lavoisier up to 1963.

Lavoisier, Antoine-Laurent. *Oeuvres de Lavoisier.* Paris, 1965. This reprint of the six volumes originally published from 1862 to 1893 is not perfectly complete, but it allows scholars and other researchers an entrée into Lavoisier's most significant publications.

Secondary Sources

Donovan, Arthur. *Antoine Lavoisier: Science, Administration, and Revolution.* Cambridge, U.K., 1996. A comprehensive biography of the scientist and public figure for general readers.

Poirier, Jean-Pierre. *Lavoisier: Chemist, Biologist, Economist.* Translated by Rebecca Balinski. Philadelphia, 1996. When this biography was published in French in 1993, some reviewers stated that it supplanted all previous biographies and became the standard treatment of Lavoisier's life and work.

ROBERT J. PARADOWSKI

LAW, THEORIES OF.

Nineteenth-century law belonged to the same intellectual culture as nineteenth-century art and nineteenth-century politics, and legal theory underwent changes typical of the period from 1789 to 1914. The French Revolution was marked by efforts at rationalization and reform, inspired by Enlightenment critiques of the *ancien régime.* By the end of the Napoleonic period a Romantic reaction had set in, which insisted on the virtues of tradition and the perils of overconfident reason. The middle decades of the nineteenth century were years of a sober materialism, and of the emergence of new social scientific traditions on the Continent. They were also years of increasingly assertive left-wing critiques of "bourgeois" law. Finally, the 1890s and after saw the efflorescence of self-consciously "modernist" theories, which were blossoming all over the Continent in the years before the outbreak of World War I. Britain, with its distinctive common law tradition, stood aloof from Continental developments in some measure, but in various ways British legal thinkers were carried along by the same cultural currents.

REVOLUTION AND LEGAL REFORM

Reformers of the French Revolution mounted a comprehensive attack on the evils of the *ancien régime* as they saw them. Those evils fell into five broad categories: problems of *authority*, problems of *legality*, problems of *systematicity*, problems of *equality*, and problems of *individualism.* The approach of the revolutionaries to these five problems set most of the agenda for nineteenth-century legal thought.

The problems of *authority* and the problems of *legality* were closely linked. Both had to do largely with the role of judges in the legal system. The judges of the pre-Revolutionary French *parlements* exercised great authority: they had the power to resist royal legislation, and they exercised considerable power of local government. These powers seemed illegitimate to Revolutionary reformers committed to the supremacy of a single sovereign. Pre-Revolutionary judges also often administered "arbitrary" punishments, that is, punishments whose measure was determined by the judge rather than specified by statute. In the eyes of reformers, such judge-made punishments violated the basic norm of *legality*, according to which all crimes and punishments had to be specified in advance by law, and applied equally to all, without discrimination. Nor were judges the only actors who violated the norm of *legality.* The king did so too, through issuing *lettres de cachet*, which ordered the imprisonment of political dissidents and wayward members of French families without notice or trial.

In response to these perceived problems, the French revolutionaries insisted on strong norms of sovereignty and legality. There was to be a single locus of sovereign power: the Nation. There was also to be a strong insistence on legality. Judges were to act simply as "the mouth of the law," mechanically applying the provisions of duly-enacted statutes. Every person who committed a given offense was to be punished in exactly the same way. The law itself was to be framed in clear and unambiguous language, easily grasped by laypeople and therefore immune to manipulation by the legal profession. The Revolutionary reformers also insisted on *systematicity.* Law was to be embodied in Codes, founded on a few fundamental principles and framed in easily comprehensible language. All cases were to be resolved by reference to rules directly deduced from such fundamental principles as the duty to repair damage caused by unjustifiable acts, or the principle of property absolutism—the principle that every thing must have a single identifiable owner with plenary rights. The Code Napoléon (1804), later renamed the Code Civil, was the most important product of this reform effort.

Revolutionary reformers further insisted on *formal equality* and *individualism.* The law of the *ancien régime* had been marked by an elaborate law of ascriptive status, which accorded differing rights and responsibilities to persons of different social orders. It also accorded rights to many collectivities, such as guilds. These doctrines were sharply attacked by Revolutionary reformers, who framed the law in the language of formal equality, making no distinctions between male persons who had reached the age of majority. The reformers also attacked the rights of collectivities, notably in the Le Chapelier law of 1791, which banned guilds and the similar institutions, acknowledging only individuals as cognizable actors in the marketplace.

French Codes embodying these principles were introduced in much of western Europe during the Napoleonic period. Many of the same principles were also defended with great vigor by the Englishman Jeremy Bentham. With the collapse of the Napoleonic empire, though, a Romantic reaction began, led in particular by the German scholar Friedrich Carl von Savigny.

THE ROMANTIC ERA REACTION

Savigny embraced many of the same ideals embraced by the French Revolution. He was strongly oriented toward individualism and formal equality. He was a great champion of systematicity in the law, believing that law could indeed be based on a few fundamental principles. He certainly believed in legality and was no advocate of the power of judges.

Nevertheless, Savigny rejected the principle that change could be made through revolutions, and opposed anything that smacked of the direct interference in the law by a putative sovereign authority. New Codes were inevitable, but they were to be made through the slow collective efforts of legal scholars with a rich consciousness of the values of the past. These legal scholars were the representatives of what German Romantics called the Volksgeist, the slowly evolving national spirit. Savigny's argument made a Europe-wide sensation, and presumably did much to halt the progress of codification. Only in the later nineteenth century did important codification programs resume, and when they did they were dominated by legal scholars, who no longer pursued the goal of drafting Codes in language easily accessible to laypeople. The most important product of this second wave of scholarly codification was the German Civil Code (1900).

By the 1830s and 1840s, other forms of opposition to the legal ideas of the French Revolution began to appear. These involved in part opposition to the fundamental principles the Revolution had established as the basis of the Code Civil. Property absolutism was attacked by Pierre-Joseph Proudhon and Karl Marx. Both men argued that the dogma of unimpaired property rights favored the interests of the rich over those of the poor. Marx also attacked the principle of formal equality, arguing that the formal equality of the law masked differences in power between workers and capitalists, and permitted exploitative labor contracts. These attacks did little at first to shake the dominance of the ideas of the Revolution. On the contrary, into the 1860s most leading figures continued to believe that the doctrines of the Code Civil represented an inevitable step in the march of human evolution—an evolution most famously characterized by Sir Henry Maine in 1851 as a "movement from status to contract."

The second half of the nineteenth century, however, witnessed more widespread and influential attacks on the legacy of the Revolution. Some of these attacks carried the initiative of Marx forward, raising doubts about both formal equality and individualism in the law. In Germany, the drafters of the German Civil Code enshrined principles of formal equality in their published draft of the 1880s. That draft was assailed by both the German jurist Otto von Gierke and the Austrian economist Anton Menger. Gierke in particular argued influentially that contracts between workers and employers could not be analyzed as contracts between abstract equals: the work relationship was more complex and socially charged than ordinary market transactions.

Labor law was not the only field in which formal equality was attacked. The same was true of criminal law, with a number of leading thinkers arguing that the law should not treat all persons as formal equals. One notable exponent of this view was the Italian Cesare Lombroso, who insisted that criminals were biologically defective and thus not to be equated with other human beings. Other important criminal law scholars, including the Frenchman Raymond Saleilles and the German Franz von Liszt, favored "individualization," the tailoring of criminal punishment to the particular circumstances of the offender.

The legal individualism of the French Revolution also came under assault. The jurists of the Revolution, determined to break the power of the guilds, had insisted that the law could not recognize collective actors. This was incompatible with later nineteenth-century efforts to unionize laborers. It was also incompatible with the formation of industrial cartels, and difficult to reconcile with the developing law of the business corporation. These concerns led a number of thinkers to insist that the law should recognize collective and corporate persons. Here again Gierke was a leading figure, deploying arguments about medieval German law to demonstrate that collectivities were cognizable in law. Of comparable importance were the so-called *Kathedersozialisten*, the German "Socialists with Tenure" who defended various forms of cartelization as healthy and appropriate in a modern economy. The *Kathedersozialisten* also argued on behalf of various early welfare state initiatives.

CONCEPTUALISM AND THE "FREE SCHOOL"

During the second half of the nineteenth century, there were also dramatic new movements in technical jurisprudence. Later nineteenth-century continental jurists generally accepted the principle of systematicity. The law, in their minds, should represent a systematic effort to give effect to certain basic philosophical commitments necessary for the maintenance of a just system. Bernhard Windscheid, for example, the principal architect of the German Civil Code, argued that law had a basic commitment to the principle that individuals should create their own rights and duties through the exercise of their free will. Individuals, jurists like Windscheid believed, must be held responsible for their freely made decisions. This was the basic concept, from which the particularities of the law should flow deductively: The decision in every particular case should flow logically from the basic commitment to individual responsibility.

This deductive approach, sometimes referred to as "conceptualism," was derided in a series of famous parodies by the German Rudolf von Jhering, beginning in the late 1850s. Jhering argued that law was a mere "means to an end," a flexible tool of social policy, to be manipulated in the service of social interests. Toward the end of the nineteenth century, Jhering's writings inspired a Europe-wide modernist movement in the law. Among the principle figures in this movement were Franz von Liszt, who argued for a criminal law based, not on principles of abstract justice, but on the pursuit of social policy goals; and Raymond Saleilles.

At the turn of the century, Jhering's parodistic attack on conceptualism was elaborated into a sustained jurisprudential theory by the Frenchman François Gény. Gény attacked the claim that it was logically possible to deduce a complete array of legal rules from any set of basic principles. There would always be gaps—cases that could not be resolved through an appeal to any basic principle. The law could never be a perfect deductive system. When the law presented a gap, judges had no choice but to make a decision through "free scientific inquiry." Such free scientific inquiry could include social scientific research as well as intuitive and theologically informed ideas of justice.

By the early years of the twentieth century, German and French scholars alike were joining in a modernist revolt against the ideal of deductive systematicity in the law. Alongside Gény, the leading figures in this movement included Hermann Kantorowicz, a medievalist and legal philosopher; Eugen Ehrlich, the founder of legal sociology; and

Ernst Fuchs, the most radical of the group. Together, these figures are generally referred to as the "Free School" of law. These self-consciously modern scholars insisted on the ultimate indeterminacy of the law, at least in some cases. They also generally idealized the law-making authority of the judge. This idealization of the judge reflected the admiration many of these scholars felt for the English common law; and it embodied their strong rejection of the jurisprudential program of the French Revolution. The ideas of the Free School were forcefully rejected by Max Weber and others, and they had fallen into eclipse by 1914. They had considerable influence in the United States, though, and experienced renewed vigor in Germany during the Weimar and Nazi periods.

All of these nineteenth-century Continental developments had echoes in Britain. For the most part, though, English legal thought developed independently and had less influence. There were major reform movements in Britain, but they were largely concerned with matters like the technical rules of common pleading, of little interest to the outside world. There were major developments in the conceptualization and characterization of the common law as well. Nevertheless, the intellectual world of English law was less lively than that of the Continent. This probably reflects the fact that the teaching of English law remained in the hands of practitioners, with university scholars mostly standing on the sidelines until the late nineteenth century.

See also **International Law; Professions.**

BIBLIOGRAPHY

John, Michael. *Politics and Law in Late Nineteenth-Century Germany: The Origins of the Civil Code.* Oxford, U.K., and New York, 1989.

Merryman, John Henry. *The Civil Law Tradition: An Introduction to the Legal Systems of Western Europe and Latin America.* 2d ed. Stanford, Calif., 1985.

Proudhon, Pierre-Joseph. *What Is Property?* Edited by Donald R. Kelley and Bonnie Smith. Cambridge, U.K., and New York, 1994.

Watson, Alan. *The Making of the Civil Law.* Cambridge, Mass., 1981.

Whitman, James Q. *The Legacy of Roman Law in the German Romantic Era: Historical Vision and Legal Change.* Princeton, N.J., 1990.

Wieacker, Franz. *History of Private Law in Europe with Particular Reference to Germany.* Translated by Tony Weir. Oxford, U.K., and New York, 1995.

JAMES WHITMAN

LEBON, GUSTAVE (1841–1931), French sociologist known for his study of crowds.

Gustave LeBon was born in a village west of Paris in 1841 and died in the Paris suburbs in 1931. Apart from holidays, LeBon never left Paris after his arrival in the French capital in 1860. LeBon obtained his medical degree in 1867 but never practiced medicine. Instead he devoted himself to a career as a popularizer and synthesizer of science, politics, and contemporary affairs, occasionally laying claims to precedence for work that was almost always initiated by others. He was a prolific writer whose books sold extremely well and was also successful as an editor, a friend of the politically powerful, and a dashing man about town. He never married but maintained a series of glamorous mistresses who helped preside over the fashionable lunches and dinners he hosted for most of his life.

For all his popular and political triumphs, LeBon was a distinct outsider in French academic life. To be a man of the right was no disqualification in French intellectual life, but LeBon's unusual combativeness and his unwillingness to bend his knee to men he regarded as his inferiors meant that all the doors to academic appointments and honors were closed to him. Positioning himself on the political right, LeBon took his revenge on the establishment by lampooning the French university and ridiculing the leftist political opinions held by much of the professoriat. In his mature writings, he explicitly linked the intellectual ideals and style of the university with socialism, national decadence, and, after 1894, the crimes of Alfred Dreyfus (1859–1935), the Jewish officer accused by the French army of treason.

Beginning in the early 1890s, LeBon published a series of popular books that linked evolutionary theory, psychology, and anthropology with national and global developments in which he posed alternatives to the bankrupt policies of the leftist political coalitions that governed France in the last few decades of the nineteenth century. Beginning with *La Psychologie des peuples* (Psychology of peoples) in 1894, LeBon published *La Psychologie des foules* (Psychology of crowds) in 1895, *La Psychologie du socialisme* (Psychology of socialism) in 1898, and *La Psychologie de l'éducation* (Psychology of education) in 1901. The gist of these books was that a vast revolt led by urban masses, colonial peoples, socialist labor agitators, and university professors was threatening to destabilize the foundations of Western civilization. Though a freethinker himself, LeBon took a highly pragmatic stance on the conservative virtues of religion, nationalism, and colonialism, which he believed could ultimately generate greater loyalty within the democratic masses than leftist causes.

LeBon's book on crowds is now regarded as a classic of the social science literature, despite being largely a synthesis of the work of other writers and scholars. The book was still in print in French at the turn of the twenty-first century and has been translated into dozens of foreign languages. The appeal of the book lay in LeBon's characterization of the end of the nineteenth century as the beginning of the "era of crowds," which was brought about by the electoral mobilization of democratic politics, the creation of national audiences by the new mass press, and the rise of radical and revolutionary working-class movements. LeBon's slender book suggested numerous ways that conservative leaders could manipulate the mentality of crowds by appealing to images deeply rooted in the popular mind: patriotism, racial and national stereotypes, and the masculine virtues of struggle. It is not surprising that the book appealed to Benito Mussolini (1883–1945), Adolf Hitler (1889–1945), and many other right- and left-wing advocates of direct action in politics in the first half of the twentieth century. The politics of the interwar years do appear to testify to a widely shared conviction that power could be gained and held only by those who grasped the essential nature of modern mass society, of which atomized and available crowds were an important component.

Since World War II, collectivities have been studied as integral elements of the surrounding social order, from which they receive their norms and behavioral cues, not as anomic entities stripped of values and goals. Researchers now assume that "emergent norms" and "value-added perspectives" drive collective action. It is thus possible to consider seriously what LeBon could never admit, namely that crowds may be said to act on the basis of "interests" and to follow well-defined strategies based on an awareness of the wider social environment. In this perspective, crowds are not guided by willful leaders or by particular images and ideological constructs but by tacit reckonings communicated by means of nonverbal signs.

LeBon evinced a certain admiration for Mussolini in the 1920s, but lent his advice and support to conservative and nationalist republican politicians like Raymond Poincaré (1860–1934) in his own country. Ultimately, LeBon was an elitist and pragmatist for whom ideology was nothing more than an instrument to be wielded in the interests of power. Only lesser mortals actually believed ideologies were true.

See also **Dreyfus Affair; France; Socialism; Sociology.**

BIBLIOGRAPHY

Barrows, Susanna. *Distorting Mirrors: Visions of the Crowd in Late Nineteenth-Century France.* New Haven, Conn., 1981.

Nye, Robert A. *The Origins of Crowd Psychology: Gustave LeBon and the Crisis of Mass Democracy in the Third Republic.* London, 1975.

Van Ginneken, Jaap. *Crowds, Psychology, and Politics, 1871–1899.* Cambridge, U.K., 1992.

Robert A. Nye

LEDRU-ROLLIN, ALEXANDRE-AUGUSTE (1807–1874), French politician.

The most prominent French left-wing republican in the revolutionary years of 1848 and 1849, Alexandre-Auguste Ledru-Rollin was born in Paris on 2 February 1807, the son of an inspector of pawn shops. Educated at the Lycée Charlemagne and at the University of Paris, he became a lawyer. He frequently defended republicans accused of political offenses, and in 1834 he published a pamphlet on the so-called massacre of the Rue Transnonain.

In 1841, Ledru-Rollin was elected a deputy for Le Mans. Reelected in 1842 and 1846, he became the leader of the small band of left-wing republicans in the Chamber of Deputies. With Godefroy Cavaignac in 1845, he also founded *La Réforme,* which became the main left-wing republican Paris newspaper. At first Ledru-Rollin and *La Réforme* were critical of the reform banquet campaign of 1847–48, which preceded the Revolutions of 1848. However, Ledru-Rollin changed his attitude and gave radical and well-publicized speeches at the reform banquets of Lille (7 November 1847), Dijon (21 November), and Chalon-sur-Saône (19 December). In another well-publicized speech (9 February 1848), he defended in the Chamber of Deputies the right of public assembly.

Following the banning of a proposed reform banquet in the twelfth *arrondissement,* or district, of Paris by the government of François-Pierre-Guillaume Guizot (1787–1874), Ledru-Rollin attended a meeting of supporters of the twelfth *arrondissement* banquet at the offices of *La Réforme* on 21 February. The meeting agreed not to support violent resistance, but after the massacre on the Boulevard des Capucines (23 February 1848), Ledru-Rollin publicly demanded major concessions from King Louis-Philippe (1773–1850): an amnesty, the liberation of all political prisoners, the recognition of the right of public assembly, and the introduction of manhood suffrage.

During the afternoon of 24 February, after Louis-Philippe's abdication, Ledru-Rollin in the Chamber of Deputies successfully demanded the formation of a provisional government. Soon afterward, at the Paris Hôtel de Ville (city hall), Ledru-Rollin joined the provisional government as minister of the interior. He introduced manhood suffrage for local and parliamentary elections, replaced the prefects with *commissaires* (commissioners), and tried to exploit government influence and propaganda to secure the election of genuine republicans in the National Assembly elections of 23 April 1848. All this associated Ledru-Rollin with political radicalism and made him unpopular. Three departments elected him on 23 April, but his electoral performance was worse than that of most of his government colleagues. Due to the insistence of Alphonse-Marie-Louis de Prat de Lamartine (1790–1869), Ledru-Rollin was included in the five-man Executive Commission that replaced the provisional government on 10 May 1848.

Following the outbreak of a working-class insurrection in Paris on 23 June, Ledru-Rollin had to resign the next day with the other members of the Executive Commission. In the parliamentary debates on the new constitution during September and October, he unsuccessfully argued for a declaration of rights and a chairman of the council of ministers rather than a president, but a single-chamber parliament was maintained, as he wished. In the presidential election Ledru-Rollin, as the left-wing republican candidate, received just 371,431 votes. After December 1848 he emerged as the leader of the extreme left-wing group of representatives in the National Assembly known as the Mountain.

When Louis-Napoleon Bonaparte (later Napoleon III; r. 1852–1871) sent a military expedition to Rome to overthrow the Roman Republic and restore papal rule, against the wishes of a majority in the National Assembly, Ledru-Rollin on 11 May 1849 voted for Louis-Napoleon Bonaparte and his ministers to be impeached. The Roman expedition was unpopular and in the elections to the new parliament, the Legislative Assembly, five departments returned Ledru-Rollin (13 May 1849). When the Legislative Assembly first met on 28 May, he argued that the government had violated the constitution by ordering an attack on the Roman Republic. On 11 June he again argued for the impeachment of the ministry, and threatened to defend the violated constitution, even by violence. Encouraged by such rhetoric, on 13 June demonstrations against the government's Roman policy turned violent.

Provoked by General Nicolas-Anne-Theodule Changarnier (1793–1877) and the army (according to the Left), or attempting to carry out a premeditated coup d'état (according to the Right), Ledru-Rollin and his supporters occupied the Conservatory of Arts and Trades in Paris. Changarnier sent troops to the Conservatory and, without any resistance, the Conservatory was captured. Ledru-Rollin managed to escape by train to Belgium and then to London, but he was tried in absentia. On 15 November 1849, he was found guilty of conspiracy and insurrection and sentenced to transportation. He did not return to France until 1870, but then, disgusted by the Paris Commune, resumed residence in England for two years. He died at Fontenay-aux-Roses on 31 December 1874. Although a powerful orator, a consistent advocate of manhood suffrage, and the leading left-wing republican in 1848–1849, Ledru-Rollin had a limited long-term influence. His brand of republicanism owed too much to the Jacobin past and too little to the socialist future.

See also **France; Republicanism; Revolutions of 1848; Socialism.**

BIBLIOGRAPHY

Primary Sources

Ledru-Rollin, Alexandre-Auguste. *Discours politiques et écrits divers.* 2 vols. Paris, 1879.

Secondary Sources

Calman, Alvin Rosenblatt. *Ledru-Rollin après 1848.* Paris, 1921.

———. *Ledru-Rollin and the Second French Republic.* New York, 1922.

WILLIAM FORTESCUE

LEIPZIG, BATTLE OF. The Battle of Leipzig (16–19 October 1813), also known as the Battle of the Nations, was the largest military engagement fought until the twentieth century. It marked the end of the Napoleonic Empire. Strategically, it was more important than Waterloo. This four-day battle was fought on a front twelve to twenty-five miles long. Napoleon I (r. 1804–1814/15) engaged 191,500 troops and seven hundred guns against the combined armies of Russia, Prussia, Austria, and Sweden: 394,000 men and almost fifteen hundred guns. Leipzig surpassed the numeric size of the other great battles of the nineteenth century (Koniggratz [1866] 206,000 versus 220,984; Gravelotte-St. Privat [1870] 112,800 versus 188,332). Leipzig destroyed the Napoleonic Empire beyond the Rhine, paved the way for an invasion of France, and created the conditions for a unified front of Great Britain, Austria, Prussia, and Russia with the war aim of reducing France to the frontiers of 1792.

Napoleon I had been at war with Great Britain since 1803 and dominated continental Europe by 1807. In 1810 Russia broke with Napoleon, ceasing to participate in the Continental System that had been designed to bring Britain to her knees by economic means. The invasion of Russia followed in 1812 with Prussia and Austria as unwilling French allies. Napoleon's armies were destroyed during that campaign. During the retreat from Russia, Prussia changed sides, making common cause with Russia and Britain. Sweden, although a minor power, entered the coalition against Napoleon as well. Austria became neutral.

By March 1813 the Russians and Prussians drove what was left of the French west of the Salle River in central Germany. During the winter of 1813 everyone raised new armies. With an army of conscripts, Napoleon drove the Allies (Russians and Prussians), back behind the Elbe, winning two inconclusive battles in April and May. Both sides were exhausted and Napoleon accepted an armistice mediated by Austria in June 1813. Both sides used the time to build up their forces; Austria mobilized its army planning to enter the war on the Allied side.

With Austria in the Allied camp, France would be fighting all of the other Great Powers simultaneously for the first time. Napoleon held a central position based on Saxony and its capital, Dresden. There would be three Allied operational fronts: northern, southern, and eastern. The Allies operated on exterior lines. Allied strategy was hammered out in July, known as the Trachenberg Plan or the Trachenberg-Reichenbach Plan. Its main components consisted of the deployment of armies on the three operational fronts. Sweden's Crown Prince Bernadotte commanded the Army of the North and protected Berlin. The Army of Bohemia under Karl Schwarzenberg (1771–1820) (who also served as titular supreme allied commander) threatened Saxony from the south. Blücher's (Gebhard van Blücher Leberecht, 1742–1819) Army of Silesia formed the eastern front linking the other two fronts. A fourth Allied army was building up in Poland under General Rudolf von Bennigsen (1824–1902), and would later reinforce central Germany. The Plan called for each army to attack the French flanking forces, while defending against or retreating from the main French effort, which would undoubtedly be commanded by Napoleon in person. This was to have the advantage of wearing down the French by attrition. The Plan also called for a concentric advance against Napoleon's lines of operation with the idea of an eventual concentration of overwhelming force against his main force and a decisive battle.

Napoleon planned to use interior lines to reinforce the three threatened sectors, concentrating and defeating each in succession. He especially wanted to concentrate toward Berlin. For the plan to work the army threatened by Napoleon's main force would have to stand and fight, while his flanking forces had to hold the enemy armies at bay until it became their turn. The Allied plan effectively contrasted with Napoleon's, by avoiding the main effort, engaging and defeating the French flanking forces.

In the past Napoleon had been able to rely on weaker or even equal detached forces to deal with enemy armies because of a qualitative superiority in French troops and their commanders. By 1813 this qualitative edge had vanished. The losses sustained by Napoleon's army in Russia had been so overwhelming that although the numbers of troops could be replaced, their qualities in performance and leadership could not. The majority of Allied troops were similarly poorly trained. On both sides, the time between recruitment and employment in the front ranks in 1813 was about six months. The Allies, to varying degrees, adopted French tactical methods. The Allied armies also adopted the army corps system pioneered by the French. This structure improved tactical command and control, as well as the integrity and cohesion of large formations. It eased the integration of corps of different states into the Allied armies.

Austria declared war on France on 12 August, ending the armistice. Napoleon deployed three armies against his enemies. The Army of Berlin, under Nicolas Oudinot (1767–1847), faced Bernadotte, while the Army of the Bober, under Étienne-Jacques-Joseph-Alexandre Macdonald (1765–1840), faced Blücher. Napoleon, with the main army, faced Schwarzenberg, but planned to maneuver among the three fronts.

A series of battles in August and September followed. Generally, the Allies followed the dictates of the Trachenberg Plan, falling back when faced by Napoleon. The flanking French forces were defeated in battles at Gross Beeren (23 August), the Katzbach (26 August), Dennewitz (16 September), and Kulm (30 August), while Napoleon indecisively defeated Schwarzenberg at Dresden (26–27 August).

The result of six weeks of fighting and maneuvering did not bring any decision, but Napoleon's forces were being ground down. Napoleon, with 260,000 troops and 784 guns, realized that contraction of the front was the only recourse, and began withdrawing his forces on 24 September.

Bennigsen's Army of Poland reinforced Schwarzenberg, and Blücher moved north, reinforcing Bernadotte. According to the Trachenberg Plan, Schwarzenberg moved his army west toward Leipzig to threaten Napoleon's communications to the Rhine. Blücher, with Bernadotte in tow, forced the Elbe River and moved west and south, threatening Napoleon from that direction.

Napoleon planned to fall back, still hoping to defeat the separate armies. The Emperor left two corps to hold Dresden to keep Saxony as an ally, a mistake considering that all troops would be needed for the forthcoming battle. The Emperor decided to concentrate at Leipzig, which was being threatened by Schwarzenberg. Part of Bennigsen's army moved to blockade Dresden.

As the French fell back toward Leipzig, Marshal Joachim Murat (1767–1815), with part of the army, faced south to delay Schwarzenberg and cover the approaches to Leipzig. In Napoleon's mind, only the Army of Bohemia was in range. In truth, all of the enemy armies were closing on Leipzig. Murat fought a battle with Schwarzenberg's advance forces on October 14 at Liebertwolkwitz, setting the southern front for the following battle of Leipzig.

Leipzig sits at the confluence of four rivers (Elster, Pleisse, Luppe, and Parthe), and a series of major roads dividing the battle area into four sectors. Most of the city is east of the Elster, Parthe, and Pleisse. The terrain between the Elster and Pliesse constricts deployment, and the rivers are almost impossible to ford. Located west of Leipzig are marshes, the banks of the Luppe and Elster, and the village of Lindenau. The terrain east of the Pleisse and Elster is open and it supported the deployment of large forces. About four miles south of Leipzig and east of the Pleisse is a line of hills and villages running west to east including the hamlets of Wachau and Liebertwolkwitz. This area formed the southern front line. The battle fought here was known as Wachau. On the east bank of the Elster, three to four miles north of Leipzig, are the villages of Möckern and Lindenthal, forming the northern front of the battle.

The French used the converging roads to concentrate in the Leipzig area. The Allies did the same, but it would take them longer to arrive. By the morning of 16 October, Napoleon had 177,500 troops with an additional eighteen thousand (Jean Louis-Ebenezer Reynier's VII Corps) en route. The French were deployed in two wings and a Reserve. The southern wing (which had been Murat's command and fought on two days earlier) consisted of three corps, the northern wing of three corps under Michel Ney (1769–1815) (including the garrison of Leipzig, which held bridgehead at Lindenau), and a central reserve of three cavalry corps, IX Corps, and the Imperial Guard Corps. The Reserve supported the southern front, while an additional cavalry corps and the XI Corps under Macdonald were approaching Leipzig from the northeast and were ten miles from the southern front.

Schwarzenberg had wanted to move his entire army west of the Pleisse and Elster in the misguided belief that those rivers were fordable; they were not. The Russian commanders objected to the tsar, who intervened directly, ordering that all the Russian and Prussian forces would attack from the south and east of those rivers. Although Schwarzenberg protested, the tsar was right. Had all of the Army of Bohemia been west of those rivers, they would have been isolated, leaving Napoleon free to move against Blücher and Bernadotte. A compromise was made: three Austrian corps would advance on Leipzig west of the Pleisse and Elster. Barclay, with 77,500 troops, would advance from the south and east of the Pleisse. Supporting Barclay were the Allied reserves of 24,000 men. His forces extended six miles, and he hoped to turn the French left. Blücher, followed by Bernadotte, would attack from the north in support. Pressure from all three fronts would prevent Napoleon from making a decisive concentration against the different armies.

The powerful Allied cavalry prevented the French from effective reconnaissance. Napoleon was unaware of the location of the armies of Blücher and Bernadotte. On the night of 15 October, seeing the enemy campfires around the Pleisse, he mistakenly believed that somehow the armies of Blücher and Bernadotte had joined Schwarzenberg and were to the west and south.

Napoleon's plan was to concentrate his forces and destroy Mikhail Barclay de Tolly's (1761–1818) wing first. The Emperor would attack with his southern wing, fixing the enemy in place; Macdonald's corps was to envelop the Allied right. Once that was underway, the powerful Reserve would attack and shatter the Allied line. The southern front was to be reinforced by the three corps of the northern wing under Ney. Auguste Marmont's (1774–1852) corps was ordered to fall back toward Leipzig, from his covering position in the north. Napoleon would bring 120,000 men against the Barclay. Barclay and the Reserves had 101,000—not enough to ensure a decisive victory.

The Army of Bohemia attacked first, coming into action on the southern front while the corps of Ignatius Gyulai von Maros-Nemeth and Maximillian Count Meerveldt, distantly supported by Austrian reserves, attacked from the western banks of the Pleisse and Elster. Gyulai hit the French bridgehead at Lindenau.

Pursuant to his orders, Marmont began to move south, but sighted Blücher's advance guard at ten in the morning. The French marshal took up a position at Möckern to defend against Blücher. Marmont had 24,000 troops facing Blücher's 54,000.

Gyulai's attack at Lindenau caused Ney to divert Henri Bertrand's (1775–1846) corps there. The French general smashed Gyulai's troops and opened up a line of retreat due west. Pressure from the north and west prevented Souham's corps from intervening effectively in the south. Meerveldt's attack managed to secure a small bridgehead over the Pleisse.

By 11:00 A.M., Barclay's attack was contained and Napoleon went on the offensive. Macdonald had reinforced the left flank of the front. The main attack began at 2:00 P.M.

The battle on the southern front (Wachau) swayed to and fro. By the end of the day the French held their former positions but the Army of Bohemia was not defeated.

In the north, Blücher attacked Marmont at Möckern. The French marshal held his position through most of the day, until borne back by superior numbers.

If Napoleon had any chance of winning this battle it was on the first day. However, the pressure provided by Blücher and Gyulai ensured that the bulk of the French northern wing never reached the critical battlefield at Wachau. The forces under Barclay, supported by the Reserves and Meerveldt, effectively tied up the French. Napoleon's numerical superiority at Wachau was slight, and the qualitative difference, which usually ensured French victories in earlier years, was gone.

During the night of 16–17 October, the numerical balance as well shifted irrevocably in favor of the Allies. The French were reinforced by an extra 18,000 men. Allied reinforcements were far greater. Bennigsen's Army of Poland came up from Dresden, reinforcing Barclay with an additional 70,000 troops, while Bernadotte was moving to the flank of Blücher with an additional 85,000 men.

Napoleon made a major mistake by not withdrawing on 17 October. He had an open line of retreat via Lindenau. Meanwhile the Allies planned a concentric attack of 300,000 men and fifteen hundred guns on 18 October. The French closed up in a defensive bridgehead early on 18 October while the army began a retreat via Lindenau. The Allied attacks on 18 October were contained, while Gyulai was driven back again, ensuring that the line of retreat remained open. A rear guard of 30,000 was to keep the enemy at bay while the rest of the army escaped. Everything went well, and the rear guard kept the enemy from pressing too closely while the army crossed the Elster. At 1:00 P.M. on 19 October, a French corporal, incredibly left in charge of blowing up the Elster Bridge, panicked and blew up it up ahead of schedule, leaving 30,000 French troops trapped on the enemy's side of the river.

The casualties of this four-day battle are estimated at 54,000 killed and wounded for the Allies, while the French sustained 38,000 casualties, plus the loss of the 30,000 soldiers trapped in Leipzig. Four thousand Saxon troops defected during the battle, for a total of 72,000.

The battle was a strategic disaster that cost Napoleon his empire. Compelled to retreat behind the Rhine, the remaining French garrisons in Germany and Poland totaling 100,000 were isolated without any prospect of relief and eventually capitulated. All of Napoleon's German allies defected or, in the case of Saxony, treated as a defeated state by the allies. The 1813 campaign cost Napoleon 400,000 troops. His prestige was damaged, and the defeat contributed to war-weariness within France. Napoleon was now clearly on the defensive, and the campaign that followed in France would lead to his abdication.

See also **Continental System; French Revolutionary Wars and Napoleonic Wars; Napoleonic Empire.**

BIBLIOGRAPHY

Bowden, Scott. *Napoleon's Grande Armée of 1813.* Chicago, 1990.

Chandler, David G. *The Campaigns of Napoleon.* New York, 1966.

Cook, Llewellyn, "Schwarzenberg at Dresden: Leadership and Command." *Consortium on Revolutionary Europe* (1994): 642–651.

Craig, Gordon Alexander. "Problems of Coalition Warfare: The Military Alliance against Napoleon, 1813–1814." *The Harmon Memorial Lectures in Military History,* No. 7. U.S. Air Force Academy, Colorado, 1965.

Esposito, Vincent J., and John Robert Elting. *A Military History and Atlas of the Napoleonic Wars.* New York, 1964.

Leggiere, Michael V. *Napoleon and Berlin: The Franco-Prussian War in North Germany, 1813.* Norman, Okla., 2002.

Maude, Frederic Natusch. *The Leipzig Campaign.* London, 1908.

Petre, F. Loraine. *Napoleon's Last Campaign in Germany, 1813.* London, 1912.

Riley, J. P. *Napoleon and the World War of 1813: Lessons in Coalition Warfighting.* Portland, Ore., 1999; London, 2000.

Schroeder, Paul W. *The Transformation of European Politics, 1763–1848.* Oxford, U.K., 1994.

ROBERT M. EPSTEIN

LEISURE. The historical development of attitudes toward leisure mirrored many of the larger currents of change witnessed by Europeans in the epoch separating the French Revolution from World War I. Indeed Europe's industrializing economy, shifting contours of class identity, rising sense of national consciousness, and commodifying market and cultural forces shaped the world of "free time" just as markedly in the long nineteenth century as they did the everyday worlds of work and domestic life. Almost without respect to geography or social position, what villagers, city folk, and anyone in between would have done—or certainly dreamt of doing with leisure—by 1914 was fundamentally far removed from what would have been the case in 1789.

BACKGROUND

Voltaire's (1694–1778) "age of Enlightenment" had cajoled its citizens in the direction of the cultivated garden, both metaphorically and literally. Still, for country people and urban artisans alike, when the pressing calendar of work relented—whether because a day was marked off as one of the many allocated to forms of festive recreation or simply because a raucous weekend was so often followed by a Saint Monday's hangover—it was the familiar rhythms of hearthside and well deserved time with one's mates that structured leisure far more than anything offered by the philosophes as counsel regarding the rational use of time away from work. In this order of leisurely things, which Samuel Smiles (1812–1904), Mathew Arnold (1822–1888), Émile Zola (1840–1902), and so many other nineteenth-century commentators of varying ideological persuasions would see as slothful and even degenerative, humble workers of the land and their artisan counterparts were scarcely without aristocratic peerage. Blessed with abundant leisure as compared to their toiling contemporaries, the socially privileged of eighteenth-century Europe hardly excelled in avoiding what later moralists of the middle class would decry as an over-interest in measuring up to some very Bacchanalian standards. As the rules of social conduct and comportment posted at Bath in the generation before the novelist Jane Austen's (1775–1817) visits there reveal, not only was the gentry's leisure deemed needful of a reformation, but indeed its practitioners were themselves largely willing to cede over governance of their time at the spa to Beau Nash (Richard Nash; 1674–1762), the English gamester and social arbiter, and to the town's other well-known social figures.

The quest for a transparent, ideological purity, installed briefly by the radical phase of the French Revolution, sought to reform and in some cases eradicate practices of leisure long associated with the different strata of social life in France and wherever else the tenets of 1789 and after held sway. But if political club meetings and a new calendar of festive days could be culturally installed or governmentally decreed, no political mapping of reformed ideas about leisure onto social life could alter fundamentally the salient and inherently conserving attributes of ideas and experiences of leisure: that people tended to travel very little; that they tended to be their own performers and entertainers; that they took their cues and clues about leisure from church, village, guild, and regional patterns; and that their great, great grandparents would have felt just as much at ease living their descendant's leisure as they had lived their own.

NEW TIME

The industrialization and urbanization of Europe during the nineteenth century—exhaustively chronicled by contemporaries and only more intensely scrutinized since by scholars—ushered in a changed encounter with the concept of time. Long pegged to an agrarian calendar and the routines of seasonal farm and proto-industrial labor, conceptions of time were already being infused with the new imperatives of the industrial clock by the later 1820s. Not only did workers now need to devote a predetermined and agreed-on amount of time to their jobs, but also the steady rise of mechanized production brought with it efforts to calibrate very precisely how much work a given producer could be expected to accomplish in a given day of labor. Being on time for work now mattered, just as a new hierarchy of bosses and factory rules combined to zealously monitor comportment, productivity, and the time allotted for pausing from one's work.

Even more generally, however, cultural forces well removed from the economic dictates of the factory helped to frame a new sense of time. Clocks were installed on town halls and churches all over Europe, just as the pocket watch would become to the bourgeoisie of the 1840s and after what Zola's working-class would later see in the bureau clock: a symbol of success, self control, and thrift.

The rise of factory time and the ubiquitous timepiece were matched in social importance by

A tennis match on the beach, Belgium, 1909. ©HULTON-DEUTSCH COLLECTION/CORBIS

other alterations in the way that people lived with time. The full festive calendar of days off from work, by the decades around the middle of the nineteenth century, had been replaced by a very few vacation days for most workers. England's five bank holidays represented a more curtailed version of this change than Continental Europe's Catholic and less quickly industrialized countries would see early in the era, but the constricted experience of holidays was a reality everywhere. Replacing the traditional array of feast and rest days were new arguments for a day away from work. Birthdays, anniversaries, honeymoons, and other personal uses for leisure were placed on the new time's calendar coincidentally with days that the state deemed critical for rest, reflection, or festive participation.

THE VACATION

Aristocrats had always had access to an experience of extended leisure that might be rightly called the proto-vacation. So did to some degree the pilgrims who sojourned all over Europe to visit Rome, Santiago e Compostela, Canterbury, and other sites of devotional interest. But new conceptions of time in the nineteenth century joined together with the rising force of the industrializing economy to mark a radical shift in who could vacation, how it was that vacationers did what they did, and where it was that they went. Improved transportation was paramount in opening up the possibilities of the vacation. Carriage travel from Paris to the watering places and spa towns favored by the seventeenth- and eighteenth-century aristocracy was a venture that took days to execute. The arrival of the railroad altered this fact dramatically and immediately. England's Blackpool and Brighton were just two of many cities whose explosive growth in the middle decades of the nineteenth century bore witness to what the railroads could efficiently deliver by way of day tripping or weekending passengers. London's Sunday trains, already by the early 1840s, were packed to Brighton and back with working-class and middle-class trippers who eagerly sought the distractions of Brighton and its famous seaside piers over another day spent in the congestion of the city. The capacity to choose a day in Brighton, whether that meant entering one of its rickety bathing machines to be dragged some distance from the shore for a trap-door drop into the cold waters or just a lazy day taking in the sights and the odd entertainers who flocked to the coast, the seaside town was something nobody's parents had grown up being able to easily visit.

Meanwhile, the more affluent, who could pay for taking longer trips away from home, flooded the great spa towns of Europe, where civic leaders fought to secure train connections and build better train stations than their rivals could boast. It was not just improved transportation, however, that drove the growth of the vacation industry in the nineteenth century. The dream of the vacation and the things one would do while vacationing had first to be crafted and well inculcated in the mentality of those who would travel for leisure. Hardly a simple matter, this, considering the negative and even terrible associations some of Europe's greatest vacation destinations had historically endured. The great Mont Blanc, for example—whose ardent English admirers would spur a veritable cult of alpinist worship that would more or less chronologically match the great dates of Romanticism as a literary and artistic genre (1795–1840)—was only "discovered" in the eighteenth century, when scientifically minded explorers tamed the mountain's fierce isolation first by mapping and measuring and then, only late in the century, by conquering the giant itself.

The same processes would colonize, safeguard, and then popularize the many beaches, including those on the French Norman coast and the Côte d'Azur, and inland watering places—or spas—of Europe. Long understood as a treacherous borderland between the safety of the shore and the turbulence of the otherworldly sea, beach areas enjoyed a tremendous cultural reformation, compliments largely of doctors, whose writings about the health benefits of sea bathing helped spur local developers to build hotels and other amenities. Not only did this partnership of doctors and developers create resort towns, but also it gave order and a cultural imperative to what one did while at these places. Would-be vacationers among Europe's bourgeoisie, in particular, had largely internalized their century's mantra of productivity by its middle decades. In the highly medicalized organization doctors gave to the beach vacation, travelers experienced a rejuvenating stay by the sea whose rhythms were carefully calibrated to produce a more healthful and hence productive person. All the while, of course, any mystery related to what one would do while on vacation was replaced by the certainty of medical authority. Spas were likewise developed by alliances between medical authorities and civic leaders, partnering guidebook writing with cleaned up bathing facilities, carefully scripted water cures, and the pleasures of exciting casinos and verdant walking parks. The success of these efforts was obvious to any observer by 1900, a year when more than half a million people in France alone were employees of the spa industry. Around the same time, more than a million annual visitors went to Lourdes on its pilgrim trains, and slightly fewer than that went to spas.

LEISURE AND GENDER

If experiences of leisure varied across the social spectrum, gender was also a categorical organizer of time-off for Europeans. For women and men of the working classes, leisure was more equally understood than was the case among the bourgeoisie and middle class. Factory employees had cafes, pubs, public parks, and the emerging places of mass cultural amusement—such as the wax museum and the café concert—where men and women were welcomed, even if even sympathetic writers like Zola would take literary pains to point out how drinking and working-class lives could intersect with tragic results. For women of the middle class and bourgeoisie, however, it was a social ideal by midcentury and after not to be associated with work outside of the home on a remunerative basis. Charity work and the almost endless tasks of making the home a representative attribute of a family's claims to social standing and respectability were taken to be more than enough work indeed. Piano playing, novel reading, working on handcrafts, hosting social functions, and embarking on well supervised spa trips loomed large among the more accepted performances of leisure among these women. So, in the latter decades of the century among the younger women of this group, did the burdensome role cast for them as invalids whose physiology as women was said to leave them prone to hysteria and other disabling nervous maladies. While tubercular beauty was depicted in countless canvases hung on the walls of bourgeois homes and made manifest in the sick rooms set up for girls of this class, the last years of the century also witnessed a pronounced interest on the part of many younger women in enjoying the social spaces and cultural places of the modernizing city. The so-called new woman—whether she went to a spa for three weeks with her girlfriends and a domestic servant as chaperone or otherwise sought out the fun of society in public with her peers—was eager to enjoy the life that her family's money and her own leisure could support.

MOBILITY AND DEMOCRATIZED LEISURE

If the long nineteenth century was ushered in to the sound of plodding horse hooves and a view of the world that for most people was limited to a farmstead, a hamlet, or a particular city, the years before World War I echoed with the hiss of steam engines taking people to the mountains, the sea, and everywhere in between. Mobility had been fused together with dreams of seeing new places and doing new things with leisure. Among workers, the great cry for "eight hours for what we will" was already current, even if the reality of the tripartite day—eight hours for work, and eight each for sleep and leisure—was still years away. Horse-racing, tennis, golf, and the bicycle would all come to compete for the leisure not just of affluent Europeans but also—over time—that of the middle class and its working counterparts. Auto racing, national bicycle contests, and the like were quickly becoming important spectator sports, together with football matches and sundry other ways of watching professionals perform either in sport or as entertainers. Package tours of southern France or the Scottish Highlands or the German Black Forest would become an international business, complete with tour brokers and veteran leisure enthusiasts from all classes who had been to places or done things with their time away from work that their grandparents might have understood but that would have seemed inexplicably strange to anyone from generations earlier.

See also **Bourgeoisie; Industrial Revolution, First; Railroads; Seaside Resorts; Secularization; Tourism.**

BIBLIOGRAPHY

Bailey, Peter. *Leisure and Class in Victorian England: Rational Recreation and the Contest for Control, 1830–1885.* London, 1978.

Baranowski, Shelley, and Ellen Furlough, eds. *Being Elsewhere: Tourism, Consumer Culture, and Identity in Modern Europe and North America.* Ann Arbor, Mich., 2001.

Cunningham, Hugh. *Leisure in the Industrial Revolution, c. 1770–c. 1880.* New York, 1980.

Mackaman, Douglas Peter. *Leisure Settings: Bourgeois Culture, Medicine, and the Spa in Modern France.* Chicago, 1998.

Douglas P. Mackaman

LENIN, VLADIMIR (1870–1924), Russian revolutionary and founder of the Bolshevik Party.

Vladimir Ilyich Lenin (born Vladimir Ilyich Ulyanov) was the first great revolutionary of the twentieth century. Lenin was born on 22 April (10 April, old style) 1870 in the western Siberian town of Simbirsk, a shipping center of thirty thousand on the Volga River. His father, Ilya N. Ulyanov, served the Russian imperial government as an inspector of schools. The elder Ulyanov eventually rose to the rank of director of public schools for Simbirsk Province, earning hereditary noble status. Lenin's parents stressed education, and the young Vladimir excelled in school.

The most important event of his youth involved the actions of his brother, Alexander Ulyanov. By his fourth year as a student at the University of St. Petersburg, Alexander had become bitterly disillusioned with the autocracy. Joining a group of student conspirators modeled on the People's Will, the terrorist wing of the populist party, which attempted to incite revolution through a campaign of political assassination, Alexander Ulyanov participated in a plot to murder the new tsar, Alexander III. Police foiled the plot and arrested Lenin's elder brother. Ignoring the pleas of his mother, Alexander refused to beg for mercy at his trial. After an impassioned speech from the dock denouncing the regime, he was hanged in 1887, one year after the death of the boys' father and the year of Lenin's graduation from the gymnasium in Simbirsk. Lenin was deeply affected by his brother's fate.

THE DEVELOPING MARXIST

While attending Kazan University to study law later in 1887, school authorities expelled Lenin following a brief imprisonment for participating in a student demonstration. Readmitted to the university in 1890, he passed the law exams in 1892 but practiced law only briefly, in Samara. This period signaled a change in Lenin's thinking, as he first began reading Karl Marx and became active in tiny revolutionary political circles. Still wedded to populist revolutionary principles of direct action, underground conspiratorial political groupings, and hatred for liberalism in all its guises, he joined the fledgling St. Petersburg Union of Struggle for the Emancipation of the Working Class. This new Marxist group devoted itself to eradicating the injustice and poverty that afflicted Russian workers.

Lenin moved to St. Petersburg in the late summer of 1893, joining a growing number of like-minded intellectuals under the influence of Georgy Plekhanov who had embraced Marxism and were active in small underground circles. It was in this period that Lenin became a full-time revolutionary, writing voluminously on economic matters. He struck his associates in St. Petersburg as having several traits that would define his career as a revolutionary and political leader: an autocratic personality, a virulent polemical style in his interactions with political opponents and colleagues alike, impressive persuasive powers, and absolute certainty in the truth of his views. At this point, Lenin had adopted the mainstream Marxist idea that Russia must pass through a reformist, "democratic-bourgeois" phase, complete with elections and a parliament, which would pave the way for the onset of the inevitable socialist revolution.

In December 1895 the twenty-five-year-old Lenin was arrested while agitating among workers and organizing the waves of strikes that would sweep over St. Petersburg in the spring of 1896. Imprisoned in St. Petersburg for more than a year, Lenin was sentenced to three years exile (beginning in 1897) in the southern Siberian town of Shushenskoye. He married his friend and political associate, Nadezhda Krupskaya, so that she could join him in exile, and they remained married until his death in 1924. In exile, Lenin wrote his first major book, *The Development of Capitalism in Russia* (1899). In this huge volume, Lenin marshaled evidence to reject populist beliefs that Russia could altogether skip the capitalist stage of development, with its vicious exploitation and social stresses, and vault directly to a socialist society based on what populists regarded as the perfect equality of the peasant commune. Lenin's book attempted to prove that capitalism had already taken deep, permanent root in Russia. According to Lenin, the spread of capitalist relations in backward Russia could be seen not only in the burgeoning of capitalist industry, but also in the sharp and growing class conflict between the wealthy and the poorer peasantry in what the populists "naively" viewed as a united, harmonious, protosocialist village. Revolutionaries must welcome rather than resist the inevitable expansion of capitalism, which would accelerate the growth of Russia's still tiny working class. Russian Marxists must therefore abandon populist strategies that combined attempts to preserve the peasant commune with acts of political assassination. Instead, revolutionaries must create a party that would educate the growing proletariat about their critical role in the forthcoming class war against an exploitative but brittle international capitalism.

Vladimir Ilyich Lenin. ©HULTON-DEUTSCH COLLECTION

Lenin returned from Siberia in 1900. He immediately became active in the leadership of Russia's first Marxist political party, the tiny Russian Social Democratic Labor Party (RSDLP), founded in 1898, and was incessantly harassed by the police. After emigrating from Russia in 1900 under threat of arrest, Lenin spent seventeen of the next eighteen years in foreign exile in Zurich, London, Brussels, and other central and western European cities. In 1901 Vladimir Ulyanov adopted his nom de guerre, Lenin, most likely in honor of the Lena River in Siberia.

THE DEVELOPMENT OF BOLSHEVISM

In 1900, Lenin helped found the newspaper *Iskra* (The spark), which was published by the RSDLP in Europe and smuggled into Russia. By this time, Lenin had begun to evince his trademark impatience with those among the radical intelligentsia who called for gradual, evolutionary change in Russian autocratic structures. In 1902 Lenin issued his famous *What Is to Be Done?* a pamphlet attacking moderates in the RSDLP who embraced this "revisionist" approach, whose champion was the German Social Democratic Party theorist Eduard Bernstein. In particular, Lenin expressed contempt for a trend in European Marxism known as "economism." This current urged workers to focus on achieving concrete economic goals rather than aspire to fundamental political change—to demand improvements to living and working conditions within the capitalist system rather than to organize to overthrow it altogether. Moderate RSDLP members—calling themselves the "Legal Marxists"—agreed, arguing that democracy for workers was not incompatible with capitalism. They maintained that Russia must pass through a "bourgeois-democratic" phase, which would result in the establishment of representative institutions, trade unions, free elections, and equality under the law. Legal Marxists declared that workers should participate fully in this process, through a large social democratic party, which would have a loose, broadly based membership comprised of any person who supported their goals.

Lenin and his followers denounced such reformist plans for creating a large, open political party on the German Social Democratic model as wholly unrealistic in the repressive conditions of the Russian police state. In the latter, according to Lenin, only a political organization that was small, highly centralized, tightly knit, and conspiratorial, comprised exclusively of an elite cadre of dedicated, full-time revolutionaries, could lead the working class and ultimately bring down the monarchy. He argued that only such a "vanguard party" could avoid infiltration by police informers while maintaining ideological purity and rigor. The goal of this party would be the overthrow of the autocracy, the only path to the liberation of the proletariat in Russia. In contrast with moderates among the Russian who were convinced that workers would acquire "revolutionary consciousness" on their own in the natural course of society's evolution, Lenin argued that workers would become aware of their revolutionary role only when that consciousness was introduced to them from outside, by an enlightened few, organized in the vanguard party. If left to their own devices, workers could achieve only "trade-union consciousness," the belief that their lives could be improved through salary hikes and other economic benefits. They would permanently remain under the influence of "bourgeois" ideology.

Disagreements over these fundamental issues of organization, party membership, and timetable, heightened by squabbles over style and personality, brought conflict into the RSDLP itself. At the contentious Second Congress of the RSDLP held in Brussels and London in 1903, the party split permanently into two wings. The Mensheviks (literally, the "minorityites"), adopted the gradualist program; the more uncompromising and impatient Bolsheviks ("majorityites"), under Lenin's direction, would take power in November 1917 (October, O.S.).

THE REVOLUTION OF 1905

During the Russo-Japanese War (1904–1905), Lenin rejoiced in the defeat of the Russian imperial navy and army, believing Asia's victory to portend the collapse of the European bourgeoisie. From exile in Geneva, he celebrated the peasant uprisings sweeping the countryside and encouraged strikes, demonstrations, and the building of barricades in the streets of Moscow and St. Petersburg. He urged armed insurrection, including violence against the police and army. Lenin returned to St. Petersburg in November 1905 (October, O.S.), leading the small contingent of Bolsheviks. Like all parties, the Bolsheviks were helpless to control the largely spontaneous activities of a strike movement that numbered in the millions. Ultimately, the Revolution of 1905 was put down by a combination of vicious repression of insurgents by the army, mass arrests of Social Democratic leaders, and an October Manifesto, issued by the tsar, that granted the creation of a Duma (parliament) and limited civil rights. Lenin's dream that the 1905 uprising would be the spark that would ignite international proletarian revolution was not realized.

Yet he did learn important lessons from the abortive revolution. Lenin became convinced that the restive peasantry held extraordinary potential as a revolutionary class; that uprisings among the unstable, oppressed national minorities scattered throughout the imperial borderlands could help to shatter the empire's cohesion; and that no compromise was possible with the "liberal-democratic" bourgeoisie, who were weak and vacillating and would certainly side with the forces of order in the face of street violence. Lenin came to believe that the working class, under the direction of the vanguard party and in alliance with the poorer sections of the peasantry, could achieve revolution quickly and without help from the bourgeoisie.

Eluding the police after the Revolution of 1905, Lenin traveled back and forth between Russia and European cities in 1906 and 1907, settling in Geneva in 1908. Lenin did not set foot in Russia again until April 1917. In the interim, the divisions between Bolsheviks and Mensheviks grew deeper, thanks not least to Lenin's constant rhetorical thrashing of his political nemeses.

By 1914, the combined membership of the Menshevik and Bolshevik parties, hounded by the police and divided by internal conflict, comprised only a few thousand people. Lenin's political fortunes were close to their nadir, with even many Bolsheviks rejecting his tactics and ideas. The outbreak of World War I gave Lenin hope as the disastrous performance of the Russian armies brought new vitality to the revolutionary movement. Understanding the weakness of the organized working class in Russia, Lenin argued that only an external catastrophe such as the European war could undermine the autocracy. Rejecting the insurgent patriotism with which European socialist parties greeted the outbreak of hostilities, Lenin—practically alone among Russian Marxists—called for the defeat of Russian armies as a necessary precondition for revolution. From exile in Switzerland, Lenin deemed World War I an inevitable dispute among imperialist thugs, each seeking advantage in a barbaric competition for colonies; the European working class would be the war's greatest loser. This analysis was expressed in his important book titled *Imperialism: The Highest Stage of Capitalism* (1917). Lenin urged the proletariat of all countries to take advantage of the conflict as an opportunity to unleash pan-European civil war against their governments. The revolutionary inferno that Lenin predicted would engulf all of war-torn Europe came to pass, however, only in the Russian Empire.

See also **Alexander III; Anarchism; Bernstein, Eduard; Bolsheviks; Marx, Karl; Mensheviks; Plekhanov, Georgy; Revolution of 1905 (Russia); Russia.**

BIBLIOGRAPHY

Fischer, Louis. *The Life of Lenin*. New York, 1964.

Pipes, Richard. *The Russian Revolution*. New York, 1990.

Service, Robert. *Lenin: A Biography*. Cambridge, Mass., 2000.

James Heinzen

LEO XIII (1810–1903), pope from 1878 to 1903.

The conclave of 1878, following the long and contentious pontificate of Pius IX (r. 1846–1878), proved difficult as conflict in the college of cardinals continued, dividing those who favored confrontation from those who sought conciliation with the modern world. Pius IX had reasserted Rome's traditionalism vis-à-vis "modern civilization," but embroiled the church in bitter conflicts with the kingdom of Italy over the loss of Rome (the Roman Question), and with the German empire in the *Kulturkampf*, or cultural struggle between the Catholic Church and the state. Papal and clerical support for a monarchical restoration in France embittered Republicans, who eventually triumphed and retaliated against the church. Pius IX's concordat with Russia was never implemented, and the persecution of Catholic Poles continued. Relations with Austria and Switzerland were little better, and in much of Europe papal infallibility provoked controversy. The Vatican appeared estranged from the working classes, and its diplomacy was deemed a colossal failure.

On 20 February 1878 the conclave, avoiding the extremes of reform and reaction, settled on the sixty-eight-year-old Gioacchino Vincenzo Rafaelle Luigi Pecci. The cardinals selected Pecci for varied reasons, with some favoring a short pontificate and interim pope after the long reign of Pius IX. Their hope for a transitional pope seemed assured by Pecci's advanced years and frail health. Their assessment proved inaccurate, as Leo XIII would have a long and momentous pontificate that figuratively and literarily brought the church and papacy into the twentieth century.

EARLY LIFE AND CAREER

Initially there was neither a positive nor negative reaction to Pecci's election, for outside of the conclave, Perugia, and Belgium, he was little known. This son of Count Luigi Domenico Pecci was born on 2 March 1810 in Carpineto (Frosinone), to a family of Sienese origin. He studied at the Jesuit College of Viterbo (1818–1824), followed by the Roman College (1824–1832) where he received a degree in sacred theology (1832), entering the Academy of Noble Ecclesiastics and preparing for a future in the Roman diplomatic service. Ordained a priest in December 1837, Pecci was appointed apostolic delegate at Benevento, and in 1841 was named papal delegate to Perugia. In 1843, Pope Gregory XVI (r. 1831–1846) dispatched him to Belgium as nuncio (1843–1846). Three years later, Gregory named him bishop of Perugia (1846–1877), where he remained even after he entered the college of cardinals in 1853. Conservatives complained that Pecci's support of the Syllabus of Errors (1864) and its condemnation of the modern age was lukewarm. However, at the Vatican Council he aligned with the majority favoring infallibility and denouncing contemporary errors, but stipulating that the condemnations did not necessarily anathematize the modern world or all progress.

Pecci transcended the limited perspective offered by rural Italy in midcentury, having been exposed to industrial Europe and its social and economic problems. In Brussels he had an opportunity to study the country's Catholic movements, and he visited London, Paris, and the Rhineland. In Perugia, Pecci showed interest in the material well-being of his flock, considering social injustice to be sinful. In a pastoral letter of 1877, he decried the abuses imposed upon "the poor and the weak," invoking legislation to correct the "inhuman traffic" of children in factories. Although he shared Pius IX's insistence on the need for the temporal power, he did not condemn all manifestations of the current age. Examining his speeches at Perugia and during the Vatican council, reformers prayed Leo XIII would be more attuned to the modern world, while others hoped he would abdicate his role as "prisoner in the Vatican" and seek reconciliation with Italy.

PONTIFICATE

Following his election, Leo showed himself sensitive to the broad social currents of the age as well as its diplomatic realities. Basing his thought on the Gospels, the new pope perceived Catholic social doctrine central to his mandate to defend humanity and preserve its spiritual heritage. Leo opened a diplomatic campaign to parallel his social one, writing the president of France seeking rapprochement with the Republic. Other letters followed: to the emperors of Germany and Russia, and the president of the Swiss Confederation, informing them of his election and paving the way for reconciliation. He reestablished diplomatic relations with Germany in 1884. The new cardinal secretary of state, Alessandro Franchi (1819–1878), dispatched George Conroy, bishop of Ardagh to Canada as apostolic delegate, reminding its conservative clergy that in condemning liberalism the Holy See did not intend to attack all liberal parties or practices. Finally, the pope personally appealed to Belgian Catholics to sustain their constitution, even though it provided for a separation of church and state, because on balance he considered it beneficial. In 1879, recognizing the immense contribution of the independent-minded John Henry Newman (1801–1890), Leo made him a cardinal. These actions, and the pope's determination to make the Vatican Archives accessible to scholars, contributed to the positive reaction to Leo's pontificate.

The optimistic expectations were somewhat diminished by Leo's first encyclical, which examined God's inscrutable design (28 April 1878) and revealed his adherence to Pius IX's traditionalism. While Leo stressed the need to have love temper exchange, he bewailed the evils of the day including civil strife and dissension within and between nations, war, and bloodshed. Like Pius IX, Leo believed these ills flowed from the fact that the voice of the church was either ignored or despised. Leo praised Pius IX's stance on the Roman Question, proclaiming that deprived of the temporal power, the head of the church was no longer free.

Determined to preserve the principles of the faith as well as the papacy's claims to Rome, Leo nonetheless sought to bring the papacy and church into some accommodation with the modern world.

Unlike Pius IX, the more pragmatic successor showed himself willing to cooperate with secular governments ranging from monarchies to republics. He softened his tone toward the German empire, and was rewarded by a lax enforcement of the Falk laws (or May laws, which regulated the church and clergy in Prussia and Germany). Eventually, most of this legislation was repealed. In turn, Otto von Bismarck (1815–1898) recognized the importance of the papacy by inviting Leo to mediate the dispute between Germany and Spain in the Caroline Archipelago in the South Seas. His settlement was accepted in December 1885. Subsequently, the Reichstag passed the "fourth law for peace," which virtually brought the Kulturkampf to a close. In 1890, provision was made to restore to the Catholic Church the entire capital formed by the confiscation of priests' salaries during the Kulturkampf.

Relations proved more difficult with Catholic Italy and France. In January 1881, the Italian government was empowered to close, confiscate, or devote to other usage church property in its dominions. Leo objected to these and other anticlerical measures, invoking prayers for the "intolerable" position of the papacy in Rome. The pope urged the Italian faithful to undertake vigorous action in provincial and municipal elections on behalf of the church, the only domain open to them in light of the papal prohibition on Catholic participation in Italian national affairs. Relations deteriorated further in July 1881 following the demonstration orchestrated against the papacy when the body of Pius IX was transported from St. Peter's to its final resting place in San Lorenzo outside the walls. Harping on the perilous position of the papacy in the eternal city, Leo pleaded for foreign intervention.

Papal relations with the French Third Republic were little better, as the pontiff protested the attempt to impose military service on French seminarians. President Jules Grévy (1807–1891) urged Leo to persuade French Catholics to abandon the royalists, thereby disarming the republican opposition to the church. Leo accepted the suggestion, having the *Osservatore Romano* criticize the ultra-legitimist trend of the *Journal de Rome,* while continuing his efforts to seek reconciliation with the Republic. Leo was seconded in his efforts for a *Ralliement*, or détente, between French Catholics and their anticlerical government by Cardinal Mariano Rampolla del Tindaro (1843–1913), who shared his vision, and the primate of Africa, Cardinal Charles-Martial-Allemand Lavigerie (1825–1892), who pressed the pope to make some dramatic move in the matter. In October 1890, Lavigerie visited Rome, where it was decided that the cardinal would appeal to French Catholics to adhere to the Republic. Meanwhile, Rampolla encouraged the faithful in France to follow the course of the Holy See, which recognized all established governments in order to defend religious interests. In 1892, Leo explained that while the anticlerical measures might be opposed, the Republic should still be respected. Difficulties remained between Catholics and the Republic, but Leo had improved relations between Paris and the Vatican, in 1894 recognizing the Third Republic and urging Catholics to rally to it.

Pope Leo also sought a rapprochement of sorts with the modern world by having Christianity address the problems raised by the economic and social revolutions. Like his predecessors in the century, Leo rejected the notion espoused by liberal economists that labor was another commodity whose price was determined by supply and demand. He displayed a Christian concern for the poor, insisting on the need to alleviate their suffering. The human dignity of the worker mandated a just wage as the first step toward distributive and social justice. For this among other reasons, he proved more sensitive to labor's plight than the archbishop of Quebec, who had condemned the Knights of Labor, an American union under the presidency of Terrence Vincent Powderly (1849–1924). Leo did not condemn organized labor, although he favored cooperation rather than confrontation between owners and workers.

In 1891, Leo revealed his sensitivity to the problems of workers in *Rerum novarum*. The best known of Leo's encyclicals, *Rerum novarum* proclaimed the workers' right to protection against economic exploitation, suggesting that when the workers could not defend their own rights, the state had to intervene on their behalf. The pope recommended societies for mutual help for the workingman and his family, as well as institutions for the welfare of the young and the aged. Concerning workingmen's leagues, Leo preferred the guilds of the past to modern industrial unions. Nonetheless, he recognized that these workingmen's associations should be organized to improve the worker's material as well as his spiritual well-being. Publication of this "social *Magna Carta* of Catholicism" earned Leo the title "workingman's pope," inspiring Catholic social action in Europe and abroad to the present.

Two of Leo's letters in 1888 and 1890 aimed to expedite the abolition of African slavery. Historians, in turn, acclaimed his opening of the Vatican Archives in 1883 (*Saepenumero*), while Catholic philosophers applauded his advancement of Thomism and the restoration of Christian philosophy in the schools (*Aeterni Patris*, 1879). Leo encouraged biblical studies (*Providentissimus Deus*, 1893) and established a permanent biblical commission in 1902. He fostered the growth of religious orders, favored missionary activity, and during the course of his twenty-five year pontificate, worked to remake the college of cardinals. There were setbacks, including his failure to resolve the Roman Question, which continued to trouble relations between the Holy See and the Kingdom of Italy.

In 1895, in his encyclical *Permoti Nos* on the social question in Belgium, Leo stressed its relationship to religion and morality. The pope invoked cooperation, with the workers trusting their employers, and the latter treating their workers with kindness and care, both aiming for the common good. The workers' plight, the pope counseled, required a Catholic rather than a socialist solution. By this time, however, some Catholics called for political action to protect the masses, considering this the proper goal of Christian Democracy. The pope disagreed. In his encyclical on Christian Democracy, *Graves de Communi Re* (18 January 1901), Leo called for cooperation rather than conflict between classes, repeating that a just solution to the social question could only be found in the precepts of the Gospel. Thus, the pope refused to see Christian Democracy as a political movement, viewing it as a beneficent Christian action on behalf of the people, without favoring one type of government over another. Furthermore, while safeguarding the needs of the working classes, the movement he envisioned embraced all groups, irrespective of rank or position, as members of the same family, redeemed by the same savior. Christian Democracy, he insisted, should flourish free of political entanglements, rejecting the efforts to create political parties that linked Christian principles to secular doctrines, and the church to any form of political organization.

BETWEEN TRADITIONALISM AND ACCOMMODATION

Seeking a Christian solution to the social question, Leo did not completely abandon the conservatism of Pius IX. He was distressed by the liberal faction that supposedly had emerged in the American church, which allegedly sought to adapt Catholicism to American culture. Conservatives called for a condemnation of this movement, subsequently known as Americanism, and the pope complied. Leo addressed the controversy in an apostolic letter (*Testem Benevolentiae*, 22 January 1899), rejecting the notion that the church in America should differ from that which prevailed in the rest of the world. Although he sought reconciliation with the Church of England in 1896, his papal bull *Apostolicae Curae* found Anglican ordinations invalid. At the same time, the pope dismissed the criticism of external spiritual direction, adhering to the Roman centralization and papal primacy championed by his predecessor. Nonetheless, this nineteenth-century figure who adhered to traditionalism prepared the church for the twentieth century. Leo's diplomatic endeavors ended papal isolation while his pontificate marks the Vatican's official effort to restate the traditional social teachings of the Catholic Church in an industrial era, representing a watershed in the history of the modern papacy.

See also **Catholicism; Catholicism, Political; Kulturkampf; Roman Question.**

BIBLIOGRAPHY

Primary Sources

Carlen, Claudia, ed. *A Guide to the Encyclicals of Roman Pontiffs from Leo XIII to the Present Day, 1878–1937.* New York, 1937.

———. *Papal Pronouncements. A Guide, 1740–1978.* Vol. 1. Ann Arbor, Mich., 1990.

O'Reilly, Bernard, ed. *Life of Leo XIII: From an Authentic Memoir Furnished by His Order.* London, 1887.

Wynne, John J., ed. *The Great Encyclical Letters of Pope Leo XIII.* New York, 1903.

Secondary Sources

Burton, Katherine. *Leo the Thirteenth: The First Modern Pope.* New York, 1962.

Gargan, Edward T. *Leo XIII and the Modern World.* New York, 1961.

Hughes, John Jay. *Absolutely Null and Utterly Void: The Papal Condemnation of Anglican Orders, 1896.* London, 1968.

Wallace, Lillian Parker. *Leo XIII and the Rise of Socialism.* Durham, N.C., 1966.

FRANK J. COPPA

LEOPARDI, GIACOMO (1798–1837), Italian poet.

The greatest Italian poet of the nineteenth century, Giacomo Leopardi was born in Recanati, a small town in the Papal States, during the turmoil of the revolutionary triennium (1796–1799). His father, Monaldo, epitomized the provincial aristocrat of reactionary political convictions. Yet he was also keenly interested in the arts and sciences and provided his son with a ten-thousand volume library and a dispensation to read books on the *Index* (the Catholic Church's list of prohibited books). A child prodigy with immense classical erudition as well as a profound knowledge of contemporary European culture, Giacomo was already a remarkable philologist in his teens. Confined within the boundaries of a provincial existence and of an oppressive family life until his early twenties, he then left his "barbaric native town" and cultivated friendships with important intellectuals in his several stays in Bologna, Florence, Pisa, Rome, and Naples, where he spent the last years of his life in the company of his fellow writer Antonio Ranieri.

The first collection of his poetic works, *Canzoni,* was published in 1824 in a style still burdened by the classical tradition. It included poems inspired by civic-patriotic sentiments ("To Italy," "On the Monument of Dante") as well as compositions that prefigured the themes of his full maturity, in particular the unhappiness of human beings unable to fulfill the very desires that nature places in their hearts. Other poems cast in a fresher language and imbued with a powerful elegiac intonation and a Romantic sensibility (most famously "The Infinite") were published in 1825 and 1826; the first collection of his poetic production, the *Canti,* came out in Florence in 1831. Leopardi composed two more poems after that year, one of which, entitled "Broom, or the Flower of the Desert," is considered his poetic testament and a testimony to his final humanism. In the mid-1820s he also began publishing his important *Operette morali,* short and elegant moral-philosophical essays mostly in the form of dialogues laying out his cosmic materialism and pessimism. A collection of aphorisms, *Pensieri* (Reflections), was published in 1845.

His other writings include "Discorso sullo stato presente dei costumi degli italiani" (1906; Discourse on the current state of the customs of Italians) and his vast *Zibaldone di pensieri* (Notebooks), written from 1817 to 1832 and first published in 1898. In this remarkable diary he confided his thoughts on a variety of subjects, from linguistics and literature to theoretical and practical philosophy to the theme of national character (in which he was clearly indebted to the writings of Madame de Staël, and particularly to *Corinne* [1807]), as well as more personal reflections on his own life and feelings.

Central themes of both his prose and poetic writings are the contrast between youthful illusions and hopes and the disappointment and tedium of human existence, the comfort (and pain) of remembering, and nature's indifference to the misery of human beings. Some have related his views to the vicissitudes of his life and especially to his physical ailments and his unfulfilled love life. As it often happens, however, there was much more than just a personal and historical experience at the roots of Leopardi's vision of the human condition. His philosophical outlook was imbued with eighteenth-century materialism and an epistemology based on sensation; his interest in the issue of human happiness was still part of that culture, while his desperation and longing bespeak the climate of early Romanticism and the Restoration.

While he did not reject progress in itself, the skepticism, if not sarcasm, with which he approached both religious fideism and the liberal faith in mankind's "magnificent, progressive destiny" (especially in his 1830–1831 satirical poem "A Supplement to the Battle of the Mice and Frogs") placed him necessarily at odds with many of his contemporaries. However, increasingly from the 1840s onward, he was recognized as a major Italian writer. Vincenzo Gioberti, one of the foremost exponents of Italian Catholic liberalism and nationalism, while rejecting Leopardi's materialism and skepticism, highly praised his poetic works. For some, Leopardi became a symbol of atheism, and as such, he was contrasted to the Catholic Alessandro Manzoni, the "organic" intellectual of Italian conservative liberalism. Others later made him into the symbol of a radical and coherent antiprovidential outlook. In France, Leopardi acquired a considerable reputation thanks to a positive portrait by Charles-Augustin Sainte-Beuve published in the *Revue des Deux Mondes* in 1844. The complete collection of his poems was translated into French in 1841. In 1850 William Gladstone made Leopardi's poetic work known to the English public with an appreciative (and moralizing) essay published in the *Quarterly Review*. Friedrich Nietzsche thought highly of Leopardi's prose writings, reflecting a more general German appreciation for his philological work.

See also **Carducci, Giosuè; Manzoni, Alessandro; Verga, Giovanni.**

BIBLIOGRAPHY

Primary Sources

Casale, Ottavio M., ed. *A Leopardi Reader.* Urbana, Ill., 1981.

Francesco, Flora, ed. *Zibaldone di pensieri.* Milan, 1997.

Rigoni, Mario Andrea, ed. *Poesie e prose: Giacomo Leopardi.* 2 vols. Milan, 1987.

Secondary Sources

Carpi, Umberto. *Il poeta e la politica: Belli, Leopardi, Montale.* Naples, 1978.

Celli Bellucci, Novella. *G. Leopardi e i contemporanei: Testimonianze dall'Italia e dall'Europa in vita e in morte del poeta.* Florence, 1996.

Damiani, Rolando. *All'apparir del vero: Vita di Giacomo Leopardi.* Milan, 1998.

Dionisotti, Carlo. *Appunti su moderni: Foscolo, Leopardi, Manzoni e altri.* Bologna, 1988.

Press, Lynn, and Pamela Williams, eds. *Women and Feminine Images in Giacomo Leopardi, 1798–1837: Bicentenary Essays.* Lewiston, N.Y., 1999.

Rigoni, Mario Andrea. *Il pensiero di Leopardi.* Milan, 1997.

Silvana Patriarca

LEOPOLD I (1790–1865; ruled 1831–1865), first king of independent Belgium.

The newly independent Belgians inaugurated Leopold I as their first king on 21 July 1831. In his inaugural oath, Leopold pledged to observe the Belgian constitution, to maintain national independence, and to preserve the territorial integrity of Belgium. Twenty-five years later, on the anniversary of his inauguration, the Belgians feted the monarch who had bestowed stability and maintained the independence of their small but industrious nation.

YOUTH

Before he was chosen to be king, Leopold of Saxe-Coburg was little known in Belgium. Leopold was born on 16 December 1790 in Coburg, the eighth child and third son of Francis Ferdinand, duke of Saxe-Coburg-Saalfeld, and Augusta Caroline Sophia of Reuss-Ebersdorff. At the age of five, Leopold was named a colonel of the Izmailovsky Imperial Regiment in Russia; he was promoted to the rank of general at the age of twelve.

In the winter of 1805, Napoleon I's troops occupied Coburg. Leopold's family emigrated to Paris. The young Leopold joined the Russian army, refusing Napoleon's offer of a position as his aide-de-camp. He fought in the battles of Lützen, Bautzen, Kulm, and Leipzig and accompanied Tsar Alexander I on his triumphal march through Paris after Napoleon's defeat. Leopold traveled with the tsar's advisors to London. There, in 1814, on the back stairs of Pulteney's Hotel, he met Princess Charlotte, daughter of the prince regent and heir to the British throne. The Russian delegation soon left London, but Leopold remained behind to court Princess Charlotte until Napoleon's escape from Elba called Leopold back to the Russian army as head of a cavalry division.

Leopold and Charlotte were married on 2 May 1816 and settled at Carlton House. Charlotte died eighteen months later giving birth to a stillborn son. Leopold remained in London for fourteen years. He enjoyed the privileges of English citizenship, a generous annual stipend, the title of royal prince, and the military rank of field marshal. In 1830 he was offered the throne of the newly established kingdom of Greece, but he refused after learning that the Greek people did not support his nomination.

BELGIAN REVOLUTION OF 1830

The successful revolution of the former Habsburg territories for independence from Dutch rule in October 1830 resulted in the establishment of a provisional Belgian government in Brussels. Five European powers, France, Britain, Prussia, Austria, and Russia, convened in London to set the boundaries and find a king for the new constitutional monarchy. They settled on Leopold, who accepted their nomination, which was confirmed by the Belgian National Congress.

Before he had even completed his inaugural tour of his new country in August 1831, Leopold received the news that fifty thousand Dutch troops were assembling along the Belgian border, ready to reclaim the territory for the Dutch king, William I. The small Belgian army was ill prepared to defend the new nation. Leopold rode into battle, at the same time appealing to England and France to intervene to protect Belgium. The threat of French military forces dispatched the Dutch troops, for the time being. Over the next eight years, however, Dutch troops continued to launch incursions onto Belgian soil.

FOREIGN AFFAIRS DURING REIGN

During the first fourteen years of his reign, King Leopold sought to be involved in every detail of Belgian foreign relations. He informed a visiting diplomat that he had decided to "allow" the Belgian parliament to manage domestic affairs, but that he would personally defend the interests of his country against foreign powers.

Leopold's family relations allowed him to dominate the direction of Belgian foreign policy. In 1832 Leopold, who had been raised a Lutheran, improved his standing in Catholic Belgium and solidified his relations with France by marrying Louise-Marie d'Orléans, the oldest daughter of King Louis-Philippe of France. Leopold arranged the marriage of his niece, the future Queen Victoria of England, with his nephew, Prince Albert of Saxe-Coburg-Gotha. Since his time in London, Leopold served as Victoria's advisor first on personal affairs and later on national and international relations. Leopold built a veritable empire through the marriages of his nieces and nephews, and his own children.

Throughout his thirty-four-year reign, Leopold corresponded with all of the European sovereigns and many of the important statesmen as well as with Belgian diplomats stationed abroad, all outside of the ministerial channels. When foreign diplomats visited Brussels, they customarily met the king before attending their official ministerial sessions.

It was reported that the Belgian king had an opinion about every issue in European politics. Leopold was concerned especially with preserving Belgium's independent status and with maintaining the peace in Europe, two questions that were not unrelated. He frequently played the role of arbiter in international conflicts. Leopold's closest advisors were the Baron Christian Friedrich von Stockmar and the Romantic historian Jules van Praet.

DOMESTIC AFFAIRS

Leopold chafed at the limitations imposed on his power by the Belgian constitution. Initially, he struggled to claim sufficient authority to promote the interests of commerce and industry, trying for example to give ministerial positions to the directors of the Société Générale bank. He took an especially active interest in the construction of the first railway on the European continent in 1835. Officially above party politics, Leopold managed to name governments of center-right coalitions until the Liberals won the election of 1847. Leopold complained about the indignities he suffered under Liberal governments and vehemently condemned revolutions and revolutionaries.

In 1848 revolution spread throughout much of Europe, toppling monarchs from France eastward, but Leopold survived the upheaval unscathed. To stave off revolt in Belgium, the government offered social and political reforms. After 1848, former skeptics praised the Belgian king and his government for preserving order in their small kingdom amidst the general unrest.

DEATH

Leopold returned from a visit to England suffering from bronchitis. He died on 10 December 1865 and was buried at Laeken after an elaborate state funeral. He would have preferred to be buried at Windsor with Princess Charlotte, but the Belgians prevailed.

Leopold had four children with Louise, and two sons with his mistress, Arcadia Claret, Baroness von Eppinghoven. He was succeeded by his oldest surviving son, who became Leopold II, second king of the Belgians.

See also **Belgium; Leopold II; Revolutions of 1830.**

BIBLIOGRAPHY

Juste, Théodore. *Leopold I: Roi des Belges.* 2 vols. Brussels, 1868.

Lichtervelde, Louis de. *Léopold I: The Founder of Modern Belgium.* Translated by Thomas H. Reed and H. Russell Reed. London, 1930.

Simon, A. *Léopold I.* Collection Notre Passe, listed in *Belgie en Zijn Koningen.* Brussels, 1990.

Stengers, Jean. *L'action du Roi en Belgique depuis 1831: Pouvoir et influence.* 2nd ed. Brussels, 1996.

JANET POLASKY

LEOPOLD II (1835–1909; ruled 1865–1909), king of Belgium and personal sovereign of the Congo Free State.

Leopold II, King of the Belgians—as his country's rulers have traditionally been known—was born in 1835. He took the throne in 1865, on the death of his father, who had been the young nation's first king. In most of western Europe, monarchs were then rapidly losing power to elected parliaments, and so Leopold did not leave a great mark on Belgium's internal politics. But he left an enormous impact overseas.

Shrewd, ruthless, ambitious, and openly frustrated with being king of such a small country, he was eager to acquire a colony. After studying how Spain and Holland had won great colonial wealth, he made a string of unsuccessful attempts to buy or lease colonies in various parts of the world. In the 1870s, as Europe rapidly began conquering almost all of Africa, he saw his chance. The Belgian government was not interested in colonies, but for the king that posed no problem.

Leopold hired the British explorer Henry Morton Stanley, and for five years, starting in 1879, Stanley served as the king's man in Africa. Essentially Stanley staked out the vast territory in the center of the continent today known as the Democratic Republic of Congo, and threatened or tricked hundreds of African chiefs into signing their land over to Leopold. Then, using these treaties as ammunition, the king managed to persuade first the United States, and then the major nations of Europe, to recognize this huge region as his own. In 1885 he christened his new possession the État Indépendant du Congo, or, as it was known in English, the Congo Free State. One-thirteenth the land area of the African continent and more than seventy-six times the size of Belgium, it was the world's only colony owned by one man.

At the beginning of his colonial rule the main commodity Leopold was after was ivory—much valued in Europe for the way it could be carved into jewelry, statuettes, piano keys, and even false teeth. Joseph Conrad unforgettably portrayed the greed and cruelty of the race for Congo ivory in his great novella *Heart of Darkness* (1902). Conrad had been a steamboat officer on the Congo River in 1890.

Soon, however, the Congo was profoundly affected by something that happened in Europe: the invention of the inflatable bicycle tire. This, followed quickly by the invention of the automobile, created a huge worldwide rubber boom by the early 1890s. Wild rubber vines grew throughout the rain forest of Leopold's Congo, and to gather it he turned much of the territory's male population into forced labor.

The king maintained a private army of some nineteen thousand soldiers, black conscripts under white officers. For some twenty years, troops came into village after village, and held the women hostage in order to make the men go into the forest and gather a monthly quota of wild rubber. As rubber prices soared, men were forced to do this for weeks out of each month. The results were immense profits for the king and a human disaster for the Congolese. Huge numbers of male forced laborers were worked to death while women hostages starved. And with women in custody and men turned into forced laborers, there were few people left to plant and harvest food and to hunt and fish. In addition, tens of thousands died in unsuccessful rebellions. Hundreds of thousands fled the forced labor regime, but they had nowhere to go but remote rain forest areas where there was little food and shelter. Famine raged, the birthrate dropped, and disease killed millions who would otherwise have survived.

From all these causes, the best demographic estimates suggest that the population of the Congo was slashed by 50 percent, from roughly 20 million people in 1880 to roughly 10 million in 1920. Belgian colonial authorities at the time, including the official Commission for the Protection of the Natives, also estimated that the population had dropped by half. The forced labor regime began to moderate only in the early 1920s, when officials realized that, without changes, they would soon have no labor force left.

Leopold II earned, at minimum, an estimated $1.1 billion in early-twenty-first-century dollars from the Congo, most of it in rubber profits. This he spent on palaces and monuments in Belgium, on clothes for his teenaged mistress, and on his vast array of properties on the French Riviera. International protests forced him to turn the Congo over to Belgium in 1908, but he managed to extract additional payments from the Belgian government for doing so. He died, unpopular at home but with his fortune intact, the following year.

See also **Africa; Belgium; Colonies; Imperialism.**

BIBLIOGRAPHY

Ascherson, Neal. *The King Incorporated: Leopold II in the Age of Trusts.* London, 1963.

Emerson, Barbara. *Leopold II of the Belgians: King of Colonialism.* London, 1979.

Hochschild, Adam. *King Leopold's Ghost: A Story of Greed, Terror, and Heroism in Colonial Africa.* Boston, 1998.

ADAM HOCHSCHILD

LESBIANISM. *See* **Homosexuality and Lesbianism.**

LESSEPS, FERDINAND-MARIE DE

(1805–1894), French entrepreneur.

Ferdinand-Marie de Lesseps oversaw the construction of the Suez Canal in Egypt, but failed in his attempt to build a canal across Panama. Neither an engineer nor a businessman, Lesseps employed his skills as a diplomat, as well as his boundless optimism and energy, to promote his plans.

The idea of a canal across the isthmus of Suez joining the Mediterranean with the Red Sea did not originate with Lesseps. Although an ancient canal system had existed in Egypt, the modern project for the Suez Canal first developed during Napoleon's 1798 expedition to Egypt. In the 1830s, a group of Saint-Simonians traveled to Egypt, and several, including Prosper Enfantin, returned with the dream of building a canal. Enfantin established the Suez Canal Study Group, which developed plans during the late 1840s.

Lesseps did not participate in the Saint-Simonian trip to Egypt or the Study Group, but he too wished to build a canal. The son of a diplomat, Lesseps began his career in the foreign service. Lesseps spent much of the 1830s as a consul in Egypt, where he befriended the young prince and future ruler Muhammad Said Pasha (r. 1854–1863). Lesseps's diplomatic career ended in 1849, during a political crisis in Rome, and he retired to a family farm. In 1854, Lesseps learned that Said, known for his support for innovation and desire to modernize Egypt, had become khedive. Lesseps drew upon their earlier friendship and convinced Said that building the Suez Canal would help preserve Egypt's independence from Europe and strengthen its position within the

Ottoman Empire. Lesseps controversially used the Study Group's plans as the basis for his own canal project.

Lesseps guided the construction process through diplomatic and logistical difficulties. The Suez Canal Company, formed in 1858, primarily included French and Egyptian employees with Lesseps at its head. Although Lesseps held no official position in France, he managed the competing interests of the French, the British, the Egyptians, and the Ottomans in the project. He maintained control over the venture despite attempts by the Study Group and the British to gain a larger stake in the canal. French investors, generally urban middle-class professionals, purchased over half the shares financing the project, at a cost of five hundred francs apiece. Digging through sand and plateaus proved a difficult but surmountable challenge. The project initially depended on the corvée, forced manual labor of Egyptian peasants. After the death of Said in 1863, however, the new khedive, Ismail Pasha (r. 1863–1879), abolished the corvée. Arbitrator Napoleon III of France required Ismail to compensate the company for this new policy. To speed progress, Lesseps implemented mechanization.

The Suez Canal opened in 1869 with much fanfare and acclaim for Lesseps. Britain primarily benefited from the canal, because it cut in half the time of the voyage from London to Bombay. Ships traveling from Europe to Asia no longer were required to travel around Africa. In 1875, when Ismail fell into financial trouble, the British government bought out his shares in the canal. The British turned Egypt into a protectorate in 1882. Although technically remaining under Ottoman rule, Egypt served British interests.

In 1879, Lesseps formed the Universal Panama Interoceanic Canal Company, which undertook the construction of a canal across Panama (then part of Colombia), linking the Atlantic and Pacific Oceans. Lesseps financed the project by raising public loans, and construction began in 1882. However, construction in Panama faced great obstacles, including tropical diseases such as malaria, which killed thousands of workers. The large difference in the sea level of the Pacific and Atlantic Oceans necessitated the use of locks, which Lesseps recognized only too late.

The Panama Canal Company bribed French politicians to continue to support the project and encourage the sale of further shares in the company. However, the company could not overcome its technical and financial difficulties. Many small investors lost their money when the company went bankrupt in 1889. The French National Assembly charged Lesseps, his son Charles, engineer Gustave Eiffel, American con artist Cornelius Herz, and others with conspiracy and fraud. Lesseps escaped imprisonment due to his ill health. The scandal demonstrated to many critics of the French Third Republic that the government was corrupt. Anti-Semitism in France was inflamed because Herz and others involved were Jewish.

The United States bought the rights to the canal in 1903, after having backed a revolution that separated Panama from Colombia. The Panama Canal opened in 1914 and considerably shortened trading distances between the two oceans.

See also **France; Great Britain; Imperialism; Trade and Economic Growth.**

BIBLIOGRAPHY

Fitzgerald, Percy. *The Great Canal at Suez: Its Political, Engineering, and Financial History. With an Account of the Struggles of its Projector, Ferdinand de Lesseps.* 2 vols. Reprint. London and New York, 1978. Includes many original documents concerning the construction of the Suez Canal.

Karabell, Zachary. *Parting the Desert: The Creation of the Suez Canal.* New York, 2003.

Simon, Maron J. *The Panama Affair.* New York, 1971

RACHEL CHRASTIL

LEVÉE EN MASSE. The *levée en masse* was decreed on 23 August 1793 as an emergency measure to raise the manpower that the generals believed they needed if they were to throw off the danger of invasion and save the *patrie en danger.* It was a law born of military necessity rather than out of deep-seated Revolutionary conviction, as French armies faced defeat at the hands of the First Coalition and panic spread among the population of Paris. The optimism engendered by early victories at Valmy and Jemappes had given way to widespread despondency when France's opponents regrouped and war was declared on a new raft of states, including Great Britain and Holland in February 1793, quickly followed by Spain a month later. Morale disintegrated in the French ranks as officers—many of whom were filled with revulsion when the republic was declared and the king put on trial—resigned their commissions or emigrated, leaving huge holes in the command structure. The early victories gave way to a succession of defeats. By March 1793 foreign forces had invaded French soil both in the northeast and in the Pyrenees; the frontiers no longer offered protection. The suspicion spread that the government had lost control of the military situation, a suspicion that became irresistible once the general and leading Girondin Charles-François du Périer Dumouriez defected on 5 April, taking his troops with him to join the war against Revolutionary France.

Above all, it was clear that existing methods of recruitment were no longer capable of producing the mass army that the situation seemed to demand. From the earliest period of the constitutional monarchy it had been evident to France's leaders that there was a contradiction between the language of liberty in which the message of revolution was framed and the ways in which the line army of the *ancien régime* was recruited, which included threats and bullying, the use of drink to win over doubters, the payment of bounties to attract the poor and disaffected, the promise of pardons to criminals, and press-gangs and *racolage* (the practice of impressing young men, often in bars and wayside taverns when they were too drunk to resist), when other methods failed. It was not only Voltaire who believed that the soldiers recruited in such ways came from the most marginal and least-dependable groups in French society, and the eighteenth-century stage routinely portrayed soldiers as thieves, pickpockets, and vagabonds. In 1791 the state called for volunteers to come forward to defend France, trying to build on the new reputation enjoyed by the National Guard in civil society, but, though the first call was met with apparent enthusiasm, by 1792 it was clear that the voluntary principle was not sufficient to meet the requirements of the armies. Besides, too many of the volunteers saw their commitment as being a short and finite one, returning to their villages after a season's campaigning.

From the spring of 1793 the government turned instead to requisitioning, insisting that every department, and every district, provide a fixed quota of men in accordance with its population, with the aim of raising 300,000 troops. But the demands of the military were such that by August the new Jacobin administration was forced to take this idea further, insisting that all citizens must be prepared to contribute to national defense, and that all were equally at the disposal of the army until the moment of national emergency had passed. The situation, they believed, required controls on individual liberty that did not pertain in peacetime. It was in this spirit that they had passed a decree, on 26 July, to outlaw speculation and repress profiteering by army contractors, making such profiteering a capital crime. In the same spirit, less than a month later, they established the *levée en masse,* which can legitimately be described as the first act of total mobilization in modern history, the mobilization of the entire community in the service of the state.

COMPONENTS OF THE LAW

The law was unambiguous. Until France's enemies had been driven from the territory of the republic, "the French people are in permanent requisition for army service." Lest that be misunderstood, its meaning was then spelled out in greater detail, its implications for every section of society carefully itemized. The words are justly famous, and they would resonate around Europe.

> The young men shall go to battle; the married men shall forge arms and transport provisions; the women shall make tents and clothes, and shall serve in the hospitals; the children shall turn old linen into lint; the old men shall repair to the public places, to stimulate the courage of the warriors and preach the unity of the Republic and hatred of kings.

It was a declaration worthy of the classical heroes whom the French Republic so much admired. Horses were to be requisitioned, too; national buildings were to be converted into barracks; gunsmiths and tailors were to be placed at the disposal of the nation.

But what did this mean in practice once the decree was disentangled from its rather grandiose rhetoric? No army actually needs the services of the entire population; it would continue to require the work of civilians to grow food, transport supplies, and stimulate the economy. And, as the law recognized, it would need public administration to continue; so officials were to remain at their posts. Indeed, the government's aim was quite precise—to create an army of three-quarters of a million men—and behind the heroic language of equality lay a measure geared to create a mass army on a scale France had not previously known. Of course, in practice, all would not serve; indeed, the decree specifically pointed to the group from whom personal military service would be required: "The levy shall be general. Unmarried citizens or childless widowers, from eighteen to twenty-five years, shall go first; they shall meet, without delay, at the chief town of their districts, where they shall practice manual exercise daily, while awaiting the hour of departure."

The *levée en masse* was not a conscription in the modern sense, whereby each annual contingent of young men has to present itself for service; for that France had to wait until 1799 and the implementation of the Loi Jourdan-Delbrel. Rather it emphasized the unity of the entire community in the sacrifice demanded for the war effort, and it maintained the myth of spontaneity, of an entire people girding itself for communal defense in the name of the republic. Service was to be personal: unlike the previous levy, and unlike the majority of the annual conscriptions to follow, there was no provision for substitution, for buying replacements to serve instead of those designated for service. Instead, military service was proclaimed to be a duty for all, a function that was inseparable from citizenship itself. This does seem to have had an effect on public opinion, because rates of desertion and draft dodging were significantly lower with this levy than in most others of the Revolutionary and Napoleonic Wars. The fact that service was obligatory at least had the advantage of making it appear less inequitable; rich and poor, bourgeois and peasant fought alongside one another in the Revolutionary battalions.

IMPACT

The *levée en masse* succeeded where previous recruitments had failed, in that it gave France the large-scale citizen-army that the Convention demanded to repel invading forces. It contributed to a change in France's military fortunes, too, because the nation-in-arms that the Jacobins created not only drove foreign troops out of French territory but also began the process of imperial conquest that, under the Directory and Consulate, laid the foundations of a French imperium across much of continental Europe.

But how far did it change the face of battle, as the Prussian general Carl von Clausewitz famously claimed, or inaugurate a new era in European warfare? It did expand the scale of war, as mass armies were pitted against one another and others responded to the challenge of the nation-in-arms by recruiting greater numbers of men into their military. Casualties inevitably rose, and it is arguable that soldiers' lives became devalued as troops became more expendable. During the Napoleonic campaigns France would lose over 900,000 men, and, even before Moscow, Napoleon was not noted for avoiding casualties in pursuit of his goals. On the other hand, the mass armies did not of themselves bring about significant changes in technology or military strategy. The advances in light artillery, for instance, were inherited from Jean-Baptiste Vaquette de Gribeauval and other reformers under the *ancien régime.*

What the *levée en masse* did do was contribute to the mythology of the Revolutionary armies among future generations. It was a myth that inspired nineteenth-century French republicans—in 1830 and 1848, during the Franco-Prussian War (1870–1871), even in the call to arms on the eve of World War I in 1914. And its impact was not limited to France alone. It would reappear in revolutions and liberation movements of later centuries, wherever the ideals of 1789 evoked enthusiasm or where French cultural influence remained strong—in the Soviet Union in 1917, in China after 1945, throughout much of Latin America during the nineteenth century, in Algeria in 1958, and in Vietnam during the long years of struggle against first France, then the United States.

See also **Armies; France; French Revolution; French Revolutionary Wars and Napoleonic Wars; Napoleon; Nationalism.**

BIBLIOGRAPHY

Bertaud, Jean-Paul. *The Army of the French Revolution: From Citizen-Soldiers to Instrument of Power.* Translated by R. R. Palmer. Princeton, N.J., 1988.

Blaufarb, Rafe. *The French Army, 1750–1820: Careers, Talent, Merit.* Manchester, U.K., 2002.

Forrest, Alan. *Conscripts and Deserters: The Army and French Society during the Revolution and Empire.* New York, 1989.

Lynn, John A. *The Bayonets of the Republic: Motivation and Tactics in the Army of Revolutionary France, 1791–94.* Urbana-Champaign, Ill., 1984.

Moran, Daniel, and Arthur Waldron, eds. *The People in Arms: Military Myth and National Mobilization since the French Revolution.* Cambridge, U.K., 2003.

Paret, Peter. *Understanding War: Essays on Clausewitz and the History of Military Power.* Princeton, N.J., 1992.

ALAN FORREST

LIBERALISM. For a good many reasons the nineteenth century may be considered the century of liberalism par excellence. Indeed the Europeans of the time took it for granted that theirs was a liberal era. The term itself and several other relatives of "liberty" ("liberal," "liberals," "liberalism," or the Italian "*liberismo,*" referring to an economic rather than a political liberalism) all date from the nineteenth century. Consequently, and even though liberalism can claim no founding programmatic statement or text, the word has come to connote almost all the great political and social changes brought by "modernity."

Four broad spheres may be identified that together make it possible to arrive at an overall picture of nineteenth-century European liberalism. One such sphere in which liberal ideas were able to develop was the judicial one, embracing the entirety of reforms and advances of a legal kind founded on guarantees made to the individual and including the right to defend oneself in court, the right to the presumption of innocence, the right to a trial by jury—in short, the right to justice, whether individual or collective (especially with respect to religious minorities). The issue here is less the "rights of man," in the sense of the French Declaration of 1789, than a set of rights, won incrementally and concretely within the judicial realm, which together solidified the rule of law (called *l'état de droit* by the French and *Rechtstaat* in German-speaking countries). This process was under way before 1789 and it continued long thereafter (as witness the belated abolition of serfdom in Russia in 1860).

A second front of advancing liberalism was that of the economic, commercial, and industrial freedoms wrested from the old economic order based on partial control of the economy by the state (mercantilism), on various kinds of corporations and monopolies, and on the last vestiges of the feudal yoke. The notion that anything that helps free up commerce and industry must be good for the individual and for society at large gained currency as early as the second half of the eighteenth century. The idea of free trade nourished the prospect of prosperity and social harmony not just within each country but also in the relations between states: commerce was supposed not merely to offer individuals the greatest possible number of opportunities, not only to reward talent and merit but also to bring peoples closer together through exchange and reciprocal enrichment.

Advances in the realms of thought and science constitute a third sphere of liberal growth. Here the notion of freedom implied the setting of great store by discussion; the spread of "enlightenment" and the creation of a "public sphere" where not only every new idea but also every new political reform, indeed every "public" innovation, could be subjected to the test of debate and argument in a multitude of circles, academies, salons, clubs, and newspapers or journals.

The fourth dimension of the spread of liberalism in Europe concerns the most decisive but also the most delicate aspect of the matter, namely the organization and the very nature of political power: free and open discussion, public control over the actions of the executive authorities, the holding of government responsible for any errors it might commit—all were cardinal for liberalism, or more precisely for liberal constitutionalism.

Separately or together, these four aspects of the rise of liberalism were responsible for an almost infinite variety of policies and moments that could be described to a greater or lesser degree as "liberal." In some cases legal and civil liberties were granted without any true loosening of the grip of an authoritarian political order (as for example in the case of the Stein, Hardenberg, and Humboldt reforms in Prussia between 1807 and 1815).

Sometimes, by contrast, economic liberalism was introduced to boost national power, especially in the military sector, without any concomitant political liberalism—without instituting such public freedoms as the right of assembly, the freedom of the press and of publication, and the right of association, or such constitutional liberties as a parliamentary system and broader suffrage.

Had it ever achieved its full expression, therefore, nineteenth-century European liberalism would have meant the fusion of all four spheres into an indivisible whole. To define a political order, the doctrine of a party, or the ideas of an individual as liberal in the fullest sense would then imply the reality or premise of an established state having adopted economic liberalism (a free market, or what the Italians call *liberismo,* implying minimal state intervention) while at the same time embracing complete freedom of the public realm and genuinely liberal state institutions (executive and legislative bodies in competition based on open debate and the principle of governmental accountability). The chances of all four strands of liberalism coming together in this way, however, were close to nil. To confront such an ideal model with the various realities of European history is to understand why liberalism was never consistently defined across the Continent. The best that may be hoped for by way of definition of nineteenth-century liberalism is a sort of scale of historical situations, ranging, say, from nearly perfect examples (Great Britain in the 1850–1890 period and a number of smaller European states such as Belgium or the Netherlands) to cases of weak and minority liberalism (Otto von Bismarck's [1815–1898] Germany, Austria-Hungary after 1867, or—and especially—tsarist Russia), with France, Italy, or Spain occupying intermediate positions as examples of an unfinished or partial liberalism.

To these fundamental obstacles in the path of a clear definition of European liberalism must be added difficulties of the linguistic, ideological, and cultural kinds. In Europe the nineteenth century was the age of rising nationalism, and the use of the terms *liberal* and *liberalism,* like the adoption by one state or another of a model considered liberal, were widely infected by national rivalries. As identified with the ideas thrown up by the French Revolution, "liberal" notions were violently denounced in the 1820–1850 period by monarchist states attached to the old European order, even though such states (including Prussia, Austria, several small German states, and Piedmont) had already undertaken civil, judicial, and administrative reforms consistent with the ideal of the rule of law. As attributed, by contrast, to France's great rival England, "liberalism" was the butt of a multitude of criticisms and caricatures from Jacobins, democrats, and republicans; from this perspective, French Republicanism, even as embodied in the Third Republic after 1875, was seen as an advance beyond liberalism, which was too "English" and too aristocratic. Lastly, in a general way, and especially in the second half of the century, liberalism came in many countries to be viewed simply as an import either from the Anglo-Saxon world or (as by Russian pan-Slavism) from the Western one; the rejection of liberalism, or the claim that liberalism had been transcended and its supposed shortcomings obviated, thus became a badge of patriotic and nationalist correctness (as in the Germany of William II).

EMANCIPATORY LIBERALISM

The features of the liberal movement that developed in the wake of the French Revolution of 1789 had little in common with the present-day conception of liberalism. The "liberalism" of that time was inseparable from violent, revolutionary events set in motion by the people, and the power of liberal ideas from the advent of the Revolution onward was grounded in their rejection of an *ancien régime* all the more intolerable because it was in decline (see Alexis de Tocqueville's *The Old Régime and the French Revolution,* first published in 1856). In every part of Europe where the reverberations of the Revolution were felt, whether directly (thanks to invasion and occupation by the French) or indirectly, the idea of liberty had as its first implication freedom from the old order. This emancipation had legal aspects (equality before the law; one justice for all; the same rights for every individual, irrespective of birth); social and economic aspects (suppression of guilds, right of free enterprise, abolition of church tithes); intellectual aspects (freedom of the press, growth of philosophical societies); and, of course, political aspects proper (the establishment of elected representative bodies capable of participating in or even seizing state decision-making powers).

Linked as they were to the French Revolution, these "liberal" ideas suffered the backlash of disillusion that the Revolution precipitated. For the Revolution did not long remain the general "idea" celebrated by European philosophy in general and by Immanuel Kant (1724–1804) in particular; as a historical reality, after all, it meant the Terror, civil war, religious persecution, anarchy, corruption—and ultimately dictatorship, in the shape of Napoleon I (1769–1821). It is here, in fact, that the real roots of liberalism are to be found: in the need to draw up a *critical* balance-sheet of modern liberal ideas, ideas that did not originate in some miraculously rational doctrine applied by an enlightened government, nor in the heads of philosophers gathered together, but which were forged in the great maelstrom of a people's revolution. European liberalism, at least on the Continent (for Great Britain was an exception in this regard), drew strength from its own contradictions, from the gulf between its philosophical agenda and the runaway course of its historical embodiment.

All the basic questions concerning European liberalism were raised during the years 1800–1820, either in the form of intellectual review (Edmund Burke [1729–1797] in Great Britain, beginning in 1790; Benjamin Constant de Rebecque [1767–1830], Germaine de Staël [1766–1817], and François Guizot [1787–1874] in France between 1790 and 1820); or else in the more concrete and pressing form of the set of dilemmas confronting the political and social elites: Should political freedoms (of assembly, the press, association, elections) be instituted at the risk of inviting excesses and anarchy among the people? Should the political responsibility of the government with respect to parliament be instated at the risk of weakening the central power of the state (so necessary in case of civil or foreign war)? Should completely free trade and exchange be allowed at the risk of creating a social void, of atomizing society by abolishing mediating bodies and spontaneous associations? Should a representative system be confined to elites alone or should the perils of universal suffrage be confronted? Seen in this light, the liberalism of the first half of the nineteenth century, as expressed by Guizot, for example, or by his Dutch counterpart Johan Rudolf Thorbecke (1798–1872), was an anxious and at times pessimistic one. It vacillated between an overarching optimism, envisioning the historical advent of liberty and reason thanks to representative government and the rise of a universal middle class, and a pessimism based on real fears (of people's uprisings, the Jacobin Terror, the specter of the guillotine, the manifest instability of post-1789 political regimes, and the extension of suffrage).

From this critical relationship to the French Revolution arose the two great contrasting traditions of European liberalism: on the one hand, a left-wing liberalism that did not confine itself to promoting the tenets of liberal philosophy but considered the people to be a historical agent, actively sought to extend the involvement of individuals in the machinery of the state, and deemed it legitimate to resort to revolution; on the other hand, a conservative liberalism, concerned with the civil and social order, which strove to protect the individual from the power of the state, feared anarchy and the people and urged reform while rejecting revolution and democracy. As early as the Restoration period in France (1814–1830), both tendencies nevertheless appeared under the banner of the liberal "party" in common opposition to reactionary monarchism. They were likewise present in Spain, where the term *liberal* was first used in connection with the regime voted in by the Cadiz Cortes (assembly) in 1812; during the three-year liberal interlude of 1820–1823, liberals were subdivided into *moderados* (moderates) and *exaltados* (ultraradicals). In Great Britain too the liberal universe tended to swing from moderation and the aristocratic tradition (the Whig party) to radical and democratic demands (followers of James Mill [1773–1836]). In Italy, the *Risorgimento,* a movement whose goal was the reunification of the nation as a free country, was split between advocates of a liberal state under whose sway reforms would be implemented from above (Count Cavour [Camillo Benso, 1810–1861] in Piedmont) and proponents of a more democratic liberalism (such as Giuseppe Mazzini [1805–1872]). In all European countries the liberal tendency initiated at the beginning of the century thus followed a narrow course between two possible "deviations," rather like a bowling ball ever in danger of veering to left or right off its lane. Liberals who tended to resist even cautious reforms out of fear of universal suffrage, of violent revolution, or of the poorer classes in general, tended to defect to conservatism; those ready to pursue democracy, voting rights, or the will of the people come what may, tended to quit the liberal realm and enlist with democrats, radicals, or republicans.

Almost everywhere, this basic split in liberalism was correlated with two distinct views of the role of religion in modern society. Thus radicals or *exaltados* espoused anticlericalism, whereas *moderados,* Whigs, or conservative liberals felt that strong religious institutions buttressed the social order. In predominantly Catholic countries this dividing line left but a very narrow space for liberal Catholicism. And the further liberal and modern ideas evolved toward democracy, lay institutions, and secularism, the further religious practice declined and the more sharply contradictory Catholics who had endorsed the liberal program of 1820–1830 felt their own positions to have become: they felt that they had played the sorcerer's apprentice.

Liberalism was precipitated and carried forward by the French Revolution, but for that very reason it was assailed by the Revolution's backwash. In the Europe of the Holy Alliance that emerged from the Congress of Vienna (1814–1815), the liberal tendency was reduced to the role of a minority opposition, at least for the time being. It was not long, however, before trends in the development of ideas, of the arts and of culture, gave liberal ideas a new lease on life. The about-face of Romanticism, a movement which began by opposing eighteenth-century rationalism but ended up exalting the freedom of the artist from the dictates of academicism, is a very typical instance. Although the expression of liberal ideas in the properly political sense was seriously hindered by authoritarian restrictions, the liberal *sensibility,* at least, continued to develop through music, opera, theater, poetry, literature, and the *genre historique.* This example of "the cunning of history" did more, perhaps, for the dissemination of liberal ideas than formal political organizations of liberals in legal and parliamentary opposition. The revolution of July 1830 in France, which opened the way to a liberal monarchy personified by Louis-Adolphe Thiers (1797–1877) and Guizot, was also a revolt of Romantic youth.

But the chief ally of the liberal idea in the Europe of 1820–1840 was unquestionably the idea of the nation. This might seem paradoxical in view of the fact that this idea would later be assimilated to that of nationalism, and hence to a rejection of liberal values. In the context of the early nineteenth century, however, the primary connotation of the idea of the nation was that of an *emancipation.* The point was liberation: either liberation from foreign occupation—be it that of the future Belgium from the Netherlands; that of Poland, largely occupied by Russia; that of Ireland from the English; or that of Greece and other Balkan countries from the Ottoman Turks—or liberation from the division of a nation into several states, an arrangement perceived as an anachronistic legacy of the past, as in the case of Germany or even in that of the Swiss confederation. Italy belonged to both categories, being partly occupied and partly shackled by divisions (between Italian states) inherited from the past. In much of continental Europe— indeed in by far the greater portion of it, considering the ease with which national demands proliferated as freedom movements spread—the cause of national freedom was thus a formidable crucible of liberal ideas.

During this first phase of the nineteenth century, for example in the philhellenist movement of the 1820s, the freedom of one European nation was felt to concern all other Europeans in accordance with an optimistic and reconciliatory outlook sustained by the liberal movement's Romantic generation. The liberals of each country should struggle for their own national freedom, but, once it was won, they should come to the aid of the liberals and patriots of other, still oppressed countries. As for the military interventions of conservative monarchies seeking to repress movements of national emancipation (such as the invasions of Spain and of Italian states during the 1820s, or the quelling of liberal-national movements in 1848, notably in Italy and Hungary), they merely reinforced the intensity of the ideas, passions, and myths of Romantic liberalism. A liberal "public opinion" came into being for the first time. Liberal tendencies in each country won many more recruits by playing on national-patriotic themes than they could ever have garnered by evoking the liberal program in its "pure" form (consider the liberal patriots in Spain, Italy, and Germany).

Even after 1850 and the first disillusions with movements of national unification, the idea of a right to freedom for every European people or nation continued to be a central plank of liberal party platforms. Right up until 1914, in fact, a not insignificant portion of Europe, from Ireland to the Balkans, and including the old Austro-Hungarian Empire, known as a "prison of peoples," continued to foster the alliance between liberalism and the idea of the nation (in Norway, the liberal-national party Venstre led the country into independence in 1905; the Greece of Eleuthérios Venizelos [1864–1936] and the Irish Home Rule struggle likewise come to mind here).

LIBERALISM IN POWER

Borne along by the whirlwind of revolutionary, emancipatory, and national ideas; by most literary and artistic trends; and by the gradual embrace by European states themselves of modern conceptions of law, the liberal movement in the first half of the nineteenth century tended to find itself fighting for social demands and against established power (authoritarian monarchies or representative systems with oligarchic tendencies where the vote was confined to the propertied classes). Liberalism derived a powerful dynamism from this oppositional role. The midpoint of the century saw the start of a new stage, that of "liberalism in power." Its divisions notwithstanding, the liberal movement became almost everywhere the chief government party or the chief political force capable of affecting the decisions of governments and states.

The best example of liberalism triumphant was Great Britain. There are five reasons for saying so. First of all, British liberalism benefited from the continuity between already ancient traditions of civil liberties (*habeas corpus*) and of local and parliamentary aristocratic rights and such modern achievements as the emancipation of Catholics and Jews, the establishment of free trade, freedom of thought, and the extension of the franchise in 1832. It was thus not necessary for British liberalism to negotiate a revolutionary crisis opening a chasm between tradition and modernity, *ancien régime* and revolution, the elites and the people, and liberal ideas and progress toward democracy. The passage of the Reform Bill of 1832 showed that the parliamentary regime was capable of reforming itself and getting into step with the march of history. The second reason for British liberalism's success was that, although confronted until the outbreak of World War I by the continued social and political power of the aristocracy and the "establishment," it was able to incorporate many radical and even populist themes (in the arguments of William Gladstone [1809–1898] himself, and later in those of David Lloyd George [1863–1945] in his campaign against the House of Lords), and thus glean support from the working classes.

In the third place, the British liberals had already gained access in the eighteenth century to the very heart of political power thanks to the presence in Parliament and in the government of the Whigs, incarnation of the struggle against absolute monarchy. British liberal constitutionalism, based on the weakening of royal prerogatives and the emergence of the cabinet as a governmental structure, became the model for liberals throughout Europe. The fourth reason for liberalism's dominance in Britain, bound up with the patriotic parliamentary constitutionalism that reached its zenith in the middle of Queen Victoria's reign (1837–1901), is that Great Britain was also the cradle of the most thoroughgoing expression of liberal political philosophy. In John Stuart Mill's (1806–1873) account (1859), liberty was at once a condition of individual accomplishment and the only possible guarantor of an independent society that could run itself (mutual aid, charity, philanthropical associations) and thus limit the reach of state power. Although it is arguable that liberal philosophy concerned only the elite, liberalism in the broad sense certainly became the core of British national identity—and that is the fifth reason for its ascendancy. Victorious liberalism in the British mold, as the final argument of British military, maritime, commercial, and industrial power—linked to the adoption of free trade (1846–1848), to the notion of an increase in wealth and an improvement in life within the reach of all (as embodied by the campaigns of Richard Cobden [1804–1865] and the Anti–Corn Law League, created in 1839), and to the prospect of stable and pacific relations between states, in the period framed by the administrations of its two great prime ministers, Robert Peel (1788–1850) and William Gladstone (1809–1898), among others—represented the true high-water mark of the entire European liberal movement.

This "moment" of governmental liberalism may certainly be discerned in other European countries, as for example in Piedmont under Cavour or Hungary under Ferenc Deák (1803–1876), but such instances are invariably less stable and less "pure" than the British one. The case of France, where the memory of the Revolution of 1789 remained present in everyone's mind, and where the experience of political revolution was in fact relived several times (in 1830, 1848, and 1870–1871), is certainly the most complicated. That liberal ideas were in power in France cannot be disputed: one need only consider the nature of the country's political institutions (French parliamentarianism was in every way comparable to British) or the establishment of public freedoms at the end of the Second Empire and under the Third Republic. There were nevertheless three impediments to the advent of a true liberal era in France. In the first place, the powerful central role of an administrative state inherited from the *ancien régime*, and from Napoleon, continued to block the complete application of civil, judicial, and political liberalism: important factors here were the existence of an administrative justice separate from the general judicial system, a number of restrictions upon public freedoms, and state controls affecting civil servants and judges. Secondly, French liberalism, now identified with the limited electoral system of the July Monarchy (1830–1848), was criticized and overtaken by a more radical conception of democracy stemming from the Revolutionary tradition (Jacobinism and the ideal of direct democracy).

Although a few republicans in the 1860s, at the beginning of the Third Republic, continued to describe themselves as liberals (Jules Ferry [1832–1893] being a case in point), the word underwent a distinct change in sense and usage in the last decades of the century, as republican, democratic, and radical ideas continued to evolve. By the beginning of the twentieth century it was being used only by those Catholics (Popular Liberal Action party) opposed to the secularizing reform efforts of left-republican governments. The third obstacle confronting French liberals was the fact that they were the first in Europe to contend with mass electoral politics, universal male suffrage having been instituted in 1848. In this connection, French liberalism simply did not have the mobilizing appeal of radicalism, socialism, or even nationalist and chauvinist forms of conservatism. This was amply demonstrated by legislative election results up until 1914. The fact was that French liberals were often distinguished individuals hailing from the professional class and having no connection with movements, trade unions, or other organizations rooted in civil society. They were therefore condemned to remain in the minority, even if their ideas influenced all their adversaries (the republicans eventually became fierce defenders of parliamentarianism—and this even in its bicameral version, a characteristic liberal cause).

As for German liberals, they did achieve political power, first in Prussia and in a number of small states (notably Baden) and later in the context of a unified Reich, but this success entailed a basic change in liberalism itself, a shift that was evident in varying degrees throughout Europe and especially in newly unified nation-states.

Until the failure of the 1848 revolution and of the Parliament of Frankfurt (1848–1849), the program of the German liberals called for German unity to be attained by liberal means. They banked on the support of an educated middle class and the leadership of liberal governments in each of the German states (such as that of Heinrich von Gagern [1799–1880] in Hesse; Gagern also presided between December 1848 and May 1849 over the government formed by the Parliament of Frankfurt). Economic exchange (Zollverein) was also expected by the liberals to play a unifying role, along with the extension of public rights, a free press, and peaceful political relations among the states. After the shattering successes of Bismarck's authoritarian policies, however, and the imposition of unity on the Germans from above (1871), the liberals were obliged to define themselves not only in terms of their own philosophy but also by reference to the national prestige of Bismarck and the new Reich. Their subsequent electoral gains and their place in parliament and government could not be attributed solely to the virtues of the liberal program, for they had effectively subordinated themselves to other political tendencies and in so doing firmly tied the liberalism to the idea of the nation. The upshot was twofold: in the first place, the liberals split into opposing camps, with Rudolf von Bennigsen's (1824–1902) Nationalliberale Partei, founded in 1879, on one side and Eugene Richter's (1838–1906) left progressives on the other; secondly, the conquest of supreme power became impossible for them inasmuch as the chancellor, Bismarck, was not answerable to the Reichstag. This shift in Germany between 1861 and 1890 had profound and long-lasting consequences for European liberalism as a whole and most particularly for countries such as Italy.

In the wake of the French Revolution of 1789 liberalism could reasonably identify itself with the movement of history itself; it seemed to be the incarnation of the modern idea of progress. Later, even its reverses and failures, including the return of conservative monarchies after 1814–1815, could be looked upon merely as temporary obstacles or delays in the ineluctable advent of a liberal regime and society. In Bismarck, however, the liberals were faced by an opponent who had won where they had lost. The German liberals of 1848 showed up the weakness and limitations of their movement, its inability to endow the Germans with a unified state, to make war on Austria and France, to create a strong and effective government. The final irony was that the very enemies thought to have been condemned by the movement of history—conservatives, sometime reactionaries, monarchists of the *ancien régime*—had retrieved a prestige and popularity among the people (Bismarck first, then William II [r. 1888–1918]) that no one could ever have imagined before 1848. In striking contrast, the liberals themselves, whether "national" or "progressive," proved incapable of expanding beyond the middle classes, the liberal professions, and the intellectual elite. Thereafter it was easy for their opponents to denounce them for defending the status quo and private property and standing for class privilege (or, in Italy, for favoring the North over the South).

LIBERALISM CHALLENGED AND SURPASSED

Between about 1890 and 1914 liberalism in Europe had to deal with the surging power of the masses and the problems of freedom in an industrial society. This watershed period was marked by the generalization of political suffrage; the achievement of literacy by the greater portion of the population; a dramatic expansion of the popular press and of all kinds of publishing; and the emergence of large organizations—patriotic associations or leagues, trade unions, and political parties. During the period from 1860 to 1880, all the main European political traditions, namely liberalism, democratic radicalism, socialism, and nationalism, were essentially at parity with respect to the coming struggle for mass support.

By 1914 the state of play as it would have appeared to contemporaries was extremely unfavorable to liberals and liberalism. How is such a failure to be explained?

A first consideration is that liberalism found it very hard to adapt to the new world of highly organized and *disciplined* political parties. At bottom, liberalism was the product of the highly restricted ("censitary") representative systems of the early nineteenth century and of circumscribed groups of intellectuals (aristocratic salons and clubs, learned societies, newspaper editorial committees, Masonic lodges in some countries, and so on). Almost everywhere in Europe, therefore, liberals were defined by their fealty to the principle of open debate and to the interplay of freely formed and expressed opinions. Factionalism and its attendant divisions alarmed them not at all.

Neither the Whigs in Great Britain, nor the liberals of the July Monarchy in France, nor their counterparts in Spain or Italy were ever unified, and they never defended political unity as needful to a "party." All these assumptions and habits became a liability with the advent of the mass era. Vis-à-vis a newly vast electorate whose opinions were formed by the great popular newspapers and by national political campaigns, liberals frequently fell prey to their own divisions and to their inability to frame a simple or indeed "demagogic" program, to adopt a single slogan (or "cry" in the traditional English sense), or to produce a leader acceptable to all their number. In parliament they were confronted by groups unified by a coherent ideology—sometimes by radical democrats but more often by agrarian parties, Catholics, nationalists, or socialists. In this context they were often ill served by their affection for open debate and free balloting.

Even where liberals succeeded in forming governments, as in Great Britain with Gladstone or Herbert Asquith (1852–1928), they were continually undermined by personal and factional rivalries. As the situation grew more perilous in Europe, as an accelerating arms race and mounting nationalist propaganda raised the specter of war, conservatives, often recycled as modern-day nationalists, had no trouble tarring liberals and parliamentary liberalism with the brush of weak government. There were even those among the liberals who "betrayed" their cause by endorsing the view that public order trumped individual liberties or that a strong executive took precedence over legislative government (as for instance in the Italy of Francesco Crispi [1819–1901]).

Some liberal parties, certainly, were organized and structured. In Great Britain, through the efforts of Joseph Chamberlain (1836–1914), who took the local model of Birmingham as his starting-point, and under the leadership of Gladstone, the Liberal Party assumed the profile of a modern political party. It drew a response from the masses (including the working class), imposed a relatively effective discipline on its members in Parliament, led coherent political campaigns at the national level, and so constructed a genuine identity for itself. Yet two facts militate against the claim that liberal "parties" enjoyed great success. In the first place, save in Great Britain and a few northern countries, partisan liberal organizations throughout Europe must be said to have failed. This is true of Italy, and most of all of France, where the liberals achieved neither parliamentary discipline nor any kind of national electoral organization (the radical-socialists, who dominated French political life in the 1900s, not being purely liberal in character).

Second, and this even in Great Britain, the philosophical tenets of liberalism continued to undermine the reality, stability, and durability of the party form. Gladstone's Liberal Party very soon suffered the secession of the Unionists (1886) over the issues of Irish Home Rule and imperialism. And even though the party continued to dominate the political scene during the Henry Campbell-Bannerman (1836–1908) and Asquith governments (1906–1914), and on through the war years, with David Lloyd George (1863–1945) and Winston Churchill (1871–1947) in the leadership, it is doubtful that the Liberals were a homogeneous and philosophically consistent grouping: internal debate raged on imperialism, on state intervention in the economy, and on the redistribution of wealth by fiscal means—all issues that put Whigs, moderate liberals, partisans of the New Liberalism, and radicals at odds with one other.

A major reason, too, for European liberalism's failure on the eve of World War I was competition from socialism, and more generally from all the new social ideas of the time (not just the Marxist or collectivist ones). Political liberalism was in a weak position relative to the model of the modern political party, but *social* liberalism—meaning the social ideas of classic liberalism—also came under fire, and was indeed ultimately overtaken. The liberal view of socioeconomic issues was based on the importance of individual merit, the achievement of personal success, free enterprise and commerce, and a minimal role for the state; these ideas had long dominated European thinking. It is arguable, indeed, that so long as socioeconomic features of the *ancien régime* persisted (such as constraints on business, the power of the landowning nobility, of corporations and guilds, or of the established church), then the ideas of the so-called Manchester liberals retained a good deal of their progressive character, that they were still revolutionary as applied to the most economically backward parts of the Continent, where agrarian reform was still unheard of and property ownership highly restricted. By the end of the nineteenth century, however, these liberal economic and social conceptions no longer tallied with majority opinion. In the mid-1870s the European economy had entered its first great cycle of depression in the modern sense. The liberal myth of a market economy founded on never-ending progress and the enrichment of all lost credibility. Most European countries aside from Britain adopted protectionist measures and turned their backs on the free-trade ideal, hitherto considered the guarantee of rapprochement and interdependence between states. By the century's end, the economy began to be perceived within European opinion as a new kind of war of conquest, of merciless competition (including the practice of dumping). This was yet another blow to the sanguine visions of economic liberalism of the Manchester variety.

Around 1900, even though Marx's bleak predictions concerning the pauperization of the working class and the total collapse of capitalism had not come to pass, the promise of generalized prosperity held out by liberalism had proved scarcely less illusory. Poverty and the extremely slow development of a middle class in the agricultural regions of southern Europe, including most of Spain and Portugal, the south of Italy, and the Balkans, were inhospitable conditions for the implantation of liberal ideas, especially in view of spreading socialist and even anarchist ideas and (as in Scandinavia) the success of agrarian-defense parties. Meanwhile, in urbanized and industrialized areas of Europe, the liberal vision of a society founded on individual merit and the disappearance of social class was given the lie by low social mobility, by the persistence of class and status differences, and by abiding feelings of fear and insecurity centered on industrial accidents, temporary or chronic unemployment, and illness. True, a new generation of liberals, spearheaded by Giovanni Giolitti (1842–1928) in Italy and by Lloyd George in Britain (with his "people's budget" of 1909 based on progressive taxation), introduced real social reforms in the 1900s (the eight-hour day in Italy in 1908; the British National Insurance Act in 1911) that laid the groundwork for the welfare states of the future. But even these measures inevitably appeared timid and incomplete, not to say hypocritical, when compared with the social solutions, pledges, and utopias outlined in the programs of the radical-democratic, social-democratic, and socialist parties.

As World War I approached, the liberals' economic and social agenda spoke only tangentially to the broad masses; only the middle and professional classes were drawn to it. The movement appeared distinctly weaker than its immediate rivals. In sharp contrast to democratic and radical parties, liberals were often reticent and suspicious with regard to universal suffrage and the political participation of the masses; they seemed pusillanimous, as compared with conservatives and nationalists, when it came to the defense of national unity and public order; and the appeal of their promises on the social front was easily surpassed by that of the socialists.

Perhaps the most striking instance of liberal failure in the 1900–1914 period is the case of Russia. During the nineteenth century, Russian liberals anticipated the conjunction of top-down reforms and the institution of liberal political representation from below (by means of the zemstvos, or local government councils, for example). When the moment finally arrived, however, under the pressure of the revolution of 1905 and the convening of a first Duma (elected national assembly), the liberals were very quickly left behind: overtaken on the left by democrats (specifically, by part of the Constitutional Democratic party) and by the various socialist tendencies, they were also challenged on the right by the authoritarian measures taken by the tsar and the conservatives in order to buttress their power. Unable to detach themselves from their nineteenth-century antecedents, the liberals were obliged to make way for the political forces that would stamp the century ahead, namely socialists, nationalists, and partisans of a strong executive arm and an interventionist state.

Up until the outbreak of World War I it was still possible to argue that, even if liberalism had missed the turning-point of political modernity (universal suffrage, organized political parties, trade unions, mass-based leagues, and associations), liberal ideas now helped define regimes and states throughout Europe. Liberals could still console themselves by recalling that their goal had never been to engage in partisan politics but simply to disseminate liberal principles within judicial systems and state administrations, to provide the other parties with constitutional rules capable of regulating their confrontations, and infuse public life with civility and general moderation. But, as some liberals clearly realized immediately, the outbreak of World War I threw liberal principles and ideals dramatically into question. War among European states meant that experimenting with free trade, so far from bringing nations closer together, had set them at each other's throats. War signaled the failure of liberal diplomacy (and the notion of arbitration) vis-à-vis military leaders; likewise the failure of parliaments vis-à-vis executive branches seeking to strengthen their grip on power. By mobilizing the economy under state control, war also showed up the limitations of liberal economics. And with war came types of propaganda, press censorship, restrictions on civil liberties, and methods of treating foreign residents that eroded liberal judicial principles considered beyond challenge in the nineteenth century. Above all, the passions and hatreds unleashed by the war challenged the most important philosophical precept of nineteenth-century liberalism, namely the idea that modern politics should be founded on judgment and reason and partake of the supposed forward march of "civilization."

See also **Asquith, Herbert Henry; Conservatism; France; Gagern, Heinrich von; Germany; Giolitti, Giovanni; Gladstone, William; Great Britain; Guizot, François; Italy; Lloyd George, David; Mill, John Stuart; Republicanism; Thiers, Louis-Adolphe.**

BIBLIOGRAPHY

Ashley, Susan A. *Making Liberalism Work: The Italian Experience, 1860–1914.* Westport, Conn., 2003.

de Ruggiero, Guido. *The History of European Liberalism.* Oxford, U.K., 1927.

Droz, Jacques. *Le libéralisme rhénan 1815–1848.* Paris, 1940.

Girard, Louis. *Les libéraux français, 1814–1875.* Paris, 1984.

Langewiesche, Dieter. *Liberalism in Germany.* Basingstoke, U.K., 2000.

Léontovitch, Victor. *Histoire du libéralisme en Russie.* 1987.

Morgan, Kenneth. *The Age of Lloyd George.* London, 1971.

Robledo, Ricardo, Irene Castells, and María Cruz Romeo. *Orígenes del liberalismo. Universidad, política, economía.* Salamanca, Spain, 2002.

Sheehan, James J. *German Liberalism in the Nineteenth Century.* Chicago, 1978.

Sykes, Alan. *The Rise and Fall of British Liberalism, 1776–1988.* London, 1997.

NICOLAS ROUSSELLIER

LIBRARIES. The political, economic, social, and cultural movements of the eighteenth century laid the groundwork for the rapid expansion and development of both public and private libraries in the nineteenth century. More numerous and varied, more public and accessible than in previous centuries, they were intimately connected to many of the broader cultural, political, and economic changes that were reshaping European societies.

In the case of public libraries, the most visible change was the accelerated transformation of princely or court libraries into public institutions. A fundamental shift occurred in the conception of such collections. They ceased to be repositories for the personal benefit of rulers and their courts. By declaring them open to the public, rulers recognized the right of a wider audience to study and enjoy their content. In addition, material support for these libraries moved from the princely purse to state or public funding.

Numerous factors contributed to this transformation. A growing sense of national identity required monuments to national culture and greatness. Opening them to the public encouraged national pride and—it was hoped—a loyal, educated citizenry.

State libraries grew through collecting, conquest, and purchase. In addition, the confiscation of ecclesiastical libraries, notably those of the Jesuit order following its dissolution in 1773 and of monasteries secularized in the wake of the French Revolution, vastly increased state library holdings. For example, the Hofbibliothek (Court Library) of Bavaria, in Munich, which opened to the public in 1790, added some 480,000 volumes, including 20,000 manuscripts, between 1799 and 1817.

Other political and cultural trends hastened the transition to state and national libraries. The foundation of learned societies and the spread of literacy to the middle classes by the mid-1700s had created a clientele for libraries. Liberal and republican ideals and the democratic revolutions of the late eighteenth and nineteenth centuries weakened monarchies and expanded the image of state libraries from symbols of national pride and culture to institutions for the service and education of citizens.

The modern sense of a national library as an institution performing national functions began to evolve during the nineteenth century with the recognition that its principal task was collecting the nation's publications. The earliest library to attempt this was the Bibliothèque Nationale (National Library) of France, which had benefited from legal deposit since 1537. It was the first library to call itself a national library, having been renamed during the French Revolution (1795).

The Reading Room of the British Museum, completed in 1857. From its inception in 1753, the department of printed books of the British Museum collected copies of most books published in Great Britain. In 1857, a lavish reading room was constructed to provide authorized users access to the vast collection. BRITISH MUSEUM, LONDON, UK/BRIDGEMAN ART LIBRARY

A British national library was proposed in 1707 but did not emerge until 1752, and then it took the form of the British Museum Library; opened to the public in 1759, it only changed its name to the British Library in 1973. By 1800, nearly all European countries had recognized national libraries.

The use of public and national libraries was at first generally restricted to scholars and then, increasingly, to the university students, whose numbers expanded dramatically during the eighteenth century. The consumer revolution of the eighteenth century had, however, created increased leisure, expectations, and demand for goods and activities (including books and reading) that denoted social status. The dramatic increase during the last third of the nineteenth century in both secondary education and literacy (which by 1900 was above 50 percent even in the less advanced countries) created an expanding reading public. To meet its needs, the number and variety of popular reading institutions increased.

Popular libraries had antecedents in the fee-based eighteenth-century circulating libraries run by booksellers and the reading rooms that emerged in coffeehouses. In addition, private citizens and social associations had started subscription libraries for the growing merchant and trade classes. These libraries continued to flourish, giving important stimulus to the book trade. By the century's end, the dramatic rise of popular literature in the form of newspapers, periodicals, and novels resulted in the creation of a new type of library: the public lending library, which emerged in 1780 in Germany. By 1800 most large cities and many smaller municipalities had libraries of this sort.

Private, commercial, and public circulating libraries persisted into the nineteenth century, expanding their scope and democratizing their appeal. Lending libraries were started not just in bookstores but in barbershops and in tobacconists', confectioners', and stationers' shops. As society industrialized, libraries for workers emerged. Nineteenth-century bourgeois national consciousness, linked as it was to moral reform, self-help, and the education of responsible citizens, shaped their development. The rich associational life of Europeans also played an important role. Educational and self-help societies like the mechanics institutes of the 1820s in England provided lectures, reading rooms, and lending libraries as a way of educating skilled workers. In France, where the public library system developed slowly, from 1862 onward the bourgeois Franklin Society advocated the formation of popular collections of "instructive works" to make French working men sober and responsible and to avoid social unrest. Chafing at restrictions on dress and on the type of literature in these libraries, however, unskilled workers often founded their own reading rooms. Cooperative societies of workers also founded libraries, and their numbers exceeded the number of public libraries before 1880. Between 1836 and 1854, the English workers of Carlisle established twenty-four reading rooms with 4,000 volumes and 1,400 members. Workers' libraries appeared in Germany during the revolutions of 1848 and again among local Socialist Party and trade union chapters in the 1890s.

Libraries for women also emerged in the late eighteenth century and expanded their scope in the nineteenth. The earliest rented, often by mail, those books deemed suitable for women. Women were avid readers of novels and the new magazines about women's issues. Despite heated debates about the propriety of women reading novels and going to public libraries to do so, by the century's end reading rooms had been established for women in public libraries and libraries for women had been established in factories.

Fueling the development of these libraries were not only the desires of working-class men and women for status and direct access to religious, political, and recreational literature, but also the anxieties of the upper classes about what they considered the dangerous classes and the upper-class desire to inculcate the values of what they considered responsible citizenship. The British Public Libraries Act of 1850 was the work of social reformers rather than the government. In France, the Ligue d'enseignement (Instructional League) persuaded employees to establish workers' libraries in factories in 1866. The Borromäus Verein was founded in Germany in 1845 as a society to promote good reading and establish libraries for Catholics of all classes. The convergence of the popular education and popular library movements resulted in the establishment of additional free, popular municipal libraries, and consequently commercial and private lending libraries declined.

Expanding access to libraries was accompanied by the steady development of ways to access library collections, from printed and card catalogs to uniform cataloguing rules and classification systems. With the professionalization of librarians, library science emerged as a distinct field of learning.

See also **Education; Literacy; Museums; Popular and Elite Culture.**

BIBLIOGRAPHY

Secondary Sources

Blasselle, Bruno. *La Bibliothèque nationale.* Paris, 1989.

Dalton, Margaret S. "The Borromäus Verein: Catholic Public Librarianship in Germany, 1845–1933." *Libraries and Culture* 31, no. 2 (1996): 409–421.

Everitt, Jean. "Co-Operative Society Libraries." *Library History* (Great Britain) 15, no. 1 (1999): 33–40.

Garrett, Jeffrey. "Redefining Order in the German Library, 1775–1825." *Eighteenth-Century Studies* 33, no. 1 (1999): 103–123.

Hammond, Mary. "'The Great Fiction Bore': Free Libraries and the Construction of a Reading Public in England, 1880–1914." *Libraries and Culture* 37, no. 2 (2002): 83–108.

Stam, David H. *International Dictionary of Library Histories.* 2 vols. Chicago, 2001. Extensive coverage of types of libraries as well as of individual libraries; useful bibliography.

Sturges, Paul. "Great City Libraries of Britain: Their History from a European Perspective." *Library History* (Great Britain) 19, no. 2 (2003): 93–111.

Tedder, Henry Richard, and James Duff Brown. "Libraries." In *Encyclopaedia Britannica: A Dictionary of Arts, Sciences, Literature and General Information.* 11th ed. New York, 1911. A detailed treatment of libraries, especially in Europe and the United States; includes statistics from contemporary sources.

SUSANNE F. ROBERTS

LIEBERMANN, MAX (1847–1935), German painter and graphic artist.

Max Liebermann was one of the most prominent figures in German art in the late nineteenth and early twentieth centuries. He began his career as an enfant terrible of realism but evolved into the most celebrated representative of German impressionism. As a founder of the Berlin Secession and its first president (1899), he was instrumental in the development of modernism in Germany, both artistically and institutionally; his world-class collection of French impressionist paintings, alongside influential writings on art, such as his monograph on Edgar Degas, augmented his significance as a champion of modern art. Although the early years of his career were marked by controversy, by the time he served as president of the Prussian Academy of Arts (1920–1932), he had become a representative of the artistic establishment. As a Jew, Liebermann has been seen as an exemplary figure for evaluating Jewish assimilation into German society and he has been a focus of debate on the role of Jews in German culture generally and as agents of modernism in particular.

Born into a wealthy Berlin family, Liebermann began his studies with the Berlin horse painter Carl Steffeck and in 1869 enrolled in the Weimar art academy. In 1871 he visited the studio of the Hungarian painter Minhály Munkácsy in Dusseldorf; this encounter inspired Liebermann's first major work, *Die Gänserupferinnen* (1872; Women plucking geese). The painting's realist depiction of poor people engaged in physical labor, rendered in a somber palette of browns, elicited scathing criticism when it was exhibited, earning Liebermann the epithet "apostle of ugliness." Liebermann's Parisian sojourns (1872; 1874–1878), exposing him to the Courbet and Barbizon school painters, coupled with his yearly trips to Holland, reinforced these tendencies. During the 1870s and 1880s, Liebermann's work was characterized by a naturalistic and sympathetic depiction of working people: the simple life of a community in harmony with nature, the dignity of peasants harvesting potatoes, tending animals, weaving and bleaching linen. These scenes were often set in Holland, a land whose painterly tradition (especially of Franz Hals and Rembrandt) and contemporary communal structure he admired. In works such as *Freistunde im Amsetrdamer Waisenhaus* (1882; Leisure hour in the Amsterdam orphanage), Liebermann depicted the exemplary way that Dutch social welfare institutions cared for the poor, orphaned, and elderly.

Liebermann settled in Munich in 1878. The following year, *Der zwölfjährige Jesus im Tempel* (1879; The twelve-year-old Jesus in the Temple) unleashed a storm of controversy when it was exhibited in Munich, eliciting anti-Semitic attacks in the press and prompting a debate in the Bavarian parliament. Liebermann's unidealized depiction of Jesus was criticized as "the ugliest, most impertinent Jewish boy imaginable." Whereas other German artists were presenting New Testament scenes with contemporary realism, a Jewish artist's interpretation of this theme proved to be too much for many Germans to tolerate. In response, Liebermann altered the painting to make Jesus look less scruffy, less unkempt, and less stereotypically Jewish; he mostly avoided Biblical subjects for the rest of his career.

In 1884 Liebermann married Martha Marckwald and returned to Berlin, eventually moving into the house at Pariser Platz 7, next to the Brandenburg Gate, which his father had acquired in 1859. He became part of a circle of early enthusiasts of French impressionism that gathered in the home of pioneering collectors Carl and Felicie Bernstein. The year 1884 also marked his first depiction of the Judengasse (Jewish quarter) in Amsterdam, a subject he would explore obsessively into the next century; it was also the year he introduced freer methods of paint handling and greater movement into his compositions. This change in style accompanied a gradual shift away from depictions of rural working people to representations of Liebermann's own class, the urban upper bourgeoisie, engaged in leisure activities: at the seashore, riding horses, playing tennis, relaxing in

Girls in the Garden of an Orphanage in Amsterdam. Painting by Max Liebermann, 1885. BILDARCHIV PREUSSISCHER KULTURBESITZ/ART RESOURCE, NY. ©2005 ARTISTS RIGHTS SOCIETY (ARS), NEW YORK/VG BILD-KUNST, BONN.

parks and beer terraces. In this choice of subjects, in his penchant for painting out of doors, and in his lightened palette and looser brushwork, Liebermann demonstrated many affinities with French impressionism without adopting the more radical innovations of color, facture, and spatial organization that characterized the French movement.

Liebermann was a passionate defender and collector of French modernism at a time when deep-seated anti-French sentiments in Prussia branded enthusiasm for French culture as antipatriotic. Although Liebermann was suspect in certain circles for his cosmopolitan and francophile tastes, by the late 1890s he had achieved official recognition. For his fiftieth birthday, in 1896, he was honored with a retrospective exhibition at the Berlin salon, received the Great Gold Medal, and was awarded the title of professor; the following year he was elected to the Royal Academy. Yet in 1898 he became one of the founders of the Berlin Secession, that major break with the officially sanctioned academic art establishment.

Liebermann had already demonstrated his organizational talents: he spearheaded (unofficial) German participation in the 1889 Paris Exposition and co-founded the independent exhibition group called the Eleven, in 1892. He was elected first president of the Berlin Secession, which was founded in 1898 as an alternative to the conservative exhibition and patronage policies of the state's art associations. Throughout central Europe at this time, artists were forming secessions in order to organize their own exhibitions, establish their own galleries and publications, and nurture a more progressive art public. Conservatives condemned the Berlin Secession's cosmopolitan values and its exhibition of foreign artists as reflecting the subversion of German culture by alien influences, namely French-influenced Jewish artists and dealers. Liebermann remained president until 1911, by which time his resistance to including the younger generation of expressionists showed that he was no longer in the vanguard. In 1920 Liebermann reached the apogee of artistic public life, becoming president of the Prussian Academy of Arts.

Liebermann's late work focused on the garden of his country home on the Wannsee, a wealthy area of villas surrounding a lake on the outskirts of Berlin. In addition, he was much in demand for his sensitive and insightful portraits of the leading figures of German society. Self-portraits constitute a large part of Liebermann's oeuvre, as they do of Rembrandt's, and they range from the slightly comic and symbol-laden *Selbstbildnis mit Küchenstilleben* (1873; Self-portrait with kitchen still life) to the debonair and self-confident artist holding a cigarette and surrounded by paintings in his studio (1909–1910), to the late self-portrait with paint brushes revealing the anxieties of old age and the political realities of Nazi Berlin (1934).

On his eightieth birthday, in 1927, Liebermann's career was celebrated with an exhibition and he was made an honorary citizen of Berlin. By 1932 Nazi attacks prompted his resignation as president of the Academy of Arts. The Nazi ascent to power in 1933 inspired a classic example of Liebermann's legendary Berlin wit: "I could not possibly eat as much as I would like to throw up." Liebermann was ostracized from public life and his art banished from Nazi Germany's museums; only a few non-Jews had the courage to attend his burial on 11 February 1935. Liebermann's widow, Martha, committed suicide in March 1943 to avoid her imminent deportation to the Theresienstadt concentration camp.

See also **Anti-Semitism; Berlin; Impressionism; Jews and Judaism; Modernism; Painting; Realism and Naturalism.**

BIBLIOGRAPHY

Achenbach, Sigrid, and Matthias Eberle, eds. *Max Liebermann in seiner Zeit.* Munich and Berlin, 1979.

Bilski, Emily D. ed. *Berlin Metropolis: Jews and the New Culture 1890–1918.* Berkeley, Calif., and New York, 1999. Especially the essays by Bilski, Paret, and Schütz.

Eberle, Matthias. *Max Liebermann 1847–1935: Werkverzeichnis der Gemälde und Ölstudien.* 2 vols. Munich, 1995–1996.

Frenssen, Birte, and Jenns Eric Howoldt, eds. *Max Liebermann: Der Realist und die Phantasie.* Hamburg, 1997.

Gay, Peter. *Freud, Jews and Other Germans: Masters and Victims in Modernist Culture.* New York, 1978.

Janda, Karl Heinz, and Annegret Janda. "Max Liebermann als Kunstsammler." *Forschungen und Berichte der Staatlichen Museen zu Berlin,* 15 (1973): 105–148.

Natter, G. Tobias, and Julius H. Schoeps, eds. *Max Liebermann und die französischen Impressionisten.* Vienna, 1997.

Paret, Peter. *The Berlin Secession: Modernism and Its Enemies in Imperial Germany.* Cambridge, Mass., 1980.

Wesenberg, Angelika, ed. *Max Liebermann: Jahrhundertwende.* Berlin, 1997.

Emily D. Bilski

LIEBKNECHT, KARL (1871–1919),

German revolutionary.

Karl Liebknicht was the son of Wilhelm Liebknecht (1826–1900), cofounder of the political branch of the German socialist movement (the Sozialdemokratische Partei Deutschland [SPD]). Despite his father's frequent absence from the family because of political activities, the senior Liebknecht largely determined Karl's education, career, and eventually his politics. Karl became a lawyer, as did two of his four brothers, and concentrated his practice in defending the poor, especially members of the working class. He delayed taking an active role in politics until after he had attained his doctorate in law and qualified for the bar, fearing that socialist activities would prejudice his chances for success in the highly discriminatory Bismarckian Reich. However, in part because Wilhelm died in 1900 and in part because Karl followed his own particular inclinations in his political career, the son cannot be said to have lived and acted in the shadow of the father.

While he was not a leader of the prewar SPD, Liebknecht did serve for a number of years in the Prussian Landstag, representing a poor working-class constituency, and in 1912 he was elected to the German Reichstag. He was neither a major theoretician nor journalist, but rather concentrated his socialist activities in two major areas, antimilitarism and the youth movement, neither of which was a significant concern of the majority of the party. Liebknecht was primarily an activist, working the streets, picket lines, strikes, and other forms of protest, rather than a theoretician, journalist, or politician who talked or wrote about the issues important to particular elements of the working-class movement. In this capacity, he won little support from the party mainstream, but seems to have generated considerable sympathy and following among the underrepresented and often-ignored elements of the pre-1914 German working class. His legal activities in support of the underprivileged considerably reinforced his reputation as a defender of the underdog in Wilhelmian Germany.

Prior to the outbreak of World War I, Liebknecht was best known for his 1907 book *Militarism and Anti-Militarism,* the most systematic and thorough critique of Prussian and international militarism made by any German socialist up to the time. His analysis of the dual and contradictory roles of the military in modern society, as both a defender of the nation from foreign attack and instrument by which the dominant class maintains its control of other classes, especially the proletariat, doubtless rang true for many young German workers who faced the prospect of serving in the military. However, to contemporary historians this study seems to be filled with contradictions and confusions (for example, Liebknecht contended that the discipline and intelligence demanded by modern industry made proletarians the best soldiers and that the proletariat was most oppressed and perverted by militarism). Despite obvious evidence of strong Marxian influences (capitalism as the "last" stage of class society, proletariat as gravediggers of capitalism, etc.), it is highly doubtful that his positions were informed as much by a systematic understanding of Marx's critique of modern capitalism as they were by a deep humanism and commitment to democracy in its most fundamental form.

Militarism and Anti-Militarism earned Liebknecht a prison sentence for treason, but this only more firmly secured his place in the left wing of the SPD where his closest ally was the fiery Rosa Luxemburg (1870–1919), with whose name he was destined to be linked forever. Though he submitted to party discipline and voted in favor of the first war credits requested by the government in August 1914, by December he moved to a militant antiwar position that once again won him a conviction for treason. Gradually, Luxemburg and Liebknecht moved ever closer together in their critique of the response of the SPD mainstream to the war and then the Russian revolution. In the end, both were executed by the notorious *Freikorps* (private paramilitary) of Gustav Noske (1868–1946) and Friedrich Ebert (1871–1925), postwar leaders of the SPD, who sought to limit and secure the gains of the German revolution of 1918.

Of all the figures of pre-1914 German social democracy, Liebknecht's legacy is perhaps the most ambiguous. Long hailed by the German Democratic Republic as one of the founders of the German Communist Party, Liebknecht slipped into relative obscurity in the west. Although he lacked the theoretical substance of Luxemburg, he was doubtless earnest and sincere in his opposition to Prussian militarism. However, he never seems to have grasped the contradiction inherent in his own antimilitarist position and his espousal of the violent overthrow of the old order.

See also **Bebel, August; Kautsky, Karl; Labor Movements; Luxemburg, Rosa; Second International; Socialism.**

BIBLIOGRAPHY

Primary Sources

Liebknecht, Karl. *Militarism and Anti-Militarism: With Special Regard to the International Young Socialist Movement.* Translated by Alexander Sirnis. Glasgow, 1917. Reprint, New York and London, 1973.

Secondary Sources

Meyer, Karl W. *Karl Liebknecht, Man Without a Country.* Washington, D.C., 1957.

Trotnow, Helmut. *Karl Liebknecht (1871–1919): A Political Biography.* Hamden, Conn., 1984.

GARY P. STEENSON

LIST, GEORG FRIEDRICH (1789–1846), German economist, journalist, entrepreneur, diplomat.

Friedrich List's life was as turbulent as the times in which he lived. Born in the first year of the French Revolution, he died just two years before the German revolution of 1848. He championed technological innovations such as railroads and telegraphs, provided a voice for the emerging middle class of bankers and industrialists, and tried his hand at academia, journalism, industry, and commerce. Known mostly as "the other notable economist," that is, "other" than Adam Smith (1723–1790) and Karl Marx (1818–1883), List took his own life—out of a sense of physical exhaustion and intellectual and professional rejection.

List began a career as professor of political economy at Tübingen University in 1817, but he left within two years to begin a life as journalist at Frankfurt. He at once made a name for himself by petitioning the German Confederation to abolish all internal tariffs and to protect the nascent German industry with tariffs against the British mass-produced goods then flooding central Europe. He was elected to the Württemberg Diet in 1819, but ran afoul of the Stuttgart government when he published a brochure calling for local self-government and open judicial procedures. He was evicted from the legislature and stripped of his citizenship. After a brief period of exile in France and Switzerland, List returned to Stuttgart and was promptly arrested and sentenced to ten months incarceration. When he promised to migrate to the United States, his sentence was reduced.

List spent several happy years in the more open and dynamic American society. He purchased a farm in Harrisburg, Pennsylvania, then an anthracite coal mine in nearby Tamaqua, and in 1829 an interest in the Little Schuylkill Navigation Railroad. In a pamphlet entitled *Outlines of American Political Economy,* List in 1827 appealed to Thomas Jefferson (1743–1826) and James Madison (1751–1836) to establish tariffs to fend off British exports. Made a citizen in 1830, two years later List supported Andrew Jackson's (1767–1845) election campaign and was reward by being appointed U.S. consul in Baden (1831–1834), Saxony (1834–1837), and Württemberg (1843–1845).

Having returned to Germany in 1834, List turned his prodigious energy and talent to lobbying for railroad construction. He was delighted when Prussia later that year—without his direct influence, as is often claimed—founded the Zollverein, a customs union of some thirty German states save Austria. For List, railroads and free trade were "symbiotic twins," ones that would eventually lead to national unification. After a three-year sojourn in Paris, he returned to Germany in 1840, where under the patronage of King Louis I of Bavaria (r. 1825–1848) he penned his major treatise, *The National System of Political Economy.* Six years later, List visited the home of Adam Smith and wrote a political pamphlet entitled *Concerning the Importance and Conditions of an Alliance between Germany and England.* It was firmly rejected by the Victorian elite.

List's influence rests on three pillars: first, as the leading advocate of railroad building; second, as an unflagging champion of a customs union; and third, as the author of the first German treatise on national economy. He renounced English free-trade theory as being too doctrinaire, too divorced from time and place. Above all, it ill suited an "underdeveloped" economy such as the German, which instead needed "educational" tariffs to protect infant industries and to allow the economy to rise (in a five-stage process) to a more "developed" level, such as that of Britain. Like Marx, List recognized the close link between economic theory and political factors; unlike Marx, he refused to reduce political economy to theoretical mathematical constructions. For List, the nation and/or state was the critical link between the individual and mankind. He cared less for the accumulation of wealth in and of itself, and more for the forces that lay behind that accumulation—public administration, communication and transportation, education, entrepreneurship, law and order, scientific discovery, self-government, and technology. He firmly anchored his theory in historical and cultural contexts.

Sometime after 1841, List, much like Alexis de Tocqueville (1805–1859) that same year, began to turn to geopolitics—well before the term had been invented. He foresaw the eventual division of the world into a few mighty empires in general, and of the rise to great-power status of the United States and Russia in particular. Thus, he called not only for an Anglo-German alliance to counterbalance the perceived American-Russian "threat," but also for a "central European" economic bloc (*Mitteleuropa*) anchored on the vast contiguous land mass that swept southeast across the Continent from Denmark down to the Danubian basin. The revival of such a notion of dominance over *Mitteleuropa* in German Chancellor Theobald von Bethmann Hollweg's (1856–1921) infamous 1914 "September program" of war aims unfairly brought List much negative publicity more than six decades after his death.

See also **Liberalism; Protectionism; Trade and Economic Growth.**

BIBLIOGRAPHY

Henderson, William Otto. *Friedrich List: Economist and Visionary, 1789–1846.* London, 1983. The best survey of List and his political economic views by the author of the standard history of the German *Zollverein.*

Roussakis, Emmanuel N. *Friedrich List: The Zollverein and the Uniting of Europe.* Bruges, 1968. A terse analysis of List, the customs union and unification—highly laudatory of the economist's role therein.

Szporluk, Roman. *Communism and Nationalism: Karl Marx versus Friedrich List.* New York, 1988.

Holger H. Herwig

LISTER, JOSEPH (1827–1912), English surgeon and scientist.

Joseph Lister was born on 5 April 1827 in the village of Upton, Essex. His father, a Quaker and fellow of the Royal Society, encouraged Lister's early interest in microscopy. In 1844 he attended University College, London. Although he joined the college's arts faculty, Lister maintained his scientific interests and, after a break to recuperate from a bout of smallpox, he entered University College Medical School in 1847. The school was unique among English medical schools in its emphasis on experimental science as the basis of good medical practice. This view informed much of Lister's subsequent career.

Lister graduated in 1851 and took a post as junior surgeon in the Royal Infirmary, Edinburgh. He continued his research under the patronage of James Syme, professor of clinical surgery, and in 1860 married Syme's daughter Agnes. In the same year Lister moved to Glasgow to take up the chair of surgery. Here he began to consider the complex problem of surgical sepsis.

At this time patients undergoing hospital surgery suffered high death rates: estimates range from 10 to 45 percent. Postoperative wound infection—the "hospital diseases" such as gangrene and erysipelas—caused most of these deaths. Many of the leading figures in the Victorian public health reform movement—such as Edwin Chadwick, author of the influential *Report on the Sanitary Condition of the Labouring Population* (1842)—blamed high mortality rates on the size and location of the hospitals themselves. Their solution was to break up the large city hospitals and replace them with smaller rural institutions. The challenge facing Lister and his colleagues was not merely to solve the problem of surgical sepsis, but to do it in a way that could vindicate both experimental medicine and hospital surgery.

Lister took as his inspirations the germ theory of disease developed by Louis Pasteur (1822–1895) and the prevailing notion that inflammation and suppuration were a necessary part of wound healing. He sought a technique that would allow the body to heal naturally through the production of "laudable pus," while keeping out airborne contaminants that he thought would lead to critical infection. In a short paper in the *Lancet* in March 1867 Lister advocated the use of carbolic acid, applied to wound dressings, as a means of preventing sepsis and described eleven cases of compound fracture that he had treated successfully with this method.

The medical profession's response to Lister's "antiseptic" method was mixed. Some older surgeons opposed the encroachment of science on the "craft" of surgery, and others argued that carbolic was unnecessary. However, his technique was widely discussed and, by 1870, widely used. Lister continually modified his method: in 1870 he introduced a steam-powered carbolic spray for use during operations. His other innovations included a lighter, more flexible gauze dressing, rubber tubes that could be inserted into wounds to drain away pus, and (perhaps his most enduring innovation) the dissolvable suture.

Lister's return to London in 1877 as professor of surgery at King's College provided an opportunity to change the theoretical basis of antisepsis, as Pasteur's germ theory was replaced by that of the German bacteriologist Robert Koch (1843–1910). After Koch showed that skin-borne rather than airborne pathogens were the major cause of infection, Lister's carbolic spray (unpopular also because it drenched surgeons in warm acid) became obsolete. Also discarded was the idea of "laudable pus": Koch had shown that all suppuration represented infection. From the early 1880s German surgeons had begun to combine Koch's and Lister's observations, using soap to clean their hands and high-pressure steam to sterilize instruments and garments. This "aseptic" method was taken up in Britain, where by 1900 it had replaced "Listerism" as the preferred method of preventing sepsis. Lister retired from King's College in 1893 and moved to Walmer, Kent, where he died on 10 February 1912. He had no children.

Lister's impact on surgical practice must be separated from public perceptions of his work. Even in his lifetime Lister was hailed as the "father of modern surgery": in 1883 he received a baronetcy and in 1897 a peerage (the first British clinician to be so honored). His early biographers credited him with both the antiseptic and the aseptic methods, and also with significant contributions to modern germ theory. Twenty-first-century historians—notably Christopher Lawrence—have challenged this view and sought to contextualize Lister's work in Victor-

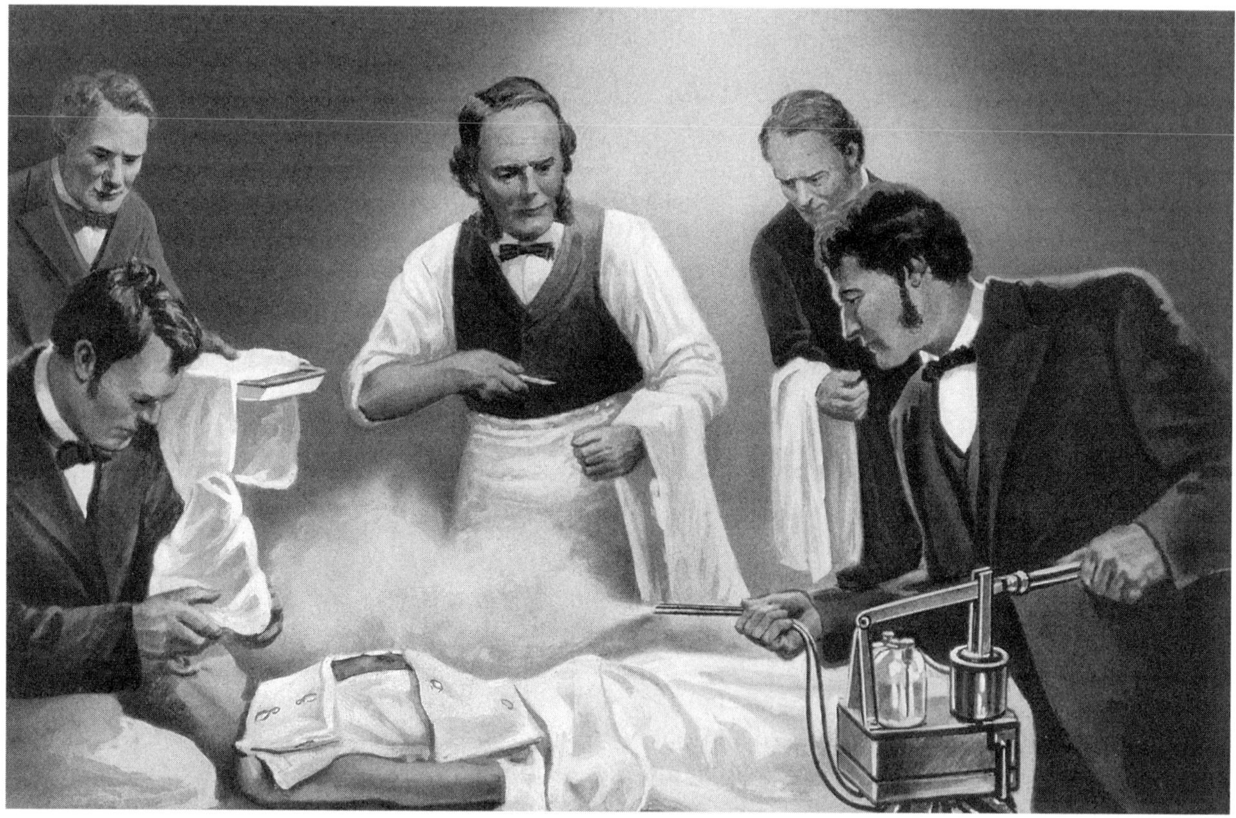

Joseph Lister (center) experiments with the use of carbolic acid spray. Nineteenth-century illustration. © BETTMANN/CORBIS

ian culture. Lister exemplified the Victorian "Great Man": a faithful husband, committed to working for the public good, he was revered by politicians and journalists. By helping to change the public image of surgery from a bloody craft to a clinical science, Lister greatly improved the standing of the surgical profession within society. This earned Lister the respect and support of his colleagues, whatever their views on the validity of his theories or his actual contribution to their practice.

See also **Public Health; Science and Technology.**

BIBLIOGRAPHY

Primary Source

Lister, Joseph. "On a New Method of Treating Compound Fractures, Abscesses, etc., with Observations on the Condition of Suppuration." *Lancet* 89 (1867): 326–329.

Secondary Sources

Gaw, Jerry L. *"A Time to Heal": The Diffusion of Listerism in Victorian Britain.* Philadelphia, 1999. Penetrating analysis of the sociopolitical context of Lister's work.

Granshaw, Lindsay. "'Upon This Principle I Have Based a Practice': The Development and Reception of Antisepsis in Britain, 1867–90." In *Medical Innovations in Historical Perspective*, edited by John Pickstone, 17–46. London, 1992. Excellent summary of current scholarship on Lister and Listerism.

Lawrence, Christopher, and Richard Dixey. "Practising on Principle: Joseph Lister and the Germ Theories of Disease." In *Medical Theory, Surgical Practice: Studies in the History of Surgery*, edited by Christopher Lawrence, 153–215. London, 1992. Superb deconstruction of the "Lister Myth."

RICHARD BARNETT

LISZT, FRANZ

LISZT, FRANZ (1811–1886), virtuoso pianist, composer, conductor, and musical producer.

Franz Liszt created an image that still endures in musical performance in Western culture. He was the first to place a grand piano lengthwise, alone, on the stage for a piano concert, and invented the form of the piano recital, which young musicians still contend with today. Liszt emulated Niccoló Paganini (1782–1840), the Italian violinist whose virtuosity was so prodigious that he was reputed to be possessed by the devil. But what, in Paganini's case, was a deviation—the solo performer defying the laws of nature in his ability to perform—became a hallmark of modernity, a perfected business, in the case of Liszt. He was one of the first musicians to tour internationally on a regular basis, and was received with an excessive enthusiasm that foreshadowed the orgiastic reactions to 1960s rock bands. What Heinrich Heine (1797–1856) called "Lisztomania" was a new and distinctly Romantic phenomenon, and Liszt was felt to be a true representative of his time. He lived a flamboyant life and had many liaisons, but never married. Opinion was split about Liszt: Was he truly a brilliant performer, or a mere showman with astonishing but empty technical abilities? Was he inspired, or did he know how to manipulate his audience through advertising, charisma, and vain effects?

Liszt was born in 1811 in Raiding, Hungary, to bourgeois parents. His life spanned the nineteenth century; he died in Bayreuth in 1886. At eight, he went to Vienna and studied with Carl Czerny. Liszt's life is enveloped in fictions. Some accounts claim, for example, that at his farewell concert in Vienna at the age of eleven, Liszt received a "kiss of benediction" from Ludwig van Beethoven himself, though evidence shows that Beethoven was not even present. In 1823 Liszt moved to Paris, where he was refused entry to the Conservatory, since foreigners were not allowed to study there. This contributed to Liszt's status as an outsider, a cause of resentment throughout his career. Determined to gain fame and glory to make up for his marginal social status—both foreigner and bourgeois—he devoted himself to performances of the musical canon and of his own compositions and adaptations of others' compositions, Paganini's, for example. Despite his prodigious popularity, many criticized Liszt's performances as mere display of technical ability. He was ridiculed, too, for his social climbing. He was awarded, for example, a bejeweled "Sword of Honor" by a group of Hungarian noblemen when he performed there in 1840. Satirists often pictured Liszt with this saber riding on his piano to the strains of his own "Grand Galop Chromatique." Liszt was a constant defender of Romantic music and moved in circles with artists and writers including Frédéric Chopin (1810–1849), Hector Berlioz (1803–1869), George Sand (Amandine Dudevant; 1804–1876), Alphonse-Marie-Louis Lamartine (1790–1869), and Eugène Delacroix (1798–1863).

Liszt retired from performance at the age of thirty-five in 1847, thus ending the period of his life most vivid in cultural memory. Taking a position as *Kapellmeister* at Weimar, Liszt devoted his efforts to composition. During this time, Liszt composed new versions of his famous piano composition: the six *Etudes d'Après Paganini,* and the twelve *Grands Ètudes d'Execution Transcendantes,* which Charles Rosen considers a masterpiece of keyboard composition. Liszt's originality as a piano composer lies in his interest in color and the musical importance of performance techniques. The technique of thematic transformation offered variations of style rather than thematic development. This technique is highlighted in the Sonata in B Minor (1852), often thought to be Liszt's greatest work. Even in composition, Liszt never lost sight of the constitutive role of musical realization. Liszt also invented the symphonic poem, of which he composed twelve during his years at Weimar, as well as the Faust and Dante symphonies. The symphonic poem is a one-movement composition that draws its inspiration from a source in literature or painting. Liszt based his symphonic poems on readings of Victor Hugo (1802–1885) and Lamartine, for example.

As *Kappellmeister* in Weimar, Liszt strongly promoted the "new music" of others, in particular of Richard Wagner (who married Liszt's daughter Cosima). Liszt produced *The Flying Dutchman* and *Tannhäuser* with great success. He wrote important introductory texts to Wagner's operas, which served as program notes in Germany and France. Liszt continued his role as musical disseminator that had begun so spectacularly on the virtuoso stage.

Liszt had a long career as a writer, which is also shrouded in controversy, especially since there are no remaining manuscripts in his own hand. As an adult, Liszt no longer spoke Hungarian and had no real first language, though he did speak French and

German. Perhaps because of his problematic relationship to language, his writing is usually read through his two major relationships: Countess Marie d'Agoult (Cosima Wagner's mother) and Princess Carolyne von Sayn-Wittgenstein. Both women are believed to have been ghost writers of Liszt texts. Among Liszt's writings are a biography of Chopin, the program notes for Wagner's operas, and a strange book. In this book, Liszt tries to find the origin of virtuosity in Magyar folk culture, as well as justify his own "Hungarian Rhapsodies," first conceived during a trip to Hungary. Although his methodology would not satisfy any scientific standards today, Liszt deserves credit for his pioneering efforts to connect popular ethnic music and high art music. The book is also the context for Liszt's late identification with Hungary. Though he had virtually no relationship to Hungary and was most strongly influenced by the French and German musical traditions, he always claimed to be Hungarian. This confusion about origin and identity is typical of the growing problems surrounding nationality in the nineteenth century.

In 1861 Liszt moved to Rome, where he took lay orders and stayed until 1868. He then traveled between Rome, Weimar, and Hungary, continuing to teach and compose until his death. At home everywhere and nowhere, a speaker of many tongues but no mother tongue, Liszt—brilliant virtuoso and manipulative showman, composer, and author—was truly a virtuoso of the nineteenth century.

See also **Chopin, Frédéric; Music; Paganini, Niccoló; Wagner, Richard.**

BIBLIOGRAPHY

Bernstein, Susan. *Virtuosity of the Nineteenth Century: Performing Music and Language in Heine, Liszt, and Baudelaire.* Stanford, Calif., 1998.

Rosen, Charles. *The Romantic Tradition.* Cambridge, Mass., 1995.

Walker, Alan. *Franz Liszt.* 3 vols. Ithaca, N.Y., 1983–1996.

Watson, Derek. *Liszt.* New York, 1989.

SUSAN BERNSTEIN

LITERACY. Reading and writing were widely taught in western Europe before the French Revolution. Demand from parents and teachers for learning aids sustained a large and diverse market for alphabets and primers. Publishers produced a range of simple texts upon which the inexperienced readers could practice their skills. Folk tales and devotional texts were carried by chapmen and colporteurs (book peddlers) through the countryside and sold for little more than the cost of a loaf of bread. If a peasant or a laborer could not read, he would know someone who did. If he owned no print himself, he would have some sense of its power, and would know some way of gaining access to it, if only as a listener at first or second hand. In the more developed northern and western countries, there were by the eighteenth century few communities entirely cut off from the written word and the skills of decoding it. The gentry, bourgeoisie, and urban artisans already had a tradition of universal literacy, at least among men, and even the laboring poor possessed in their midst a scattering of educated or self-educated readers. Only on the eastern and southern fringes of Europe were there to be found men in possession of property but deprived of the ability to compile and use the documents upon which their power was increasingly dependent.

Literacy was an invention of the nineteenth century more as a concept than a practice. The skills of reading and writing were separated from the broader spiritual and practical elements of education, and subjected to quantification. Historians have found ways of counting literacy in the early modern and medieval eras, but except in the Swedish church registers from the seventeenth century, this knowledge was denied to contemporaries. Literacy as it is now understood was a product of the rise of the modern state. The French Revolution produced little lasting educational reform either in France or in the countries influenced by its ideas. It did, however, give birth to the ideal of a universally schooled society, sustained and policed by governments and their bureaucracies. The emphasis given to the official curriculum was at the expense of the agencies that had borne the burden of instruction in previous centuries: the church, the educational marketplace, and the family. Even in the more developed countries it took most of the nineteenth century for the state to achieve effective control over elementary education. In this struggle, counting literacy became a key weapon. The case

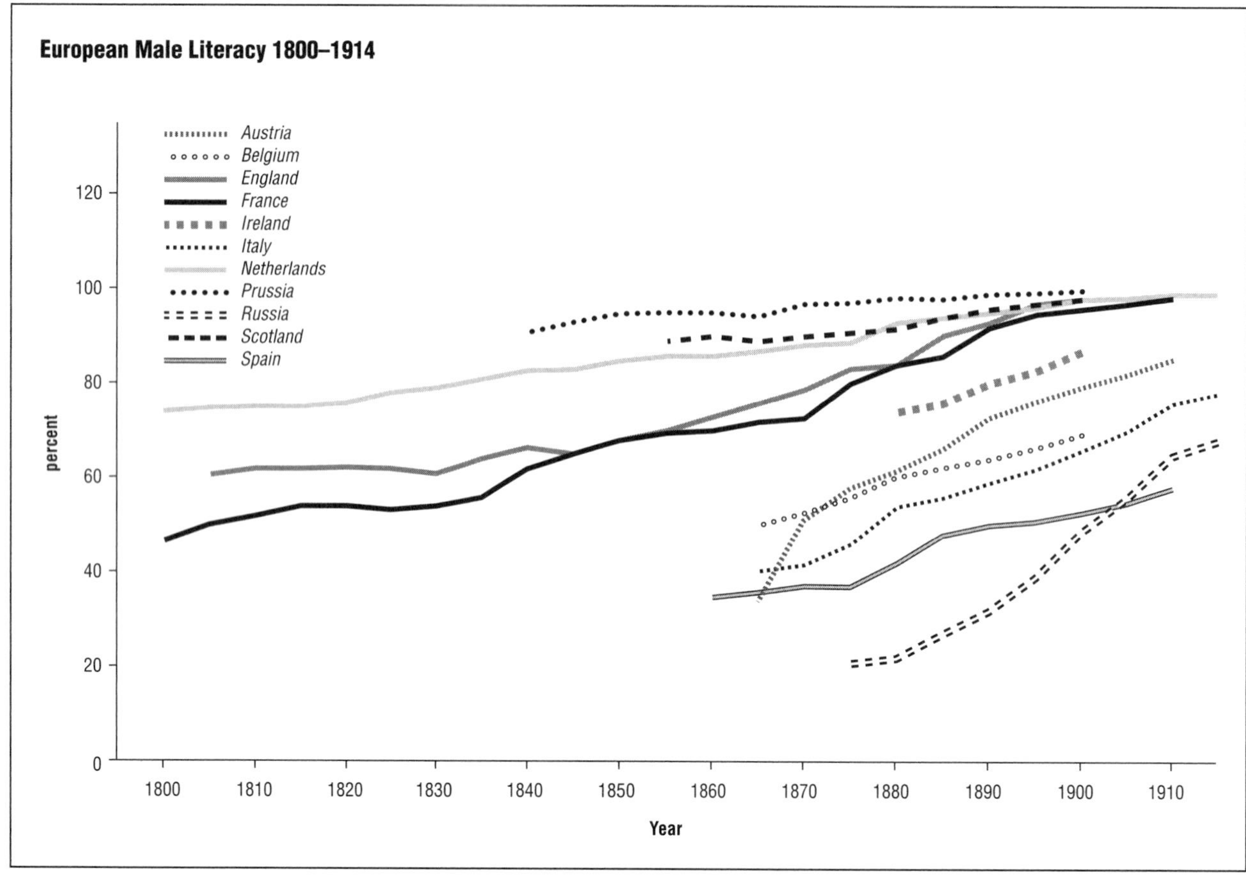

for government intervention was displayed by literacy tables that demonstrated the scale of the task. Even the sprawling, barely governed Russian Empire knew where it stood in the European league table, although it was incapable of doing much about it. The criticism of the rival church structures, and still more of the long-standing informal systems of instruction, focused on their inability to count the effect of their labors. Literacy tables stood at the center of the transaction between the emergent state and taxpaying electors. The product of public expenditure could be measured in columns of marriage register signatures and marks or in the census returns. Literacy was a performance indicator. It simplified the meaning of education, but also for the first time enabled contemporaries and subsequent historians to measure change over time within and between countries.

The first attempts at counting literacy demonstrated that in terms of the capacity to sign a name, northern and western Europe began from a base of 50 percent or more for men, and embarked on a fairly even course of improvement during the nineteenth century, arriving at virtually universal nominal literacy in the years immediately before World War I. To the east and the south the first attempts at counting literacy rates were made around the middle of the nineteenth century. They demonstrated a much greater challenge and often initiated a steeper rate of improvement. As Figure 1 indicates, relative literacy levels remained much the same across Europe, but the gaps between the top and bottom countries narrowed as the decades passed. By 1914 even the more backward countries had universal literacy in sight, although in Spain, Italy, and even more so Russia and the Balkans, it would take a generation or more before some kind of victory could be claimed.

At one level, the statistics reveal a process of European cultural homogenization. In this key area of communication, countries were increasingly coming to resemble each other as the twentieth century commenced. All appeared to be embarked on the same journey, passing through the same stations, heading for the same destination. Behind the statistics were national school systems whose

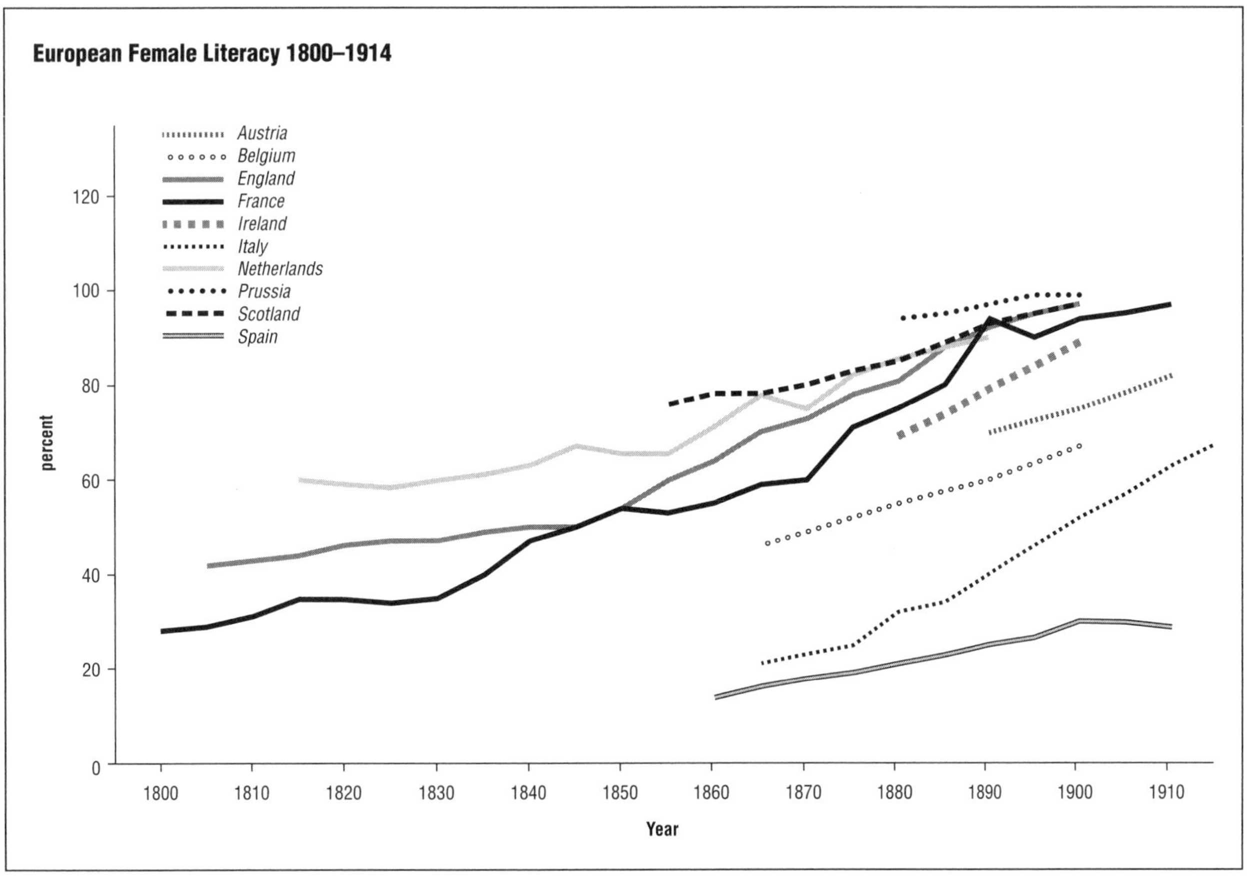

differences were less important than their similarities. Educational reformers visited other countries, bringing back an enthusiasm for trained teachers, inspected classrooms, and systematic curricula. In most countries, conflicts with the families of pupils and with the churches led to compromises on the state's terms. Adjustments were made to the ambitions of parents and the power of religious institutions in return for an acceptance of a centrally subsidized and policed drive to mass literacy.

Figure 2 suggests that the growing homogeneity embraced gender as well as national origin. Women were everywhere behind men in the early returns, by around ten points in the more advanced countries and often much more where any kind of literacy was still uncommon. But unlike higher education, which remained almost exclusively a male preserve in this period, there was a growing equality of opportunity in elementary education. The same profile of descent from nominal illiteracy is present in both sets of figures. In many countries the rate of progress for women was often more rapid than that of men and in some cases, as in parts of midcentury England, brides were on average more literate than grooms. In informal educational systems, scarce cultural resources tended to be allocated first to boys, but when governments embraced the goal of universal schooling they tended to commit themselves to equal if frequently separate provisions for the sexes. Pressures within family economies undermined the attendance of girls, and the widespread absence of opportunities beyond elementary schooling profoundly affected the meaning of the lessons in the inspected classroom. But if a wide view is taken of the distribution of privilege, power, and status between men and women over their lifetimes, the provision of basic literacy stands out in this era as an area of relative equality.

In other respects, the sense that the growth of mass literacy was collapsing the differences in European societies is profoundly misleading. At any point in this period of change, the lineaments of entrenched inequalities are still visible. For instance, the Geneva–Saint-Malo line that divided the better-educated north and east of France from the south and west remained apparent throughout the nineteenth century. Towns had always been and remained centers not only of education but also of access to the benefits that education created. The surrounding countryside was less literate, and tended to take its lead from the towns as to when and at what rate it improved. While the traditional gulf between the nominal attainments of artisans and laborers was closing, occupation remained the most powerful predictor of literacy throughout the period. A more significant gulf was that of age. A period of fundamental change in the possession and use of communication skills separated the generations. Gaps of twenty points or more are visible between children and parents in countries such as England, where population growth was steady over a given period, and by twice as much where there was a sudden population expansion, as in late-nineteenth-century Belgium. The pre-1914 victory over illiteracy in northwest Europe applied only to the young. Their less-educated parents and grandparents were still present in large numbers in the postwar societies. It was a difference not only of attainment but also of authority. With print, as later with computers, the instructed became the instructors. Those born too late to learn found themselves dependent upon their children for such access as they could gain to the benefits of the new mode of communication.

The greatest variation of all was in the range of skills measured by the single test of signing a marriage register or completing a census form. Comparative analysis of different modes of recording literacy suggests that the tests were a fairly consistent measure of a basic capacity to make a few words with a pen, which for the majority of the laboring poor corresponded to all the use they would be likely to make of writing. They underestimated to varying degrees the distribution of the ability to read. In Sweden, for instance, which before the nineteenth century taught reading efficiently and largely ignored writing, the early statistics said nothing at all about access to print. In many countries, such as France, classroom reading lessons started a couple of years before writing, and pupils had often left for the fields before they attempted to form letters. Even in England, where the official curriculum taught the skills alongside each other, reading ability may have been 50 percent higher than writing at the beginning of the period.

The neat tables of attainment floated on a sea of improvisation. This was true of the basic question of capacity. The statistics counted individuals, but the ceremonies and households from which they were derived lay at the heart of the social lives of the laboring poor. As with all other material and culture possessions, the dispossessed begged, borrowed, and shared the skills and artifacts they needed. The more literate read to the less literate, the fully literate wrote and deciphered letters for their neighbors. Books were loaned or sold on through a flourishing secondhand market. This meant that until the arrival of cheap reprints at the end of the nineteenth century, poor readers lived their intellectual lives several decades behind those of their wealthier counterparts. The key forms in the transition from the possession to the use of literacy in this period were the mass circulation newspaper and the picture postcard. The former meant that for the first time the poor could purchase and privately consume up-to-date print. The latter meant that for the first time the barely literate began to use writing with some regularity. Both innovations had their origins in the middle decades of the nineteenth century, when steam power was applied to the printing presses and facilitated the flat-rate postal systems. But they only began to engage with the newly educated on a large scale around the turn of the nineteenth and twentieth centuries.

This culture of appropriation challenges the association of literacy and progress that the decreasing rates of illiteracy shown in the figures helped to reinforce. Historians have now dispensed with much of the conceptual framework that informed the compilation and interpretation of those statistics. The contrast between a backward oral and an advanced literate culture has been undermined partly by a closer examination of the statistics, which reveals how rare wholly illiterate communities were in most of late-eighteenth-century Europe, partly by a recognition of how literacy skills were shared, and partly by a critical examination of the association of literacy with rationality and illiteracy with superstition. Ironically, mass education facilitated the expansion of many emblematic irrational vices, such as gambling and the consumption of unlicensed medicine. At the same time, the sharp division between elite and popular or mass cultures fades as attention is paid to the complexities of how access was gained to and meaning derived from the printed word.

The European governments that set about creating mass education systems took a gamble that a combination of disciplined schooling, capitalist cultural production, and variable levels of censorship would eventually produce voters who would accept the rules of orderly political debate. There was no guarantee of success, but the extremities of political stability and crisis in this period cannot of themselves be explained by the growth or distribution of literacy. Just two generalizations survive. The first is that the greatest use made of the skills taught by the nineteenth-century schools was in the consumption of fiction. Whatever else, mass literacy expanded the realm of popular relaxation. The second is that material deprivation was the single most potent force in shaping the potential of the written word to transform the lives of the newly educated. Not until the rise of credentialed and bureaucratized employment after 1914 did the potential for schooling to challenge inherited inequalities begin to become evident.

See also **Education; Libraries; Popular and Elite Culture.**

BIBLIOGRAPHY

Brooks, Jeffrey. *When Russia Learned to Read: Literacy and Popular Literature, 1861–1917.* Princeton, N.J., 1985. The standard account of change in Russia.

Chartier, Roger. "Culture as Appropriation: Popular Cultural Uses in Early Modern France." In *Understanding Popular Culture: Europe from the Middle Ages to the Nineteenth Century,* edited by Steven L. Kaplan, 229–253. Berlin, 1984. Important conceptual discussion.

Cipolla, Carlo M. *Literacy and Development in the West.* Harmondsworth, U.K., 1969. The first major European study, still influential.

Furet, François, and Jacques Ozouf. *Reading and Writing: Literacy in France from Calvin to Jules Ferry.* Cambridge, U.K., 1982. The standard work on France.

Graff, Harvey J. *The Literacy Myth.* London, 1979. Influential iconoclastic study.

———. *The Legacies of Literacy.* Bloomington, Ind., 1987. Detailed and thorough survey of Europe and the United States.

James, Louis. *Print and the People 1819–1851.* Harmondsworth, U.K., 1978. Sparkling anthology of the materials produced for new readers in England.

Johansson, Egil. "The History of Literacy in Sweden." In *Literacy and Social Development in the West,* edited by Harvey J. Graff, 151–182. Cambridge, U.K., 1981. The standard study of Sweden.

Maynes, Mary Jo. *Schooling in Western Europe.* Albany, N.Y., 1985. Best short survey.

Schofield, Roger. "Dimensions of Illiteracy in England 1750–1850." In *Literacy and Social Development in the West,* edited by Harvey J. Graff, 201–213. Cambridge, U.K., 1981. The standard statistical analysis of English literacy.

Vincent, David. *Literacy and Popular Culture: England 1750–1914.* Cambridge, U.K., 1989. In-depth study of the British case.

———. *The Rise of Mass Literacy.* Cambridge, U.K., 2000. Survey of modern European development.

David Vincent

LITHUANIA. In the course of the nineteenth century, the general understanding of the name *Lithuania* underwent significant transformation as the twin doctrines of national self-determination and popular sovereignty spread throughout Europe. Before the partitions of the Polish-Lithuanian Commonwealth, the Grand Duchy of Lithuania had been a large multinational political entity. In the nineteenth century, "Lithuania" had no clear administrative identity, and the Russian government did not recognize the name *Litva* (Lithuania). In the twentieth century an independent Lithuanian state emerged, significantly smaller than the grand duchy had been, but with a clear eponymous ethnic majority. This evolution left behind the material for considerable controversy as to Lithuania's proper geographic boundaries.

After the Congress of Vienna (1814–1815), the territory on the southeastern shore of the Baltic Sea that now makes up Lithuania lay divided under three administrations. The bulk of it became part of the Northwest Region of the Russian Empire, a region that the tsarist government insisted was historically Russian. The southwestern part of the territory was included in the Congress Kingdom of Poland, also ruled by Tsar Alexander I of Russia. The western part, including the port then known as Memel but now called Klaipėda, had been a part of East Prussia since the fifteenth century.

NATIONAL DIVERSITY

The administrative center of the Northwest Region and the cultural center of the region was the city of Vilnius (in Polish, Wilno; in Russian and Yiddish, Vilna), which historically had a mixed population. Although it became an important railroad hub, it did not share in the industrialization of the Russian Empire. It stood close to the border between the Russian and German empires, and therefore tsarist authorities deliberately limited its economic growth. Estimates of the ethnic makeup of the city have varied widely. According to the Russian census of 1897, Jews constituted a plurality of the population (40 percent); a German census in 1916 reported a Polish majority (50.1 percent). For Lithuanians, the city was their historic capital; for Jews it was the "Jerusalem of the North"; for Poles it was a regional center of Polish culture. Eventually Belarusans also raised claim to the city. As thoughts of national self-determination developed at the end of the nineteenth century, the city inevitably became an apple of discord.

At the beginning of the nineteenth century, Polish culture dominated among the nobility of the region, the cities, and the Roman Catholic hierarchy. If somehow called upon to explain their identity, upper-class inhabitants of the region would probably have called themselves "Lithuanians who speak Polish." The population offered strong support to the Polish risings of 1830–1831 and 1863 against Russian rule. After 1863 the Russian administration in the Northwest Region devoted considerable effort to encouraging and pushing Lithuanians to reject traditional Polish influences. Nevertheless Poles remained, to the eve of World War I, a significant political, economic, and cultural force in Lithuanian affairs.

Standing rather apart from the power struggles between Russian administrators and Polish nobility and church hierarchs was the Jewish population of the region, concentrated mostly in cities and villages. Jews had been migrating to this region since the thirteenth century, and Vilna had become a focal point for a distinctive "Litvak" culture, with its own traditions and speaking Yiddish. In the nineteenth century, this region constituted the northern part of the Pale of Settlement, the area to which the Russian government sought to restrict the Jewish population; Jews needed special permission to live in Russian cities outside the Pale. In the middle of the century, many Jews attempted to assimilate into Russian culture, but by the end of the century, stimulated by the growth of the government's anti-Jewish policies, new political-cultural trends were developing, in particular a Jewish working-class movement and Zionism, the idea of creating a new Jewish homeland in the Middle East.

Over the previous centuries ethnic Lithuanian culture had survived basically among the peasantry, most of whom worked as serfs until their emancipation in 1861. A modern national consciousness developed among some lesser nobles in the first half of the century, but a mass movement could take root only after the emancipation. In the aftermath of the rising of 1863, the Russian government encouraged Lithuanian peasants by granting them relatively favorable terms in acquiring land and also by awarding places to the children in schools previously open only to Poles.

At the same time, in an effort to draw the Lithuanians away from Polish influences, in 1864 the authorities banned the publication of Lithuanian texts in Latin characters, demanding instead the use of Cyrillic characters. When the Lithuanians resisted, this amounted to a ban on the publication of Lithuanian books and newspapers. The Russian government lifted the ban only in 1904, after it had become clear that smugglers, enshrined in Lithuanian memory as "book carriers," had undermined whatever hopes the tsarist authorities had placed in the measure. The language and the Roman Catholic religion became fundamental pillars of the growing Lithuanian national consciousness.

The life of Jonas Basanavičius (1851–1927), hailed as the "Patriarch of the Lithuanian National Renaissance," illustrated the development of Lithuanian national consciousness and at the same time typified the consequences of tsarist policies. As a student, Basanavičius attended a school previously closed to Lithuanians; he studied medicine at Moscow University on a special scholarship for Lithuanians; he then served the Russian government by working as a doctor in the new state of Bulgaria. In 1883 he published the first Lithuanian national newspaper, *Aušra* (The dawn), which was printed in East Prussia (then part of the German Empire) and then smuggled into Lithuania.

Vilnius, Lithuania, and the Neris River. Photograph by Sergei Prokudin-Gorsky, 1912. The Library of Congress

As Basanavičius's service in Bulgaria showed, the Lithuanian intelligentsia that emerged after the emancipation of the peasants had only limited possibilities for working within their native region. A typical peasant household might well plan that the first son would inherit the land and the second son should become a priest. The priest could work in Lithuania, and having no children, in turn could contribute to the education of nephews and nieces. In order to remain in Lithuania, however, the nephews and nieces might have to plan to be free-practicing doctors or lawyers. Even artists might not find an audience and therefore have to seek it elsewhere, as did the composer-painter M. K. Čiurlionis (1875–1911), who went to St. Petersburg to make his career.

SOCIAL AND POLITICAL DEVELOPMENT

The cities and towns of Lithuania had no significant industry to draw the young people wanting to leave the land. Tsarist policies limited the region's industrial development, and therefore to find work migrants had to travel to other cities in the empire or even go abroad. After 1880, the expanding industrial society in the United States attracted a growing number of immigrants from Lithuania, including Jews. About one-fifth of the Lithuanians who traveled to the United States eventually returned to the homeland, whereas the Jewish migrants, who tended to come to the United States as families, had no intention of returning. The Lithuanian immigrants in the United States contributed extensively to the flow of illegal literature into the homeland, but the new intelligentsia there expressed great fears that the nation was losing its dynamic young power.

By the beginning of the twentieth century, a kaleidoscope of political parties and groupings existed in the region. Lithuanians participated actively in the Russian Duma, even forming a voting coalition with Jews in the Kovno (Kaunas) *gubernija* (administrative unit) to assure the election of Lithuanian and Jewish deputies. The Lithuanians favored social and economic reform and tended to split as much over attitudes toward the role of priests in society as over any other question. Lithuanian Poles split along the same lines as their fellow nationals in the Kingdom of Poland, while Lithuanian Jews tended to split between conservatives, emphasizing religious considerations and the use of Hebrew, and socialists, who favored a more secular life and the use of Yiddish.

When war came in 1914, very few anticipated that in the next four years all three empires that had participated in the partitions of the Polish-Lithuanian Commonwealth would collapse, and that an independent Lithuanian state would rise. Poles, seeking their own independence, believed that Lithuania should be a part of their new creation. Some Lithuanians at first considered the possibility of recreating a multinational state along the lines of the pre-partition grand duchy, but eventually, while still under German occupation, a distinctively Lithuanian national administration began to take form.

The exact boundaries of the Lithuanian national state became a matter of controversy. There had been no clear political-social-economic-cultural unit identified as Lithuania in the nineteenth century, and therefore, in the restructuring of eastern Europe after the war, Lithuania found itself in a bitter clash with Poland, particularly over the city of Vilnius and its environs. Lithuanians claimed to have the support of the Jewish population in the city, but the Poles had the superior military force and seized the city. The controversy became a major factor in the political instability in eastern Europe throughout the period between the world wars.

See also **Finland and the Baltic Provinces; Nationalism; Poland; Russia; Ukraine.**

BIBLIOGRAPHY

Aleksandravičius, Egidijus, and Antanas Kulakauskas. *Carų valdžioje: XIX amžiaus Lietuva.* Vilnius, Lithuania, 1996. A major study by two Lithuanian historians that won a Polish historical prize in 2004; also available in a Polish translation.

Atamukas, Solomonas. *Lietuvos žydų kelias.* Vilnius, Lithuania, 1998. A scholarly history of the Jews in Lithuania.

Senn, Alfred Erich. *The Great Powers, Lithuania, and the Vilna Question, 1920–1928.* Leiden, Netherlands, 1966. Deals with the Polish-Lithuanian rivalry for the possession of the city of Vilnius.

———. *Jonas Basanavičius: Patriarch of the Lithuanian National Renaissance.* Newtonville, Mass., 1980. A biography of a key figure in the development of Lithuanian national consciousness.

Wandycz, Piotr S. *The Lands of Partitioned Poland, 1795–1918.* Seattle, Wash., 1974. Offers a Polish interpretation of Lithuania's history in the nineteenth century.

ALFRED E. SENN

LLOYD GEORGE, DAVID (1863–1945),

British politician.

David Lloyd George, perhaps best known as Great Britain's prime minister from 1916 to 1922, was already recognized in 1914 as a leading politician and statesman. Born in Manchester, England, in 1863 to poor but respectable Welsh parents and fatherless by the age of two, Lloyd George seemed destined to lead an obscure life. But robust encouragement from family members and dedicated teachers, combined with native intelligence and natural oratorical skills, created in the young Lloyd George an ambition far beyond what his station in life promised.

Articled to a law firm in 1879, Lloyd George qualified as a solicitor in 1884, and a year later he established his own law firm. His legal aspirations, however, soon lagged behind his political ambitions. His cases in law challenged the perquisites enjoyed by both the Church of England and the landed class in Wales. He denounced rank and privilege at temperance meetings and nonconformist gatherings. In addition, he honed his critical skills in a local debating society and writing for the *North Wales Express*—an experience that taught him how the press could influence public opinion.

In 1890, at the age of twenty-seven, Lloyd George was elected Liberal member of Parliament (MP) at a by-election for Caernarvon Boroughs, a constituency he held for the remainder of his lengthy political career. In his early days in the House of Commons, Lloyd George's radical and inflammatory voice represented an emerging Welsh democratic nationalism, firmly established among farmers as well as the urban middle class. Gradually, however, Lloyd George took tentative steps toward the center of the Liberal Party. He engaged in constructive reform, especially as it related to social welfare and education. He also defended the threat to free trade posed by Joseph Chamberlain's tariff reform scheme. Yet his radical credentials had not been put aside. He courageously criticized the Boer War (1899–1902) as an irresponsible imperial adventure, especially attacking its faulty strategy and exorbitant expense.

David Lloyd George (left) with Winston Churchill, 1910.
© HULTON-DEUTSCH COLLECTION/CORBIS

Although he antagonized even some members of his own party by his radical views, his talent could not be ignored. When Sir Henry Campbell-Bannerman won a landslide victory at the general election of January 1906, Lloyd George was brought into the cabinet as president of the Board of Trade. From this relatively minor position, he enhanced his reputation as a reformer and added to his stature by his sensible and even-handed negotiations during industrial disputes. Speaking directly with both masters and men during the railway dispute of 1907, for example, he prevented a potentially crippling strike. He was also quite willing to sponsor pro-business legislation, such as the Patents and Designs Act (1907) and the Companies' Act. Even when unsuccessful, he earned wide respect as a man unafraid to tackle difficult problems. Thus, it was not surprising that Lloyd George should replace Herbert Henry Asquith as chancellor of the Exchequer when Asquith became prime minister in April 1908.

In his early years at the Exchequer, four important issues captured his attention: the passage of the old-age pension scheme in 1908; the so-called People's Budget of 1910; the Parliament Act of 1911; and the National Insurance Scheme of that same year. Support for a pension plan had been developing for some time, and Lloyd George easily carried the bill through Parliament. The People's Budget was an altogether different affair. New taxes on inherited wealth, unearned incomes, and profits derived from the increasing value of land created a furor among the wealthy. When the conservative House of Lords, in an almost unprecedented move, rejected the budget in November 1909, Lloyd George denounced them in scathing speeches in and out of Parliament. After months of political acrimony and a general election, the Lords finally capitulated in April 1910. The Lords' delaying tactics over the budget was the last straw for the Liberals. Since they had come to power four years earlier, the Liberals had seen their legislative programs time and again vetoed by the upper house. For the Liberals, the issue was no longer merely partisan, but constitutional. To trim the power of the Lords, the Liberals introduced a Parliament bill limiting the Lords to a suspensory veto only. A year of fierce partisan strife, including a second general election, ended with its passage in 1911.

While still engaged in the struggle against the House of Lords, Lloyd George began work on the capstone of his social reform policy. A national insurance system—protecting low-income workers from the misfortunes of both ill health and unemployment—was a logical extension of old-age pensions. In piloting the bill through parliament, Lloyd George not only allayed the fears of vested interests such as friendly societies, private insurance companies, and doctors, he also convinced the insured to participate in a contributory plan. Along with old-age pensions, this bill helped to establish in Britain the cooperative principle by which the state, employers, and the employed all participated in social benefit programs.

Though Lloyd George's radical reputation was enhanced by his reform policies, his moderate tendency was increasingly evident in his approach to foreign policy after the Boer War. During cabinet controversies over naval estimates, for example, Lloyd George (if sometimes under duress) invariably found the money to insure British supremacy of the seas, especially over its nearest competitor, Germany. Particularly notable—and shocking to many of his radical Liberal colleagues—was Lloyd George's surprising and influential speech during the Agadir crisis between Germany and France in July 1911, when he warned Germany that Britain was determined to maintain its dominance in the world.

The year 1911 was the high point of Lloyd George's prewar career. For the next few years, his reputation suffered from a series of political and financial misjudgments. His purchase of shares in the American Marconi Company at a time when its British counterpart was contracting with the British government to build wireless stations throughout the empire created the outward impression of a conflict of interest. His parliamentary initiatives involving land reforms in 1913 and the budget in 1914 were unsuccessful. His attempts to enact some form of women's suffrage failed. Strains in his family and personal life were occasioned by his growing intimacy with Frances Stevenson, the young woman who in 1912 became his secretary and shortly thereafter his mistress.

Criticism began to emerge, though much of it was based on partisan rancor. Some maintained that Lloyd George's vaunted negotiating skills indicated a lack of fixed principles, and that his compromises were merely designed to gain any convenient outcome. His most visceral opponents portrayed him as an ill-bred country solicitor far too enamored of golf, travel, and the good life. There is something to these criticisms; but the reasons lay not in a failure of character. His inclination for changing course, seeking compromise, and occasional grandstanding behavior was more likely rooted in an unexplored psychological need that sometimes intruded upon his public life. In fact, Lloyd George frequently manifested an almost obsessive desire for popular approval, even adulation. Evidence for this exists in his private letters to his family and in unguarded remarks to close friends. With all the doubts about his behavior, however, Lloyd George displayed enormous potential as a political leader in the years before 1914. No one could have foretold that a brutal war and divisive peace would provide the opportunity for Lloyd George to recoup his reputation as a man of vision and energy—at least for a time.

See also **Great Britain; Labour Party; Suffragism.**

BIBLIOGRAPHY

Gilbert, Bentley Brinkerhoff. *David Lloyd George: A Political Life.* Vol. 1: *The Architect of Change, 1863–1912.* Columbus, Ohio, 1987.

———. *David Lloyd George: A Political Life.* Vol. 2: *Organizer of Victory, 1912–1916.* Columbus, Ohio, 1992.

Grigg, John. *The Young Lloyd George.* Berkeley and Los Angeles, 1973.

———. *Lloyd George: The People's Champion, 1902–1911.* Berkeley and Los Angeles, 1978.

———. *Lloyd George: From Peace to War, 1912–1916.* Berkeley and Los Angeles, 1985.

Packer, Ian. *Lloyd George.* London, 1998.

Rowland, Peter. *The Last Liberal Governments: The Promised Land, 1905–1910.* New York, 1968.

———. *The Last Liberal Governments: Unfinished Business, 1911–1914.* London, 1971.

Travis L. Crosby

LOMBROSO, CESARE (1835–1909), Italian criminologist.

Often called the "father of criminology," Cesare Lombroso was a pioneer in establishing criminology as a social science. Born into a Jewish family of Verona, Italy, he studied medicine and psychiatry at universities in Italy and Austria. While volunteering as a military doctor in the new Italian army (1859–1863) he began to collect data on the physical and psychological characteristics of recruits. He subsequently transferred his methodology, based on measurement of the body and clinical interviews, to the insane and then to criminals. During his long career as a professor at the University of Turin he founded the discipline of criminal anthropology, which traced the causes of crime to abnormal physical and psychological characteristics in offenders. He thus challenged the reigning orthodoxy in legal thought that attributed criminal behavior to free will, arguing instead for the important role of biological determinism in lawbreaking.

Lombroso is best known for his concept of the "born criminal," an atavistic throwback on the evolutionary scale who can be identified by physical and psychological "anomalies." Using a social Darwinist framework, Lombroso likened these anomalies in criminals to typical traits of "savage" man, animals, and even plants. Physical anomalies included small heads, low foreheads, jug ears, and large jaws; abnormal psychological traits included vindictiveness, vanity, lack of probity, and, in the case of women, lack of modesty and of maternal feelings. Despite his emphasis on innate and hereditary causes of crime, Lombroso did not ignore the importance of social factors like poverty, illiteracy, and overcrowded housing that could lead to "occasional" criminality. The humanitarian streak in his work led him to join the Italian Socialist Party, where he found a following among those who compared his materialistic explanations of crime favorably to Karl Marx's economic determinism.

Lombroso went beyond theory to enumerate practical policies to protect society from crime. Contrary to the "classical school" of penology, which traced its philosophy back to Cesare Beccaria's famous Enlightenment tract *On Crimes and Punishments* (*Dei delitti e delle pene;* 1765), criminal anthropology argued that degrees of punishment should correlate with the dangerousness of offenders rather than the severity of their crimes. From this perspective, born criminals, whose atavistic constitution denied any possibility of reform, deserved perpetual separation from society in special prisons for incorrigibles or, in the case of the most violent recidivists, capital punishment. Lombroso discouraged incarceration for occasional criminals because prisons tended to corrupt rather than reeducate their inmates and instead recommended probation or suspended sentences. Believing that only criminal anthropologists could accurately identify and classify criminals, Lombroso sought to place his disciples in key positions within the police, courts, and prisons.

Lombroso expounded his criminological theory in a series of books, including his classic companion works *Criminal Man* (*L'uomo delinquente;* five editions from 1876 to 1897) and *Criminal Woman, the Prostitute, and the Normal Woman* (*La donna delinquente, la prostituta e la donna normale;* coauthored with Guglielmo Ferrero, 1893). Founding editor of the journal *Archivio di antropologia criminale, psichiatria e medicina legale* (Archives of criminal anthropology, psychiatry, and legal medicine), he gained national and international fame as the leader, along with Enrico Ferri and Raffaele Garofalo, of the "Italian" or "positivist" school of criminology. While the Italian school dominated debates at the first international Congress of Criminal Anthropology held in Rome (1885), Lombroso's ideas soon came under attack for emphasizing atavism at the expense of other biological determinants of crime and for underestimating the role of "social milieu" in shaping human behavior. In response to his critics Lombroso expanded his theory of the etiology of crime to include "moral insanity," degeneracy, epilepsy, and a host of sociological factors while never abandoning his primary allegiance to atavism.

After many years of neglect, the theories of Lombroso have elicited a revival of scholarship since the 1990s. These studies have been concentrated in three areas. First, Italian historians have been reevaluating Lombroso's importance to the intellectual and institutional history of his own nation. Once considered marginal and simplistic, criminal anthropology is now being recognized as consonant with many mainstream scientific and legal developments of its day. Second, international scholars are reevaluating Lombroso's influence in shaping late-nineteenth-century criminology in Europe and the Americas. Even in nations like France, where individual criminologists conducted highly public feuds with Lombroso, theories of crime were permeated with biological and deterministic rhetoric. Finally, historians of gender and racism have had to come to terms with Lombroso's voluminous data purporting to prove the inferiority of women to men and establish a hierarchy of races. Research remains to be done on his contributions to the development of sexology, the study of prison culture, and the establishment of criminological museums.

See also **Crime; Darwin, Charles; Degeneration; Durkheim, Émile; Positivism.**

BIBLIOGRAPHY

Primary Sources

Lombroso, Cesare. *Criminal Woman, the Prostitute, and the Normal Woman.* Edited by Nicole Hahn Rafter and Mary Gibson. Durham, N.C., 2004.

Secondary Sources

Frigessi, Delia. *Cesare Lombroso.* Turin, Italy, 2003.

Gibson, Mary. *Born to Crime: Cesare Lombroso and the Origins of Biological Criminology.* Westport, Conn., 2002.

Villa, Renzo. *Il deviante e i suoi segni: Lombroso e la nascita dell'antropologia criminale.* Milan, 1985.

MARY GIBSON

LONDON. London is located in southeast Britain, inland from the North Sea at a point where the Thames River could be bridged. Founded by the Romans in the first century C.E. as a trading center, London provided easy communications by water and land, and it quickly became an important marketplace. London's fortunes have always been linked to empire, first that of the Romans, and much later, that of the British crown. Connected by sea to colonies in the Americas, Africa, Asia, and the South Pacific, it is the most international of Britain's cities, leading a worldwide exchange of goods, people, and information. A spiderweb of turnpikes, canals, and, after 1840, railroads made London the kingdom's central place. In 1800, London was Britain's biggest city, its most important port, its political and cultural capital, and its largest manufacturing center. To quote the novelist Henry James (1843–1916), "for the real London-lover the mere immensity of the place is a large part of its savour." Its dominance of Great Britain, combined with the political and economic importance of the United Kingdom, made London the most influential city in the world during the nineteenth century.

POPULATION GROWTH AND EXPANSION

Between 1800 and 1900, Greater London's population rose from over 1,000,000 to 6,600,000; by 1900, one of every five people in England and Wales lived in the capital. Early in the century, growth rates reached 20 percent per decade, an explosive pace of increase by any standard. By 1810, London had become the world's largest city, outstripping the Japanese capital of Edo. Inhabitants found it impossible to know all London's different neighborhoods and districts.

London's rapid expansion was all the more remarkable because of the capital's high death rates. In the eighteenth century, the capital served as "the national reservoir of infections." People, especially infants, died from smallpox, fever, measles, and consumption at a higher rate than those living in rural areas or smaller towns; Londoners born in the first half of the eighteenth century had an average life expectancy of only thirty-five years. But after 1750, improved nutrition and cleanliness, as well as inoculation against smallpox, led to slow declines in mortality, and the trend continued. Births approximately balanced deaths in the metropolis by 1800, and outnumbered them after 1810. In later decades, advances in sanitation and water cleanliness cut the death rate still more. Even without major advances in medical care, improvements in living conditions in the capital made it no longer a deathtrap for its residents.

Much of London's growth, however, came through migration. Thousands of young people walked or rode into the metropolis every year, most coming from the south and east of England, although the capital attracted northerners, Scots, and Welsh, too. Almost 50,000 Irish came to London during the 1840s, the decade of the Potato Famine. London attracted aristocrats and actors, bricklayers and beggars. Foreign sailors jumped ship in the port; Irish arrived to work as servants or dock laborers. Merchants from around the world settled in London to trade. Because many passed through too quickly to be counted in any statistical record, the total number of immigrants and emigrants to the capital is unknown. But between 1851 and 1861, around 286,000 new residents arrived and remained long enough to be counted in a census, representing about 10 percent of the metropolitan population. Because migrants tend to follow kin or neighbors, London sheltered a string of migrant communities of British, as well as foreign, origin. Irish enclaves grew up in the East End, in Central London, and in Bermondsey. Italians congregated in Holborn, and the French in Soho. When East European Jews flocked to London in the late nineteenth century, most settled in Whitechapel, in the East End. In 1891, over 3 percent of the London population was foreign born, and an additional 3 percent came from Scotland or Ireland.

But the outflow was high too. Between 1851 and 1861, over 100,000 people born in London left to settle in other parts of England and Wales; tens of thousands of others moved from the capital overseas. Some people lived in London seasonally; others came for a few years to study or to work before marriage. The flow of people in and out of the metropolis never ceased, making London residence something shared by a substantial proportion of the British population.

This rapidly growing population needed housing. By 1800, the rush to build for newcomers had already produced suburbs of largely middle-class residents. Businessmen commuted daily from villas on the outskirts of the city to offices in the center. Aristocratic landlords worked with developers to cover their estates with terrace housing. Thomas Cubitt (1788–1855), the greatest builder of the Victorian period, worked with the Duke of Westminster to lay out Belgravia and Pimlico. Royal land converted into public parks encouraged development of the West End, London's most fashionable address.

Changes in transportation made possible the rush from the center, which by century's end included workers as well as the middle class. Horse-drawn stage coaches, omnibuses, and, later, trolleys brought thousands into town daily. By the 1870s, routes crossed London north to south and east to west. The railways provided a second mode of intra-London travel after the major railway lines completed their London stations. During the second half of the nineteenth century, companies built new approach lines into the metropolis and new bridges to bring trains into central London stations. Adding the tracks, however, meant subtracting scandalous amounts of workers' housing, for which few replacements were built. Over 100,000 people found themselves displaced by railway construction in London during the second half of the century, and many could not afford to relocate into outer areas. The fever to expand the metropolis came at a high cost.

TABLE 1

Population of Greater London, 1801–1921

	1801	1851	1901	1921
London	1,117,000	2,685,000	6,586,000	7,488,000
England and Wales	8,893,000	17,928,000	32,528,000	37,887,000

SOURCE: Mitchell, pp. 25, 30, 33

London's growth outran the capital's ability to cope with added numbers. Foul air, tainted water, stinking refuse heaps, and legions of street-people shocked respectable visitors. In 1819, the poet Percy Bysshe Shelley (1792–1822) wrote "Hell is a city much like London." It took much of the second half of the century to clean up the mess. Sir John Simon (1816–1904), Medical Officer of Health for the City of London, attacked cesspits and substandard housing. He succeeded in increasing water supplies, combatting dirt and stinks. By the mid-1850s, all metropolitan districts had hired similar medical officers to improve local sanitation. They inspected lodging houses, quarantined the contagious, and tried to close down sources of pollution. Slowly local government cleaned up the capital.

LONDON'S ECONOMY

During the period when the British economy industrialized, London kept its position as the country's largest manufacturing center. Although not a conventional factory town, the capital housed the country's largest stock of highly skilled workers. They produced luxury goods for the elite, staples for the metropolitan population, and industrial goods linked to the port and its trade. Artisans, who had been the core of the old regime economy, kept their importance in many crafts, giving London a competitive edge in fields as diverse as printing, watchmaking, tailoring, and hat making. Luxury goods—silk textiles, fine clothing, silver products—poured from London workshops. If London was a vast department store, the river was its service entrance, where thousands spent their days loading and unloading to meet deadlines.

London had an enormous service sector. The capital needed office workers, clerks, and administrators, and it attracted increasing numbers of professionals. The metropolis remained the world's financial and trading capital until the 1940s, when New York took over that primary position. The central players in the London economy were not the manufacturers, but the "gentlemanly capitalists"—directors of the East India Company or bankers such as Alexander Baring (1774–1848) and Nathan Meyer Rothschild (1777–1836). Commerce and trade outranked the city's contribution to British industrial production. The special quality of the metropolitan economy is most easily seen by measuring the capital's contribution to national employment. In 1851, when workers in the capital accounted for only 13.7 percent of the employed population of England and Wales, Londoners dominated the banking industry (41 percent), the professions (27 percent), and government service (27 percent).

Women's trades differed significantly from those of their male relatives. For the most part, females produced clothing—dresses, hats, shirts, and shoes—or small home-produced goods. Excluded from apprenticeships and the guilds, women worked in skilled occupations alongside their husbands or made simple goods in their homes for middlemen who paid starvation wages. The most common women's job in the capital was that of domestic servant, which gave women room, board, and a tiny wage in return for unregulated hours of household drudgery. Those few with a secondary education could become teachers or governesses. Not until late in the century did many administrative or clerical positions become open to women.

TABLE 2

London Occupations among Employed Population, 1861

Occupation	Males Percent	Females Percent	Total
Agriculture	2.9	0.7	2.4
Commerce	7.2	1.7	6.0
Construction	11.4	0.0	8.9
Food	7.8	2.7	6.7
Labor (Unspecified)	6.0	0.0	4.7
Manufacturing	31.2	47.6	34.7
Professional, Administrative	7.9	4.1	7.1
Service	4.6	43.1	13.0
Transport, Distribution	18.7	0.1	14.7
Other	2.3	0.0	1.8
Total	100	100	100

SOURCE: Green, p. 18.

Manufacturers in the metropolis had to confront rising costs and competition from northern British firms, as well as European and North American rivals. London was a high wage, high rent site in which to produce goods. Moreover, technological changes favored mass production, which required more space, always at a premium in central London. To cut costs, some firms moved farther out; others left London for provincial cities. Between 1870 and 1914, the London economy experienced steady economic decline. Clothing and furniture manufacturers coped by lowering wages and quality, pushing production of cheap and shoddy goods into workers' homes, thereby eliminating the expense of rent, heat, and light.

The Second Industrial Revolution, built on electricity and internal combustion engines, helped the London manufacturing economy to modernize in the late nineteenth century. London's comparative advantage in skilled labor and ready consumers encouraged entrepreneurs to locate in the southeast, and the new technology provided power. Electrified, underground railway lines reached far outside central London to offer commuters easy access to the center at low cost. Electric trams, which were cheap, fast, and large, supplanted horse-drawn omnibuses. With better transport services, the effective metropolitan area exploded again in size. The capital became "Greater London," stretching northward into the Lea Valley, westward through the county of Middlesex, and beyond Greenwich to the east. In rapidly growing outer regions, new firms producing cars, tools, and chemicals multiplied. The southeast became a national center for electrical and general engineering. Linked by road, canal, and sea to the rest of the country and the empire, a London location again made sense for the savvy entrepreneur. By 1914, London and the southeast had again become the most prosperous, progressive region of Great Britain.

SOCIETY

London had a social geography that paralleled its physical divisions. As the city grew, more and more of the middle classes, who could afford to commute to work and who preferred privacy to overcrowded central districts, left central and eastern parishes for western areas or the suburbs. The fashionable West End was launched by a spectacularly successful town planning scheme paid for by the central government. In the eighteenth century, George III (r. 1760–1820) traded royal lands in West London for cash, and the Commissioners of Woods and Forests, encouraged by George IV (r. 1820–1830), decided to support building in the area by improving access and adding greenery. John Nash (1752–1835), a government architect, produced the grand design, which resulted in an elegant north-south street, a park, a canal, as well as Trafalgar Square and Buckingham Palace. Built around 1820, Regent Street blocked access to the west from the slums of Soho and gave fashionable London a place to shop. Speculative builders, recognizing a growing demand for upscale housing, rushed to develop vacant land to the west.

Meanwhile, the East End became an industrial area and disproportionately the residence of the poor. Immigrants and people practicing nasty trades crowded into crumbling houses on mean streets. After surveying the population of the East End in the late 1880s, Charles Booth (1840–1916), ship owner and sociologist, decided that 35 percent had incomes either on the poverty line or so low that "decent life is not imaginable." Districts to the east of the Tower of London had the highest death rates and the worst housing in London. Smells from tanneries and noise from street vendors drove out the genteel, leaving behind workers who needed to be close to their jobs. Slaughterhouses shared space with railway tunnels and tumble-down tenements. Many contemporaries compared eastern districts to the unknown territories of the British Empire and their inhabitants to "savages." Such comments reflected the increasing social distance of rich and poor, as distance bred fear and condemnation. Contemporaries identified the East End with crime and prostitution. The century's most famous murders, the stabbing deaths by Jack the Ripper, took place in Whitechapel in 1888. During the nineteenth century, the contrast between slum and suburb had moral connotations, in addition to economic ones.

Crime, however, could not be confined to the East End. Streetwalkers and burglars could be found in every London district. Pickpockets frequented West End theaters and the railway stations. Riverside areas sheltered smugglers, river pirates, and mudlarks—thieving children who stole from ships. Londoners feared that the city sheltered a "criminal class," or a criminal subculture whose members shunned honest work in favor of preying upon the unwary. Criminals were those who would not work, and they needed to be punished.

Early in the nineteenth century, London had many criminals but no organized police force outside the City and the Thames River. For the most part, people were supposed to protect themselves. By prescribing the death penalty for over two hundred offenses, the criminal code was designed to frighten people into good behavior, but the chances of being caught were slim. The establishment of the Metropolitan Police Force in 1829 proved a turning point. Uniformed, trained constables began to patrol the streets. One central authority took responsibility for keeping order within the capital, and crime rates decreased. Initially resented as a threat to local liberties, the force provided a model for modern policing that was copied quickly throughout Britain.

METROPOLITAN CULTURE

London houses the largest collection of museums, theaters, clubs, and societies in the United Kingdom. The British government established the British Museum in the 1750s. Archaeological expeditions around the empire added to its vast store of

A view of London rooftops. Engraving by Gustave Doré c. 1870. Doré's view clearly shows the crowding that had become characteristic of poorer London neighborhoods. ©STAPLETON COLLECTION/CORBIS

artifacts, which included the Parthenon statuary brought back by Lord Elgin (1766–1841) from Greece in 1801. Trafalgar Square became another center of cultural pilgrimage with the building of the National Gallery of Art in 1837 and the National Portrait Gallery in 1856. Profits from the Crystal Palace Exhibition of 1851 financed new centers for study of British art and science. Opening in 1857, the South Kensington Museum eventually split into the Victoria and Albert Museum for applied art and the Science Museum. In order to bring contemporary art to workers, Samuel Augustus Barnett (1844–1913) and his wife Henrietta founded the East End Gallery in Whitechapel, which opened in 1901. As British wealth increased, so did the impulse to collect and to display the results to people of all ranks and social statuses.

Intellectuals, scientists, and the highly skilled congregated in London, and they became more highly organized and vocal during the eighteenth and nineteenth centuries. The crown chartered a variety of scientific societies, starting with the Royal Society in 1662. By the mid-nineteenth century, groups of specialists such as the Royal Society of Chemistry, the Geological Society, and the Royal Statistical Society abounded in the capital. As medicine and law became more highly professionalized, new societies such as the Royal College of Surgeons, the Worshipful Society of Apothecaries, and the Law Society brought

Fleet Street c. 1890. Fleet Street was the seat of the publishing industry in London, beginning in the sixteenth century when early printing presses were established there. ©CORBIS

added respectability and visibility to their members. A London association, chartered by the government and provided with rules of admission and conduct, became a rite of passage for aspiring professionals.

To challenge the Anglican monopoly of university education, radical intellectuals founded University College, London in 1827. No religious barriers to entry were erected, and the curriculum concentrated on modern subjects largely ignored by Oxford and Cambridge. It joined with the Anglican King's College to form the University of London in 1837—male-only until it opened examinations to women in 1878. The University expanded to include Bedford and Royal Holloway Colleges for women. Institutions like the London School of Economics, organized by Fabian socialists in 1895, made the capital a center of training in the social sciences. Art, music, and drama schools flourished in London, as well.

London was also the center of the British entertainment world. Royal licenses dating from the 1660s restricted theatrical productions to two great playhouses, Drury Lane and Covent Garden, but they had many unlicensed competitors. By the time the industry was opened to all comers in 1843, several dozen theaters operated all over the capital. In the second half of the nineteenth century, entrepreneurs built new theaters and music halls for audiences of all social classes and ages. The East End had "penny gaffes" where melodrama flourished. Regulation remained, however, in the person of the Lord Chamberlain, who retained the right to block productions and institutions "in the interest of good manners, decorum, or the public peace." His censorious gaze ended performances of Oscar Wilde's *Salome* in 1892.

For less formal entertainment, Londoners walked to pleasure gardens, where they saw open air shows and fireworks in tree-lined, suburban settings. In central London, song and supper rooms developed into music halls where patrons drank and listened to the rock stars of the time. From the 1820s, Regent's Park in London hosted a zoo and a diorama of the city as seen from the top of St. Paul's Cathedral. Sporting enthusiasts could attend wrestling matches or cockfights, until the latter were banned in 1849. Spectator sports drew large crowds to cheer and to bet on favorites. Boxing and cricket were popular in the late eighteenth century, and by 1900 this list expanded to include soccer and rugby. The best show of all proved to be the Crystal Palace Exhibition of 1851, visited by six million people who came to look at Indian crafts, French art, and British manufactured goods.

London fostered a culture of consumption, fed by changes in marketing. New technologies transformed stores into seductive places. Drapers' stores used bright lights and huge plate glass windows to lure customers inside. In 1863, William Whiteley (1831–1907) built the country's first department store in the West End, and it soon spawned even more successful imitators. Oxford Street became a shoppers' Mecca, particularly after 1909, when Selfridges' palace of merchandise drew thousands to gaze at its decorations and to lunch in its fashionable dining rooms. Central London encouraged many forms of consumption. Thousands of coffeehouses, cookshops, street vendors, and chophouses proved that fast food was not a modern invention. To provide high-status men with meeting places, social clubs where members could drink and dine, unencumbered by wives, multiplied in the West End. By the 1860s, middle-class women founded clubs of their own to ease female expeditions around the town.

Much of London's cultural life was divided according to social status and gender. High culture was less open to poorer Londoners than popular culture was to the affluent. Museums limited weekend hours, restricting workers' access, and respectable clothing was necessary for entry into London parks. Men dominated London's public spaces, risky places for unchaperoned middle-class women, who were expected to stay at home. By the 1880s, however, the rules loosened, as expanded urban opportunities for women coincided with their increasing demands for access.

GOVERNANCE

Not until 1889 did London have an effective structure of government. What became officially "London" in the late nineteenth century combined a jumble of local authorities, conflicting jurisdictions, and rival centers of power. The metropolis grew from three centers: (1) the City of London, a square mile of territory north of the river; (2) Westminster, the seat of court and Parliament; and (3) Southwark on the south bank of the Thames. Rudimentary county institutions ruled in parts of Middlesex, Kent, and Surrey, while parish vestries controlled Hammersmith, Chelsea, Paddington, Marylebone, St. Pancras, and much of Westminster. The City of London had a particularly complicated and arcane set of institutions. A Lord Mayor and two Sheriffs were elected annually, but policies were set by the Court of Aldermen, the Court of Common Council, the Court of Common Hall, and the Court of Wardmote, which operated alongside eighty-nine craft guilds or companies, whose members became "freemen" and therefore voters in the City. While the City operated as a democracy for males with property, real power lay in the hands of the Aldermen, a group of rich, elderly merchants appointed for life. City officials had also amassed power far beyond the ancient walls of the town. They governed the river Thames, as well as the Port of London, local markets, and prisons. In the crowd of metropolitan administrators, the City stood out as a giant among dwarfs.

In 1800, a crazy-quilt of tiny units and overlapping jurisdictions offered services to inhabitants. Turnpike trusts ran the main roads, while sewer commissioners looked after the drains. The Bow Street Magistrates' Court and its small staff of detectives attempted to control crime. Around two hundred parishes independently subsidized the poor within their boundaries, and paved, lit, and cleaned streets. In addition, Parliament authorized hundreds of local improvement trusts. Nine different trusts looked after the lighting of the Lambeth parish alone. With little coordination other than that provided by the market, London institutions and voters ignored their neighbors and guarded their own turf.

Reform came piecemeal throughout the nineteenth century. A string of cholera epidemics paved the way for the Metropolitan Board of Works,

Pedestrian and carriage traffic on London Bridge, c. 1904. Built in 1831 to replace a bridge of the same name that had stood since 1209, London Bridge served as a major thoroughfare in the nineteenth century. In the early twentieth century, an attempt to widen it to facilitate traffic flow undermined the structure and led to its eventual replacement. ©HULTON-DEUTSCH COLLECTION/CORBIS

founded in 1855 to build sewers and new streets. Elected by the City Corporation and parish vestries, the Board managed to centralize control of waste management, street improvements, and parks while leaving the ancient, archaic structures of local government intact. By the 1880s, demonstrators on the streets and reformers in Parliament called for its replacement.

The Local Government Act of 1888 established the London County Council (LCC), which had jurisdiction over 117 square miles. Only a minority (about one in ten Londoners) could vote for the new council, but property-owning women were included in the electorate. They chose a central council and twenty-nine borough councils, who ran the metropolis until 1965, when the LCC expanded into the Greater London Council and was responsible for an even larger territory. Under the leadership of the Liberals and Radical Progressives who controlled the group until 1907, the LCC launched an ambitious program of social reform. It took responsibility for fire service, housing, and trolley transport; it launched steamboat service on the Thames. After 1904, the LCC managed state-funded primary and secondary education, while moving London teachers onto the municipal payroll. By 1914, the LCC was London's largest employer. Its staff built schools and monitored midwives, music halls, and lodging houses. Influenced by Fabian socialists, the council erected large, publicly owned housing estates for workers on the outskirts of the city. These model

A match-seller outside the church of St. Martin-in-the-Fields, central London, 1912. In his landmark study *London Labour and the London Poor* (1861), Henry Mayhew noted that match-sellers, among the poorest of street peddlers, were often elderly men who were no longer able to work but too proud to beg.

estates provided workers with far better sanitation—indoor plumbing and bathrooms, for example—in a relatively drab, restricted social setting. Municipal collectivism made its mark in London during the two decades before World War I, when activist politicians had the votes to "expand the sphere of the civic." London government shifted from retrograde to reforming at the end of the nineteenth century.

By the outbreak of World War I, London had become a "modern" city with effective government, well-functioning infrastructures, and a booming cultural life. Although the region had reestablished its economic hegemony, social inequalities remained deep and unresolved.

See also **Cities and Towns; Great Britain; Paris.**

BIBLIOGRAPHY

Primary Sources

Besant, Walter. *London in the Nineteenth Century.* London, 1909. Reprint, New York, 1985.

Booth, Charles. *Life and Labour of the People of London.* 17 vols. London, 1902.

Doré, Gustave, and Blanchard Jerrold. *London, A Pilgrimage.* London, 1872. Reprint, New York, 1968.

James, Henry. *English Hours.* Boston, 1905.

Mayhew, Henry. *London Labour and the London Poor,* 4 vols. London, 1861–1862. Reprint, New York, 1968.

Secondary Sources

Dennis, Richard J. "Modern London." In Vol. 3 of *The Cambridge Urban History of Britain,* edited by Martin Daunton, 95–132. Cambridge, U.K., 2000.

Fishman, William J. *East End, 1888: Life in a London Borough among the Labouring Poor.* Philadelphia, 1988.

Green, David R. *From Artisans to Paupers: Economic Change and Poverty in London, 1790–1870.* Aldershot, U.K., 1995.

Jones, Gareth Stedman. *Outcast London: A Study in the Relationship between Classes in Victorian Society.* Oxford, U.K., 1971.

Lees, Lynn Hollen. *Exiles of Erin: Irish Migrants in Victorian London.* Ithaca, N.Y., 1979.

Mitchell, B. R. *British Historical Statistics.* Cambridge, U.K., 1988.

Nead, Lynda. *Victorian Babylon: People, Streets and Images in Nineteenth-Century London.* New Haven, Conn., 2000.

Olsen, Donald J. *The Growth of Victorian London.* New York, 1976.

Pennybacker, Susan D. *A Vision for London 1889–1914: Labour, Everyday Life, and the LCC Experiment.* London, 1995.

Porter, Roy. *London: A Social History.* Cambridge, Mass., 1994.

Rappaport, Erika Diane. *Shopping for Pleasure: Women in the Making of London's West End.* Princeton, N.J., 2000.

Schwarz, L. D. *London in the Age of Industrialisation: Entrepreneurs, Labour Force and Living Conditions, 1700–1850.* Cambridge, U.K., 1992.

Sheppard, Francis. *London, 1808–1870: The Infernal Wen.* Berkeley, Calif., 1971.

Walkowitz, Judith R. *City of Dreadful Night: Narratives of Sexual Danger in Late Victorian London.* Chicago, 1992.

LYNN HOLLEN LEES

LOOS, ADOLF (1870–1933), Austrian architect and cultural critic.

Adolf Loos was an influential figure in European avant-garde circles in the early twentieth century and has continued to fascinate architects, architectural historians, and philosophers of architecture ever since.

In 1889–1890 Loos attended the Technical University in Dresden, where he became a member of the Architects' Association. He then spent two years in military service before returning to Dresden to continue his studies. In 1893 he embarked upon a three-year trip to the United States. On his return to Vienna, Loos went to work with the architect Karl Mayreder, and also began publishing in leading newspapers such as the *Neue Freie Presse.* In 1898 he published a series of critical articles on the Kaiser Franz Josef Jubilee Exhibition, which were subsequently collected and published under the title *Spoken into the Void* (1921). In these articles, Loos drew on his American experiences to provide a critique of everyday culture in Austria in the early twentieth century.

Loos's first architectural commission—the renovation of the interior of the Café Museum in Vienna—dates to 1899. His design, later nicknamed "Café Nihilism," brought him to the attention of prominent art critics, who noted that although Loos's style was entirely modern, his modernism was very different from that of the Viennese Secession. From this point onward, Loos defined his architectural work in opposition to the Viennese Arts and Crafts movement and its central representatives, Josef Hoffmann (1870–1956) and Joseph Maria Olbrich (1867–1908).

In a number of articles published in leading German avant-garde journals such as *Der Sturm* and, from 1909 onward, in public lectures delivered throughout Europe, Loos developed his critique of the Viennese Arts and Crafts movement and everyday Austrian culture in general, in order to ground a prescriptive view of modern Western culture. In influential and controversial texts such as "Ornament and Crime," which was delivered as a lecture as early as 1909 but was not published in German until 1929, Loos also provided insight into the paradoxical culture of Vienna in the early twentieth century. In characteristically polemical style, Loos's "Ornament and Crime" invokes the fashionable doctrine of social evolutionism to suggest that anyone resorting to ornamentation in the modern world was either a degenerate or an aristocrat. At the same time, he provided an insightful treatise on the social relations of architectural production.

Texts such as "Ornament and Crime" also served to educate a wider public to receive his architecture—which was no less controversial than his cultural criticism. In 1910 Loos was commissioned to build a business premises for Goldman and Salatsch, a firm of Viennese tailors, on a prominent site opposite the Imperial Palace on the Michaelerplatz in Vienna. The façade of his rationalist design differentiated sharply between the lower floors, clad in green and white marble and dominated by four Doric columns, and the unornamented whitewashed form of the upper floors. The controversy that surrounded the "House without Eyebrows" in 1910–1911 was sparked off by the sharp contrast between the plain upper facade of Loos's design and the ornamented facade of the wing of the Imperial Palace designed by Johann Bernhard Fischer von Erlach (1656–1723) facing it, but soon developed into a full-blown argument about the modernity of Loos's design. More recent analyses of the building continue to debate its modernity.

In the immediate aftermath of World War I, Loos played a role in the development of "Red Vienna," being appointed chief architect to the municipal settlement office in 1921. Two years later, however, frustrated by problems faced by the settlement office, Loos left Vienna for Paris, where he lectured at the Sorbonne and continued designing private villas, as he had done in prewar Vienna, including that of Josephine Baker (1906–1975). He also continued to work in Austria and the Czech Republic, designing mainly settlement houses and private villas in which he could showcase his influential spatial theory, the *Raumplan*.

Loos is an architect arguably better known for his writings than for his architecture, although until the late twentieth century his teachings had not been adequately analyzed. From the 1980s, however, architectural historians began to recognize the role that articles and lectures played in disseminating Loos's architectural ideas, whereas philosophers, philologists, and sociologists set out to examine his texts in their own right. Loos is no longer understood as the predecessor of 1920s rationalist modern architecture but as a more complex figure whose concern to communicate an ideal form of everyday culture, articulated in his architecture and his texts, provides us with insight into aspects of modernity.

See also **Furniture; Housing; Vienna.**

BIBLIOGRAPHY

Primary Sources

Loos, Adolf. *Trotzdem.* Innsbruck, 1931.

———. *Spoken into the Void: Collected Essays 1897–1900.* Translated by Jane O. Newman and John H. Smith. Cambridge, Mass., 1982.

———. *Ornament and Crime. Selected Essays.* Edited by Adolf Opel and translated by Michael Mitchell. Riverside, Calif., 1998. Accurate translation of key essays from *Ins Leere gesprochen* and *Trotzdem* but omits bibliographical details.

Secondary Sources

Cacciari, Massimo. *Architecture and Nihilism: On the Philosophy of Modern Architecture.* Translated by Stephen Sartarelli. New Haven, Conn., 1993.

Colomina, Beatriz. *Privacy and Publicity: Modern Architecture as Mass Media.* Cambridge, Mass., 1994.

Rukschcio, Burckhardt, and Roland Schachel. *Adolf Loos: Leben und Werk.* Salzburg, 1982. The most comprehensive life and work study on Loos, cataloging the Adolf Loos Archive in the Albertina in Vienna.

Schezen, Roberto. *Adolf Loos: Architecture 1903–1932.* New York, 1996. Collection of photographs of Loos's main architectural works.

Stewart, Janet. *Fashioning Vienna: Adolf Loos's Cultural Criticism.* London, 2000.

Tournikiotis, Panayotis. *Adolf Loos.* Translated by Marguerite McGoldrick. New York, 1994.

JANET STEWART

LOUIS II (in German, Ludwig II, 1845–1886; ruled 1864–1886), king of Bavaria.

Louis II, popularly known as "Mad King Ludwig," came to the throne of Bavaria upon the death of his father, Maximilian II, on 10 March 1864. Louis's ill-starred rule ended with his own controversial death on 13 June 1886.

"Max died too soon," wrote Louis's mother when her son inherited the throne at age eighteen. She meant by this that Crown Prince Louis was too innocent and unworldly for his royal duties. He had spent his childhood and early adolescence under the lax tutelage of his art-loving grandfather, King Louis I, who was forced to abdicate the throne over his infatuation with the self-proclaimed "Spanish dancer" Lola Montez in 1848. Louis learned nothing about statecraft from either Louis I or his cold and distant father, and his later problems as king were forecast by his childhood passions for dressing up as a nun and constructing elaborate edifices out of toy bricks. At age thirteen he became obsessed with the operas of

Richard Wagner and devoted endless hours to acting them out.

Louis's first act as king was to invite Wagner, then fifty-three, to move to Munich as composer-in-residence. Like Lola Montez before him, Wagner soon incurred the wrath of the citizens of Munich by living grandly at state expense, engaging in sexual scandal, and meddling in royal affairs. Oblivious to popular sentiment, Louis promised to build the composer a magnificent new theater in Munich for the exclusive performance of Wagner's own works. Louis's ministers became convinced that the king might be forced to go the way of his grandfather if he did not rescind the theater plan and send the freeloading Wagner packing. In December 1865 Louis tearfully dismissed Wagner from his service, but he continued to subsidize the composer and eventually provided part of the funding for the creation of Wagner's festival theater at Bayreuth.

Louis never forgave the people of Munich for forcing him to jettison Wagner. He got his revenge by avoiding his capital for the rest of his life. He spent the bulk of his time in the nearby Alps, where he built, at enormous state expense, his spectacular rural retreats: Linderhof, Herrenchiemsee, and Neuschwanstein. Considered "holy places" by Louis, the castles were inaccessible to the public.

In 1866, when Prussian Prime Minister Otto von Bismarck coerced Austria into war in hopes of making Prussia the primary arbiter in German affairs, Louis, who despised Prussia, cast Bavaria's lot with Austria. (He refused, however, to march with his troops, insisting that wearing a helmet would ruin his coiffure.) The Bavarians were routed along with the Austrians after only seven weeks of fighting. Embittered, Louis retreated ever more thoroughly into his reclusive dream world in the Alps, where, rumor had it, he engaged in increasingly bizarre behavior—conversing with imaginary guests at dinner; forcing his valet to wear a bag over his head; and taking moonlit sleigh rides accompanied only by a retinue of young boys. In 1866 he became engaged to a cousin, Sophie, but as the wedding approached he insisted he would rather drown himself than marry, and the nuptials were called off.

Louis was in the mountains when France declared war on Prussia in 1870. He had no interest in the war, but this time he consented to Bavaria's joining the alliance of German states in their victory over France, which set the stage for the unification of Germany. Louis signed an "imperial letter" inviting King William I of Prussia to become Emperor William I of Germany. In return, Bismarck saw to it that Louis secretly received imperial funds to continue his building projects.

While Bismarck and Emperor William I presided over the consolidation and material growth of the new German state, Louis, secluded in the Alps, worked on the decoration of his châteaux and indulged his passions for historical drama, neo-medieval poetry, and romantic painting. He used imagery from Wagner's operas as the main themes in decorating his castles. He commissioned dozens of historical paintings based on his readings in medieval literature and poetry. Unlike his grandfather, however, whose collections enriched the museums of Munich, Louis bought paintings only for himself.

Increasingly, Louis refused to conduct any of the mundane duties expected of a king; he rarely held royal audiences, neglected to read state documents, and almost never let himself be seen by his people. In the mid-1880s, word had it that he was planning to build yet another mega-castle above Neuschwanstein. Concluding that the king was a dangerous liability to the Bavarian state and to the continuing rule of the Wittelsbach dynasty, Louis's ministers now decided to have him declared mentally unfit to carry on his royal duties. An "alienist" (psychiatrist), Dr. Bernhard von Gudden, was appointed to collect the data necessary to confirm the king's insanity. Von Gudden interviewed a number of court lackeys and household servants, but not the king himself, before duly drawing up a "medical report" stating that Louis suffered from an incurable mental disturbance. In June 1886 Louis's cabinet sent a delegation of medical men, accompanied by soldiers, to Neuschwanstein to seize the king and convey him to a smaller castle on Lake Starnberg near Munich, where he could be put away for life. Before locking him up in his gilded cage, however, his minders allowed him to go out for a walk along the lake with von Gudden. The two men never returned. Searchers eventually found the bodies of Louis and his doctor floating face down a few meters from the shore. To this day, nobody knows exactly what happened.

Was Louis indeed "mad," or just wildly eccentric? The question of the king's sanity continues to be debated, but even those who insist he was sane concede that he was not a very effective monarch. On the other hand, the Bavarian state can be thankful for the building mania that got Louis into so much trouble during his lifetime. These days, Neuschwanstein is the most heavily visited tourist site in Europe after the Notre-Dame cathedral in Paris.

See also **Austro-Prussian War; Franco-Prussian War; Germany; Romanticism; Wagner, Richard; Willam I.**

BIBLIOGRAPHY

Blunt, Wilfred. *The Dream King: Ludwig II of Bavaria.* New York, 1970.

Hüttl, Ludwig. *Ludwig II, König von Bayern: Eine Biographie.* Munich, 1986.

Prinz, Friedrich. *Ludwig II: Ein königliches Doppelleben.* Berlin, 1993.

DAVID CLAY LARGE

LOUIS XVI (1754–1793), ruled as king of France, 1774–1792.

Louis-Auguste, duc de Berry, the third son of the dauphin, Louis (1729–1765), and Marie-Josèphe of Saxony, was born at Versailles on 23 August 1754. He never expected to be king, but the high childhood mortality of the age that had bedeviled the Bourbon successions since the reign of Louis XIV (r. 1643–1715) intervened. His two older brothers died before him, and his father died young in 1765. The following year the unexpected heir apparent, at the age of twelve, began his diary. It reveals a limited intelligence, a mind little exercised, and a young man ill at ease with the demands of a public, ceremonial life.

The education of the new dauphin was given over to the duc de La Vauguyon, who surrounded his pupil with priests noted for their learning (the Jesuit abbé Soldini and the abbé Nollet). The boy proved a diligent but unimaginative pupil. In 1770, Louis was married by arrangement of Étienne François, duc de Choiseul (1719–1785), who headed the Austrian party at court, to Marie-Antoinette (1755–1793), the daughter of the Austrian Emperor Francis I (r. 1745–1765) and Marie-Thérèse (1717–1780).

The young couple were ill-matched. The Austrian princess had been wretchedly educated, wrote French slowly and with difficulty, and shared none of her husband's interests. Louis-Auguste was pedantic but well-read—his favorite Latin author was Tacitus, obviously not principally appreciated for his anti-imperial ideas—and even taught himself English. His taste ran to practical rather than imaginative or philosophical works. There were only two novels in his library, of which *Robinson Crusoe* was one. He was passionately interested in locksmithing, and had also had a telescope installed above his workroom at Versailles, where he enjoyed watching the comings and goings in the gardens of the great palace.

His marriage was celebrated in 1770 when Louis was sixteen and his bride fifteen. It was not consummated for seven years. Louis was not impotent, as was his brother the comte de Provence (the future Louis XVIII, r. 1814–1824), but he was unable to ejaculate until—and here there is some murkiness—an operation was performed at the urging of Marie-Antoinette's brother, Joseph. His affliction, in contrast to the libidinous excesses of his grandfather, Louis XV (r. 1715–1774), made the young heir a subject of private ridicule. The couple would eventually have four children. Only Marie-Thérèse Charlotte (called Madame Royale, who became the duchess d'Angoulême) survived the French Revolution.

In 1774, Louis XV died suddenly of smallpox and Louis-Auguste succeeded to the throne, a place where he was never comfortable. The young king made the seventy-four-year-old Count Jean-Frédéric Phelypeaux de Maurepas (1701–1781) his principal advisor. The count, earlier disgraced by Louis XV, now surrounded himself with capable men, most notably the philosophe Anne-Robert-Jacques Turgot (1727–1781) and Count Charles Gravier de Vergennes (1719–1797), and tried to shield his master from the poisonous court intrigue. But the reforming promise of the new monarchy soon evaporated and the king was overwhelmed by the accumulated structural ills of the kingdom, the ferocious and destructive factional fighting at court, the cynical legacy of his grandfather, all intensified by bankruptcy caused by the French backing the American rebels in their war for independence.

Despite his intellectual limitations, his indecisiveness, and his timidity that often took refuge in stubbornness, Louis had the good fortune to be served by ministers of talent; but he was incapable of pursuing a consistent policy of needed reform, and perhaps it was too late. The historian Jules Michelet (1798–1874) asserts the monarchy was dead by the final years of Louis XV's reign; certainly Louis XVI was unable to revive it.

The first so-called budget of the kingdom, the *Compte rendu* prepared by the new finance minister Jacques Necker (1732–1804) in 1781, falsely suggested there was a surplus. But the nation continued to borrow until servicing the growing debt soon surpassed the original sums borrowed. Later that year, Maurepas died and Louis began his personal rule and spent extravagantly on Marie Antoinette—he purchased the château of Saint-Cloud for her in 1784, without consulting his ministers—and drew ever closer to the queen whose mostly harmful influence increased.

By late 1786, it was clear that without some fundamental reform in the tax system the kingdom could not pay its bills. Charles-Alexandre de Calonne (1734–1802), the comptroller general (1783–87), drew up an elaborate and radical proposal that Louis embraced. The king and his comptroller called to Versailles an Assembly of Notables (1787), drawn from the most distinguished nobility and church officials in the land. They were offered concessions in exchange for abandoning their privilege of exemption from the *taille,* the chief direct tax of the kingdom. The negotiations failed, Louis was depressed, took to more and more hunting and overeating, and increasingly relied on his politically inept wife. He was forced to dismiss Calonne and replace him with his rival, Étienne-Charles de Loménie de Brienne (1727–1794), who called a second Assembly of Notables (1788). This group also rejected the king's proposed reforms and insisted the Estates-General be called. Louis governed briefly by decree and extracted forced loans, but he had no choice but to call the Estates-General, which had not met since 1614.

As the election writs went out, censorship was lifted. France found a direct outlet for its political voice, long stifled. Thousands of pamphlets accompanied the electioneering, and *cahiers de doléances,* the grievances solicited by the king, were drawn up and submitted to Versailles. When the representatives of the three estates (clergy, nobility, and everyone else) met at Versailles on 5 May 1789, it turned out to be the official beginning of the French Revolution.

On 3 June 1789, Louis's oldest son, the dauphin, died. The king was inconsolable as the first dramatic events of the Revolution unfolded. In his grief and disappointments, he became increasingly dependent upon his wife. He addressed the Estates on 23 June in a *séance royale,* but seemed distracted as his dry, authoritarian speech was read out. Whatever energy he had, as he assembled troops at Versailles to disperse the National Assembly and perhaps attack Paris—at least this was widely believed in the capital—was quickly exhausted with news of the fall of the Bastille, whose significance he never grasped. The entry in his diary for 14 July was "*Rien*"—"nothing."

Through the summer the court intrigued until, on 5–6 October 1789, the king was forcibly taken to Paris by women of the city who had trudged through the rain to confront him about soaring bread prices. The Tuileries Palace, unoccupied by a French king since 1680 when Louis XIV moved to Versailles, was hastily cleaned to receive Louis XVI. After much dilatoriness and indecision, he took the advice of his wife that the royal family should flee Paris. (Apparently the epistolary advice of comte de Mirabeau [1749–1791] urging such action was never read by Louis.) Sometime after midnight on 21 June 1791, the king and queen, their two children, and the Marquise de Tourzel (the royal governess) and her daughter left the palace in disguise, carrying false passports, and set out for the eastern frontier. At the town of Varennes, long after their incognito had been exposed, their coach was stopped. The mournful procession back to Paris, which the royal family reentered on 25 June, has been called a coronation in reverse. The king's flight was his betrayal of the Revolution.

Under the new constitution Louis had spurned by fleeing, the king had a suspensive rather than an absolute veto. This he exercised on laws against those who had emigrated and priests who refused to swear an oath to the constitution. On 20 June 1792, a mob penetrated the Tuileries and tried to get him to rescind his vetoes. This proved the dress rehearsal for overthrowing the monarchy on 10 August 1792. Before the attack on the Tuileries began, Louis and his family walked across the gardens to take refuge in the riding academy (the Manège), where the rump of the National Assembly was meeting. On 13 August, the victorious Paris Commune claimed Louis as their prisoner and locked the royal family up in the tower of the Temple. He would leave only to appear at his trial and to go to the guillotine.

The king's trial, to be conducted by the 745 elected members of the new National Assembly (the Constituent Assembly) who had arrived in Paris, began on 13 November 1792. The trial was unprecedented. Louis was the first French king to be held accountable by the nation. More than 400 speeches were delivered and/or published before the voting began on 16 January 1793. There were four separate votes, all taken by roll call. Louis was found unanimously guilty; the Assembly voted not to send the decision to the primary assemblies of the country for ratification; 387 deputies voted for death (the absolute majority was 361); and on 20 January they voted overwhelmingly not to delay execution.

The following day, 21 January, at 10:20 A.M., the king was beheaded in the former Place Louis XV (renamed the Place de la Révolution, now the Place de la Concorde). He was quickly buried in a common grave with other victims of the guillotine.

The supposed royal remains were exhumed by the restored Bourbon monarchy in 1816 and buried in the traditional crypt of French kings, in the Cathedral of St. Denis. The restored monarchy exiled all those they considered regicides and built an Expiatory Chapel in Paris to honor the martyred king. So long as the Bourbons sat on the throne, royalists marked 21 January as a solemn national day of mourning.

See also **French Revolution; Marie-Antoinette.**

BIBLIOGRAPHY

Furet, François. "Louis XVI." In *Critical Dictionary of the French Revolution*, edited by François Furet and Mona Ozouf, 234–243. Cambridge, Mass., 1989.

Hardman, John. *Louis XVI.* New Haven, Conn., 1993.

Jordan, David P. *The King's Trial: The French Revolution vs. Louis XVI.* Berkeley, Calif., 1979.

Vovelle, Michel. *The Fall of the French Monarchy, 1787–1792.* Translated by Susan Burke. Cambridge, U.K., 1984.

DAVID P. JORDAN

LOUIS XVIII (1755–1824; ruled 1814–1815, 1815–1824), king of France.

Born Louis-Stanislas-Xavier, the Count of Provence, at Versailles on 17 November 1755, Louis XVIII ruled France after the abdication of Napoleon I (1769–1821) in April 1814 until his own death in Paris on 16 September 1824. Working to reform the monarchy in the 1780s, fighting against the Revolution while in exile between 1791 and 1814, and ruling France as a reluctant constitutional monarch from 1814 to 1824, Louis XVIII negotiated the competing legacies of the Old Regime and the French Revolution.

Louis XVIII favored projects to reform the monarchy at the Assembly of Notables (1787). Unlike his younger brother, Charles (the Count of Artois, and future Charles X; r. 1824–1830) who left France immediately after the fall of the Bastille (14 July 1789), Louis remained with the royal family until his older brother, Louis XVI (r. 1774–1792), and Marie-Antoinette (1755–1793) tried to escape and were captured at Varenne on 21 June 1791. While in exile Louis worked with Charles to persuade the European powers to invade France and to restore the monarchy. Upon Louis XVI's execution on 21 January 1793, Louis declared himself regent for the young captive Louis XVII (1785–1795). When the latter died, Louis was recognized by émigrés as the king of France. While in exile Louis married Marie-

Josephine (1753–1810), who died in England in 1810, leaving no direct heirs to the throne.

When Louis was recalled to the throne in 1814 (First Restoration), it was by the Allies who had just defeated France, leaving the Bourbon monarch with the difficult task of reasserting his legitimate right to rule in a nation that had lived for twenty-five years under the tricolor flag and with a bureaucracy and legal structure that consolidated the liberal gains of the Revolution. Upon his arrival in France Louis XVIII "granted" a Charter that promised careers open to talent, the validity of *biens nationaux* (national properties sold off during the Revolution), and a representative government and the protection of basic individual rights; but he also delivered a speech at Saint-Ouen proclaiming the contradictory principle of his divine and historic right to the throne. Waving the white Bourbon flag, restoring honorific offices of the ancient court, and favoring returning émigrés while shunting one hundred twenty thousand of Napoleon's soldiers to half-pay, Louis XVIII gave his subjects reason to fear the return of the Old Regime. This fear was exploited by Napoleon, who escaped from Elba, rallied the nation around the tricolor flag, and sent Louis XVIII into exile until the Allies' definitive defeat of Napoleon at Waterloo (this period, March 1815–July 1815, was known as the Hundred Days).

During the first years of the Second Restoration (July 1815–July 1830) Louis XVIII reassured the nation of his commitment to reconciling the legacies of the Old Regime and the Revolution. To ensure the security of the monarchy, the bureaucracy was purged of Napoleonic officials. But the king also took measures against foes on the Right; when the election of 1815 produced a resounding victory for the ultraroyalists clustering around his brother, Louis XVIII dissolved the lower chamber and called for a new election. While the king reintroduced some minor Old Regime feast days, such as Saint Louis (25 August), he never held a public coronation; while he ruled a nation whose religion was officially Catholicism, he presided over a bureaucracy that protected the freedom of religion and the *biens nationaux.*

After the assassination of Charles Ferdinand, the Duke of Berri (1778–1820), in February 1820, in what was presumed to be a liberal plot, Louis XVIII curtailed freedom of the press and redoubled surveillance of critics of the regime; he passed a law doubling the votes of the richest, most conservative electors in the nation; he called for military intervention against the liberal regime in Spain (1823), allying France with the most counterrevolutionary nations of the Restoration period. Yet these measures paled before the counterrevolutionary thrust of his successor Charles X's reign (1824–1830). The Sacrilege Law, the coronation at Rheims, the law indemnifying nobles and clergymen for the *biens nationaux,* and the July Ordinances, abrogating all of the freedoms promised in the Charter, sent French men and women to the barricades (Revolution of 1830) in defense of the moderate liberal legacies of the Revolution that Louis XVIII preserved, albeit reluctantly.

See also **Charles X; French Revolution; Restoration.**

BIBLIOGRAPHY

Bertier de Sauvigny, Guillaume de. *La Restauration.* Paris, 1955. Translated as *The Bourbon Restoration* (Philadelphia, 1966). Standard work on the French Restoration, with detailed attention to the political controversies defining the reigns of Louis XVIII and Charles X.

Kroen, Sheryl. *Politics and Theater: The Crisis of Legitimacy in Restoration France, 1815–1830.* Berkeley, Calif., 2000. Cultural history of the Restoration highlighting the contrast between Louis XVIII's effort to reconcile with the revolutionary legacy and the more counterrevolutionary efforts of Charles X, and the popular response to both.

Mansel, Philip. *Louis XVIII.* London, 1981. Good biography of the king, covering his whole life, before and during his reign.

SHERYL KROEN

LOUIS-PHILIPPE (1773–1850; ruled 1830–1848), king of the French; known as the duc d'Orléans before accession to the throne.

Louis-Philippe d'Orléans was the eldest son of the liberal prince who became Philippe Égalité. An enthusiastic supporter of the Revolution of 1789, Louis-Philippe had risen to the rank of lieutenant general in the army by 1792. When the monarchy fell that year, he embraced the new republic and fought at the victorious battles of Valmy and Jemappes. In the wake of escalating political violence and problems of discipline within a volunteer army, he lost his enthusiasm for the republic. His father's vote in the National Convention to execute Louis XVI outraged him, and he approved of General Charles-François Dumouriez's military conspiracy to restore the monarchy. The government's interception of an incriminating letter led to an order for his arrest and his flight into exile on 5 April 1793. His flight precipitated the Convention's vote to imprison his father and two younger brothers. Philippe Égalité was guillotined seven months later, at which time Louis-Philippe became duc d'Orléans. His siblings remained in prison until 1797, when the Directory agreed to release them in return for a pledge that all three brothers leave Europe for the United States. In 1800 the duc d'Orléans found asylum in England and swore allegiance to Louis XVIII. His brothers died of ailments contracted while in prison. Suspicions that his father and later he, himself, aspired to the throne of France fed endless rumors among Bourbon supporters and republicans alike of an Orléanist plot. No reliable historical evidence supports that accusation.

ROAD TO THE THRONE

This troubled past with its tragic personal dimension gave Louis-Philippe's political career its distinctive features. In exile, he refused to join the prince de Condé's army of aristocratic émigrés made up of his family's bitterest enemies. Politically, he became an advocate of constitutional monarchy. He blamed its failure in France on the aristocratic emigration and Louis XVI's own irresolution. He attributed the violence of the Revolution to democracy. In 1809 he married Marie-Amélie de Bourbon, daughter of the king of the Two Sicilies. Implacable in his opposition to Napoleon I, the duc d'Orléans sought military commands in Spain and Sicily to fight the French. Fortunately for his subsequent career, he did not succeed.

Napoleon's defeat in 1814 made it possible for the duc d'Orléans to return to France until Napoleon's Hundred Days drove him into exile again in 1815. This time he refused to settle with his family in France until 1817, when the reactionary political climate that followed the second Bourbon Restoration had subsided. He had already established a reputation for liberal political views that he intended to protect. Both Louis XVIII and Charles X denied him any official function throughout the Restoration Monarchy. This official marginalization had the paradoxical effect of making him more popular with the liberal opposition. His popularity increased after he demonstrated his support for a meritocratic social order by sending his sons to a state secondary school. In July 1830 Charles X's four edicts that dissolved the Chamber of Deputies and disenfranchised many liberal voters touched off a popular revolution in Paris. To end the political crisis, liberal royalists prevailed on the duc d'Orléans to accept an offer from the legislature to replace the Bourbon family on the throne of France. The marquis de Lafayette's endorsement guaranteed him popular support.

KING OF THE FRENCH

Louis-Philippe knew that his decision would brand him as a usurper in the eyes of Bourbon loyalists. But he believed that only he could halt the civil war, shore up the monarchy, and prevent another foreign invasion of France. As "king of the French," he swore absolute fidelity to a liberal constitution that abolished censorship. A revised electoral law increased the number of male taxpayers eligible to vote from 90,000 to 170,000. Hereditary peers were abolished. The principle of merit was to regulate access to all public offices except the throne. Louis-Philippe hoped to consolidate a constitutional monarchy through economic growth, expanded public schooling, and a diplomatic alliance with England that would guarantee peace in Europe.

Over the course of his reign, known as the July Monarchy, Louis-Philippe oversaw the execution of these policy objectives. The number of public primary schools increased by a third for boys and a fifth for girls. After 1840, the French economy entered a period of rapid growth. Though France went to war with Holland to defend Belgium's internationally recognized boundaries in 1832, the king prevented a diplomatic crisis precipitated by his premier and minister of the interior, Adolphe Thiers, from escalating into war with England in 1840. To unite the French around a glorious image of themselves while avoiding war in Europe, the king created a new museum at Versailles celebrating French achievements. He approved the return from St. Helena of Napoleon's ashes, and he continued the conquest of Algeria begun by Charles X. Four of his five sons served in Algeria to prove their value to the nation.

Throughout his reign, Louis-Philippe retained considerable support from government officials and business elites. Popular approval for the July Monarchy waned, however, as supporters of the Bourbons (Legitimists) and republican advocates of universal suffrage and workers' rights discredited the regime in the popular press. Within five years, several short-lived insurrections and attempted assassinations of the king had prompted repressive laws that by limiting freedom of association and the press, belied the monarchy's liberal origins. Unstable majorities in the Chamber of Deputies made for a succession of fragile ministries in the 1830s. François Guizot managed to guarantee his own survival as chief minister in the 1840s through a combination of electoral manipulation and patronage for elected deputies. Despite the accidental death of the heir apparent in 1842, the regime appeared solid if unpopular in the 1840s.

Les Poires. Engraving by Charles Philipon from the French journal *Le Charivari,* 1834. Philipon shows the jowly king evolving into a pear. The comparison was so apt that the pear afterward became a common symbol for the king. MUSÉE DE LA VILLE DE PARIS, MUSÉE CARNAVALET, PARIS, FRANCE/BRIDGEMAN ART LIBRARY/ GIRAUDON

REVOLUTIONARY END TO REIGN

The rhetorical strategy adopted by republicans to discredit the regime pitted a greedy, self-interested bourgeoisie, out to profit at the expense of public interest, against a selfless working class of honorable men. Caricatures carried the message to even the illiterate. Louis-Philippe appeared the worst offender when he claimed that despite his enormous personal fortune, he could not afford to dower and support his numerous offspring in keeping with their stature as French royals. The Spanish marriages in 1846 that sacrificed the Anglo-French alliance for a dynastic triumph allowed his enemies to repeat the charge. In 1846 and 1847, a severe economic downturn amplified the persuasive power of this morality tale for elite and populace alike.

The final crisis of the regime originated in Louis-Philippe's refusal to consider any electoral reform for fear that populists would stir up popular passions. The decision to ban a political banquet in Paris in support of electoral reform set the stage for violent confrontation. On 23 February 1848 municipal guards fired on a chanting crowd in front of Guizot's ministry. Popular anger led to an insurrection the following day that made any compromise by the regime arrive too late. Louis-Philippe abdicated in favor of his grandson. After revolutionaries declared France a republic, he escaped to England, where he died on 26 August 1850.

See also **Charles X; France; Guizot, François; Restoration; Revolutions of 1830; Revolutions of 1848; Thiers, Louis-Adolphe.**

BIBLIOGRAPHY

Collingham, H. A. C. *The July Monarchy: A Political History of France, 1830–1848.* London, 1988.

Kenney, Elise K., and John M. Merriman. *The Pear: French Graphic Arts in the Golden Age of Caricature.* South Hadley, Mass., 1991.

Margadant, Jo Burr. "Gender, Vice, and the Political Imaginary in Postrevolutionary France: Reinterpreting the Failure of the July Monarchy, 1830–1848." *American Historical Review* 104, no. 5 (1999): 1461–1496.

Marrinan, Michael. *Painting Politics for Louis-Philippe: Art and Ideology in Orléanist France, 1830–1848.* New Haven, Conn., 1988.

Maza, Sarah. *The Myth of the French Bourgeoisie: An Essay on the Social Imaginary, 1750–1850.* Cambridge, Mass., 2003.

Pilbeam, Pamela. *The Constitutional Monarchy in France, 1814–1848.* Harlow, U.K., 1999.

Pinkney, David H. *Decisive Years in France, 1840–1847.* Princeton, N.J., 1986.

JO BURR MARGADANT

LOVETT, WILLIAM (1800–1877), British radical reformer.

Unable to find employment in the rope-making trade, William Lovett left his native Cornwall (and strict Methodist upbringing) for London to learn a second trade, subsequently gaining admittance to the elite West End Cabinet-makers Society, of which he was later elected president. The inadequacies of his formal education notwithstanding, he soon also progressed to a leading position within metropolitan artisan radicalism. In the heady days of the late 1820s and early 1830s he was in the vanguard of advanced radicals—along with Henry Hetherington and John Cleave—who adopted Robert Owen's (1771–1858) cooperative vision of a new moral world but eschewed his denigration and proscription of political reform.

While storekeeper of the First London Co-operative Trading Association and secretary of the British Association for Promoting Co-operative Knowledge, Lovett followed a militant "rational republican" line in successive radical reform organizations. Although renowned for organizational skills (he was often later described as the perfect political secretary), Lovett first came to notice for his hard-line stance against concessions to constitutionalism, gradualism, and middle-class leadership (hence his designation by the police as "a dangerous man"). In the midst of the Reform Bill crisis, he helped to draft the uncompromising rules and declaration of the significantly titled National Union of the Working Classes. The defeat of radical reform, compounded by the collapse of cooperative trading, prompted Lovett to revise his ways and means. In the disillusioning aftermath of the Reform Act of 1832, he began to move away from militant agitation and Owenite socialism toward the politics of improvement, a liberal project based on working-class education and mutual improvement, aided and facilitated by middle-class patronage—and with a strong commitment to international struggles for freedom and reform. The new alignment was evident in the London Working Men's Association (LWMA), an artisan's forum of mutual self-improvement founded in 1836 with Lovett (inevitably) as secretary: membership was restricted to "the *intelligent* and *useful* portion of the working classes" with honorary members elected from the middle class.

On behalf of the LWMA, Lovett, assisted by Francis Place (1771–1854), undertook the task (originally intended for a committee of six working men and six radical members of Parliament) of drafting a six-point parliamentary bill for democratic reform, on the agreed understanding that it would neither attack the Poor Law nor advocate socialism. At first, Feargus O'Connor (1796–1855) and the "fustian jackets, blistered hands and unshorn chins" whom he mobilized in the "factory" north regarded this "people's Charter" with suspicion, as a diversionary ploy by those opposed to the working-class thrust and tone of the anti–Poor Law agitation. However, once linked to schemes for a national petition and national convention (of which Lovett was the unanimous choice as secretary), the Charter became the symbol and focus of radical endeavor. Although scathing in criticism of O'Connor's "demagogic" leadership and "physical force" oratory, Lovett committed himself wholeheartedly to the first great Chartist agitation. Following the convention's move to Birmingham, his condemnation of police brutality toward Chartist demonstrators led to a year's imprisonment for seditious libel. Having outlined his plans in a short book coauthored with John Collins in prison, *Chartism: A New Organization of the People* (1840), Lovett placed himself at the head of the "new movers" on his release from Warwick Gaol, defiantly apart from vainglorious demagogues, fickle crowds, and illegal organizations of mass agitation such as the National Charter Association, which he declined to join.

By eradicating ignorance, drunkenness, and thraldom, his rival National Association for Promoting the Political and Social Improvement of the People offered the working class the self-respect necessary for the attainment and exercise of the franchise, "knowledge Chartism" to be promoted through a projected network of halls, schools, and libraries. The means, facilities, and methods of instruction in the virtues of working-class self-reliance, however, were assisted by middle-class patronage, at times exercised in a manner that tended to subvert the democratic ethos of collective self-help. It was this unthinking arrogance, the assumption of leadership and control, that prompted Lovett (with O'Connor in support) to reject the proposed "Bill of Rights" offered by the middle-class leaders of the Complete Suffrage Union in 1842 in place of the Charter. Thereafter, Lovett scraped a living as teacher and writer on the virtues of individual effort and personal morality, moving into a respectable Victorian liberalism, a perspective that infuses his autobiography (used rather uncritically by historians) at the expense of adequate acknowledgment of his initial militancy (or of the contribution of his wife, Mary, in sustaining his lengthy political career).

See also **Chartism; Labor Movements; O'Connor, Feargus; Owen, Robert.**

BIBLIOGRAPHY

Primary Sources

Lovett, William. *The Life and Struggles of William Lovett, in His Pursuit of Bread, Knowledge, and Freedom.* London, 1876.

Secondary Sources

Goodway, David. "William Lovett." In *Oxford Dictionary of National Biography.* Oxford, U.K., 2004.

Wiener, Joel. *William Lovett.* Manchester, U.K., 1989.

JOHN BELCHEM

LUDDISM. The Luddites were early-nineteenth-century English machine-breakers, so named after their mythical leader, Ned (later "King" or "General") Ludd, who according to legend smashed the needles of a stocking-frame in Anstey in Leicestershire sometime in or around 1779. Essentially an expression of working-class resistance to industrial technology, Luddism proper began on 11 March 1811, when a crowd of stockingers—hosiery knitters—destroyed some sixty-three frames in the small town of Arnold in Nottinghamshire. From there the violence spread to neighboring Derbyshire and Leicestershire and assumed the characteristics of an insurrectionary movement: pseudonymous letters, torch-lit raids, secrecy, and oath-taking. There was the occasional riot and the occasional injury or even loss of life. But for the most part, the Luddites reserved their fury for the machines that in their minds threatened their artisanal independence and way of life. They did not destroy machinery randomly or wantonly. Rather, they targeted those specific master hosiers who either charged excessive rents for the stocking frames or unscrupulously adapted them to the purpose of mass, low-quality production. To that extent, Luddism at its origin was less about machinery per se than its fair and responsible use; it was a movement in defense of traditional standards of employment and production.

After a lull through the summer of 1811, Luddism revived strongly across the Midland counties in November. Some 250 frames were destroyed in November and December, and another 300 in January 1812 alone. By now the authorities were seriously alarmed and suspected some sort of seditious French connection. The prince regent issued a proclamation offering a reward of £50 for information leading to the conviction of anyone involved in machine breaking, the home secretary dispatched nine troops of cavalry and two troops of infantry to the affected region, and the government of Prime Minister Spencer Perceval (1762–1812) introduced into Parliament a bill to make frame-breaking, hitherto a minor felony, a capital offense. By the time the bill became law in March (over the furious objections of Lord Byron, among others), Luddism in Nottinghamshire had largely died away.

Extract of a threatening letter from "Ned Ludd" to "Mr. Smith Shearing Frame Holder at Hill End Yorkshire," reproduced in W. B. Crump, ed., *The Leeds Woollen Industry* (Leeds, 1931), p. 229:

Sir. Information has just been given in that you are a holder of those detestable Shearing Frames, and I was desired by my Men to write to you and give you fair warning to pull them down, and for that purpose I desire you will now understand I am now writing to you. You will take Notice that if they are not taken down by the end of next week, I will detach one of my Lieutenants with at least 300 Men to destroy them and furthermore take Notice that if you give us the Trouble of coming so far we will increase your misfortune by burning your Buildings down to Ashes and if you have Impudence to fire upon any of my Men, they have orders to murder you, & burn all your Housing, you will have the Goodness to your Neighbours to inform them that the same fate awaits them if their Frames are not speedily taken down as I understand there are several in your Neighbourhood, Frame holders. . . .

Signed by the General of the Army of Redressers
Ned Ludd Clerk
Redressers for ever Amen.

To the north, however, in the textile districts of Lancashire and Yorkshire, Luddism still raged, and here the workers were far less particular about what they destroyed. In Leeds, an entire finishing mill went up in smoke; in Manchester, a whole warehouse stocked with machine-woven cloth. On 14 March 1812, a crowd of weavers in Stockport attacked several factories, destroyed power looms, and for good measure burned down the home of a local mill owner. The climax came on 12 April 1812, when one hundred workers attacked a strongly defended shearing mill near Huddersfield—the central incident in Charlotte Brontë's novel *Shirley* (1849). From this point, it becomes difficult to separate Luddism out from the general social turbulence of the time and the struggle for constitutional reform. Machine breaking continued in sporadic fashion throughout the nineteenth century. But the last explicit invocation of General Ludd's authority, the last record episode of machine breaking in the name of Ludd, came in January 1813, when fourteen stocking frames were destroyed in Nottinghamshire, where it all began.

What the Luddites had achieved is difficult to say. They had destroyed about £100,000 worth of machinery and delayed briefly the advent of the industrial age in a few isolated places. Their more lasting achievement, though, was to have made so enduring an impression on history that to this day technological skeptics describe themselves as Luddites. *Luddite* has become, that is to say, a generic term for anyone doubtful of the social benefits of innovative technology. Historians, meanwhile, continue to argue over the scope and bearing of the original revolt. Where one sees pointless physical violence and blind vandalism, another sees "collective bargaining by riot." Where one sees a reactionary hankering after the lost village community, another sees a progressive struggle for industrial democracy. The Luddites themselves, unfortunately, left no tracts or manifestos behind: the question of their ultimate intention will never be resolved. But in the evidence of their actions we discern, at the very least, a historically compelling refusal to submit to the arbitrary tyranny of the machine.

See also **Captain Swing; Industrial Revolution, First; Machine Breaking.**

BIBLIOGRAPHY

Hammond, J. L., and Barbara Hammond. *The Skilled Labourer, 1760–1832.* London, 1919.

Hobsbawm, Eric. "The Machine-Breakers." In *Labouring Men.* London, 1964.

Thomis, Malcolm I. *The Luddites: Machine-Breaking in Regency England.* Newton Abbott, U.K., 1970.

Thompson, E. P. *The Making of the English Working Class.* London, 1963.

STEWART WEAVER

LUDWIG II. *See* **Louis II.**

LUEGER, KARL (1844–1910), Austrian politician.

Karl Lueger was arguably the most consequential mayor of Vienna from 1848, the year of European revolution, till 1938, the year of *Anschluss.* His rule lasted nearly thirteen years (1897–1910), longer than any other Viennese mayor during the sixty-eight-year reign of Francis Joseph I, emperor of Austria-Hungary. As mayor, Lueger occupied the highest elective position in the Habsburg Empire, and he was at the same time the leader of the Austrian Christian Social Party.

Lueger remains a controversial figure and his is a dual legacy. He socialized and improved many of Vienna's municipal services, and built schools, parks, and public facilities. But some consider his ideas to have had an ominous impact on Adolf Hitler, who acknowledged him in *Mein Kampf* as "the greatest German mayor of all times." Lueger, however, was an unsystematic anti-Semite whose most remembered words—"I decide who is a Jew!"—were echoed both by Hitler and one of Hitler's most important followers, Hermann Göring. Lueger led Austria's first successful mass political party, having formed a coalition comprised of many interest groups. According to the American historian Richard S. Levy, creating such a coalition was perhaps Lueger's most important contribution to Hitler's political education. The Christian Social Party came into its own during Lueger's mayoralty and extended its influence into imperial politics as the leading party in the Austrian parliament from 1907 to 1911.

Coming to the fore during the waning years of Austrian Liberalism, Lueger built on its foundations just as the Social Democrats would carry on some of the Christian Socialists' unrealized projects. His family background marked Lueger as a man of the people, but it was somewhat unusual for the pre-1918 period that he achieved a significant leadership role belying his lower-middle-class origins. It was said that no prime minister could be appointed without his approval, and Lueger was dubbed "the uncrowned king of Vienna." In spite of his personal background, Lueger received an elitist education at the exclusive Theresianum preparatory school, where his father was a custodian, and at the University of Vienna. He received his doctor of law degree in 1870.

THE CATHOLIC POLITICIAN

Lueger was an important champion of fin-de-siècle Austrian political Catholicism. Pope Leo XIII (r. 1878–1903) thought well enough of him during his struggle for the mayoralty to display Lueger's picture on his desk. Some aristocratic Austrians, including Emperor Francis Joseph himself who three times denied Lueger the necessary sanction of his election to mayor, disliked his anti-Semitism. But other Catholic conservatives saw Lueger and his movement as important bulwarks against "godless socialism," a concern that Lueger and his propagandists skillfully exploited. Lueger made a show of religious devotion, but this may well have been calculated to create an image of himself as a defender of traditional religious values. His relationship with certain radical priests attempting to win back their wandering flocks was thus of mutual advantage, because the priests stumped for Lueger from their pulpits.

THE ANTI-SEMITE

Surprisingly, one of Lueger's early friends, the physician and politician Ignaz Mandl, was Jewish. As early as 1877 Mandl's party campaigned against a rival on the grounds that he was a Jew. Though out of office at the time, Lueger nonetheless assisted Mandl's party. This may have been Lueger's first initiation into the tactics of expedient anti-Semitism, a technique that later played a major role in defining his politics. During most of the 1880s Lueger's anti-Semitism was more implied than overt, but he did cooperate with a number of outspoken anti-Semites, including the racist Georg von Schönerer, whose Jewish exclusion bill Lueger supported in 1887. During that same year Lueger began to make anti-Semitic speeches and thus contributed to the increasing radicalization of Austrian politics. While some of Lueger's anti-Semitic activities were doubtless opportunistic and calculated to capitalize on popular sentiment, there is no denying that, as a "respectable" politician with an elitist education in the eyes of his followers, he legitimized anti-Semitism in Austrian politics. His successors had their work done for them.

Lueger avoided violating the letter of the law: Jews had been granted legal equality together with most other religions in the empire, so anti-Semitic Austrian politicians eschewed the older religious line of attack. Instead, anti-Semitism assumed a

Karl Lueger, seated at far right, with a group of supporters. © AUSTRIAN ARCHIVES/CORBIS

racial or political shape and would in the century to come aim at depriving Jews of the franchise, their civil rights, and ultimately their lives. Schönerer was one of the new school of extremist anti-Semites. He possessed a violent and unsavory reputation after he led his followers in wrecking the editorial office of the *Neues Wiener Tagblatt* (New Vienna daily) in 1888. Schönerer believed this newspaper had prematurely reported the death of William I, emperor of Germany, in order to manipulate stock prices. Schönerer was arrested, tried and found guilty of assault, and sentenced to jail and forfeiture of his political rights until 1893. He also lost his patent of nobility. Lueger defended Schönerer in parliament, stating that one of his constituents had told him at a party meeting that there were "enough Jewish journalists in Vienna, but only one Schönerer" (Geehr, 1990, p. 74).

In 1889 Lueger broke with Mandl. Thereafter, until he died in 1910, Lueger continued to make anti-Semitic remarks in parliament, the Lower Austrian diet, and the municipal council, and to his local constituents. Sometimes his remarks anticipated those heard later in Germany. Thus Jews were "the destructive element" wherever they settled. Jews in Austrian education became a favorite target, as was "the Liberal Jewish Press." Both before and after he became mayor, Lueger asserted in parliament that Jewish sects murdered Christians for their blood for use in ritual practices.

But Lueger's anti-Semitism included more than verbal abuse. During his mayoralty Jewish teachers were denied promotion and sometimes fired. And during this same period there are recorded instances of anti-Semitic violence. From 1898 to 1903 the Vienna municipal government supported an anti-Semitic theater, the Kaiserjubiläums-Stadttheater, now the Volksoper, second only in seating capacity to the national Burgtheater. According to its bylaws, the Stadttheater, or "Aryan Theater" as it was sometimes called, was prohibited from employing Jews in any capacity or performing plays by Jewish authors. The Aryan Theater actually produced anti-Semitic agitational plays and only the imperial censor prevented production of more violent works. Undaunted, the theater director Adam Müller-Guttenbrunn published some of the unperformed dramas at his own expense and distributed them in thousands of copies.

Lueger was aware of anti-Semitic pogroms in Russia during the revolutions of 1905. At an electoral assembly toward the end of 1905 he warned Jews in Vienna that if they behaved as had their "co-religionists in Russia" and agitated for revolution, "if the Jews should threaten our fatherland then we will show no mercy" ("Grosse Wählerversammlung" [Large electoral meeting], p. 5). Three days later in a municipal council meeting, one of Lueger's opponents charged him with "legally prohibited incitement against a religious community." Lueger treated the charge as an irritation and replied with racist slurs against Viktor Adler, the leader of the Austrian Social Democratic Party.

But perhaps the most damaging aspect of Lueger's anti-Semitism was its legacy to his Christian Social successors, some of whom remained lifelong anti-Semites, even after the Holocaust. Many years before that event the Hungarian Zionist leader Theodor Herzl saw Lueger outside a polling place in 1895. He heard one of Lueger's supporters remark "That is our Führer!" This taught Herzl more than any tirade how deeply rooted anti-Semitism was among Lueger's followers. Lueger nourished the growth of this pernicious tendency.

LUEGER IN THE POLITICAL CONTEXT OF FIN-DE-SIÈCLE AUSTRIA

Awakening mass political consciousness, the extension of the franchise, and his charisma facilitated Lueger's rise to power. An erstwhile Liberal from 1875 to 1882 seeking a direction, he flirted with a number of parties including the Socialists, before settling in the newly created Christian Social Party in the late 1880s. Lueger was more than a clever demagogue. He instinctively and accurately gauged the mood of his audience and played on or reinforced existing prejudices—hallmarks of the master propagandist.

As an inventor of mass politics, Lueger exploited his stately appearance and lifelong bachelor status. He persuaded women who were denied the franchise to influence their male relatives to vote for him. The mayor created a party organization, the Christian Viennese Women's League, for this express purpose. Most agree that Lueger owed a substantial measure of his early success to his female supporters.

If Lueger drew significant strength from women, normally a nontraditional source of political power, he also won early support from a youth organization named after him. This won the young Hitler's admiration. Other important Lueger bodies included a Christian Social workers association and groups of publicist priests. Lower-middle-class property owners also saw him as their champion, and the shopkeepers, artisans, cab drivers, and small grocers—all of them plentiful in Vienna—and later rural conservatives as well, came to form his voting base. Lueger did not set out to invent mass politics, but he understood early on the significance of the widening franchise and the political awakening of those he represented. A keen observer, he selected the precise moment for directing his appeal to as many groups as possible, rather than concentrating on any one large group such as unskilled laborers or pan-German nationalists, whose political hour, he sensed, had not yet arrived. When it did, Lueger's creation was replaced by yet more radical politics. Lueger left Vienna a better place to live, with its improved transportation, parks, schools, and other public amenities, but a question remains as to the true cost of these achievements.

See also **Anti-Semitism; Austria-Hungary; Francis Joseph; Socialism, Christian; Vienna.**

BIBLIOGRAPHY

Primary Sources

"Grosse Wählerversammlung." *Deutsches Volksblatt.* 6 December 1905, 5.

Secondary Sources

Beller, Steven. *Vienna and the Jews, 1867–1938.* Cambridge, U.K., 1989.

Boyer, John W. *Political Radicalism in Late Imperial Vienna: Origins of the Christian Social Movement, 1848–1897.* Chicago, 1981.

———. *Culture and Political Crisis in Vienna: Christian Socialism in Power, 1897–1918.* Chicago, 1995.

Geehr, Richard S. *Adam Müller-Guttenbrunn and the Aryan Theater of Vienna, 1898–1903.* Göppingen, West Germany, 1973.

———. *Karl Lueger: Mayor of Fin de Siècle Vienna.* Detroit, Mich., 1990.

Pauley, Bruce F. *From Prejudice to Persecution: A History of Austrian Anti-Semitism.* Chapel Hill, N.C., 1992.

Schorske, Carl E. *Fin-de-Siècle Vienna: Politics and Culture.* New York, 1979.

Richard S. Geehr

LUMIÈRE, AUGUSTE AND LOUIS.

Contrary to common beliefs about the invention of motion pictures, Auguste Lumière (1862–1954) and Louis Lumière (1864–1948) were not the first to devise and project moving images on a screen. However, their synthesis of late-nineteenth-century discoveries by Etienne-Jules Marey (1830–1904), Émile Reynaud (1844–1918), and William Dickson (1860–1935, under Thomas Edison [1847–1931]), to name a few, resulted in the Cinématographe, the most practical and ingenious motion picture camera and projector.

A deceptively simple box of wood and copper, the Cinématographe weighed in at ten pounds, making it a truly portable combination camera, contact printer, and projector. Edison's camera, the Kinetograph, weighed more than 1,100 pounds. It was impractical for shooting outside away from an electrical power source. Edison filmed in his West Orange, New Jersey, studio, known as the "Black Maria," while the Lumières' hand-cranked camera filmed life in the streets.

On 28 December 1895, barely thirty-five passers-by braved a glance at the Cinématographe's first public film projection in the converted billiards room known as the "Salon Indien" of Paris's Grand Café. Each customer paid a franc and watched enthralled as flickering black and white images were projected: a group of workers leaving the Lumière photography factory in Lyon; Auguste Lumière feeding his baby daughter; a boy stepping on a garden hose—to our delight and the dismay of the gardener. The entire program, with time out to change the fifty-second reels, lasted fifteen minutes.

The receipts for the evening were not even enough to pay for the room rental and the hired help, but word of mouth would change that the very next day. No major daily newspaper covered the event, but a local gazette, *Le Radical,* exalted: "We have already recorded and reproduced spoken words. We can now record and play back life. We will be able to see our families again long after they are gone."

Within days, lines trailed down the Boulevard des Capucines. The Lumière Company raked in 2,500 francs a day by mid-January 1896. From 1896 to 1900, the Lumières earned 3 million francs (the equivalent of approximately $20 million in 2006). Not bad for "a simple scientific curiosity," as Antoine Lumière had described his sons' invention to prospective buyer Georges Méliès (1861–1938).

Both Auguste and Louis Lumière were born in Besançon, France. They were close throughout their childhood growing up in Lyon. During a vacation on the Brittany coast in 1877, they built a portable laboratory and darkroom and vowed that they would work together in the future. Auguste received a diploma in chemistry; Louis, at sixteen, earned top honors in math, drawing, and chemistry.

By Louis's eighteenth birthday, Antoine Lumière's photography company was on the verge of bankruptcy. Louis and Auguste convinced their father to let them take over the business, and within a year they had righted the situation. Louis Lumière invented an instantaneous photograph known as "extra-rapides à etiquette bleue" which would remain on the market for eighty years and make the Lumières wealthy.

In fact, by 1890, the Lumière factories in Lyon were the largest manufacturers of photographic products in Europe, second only in the world to George Eastman in Rochester, New York. Edison's Kinetoscope, devised for viewing 35 mm Kodak filmstrips shot with a motion picture camera that Dickson invented for Edison in 1893, was commercialized in Paris in the summer of 1894. Louis and Auguste Lumière were amused by the projections that were confined to a box designed for a single viewer, but the Lumières were determined to capture motion and project it on a screen.

Both brothers suffered from terrible migraine attacks. It was supposedly during one painful sleepless night that Louis Lumière thought up a means of advancing film through the camera with a hand

The Lumière brothers in their laboratory. Undated photograph. ©BETTMANN/CORBIS

crank mechanism similar to the foot pedal on a sewing machine. He built a prototype camera, applied for a patent for it on 13 February 1895, and in March, filmed the workers leaving the factory. A few days later on 22 March, the Lumières presented their film to a group of scientists in Paris. Throughout that year they perfected the camera and named it the *Cinématographe* from the Greek words for "to write with movement." Jules Carpenter, an engineer, worked with them and eventually built the Cinématographe in quantity. A dozen cameras were ready by March 1896, and Louis Lumière began training cameramen to be sent around the world. Within two years, Lumière cameramen filmed some 2,000 shorts in most corners of Europe, Africa, Asia, and South and North America.

Two theaters flourished in Paris where people were amazed to see the sights of the world without budging from their chairs. Within two years, however, the novelty wore off and audiences dwindled. Meanwhile, Méliès, Charles Pathé (1863–1957), and Léon Gaumont (1864–1946), who had all begun producing fictional films, were forging France into the world's leader in motion picture production, a distinction it would hold until World War I.

Louis Lumière dreamed up other inventions. A wraparound screen twenty feet high and sixty-five feet in diameter enveloped visitors to the 1900 World's Fair in Paris with Photorama views of European cities. Lumière had devised a carousel-shaped still camera with a revolving lens that covered a 360-degree field of view. There were daily Photorama viewings in Paris for two years thereafter.

Auguste and Louis Lumière both worked night and day to create a color photo process. By 1905, experimenting with potato flour and dyes, they had invented the Autochrome, a photograph broken into little colored dots like a painting by Georges Seurat (1859–1891). By 1914, the Lumière factories were manufacturing 6,000 Autochrome plates a day. They also built a special projector for Autochrome glass slides. Louis Lumière naturally saw the possibilities for color motion pictures, but the large grain and the lack of sufficiently sensitive film delayed a practical process until the early 1930s.

Louis Lumière patented a speaker for phonographs and radios made from corrugated paper. During World War I, he invented and patented an artificial jointed hand for disabled veterans as well as a catalytic gas heater that was installed in airplanes and many apartments. He devised a stereoscopic photo process in the 1920s that resembles later holograms. In 1935, Louis invented a stereoscopic 35 mm movie camera. Viewers had to wear glasses with one blue lens, the other green, to view the 3-D movies.

As for Auguste, the study of biology took precedence in his professional life. As soon as x-rays were discovered in Germany, Auguste Lumière began similar experiments in Lyon, and was the first in France to use x-rays for medical research. Later he built his own pharmaceutical company, developing homeopathic remedies and inventing a nonsticking bandage that is still sold today.

Louis Lumière died in 1948, a few years short of seeing a 3-D process similar to his own refined and commercialized in the United States. Auguste Lumière died in 1954 at the age of ninety-two.

The Lumière brothers, like Edison, were great industrialists and proselytized the cinema(tographe) worldwide. That certainly helps explain why their names are remembered and not those of Marey, Reynaud, or Dickson. For the Lumière centenary celebration in 1995, the Banque de France printed approximately seventeen million 200 franc notes with the Lumière brothers' effigy on it. However, in a rare showing of posthumous retroactive political correctness, the French government recalled the bills and destroyed them when a public outcry accused the Lumière brothers of collaborationist activities in Lyon during the German Occupation. Gustave Eiffel replaced the brothers on the 200 franc note while Paul Cézanne (1839–1906) replaced Eiffel on the 100 franc note; of course, the rest is monetary history, since barely six years later, France converted to the Euro.

See also **Cinema; Fin de Siècle; France; Méliès, Georges.**

BIBLIOGRAPHY

Aubert, Michelle, and Jean-Claude Seguin. *La Production cinématographique des Frères Lumière.* Paris, 1996.

Chardère, Bernard. *Les Lumière.* Paris, 1985.

Musser, Charles. *The Emergence of Cinema: The American Screen to 1907.* New York, 1990.

Rittaud-Hutinet, Jacques. *Le Cinéma des origines: les frères Lumière et leurs opérateurs.* Paris, 1985.

Sadoul, Georges. *Lumière et Méliès.* Paris, 1985.

Sauvage, Léo. *L'affaire Lumière: du mythe à l'histoire: enquête sur les origines du cinéma.* Paris, 1985.

GLENN MYRENT

LUXEMBURG, ROSA (1871–1919), socialist activist.

Rosa Luxemburg was one of the great intellects and militants of pre-1914 European socialism. Her life's work spanned the Russian, Polish, and German socialist movements as well as the Second International, the worldwide organization of socialist parties. She made major contributions to Marxist theory and to debates on political strategy within the socialist movement. Marxist analysis and faith in the creative activism of workers were her unwavering guideposts.

EARLY YEARS

Luxemburg was born in 1871 into a middle-class Jewish family in Zamość, Poland, at the time a part of the Russian Empire. Her background, like her future politics, reflected the multiethnic and multilingual world of central and eastern Europe. The family was not religious. Her parents spoke Polish at home and read and admired German literature. Luxemburg herself would move easily in three languages, Russian, Polish, and German, and read and understood French and English.

When Luxemburg was still very young the family moved to Warsaw. Admitted to an elite girls' high school, she quickly became involved in the revolutionary movement. Warsaw and other parts of Poland were experiencing the early stages of

Rosa Luxemburg addresses the Internationale in Stuttgart, 1907. GETTY IMAGES

industrialization and the oppressive social conditions it created. Many Poles resented the discrimination and repression they suffered under imperial Russian control. The revolutionary movement was highly diverse; Luxemburg was finding her way to its most radical wing.

Already as a teenager Luxemburg had come to the attention of the police. Threatened with arrest, she fled in 1889 to Switzerland, a safe haven for socialists from all over Europe and especially for those from the Russian Empire. Switzerland was also pathbreaking in allowing women to enter the university. Luxemburg matriculated at the University of Zurich, where she studied law, political economy, and biology. She received a doctorate in 1897 with a dissertation called "Die industrielle Entwicklung Polens" (The industrial development of Poland).

Alongside her formal studies, Luxemburg read intensively in the works of Karl Marx (1818–1883) and Friedrich Engels (1820–1895) and other socialist theoreticians. In Switzerland she began to write for socialist newspapers and quickly acquired a reputation for her sharp pen and radical ideas. She became a leading figure in the Social Democratic Party of the Kingdom of Poland and Lithuania (SDKPiL). In opposition to virtually every other political movement in Poland, the SDKPiL decisively opposed Polish and every other form of nationalism. That position, which placed the SDKPiL at odds with many other socialist parties as well, would remain a lodestar of Luxemburg's politics. But her ambitions were large, too great to be contained by the small Polish socialist movement.

GERMANY AND THE REVISIONISM DEBATE

In the late nineteenth and early twentieth centuries, Germany's Social Democratic Party (SPD) was the largest and best-organized socialist party in the world. It also claimed moral stature as the party of Marx and Engels. It occupied pride of place in the Socialist International. To have a decisive influence on the future of the socialist movement, Luxemburg knew that she had to participate in the German party.

In 1898 she moved to Germany and through an arranged marriage, obtained German citizenship. Her timing was auspicious. Eduard Bernstein, one of the leading figures of the SPD, had just published a number of articles that would unleash the "revisionism debate" among socialists. Bernstein argued that socialists had to update their Marxism. They had to realize that capitalist society was not dividing into two classes, a massive impoverished proletariat and a tiny group of wealthy capitalists. Instead, living standards in general were improving and the middle class was expanding exponentially. Socialists had to find a way to appeal to the middle class. They had to abandon the fire and brimstone of revolution and work through the electoral systems of bourgeois democracy. The end goal of socialism would come gradually through the daily work of the party and the extension of democracy.

Luxemburg reacted with fury. In a series of articles in the SPD press and in a short book, *Sozial reform oder Revolution?* (1899; *Social Reform or*

Revolution), she attacked Bernstein for abandoning the principles of Marxism. She reaffirmed the Marxist fundamentals that capitalism was a system destined for collapse. It would be overthrown by the revolutionary action of the proletariat around the world, who would then install a socialist system. Luxemburg won the theoretical debate, but it was a pyrrhic victory. The SPD and many other socialist parties outside the Russian Empire were on a slow march to a gradual form of politics that more closely reflected Bernstein's position than her arguments.

MARXIST THEORY

Moreover, like many Marxists, Luxemburg would never be able to resolve intellectually the key theoretical issue concerning the collapse of capitalism: would the decisive blow come from the systemic contradictions of capitalism, or from the revolutionary action of the proletariat? (She would have responded that the very question is undialectical and therefore non-Marxist.) In her major theoretical work, *Die Akkumulation des Kapitals* (1913; *The Accumulation of Capital*), she argued that as capitalism came to encompass every region of the globe, it would lose the advantages of uneven development, that is, capital's constant search for the sites with the cheapest costs of labor and materials, which therefore engendered the greatest profit margins. The moment at which capital became truly global would also be the moment of its demise. Such a position could and did inspire a politics of passivity: socialists only needed to wait for that moment and then the new system would emerge. But Luxemburg was also a forceful advocate of decisive revolutionary action. She wrote and spoke about the need for the proletariat and the party to engage unceasingly the capitalist enemy—through strikes, demonstrations, rallies, and elections, and, if necessary, at the barricades in armed conflict. Theoretically, she could never resolve the tension between her understanding of the workings of capitalism as a system and her promotion of revolutionary activism.

MASS ACTION AND DEMOCRACY

The Russian Revolution of 1905 provided the opportunity for her to develop further her thoughts on socialist strategy. The socialist parties had been taken by surprise when workers set loose a strike wave that reached all the industrializing areas of the Russian Empire, including Poland. Workers demanded better wages and working conditions, but the strikes quickly escalated into overtly political affairs with calls for democratization. Ignoring the advice of many of her comrades, Luxemburg traveled to Warsaw and quickly plunged into a swirl of meetings and writings. Against more moderate socialists and nationalists of all stripes, she promoted the two major positions she had already staked out: internationalism and revolution. But by the time she arrived in Poland, the revolutionary movement was already on the ebb. She was caught and imprisoned (not for the first time), and only the most strenuous efforts of her family and friends secured her release.

During the Revolution, she wrote one of her most important works, the long essay, *Massenstreik, Partei und Gewerkschaften* (1906; *Mass Strike, Party, and Unions*). Luxemburg delivered a withering critique of the growth of bureaucracy within the SPD and the trade unions. She argued that to its officials, the party and unions as organizations had become more important than the goal of the revolutionary transformation of capitalism. She based her alternatives on her observations of Russian and Polish workers in 1905. They had launched the Revolution spontaneously. They had not waited for directives from shop stewards or party bosses. In Luxemburg's radical view, the party and the unions had become obstacles to revolutionary action. In the future, the SPD and the unions should follow the workers rather than the other way around. The role of the formal organizations of the labor movement should be to agitate and educate, and to help elevate the spontaneous activism of workers into revolutionary assaults on the existing system.

Luxemburg's views stimulated another great debate within the SPD and the International, but they were hardly embraced. Many leaders and mid-level functionaries had spent years building up the institutions of the labor movement, often at great personal sacrifice. The unions and the party were their proud creation. They viewed Luxemburg as a starry-eyed, irresponsible radical. Less charitably, they said among themselves that she was a female Polish-Jewish intellectual with no real experience of the working class. Those party and union officials who were themselves workers, at least by background, where far less inclined to idealize the spontaneous activism of their class comrades.

Luxemburg's emphasis on spontaneity led her into another great conflict, this time with Vladimir Lenin (1870–1924). Luxemburg and Lenin shared the commitment to revolutionary activism, but came to opposite strategic conclusions. While Luxemburg cherished spontaneity, Lenin idealized the revolutionary party. Left to their own devices, workers, according to Lenin, would never become revolutionaries. They needed the guiding hand of the party with its cadre of disciplined, professional revolutionaries. Luxemburg had attacked Lenin's views even before the Revolution of 1905 and the dispute between them continued. In 1918, while she languished in a German prison, she wrote a sharp-eyed critique of the Bolshevik Revolution. In all of these writings, filled with evocative prose, she argued for the importance of free speech within the party and society at large. Socialism was the fulfillment of democracy; it could not flourish without democratic procedures. Lenin's organizational fetishism, she suggested, threatened to undermine the very meaning of socialism.

These were prescient words, and her conflict with Lenin and the Bolsheviks has given her a well-deserved reputation as a democrat. She is admired by feminists and socialists around the world, who look to her ideas as an alternative to the repressive and dictatorial form of socialism that came to prevail in the communist world in the twentieth century. Her combination of political commitment with deep personal friendships and love relationships, notably with her fellow Polish revolutionary Leo Jogiches, is expressed eloquently in her letters and has won her flocks of admirers. Yet Luxemburg never squarely faced the inherent contradictions of her own politics. As a Marxist she was convinced that there existed a correct path to an inevitable socialist future. But what if people, and the proletariat in particular, chose a different path? What if other futures were possible? What sense does democracy make when the future is already known?

World War I brought great tragedies, personal and political, to Luxemburg. It also unleashed her revolutionary hopes and optimism, which were dashed by her brutal assassination in January 1919.

See also **Bebel, August; Germany; Kautsky, Karl; Labor Movements; Lenin, Vladimir; Russia; Socialism.**

BIBLIOGRAPHY

Primary Sources

Ettinger, Elzbieta, ed. and trans. *Comrade and Lover: Rosa Luxemburg's Letter to Leo Jogiches.* Cambridge, Mass., 1979.

Waters, Mary-Alice, ed. *Rosa Luxemburg Speaks.* New York, 1970.

Secondary Sources

Abraham, Richard. *Rosa Luxemburg: A Life for the International.* Oxford, U.K., 1989.

Nettl, Peter. *Rosa Luxemburg.* Abridged ed. Oxford, U.K., 1969.

Schorske, Carl E. *German Social Democracy, 1905–1917: The Development of the Great Schism.* Cambridge, Mass., 1955.

Weitz, Eric D. *Creating German Communism, 1890–1990: From Popular Protests to Socialist State.* Princeton, N.J., 1997.

ERIC D. WEITZ

LYELL, CHARLES (1797–1875), Scottish geologist and man of letters.

Charles Lyell was brought up and educated in the south of England, ultimately graduating in classics from Exeter College, Oxford, in 1819. He then entered Lincoln's Inn, and became a barrister in 1822, but by then much of his time was taken up by science. The son of a wealthy botanist, Lyell had early been fascinated by natural history, and like many other young gentlemen at Oxford he had been spellbound by the geological lectures of the charismatic William Buckland (1784–1856).

Buckland was an important figure in the genteel Geological Society of London, founded in 1807 with the aim of reinventing geology as an empirical discipline focused on the strata. Such geologists rejected what they saw as the unbridled speculations of eighteenth-century "theories of the earth," and they shared Lyell's determination to "free the science from Moses" (the putative author of the Book of Genesis). By the 1820s many geologists agreed that the earth had supported life long before the creation of man. Buckland himself promoted a progressive vision of earth history, and his sensational research on cave fossils vividly demonstrated the value of present-day evidence (such as bones chewed by Buckland's pet hyena Billy) in picturing the remote past. For Lyell this approach soon hardened into a fundamental principle: processes observed in the present world were, he claimed, sufficient to account for all existing traces of the past.

In 1825 Lyell's first scientific paper was published, based on geological fieldwork undertaken near his family seat in Scotland. By now he was moving in the uppermost scientific circles in London and Paris, becoming secretary of the Geological Society of London in 1823 and a fellow of the Royal Society in 1826. The modest income from his sporadic legal work was soon supplemented by literary activity: in 1825 the Tory publisher John Murray invited him to write for the prestigious *Quarterly Review*. A moderate Whig and theologically liberal, Lyell used this platform to promote reform among the Tory intelligentsia, protesting against the clerical domination of English intellectual life and (encouraged by clerical geologists like Buckland) contesting the Bible's authority over scientific matters. However, Lyell was so concerned to distance himself from the rising tide of evolutionary speculation that he even denied any directional element to the history of life on Earth, viewing the world instead as a self-sustaining system shaped by uniformly acting natural processes. Here he took his cue from older Scottish Enlightenment models, and from contemporary research on the Continent. Massive cataclysms—such as the "geological deluge" proposed by Buckland and others to explain what we call glacial phenomena—had no place in this vision of stability and regeneration, which Lyell set out with a wealth of empirical evidence (most of it gathered from the work of others) in his literary masterpiece, *Principles of Geology* (1830–1833).

This book is sometimes credited with having introduced into British earth science such concepts as the great antiquity of the earth, though this idea had long been a tacit commonplace among geologists. Lyell's greatest achievements did not lie in matters of geological theory: his most cherished claims never caught on, such as his denial of progression in the history of life on Earth and his insistence that no past cataclysm could have been greater than present-day equivalents. His true importance lay in his ability to synthesize and deploy vast quantities of abstruse scientific data within an elegant, rhetorically compelling work of literature. Aimed at a dual readership of specialists and nonspecialists, the *Principles* transformed the public profile of geology and its genteel practitioners at a critical stage in the science's development. As a confident statement of geology's authority as a secular discipline, blazoning its independence from biblical scholarship, the *Principles* played a major role both in ongoing boundary disputes between science and theology, and in wider debates about man's place in nature. In such matters, the pen proved mightier than the geological hammer.

The *Principles* sold well and was widely read: among its more celebrated admirers was the young Charles Darwin. New and cheaper editions (often substantially revised) followed, as did translations into French and German. The sometime barrister had found his vocation as a scientific author and advocate for science; he also served briefly as professor of geology at King's College, London (1831–1833), and was much in demand as a visiting lecturer both in Britain and in the United States. Lyell was knighted in 1848 and became a baronet in 1864; his wife, Mary (née Horner), whom he had married in 1832, was now a prominent hostess in London intellectual society. Lyell's later publications included *Elements of Geology* (1838), two sets of *Travels in North America* (1845 and 1849), and *The Antiquity of Man* (1863), in which he summarized the recently unearthed evidence for the coexistence of fossil humans with extinct mammals. In the tenth edition of the *Principles* (1867–1868) Lyell at last gave his qualified and reluctant approval to Darwin's theory of evolution. Mary died in 1873, and Lyell survived her by less than two years. He is buried in Westminster Abbey.

See also **Cuvier, Georges; Darwin, Charles; Evolution; Science and Technology.**

LEISURE

Horse Races and Amusements on the Frozen Neva in St. Petersburg. Nineteenth-century French print, 1846. Russian leisure activities are depicted in a picturesque manner for French viewers. SNARK/ART RESOURCE, NY

RIGHT: ***At the Start.*** Painting by Henry Alken, mid-nineteenth century. Alken is renowned for his realistic paintings of fox hunting, which was enormously popular among British elites in the nineteenth century. FINE ART PHOTOGRAPHIC LIBRARY, LONDON /ART RESOURCE, NY

BELOW: ***Garden Café Moritzhof in Berlin.*** Painting by Adolf von Menzel, 1865. As the population of European cities grew dramatically during the nineteenth century, residents sought refuge in large parks and gardens. BILDARCHIV PREUSSISCHER KULTURBESITZ/ART RESOURCE, NY

LEFT: *At the End of the Day.* Painting by Hans Thoma, 1868. Thoma celebrates the simplicity and piety of the rural people of his native Black Forest region. BILDARCHIV PREUSSISCHER KULTURBESITZ/ART RESOURCE, NY

BELOW: *The Beach at Trouville.* Painting by Eugène Boudin, 1864. Wide belief in the health benefits of bathing in the sea and a growing appreciation of natural landscapes led to the development of seaside resorts beginning at the end of the eighteenth century. The fishing village of Trouville, on the Normandy coast, became a popular travel destination for Parisians during the mid-nineteenth century, spurred in part by the construction of a railway line in 1863. ERICH LESSING/ART RESOURCE, NY

RIGHT: ***Café Terrace, Place du Forum, Arles.*** Painting by Vincent van Gogh, 1888. Outdoor cafés such as the one depicted here became a feature of European life during the last quarter of the nineteenth century, inviting patrons to linger over food or drinks while observing activities in the surrounding environment. RIJKSMUSEUM KROLLER-MULLER, OTTERLO, NETHERLANDS/BRIDGEMAN ART LIBRARY

BELOW: ***Dance at the Moulin de la Galette.*** Painting by Pierre Auguste Renoir, 1876. Renoir depicts a favorite gathering spot of working-class Parisians, a lively café in the Montmartre neighborhood where Sunday afternoon dances were held. ERICH LESSING/ART RESOURCE, NY

LEFT: *A Game of Ninepins.* Painting by Philippe Jolyet, 1894. Jolyet evokes the pastoral pleasures of an outdoor game at a time when the daily life of most Europeans was becoming more hectic. RÉUNION DES MUSÉES NATIONAUX/ART RESOURCE, NY

BELOW: *Boating on the Epte.* Painting by Claude Monet, c. 1890. Monet depicts two of his step-daughters enjoying an excursion on the river near his home at Giverny. MUSEU DE ARTE SÃO PAULO, BRAZIL/BRIDGEMAN ART LIBRARY

TOP RIGHT: **Advertising poster by Paul Berthon, 1898.** Berthon's classic art nouveau advertisement exemplifies the common perception of music education as a means of refinement for young women. © SWIM INK/CORBIS

BELOW: **Motorcycle advertising poster.** By Théophile-Alexandre Steinlen, 1899. By the end of the nineteenth century, bicycling had become a hugely popular form of recreation. Motorized bicycles were introduced about 1885, and within twenty years they were widely available in western Europe. BILDARCHIV PREUSSISCHE KULTURBESITZ/ART RESOURCE, NY

BOTTOM RIGHT: **Cover of the French magazine *Les Sports Modernes*, July 1905.** A lithograph by Cecil Aldin, who was a leading force in the revival of sporting art in Britain, shows two polo players. Originating in the Far East, the game was quickly adopted by British soldiers serving in India during the mid-nineteenth century, and it thereafter gained wide popularity in a number of Western countries. COLLECTION KHARBINE-TAPABOR, PARIS, FRANCE/BRIDGEMAN ART LIBRARY. © ANN NORMAN. REPRODUCED BY PERMISSION.

TOP LEFT: Advertising poster of dancer Jane Avril by Henri de Toulouse-Lautrec, 1899. Jane Avril was one of the most popular attractions at the Moulin Rouge, the infamous Montmartre dance hall and cabaret where Parisians of all classes gathered to enjoy lively entertainment. MUSÉE TOULOUSE-LAUTREC, ALBI, FRANCE/BRIDGEMAN ART LIBRARY/LAUROS /GIRAUDON

BOTTOM LEFT: Poster for a masquerade ball, Zurich, 1907. During the nineteenth century, pre-Lenten masquerade balls, long a tradition among wealthy and aristocratic Europeans, became more widespread among other classes, despite claims that the dances facilitated immoral behavior. © SWIM INK/CORBIS

BELOW: Russian circus poster, 1910. Improvements in roads and transportation at the end of the nineteenth century facilitated the movements of traveling circuses, which reached the height of their popularity between 1880 and 1920. © BOJAN BRECELJ/CORBIS

TOP RIGHT: ***Tennis Court with Players in Noordwijk, Netherlands.*** Painting by Max Liebermann, 1913. Tennis, which evolved from an indoor game to an outdoor one late in the nineteenth century, quickly became a favorite pastime of wealthy Europeans. ERICH LESSING/ART RESOURCE, NY

BELOW: ***The Village Fair.*** Painting by Boris Kustodiev, 1908. Throughout European history, fairs provided an opportunity for rural dwellers to gather to exchange news and ideas and to enjoy a brief respite from difficult labor. SCALA/ART RESOURCE

BOTTOM RIGHT: **Advertising poster for the Norddeutscher Lloyd shipping company, 1914.** Founded in 1857 in the port city of Bremen, Norddeutscher Lloyd soon became one of the primary providers of transatlantic service. In addition to transporting large numbers of emigrants, Norddeutscher Lloyd ships also provided luxury leisure travel to wealthy Europeans.

BIBLIOGRAPHY

Primary Sources

Lyell, Charles. *Principles of Geology.* Introduced by Martin J. S. Rudwick. 3 vols. Chicago, Illinois, 1990–1991. Facsimile reprint of 1st edition (1830–1833) with excellent introduction.

———. *Principles of Geology.* Edited and introduced by James A. Secord. London, 1997. Convenient one-volume abridged edition with a superb introductory essay on Lyell and his cultural context.

Secondary Sources

Rudwick, Martin J. S. "The Strategy of Lyell's *Principles of Geology.*" *Isis* 61 (1970): 5–33. Groundbreaking analysis of the rhetorical structure of the *Principles.*

Wilson, Leonard G. *Charles Lyell: The Years to 1841: The Revolution in Geology.* New Haven, Conn., 1972. The first part of a still-uncompleted biography: an essential (if somewhat adulatory) reference-point for Lyell's early career.

———. *Lyell in America: Transatlantic Geology, 1841–1853.* Baltimore, Md., 1998. The second part of the biography, covering Lyell's years as an international celebrity.

RALPH O'CONNOR

LYON. "Lyon has declared war on Liberty. Lyon is no more." This decree by the Convention of 12 October 1793 placed France's "second city" at cross-purposes with modernity, since its inhabitants, unlike the majority of French people, did not join the Revolution. As a city without a parliament, Lyon shared in the period's hopes and its fears, including the price of bread and the cuts in state subsidies. However, the Lyon Consulate (the name of Lyon's municipal administration, not to be confused with the Consulate that ruled the entire country starting in 1798) relied on a Swiss regiment to bring the popular uprising under control no later than the spring of 1789. At the same time, the first monarchist plots were being hatched there, encouraged in early 1790 by the Comte d'Artois, who led the Lyonnais to believe he would return from Turin and protect Louis XVI, then a prisoner in Paris. The king's flight to Varennes in June 1791 heightened this opposition at a time when the entire southwest region of France seemed on the verge of tipping over into counterrevolution.

From mid-August 1792 into fall 1793 a number of political battles failed to sharpen the city's social divisions to the breaking point, although a Committee for Popular Rescue, formed in April under the direction of Joseph Chalier, called for the implementation of measures—mainly concerning taxation—that were copied from the Parisian sans-culottes. The conflict became acute, however, on 28–29 May, days of veritable civil war. The committee was disbanded and Chalier and his cohorts were arrested and scheduled to be guillotined on 16 July, at the same time that a Lyonnais army was being formed under a monarchist officer, the Comte de Précy. The stage was set for the tragedy to begin. Although they were against the convention, not all Lyonnais were monarchists. They did apparently subscribe however to the Girondins' federalist tone, which resonated deeply with the age-old Lyonnais dream of autonomy. On 7 August 1792, Republican troops laid siege to the city, which they simultaneously bombarded and blockaded on 12 May, just prior to taking it by force on 9 October. Thus began a period of bloodletting that would drain the population for many years to come, lasting until the arrival of Napoleon. At first the Terror was carried out by the Jacobins, whose excesses left permanent scars in the memories of many: nearly 2,000 real or supposed insurgents (1,896 to be exact) were killed, either guillotined or shot on the Brotteaux Plain. The houses of the "rich" were razed to the ground, and the city itself threatened to disappear as its population plummeted to about 100,000 inhabitants. After a general amnesty put an end to these excesses between the end of 1794 and February 1795, a new era of "white" terror began, itself reminiscent of the worst moments of 1793–1794, when the throats of prisoners were routinely slit. In the years that followed, the deeply divided people of Lyon waged an undeclared civil war, and on 20 February 1798 the order came to lay siege once more in order to subdue the "city in revolt."

SILK INDUSTRY AND THE SECOND EMPIRE

The Lyonnais rebellion was short and the economic crisis it provoked quickly surmounted, a tiny wrinkle in an otherwise steady trend of growth that lasted from the beginning of the eighteenth century until the years 1875 and 1876. Indeed, despite the periodic setbacks faced by every luxury industry, silk weaving (in Lyon called simply "the Industry") grew so quickly that the city became the predominant silk-producing city Europe, up to and including the apex of its production beginning with the Second Empire (1856–1870). The Lyonnais were not only the period's best makers of finished fabrics, including the "dyed" and "tailored" materials produced by the Jacquard looms invented at the beginning of the century; they also ruled the market in raw materials. The silkworks of Lyon penetrated countries far and wide, including London and the United States. Their success was based on Lyon's large population of colorists and designers and on a well-developed financial system with bankers and brokers. The entire system depended on a productive apparatus highly adapted to the succession of economic peaks and troughs by exploiting the flexibility of a work process requiring minimal fixed capital investments. Lyon's population, which was just 130,000 at the end of the *ancien régime*, was still only 150,000 at the beginning of the July monarchy and 177,000 in 1851. However, Lyon is only one part of an agglomeration constituted by the annexation of three outlying counties in 1852, two of which (La Croix-Rousse and La Guillotière) were highly active textile zones. At that point the aggregate population grew to 290,000 and then to 384,000 in 1876.

The systemic flexibility that underpinned the industry's success was based on the organization of its production. In Lyon proper at least, instead of factories there was a burgeoning of small workshops, each housing one to five professionals in a quasi-familial setting and blended into the city's existing buildings. In the eighteenth century they sprouted on the right bank of the Saône side of the "almost island" Presquile and scaled the hills of the Croix-Rousse. By the nineteenth century they occupied its plateau and had spread out over the left bank of the Rhône, reaching into ever-larger swaths of the surrounding countryside. In the 1860s the city boasted the highest concentration of workers devoted to the same industry in Europe, even though they remained organized according to a mode that adapted the domestic system to a large-scale city. At the heart of the industry, therefore, was a small kernel of "producers" (who in fact produced nothing) and a great mass of workshop foremen and their apprentices, marked by an ever-present debate concerning "rates," meaning the calculation of salaries. This debate degenerated into open revolts in February 1831 and November 1834, which, at the dawn of the Industrial Age, marked the first exclusively working-class uprisings waged in the name of workers' dignity. Although it took a veritable army at the city walls firing cannons into the working-class neighborhoods to subdue the uprisings, the losses in human life and materials were minor: Lyon was retaken with little difficulty, handed over by the rebellious *canuts* (silk weavers) themselves. Nevertheless, the revolts marked a turning point stretching far beyond Lyon itself, aptly phrased in the expression "Live by working, die by fighting."

The decades that followed enjoyed a relative calm. Despite the fear provoked by the radical and militant workers' organization known as Les Voraces (the devourers), the only specific action taken was by gangs of *canuts* who burned down several welfare convents where the nuns made the interns work to earn their keep. Still, somehow the city earned a reputation for being a "mecca of socialism" whose revolution was awaited with either intense anticipation or dread. (It did not come.) Under the Second Empire, the city's unfortunate reputation earned it a massive military presence and overt police surveillance, even as its prefect Vaïsse sought to refashion it in the image of Georges-Eugène Haussmann's Paris. The events of 1831 and 1834 made Lyon in the mid-nineteenth century an active center of cooperation and mutualism, with a highly literate population. This fact no doubt furnished the crucible for another, less violent sort of dissidence. Arms were no longer taken up inside or outside the Croix-Rousse, even though 1870–1871 did see some agitations. Instead, in 1852 the moderate Republican Hénon was elected to the assembly, where he was joined in 1857 by another moderate, Jules Favre. In 1869 they were turned out by more radical candidates (Bancel and Raspail). These elections, tinged as they were with an atmosphere of popular anticlericalism, were the countercurrent to Lyon's strongly pro-Catholic element, which took no pains to hide its hostility to the spirit of the age and which erected a basilica at Fourvière near the end of the century that strove to match Paris's Sacré-Coeur, a structure whose significance is well known.

This religious revival is the other great occurrence in Lyon during the nineteenth century. It emerged as early as the First Empire, when the Catholic Church was restored and strengthened by the long reign of the Bishop Monsignor de Bonald, which lasted from 1833 to 1870, and counted a Catholic fundamentalist "Congrégation des Messieurs" among its ranks. Even more striking was the fervor evinced by common people. The appeal launched by Pauline Jaricot, who died in 1861, turned Lyon into the French capital of a great missionary awakening. On the eve of the outbreak of World War I, 343,751 copies of the *Annals of the Spreading of the Faith,* published in Lyon, were printed in several languages.

A NEW ERA

The new era began, however, badly for Lyon. An economic recession in the silkworks took hold, reducing productive activity industry-wide. The heavy silk fabrics of old were rejected by a clientele demanding lighter and more marketable materials. Colors and patterns were beginning to play a more important role in catering to the whims of ever-changing fashions. Weaving itself became mechanized. Furthermore, Lyon's status as a center of banking was ruined in 1882 by the crash of its premier commercial bank, the Union Générale, whose capital was instrumental to the industry's functioning. Lyon would never regain its status as a financial center, and even Crédit Lyonnais, founded in 1863, moved its headquarters to Paris. When the silk industry finally did recover at the height of the belle epoque, it did so only at the cost of the disappearance of thousands of artisanal workshops, displaced by mechanized looms operating in the countryside. On the other hand, the chemical industry that accompanied the boom in colors and patterning boded well for the future. The same was true of the local metallurgy industry, which had always been present in Lyon but whose orientation toward the production of iron materials was converted to the production of components for the electric industry and, above all, automobiles, for which Lyon became one of the first centers as early as 1914.

Outside of the occasional stir caused by anarchist agitation during the 1880s and 1890s, political debate in Lyon was framed by democratic principles and flowed through electoral channels. The Croix-Rousse had long since ceased to be synonymous with revolutionary expectations; the "Mountain of Work" squared off against the grand hill of Fourvière, the "Mountain for Prayer." Although the union brotherhoods and socialist political groups were more visible in the last years of the century, the still-active cooperative, arbitration-oriented associations truly held sway. Through them was born and nurtured a "Lyonnais radicalism"—radicalism, that is, in the French sense of the word meaning willingness to roll up one's sleeves and get things done. This radicalism brought together Republicans of all stripes (those who found themselves on the same side in moments of crisis like the Dreyfus affair) and those Socialists who could only be called "Independents" for lack of a better label. In 1881 Lyon won back the right to a mayor's office, which had been lost because of the city's history of insurrection. The post was first occupied by the "radical" Dr. Antoine Gailleton in 1882, who was later replaced by the Independent Socialist Victor Augagneur in 1900. In 1905 Édouard Herriot, a thirty-three-year-old professor who was an outsider with a reputation for being a Red, won back the spot for the radicals. At the outset of his tenure he surrounded himself by technical experts such as the architect Tony Garnier and the doctor Jules Courmont in order to build the Gerland battery in 1914 and draw up plans to build a hospital and a stadium. These turned out to be just the opening acts in a princely reign destined to last until 1957, by which time Herriot had long since become above all a man of state, whose core principles could be said to have embodied those of the Republic at large.

See also **Cities and Towns; France; Paris.**

BIBLIOGRAPHY

Bezucha, Robert J. *The Lyon Uprising of 1834: Social and Political Conflict in the Early July Monarchy.* Cambridge, Mass., 1974.

Garden, Maurice. *Lyon et les lyonnais aux XVIIIe siècle.* Paris, 1970.

Latreille, André, ed. *Histoire de Lyon et du lyonnais.* Paris, 1975.

Lequin, Yves. *Les ouvriers de la région lyonnaise (1848–1914).* Lyon, 1977.

Saunier, Pierre-Yves. *L'esprit lyonnais XIXe–XXe siècle.* Paris, 1995.

Sheridan, George J., Jr. *Social and Economic Foundations of Association among the Silk Weavers of Lyons, 1852–1870.* New York, 1981.

YVES LEQUIN

MACAULAY, THOMAS BABINGTON

(1800–1859), British politician and historian.

Thomas Babington Macaulay was the precocious eldest son of a Quaker, Selina Mills Macaulay, and the notable Evangelical reformer Zachary Macaulay. A playful, affectionate, humorous man, Macaulay the public figure was combative, cocksure, and fond of exaggeration.

He is best known for his *History of England from the Accession of James II.* Volumes one and two were published in 1848, three and four in 1855, and the last volume posthumously in 1861. Macaulay thought history should be as interesting as fiction, and his *History* became nearly as popular as Dickens's novels. It was widely read in the United States and on the Continent. Believing that the lives of ordinary people were as relevant to historical writing as battles, treaties, and great deeds, Macaulay brought to life dramatic, picturesque scenes of the past. As a social historian, he used a range of material besides archival sources, including ballads, pamphlets, and diaries.

The story of seventeenth-century England exemplified for him the gradual progressive movement of history, not only in material improvement but also in extensions of liberty. The timely arrival of William III (r. 1689–1702) represented a "preserving revolution," whereby William became the instrument for restoring both English liberty and English Protestantism. This inherently dramatic story involving the downfall of King James II (r. 1685–1701) lacks the analytic power, however, that the critic Macaulay had recommended in his 1828 *Edinburgh Review* essay "History."

Macaulay was elected to Parliament in 1830 as a Whig. The party that abolished the slave trade occupied a middle ground between Tories and Radicals that suited him. In eloquent speeches in the House of Commons, Macaulay defended the Reform Bill (that extended political power to the middle class) and advocated grants to a Catholic institution in Ireland, factory legislation, and equal rights for Unitarians and Jews. He also opposed universal suffrage and supported capital punishment.

As a legal member of the Supreme Council of India from 1834 to 1837, Macaulay expressed a comparable range of opinion, disparaging Indian culture, for example, but also supporting a uniform justice system that treated rulers and the ruled alike, and advocating an end to press censorship. He believed India would eventually be free of British rule and acknowledged that coercion was needed to maintain it.

Macaulay's *Minute on Indian Education* (1835) argued that English should be the language of instruction in India, against Orientalists, who favored Arabic and Sanskrit rather than vernacular languages. Late-twentieth-century postcolonial studies have revived interest in Macaulay's role in this debate. The best account of Macaulay is given by John Clive in the last four chapters of *Macaulay: The Shaping of the Historian.*

Macaulay's essays fall into two groups: arguments and narratives. His 1825 *Edinburgh Review* essay on John Milton made him famous. Other polemical essays demonstrate more skill in treating concrete, practical subjects than at analyzing abstract subjects such as political economy. Macaulay used contrasts, allusions, historical analogies, hypothetical cases, and metaphor to make his points. His language was vivid and forceful. "Gladstone on Church and State" (1839), one of his best argumentative essays, cautions against too close a link between the two institutions.

Three notable, long narrative essays are "Lord Clive" (1840), "Warren Hastings" (1841), and "Frederic the Great" (1842). Of the five essays Macaulay contributed to the *Encyclopaedia Britannica* in the 1850s, "Samuel Johnson" best illustrates his mature style, marked by careful judgments and the ability to sustain a complex narrative.

The antithetical style of Macaulay signals more than word arrangement: it was a way of perceiving, one that showed a strong affinity for order and balance, and an eighteenth-century sensibility. He was also influenced by the Romantic movement. Though sometimes rigid and oversimplifying, his antithetical style imparted special force to aphorisms: for example, "An acre in Middlesex is better than a principality in Utopia."

Macaulay's impressive accomplishments in several fields, including colonial administration, are remarkable. In his own day the preeminent Victorian, Macaulay today is less read than other great nineteenth-century English writers—George Eliot (Mary Ann Evans; 1819–1880), Matthew Arnold (1822–1888), John Ruskin (1819–1900), and John Stuart Mill (1806–1873). One reason is that he often has been represented in texts and anthologies by his poorest work, and by excerpts, rather than whole essays, that obscure his humanism. In addition, modern specialization has made his concept of history as a branch of literature seem obsolete. Nonetheless, some of his opinions, such as his support of women's education, bring him closer to the present. What Macaulay did best, historical narration, he did incomparably well.

See also **History; Liberalism; Whigs.**

BIBLIOGRAPHY

Primary Sources

Clive, John, and Thomas Pinney, eds. *Thomas Babington Macaulay: Selected Writings.* Chicago, 1972.

Secondary Sources

Clive, John. *Macaulay: The Shaping of the Historian.* New York, 1973.

Edwards, Owen Dudley. *Macaulay.* New York, 1989.

Rau, Uma Satyavolu. "The National/Imperial Subject in T. B. Macaulay's Historiography." *Nineteenth-Century Contexts* 23, no. 1 (2001): 89–119.

Thomas, William. "Macaulay, Thomas Babington." In *Oxford Dictionary of National Biography.* Vol. 35. Oxford, U.K., 2004.

MARGARET CRUIKSHANK

MACH, ERNST (1838–1916), Austrian physicist and philosopher.

Ernst Mach was born on 18 February 1838 into a German-speaking family with some Slavic roots, in Chirlitz/Chrlice in Moravia, in what is now part of the Czech Republic. He is best known as a critic of Newton and as the namesake for the terms "Mach One," "Mach Two," and so forth. Mach studied physics at the University of Vienna from 1855 to 1860 and taught that subject in Vienna (1861–1864), mathematics and later physics in Graz (1864–1867), and physics again in Prague (1867–1895).

Mach's experimental approach was based on an empiricism so narrow that it denied the reality of atoms and molecules. He applied the approach to problems in psychology and physiology as well as physics, and defended his phenomenalism on the grounds that it enabled him to work in both psychology and physics without having to change worldviews. In 1865, he discovered what are now called "Mach Bands" (that is, subjective color intensity on both sides of a boundary between two colors, which acts to make the boundary more conspicuous) and, in 1873, the equilibrium function of the inner ear. In the 1870s and 1880s he studied spark and ballistic shock waves. Possibly in reaction to the lack of attention paid before 1900 to this work, he seems to have turned to philosophy of science to help justify what some of his opponents considered an unduly narrow approach.

Mach became influential among physicists with the publication of his book *Die Mechanik in ihrer Entwicklung* (1883; *The Science of Mechanics,* 1893), which criticized Newton's theories of absolute space, time, and motion because they seemed to lack observable relations. He followed that work with his *Beiträge zur Analyse der Empfindungen* (1886; *Contributions to the Analysis of the Sensations,* 1897), which defended his rejection of a transconscious physical world in a way that he hoped would attract psychologists, physiologists, and philosophers.

Mach's new reputation made it possible for him to become the first professor in the history and philosophy of science in Vienna in 1895. However, three years later a stroke paralyzed the right side of his body, and he was forced to resign in 1901. He moved in 1913 to Vaterstetten, a village near Munich in Bavaria, where he died on 19 February 1916.

The first decade of the twentieth century saw both the highpoint of Mach's philosophical influence and criticism of the most severe kind against his phenomenalism and extreme form of positivism. His philosophical allies included William James, Karl Pearson, Wilhelm Ostwald, Otto Neurath, and other members of what would later be called the Vienna Circle who were associated with logical positivism, including Rudolf Carnap. But the most famous of his followers were Max Planck and Albert Einstein, who supported Mach's work in the 1890s.

Mach's opponents were numerous. Edmund Husserl accused him of "psychologism," or working from the premise that formal logic and mathematics had psychological roots. Vladimir Lenin (1870–1924) attacked him and positivists everywhere for denying the existence of the external physical world. In the 1910s, in light of Einstein's work on relativity and Jean-Baptiste Perrin's work on Brownian motion and the random movement of molecules, a more mature Max Planck argued that Mach's anti-atomism was detrimental to science. Conscious sensations may seem or may be subjectively certain, but physics was relying more and more on objective measurement of transconscious physical objects and processes using instruments and machines.

Mach was so offended by Planck's criticism that he threatened to "leave the church of physics" if belief in the reality of atoms were required. Einstein also criticized Mach for his position on the atomic theory, and it appears that Mach did in fact leave "the church" in 1913. A few months later Mach seems to have written the preface to his posthumously published book *Die Prinzipien der physikalischen Optik* (1921), in which he rejects Einstein's theory of relativity, which had included ideas from Mach.

Mach's criticism of Newtonian absolutes influenced Einstein's special theory of relativity (1905). Also, Einstein's general theory of relativity (1915) initially contained "Mach's Principle" that the totality of the stars have an influence on local inertia. But Einstein eventually dropped it, because it could not be deduced from the general theory. Starting in 1917 Einstein increasingly rejected Mach's epistemology, which he found too restrictive. Like Planck, Einstein often found it necessary in physics to make inferences beyond what could be sensed or made conscious. Nor could he accept Mach's notion that all theories were merely temporary.

In the late twentieth century, some philosophers traced some of Mach's views back to the psychological ideas of Johann Friedrich Herbart (1776–1841) and Ewald Hering (1834–1918). This view minimizes Mach's debt to the Irish philosopher George Berkeley (1685–1753), the German philospher Immanuel Kant (1724–1804), and epistemological idealism. It suggests that, rather than a phenomenalist or even a physicist, Mach was primarily a psychologist closer to direct realism, which held that external physical objects existed but could be directly sensed at least in principle. These philosophers also point out that Mach's emphasis on so-called mathematical functions as a substitute for laws and powers to relate sensory objects or impressions did not require the existence of space, which if true might help make it seem more plausible that distant stars could indeed influence local inertia in accord with Mach's Principle.

While there are few self-declared "Machists" in philosophy in the early twenty-first century, Mach's ideas live on in much of analytic philosophy and in some interpretations of physical theory. Indeed, many of his long minimized or overlooked experimental contributions to psychology, physiology, and physics show signs of becoming the best appreciated and least controversial aspects of his work.

See also **Einstein, Albert; Husserl, Edmund; Physics; Planck, Max; Science and Technology.**

BIBLIOGRAPHY

Banks, Erik C. *Ernst Mach's World Elements.* Dordrecht, Germany, 2003.

Blackmore, John T. *Ernst Mach: His Life, Work, and Influence.* Berkeley and Los Angeles, 1972.

———. *Ernst Mach: A Deeper Look.* Dordrecht, Germany, 1992.

Blackmore, J., R. Itagaki, and S. Tanaka, eds. *Ernst Mach's Vienna, 1895–1930; or, Phenomenalism as Philosophy of Science.* Dordrecht, Germany, 2001.

Hoffmann, Christoph, and Peter Berz, eds. *Über Schall: Ernst Machs und Peter Salchers Geschoßfotografien.* Göttingen, Germany, 2001.

Ratliff, Floyd, *Mach Bands: Quantitative Studies on Neural Networks in the Retina.* San Francisco, 1965.

JOHN T. BLACKMORE

MACHINE BREAKING. Machine breaking has a long, sporadic history in Europe stretching back to the middle ages, but as a modern form of protest against technological innovation, it dates essentially to the early years of the Industrial Revolution. Sir John Kay's flying shuttle, a device by which a weaver could send the yarn through the web of a loom without assistance, met with violent resistance on its appearance in England in the 1760s, as did James Hargreaves's spinning jenny, a portentous invention that made it possible to turn up to a hundred spindles with the same single wheel that had traditionally turned one. Custom and (in some cases) statute expressly forbade such innovations, but increasingly, as the mercantile state gave way to the liberal state in the age of Adam Smith (1723–1790), custom and statute both yielded to the march of progress. In 1780, for instance, four years after the publication of *Wealth of Nations,* the British Parliament refused a petition asking for a ban on cotton spinning machinery. Five years later, with the successful application of steam power to spinning and the advent of the power loom, cotton textiles became the world's first factory-based industry, and incidents of machine breaking naturally quickened. Wool, England's traditional textile fiber, was less amenable than cotton to industrial production, but here too technological innovation met with furious resistance, notably in Wiltshire, where the appearance of the gig mill—a machine for raising the nap of the cloth preparatory to shearing—provoked destructive riots in 1802.

By far the most famous early episode of machine breaking, however, was the so-called Luddite Rebellion. Starting in the hosiery districts of Nottinghamshire, and then moving north to the Pennine valleys of Yorkshire and Lancashire, loosely organized groups of anonymous workmen, acting on the mythic authority of one Ned (variously "King" or "General") Ludd, demolished thousands of stocking-frames, power looms, gig mills, and the like, in 1811 and 1812. The Luddites made a tremendous impression on their contemporaries (including Lord Byron, who famously defended them in his maiden speech to the House of Lords, and Charlotte Brontë, who made a Luddite riot the central incident of her novel *Shirley*), and historians continue to argue over their social and political significance. Were they, as some contend, simple rioters, lashing out randomly and incoherently at industrial forces beyond their control? Or were they, as others contend, a well-organized and disciplined "army of redressers" acting according to the traditional logic of the moral economy? Did they feel a visceral aversion to machinery per se? Or did they mean only to regulate and control the terms of its use? Were they purely social rebels? Or did their actions express a wider, democratic yearning? Existing evidence points in all of these directions and more. Whatever else one might claim for them, the Luddites certainly conferred an idea and a word on the language. They were, in effect if not in fact, the original machine-breakers, and to this day, those skeptical of the benefits of industrial technology describe themselves proudly as "Luddites."

Across the English Channel in France, machine breaking was never as deliberate or extensive as in

Great Britain, the "first industrial nation," but it was not unknown. A few of the Enlightenment philosophes—Jean-Jacques Rousseau (1712–1778) and Montesquieu (1689–1755) especially—had worried about the degrading effects of mechanization on the lives of workers, and with the French Revolution, their misgivings assumed concrete form. The *cahiers de doléances* (lists of public grievances drawn up for the Estates General in the spring of 1789) of the Rouen district are full of denunciations of the new spinning technology, all of it imported from Great Britain. "Let us forget the very name of these spinning machines which have stolen the bread from innumerable poor citizens who have nothing but cotton spinning as their sole resource," read Article 7 of the *cahier* of Saint-Jean-sur-Cailly, for instance (Reddy, p. 58). Machine breaking featured far less than grain rioting in the French Revolution, but on 14 July 1789, even as the crowds of Paris stormed the Bastille, workers in Rouen were demolishing spinning machines in the cotton factory of MM. Debourge and Callonne. Similar episodes took place over the next few years among the carders of Lille, the spinners of Troyes, and the cutlery-workers of Saint-Étienne, but historians impute them more to the general revolutionary fever than to a particular hostility to machines. The Napoleonic period saw the rapid extension of the factory system in France and, with it, machine-breaking riots in Sedan, Vienne, and Limoux. But it was with the Restoration, and the arrival of machinery in the woolen centers of the south, that French Luddism came of age. Anonymous shearmen, often acting in connivance with small, sympathetic masters and shop owners, destroyed shearing machines in Vienne and Carcassone in 1819 and in Lodève in 1821. Thereafter, as the French textile industry expanded and workers found ready employment in spite of the new machines, the hostility faded. Machine breaking recurred in Paris and other northern centers in the early years of the July Monarchy, but by then it reflected not hostility to the machine as such but a deeper demand for fundamental changes in the nature and organization of labor.

The year 1830 saw a dramatic recurrence of machine breaking in England, this time, unusually, in the agricultural counties of the south and east. Here the hated object was the thresher, a machine for separating the grain from the chaff that was thought to deprive agricultural laborers of much-needed winter work. Starting in east Kent in August 1830, rioters acting in the name, this time, of the mythical Captain Swing, combined demands for higher wages and tithe reductions with destructive attacks on threshers. More than 1,400 incidents have been attributed to the "Swing Riots," in the repressive wake of which nineteen people were executed, 481 transported, and more than 700 imprisoned. Machine breaking returned to the north of England in the 1840s, with the first widespread adoption of the power loom. Thereafter, as the "hungry forties" gave way to the prosperous 1850s, English workers increasingly accepted the inevitability of the machine and turned their attention, by way of trade unionism, to securing for themselves a greater share of the profits it generated.

Though industrialization came relatively late to central and eastern Europe, machine breaking appeared there as early as March 1819, when a group of 150 relatively comfortable but precariously positioned domestic textile workers (possibly influenced, in this case, by news of recent "Luddite" riots in southern France) destroyed spinning machines in the Moravian town of Brno. Linen workers in the Ruhr Valley towns of Krefeld and Aachen rioted in 1828 and 1830, on both occasions unremarkably provoked by the introduction of power looms and the increasing employment of female and unskilled labor. The 1844 revolt of the weavers of Silesia against the power loom would later be immortalized by Gerhart Hauptmann in his play of 1892, *The Weavers,* and it seems to have inspired within a few days a most impressive series of deliberate and concerted attacks on machinery at six different cloth printing factories in and around Prague over a period of a week in mid-June 1844. In each case in Prague, the targeted factory owner was Jewish, and historical commentators on the *Prager Maschinensturm* have consistently noted an anti-Semitic tinge to the proceedings. For the most part, however, machine breaking in Germany and the Austrian Empire reflected the same standard fearfulness in the face of technological change that it did in Great Britain and France. Luddism everywhere was the response of skilled workers and artisans to something new that threatened their livelihood, their independence, and their proudly held standard of craft production.

The 1848 Revolution in Germany brought with it widespread machine breaking, most notably among the steel and cutlery workers of Solingen. Thereafter, as revolutionary passions cooled and workers in Germany, like those in Great Britain before them, adapted to the new technological dispensation, machine breaking became a thing of the past. Industrial sabotage in the more limited sense of slowing, stopping, or disabling machines remained a problem, from the employer's point of view, right through the nineteenth century, especially in syndicalist France (where the very term *saboteur* derives). And sporadically across the less-industrialized parts of Europe, classic machine breaking recurred, as in the famous case of the carpet weavers of Anatolia in 1908. But in the main, it is a feature of early nineteenth-century European history, a dramatic social aspect of Europe's painful transition to the industrial age.

See also **Captain Swing; Industrial Revolution, First; Luddism.**

BIBLIOGRAPHY

Hammond, J. L., and Barbara Hammond. *The Rise of Modern Industry.* London, 1925.

Herzig, Arno. "Die Reaktion der Unterschichten auf den technologischen Wandel der Proto-und Früh-industrialisierungsphase in Deutschland." *Archiv für Sozialgeschichte* 28 (1988): 1–26.

Hobsbawm, Eric. "The Machine-Breakers." In *Labouring Men.* London, 1964.

Manuel, Frank. "The Luddite Movement in France." *Journal of Modern History* 10, no. 2 (1938): 180–211.

Nuvolari, A. "The 'Machine Breakers' and the Industrial Revolution." *Journal of European Economic History* 31, no. 2 (2002): 393–428.

Quataet, Donald. "Machine Breaking and the Changing Carpet Industry of Western Anatolia, 1860–1980." *Journal of Social History* 19, no. 3 (1986): 473–489.

Reddy, William M. *The Rise of Market Culture: The Textile Trade and French Society, 1750–1900.* Cambridge, U.K., 1984.

STEWART WEAVER

MADRID. In comparison with other European capitals, nineteenth-century Madrid was a small city. In 1900 Paris had three million inhabitants, Berlin had two million, and Madrid, the capital of a formerly great empire, had only half a million and covered only seventeen acres. Growth was slow during the nineteenth century. In 1798 the population was 180,000; in 1804, 176,000; in 1825, 200,000; in 1845, 230,000; in 1857, 281,000; in 1872, 334,000; and in 1910, 540,000.

The countryside surrounding Madrid was dry and poor, and the city was located far from the seas and both the French and Portuguese borders. Having been the seat of the Spanish court since 1561, the land within the city was owned by aristocrats, churches, and monasteries. The boroughs, or central neighborhoods, were built between the seventeenth-century Buen Retiro Palace in the east and the eighteenth-century Royal Palace in the west. When Napoleon's army invaded the city in 1808, the city had only two squares, the Plaza Mayor and the Puerta del Sol, and one boulevard, the Paseo del Prado. The remainder of the city was made up of narrow streets running between the palaces of the nobility and the buildings of Catholic Church.

The river Manzanares could not provide enough water for the city and the city's water was provided by underground aqueducts that had been built by Muslim engineers in the Middle Ages. Garbage was cleared out only once a week. Consequently the sanitary situation was dire. In 1834 the plague killed no less than four thousand people. Cholera outbreaks killed five thousand in 1855 and three thousand in 1865. In 1890 three epidemics struck the city: cholera, flu, and smallpox. In 1900 the yearly mortality rate was still forty-five out of a thousand, much higher than in other European capitals. Despite the creation of new neighborhoods within the limits of the city, workers and other poor people lived in outlying shanty towns. In the older parts of the city, especially in southern and eastern Madrid, many neighborhoods were unhealthy, miserable, and crowded with immigrants from the countryside.

Until the end of the century, the demographic economy of Madrid was similar to that of the *ancien régime* in France. Population growth was exclusively due to immigration, since the infant mortality rate remained horrendously high.

During the first decades of the nineteenth century, more than 1,600 plots of land owned by the

The Palacio de Cristal, Madrid. ©PETER M. WILSON/CORBIS

Church were sold. The construction of the Queen Isabel II Canal—a massive project—was finished in 1858. The first railway between Madrid and the royal residence at Aranjuez opened in 1857. Nonetheless, no urban restructuring was done until the 1860s, when Carlos María de Castro designed an enlargement (*ensanche*) of Madrid. Castro planned his blocks to make optimum use of light and included interior gardens and courtyards for the houses, which would not be taller than three stories. The project was inspired by Spanish-American towns, with an orthogonal organization of streets, which were to be larger than those in old Madrid. Yet the criteria he specified seemed too restrictive to investors and after 1864 several of the plans were abandoned.

The Cortes passed a number of bills enforcing private investment in the new boroughs. Nevertheless, investment was disappointing. After the Revolution of 1868, the liberal Ángel Fernández de los Ríos came back from his exile in Paris and was put in charge of urban reformation. He used Georges-Eugène Haussmann's work rebuilding Paris as his model. After the restoration of the Bourbon dynasty, the Recoletos y Castellana area, between old Madrid and the eastern *ensanche,* became the most fashionable neighborhood for the new bourgeoisie and the financial aristocracy.

Madrid's first iron buildings were built in the 1880s; they included food markets and the railway stations of Norte, Delicias Atocha, and the Palacio de Cristal, a remarkable example of iron and glass architecture, which opened in Retiro Park in 1883. Before the twentieth century, Madrid had no industrial belt. The factories grew at the same rate as the population, with no significant surge and no technological revolution. In 1885 Spanish steam engines had an average of 2,500 horsepower and in 1900 25,000, which was very low by European standards.

As urban populations did in other European capitals during the nineteenth century, Madrid's population became protagonists in political actions and the National Militia was a usual way for ordinary citizens to mobilize themselves, since the parties, Liberal and Moderate, were exclusive clubs for lawyers and the educated elite. Madrid swept up by the romantic literary fashion, and theaters became the most active forums for liberal movements. In famous cafes, such as the Fontana de Oro, liberal journalists met playwrights and politicians such as Francisco Martínez de la Rosa and Ángel Saavedra, the Duke de Rivas, whose plays were lively symbols of liberalism against absolutist and conservative governments. Italian opera was popular among the aristocracy and a gentrified bourgeoisie; its temple was the Teatro Real. For a broader public, Federico Chueca re-created the zarzuela, or popular opera, partially inspired by the works of Offenbach. The zarzuela and the *genero chico,* its lightest expression, became vehicles for patriotic emotions and mobilization in the second half of the century. After the fall of the First Republic (1868–1874), the intellectuals and artists behaved more cautiously and did not become involved in politics.

After the restoration of the Bourbon dynasty in 1874, the administration tried to make Madrid a real capital for the nation. After three centuries of negotiations with the Holy See, Madrid-Alcalá became a diocese for the first time in 1885. The Church of Spain started building Almudena Cathedral in 1883, which was finally inaugurated by Pope John Paul II in 1983. An equestrian statue of King Philip III was erected in the middle of the Plaza Mayor, and an equestrian statue of Philip IV in front of the Royal Palace. During the last decade of the nineteenth century, Madrid gained electric lighting in the streets and the trams were electrified. The Lumière brothers' movie machine was exhibited in 1896. The first soccer club was opened in 1897, and the emblematic club, Real Madrid, in 1902. This new form of entertainment quickly challenged bullfighting as recreation for the masses. In 1898, as the capital city was in the process of modernization, the news of Spain's defeats in the Philippines and Cuba provoked a deep crisis of self-confidence among the Spanish population, the elite, and the administration. The beginning of the twentieth century found Madrid in a melancholy mood.

See also **Cities and Towns; Spain.**

BIBLIOGRAPHY

Cruz, Jesús. *Gentlemen, Bourgeois, and Revolutionaries: Political Change and Cultural Persistence among the Spanish Dominant Groups, 1750–1850.* Cambridge, U.K., 1996.

Díez de Baldeón, Clementina. *Arquitectura y clases sociales en el Madrid del siglo XIX.* Madrid, 1986.

Juliá, Santos, David Ringrose, and Cristina Segura. *Madrid: Historia de una capital.* Madrid, 1994.

JEAN-FRÉDÉRIC SCHAUB

MAFIA. Following their restoration in 1815, the Neapolitan Bourbons, rulers of Sicily, attempted to abolish feudalism and enclose common holdings, subordinating collective pasture rights to "improved" private cultivation. Their parallel effort to establish seven provincial prefectures suffered from a paucity of roads and financial resources. Poorly managed by governmental authority, the agrarian transformation produced conditions—banditry, rebellion, and political corruption—that nurtured mafia formation.

The land reform was intended to create a class of smallholders, but instead it privileged an emergent group of *civile* owners whose newly minted titles, marriages with aristocrats, and acquisitions of vast estates (*latifundia*) reproduced the landlordism of the past. Displaced from promiscuous access to land, peasants rebelled, encouraged by the secret societies of liberal intellectuals and Freemasons plotting insurrection against the Bourbon *ancien régime.* The rebels spawned bands that kidnapped landlords, rustled livestock, and pirated commodities moving through the countryside. Although it is tempting to distinguish among revolutionary "*squadre*" aimed at state power, "bands" of rural thieves and kidnappers, and "gangs" of persons escaping arrest, these categories were inherently ambiguous, subject to manipulation by bandits, gangsters, revolutionaries, and repressive authorities alike.

Peasant disturbances were particularly violent in the western provinces, a reflection of the greater presence in these provinces, when compared to eastern Sicily, of latifundist great estates. As the Bourbon reforms abrogated rights of common pasturage, and as Sicily's population grew in the nineteenth century, this forbidding territory became a "brigand corridor"—a highway for abusive grazing, animal theft, and the clandestine movement of stolen beasts to city markets. The lawlessness of the corridor was one reason the mafia would gain a particular foothold in western Sicily. Another factor concerns the significance of Palermo, seat of the viceroyal government, as the fulcrum for both insurrection and repression. Each uprising consolidated relationships between the rural and urban forces of disorder in the western half of the island.

The first official reference to groups that would later be defined as *mafias* dates to an 1838 report of a Bourbon magistrate who noted that in the western province of Trapani, many local communities supported "types of sect called *partiti*" that had powerful patrons and deployed common funds to influence judicial proceedings. This phenomenon was not labeled *mafia* until the early 1860s, when Sicilian dramatists Giuseppe Rizzotto and Gaspare Mosca produced a play called *I Mafiusi di la Vicaria* (1863), in which the word "mafiusi" referred to a group of prisoners in a Palermo jail who defined themselves as "men of respect" and exacted deference from other prisoners. Shortly after, in 1865, the prefect of Palermo Province, Filippo Gualterio, referred to the "so-called Maffia" in a government document, defining it as an increasingly audacious criminal association.

Mafia formation continued in the 1860s, now in the context of the landing of Giuseppi Garibaldi (1807–1882), the Bourbons' surrender, and the plebiscite favoring adherence to the constitution of Piedmont. Not only did Sicily receive Piedmont's flag and currency, the Piedmontese also imposed their tax code, anticlerical legislation, and, most controversially, a military draft. Like an occupying power, in 1866 they declared a state of siege in Sicily, rounding up alleged draft dodgers for trial in military courts, placed suspicious persons under surveillance, and suspended freedoms of association and press.

After 1862, 163,000 hectares of ecclesiastical holdings plus 37,000 hectares of royal land were sold at auction to pay off debts incurred by the new nation state. As with the Bourbon reforms, local councils administered the land sales, favoring elite cliques. A parliamentary inquest of 1878 determined that 93 percent of the distributed land went to those "who were already rich," leaving thousands of peasants precariously closer to landlessness than they had been before. The colossal problem of peasant unrest worsened and with it the confusing mix of criminal and revolutionary activity. By the late 1860s, banditry had become endemic to property relations.

The new Italian state did not conduct a "brigand war" in Sicily comparable to its military campaign in southern Italy; even the most audacious bandits continued to enjoy the support of kin and neighbors, landed elites and notables, and the police. To the national government's authorities, all Sicilians seemed impenetrably "barbarian" and "criminal."

In 1876, however, the more democratic forces of the Risorgimento—the "Historic Left"—took power, expanding the presence of southern and Sicilian notables in the national government and altering the dynamics of local governance. As restricted parties of "liberal" elites and "democrats" competed for ministerial positions, parliamentary deputies from Sicily made themselves clients of ministers who dispensed the state's patronage, while local "grand electors" both distributed this patronage and delivered the deputies' votes.

The new regime also supported initiatives for public welfare and economic growth, including the development of citrus crops, mineral exports, and shipping facilities. At last acknowledging the need for effective police action against brigandage, it brought about a decline in kidnappings. But crimes against property continued: the lucrative new crops invited theft, and animal rustling flourished with the growth of urban markets. Opportunistically, local "mafias" transformed themselves into full-fledged protection rackets.

The racketeers arose, it seems, among an incipient entrepreneurial class of carters, muleteers, merchants, bandits, and herdsmen who, in the rural towns and suburbs of Palermo, joined *fratellanze* or "brotherhoods," also called *cosche* (singular, *cosca*) after the tightly bundled leaves of the artichoke. Claiming to restore order, members of these groups "offered" landowners the service of protection and/or forced them, against the menace of violence, to employ particular clients as estate guards, rentiers, and all-around henchmen. At the same time, they extorted a tribute or *pizzo*—literally, a "beakful"—from business activities in the cosca's territory. Amid the spreading orchards around Palermo, racketeers also deployed violence to gain monopoly control of produce markets and water for irrigation. In each case, racketeering advanced with the collusive knowledge of public officials and policemen and in the context of an inadequate state investment in policing and criminal justice. Distributing employment opportunities, mafiosi won at least grudging admiration in poor communities, enough so that silencing witnesses to their crimes did not have to depend on fear alone. When arrests and convictions did occur, the cosca functioned as a mutual aid society, using its accumulated funds to support the families of imprisoned members.

Post-1870s police reports index the mafia's growing influence, defining it as a monopolistic network of "politically protected extortion rings" or "groups of criminals who terrorized a local community, living off extortion and other illegal gains, and controlling access to jobs and local markets." In a 500-page report of 1898 to 1900, the police chief (*questore*) of Palermo, Ermanno Sangiorgi, referred to a "vast association of evildoers, organized in sections, divided into groups, each group regulated by a capo." Mafiosi, by contrast, represented themselves as "men of honor" who solved problems (their own and others') without resort to state-sponsored law.

The Sangiorgi and subsequent reports, amplified by the occasional autobiographical or observer's account, and, in the late twentieth century, by the depositions of justice collaborators in the antimafia trials of the 1980s and 1990s, are remarkably consistent regarding several features of the mafia's social organization and culture. Territorial in scope, most cosche bear the name of the rural town or urban neighborhood over which they hold sway. Also referred to as "families," they are to some extent kin-oriented, with membership extending from fathers to sons, uncles to nephews, and through the fictive-kin tie of godparenthood. Yet, becoming a mafioso is also a matter of talent. Sons of members believed to lack "criminal reliability" are passed over in favor of impressive young delinquents from unrelated backgrounds.

Applied to the cosca, the term *family* is metaphorical—an evocation of the presumed solidarity of kinship. Mutual good will is further induced by idiosyncratic terms of address and linguistically playful nicknames. In a symbolically laden rite of entry, possibly learned from Freemasons in nineteenth-century prisons, the novice holds the burning image of a saint while his sponsor pricks his finger and, mixing the blood and ashes, has him swear an oath of lifelong loyalty and *omertà,* or silence before the law.

The mafia cosca is a male organization; women are habitually excluded not only from meetings but also from events like banquets and hunting parties where masculine identity is asserted. These events have implications for socializing novices into the practice of violence, and women's absence from them may be fundamental to the bonding that takes place. Nevertheless, the women of mafiosi are themselves from mafia families. A mafia wife basks in the refinements that her husband's money and status can provide and knowingly shelters his assets from the confiscatory power of the state. Her sons will most likely join the company, her daughters marry into it, and she participates in preparing them for these futures.

The mafia cosca is a largely autonomous group, structured internally along lines of age and privilege, with new recruits, the "soldiers," expected to take greater risks and receive lesser rewards. Generally, the senior bosses monopolize the elected leadership positions, but there are notable cases of ambitious upstarts seizing power. Although each cosca stands alone, members share in an island-wide subculture fostered by the standardized initiation, ideology of honor and omertà, and secret signs of mutual recognition, not to mention collaboration in specific trafficking ventures. Anticipating the Commission that united mafia groups in and around Palermo in the 1960s through 1980s, leaders of several cosche attempted a common command structure, the *Conferenza,* at the turn of the twentieth century.

The mafia's *intreccio* or dense interweaving with national as well as local and regional governments was already in place by that time. The most powerful mafiosi served as grand electors of parliamentary deputies; reciprocally, these political patrons made it easy for racketeers to acquire weapons and fix trials. Older, established *capi* rarely went to jail, while younger "soldiers" experienced incarceration as no more than a perfunctory interruption of their affairs. Populating the murky moral universe of the mafia and politics were the figures of the *mandante,* who orders crimes, and the *mestatore* or scandalmonger, who brings rivals down through accusations of "sponsored criminality." For many scholars of the mafia, the notorious murder of Emanuele Notarbartolo was diagnostic of these ills.

On 1 February 1893, Notarbartolo, an aristocrat allied with the Historic Right, former mayor of Palermo (1873–1876) and director general of the Bank of Sicily (1876–1890), was stabbed to death on a train en route to a town southeast of Palermo. Suspicion fell on two mafiosi from the nearby cosca of Villabate, yet no one thought that responsibility for the crime ended with them. Another bank director and prominent notable, Raffaele Palizzolo, was eventually indicted and convicted as the organizer of the murder, but his conviction was annulled by the appeals court, and he was eventually acquitted after a retrial. All told, the Notarbartolo affair was a script for later developments, from the powerful intreccio between the mafia and politics, to the divided role of the judiciary in prosecuting mafia crimes.

The investigation of the Notarbartolo case also unearthed a geographical fault line that would reappear in subsequent mafia conflicts. The cosche of the orchards to the north and west of Palermo were geographically closer to, and heavily involved in, the city's produce markets and port. Strongly territorial in orientation, their members specialized in guarding crops, commercial mediation, and the control and distribution of water; extortion was their premier crime. Supporting politicians electorally, they received protection from them, but they organized their own intercosca relations more or less independently of this political shield.

In contrast, the cosche to Palermo's south and east were less coherent. Much of this zone was also given over to orchards and gardens, but these were interspersed with large towns of the sort that characterize the latifundist interior. Moreover, the entire zone was a gateway to the interior—the main pathway over which rustlers drove stolen livestock for clandestine butchering and sale in Palermo. Significantly, robbery, kidnapping, and animal theft were the premier crimes of this zone. Elastic relationships between local mafias articulated well with these offenses, as did the lesser concern of mafiosi with strictly territorial activity. At another level, political figures like Palizzolo enabled a certain degree of integration among cosche. In the early twentieth century, these divergent tendencies deepened as the coastal and orchard mafias gained advantage from their greater commercial interaction with relatives in the United States. Constituting an economic and ecological substrate of mafia formation, the factionalism would resurface after World War II in the "mafia wars" related to urban construction and narcotics trafficking.

Understanding the mafia is rendered difficult not only by the ambiguities inherent in its relationships with society and state but also because of the contradictory discourses that surround it. For, at the same time as police reports began to depict a secret, conspiratorial association sworn to omertà, they were countered by theories of a mafia-friendly Sicilian character, diffuse and age-old. Positing Sicilian culture as the locus of the mafia took two different forms, however. One was explicitly racist—all Sicilians are *delinquenti* at heart. The other amounted to a defensive attempt to render the mafia benign and romantic—"not a criminal association but the sum of Sicily's values" that outsiders can never understand. Folding the mafia into a generalized cultural "atmosphere," blurring its definition by assimilating it to Sicilians' presumed exaggeration of individual force or efficacy, constitutes a kind of *Sicilianismo* that for many years obstructed any concerted mafia historiography. It is one of the most significant achievements of the late twentieth century antimafia process that there are now Sicilian historians working on the reconstruction of this much misunderstood institution.

To a large extent, the new research both uses and validates police reports such as that of Sangiorgi while at the same time faulting police and prosecutorial models for hyper-coherence. Representing the cosca and the coordinating bodies as super-secret, clearly bounded, and conspiratorial, these models underplay the systematic practice of single mafiosi to cultivate friends, and friends of friends, in wider social and political fields. This reality, and the mafia's intreccio with politics, tells us that the prototypical nucleus of Sicilian organized crime, and the key to its economy and system of power, is not the overly conjured cosca, Conferenza, or Commission, but shifting coalitions of select capi and corrupt elites.

See also **Crime; Sicily.**

BIBLIOGRAPHY

Blok, Anton. *The Mafia of a Sicilian Village, 1860–1860: A Study of Violent Peasant Entrepreneurs.* New York, 1974.

Lupo, Salvatore. *Storia della mafia; dalle origini ai giorni nostri.* Rome, 1993.

Pezzino, Paolo. *Mafia: industria della violenza. Scritti e documenti inediti sulla mafia dalle origini ai giorni nostri.* Florence, 1995.

Riall, Lucy. *Sicily and the Unification of Italy: Liberal Policy and Local Power, 1859–1866.* Oxford, U.K., 1998.

JANE SCHNEIDER, PETER SCHNEIDER

MAHLER, GUSTAV (1860–1911),

Bohemian-born composer and conductor.

Gustav Mahler is often thought to have brought the Austro-Germanic tradition of nineteenth-century music to its conclusion and to have ushered in aspects of musical modernism. Along with Arthur Nikisch and Arturo Toscanini, Mahler was one of the most important conductors of his day.

Brought up in a German-speaking Jewish community in Iglau, Moravia, Mahler was accepted in 1875 as a student to the Vienna Conservatory, where he identified himself as a Wagnerian (and thus, for the times, a modernist) and developed interests in socialism, pan-Germanicism, and the philosophy of Friedrich Nietzsche. He was also close to the important lieder composer Hugo Wolf and attended some of the lectures of the composer Anton Bruckner, who was then teaching at the conservatory.

In 1880, Mahler began an incredibly successful career as a conductor that was to last his whole life; financial restrictions meant that he was never able to devote himself solely to composition, which had to be squeezed in during the summer months between the concert and opera seasons, when Mahler would retire to the countryside. Taking up the position of a conductor of operetta in Bad Hall, near Linz, Mahler then passed rapidly through a series of increasingly prestigious positions leading eventually in 1897 to one of Europe's most coveted posts: conductor and artistic director of the Imperial Court Opera in Vienna, whose orchestra was the famed Vienna Philharmonic. However, as a Jew in the deeply ingrained anti-Semitic culture of fin-de-siècle Vienna, it was necessary for Mahler to convert to Roman Catholicism before he could take up the position.

His years at the opera in Vienna were full of controversy, in part because of the rife anti-Semitic atmosphere, but also because of the incredibly high standards that Mahler demanded of his performers, which he was often brutal and insensitive in achieving (Mahler was a seminal figure in the establishment of the twentieth-century paradigm of the conductor as tyrannical idealist). But they were also years when Mahler was responsible for some of the landmark productions of operatic history. Compositionally, the period saw Mahler developing toward more evidently modernist modes, starting with the Fifth Symphony (1901–1902), and briefly, as a result of connections produced by his marriage in 1902 to Alma Schindler, Mahler directly associated with the modernists and the next generation of radical composers, particularly Arnold Schoenberg. Eventually, in 1907, the strain of his conducting position at the opera would lead Mahler to resign, and later that year—after the tragic death of his daughter Maria, and the diagnosis of his own fatal heart condition—he would leave for New York. There he was to take up directorship of the Metropolitan Opera Company, and then the New York Philharmonic, before he finally returned to Europe in 1911 and died in Vienna on 18 May.

If Mahler's life was problematically split and suspended between the practical realities of life as a conductor and a man of the theater and the more seemingly idealistic world of composition, it is likewise true that his compositions also vacillate between idealism and realism and related pairings—for example, between the high and the low stylistically, and the organically fully formed and the open-ended and broken aesthetically. Furthermore, it has been common to interpret this bipolar split in Mahler's music as a profound illustration of similar tensions both within the Habsburg empire at the fin de siècle as it balanced precariously between the passing nineteenth century and the uncertainties of the century to come, and within pre–World War I Europe in general.

On the one hand, Mahler's music is symphonic in the nineteenth-century mold: primarily Beethovenian, but also Wagnerian, in its monumental drive toward totalizing synthesis and transcendent conclusions, particularly as witnessed in the Second (1888–1894, revised 1903), Third (1893–1896, revised 1906), Seventh (1904–1905), and Eighth Symphonies (1906–1907). Mahler's nineteenth-century inheritance also finds expression in the use of massive sonorities requiring enormous orchestral and often also vocal forces for their production, and in a tendency toward grand music-historical summation in the strong tradition of historicism within Austro-Germanic music since Beethoven—references abound not only to Beethoven and Wagner, but also Haydn and Mozart (for example, in the Fourth Symphony [1899–1900, revised 1901–1910]), the music of Johann Sebastian Bach (from around the time of the Fifth Symphony), and even eighth-century church music, with the use of the hymn-tune *Veni, creator spiritus* in the first movement of the Eighth Symphony. Finally, the deeply autobiographical element in Mahler's music, manifesting itself specifically in the network of telling self-quotations between works (for example, the famous quotation from his *Kindertotenlieder* [Songs on the death of children; 1901–1904] in the finale of the Ninth Symphony [1908–1909]), is reminiscent of the composer Robert Schumann and the tendency toward self-reference in Romantic music.

On the other hand, Mahler's music acts as a radical critique of this very inheritance. As Mahler famously asserted to the Finnish composer Jean Sibelius in 1907, the symphony "must be like a world. It must embrace everything"—by which he meant not just "everything" in its absolute, idealist sense, but also everything that has been excluded from nineteenth-century symphonic discourse by such idealist underpinnings. Thus, in line with then-emergent strains of modernism in the arts in general, Mahler's music acted to challenge various, particularly bourgeois, taboos regarding what was considered aesthetically appropriate, both formally and content-wise, in works of art. In doing so he was formative in the creation of one of the defining functions of twentieth-century musical art, which was to question our assumptions as to what constitutes music in the first place. From an expressive and formal perspective, in Mahler's music this manifested itself in violent disruptions to the expected unfolding of his music and also in the undermining of the usual narrative trajectory of symphonic music toward triumphant conclusions—as, for example, in the bleakly negative ending of the Sixth Symphony (1903–1904, revised 1906) or the diffuse endings of the Ninth Symphony and *Das Lied von der Erde* (The song of the earth; 1908–1909). From a stylistic perspective Mahler was to question his nineteenth-century inheritance through jarring and, in the elevated realm of symphonic composition, inappropriate juxtapositions of musical types; the slow movement of the First Symphony (1888) includes a bizarre reworking of the nursery tune *Frère Jacques* as a funeral march alongside deliberately crude-sounding street music and more traditional lyrical material. Such stylistic pluralism and formal disruptiveness and openendedness has led to Mahler being particularly valorized by postmodernists, who see in his music a reflection of their own discomfort with the values associated with idealist, nineteenth-century, Germanic decrees that works of art should be stylistically and formally self-contained, autonomous wholes, as if they were organisms. However, as Theodor Adorno and others have asserted, there is a critical aspect to Mahler's music and life, he is no mere revolutionary; like many other Viennese in the period preceding World War I, his relationship to the very traditions that were his seeming objects of criticism was dialectical and thus beholden unto them as well.

See also **Beethoven, Ludwig van; Modernism; Nietzsche, Friedrich; Romanticism; Schoenberg, Arnold; Wagner, Richard.**

BIBLIOGRAPHY

Cooke, Deryck. *Gustav Mahler: An Introduction to His Music.* Cambridge, U.K., and New York, 1980.

Mitchell, Donald. *Gustav Mahler: The Wunderhorn Years: Chronicles and Commentaries.* London, 1975.

———. *Gustav Mahler: The Early Years.* Revised and edited by Paul Banks and David Matthews. Berkeley and Los Angeles, 1980.

———. *Gustav Mahler: Songs and Symphonies of Life and Death: Interpretations and Annotations.* Berkeley and Los Angeles, 1985.

Mitchell, Donald, and Andrew Nicholson. *The Mahler Companion.* Oxford, U.K., and New York, 1999.

JAMES CURRIE

MAHMUD II (1785–1839), Ottoman sultan (ruled 1808–1839).

Mahmud II succeeded his brother Mustafa IV (r. 1807–1808), who had been enthroned by the leaders of a powerful coalition that eliminated the reform-minded sultan Selim III (r. 1789–1807). The latter had initiated a series of reforms aimed at modernizing the army, a program known as the *Nizam-i jedid* (New Order), and at increasing the power of the central government. These measures led to the resentment of the Janissaries as well as that of the *Ayan* (notables) and the *Ulema* (religious establishment). Selim III was deposed as a result of a military coup led by this coalition and was replaced by his cousin Mustafa IV. This setback prompted the reformists to rally around Bayrakdar Mustafa Pasha (1775–1808), the notable of Ruse (Ruschuk) in Bulgaria. In 1808 Bayrakdar and his forces marched on Istanbul with the aim of reinstating Selim to the sultanate. Upon gaining control of the capital on 28 July 1808, Bayrakdar installed Mahmud (Mustafa's brother and Selim's cousin) as the new sultan, since Selim had been assassinated before his victorious supporters could reach him.

Although Mahmud II was determined to carry out the modernization of the empire, he also drew a lesson from the failure of Selim III and decided to proceed with caution, particularly with regard to the Janissaries, the centuries-old military institution that felt threatened by the reform and whose members were prone to revolt. In November 1808, rumors circulated among the Janissaries that they were to be disbanded. The ensuing riots resulted in the accidental death of Bayrakdar. In 1826 the sultan was able to overcome the stumbling block represented by the Janissaries: he reacted to their rioting by ordering a bloody massacre and decreeing their dissolution. As was the case in Egypt under his contemporary Mehmet Ali (r. 1805–1848), the cornerstone of the reform was the training of a modern army with the help of European advisors and instructors. The financing of these reforms necessitated the increase of the state funds and of the power of the central government at the expense of the local notables. Mahmud II curbed the power of the notables, directly appointed provincial governors, and took away from the religious hierarchy the supervision of the funds of the bureau of inheritance. In addition, he abolished the *Timar* system (1831), the land grant to the cavalry in exchange for military service. Overall, this sultan initiated the reforms that effectively placed the Ottoman Empire on the path to modernization and Westernization.

Mahmud II faced increased European intervention in Ottoman affairs, especially by Russia, Britain, and France, and the rise of nationalism among his subjects in the Balkans. In the Middle East, the ambitions of Mehmet Ali of Egypt, his nominal vassal, led to protracted warfare, hence furthering European interference in the region. In North Africa, the Ottomans lost Algeria to France (1830), but were successful in regaining direct rule over Tripoli from the Karamanlı dynasty (1835).

In Europe, war was still dragging on with Russia since its invasion of the Danubian Principalities, Moldavia and Wallachia, in 1806. The Treaty of Bucharest (28 May 1812) restituted these two principalities to the Ottomans but allowed Russia to keep Bessarabia. Also in Europe, the intermittent risings in Serbia against Ottoman rule from 1804 onward eventually forced the sultan to recognize Serbian autonomy (although still under Ottoman suzerainty) and the signing of the Treaty of Edirne (or Adrianople) on 14 September 1829 following a second war against Russia (1828–1829) gave more autonomy to Moldavia, Wallachia, and Serbia, and recognized the full autonomy of Greece. The Greek uprising that had begun in 1821 achieved full independence in 1830. Unable to quell this insurgence, Mahmud II sought the help of Mehmet Ali and his superior Egyptian army. The success of the Egyptian troops in the Morea (the Peloponnese peninsula in southern Greece) in 1825 prompted the intervention in favor of Greek autonomy of the Ottomans' traditional European rivals: Russia, Britain, and France. On 20 October 1827, a Franco-British fleet destroyed the combined Ottoman and Egyptian fleet at Navarino.

Mahmud II relied on the service of Mehmet Ali of Egypt to pacify western Arabia. There, Egyptian troops were engaged in a long campaign (1811–1818) to dislodge the Wahhabi warriors from the Hejaz (western Arabia), including the holy cities of Mecca and Medina. Mehmet Ali laid claim to Syria as a reward for his services to the Ottomans and in 1831 his son Ibrahim (1789–1848) headed a campaign for the occupation of this province. By the end of 1832, the Egyptian army overran Syria and crossed into Asia Minor, where they defeated the Ottomans near Konya and pressed their advance toward the capital Istanbul. The arrival of a Russian naval force in the Bosporus in April 1833 and the pressure exerted by France and Britain led to the conclusion of the Peace of Kutahiya (May 1833) that allowed Mehmet Ali's son to keep Syria in exchange for an annual tribute. Shortly before his death on the first of July 1839, Mahmud II failed in his attempt to regain control of Syria from Mehmet Ali when his army was defeated at Nizip (24 June 1839) and his naval commander defected to the Egyptians with his fleet.

See also **Egypt; Greece; Ottoman Empire.**

BIBLIOGRAPHY

Inalcık, Halil, and Donald Quataert, eds. *An Economic and Social History of the Ottoman Empire.* Vol. 2. Cambridge, U.K., 1994.

Levy, Avigdor. "The Officer Corps in Sultan Mahmud II's New Ottoman Army, 1826–39." *International Journal of Middle East Studies* 2 (1971): 21–39.

———. "The Ottoman Ulema and the Military Reforms of Sultan Mahmud II." *Asian and African Studies* (Jerusalem) 7 (1971): 13–39.

Lewis, Bernard. *The Emergence of Modern Turkey.* 2nd ed. New York, 1968.

Shaw, Stanford J. *Between Old and New: The Ottoman Empire under Sultan Selim III.* Cambridge, Mass., 1971.

Zakia, Zahra. "The Reforms of Sultan Mahmud II (1808–1839)." In *The Great Ottoman-Turkish Civilisation,* vol. 1, edited by Kemal Çiçek, 418–426. Ankara, 2000.

Zürcher, Erik J. *Turkey: A Modern History.* 3rd ed. London, 2004.

Adel Allouche

MAISTRE, JOSEPH DE (1753–1821),

Savoyard writer and diplomat.

A provocative and controversial opponent of the Enlightenment and the French Revolution, the Comte Joseph-Marie de Maistre was as often reviled by nineteenth-century liberals as an unscrupulous apologist of the executioner and the Inquisition as he was praised by French royalists and ultramontane Catholics as a steadfast and loyal monarchist and Catholic. It has only been since the late twentieth century, with the appearance of revisionist interpretations of the Enlightenment and the French Revolution and access to Maistre's private papers, that scholars have been able to formulate a reasonably objective assessment of this important and original counter-Enlightenment writer.

A native of Savoy, then a province of the Italian kingdom of Piedmont-Sardinia, Maistre served that state all his life as a magistrate and diplomat. Born in Chambéry, where he received his early education (in part from the Jesuits), he did his legal training in Turin. Maistre's early career (1772–1792) was in the senate of Savoy (a law court), where he was named a senator in 1788. When the French invaded Savoy in 1792, he fled, at first to Turin, and then to Lausanne, where from 1793 to 1797 he took up a new career as the Piedmontese consul and a counterrevolutionary propagandist. After an interlude as a refugee in northern Italy, and three years (1799–1803) as regent (head of the court system) in Sardinia, he served as the Piedmontese ambassador in St. Petersburg from 1803 to 1817. After his recall to Turin, he ended his career as regent (justice minister) of Piedmont-Sardinia (1818–1821).

Though Maistre had inherited a substantial legal library and followed a legal career for more than half his working life, his notebooks, works, and correspondence suggest that he was always much more interested in broad humanistic subjects than in narrow legal questions. The beneficiary of an excellent classical education, he read Latin, Greek, Italian, English, Spanish, Portuguese, and German as well as his native French. Well-versed in the Scriptures, the church fathers, Greek and Latin classical authors, and Renaissance and seventeenth-century authors, he was also thoroughly familiar with all the major authors of the Enlightenment.

Maistre's first major work, which won him immediate renown as a theorist of throne and altar, was *Considérations sur la France* (Considerations on France), published anonymously in 1797. Construing the Revolution as both a divine punishment and as a providently ordained means for the regeneration of France, Maistre was able to condemn the

Revolution and the ideas that it embodied, and, at the same time portray it as a necessary prelude to the restoration of the monarchy. Maistre had read Edmund Burke's *Reflections on the Revolution in France* soon after that work appeared in 1790, and he shared Burke's reaction against the violence, "immorality," and "atheism" of the Revolution. Maistre's work echoed Burkean themes, including reverence for established institutions, distrust of innovation, and defense of prejudice, aristocracy, and an established church. Maistre differed from Burke primarily in his providentialism, and in his adamant defense of traditional Roman Catholicism and papal authority.

Maistre's later works reveal a shift from politics to fundamental philosophical and theological issues. His *Essai sur le principe générateur des constitutions politiques* (written in 1807 and published in 1814; Essay on the generative principle of political constitutions) generalized the constitutional principles he had enunciated in his *Considérations sur la France. Du Pape* (1819; On the pope) argued forcefully for infallible papal authority as a prerequisite for political stability in Europe. *Les soirées de Saint-Pétersbourg* (1821; St. Petersburg dialogues) published shortly after Maistre's death, explored a host of philosophical and theological issues in witty dialogue form, while an appendix, called an "Enlightenment on Sacrifices," developed Maistre's ideas about suffering and violence. Finally, an *Examen de la philosophie de Bacon* (published in 1836; Examination of the philosophy of Bacon) located the origins of Enlightenment scientism and atheism in the works of the English writer. Maistre's writings, all distinguished by a vigorous French literary style, include a number of other minor works, some published only long after his death, and an extensive correspondence, most of which has also been published.

Maistre has been criticized for his extremism, and in particular for his reflections on the social role of the executioner, on war, and on bloodshed. His speculations were certainly original; rejecting what he castigated as naive Enlightenment forms of rationality, Maistre struggled to comprehend the irrational and violent dimensions of social and political life. Though his ideas shocked many, he should probably be regarded as an innovative theorist of violence, rather than its advocate.

See also **Bonald, Louis de; Burke, Edmund; Conservatism; French Revolution; Papal Infallibility.**

BIBLIOGRAPHY

Primary Sources

Maistre, Joseph de. *Works.* Selected translated and introduced by Jack Lively. New York, 1965.

———. *Oeuvres complètes contenant ses oeuvres posthumes et toute sa correspondance inédite.* Hildesheim, Germany, and New York, 1984.

Secondary Sources

Benoist, Alain de. *Bibliographie générale des droites françaises.* 4 vols. Paris, 2005. See vol. 4, pp. 13–131 for a complete bibliography of works by and about Maistre.

Bradley, Owen. *A Modern Maistre: The Social and Political Thought of Joseph de Maistre.* Lincoln, Neb., 1999.

Lebrun, Richard A. *Joseph de Maistre: An Intellectual Militant.* Kingston, Ont., 1988.

RICHARD A. LEBRUN

MAJUBA HILL. The vexed question of taxation led to a declaration of independence from British rule by the South African Boer states on 16 December 1880. Four days later at Bronkhorstspruit Commandant Frans Joubert intercepted and destroyed a British army column. Major-general Sir George Pomeroy-Colley (1835–1881), the British governor, was sent reinforcements and by 24 January 1881 the newly formed Natal Field Force numbered 65 officers and 1,397 men and was ready to move north from the town of Newcastle.

Boer military organization was based on the commando, a unit drawn from a given locality in which all males between sixteen and sixty years of age were obliged to serve, bringing their own horse and rations and often their own rifle. These ad-hoc formations elected their own officers and when given orders might cooperate or not, as they deemed prudent. All were skilled in their use of arms.

The border between Natal and the Transvaal is north of the pass called Laing's Nek, which is overlooked from three miles to the southwest by the mountain, some 2,000 feet higher, called Majuba Hill and from the east by a feature called, in British reports, Table Mountain. About four miles southeast of Majuba, the road to the north runs past a place named Mount Prospect. On 1 January 1881 the Boers, under Piet Joubert (1831–1900), occupied and fortified Laing's Nek. General Colley's force moved out of Newcastle on 24 January and arrived in rain and mist at Mount Prospect two days later. The weather prevented movement on 27 January. By that time Joubert had some 1,000 men on the high ground on either side of the Nek. On 28 January the British attacked Table Mountain, but the Boer left easily repulsed the Mounted Squadron, while the red-coated 58th Regiment found themselves facing the Boer trenches, from which volleys of rifle fire raked them. The colors were saved and the retreat was made in good order, but 84 men had been killed and 110 wounded. Colley's staff, ostentatiously riding into action, had been almost completely destroyed.

On 8 February the Boer forces of Nicolaas Smit (1837–1896) attacked a supply column's escort between Newcastle and Mount Prospect and inflicted serious losses on them with accurate and persistent rifle fire. The action was broken off when thunderstorms broke out, and during the night the British managed to withdraw in silence. Next day Smit returned to find his enemy gone.

As fresh British forces arrived from India, Colley was, to his disgust, instructed to negotiate an armistice. Joubert agreed, but the news failed to arrive before the next battle. In the meantime Colley had decided to occupy Majuba, presumably in order to dominate the Nek.

As midnight approached on 26 February, Colley himself led a force of 595 officers and men out of Mount Prospect and up the flank of Nkwelo Mountain to gain the ridge leading to Majuba. He secured the line of communication as they climbed and 405 men reached the dished summit of Majuba in darkness. Dawn broke to reveal that the full perimeter had not been occupied, a stony ridge having been mistaken as the northern edge. The 92nd Highlanders pushed forward, thinning the line further and establishing an exposed post on Gordon's Knoll, a hillock dominating the northern side. Colley and his staff made a leisurely inspection as the sun rose and made no further provision for the defense of the position.

The Boers reacted by sending men both to Majuba and the Nek, but when they found the pass peaceful, they concentrated on the mountain. While the older men maintained fire from below on their enemy silhouetted on the skyline, the younger, in two groups, worked their way up the gullies that shielded them from observation. In spite of warnings, nothing was done to strengthen the five-man outpost on the Knoll, which was taken by seventy Boers at 12:45 P.M. Their covering fire allowed their comrades to secure the northern slope. A counterattack by the British reserves collapsed and the stony ridge became the front line. Scattered thinly over the terrain, the soldiers' will to resist evaporated. The end came when, threatened by a Boer flanking movement, a wild rush took the survivors back off the mountain, allowing the Boers to pick them off from above. Only the 92nd (later the Gordon) Highlanders stood on the left of the line, commanded by the defiant Lieutenant Hector Archibald MacDonald (1853–1903) who, when he was one of only two men left unwounded, resorted to his fists in a final act of defiance. Colley was killed and thus spared the disgrace of having commanded the British in a humiliating defeat in which they suffered casualties of 85 killed, 119 wounded, and 35 missing or taken prisoner. The fieldcraft and marksmanship of the Boers, who lost one man killed and six wounded, had revealed the weakness of tactics devised to overcome poorly-equipped foes. Peace was agreed on 21 March.

See also **Boer War; Imperialism; South Africa.**

BIBLIOGRAPHY

Bond, Brian, "The South African War 1880–1881." In *Victorian Military Campaigns.* London, 1967.

Castle, Ian. *Osprey Campaign Series 45: Majuba 1881.* London, 1996.

Lehmann, Joseph H. *The First Boer War.* London, 1972.

Troup, Freda. *South Africa: An Historical Introduction.* London, 1972.

MARTIN F. MARIX EVANS

MALATESTA, ERRICO (1853–1932), Italian anarchist.

One of the most influential figures in the anarchist tradition, Errico Malatesta was born in 1853 at

Santa Maria Capua Vetere near Naples, Italy. After enrolling in the faculty of medicine at the University of Naples, Malatesta soon devoted himself entirely to politics, abandoning his studies and medical career.

Initially, Malatesta was drawn to the ideas of Giuseppe Mazzini, the radical revolutionary and father of Italian nationalism. The Paris Commune of 1871, however, decisively transformed Malatesta's political direction. For Malatesta, the Commune seemed to embody the ideals of Italian radicals. It was a revolutionary movement of ordinary men and women who attempted to liberate themselves and to build a democratic and egalitarian society. It was profoundly disillusioning, and indeed somewhat surprising, therefore, that Mazzini condemned the Commune and welcomed its suppression.

Immediately after the events in Paris, therefore, Malatesta turned to the Russian anarchist Mikhail Bakunin. In those years Bakunin was active in Naples, where he founded an Italian section of the International Workingmen's Association (IWA) established by Karl Marx. Malatesta accepted Bakunin's critique of the authoritarianism of Marx's leadership. He also agreed with Bakunin that the social and economic structures of Italy precluded a revolution based on the Marxian notions of an industrial proletariat. In an agrarian society like Italy, the social groups likely to lead a revolution were peasants in the countryside and artisans in the cities. The actions of Parisian craftsmen in 1871 and of southern Italian peasants during the 1860s revolt, known as "banditry," suggested that Bakunin had provided a more realistic assessment of Italian revolutionary possibilities than Marx. Furthermore, Malatesta opposed the elaboration of a complex theory such as Marx's on the grounds that a doctrine beyond the grasp of the movement's members was inherently authoritarian. He also anticipated that the precise structures of the future egalitarian society would be determined spontaneously after the revolution. Thus, with the establishment of the IWA, the first form of organized socialism in Italy was anarchism rather than Marxism.

Although the anarchists had many initial advantages over Marxism in attracting a popular following, their dominant role in Italy proved fleeting. One problem was the overly simple anarchist theory of revolution itself—that all that was needed was the example of selfless intellectuals who practiced the "propaganda of the deed." The masses, the theory held, would follow. In keeping with this perspective, Malatesta and his comrades attempted to ignite insurrections in 1874 and 1877. Unfortunately for them, the masses remained indifferent on both occasions. The only enduring result was that the police unleashed a lasting campaign to suppress the anarchist movement, outlawing the International and targeting its members for mass arrests, the dissolution of party branches, a ban on meetings, and administrative banishment. Malatesta suffered imprisonment and then fled abroad. For most of the remainder of his life—from his first exile in 1879 until his definitive return to Italy in 1919—Malatesta lived outside of his native country.

With the foundation of the Italian Socialist Party (PSI) in 1892, the anarchists permanently lost their leadership of the workers' movement. The establishment of the PSI formalized a permanent split in Italian socialism between legalitarian social democrats and anarchists, and the anarchists failed to keep pace with the PSI in competing for mass support. In the course of this schism, some anarchists defected to the cause of legalitarian socialism, the most clamorous example being that of Andrea Costa. Malatesta, however, never wavered in his commitment to the anarchist cause. For three decades after 1892 he tirelessly preached the cause of antiauthoritarian communism, arguing for the rejection of elections, parliaments, and any approach to socialism that involved the use of state power for its realization.

Within the anarchist cause, Malatesta established a distinctive and coherent current of thought. Malatesta was committed to building a broad base for revolution, and for that purpose he accepted the necessity for organization and for anarchist participation in party structures, chambers of labor, trade unions, and newspapers. For that reason, too, he rejected the temptations of libertarian individualism in the manner of Max Stirner, and of the practice of terrorism, which he thought alienated the masses and dehumanized revolution. The anarchist cause, he argued, was not the property of individuals or even of the working class. Anarchy—the abolition of coercive state power—was the means to liberate all of humanity. At its height, Italian anarchism attracted a following variously estimated at between eight thousand and twenty thousand members concentrated primarily in central Italy.

A sworn enemy of militarism, Malatesta opposed World War I and Italian entry into the conflict. After the war he returned to Italy in 1919 and played an active role in the political ferment marking the "Red Years" in Italian history—1919 and 1920—even founding an anarchist newspaper, *Umanità Nuova*. With the fascist seizure of power in 1922, however, Malatesta again faced rigorous repression. His paper was closed, and he himself, by now in failing health, was placed under house arrest from 1926 until his death in Rome in 1932.

See also **Anarchism; Bakunin, Mikhail; Italy; Mazzini, Giuseppe.**

BIBLIOGRAPHY

Berti, Giampietro. *Errico Malatesta e il movimento anarchico italiano e Internazionale: 1872–1932.* Milan, 2003.

Levy, Carl. "Italian Anarchism, 1870–1926." In *For Anarchism: History, Theory, and Practice*, edited by David Goodway, 25–78. London and New York, 1989.

Nettlau, Max. "Errico Malatesta: Vita e pensieri." New York, 1922.

Pernicone, Nunzio. *Italian Anarchism, 1864–1892.* Princeton, N.J., 1993.

Woodcock, George. *Anarchism: A History of Libertarian Ideas and Movements.* New York, 1962.

FRANK SNOWDEN

MALTHUS, THOMAS ROBERT

(1766–1834), English economist and sociologist.

Thomas Robert Malthus was the son of an unusual Surrey country gentleman who personally knew, and was deeply influenced by, both Jean-Jacques Rousseau and David Hume. Young Robert was educated at home (Rousseau opposed formal schooling) and then at Jesus College, Cambridge. Malthus's many writings can be viewed as sustained critiques of Enlightenment spirit of optimism and utopian reform within which he had been reared.

Some "know" Thomas Robert Malthus as the Briton who predicted the population explosion of the nineteenth and twentieth centuries. Malthus actually argued the opposite, that "population is necessarily limited by the means of subsistence." He identified many "positive checks" that ensured that population did not outrun food supply (by periodically eliminating unsustainable numbers, mostly among the "lowest orders of society"). These included famine, epidemics, wars, and—new to early-industrial Britain—"the silent though certain destruction of life in large towns and manufactories." The misunderstanding perhaps arises from Malthus's speculation that population, *left to itself* would grow faster (geometrically, i.e., 2, 4, 8, 16, 32 ...) than food production (which would grow arithmetically, i.e., 2, 4, 6, 8, 10 ...). Malthus clarified that population is never left to itself, except on a newly discovered island.

Malthus admitted a small ameliorative role for "preventive" (voluntary) checks like late marriage and systematic sexual denial. (An ordained Anglican clergyman, Malthus did not endorse contraception.) By inducing the libidinous "hare" to sleep, "the tortoise [of food production] may have some chance." But broadly, humankind was doomed, by an immutable "law of misery," to bare subsistence.

MALTHUS AND POLITICAL CONSERVATISM

The *Essay on the Principle of Population* was a widely read work that went through six editions by 1826. Ten of the first edition's nineteen chapters are polemical attacks on the optimism of radical contemporaries—William Godwin, Dr. Price, and the French revolutionary Marie-Jean de Caritat, marquis de Condorcet. They had argued that unlimited progress and the elimination of inequality was possible, once antiquated political institutions were swept away. Malthus, a political conservative, countered that revolution, or even institutional reform, would not help. Poverty stemmed from *natural* (not man-made) scarcities and hence could never disappear.

Malthus opposed state intervention to relieve poverty—making him a founder of modern-day conservatism. In his view, even parish charity and the Speenhamland bread subsidies (instituted in 1795 to save Britain from food riots) would only encourage paupers to start families, which would ultimately become victims of famine, or wards of the state. Malthus provided the British landed gentry "scientific" arguments against higher local taxes ("poor rates")—provoking Karl Marx to call him a "shameless sycophant of the ruling classes"—and provided future conservatives ammunition against the welfare state. In the short term, "Malthusianism" led indirectly to Britain's harsh Poor Law of 1834. Yet Malthus insisted that his prescriptions increased "the aggregate mass of happiness among the common people." Absence of poor relief may create a few cases of "very severe distress" but food-for-work programs for the unemployed would hurt the entire working population, by raising food prices and lowering wages.

The perceived coldness of Malthus's policy prescriptions earned him the ire of his contemporaries, the Romantic poets. Lord Byron condemned Malthus for "turning marriage into arithmetic" and ridiculed him on four occasions in *Don Juan* (1821). Even Tories like Robert Southey and Samuel Taylor Coleridge joined the more progressive William Hazlitt and William Wordsworth in denouncing Malthus's heartlessness. Malthus countered that *he* was painting the true face of rural poverty, wryly noting that the "daughters of peasants will not be found such rosy cherubs in real life as described in romances."

MALTHUS, SOCIAL HISTORY, AND THE BIRTH OF THE SOCIAL SCIENCES

Complaining that "the histories of mankind that we possess are, in general, histories only of the higher classes," Malthus called for "a faithful history" that would record changes in marriage age, fertility, and wages of agricultural labor. Malthus argued that such statistics were crucial because these poorer classes bore the brunt of nature's "positive checks," and in 1834 he cofounded the Statistical Society of London. If social, family, and agrarian history took another 150 years to emerge, the fault was scarcely Malthus's.

Second and subsequent editions of Malthus's *Essay* carefully documented "checks to population" recorded across many societies over many time periods—from ancient Greece to modern Siberia. Universal, timeless laws were derived from this quantitative or anthropological evidence, and predictions and policy prescriptions offered. Arguably, this made Malthus the world's first systematic social scientist. Errors can plausibly be attributed to poor data quality rather than deficient method. Barring Sweden, there were no *regular* censuses in 1800, and if they soon became the norm in Europe and America it was because Malthus highlighted their importance.

Though Malthus collected no data on nonhuman populations, his most enduring contribution, ironically, is to biological rather than social science. His population theory works far better for animal habitats (and is enshrined in the ecological concept of "carrying capacity") than it has done for human societies, capable of innovation. As Charles Darwin acknowledged in his *Autobiography* (1887), a chance encounter with Malthus's book in 1838 provided him the crucial mechanism for biological evolution—natural selection. Darwin, in his *Origin of Species* (1859), extrapolated the Malthusian "struggle for existence" to all species. The best-adapted members survive this struggle, and procreate; the least-adapted die.

It is scarcely known that Malthus was the world's first professional economist. Appointed in 1805 to the first-ever economics professorship (at the East India College, Haileybury), he held it till his death. While the Scottish economist Adam Smith's pioneering *Wealth of Nations* (1776) had promised growing prosperity through free trade and division of labor, Malthus's *Principles of Political Economy* (1820) recast economics as a "dismal science" struggling to reconcile unlimited needs with scarce resources. Though witnessing the tremendous productivity gains of the First Industrial Revolution, Malthus (and his friend David Ricardo) predicted declining wages and profits, higher food prices, and threats from grain imports—a declining, or at best a steady-state, economy.

THE VERDICT OF HISTORY

The nineteenth and twentieth centuries appear to have borne out Enlightenment optimism, not Malthus. Food production and living standards more than kept pace with rapid population growth—even if famines and epidemics in nineteenth-century India and Ireland and, more recently, sub-Saharan Africa, have periodically vindicated Malthusian pessimism in specific locales. Some environmentalists, however, maintain that the jury is still out: Malthus's dire prophecies have not been refuted but merely postponed, because of unprecedented (and unsustainable) technological progress. For others like Amartya Sen, two centuries afford ample time to test any theory, and most famines have had political, not natural, causes. While it is tempting to see Malthus as a protoenvironmentalist, it should be remembered that his focus on the scarcity of natural resources influenced, without doubt, the nineteenth-century scramble for colonies.

As has been argued above, however, Malthus's historical significance does not rest on the validity of his demographic pronouncements. It is by shaping the early contours of conservatism (political *and* sexual), economics, and social science at large, that Malthus cast his shadow into, and beyond, the nineteenth century.

See also **Economists, Classical; Great Britain; Industrial Revolution, First.**

BIBLIOGRAPHY

Primary Sources

Malthus, Thomas Robert. *An Essay on the Principle of Population. 1798.* 1st edition. Edited by Anthony Flew. Harmondsworth, U.K., 1982.

———. *An Essay on the Principle of Population. 1826.* 6th edition. London, 1973.

Secondary Sources

Brown, Lester R., et al. *Nineteen Dimensions of Population Challenge.* New York, 1999.

Himmelfarb, Gertrude. *The Idea of Poverty.* New York, 1985.

Sen, Amartya. "Malthusian Delusions?" *Nation* 271, no. 17 (November 27, 2000).

Winch, Donald. *Malthus.* Oxford, U.K., 1977.

Cyrus Vakil

MANCHESTER. Manchester is forever associated with the Industrial Revolution. From the late eighteenth century, the factory production of cotton goods made the Manchester region of northwestern England a center of sustained economic growth, the like of which the world had never seen before. Cotton was central to British industrialization. However, the importance of Manchester was not confined to the steam-powered mechanization of cotton production and the transport revolution that accompanied it. Manchester was the greatest of the trading cities to emerge from the Industrial Revolution, the center of the global market for cotton goods. It was also the political home of free trade and became associated across Europe with the British ideology of economic individualism. By 1850 the name of Manchester was known around the world and was synonymous with cotton, commerce, and industrial strength. The hundred years following 1850 was a period of gradual decline as other cities and other countries caught up with the pioneers of industrialization.

COTTON AND THE INDUSTRIAL REVOLUTION

The transformation of Britain into the world's first industrial nation was centered in a small number of industries: coal, iron, and cotton. Of these it was cotton that was to have the most profound effect and make the most important contribution to the process of industrialization. Cotton was central to British industrialization, and cotton meant Manchester and its region. Even before the end of the eighteenth century Manchester had emerged as the foremost urban center of the first power-driven factory industry. Britain's cotton industry was centralized in one region of the country. As early as the 1790s, 70 percent of the British cotton industry was concentrated in the district of southeast Lancashire and northeast Cheshire; by 1835 the figure had risen even further to 90 percent. For more than a century, the cotton industry of this region was the world's premier example of mechanized factory production. Raw cotton, which had been imported in insignificant quantities before the 1770s, became one of Britain's principal imports, increasing from 1,900 metric tons in the period from 1772 to 1774 to 205,000 metric tons in 1839 to 1841. Manchester played a central role in this revolution. Although the factory production of textiles and the industrial use of steam power first occurred elsewhere, the application of steam power to cotton spinning in Manchester in the

1780s and 1790s enabled factories to become urban based and secured the role of the factory in industrialization.

To the nineteenth-century mind Manchester was "Cottonopolis," the very essence of industrialism, the archetypal manufacturing town, and the model of all the other Lancashire mill towns, themselves sometimes referred to as "Little Manchesters." But research since the 1980s (especially by Roger Lloyd-Jones and M. J. Lewis) suggests that this impression is misleading, for Manchester was never merely a mill town. For centuries it had offered marketing facilities for linens and woolens, and during the eighteenth century had become the regional market center for cotton mixtures. Thus, before the first factory was erected in the 1780s, Manchester was already the commercial hub of its region. Transport developments during the canal era and later the railway age strengthened its position. Beginning with the Duke of Bridgewater's canal in 1762, Manchester soon became the focus of a complex of canals that greatly aided its trade, and in 1830 the Liverpool to Manchester Railway provided the first passenger rail service in the world.

The commercial warehouse continued to play a vital role in Manchester's economic life. But the importance of the warehouse to the local economy is most tellingly revealed by the striking imbalance of investment between the town's warehouse and factory sectors. Total capital investment in factories was considerably less than in warehouses. Warehouses absorbed over 48 percent of property asset investment by 1815, as opposed to a mere 6 percent in factories. Even public houses and inns attracted a larger proportion at almost 9 percent. This does not allow for machinery or the power to drive it. But even assuming a doubling of the value of the fixed assets of factory plant and buildings, the dominance of warehouse investment remains clear. Investment in cotton mills increased, especially as weaving was mechanized in the 1820s, but Manchester's business structure still leaned heavily toward its commercial sector. While the proportion of all capital tied up in cotton factories had increased to some 12 percent by 1825, that invested in warehouses remained much higher at nearly 43 percent.

Indeed, Manchester's symbolic role as the focus of the factory system may be best understood in terms of labor rather than capital. Workers flocked to the mills. In 1815 Manchester's cotton factories employed approximately 11,500 men, women, and children. By the time of the 1841 census, there were 19,561 working in all branches of cotton manufacture in Manchester. This was a huge workforce. In size it approached the total for the combined cotton workforces of Oldham, Blackburn, and Ashton-under-Lyne (21,615). But these figures can be misleading. Although cotton manufacture was a major source of work in Manchester, it did not dominate the local labor market, as was the case in the surrounding cotton towns. As a proportion of total occupied persons in 1841, cotton employed 18 percent of Manchester's labor force, compared with the respective figures of 50 percent in Ashton, 40 percent in Oldham, and 40 percent in Blackburn. These were the mill towns proper.

WORLD'S MARKETPLACE FOR COTTON GOODS

Manchester's historical significance owes as much to its role in the development of world trade as it does to its place in the history of the factory system. The mechanization of cotton spinning transformed world trade. It enabled British producers to undercut competitors producing by traditional handicraft manufacture. Thus it was as early as the 1790s that India was overtaken by Britain as the leading exporter of cotton goods, and in the process the sheer scale of production by this new low-cost producer created the first truly global market of the modern industrial era. Manchester's nineteenth-century commercial preeminence depended upon the phenomenal growth in the production of cotton cloth. As early as the first decade of the nineteenth century cotton goods constituted half of total British exports (by value), and this level of contribution was maintained for much of the nineteenth century. Thus cotton was the main contributor to the export trade at the height of Britain's economic power and global influence. Manchester was the commercial lynchpin of this trade: the world's central market for the sale of cotton goods. The Royal Cotton Exchange was the venue for the myriad commercial transactions involved, and the city center streets were lined with warehouses for the display as well as storage of goods.

The name *Manchester* became symbolically linked with cotton and commerce. *Manchester goods* became

Millinery workers at the Sutton and Torkington factory in Manchester, 1909. Long the center of the English textile trade, Manchester became the site of increasing industrial diversification during the latter half of the nineteenth century. © HULTON-DEUTSCH COLLECTION/CORBIS

a synonym for all textiles, not just cotton. But equally important, it was linked in the mind of the world with the political ideology of free trade. By the mid-nineteenth century, in part through the efforts of the Manchester-based Anti–Corn Law League, the principles of free trade had become national policy of the leading industrial nation. This achievement was symbolized in Manchester in the naming of the city's premier public building not after a saint, a national hero, or a monarch but after an idea: the Free Trade Hall. As the first industrial city and the home of the Anti–Corn Law League, Manchester was characterized by nineteenth-century German critics in the abstract noun *das Manchestertum* to represent the British ideology of economic individualism. Thus *Manchester* itself became abstracted as the symbol both of Britain's economic power and of the industrial middle class.

"SHOCK CITY" OF ITS AGE

By the 1840s more than half a century of revolutionary change had made Manchester the "shock city" of its age. Manchester symbolized more than an economic revolution. A major reason for Manchester's prominence was the enormous urban growth revealed by the national census in 1831 and 1841, which made contemporaries accept that theirs was the "age of great cities." It was not just the rising national population figures that impressed contemporaries but the concentration in large towns, especially certain provincial centers, which were growing at an unprecedented rate. While between 1801 and 1841 the population of London had doubled, that of Manchester had more than trebled and by 1851 was more than four times larger than fifty years before. Manchester was not alone in this; among the larger English towns Liverpool had also multiplied fourfold, and Bradford's population was eight times greater than in 1801. But there was a difference of scale: Manchester and Liverpool were three times the size of Bradford; outside London they were the biggest towns in England. The environmental and social problems created by rapid urban growth were most marked in the biggest centers and, for a while, Manchester became a symbol for the nation of twin developments. It combined massive urban growth with factory production and acquired almost mythical status as the emblem of a new order of things.

To contemporaries, Manchester represented new social classes and unleashed political forces: trade unionism, Chartism, and socialism. Working-class politics demanded democracy and appeared to threaten property. If it was to be contained, it had to be understood, and Manchester seemed to hold the key to this knowledge. Moreover, if urban industrial living was the pattern of the future, then Manchester seemed to be its herald. Manchester's economic miracle, which made it seem heroic to some, was overlaid by living conditions that offered instead the prospect of social catastrophe. While the future prime minister Benjamin Disraeli felt able to make comparisons with the classical world, claiming that industrial Manchester was "as great a human exploit as Athens" (in his novel *Coningsby, or, the New Generation;* 1844), such optimism was more qualified in the observations of other contemporaries. Manchester generated great wealth but also great squalor. Massive urban growth brought enormous problems of organization, provision of amenities, and maintenance of public order. The environmental consequences of dramatic and continuous growth for more than fifty years were on the debit side of the balance sheet of industrialization. During the first half of the nineteenth century Manchester was one of the most overcrowded and unhealthy places in Europe. Moreover, the modern urban pattern of residential zoning by function and by social class, including the gulf between the suburb and the slum, found its early expression in Manchester. Such a degree of social segregation made Manchester central to Friedrich Engel's analysis of conditions under industrial capitalism in *Die Lage der arbeitenden Klasse in England* (1945; *The Condition of the Working Class in England in 1844*), a book that had a great influence on Karl Marx. The town also provided much of the context for many of the social-problem novels of the 1840s and 1850s, most notably *Mary Barton: A Tale of Manchester Life* (1848) by Elizabeth Gaskell.

COTTONOPOLIS?

The overworked sobriquet "Cottonopolis" masks Manchester's more complex industrial character. Manchester was also an important center of engineering. Scientific engineering developed out of the work begun by its millwrights and mechanics in the early part of the Industrial Revolution. Manchester engineers placed the town at the cutting edge of one of the defining sectors of the modern industrial economy: the manufacture of machine tools. This was epitomized by James Nasmyth, whose steam hammer (1839) was one of the principal engineering inventions of the nineteenth century, and Joseph Whitworth, whose name was synonymous with precision engineering and standardization around the world. Underpinning this was the city's cultural climate of inquiry and practical learning, a prime example of the city as "innovative milieu" (Hall) exemplified by the Manchester Literary and Philosophical Society, the oldest enduring English institution, apart from the Royal Society, devoted to scientific discourse and publication. From its foundation in 1781 an impressive sequence of major scientific figures passed through its portals, including John Dalton, William Henry, William Sturgeon, and James Prescott Joule, together with "practical scientists": engineers and inventors such as Richard Roberts and William Fairbairn.

The Industrial Revolution had made Manchester one of the world's most famous cities. Apart from London, it was the foremost commercial, banking, and transport center in what was the most economically advanced country in the world. If Manchester's comparative importance was to decline during the second half of the nineteenth century, as other cities and other industries caught up, it nonetheless remained one of the great trading cities of the world. It certainly dominated the commercial life of the cotton district of Lancashire and Cheshire. The challenge to Lancashire's domination of the cotton trade in the decades following the "cotton famine" caused by the loss of raw cotton imports during the American Civil War of 1861–1865 was met in characteristic fashion by the construction of the Manchester Ship Canal (1894), which turned a city thirty miles from the sea into an international port with extensive docks. By 1914 Manchester was ranked as one of Britain's leading commercial ports, with the world's first industrial estate at Trafford Park. The twentieth century was to be a story of steady and relentless industrial decline. Finally, after 1950, the decline of the cotton industry turned into a collapse, and subsequently, like many former industrial giants, Manchester's fortunes have depended upon other industries and upon the nonindustrial sectors of the local economy.

See also **Cities and Towns; Great Britain; Industrial Revolution, First.**

BIBLIOGRAPHY

Primary Sources

Engels, Friedrich. *The Condition of the Working Class in England in 1844.* Edited by David McLellan. Oxford, U.K., 1993.

Gaskell, Elizabeth. *Mary Barton: A Tale of Manchester Life.* Edited by Stephen Gill. Harmondsworth, U.K., 1985.

Secondary Sources

Briggs, Asa. *Victorian Cities.* London, 1963. See chapter 3, "Manchester: The Symbol of an Age."

Farnie, D. A. *The English Cotton Industry and the World Market, 1815–1896.* Oxford, U.K., 1979.

Fishman, Robert. *Bourgeois Utopias: The Rise and Fall of Suburbia.* New York, 1987. See chapter 3, "The Suburb and the Industrial City: Manchester."

Hall, Peter. *Cities in Civilization: Culture, Innovation, and Urban Order.* London, 1998. See chapter 10, "The First Industrial City: Manchester, 1760–1830."

Kidd, Alan J. *Manchester.* 3rd ed. Edinburgh, 2002.

Kidd, Alan J., and K. W. Roberts, eds. *City, Class, and Culture: Studies of Social Policy and Cultural Production in Victorian Manchester.* Manchester, 1985. Contains an extensive bibliography.

Lloyd-Jones, Roger, and M. J. Lewis. *Manchester and the Age of the Factory.* London, 1988.

Manchester Region History Review (1987–). Publishes an annual bibliography.

Alan J. Kidd

MANET, ÉDOUARD (1832–1883), French realist painter.

Édouard Manet was born on 23 January 1832, in Paris. His father, Auguste Manet, began his career in the French Ministry of Justice and was, for sixteen years, a civil judge for the Tribunal de la Première Instance, the entry-level court in Paris. Manet's mother, born Eugénie-Désirée Fournier, was the daughter of the vice-consul of France in Sweden, as well as the goddaughter of the king of Sweden, the French-born Jean Baptiste Bernadotte (r. as Charles XIV John, 1818–1844). Both parents were descendents from an aristocratic lineage of so-called *gens de robe* (nobility acquired through venal offices such as regional treasurer). Auguste's father and grandfather were both mayors of the town of Gennevilliers, a town north of Paris where the Manets owned extensive property, and where Manet spent family vacations. The income from this property guaranteed that Manet and his family remained extremely comfortable.

The young Manet was an indifferent student whose interest in drawing had been aided and encouraged by his maternal uncle Edmond Fournier, who lived with the Manets until Édouard was sixteen. It was determined that a naval career would be appropriate for him, and after Manet failed his entrance exam, he undertook a sea voyage to South America in 1848–1849 as a qualification for naval service. By the time of his return to Paris, however, Manet was determined to study painting, and he enrolled in the studio of Thomas Couture (1815–1879) in Paris, where he remained for six years. Couture was a respected teacher who earned official recognition; he had other illustrious pupils such as Pierre-Cecil Puvis de Chavannes (1824–1898). However, it is significant that Manet, whose career would be marked by dramatic breaks with the art establishment of his time, chose not to study at the official art school of the Academy, the École des Beaux-Arts, sited across the Rue des Petits-Augustins in Paris from the house of Manet's birth.

In 1859, Manet submitted his first entry to the Salon exhibition juried by members of the French Academy, and not surprisingly, it was rejected. *The Absinthe Drinker* (1858–1859) was a sketchy but full-length representation of a homeless drunkard—a type known in popular prints and legends of the *chiffonnier*

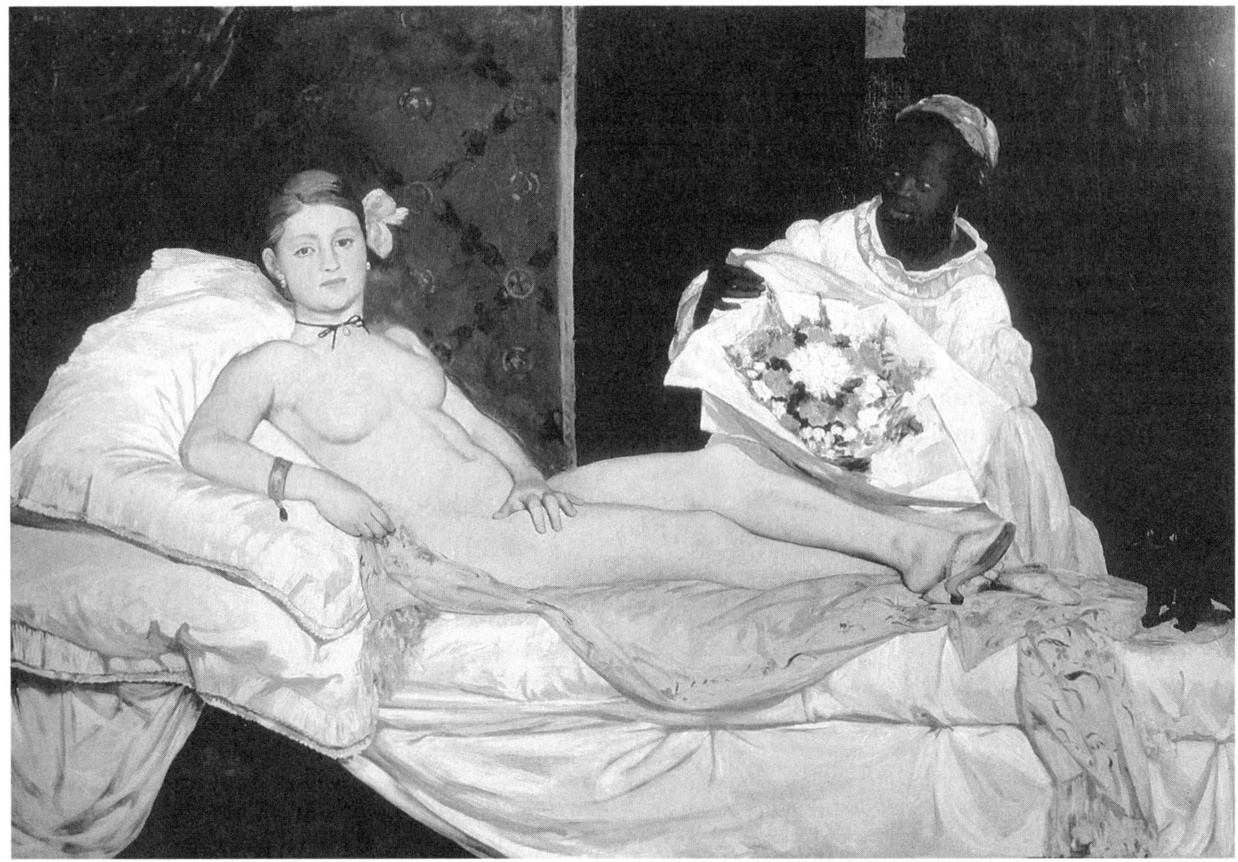

Olympia. Painting by Edouard Manet, 1865. ©FRANCIS G. MAYER/CORBIS

or ragpicker, and found on the outskirts of Paris. The *chiffonnier* was also notorious, as the character had figured in several poems in Charles Baudelaire's *Les Fleurs du mal*, which was published in 1857 and immediately put on trial for offending public morality. (Baudelaire was found guilty and fined; the court ordered six poems removed from the edition.) Manet and Baudelaire became friends, and Manet's early work frequently featured the kinds of urban characters—gypsies, ragpickers, street entertainers, prostitutes—that populate the poems of Baudelaire.

Although Manet shocked the public with his representations of wayward Baudelairean types, he was equally at home painting his fashionable and well-to-do friends. Until the late 1860s, Manet frequently painted the working poor, or at least models posing as such types, as well as a number of well-known artists, musicians, and writers who are also recognizable figures in his paintings. In a single painting, *Music in the Tuileries Gardens* of 1862, one can identify the critic Zacharie Astruc (1833–1907), painter Henri Fantin-Latour (1836–1904), poet Théophile Gautier (1811–1872), composer Jacques Offenbach (1819–1880), collector Baron Isidore-Justin-Severin Taylor (1789–1879), Baudelaire, and many other personages who form a cadre of the Parisian cultural elite.

In 1863, more than half of the over 5,000 submissions to the Salon were rejected by the Academy, and there was an outcry from the artists that the judging had been harsh. Emperor Napoleon III (r. 1852–1871), in consideration of the excessive complaints, proclaimed that there would be an exhibition of the works rejected by the jury. In this unprecedented Salon des Refusés, Manet exhibited three paintings, including *Le Déjeuner sur l'herbe* (1863). Entitled *Le Bain* (*Bathing*) at the exhibition, the painting was loosely based on a Venetian Renaissance idyll, but featured two men dressed in contemporary attire, one woman bathing in the river, and a nude woman—the model Victorine Meurent—gazing actively out of the painting and at the beholder.

The painting bewildered critics and visitors and remains the subject of intense scholarly debate.

Although *Le Déjeuner sur l'herbe* shocked critics and viewers, it was in some ways insulated from the harshest of critical responses by being in the Salon des Refusés; the Academy had, after all, not accepted it for the Salon. But in 1865, it accepted *Olympia* (1865), a work modeled on Titian's *Venus of Urbino* (1538). In place of the Renaissance Venus, however, *Olympia* featured a contemporary nude woman in jewelry and satin mules; she gazes directly out at the viewer as a black cat arches its back, and as a female servant of African descent brings in a bouquet of flowers, still in their street wrapper. The picture, with its stark lighting, abbreviated modeling, and references to prostitutes who sometimes rented jewelry and other accessories, or who accepted gifts in lieu of cash, caused an enormous scandal. More than seventy critics showered the picture with hostile commentary: a few associated the painting with Francisco de Goya (1746–1828) and Baudelaire, but most expressed utter shock at both the subject and the manner of painting.

Manet exhibited *Olympia* again in 1867 in an enormous, self-funded, solo exhibition near the Pont de l'Alma in Paris during the Universal Exposition. In doing so, Manet was following the lead of Gustave Courbet (1819–1877), who had erected a similar pavilion in 1855 during that world's fair, and did so again in 1867. The novelist and journalist Émile Zola (1840–1902) would be one of *Olympia*'s defenders in 1867. In a pamphlet and in his published reviews, he asked viewers to look only at Manet's bold manner of painting rather than at the subject matter.

Manet's work in the 1870s took on a lighter palette, and like the impressionists who were inspired by his example, frequently featured the subject matter of modernity in Paris: cafés, fashionable men and women, the opera ball, conservatories. For instance in *The Railroad* (1873), Manet's model Victorine Meurent and a young girl pose near the Pont de l'Europe and the Gare St.-Lazare—landmarks of a Parisian neighborhood of rapid growth and prominence in the 1870s. In *Argenteuil, Les Canotiers* (1874), a man and a woman pose on a river dock in a town that was becoming almost a suburb of Paris in the period. In both paintings, the woman looks away from her companion and gazes out of the painting and at the viewer. The effect is arresting in comparison with the typically tidy narratives of mid-nineteenth-century genre painting: the viewer is put into a position of thinking critically about the subject. Manet's last masterpiece, the *Bar at the Folies-Bergère* (1882), makes use of the mirror behind the bar at a glamorous café-concert that was part of the changing urban landscape of Paris in the period: the mirror is used to suggest both the complexity of the subject and the deceptiveness of the viewer's trust in fleeting appearances. Despite his friendship with many of the impressionists, especially with Berthe Morisot (1841–1895), who married Manet's brother Eugène in 1874, he never exhibited at their independent exhibitions; instead, he preferred to risk rejection from the Salon, or he exhibited at private galleries or directly from his studio.

Manet married the Dutch-born Suzanne Leenhoff, a musician and piano teacher, in 1863. The couple had no children of their own, although Suzanne was the mother of Léon Koëlla-Leenhoff, referred to in polite society as Suzanne's younger brother. Questions still surround the paternity of Léon. Manet probably suffered from syphilis, and his health worsened considerably by 1880. His left leg was amputated in 1883, and he died shortly after, in Paris.

Édouard Manet has been considered by many critics and historians as the first modernist artist; that is, the first artist to impart a particular consciousness of modernity to subjects drawn from modern life, at a time when most artists still depended on recognized subjects from classical history and mythology. In Manet's work, this awareness of the particularity of the present moment is at times critical, and at times celebratory; indeed, many see it as crucial to modernism that the artist's attitude somehow oscillates between the two or even embraces both stances. As Manet gained notoriety by drawing on modern subjects and by painting them in a more sketchlike and abstract way than his contemporaries, he has been seen as paving the way for the developments in abstractions and modernism that followed, from impressionism to cubism and on into twentieth-century nonrepresentational art. Because of the complex nature of his subjects, the boldness of his style, and his continued

A Bar at the Folies-Bergère. Painting by Edouard Manet, 1881–1882. SAMUEL COURTAULD TRUST, COURTAULD INSTITUTE OF ART GALLERY/BRIDGEMAN ART LIBRARY

interest in Old Master compositions, art historians and commentators from a wide variety of perspectives, from formalism to Marxism, from feminism to psychoanalysis, continue to debate ways of seeing Manet, but agree on his fundamental importance for the history of modern art.

See also **Absinthe; Baudelaire, Charles; Courbet, Gustave; France; Impressionism; Painting; Paris; Realism and Naturalism.**

BIBLIOGRAPHY

Cachin, Françoise. *Manet 1832–1883.* New York, 1983.

Clark, T. J. *The Painting of Modern Life: Paris in the Art of Manet and His Followers.* New York, 1984.

Locke, Nancy. *Manet and the Family Romance.* Princeton, N.J., 2001.

Reff, Theodore. *Manet and Modern Paris.* Washington, D.C., 1982.

Rouart, Denis, and Daniel Wildenstein. *Édouard Manet: catalogue raisonné.* 2 vols. Lausanne, 1975.

Tabarant, Adolphe. *Manet et ses oeuvres.* Paris, 1947.

NANCY LOCKE

MANN, THOMAS (1875–1955), German writer.

Thomas Mann's standing as a modern classic rests securely on his singular accomplishments as a writer. Contributing to his pre-eminence was his role, first in Germany, later in the United States, as incisive public intellectual during the most tortured period of the twentieth century. Mann was the head of a family of six children, three of whom achieved fame in their own right: Erika as cabaret performer and journalist; Klaus as author and essayist; Golo as historian. In 2001, *Die Manns* became a popular television series in Germany—the most visible sign of a growing recognition that the members of the Mann family, including Heinrich, Thomas's older brother, embodied in their lives and works much of the genius, spirit, and unrest of recent German culture and history.

LIFE

Paul Thomas Mann was the second of the five children born to Johann Heinrich Mann, the owner of a grain trading firm and a senator from the Hanseatic city of Lübeck, and Julia, *née* da Silva-Bruhns, his wife of Brazilian-German descent. After attending a performance of *Lohengrin* in 1893, Mann's love of music, kindled by his mother, grew into a passionate and lifelong interest in everything Wagnerian. Mann was a poor student who never obtained the high school diploma required for formal university study. He rather became a formidable autodidact, as evidenced in all his literary work, and outstandingly in *Joseph and His Brothers.*

In 1894, Mann moved to Munich, where he remained until 1933. Briefly, while Heinrich was its editor, he wrote for the nationalist journal *Das zwanzigste Jahrhundert*; he then held a job for two years with the satirical weekly *Simplicissimus.* Having established himself as a major writer in 1901, he married, in 1905, Katia Pringsheim (1883–1980), the daughter of a distinguished Jewish family. Although Mann was profoundly shaped by the homosocial culture prevalent in artistic circles of the day, the marriage was by all standards a success. Nonetheless, his essentially homoerotic imagination remained a most profound source of his creativity, as evidenced in nearly all his works, and notably in *Death in Venice.*

When war broke out in 1914, Mann was carried away by the prevailing nationalist fever. In an inspired five-hundred-page essay, *Reflections of a Nonpolitical Man* (1918), part intellectual autobiography, part analysis of German culture, he aggressively defended Germany's right to preserve its unique music-centered culture and, pitting Western *Zivilisation* against German *Kultur*, to reject Western-style democracy. The book made him a hero in conservative circles. However, by entering the political arena Mann began a learning process that soon led him to revise his wartime views of France and the West. In 1922, in one of his most consequential public interventions, he irritated his conservative admirers by enjoining German youth to support the unloved Weimar Republic. Much of Mann's spiritual journey of those years is reflected in *The Magic Mountain.*

As an early critic of fascism (*Mario and the Magician*, 1929) and of National Socialism (*An Appeal to Reason*, 1930), Mann was forced to leave Germany in 1933 when, in the wake of the powerful speech he gave to commemorate the fiftieth anniversary of Richard Wagner's death, an opportunistic alliance of prominent cultural figures and Nazis singled him out for denunciation as un-German and unwanted in the new Germany. During the first three years of his exile (in France and Switzerland), he maintained a tactical silence about the Nazi regime, largely to protect his publisher. When he did begin to speak out, in February 1936, Mann rose from the German exiles as the most implacable foe of Adolf Hitler and the Third Reich, expressing himself nowhere more effectively than in the open letter to the University of Bonn in response to having been stripped of his German citizenship and honorary doctorate.

In 1938, Mann moved to the United States, first to Princeton, New Jersey, where he was a lecturer at the university, then, in 1941, to Los Angeles, where he became the central figure of an illustrious German exile community (the so-called Weimar on the Pacific) that included Bertolt Brecht, Arnold Schoenberg, and Theodor W. Adorno. Long before the Japanese attack on Pearl Harbor, in speeches across the country, Mann sought to convince a reluctant America of the necessity to go to war against Germany. With Albert Einstein and Arturo Toscanini, he was one of the politically most outspoken intellectuals in America, broadcasting, from 1940, monthly radio messages to Germany (*Listen, Germany!*).

Having entered the country on a Czech passport, Mann became an American citizen in 1944. In 1945, after the defeat of the Third Reich, he was asked to return to Germany to help to heal the wounds. He refused to do so, citing his "national excommunication" of 1933 and rebuking his colleagues for having continued to publish under the Nazi regime. This only deepened the rift between Germany and its most prominent writer. Dismayed by the policies of the Truman administration and publicly branded as a communist dupe, Mann left America in 1952 to spend the last years of his life in Switzerland. He lies buried in Kilchberg, near Zurich.

WORK

Mann's work embraces short fiction; novels; a play; essays on literature, music, and philosophy; and political commentary. He left thousands of letters and ten volumes of diaries covering the years from 1918 to 1921 and 1933 to 1955, all others having been destroyed by the author.

At first, Mann considered the short story in the manner of Guy de Maupassant and Anton Chekhov to be his particular forte. In fact, all his novels were conceived as novellas, including *Buddenbrooks* (1901), a family saga spanning four generations and tracing the decline of a once robust Hanseatic merchant family as its members display a growing interest in matters of the mind, music in particular. With the death of sixteen-year old Hanno, intoxicated by the music of Wagner and unfit for the harsh realities of life, the family becomes extinct, thus making room for the rise of a rival Jewish family. Drawing on Theodor Fontane's late novels and Wagner's *Ring of the Nibelung*, philosophically shaped by Arthur Schopenhauer and Friedrich Nietzsche, *Buddenbrooks* remains Mann's most popular novel. It was this book that earned him the Nobel Prize in 1929. The theme of the artistically inclined outsider, personified by Hanno, is continued in several early novellas, most felicitously in *Tonio Kröger* (1903), a portrait of the artist as a young man. The competing claims of art and society long remained at the center of Mann's work; however, under the weight of historical experience he both broadened and sharpened his vision with a focus on the nexus of culture and politics that eventually produced *Doctor Faustus*.

Mann's second novel, *Royal Highness* (1909), an allegorical romance set at the court of a small German principality, proved to be a artistic dead end. It was the polished, neoclassical form of *Death in Venice* (1912) with its elaborate mythological subtext that opened the way to the future. The story's hero, Gustav von Aschenbach, bears more than a superficial resemblance to its author; but while Aschenbach's life is tragically destroyed by his passion for a fourteen-year-old Polish boy, Mann himself emerged from writing *Death in Venice* artistically strengthened. Conceived in 1912 as a comic and satirical counterpart to the tragedy of Aschenbach, *The Magic Mountain* (1924) grew into a modernist bildungsroman and an epic exposition of prewar European cultural issues. Set in a Swiss sanatorium, the novel traces the emotional and intellectual adventures of an engineering student from Hamburg and concludes with the "thunderclap" of the outbreak of war.

For most of the sixteen years from 1927 to 1943, Mann was preoccupied with his four-part epic, *Joseph and His Brothers*, a meticulous, often humorous retelling of the biblical story through the lens not only of modern scholarship but also of Freudian and Jungian psychology. Part III, *Joseph in Egypt*, contains what may well be the most elaborate and moving erotic scene in all modern literature. Part IV, *Joseph the Provider*, written entirely in the United States, contains a covert tribute to Roosevelt's New Deal. *Joseph and His Brothers* is above all a loving tribute to the exemplary humanity and spirituality of the Jewish people at a time when they were under assault from Mann's native country.

A tribute of a different sort—to Goethean humanism—is manifest in *Lotte in Weimar* (1939), a lovingly amplified episode drawn from the life of Charlotte, the real-life model of Goethe's *Young Werther*, who, forty years after the events immortalized in the novel, comes to Weimar to visit the now famous, emotionally distant author.

In 1943, as it became evident that Germany would be defeated, Mann began to write *Doctor Faustus*, a largely self-critical probing into the psychological and cultural root causes of the "German catastrophe." Designed as a biography of a fictitious composer as narrated by a friend, the novel draws on the Faust myth and on the invention, by Schoenberg, of twelve-tone composition; it suggests that the "German catastrophe" may be traced to the Faustian hubris of German aspirations to translate musical supremacy into political hegemony. Despite expert help from Adorno, Mann became embroiled in a public spat with Schoenberg about the true authorship of the method of composition with twelve tones. The book remains controversial for its apparently wholesale implication of German music in the failure of German culture.

The Holy Sinner (1950), a linguistically virtuosic retelling of the medieval story of Pope Gregory, was eclipsed by the popular success of *Felix Krull* (1954), one of the great comic novels of modern literature, the origins of which date from 1905. Mann had returned to the story intermittently but was unable to complete it until the final years of his life.

CONTROVERSY

Mann's career was punctuated by rivalries and occasional clashes with other writers. Stung by his politically more conscious brother's criticism of his lack of political awareness, Mann caricatured, in *Reflections*, Heinrich as a *Zivilisationsliterat* (a politicizing *littérateur*). Relations with Gerhart Hauptmann, the uncrowned king of German literature at the time, were equally complex. Mann's caricature of Hauptmann as Peeperkorn in *The Magic Mountain* may well have been motivated by his regicidal desire to take Hauptmann's place. Mann and Brecht were ideological opposites, and no love was lost between them; in Los Angeles, in 1943, they clashed over a political manifesto concerning the future of Germany. Virtually all of Mann's colleagues who remained in Nazi Germany resented him for his harsh criticism of their comportment.

Mann admired Kafka when he discovered him posthumously and was moved to learn that Kafka had wept over *Tonio Kröger*. Relations with Hugo von Hofmannsthal and Arthur Schnitzler were cordial and mutually respectful. He enjoyed a lasting, warm friendship with Hermann Hesse who, in a brief obituary, offered this generous thought about Mann:

> Beneath his irony and virtuosity—and completely unappreciated for decades by the German public—he possessed great courage, loyalty, a sense of responsibility, and a capacity to love that will keep both his work and memory alive far beyond our own confused times. (13 August 1955)

See also **Einstein, Albert; Germany; Hofmannsthal, Hugo von; Kafka, Franz; Modernism; Schnitzler, Arthur.**

BIBLIOGRAPHY

Fetzer, John F. *Changing Perceptions of Thomas Mann's Doctor Faustus: Criticism 1947–1992.* Columbia, S.C., 1996.

Hamilton, Nigel. *The Brothers Mann: The Lives of Heinrich and Thomas Mann, 1871–1950 and 1875–1955.* New York, 1979.

Koopmann, Helmut. *Thomas-Mann-Handbuch.* Stuttgart, 1990; 3rd ed., 2001.

Kurzke, Hermann. *Thomas Mann: Life as a Work of Art,* translated by Leslie Wilson. Princeton, N.J., 2002.

Lehnert, Herbert, and Eva Wessel, eds. *A Companion to the Works of Thomas Mann.* Rochester, N.Y., 2004.

Lubich, Frederick A. "Thomas Mann's Sexual Politics: Lost in Translation," *Comparative Literature Studies* 31 (1994): 107–127.

Minden, Michael, ed. *Thomas Mann.* London, 1995.

Reed, T. J. *Thomas Mann: The Uses of Tradition.* Oxford, U.K., and New York, 1974. 2nd ed., 1996.

Robertson, Ritchie, ed. *The Cambridge Companion to Thomas Mann.* Cambridge, U.K., and New York, 2002.

Shookman, Ellis. *Thomas Mann's Death in Venice: A Novella and Its Critics.* Rochester, N.Y., 2003.

Vaget, Hans Rudolf. "National and Universal: Thomas Mann and the Paradox of 'German' Music." In *Music and German National Identity,* edited by Celia Applegate and Pamela Potter, 155–177. Chicago, 2002.

HANS RUDOLF VAGET

MANNERS AND FORMALITY. Across the societies of Europe, manners drew intense and growing interest throughout the nineteenth century. While the elaborate courtly rituals once associated with the aristocracy were generally simplified, the subtle shades of etiquette preoccupied the ranks of an expanding bourgeoisie bent on upward social mobility. The hurrying throngs that jostled for space on crowded thoroughfares and modern forms of transport posed new challenges to public order. Not surprisingly, the period saw an explosion of guides to the manners and usage of good society and rules to govern conduct in public places.

ARISTOCRATIC EXCLUSIVENESS

After 1789 the economic and political dominance of the aristocracy throughout Europe was challenged by the rapid expansion of industrial, mercantile, and commercial wealth. Thrown on the defensive, the nobility were affronted by the efforts of the vulgar to break into their exclusive social circles. But many were forced to adopt a conciliatory attitude in the interests of survival, some positively allured by the prospect of repairing battered patrician fortunes through strategic alliances. Regional variation between and within European countries saw some enclaves of hereditary aristocracy hold aloof from the upper bourgeoisie and survive as a distinct and influential element in society while others sought fusion with the wealth and power of a new plutocracy. Treading the fine line between social distinctiveness and economic survival, the aristocracy invoked an arsenal of manners. Formal observance of etiquette was the price they demanded for their toleration of the aspirational classes; innate courtesy was the ground on which they proclaimed their own indefinable but immutable superiority. For the French nobility, the difference was between *savoir-vivre* (literally, knowing how to live)—which anyone might acquire with study—and *savoir-être* (knowing how to be), which must be instilled from birth.

BOURGEOIS ASPIRATIONS

Manners held a different significance for the bourgeoisie. It was they who sought to define the indefinable, to convert the innate refinement of the cultivated elite into a series of rules to guide conduct. If manners could be reduced to rules, then the rules could be learned by heart and systematically applied. Guides to etiquette proliferated throughout the century and were avidly consumed by an expanding middle class. But to gain admission to an elite circle meant little unless that circle still remained ostensibly exclusive. Despite a rhetoric of liberalism, the bourgeoisie was riven by an obsession with social hierarchy, and the desire to believe that the rules could never be successfully learned by those below them in the social scale. The same person might simultaneously embody the "parvenu," eagerly reaching for acceptance in the social elite, and the "snob," fastidiously preserving social distance from the masses. An ostentatious display of formal manners equally served both ends.

The codification of conduct served another purpose too. The expansion of the middle class was accompanied by a new profusion of things. The home of a wealthy tradesman or burgher could be crammed with china and ornaments, pictures, screens and occasional tables, and elaborate sets of cutlery and crockery for family or hospitable use. The rituals of tea-drinking demanded a bewildering array of pots and jugs, spoons and strainers, cups and saucers. Should sandwiches be offered? How should they be presented? Should a doily be used on the plate? How might a hapless guest manage cup, saucer, plate, cake-fork, and gloves all at the same time? Should she remove her hat before attempting the challenge? Daily life had never been so complicated for the middle classes, and etiquette books offered a reassuringly authoritative guide to dealing with its unfamiliar complexities.

GENDER AND PROPRIETY

While the thirst for upward social mobility produced a widespread obsession with formal etiquette, it was complicated by the introduction of specifically bourgeois values: an ideal, if not actual, segregation between public life and the intimate concerns of family, a separation of the responsibilities of men and women, and a preoccupation with the propriety of bodily behavior. Increasingly the formal manners of nineteenth-century high society were infused with moral preoccupations bordering on prudishness. Etiquette manuals warned young ladies not to blush when a "warm" joke was told in their hearing: it was wiser to pretend to incomprehension or, if that were impossible, to deafness.

For it was women who primarily had to enact and police manners and propriety. On women fell many time-consuming social duties that were impractical for men preoccupied with their professional lives. The elegant fripperies adorning women's homes and attire proclaimed their status and that of their families; they monitored and protected social position through the guarded inclusion implied by a call returned, or the polite snub conveyed by a card. They protected the visible purity of their own sexual conduct and that of their daughters, while their gossip policed and condemned the moral lapses of those around them. For men, reputation was less incompatible with sexual experience. To them fell the duty of defining

An English couple at afternoon tea, 1909. The tradition of the afternoon tea developed in England during the mid-nineteenth century and quickly became incorporated into the rigid conventions of Victorian social life. ©HULTON-DEUTSCH COLLECTION/CORBIS

and redefining the world of masculine honor and the rules of engagement governing political and personal strife. By the early years of the twentieth century an ideal of virile masculinity was increasingly at war with the convention of women's prudishness and obsession with the social "littleness" of manners. The tensions gradually forced new accommodations over the standards demanded of both sexes.

WORKING-CLASS SOCIABILITY

Formal manners remained the preserve of the wealthy. Elaborate domestic rituals implied the presence of a plethora of equipment that lay well beyond the means of the average working-class family; the mannered exchanges of calls depended on a leisure time equally unattainable. But if formal manners were an instrument of exclusion, the bourgeoisie had a vested interest in extending throughout society their rigidly moral codes of conduct and comportment. In rural communities the peasantry sustained a plethora of careful domestic rituals, but in the spaces of the growing cities a less structured working-class culture emerged. Here, too, alternative codes of conduct regulated social exchange, but to the affronted eyes of the bourgeoisie, working-class sociability was most notable for its rowdy camaraderie and free association between the sexes. More troubling still in this urban scene were the bohemians and demimonde, to whom the boundaries of an ordered society were meaningless and the rules of good conduct merely a source of mirth.

At stake was not only the maintenance of public order, not only the regulation and discipline of the bodies that constituted the labor force. The language of orderly, *civilized* behavior had particular resonance in European countries with imperial ambitions. In the colonies, the idea of a "civil" society was extended to demarcate the boundaries of white society and to shore up the racial identification and exclusion of the "savage." At home, concepts of savagery and civility were simultaneously and ambiguously present in the language of class distinctions and the language of racial unity. Like the lore of "good manners" and formal usage, such terms could be employed strategically to include or to exclude, as occasion seemed to demand.

See also **Aristocracy; Body; Bourgeoisie; Dueling; Imperialism; Leisure; Working Class.**

BIBLIOGRAPHY

Bramsted, Ernest K. *Aristocracy and the Middle-Classes in Germany: Social Types in German Literature, 1830–1900.* Chicago, 1964.

Cannadine, David. *The Decline and Fall of the British Aristocracy.* New Haven, Conn., 1990.

Cardoza, Anthony L. *Aristocrats in Bourgeois Italy: The Piedmontese Nobility, 1861–1930.* Cambridge, U.K., 1997.

Davidoff, Leonore. *The Best Circles: Society, Etiquette, and the Season.* London, 1973.

Elias, Norbert. *The Civilizing Process.* Translated by Edmund Jephcott. 2 vols. New York, c. 1978.

Haine, W. Scott. *The World of the Paris Café: Sociability among the French Working Class, 1789–1914.* Baltimore, Md., 1996.

Russell, Penny. *A Wish of Distinction: Colonial Gentility and Femininity.* Melbourne, 1994.

Stoler, Ann Laura. *Race and the Education of Desire: Foucault's History of Sexuality and the Colonial Order of Things.* Durham, N.C., 1995.

Veblen, Thorstein. *The Theory of the Leisure Class: An Economic Study in the Evolution of Institutions.* New York, 1899. A classic for his development of the idea of "conspicuous consumption" and "conspicuous leisure."

PENNY RUSSELL

MANNING, HENRY (1808–1892), English Roman Catholic convert and cardinal-archbishop of Westminster.

Henry Edward Manning was born in Totteridge, England, to affluent parents; his father was a Tory MP (member of Parliament) and governor of the Bank of England. In April 1827 Manning entered Balliol College, Oxford. Manning married Caroline Sargent in November 1833, the same year in which he was ordained a priest in the Church of England. She died unexpectedly on 25 July 1837, having produced no children.

In the 1830s, Manning became involved with the controversial Oxford Movement, a widening group of religious thinkers led by theologian John Henry Newman (1801–1890) that sought to return the Church of England to the High Church ideals of the seventeenth century. He distributed the movement's *Tracts for the Times* in his locality and in 1836 lent his own name to Tract 78, which treated the subject of Catholic tradition.

Manning was appointed archdeacon of Chichester in December 1840. He became a prominent figure as his compelling pronouncements were followed nationwide. He called attention to the condition of the impoverished and the socially marginal, sympathized with the working class, condemned the abuses of landowners and employers, and promoted the education of the poor and the independence of the church from secular interference.

While convalescing from illness in Rome in 1847, Manning studied Catholic theology, met with Pope Pius IX (r. 1846–1878), and returned to England to endure three years of spiritual distress. He was troubled when in 1850 the Privy Council overruled the refusal of a bishop to institute an Anglican divine on grounds of unorthodoxy. Manning saw this as an unacceptable invasion by the state upon the independent authority of the church.

On 6 April 1851 Manning entered the Roman Catholic communion at a Jesuit church.

Manning intensified his radical social work as a Catholic priest and founded a community of mission priests (the Oblates of St. Charles) to work in the poorest quarters of London. In 1857, he established a major Catholic congregation in Bayswater. Over the next eight years, he built three new churches in the neighborhood, as well as four convents and eight schools.

On 8 June 1865, Manning was appointed archbishop of Westminster, the leading clerical Roman Catholic post in Britain—just fourteen years after his conversion. He was named a cardinal on

29 March 1875. His years as archbishop began with efforts to fund Catholic schools throughout Britain. As an ultramontanist, he defended the doctrine of papal infallibility at the Vatican Council of 1869–1870, though the council's final definition gave less authority to the papacy than he had advocated. Manning consistently sought to protect the pope's independence from secular control.

Manning insisted that the church should help protect workers against exploitation by employers and that labor should fight for fair wages and reasonable hours of work. He personally intervened in the London Dock Strike of 1889, breaking the deadlock and earning the gratitude of the labor force nationwide.

Manning died in London on 14 January 1892, following an attack of bronchitis. Crowds thronged his funeral procession—an event that would have been unthinkable for a Catholic in Britain just two generations earlier. His body was reinterred at Westminster Cathedral.

See also **Catholicism; Newman, John Henry.**

BIBLIOGRAPHY

Gray, Robert. *Cardinal Manning: A Biography.* London, 1985.

McClelland, V. A. *Cardinal Manning: His Public Life and Influence, 1865–1892.* London, 1962.

Newsome, David. *Convert Cardinals: John Henry Newman and Henry Edward Manning.* London, 1993.

Pereiro, James. *Cardinal Manning: An Intellectual Biography.* Oxford, U.K., 1998.

STEPHEN VELLA

MANZONI, ALESSANDRO (1785–1873), Italian novelist and poet.

Alessandro Manzoni was the author of the most important historical novel of nineteenth-century Italy. He was the son of Giulia Beccaria (daughter of Cesare Bonesana, Marchese di Beccaria, the Enlightenment legal reformer) and Pietro Manzoni, a member of the lesser Lombard nobility (at least nominally; Alessandro's father was probably another man). When his mother legally separated from Pietro after seven years of marriage, Alessandro was sent to Catholic boarding schools, an experience that contributed to his anticlericalism. In 1805 he joined his mother in Paris, where he lived until 1810 and met important intellectuals in the circle of the idéologues. In 1808 he married sixteen-year-old Henriette Blondel, who died in 1833. They had ten children, eight of whom died before their father. He returned to Catholicism in 1816 after his Calvinist wife converted under the spiritual direction of a priest close to Jansenism. As a result, his own brand of Catholicism remained imbued with an austere morality. An ardent supporter of Italian unification, he was appointed senator of the kingdom in the first parliament of 1860 and was named an honorary citizen of Rome in 1872. Prince Umberto of Savoy (who would become king of Italy) was present at his funeral in 1873.

With close links to Romantic circles in Milan, in his early literary career Manzoni composed poems inspired by religious themes, such as *Inni sacri* (1815; The sacred hymns), tragedies based on historical figures and situations (*Adelchi* [1822] and *Il conte di Carmagnola* [1821]), patriotic verses (*Marzo 1821*), and a famous ode on the death of Napoleon, "Il Cinque Maggio" (1822; The fifth of May). His interest in history, kindled by the influence of French Restoration culture (and especially the work of historian Augustin Thierry) and already visible in early writings such as *Discorso sopra alcuni punti della storia longobardica in Italia* (1822; Discourse on some aspects of Lombard history in Italy), was fully deployed in the work that gave him a place in the Italian literary canon: *I promessi sposi* (1825–1827; The betrothed). Following in the path of Sir Walter Scott, Manzoni's *I promessi sposi* is set in Spanish Lombardy around 1630 and features the vicissitudes of two peasants whose wedding plans are disrupted by the arrogance of an abusive provincial nobleman. In contrast to the tradition of the historical novel, however, lengthy digressions on events and figures of the period are included to paint a broad picture of seventeenth-century Italian society.

Manzoni intended *I promessi sposi* to be a serious work approaching "historical truth" and carrying a moral message. It dealt with themes that were implicitly patriotic (the moral decadence of Italian society under the rule of corrupt foreign rulers), condemned the abuses of power (both civil and clerical), and emphasized the role of divine providence, which alone is able to provide solace to the victims of human injustice. Although, as critics have observed, ordinary men and women became the protagonists of a major work of Italian literature for the first time, the author had no interest in making these people speak for themselves, nor was he prey to romantic populism.

Translations into French and English appeared very soon. Critics' reactions varied, ranging from praise for its moral lesson (an "elementary catechism" according to one Italian admirer) to questions about the choice of protagonists and the length of the historical digressions. *I promessi sposi* went through a linguistic revision in the following years as the author tried to make it conform to his idea of what the Italian language should be like: the Tuscan dialect spoken by the Florentine upper classes. To this end Manzoni went to the Tuscan capital to enlist the collaboration of some friends for a second edition, eventually published in 1840–1842. More than a hundred editions had appeared by 1875 as the book was canonized in the new state as a masterpiece of Italian literature.

Having developed profound doubts about the possibility of being truly faithful to history while writing fiction, doubts which he explained in an essay published in 1850, *Del romanzo storico, e in genere, de' componimenti misti di storia e d'invenzione* (On the historical novel and in general on writings mixing history and invention), Manzoni never wrote another novel, and he soon also exhausted his poetic inspiration. In his later years he devoted his time to essays on philosophical, aesthetic, and historical issues. Although as a liberal Catholic he was a critic of the church's temporal power, in his works he offered a defense of the role of the church in Italian history that provided the bases for the Neo-Guelf school of historiography. Until his death, he also continued to contribute to the important *questione della lingua,* the discussion on how to shape a viable language for the new Italian nation.

See also **Catholicism; Italy; Nationalism; Romanticism.**

BIBLIOGRAPHY

Brand, Peter, and Lino Pertile, eds. *The Cambridge History of Italian Literature.* New York, 1999.

Dionisotti, Carlo. *Appunti su moderni: Foscolo, Leopardi, Manzoni, e altri.* Bologna, 1988.

Ghidetti, Enrico. *Alessandro Manzoni.* Florence, 1995.

Manzoni, Alessandro. *Tutte le opere di Alessandro Manzoni.* Edited by Alberto Chiari and Fausto Ghisalberti. 7 vols. Milan, 1957–1991.

———. *The Betrothed.* Edited by David Forgacs and Matthew Reynolds. London, 1997.

SILVANA PATRIARCA

MARAT, JEAN-PAUL (1743–1793),

French revolutionary political journalist, physician, and leader of the Jacobin Mountain.

Jean-Paul Marat is best known to posterity for two things: first, his populist, not to say rabble-rousing, journal, *L'ami du peuple* (Friend of the people), which phrase he also adopted for his revolutionary sobriquet; and second, Jacques-Louis David's painting of his assassination, at the hands of Charlotte Corday, while lying naked in his oily bath, wherein he found slight relief from the eczema that covered his unsightly skin and exacerbated his already acerbic soul.

Born on 24 May 1743 in Boudry, Neuchâtel, and thus a francophone Prussian subject in his youth, Marat took only peripheral interest in politics prior to the convening of the Estates-General in May 1789. Medicine was his intended vocation. He began following courses in Paris in 1762 and in 1765 moved to London, where he treated venereal disease. The University of St. Andrews, Scotland, a diploma mill for higher degrees, awarded him a doctorate in 1775. Thereupon he returned to Paris and opened a general practice, not without some success. Among his clients was a noted lady, the marquise de Laubespine, and he was named physician to the Garde du Corps of the comte d'Artois, brother of King Louis XVI (and the future Charles X).

Two early writings, *A Philosophical Essay on Man* (1773) and *Chains of Slavery* (1774), were respectively philosophical and political. Denouncing tyranny, the latter gave a foretaste of what was to come. Such was the prestige of science in the late Enlightenment, however, that Marat thought to rise above minor bourgeois status rather through that route than through letters, medicine, or public affairs. Between 1778 and 1789 he sought election to the Paris Academy of Science and besieged it with a series of experimental memoirs on fire, heat, light, color, and electricity. Certain effects he produced by means of shining a beam of sunlight through a modified microscope were neither known nor empty, but they were of minor interest at best and held nothing of the cosmic and anti-Newtonian significance he claimed for them. Academic commissions reviewed the early submissions in correct if mildly dismissive fashion, after which the academy ignored him—for Marat made a pest of himself. Of paranoid disposition, he always attributed reverses to persecution and to plots. The chance for revenge came with the Revolution. His diatribe *Les charlatans modernes* (1791; The modern charlatans) excoriates his oppressors of the scientific establishment, foremost among them Antoine-Laurent Lavoisier and Pierre-Simon Laplace. It had a major influence preparing public opinion for the suppression of the Academy of Science on 8 August 1793 in the wave of hostility to privilege and authority of every sort that accompanied the Terror.

Persecuted by the Academy of Science, Marat wrote not long before his death that he had welcomed the Revolution for the opportunity to reach a proper place in the world. Marat was a vivid writer and became a polemical journalist, externalizing his own resentments to champion the poor, the downtrodden, the wretched of the earth, in short, the proletariat. The first issue of *L'ami du peuple* appeared in September 1789. Marat opened with praise of the prospect for a just society. Such was his suspicious nature that successive issues soon took to denouncing the infidelity, indeed the perfidy, of the institutions and persons in power: the Commune of Paris and its mayor, Jean-Sylvain Bailly; the Constituent Assembly and its early spokesman, the comte de Mirabeau; the National Guard and its commander, the marquis de Lafayette; the royal family and its prospective treachery; the Legislative Assembly and its subservience to moderates and ministers of state; and the army and its initially victorious commander, Charles-François du Périer Dumouriez. Paranoids are not ipso facto wrong, however. Such was the irreconcilability of factions that Marat's suspicions were often accurate, as in the instances among others of the royal family, Mirabeau, and Dumouriez.

Marat owed his effect not to the cogency of his political ideas, banal in themselves, but to the brilliance of his style. His was an invective genius in a time of latent hatreds burst into the open. His inflammatory writing earned him several arrests and detentions. He frequently had to go into hiding while continuing to publish at irregular intervals. On two occasions he took refuge in London. There is no way to measure the extent of his influence in summoning the mob into the streets on the insurrectional days of October 1789, which brought the royal family from Versailles to virtual captivity in Paris; for the rising of 10 August 1792 that overthrew the monarchy; and for the massacres that followed in September. But there is no doubt that his incitement was an effective factor.

Only with election to the National Convention in September 1792 did Marat hold political office. In the struggle between the Gironde and the Jacobin Mountain that defined the first phase of that body's history, Marat sided polemically with the latter. So vicious did his attacks become, calling for something like a dictatorship of the people, that the Girondist faction, barely dominant throughout the winter and early spring of 1792 to 1793, voted his indictment for incendiary acts. Theirs was a Pyrrhic victory. Acquitted on 14 April, Marat was borne from the courtroom on the shoulders of the crowd. His triumph led directly to the rising of 31 May that forced the expulsion of the Girondist deputies from the Convention and opened the way to the Jacobin dictatorship of the Terror. On 13 July, the eve of Bastille Day, Charlotte Corday, daughter of a devout and royalist Norman family, gained access to Marat's dwelling and stabbed to death the incarnation of the godless Revolution.

See also **France; French Revolution; Jacobins; Reign of Terror.**

BIBLIOGRAPHY

Coquard, Olivier. *Jean-Paul Marat.* Paris, 1993. Supersedes all earlier biographies.

Gillispie, Charles C. *Science and Polity in France at the End of the Old Regime.* Princeton, N.J., 1980. 2nd ed., published as *Science and Polity in France: The End of the Old Regime,* 2004. Includes a chapter (pp. 290–329) on Marat's scientific endeavors.

CHARLES C. GILLISPIE

MARCONI, GUGLIELMO (1874–1937), Italian physicist and inventor.

Guglielmo Marconi was born in Bologna on 25 April 1874, son of an Italian father (Giuseppe, a wealthy landowner) and an Irish mother (Annie Jameson). Because of frequent family moves during the winter months, first to England and then to Tuscany, Marconi did not receive traditional schooling. As a boy, Marconi developed a great interest in electrical science, which he furthered with Vincenzo Rosa, his tutor in Leghorn in the early 1890s, the only "teacher" figure Marconi later recognized. In the laboratory set up in his father's home in the Bolognese countryside, Villa Griffone, Marconi dedicated his time to experiments and readings and soon developed the ambition to become an inventor. Even his very first technical projects reflect his interest in real technological applications and their commercial potential.

In 1894 Marconi started experimenting with electromagnetic waves (the subject of research in many European research labs at that time) with the aim of signaling across space without wires. Following much experimentation, he managed to send signals over a distance of 2 kilometers (1.2 miles), beyond a hill situated between the transmission equipment (to which Marconi had added a grounded vertical antenna) and the reception apparatus (characterized by an extremely sensitive coherer, a device designed to pick up radio signals). These first wireless telegraphy experiments, in 1895, marked the beginnings of radio communications.

With the aim of developing his promising invention, Marconi decided to move to England, a country with a great interest in improving communication networks and home to his mother's family who were a great help in making the right contacts when he arrived in London in February 1896. Marconi had his first patent drawn up by top legal experts in June 1896 and began collaborating with William H. Preece, the chief engineer of the General Post Office, but after a long list of contacts and demonstrations decided to found a private company. In July 1897 the Wireless Telegraph and Signal Company (later known as Marconi's Wireless Telegraph Company) was registered in London.

In his role as technical director of the company, Marconi recruited top-class collaborators (among whom John Ambrose Fleming stands out, the future inventor of the diode valve) who worked with him on two main projects, increasing transmission capabilities and solving interference problems between stations. This latter issue was resolved with the renowned British patent No. 7777 for "Improvements in Apparatus for Wireless Telegraphy" (granted in 1900 and followed by lasting litigation), which covered a syntonic tuning device that considerably improved the communicative capabilities of radio.

Marconi proved adept at deciding which demonstrations to carry out and in making sure his every success was publicized. For example, the first radio-telegraphic media-oriented transmissions had a great success, carried out at two yachting events: the Kingstown Regatta near Dublin (1898) and the America's Cup competition off Sandy Hook, New Jersey (1899).

Among the fundamental milestones gained in the "distance conquest" (Marconi's main goal) were the setup of communication between England and France (50 kilometers [31 miles] in 1899) and the first transatlantic transmission (between England and Newfoundland, over 3,000 kilometers [1,860 miles] in December 1901). This last project was a real challenge for the scientific understandings of that time and involved a considerable economic gamble. Its success earned Marconi a great deal of fame and, at the same time, a great deal of hostility from cable companies who felt threatened by the enormous developments made in radiotelegraphy, and from a number of skeptics (many of whom were from the scientific community itself). Marconi defended himself by continuing to produce positive results, even as early as 1902, first from experiments conducted during a transatlantic voyage aboard the *Philadelphia,* and then onboard the Italian naval warship *Carlo Alberto.* That same year, Marconi completed a new kind of magnetic detector, which then became the standard wireless receiver for many years, replacing the coherer. In December 1902 he transmitted the first complete messages to Poldhu (located in Cornwall, England) from stations at Glace Bay, Nova Scotia, and later Cape Cod, Massachusetts. The transatlantic project culminated in

1907 with the opening of the first transatlantic commercial service between Glace Bay and Clifden, Ireland. One of the invention's main applications was for seafaring safety, and it is a well-known fact that the *Titanic* (1912) was fatefully fitted with Marconi wireless communication equipment.

From the beginning of World War I, Marconi began investigation of shortwaves (which he had used in his very first experiments), setting up new research projects that were mainly carried out onboard the *Elettra,* the yacht Marconi purchased in 1919, and transformed into a floating laboratory. Important experiments in 1923 led him to the establishment of the new high-speed beam system for long-distance communication: agreement was reached in 1924 to adopt this system throughout the British Empire. In 1926 his company built the first beam station, linking England and Canada, followed by further stations in subsequent years.

In 1923 Marconi joined the Fascist Party, and this led him to be given various prestigious public offices: in 1928 he was named as the National Research Council president, and in 1930 he took over the presidency at the Royal Italian Academy. Just a few years later his relationship with the Fascist Party started to weaken: Marconi was certainly among those who tried to dissuade the pro-German and anti-Jewish tendencies within the party and was one of the supporters of an alliance with Britain.

In 1931, having set up a shortwave station for the Vatican, Marconi supervised the pope's first broadcast to Catholics worldwide. In this same period he started studying microwaves, research on which the majority of modern radio systems are still based in the early twenty-first century. In 1934, at sea, aboard the *Elettra,* he used this technique for blind navigation by radio beacon.

Marconi was invited by many countries worldwide to demonstrate developments in radio communications—projects for which he had become a living icon. Among the numerous international honors and awards given to Marconi were sixteen *honoris causa* degrees and the Nobel prize for physics, which he shared with Karl Ferdinand Braun in 1909.

Marconi died in Rome on 20 July 1937. The world commemorated his death with an exceptional event: all radio stations observed a two-minute silence, during which time the ether fell silent—just like it had been in the pre-Marconi era.

See also **Italy; Physics; Science and Technology.**

BIBLIOGRAPHY

Bussey, Gordon. *Marconi's Atlantic Leap.* Coventry, U.K., 2000.

Dunlap, Orrin E., Jr. *Marconi: The Man and His Wireless.* New York, 1937. Reprint, New York, 1971.

Jensen, Peter R. *In Marconi's Footsteps, 1894 to 1920: Early Radio.* Kenthurst, N.S.W., Australia, 1994.

Jolly, W. P. *Marconi.* New York, 1972.

Weightman, Gavin. *Signor Marconi's Magic Box: The Most Remarkable Invention of the Nineteenth Century and the Amateur Inventor Whose Genius Sparked a Revolution.* Cambridge, Mass., 2003.

BARBARA VALOTTI

MARIE-ANTOINETTE

MARIE-ANTOINETTE (1755–1793), ruled as queen of France, 1774–1792.

The queen of Louis XVI (r. 1774–1792) has been associated with unwittingly contributing to the outbreak of the French Revolution of 1789 and the overthrow of the monarchy in 1792. She has also been viewed as one of the Revolution's most tragic victims.

The daughter of Holy Roman Emperor Francis I (r. 1745–1765) and Maria Theresa (r. 1745–1780) of Austria, Maria Antonia was scarcely in her teens before she was apprenticed by her parents into becoming the partner of the French Dauphin, surviving heir of Louis XV (r. 1715–1774). By the Diplomatic Revolution of 1756, France had allied itself with Austria, its perennial foe since the fifteenth century, and the marriage was designed to strengthen the alliance. The wedding took place in 1770, when she was fifteen years old. Henceforth Maria Antonia was Marie-Antoinette. Although the engagement and marriage sparked wide rejoicings within France, a bad augury occurred when, during celebrations in Paris, a crowd panic led to a major incident in which over a hundred people died.

Marie-Antoinette never really recovered the popularity that she had enjoyed in the context of her marriage. Indeed, she became increasingly unpopular as time went on. Maria Theresa and her advisers saw her as a conduit for pro-Austrian sentiment at the French court and as an intelligence source to buttress Austrian diplomacy. The Austrian envoy in Paris, Florimond Claude Mercy-Argenteau (1727–1794), was the hub of this operation that stimulated attacks on the newcomer by court factions antagonistic to the Austrian alliance. In addition, the initial failure of Louis to consummate their marriage—possibly due to a malformation of his penis, but more likely as a result of uncertain psychosexual problems—also caused whispering against her. A pornographic pamphlet campaign emerged, blackening her character by attributing to her every sexual vice, even after she became queen in 1774. The sensitive and rather exposed position that Marie-Antoinette came to inhabit was made even more problematic by the fact that, almost alone among French kings, Louis declined to take a mistress. This upset the informal system of political checks and balances in the king's entourage and attracted to the royal couple hostilities that in other reigns would have been channeled against the royal mistress and her cronies.

Court tittle-tattle aimed against Marie-Antoinette was not stilled by the resolution of her husband's sexual problems and by the appearance of children: a daughter in 1778, a son and royal heir in 1781 (who was to die in 1789), a further son in 1785 (the ill-starred "Louis XVII," who died in prison in 1795). The antagonisms she aroused never went away. Her impatience with court ceremonial, her insouciant meddling at the fringes of court politics, her cozy relations with male and female favorites, her delight in fashion and shopping were all held against her. Although she appears to have been completely blameless in the so-called Diamond Necklace Affair of 1784–1786 (when a cardinal, hoping to win her favor, offered her a fabulously expensive necklace of diamonds that was then stolen by plotters who had tricked the prelate), this scandal further promoted allegations about her sexual conduct and general waywardness. As the grave state of the government's financial problems became increasingly clear in the late 1780s, moreover, *l'Autrichienne*—a denigratory sobriquet that denoted "Austrian woman" but also evoked "bitch" (*chienne*)—was believed to have contributed to impending bankruptcy through extravagant spending. To what was already a somber charge-sheet against "Madame Déficit," as the scandal-sheets were now calling her, was added the accusation of having contempt for the people of France. She almost without doubt never uttered the famous phrase "let them eat cake" when told of the generalized hunger throughout the country in the years 1788 and 1789—but she was widely believed to have done so. Her unpopularity by 1789 has often been held to have compromised the respect felt for the monarchy at this difficult time.

In 1789, Marie-Antoinette sided with reactionary court factions against the Revolutionary cause—a fact that almost triggered her lynching by rioting crowds in the "October Days," an event that led to the royal family relocating away from Versailles to the Tuileries palace in central Paris. In following years, she continued to be widely attributed a nefarious, counterrevolutionary and pro-Austrian role. The fact that Louis XVI, never a decisive character, had been virtually paralyzed into depression and vacillation by events since late 1787 made her role in shaping royal policy appear more important. When the royal family, seemingly fleeing the country, was captured at Varennes in June 1791, she again bore the brunt of attacks. Subsequently she supported the country's drift into war against Austria and *ancien régime* Europe, confidently expecting the European powers to rescue Louis XVI from his predicament. Once war had broken out, however, the position of *l'Autrichienne* became even more exposed. Rumors of treasonous machinations at court had some foundation, moreover: she passed secret intelligence about French strategy and troop dispositions to the Austrian emperor.

The overthrow of the monarchy on 10 August 1792 led to the royal family being incarcerated in the Temple prison. The king's execution in January 1793 left the revolutionaries in a quandary as to the position of the ex-queen. Her fate became caught up in waves of radicalism in the summer of 1793 caused by civil and foreign war and worsening economic crisis. She was separated from her son, Louis XVII, placed in the Conciergerie prison, by this time an antechamber to the scaffold, and on 14 August 1793 brought to trial before the Revolutionary Tribunal. Oddly, the public prosecutor, Antoine-Quentin Fouquier-Tinville (1746–1795), almost overlooked her treason during the 1792 campaigns and rested his case on Marie-Antoinette's alleged role in the flight to Varennes and other events in which she had often in fact played only a peripheral role. Fouquier-Tinville also accused her of committing incest with her son—a charge in line with earlier political pornography, but in reality so preposterous that it almost triggered a wave of sympathy for the ex-queen in the courtroom. Yet her fate was predestined, and on 16 October she was guillotined.

The vertiginous scale of Marie-Antoinette's fall from grace, her ignominious end, and the dignity with which she comported herself in the last months of her life gave undeniable pathos to a personage arguably less important than the myths that she unwittingly generated.

See also **French Revolution; Louis XVI.**

BIBLIOGRAPHY

Fraser, Antonia. *Marie Antoinette: The Journey.* London, 2001.

Goodman, Dena, ed. *Marie-Antoinette: Writings on the Body of a Queen.* London, 2003.

Lever, Evelyne. *Marie Antoinette: The Last Queen of France.* London, 2000.

Thomas, Chantal. *The Wicked Queen: The Origins of the Myth of Marie-Antoinette.* New York, 1999.

COLIN JONES

MARKETS. Markets, defined as physical locations at which individual vendors come together to sell foodstuffs and other commodities, appeared around the world as one of the earliest organizational models for commercial exchange. Through the early modern period, Europe's markets operated as key urban institutions for the distribution of food, while functioning in symbiotic relationship to local and longer distance supply networks, demographic expansion or contraction, and to other commercial entities such as shops, rural fairs, and more formalized exchange houses, or bourses.

The long nineteenth century was a particularly crucial period in the history of Europe's markets. In the regions most transformed by the processes of industrialization and urbanization, markets grew dramatically in size and number. Other forces such as the revolutionary movements of the century, the process of municipalization, and the consolidation of the urban bourgeoisie contributed to greater levels of public intervention in the management and rationalization of food market trade. While eastern Europe experienced less frequent and significant changes in the nature and organizational strategies of markets through the nineteenth century, western Europe was more generally characterized by a flurry of new urban market hall construction beginning in the 1850s. Quite a number of these structures, though unprecedented in scale, complexity, and attention to aesthetic detail, had only a relatively brief heyday; on the eve of World War I, many of the biggest retail market halls in western Europe had been eclipsed by larger high street shops, department stores, cooperatives, and chain or multiple operations. In many southern European cities, urban market halls proved more enduring institutions for food retailing through the early and mid-twentieth centuries.

As had long been the case, Europe's late eighteenth century markets were mainly held in the open air. Unlike fairs, markets were characteristically urban institutions; towns and cities featured a range of such commercial gatherings that met on a daily, weekly, or sometimes more intermittent basis. Typically regulated by competing civil and religious authorities, individual vendors paid fees to operate stalls selling comestible and noncomestible oods while most markets involved some combination of retail and wholesale functions. Because shops typically sold a fairly narrow range of foodstuffs, and the facilities for food storage and preservation were limited in most urban households, marketing was one of the main everyday activities for married women from all but the highest-ranking families. At the upper end of the social orders of Europe, female servants assumed this important responsibility. Moreover, with market trade often constituting a relatively marginalized commercial specialization, it is not surprising that women worked in large numbers as vendors in most regions of Europe. So while the authorities governing market trade were overwhelmingly male, many men worked in market wholesaling, and family economy arrangements were a commonplace, markets were largely feminized commercial spaces characterized by intense and repeated social, economic, and cultural exchange among women.

The late eighteenth and early nineteenth century open-air urban marketplaces of Europe often acted as tinderboxes for revolutionary mobs. Women buying and selling food in the markets exchanged much more than money and provisions. They also traded information, news, and gossip, while asserting or confirming their place within the urban social order through displays of acquisitive power, dress, language, and gesturing. Such exchanges among women typically took place within formalized legal frameworks but also within the context of a common set of cultural ideas about fairness embodied in the concept of the moral economy. In times of food shortage and inflation, discontent among consumers could easily spill beyond the amorphous boundaries of open-air markets to spark demonstrations that led to wider-spread mobilizations and outbreaks of violence against public and ecclesiastic authority. Through the first half of the nineteenth century, the growing threat posed by revolutionary urban crowds compelled civil authorities to seize greater control over food marketing. Competing municipal, regional/departmental, royal, and emerging liberal-nationalist authorities exercised increasing degrees of power in regulating food market sales through Europe's Age of Revolution.

While continuing to serve as the premises for later public approaches to urban food retailing, concerns related to the maintenance of order constituted a key force driving the first phase of market expansion in nineteenth-century Europe. As long as fortifications continued to limit urban growth, legal markets could only expand where political authorities issued new patents and permits and increased the number of stalls and space along streets and squares devoted to market trade. The erosion of guild controls and the increasing liberalization of the economy through most of western Europe did much to facilitate this process. Every town or city that experienced significant population growth had little choice but to pursue a set of strategies that would facilitate the expansion of market trade. Yet, in response to such forces, markets in many locations across Europe became ever more crowded places occupying larger and larger portions of urban space. These circumstances meant that food markets remained centers of ongoing social tension. This despite the fact that increases in agricultural production and improved distribution of grains, combined with augmented policing, had helped to reduce incidents of bread rioting in much of Europe by midcentury.

In the second phase of market expansion in Europe, which dates from the mid-1850s to the end of the century, municipal authorities and private interests won out in the struggle for control of markets, and of urban food retailing more generally. With the demolition of urban fortifications and the extension of the rail network, cities throughout western Europe faced the challenge of providing urban services to newly built peripheral districts of varying social composition. Many municipal governments embraced ambitious market hall building programs as a part of their urban expansion and renovation endeavors. The Hausmannization of Paris and the building of Barcelona's *Eixample* are two of the best illustrations of this process of which market building constituted an important element. No less than broad boulevards, statues to national heroes, and monumental public buildings, the large-scale urban market halls of nineteenth-century Europe carried heavy symbolic loads. They were characterized in the press and through public ceremony and ritual as tangible evidence of the power of the state in its various guises, and of the commitment of urban authorities to the welfare of the population.

While market hall building was all the rage in the last quarter of the nineteenth century in western Europe, open air markets did not face complete extinction. Some cities, such as London, mainly designated its new market halls for wholesaling purposes while continuing to permit customary street markets to take place on designated days to handle the bulk of retail sale in produce and some other items. Luxury foods, on the other hand, in London and elsewhere, were increasingly sold from shops. Grocers specializing in coffee, tea, chocolate, sugar, and the new pre-packaged and branded items expanded their lines to compete more handily with both open air and market hall vendors as the nineteenth century came to a close. Other forms of competition, such as the chain and the cooperative, played significant roles in eroding public market hall clientele in England and other parts of northern Europe by the end of the century.

Les Halles, the central market in Paris, photographed in 1860. GETTY IMAGES

Technologies such as the telephone, used by women to call in orders to grocers for home delivery, also undermined the customer base of market halls in cities such as Paris. The pattern in much of northwestern Europe in the decade preceding World War I featured a decline in the rate of large-scale retail market hall construction as well as a contraction in market sales alongside the growth of other types of competing food retailing enterprises. This was much less the case for southern Europe, and especially for cities such as Barcelona, where public market building and renovation projects continued until much later. Likewise, large numbers of open air markets worked by producer vendors in both eastern and western Europe continued to survive the competition posed by the expanding number of shops and stores, especially among a working-class consumer base.

By the early twentieth century, the flowering of consumerist culture, of branding, and of advertising, had acted to undermine the long-term survival of public retail markets in major cities such as Paris and Berlin, while taking place within markets themselves in many other highly urbanized regions. For women on the lowest rungs of the social orders of Europe, markets continued to constitute daily destinations in food shopping routines, and stall displays were often elaborately designed to appeal to popular consumerist fantasies. This was the case in parts of rural Britain, southwest Europe, and in some other areas of the Continent. With department stores and upscale high street shops generally beyond the socioeconomic reach of the urban poor, markets remained the main source for most food and cheap semi-durable manufactured goods in working and lower-middle class neighborhoods. While the historical literature on retailing and consumerism mainly focuses on non-food items sold in shops, galleries, and department stores, there is little doubt that the urban market halls of Europe were also transformed by such crucial economic and cultural developments. In early twentieth century Europe, urban markets faced new and sometimes fatal challenges to compete with other types of retailing enterprises. Yet significant numbers of food markets survived, and where they did so they remained centers for sociocultural exchange among women as well as sources for relatively inexpensive food and manufactured goods that were no less a part of consumer culture than the fare for sale at the fanciest department stores on the Continent.

See also **Consumerism; Trade and Economic Growth.**

BIBLIOGRAPHY

Horowitz, Roger, Jeffrey M. Pilcher, and Sydney Watts. "Meat for the Multitudes: Market Culture in Paris, New York City, and Mexico City over the Long Nineteenth Century." *American Historical Review* 109 (October 2004): 1055–1083.

Lohmeier, Andrew. "Burgerliche Gesellschaft and Consumer Interests: The Berlin Public Market Hall Reform, 1867–1891." *Business History Review* 73 (spring 1999): 91–113.

Miller, Montserrat. "Mercats nou-centistes a Barcelona: Una interpretació dels seus origens i significant cultural." *Revista de l'Alguer: Anuari academic de cultura catalana.* 4 (December 1993): 93–106.

Schmiechen, James, and Kenneth Carls. *The British Market Hall: A Social and Architectural History.* New Haven, Conn., 1999.

Tangires, Helen. *Public Markets and Civic Culture in Nineteenth-Century America.* Baltimore, Md., 2003.

Thompson, Victoria E. *The Virtuous Marketplace: Women and Men, Money and Politics in Paris, 1830–1870.* Baltimore, Md., 2000.

Montserrat Miller

MARRIAGE AND FAMILY. European social theorists of the nineteenth century were keenly interested in the impact of modern industrial society and changing forms of government on the family, which they all regarded as a key institution of social life. Conservatives like Frédéric Le Play (1806–1882) of France (author of many books including *La réforme sociale en France,* published in 1864) developed pioneering new techniques of social science research to study household and family life, even though their goals were to preserve tradition. They sought to call attention to the forces of modern society that threatened the type of family they idealized. Le Play, for example, hoped to strengthen the three-generational peasant "stem family system," in which the family farm was passed down to one son who lived together with his parents, along with his own wife and children. Le Play worried that the tendency of law and practice in France since the Revolution toward favoring an egalitarian division of inheritance among all children undermined both parental authority and the viability of family farms based on this stem family type inheritance.

However, concerns and theories about changing family life did not just come from conservative thinkers. Liberal and socialist reformers also criticized the conditions of family life in rapidly growing urban centers. Liberals tried to reconcile their faith in human progress through market capitalism with their anxieties about "the social question"—poverty, unrest, and moral decay among the families populating new industrial cities. Their concerns would eventually lead to private and state initiatives in the new arena of social reform.

Socialists formulated a distinctive analysis of the problem of the family under industrial capitalism. Perhaps the most famous among them, the German socialist Friedrich Engels (1820–1895), spent time as a young man in the English industrial city of Manchester and used his observations there among other sources to develop his theory on the historical evolution of the family presented in his pathbreaking book *The Origin of the Family, Private Property, and the State,* which was first published in 1884. Engels drew on the changes in family life that he observed—he noted for example that in some homes in Manchester's slums men could not find paid labor and women could, thus leading to a reversal of usual roles of gender dependency—to make the point that family, gender, and generational relations were rooted in economic conditions, and were therefore human, not natural, institutions. Although Engels was very critical of what he saw around him, his historical argument looked toward a possible socialist future where the ties that bound men and women, parents and children, would not be built around inequalities and dependency.

From a quite different direction, the modern family was also scrutinized by critics who imagined still other possible models of gender and even sexuality. "First-wave" feminists challenged aspects of family law and practice, the gender division of labor, and female political subservience all across Europe in the decades between 1880 and World War I. And sexologists such as Havelock Ellis (1859–1939) in England and Max Hirschfeld in Germany brought the subject of homosexuality into public discussion for the first time, even as openly gay cultures were appearing in some of Europe's metropolitan centers by around 1900.

All of these observations, debates, and theoretical claims were enmeshed in political controversies about the family that that these theorists confronted in their own times. Since these ideas fed into emerging disciplines such as sociology, psychology, and social work, subsequent social scientific theories of the family and also state policies have been informed by the historical conditions of families in industrializing Europe.

Similarly, theoretical and political concerns about the present, past, and future of the family motivated the outpouring of research and scholarship about the history of marriage and the family in modern Europe that began with "new social history" and feminist history in the 1960s. This research has emphasized several themes including: changing family strategies and gender relations in the face of massive social and economic transformations; the impact on family life of demographic transformation (especially lowered mortality and fertility and vastly increased rates of migration); the emergence of the modern nuclear family and the "private sphere" of domestic life and its relationship to class formation; and the impact of law, political conflict, and the state on marriage, reproduction, and the socialization of children. Research in all of these realms points to crucial connections between family history and other domains of historical transformation.

CHANGING FAMILY STRUCTURE

Before exploring some of these dimensions of modern European family history, it is useful to place European family patterns in a wider frame. In certain respects, the European families were distinctive in the early modern period when compared to those of other world regions. One of the striking peculiarities of central and western European family history that had developed before the seventeenth century was that men and women married relatively late, and a substantial minority never married. This pattern was connected historically with norms that discouraged marriage before the couple could establish the basis for a solid household economy—either plots of land or an artisanal shop. It was the responsibility of the family and the community to oversee courtship, betrothal, and marriage to assure that these conditions were met. Late marriage was also rooted in the common though by no means universal practice of *neo-locality*—that is, the expectation that a bride and groom would set up their own household at or soon after marriage. This expectation was far more common in northern and western Europe than in other regions of Europe and throughout the rest of the world.

Moreover, in connection with this marriage pattern, European young people of both sexes experienced a relatively long hiatus between puberty and marriage. Unmarried young adults played a distinctive role in economic life (as well as social, cultural, and political life) through such institutions as guilds, rural youth groups, domestic service, and universities. Young men and women were available for employment outside the familial household to a degree uncommon elsewhere. In part as a result of these patterns, Europeans, especially the young, were frequently on the move. Initially, they typically spent part of their youth working on nearby farms or in towns of their region, but industrialization and the growth of enormous new industrial cities drew them further from home. In addition, the huge upsurge in population growth that began at the end of the eighteenth century, along with the development of new technologies of transportation and communications, helped to turn temporary and regional migration streams into massive overseas emigration by the second half of the nineteenth century, as hundreds of thousands of Europeans went abroad, especially to the Americas, in search of new opportunities. All of these changes in the ways in which young people prepared for and entered the workforce, and in migration patterns, transformed family life and intergenerational relations.

The demands of modern industrial society not only changed prior patterns of setting up young people for marriage and economic life, they also encouraged different types of personalities, and hence different methods of socialization. Theorists and historians since the nineteenth century have discussed this phenomenon of the creation of the modern individual. Pavla Miller, in her book *Transformations of Patriarchy in the West, 1500–1900*, pulls together diverse strands of theoretical argument and historical evidence. She suggests that the changes associated with the development of capitalism and the modern state were built on and reinforced accompanying changes in family life, socialization, and gender relations. According to Miller, modern forms of political and economic organization were premised on the emergence of individuals who did not need to be coerced into working or behaving in a certain way, but rather were capable of self-discipline or, as she terms it, "self-mastery." Self-mastery entailed emotional and physical self-control, and the ability to learn and abide by normative rules of social behavior and conduct.

Accomplishing self-mastery entailed new and more intensive forms of child socialization and discipline both at home and in institutions like the churches and schools. It rested on a new gender division of labor and new intergenerational relations—indeed, on a new human psychology. The modern European family of the nineteenth century was more capable of producing such individuals than earlier family forms had been. Beginning in the late eighteenth century, initially under the tutelage and example of the urban middle classes, new notions of family life and childrearing were established throughout much of Europe; this project of creating a new type of family life, while never unchallenged, was increasingly reflected in and disseminated through the various economic, political, and social institutions over which urban elites held sway—for example, through lay and religious philanthropic ventures, private and state schools, factories, and domestic service—as well as in literature, and the arts, and consumer culture.

BOURGEOIS DOMESTICITY AND ITS APPEAL

What was this new family ideal? The reinvention of family life, within the private bourgeois home as its spatial and emotional center, was among the most innovative accomplishments of nineteenth-century Europe. The ideal modern family as portrayed in prescriptive literature, graphic images, and literature was based on close and loving relations between husband and wife and parents and children; it was lived out in the serene and thoughtfully planned and regulated spaces of the home, protected from the harsh realities of the outside world; it was based on new definitions of fathering, and especially mothering, and on a revised and highly polarized notion of gender differentiation.

From a spatial perspective, the modern European family took for granted the establishment of a morally superior and distinct "private" domestic realm in which a new style of family life and family relations could flourish. Family life in the domestic realm complemented the new institutions of public life (coffeehouses, public parks and gardens, stock markets, polling places) and was equally crucial for the establishment of bourgeois political and cultural predominance beginning in the late eighteenth century. Public space was, in theory at least, a realm of open and democratic access, even if in actuality it was dominated by men of property and education. In contrast with the public spaces of economic and political life, the domestic realm was apolitical and anticompetitive, and ideally segregated from the workplace, whereas in earlier eras households had been taken for granted as the sites of most economic activity (which was still true in peasant and artisanal households even in the nineteenth century). Separating private from public conveniently provided a solution to the moral neutrality of the capitalist marketplace. According to those who exalted its virtues, the private realm of the idealized modern family was a world dominated by women and children rather than by men, by emotion rather than by reason, by love rather than by economic considerations. Indeed many literary, artistic, and prescriptive representations of nineteenth-century family life self-consciously construct the domestic realm so as to emphasize its spatial and moral separation from the world of business and politics.

To some extent, these new ideals could take hold because of the reorganization of space that resulted from industrialization. Industrial capitalism moved people from rural areas into towns and cities, and reclassified urban space. It increased the functional specialization of space (industrial zones, residential zones, and commercial zones) and segregated residential areas to an extent previously unknown. New urban patterns also brought more highly class-segregated residential neighborhoods—best exemplified by the working-class tenement slum on the one hand and the upper-class residential square or suburb on the other. Even though most urbanites continued to live in city centers, and most continued to rent their homes, the tone of modern bourgeois domesticity was set in the newly constructed posh neighborhoods around residential urban squares and in the suburbs, and then imitated to one degree or another elsewhere.

Where space was available, as in new suburbs, single-family or semidetached homes and gardens served as both status symbol and aesthetic frame around the domestic space within. The desire for privacy "marked property boundaries with gates, drives, hedges and walls around house and garden. Humphrey Repton strikingly demonstrated the effect in his paper model of the space in front of his Essex 'cottage' where the view of shops, road and passing public was cut off by fencing, shrubbery and trees, a strong contrast to the communal squares and terraces of Georgian style" (Davidoff and Hall, pp. 361–362). If this new topography of domesticity was first elaborated in England, other bourgeoisies followed suit, with national variations, later in the nineteenth century.

Still, despite the domestic ideology, the boundaries that separated private from public space were far more porous than the rhetoric of domesticity and privacy suggested. Since the creation of a new style of domestic life accompanied middle-class assertions of political superiority, the virtues of bourgeois domestic life had to be apparent outside the walls of the home. One history of the Swedish middle class argues explicitly that, ironically, "for the bourgeoisie, the home was both a showcase for the world and a shelter against it" (Frykman and Löfgren, pp. 127–131).

Moreover, the two realms of public and private could not really be disconnected from one another. Housewives had to be clever consumers, hence they remained in touch with the rules and prices of traditional markets and shops and new commercial outlets such as department stores. The proper management of a middle-class household required, at least until the end of the nineteenth century, the hiring and supervision of household servants. Thus the "angel of the house"—the wife and mother—was required to be an employer and manager of paid labor. Her economic activities sustained family life but undercut the claim that the home could be a realm of love rather than of market relations. In addition, family capital such as dowries and inheritances fed business ventures, and domestic desires, rooted in the search for the perfect family life, served to motivate and justify businessmen's drive to earn profits and accumulate wealth.

In addition to reorganizing domestic space, modern family life also entailed a reorganization of gender relations and notions about sexuality. Accompanying the idealized separation of space into public and private realms was the gender division of labor that charged women with sustaining private virtue and with the care of the home and children, and men with the public realm of work and politics.The establishment of the norm of companionate marriage among the English upper classes already in the early modern era has been documented; the norms were fully established by the beginning of the nineteenth century. Close emotional ties between husband and wife supposedly cemented their complementary (separate but equally important) realms; the emphasis on companionate marriages contrasted with older understandings according to which men were put in control over their unruly wives, and parental preferences and family strategies weighed heavily in the choice of marriage partners. In some regions, such as Baden, Germany, in the early nineteenth century the assertion of the ideal of a strong heterosexual bond between husband and wife in marriage was closely tied to the development of liberal parliamentary politics, new forms of urban associational life, and criticism of conservative Catholic clerical preference for celibacy.

But underlying pressures of economic interest that also drove family life could never be fully denied. Authors of domestic novels, a literary genre that emerged in the late eighteenth century along with the new family norms (which they also played a large role in disseminating), wrote stories whose plots pivoted on both fulcrums—love and fortune. Their heroines, whose efforts to negotiate successful matches have comprised the novel's most common plot line since its birth as a genre, were quite aware of the workings of property behind the drama of falling in love, the inseparability of economic interest from ties of affection, the intricate rituals and taboos evolved for working out this balance in the courtship rituals of the propertied classes.

The emphasis on love versus interest in marital matches varied regionally and according to class. Among the bourgeoisies of northern France, for example, economic negotiations drove marriage strategies until the end of the nineteenth century—arranged marriages were still quite common, and love matches were suspect, even at the century's

Thanks to the Dowry. **Lithograph by Frederic Bouchot c. 1830.** Bouchot comments on the practice of marrying for money. BIBLIOTHÈQUE DE ARTS DECORATIFS, PARIS, FRANCE/THE BRIDGEMAN ART LIBRARY

end. The bourgeois women seem to have seen no contradiction between the rhetoric of a domestic realm driven by love and the practical requirements of arranging respectable marriages. Similarly, the Athenian middle classes of the mid-nineteenth century considered love a "luxury." However, in something of a contrast, more discretion was beginning to be allowed to children in these milieus in the selection of their spouses. It should be noted, however, that even where children exercised such options, parents still exerted sufficient indirect control through their careful engineering of the circles in which their offspring circulated.

After marriage, middle-class family life centered on a reconfigured and intensified parent-child, in particular mother-child, relationship. Beginning with Enlightenment-era ideals of pedagogy and parenting, modern understandings of psychology and child development emphasized that children needed to be under the surveillance of trustworthy adults; their impressionable minds needed to be shaped by exposure to tasks commensurate with their developmental capacities. The practices and discourses of parent-child relations in Germany in the late eighteenth and nineteenth centuries offer clear evidence of the marginalization of fathers and the increasing prominence of mothers. The debate about mothering, "was shaped by changing ideas of the state, of citizenship, and of public-private boundaries. The most striking change, centrally illustrated by the works of Johann Heinrich Pestalozzi (1746–1827), was the shift from father-centered to mother-centered theories of child-rearing" (Allen, p. 17). Pestalozzi was a Swiss theorist of pedagogy who popularized his theories in novels like *Leonard and Gertrude* published in 1781, in which the loving and devoted mother was exalted as both the center of domestic virtue and morality, and also as the guarantor of society's future through her raising of model children. If such ideas appeared earliest in England, the Netherlands, Germany, and France, and were slower to permeate in regions of Europe where urban middle-class readerships were weaker, new ideals of family life and child rearing nevertheless began to appear by the beginning of the nineteenth century, even, for example, in publications aimed toward the literate urban classes of eastern and southern Europe.

WORKING-CLASS AND PEASANT FAMILIES

The exaltation of domesticity and the celebration of the family that was so much a hallmark of European middle-class life in the nineteenth century was thus a product of several factors: the idealized separation of space into public and private realms governed by different rules and associated with different genders; technological change that enlarged workplaces and separated them from home; and political changes that brought middle-class men into political predominance in a new way even as they continued to exclude poorer men, and virtually all women, from participation in public life. Ironically, these new conditions also made it harder than ever for lower-class families to maintain a viable family life at all, let alone to follow the norms and prescriptions for ideal family life that were circulating around them.

In the realm of lower-class marriage, historians' assessments of the role of interest and emotion vary considerably. It has been argued that the practice of marrying for love was in fact the invention of the lower classes, not the upper classes, precisely because the poor were not subject to the same constraints on choice of partner imposed on the wealthy by considerations of property. Many middle-class observers shared this assessment; it was a matter of some concern to them that propertylessness, in their view, bred carelessness with respect to marriage and family formation. Several key features of working-class family life struck nineteenth-century French moral economists as problematic. Their concerns "centered on problems of early marriage and lack of sexual self-control, the weakness of both financial and affective bonds between parents and children, and the apparent inability of workers to create nuclear households that were financially self-sufficient" (Lynch, p. 55).

Indeed, many of the innovative practices of middle-class family life bore little relation to habits in lower-class milieus. In the first place, lower-class mothers engaged in a variety of economic activities that varied in intensity according to regions and occupation. It was rarely possible or even imaginable for lower-class women to devote themselves exclusively to child rearing and housework. Indeed, in many regions of Europe changes associated with proto-industry and the commercialization of agriculture brought intensification of women's work, the move of paid employment for women out of the home, and diminished time spent on childcare. Moreover, segregating children from the adult world of work, as modern models of childhood demanded, was inconsistent with the family economy of peasants and industrial workers in the nineteenth century. Children still worked alongside adults and were central to their economic activities; young children disappeared from the European labor force only toward the century's end, and in many regions of Europe, even later. Only with the triumph of the "male-breadwinner" norm and increasing adult male real wage levels was it possible for families to imagine living without the supplemental wages of children or mothers. One-earner families became a possibility in most of Europe only during the last quarter of the nineteenth century, and then only for the highest-paid echelons of the working class.

Demographic conditions also made it extremely difficult to follow the prescriptions for a new style of family life in most of Europe. The new model—centered as it was on attention lavished on even very young children—made most sense when birth rates and infant and child death rates were low. With the exception of peasant and petit bourgeois France, where fertility had declined by the early nineteenth century, family size among the European popular classes remained high until the early twentieth century. High levels of infant and child mortality among the poor also persisted despite the overall mortality decline. In many regions including areas of Germany and northern Italy, demographic differentials between classes in fact widened as death rates declined, before they converged in the twentieth century.

Even where new family ideals were difficult to accomplish, however, evidence suggests that these ideals were known and could serve as a source of frustration and even anguish because they were so elusive. European working-class autobiographers who grew up in the nineteenth century called on normative ideals of childhood with which they were familiar even as they claimed that these ideals did not apply to their own experiences. They used common metaphors to describe what they had missed: the carefree "golden years" of childhood centered on the mother as "warming sunshine" or "bright spirit of the home." Adelheid Popp, who was born in 1869 into a family of village weavers in Austria, began her memoirs with a litany of what her childhood had lacked:

> No bright moment, no sunbeam, no hint of a comfortable home where motherly love and care could shape my childhood was ever known to me. . . . When I'd rush to work at six o'clock in the morning, other children of my age were still sleeping. And when I hurried home at eight o'clock at night, then the others were going to bed, fed and cared for. While I sat bent over my work, lining up stitch after stitch, they played, went walking or sat in school.

THE WELFARE STATE AND FAMILY LIFE

The flash points—points of contradiction between norms of proper family life and the real conditions faced by most families—were numerous. However, criticisms of imprudent marriages or deficient parenting among the poor could be turned around to criticize in turn the social and economic system that made the idealized family life impossible for the poor. It was these contradictions that led state authorities, social reformers, and socialist critics, all from different motives, to turn their attention to the conditions of modern family life. In so doing, they laid the groundwork for modern welfare state systems. Take living space, for example. Access to proper domestic space had become a politically charged issue in many regions of Europe by the late nineteenth century. The very structural transformations brought by industrial capitalism both encouraged the new domesticity and set up conditions in growing industrial cities that made it impossible for all but the very well off to find spaces suitable for family life. The internal migrations in Europe in the nineteenth century brought hundreds of thousands of migrants into crowded urban areas. Escape to the suburbs was hardly an option for most. In contrast with the relatively secluded domestic space of the propertied, protected from unwanted intrusion, the porosity of domestic space in urban working-class neighborhoods was apparent. Working-class men and boys, but also many women and girls, were (almost literally) at home in the streets. Moreover networks of kin, neighbors, and boarders figured prominently in working-class interior spaces and domestic strategies, and working-class mothers often helped their families to survive by doing "sweated" labor at home.

But the circulation of middle-class domestic models converted such contradictions into a possible focus of political mobilization or state intervention. The housing crisis that characterized many turn-of-the-century European cities inspired the political imagination to search for alternatives that eventually fed, for example, into the working-class experimentation with municipal housing projects that appeared in cities throughout Europe by the early twentieth century. Whether in the form of arguments for municipal housing in Berlin or Lyon or home loans for working-class families in Stockholm, or public health measures to lower infant mortality in working-class slums in Bologna, or milk depots in workers' neighborhoods in Paris, reformist and socialist political organizations used the new norms of bourgeois family life and their inattainability as a political weapon in efforts to improve living conditions for poor families. Many of these redeployments of the models of middle-class domesticity by workers' movements involve tacit or even explicit endorsement of middle-class ideals. If such arguments proved very potent politically, they also, of course, suppressed the opportunity to offer a critique of or alternative to those ideals. That many workers' movements chose to demand rather than critique the comforts of home attests to the wide circulation not just of the images and artifacts of domesticity, but also of their powerful emotional appeal. By the same token, these new programs also gave opportunities to state authorities and social workers to intervene in the family life of the lower classes. Sometimes these interventions could provide welcome resources to family members. But they could also serve more sinister ends, as, for example, when harried working-class mothers were criticized for not living up to middle-class norms, and might even be threatened with loss of custody over their children for their "failings" as mothers.

EUROPEAN FAMILIES IN A GLOBAL CONTEXT

Europe's modern family, it cannot be forgotten, also evolved in a global context. On the one hand, there were new migration streams. Well-established patterns of life-cyclic migration, especially of young men and women, to nearby rural regions or cities, altered dramatically with the huge increase in overseas migration. Millions of Europeans migrated abroad in the nineteenth century, and this massive out-migration held equally massive implications for family life among the transplanted and those left behind. Secondly, the global competition and imperialist expansion of European states that heightened in the second half of the nineteenth century affected the family life of Europeans and of those people they colonized.

The impact of overseas migration varied tremendously by region, of course. In some areas of heavy out-migration such as southern and western Germany in the early to mid-nineteenth century and Italy and Ireland in the mid to late nineteenth century, migrant flows could carry away 20 percent or more of a region's population in a decade, largely concentrated among young adults. Although this massive outflow could devastate a region, there is also evidence pointing to the continuation of transnational family ties. Many migrants did return home, sometimes disillusioned, but sometimes with a small capital to start a farm or business. Even those who did not return often sent money home, and thus helped family in the home country to keep small farms going that might otherwise have been unviable. Patterns of chain migration that reunited separated family members in areas of settlement are also evidence of the persistence and strength of family ties despite long-distance migration. Nevertheless, it is ironic that the era of heightened emphasis on the emotional ties of family life was also the era of maximum migration around and out of Europe, and thus maximum stress on family ties for the huge numbers of migrants.

Imperialism brings out other dimensions of modern European family history. The economic and political histories of imperialism are relatively well known. But the ways in which family and gender relations were implicated in imperialist projects are just beginning to be recognized. Recent scholarship suggests the extent to which European empires of the late nineteenth and early twentieth centuries aimed to reconstruct family life along with political and economic life in the colonies. Moreover, the family history of European colonies demonstrates how, in the context of imperialism, global power systems, race relations, and family and gender history of both colonizers and colonized are bound together. For example, critical reading of the sources has debunked the once-prevalent myth that sexual liaisons between colonizing men and colonized women gave imperialism a "human side" that was disrupted with the arrival of European women in the colonies. Feminist histories of colonialism have pointed to the sexual regimes that were a component of imperial rule.

New histories of relationships between missionaries and colonial administrators and the peoples who lived in colonized areas also point to subtle interplays between strategies of rule and resistance, on the one hand, and family, gender, and generational relations, on the other. For example, varying responses to missionary activities in the Gikuyu region of Kenya in the early twentieth century could often be accounted for by people's varying positionalities in gender and generational hierarchies of the precolonial and early colonial family system.

The history of imperialism is just one of the more recent realms of modern European history in which attention to marriage and family is pushing us toward new understandings of the past. It has become clear that in order to analyze such major historical transformations as industrialization, the development of modern welfare state systems, or the imperialist world order, the historian's gaze cannot stop at the door of the cottage, townhouse, or hut, but has to take in domestic interiors as well.

See also **Childhood and Children; Cities and Towns; Demography; Gender; Public Health; Sexuality.**

BIBLIOGRAPHY

Allen, Ann Taylor. *Feminism and Motherhood in Germany, 1800–1914.* New Brunswick, N.J, 1991.

Ariès, Philippe. *Centuries of Childhood: A Social History of Family Life.* Translated from the French by Robert Baldick. New York, 1962.

Davidoff, Leonore, and Catherine Hall. *Family Fortunes: Men and Women of the English Middle Class, 1780–1850.* Chicago, 1987.

Foucault, Michel. *The History of Sexuality*. Translated from the French by Robert Hurley. New York, 1978–1986.

Frader, Laura M., and Sonya O. Rose, eds. *Gender and Class in Modern Europe*. Ithaca, N.Y., 1996.

Frykman, Jonas, and Orvar Löfgren. *Culture Builders: A Historical Anthropology of Middle-Class Life*. Translated by Alan Crozier. New Brunswick, N.J., 1987.

Gillis, John. *Youth and History: Tradition and Change in European Age Relations, 1770 to the Present*. New York, 1981.

Gray, Marion W. *Productive Men, Reproductive Women: The Agrarian Household and the Emergence of Separate Spheres during the German Enlightenment*. New York, 2000.

Hajnal, John. "European Marriage Patterns in Perspective." In *Population in History: Essays in Historical Demography*, edited by D. V. Glass and D. V. Eversly, 101–140. Chicago, 1965.

Heywood, Colin. *Childhood in Nineteenth-Century France: Work, Health, and Education among the Classes Populaires*. Cambridge, U.K., 1987.

Kertzer, David I., and Marzio Barbagli, eds. *Family Life in the Long Nineteenth Century, 1789–1913*. New Haven, Conn., 2002.

Lynch, Katherine. *Family, Class, and Ideology in Early Industrial France: Social Policy and the Working-Class Family, 1825–1848*. Madison, Wis., 1988.

Maynes, Mary Jo. *Taking the Hard Road: Lifecourse and Class Identity in Nineteenth-Century French and German Workers' Autobiographies*. Chapel Hill, N.C., 1995.

Maynes, Mary Jo, and Ann Waltner. "Family History as World History." In *Women's History in Global Perspective*, edited by Bonnie Smith. Champaign-Urbana, Ill., 2004.

Miller, Pavla. *Transformations of Patriarchy in the West, 1500–1900*. Bloomington, Ind., 1998.

Mitterauer, Michael, and Reinhard Sieder. *The European Family: Patriarchy to Partnership from the Middle Ages to the Present*. Translated by Karla Oosterveen and Manfred Hörzinger. Chicago, 1982.

Peterson, Derek. *Creative Writing: Translation, Bookkeeping, and the Work of Imagination in Colonial Kenya*. New York, 2004.

Ross, Ellen. *Love and Toil: Motherhood in Outcast London, 1870–1918*. Oxford, U.K., 1993.

Sabean, David Warren. *Property, Production, and Family in Neckarhausen, 1700–1870*. Cambridge, U.K., 1990.

Sant Cassia, Paul, with Constantina Bada. *The Making of the Modern Greek Family: Marriage and Exchange in Nineteenth-Century Athens*. Cambridge, U.K., 1992.

Seccombe, Wally. "Patriarchy Stabilized: The Construction of the Male Breadwinner Wage Norm in Nineteenth-Century Britain." *Social History* 2 (1992): 53–76.

Shorter, Edward. *The Making of the Modern Family*. New York, 1976.

Sinha, Mrinalini. *Colonial Masculinity: The "Manly Englishman" and the "Effeminate Bengali" in the Late Nineteenth Century*. New York, 1995.

Smith, Bonnie. *Ladies of the Leisure Class: The Bourgeoises of Northern France in the Nineteenth Century*. Princeton, N.J., 1981.

Stone, Lawrence. *The Family, Sex, and Marriage in England, 1500–1800*. New York, 1977.

Strobel, Margaret. *European Women and the Second British Empire*. Bloomington, Ind., 1991.

Tilly, Louise A., and Joan W. Scott. *Women, Work, and Family*. New York, 1987.

Wildenthal, Lora. *German Women for Empire, 1884–1945*. Durham, N.C., 2001.

MARY JO MAYNES

MARTINEAU, HARRIET (1802–1876),

English writer and journalist.

Harriet Martineau was born in Norwich on 12 June 1802, the sixth of eight children of Thomas Martineau, a textile manufacturer of Huguenot descent, and his wife, Elizabeth. Well educated at home and, briefly, in schools in Norwich and Bristol, she nevertheless recalled her childhood as unhappy. Often in ill health, she suffered from deafness that became total by age twenty, necessitating the use of an ear trumpet.

The Martineaus belonged to the religiously liberal and politically radical circle centered on the Octagon Chapel, Norwich, originally Presbyterian but by then Unitarian. Religious fantasies had brought solace in her early unhappiness, but as a young woman she became convinced by Necessarianism—the deterministic philosophy derived from the physician David Hartley (1705–1757) and the minister and scientist Joseph Priestley (1733–1804)—which by then was dominant among English Unitarians. With family encouragement, she contributed to the *Monthly Repository*, the leading Unitarian periodical, and when the family business foundered in 1825 and failed in 1829, she turned to writing as a career. In 1827, the minister William Johnson Fox (1785–1864)—later an important journalist and politician—had become editor of the *Monthly Repository*; he offered her a small stipend and encouraged her to explore a wide range of subjects.

In 1831 she began *Illustrations of Political Economy,* twenty-three tales that appeared in twenty-five monthly parts between 1832 and 1834, catching current enthusiasm for both economic science and popularization; two shorter, commissioned sets of tales followed, on the poor laws (1834) and taxation (1835). An almost instant celebrity in 1832, she moved to London and was thereafter rarely out of the public eye. In the years 1834 to 1836, she traveled widely in the United States, and wrote two books based on her experiences, notably *Society in America* (1837). Back in London, she contributed to various periodicals and published a revealing but not particularly successful novel, *Deerbrook* (1839), as well as a long-popular series of children's stories, *Playfellow* (1841–1842).

In 1840, suffering from complications of an ovarian cyst, she retreated to Tynemouth, near Newcastle, where for an extended period she was bedridden, an episode memorialized in *Life in the Sickroom* (1844). Turning to the much-discussed pseudoscience of mesmerism, she soon claimed a complete cure; *Letters on Mesmerism* (1844), originally published in the *Athenaeum,* aroused much medical controversy and brought her considerable notoriety. She settled in the Lake District, where she farmed, walked great distances, and wrote a guidebook, socialized with famous neighbors and a stream of visitors, and engaged in extensive philanthropy. She resumed her travels, most importantly to the Near East in 1846 and 1847.

After her fiancé, a college friend of her brother James, died in 1827, she determined with evident relief to remain single. She had long been close to James (1805–1900), who emerged by the 1830s as a leading minister, philosopher, and teacher, but they grew apart as his mounting attack on Unitarian organization and theology led him to reject determinism for free will; when he savagely reviewed her *Letters on the Laws of Man's Nature and Development* (1851), written in collaboration with Henry George Atkinson, a close friend from her mesmeric years, the break became irreparable.

While she never abandoned Necessarianism, she came to reject Unitarianism and all religion, proclaiming her atheism in *Eastern Life, Present and Past* (1848), a reflection on her travels, and in an important translation and abridgment, *The Positive Philosophy of Auguste Comte* (1853), though she could not follow Comte in his later political speculations. In 1852 she began writing leading articles for the radical London paper, the *Daily News,* contributing over 1,600 editorials before her retirement in 1866. She continued to publish widely in British and American periodicals and also wrote a brilliant annalistic account of her own times, the *History of the Thirty Years' Peace* (1849–1850). Widely recognized as an expert on America, she was a passionate follower of the American abolitionist William Lloyd Garrison (1805–1879) and formed a close friendship with Garrison's disciple Maria Weston Chapman (1806–1885), who became her first biographer.

Martineau died on 27 June 1876, of heart failure induced by the ovarian cyst that had brought on her illness in the 1840s. In 1877 a magnificent autobiography appeared, published unchanged from its composition in 1855, when she had been expecting imminent death. Its unsparing frankness caused her reputation to decline, as did her increasingly unfashionable advocacy of classical economics, but since the mid-twentieth century her reputation has soared, as her works and her many contributions to Victorian life, notably her idiosyncratic feminism, have been newly assessed.

See also **Economists, Classical; Feminism.**

BIBLIOGRAPHY

Primary Sources

Arbuckle, Elisabeth Sanders. *Harriet Martineau's Letters to Fanny Wedgwood.* Stanford, Calif., 1983.

———. *Harriet Martineau in the London* Daily News: *Selected Contributions, 1852–1866.* New York and London, 1994.

Sanders, Valerie. *Harriet Martineau: Selected Letters.* Oxford, U.K., 1990.

Secondary Sources

Hoecker-Drysdale, Susan. *Harriet Martineau: First Woman Sociologist.* Oxford, U.K., and New York, 1992.

Sanders, Valerie. *Reason over Passion: Harriet Martineau and the Victorian Novel.* London, 1986.

Webb, Robert K. *Harriet Martineau: A Radical Victorian.* London and New York, 1960. Biographical study emphasizing her intellectual concerns.

R. K. WEBB

MARTOV, L. (1873–1923), Russian Marxist and leader of the Mensheviks.

A prominent Russian Marxist, an early leader of the Russian Social Democratic Labor Party (RSDLP), and an important theoretician of its Menshevik faction, L. Martov occupies a special personal position in the historiography of Russian socialism. Contemporaries and historians have remarked on his uncompromising moral stances, his attractive personality, and his fate as one of the first socialist victims of the Russian Revolution.

Born Yuli Osipovich Tsederbaum into a Russified middle-class Jewish family, Martov grew up in Odessa and St. Petersburg. He adopted the pseudonym Martov in 1901 because, as he put it, he considered March to be a particularly revolutionary month. He chose the initial "L." out of affection for his sister Lidia, a revolutionary activist married to Fyodor Dan, another prominent Russian Social Democrat and Martov's successor as leader of the Mensheviks in exile after Martov's death in 1923. Several other Tsederbaum siblings were also deeply involved in the revolutionary movement and later suffered under the Soviet regime.

Like many of his generation, Martov turned to politics under the impact of the famine of 1891. He was first arrested in 1892 and first sent into internal exile in 1897. He was to spend much of his life in exile abroad. Martov's earliest significant political experience was among Jewish workers in Vilna in 1893. In the tract "On Agitation" (1894), cowritten with Arkady Kremer, Martov argued for a strategy that contrasted grassroots "agitation" among the working masses with "propaganda" among a workers' elite. He temporarily adhered to Vladimir Lenin's elitist conception of party organization, as presented in Lenin's "What Is to Be Done?" (1902), but a belief in workers' autonomous activity returned to the center of Martov's thinking.

Martov and Lenin were the closest of collaborators, first in the St. Petersburg Union of Struggle for the Emancipation of the Working Class and then on the journal *Iskra* (The spark), published abroad from 1900 to 1903. It was during the latter period that the RSDLP defined itself both organizationally and ideologically. Collaboration came to an abrupt close at the Party's Second Congress in 1903 with the break between Lenin and Martov, one that was to give rise in time to "Menshevik" and "Bolshevik" currents or factions within the RSDLP. The reasons for the break were both personal and ideological. Some historians have emphasized the moral revulsion that Martov experienced in reaction to Lenin's tactics. Others have pointed out that Martov had gone along with such tactics, up to and during the Second Congress itself. In years to come Martov was probably more implacably hostile to Lenin than Lenin was to him.

Although all Party theoreticians considered themselves faithful to Marxist doctrine, Martov had more reason than many others to claim that title. Even in the heady days of the Revolution of 1905, he adhered closely to the classical view that the situation called for a bourgeois revolution, with the participation of the Russian bourgeoisie, rather than a proletarian revolution that would rely on an alliance with the peasantry, as others were arguing. In 1905 many revolutionaries, both Bolsheviks and Mensheviks, entertained unconventional non-Marxist scenarios, founded, for example, on hopes of proletarian revolution abroad. Martov resisted such temptations better than most of his comrades. Martov's confidence in the proletariat's capacity for spontaneous and autonomous activity in the circumstances of 1905, as witnessed by the rise of the soviets or workers' councils, was exaggerated but it was consistent with Martov's earlier views and it was not incompatible with the belief that a bourgeois revolution was the order of the day.

In the period from 1905 to 1914, during most of which time he lived in the West, Martov addressed the two important issues confronting Russian Social Democrats—the overcoming of the Menshevik/Bolshevik division and the proper form of Party organization in Russia's new political circumstances. Martov appears to have given up hopes of real Party reunification early on, although preeminence within the Party seesawed back and forth between Mensheviks and Bolsheviks for several years. One could argue that a final split did not take place before the October Revolution in 1917. In these years of revolutionary disenchantment among the intelligentsia and the growth of a nonrevolutionary-minded Russian working class, Martov was prepared to adapt party structures, thus incurring the accusation of seeking to "liquidate" the Party. He also consistently urged Party participation in Duma or parliamentary elections. Martov's distrust of Leninist principles of strong, even dictatorial, leadership within an elitist underground Party provided the impulse and the element of continuity in the positions he took.

When war broke out in 1914, Martov was traveling abroad to a socialist congress. In contrast to most Western socialists but like Lenin and many other Russian Social Democrats, Martov came out firmly against the war and worked to create an international socialist opposition to it. He returned to Russia during the period of the Provisional Government in 1917.

As the leader of the Menshevik Internationalists, Martov found himself in a minority within his own party. Only after the Bolshevik coup in November 1917 did Martov establish his personal hegemony within the Menshevik Party. In the following years he practiced what amounted to an increasingly desperate policy of loyal opposition, criticizing the regime fiercely, but participating, to the extent possible, in the Bolshevik-controlled soviets. In August 1920 Martov went abroad to attend a German socialist congress. He left legally and, in principle, temporarily. In fact, he never returned to Russia, dying in Berlin on 4 April 1923 after a prolonged illness. In his last years in Germany Martov founded and contributed to *Sotsialistichesky vestnik* (Socialist herald), which was to be the flagship publication of the exiled Mensheviks for over forty years.

See also **Lenin, Vladimir; Mensheviks; Revolution of 1905 (Russia).**

BIBLIOGRAPHY

Getzler, Israel. *Martov: A Political Biography of a Russian Social Democrat.* Cambridge, U.K., 1967.

Martov, Yuli. *Zapiski sotsial-demokrata.* Berlin, 1922. Reprint, with a new introduction by I. Getzler, Cambridge, Mass., 1975.

Urilov, I. Kh. *Iu. O. Martov: Politik i istorik.* Moscow, 1997.

ANDRE LIEBICH

MARX, KARL (1818–1883), German social and political theorist.

Karl Marx is recognized as one of the most influential social and political thinkers of all time and possibly the first thinker of nonreligious significance to become a truly global influence. He has been known since the late 1880s as the eponymous founder of Marxism, a doctrine of revolutionary communism. In one form or another, it has been supported by and has held sway over considerable portions of the world's population. Great political leaders such as Vladimir Lenin (1870–1924), Joseph Stalin (1879), Mao Tse-tung (1893–1976), and Ho Chi Minh (1890–1969) have attributed their success to the inspiration they derived from his works and from those of his lifelong friend and colleague, Friedrich Engels (1820–1895).

MARX, ENGELS, AND MARXISM

Initially, Marx lived a life of considerable intellectual and personal obscurity. Both his fame and his notoriety were confined to narrow circles, even when he became known (briefly) in the early 1870s as the Red Terror Doctor. The books and pamphlets he published in his own lifetime divide roughly equally between political polemic against rival socialists (mostly long forgotten) and an astoundingly grandiose project: a savage critique of capitalist commodity production as a globalizing force, based on historical investigation and a unique philosophical insight. His overtly political activities were confined to editorial work on short-lived newspapers and international "correspondence committees," although during the revolutionary events of 1848 he addressed public meetings in Germany. For many years he also worked as an international journalist, commenting on political events and issues. Throughout his life, he promoted socialist political principles in contemporary politics, whether revolutionary or electoral, but he was never the leader of an organized movement or party as such, and indeed was said to have denied late in life that he had ever been a Marxist.

From late 1844 until his death, Marx was shadowed by Engels, who shared his socialist commitments and complemented his relentless analytical and satirical skills with an easier, synthesizing mode of writing and more accessible writing style. Engels was Marx's first biographer and bibliographer and his only significant collaborator, although they coauthored only three important works. The issue of authorship and interpretation has become more important in retrospect than it was in their lifetimes, when they had little visibility and were generally grateful for what attention they got.

Engels was also the biographer of their partnership, and from 1859 onward he framed his summary accounts of Marx's work, methods, and importance in this authoritative way. Moreover, after Marx's death, Engels's works, particularly those of the late 1870s through the mid-1890s, acquired far more fame and readership in socialist circles than those by Marx alone. However, after Engels's death, a certain skepticism concerning the relationship between Engels's popularizing works, which were avowedly based on Marx's ideas, and the original (and updated) import of Marx's published and unpublished writings began to emerge. This textual and scholarly work continues, and the projected complete works of the two will run to approximately 130 double volumes (printed text in the original languages with accompanying scholarly commentary) and is expected to be complete in the early decades of the twenty-first century.

In the decades between the death of Engels and World War I, Marxists became the most intellectually influential tendency within the broad socialist movement in continental Europe. This was largely based on the jointly written *Communist Manifesto* (1848), and on Engels's works, especially *Anti-Dühring* (1878) and *Socialism: Utopian and Scientific* (1880), which provided an apparently authoritative point of access to Marx's thought. Engels's works were generally perceived to be less challenging and more suited to political agitation than Marx's more elaborately historical and philosophically analytical works, such as *A Contribution to the Critique of Political Economy* (1859), *Capital*, volume 1 (1867), and even *The Eighteenth Brumaire of Louis Bonaparte* (1852), a political broadside against a highly visible dictator.

Engels's German-language works went through numerous editions, reprintings, and translations and in general reached far more readers than Marx did in his individually authored works. *Capital*, volume 1, though, eventually acquired minor fame as a (generally unread) classic. Even Marx's English-language lectures, posthumously published as *Value* [or *Wages*], *Price, and Profit* (1898), never had the circulation, fame, and cachet of Engels's works, through which the concepts of a materialist interpretation of history, dialectics, and scientific socialism became a defining catechism of what it means to be Marxist.

Marx became something of a legend after his death, particularly in relation to the intellectual and political development of Marxism in the later nineteenth and early twentieth centuries. It is thus of profound importance in examining his actual life, works, and career that the legend should not be read back into any scholarly consideration of the books and manuscripts that have been preserved, unless a clear link between Marx's thought and events following his death can be established. It is possible, however, to undertake this historical task and thus renew Marx as an intellectual figure in social, political, economic, historical, and philosophical studies, particularly since far more of his work is available in reliable editions in the twenty-first century than was ever the case in the past.

This renewal is possible for political reasons. More than one hundred years have passed since the heyday of Marxism in Europe, and the particular kind of mass working-class politics associated with it is now attenuated. More importantly, enough time has passed since Soviet communism imploded that its claim of descent from Engels and Marx via Lenin and Stalin looks far less threatening and historically less plausible. Marxist and anti-Marxist political framing has dogged all assessments of Marx and has interfered with earlier scholarly presentation and assessment of his ideas. Moreover, the ways that his ideas influenced mass politics, particularly after his death, have been hagiographically recounted and politically demonized. The irony is that in his lifetime Marx courted controversy and sought mass adherence to his views (although not under his own direction), yet when these things arrived in his name, their relationship to his actual ideas and ambitions was highly questionable.

EARLY YEARS

Karl Marx was born into a Jewish family in Trier, in Rhenish Prussia. His father was a lawyer and converted Lutheran and his mother came from a rabbinical background, although Karl's upbringing was not unduly religious in any way and the family ambience is generally portrayed as one of Enlightenment liberalism. This outlook derives from moderates in the French Revolution, who favored individual rights, limited government, representative institutions, middle-class suffrage, free trade, and religious disestablishment. The Napoleonic regime introduced an element of this political ethos into the Rhineland, and the incorporation of the region into the much more authoritarian Kingdom of Prussia after 1815 was a blow to local liberals.

Marx had an unremarkable classical education and was sent to university, first to Bonn in 1835 and then Berlin in 1836 after some student scrapes. He was supposed to study law and follow a professional career but instead became interested in liberal, activist politics, albeit of a rather intellectual sort. During this period, he was deeply in love with Jenny von Westphalen (1814–1881), a childhood sweetheart from a family that was more aristocratic than the Marxes but still liberal and more intellectually adventurous.

Marx's initial political engagement was with the Young Hegelians, a movement based in liberal university faculties. Although it had an obvious intellectual appeal given his interests in history and philosophy (as he explains in his autobiographical sketch of 1859 in the preface to *A Contribution to the Critique of Political Economy*), the political context for this movement—authoritarian, semifeudal, and highly militarized Prussia—may be less obvious to the modern observer. Prussia had no elected representative institutions; no constitutional guarantees of rights to free speech, expression, or assembly; and the regime employed an apparatus of police spies, detention, deportation, and harassment of anyone deemed a radical. In these circumstances, political activism—and even discussion of the commonplace elements of democracy or peaceful liberalizing change—were

Karl Marx, 1880. GETTY IMAGES

dangerous enterprises, and the universities were always under surveillance. In the absence of any commitment to academic freedom, the royal government felt empowered to intervene in academic appointments, particularly those in philosophy and made it a duty for all to safeguard the supposed sureties of Christian belief from which the monarchy claimed a mandate to rule.

Crucially at issue in Prussia in the 1830s was the mammoth philosophical legacy of Georg Wilhelm Friedrich Hegel (1770–1831) and its interpretation of Christian doctrine; this was a public political matter, since religion was not merely a private matter for individuals. Hegel (in his view and in the view of his disciples) had produced vast works of philosophical synthesis, reconciling history, religion, philosophy, science, logic, aesthetics, and politics with reason and the progressive development of human freedom. However, the relationship between his highly ambiguous writings on the one hand and contemporary politics and doctrinal Christianity on the other was difficult to discern, and two schools of interpretation developed: Old

Hegelians, emphasizing the conservative side (i.e. alignment with the Prussian monarchy and its claimed relationship to the established churches), and Young Hegelians, emphasizing a further political development in history toward liberalism in politics, including skepticism about supernatural phenomena in general and Christianity in particular.

Characteristically, Marx took his Young Hegelian analysis into a recondite doctoral dissertation on the ancient Greek philosophies of Democritus and Epicurus (submitted by mail to the University of Jena in 1841), but his connections with radical professors cost him the chance of a university post. He obtained a job in journalism on a liberal Rhineland paper in Cologne, and then unexpectedly became its editor in 1842. This coincided with a period of nervous and short-lived governmental liberalization, but the paper was suppressed in March 1843, after which Marx ended his long engagement and got married.

Although little noticed at the time, Marx's early journalism contains the key to all his later work. On the one hand, he was a recognizable liberal in the French revolutionary tradition, writing to defend freedom of the press and religion within secular institutions (including civil marriage and divorce), all of which were dangerous, radical ideas in the Prussian context. On the other hand, he was highly radical compared with most liberals in that he highlighted economic issues in a class-structured way, suggesting that a reformed government should intervene and not leave poverty and working conditions simply to the market and individual enterprise or charity. This angle was identified as socialist or communist (terms that were largely interchangeable at the time) and was vilified as foreign (the ideas were generally of recent French currency) and incipiently revolutionary (middle-class liberals feared that the working classes were a threat to their property, investments, and livelihoods). Marx had absorbed some of this outlook from other associates on the *Rheinische Zeitung*, including Moses Hess (1812–1875), who praised him at the time as, "Rousseau, Voltaire, Holbach, Lessing, Heine, and Hegel fused into one person" (quoted in McLellan, p. 47).

As Marx writes in his autobiographical sketch, he suffered "the embarrassment of having to discuss so-called material interests," by which he meant matters of economic fact and theory (*Later Political Writings*, pp. 158–159). While in the Rhineland, he was concerned with the plight of vineyard workers when the markets failed and with peasants whose landlords were removing their traditional rights by legal means. But he was also aware of the increasing industrialization of other areas in Europe (notably France and Belgium), where concentrations of disadvantaged workers (in many instances German émigrés) had formed. Allying himself with other intellectuals of similar views, first in Paris and then in Brussels, he began to publish the first installments of what was for him an important political project: the critical destruction of Old Hegelian political conservatism and the Young Hegelian defense of historical change, albeit in a highly unusual way. Building on the historical critique of Christianity unwittingly accomplished by David Friedrich Strauss (1808–1874) and the philosophical critique of religion accomplished by Ludwig Feuerbach (1804–1872), both of whom were driven from German intellectual life as a result, Marx embarked on a demystification of Hegel's philosophical system. The goal was to turn the (necessarily covert) world of Prussian politics around, away from conservative reaction and Christian orthodoxy, toward an enlightened world of liberal democracy and rationalistic atheism.

Although any number of Young Hegelians could have appreciated this project, it had two further dimensions that were Marx's own, or were at least not widely shared at that point: the first was a commitment to the class politics of socialism or communism, through which mankind was to be united in a non-exploitative society where production and consumption would be shared according to needs and abilities; the second was a commitment to working-class activism as a practical matter, promoting self-determination and suffrage for the vast unpropertied majority of men (political rights for women was a further radicalism not generally discussed in these circles). Both of these went well beyond the interests of contemporary middle-class liberals, and the commitment to hands-on activism among the working classes was alien to the intellectualized university politics of most Young Hegelians. Marx's work and activities at the time represented, in theory at least, an ambitious union of philosophy and politics together with a vision of the good society. This recouped the achievements of previous figures of the liberalizing Enlightenment, whether materialists and empiricists or idealists and rationalists, and promised to give it overwhelming political might. In his short work *A Contribution to the Critique of Hegel's Philosophy of Right: Introduction* (1844) Marx (using the French socialist term *proletariat,* meaning "urban working class") announced that the philosophy of freedom and the emancipation of the proletariat must mutually merge.

POLITICS AND CRITIQUE, 1845–1850

Having moved to the more liberal political climate of Brussels, Marx (in conjunction, from time to time, with Engels) worked with both the middle-class liberal Democratic Association and a communist group that was made up mostly of German émigrés, both of which were loosely allied to similar associations in France, England, and elsewhere. Marx published his short book *The Poverty of Philosophy* in French in 1847, attacking the French socialist Pierre-Joseph Proudhon and broadening the scope of his critique of the forms of socialism that he considered economically naïve and out of touch with working-class political organizations. Throughout his life, these remained common points of self-created division between Marx and other socialists, and he had few stable political associates during his career other than Engels. However, during this period he and Engels were asked by the nascent Communist League to draft a defining document for international socialism, and the resulting pamphlet, *The Communist Manifesto,* was accepted at a conference in London in late 1847.

More than any other document, *The Communist Manifesto* conveys the essence of Marx's outlook on history, politics, and society. Although Engels played a major role in drafting it, it makes no mention of the core concepts that he later used to define Marxism: dialectic, materialism, determinism, metaphysics, idealism, interaction, contradiction, and reflection, and although the work was written to satisfy an executive committee and may thus contain an element of compromise and pastiche, little of its content could count as radically inconsistent with Marx's more detailed and thorough later writings. *The Communist Manifesto* is divided into four sections. The first is a magnificently sweeping historical account of the development of industrial production and commercial relations by the European "bourgeoisie" (again a French term, meaning the manufacturing and trading classes). As this broad social movement progresses, it disposes of feudal relations and structures, forces the peasantry to seek work as wage laborers, and spreads beyond Europe, destroying older cultures and creating exploited colonies. Predicting ever-worsening economic crises of overproduction and ever-increasing exploitation and misery for the proletariat, *The Communist Manifesto* maintains that the social structure of industrial societies will simplify into two great opposing classes and that the proletariat will gain consciousness of itself politically as a vast majority. A more or less veiled civil war between these two classes will break out openly into revolutionary conflict and socialists will eventually establish a classless society that will transcend national borders.

The second section explains the relationship between proletarians and communists, stating that they have identical interests but that communists have a role in unmasking bourgeois hypocrisy. In that way, the document claims, communists are more theoretically advanced than most workers but have no sectarian, partisan principles other than those of the workers' movement itself. Proletarian revolution will win "victory for democracy" while also mandating "despotic incursions into the rights of private property," since that is where exploitation originates. The section closes with a ten-point checklist of typical communist demands (most of which were institutionalized in the twentieth century by social democratic regimes).

The third section is an analytical and critical review of other popular theories of socialism and communism of the time, establishing clear points of differentiation from the views and methods of the Communist League, and the fourth section is a more detailed (and obviously ephemeral) statement of contemporary tactics in various countries such as France, Switzerland, Poland, and Germany. *The Communist Manifesto* promises a society in which "the free development of each is the condition for the free development of all" and closes with the clarion call, "*Proletarians of all countries unite!*" (*Later Political Writings,* pp. 19, 30; emphasis in original).

The Communist Manifesto was printed in London in early 1848 and distributed just as revolution broke out in Paris and then spread swiftly to other European capitals. Conservative monarchies and aristocratic establishments were routed and democratic assemblies inaugurated throughout the Continent. Marx was welcomed into France by liberal revolutionaries of his acquaintance, and he journeyed from there to Cologne when revolution spread to the Rhineland. With others, he started a new version of his former liberal newspaper, and for the duration of the revolution he urged the democratic process forward, particularly on economic issues and working-class political participation, even making some speeches. As the revolutionary democrats were rolled back by conservative forces, and reaction and repression became the order of the day, he fled with his family (he and his wife now had two daughters) to London, as did many other political refugees. Engels followed and set himself up in Manchester with a job at one of his father's factories. For the remainder of what became a lifetime exile for the two of them, Engels supported the Marx family (another daughter was born in London; three other children, a daughter and two sons, did not survive beyond infancy or childhood).

THE INTERNATIONAL DIMENSION, 1851–1883

Writing almost always in German for an audience back in Germany (when he could reach them through the censorship) and in exile all over Europe and in America, Marx's thought and politics were necessarily international but also focused primarily on a German target group except in rare cases when translations could be arranged. His pamphlets *The Class Struggles in France, 1848–1850* (1850), *The Eighteenth Brumaire of Louis Bonaparte* (1852), and *The Cologne Communist Trial* (1853) were typical of his interest in saving something of the spirit of 1848 while pouring scorn on the conservative and reactionary political forces aligned with the rich, powerful, and well armed. Notably, he dismissed his former communist political associates as "jackasses," swearing he would never involve himself in partisan struggle again.

With Engels's help, Marx had a stop-gap career as an English-language journalist for the New York *Tribune* and various encyclopedias, but this was never enough to pay the bills and he resented the time it took away from what he defined as his lifework and major contribution to the socialist struggle: a critique of the categories of political economy. This multi-volume project went through numerous changes of plan, but the main thrust remained clear. Marx aimed to rewrite the economics of his day, known as political economy, by producing a new account of the production, consumption, distribution, and exchange of goods and services in any commodified and industrialized society where the capitalist mode of production prevails. He published a short installment in 1859 (*A Contribution to the Critique of Political Economy*) and the first volume (*Capital*) in 1867, leaving a vast mountain of notebooks, manuscript drafts and critical commentary behind at his death.

Marx's targets were the political economists Adam Smith (1723–1790) and David Ricardo (1772–1823), together with their numerous precursors and followers. Their work differs somewhat from that of later marginalist economics of the 1870s onward, which defines value as market prices that result from calculations of utility "at the margin" of any individual's preferences to consume goods and services. The methods of the political economists were more philosophical than mathematical, and in particular they considered value itself (rather than merely numerical prices) to be the key to understanding and (minimally) directing the economies of their day. Value, they hypothesized, must rest in some way on labor, and Marx rightly argued that their ideas on this point were analytically inconsistent. Moreover he maintained that their work was politically biased toward the interests of the propertied classes and that their theory made the obvious exploitation of the working classes disappear as a (supposedly) fair exchange. Thus Marx accepted much of the project and methodology of the political economists while rejecting what he took to be their politics and certain details of their theories.

Marx's critique of political economy led rigorously to quite different political conclusions, namely that capitalism could not be a self-sustaining system but would instead be subject to crises of increasing severity; that it would proletarianize the middle classes rather than remedy the exploitation of the workers; and that it would thus represent an increasingly pale alternative to the obvious attractions that socialism would hold for the vast

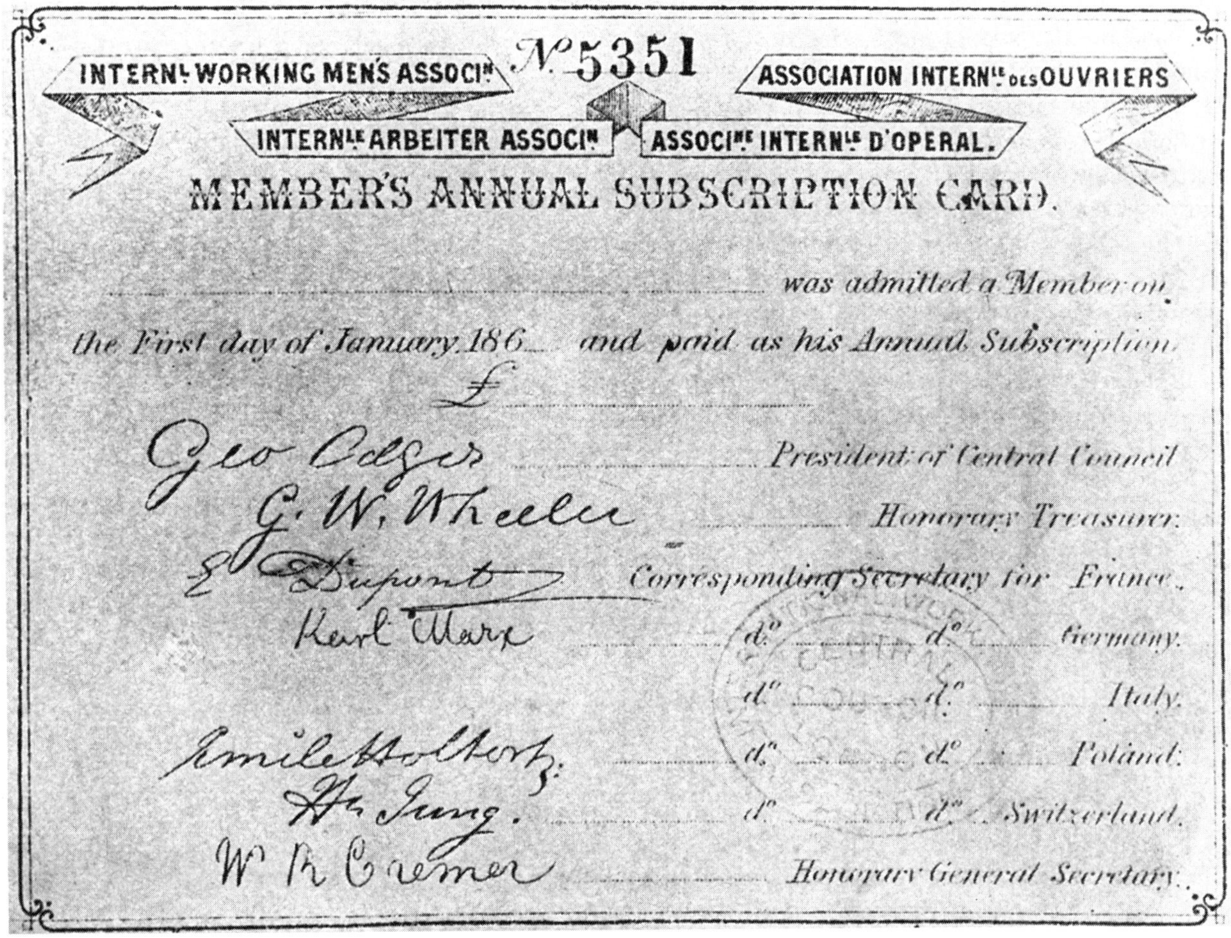
No 5351
INTERNL WORKING MEN'S ASSOCIN
ASSOCIATION INTERNLE DES OUVRIERS
INTERNLE ARBEITER ASSOCIN
ASSOCINE INTERNLE D'OPERAL.
MEMBER'S ANNUAL SUBSCRIPTION CARD.
.... was admitted a Member on
the First day of January 186_ and paid as his Annual Subscription
£ ....
Geo Odger .... President of Central Council
G. W. Wheeler .... Honorary Treasurer.
E Dupont .... Corresponding Secretary for France.
Karl Marx .... do. do. Germany.
.... do. do. Italy.
Emile Holtorp .... do. do. Poland.
H. Jung. .... do. do. Switzerland.
W. R. Cremer .... Honorary General Secretary.

Membership card of the International Working Men's Association, c. 1865. Marx signed the card in his capacity as corresponding secretary for Germany. ©HULTON-DEUTSCH COLLECTION/CORBIS

majority. His solution to the question of value was to argue that human labor time was itself (in its abstract or generic form) the origin of value for mass-produced commodities and thus ultimately the regulator of their exchange ratios (as measured by their long-term price levels relative to each other). However, the system as a whole was not one of equal exchange between, for example, wages and labor time, because wages paid only for the labor time required to purchase subsistence goods and services to maintain the worker. He posited that human labor power has a unique property: it can produce more output in terms of labor time than is required for its own renewal and subsistence, thus allowing capitalists (who pay wages) to collect a surplus, from which their profits derive.

At a stroke, Marx had (apparently) solved a long-standing puzzle and generated a rigorous theory of exploitation that established it as a fact. Although his reasoning has since been faulted, his theory was bypassed rather than refuted. After the 1870s, economists reoriented their profession around an acceptance of monetary prices as the principal reality in their increasingly mathematical studies, rather than treating prices as something epiphenomenal to value. For Marxists, however, acceptance of the Marxist economics in *Capital* was doctrinal, although it was not of much political value other than as a (supposed) proof that capitalism was incontrovertibly exploitative and doomed to collapse.

Marx was instrumental in founding the International Working Men's Association in 1864 as a correspondence committee and an organ of socialist publicity; this organization was generally known as "The International" and later "The First International." Perhaps predictably, this kind of organization, which was by definition remote from national politics and prone to doctrinal factions, could never be rated a complete success, although it did give encouragement to many individuals and groups. Through it, socialists struggled together across national boundaries to get trade unions and working-class political parties properly represented and legally defended within the democratizing structures of industrial capitalist nations. Marx withdrew from the organization after bitter battles with anarchists and others whom he considered politically naïve and intellectually retarded. Perhaps his swan song was the (English-language) address to the International, published as *The Civil War in France* (1871), in which he defended and perhaps romanticized the struggles of ordinary Parisians against conservative forces. The French counterrevolution from the countryside was backed by the occupying Prussians, and neither group wanted any communal experiments in mass democracy and cooperative economic management. The communards were massacred in their thousands, and Marx's testimony still makes moving reading, although at the time he was vilified in the anglophone press for memorializing the communards.

LAST YEARS AND HERITAGE

Marx's later years were spent largely in ill health and unhappiness, working on the later volumes of his unfinished masterpiece, *Capital,* itself a truncated version of his original scheme from the 1850s. The inspiration for *Capital,* however, dates all the way back to his earliest journalism in alliance with liberals, his relentless insistence on the importance of economic structures in constraining and empowering political change, and his conviction that collective, cooperative sharing of social resources through democratic means was compatible with the globalization of modern industry. Although a good deal of this vision remains in the posthumously established variations of Marxism that endure into the twenty-first century, they also contain, of necessity, many tenets and tactics that derive from other minds. Whether or not these adaptations of Marx's work are faithful is a matter for scholarly investigation and individual judgment.

See also **Communism; Engels, Friedrich; First International; Germany; Hegel, Georg Wilhelm Friedrich; Labor Movements; Proudhon, Pierre-Joseph; Socialism; Young Hegelians.**

BIBLIOGRAPHY

Primary Sources

Marx, Karl. *Early Political Writings.* Edited and translated by Joseph O'Malley and Richard A. Davis. Cambridge, U.K., and New York, 1994.

———. *Later Political Writings.* Edited and translated by Terrell Carver. New York, 1996.

Marx, Karl, and Frederick Engels. *Collected Works.* 50 vols. London, 1975–2004.

Secondary Sources

Berlin, Isaiah. *Karl Marx: His Life and Environment.* 5th ed. New York, 2002.

Callinicos, Alex. *The Revolutionary Ideas of Karl Marx.* 2nd ed. London, 1995.

Carver, Terrell. *The Postmodern Marx.* Manchester, U.K., and University Park, Pa., 1998.

Carver, Terrell, ed. *The Cambridge Companion to Marx.* New York and Cambridge, U.K., 1991.

Cohen, G. A. *Karl Marx's Theory of History: A Defence.* Princeton, N.J., 1978.

Fine, Ben. *Marx's Capital.* 3rd ed. Basingstoke, U.K., 1989.

Graham, Keith. *Karl Marx Our Contemporary: Social Theory for a Post-Leninist World.* New York, 1992.

Kitching, Gavin. *Karl Marx and the Philosophy of Praxis.* London, 1988.

McLellan, David. *Karl Marx: His Life and Thought.* 2nd ed. Glasgow and New York, 1986.

Wheen, Francis. *Karl Marx: A Life.* London, 2000.

Wolff, Jonathan. *Why Read Marx Today?* Oxford, U.K., and New York, 2002.

TERRELL CARVER

MASARYK, TOMÁŠ GARRIGUE

(1850–1937), prominent Czech scholar and statesman.

Born to a Slovak father who was a coachman on an imperial estate and a German mother, Tomáš Masaryk gained his primary and secondary education in Moravia and Vienna. After completing his doctorate in philosophy in 1876 at the University of Vienna with a dissertation on Plato, he continued his studies at the University of Leipzig, where he met a young music student, Charlotte Garrigue, from Brooklyn, New York. They married in 1878 and, as a symbol of his esteem, he took her family name as his middle name. His marriage brought him into contact with the United States, and he made several visits there in the prewar years.

To secure a teaching post at the University of Vienna, Masaryk submitted a required second dissertation, or habilitation, entitled *Suicide as a Social Mass Phenomenon,* that employed modern tools of sociological analysis to correlate the rise in suicides with a decline in religious faith. His work was accepted and he became a privatdozent at the university, a poorly paid position that was a necessary first step to a professorship. Around the same time, he converted from Roman Catholicism to Protestantism, a decision motivated in part by a sense of national identity, since the Hussites, the early Protestants who were suppressed by the Catholic Habsburgs in the seventeenth century, held a place of honor in the pantheon of Czech national heroes.

In 1882, following the division of Charles University in Prague into separate Czech and German entities, he took a position as professor extraordinarius of philosophy at the Czech university. His appointment to the more prestigious "ordinarius" rank was delayed until 1896, in part because of his involvement in a bitter dispute about the authenticity of two medieval manuscripts, discovered early in the century, that described life among the early Czech tribes and were a source of national pride. In the 1880s, a prominent Czech philologist unleashed a furor in the national community when he proved that they were forgeries. Masaryk supported his findings, arguing that national pride must be founded on truth, and although excoriated as a traitor in the popular press, he won the support of a younger generation eager to escape the narrow confines of national chauvinism.

In 1890, Masaryk joined the Young Czech Party and was elected to both the Imperial Parliament and the Bohemian Diet, but left the party and abandoned both mandates in 1893, following a dispute with the party's leadership. In numerous publications from the 1890s, he articulated his understanding of the Czech national mission, arguing that the meaning of Czech history was the ideal of humanity, which was embodied in religious faith and manifested in the Hussite movement and in the Czech National Revival of the nineteenth century. Expanding this perspective to contemporary issues, he supported the drive for workers' rights, women's equality, and universal suffrage. He was one of the few Czech leaders to reject the historic state rights argument, which based the demand for autonomy on the traditional privileges of the old Kingdom of Bohemia. Arguing that it abandoned the Slovaks, who lived under Hungarian rule and whose territory had never been part of the Bohemian Kingdom, he instead pioneered the concept of Czech and Slovak unity, and was supported in this effort by a group of young Slovak intellectuals.

Masaryk gained international renown for his principled stands in two widely publicized legal proceedings. In 1899, he defied popular opinion to defend a poor Bohemian Jew, Leopold Hilsner, who had been convicted of ritual murder, and in 1909, he supported Croats and Serbs who were being tried for treason on the basis of trumped-up evidence. In 1900, he founded a political party, popularly known as the Realists because its platform emphasized reason and facts over Romantic notions and national illusions. Although his party was small, Masaryk acquired a seat in parliament in 1907, following the introduction of universal male suffrage for elections to that body.

The Russian Revolution of 1905 inspired Masaryk to undertake his most extensive scholarly work, an analysis of the Russian intellectual tradition entitled *Russia and Europe,* which appeared in 1913. Masaryk left the country during World War I to work abroad for the creation of a postwar state of Czechs and Slovaks, and in 1918 was acclaimed "President-Liberator" of the new country he helped to found. He died in 1937, two years after resigning the presidency.

See also **Nationalism; Young Czechs and Old Czechs.**

BIBLIOGRAPHY

Capek, Karel, ed. *Talks with T. G. Masaryk,* translated and edited by Michael Henry Heim. New Haven, Conn., 1995.

Skilling, H. Gordon. *T. G. Masaryk: Against the Current, 1882–1914.* University Park, Pa., 1994.

Winters, Stanley B., Robert B. Pynsent, and Harry Hanak, eds. *T. G. Masaryk, 1850–1937.* 3 vols. London, 1989–1990.

Zeman, Zbyněk A. B. *The Masaryks: The Making of Czechoslovakia.* New York, 1976.

Claire E. Nolte

MASCULINITY. Scholarship on masculinity has moved away from the concerns that were central to second-wave feminist analysis of the history of patriarchy and the oppression of women. In the older perspective, scholars focused on the competition between males and females as the dynamic source of men's historic efforts to keep women confined to the domestic sphere as child-bearers and out of the public sphere monopolized by men. Economic and political analysis and the evolution of institutions and law have been the chief means scholars have used to study male gender dominance. Early-twenty-first-century work pays tribute to the older scholarship but emphasizes the power imbalances between men and considers the masculine oppression of women to be a by-product of those imbalances. In this perspective, masculinity is a protean quality that is constantly in crisis, requiring reconfiguration and stabilization. Hegemonic forms of masculinity invite assimilation or challenge from competing masculine "others," and these essentially cultural struggles are as much about the performance of gender as they are about political or economic status. The great irony of the history of masculinity is the fact that masculine ideals have not been constructed against women, but against features in other men that are thought to be feminine. That is why masculinity is an exceedingly precarious condition. One does not simply achieve manhood as a function of age; one must struggle to remain *not* feminine throughout the life course or forfeit the "patriarchal dividend" that comes with being a man.

MASCULINITY AND ECONOMIC INDEPENDENCE

Some historians such as Thomas Laqueur have argued that a "two-sex" model of gender developed in the medicine and science of the mid-eighteenth century in part to permit rational, courageous males to lay claim to the emergent civil and political rights envisioned by Enlightenment philosophers and to exclude women, who were judged to be uniquely suited for childbearing and domestic duties. But though women were legally excluded on "natural" grounds from political life in the French Revolution, so were men without the "capacity" to fulfill roles as full citizens: criminals, the insane, and men without residence or who paid no taxes. Likewise, in the Napoleonic Code all men had particular rights vis-à-vis their wives and children, with respect to marriage, divorce, and property, but statutory law and custom gave men of independent means decided advantages in citizenship rights and access to political power over illiterate, impoverished, or dependent men. Similar distinctions, particularly in electoral law, flourished everywhere in Europe until the twentieth century. These were not simple economic distinctions, but judgments about a man's ability to participate in public life as an independent actor who was free of obligations to other men, which was not true of many men in the semifeudal societies of central and eastern Europe in the nineteenth century, or men serving as apprentices in traditional crafts. Citizenship was decidedly connected to men in all those places where Napoleonic conquest carried French institutions and laws, and the emerging political public sphere was thoroughly male in character, but for much of the century public life was dominated by a masculine elite of economically and legally independent men.

The clear demarcation in industrializing Europe between public and domestic spheres had important implications for the masculinization of work. Beginning in the British Isles, the domestic system of textile production was gradually replaced by factory assembly lines. This development definitively separated home from work; however, following an era when women and children initially worked in the new factories alongside men, male labor unions and reforming politicians agitated for laws restricting the duration and time of their work and eventually the kind of work they could do. As factory organization was extended to heavy industry in Britain and elsewhere on the Continent, workspaces became masculine spaces and women's work could be found only in gender-segregated sweatshops. As industrial wages rose, it became a point of masculine pride for a man to support his wife and children alone and keep his wife at home like a gentleman was expected to do. The independence of a man selling his labor on the market was thus the working-class equivalent of the bourgeois property-owner, businessman, or professional who controlled his own economic destiny. Throughout the nineteenth century, most labor unions were all-male organizations, and however radical or socialist their politics, they were resolutely patriarchal in their views of the place of women in the workplace and on the priority of male authority at home. Women continued to work in significant numbers, but in low-paying jobs spurned by men or in domestic service.

MASCULINE DOMAINS

In the middle class and in the better off working-class families, women were effectively confined to the responsibilities of domestic management and the care of children. But even here they were obliged to undergo some degree of masculine management. Men often kept the account books, made executive decisions about the hiring and firing of domestic staff, and made key decisions on schooling and activities for children. The rhythms of the household were often masculine ones that followed the man's routines in work and leisure; male children were exposed early to their future duties in the father's line of work. The moral framework that governed life in the nuclear family of the industrial age owed much to a masculine ideology of sexual purity, not so much the chastity of the patriarch, though that was also assumed, but of his wife and future heirs. A genuine fear of venereal disease, complicated by widespread uncertainty about how such things were transmitted, a belief in the degenerative effects of masturbation, and a hard-headed concern about the financial hazards of illegitimate children and otherwise-marriageable daughters compromised by scandal led many men to engage in the active sexual surveillance of their households. They were aided in this by the proliferation of middle-class and skilled working-class purity crusaders of various kinds that were intent on stamping out pornography, lewd entertainments, prostitution, and strong drink in the name of keeping the family pure.

The Thinker. Bronze sculpture by Auguste Rodin, 1880–1881. Known for the Romantic expressiveness of his sculptures, Rodin here conveys a sense of masculine power as manifested in the intellectual creativity of the mind. BURRELL COLLECTION, GLASGOW, SCOTLAND/BRIDGEMAN ART LIBRARY/GLASGOW CITY COUNCIL (MUSEUMS)

Another all-masculine domain in nineteenth-century life was the private club. Beginning with Freemasonry in the eighteenth century, a variety of clubs modeled on the secret society grew rapidly throughout Europe. There were clubs affiliated with professional groups, with commercial specialties, and with academic or artistic interests. Many clubs did charitable works or engaged in civic activities, but many were simply private leisure organizations for men with particular class and occupational affiliations or recreational interests. Men's clubs typically organized themselves according to rules of admission and expulsion and self-governance that were ordinarily explicit about admitting only gentlemen. Political or religious discussions were sometimes forbidden, but in any case men were expected to govern themselves by a prevailing code of honorable comportment that discouraged talk about families, moral or business failings, or any discourse that might give rise to personal offense. When such instances did occur, clubs attempted to mediate them, and, failing that, to assure that the subsequent duel took place in private circumstances.

Duels were remarkably frequent in all-male organizations and meetings in the nineteenth century, particularly in France, Italy, Spain, and the German lands. Hundreds of duels each year were reported to the public in the press, and many more took place in private venues. The old aristocratic honor code that required a man to demonstrate his courage in personal combat to efface an insult struck deep roots in the soil of middle-class society. Middle-class men learned the rules of the point of honor, and, if they had the time and energy, took fencing lessons in the event they were offered a challenge they could not refuse. The masculine style of men who were eligible to duel was a friendly but discreet manner that respected the private lives of others but that radiated the confidence of one willing to defend his personal honor or that of his family or corporation. An unwillingness to give or accept challenges, or a display of treachery or cowardice on the field of honor, could effectively eliminate a man's ability to participate in public life. Honorable men, or those who aspired to honor, simply shunned him. Not many men died in these encounters, but an atmosphere of tense readiness and of caution in word and gesture permeated all-male societies in the nineteenth century, making these environments unwelcoming to men who did not know or care to learn the rules of the point of honor, and positively poisonous to women. The adoption by middle-class men of a code of behavior borrowed from the ancient nobility was not as surprising as it appears. It was a survival of old ways that flattered the social remnants of the Old Regime and a token of upward mobility for the ambitious.

MASCULINITY AND IMPERIALISM

The end of the period of warfare that marked Italian and German unification did not end national rivalries but pushed them into the arena of imperial competition. The process of exploring, subduing, and ostensibly civilizing native peoples was characterized by the newspapers and pitched to the general public as a task for courageous and resourceful men. The exploits of Henry Morton Stanley, David Livingstone, and Captain Jean-Baptiste Marchand placed an unusual emphasis on their courage and masculine qualities and framed the imperial quest as a contest of national virilities. A new generation of young men, apparently eager to avoid the domestic cocoons of their fathers, graduated from elite schools in the 1870s and 1880s in the mood for adventure and fame. In the colonial service of their respective nations, many found opportunities to dominate native peoples and enjoy a freebooting sexual liberty with exotic colonial women while doing good work in the national cause. In the course of this manly enterprise, colonial peoples came to be gendered feminine, and their domination justified by the "natural" gender order that prevailed in European political and domestic spheres. Thanks to the popularity of Darwinian explanations of social arrangements, the masculine superiority of European civilization and the rational precedence of European males in their own households and polities could all be explained in irrefutable evolutionary logic.

The apogee of this imperial style also marked the first signs of an unraveling that exposed many of its contradictions. First, psychiatrists and medical doctors identified a number of illnesses that appeared to be characteristic of late industrial civilization. Hysteria was a debilitating nervous condition shared by men and women alike; neurasthenia, characterized by emotional instability and morbid sensitivity, particularly afflicted upper-class urbanites; and there emerged a growing concern with male impotence, which was as much as anything a partial explanation for the rapidly falling European birth rate, and the fear, in France particularly, of national depopulation. As Sigmund Freud pointed out in his essay, "The Most Prevalent Form of Degradation in Erotic Life" (1912), a man's potency with his wife was in inverse relation to his (and society's) idealization of her. All these afflictions, whether real or imagined, were believed to be symptoms of degeneration, a kind of reverse evolution that seemed to account for the growth of any number of pathologies in European life: crime, alcoholism, venereal diseases, and the falling birth rates. The concept of a European man weakened, impotent, and emasculated by the anxieties of modern life seriously undermined the image of aggressive manhood of the previous generation of imperial heroism.

Second, what historians have begun calling the "crisis of masculinity" of the fin de siècle was exacerbated by the rise of feminist movements in all the major European countries. These movements produced a "new woman" who wanted education, a career of her own, and reforms in the legal and political disadvantages that women still experienced everywhere in Europe. As politicians dug in their heels to resist, dramatists, artists, and writers began to characterize women as willful, castrating vampires intent on bringing men down by a combination of seductive power and guile. The cultural "sex wars" of this era were unprecedented and were inflamed by the incessant battles in every educational and professional field to bar or limit women's access to domains previously monopolized by men. The enormous scandal that greeted the first performances of Henrik Ibsen's *A Doll's House* (1879) is testimony to the fact that the European public, and male critics in particular, found it inconceivable that a woman could leave her husband and children for what seemed to be trivial marital peccadillos.

Finally, European military elites were dismayed by some of the stumbling blocks imperial armies had experienced on the road to empire. Chief among these was the Boer War (1899–1902), but the rapid defeat of the Russian Navy by Japan in 1905 also added to concerns that the European expansion was beginning a slow retreat. For many contemporaries, scouting movements, sport, and a reconnection with nature offered the best hopes for a renewal of masculine vigor in modern societies. The reinvention of the modern Olympic Games under the aegis of Pierre de Coubertin in 1896 put the focus squarely on the bodies and skills of men and emphasized the national aspect of the competition. Every European nation underwent a nationalist revival in the alliance-building years prior to 1914. Military establishments received virtually everything they demanded in terms of new technologies, armaments, and increased manpower. A distinctly military style of masculinity became the hegemonic masculinity for this entire generation, despite the extraordinary growth in commerce, the arts, and science, where less aggressive masculine styles prevailed. The clearest testimony to the success of this essentially compensatory masculinity was the enthusiastic, if delusional, response in 1914 to the call to war. The socialist Second International, which had promised resistance to a European war, adapted easily to war chauvinism, and pacifists were unable to convince any of their contemporaries that restraint and negotiation were masculine virtues.

By 1914 biologists and medical men had established that masculinity was a natural feature of a man's body. The courage, aggressiveness, and stoic calm required of the fighting man had become a universal trait of males; the man who lacked any of these qualities fell short, not only of the gender ideal, but also of full physical and psychic health. It is not surprising that the shell-shock victims who appeared in the early stages of the war were described by most medical men as functionally unmanned, impotent, and ruined. In the course of the century, ideals of masculinity that reflected the varying standards of class and culture had been subsumed into a definition that was believed to apply to all men, but that was virtually impossible to fulfill.

See also **Dueling; Feminism; Gender; Homosexuality and Lesbianism; Sexuality.**

BIBLIOGRAPHY

Braudy, Leo. *From Chivalry to Terrorism: War and the Changing Nature of Masculinity.* New York, 2003.

Connell, R. W. *Masculinities.* Berkeley, Calif., 1995.

Grogan, Susan. *French Socialism and Sexual Difference: Women and the New Society, 1803–1844.* London, 1992.

Hunt, Lynn. *The Family Romance of the French Revolution.* Berkeley, Calif., 1992.

Mangan, J. A. *The Games Ethic and Imperialism: Aspects of the Diffusion of an Ideal.* Harmondsworth, U.K., 1986.

Mosse, George L. *The Image of Man: The Creation of Modern Masculinity.* New York, 1996.

Nye, Robert A. *Masculinity and Male Codes of Honor in Modern France.* Oxford, 1993.

Roper, Martin, and John Tosh, eds. *Manful Assertions: Masculinities in Britain since 1800.* London, 1991.

Stoler, Ann Laura, and Frederick Cooper, eds. *Tensions of Empire: Colonial Cultures in a Bourgeois World.* Berkeley, Calif., 1997.

Robert A. Nye

MATISSE, HENRI (1869–1954), French painter.

Henri-Émile-Benoît Matisse was born in Le Cateau-Cambrésis, a village in Picardy, into a petit bourgeois family of the Aisne département in northern France. After law studies, while working as a legal clerk in Saint-Quentin, he fell ill. It was during his convalescence, at the age of twenty-one, that he took up drawing and painting. In 1892 he settled in Paris, where he enrolled at the Académie Julian and joined the atelier of Gabriel Ferrier (1847–1914). After attending the École Supérieure des Arts Décoratifs, he decided to enter the École des Beaux-Arts. There he studied under Gustave Moreau (1826–1898), who told him, prophetically, that he was destined to "simplify painting." Two paintings stand out from Matisse's years of training: *Nature morte aux livres* (1890; Still life with books) was inspired by Jean-Baptiste-Siméon Chardin (1699–1779); *La desserte* (1897), done in lighter colors, would undergo several modifications in subsequent years. The influences of Gustave Moreau and Paul Cézanne (1839–1906) were unmistakable in Matisse's work up to 1903; these two predecessors gave him the wherewithal to think in and through color.

Gustave Moreau died in 1898; to aid his family, Matisse collaborated with Albert Marquet (1875–1947) on the decoration of the Grand Palais for the upcoming Universal Exposition. Matisse's work began attracting attention from 1901; he exhibited at the Salon des Indépendants and at the Salon d'Automne, and mounted a one-man show at the Ambroise Vollard gallery. In 1904 the directors of the Beaux-Arts acquired his copy of *Balthazar Castiglione,* a painting by Raphael (1483–1520). In the same year, during a summer stay with Paul Signac (1863–1935), Matisse offered his own interpretation of divisionism in the shape of his painting *Luxe, calme, et volupté.* The following summer he spent with André Derain (1880–1954) in the small Mediterranean town of Collioure in French Catalonia, abandoning the pointillism of Signac and Georges Seurat (1859–1891) under the influences first of Paul Gauguin (1848–1903) and then of Vincent van Gogh (1853–1890). He painted *La femme au chapeau* (1905; Woman with a hat), *Le portrait de Derain* (1905; Portrait of Derain), and *La fenêtre ouverte à Collioure* (1905 The open window, Collioure)—all major works that were to cause an uproar at the Salon d'Automne in Paris and propel Matisse to leadership of the fauvist movement. Another fauve canvas of his, *La joie de vivre* (1905–1906), was bought by Leo Stein.

In 1906 and 1907 Matisse traveled a good deal, notably in Algeria and Italy, but little sign of this is to be discerned in his work of the time, save for the mild exoticism of the palm trees in the background of *Nu bleu (Souvenir de Briska)* (Blue nude [Memory of Briska]), painted in 1906. This picture marked an important stage in the artist's development, for it corresponds to the moment when Matisse turned to simplified forms and to the systematic use of flat areas of paint, a shift clearly discernible, too, in the evolution from *Luxe I* to *Luxe II* (1907–1908). Both paintings have as their subject three women bathers against a marine background, and they encapsulate Matisse's stylistic development at that time. The theme of the nude recurred throughout the artist's work, ending only in 1952. It was embodied in the sculpted series of *Dos* (back views), extending from 1908 to 1931, and in the *Blue Nudes* created by means of gouache on paper cut-outs. The various versions of *Nu de dos* (*Dos I, Dos II, . . .*) bore witness to Matisse's continuing research, which also had an impact on his painting, as discernible notably in *La musique* (1910) and *La danse* (1909–1910). These two canvases were commissioned by the Russian collector Sergei Shchukin, who had just bought another major painting by Matisse, *La desserte rouge/Harmony in Red* (1909).

From 1907 to 1909 Matisse ran an art academy, but his pedagogical activity was short-lived. All the same, it bore witness to his desire to disseminate his theory of color as sensation. In December 1908, he published "Notes of a Painter" in *La grande revue,* a text in which he developed his notion of an art of balance. In the still lifes that he painted in Tangier in 1913, Matisse worked with space, complicating it, and played with and around motifs, incorporating the decorative aspect of fabric into his disposition of planes. In 1913, too, Matisse took part in the Armory Show in New York and Chicago, showing a sculpture, three drawings, and thirteen canvases, including *Blue Nude (Memory of Briska),* which thoroughly outraged the critics.

After World War I, Matisse's work came under the sway of a powerful Oriental exoticism that gave rise to a series of paintings of odalisques—*L'odalisque au fauteuil turc* (1928; Odalisque on a Turkish sofa), for example—and to works like

La Danse. Painting by Henri Matisse, 1909. AP/Wide World Photos

Les Marocainsi (1916; The Moroccans). These pictures, distinctly less innovative in their composition, won plaudits for Matisse from the very critics who had earlier disparaged him.

Matisse's first gouache paper cut-outs (paper painted with gouache, which was then cut and glued onto a new canvas) were produced in 1927 for the magazine *Verve*. This was an approach that enabled him to sculpt in and through color, using scissors; in this way he set about redefining the issues associated with line and volume. Eventually the new technique generated such major works as *Deux danseurs* (1937–1938; The two dancers), *La piscine* (1952; The swimming pool), where the blue gouache is applied to human and animal forms, or the album *Jazz,* published in 1947. Also in 1947, Matisse was named a commander of the Legion of Honor. From 1948 to 1951, he devoted himself to the decoration of Saint Mary's Chapel of the Rosary in Vence, contributing to architectural decisions as well as designing stained-glass windows and frescoes.

Matisse's artistic career was not confined to painting and sculpture. He was also an engraver (illustrating works of Charles Baudelaire, James Joyce, Stéphane Mallarmé, and Henri de Montherlant), a tapestry maker, and a set designer for the ballets *Song of the Nightingale* (1920) and *The Red and the Black* (1939). Two years before his death, Matisse was present at the inauguration of the museum that bears his name in his home town of Le Cateau-Cambrésis.

See also **Fauvism; Painting.**

BIBLIOGRAPHY

Benjamin, Roger. *Matisse's "Notes of a Painter": Criticism, Theory, and Context, 1891–1908.* Ann Arbor, Mich., 1987.

Bock-Weiss, Catherine C. *Henri Matisse: A Guide to Research.* New York and London, 1996.

Clement, Russell T. *Henri Matisse: A Bio-Bibliography.* London, 1993.

Elsen, Albert E. *The Sculpture of Henri Matisse.* New York, 1972.

Fourcade, Dominique. *Henri Matisse, Ecrits et propos sur l'art.* Paris, 1972.

Golding, John. *Matisse and Cubism.* Glasgow, 1978.

Greenberg, Clement. *Henri Matisse.* New York, 1953.

Herrera, Hayden. *Matisse: A Portrait.* London, 1993.

Schneider, Pierre. *Matisse.* Paris, 1984.

Spurling, Hilary. *The Unknown Matisse: A Life of Henri Matisse: The Early Years, 1869–1908.* New York, 1998.

CYRIL THOMAS

MAURRAS, CHARLES (1868–1952),

militant nationalist, monarchist, and self-styled representative of "French intelligence."

Charles Maurras became one of the most influential figures on the French political and intellectual scene in the first half of the twentieth century. His name first came to public attention during the Dreyfus affair, when he penned a highly provocative tract that defended the forging of incriminating evidence against Jewish army officer Alfred Dreyfus as a heroic act in the service of the French nation. Not long afterward, Maurras joined the ideologically inchoate and fledgling Action Française and, by the eve of World War I, he had not only provided the movement with a doctrinal base but had helped establish it as the cutting-edge force of a resurgent nationalist right. Maurras's political doctrine was eclectic, mixing older strains of counterrevolutionary thought, including monarchism, with the violent activism and anti-Semitism of fin-de-siècle nationalism. The latter was the most visible side of the Action Française before 1914, when its gang of young street-brawlers, the Camelots du Roi, defaced statues, assaulted republican dignitaries, and disrupted university classes.

Yet despite the notoriety created by its public theater, the Action Française under Maurras's leadership was an essentially pedagogical enterprise. The main conduit for the Maurrassian message was the movement's daily newspaper, *L'Action française*, launched in 1908. Here Maurras and his fellow editorialists expanded the campaign against Dreyfus into a broad-front attack against the "Dreyfusard" Republic. From his front-page editorial perch, Maurras managed to infuse new energy into the nationalist camp in the aftermath of the victory of the Dreyfusards and helped set the stage for the nationalist revival on the eve of World War I.

This was achieved in no small part because Maurras presented an overarching historical vision, one that separated his nationalist politics from the more mundane forms of nationalism circulating in fin-de-siècle France. The point of departure was his obsession with decadence. At one level, he viewed the decline of France—evident in its defeat at the hands of Prussia as well as its internal division and loss of purpose—as the result of larger historical forces. Most immediately, decadence could be traced to the twin evils of Romanticism and revolution: the first, which rejected classical notions of harmony, balance, and reason, resulted in the aesthetic vagaries of modernist art; the second, which renounced the sound political principles of order, authority, and hierarchy, produced a republican regime that neglected the national interest. But decadence, for Maurras, had even deeper historical sources in the individualist revolt of the Reformation and, more distantly, in the "Oriental spirit"—acting in the name of unchecked and chaotic passions. Civilization's history, for Maurras, was essentially the record of the long struggle waged against the Oriental spirit, a struggle in which France had assumed the historic burden of carrying forward the heritage of the classical world.

According to Maurras, although decadence had its origin in these abstract historical forces, it was exacerbated by the machinations of concrete "enemies." Clearly Germany stood as France's most obvious enemy. But no less dangerous, for Maurras, was a host of internal enemies—Protestants, foreigners, freemasons, and especially Jews. In order to defeat these internal enemies, France's elites needed to be mobilized against the institutions that provided them with a safe harbor for their activities—most notably, democracy. Not only had the practice of democracy fatally weakened France and given shelter to its enemies, but its core principle—egalitarianism—was antithetical to civilization, which, by its very nature, demands recognition of inequality and the construction of necessary hierarchies. The imprint of this species of cultural politics on generations of nationalist intellectuals in France was palpable, largely justifying the claim that Maurras provided an overarching worldview for the French right akin to that which Karl Marx (1818–1883) had given the French left.

Maurras's support of the wartime "sacred union," combined with the increased popularity of his anti-Germanism and intransigent nationalism, made him a political force to be reckoned with in the immediate period following World War I when his movement reached its apogee. However, when Maurras and the Action Française were condemned by the Vatican in 1926, thus losing the support of many Catholics, the movement went into a period of decline. This decline, which continued through the 1930s, was temporarily reversed with the arrival of the reactionary Vichy regime under Philippe Pétain (1856–1951) in 1940. The revival was short-lived, however, and Maurras, who supported Pétain to the end, shared in the discredit that increasingly haunted the Vichy regime after 1942. Arrested in late 1944, tried for "intelligence with the enemy" in January 1945, Maurras was condemned to life imprisonment and "national degradation."

See also **Action Française; Anti-Semitism; Dreyfus Affair.**

BIBLIOGRAPHY

Primary Sources

Maurras, Charles. *Mes Idées politiques.* Paris, 1937.

Secondary Sources

Carroll, David. *French Literary Fascism: Nationalism, Anti-Semitism, and the Ideology of Culture.* Princeton, N.J., 1995.

Weber, Eugen Joseph. *Action Française: Royalism and Reaction in Twentieth-Century France.* Stanford, Calif., 1962.

PAUL MAZGAJ

MAXWELL, JAMES CLERK (1831–1879), Scottish physicist and natural philosopher.

The natural philosophy of James Clerk Maxwell includes both his physics and his inseparable broader philosophical views on science and the world and reflects a historical transition in Great Britain from the culture of Scottish Enlightenment (he was born in Edinburgh) and the gentlemanly generalism of his family to the combined culture of the Industrial Revolution, Cambridge physics, German philosophy, empire, and the Victorian era. Maxwell's natural philosophy also reflects the rich intersection of a number of fields of inquiry that have since become distinct: mathematics, experimental physics, logic, philosophy of language, rhetoric, cognitive psychology, aesthetics, natural and personal theology, engineering, political economy, and muscle and optical physiology. His contributions to physics span the areas of color theory and optics, elastic solids, geometry, mechanics, physical astronomy, molecular physics, and electromagnetism. They are characterized by a combination of abstract mathematical sophistication, methodological and linguistic awareness and rigor (in the form of the methods of scientific analogy, metaphor, and illustration), theoretical unification and cross-fertilization, and the engagement of concrete imagination in the service of understanding in the form of geometrical and mechanical models and analogies.

Maxwell attended Edinburgh Academy with future fellow researches Peter G. Tait and Fleeming Jenkin. He became a skilled draftsman, poet, and amateur scientific experimenter. In 1847 he entered the University of Edinburgh, where he studied literature and natural philosophy for three years, became the protégé of natural philosopher James Forbes, and studied philosophy with William Hamilton. With recommendations from Forbes, Blackburn, and William Thomson (his cousin's husband), he moved to Cambridge in 1850, studying, like Thomson and Stokes before him, with a private tutor (the physical geologist William Hopkins), as well as under the supervision of the master of Trinity College, the scientist, philosopher, and educator William Whewell. In 1856 he took a post at Marischal College, in Aberdeen, where he married the principal's daughter, Katherine Dewar. In 1860 he moved to London to take a position at King's College London, and in 1861 he became a fellow of the Royal Society. He also joined the efforts to establish new electrical units, which were crucial to the new telegraphic cable networks that sustained the British Empire. In 1865 he retired to Glenlair and he remained there until 1871, when he was appointed professor of experimental physics at Cambridge and designer and director of the Cavendish Laboratory. In 1873 he became the physics editor of the ninth edition of the *Encyclopaedia Britannica.*

In the area of color theory, Maxwell established a coordinate system and an algebraic equation in terms of quantities for three primitive colors: red, green, and blue. He also designed a spinning color disk to study the mixture of colors and a color box to compare different colored lights, and he elaborated a theory of optical instruments. It is against this background that he developed his interest in the optical properties of elastic systems under mechanical stress. The combination of mechanics and optics reappeared in his best known contribution to science, his theory of electromagnetism. Maxwell borrowed Michael Faraday's experimental results about the relation between electricity and magnetism and the rotational nature of magnetism shown by its effect on light and his notion that electric and magnetic forces act contiguously and along curved lines of force between polar opposite states. In order to capture mathematically the physics of contiguous action, which is opposed to the Newtonian model of action at a distance, Maxwell also borrowed the differential calculus that William Thomson, first baron Kelvin, applied to analogies between heat flow and the mechanics of continuous systems on the one hand and electric and magnetic action on the other. He thus formulated a unified mathematical theory of electromagnetism based on the notion of fields and of a mechanical ether that pervades the universe and can store and communicate energy. A famous paper from 1861 presents a molecular model of the electromagnetic ether with rotating vortices in rolling contact. To incorporate the connotation of an imaginary mechanical model illustrating electromagnetic phenomena and quantities, Maxwell introduced scientific metaphors such as "electric tension." The theory predicted the existence of electromagnetic waves and the value of their velocity of propagation, which was very close to the adopted value of the velocity of light. On this basis Maxwell asserted the electromagnetic nature of light and the reduction of optics to electromagnetism. His ideas appeared in the survey *Treatise on Electricity and Magnetism* (1873).

Maxwell's application of mechanics, or dynamics (with force and energy) in the form of molecular physics, extended to macroscopic astronomy and microscopic molecules. He explained the stability of Saturn's rings in terms of the velocity of an indefinite number of small independent particles orbiting the planet at different distances. This model strengthened his interest in statistical models of macroscopic, apparently non-mechanical properties such as temperature, pressure, and viscosity, and led him to his dynamic theory of gases. He explained the viscosity of gases as the diffusion of momentum between layers of spherical elastic particles in collision, independent of their density. His successful predictions and experiments supported belief in the existence of molecules of matter and helped establish some of their properties. They also cemented the use of a statistical method, describing only the group properties of populations of identical molecules. By contrast, the historical method describes the properties and evolution of individuals. Maxwell's "demon" is a thought experiment intended to show that the possibility of reversing the flow of heat from hot to cold at the molecular level establishes the uncertain and incomplete nature of statistical knowledge, including that of the irreversibility of macroscopic processes described by the second law of thermodynamics. Maxwell's contributions to physics, then, represent the grand culmination of the mechanical view of the world on the brink of its collapse in the early twentieth century.

See also **Physics.**

BIBLIOGRAPHY

Primary Sources

Maxwell, James Clerk. *Treatise on Electricity and Magnetism.* Oxford, U.K., 1873.

———. *The Scientific Papers of James Clerk Maxwell.* 2 vols. Edited by W. D. Niven. Cambridge, U.K., 1890.

Secondary Sources

Campbell, Louis, and William Garnett. *The Life of James Clerk Maxwell.* 1882. New York, 1969.

Cat, Jordi. "On Understanding: Maxwell on the Methods of Illustration and Scientific Metaphors." *Studies in History and Philosophy of Modern Physics* 32B, no. 3 (2001): 395–442.

Goldman, Martin. *The Demon in the Aether: The Life of James Clerk Maxwell.* Edinburgh, 1983.

Harman, P. M. *The Natural Philosophy of James Clerk Maxwell.* Cambridge, U.K., 1995.

Siegel, Daniel M. *Innovation in Maxwell's Electromagnetic Theory: Molecular Vortices, Displacment Current, and Light.* Cambridge, U.K., 1991.

Jordi Cat

MAZZINI, GIUSEPPE

MAZZINI, GIUSEPPE (1805–1872), the most inspirational figure of the Italian Risorgimento.

Giuseppe Mazzini was born in Genoa on 22 June 1805 to a family of the upper middle class, the third of four children and the only male. His father was a successful medical doctor and university professor, his mother a well-educated woman who shared her son's interests and convictions. Both parents were religious, but it was the Jansenist inclinations of the mother that had the greatest impact on the son. Jansenists were Catholics who took their religion in pure form, with little ritual and much moral commitment. So did the mother and the son. After experiencing a personal crisis in his youth, the son insisted that there could be no true commitment to worldly causes without a religious foundation. Precociously intelligent and a quick learner, the young Mazzini was educated at home by private tutors, entered the University of Genoa at age fourteen, and graduated with a law degree in 1827. But the law was not his calling. Like many of his generation, he was drawn to the literature of Romanticism, which satisfied the need for passionate expression.

Love of country became the passion of Mazzini's life after an encounter with the destitute victims of the failed revolution of 1821 begging in the streets of Genoa on their way into exile. It was on that occasion, he claimed, that he first perceived that one could, and that therefore one should, fight for the ideals of *patria* and *libertà*. The ideals of homeland and liberty were the two anchors of his creed. God was at the root of the creed, but Mazzini's attention was on the affairs of this world and his theology was nonconformist. His experience of a warm and supportive family life may have had something to do with the notion that love is the most sublime human passion, for he attributed to the capacity for love the ability of individuals to transcend their egoism and reach out in broadening circles of empathy toward the whole human race. Attachment to family and nation were part of that continuum. God was the driving force of history. Mazzini's motto "God and the People" summed up his view that human agency followed a divine script. The name of that script was Progress.

A people divided and under foreign control had a duty to become free and united so that they could fulfill the earthly mission that God assigned to them for the benefit of humanity. A people deprived of their freedom had no choice but to revolt. Mazzini was not loath to accept the legitimacy of violence when the means of peaceful change were denied. Monarchy was the target of his revolutionary violence. Monarchies in any shape or form were corrupt because they existed to protect dynastic interests rather than the public good. Mazzinianism thus revolved around the political postulates of republicanism, democracy, national independence, and unity.

Deeming it immoral not to act on one's convictions, Mazzini coined the motto "Thought and Action" to emphasize that principled action was a duty. The concept of duty loomed large in Mazzini's thinking, and often trumped the concept of individual rights. The moral imperative to act on his convictions made him a leader of student protests and a member of the secret Carboneria society, which he joined the same year that he graduated from university. He was a zealous Carbonaro, recruiting near and far and making a nuisance of himself with less zealous fellow conspirators. He could not abide the hocus-pocus of secret rituals and did not share the Carbonari's faith that they could work with constitutional monarchs. Absolute or constitutional, all monarchs were unacceptable to Mazzini. Someone from inside the secret society set him up. Arrested, imprisoned, and tried on charges of sedition, he was given the choice between confinement at home and expatriation.

Mazzini chose to go abroad and left for France in January 1831 to begin life as a political exile. He hoped that the July Revolution that had succeeded in France would also succeed in Italy. When that did not happen, he founded his own organization to take up where the secret societies had left off.

Giuseppe Mazzini. Undated portrait. SCALA/ART RESOURCE, NY

Young Italy openly proclaimed its republicanism, commitment to revolution, democracy, and social justice. Harassed by the French police, Mazzini moved to Geneva in July 1833, but nothing went as planned. In February 1834 incursions into the region of Savoy by armed bands of exiles failed to ignite the popular revolts that Mazzini counted on to start the revolution. Young Italy never recovered from these setbacks. Undeterred, Mazzini launched Young Europe in April 1834 with a few other Italian, German, and Polish exiles to unify the revolutionary forces of Europe. Young Europe also foundered, but the notion of forming a unified revolutionary front lived on.

Forced to leave Switzerland, Mazzini settled in London in January 1837. In the English capital he wrote for British publications, made friends with Thomas Carlyle (1795–1881) and John Stuart Mill (1806–1873), opened a school for Italian workers, revived Young Italy, and gained recognition as the voice of the Italian national movement. Living in a cosmopolitan city broadened Mazzini's vision. He became more aware of the problems of industrial society, showed renewed interest in workers, and made room for them in Young Italy. He insisted that workers be part of the national movement and exhorted middle-class Italians to help their less fortunate brothers for the sake of national solidarity. To workers he held out the prospect of full political participation in republican Italy. The right to vote would guarantee workers their rights.

By the time the revolutions of 1848 broke out, Mazzini had to contend with competitors. Charles Albert (r. 1831–1849) was one. The administrative reforms of this enigmatic monarch and his covert expressions of support for Italian independence appealed to liberals. Liberal Catholics and their Neo-Guelph movement were invigorated by the election of the reputedly liberal Pope Pius IX (r. 1846–1878) in 1846. According to the leader of the Neo-Guelphs, Vincenzo Gioberti (1801–1852), the pope was the natural leader of the movement for Italian independence, a view that Mazzini found abhorrent. Mazzini returned to Italy in April 1848 after an absence of seventeen years to find popular acclaim and opposition. Even republicans were no longer united behind him. In Milan he clashed with Carlo Cattaneo (1801–1869), a republican federalist who did not share Mazzini's enthusiasm for centralized government, and with Giuseppe Ferrari (1811–1876), a federalist and a socialist.

Mazzini found a friendlier reception in Rome. The short-lived Roman Republic of 1849 gave Mazzini the opportunity to put his ideas to the test. He worshipped the name of Rome and believed that democratic government was destined to spread from Rome to the rest of Europe. He was principally responsible for the experiment in republican government as the leading figure of a governing triumvirate. He set out to show the world that republicans could live up to their ideals and govern responsibly. The republic adopted universal suffrage, organized popular clubs to involve ordinary people in public affairs, staged rallies and ceremonies, provided relief for the unemployed, curtailed clerical privileges, declared an end to the pope's temporal rule, and maintained public order—all to no avail. A coalition of powers led by France evicted the insurgents and restored Rome to the pope.

Mazzini continued to fight monarchy and rely on popular revolution when others lost faith in his ways. From London he plotted insurgencies in Italy that failed and cost his dwindling followers dearly. Abandoned by the middle classes that turned increasingly toward the charismatic Giuseppe Garibaldi (1807–1882) and the adroit Count Cavour (Camillo Benso, 1810–1861), Mazzini pinned his hopes on workers. His book *The Duties of Man* (1860) exhorted workers to be mindful of their rights and duties, reject class warfare, and remain loyal to the ideal of a republican Italy. Many listened, and not only in Italy, but his condemnation of the Paris Commune and socialism alienated militant radicals, who rejected him. A sense of isolation and failure marked the last years of his life. He died in Pisa under an assumed name, for he was still officially banned from the country. His acceptance as a founder of the nation came some thirty years after his death, when the passage of time defused the passions that made him controversial.

See also **Carbonari; Cavour, Count (Camillo Benso); Garibaldi, Giuseppe; Italy; Pius IX.**

BIBLIOGRAPHY

Primary Sources

Mazzini, Giuseppe. *Selected Writings.* Edited by N. Gangulee. London, 1945.

———. *Life and Writings of Joseph Mazzini.* 6 vols. London, 1864–1870.

Secondary Sources

Mack Smith, Denis. *Mazzini.* New Haven, Conn., 1994.

Sarti, Roland. *Mazzini: A Life for the Religion of Politics.* Westport, Conn., 1997.

ROLAND SARTI

MEDITERRANEAN. The Mediterranean Sea has held huge economic importance for millennia. This virtually landlocked sea, bordered by three continents, has been a vital bridge for economic and cultural commerce over centuries. In the ancient period it gave rise to the world's first great civilizations, most notably the Phoenicians and the Minoans. In later periods it fostered major global developments such as the rise and dissemination of Christianity and Islam. While following the Middle Ages the Mediterranean went into decline, largely as the result of the so-called Age of Discovery and Europe's new orientation toward the Americas, it remained critical to the imperial regimes of the Venetians, Ottomans, and Habsburgs. In the early twenty-first century, following the initiation in the 1990s of the Barcelona Process, it has regained importance as a critical cultural and economic intersection between Europe, Africa, and Asia.

States along the Mediterranean's shores in the early twenty-first century include Spain, France, Monaco, Italy, Slovenia, Croatia, Bosnia, Serbia and Montenegro, Albania, Greece, Turkey, Syria, Israel, Palestine, Egypt, Libya, Tunisia, Algeria, and Morocco. Two further states—Cyprus and Malta—are islands within it. Most of these polities were shaped by the nineteenth-century transition from Ottoman regional dominance to the establishment of separate nation states in the area. Traditionally, the Mediterranean Sea has had a unifying, rather than a dividing effect, and has served far more as a conduit for communication and cultural diffusion than as a boundary between different geographic regions. This unity notwithstanding, the region has over the course of millennia been a site of intense international and regional competition and warfare. The events of the "long nineteenth century" are a case in point.

At the time of the French Revolution the Mediterranean was divided up largely between the Ottoman Empire, the Russian Empire, and the Venetian Republic; by the end of World War II none of these empires existed. The most dramatic changes of fortune during the period were dealt to the Ottomans and to the Venetian Republic; struggles within the Mediterranean were the direct cause of the latter's decline, and a key component of the Ottoman Empire's ultimate demise.

During the French Revolutionary period and on into the nineteenth century, the Russians, French, and British were the primary contenders for control in the region. Following the Treaty of Kuchuk Kainardji (1774), the Russians were granted large latitude in Mediterranean seagoing trade within Ottoman waters and gained control of the Dardanelles, a narrow strait that links the sea in the northeast to the Black Sea. The treaty also gave Russia a protectorate of sorts over Greek Orthodox subjects of the Ottoman Empire and as such contributed greatly to the growth of Greek dominance in Mediterranean trade.

The Ionian Islands, off the northwest coast of today's Greece, were the site of conflict between Venice, France, and Britain. Corfu, the largest of the island chain, was under Venetian control until Napoleon wrested it from Venice, effectively bringing about the end of the Venetian overseas empire. Some years later the islands came under a British protectorate, before being joined with Greece in 1864. The rapid growth of Napoleonic power in Europe made the Mediterranean a strategically vital site in the efforts of British, Habsburg, and Russian powers to stem the growth of France. The Congress of Vienna (1814–1815), the basis for modern-day concepts of the balance of power, laid a plan for maintaining equilibrium between the Great Powers; equitable division of the Mediterranean was one of its core components. Over the course of the century, Britain and France took control of most of formerly Ottoman North Africa, most notably with France taking Algeria in 1830 and Great Britain taking Egypt in 1882.

Internal conflicts as well as international ones also led to significant changes in the region. Under Mehmet Ali (1769–1849), Egypt was modernized over the course of the first half of the nineteenth century, and the port city of Alexandria emerged as the Mediterranean city par excellence. In 1848 revolutions within the Habsburg Empire, France, and particularly the Italian States further destabilized the region.

With the exponential growth of trade and industry in the wake of the Industrial Revolution, the nineteenth century saw the rise of a number of important port cities, known for their markedly high levels of liberal cosmopolitanism, cultural diversity, and multilinguality. Such cities as Izmir on the Asia Minor coast, Alexandria in Egypt, Salonika in Greek Macedonia, Trieste on the Adriatic in northeastern Italy, and Marseilles and Toulon on the French coast are prime examples. At the same time, vast engineering projects reclaimed some of the Mediterranean's earlier centrality to global seagoing trade. The Suez Canal, which opened in 1869, linked the Mediterranean to the Red Sea, and thus to the Arabian Sea, while the Corinth Canal (1893) linked the Aegean and Ionian Seas within the Mediterranean. With this renewed economic importance, struggle for control of the region intensified further.

See also **Africa; France; Italy; Ottoman Empire.**

BIBLIOGRAPHY

Abulafia, Daniel, ed. *The Mediterranean in History.* London, 2003.

Bradford, Ernle Dusgate Selby. *Mediterranean: Portrait of a Sea.* London, 1971.

Braudel, Fernand. *The Mediterranean and the Mediterranean World in the Age of Philip II.* Vol. 2. Translated from the French by Siân Reynolds. Berkeley, Calif., 1995.

Kurth, James, and James Petras, eds. *Mediterranean Paradoxes: Politics and Social Structure in Southern Europe.* Providence, R.I., 1993.

Swain, James E. *The Struggle for the Control of the Mediterranean Prior to 1848: A Study in Anglo-French Relations.* Boston, 1933.

K. FLEMING

MÉLIÈS, GEORGES (1861–1938), French filmmaker.

Georges Méliès made approximately 520 films between May 1896 and 1912. He was the first to envision film as a medium for fiction, for fantasy, and for grand spectacle: he viewed the cinema as art as opposed to science. In further contrast to the brothers Auguste and Louis Lumière, he incorporated all forms of popular entertainment in his oeuvre, including the music-hall, the magic theater, fairground attractions, and the magic lantern. Méliès's films in fact deploy the mode of presentation typical of the music hall, circus, and fairground—the attraction—theorized by Sergei Eisenstein in 1923 and proposed by André Gaudreault and Tom Gunning as a fundamental principle of early cinema.

Méliès was trained as a visual artist before pursuing a career as a prestidigitator (juggler) in the magic theater. Both of these talents would serve him admirably when he became a filmmaker in 1896. The first talent was employed in the painting of the decor for his films, in costume design, and in making the preparatory sketches for the characters and mise-en-scène. The second talent is equally visible in his films. Méliès took over Robert Houdin's magic theater in 1888. As its director, he not only created perceptual illusions but also incorporated them in narratives, diabolical apparitions, or scenes of burlesque comedy, often based on the character of a mad scientist or hypnotist. Méliès's continuing preoccupation with hypnosis, illusion, and hallucination in film—the medium that would prove most apt to reproduce them—is part of the cultural context of late-nineteenth-century experimentation with these phenomena in psychology.

The importance of Georges Méliès's work as a magician for his later cinematic production has been studied by many scholars, most fully by Jacques Malthête. The theatrical illusions of sudden appearances, disappearances, and decapitations were recreated by purely cinematic means through techniques that Méliès called trick shots or *trucs*: stop-action filming enabled him to create the trick of substitution with its astonishing transformations of people into objects or animals, perfectly accomplished with the aid of montage: cutting and gluing frames. He then pioneered speeded-up filming, and invented the dissolve and superimpressions by means of double exposure and multiple exposures (seven Georges Mélièses perform simultaneously in the 1900 *L'homme-orchestre*). In short, Méliès (with the exception of stop-action) is the inventor of special effects in the cinema.

Méliès was not only author, director, designer, and painter and constructor of his own sets and props, but he also acted in nearly all of his films. This aesthetic of total involvement and control was elevated to a principle for making films in his important text "Les vues cinématographiques," published in 1907 in *L'Annuaire general and international de la photographie*. As actor, he most often played the role of Mephistopheles, a zany scientist, or a magician: in each film he exhibits an unbelievable vitality of acrobatic movement and gesticulatory exuberance. For Méliès, the art of film was distinct from that of the theater: in cinema, "the word is nothing, gesture everything." Constant movement of the actors compensates for an immobile camera, an aesthetic choice Méliès made and held to throughout his career. The most well-known of his films is the 1902 *Le Voyage dans la lune* (Voyage to the Moon); it contains many traits that characterize the filmmaker's style, including the panoply of special effects, the whirlwind of movement, scores of lovely music-hall dancers in tights, and a fairy-tale decor for the Selenite King's palace worthy of a spectacular *Féerie* at the Châtelet Theatre (the *Féerie* employed complex stage machinery and was constituted of several tableaux representing a fairy-tale realm of the marvelous involving scores of extras). Many of the films were hand-colored, and those that have been found again are extraordinarily beautiful (for example, *Le Chaudron infernal*, 1903; The diabolical cauldron). The imaginary universe of the marvelous or of the irrational created by Méliès—visions that earned him the admiration of the surrealists—bear the indelible stamp of his personality and style. Although he is associated with trick films and the genres of comedy, the fantastic, and the fantasy of the *Féerie* (represented in 1903 by, among others, *Bob Kick, Le Mélomane, Le Monstre* [The monster], and *Le royaume des Fées* [The fairy realm]), his work encompassed all of the genres present in early cinema, including dramatic reconstitutions of historical figures such as that of *Jeanne d'Arc* (1900; Joan of Arc), and of current events such as the Dreyfus trial (1899; *L'Affaire Dreyfus*).

In 1897 Méliès built a film studio on the family's property in Montreuil, enabling him to shoot indoors and to perfectly manipulate lighting. He became the first filmmaker to shoot with electric light, also in 1897, but this time in his Passage de l'Opéra laboratory. The popularity of his films resulted in constant plagiarism of them; he thus began using a star as trademark in 1896, and the name Star-Film in 1901. His production surpassed the giants Pathé and Gaumont until around 1906; Georges Méliès was responsible for making the French film industry first worldwide. Late-twentieth- and early-twenty-first-century scholarship on Méliès includes the study of scenarios and descriptive texts in the Star-Film catalog, accompaniment to the films by a live narrator, parallels with cubism, futurism, and avant-garde cinema, and the forms and signification of gesture in Méliès.

Méliès's films enjoyed great popularity until around 1909. Discouraged and in debt, he destroyed the negatives of his films in 1923. Georges Méliès was then only able to survive thanks to his second wife's tiny toy and candy shop in the Gare Montparnasse. In 1929 several old reels of film were found, and eight of these were screened that year at the Gala Méliès, which enabled a new generation to discover the filmmaker. It is largely thanks to his granddaughter, Madeleine Malthête-Méliès, that so many of his films have been recovered. Film archives around the world have since added substantially to their number. In a trick of fate, the filmmaker, who could well be called the inventor of cinema as aesthetic and fictional spectacle, died on the same day as another visionary French genius, the European inventor of animated film animation, Émile Cohl.

See also **Cinema; Lumière, Auguste and Louis.**

BIBLIOGRAPHY

Cherchi-Usai, Paolo, ed. *A Trip to the Movies: Georges Méliès, Filmmaker and Magician (1861–1938)*. Rochester, N.Y., 1991.

Ezra, Elizabeth. *Georges Méliès*. Manchester, U.K., 2000.

Gaudreault, André. "Theatricality, Narrativity, and 'Trickality': Reevaluating the Cinema of Georges Méliès." *Journal of Popular Film and Television* 15, no. 3 (1987).

Gunning, Tom. "Now You See It, Now You Don't: The Temporality of the Cinema of Attractions." *The Velvet Light Trap* 32 (fall 1993).

Malthête, Jacques, and Laurent Mannoni, eds. *Méliès, magie et cinéma: Exposition Electra*. Paris, 2002.

Malthête, Jacques, and Michel Marie, eds. *Georges Méliès: L'illusionniste fin de siècle?* Paris, 1997.

Rae Beth Gordon

MENDEL, GREGOR (1822–1884),

Austrian monk and researcher on plant hybridization and heredity.

Gregor Mendel is widely regarded as the father of genetics because he laid the foundations of that science with his classic study of hybridization. Born on 22 July 1822 and christened Johann, the future Gregor Mendel was the first son of the peasant farmer, Anton, and his wife, Rosine née Schwirtlich. Growing up in rural Silesia in the village of Heinzendorf, and encouraged by the local priest, Father Johann Schreiber, young Mendel became familiar with the practical skills of the farmer, fruit grower, and beekeeper. Naturally the expectation was that he would one day take over the running of his father's farm. Then in 1833 the village schoolmaster, Thomas Makitta, advised sending Mendel away to the Piarist Central School in Leipnik. This set young Mendel on a different course. The next six years found Mendel in the gymnasium at Troppau.

To continue his studies, Mendel moved to Olmütz, where at the Philosophical Institute he entered the two-year program to prepare for entry to the university. Among his teachers was the mathematician, Johann Fux, and the physicist, Friedrich Franz. Unfortunately, his studies both at Troppau and at Olmütz were compromised by several breakdowns in his health, caused, it seems, by the stress of studying and tutoring to raise the needed funds for his education—needed because of the declining state of the family finances. In 1838 his father had suffered an accident that impaired his ability to run the farm, making it impossible for the family to send their son any support. Advised of the situation, Professor Franz suggested Mendel might consider becoming a candidate for the Augustinian Monastery of Saint Thomas in Brünn, Moravia. Mendel applied to join the order, a change of social status, he explained, determined by his need to be freed "from the bitter struggle for existence," (Orel, p. 44) that was involving him in exertions that he could no longer endure.

GREGOR THE AUGUSTINIAN

We have no reason to doubt the sincerity of Mendel's support of the Christian religion, but clearly he would not have become a monk had his financial situation been different. Given the name "Gregor," he was to serve the monastery loyally, but as priest to the monastery parish he proved unsuited, for close encounters with the dying proved too much for him. Fortunately, the monastery had a teaching role in the schools and institutes in Moravia. Thus began Mendel's career as an unqualified adjunct teacher in 1849 at the Gymnasium in Znaim.

Qualification would involve an examination in Vienna. This he took in 1850, but failed. The remedy taken by Mendel's abbot, Cyrill Napp, was to send Mendel to Vienna University for four semesters from 1851 to 1853. Among his teachers were the physicist Christian Doppler and the botanist Franz Unger. The latter introduced him to the cell theory, the work of plant hybridists, and species transmutation.

Strangely, it was not until he was forced to retake the teacher qualification in 1855 that he returned to Vienna. Then the ordeal of the oral examination upset him so badly that he returned to the monastery seriously ill and unsuccessful. Fortunately, he was able to continue teaching as an unqualified adjunct at the newly established Modern School (*Oberrealschule*).

Mendel's teaching career came to an end in 1868 with his election as Cyrill Napp's successor as abbot. His new duties gave him little time for his research and his latter years were clouded by his dispute over the taxation of monasteries to support the state's religious fund. Only with his death on 6 January 1884, was this dispute resolved by his successor.

SCIENTIFIC RESEARCH

Mendel's scientific interests were many, but for him there was no strict separation between fundamental and applied research. He was as concerned about the quality of the grape for wine making and the beauty of the fuchsia for decoration as he was for seeking an understanding of the nature of hybridization. Besides beekeeping, gardening—including the study of insect pests—and botanizing he was especially devoted to meteorological observation. His Vienna experience had taught him the value of experimental design, and the statistical character of the physical world. Speculation about species transformation, though couched in the language of the still popular Nature-philosophy (*Naturphilosophie*), brought into question the supposed fixity of species. Could the hybridization of existing forms have led to species multiplication? Equally, would an understanding of the nature of the hybridization process aid the breeders of animals and plants in their pursuit of commercially attractive varieties? Hybridization thus held out potential economic benefits and at the same time might reveal how novel combinations of characters are transmitted in heredity and new species formed. Following his return from Vienna University in 1853, he began to plan an experiment to address the question, for as he notes, "among the numerous experiments not one has been carried out to an extent or in a manner that would make it possible to determine the number of different forms in which hybrid progeny appear, permit classification of these forms in each generation with certainty, and ascertain their numerical relationships" (Stern and Sherwood, p. 2). This passage expresses the originality of his experimental design. The need for classification of hybrid progeny led him to choose hybridizations between forms differing in traits that "stand out clearly and decisively in the plants." The determination of numerical relations meant growing large populations and treating them in a statistical manner. In tracing descent from generation to generation he followed the individual traits rather than the old practice of treating the species as a whole.

By 1854 he had obtained thirty-four varieties of the garden pea (*Pisum sativum*) that he tested for constancy of type over a two-year period. Twenty-two of these he retained as controls, growing them for the duration of the experiments to confirm their constancy. Having selected clearly distinguished traits like plant height, for example—either six to seven feet or ¾ to 1 ½ feet—he arrived at the conception of "character pairs," seven of them in all. Some pairs, like round or wrinkled seeds, were characteristics of the embryo within its seed coat. Others, like the shape of the ripe pod—constricted or unconstricted—were characteristics of the grown plant.

Next he noted that in the hybrids yielded by crossing forms differing in each of the seven traits, only one of the contrasting expressions of each trait was expressed in the hybrid. Such characters he called "dominant." The hidden characters he called "recessive." When he grew the succeeding generation, however, the recessive characters reappeared, and the ratio between the numbers of dominants to recessives approximated to 3:1. Here was a statistical regularity holding for all seven traits. Breeding a further generation of offspring revealed to him the constitution of the dominant parents as one third pure-breeding and two-thirds hybrid. The ratio 3:1 in constitutional terms was really 1:2:1, reminding him of the terms in the binomial equation: $(A + a)^2 = A^2 + 2Aa + a^2$.

Mendel went on to show how several traits could be combined in the same hybridization, but each behaved separately from the others, yielding novel combinations of characters. Mendel interpreted his results as suggesting that hybrids form germ cells, the composition of which is representative of either the dominant or the recessive character. When therefore large numbers of the pollen and egg cells in a hybrid unite in fertilization all combinations of these cells are realized just as in the expansion of the binomial equation—hence the ratio 1:2:1, obscured by dominance as 3:1.

This study with the edible pea took Mendel from 1854 to 1863, after which he reviewed his analysis of the results and wrote the paper "Versuche über Pflanzen-Hybriden" (Experiments on plant hybrids), presenting the work in two lectures to the Natural Science Society (*Naturforschender Verein*) in Brünn on 8 February and 8 March 1865, and published in the Society's *Proceedings* (*Verhandlungen*) for that year.

AFTERMATH

Nineteen citations of Mendel's paper of 1865 have so far been found in the literature of the nineteenth century. However, only one of these gave an adequate account of the paper and that was in a Russian doctoral dissertation. Of the 115 copies of the *Proceedings* sent out, fifty-four went to institutions that have been identified as recipients, but who read them we have no idea. While "obscure" may not be the appropriate word to describe this publication, well known or widely read it certainly was not. The one scientist who took Mendel's work seriously was Carl Wilhelm von Nägeli. Mendel's letters to him reveal the extent of his continuing hybridization research to seek the extent of validity of his theory of hybridization for other plant species. Also they speak to his search for hybrids in which there is no separation of the contrasted characters in germ cell formation, hence they would reproduce their like—be "constant hybrids." Such could be treated as new species. This interest led him to his very difficult and unresolved work on the hawkweeds (*Hieracium*). In this work Nägeli encouraged him, but contrary to the widely held view, Nägeli had not initiated this choice by Mendel.

Several issues concerning Mendel's contribution continue to be debated. Were his data too good to be true, as Ronald Fisher claimed in 1936? Franz Weiling has rejected this claim on the grounds that the situation in which germ cells are formed and fertilizations occur is not of the statistical character that Fisher assumed in his analysis. Fisher also expected there to be some misallocation of progeny to the class of pure dominants when in fact they were hybrid dominants. But he did not allow for ways in which despite the presence of dominance the two classes might be distinguished. There continues, too, to be disagreement over the context of Mendel's work. L. A. Callendar situates the work in the context of discussions of the origin of species. Vítězslav Orel and Roger Wood have explored the economic circumstances in Moravia that caused attention to be focused on hybridization.

When in 1900 the three hybridists, Hugo de Vries, Carl Erich Correns, and Erich Tschermak von Seysenegg, perceived the ratio 3:1 in their own data, Mendel's work at last became widely known. It is appropriate that he is regarded as the founder of the science of genetics, although it is surely an exaggeration to claim the concept of the gene to be present in his paper of 1865.

See also **Darwin, Charles; Science and Technology.**

BIBLIOGRAPHY

Primary Sources

Mendel, Gregor. "Versuche über Pflanzen-Hybriden." Reprinted in *Fundamenta Genetica: The Revised Edition of Mendel's Classic Paper with a Collection of Twenty-Seven Original Papers Published during the Rediscovery Era,* edited by Jaroslav Kříženecký and Bohumil Němec, 57–92. Brno, 1965.

Stern, Curt, and Eva R. Sherwood, eds. *The Origin of Genetics: A Mendel Source Book.* San Francisco and London, 1966.

Secondary Sources

Callender, L. A. "Gregor Mendel: An Opponent of Descent with Modification." *History of Science* 26 (1988): 41–75.

Fisher, Ronald A. "Has Mendel's Work Been Rediscovered?" *Annals of Science* 1 (1936): 115–137. Reprinted in Stern and Sherwood, 1966, pp. 139–172, see above.

Henig, Robin. *The Monk in the Garden: The Lost and Found Genius of Gregor Mendel, the Father of Genetics.* Boston, 2000.

Iltis, Hugo. *Life of Mendel.* London, 1932. 2nd impression, 1966. Abridged translation of *Gregor Johann Mendel: Leben, Werk, und Wirkungl.* Berlin, 1924.

Olby, Robert. *Origins of Mendelism.* 2nd ed. Chicago, 1985. Includes reprint of "Mendel no Mendelian?" *History of Science* 17 (1979): 53–72.

Orel, Vítězslav. *Gregor Mendel: The First Geneticist.* Translated by Stephen Finn. Oxford, U.K., 1996.

Piegorsch, W. W. "The Gregor Mendel Controversy: Early Issues of Goodness of Fit and Recent Issues of Genetics." *History of Science* 24 (1986): 173–182.

Weiling, Franz. "Historical Study: Johann Gregor Mendel, 1822–1884." *American Journal of Medical Genetics* 40 (1991): 1–25.

ROBERT OLBY

MENSHEVIKS. The Mensheviks constitute a faction and a current within the prerevolutionary Russian Social Democratic Labor Party (RSDLP). The term *menshevik* may be translated as minoritarian and, as such, it is naturally opposed to its counterpart *bolshevik,* or majoritarian. After 1917, the Bolsheviks were to abandon the Social Democratic label, making the Mensheviks the sole bearer of the original party name. Before this, however, Mensheviks and Bolsheviks competed for leadership within what was widely considered to be still a single Social Democratic party.

SPLIT WITH BOLSHEVIKS

The original division between Mensheviks and Bolsheviks is commonly situated at the Second Congress of the RSDLP held in 1903. The disagreement is traced to divergence over conceptions of party membership, the future Mensheviks supporting L. Martov's broader definition (someone who renders the party assistance) and the future Bolsheviks defending Vladimir Lenin's narrower definition (someone who personally participates in a party organization). In fact, on this issue, which corresponded to article one of the party statutes, it was the Mensheviks who obtained a majority. The Party therefore adopted the Menshevik variant of article one, until 1907 when the Mensheviks themselves voted against it.

The majority/minority split actually took place over the question of culling the editorial board of the party journal, *Iskra* (The spark). Although Lenin was not proposing to eliminate Martov, the latter opposed Lenin ferociously. Lenin won because a number of delegates from the Jewish Bund had walked out in protest earlier. The bitter split between Lenin and Martov caused bewilderment in the party, as the two leaders had enjoyed the closest of personal and political relations. Indeed, the Second Congress had been called to confirm their joint victory over "economist" currents in the party, which, according to both Lenin and Martov, wrongly played down the importance of politics, party leadership, and party organization.

By October 1903 the Mensheviks had reversed the outcome of the Second Congress and were in control of the party and the party journal. The prestigious father of Russian Marxism, Georgy Plekhanov, allied to Lenin at the Second Congress, had switched sides to become a Menshevik, permanently and unconditionally. In the course of the Revolution of 1905 neither faction behaved consistently. Some Mensheviks, such as Fyodor Dan, were occasionally more radical than Bolsheviks, with respect to the burning issues of that year, such as the question of an armed uprising, the role of the newly created soviets, and the hopes of transcending the boundaries of a purely bourgeois revolution. In 1905, both factions were subjected to strong pressure from the party grassroots to bridge their differences. After creation of a unified central committee a "reunification" party congress, dominated by the Mensheviks, took place in Stockholm in 1906. Its efforts soon unraveled. A formal reunification agreement in 1910 also proved stillborn. In the same year in Vienna, Leon Trotsky sought, also unsuccessfully, to transcend the Menshevik/Bolshevik split by gathering party forces around his journal *Pravda.* In 1912 the Bolsheviks called a party conference in Prague, which the Mensheviks refused to attend. Some historians date the division into two separate parties from that moment. On the eve of World War I, the Socialist International was showing impatience with the bickering of the Russians and was threatening to impose unity. Even in 1917 hopes for a united party remained strong.

POLICY AND PERSONAL DIFFERENCES

Both the Mensheviks and the Bolsheviks were orthodox revolutionary Marxists. They quarreled, in 1905 as in 1917, about the role of the bourgeoisie and of the peasantry in the coming revolution. Generally speaking, the Mensheviks were less harsh toward the bourgeoisie and more suspicious of the peasantry than the Bolsheviks. The Mensheviks proposed municipalization of land, whereas the Bolsheviks called for nationalization. Fundamentally, however, both factions were working within the same Marxist framework. Until 1917 the party program was common to both factions. In terms of the number and class origins of rank-and-file members, the factions were roughly comparable. In 1907, for instance, there were 46,000 Bolsheviks and 38,000 Mensheviks. The Mensheviks counted more members of national minorities, Jews, and, in particular, Georgians.

Policy differences between 1905 and 1917 both fueled and reflected divergences between the factions. From the outset the Mensheviks looked favorably upon RSDLP participation in elections to the newly created Duma, whereas Lenin came around to endorsing participation only belatedly. When discouragement among revolutionaries set in after 1907, the Mensheviks supported workers' activity in social and professional organizations outside the party. Lenin denounced them as "liquidators," that is, guilty of liquidating the underground party. The Mensheviks were shocked, as were many foreign socialists, by Bolshevik tactics of "expropriation," such as bank robberies. Menshevik strategies appeared to be rewarded with the emergence of a new stratum of Menshevik-inspired "workers' intelligentsia" or trade-union "practicals" during the period of reaction after 1905. In the years immediately preceding World War I, however, it was the Bolsheviks who appeared to reap advantage from the upsurge of worker discontent.

From the very beginning, there was a significant personal dimension to the Menshevik/Bolshevik division. The Bolsheviks were always identified with Lenin, though he did not always control his own faction. No single individual represented Menshevism in this way, although Martov, Pavel Axelrod, and Plekhanov shared intellectual leadership of the Mensheviks. This personal difference was construed, first by Axelrod but then by many others, as a fundamental theoretical opposition. The Bolsheviks were the faction of one-man leadership; they were authoritarian, conspiratorial, and hierarchical. The Mensheviks were the faction of democratic and autonomous workers' spontaneity. Over time and in retrospect, both factions and, in particular, postrevolutionary historiography transformed Bolshevism and Menshevism into ahistorical qualities. Hard, narrow, closed Bolshevism confronted soft, broad, open Menshevism. To Menshevik charges of reckless adventurism, the Bolsheviks retorted with accusations of reformist pusillanimity. Stereotypically, Menshevik moderation stood opposed to Bolshevik maximalism.

Both factions eventually became defined as reverse images of each other. In the Soviet Union, such definition served Bolshevik myths. In the West, it responded to the need for self-justification among surviving Mensheviks and historians seeking an alternative to the outcomes of 1917. There is debate about the extent to which the differences between the factions were so fundamental as to effectively engender two separate parties already before 1917. Clearly, the differences become sharper as one looks at them from a distance than they appeared in their own day.

See also **Bolsheviks; Martov, L.; Plekhanov, Georgy.**

BIBLIOGRAPHY

Ascher, Abraham, ed. *The Mensheviks in the Russian Revolution.* Ithaca, N.Y., 1976.

Dan, Theodore (Fyodor). *The Origins of Bolshevism.* Edited and translated by Joel Carmichael. London, 1964.

Haimson, Leopold H. *The Russian Marxists and the Origins of Bolshevism.* Cambridge, Mass., 1955.

Schwarz, Solomon M. *The Russian Revolution of 1905: The Workers' Movement and the Formation of Bolshevism and Menshevism.* Translated by Gertrude Vakar. Chicago, 1967.

Swain, Geoffrey. *Russian Social Democracy and the Legal Labour Movement, 1906–1914.* London, 1983.

ANDRE LIEBICH

MENZEL, ADOLPH VON (1815–1905),

German realist painter.

Adolph Friedrich Erdmann von Menzel began his artistic work in the Biedermeier period during the first half of the nineteenth century, particularly

1820–1850; by the time he died, the expressionist painters of Die Brücke had joined forces in Dresden. Both the democratic progress of the 1830s and the 1848 Revolution formed the young painter. In his countless representations of scenes from German history, connections to the contemporary time are also discernible. Menzel's paintings were created on the foundation of an enormous graphic corpus. Both his paintings and drawings testify to his interest in the inconspicuous, in surprising details, and in lighting effects.

Menzel was taught in his father's lithographic workshop, which he carried on after his father's death, producing functional merchandise such as greeting cards and advertisements. For a short time, he attended the Berlin Kunstakademie (Academy of Arts) on the side, but was largely an autodidact. In 1833 he had his first public exhibition as an independent artist with lithographs for *Künstlers Erdenwallen* (The artist's life on Earth) by Johann Wolfgang von Goethe (1749–1832). From 1839 to 1842 he created, on the basis of meticulous studies of the historical situation, 400 drawings for woodcut illustrations to the comprehensive *Geschichte Friedrichs des Grossen* (History of Frederick the Great) by Franz Kugler (1808–1858), an assignment affecting him deeply. It was above all his illustrations that popularized the work. Not only do they show Frederick II (r. 1740–1786) as the successful military strategist but also as an art aficionado seasoned with wit, a friend of the philosopher Voltaire (1696–1778), and a reformer. The eighteenth-century king had become an ideal.

Between 1850 and 1860 paintings dealing with the times of Frederick II took shape, starting with *Flute Concert with Frederick the Great in Sanssouci* (1850–1852) and *Flute Concert of Frederick the Great at Sanssouci* (1852), a work that is courtly and intimate at the same time. The king is performing a solo on the transverse flute; at the harpsichord is Carl Philipp Emanuel Bach (1714–1788), the great church musician's son; and Frederick's favorite sister, Wilhelmine von Bayreuth (1709–1758), is sitting on the sofa listening. Above and beyond the theme, the *Flute Concert,* like Menzel's other paintings, attained fame because of its coloristic and artistic appeal. Yet initially the paintings on the life of Frederick II were also controversial. Though distinguished by historical accuracy and unconditional realism, they avoid any dramatic overstatement. Menzel depicts the protagonists without any significant characteristics. Menzel's art was only officially recognized with the commission in 1861 to paint the coronation of William I (r. 1861–1888) in Königsberg. Subsequently, he received numerous tributes and was named to the nobility in 1898.

Even before Menzel created the paintings dealing with Frederick II's life, he started his series of rather private paintings especially fascinating to twenty-first-century viewers. In 1839, Menzel admired works by the English landscape painter John Constable (1776–1837), exhibited in Berlin at the time. Constable's novel, natural way of observation still reverberated in Menzel's studies of everyday life in the 1840s. These works, featuring casual brushstrokes in which airiness and atmosphere dominated, helped him develop his fondness of lighting effects. The group of works only became widely known through the commemorative exhibit featuring unpublished works in 1905 at the Nationalgalerie in Berlin, securing Menzel posthumous fame. To many viewers he suddenly appeared as a bold precursor of the impressionists. *Balcony Room* (1845) reveals the kind of artistic ability Menzel was developing at the time. *Balcony Room* represents neither a genre painting nor an interior but instead an artistic and atmospheric appearance. Without preconceptions, Menzel also included entirely new motifs in his studies: the consequences of urbanization and industrialization. In 1847 he painted the Berlin-Potsdam Railway, the first railroad line in Prussia.

In the years 1872 to 1875, Menzel once again turned, on his own commission, to a subject rarely represented until then: on a grand format, he executed the *Iron Rolling Mill.* Menzel familiarized himself with the new world of modern industry by means of numerous studies in Upper Silesian ironworks and Berlin factories. Once again, the outcome was an atmospheric work and complex event-centered painting connecting the exact description of the production process with the social interaction of the people working there.

Highly influential, too, were Menzel's sojourns in Paris in 1855, 1867, and 1868. There he visited Gustave Courbet (1819–1877) and befriended the historical painter Ernest Meissonier (1815–1891). Works by Menzel making reference to the city, such as the *Théâtre du Gymnase* (1856), appear astonishingly modern with their bold angle toward auditorium and stage. The *Ball Souper,* painted in 1878, was in turn copied by Edgar Degas (1834–1917).

Menzel was one of the few German painters also famous abroad in his own lifetime. However, Menzel had no immediate effect on contemporary artistic production, lacking any actual successors. His forward-looking achievements were overtaken by impressionism. Yet his rich and multifaceted oeuvre continues to preoccupy and fascinate scholars and art lovers to this day. In the last decades of the twentieth century, it was the subject of countless dissertations, books, and exhibits.

See also **Constable, John; Courbet, Gustave; Painting; Realism and Naturalism.**

BIBLIOGRAPHY

Fried, Michael. *Menzel's Realism: Art and Embodiment in Nineteenth-Century Berlin.* New Haven, Conn., 2002.

Jensen, Jens Christian. *Adolph Menzel.* Cologne, Germany, 1982.

Keisch, Claude, and Marie Ursula Riemann-Reyher, eds. *Adolph Menzel, 1815–1905: Between Romanticism and Impressionism.* New Haven, Conn., 1996.

Tschudi, Hugo von. *Adolph von Menzel.* Munich, 1905.

ANGELIKA WESENBERG

MESMER, FRANZ ANTON (1734–1815), German physician who developed mesmerism.

Mesmerism, or animal magnetism, was a practice developed in the late eighteenth century by the physician Franz Anton Mesmer in which one person was thought to dramatically affect another's mind and body through a subtle influence. Mesmer speculated that the Newtonian forces that operated in the physical world must have an influence on the body: the subtle fluids of magnetism, he thought, must play a key role in the regulation of health, and by manipulating the movement of these fluids in the human body one could develop new ways of treating illness. His doctoral dissertation at the University of Vienna discussed the influence of the moon and other heavenly bodies on human physiology, arguing that the body's state of health depended on the quantity and rhythm of ethereal movement. He initially developed the practice of "animal magnetism," which sought to alter this rhythm in the hope of curing disease, in the early 1770s. He claimed that applying magnets to the surface of the body established a health-giving "artificial tide" in a patient, who initially responded to the treatment with excitement and/or pain, and then, after a magnetic "crisis," with relief. Mesmer developed a round tub or baquet from which several metal handles protruded, from which several patients could take their treatment at the same time.

His therapy became very fashionable in 1770s Vienna, until scandal drove him out of the city and he relocated to Paris. Mesmer became extraordinarily successful in France, and magnetic clinics were founded across the country in the new practice. The practice itself changed, as Mesmer and others found that magnets were not necessary to produce the effects: it was possible to create them by making "magnetic passes" over the patient's body using one's hands, or to "bottle" the influence in some object, or, perhaps, in a glass of water. Several of Mesmer's protégés—Nicholas Bergasse, Charles Deslon, and Guillaume Kornmann among them—established their own clinics and became magnetic celebrities in their own right, and the practice began to spread to other European countries and, within a few decades, farther afield, including to the United States and India.

Mesmer's success drew the attention of the Royal Academy of Sciences and the Faculty of Medicine in France, and both groups appointed a commission to investigate Mesmer's claims. The commissioners attended a magnetic clinic, tried the baquet, and used their own instruments to test Mesmer's claims of magnetic influence. Some commissioners experienced effects; others claimed that nothing happened. Some of them suspected that patients' imaginations were at the root of the phenomena, and to test this, they persuaded a number of patients to think they were being treated with magnetism when in fact they were not, and vice versa. They found that individuals who believed they were being magnetized displayed the expected phenomena, and those who were indeed given the treatment (but were ignorant of receiving it) did not. A majority of the commissioners (though not all) concluded that imagination, not magnetism, was the root cause of the phenomena, and since imagination was not at this time considered to be a legitimate cause of natural phenomena, assigning it as the cause of magnetic effects amounted to a dismissal of Mesmer's claims. The term *mesmerism* was coined as a kind of mocking rebuttal (meaning that no magnetism was involved, just "Mesmer-ism").

Despite this formal rejection, mesmerism spread and diversified in the late eighteenth and early nineteenth centuries. A significant change came with the work of the Marquis de Puysegur (1751–1825), who changed the practice and effects. In Mesmer's practice, the effects had been brief and violent, producing a sudden "climax." But Puysegur developed a very different phenomenon, a trance state that was characterized by an altered set of mental functions. During this time patients spoke and acted in new ways, claimed to be able to diagnose their own diseases and those of other people, spoke languages they had never learned, and "traveled" to other places mentally.

The new form of magnetism transformed the practice into a new experimental tool and phenomenon, and in this new form it became extremely widespread during the nineteenth century, particularly in Europe and the United States, and in the 1840s and 1850s, in colonial India. Mesmeric journals, societies, and lecture tours proliferated, ranging from the formal and fairly elite (such as *The Zoist* in England, founded and run by physician John Elliotson, and the *Journal du Magnetism* in Paris, run by Charles Dupotet). It flourished in Germany and Switzerland, encouraged by such intellectual leaders as Christoph Wilhelm Hufeland, Carl Kluge, and Johann Kaspar Lavater; in England it proliferated widely, becoming the most widespread experimental practice of the nineteenth century, and the first widespread surgical anesthetic (in 1842), but it was intensely controversial, and it was professionally risky for elite doctors to practice it.

Mesmerism declined as a challenging, promising, and medically ambitious practice in the second half of the nineteenth century, though it continued to be practiced and flourished as an accompaniment to popular scientific lectures and shows. One reason for its decline was the rise of competing practices. Inhalation anesthesia became widespread in the late 1840s, promoted by surgeons motivated to find an alternative to mesmeric anesthesia; hypnosis was developed in 1842 as an alternative to mesmerism (it avoided certain features of the practice and attributed the effects to imagination, rather than to a subtle physical influence); and the rise of spiritualism, beginning in the 1850s, eclipsed mesmerism as an experimental practice. By the twentieth century, mesmerism as a practice had largely disappeared.

See also **Freud, Sigmund; Gall, Franz Joseph; Popular and Elite Culture; Psychology; Vienna.**

BIBLIOGRAPHY

Crabtree, Alan. *From Mesmer to Freud: Magnetic Sleep and the Roots of Psychological Healing.* New Haven, Conn., 1993.

Darnton, Robert. *Mesmerism and the End of the Enlightenment in France.* Cambridge, Mass., 1968.

Ellenberger, Henri F. *Discovery of the Unconscious: The History and Evolution of Dynamic Psychiatry.* New York, 1970.

Gauld, Alan. *A History of Hypnotism.* Cambridge, U.K., 1992.

Winter, Alison. *Mesmerized: Powers of Mind in Victorian Britain.* Chicago, 1998.

Alison Winter

METTERNICH, CLEMENS VON

(1773–1859), Austrian statesman and diplomatist.

Prince Clemens von Metternich was a statesman who guided Austria's foreign policy for forty years, played a leading role in defeating Napoleon I, and made the Austrian Empire for a time the leading power in Europe and himself its foremost statesman.

EARLY YEARS

The future chancellor of the Austrian Empire was born in Koblenz in the Rhineland on 15 May 1773. He was the son of Francis George, Count von Metternich-Winneburg, one of the autonomous

German nobles who held a fief directly from the Holy Roman Emperor, whom he also served as a diplomat. Young Clemens studied diplomacy at the Universities of Strasbourg and Mainz, but his studies were interrupted by the spread of the French Revolution. In 1794 a French army conquered the Rhineland and seized the family estates. The Metternich family, after a brief stay in England, was forced to flee as refugees to Vienna. There in 1795 he married Eleonora von Kaunitz, granddaughter of Wenzel Anton von Kaunitz, the former Austrian chancellor. The marriage linked him with the high nobility and opened the door to his future career.

After performing diplomatic missions for Austria and various German princes, in 1801 he entered the Austrian diplomatic service. His abilities and his connections brought him rapid promotion: minister to Saxony in 1801, to Prussia in 1803, and finally in 1806 to the most important diplomatic post in Europe, Paris. He was able to become on good terms with Napoleon and acquired a thorough knowledge of the all-powerful emperor's character, strengths, and weaknesses.

THE STRUGGLE WITH NAPOLEON

By 1806, Austria had fought and lost three wars with Napoleon, each time losing more territory. Encouraged by the success of the Spanish guerrillas against the French, Austrian leaders decided that they too could defeat Napoleon by arousing a German popular uprising. Metternich was also impressed, and his overly optimistic reports helped to precipitate Austria into another losing war in 1809.

In this critical moment, Emperor Francis I (r. 1804–1835) entrusted the fate of Austria to Metternich, appointing him foreign minister in October 1809. Metternich rose to the challenge. He could not prevent Napoleon from imposing a harsh peace and threatening further demands, but he cleverly played on Napoleon's vanity, his desire to be on a par with the old dynasties of Europe, to score a diplomatic triumph. In 1810 his patient, skillful diplomacy persuaded Napoleon to marry Marie Louise, the daughter of Francis I. He thus saved Austria from any further encroachment on its territory and independence and won it breathing space to recover from defeat. For the next two years he was careful to remain on good terms with Napoleon, even agreeing to send an Austrian force to accompany his invasion of Russia in 1812, though the force was independent and had secret instructions to avoid fighting. The destruction of Napoleon's army in Russia came as a surprise to Metternich, but he realized that it opened up new possibilities of revival for Austria.

The next two years saw one of the most skillful diplomatic performances of his career. In 1813 Britain and Prussia were now allied with Russia to fight Napoleon. Both sides sought Austria's alliance, knowing it would probably decide the outcome. Metternich maneuvered between them with great skill. He knew it would be foolish to enter the war until the Austrian army, at a low ebb after many defeats, had been rebuilt to the point at which it was again fit to play a major role in the war.

More important, he would not commit Austria to either side until he could be sure that, whoever won, the resulting peace settlement would safeguard its interests. Austria's most obvious interest was to regain territory equal to that which it had had before the revolutionary wars, so that it would once again have the strength necessary to act as a great power. More important, however, the peace must also create a balance of power in Europe. Metternich saw clearly the weaknesses of Austria: its multinational character, its lack of strong natural frontiers, its central position open to invasion on every side. Austria could survive only in a Europe in which power was balanced—or, as he would come to see, restrained in some other way. To achieve a balance, it was clear that the power of Napoleon must be reduced, but that was no longer Metternich's only concern. He was equally worried by the growing strength of Russia. A Europe dominated by Russia would be no safer for Austria than a Europe dominated by France. In 1813 his ideal arrangement would have been a Europe in which a Napoleonic Empire west of the Rhine, weakened but still strong, balanced Russia in the east. With this in mind, he proposed an armed mediation by Austria between the two sides. Both accepted, and an armistice was arranged in June 1813. Negotiating with the Allies, Metternich agreed to join them, but only if they offered Napoleon generous peace terms. Generous terms were offered, and Metternich did his best to persuade the emperor to accept them. Napoleon, however, still confident of total victory, rejected the offer.

Metternich now had no alternative but to join the war against France. His skillful diplomacy, however, had already won for Austria a leading role in the war and assurances that Austria would recover its prewar strength and position of leadership in Germany. An appreciative Francis I bestowed upon him the hereditary title of prince.

He continued to safeguard Austrian interests during the war, in particular by arranging treaties with the south German states guaranteeing their independence. He thereby thwarted the plans of the Prussian minister Baron vom Stein for a unitary Germany under Prussian hegemony that would have ended Austria's traditional influence there. Metternich also continued to seek a peace that would preserve a weakened Napoleon as a balance against Russia. In February 1814 his insistence on a new peace offer led to a crisis with the tsar, who wished to push on to total victory. The crisis was defused by the arrival of the British foreign secretary, Lord Castlereagh. He and Metternich soon agreed on the dangers of Russian power and the need for a balance; they also agreed that if Napoleon were overthrown, the French throne must go to a restored Bourbon king, not to a protégé of the tsar. A new peace offer to Napoleon was then made, but once again, rejected, and the war went on until the final defeat of Napoleon in April 1814.

THE CONGRESS OF VIENNA

The leading statesmen of Europe met in September at the Congress of Vienna, to begin the task of restoring peace and order to a Europe devastated by a generation of war. Though the congress was a splendid social occasion, in which Metternich took a leading part, there was serious work to be done. Frightened by the unprecedented duration and destruction of the generation of war since 1792, the statesmen believed that a new international order, based on something better than the cutthroat power politics of the eighteenth century, was essential. The result was the "Concert of Europe," which was to give Europe a century of relative peace. This concept implied that it was in the interest of all the powers to maintain peace, even at the cost of limiting their ambitions to some degree; when disputes arose, they should be settled by consensus, not confrontation, with noninvolved powers acting as mediators. Metternich was its strongest supporter, for he saw that only in a peaceful Europe could Austria with all its weaknesses hope to survive.

Consensus was nevertheless not easily achieved. The most intractable problem arose from the determination of Tsar Alexander I (r. 1801–1825) to take over the Grand Duchy of Warsaw, a revived Polish state created by Napoleon from lands taken from Austria and Prussia, and to allow Prussia as compensation to annex Saxony. This plan posed a major threat to the balance of power, and to Austria's security. Russian domination of Poland would bring its power into the heart of central Europe. Prussian control of Saxony would remove the chief buffer between Austria and Prussia and give the latter control of the natural invasion route into the Austrian Empire. To defeat the plan, Metternich first attempted to detach Prussia from its alliance with Russia, but without success. He then forged an alliance with Castlereagh and the French foreign minister, Charles-Maurice de Talleyrand, who were also alarmed at the threat to the European balance. In the long struggle that followed, Metternich was only partly victorious. Russia returned parts of the grand duchy to Austria and Prussia, but kept most of it. Prussia, however, gained less than half of Saxony, so that buffer remained.

Napoleon's dramatic return from exile in March 1815 spurred the congress to finish its work. The Final Act of Vienna was signed on 9 June 1815. In the end, all the major problems at the congress were settled in ways that left all the powers reasonably content, and none so dissatisfied that it was willing to go to war to upset the settlement. Metternich secured his main concerns: restoration of Austria to its prewar size, and predominance in Germany and Italy. It was the high point of his career.

THE RESTORATION

The five years after the congress were generally tranquil. Since 1811, Metternich had been urging the Austrian emperor to abandon the centralizing policies of the late eighteenth century in favor of a federal approach, without success. He renewed his efforts after 1816, arguing the need to recognize and conciliate the ethnic groups of the monarchy, and so counteract the growing force of nationalism that was the greatest threat to its survival. He was especially concerned to give Lombardy and Venetia, where Italian nationalism was strong, greater local autonomy and a native administration. Francis I would not listen. Instead, he reorganized the empire on absolutist and centralized lines, relying on paternalism, censorship, and the police to prevent discontent. Because loyalty to the emperor forced Metternich to acquiesce, the result was often called by contemporaries the "Metternich system," though he disapproved of it. In reality, though Francis gave Metternich steady support in foreign policy, he allowed him little voice in domestic affairs.

Metternich was more successful in foreign affairs. At the congress, he had secured the establishment of a German Confederation, basically a defensive military alliance through which Austria could balance the power of Russia and France. Austria's position, however, was challenged by Prussia and the south German states. To defeat their challenge, Metternich seized upon a minor flurry of revolutionary activity, climaxed by political assassinations in 1819, to call a conference at Carlsbad. Exaggerating the revolutionary threat (which he knew was still minor), he led the German rulers to pass measures establishing press censorship and surveillance of universities. More important from his point of view, he also frightened them into seeing cooperation with Austria as their best defense against revolution. In this way he consolidated Austrian predominance over Germany for the next two decades.

In Italy, too, he cemented Austrian predominance. Lombardy and Venetia had been given to Austria at the congress. As for the independent Italian states, he had planned to organize an Italian confederation, but opposition from the Italian rulers and from the tsar defeated him. Nonetheless, he managed for three decades to control the Italian states, using adroit diplomacy, Habsburg family connections, and promises of protection against revolution.

NEW REVOLUTIONS

The first great challenge to Metternich's achievements came with the revolutions of 1820. The revolution that broke out in July 1820 in Naples threatened Austria's hold on the Italian peninsula. A liberal Naples would surely reject Austrian tutelage; moreover, the example of its success would inspire imitation elsewhere in Italy. Austrian forces could easily suppress the revolution, but there were international complications. France was inclined to sympathize with the rebels, hoping to replace Austria's influence with its own. The tsar, who had been flirting with liberal ideas, was unwilling to give Austria a free hand. In a series of brilliant maneuvers, Metternich was able to overcome his opponents and win the support of the powers at the Congresses of Troppau (1820) and Laibach (1821). While Austrian troops were suppressing the Neapolitan revolution in March 1821, another revolt broke out in Piedmont, but this too was easily suppressed. Austrian power was once again supreme in Italy. An appreciative Francis I appointed him state chancellor, the highest post in the empire.

From this high point, Metternich's position began to deteriorate. After Castlereagh's death in 1822, Britain, increasingly under liberal rule, tended to distrust Metternich. A greater blow was struck by the Greek revolt of 1821, for it split the conservative front. This revolt of Orthodox Christians aroused great sympathy in Russia; moreover, it offered Russia an excuse to expand at Turkish expense. Though able to restrain Alexander I, Metternich was unable to prevent his successor, Nicholas I (r. 1825–1855), from going to war with Turkey in 1829 to liberate Greece—the first successful revolution since 1815, and the greatest defeat Metternich had yet suffered.

DECLINING INFLUENCE

Metternich was able to rescue Austria from diplomatic isolation when a new wave of revolutions in 1830 brought the conservative powers together again in alliance. The cost was high, however, for the revolution brought the liberal July Monarchy to power in France—a new adversary for Austria. Moreover, in the revived conservative bloc, it was Russia, not Austria, that was the dominant partner, for Metternich could not manage Nicholas I as he had managed Alexander I, and he could no longer look to Britain or France for support. The years after 1830 therefore saw a gradual decline in Austria's international position. He was able to maintain Austria's hegemony in Germany and Italy, but his growing dependence on Russian backing inevitably eroded Austria's freedom of action and his own importance.

At home too his influence was in decline. In 1826 Franz Anton, Count von Kolowrat, was given charge of Austria's finances. His financial skill won him growing influence over Francis I, and Kolowrat and Metternich became bitter rivals. In an apparent effort to reverse his decline, the chancellor advised Francis I to recognize his feebleminded son Ferdinand as heir, by a will directing the latter to follow Metternich's advice. It seemed as if Metternich would at last be in a position to reorder the government according to his own ideas. Kolowrat, however, was able to mobilize the support of the Habsburg family to defeat him. In the resulting regency, the powers of Kolowrat and Metternich were evenly balanced. Their constant rivalry tended to paralyze the government, so that no effective action could be taken to head off the revolutionary pressures that were growing in the empire. When revolution broke out in Vienna in March 1848, Metternich, now widely if somewhat unfairly seen as responsible for the repressive and reactionary policies of the government, was forced to resign and go into exile.

EXILE AND DEATH

After three years of exile in London, he returned to Vienna. He held no office thereafter, but gave the government frequent advice, which was usually either misunderstood or ignored. He died in Vienna on 11 June 1859.

See also **Austria-Hungary; Carlsbad Decrees; Concert of Europe; Congress of Vienna; French Revolutionary Wars and Napoleonic Wars; Napoleonic Empire.**

BIBLIOGRAPHY

Primary Sources

Metternich-Winneburg, Richard von, ed. *Memoirs of Prince Metternich.* Translated by Alexander Napier and Gerard W. Smith. 5 vols. London, 1880–1882.

Secondary Sources

Billinger, Robert D. *Metternich and the German Question: States' Rights and Federal Duties, 1820–1834.* Newark, Del., 1991.

Emerson, Donald E. *Metternich and the Political Police.* The Hague, 1968.

Haas, Arthur G. *Metternich: Reorganization and Nationality, 1813–1818.* Knoxville, Tenn., 1964.

Kraehe, Enno. *Metternich's German Policy.* 2 vols. Princeton, N.J., 1963–1983.

Palmer, Alan. *Metternich.* London, 1972.

Radvany, Egon. *Metternich's Projects for Reform in Austria.* The Hague, 1971.

Reinerman, Alan J. *Austria and the Papacy in the Age of Metternich.* 2 vols. Washington, D.C., 1979–1989.

Schroeder, Paul W. *Metternich's Diplomacy at Its Zenith, 1820–1823.* Austin, Tex., 1962.

Alan J. Reinerman

MEYERHOLD, VSEVOLOD (1874–1940), Russian theatrical director and producer.

One of the most innovative and influential theatrical directors and pedagogues of the twentieth century, and a central figure in the history of modern Russian culture, Vsevolod Meyerhold worked in Russia during a particularly exciting and turbulent period in the country's history. His career began in the promising decades just before the 1917 Bolshevik Revolution (which he embraced with enthusiasm) and ended in tragic repression under the regime of Soviet dictator Joseph Stalin. Born on 9 February (28 January, old style) 1874 into a Russified German family in the provincial city of Penza, Meyerhold went to Moscow in 1895 to study law, but soon gravitated to the world of theater. Like many aspiring actors, he enrolled in the legendary classes taught by the director and playwright Vladimir Nemirovich-Danchenko at the drama school of the Moscow Philharmonic Society.

In 1898 Meyerhold was invited to take the role of the neurotic writer Treplev in a production of Anton Chekhov's *The Seagull* for the first season of the new Moscow Art Theater, founded by Nemirovich-Danchenko and Konstantin Stanislavsky. This groundbreaking interpretation established Chekhov as a successful playwright, and introduced the basic elements of what became known as the Stanislavsky "method": creation of evocative atmosphere (through sound effects, scenery, costumes, music) and psychological realism in acting style (achieved through the actor's use of personal memory and experiences). Meyerhold later vehemently rejected Stanislavsky's psychological and realistic approach, but the two men remained friends and colleagues until the end of Stanislavsky's life.

In 1902 Meyerhold founded the Company of Russian Dramatic Artists and began his prolific career as a director, which eventually included nearly three hundred productions. He began to move away from realism in several productions for the Studio of the Moscow Art Theater in 1905, and even more so at a theater in St. Petersburg founded in 1906 by the actress Vera Komissarzhevskaya. There Meyerhold began to develop a new "symbolist" theater, particularly with his staging of *Balaganchik* (The fairground booth), by the symbolist poet Alexander Blok, which uses the familiar masks and conventions of the Italian commedia dell'arte to create an abstract and highly artificial theatrical environment that rejects logical psychological motivation and breaks down the barrier between audience and performer.

Despite his strong avant-garde and iconoclastic leanings, Meyerhold was appointed in 1908 as an assistant to the director of the conservative imperial theaters in St. Petersburg, a post he held until the collapse of the tsarist government in 1917. In this capacity, he assisted other directors and staged his own productions, including the operas *Tristan and Isolde, Boris Godunov, Elektra, The Nightingale, Orpheus and Eurydice,* and *The Queen of Spades.* Music was an essential part of Meyerhold's work as a director. He incorporated music into his productions in unusual and aggressive ways, sometimes matching the emotional mood and rhythm of the stage action, sometimes contradicting it, in highly self-conscious counterpoint. He also worked closely with leading composers. With Sergei Prokofiev (to whom he gave the idea for the opera *Love for Three Oranges*) and Dmitri Shostakovich he enjoyed particularly close relationships.

Like most progressive Russian artists, Meyerhold welcomed the 1917 Bolshevik Revolution and the foundation of the world's first socialist state as a unique opportunity to (in Blok's words) "redo everything." But much more than most, he participated in the actual building of the new Soviet culture, by opening new theaters and institutes for training theater people in a new way of working. A Communist Party member from 1918, Meyerhold held numerous high-ranking positions in the cultural bureaucracy and engaged vigorously in the bitter ideological conflicts that raged within the Soviet leadership over the role of theater in the new utopian society.

In 1926 Meyerhold was rewarded with a state-supported theater in Moscow bearing his name. There, as he had done throughout his career, Meyerhold trained actors in his method of "biomechanics," a system that emphasized specific physical techniques related both to the non-realist traditions of commedia dell'arte and the highly stylized gestures of Kabuki. Biomechanics was also closely linked to the ideas of constructivism, which reached its peak in the Soviet Union in the 1920s and viewed humans as cogs in a giant social machine. One of Meyerhold's most celebrated constructivist productions was *The Magnificent Cuckold* by Fernand Crommelynck, with sets by Lyubov Popova (1922).

With Stalin's ascent to power in the 1930s, Meyerhold's position worsened, as the ideas of the Soviet revolutionary avant-garde were discarded in favor of the conservative totalitarian doctrine of socialist realism. To his credit, Meyerhold was one of the very few who refused to disown his outspoken convictions, even in the face of overwhelming pressure and danger. In June 1939 he was arrested and charged with being a "wrecker" of the Soviet theater. He was executed in Moscow on 2 February 1940.

See also **Blok, Alexander; Chekhov, Anton; Russia.**

BIBLIOGRAPHY

Braun, Edward. *Meyerhold: A Revolution in Theatre.* Iowa City, 1995.

Leach, Robert. *Vsevolod Meyerhold.* Cambridge, U.K., 1989.

Schmidt, Paul, ed. *Meyerhold at Work.* Translated by Paul Schmidt, Ilya Levin, and Vern McGee. Austin, Tex., 1980.

Harlow Robinson

MICHEL, LOUISE (1830–1905), French anarchist and revolutionary.

Louise Michel was the daughter of Marianne Michel, chambermaid to the mayor of Vroncourt

Who am I, Louise Michel? Don't make me out to be better than I am—or than you are. I am capable of anything, love or hate, as you are. When the Revolution comes, you and I and all humanity will be transformed. Everything will be changed and better times will have joys that the people of today aren't able to understand. . . . Beyond this cursed time will come a day when humanity, free and conscious of its powers, will no longer torture either man or beast. That hope is worth all the suffering we undergo as we move through the horrors of life.

Source: *The Red Virgin: Memoirs of Louise Michel,* edited and translated by Bullitt Lowry and Elizabeth Ellington Gunter (University, Ala., 1981), p. 197.

in Haute-Marne. Her father was most likely the mayor's son, Laurent Demahis. Her paternal grandparents gave her a good education and she became a schoolteacher. In 1855 she moved to Paris, opening her own school there in 1865.

In Paris, Michel helped found the Association for the Rights of Women in 1870. She also had links with free-thought groups, the banned International Working Men's Association, and followers of the revolutionary Auguste Blanqui. During the Franco-Prussian War of 1870–1871, Michel joined both the women's and men's Vigilance Committees of the Eighteenth Arrondissement of Paris, which espoused Blanqui's revolutionary socialism.

Michel welcomed the Paris Commune (18 March–28 May 1871), supporting its democratic and anticlerical agendas. She participated in political clubs, drove ambulances, and fought as a combatant with the Sixty-first Montmartre Battalion where she gained a reputation for fearlessness. After the defeat of the Commune she was arrested and deported to the Pacific island of New Caledonia. There she befriended the indigenous Kanaks, supporting them in their 1878 uprising and becoming an enduring critic of French colonialism. After the amnesty of 1880, Michel returned to France a popular hero in leftist circles.

The Commune and its repression by Republicans confirmed Michel's conversion to anarchism. She envisaged a society without government and regarded suffrage as irrelevant. Grassroots resistance was the key to change, and the general strike would produce a social revolution. For this reason Michel rejected Marxism, which accepted parliamentary politics, although she shared speaking platforms with Marxist leaders on occasion. Women's rights were also defended within an anarchist framework. Michel supported "free marriage," equal education, and women's right to work but declined to support female suffrage.

The political scandals of the 1880s and 1890s strengthened Michel's criticism of the Third Republic. She refused to take the Republican side in the Boulanger affair (1887–1889) and the Dreyfus affair (1898–1900), regarding the Republicans as no better than other bourgeois governments. Her attacks on the Republic's failings resembled those of the extreme Right, although she did not support their monarchism. She was not enthusiastic about the anarchist bombings in Paris in 1892 but regarded "propaganda by the deed" as a justifiable revolutionary tactic.

Michel's key contribution to the revolutionary movement was as an inspiring speaker. She was the subject of constant surveillance in France and London, where she spent considerable time from 1890. Michel's uncompromising views brought several terms of imprisonment. She was jailed briefly in 1882 and served two years of a six-year sentence in 1884–1886 for defending striking miners. Later in 1886 she was jailed for a further four months, and she spent two months in prison in 1890 before being released without charge. Michel's radicalism also brought an attack on her life (1888), even her political enemies praised her compassion and generosity.

Louise Michel died in Marseilles on 9 January 1905. She left a large literary legacy, including novels, poetry, and children's stories, as well as her memoirs (1886) and a valuable history of the Paris Commune (*La Commune,* 1898). Her historical significance derives principally from her political role, especially during the Commune. She has been seen as an archetypal revolutionary woman, one of the few women generally included in studies of anarchism. Her status as a feminist, however, is debated. While Michel condemned women's oppression and mixed with feminists of

Personification of the French Republic as Louise Michel trampling Louis Adolphe Thiers and Napoleon III. Musée de la Ville de Paris, Musée Carnavalet, Paris, France/ Bridgeman Art Library/Archives Charmet

every stripe, her hostility to parliamentary politics and reformism meant that she rejected both republican feminism and the socialist women's movement. Instead Michel envisaged a social revolution that would end both women's and men's oppression.

See also **Anarchism; Franco-Prussian War; Paris Commune.**

BIBLIOGRAPHY

Primary Sources

Michel, Louise. *The Red Virgin: Memoirs of Louise Michel.* Edited and translated by Bullitt Lowry and Elizabeth Ellington Gunter. University, Ala., 1981.

———. *Souvenirs et aventures de ma vie.* Edited by Daniel Armogathe. Paris, 1983.

Secondary Sources

Albistur, Maïté, and Daniel Armogathe. *Histoire du féminisme français.* Paris, 1977.

Barry, David. *Women and Political Insurgency: France in the Mid-Nineteenth Century.* Houndmills, U.K., and New York, 1996.

Eichner, Carolyn J. *Surmounting the Barricades: Women in the Paris Commune.* Bloomington and Indianapolis, Ind., 2004.

Gullickson, Gay L. *Unruly Women of Paris: Images of the Commune.* Ithaca, N.Y., and London, 1996.

Johnson, Martin Phillip. *The Paradise of Association: Political Culture and Popular Organizations during the Paris Commune of 1871.* Ann Arbor, Mich., 1996.

Maitron, Jean. *Le mouvement anarchiste en France.* Vol. 1: *Des origines à 1914.* Paris, 1975.

Moses, Claire Goldberg. *French Feminism in the Nineteenth Century.* Albany, N.Y., 1984.

Mullaney, Marie Marmo. *Revolutionary Women: Gender and the Socialist Revolutionary Role.* New York, 1983.

Offen, Karen. *European Feminisms, 1700–1950: A Political History.* Stanford, Calif., 2000.

Schulkind, Eugene W. "Le rôle des femmes dans la Commune de 1871." *1848: Revue des révolutions contemporaines* 42, no. 185 (1950): 15–29.

———. "Socialist Women during the 1871 Paris Commune." *Past and Present* 106 (1985): 124–163.

Sonn, Richard. *Anarchism in Cultural Politics in Fin-de-siècle France.* Lincoln, Neb., 1989.

Thomas, Edith. *The Women Incendiaries.* Translated by James and Starr Atkinson. New York, 1966.

———. *Louise Michel.* Translated by Penelope Williams. Montreal, 1980.

Susan K. Foley

MICHELET, JULES

MICHELET, JULES (1798–1874), often considered France's greatest historian and the country's preeminent Romantic historian.

Jules Michelet was born and educated in Paris, the only child in a loving family of poor printers. Largely self-taught in his early years, the apprentice turned student entered the prestigious Charlemagne College in 1813 and had to repeat his first year. Then he sped forward. Baccalaureate in 1817, doctor of letters from the Sorbonne in 1819, and lycée professor in 1821, Michelet launched a brilliant academic career, and he lived up to his promise. Thus Michelet is sometimes presented as a sort of nouveau riche, a man who entered the bourgeoisie by profession, income, and social contacts. Yet

Michelet always claimed that he remained true to the common people, and a careful reading of his life and work confirms his self-definition.

The young Michelet was strongly influenced by the still largely ignored Italian philosopher Giovanni Battista Vico (1668–1744), who viewed history as the development of societies and human institutions, as opposed to the biography of great men or the work of divine providence. Translating and commenting on the Italian's work in an 1827 publication and thereby contributing to Vico's discovery in the nineteenth century, Michelet wrote introductions to both modern and universal history and was rewarded with an appointment to the École Normale Supérieure. Then, after completing a two-volume *History of the Roman Republic* (1831), Michelet turned his focus from antiquity to medieval France. Motivated by the Gothic revival and Romantic nationalism, Michelet's decision also reflected his appointment as director of the historical section of the National Archives shortly after the Revolution of 1830. This allowed him to combine teaching and writing with intense research in still largely unexplored documentary collections and tell what he believed would be the genuine history of his country and its people. Many historians, though not Michelet himself, believe that his history of France in the Middle Ages, published between 1833 and 1844 and becoming the first six volumes in his multivolume *History of France* (1833–1867), is his most solid, useful, and lasting accomplishment. They single out his vast knowledge of the sources, his uncanny evocation of times and places, and his empathetic and balanced understanding of different views and individuals. Michelet explained in 1835, "it is an indispensable condition for the historian to enter into all doctrines, to understand all forces, and to be passionately involved in every state of mind" (quoted in Monod, p. 30). His treatment of the national revival under Joan of Arc in the fifteenth century is a famous example of his early work.

As Michelet was finishing his history of the Middle Ages, he experienced personal challenges, and he became increasingly impassioned and partisan. Moving from the École Normale in 1837 to teach at the Collège de France, he left working closely with a small elite to lecturing to a large, excitable crowd that preferred eloquent language and sweeping synthesis to precise analysis. Increasingly France's past seemed important to Michelet as the long, difficult preparation for the French Revolution, when the French people reached maturity and began the liberation of mankind. Committed historian and man of the people, he would now concentrate his feelings on the side of popular forces and guard against his earlier generous, but impartial and therefore superficial, sympathy for all.

This critical turning point in the historian's development is reflected in Michelet's *The People* (1846), written just before Michelet jumped from the Middle Ages to his white-hot *History of the French Revolution* (1847–1853). Drawing in *The People* upon personal experience, history, and contemporary debates, Michelet paints a vivid picture of French society and the social dislocation that afflicts all classes. Then, after rejecting socialism, he offers a solution in the form of republican nationalism and egalitarian secular education that will teach the Revolution of 1789 and heal a fractured France. Sickened by the failure of the Revolution of 1848 and refusing to swear allegiance to Louis-Napoleon Bonaparte (later Napoleon III; r. 1852–1871), Michelet lost his government positions and turned to full-time writing. He completed his seven-volume history of the French Revolution, filled in the early modern period history of France with another eleven volumes, and wrote popular impressions of nature and anticlerical polemics. Michelet's later history is often criticized for being overly emotional and biased against the monarchy, the nobility, and the clergy, while idealizing popular forces and revolutionary upheaval. A great individualist, Michelet had many admirers but few disciples. He survives as a gifted writer with a grand, heartfelt historical narrative of compassionate nationhood for a noble people.

See also **France; Revolutions of 1848; Romanticism; Tocqueville, Alexis de.**

BIBLIOGRAPHY

Primary Sources

Michelet, Jules. *The People.* Translated with an introduction by John P. McKay. Urbana, Ill., 1973.

Secondary Sources

Fauquet, Eric. *Michelet, ou, La gloire du professeur d'histoire.* Paris, 1990.

Mitzman, Arthur. *Michelet, Historian: Rebirth and Romanticism in Nineteenth-Century France.* New Haven, Conn., 1990.

Monod, Gabriel. *Jules Michelet.* Paris, 1875.

JOHN P. MCKAY

MICKIEWICZ, ADAM (1798–1855), Polish Romantic poet.

Adam Mickiewicz was born on 24 December 1798 in or near Nowogródek (Novogrudok), a town in historical Lithuania, with Polish high culture, inhabited by Jews, surrounded by Belarusian peasants, featuring a mosque for Tatars, in the Russian Empire. Although the Polish-Lithuanian Commonwealth had been partitioned out of existence by Russia, Austria, and Prussia three years before Mickiewicz's birth, Polish culture remained dominant in historical Lithuania. From 1815 to 1819 Mickiewicz studied philology at the University of Vilnius, a center of Polish culture. He published Romantic manifestos in his *Poetry* in 1822 and two further works in 1823. In 1824 he was exiled for membership in secret student organizations. He spent five years in St. Petersburg, Moscow, Odessa, and Crimea, came to know Russian poets, and befriended Alexander Pushkin. In 1826 Mickiewicz published his *Sonnets,* which included erotic poetry and descriptions of steppe, sand, and sea. In 1828 followed *Konrad Wallenrod,* which included poetic formulations of the Romantic ideas of durability ("As butterflies drown in golden amber/Let us remain dear as we once were" or "O folk song! Ark of the covenant between days of old and these days of ours!"). The hero was a medieval Lithuanian who became a Teutonic Knight to rescue his people; Wallenrodism (apparent treason as national rescue) became an enduring political idea.

In the November Uprising of 1830, it appeared that Poland and Lithuania might liberate themselves from Russian rule. Mickiewicz was in Rome in 1830, and he failed to reach Russian Poland before the uprising was crushed. Like many refugees from Poland, he settled in Paris. There he quickly published three further works: the third book of *Forefathers' Eve* (1832), the *Books of the Polish Nation and of Polish Pilgrimage* (1832), and finally *Pan Tadeusz* (1834). The first two of these defined the current of messianism, articulating the special place of the poet in the life of the nation, and that of Poland in the general revival of European civilization. *Pan Tadeusz,* a gorgeous novel in poetry, was Mickiewicz's greatest technical achievement, and one of the most impressive poems of the nineteenth century. The hero, a humble young nobleman, disappears into his environment, the historic Lithuania of the early nineteenth century. The action is of little significance, while the descriptions of the habits of the petty gentry and the beauty of the land are, in addition to their limpid elegance, of anthropological and even botanical interest. The realism, the attention to private life, and the melancholy of the ending anticipate the end of Romanticism. It was Mickiewicz's last major poetic work.

In 1840 Mickiewicz was awarded the chair in Slavic literatures at the Collège de France. His lectures displayed a professional competence, as well as a particular affection for the Lithuanian and Belarusian languages. The "Springtime of the Peoples"—the Revolutions of 1848—found Mickiewicz in Rome. He gained an audience with Pope Pius IX, whom he is supposed to have told that the Holy Spirit was to be found in the blouses of the workers of Paris. Mickiewicz's heresy guaranteed that he was never in favor with the Roman Catholic Church. In Italy he organized a legion, which he provided with a list of *Principles:* among them equal rights for Jews, "our elder brothers in the faith." This formulation endured; it was employed, for example, by Pope John Paul II in the late twentieth century. In 1849 Mickiewicz published, in Paris, the journal *La tribune des peuples* (Peoples' tribune). The Crimean War (1853–1856) provided Mickiewicz with his last occasion to realize what he regarded as his mission. He traveled to Istanbul, with the intention of raising a Jewish legion to fight against the Russian Empire. There he died suddenly on 26 November 1855.

In his day, Mickiewicz was regarded as one of the greatest European poets. The French scholar Ernest Renan remembered him as part of the French heritage, associating him with the radical democrats Edgar Quinet and Jules Michelet. Michelet called Mickiewicz "the greatest of us all." Poles remember him as a national "bard," a term that reveals the special role of poetry in Polish national consciousness during the partition period of the nineteenth century. The Poland that Mickiewicz imagined was the plural society of the Polish-Lithuanian Commonwealth. His poems were dear to Polish socialists who wished to create a federation with Poland's eastern neighbors, and to Lithuanian and Belarusian patriots. Polish nationalists treated the poetry as pedagogical texts of the Polish language. Mickiewicz himself was of mixed national origins, likely both Belarusian and Jewish, and was concerned with the rejuvenation of Europe.

See also **Chopin, Frédéric; Nationalism; Poland.**

BIBLIOGRAPHY

Mickiewicz, Adam. *Pan Tadeusz; or, The Last Foray in Lithuania*. Translated by Kenneth Mackenzie. New York, 1966.

Weintraub, Wiktor. *The Poetry of Adam Mickiewicz*. The Hague, Netherlands, 1954.

TIMOTHY SNYDER

MILAN. When Napoleon I (r. 1804–1814/15) entered Milan in May 1796, he came into a walled city of some 140,000 inhabitants. The Lombard countryside began just outside the city walls and there was little industry of note inside. Milan was a trade and religious center—above all for the crucial silk industry—as well as a place of strategic and cultural importance. By the time Italy entered World War I in 1915, the city's population had risen to more than 500,000 and was to be boosted further by the conflict. Milan's walls had been demolished and the urban periphery was beginning to dominate the city center. Smokestacks dominated the first industrial belt and the city possessed a powerful socialist movement, a Socialist Party mayor, a burgeoning working class, and a trade fair of worldwide importance. This rapid development had taken place against the background of occupation by two foreign powers, the Risorgimento, and the slow growth of local and national democracy. By 1915, Milan could lay full claim to being the "moral capital" of Italy, a city where production, work, and exchange were such as to make it the economic and financial powerhouse of the new Italy.

NAPOLEON'S INFLUENCE

Napoleon's rule over Milan was brief but revolutionary. The presence of the French encouraged patriot groups to organize and spread propaganda. The semi-autonomous powers Napoleon granted Milan under the Cispadane and Cisalpine Republics encouraged self-rule and helped to create a domestic political class. Moreover, Napoleon intervened to reshape the urban fabric of the city. The French built an amphitheater—the Arena—that would later host the first game of the Italian football team in 1910, as well as modern palaces (above all the vast Foro Bonaparte complex). The world-famous Brera Art Gallery was enriched by Napoleon by raiding churches and galleries in Italy and even the Louvre, and his statue still stands in its courtyard.

After the French were briefly thrown out of Italy in 1799, Napoleon returned in 1800 and made himself king of the Kingdom of Italy in 1805 in a pompous ceremony held in the city's cathedral (whose facade he had completed). The capital of this kingdom was Milan, and Napoleon set himself up in the Royal Palace. Construction of a triumphal arch facing Paris, through which Napoleon could enter the city, was begun; unfortunately for Napoleon, the arch was not completed until 1838 under the Austrians, although Napoleon III (1808–1873) and the new king of Italy were able to pass through it on their own entrance into Milan in 1859. French rule modernized Milan in other ways. Administrative and legal systems were instituted that are still, in part, in place, especially the prefects that link national and local government.

NATIONALISM AND REVOLUTION

Napoleon's reign ended in 1814, and the Austrians then ruled over Milan for the next fifty-five years. The 1820s saw the genesis of the nationalist movement in Milan, particularly around the brilliant historian and political activist Carlo Cattaneo (1810–1869) who advocated a federalist version of an Italian nation-state while identifying the roots of the city's industrial revolution in the rural resources of Lombardy that linked organically with the services, markets, and technical expertise of the city. After a series of abortive and sometimes farcical attempts at patriotic rebellion, the Milanese rose up against the Austrians in March 1848. The spark for the revolt was a monopoly over tobacco and snuff, which was merely symptomatic of the way the Austrians taxed the Milanese to the hilt. As revolution spread across Italy and Europe, the Milanese defeated the 13,000-strong Austrian army on the streets and liberated the city during the Five Days; an event still celebrated every March in Milan and marked by a huge monument and ossuary in the city center. Some four hundred Milanese were killed in the fierce fighting, and Cattaneo himself was right at the center of events. The Austrian field marshal Joseph Radetsky (1766–1858) regrouped and re-took Milan after a series of battles some five months later. The movement's failure to link up with the countryside, and the lack of a powerful and radical social base, had proved to be its undoing. Nonetheless, the Milanese would not have long to wait. In 1853 an abortive rising inspired by Giuseppe Mazzini (1805–1872) was brutally repressed, but in the years 1859 to 1861, the city's hinterland was at the center of a series of battles that eventually led to its incorporation in a unified Italy under the Savoy monarchy.

ITALY'S "MORAL CAPITAL"

Italian Milan began to lay the foundations for its future role as an industrial powerhouse. Water power in the countryside was utilized for agricultural production and later as a crucial energy source: "white coal." Impressive engineering works to tap into this potential were constructed across Lombardy, particularly in the Adda and Ticino valleys. In the 1870s, the first important industries began to form in Milan. Pirelli set up its first factory in 1872, and by the 1890s had become an enormous concern producing rubber and other goods on the northern edge of the city. The creation of a commuter railway service—the northern railways—with Swiss investment helped with the mobility of freely available cheap rural labor from the countryside. Meanwhile, a building boom in the city attracted investment and thousands of construction workers. Milan also consolidated its position as a market and commercial center. Five international exhibitions held in the city between 1871 and 1906 helped to create a dynamic entrepreneurial class linked to European markets. Technical and scientific advances were stimulated by the milieu around the city's highly modern Politecnico—a kind of technical university first set up in 1863—and the private Università Commerciale Luigi Bocconi, opened in 1901.

In the 1880s, what literary critic Vittorio Spinazzola has called "the only serious ideological myth, not empty and rhetorical, elaborated by the Italian bourgeoisie after unification, the myth of Milan, the myth of the 'moral capital,' began to take shape" (p. 317). The 1881 Expo was a key component of this myth. This huge explosion into the public sphere covered an area of 162,000 square meters, and more than eight thousand businesses were represented in rooms of "new machines" and "galleries of work." But what was the content of the idea of a "moral capital"? On the one hand, Milan was the true capital because Rome was not—the myth was a negative assessment of the contribution of Rome and the south to Italy's industrial progress. Milan was modern, industrious, hardworking, honest, productive; Rome was corrupt, unproductive, lazy, and premodern. Rome was the political capital, Milan the real driving force of the nation, its moral heart. On the other hand, the myth was also a celebration of these values in themselves—a series of character traits and concrete realities pertaining to the Milanese worker, entrepreneur, and industrialist—modernity, hard work, thrift, legality, the self-made person. In Milan, D. Papa wrote that "here by day there is always much to do: people go, come back, rush, make themselves busy, they study and they work" (cited in Rosa, p. 42). In addition, Milan was a moral capital because of its cultural strength: it was home to the greatest opera house in the world—La Scala—and the intellectual establishments and classes, including the newspaper *Corriere della Sera,* the publishing houses and universities, the writers and poets, and scientists and engineers.

Milan was seen as a city of urban planning, of order, of productive intellectuals, the only real Italian *city* and the only *European* city in Italy—a city not of no government, but of *good* government. That not everything was reduced to money and work and the moral "correctives" introduced by the most powerful urban socialist reformist movement in

Galleria Vittorio Emanuele II, Milan. Designed by Giuseppe Mangoni and built between 1865 and 1877, the enclosure forms an arcade linking the plazas of the Milan cathedral and the opera house. ©AUSTRIAN ARCHIVES/CORBIS

Italy—with its vast network of welfare and educational institutions such as the Società Umanitaria—meant that capitalism, it was argued, had a human face in Milan. The moral capital ideal was thus an organic mix of dynamism, modernity, gesellschaft-values, paternalism, collective enterprise and humanity. For all these reasons, and despite the dark side of Milan revealed in journalistic inquests, "Milan," as historian Giovanni Rosa has written, "was convinced, just twenty years on from Unification, that it really was the 'moral capital of Italy'" (p. 21).

Milan also played a key role as a financial center, with the institution of modern investment banks such as the Credito Italiano, whose sumptuous offices dominated the new financial district near Piazza Cordusio. Milan's stock exchange—the most important in Italy—was opened nearby in 1808 and moved to large premises in 1809 before a special palace was built to accommodate it, also in Piazza Cordusio, in 1901. Milan's commercial mix was complemented by its extraordinary network of small, specialized shops and by the highly popular consumer cooperative movement.

URBAN GROWTH

The city was also freed up and expanded in the nineteenth century. Huge walls (extending eleven kilometers) had been constructed around Milan in the mid-sixteenth century and remained the boundaries of the *Comune di Milano* until 1873 when the *Corpi Santi,* so-called because the bodies of the first Christian martyrs were buried in the ring outside the city walls, was incorporated into the city. Immigrants flooded into the city from the hinterland and across Lombardy, as well as from as far away as Apulia, to work in the new factories that mushroomed across the city. More than 250,000 immigrants came to Milan between 1871 and 1914. Industrial development after the 1890s was rooted in the key areas of metalwork and mechanical industries (Falck, Breda), rubber (Pirelli), munitions (Ansaldo), cars (Alfa Romeo), and chemicals (Carlo Erba). As a result, Milan was a workers' city at the outbreak of World War I. The 1911 census showed that out of an "active" population of 153,000, some 103,000 were workers.

This rapid expansion was not without its problems. Poverty and frustration led to violent bread riots in May 1898 that were put down with cold brutality by the cannons of General Fiorenzo Bava-Beccaris. A state of siege was declared, and indiscriminate arrests hit the reformists—who had opposed the riots—and even some local priests. Alongside the capillary organizations of the reformist movement—inspired by the trade unions and Socialist leaders Filippo Turati (1857–1932) and Anna Kuliscioff (1854–1925)—a revolutionary syndicalist movement began to emerge. September 1904 saw the first general strike in Italy originate in Milan, called by the Chamber of Labor that had briefly fallen under control of syndicalists. Milan had been the first Italian city to set up a Chamber of Labor in 1891. General strikes also swept across Milan in 1906 and 1913. "Red Week" of June 1914 found strong support in the city, and the revolutionary interventionists of the "Radiant May" in 1915 took to the streets to demand—successfully—Italian entry into the war.

The reformists were also very active. Socialists and trade unionists set up local libraries, employment offices, credit associations, "popular" universities, schools, mutual-aid societies, cooperatives, theaters, and newspapers, and constructed working-class housing and formed unions. This organic and hegemonic activity built on the Milanese traditions of craft organizations, skilled work, and artisan socialism. Milan was the innovative urban center of reformist strength from the 1890s onward, the "jewel in the crown" of the gradualist movement. The roots of these ideas of gradualism and integration both formed and built upon such trends in the Milanese working class and middle classes.

CULTURE

Culturally, Milan also played a central role. Apart from La Scala, where many operas by Giuseppi Verdi (1813–1901) and Giacomo Puccini (1858–1924) were premiered and which remained the most celebrated opera house in the world, there were the publishing industries and newspapers. The city created the most important newspaper in Italian history, *Il Corriere della Sera.* Founded in 1876 by textile magnates the Crespi family, the *Corriere* became a model for all other newspapers and a school of journalism for all the most important writers who worked for the press. The journalistic milieu in the city center, near the paper's head offices, was matched by the cultural and literary milieu elsewhere, ranging from Alessandro Manzoni (1785–1873) and Stendhal (1783–1842) in the early to mid-nineteenth century, to the futurist painters, poets, and architects who worked in Milan in the early part of the twentieth century. Milan also set up one of Italy's first silent film industries on the edge of the city in the same period.

CHANGING CITY

The city's infrastructure matched its economic wealth, with modern electric power, extensive tram commuting systems, train networks, and the canals, which were still a key part of urban transport. Urban growth ate up the countryside, absorbing into the city's fabric the rural buildings that had marked the plains. Villages became part of Milan in a matter of years, and rural work coexisted alongside Fordist factory production. By the time of the outbreak of war in 1915, the city was a heaving mass of workers and worker-peasants, many of whom had maintained their links with the countryside. Political ferment in the city was to transform Italy (and Europe) in the wake of the conflict, as Benito Mussolini (1883–1945) set up his pro-war and revolutionary nationalist paper in the city in 1915: *Il Popolo d'Italia.* The world's first fascist movement was to be formed in the city in March 1919 under his leadership, and Mussolini himself would take control of the whole country in 1922.

See also **Naples; Rome; Trieste; Venice.**

BIBLIOGRAPHY

Antonioli, M., et al., eds. *Milano operaia dall'800 a oggi.* Rome-Bari, 1993.

Bell, Donald Howard. *Sesto San Giovanni: Workers, Culture and Politics in an Italian Town, 1880–1922.* New Brunswick, N.J., 1986.

Borghi, F. *Milano negli ultimi cinquant'anni di storia italiana, 1871–1921.* Milan, 1923.

Cattaneo, C. *L'insurrezione di Milano e la successiva guerra,* edited by L. Ambrosoli. Milan, 2001.

Consonni, G., and G. Tonon. "Alle origini della metropoli contemporanea." In *Lombardia: il territorio, l'ambiente, il paesaggio.* Vol. 4: *L'età delle manifatture e della rivoluzione industriale,* edited by C. Pirovano, 89–164. Milan, 1984.

Davis, John A. *Conflict and Control: Law and Order in Nineteenth Century Italy.* London, 1988.

Davis, John A., ed. *Italy in the Nineteenth Century.* Oxford, U.K., 2000.

Decleva, E. "L'Esposizione del 1881 e le origini del mito di Milano." In *Dalla stato di Milano alla Lombardia contemporanea,* edited by S. Pizzetti, 181–211. Cisalpino-La Goliardica, 1980.

Della Peruta, F. *Milano: Lavoro e fabbrica, 1815–1914.* Milan, 1987.

Foot, John. *Milan Since the Miracle: City, Culture, Identity.* Oxford, U.K., 2001.

Ginsborg, Paul. "Peasants and Revolutionaries in Venice and the Veneto, 1848." *Historical Journal* 17, no. 3 (1974): 503–550.

Granata, I., and A. Scalpelli, eds. *Alle radici della democrazia: Camera del Lavoro e Partito Socialista nella Milano di fine Ottocento.* Rome, 1998.

Laven, David, and Lucy Riall, eds. *Napoleon's Legacy: Problems of Government in Restoration Europe.* Oxford, U.K., 2000.

Lyttelton, A. "Milan, 1880–1922: The City of Industrial Capitalism." In *People and Communities in the Western World.* Vol. 2, edited by Gene Brucker, 256–257. Homewood, Ill., 1979.

Meriggi, M. *Amministrazioni e classi sociali nel Lombardo-veneto 1814–1848.* Bologna, 1983.

Morris, Jonathan. *The Political Economy of Shopkeeping in Milan, 1886–1922.* Cambridge, U.K., 1993.

Rosa, G. *Il mito della capitale morale: Letteratura e pubblicistica Milano fra Otto e Novecento.* Milan, 1982.

Spinazzola, V. "La 'Capitale Morale': Cultura milanese e mitologia urbana. *Belfagor* 3 (1981): 317–327.

Tilly, Louise A. *Politics and Class in Milan, 1881–1901.* New York, 1992.

JOHN FOOT

MILITARY TACTICS.

MILITARY TACTICS. Until the French Revolution, the distinction between military strategy and tactics was so obvious that even feckless salon generals—an abundant species before the revolution—could grasp it. Strategy, as the Prussian military theorist Carl von Clausewitz put it in 1830, was "the use of battles to attain the object of war." Tactics referred to "the use of armed forces in battles." This distinction began to blur as armies expanded after 1789. Flush with draftees from conscription, such as the French *levée en masse,* and new national guard levies, such as the Austrian *Landwehr,* all the European powers found themselves deploying not one but *many* armies comprised of multiple divisions or corps. This created an intermediate level of warfare, between strategy and tactics, which was generally called "operations."

Given that tactics and operations have always been interrelated, this entry discusses the development of both concepts in the years between the French Revolution in 1789 and the outbreak of World War I in 1914.

FRENCH REVOLUTIONARY WARS PERIOD

The revolutionary military tactics unleashed by the Jacobins in the French Revolutionary Wars had their roots in the old regime. Already in the 1770s several French military philosophes had wrestled with the demands of modern war. Impatient with the inconclusive methods of the age of Frederick the Great (r. 1740–1786), when small, poorly supplied professional armies maneuvered in vast spaces and habitually refused battle, a number of uniformed French reformers (Pierre de Bourcet, Jean de Gribeauval, and Jacques de Guibert) pressed for the introduction of all-arms "divisions"—12,000-man units that would include infantry, cavalry, and artillery and move faster and hit harder; additional artillery with standardized calibers in mobile six- and eight-gun batteries; and a modern general staff that would coordinate the operations of a multipart army and drive it forward to live off the land and, according to Guibert, hit "pitilessly, drowning the enemy in flame and steel."

In a series of campaigns from 1796 to 1800, the young French generals formalized the changes begun in the 1770s. The French embraced the division of 12,000 men with thirty-eight guns. The French line infantry—filled with conscripted peasant louts—increasingly resorted to bayonet charges by "shock columns" shielded up to the point of attack by dispersed companies of *tirailleurs* (sharpshooters). In theory, the celerity of the shock columns compensated for their clotted vulnerability to volley fire from lines of waiting gunners and musketeers. In practice, the early French shock columns—which would be vastly improved under Napoleon—merely released what one Austrian onlooker called "un mer de sang" (a sea of blood). At Jemappes (1792) and Wattignies (1793), the French infantry suffered 30 percent casualties, which were sustainable only because France alone had universal conscription, and manpower was therefore plentiful and cheap.

French operations on multiple fronts in all weather worked chiefly because the French systematized what they called supply *à la maraude* (marauding). The army often marched without heavy impediments such as tents and field kitchens, preferring to requisition food, drink, fuel, and shelter from enemy populations. Paradoxically, heavy requisitioning *eroded* the fighting effectiveness of the French army. Dependent on scrounging and pillage, French units literally dissolved in Spain, Russia, and Germany in their mad scramble for food and drink. That became a characteristic of the French Grand Army that the Allies learned to exploit.

General Napoleon Bonaparte refined the French military reforms. He folded two or three divisions into a corps. Napoleon increased the ratio of French guns to infantry faster than his enemies, from 2 per 1,000 at Austerlitz in 1805, to 3 per 1,000 at Bordino in 1812, to 3.5 per 1,000 at Leipzig in 1813. Shock tactics under Napoleon were fused with linear tactics in a package called *l'ordre mixte:* a smooth, devastating tactical transition from firing lines to bayonet charges. Bonaparte attached a brigade of cavalry to every corps and insisted on active scouting and pursuit: "No rest! Pursue the enemy with your sword in his back." Napoleonic operations strove for the *manoeuvre sur les derrières* (the enveloping attack), in which the French would fix the enemy in place before swinging detached units into his flanks. Clausewitz's *On War,* largely completed by 1830 but not published until 1833, owed its emphasis on annihilating battle to Napoleon and his brusque methods.

TECHNOLOGICAL CHANGES

The next great changes in military operations and tactics in the mid-nineteenth century were driven by technology. The French changes of the late eighteenth century had been more political and social: a determination to apply Enlightenment ideals to armed force and a need to equip a mass army of peasants and sans-culottes for war. Starting in the 1850s, the Prussians refined warfare further, as they sought ways to knit railroads, telegraphs, and improved firearms—rifled muskets and artillery—into the modern campaign. Prussian General Helmuth von Moltke (1800–1891) was the maestro.

Moltke understood that Prussia—derided by Voltaire in the eighteenth century as a "kingdom of border strips"—had to defeat its peculiar geography before it could defeat anyone else. Railroads and telegraphs would be the essential bridge between Prussia's eastern heartland—Berlin, Breslau, and Königsberg—and its rich, western industrial districts in the Rhineland and Westphalia. Under Moltke's prodding, Prussia increased its railways from 3,860 kilometers (2,400 miles) of track in 1850 to 11,580 kilometers (7,200 miles) in 1870. Prussia also militarized the railroads, double-tracking lines, adding large platforms and sidings, and building dual-use carriages that could be rapidly converted from passenger wagons to troop, horse, and artillery carriers. With a dedicated general staff railroad and telegraph section, Prussia was poised to mobilize and strike faster than any other Great Power. When Otto von Bismarck picked a fight with the Austrian Empire in 1866, Moltke swung into action.

The Austro-Prussian War of 1866 was the first look at the Prussian military revolution, which was as significant operationally and tactically as the Napoleonic revolution. Speeding on trains to the Austrian border, three Prussian armies invaded Habsburg Bohemia before the Austrian army had even completed its mobilization. Moltke grasped that the new mobility of the industrial age degraded the old Napoleonic advantage of "internal lines," that is, of a well-supplied position *between* converging enemies. If the enemies converged *fast* enough, they could throttle the central army before it had properly deployed. "An army hit in the front and flank finds that its strategic advantage of internal lines has been beaten tactically," Moltke later summarized.

Of course the tactics themselves had to be sound, and Moltke's were the best. Prussia in 1866 was the first European Great Power to arm its entire infantry establishment with breech-loading rifles. Although the other powers had switched in the course of the 1850s from muskets to rifles, they all preferred muzzle-loaders because of the problem of fire control. Excited troops in the heat of battle tended to shoot wildly. Provided with a breechloader, they might fire off all of their ammunition—typically sixty rounds—in just fifteen minutes. A rifleman with a muzzle-loader would need an hour, and would be more easily regulated by his noncommissioned officers, who would have time to cool emotions, call out ranges, and align front and back sights.

Moltke never solved the problem of fire control. No army ever has. Only one out of every 250 rounds fired by a Prussian infantryman in 1866 actually struck an Austrian. But that was not bad by nineteenth-century standards. Union troops in the American Civil War required 1,140 pounds of lead and powder to kill a single Confederate. In every battle of 1866, scrambling Prussian infantry companies defeated lumbering Austrian shock columns. By the end of the war, whole Austrian units dissolved at the approach of the Prussians.

In the Franco-Prussian War (1870–1871), the French army rearmed with its own breech-loading rifle—the "Chassepot"—and discarded the aggressive shock tactics that they had employed since the French Revolution. Instead they emphasized defensive fire from prepared positions. Moltke met this challenge with a second technological leap. Between 1866 and 1870 the Prussians took delivery of new field artillery: rifled, steel, breech-loading six-pound Krupp cannon. The new Prussian field guns outranged France's obsolete muzzle-loading bronze four-pounders, were more accurate, and had a higher rate of fire. Although they stumbled initially, by the last battles of the war—beginning with the great victory at Sedan (September 1870)—the Prussians had learned the tactical rule that would apply in the Russo-Japanese War and World War I: never send infantry to do a job that artillery can do. Squeezed into a narrow pocket around Sedan, the French army was pulverized by a closing ring of 700 Krupp cannon.

Sedan also enshrined the modern operational ideal: the *Kesselschlacht* (cauldron battle). An extended version of the Napoleonic *manoeuvre sur les derrières,* the *Kesselschlacht* would be handed down from Moltke to Alfred von Schlieffen. Advancing quickly by road or rail, aggressor armies would fix a flat-footed enemy in place and swarm around his flanks, enveloping him, cutting off his lines of retreat, and demolishing him in a cauldron of fire.

MODERN, EARLY-TWENTIETH-CENTURY WAR

The Russo-Japanese, or Manchurian, War (1904–1905) should have put European armies on their guard. It was the first clash of Great Powers armed with the latest military technologies, which represented a geometric increase in killing power over the arms of the early 1870s. The new technologies of the new century had been demonstrated on a small scale in the Boer War (1899–1902). Boer troops armed with magazine rifles, quick-firing cannon, and automatic weapons had torn the overconfident British to pieces. At the battle of Colenso in 1899, the entrenched Boers had killed or wounded 1,143 British troops against just fifty casualties of their own.

Those results had seemed to confirm the prediction of the Polish banker Jan Bloch, who in 1897 had famously argued that war was no longer possible because of technological advances: "any advance in force along a front swept by the enemy's fire has become impossible." By 1904 a modern brigade of 3,000 men with artillery was capable of spewing more shells and bullets in a single *minute* than the Duke of Wellington's entire army of 60,000 had fired in the daylong battle of Waterloo in 1815. In the siege of Port Arthur, attacking Japanese troops sustained 60,000 casualties. Artillery was the chief agent of death. Guns and howitzers fired faster, and also struck harder because new chemical bursting charges permitted increased shell weights. Russian and Japanese officers at Mukden noted the first cases of a new affliction called "shell shock."

Why the European armies marched off to impale themselves on these deadly technologies in 1914 is a complex question. There were strategic disputes beyond the scope of this article, but the soldiers were driven chiefly by their own operational requirements. The German army, led by Helmuth von Moltke (1848–1916)—the great Moltke's pallid nephew—provoked the war to implement the Schlieffen Plan. Named for Field Marshal Alfred von Schlieffen (1833–1913), who had been German general staff chief from 1891 to 1905, the plan proposed to envelop and destroy the French, then turn on the Russians. It aimed to use speed and initiative to encircle slower-moving foes before they had completed their mobilizations. But the younger Moltke failed to reckon with French and Russian advances in doctrine and infrastructure. Both armies had studied the elder Moltke and the German way of war since 1870, and had developed their own strategic railroads and offensive war plans. Thus, the Schlieffen Plan ran into a wall in September 1914 at the Battle of the Marne, where French troops and artillery blunted the German advance and pressed it back. The same fate awaited the Germans in the east. After an initial victory at Tannenberg, the Germans and their Austrian allies were forced into trench warfare. "Schlieffen's notes do not help any further, and so Moltke's wits come to an end," the German war minister scathingly observed.

Only the Germans in 1914 really understood modern war. They endowed their units with light and heavy artillery and sufficient ammunition to fight a multiday battle. Every other army—French, Russian, British, Austrian, and Italian—entered the war with little heavy artillery and suffered crippling shell shortages. The Schlieffen Plan failed chiefly because the largely horse-drawn German army simply could not transport all of the material needed to beat the French and Russians in a sequence of lightning campaigns. The Allied (and Austro-Hungarian) failures were intellectual. They sincerely believed, as French General Joseph Joffre put it in 1913, that "battles are above all moral struggles." Repressing the gory results of the Boer, Russo-Japanese, and Balkan Wars, the generals of 1914 hoped, merely hoped, that things would go better in World War I by doing the same things on a larger scale.

See also **Armies; Clausewitz, Carl von; Moltke, Helmuth von; Napoleon; Schlieffen Plan.**

BIBLIOGRAPHY

Best, Geoffrey. *War and Society in Revolutionary Europe, 1770–1870.* Leicester, U.K., 1982.

Bond, Brian. *War and Society in Europe, 1870–1970.* New York, 1983.

Falls, Cyril. *The Art of War: From the Age of Napoleon to the Present Day.* New York, 1961.

Liddell Hart, B. H. *The Real War, 1914–1918.* London, 1930.

McElwee, William. *The Art of War: Waterloo to Mons.* Bloomington, Ind., 1974.

Wawro, Geoffrey. *The Austro-Prussian War: Austria's War with Prussia and Italy in 1866.* Cambridge, U.K., 1996.

———. *Warfare and Society in Europe, 1792–1914.* London, 2000.

———. *The Franco-Prussian War: The German Conquest of France in 1870–1871.* Cambridge, U.K., 2003.

GEOFFREY WAWRO

MILL, HARRIET TAYLOR (1807–1858), English writer.

Harriet Hardy was born in 1807 on Walworth Road, London, married John Taylor in 1826, and bore three children, Herbert, Algernon, and Helen. After being widowed, Harriet married John Stuart Mill in 1851. Their marriage ended with her death in 1858 in Avignon, France. (Harriet Taylor Mill will hereafter be Harriet and John Stuart Mill will hereafter be John.)

Unfortunately, Harriet is now known more for her biography than her writing, but controversy surrounds both her life and her work. First, her love affair with John for more than twenty years while married to Taylor resulted in the kind of intellectual gossip that still intrigues. The academy continues to argue about whether they were as chaste as John presents their relationship in his *Autobiography* (1873) and if they were, why? Some speculate that they were merely cautious or considerate of Harriet's husband. Others suggest that John may have wanted to spare his reputation as a scholar. Yet others blame Harriet for her "masochism" or frigidity. One argued for the possibility that she had syphilis, which she contracted from her husband and did not want to spread to John. Whatever the cause, the consequence is that Harriet and John devoted nearly twenty years before marriage and seven years in marriage spending much of their time together both in England and traveling in Europe. They enjoyed a passionate commitment to each other throughout these years as witnessed by the erotic letters they exchanged when separated.

The second question hovering around Harriet concerns her collaboration in the writing that bears John's name as author. John expressed his high opinion of Harriet and acknowledged her coauthoring some of their ideas and texts in private letters to her, in dedications, in letters, and in person to others, in his *Autobiography,* and even on her tombstone. From his death until the late twentieth century many scholars have simply disagreed with John. Many justifications for denying cooperation when it exists spring to mind, but why someone would declare work is joint when it is not is less obvious. Historians of philosophy have generally characterized John as "besotted" or "bewitched" by Harriet. They picture John as a man either so desperately in love or so in need of a strong personality to replace his father that he would do anything for Harriet, including misrepresenting her contribution to his work. Another approach to Harriet's role is to blame her for the ideas with which a particular historian disagrees. For example, Gertrude Himmelfarb accuses Harriet of pulling John toward socialism in his *Principles of Political Economy* (1848). Others accuse Harriet of seducing him to support atheism. So, either Harriet had no effect of John's ideas, or she was the source of the wrong ideas he had (the correct ones were his alone).

Beginning in the 1970s, feminists argued that this analysis of Harriet and John's alleged coauthorship is sexist. Harriet and John did work together, but the ideas they produced together were not "bad" ideas. A careful look at the letters, diaries, and manuscripts demonstrates their ongoing communication regarding specific texts, revisions, and ideas to be included in texts. An understanding of the activities that result in coauthorship helps to clarify how they might have worked. Evidence that both Harriet and John collaborated with other authors in both acknowledged and unacknowledged ways adds support. Finally, their joint work exemplifies the two issues they both found to be central to their age: feminism and socialism.

If we grant their collaborative working style, it is particularly difficult to discuss Harriet's contribution to the history of ideas. She wrote a number of articles and poems for the *Monthly Repository,* an article for the Society for the Diffusion of Useful Knowledge, and a number of private essays on marriage, women's education, women's rights, ethics, religion, and the arts. She coauthored with John a series of newspaper articles on domestic cruelty. And, if John is to be trusted, was the coauthor of *On Liberty* (1859) and the author of "On the Probable Futurity of the Working Classes" in his *Principles of Political Economy.* Her best-known work is "The Enfranchisement of Women," published in 1851 (although there is also a question of what role John played in this essay). From Friedrich Wilhelm Nietzsche (1844–1900), Charlotte Brontë (1816–1855), and Sigmund Freud (1856–1939) to American and Australian feminists, the Enfranchisement essay has roused passionate admiration and condemnation. It is more radical and more consistent than John's longer *Subjection of Women,* published in 1869. Readers of this essay and Harriet's others continue to admire her courage in uncovering domestic violence, demanding the right to divorce an abusive husband, insisting that women have the right to be educated and have a profession even while married, and pointing to the inequities of household chores as the base for larger public inequities.

See also **Feminism; Mill, John Stuart.**

BIBLIOGRAPHY

Primary Sources

Mill, Harriet Taylor. *The Complete Works of Harriet Taylor Mill.* Edited by Jo Ellen Jacobs and Paula Harms Payne. Bloomington, Ind., 1998.

Secondary Sources

Hayek, Friedrich August. *John Stuart Mill and Harriet Taylor: Their Correspondence and Subsequent Marriage.* New York, 1951.

Jacobs, Jo Ellen. *The Voice of Harriet Taylor Mill.* Bloomington, Ind., 2002.

Jo Ellen Jacobs

MILL, JAMES (1773–1836), Scottish philosopher.

Famous as the father of John Stuart Mill (1806–1873), James Mill was an important thinker in his own right. Trained during the Scottish Enlightenment at the University of Edinburgh, he studied Greek and philosophy, taking a degree in theology in 1798. Instead of becoming a preacher, he went to London in 1802 to become a journalist. An agnostic by 1808, as a writer he analyzed problems confronting the Anglican Church, education, economics, and government. His articles frequently appeared in the *Anti-Jacobin Review,* the *British Review,* the *Eclectic Review,* and the *Edinburgh Review,* and in 1811 he became one of the editors of the *Philanthropist.* He was also a regular contributor to the *Encyclopaedia Britannica.* Despite numerous journalistic pursuits, Mill could not provide a comfortable living for his large family until he was appointed an Assistant Examiner in the India House in 1819, a result of his most important work, *History of British India,* begun in 1806 and published in 1817. He later became Chief Examiner of the India House in 1830.

Significantly, in 1808 Mill became a disciple, friend, and assistant to Jeremy Bentham (1748–1832), helping to popularize the ideas of utilitarianism (also known as Benthamism or radical philosophy). Mill is known for being the organizer of Bentham's followers, who included David Ricardo (1772–1823) and Joseph Hume (1777–1855). In 1821 Mill, an advocate of the Banking School theory, helped establish the Political Economy Club in London, a precursor to the establishment of economics as a profession and university discipline. Thomas Robert Malthus (1766–1834), Ricardo, and others frequented these meetings. Mill's utilitarian tome on economics, *Elements of Political Economy,* was published in 1821.

As a utilitarian, Mill believed in seeking "the greatest happiness of the greatest number"; assumed that human beings are only motivated by self-interest and that they will always seek pleasure and avoid pain; sought to educate citizens to understand what was truly in their self-interest; and focused on training individuals to choose behavior that would result in the greatest happiness for the whole society. For Mill, utilitarianism was not a self-indulgent philosophy but one that required individuals to be self-disciplined and ethically exacting. In fact, he once noted that "under a bad government there is no common interest. Every man is governed by his private interest" (cited in Burston, p. 15). Mill explains the ethical foundations of utilitarianism in his *Fragment on Mackintosh* (1835). Indeed, like the prolific Bentham, Mill systematically articulated utilitarian ideas that are important in the history of thought about education, psychology, economics, ethics, and government.

IDEAS ON GOVERNMENT

Mill's 1820 article "Essay on Government," which appeared in the *Encyclopaedia Britannica,* laid out the utilitarian notion that good governments are representative in form. His rationale was that the more people have political power, the more their government is obliged to seek what is in the people's self-interest. Utilitarians distrusted the aristocracy and monarchy, assuming that aristocrats and monarchs wanted to aggregate all power and benefits to themselves. In this influential article, Mill concluded that a large portion of the citizenry would need to have the vote and that the House of Commons was the best locus of governmental power because it represented a majority of the people and could provide adequate checks to the monarch and aristocracy. This article also asserts that in order to ensure the greatest happiness to the greatest number, men must be guaranteed the highest compensation for their work and that a representative system could best fulfill this need.

Writer and politician Thomas Babington Macaulay (1800–1859) famously lambasted Mill's article on government, saying it was hardly the scientific document Mill claimed it was. Contemporary critics note numerous problems with the utilitarian philosophy. Nevertheless, it is generally accepted that his "Essay on Government" helped to create a climate in which the first Reform Bill of 1832 was passed, enlarging the voter rolls to include some of the middle and lower classes. The second (1867) and third (1884) Reform Acts would gradually add more unrepresented citizens to the voter rolls.

Even though Mill never went to India, he spent more than a decade writing his masterwork, *The*

History of India. As an examiner in the India House, the headquarters of the East India Company in London, reviewing incoming dispatches and preparing preliminary dispatches in return for almost two decades, he was able to put into practice some of his ideas about governing India, otherwise known as "the jewel in the crown" of England's colonies. Using a utilitarian rationale, he suggested that it was actually a positive that he had never been to India because he could be more objective about the people and the culture rather than sentimentalizing them as he thought other writers had done.

In the nineteenth century, Ricardo critiqued Mill's India politics, noting that one universal form of government might not be good for all cultures. He added that it was, at the very least, inconsistent to support representative government in general while also insisting that India be governed by England.

Modern critics differ on *The History*. Many have pointed out that it is in keeping with the work of postcolonial theorist Edward Said and others who argue that those who colonized the East in the nineteenth century viewed it and its peoples as inferior and as in need of the civilizing influence of the British. Javeed Majeed, however, suggests that *The History* is ambivalent about maintaining an imperial presence in India (it was not economical, for one thing), and that it is important to note that Mill wrote the work in order to critique British governmental practices at home and abroad so as to call for reform through establishment of utilitarian principles. Others find that in *The History* Mill attacks an Orientalist approach to India typical of his time—that is, an approach that stereotypes India as an exotic, romantic site of vast economic and aesthetic riches for the use of Britain.

IDEAS ON EDUCATION

In keeping with the utilitarian optimism about the potential to change human behavior so as to create a society in which the greatest happiness was to be had by the greatest number, Mill asserted that differences between human beings could be explained by their difference in education. Reflecting the influence of John Locke (1632–1704), he added that people could be educated through "association of ideas" to learn the behaviors that would be in their own and society's self-interest. That is, he assumed, with David Hartley (1705–1757), that human beings are like a blank slate (tabula rasa), and their knowledge of the world occurs only through sense experiences. Thus Mill reasoned that through a utilitarian education of systematic rewards and punishments people could be trained to truly know and act upon what was best for themselves and their society. For example, Mill writes, "Under the guidance and stimulus of desire to obtain Pleasure and to avoid Pain, we can associate beneficent means of attaining these ends, and become morally good people, or we can find such ends associated with causing pain to others, with corruption and so forth, and be morally bad" (cited in Burston, p. 231). Laying out "associationist" ideas and strongly critiquing the imagination, Mill's *Analysis of the Phenomena of the Human Mind* (1829) is seen as important to the history of psychology.

Though Mill and his utilitarian friends abandoned efforts to establish such a system for the lower classes in London, Mill did train his own nine children according to the associationist method, combining it with the monitorial method used in Scotland. To Mill this seemed an efficient, cheap, and scientific educational model: the teacher directly educated the best students, who were then required to teach the younger children, thus reinforcing their own education while easing the strain of teachers having to work with large groups of students.

Though Mill's pedagogy produced his brilliant son John Stuart Mill, it was at a high emotional cost. As John Stuart later wrote, his father was overly strict, providing his children more punishments than rewards and little emotional support. For example, Mill made his son start learning Greek in demanding doses when John was just three years old. Dedicated to logic, the elder Mill also derided the imagination, fiction, and literary writing. As an adult, John Stuart Mill realized that this lack of the poetic had all but destroyed his ability to feel.

In *Hard Times* (1854), Charles Dickens (1812–1870) fiercely lampooned the teaching paradigm that had so badly affected John Stuart Mill by featuring utilitarian educators named Gradgrind and McChoakumchild who only focus on "Facts." Likewise, Immanuel Kant (1724–1804) and Romantic writers, including William Blake

(1757–1827) and William Wordsworth (1770–1850), attacked Hartley's associationist ideas. They argued that the human mind is not just a passive receptor of sensations from the outside world but also actively engages with and changes reality.

Dedicated to putting into practice utilitarian ideas about schools, Mill actively helped to establish the University of London in 1825 as a means of democratizing education. At the time, Oxford and Cambridge only admitted upper-class men who were members of the Anglican Church. Mill ensured that the University of London would serve children of the middle and lower classes who were of all denominations as well as those who were nonbelievers.

See also **Bentham, Jeremy; Economists, Classical; Malthus, Thomas Robert; Mill, John Stuart; Utilitarianism.**

BIBLIOGRAPHY

Burston, W. H. *James Mill on Philosophy and Education.* London, 1973.

Leung, Man To. "James Mill's Utilitarianism and the British Imperialism in India." Political Studies Association Conference (1998), 1–15. Available from http://www.psa.ac.uk/cps/1998.htm.

Majeed, Javed. *Ungoverned Imaginings: James Mill's* The History of British India *and Orientalism.* Oxford, U.K., 1992.

Milgate, Murray, and Shannon C. Stimson. *Ricardian Politics.* Princeton, N.J., 1991.

Stokes, Eric. *The English Utilitarians and India.* Oxford, U.K., 1959.

Thomas, William. *Mill.* Oxford, U.K., 1985.

Zastoupil, Lynn. *John Stuart Mill and India.* Stanford, Calif., 1994.

Gail Turley Houston

MILL, JOHN STUART (1806–1873), British philosopher.

John Stuart Mill was the most influential British philosopher of the nineteenth century. He made significant contributions to philosophy, economics, political theory, and women's liberation.

Mill was born on 20 May 1806 at Pentonville, London. His father was James Mill (1773–1836), an important philosopher in his own right, as well as a prominent leader of the Philosophic Radicals, the author of *A History of India*, and a high-ranking employee of the East India Company. The Philosophic Radicals was a political group intent upon reforming all aspects of British society in the transition from a feudal and agrarian economy to an industrial economy. They generally opposed the conservative Tory landholders, the Church of England, and slavery. Under the influence of Adam Smith (1723–1790) and David Ricardo (1772–1823) they advocated free trade. They also advocated birth control and education as means of improving the condition of the working class. The other prominent leader of the Philosophic Radicals and a family friend was Jeremy Bentham (1748–1832).

Both James Mill and Bentham exercised an enormous influence over Mill.

James Mill had adopted the Enlightenment view that a carefully controlled environment, especially in education, could mold human beings to achieve extraordinary heights. These educational views were rigidly imposed on Mill who, in his *Autobiography*, describes his remarkable intellectual achievements. By the time he was sixteen, he had read and studied practically everything now considered part of a classical liberal education. Mill also developed from this rigorous training a keen analytical mind and the virtue of being highly self-critical in the Socratic sense. At the same time, Mill describes the negative effects of this educational system: a total emotional dependence upon his father, and a starved emotional life. Mill was involved in editing Bentham's writings and as a result became an early proselytizer of the Philosophic Radical position.

Mill briefly studied law with another neighbor, the famous jurist Charles Austin, but at the age of sixteen Mill entered the employment of the East India Company under his father's watchful eye. He remained in the employ of the Company until its dissolution in 1858, having succeeded to his father's position as chief examiner. He was responsible for correspondence with high-ranking Indian civil servants. The Company during Mill's tenure was concerned largely with the administration of India. His position, along with his self-discipline, allowed him to maintain a prolific writing career and correspondence.

From 1826 to 1830 Mill underwent a severe personal crisis. Part of it was intellectual, in that he came to see the shortcomings of the positions that James Mill and Bentham so prominently advocated. Part of it was psychological, as he struggled to achieve independence from his father's domination. Part of it was emotional, as he sought to fill the emotional vacuum of his early educational upbringing.

Four things enabled Mill to resolve his crisis. First, he read and met prominent Romantic poets such as William Wordsworth (1770–1850) and Samuel Taylor Coleridge (1772–1834), initially through his friendship with the poet John Sterling (1806–1844). Second, he was exposed to Continental thought, especially the works of Henri Saint-Simon (1760–1825) and Johann Wolfgang von Goethe (1749–1832) through another close relationship this time with Thomas Carlyle (1795–1881). Carlyle also encouraged Mill's critique of the thought of James Mill and Bentham. Third, Mill met and fell in love with Harriet Taylor (1807–1858) in 1831 through his association with a Unitarian group under the leadership of William Fox. What ensued was a celibate but scandalous romantic relationship that lasted until the death of Taylor's husband in 1849 and the subsequent marriage of Mill and Taylor in 1851. Harriet Taylor Mill exercised an enormous influence on Mill, comparable to that of his father, but more positive. In addition to encouraging the cause of women's liberation, she helped Mill gain a deeper appreciation of perhaps his most important idea, personal autonomy.

In 1835 Mill became the nominal editor of the *London Review*, the official organ of the Philosophic Radicals meant to rival the Whig *Edinburgh Review*. The fourth crucial event in Mill's own liberation was the death of his father, James Mill, in 1836. From 1836 to 1840 Mill was the owner and editor of the *London and Westminster Review*. During that time he published two significant reviews of the two volumes of Alexis de Tocqueville's *Democracy in America* (1835 and 1840). It was during this time that Mill was heavily influenced by the conservative views of Carlyle and Coleridge, and he tried to use his editorship to achieve a new synthesis, both intellectual and political, of both liberal and conservative views. By his own admission he failed. It was during this time that he wrote two essays, one on Coleridge and the other on Bentham, the latter serving both as a stinging critique of the views of the Philosophic Radicals and a catharsis.

Mill achieved fame in 1843 with the publication of *A System of Logic*. In addition to its discussion of technical topics in philosophy, it expressed both the hope and the limitations of producing a social science that could be the basis of sound public policy. The work was influenced by a long correspondence with Auguste Comte (1798–1857). Mill would eventually renounce his relationship with Comte because of the latter's views on the inherent inferiority of women, a narrow positivism, and what Mill saw as the totalitarian implications of positivism.

Mill achieved even greater fame in 1848 with the publication of the *Principles of Political Economy,* which dealt with all of the economic, social, and political problems created by an industrial and market economy. The work became the standard text in economics for the next fifty years.

Harriet Taylor Mill died in 1858. Thereafter Mill published a series of essays to honor her memory: "On Liberty" (1859), which was heavily influenced by Wilhelm von Humboldt (1767–1835); "Considerations on Representative Government" (1861); and "Utilitarianism" (1863). Mill served in Parliament (1865–1867), where he was generally supportive of William Ewart Gladstone (1809–1898), and he was elected rector of St. Andrews University (1866). Stefan Collini has characterized his life as that of a public intellectual, a man who, like Matthew Arnold (1822–1888) and others, saw himself as the Socratic questioner of Victorian England's fundamental beliefs. After Harriet's death, Mill spent much time at Avignon in a house overlooking the cemetery where they are now both buried. Among his social acquaintances at this time were John Russell, Lord Amberley (1842–1876) (for whose son, Bertrand Russell [1872–1870], Mill stood as godfather), Herbert Spencer (1820–1903), and John Morley (1838–1923). He published *The Subjection of Women* in 1869. His carefully orchestrated posthumous publications include the *Autobiography* (1873), *Nature, the Utility of Religion, Theism, Being Three Essays on Religion* (1874), and *Chapters on Socialism* (1891). Mill died at Avignon on 8 May 1873.

Just about every aspect of Mill's thought is subject to scholarly debate. For many years Mill's works *System of Logic* and *Political Economy* achieved textbook status in British universities, but this was followed by a long period in which Mill became a straw man accused of multiple inconsistencies. Late-twentieth and early-twenty-first-century scholarship has stressed the continuity in his work (Fred Berger, John Gray, John Robson, and Alan Ryan), the periodization of his work (Gertrude Himmelfarb), or the historical development in his work (Nicholas Capaldi). In philosophy he has generally been viewed as the inheritor of the British Empirical tradition that originated with John Locke (1632–1704) and David Hume (1711–1776) (T. H. Green, F. H. Bradley, and John Skorupski), but later he was interpreted as a Romantic and precursor of idealism (Bernard Semmel and Capaldi). In ethics he was routinely characterized as a simplistic utilitarian follower of Bentham (G. E. Moore), but later scholarship emphasized his sophistication (J. O. Urmson) and distance from utilitarianism. With regard to religion, he has been identified as an atheistic follower and advocate of Comte's religion of humanity (Linda Raeder), but others see Mill as a sincere progressive (Eldon J. Eisenach, Robert DeVigne). In politics, he has been widely hailed as the epitome of liberalism (C.L. Ten and Nancy Rosenblum), as a consistent proponent of democracy (J.H. Burns), and as someone who never abandoned radicalism (Alan Ryan and William Thomas); but others (Maurice Cowling, Joseph Hamburger, and Shirley Letwin) see Mill as an elitist authoritarian. Until the publication of the work of Lynn Zastoupil in the 1980s there was little discussion of Mill's views on colonialism.

Much controversy surrounds Mill's economic views, with some seeing him as a kind of socialist (R. Ashcraft, Jonathan Riley; Himmelfarb claims this is true only under Harriet's influence), while others view him as a defender of capitalism (Pedro Schwartz, Samuel Hollander, and Lewis Feuer). Mill's relationship with members and leaders of the working class (aside from Feuer) needs more work. In social philosophy, he has been criticized for encouraging a destructive form of self-expression (Willmore Kendall and Himmelfarb) and hailed for defending a sophisticated form of autonomy (Capaldi). Mill's views on women's issues has been criticized by some feminists (Julia Annas and S. M. Okin) and praised by others (Ruth Abbey, Wendy Donner, and Mary Lyndon Shanley).

There is of course endless fascination with Mill's life and his relationship with Harriet. The *Autobiography* has been treated by Bruce Mazlish as a form of psychohistory; Janice Carlyle raises important questions about the truthfulness of the whole; Capaldi treats it as a self-conscious exercise in Bildung. The relationship with Harriet has been viewed as negligible (Alexander Bain, Mill's first biographer), and as substantial (F. A. Hayek and Michael St. John Packe); her influence has been described as negligible (H. O. Pappe), as negative (Himmelfarb), and as positive (Capaldi and Jo Ellen Jacobs).

The *Collected Works* in thirty-three volumes, including extensive correspondence with many major nineteenth-century figures, was edited by John Robson and published by the University of Toronto Press (1980–1991). Nicholas Capaldi published a biography on Mill in 2004; older useful biographies include works by Alexander Bain and Michael St. John Packe.

See also **Carlyle, Thomas; Coleridge, Samuel Taylor; Comte, Auguste; Mill, Harriet Taylor; Saint-Simon, Henri de; Wordsworth, William.**

BIBLIOGRAPHY

Primary Sources

Mill, John Stuart. *Collected Works.* 33 vols. Toronto, 1963–1991.

Secondary Sources

Capaldi, Nicholas. *John Stuart Mill.* Cambridge, U.K., 2004.

Eisenach, Eldon J., ed. *Mill and the Moral Character of Liberalism.* University Park, Penn., 1998.

Hollander, Samuel. *The Economics of John Stuart Mill.* 2 vols. Oxford, U.K., 1985.

Schneewind, Jerome B., ed. *Mill: A Collection of Critical Essays.* Garden City, N.Y., 1968.

Semmel, Bernard. *John Stuart Mill and the Pursuit of Virtue.* New Haven, Conn., 1984.

Skorupski, John. *John Stuart Mill.* London, 1989.

NICHOLAS CAPALDI

MILLET, JEAN-FRANÇOIS (1814–1875), French realist painter.

The artistic and political position of Jean-François Millet has never been very stable. Born a landed peasant in Gruchy (Normandy), he spent most of his life from 1849 in the village of Barbizon on the edge of the Forest of Fontainebleau. After studying art in Cherbourg, Millet moved to Paris in 1837 where he enrolled in the École des Beaux-Arts. There, painting conventional biblical and mythological subjects, he refined his skills in figure painting, competed for academic awards, submitted works to annual government-sponsored exhibitions, and sought state commissions. Returning to Normandy in 1840, Millet took up a commercially viable mix of portraiture, mildly erotic themes, and pastorals, while continuing to seek official recognition by sending mythological, biblical, and rustic subjects to the Paris Salons.

Study for *Summer: The Gleaners.* By Jean-François Millet, before 1853. HIP/ART RESOURCE, NY

With the outbreak of the revolution in Paris in February 1848 and the formation of a provisional republican government, Millet's artistic career took a decided turn. On the strength of substantial critical acclaim for a mythological subject that he exhibited at the 1847 Salon, Millet submitted a religious painting along with a peasant subject (*The Winnower*, 1847–1848) to the 1848 Salon. By late June 1848, when popular uprisings in support of the left-wing provisional government were harshly suppressed, it was Millet's monumental naturalist depiction of a peasant that was purchased by the interior minister of the new republic and won him an important government commission. Yet, despite *The Winnower*'s massive scale, its generalized pictorial treatment, and the allusion to the revolutionary flag in the figure's color scheme, Millet's intent in representing this solitary peasant was entirely unclear. While the dramatic events of 1848 prompted many artists to take up overtly political subjects, and although Millet counted many republicans among his immediate associates, his own attitude toward the revolution remains uncertain. He participated briefly in the June riots, but in which faction is unknown. In 1849, Millet fulfilled his state commission with another rustic theme, *The Harvesters*, and moved with his family to Barbizon, escaping the civil turmoil of Paris. Here, he would concentrate almost all of his public works on contemporary peasant subjects. Rendered in a style of heroic or "epic naturalism," and often incorporating traditional French and Italian artistic conventions, Millet infused his scenes with an elevated content that had traditionally been the reserve of biblical, mythological, and history painting. Critics' interpretations thus easily moved between reading his peasant scenes as signs of social inequities or urban disillusionment to seeing them as symbols that could carry much broader religious and mythological allusions.

During the Second Empire, critical debate focused sharply on the antagonism between an "official" realism that was anchored in conventional and academic aesthetic values, and the new realist school that fiercely challenged them. The increased ideological importance that republican cultural elites placed on boldly unidealized depictions of the peasants and working class pulled the debates over realist subjects and their pictorial treatment in markedly political directions. During the 1850s and 1860s, Millet's paintings met with considerable hostility from conservative opponents of the new realism who perceived in his brutal depictions of rural life the transgression of aesthetic values that sustained an idealized illusion of peasant society as a whole. Interpreted as having distorted the hardships of peasant life and of exaggerating their social and economic conditions, conservatives accused Millet of transforming reality to preach radical political ideals. The force of this antirealist campaign was borne by paintings such as *The Gleaners* (1857) and *Man with a Hoe* (1860–1862). The visual immediacy and heroic scale of the *Gleaners,* whose brutal, swollen features accentuate their weighty poses, in conservatives' eyes patently exaggerated the stark distinction between the poorest strata of peasant society gleaning in the picture's foreground, and the actions of the thriving harvesters in the distance. Attacks such as these garnered Millet unequivocal support among liberal and left-wing critics. Opposed to the Second Empire's political and social initiatives, liberal critics' defense of realist painting assailed the state's aesthetic prerogatives as counterparts to its social contradictions. The debate, then, over Millet's depiction of rural life was part of a much larger struggle to appropriate the peasant into a symbolic vocabulary with broader ideological and political implications.

With the consolidation of the Third Republic in the 1880s, and the ascension of the Empire's republican opposition to positions of institutional power, Millet's reputation again transformed. Posthumous biographies and the retrospective exhibition in 1887 held at the École des Beaux-Arts repositioned Millet's peasant imagery to a central place in a newly defined version of French national art. Cleansed of reminders of radical political associations, Millet's realism was discursively reshaped to embody the essential Frenchness of the nation's artistic heritage.

See also **Courbet, Gustave; Painting; Realism and Naturalism; Revolutions of 1848.**

BIBLIOGRAPHY

Clark, T. J. *The Absolute Bourgeois: Artists and Politics in France, 1848–1851.* London, 1973.

Herbert, Robert L. *Jean-François-Millet.* London, 1976.

———. *From Millet to Léger: Essays in Social Art History.* New Haven, Conn., 2002.

Parsons, Christopher, and Neil McWilliam. "Le Paysan de Paris: Alfred Sensier and the Myth of Rural France." *Oxford Art Journal* 6, no. 2 (1983): 38–58

Michael R. Orwicz

MILLET SYSTEM. At the height of its expansion, the Ottoman Empire consisted of a diverse population in terms of religion, ethnicity, and language. The *millet system* is the term traditionally used to describe the process through which the Ottomans governed their non-Muslim subjects. Prior to their conquest of Egypt in 1517 and their subsequent expansion in the Middle East and North Africa, the Ottomans, as Muslims, were a minority ruling over an overwhelmingly Christian majority, especially in their European provinces. The designation *system* has been questioned by Benjamin Braude, who posits that this term suggests "an institutionalized policy toward non-Muslims" when in fact "it was a set of arrangements, largely local, with considerable variation over time and place" (1982, p. 74). This argument is valid, but for the lack of a better word we will continue to adopt the traditional terminology to refer to the various arrangements the Ottomans had with their non-Muslim subjects.

The millet system is deeply rooted in the Islamic legal tradition. The term *millet* is the Turkish rendering of *Millah,* the Arabic word that occurs in the Koran in three contexts. The first refers to the religion of Abraham and of the ancient prophets (for example, Koran 2:130, 135; 3:95; 12:38; 7:88). The second specifies the religion of the Christians and the Jews (Koran 2:120). The third affirms that Islam is the continuation of the religion of Abraham (Koran 22:78). The term *Millah* is generally understood to mean "religion." The plural *Milal* appears in several medieval Arabic works and in the titles of at least two well-known works on religions and sects by Ibn Hazm (994–1064) and Shahrastani (d. 1153). In matters of governance, *millet* refers to a non-Muslim religious community and from the 1600s it is often extended to ethnic or foreign communities.

The millet system is modeled after the centuries-old Muslim legal practice related to *Ahl al-Dhimmah* (The Protected People), the non-Muslim subjects of the Islamic state. Often, they are mentioned as *Ahl al-Kitab* (People of the Scriptures), a Koranic term that refers to Christians and Jews. The first Arab expansion beyond Arabia in the seventh century resulted in the inclusion of former Byzantine and Sasanian dominions within the nascent Islamic empire. Non-Muslim subjects were not pressured to convert. On the contrary, they were left to practice their religion and had their personal safety guaranteed and functioned as an autonomous community. In exchange for this tolerance (in a medieval context) they had to abide by a number of restrictions and impositions, among which the payment of the poll tax by their able-bodied males (Arabic: *Jizyah*; Turkish: *Cizye*). The set of regulations pertaining to the *Dhimmi* (Turkish: *Zimmi*) are stated in the *Covenant of Umar* (also known as the *Pact of Umar*), the third Muslim caliph (r. 634–644). Historically, and with the probable exception of the poll tax payment, the additional regulations and restrictions, particularly those related to distinctive clothing and public behavior, were enforced unevenly and their application depended on the whim of individual rulers and of the prevailing sociopolitical conditions. An early documentary evidence of such arrangements dates from the first century of Islam during the governorship of Qurrah ibn Sharik in Egypt (r. 709–714). These papyri indicate payment of the poll tax, payment of a tax in kind on crops, and the rendering of other services by Coptic villagers.

It is difficult to document the very beginning of the millet system in the Ottoman Empire. The assumption is that the Ottoman state adhered to the precepts of Islamic law regarding its non-Muslim subjects from its inception. This system enabled non-Muslim subjects to enjoy a considerable degree of autonomy: they were not coerced to convert to Islam, and the state allowed local communities to settle their legal problems (primarily in matters of civil law) according to their own law or custom, as long as no Muslim subjects were involved. In the European provinces of the empire, this system helped preserve the ethnic, linguistic, and religious identities of their respective populations. By the nineteenth century, the millet system became an unintended contributing factor to the disintegration of the empire following the success of the nationalistic movements among the Ottoman subjects in the Balkans and central Europe. From about the same period, the term *millet* acquired an additional meaning, that of "nation"; a meaning that is now prevalent in modern Turkish.

The Ottoman reforms initiated in the nineteenth century and commonly known as the *Tanzimet* promised the equal treatment of all subjects, regardless of their *millet*. This resulted in the gradual weakening of the millet system and the rise of the laity at the expense of the power of the clergy. The millet system was finally abolished when the new Turkish republic ratified the Peace Treaty of Lausanne (24 July 1923).

See also **Minorities; Ottoman Empire.**

BIBLIOGRAPHY

Abu-Jaber, Kamel S. "The Millet System in the Nineteenth-Century Ottoman Empire." *Muslim World* 57 (1967): 212–223. A useful article despite some generalizations.

Braude, Benjamin. "Foundation Myths of the *Millet* System." In *Christians and Jews in the Ottoman Empire: The Functioning of a Plural Society,* vol. 1, edited by Benjamin Braude and Bernard Lewis, 60–88. London and New York, 1982. This two-volume work contains a number of relevant articles.

———. "The Strange History of the Millet System." In *The Great Ottoman-Turkish Civilisation,* vol. 2, edited by Kemal Çiçek, 409–418. Ankara, 2000.

Gibb, Hamilton A. R., and Harold Bowen. *Islamic Society and the West: A Study of the Impact of Western Civilization on Moslem Culture in the Near East.* London and New York, 1957. Vol. 1, pt. 2, pp. 207–261.

Shaw, Stanford. "The Jewish Millet in the Ottoman Empire." In *The Great Ottoman-Turkish Civilisation,* vol. 2, edited by Kemal Çiçek, 447–462. Ankara, 2000.

Tritton, Arthur Stanley. *The Caliphs and Their Non-Muslim Subjects: A Critical Study of the Covenant of 'Umar.* London, 1970, reprint of 1930 edition. A useful work despite some shortcomings.

Adel Allouche

MILYUKOV, PAVEL

MILYUKOV, PAVEL (1859–1943), Russian historian and politician.

One of late imperial Russia's most influential and widely read historians, Pavel Nikolayevich

Milyukov is best known in the early twenty-first century as a principal theoretician of liberalism in Russia and as the founder and leader of the liberal Constitutional Democratic Party, known as the Kadets. The author of some sixteen books and hundreds of articles on historical and topical themes, he twice served as a deputy to the Duma, the lower house of the Russian legislature, organized its wartime coalition known as the Progressive Bloc, and, in the February 1917 revolution, helped organize the Provisional Government, serving as its first minister of foreign affairs. He participated in the anti-Bolshevik movement in the Russian civil war, and, after 1920, he was a controversial leader of the Russian émigré community in Paris and editor of the widely read newspaper *Poslednie novosti* (Latest news). He married Anna Sergeyevna Smirnova in 1887; they had three children.

EARLY CAREER AS HISTORIAN AND TEACHER

Milyukov was born in Moscow on 27 January (15 January, old style) 1859 to an educated family. He received his undergraduate and advanced (*magister*) degrees in history from Moscow University, where he taught from 1886 to 1895. A self-proclaimed positivist, Milyukov, with his teachers Vasily Osipovich Klyuchevsky, Pavel Vinogradov, and Maxim Kovalevsky, helped create and disseminate the sociological and archive-based approach to history known as the Moscow (or Klyuchevsky) school of historiography. Milyukov's most important historical works include his 1892 dissertation, *The Russian State Economy in the First Quarter of the Eighteenth Century and the Reforms of Peter the Great,* in which he provocatively argued that the socioeconomic costs of making Russia a great power had nearly ruined the country, and his popular three-volume *Studies in the History of Russian Culture,* which went through numerous editions between 1896 and 1917. Several theses of this work provided a foundation for his mature political conviction that Russia could and would become a constitutional state. These include his emphasis on the enormous, dynamic role of the state in shaping Russian society; his contention that Russia, despite important singularities, had followed a "European" path of development; and his arguments concerning the adaptiveness of the Russian "national type" and the extent to which even putatively traditional Russian institutions were actually borrowed.

Milyukov's university career in Russia ended in January 1895 when he was dismissed from Moscow University and sent into internal exile for his critical views of autocracy. He then spent several years in the Balkans, teaching and participating in archaeological expeditions. Returning to Russia in 1899, Milyukov settled in St. Petersburg and increasingly became involved in publicistic writing and oppositional groups, primarily around the socialist journal *Russkoe bogatstvo* (Russian wealth). He was jailed for his political speeches and writings three times between 1901 and late 1905, which had the effect of enhancing his public reputation.

In spring 1902 Milyukov became involved with a group of urban intellectuals and activists in provincial (zemstvo) government, who planned to produce a journal to be published abroad and smuggled into Russia, for the purpose of organizing a liberation movement. Milyukov contributed thirteen articles between 1902 and 1905 to *Osvobozhdenie* (Liberation); these articles, along with those of the journal editor, Peter Struve, decisively shaped the liberation movement's program and a new kind of Russian liberalism. This liberalism, democratic, activist, and social reformist in its program, had much in common with the "new liberalism" contemporaneously being worked out in Britain and France by such thinkers as J. A. Hobson, L. T. Hobhouse, and Alfred Fouillée. Milyukov most fully articulated his liberal views in the book *Russia and Its Crisis* (1905), based on lectures he gave in the United States in 1903 and 1904, in which he traced Russian liberalism's "intellectual" rather than bourgeois origins, the broadening of its social basis, and its rapprochement with socialism. Liberals, he maintained, had come to realize that individual freedom and political rights are only the first goals of the liberal program, not its end; liberals and socialists could work together for the foundation of a democratic Russia and broad social reforms.

FOUNDER AND LEADER OF THE KADETS

From early 1905, as the revolutionary situation in Russia intensified, Milyukov devoted himself to full-time political activity. Initially he drew on his personal connections in both moderate and socialist camps to promote a broad-based, united political front through the union movement, but as he became disenchanted with the growing radicalism of the unions and the revolutionary parties, he began working to organize a formal liberal party, one that would cooperate with but be distinct from the Left. He helped draft the program of the Constitutional Democratic Party—popularly known as the Kadets—which held its founding congress in October 1905. In addition to calling for a constitution granting individual rights and full equality for all citizens of the empire, and the creation of a legislature elected by universal suffrage, the party program contained sweeping social provisions, including the right to unionize and strike, introduction of state-supported health insurance and old-age pensions, and partial redistribution of land to the peasantry. By virtue of his theoretical and publicistic talents, organizational skills, and ability to mediate between left and right wings of the new party, Milyukov naturally emerged as its de facto head, from 1907 to 1917. He was also able to shape liberal views through his position as coeditor of the party's unofficial newspaper, *Rech* (Speech), from 1906 to 1917.

The Constitutional Democrats were the largest single party in both of the first two State Dumas, in 1906 and 1907. Although the authorities barred Milyukov from standing for election, he played an important role in defining Kadet strategy and tactics. Overestimating governmental weakness, he shared responsibility for the confrontational nature of Kadet tactics in the First Duma, which contributed to the legislature's swift dissolution in July 1906. Milyukov was elected from St. Petersburg to the Third and Fourth Dumas, in 1907 and 1912, respectively. As head of the Kadets' Duma deputation, which had been greatly reduced in size thanks to restrictive changes to the franchise, Milyukov strove to create a meaningful legislative role for the party as a constructive opposition. Beyond this general goal, Milyukov's interests in the Dumas were education, foreign policy, defense reforms, and the nationality question. Here, his concerted efforts to protect the rights of Finns, Jews, Armenians, and other minorities from chauvinistic legislation caused nationalists to excoriate his and the Kadets' patriotism, as well as making him the target of physical assaults and death threats from the extreme Right. On the central committee of the party itself, Milyukov worked to combat disunity and disillusionment among Kadets in an increasingly repressive political climate.

Milyukov's convinced pacifism was reflected in his writings on the arms race and the Balkan Wars (1912–1913), and particularly in his stand against Russia's taking action on behalf of Serbia in summer 1914. This position—courageous as it was unpopular—has been overshadowed by his subsequent, ardent support of Russia's war effort and interests as a Great Power, once Germany formally declared war. Milyukov and the Kadets' patriotism and war work did much to restore the liberals' reputation, also opening the door for closer cooperation with other parties. In summer 1915, military debacles and rising public dissatisfaction with the conduct of the war prompted Milyukov to organize a broad coalition in the Duma, the Progressive Bloc, which pressed for a ministry enjoying public confidence and other measures intended to restore national unity and morale. The government's refusal to cooperate with the bloc, and rising public discontent, prompted Milyukov's influential denunciation in the Duma of government failures. His November 1916 speech in which he asked "Is this stupidity or treason?" is often characterized as the opening salvo of the Russian Revolution.

ROLE IN RUSSIAN REVOLUTION AND ITS AFTERMATH

Though he had not desired the outbreak of revolution, once it began Milyukov played the lead role on the Duma's side in negotiating establishment of a Provisional Government with representatives of the new Petrograd Soviet of Workers' and Soldiers' Deputies, from 13 March (28 February, O.S.) to 14 March (1 March, O.S.). Milyukov was named minister of foreign affairs, and expected that he and his party would dominate the new government. Instead, he held his position for only two months, thanks in part to the unpopularity of his insistence that Russia obtain Constantinople and the Straits after the war: street demonstrations in Petrograd (formerly St. Petersburg) precipitated his resignation from the cabinet on 15 May (2 May, O.S.) and the formation of a new coalition government. In the following months, though he remained one of the most prominent political figures in Russia, he was powerless to stem his party's declining influence or the disintegration of the state.

Declared an "enemy of the people" shortly after the Bolshevik seizure of power in October (November, new style) 1917, Milyukov joined forces with the anti-Bolshevik (White) Volunteer Army in southern Russia. From November 1918, he worked on behalf of the anti-Bolshevik cause from abroad, despite his misgivings about the conservatism of the White generals. Following the Red victory, Milyukov first settled in Paris, little suspecting he would never see his homeland again. He died in poverty in Aix-les-Bains, France, on 3 March 1943, at the age of eighty-three.

See also **Kadets; Liberalism; Revolution of 1905 (Russia); Russia.**

BIBLIOGRAPHY

Primary Sources

Milyukov, Pavel N. *Gosudarstvennoe khoziaistvo Rossii v pervoi chetverti XVIII stolietiia i reforma Petra Velikogo.* St. Petersburg, 1892.

———. *Ocherki po istorii russkoi kul'tury.* 3 vols. St. Petersburg, 1896–1903. Followed by 6 subsequent editions.

———. *Russia and Its Crisis.* Chicago, 1905. Reprint, with a foreword by Donald W. Treadgold, New York, 1962.

———. *Vospominaniia.* 2 vols. 1955. Reprint, Moscow, 1990.

Secondary Sources

Makushin, A. V., and P. A. Tribunskii. *Pavel Nikolaevich Miliukov: Trudy i dni (1859–1904).* Ryazan, Russia, 2001.

Stockdale, Melissa Kirschke. *Paul Miliukov and the Quest for a Liberal Russia, 1880–1918.* Ithaca, N.Y., 1996.

Melissa K. Stockdale

MINORITIES. In approaching the history of ethnicity in nineteenth-century Europe, one must immediately consider it in the context of two other social concepts, *nation* and *race.* All three gained significance during this period from a central fact of European life: the rise of state units based on citizenship and internally united not just by a single ruler but by language, history, and culture. This shift from multinational empire to homogeneous nation-state would dominate much of nineteenth-century life, culminating in the 1919 Paris peace settlement. It produced the modern idea of the nation as a sovereign entity that aligned political and cultural boundaries to emphasize the unity of the people who composed it. At the same time, European concepts of race became more sharply defined and more prominent. While the Enlightenment had pioneered the classification of different peoples according to physical characteristics, during the nineteenth century the idea of human races as unchanging and completely separate gained popularity, spurred on by new theories in anthropology and the physical sciences. By the end of the century, concepts of nation and race had merged to an important extent, so that references to "the British race" or "German race" had become common in educated European discourse.

Between two such massive conceptual frameworks, what was the place of ethnicity in nineteenth-century Europe? Unlike *nation* and *race,* the term *ethnicity* did not appear widely, owing more to twentieth-century American social science. And yet ideas of ethnicity played a significant role in the development of modern European society and culture. Let us start with definitions. *Ethnicity* refers to a sense of commonality between individuals based on several factors, including at times language, history, biology, a common territory, family ties, and rituals. Scholars have generally differentiated between ethnicity and race, the latter based on major hereditary physical differences, and between ethnicity and religion, although both religion and race can play a role in defining ethnic identifications. Ethnic groups, like other social units, define themselves by both inclusions and exclusions. They can be very small or very large, as large as (or larger than) nation-states. As late-twentieth-century scholarship has made clear, ethnic groups (like nations and races) arise from historical conjuncture and evolve over time. Essentialist ideas of ethnicity are not literally true, but rather represent strategies of self-definition on the part of ethnic groups.

In nineteenth-century Europe ethnicity became, more than ever before, a function of the nation-state. The creation of the modern nation-state to a large extent centered on the struggle for ethnonational homogeneity, or what some call ethnic nationalism. States strove to enforce a common language and history over their entire territory, bringing together the political and cultural boundaries of the nation. Paradoxically, nations that achieved this goal ceased to regard their dominant cultures as ethnic, but rather as national and hegemonic. The elevation of certain dialects to the status of national languages, underscored by the rise of mass education in the nineteenth century, is perhaps the clearest example of this. This process did not destroy ethnicity, however, but rather made it more and more synonymous with cultural difference, relegating it to the margins of the nation-state. Therefore, the rise of ethnic nationalism was complemented by the rise of ethnic minorities, peoples whose cultures lay at variance with the increasingly homogeneous culture of the nation. Peoples, like the Irish, the Gypsies, the Jews, and most of the peoples of eastern Europe, who had existed as subject nations in multinational empires, became increasingly viewed not as separate entities but as foreign bodies within the nation-state. This was especially true of groups that, through either migration or involuntary displacement, had left their traditional homelands for a diasporic mode of existence.

This entry will consider the history of both ethnic nationalism and ethnic minorities in Europe during the nineteenth century. It will outline the ways in which the rise of state power and the increasing importance of both political and cultural unification in the formation of ethnic groups and nations transformed European society in the era between 1789 and 1914. It will argue that ethnicity in nineteenth-century Europe arose both at the behest of the nation-state and in reaction to (sometimes against) it. Throughout European society, from the elites to the peasantry, ethnicity gradually became a key component of collective and individual identity. The fact that ethnic customs and cultures were often portrayed as traditional and unchanging should not be taken at face value, but rather as an indication of the powerful shock of the new in a rapidly changing continent.

ETHNONATIONALISM AND THE NATION-STATE

The rise of national cultures in the nineteenth century gave a new significance to ideas of ethnicity. The elevation of certain ethnic or regional traditions at the expense of others both underscored the importance of cultural traditions and challenged minority ethnic groups and the legitimacy of ethnic difference as a whole. As with so many other aspects of the history of modern Europe, there is perhaps no better place to start than the French Revolution. Not only in France but throughout Europe the Revolution fostered the idea of national cultures, even while it in theory rejected them in favor of an internationalist liberalism. Whereas in France itself the heritage of the Revolution became a powerful aspect of national identity, in other countries, notably Germany, the resistance to revolutionary occupation and ideology proved decisive in the constitution of ethnonationalism.

France In France the French Revolution fostered two paradoxical (even contradictory) ideas of the nation and national unity. The most prominent was the universalist tradition, the belief that the core of national identity resided in the ideological principals of liberty and citizenship enshrined in the Declaration of the Rights of Man and of the Citizen (1789). To be French (as opposed to a member of the internationalist aristocracy) meant to subscribe to these principles and, if need be, to dedicate one's life to championing them. Frenchness resided in the acceptance of core beliefs, not in one's ancestry nor culture. It therefore followed that anyone who accepted these beliefs could become French. This universalist ideal, historically grounded in the experience of the Revolution, defined the nation around citizenship and equality before the law, and has remained a key component of what it means to be French down to the present. At the same time, the Revolution also spurred the creation of a specific national identity based on language and culture. For example, during its most radical phase the Revolution elevated Parisian French to the status of the national language, suppressing Alsatian German, Provençal, and other languages as counterrevolutionary. In this way languages became dialects, reducing ancient regional cultures to subnational ethnic minorities. The revolution thus produced a specifically French universalism, a phrase that accurately expresses its contradictory vision of the nation. All men could share in the benefits of Enlightenment and liberty, but in order to do so fully they must in effect become French. Napoleon I's conquest of Europe thus represented both the extension of liberty to the peoples of the Continent, and the aggrandizement of the French nation.

The paradox of revolutionary nationalism survived both the Bourbon and Orleanist restorations to become the dominant approach to national identity in nineteenth-century France. In many respects, the political aspect of French identity seemed most important, both because nationalists throughout Europe and beyond hailed the French Revolution as the great symbol of liberty, and because until the late nineteenth century conservative and reactionary forces tended to oppose both liberalism and nationalism. No one expressed this idea of French and modern nationalism better than the historian Joseph-Ernest Renan in his 1882 Sorbonne lecture "What Is a Nation?" Rejecting the idea of a racial basis to national identity (an idea that was in fact growing more powerful in Europe) Renan portrayed the modern nation as a political and historical construct, a deliberate creation of citizens rather than a natural entity. And yet, while Renan emphasized the importance of politics and ideology in constituting a nation, he also acknowledged the significance of culture. "A community of interest is assuredly a powerful bond between men. Do interests, however, suffice to make a nation? I do not think so. Community of interest brings about trade agreements, but nationality has a sentimental side to it; it is both soul and body at once; a *Zollverein* is not a *patrie*" (p. 18). As the legacy of the Revolution itself became not just one of principles but also one of historical triumphs and collective memories, so did the idea of national universalism become the cornerstone of French identity.

The prime mover in this process during the nineteenth century was the French state. The triumph of republicanism, first in 1848 and then more definitively after 1870, made the principles of 1789 the leitmotiv of national politics. At the same time the Third Republic in particular completed the Revolution's mission of transforming France into an internally unified nation of citizens equal before the law. The expansion of state power also took the form of the homogenization of regional traditions into a synthetic national culture. In his celebrated study *Peasants into Frenchmen: The Modernization of Rural France, 1870–1914*, Eugen Weber has outlined the ways in which the French state integrated the provinces into its own vision of the nation. A variety of institutions paved the way for the conquest of rural France, frequently viewed by Parisians at the beginning of the century as a land of savages. The establishment of a state railway network centered around Paris both enabled people to travel around the country more easily and helped create national economic markets. The establishment of mandatory national military service brought together young men from different regions, training them in the defense of a common motherland. Most important, the republic created a system of obligatory primary education that not only taught an awareness of France's history, geography, and common culture (complete with national flags and maps in classrooms) but also created the mass literacy necessary for an appreciation of French identity. Finally, the republic's renewal of France's overseas empire, especially under Prime Minister Jules Ferry in the 1880s, also fostered an ethnic sense of national identity. Although in theory the principles of the Revolution applied wherever the French flag flew, in reality France's civilizing mission reinforced the idea that only those who adopted French culture, not just French politics, could be full-fledged citizens. The practices of republican empire distinguished the French from their colonies on the basis not only of ethnicity but of race as well, since in large part greater France was an empire of nonwhite colonial subjects dominated by white citizens in the metropole.

Germany If in France the state drove the creation of an ethnically unified nation, in Germany almost the reverse occurred in the nineteenth century. In contrast to France, in Germany the existence of a distinct national culture preceded the 1871 final unification of the German state by several decades. After 1871 the imperial government did pursue policies to unify the German population ethnically, in a manner comparable to France's Third Republic. Yet not until well into the twentieth century did Germany achieve a similar level of cultural unification in the context of the nation-state. For Germany, the French Revolution (in particular the Napoleonic occupation) also played a key role in fostering a sense of German national identity, although in a very different way from France. Napoleon's rationalization of German state structures, in particular his reduction in the number of German states from over three hundred to less than fifty, began to create a more regionally and even nationally based sense of German identity. Perhaps more important was the resistance movement against the French that the Germans created. Many young German intellectuals had originally embraced the ideals of the French Revolution and supported the victories of the revolutionary armies against aristocratic Europe. Napoleon's occupation, however, revealed the extent to which the universalism of the Revolution had degenerated into the imperialism of the French state. In doing so, it helped spawn a nationalist revolt, of German particularism against French universalism. The German philosopher Johann Gottlieb Fichte (1762–1814) called on all Germans, by which he meant all those who spoke the German language, to rise up in the struggle for a free Germany. The playwright Johann Christoph Friedrich von Schiller's *William Tell* (1804) transformed a Swiss legend into an allegory of national resistance. The guerrilla wars of liberation against France not only helped create a sense of common German identity against the invader, but also became over time a central myth of national glory.

The wars of liberation came at a time when Germans had begun to elaborate a new sense of cultural nationalism. By the late eighteenth century German intellectuals had begun writing in German and seeing *hoch Deutsch* (High German) in particular as key to the nation's culture. This also represented a reaction against the Enlightenment and the intellectual predominance of French. This concern with language gradually developed into an interest in folklore and mythology, as researchers began to investigate local traditions and customs to understand what was unique about the German character. In 1812 the brothers Jacob Ludwig Carl Grimm (1785–1863) and Wilhelm Carl Grimm (1786–1859) published the first volume of their famous *Grimm's Fairy Tales,* which not only became a classic of children's literature but also sought to revive a forgotten part of the nation's heritage. Such concerns with national culture both arose out of and fostered the idea that each nation had a particular character, even "soul." Starting in the 1780s, the Protestant pastor Johann Gottfried von Herder argued that the essence of Germanness was the *Volksgeist,* or culture and spirit of the common people. By the beginning of the nineteenth century the burgeoning Romantic movement gave added weight to the idea of national consciousness and culture. In particular, Romanticism emphasized the crucial role of history in shaping national identity, arguing that each nation had its own specific history. The idea of the nation as organic rather than contractual would become a powerful aspect of mystical nationalism in Germany, distinguishing it in the eyes of many from the more classical national idea of France.

Yet while German Romanticism may have championed the national soul, it did not create the German nation-state. Ultimately the idea of unifying Germany along the lines of liberal nationalism failed, signaled by the collapse of the Frankfurt Parliament in 1849. Instead national unification came from above, in the shape of the authoritarian Prussian state. This state-driven idea of nationhood, championed above all by Otto von Bismarck (German chancellor, 1871–1890), regarded Germany primarily as a political creation, subject to the kaiser, rather than as an expression of cultural nationalism. In fact large numbers of ethnic Germans, including the populations of Austria and the Sudetenland, were excluded from membership in the Second Empire. However, though it did not exercise state power, the ethnocultural image of Germany remained a powerful force to be reckoned with in the life of the new nation-state.

Some have overemphasized the contrast between French and German notions of nationhood, seeing it as a conflict between "civilization" and "culture." In both countries, and throughout most of Europe in the nineteenth century, political and cultural ideas of national identity coexisted. Nonetheless, in general German nationalism gave its ethnic and cultural component greater weight, at least in theory, than did that of the French. By the early twentieth century the definition of citizenship based on *jus soli,* or birthplace, in France, versus *jus sanguinis,* or blood, in Germany, would highlight these different approaches to national identity. In different ways, the cases of France and Germany demonstrated the pressure toward the ethnicization of European ideas of the nation-state during the nineteenth century.

ETHNICITY, IMMIGRATION, AND NATIONAL MINORITIES

The idea of ethnic minorities developed in tandem with the ethnic nation state in nineteenth-century Europe. The rise of dominant national cultures reduced those communities that did not share (or refused to embrace) those cultures to the status of minority groups. Moreover, the rise of ethnonationalism gave a new character to migration, especially that across national boundaries. The extent to which immigrants adopted dominant national cultures became an important index of the unity of nation-states, while the immigrants themselves had to contend not only with the difficulties of displacement, but also new pressures to assimilate. Therefore, in studying the history of ethnicity in Europe between the French Revolution and World War I, one must consider both insiders and outsiders, ethnic nations and ethnic minorities. The rest of this entry will focus on two particular groups: Irish immigrants in Britain, and Jews in the Austrian-Hungarian Empire. While at first glance one of Europe's most unified nations would seem to differ markedly from the rambling multinational empire of the Habsburgs, these two ethnic minorities in fact had much in common. In both cases large numbers of people migrated from imperial hinterlands to metropolitan centers, balancing between assimilation into the minority culture and the establishment of distinctive ethnic minority traditions. And in both cases, ethnicity interacted with class, gender, and especially religion in shaping the immigrants' experiences in their new homelands. As culturally unified nation-states became more normative in nineteenth-century Europe, these and other immigrant minorities gradually came to symbolize the very meaning of ethnicity.

The Irish in Britain and the Jews of Austria-Hungary were of course only two of the many ethnic groups in nineteenth-century Europe. Most minority groups came from elsewhere in Europe; however, the nineteenth century also witnessed the growth of small non-European communities. The presence of peoples from Africa, Asia, and the Caribbean on European soil reflected the growth of European colonial empires and existed before the French Revolution. Eighteenth-century Paris had a small but visible black community, for example. But the dramatic imperial ventures of Britain, France, and other European powers in the late nineteenth century sharply increased the nonwhite population of Europe, a trend that would only accelerate during the twentieth century.

This phenomenon appeared most noticeably in Britain, the heart of the world's greatest empire. While precise statistics are rare, it seems that by 1900 Britain was home to several thousand "blacks," or people of color. London alone had nearly 4,000 by the 1870s. Colonial migrants to Britain generally fell into one of two groups: members of the elite in search of education and immigrant workers in search of jobs. Mohandas Gandhi studied law in London during the 1880s and by 1910, 700 Indian students were enrolled in British universities. In 1913 colonial students founded the African Students Association. At the same time large numbers of colonial immigrants worked in British ports as sailors and longshoremen. By the end of the nineteenth century, London and Liverpool were home to a few hundred Chinese immigrants; although a tiny population, they nonetheless became targets of racist fears of cheap labor.

Irish in Britain The impact of colonial migrants paled in comparison with the huge Irish immigration into nineteenth-century Britain. Many have termed Ireland Britain's first colony, and the Irish presence in Britain goes back to the medieval beginnings of English imperial domination. The nineteenth century brought a massive increase in travel across the Irish Sea, however, thanks to the cataclysm of the Irish famine. This disaster, which killed a million Irish and forced the flight of many more, is best known for having brought a huge new immigrant population to the United States. Many Irish refugees from hunger traveled to Britain as well, either to await transport to North America, or else to settle there permanently. For example, 300,000 Irish arrived in Liverpool alone during 1847, and while 130,000 subsequently left, the rest stayed. Irish immigration constituted the greatest migration to Britain since the Norman Conquest, so that by the 1860s the Irish-born population of the island numbered over 800,000 people, by far the largest immigrant group in the country.

Forging an Irish community overseas did not happen automatically. The Irish population in Britain was not only large but also diverse. Not all of it settled there permanently: earlier patterns of seasonal migration continued, although now dwarfed by the postfamine exodus. Large numbers of Irishwomen migrated, more than traditionally the case for nineteenth-century European migrants, and significant numbers of middle-class and of Protestant Irish came to Britain as well. However, the

Irish population in Britain was dominated by poor people from the countryside, for whom migration to Britain constituted not just displacement but also their first experience with urban industrial life. Once arrived in Britain, the Irish generally set up autonomous communities, Irish urban villages in the heart of British cities. The majority of Irish inhabitants of London, Manchester, and Liverpool lived in predominantly Irish streets and neighborhoods. This segregation facilitated the establishment of ethnic community networks. By the end of the nineteenth century, Britain's Irish had developed a wide range of community associations, ranging from music societies to political clubs to celebrations of Saint Patrick's Day. No organization played a greater role in creating Irish community life than the Catholic Church. Irish immigrants effectively took over Catholicism in Britain, transforming it from a small elite organization to a mass-based one. The church not only performed missionary work among the Irish poor, but also established schools, boys' and girls' clubs, and a variety of other social organizations.

The development of Irish community life in nineteenth-century Britain constituted not only an attempt to preserve Irish culture, but also a defensive reaction against British hostility and prejudice. Anti-Irish bigotry in Britain has a history as long as the Irish presence there, but it reached its most virulent levels in the nineteenth century. British hostility to the Irish had numerous roots, including anti-Catholicism, a colonial sense of superiority to a subject people, and a tendency to blame Irish workers, some of the poorest people in Britain, for their own misery. Stereotypes of "Paddy" as lazy, dirty, stupid, violent, and criminal abounded, often drawing on racist images of blacks and other nonwhite groups. Enmity often led to violence, as Irish communities faced attacks by British mobs during the 1850s and 1860s in particular. Community solidarity and ethnic cultural assertion was one response to British antagonism. At the same time, however, Irish immigrants did gradually assimilate into British society, winning a greater level of acceptance by 1914 and the advent of Home Rule in 1922. This generally did not mean a loss of Irish identity, but rather a sense of hybridity, of being both British and Irish at the same time. Over the course of the nineteenth century, therefore, the Irish evolved from foreign immigrants to an ethnic group in Britain.

Jews in Austria Like the Irish in Britain, the Jews in Austria went from being immigrants to creating distinctive communities in the nineteenth century. Not only did migration mean for them going from imperial borderlands to urban centers, it also entailed leaving the traditional Jewish ghetto and assimilating into mainstream European society. Both groups were variously described in terms of ethnicity, nationality, religion, and race, and both ultimately experienced a certain amount of assimilation while at the same time creating well-defined community cultures. However, a crucial difference between them was the contrast between Britain and Austria (Austria-Hungary after 1867). Austria was a multinational empire, not a state, and its central institutions made no claims to representing the culture of all the empire's subjects. Yet it was also an empire increasingly battered by the forces of ethnonationalism, as the nations that composed it demanded more and more cultural and political autonomy. For the Jews of Austria-Hungary, especially those living in urban centers like Vienna, Budapest, and Prague, the tension between waning imperial control and waxing ethnonationalism shaped their ability to choose either assimilation or ethnic separatism in the nineteenth century.

Jewish migration into Austria's urban centers took place in the broader context of nineteenth-century Jewish emancipation. The revolution of 1848, in which Austrian Jews participated heavily, made them citizens of the empire and lifted residential restrictions on them, freeing them to travel. Over the next few decades hundreds of thousands migrated from the hinterlands, especially Galicia, Bukovina, Bohemia, and Moravia, to the cities. By the end of the century Vienna had a Jewish population of 175,000, Prague 13,000, and Budapest 200,000. They came drawn by not only greater economic opportunities but also the lure of German culture, the means by which many eastern European Jews had come into contact with Enlightenment modernity. Many assimilated successfully into Austro-German culture, to the extent that they often abandoned Yiddish for German and looked down on their more recently arrived brethren from Galicia. Yet although a few became so Austrian as to convert to Christianity, most retained a strong sense of Jewish identity, forging a new sense of themselves as modernized Austrian Jews. This included the creation of numerous community institutions, such as synagogues, community and charitable societies, and political organizations. In Vienna, for example, most Jews lived in Jewish neighborhoods, attended mostly Jewish schools, and married other Jews. Although the Habsburg imperial administration formally considered the Jews of Austria a religion, in actual fact they functioned as both a religious and an ethnic community.

As with the Irish in Britain, prejudice from the dominant society reinforced Austrian Jews' own sense of separateness. Unlike Britain, however, Austria was a multinational empire, not a nation-state, one in which the imperial forces strove to keep in check the nationalist desires of Hungarians, Czechs, Slovaks, and other groups. The nationalist revolutions of 1848 that emancipated Austria's Jews had also produced major popular anti-Semitic movements, and anti-Semitism continued to exist as a potent political force during the nineteenth century. The reaction of the Jewish community to this situation took different forms. It is perhaps no accident that modern Zionism arose in Austria, as some Jews responded to the assertiveness of other peoples in the empire by arguing that they, too, constituted a subject nation. In fact, one strand of Austrian Jewish nationalism advocated the creation of a Jewish state in central Europe, not Palestine. The majority of Austria's Jews rejected both Zionism and popular nationalism, preferring to view themselves as Austrians of Jewish faith and heritage. They clung to the institutions of the Habsburg Empire, seeing in it a political force that, by resisting the pressure of potentially anti-Semitic popular nationalism, could assure a place for them. Only in a state where no one culture dominated completely could the Jews feel truly at home. They therefore asserted the idea of themselves as an ethnic group in a multinational empire, engaging in ultimately futile resistance against the nationalist forces that would soon tear the empire apart.

For both insiders and outsiders, therefore, ethnicity represented an increasingly important component of both individual and national identity in Europe between the French Revolution and World War I. The idea of ethnic community was most important in relationship to nations and nationalism: ethnonationalism reinforced the power of the nation-state, whereas ethnic minority communities called its unity into question. Like nationalism and race, nineteenth-century ethnicity paradoxically championed "ancient" traditions with mass literacy, state intervention, and other aspects of modernity. Ethnicity represented a kind of intermediate level of community between the family and the nation. As life in Europe became more and more complex, ethnic groups both provided a sense of familiarity in an alien world and exemplified the extent to which the traditional worlds they so often celebrated had vanished.

See also **Citizenship; Colonialism; Immigration and Internal Migration; Imperialism; Jews and Judaism; Nationalism; Romanies (Gypsies).**

BIBLIOGRAPHY

Primary Sources

Clare, George. *Last Waltz in Vienna.* New York, 1983.

Renan, Ernest. "What Is a Nation?" Translated by Martin Thom. In *Nation and Narration,* edited by Homi K. Bhabha. London and New York, 1990.

Secondary Sources

Brubaker, Rogers. *Citizenship and Nationhood in France and Germany.* Cambridge, Mass., 1992.

Gellner, Ernest. *Nations and Nationalism.* Oxford, U.K., 1983.

Hobsbawm, Eric. *Nations and Nationalism since 1780: Programme, Myth, Reality.* Cambridge, U.K., and New York, 1992.

Lees, Lynn Hollen. *Exiles of Erin: Irish Migrants in Victorian London.* Ithaca, N.Y., 1979.

MacRaild, Donald M. *Irish Migrants in Modern Britain, 1750–1922.* New York, 1999.

Mosse, George. *Toward the Final Solution: A History of European Racism.* Madison, Wisc., 1985.

Panayi, Panikos. *Outsiders: A History of European Minorities.* Rio Grande, Ohio, 1999.

Rex, John. *Race and Ethnicity.* Milton Keynes, U.K., 1986.

Rozenblit, Marsha L. *The Jews of Vienna, 1867–1914: Assimilation and Identity.* Albany, N.Y., 1983.

Weber, Eugen. *Peasants into Frenchmen: The Modernization of Rural France, 1870–1914.* Stanford, Calif., 1976.

Weil, Patrick. *Qu'est-ce qu'un Français?: Histoire de la nationalité française depuis la révolution.* Paris, 2002.

Wicker, Hans-Rudolf, ed. *Rethinking Nationalism and Ethnicity: The Struggle for Meaning and Order in Europe.* Oxford, U.K., and New York, 1997.

TYLER STOVALL

MISSIONS. Christian missionary activity reached its apex during the long nineteenth century. The movement emerged in the late eighteenth and early nineteenth centuries in response to the growing influence of evangelical Protestantism and the expansion of European commercial and political interests around the globe. During this period evangelical Protestants in particular developed a greater sense of urgency about the Christian obligation to spread the knowledge of the gospel. While the suppression of the Jesuits on the Continent throughout the eighteenth century weakened Roman Catholic missions, English and German Protestants initiated the first significant Protestant missionary activity during the early 1700s. German Pietists, especially the Moravians, established mission stations in India, Africa, and the Caribbean. Anglicans, strongly influenced by the Pietist movement, founded the Society for the Promotion of Christian Knowledge and the Society for the Promotion of the Gospel to work in British colonies. At the end of the century, the fall of Catholicism during the French Revolution inspired British evangelicals to organize missions to France in the hope of encouraging the growth of Protestantism there. Protestant missionaries were also sent to various parts of Russia.

The most significant factor in the expansion of Protestant missions, however, was the invention of the missionary society, a voluntary organization of ministers and laypersons dedicated to the support of foreign missionary activity. Throughout the first half of the nineteenth century these institutions established their missions in India, the South Pacific, Africa, and the Caribbean, and became the defining characteristic of the missionary movement. The first societies appeared in Britain during the 1790s. The Baptist Missionary Society, established in 1792, was quickly followed by the predominantly Congregationalist London Missionary Society (LMS) in 1795, and the Anglican Church Missionary Society (CMS) in 1799. The British example inspired the formation of similar institutions on the Continent, including the Netherlands Missionary Society (1797), and German societies in Basel (1815) and Berlin (1824). Cooperation between the British and Continental societies was common. The Dutchman Johannes Van der Kemp, active in the creation of the Netherlands Missionary Society, eventually established the first LMS mission in the Cape Colony. John Philip, a director of the LMS missions in southern Africa, helped to establish mission stations for the Paris Evangelical Mission during the 1830s in present-day Lesotho. The CMS drew many of its first missionaries from the graduates of Lutheran seminaries in Germany.

MISSIONARY ATTITUDES AND PRACTICES

The missionary impulse sprang from more than a mere concern for the salvation of so-called heathen souls. Evangelical Protestants understood human history as the unfolding of divine ordinances and the fulfillment of God's purposes, chief among them the spread of Christianity throughout the world. The providential expansion of European commercial power added to the obligation of Christians to evangelize the far corners of the globe. Commerce and Christianity became increasingly linked as necessary elements of the process of civilization and were celebrated by prominent missionaries such as David Livingstone.

During the first half of the nineteenth century, missionaries approached their work with a strong belief in the divine purpose and in the Enlightenment ideal of human progress. They assumed that introducing non-Christians to the gospel would lead them to convert, and set them on the path toward civilization. They believed that with salvation came civility and respectability. The adoption of Western manners and styles of dress by converts were taken as outward signs of the authenticity of their Christian faith. Missionaries also focused intensely on the translation of the Bible into indigenous languages, and in many cases the training of indigenous evangelists to assist their work. The missionary societies encouraged the creation of self-sustaining, indigenous, Christian communities, which might free missionaries and resources to be directed into new unevangelized areas of the globe. These communities, however, were slow to develop, and the societies remained dependent on the continued support of the religious public in Europe to finance their work.

The second half of the century saw the emergence of new attitudes, and important changes. In the 1860s, J. Hudson Taylor, founder of the China Inland Mission, argued that missionaries should do more to appreciate and to assimilate themselves to indigenous cultures. Taylor created controversy by dressing himself in Chinese style clothing, but his mission converted more than one hundred thousand Chinese by the end of the century. The relative lack of success in other mission fields, especially Africa, increased skepticism within the missionary movement about the potential for large-scale conversions before non-Christians had been exposed to all of the benefits of Western civilization. Missionary activity shifted away from merely proselytizing, and placed greater emphasis on medical care, education, social welfare, and even industrial training. Most significantly, women began to play a much greater role in missionary work after 1850. Unmarried women, in particular, entered the mission field in large numbers as evangelists, doctors, and teachers. So much so that by the end of the century women missionaries outnumbered men by two to one.

The dramatic expansion of Protestant missions during the first half of the nineteenth century also sparked a resurgence of interest in Roman Catholic missions. In Restoration France, mission crosses planted throughout the countryside were symbolic of the renewed efforts of Catholic missionaries to revive the French church. Foreign missions were also revived, especially during the second half of the century. Among the most prominent organizations was the Society of Missionaries of Africa, more commonly known as the White Fathers, founded in 1868 by the archbishop of Algiers, Charles-Martial-Allemand Lavigerie. Beginning its work in northern Africa, the society eventually sent missionaries south of the Sahara by the later 1870s. Lavigerie instructed his missionaries to also concentrate their efforts on establishing Christian communities among orphans and emancipated slaves, while developing good relations with local indigenous authorities. Additionally, missionaries focused on training indigenous catechists to aid their work. The White Fathers suffered severely from the persecution of Christians in Uganda during the late 1880s, but by the twentieth century had made significant progress in Central Africa developing parishes and diocese under the leadership of African clergy.

Cover of French textbook c. 1880–1890. The work of the White Fathers, created by French cardinal Charles Lavigerie to spread Catholicism among the Muslims of North Africa, is celebrated in this illustration for children. PRIVATE COLLECTION/ BRIDGEMAN ART LIBRARY/ARCHIVES CHARMET

MISSIONS AND COLONIALISM

Historians frequently interpret the surge of missionary activity as a central component of nineteenth-century European colonial expansion. Missionaries appear in these accounts as advance forces of colonial authority, transporting the values of bourgeois society and paving the way for European domination. Others, more sympathetic to the missionary movement, emphasize the positive contributions of the humanitarian and educational efforts of the missionaries. The relationship between missions and colonial authorities was complex. Colonial governments tended to support missions wherever they felt religious expansion might strengthen their influence, and missions sometimes opened the doors through which colonial authority followed. Supporters of the missionary movement celebrated the use of force to open China to Western trade in 1850s, because it also opened China to the gospel. In other instances, however, missionaries' concerns for the well-being of indigenous or slave populations directly conflicted with the interests of settlers, slave owners, and colonial officials. The popularity of missionary work, especially in Britain, gave the movement considerable political clout, as in the early-nineteenth-century debates over the abolition of slavery. Over time, the relationship between missions and colonial government became less antagonistic and more cooperative. Another of the most powerful legacies of the missionary movement, however, was its tendency to cultivate resistance among indigenous populations. For all of the missionary movement's contributions to the expansion of European culture and colonial power, it made an equally significant contribution to the development of opposition to colonial rule.

See also **Catholicism; Imperialism; Protestantism; Religion.**

BIBLIOGRAPHY

Ajayi, J. F. A. *Christian Missions in Nigeria, 1841–1891: The Making of a New Élite.* London, 1965.

Comaroff, Jean, and John Comaroff. *Of Revelation and Revolution: Christianity, Colonialism, and Consciousness in South Africa.* Vols. 1 and 2. Chicago, 1991 and 1997.

LaTourette, Kenneth Scott. *A History of Christianity.* Vol. 2. New York, 1975.

Neill, Stephen. *A History of Christian Missions.* New York, 1986.

Stanley, Brian, ed. *Christian Missions and the Enlightenment.* Grand Rapids, Mich., 2001.

Walls, Andrew. *The Missionary Movement in Christian History: Studies in the Transmission of Faith.* Edinburgh, 1996.

MICHAEL A. RUTZ

MODERNISM. Modernism emerged in the second half of the nineteenth century as a means of reimagining and ultimately securing art's role within a culture progressively detaching itself from the institutions and practitioners of aesthetic culture. Amid the growing influence of mass media, popular entertainment, and widespread consumerism, two phenomena in particular were pivotal in establishing the conditions under which the new forms of modernist practice developed: the waning influence of the official academic Salons, and the pressure exerted on individuals by increasingly technologically mediated modes of experience. Threatened with obsolescence in the face of a dissolving system of state-sponsored patronage, art had to find new forms of address and alternative modes of expression. Modernism, then, names a set of relentlessly self-critical formal strategies that surfaced in response to art's contingent status in the wake of the rapid industrialization ushered in by the expanding social strata of the urban bourgeoisie. This quest for criticality through formal analysis was intended to reflect on the terms of art's shifting terrain while continuing to offer a realization of the potential left to art under such conditions.

Artists and writers reacted to these circumstances by updating both the forms and the subjects of their works in an attempt to adequately represent their new urban experiences. With his article "The Painter of Modern Life" (1863) the poet and critic Charles Baudelaire (1821–1867) emerged as a leading theorist of modernism, championing the creation of new styles of artistic production suited to capturing the texture and feel of life in the swelling metropolis. He embodied these ideals in his own poetry, most notably in his collection *Les Fleurs du mal* (1857; *The Flowers of Evil*), which evinced new symbolic relationships between language and the sensory phenomena elicited by the city.

Baudelaire's literary influence gave rise to the symbolists, a diverse group of writers working in France at the end of the nineteenth century. Poets like Stéphane Mallarmé (1842–1898) and Arthur Rimbaud (1854–1891) were united by a desire to evoke the nature of their urban perambulations via imaginative free-verse passages. The symbolists eschewed earlier modes of naturalism and realism, giving primacy instead to the often-arbitrary associations of the mind stimulated by the dizzying and sometimes dreamy character of life in the burgeoning metropolis.

Symbolism rippled across national borders as well, with an important variant cropping up in Germany under the leadership of the poet Stefan George (1868–1933). Borrowing from the symbolists' revolt against naturalism, George theorized a program for literary production that drew heavily on the writings of Friedrich Nietzsche (1844–1900). Meanwhile, removed from life in the frenzied urban centers, the poet Rainer Maria Rilke (1875–1926) expanded the boundaries of lyric poetry, using rhymed, metered composition to survey previously unexamined subjects. He is best known for his "object poems," which were modeled after the work of the sculptor Auguste Rodin (1840–1917) and attempted to crystallize the reality of physical objects.

In the visual arts, modernism arrived via a picnic in the park. In 1863 a group of artists and their supporters created the *Salon des Refusés,* a democratically run alternative to the juried Salon exhibitions of the academy of fine arts, which had dominated official painting in France since the seventeenth century. In its inaugural show, Édouard Manet (1832–1883) exhibited his *Le Déjeuner sur l'herbe* (Luncheon on the grass), which appropriated and radically reworked the subjects and technique of Old Master painting, offering an uncompromising representation of a classically inspired female nude recontextualized in the space of a park luncheon with two contemporary bourgeois gentlemen. Manet's handling of paint, which employed flat, untransitioned patches of color, also engaged with the new forms of mechanical reproduction to create the flash-like visual fields characteristic of photography.

The impressionist painters furthered Manet's concern with absorbing the look of ready-made technology within the medium of painting. Artists such as Claude Monet (1840–1926) created canvases filled with tiny brushstrokes that when viewed from a distance produced optical sensations that mirrored the effects of naturally illuminated landscapes. Other artists, like Edgar Degas (1834–1917) and Gustave Caillebotte (1848–1894), rose to Baudelaire's demands by taking to the streets to create works that were produced from everyday encounters. The so-called neo-impressionists, who included Paul Signac (1863–1935) and Georges Seurat (1859–1891), updated the science behind impressionism's reformulated color theories by further atomizing their predecessors' tactile brushwork. Elsewhere, post-impressionists including Paul Cézanne (1839–1906) and Paul Gauguin (1848–1903) built on the tradition of landscape by undertaking to represent a remote, removed vision of the world. The flatness and discontinuous composition of canvases like Cézanne's Mont Sainte-Victoire series and Gauguin's works from Brittany and Tahiti gave form to an alienated subjectivity that longed to reassert itself through mining the bare materiality of the painted surface itself.

In Vienna artists previously operating under state-controlled academies similarly broke with the more traditional exhibition sites and societies for art. In 1897, led by the painter Gustav Klimt (1862–1918), a group calling themselves the secessionists formally split with these institutions of high art. Their work drew heavily on the design language of art nouveau to create large mural-size pieces that fused erotically depicted subjects in the context of highly ornamental decorative programs.

The early twentieth century witnessed an eruption of formal variants to the issues linking modernism to ideas of the self. Liberated from the burden of a purely mimetic correspondence to the world, the assertion of flatness as a structural limit to painting enabled artists to imagine and realize new visions of the world. Movements like fauvism, exemplified in paintings like Henri Matisse's (1869–1954) *The Red Studio* (1911), actively obliterated form through areas of wild, violent color. In Germany, expressionism—colorful street scenes and distorted perspectives first popularized by a collective known as Die Brücke (The bridge)—became the dominant style in the visual arts. Der Blaue Reiter (The blue rider), a group of German artists that included Wassily Kandinsky (1866–1944) and Paul Klee (1879–1940), updated the ambitions of the earlier expressionists, connecting the inner vision of the artist, through painting, to a more transcendental theosophical worldview.

In France, Pablo Picasso (1881–1973) and Georges Braque (1882–1963) developed the technique they called cubism, which fused abstraction and figuration within a single painted register. This radical analysis of form reworked the traditional subjects of still life and portraiture according to the parameters of the two-dimensional picture plane. In later variations, cubist painters also employed synthetic collage elements like pasted paper in order to further scrutinize the relationship between everyday objects and the flat surfaces native to painting.

Futurism, spawned in Italy shortly before the outbreak of World War I, denounced the dominant paradigm of expressionistic, subject-oriented artistic production. According to the group's 1909 manifesto, penned by the poet Filippo Tommaso

Marinetti (1876–1944), futurism's overarching ambition was to bring art into direct conversation with the character of urban experience. Artistically, this translated into a repudiation of the traditional subjects and contexts for art in order to adequately capture the movement and dizzying speed of modern technology.

After the start of World War I modernism continued to develop and explore new aesthetic terrain. As technology and mass media increased their hold on popular culture, questions surrounding art's function in Europe's rapidly changing societies became essential to a sustained engagement with modernism. This self-reflexivity, born in response to modernism's self-imagined obsolescence, has given rise to a tradition of relentless formal innovation that has sustained modernist aesthetic production throughout the twentieth century and beyond.

See also **Baudelaire, Charles; Cézanne, Paul; Gauguin, Paul; Manet, Édouard; Matisse, Henri; Monet, Claude; Picasso, Pablo; Seurat, Georges.**

BIBLIOGRAPHY

Primary Sources

Baudelaire, Charles. *The Painter of Modern Life and Other Essays.* Translated and edited by Jonathan Mayne. London, 1964.

Kandinsky, Wassily. *Concerning the Spiritual in Art.* New York, 1947.

Nochlin, Linda, ed. *Impressionism and Post-Impressionism, 1874–1904: Sources and Documents.* Englewood Cliffs, N.J., 1966.

Secondary Sources

Birkett, Jennifer, and James Kearns. *A Guide to French Literature: Early Modern to Postmodern.* New York, 1997.

Frascina, Francis, et al. *Modernity and Modernism: French Painting in the Nineteenth Century.* New Haven, Conn., 1993.

Harrison, Charles, Francis Frascina, and Gill Perry. *Primitivism, Cubism, Abstraction: The Early Twentieth Century.* New Haven, Conn., 1993.

Travers, Martin. *An Introduction to Modern European Literature: From Romanticism to Postmodernism.* New York, 1998.

Wellbery, David E., ed. *A New History of German Literature.* Cambridge, Mass., 2005.

COLIN LANG

MOLTKE, HELMUTH VON (1800–1891), Prussian/German army officer and architect of the Wars of German Unification.

Born in 1800 in Parchim, Mecklenburg, Helmuth von Moltke stands alongside Otto von Bismarck as a symbol of Prussia/Germany's emergence as a Great Power. He is also generally recognized as the first master of modern industrial war: the administrative aspects epitomized in the general staff system and the technological elements manifested in the railroads.

Moltke, who began his military career in the army of Denmark, transferred to Prussian service in 1822—still a common pattern for officers from small states seeking wider professional opportunities. Graduating from the Prussian War Academy in 1826, he first made his mark in the embryonic general staff as a cartographer, simultaneously establishing a reputation as a freelance writer and translator. In 1835 he was seconded to the Turkish army, where he exercised the only field command of his career: of the sultan's artillery in a losing battle.

Returning to Berlin in 1840, Moltke served in a series of staff appointments that exposed him to the technological developments reshaping the face of war in Europe. As early as 1841 he served on the board of directors of a proposed Berlin–Hamburg railway line and put most of his assets into company stock: entrepreneurial behavior setting him apart from many of his Junker counterparts. He continued to evaluate and cultivate railroads' military prospects, particularly for integrating rail transport into local maneuvers. He also paid attention to the tactical and operational implications of rifled weapons, with their increased range and firepower.

Appointed chief of the general staff in 1857, Moltke worked to improve Prussia's mobilization system as a counterweight to the state's exposed geographic position. He developed the general staff as the brain and nervous system of the Prussian army, providing centralized planning and decentralized control. He cultivated positive relations with civilian ministries whose functions influenced mobilization: war, commerce, and interior. And he worked to increase harmony with Bismarck, appointed minister-president (prime minister) of Prussia in September 1862.

From the beginning of his career Moltke was concerned with reestablishing the limitations on war that had been so profoundly challenged during the revolutionary/Napoleonic era. The mass armies created in those years were heavy, blunt instruments increasingly unable to decide either battles or wars. Moltke believed decisive victories were still possible, but only by combining systematic, comprehensive operational planning with effective use of the railways that enhanced strategic mobility—and synergizing both with state policy.

Moltke was anything but a nuts-and-bolts technocrat. For example, the precondition of his operational plan in 1866 for the Austro-Prussian War was guaranteed French and Russian neutrality, thereby obviating the need to secure Prussia's eastern and western frontiers. The chief of staff's often-cited insistence that once war broke out, its conduct must be determined by military considerations is best understood in the context of his conviction that the Prussian army best served Prussia's interests by winning battles convincingly enough to compel its foes to sue for peace. And at that point by Moltke's own logic the soldier in turn withdrew in favor of the statesman.

Moltke's emphasis on the importance of limits to war making was even more clearly demonstrated during the Franco-Prussian War (1870–1871). France's initial victories left it without a government willing to negotiate peace on terms acceptable to Prussia. Instead the revolutionary Republic extended the conflict to a point at which the equally newly created German empire was desperate to find an exit from the resulting domestic and international problems.

A frustrated Moltke called briefly for the complete destruction of France—an objective he never took seriously. Instead, between 1871 and his resignation in 1888, Moltke concluded soberly that Germany's geostrategic position, sandwiched between France and Russia, worked against fighting any future wars to total victory. He correspondingly understood that the cabinet wars that had made his reputation were becoming obsolete. Governments might initiate wars; now citizens sustained them.

In that environment any protracted conflict ran the risk of becoming general—the kind of war most contrary to Germany's interests. Even preemptive war offered such limited prospects that Moltke came to stress deterrence as preferable to conflict. The next war, he declared in 1890, might last for thirty years, and "woe to him who sets Europe ablaze."

Unfortunately, Moltke did not impose this realism on either the general staff or the army at large. Instead he presided over a system that increasingly sought strategic salvation in developing a technical and bureaucratic orientation that eventually led to the kind of all-or-nothing gamble he sought to avoid. Ironically, Moltke's own creation escaped his control as Germany careened down the road to total war.

See also **Armies; Austro-Prussian War; Bismarck, Otto von; Franco-Prussian War; Germany; Military Tactics.**

BIBLIOGRAPHY

Bucholz, Arden. *Moltke and the German Wars, 1864–1871.* Basingstoke, U.K., 2001.

Meyer, Bradley J. "The Operational Art and the Elder Moltke's Campaign Plan for the Franco-Prussian War." In *The Operational Art: Developments in the Theories of War,* edited by B. J. C. McKercher and Michael A. Hennessy, 29–49. Westport, Conn., 1996. This is a model case study of Moltke's greatest campaign.

Showalter, Dennis. *The Wars of German Unification.* London, 2004.

DENNIS SHOWALTER

MOMMSEN, THEODOR (1817–1903),

German historian and legal scholar.

Theodor Mommsen was the most productive and influential German historian of Rome and legal scholar of the nineteenth century. Mommsen, the son of a Protestant pastor, studied history and law at the University of Kiel, earning his doctorate at age twenty-five with a dissertation on Roman law. His legacy lies in his publications, the organizing of scholarly projects, and the politics of his time. After several years gathering ancient inscriptions in Italy, he became professor of jurisprudence at Leipzig

(1848). He was dismissed in 1851 with his colleagues Otto Jahn (1813–1869) and Moriz Haupt (1808–1874) for protesting against the Saxon monarch. He received asylum at Zurich in Switzerland, continued to Breslau as professor in 1854, and in 1858 became research professor at the Berlin Academy. He was secretary of the Academy from 1874 to 1895. In 1861 he became professor of Roman antiquities at the Friedrich Wilhelm University (now the Humboldt University) in Berlin, where he remained for the rest of his life. He divided his time between research, the direction of international scholarly projects, and teaching—a duty, not a pleasure.

Mommsen's most widely known major work is his three-volume history of Rome from its beginnings until 46 B.C.E. (1854–1856), with a further volume on the provinces appearing first in 1885. There are some sixteen editions and translations in many languages. In 1902, this work won him the Nobel prize for literature. Not until Winston Churchill (1874–1965) would another historian be so honored. A lively narrative did much to make a remote subject attractive. The unification of Italy under Rome anticipated the unification of Germany under the Prussian Emperor. Mommsen was a convert to the *Totatitätsideal,* the conviction that one must master and use all extant evidence to reconstruct what had really happened. This meant not just ancient historians but ancient inscriptions, archaeology, numismatics, and topography (he walked through most of Italy). He lived at a time when scientific excavations were beginning and masses of new material becoming available. Philosophy plays a decisive role in Greek history. Mommsen saw that for Rome it was rather constitutional law. He began the modern, systematic study of Roman law with his *Römisches Staatsrecht* (1871; Roman civil law) and *Römisches Strafrecht* (1899; Roman penal law). Mommsen's biographers have been puzzled about why he never published a history of the Roman Empire. He writes that he lacked in old age his youthful naivete that he knew everything. And surely the inescapable fact that the innovating force of the empire was Christianity was repugnant to the apostate pastor's son. A fortunate discovery of careful lecture notes taken by an assiduous student has allowed Alexander Demandt to restore work Mommsen never published.

A brilliant organizer, Mommsen won funding that encouraged international cooperation on vast projects. With his colleague, the church historian Adolf von Harnack (1851–1930), he introduced the concept of "the big business of scholarship," that is, enlisting teams from various nations for projects that one person could never accomplish alone. After 1853 he directed the precise, scientific publication of thousands of Roman inscriptions, indispensable for understanding the Roman past. This became the *Corpus Inscriptionum Latinarum,* repeatedly cited by scholars. He invigorated the *Monumenta Historiae Germanica,* a collection of writers and documents that form modern knowledge of medieval German history. In 1890, supported by William II (1859–1941), he successfully urged the foundation of the Römisch-Germanische Kommission, to consolidate research on Roman remains within Germany. This resulted in the careful study of the *limes,* the wall separating Roman Germany from the barbarians. He began the *Prosopographia Imperii Romani,* an invaluable collection of all known Romans in the empire with the evidence attesting them. This allows reconstruction of political networks, ethnic studies, and much else. His contributions to the study of Roman law were lasting, especially his *Corpus Juris Civilis* and *Codex Theodosianus.* With the liberal theologian von Harnack, he began in 1891 the Church Fathers Commission, for editing the work of the Greek Church Fathers.

Like many great historians, Mommsen took an active part in the politics of his day. He served in the Prussian Landtag and the Reichstag. He gained national prominence through his conflicts with Otto von Bismarck (1815–1898) and his defense of German Jews against the nationalistic anti-Semite Heinrich Gotthard von Treitschke (1834–1896). He was a talented poet, a friend of Theodor Storm (1817–1888). And he sired sixteen children, twelve of whom survived him and whose descendants have kept the Mommsen name famous in modern historical scholarship. His wife was Marie Reimer, daughter of Mommsen's publisher. His industry and brilliance inspire all who read his books.

See also **History; Philhellenic Movement; Ranke, Leopold von; Treitschke, Heinrich von.**

BIBLIOGRAPHY

Primary Sources

Mommsen, Theodor. *Römische Geschichte.* 5 vols. Berlin, 1854–1885. Numerous reprints and translations.

———. *Römisches Staatsrecht.* Leipzig 1871.

———. *Römisches Strafrecht.* Leipzig, 1899.

———. *Reden und Aufsätze.* Berlin, 1905.

———. *Gesammelte Schriften.* 8 vols. Berlin, 1905–1913.

———. *A History of Rome under the Emperors.* London, 1996.

Secondary Sources

Calder, William M., III, and Robert Kirstein, eds. *"Aus dem Freund, ein Sohn": Theodor Mommsen und Ulrich von Wilamowitz-Moellendorff Briefwechsel 1872–1903.* 2 vols. Hildesheim, 2003. The annotated correspondence between Mommsen and his son-in-law the Hellenist, Ulrich von Wilamowitz-Moellendorff.

Demandt, Alexander. "Theodor Mommsen." In *Classical Scholarship: A Biographical Encyclopedia,* edited by Ward W. Briggs and William M. Calder III, 285–309. New York, 1990. The best treatment in English.

Wickert, Lothar. *Theodor Mommsen: Eine Biographie.* 4 vols. Frankfurt, 1959–1980. The standard biography.

Zangemeister, Karl. *Theodor Mommsen als Schriftsteller: Ein Verzeichnis seiner Schriften.* Hildesheim, 2000. The comprehensive bibliography of all writings by and about Mommsen.

William M. Calder III

MONET, CLAUDE (1840–1926), French painter.

Claude Monet is arguably the best known of the impressionists, a group of largely French artists who challenged conventions in painting that had developed since the Renaissance and that laid the foundations for modern trends in the arts. Radical in both their techniques of painting and their choice of subject matter, Monet and his impressionist companions like Frédéric Bazille (1841–1870), Berthe Morisot (1841–1895), Camille Pissarro (1830–1903), Pierre-Auguste Renoir (1841–1919), and Alfred Sisley (1839–1899) exhibited at eight independent exhibits between 1874 and 1886. These artists painted out-of-doors, contended that they were not painting objective reality, but momentary perceptions of light reflected from objects under constantly changing climatic conditions, and painted scenes of "modern life" in contemporary France. Although an ardent proponent of impressionism, Monet had a larger and more complex career, and his corpus of approximately two thousand paintings reveals an artist whose lifework evolved through three major phases, each with its own distinctive character.

In 1926, the last year of his life, Monet looked back on his career as an artist and commented in a letter to Evan Charteris: "I have always had a horror of theories.... My only virtue is to have painted directly in front of nature, while trying to render the impressions made on me by the most fleeting effects."

Source: Letter from Monet to Evan Charteris, 21 June 1926 (Wildenstein 2626), quoted in: John House, "Monet: The Last Impressionist?" In *Monet in the Twentieth Century,* edited by Paul Hayes Tucker and others. London and Boston, 1998, p. 3.

MONET BEFORE IMPRESSIONISM

Claude Monet was born in Paris on 14 November 1840, but he spent much of his early life in Le Havre and along the Normandy coast. Local renown as a caricaturist brought him the attention of the landscape painter Eugène Boudin (1824–1898) in the mid-1850s, and it was Boudin who introduced Monet to outdoor landscape painting. After his mother's death in 1857, Monet went to Paris, where he studied at the Académie Suisse and encountered other young artists like Camille Pissarro. Following a brief period of military service, Monet studied with the academic painter Charles Gleyre (1806–1874) and met, among other artists, Frédéric Bazille, Pierre-Auguste Renoir, and Alfred Sisley. He spent the summer of 1862 at Sainte-Adresse painting with Boudin, and there he encountered the Dutch landscape artist Johan-Barthold Jongkind (1819–1891), who together with Boudin had a decisive influence on Monet's career. Accordingly, most of Monet's works in these early years were landscapes and seascapes, many of which were painted out-of-doors, and they demonstrated an interest in light and its impact on the perception of objects. With painting excursions to the Forest of Fontainebleau and Honfleur behind him, Monet moved to Paris in 1865. That year he debuted at the Salon with two works, *The Mouth of the Seine at Honfleur* and the *Pointe de la Hève at Low Tide,* and he subsequently exhibited at the Salons of 1866 and 1868. Meanwhile he failed to complete a huge *Déjeuner sur l'herbe,* which exists today only in fragments.

After 1868, his submissions to the Salon were rejected. Perhaps stimulated by the rebuilding of Paris by Baron Georges-Eugène Haussmann (1809–1891) in the 1850s and 1860s, Monet began to take an interest in urban life and he painted three cityscapes in 1867, including *The Church of Saint-Germain l'Auxerrois.* Personal problems, including poverty and the pregnancy of his mistress Camille-Léonie Doncieux, plagued Monet during the late 1860s. Nonetheless, he continued painting, producing among other works the celebrated *Terrace at Sainte-Adresse* (1867). In 1870 he married Camille and, because of the outbreak of the Franco-Prussian War (1870–1871), left France for London, where he met Paul Durand-Ruel (1831–1922), who later became his dealer. Returning to France, he rented a house in Argenteuil-sur-Seine, where he resided until 1878.

THE YEARS OF IMPRESSIONISM

In 1873 Monet painted *Impression: Sunrise,* an atypical work that he exhibited with others at the first exhibition of impressionist art in 1874, an exhibition that was independent of the government-sanctioned Salon that had previously rejected the work of Monet and his fellow exhibitors. Reviewing the exhibition, the hostile critic Louis Leroy (1812–1885) commented on this painting, labeling the exhibitors as "impressionists." Monet's work in the 1870s depicts scenes around his home at Argenteuil, particularly *The Road Bridge at Argenteuil* (1874) and *The Railway Bridge at Argenteuil* (1874). He exhibited eighteen works at the second impressionist exhibition in 1876. The next year, he painted twelve views of the Gare Saint-Lazare, a modern Parisian railroad station, the first of Monet's ventures of devoting a series of paintings to the same object, depicting it under different climatic conditions. He showed thirty works at the third impressionist exhibition in 1877. The Monets moved to Vétheuil in 1878, and his wife, Camille, died there the next year. He continued to exhibit at most of the impressionist exhibitions, although not at the final one in 1886. Painting excursions took him to the Normandy coast and elsewhere, and he executed a prodigious number of seascapes and other works, including views of the rock arch at Etretat. Meanwhile, his paintings began to sell, and in 1883 he rented the house at Giverny, which he bought in 1890 and where he lived for the remainder of his life.

Works by Monet and others exhibited at the impressionist exhibitions, particularly the early ones, attracted much criticism. Behind this hostility was the challenge the impressionists made to the government-sanctioned Salons. There were exhibited paintings by academically trained artists, and they often depicted historical, mythological, or literary scenes. Impressionist paintings, in contrast, depicted modern urban scenes like the Gare Saint-Lazare, tourist sites like the Normandy coast, and the modern leisure activities of the middle classes. Moreover, Monet and the impressionists did not paint "reality." They sought to depict instead the fleeting perception of light reflected from objects under differing climatic conditions. The resulting paintings, critics charged, resembled rough sketches rather than carefully finished paintings. The world of Monet was thus a subjective one. For this reason, some historians place him in the context of a profound transformation of the Western intellectual tradition called the "Crisis of European Thought." This "crisis" involved, among others, challenges to the Newtonian world-view by scientists like Max Planck (1858–1947), assaults on traditional morality by critics like Friedrich Nietzsche (1844–1900), and reevaluations of conventional notions of human nature by Sigmund Freud (1856–1939). In short, a world of objective certainties was being replaced by one of uncertainty and subjectivity. Characteristic of Monet's subjective view of the world was his later series of thirty paintings of the west façade of Rouen Cathedral. Monet's interest was not the monumental cathedral itself, but the appearance of the cathedral at different times of day and under varying conditions of weather. Accordingly, a view of the façade in the morning appears dark and restrained, while a view painted in the late afternoon reveals the full impact of the sun on the building, making it brilliantly and

The Bridge at Argenteuil. Painting by Claude Monet, 1874. MUEÉE D'ORSAY, PARIS, FRANCE/BRIDGEMAN ART LIBRARY

variously colored. Monet has dematerialized the façade of the cathedral and transformed it into a surface upon which there is an endless play of light. Unfortunately, Monet did not write much about the ideas behind his paintings, so his intentions must be surmised rather than demonstrated.

MONET AFTER THE IMPRESSIONIST DECADE

Monet's annual painting excursions largely ceased when he bought the house at Giverny and married Alice Hoschedé. In the late 1880s and early 1890s, he worked on the series paintings, *The Grainstacks,* the *Poplars on the Epte,* the *Façade of Rouen Cathedral,* and the *Mornings on the Seine.* For the remainder of his life, with a few notable exceptions like his three trips to London (1899–1904), where he painted views of the Thames and its vicinity, Monet focused his attention on Giverny and making his garden, with its pond, Japanese bridge, and water lilies into a work of art. He then repeatedly depicted this garden, often with a cool detachment. He also isolated himself from contemporary movements in painting, like the postimpressionism of Paul Cézanne or Vincent van Gogh (1853–1890). Late in his life, his eyesight began to fail, and he struggled to continue painting. Monet's renderings of his gardens became more and more abstract, the colors appear more blurred and intermingled, and the paintings grew ever greater in size. Indeed, the acclaimed water lily murals required for their installation in Paris the construction of a special museum in the Orangerie of the Tuileries. Monet died at Giverny on 5 December 1926.

INTERPRETATIONS OF MONET

Early studies of Monet were primarily biographies and collections of letters and documents by authors who had known him. Virtually all are in French and have not been translated. Modern studies begin with the rediscovery of Monet after World War II. Many combined a brief biographical sketch with a rich selection of plates, each with detailed commentary. Representative of such works are William C. Seitz, *Claude Monet* (1960) and Joel Isaacson, *Claude Monet: Observation and Reflection* (1978). Robert Gordon and Andrew Forge, *Monet* (1983) provide, in addition to the reproductions of paintings, a useful collection of photographs, selections from Monet's letters, and passages from contemporary reviews. More recently, scholars like Robert J. Herbert, Virginia Spate, and Paul Hayes Tucker have attempted to situate Monet within the social, political, and cultural context of Third Republic France. Making their task challenging is the absence in Monet's letters of references to contemporary events.

See also **Cézanne, Paul; Degas, Edgar; Fin de Siècle; France; Impressionism; Manet, Édouard; Renoir, Pierre-Auguste; Van Gogh, Vincent.**

BIBLIOGRAPHY

Primary Sources

Wildenstein, Daniel. *Claude Monet: Biographie et catalogue raisonné*. 5 vols. Lausanne, 1974–1991.

Secondary Sources

Gordon, Robert, and Andrew Forge. *Monet*. New York, 1983. Biography mixed with analytical study of the paintings.

Herbert, Robert L. *Impressionism: Art, Leisure, and Parisian Society*. New Haven, Conn., 1988.

House, John. *Monet: Nature into Art*. New Haven, Conn., 1986. A study of Monet's painting techniques, emphasizing the 1870s–1890s.

Isaacson, Joel. *Claude Monet: Observation and Reflection*. Oxford, U.K., 1978. Decade-by-decade study of Monet.

Moffett, Charles S., et al. *The New Painting: Impressionism, 1874–1886*. San Francisco, 1986. Catalog of an exhibit that recreated the eight impressionist exhibitions.

Rachman, Carla. *Monet*. London, 1997.

Seitz, William C. *Claude Monet: Seasons and Moments*. New York, 1960. Brief biographical sketch with reproductions of famed paintings.

Spate, Virginia. *Claude Monet: Life and Work*. New York, 1992. Effectively blends biography with social history and the formal analysis of the paintings.

Tucker, Paul Hayes. *Claude Monet: Life and Art*. New Haven, Conn., 1995.

Robert W. Brown

MONETARY UNIONS. The European nineteenth century was a century of nation building and of the gradual Europeanization of the international economy. Both were conducive to a very rapid growth in international trade. At the same time, monetary policies became central to economic policies. The century saw the creation of national central banks, charged with managing monetary policy and supervising private banks. In a major debate among economists, the "banking school," which favored the convertibility of notes in gold to avoid inflation, won out over the "currency school," which supported free banking. European countries searched for monetary stability in a context of "laissez-faire," and a general acceptance of gold and silver standards amid strong political pressures toward free trade (leading, for example, to the Cobden-Chevalier Treaty of 1860, essentially establishing free trade between France and Great Britain). New nation-states—Belgium, Germany, Greece, and Italy—had to build or adjust their economic structures and institutions to the concert of nations.

MAJOR IMPLEMENTED UNIONS

Within this general framework, ideas for a worldwide monetary system were developed. Several continental European states decided to link their currencies. Their goals were to improve economic stability, bring about a larger fluidity of trade, and protect themselves against pressures on their economies from the growth of international trade and from British economic and colonial domination. They also sought solutions to the economic disequilibria created by the unstable supply of gold and silver. Two of the monetary unions were linked to the unification of Italy (1860–1870) and Germany (1871–1873). Two others were international monetary unions: the Latin Monetary Union (1865) and the Scandinavian Monetary Union (1872).

After the Congress of Vienna in 1815, both Italy and Germany consisted of many sovereign states using different currencies and monetary systems. In 1865, seventeen different systems for gold coins and sixty-six for silver existed in the German states, and on the Italian peninsula until 1860, twenty-two gold and forty silver systems were in use. In both the German and Italian states, a process of political, economic, and monetary unification began in the 1820s. The German states finalized a monetary unification through a customs union (the Zollverein, 1834), a monetary association of the southern states (the Munzverein, 1837), and a monetary agreement between northern and southern states (the Dresden Convention, 1838). The 1866 Austro-Prussian War accelerated political and monetary unification. The mark was created on 4 December 1871, almost a year after the formal unification of Germany. In Italy the Kingdom of Sardinia adopted the French monetary system in 1820, calling their monetary unit the lira, instead of the franc. Upon unification (1860–1870), this system was extended to all parts of the Kingdom of Italy.

France, Belgium, Italy, and Switzerland formed the Latin Monetary Union (LMU) in 1865, joined by Greece in 1868. Each had previously adopted the French monetary system (including decimalization), but not the uniformity of coin weights and metallic fineness. This had led to erratic inflows and outflows of species. On 23 December 1865, in Paris, the parties signed a convention for fifteen years. Spain, Austria-Hungary, Serbia, Romania, Bulgaria, Russia, and even Chile adopted the French monetary system, although they were not included in the formal LMU agreement. The convention was renewed in 1878–1879, and survived despite the gold-silver crisis, the lack of coordination of monetary policies, and the refusal of France to abandon its bimetallistic system. The convention formally ended in 1927.

The Scandinavian Monetary Union (SMU) had similar origins and provisions. It was created by Sweden and Denmark (via the Copenhagen Convention, 18 December 1872). Norway joined in 1875. Coins with identical weights and fineness were introduced and became legal tender throughout the union. The SMU worked smoothly up to the secession of Norway in 1905. It did not survive World War I.

INTERNATIONAL MONETARY CONFERENCES AND PROJECTS FOR A WORLDWIDE CURRENCY

At the same time, on the initiative of French Emperor Napoleon III, and with the backing of the United States, international conferences took place in Paris (1867, 1878, 1881, and 1892) with the goal of considering the possibility of a uniform world gold coinage and the adoption of the French decimal system worldwide. Discussions brought the boldest proposals ever made for a worldwide monetary union. Great Britain, however, refused to adapt its monetary system, or to accept the bimetallistic system and the decimalization of its currency. Moreover, France refused to abandon the silver system and bimetallism (the latter being a monetary system based simultaneously on gold and silver value, with, in this case, a fixed ratio between them of one to fifteen). The discovery of large silver mines in America brought about the loosening of the U.S. position, isolating France.

Two important proposals discussed during these conferences would have to wait nearly a century to be put into practice. Julius Wolf, a German economist, supported by the French representatives Jacques Chevalier and Joseph Garnier, suggested creating in a neutral country a "Universal Bank," where international gold reserves would be deposited to back the issue of international banknotes. This would occur in 1944 with the creation of the International Monetary Fund (IMF), although in a partial form, because the IMF never issued international notes or money with legal tender. Furthermore, in 1867 the French negotiator Esquiriou de Parieu proposed the creation of a European federation of states called the "European Union" that would be governed by a European Commission composed of representatives of the member states and a European Parliament. Its goal would be to impede European wars; to create a common currency, a common market, and Continent-wide postal and transport systems; and to provide a structure for common international negotiations. Such a process began with the creation of the European Coal and Steel Community in 1951 and the European Monetary Institute in 1992, and with the signing of the European Union Constitutional Treaty, scheduled for ratification votes by 2006.

See also **Banks and Banking; Cobden-Chevalier Treaty.**

BIBLIOGRAPHY

Dowd, Kevin, and Richard H. Timberlake Jr., eds. *Money and the Nation State: The Financial Revolution,*

Government, and the World Monetary System. New Brunswick, N.J., 1998.

Einaudi, Luca L. "From the Franc to the 'Europe': The Attempted Transformation of the Latin Monetary Union into a European Monetary Union, 1865–1873." *Economic History Review* 53, no. 2 (2000): 284–308.

Helleiner, Eric. *The Making of National Money: Territorial Currencies in Historical Perspective.* Ithaca, N.Y., 2003.

Kindleberger, Charles P. *A Financial History of Western Europe.* 2nd ed. New York, 1993.

Reti, Steven P. *Silver and Gold: The Political Economy of International Monetary Conferences, 1867–1892.* Westport, Conn., 1998.

Vanthoor, Wim F. V. *European Monetary Union since 1848: A Political and Historical Analysis.* Cheltenham, U.K., 1996.

THIERRY L. VISSOL

MONTENEGRO. Montenegro, meaning "black mountain," has been shaped by its rugged mountainous terrain, which facilitated the existence of its tribal social structure, long impeded the development of centralized political authority, shaped its economy, and enabled it to evade foreign domination. In the nineteenth century, Montenegro was a small province on the border of the Ottoman and Habsburg empires. Population statistics vary, but estimate 60,000 to 80,000 inhabitants in midcentury, climbing to 185,000 in 1900.

SOCIAL STRUCTURE AND ECONOMIC LIFE

Montenegrin society was largely patriarchal and militaristic. It was divided into family-based clans that warred against each other and engaged in ritual blood feuds. If one member of a clan killed a member of another, this murder had to be avenged by taking the life of one of the murderer's fellow clansmen, often spurring a chain reaction of revenge deaths and creating lawlessness. This lack of cooperation among clans also inhibited the development of trade, contributing to the generally poor economic situation. Other problems included a paucity of arable land that created a persistent problem of hunger and the lack of adequate infrastructure. The principal source of national income was animal husbandry, and people used pack animals for travel and communication. These poor conditions led to the raiding of neighboring territories and cattle rustling. Many Montenegrins also emigrated to Serbia, Russia, or Austria-Hungary. As education was not readily available, Montenegrin leaders encouraged working and studying abroad. They also moderately improved economic and cultural conditions by developing a trading class and schools.

INTERNAL POLITICAL LIFE

Political life was dominated by the attempt of its leaders to establish a centralized state, to which Montenegro's social structure posed a substantial obstacle. Only two central authorities existed: the office of civil governor, held by the Radonjić family, and the bishopric of Cetinje, held by the Petrović family and passed from uncle to nephew. The power of both was limited by the lack of an army, administration, justice system, and ability to collect taxes. Their quest to establish central authority and institutions met with resistance from clan leaders, whose only motivation to accept a single authority stemmed from the constant threats of invasion and domination by the Ottoman Empire. The tribal leaders, who enjoyed the loyalty of the people, successfully evaded centralization for much of the century.

The first steps toward centralization were taken in the eighteenth century by Bishop Peter I (1782–1830), who tried to create peace among the clans, establish a judiciary, and gather taxes. In 1798 he convened an assembly of tribal chiefs in Cetinje, which adopted Montenegro's first code of laws (written by Peter I) and established a central court to carry out administrative and judicial functions. However, the tribes refused to pay the taxes necessary to support these measures. Thus, centralization was not achieved, and tribal warfare, raiding, and looting continued. When Peter I died in 1830 a power struggle erupted between the Petrović and Radonjić families over the successor of the bishopric. Arguing that Peter I's nephew, Rade (1813–1851), was not a suitable heir as he was a minor, was not a monk, and had no formal education, the Radonjićs tried to establish superiority of the governorship to the bishopric. However, they were unable to win the support of clan chiefs, who preferred an

Montenegrin soldiers. Late-nineteenth-century photograph. After centuries of tribal factionalism, Prince Danilo I was finally able to create a unified military force in Montenegro in the mid-nineteenth century. ©HULTON-DEUTSCH COLLECTION/CORBIS

ecclesiastical leader to a governor. The Petrović family ultimately prevailed and abolished the office of the governor, killing or banishing the members of the Radonjić family. The bishop thus became the undisputed secular and religious leader of Montenegro. Rade eventually became a monk and adopted the name Peter II Petrović Njegoš. He took steps to establish a regular administrative apparatus and to limit the power of the tribes by creating a senate and a guard to serve police and judicial functions. However, he too lacked a military to enforce these measures. Clans continued to revolt, sometimes even forming alliances with foreign leaders in neighboring territories. Peter II kept the country together, but did not succeed in establishing the supremacy of the central government. He is perhaps better remembered as a poet and for his most famous work, *The Mountain Wreath* (1874).

Peter II died in 1851 and was succeeded by his nephew Danilo. Danilo II (1826–1860) secularized the office of bishop and proclaimed himself prince in 1852. After enduring an attack from local Ottoman authorities, Danilo overcame opposition from his senate to build a stronger, unified military. In 1855 he promulgated a law code based on principles of equality before the law and protection of rights of private property. When Danilo was assassinated in 1860 Nicholas I (1841–1921) assumed the throne. He proclaimed himself king in 1910 and ruled until the end of World War I. Under his reign, Montenegro doubled in size and gained access to the Adriatic Sea. Even though each successive Montenegrin ruler succeeded in securing greater central authority, the tribes remained a strong, even dominant, force in the land.

FOREIGN POLICY

While struggling to establish authority at home, Montenegrin leaders concurrently contended with securing the province's borders, which were not formally recognized. The Porte (as the Ottoman Empire was known in diplomatic circles) claimed that Montenegro was an integral part of its empire, but was not able to collect taxes or to influence internal administration. Montenegro's mountainous terrain helped it to defy foreign occupation. The province enjoyed quasi independence and an ambiguous status with relation to the Ottoman Empire, which persistently battled to subjugate the territory. Peter I fought against Ali Pasha of Janina (1819–1821) during the Ottoman campaign and continued to battle the Porte during the Russo-Turkish War of 1828–1829. Peter II battled Ottoman troops in 1832; Danilo II did in 1852 and 1858; and Nicholas I constantly entered into conflicts with the Porte. Montenegro also actively pursued its own foreign policy ambitions of securing an outlet to the Adriatic Sea and expanding its territory to the neighboring Herzegovinian and Albanian lands, where it often encouraged uprisings.

Both Montenegro's foreign and internal policies were inextricably linked to the interests and actions of the Great Powers. Montenegro's role in great-power politics was disproportionate to its size and economic weight. Especially important was its close and advantageous relationship with Russia, dating to 1715. Russia supported Montenegrin leaders in their battles against the Ottomans and their quest to centralize power at home. Russian financial subsidies were one of the leaders' few resources in the absence of tax collection. Russian wheat often fed the starving Montenegrin population. Russian envoys also assisted in the establishment of stronger centralized institutions. During Peter II's reign, Russia's influence in Montenegrin affairs became particularly significant. Peter II visited the Russian tsar several times during the 1830s, where he was even named bishop. Russia's support allowed Montenegrin rulers to take strides toward centralizing their authority.

Danilo II shifted orientation to Austria after a Habsburg ultimatum to Constantinople resulted in the return of Montenegrin territory captured during an 1852 attack by the Bosnian governor Ömer Pasha Latas (1806–1871). However, during the Crimean War (1853–1856), Austria-Hungary thwarted an opportunity to capture Ottoman territory. Montenegro made territorial gains during an uprising in Herzegovina in 1858, which it retained with the support of France and Russia. It also won the Porte's recognition of the boundary between the principality and the empire. During the Bosnian uprising of 1875 Nicholas I and the Serbian Prince Milan (1854–1901) were under pressure from the public and Pan Slav circles to take advantage of Ottoman weakness for further territorial gains. Montenegro and Serbia both desired liberation from the Ottoman Empire and territorial expansion. The countries were natural partners due to their shared Serbian nationality and Orthodox religion. Peter I encouraged Montenegrin tribes to aid the Serbian leader Karadjordjević during the Serbian national uprising. Peter II Njegoš advanced a sense of wider Serbian identity, drawing on the legend of the Battle of Kosovo (1389) and the common mission of expelling local Turks, expressed in *The Mountain Wreath*. Likewise, Serbia's national objectives aimed at union with Montenegro. However, despite their common political objectives and cultural identity, an undercurrent of rivalry existed between the two for control of South Slav affairs.

In 1876 Serbia and Montenegro waged war against the Porte. When their defeat became imminent, Russia came to their aid, leading to the Russo-Turkish War of 1877–1878. As a result of this conflict, Montenegro's territory more than tripled with the Treaty of San Stefano. Fearing the upset of balance of power and opposing strong Russian influence in the Balkans, Great Britain and Austria-Hungary called for the revision of the treaty at the Congress of Berlin (1878). Although it did not receive as much territory as it had wanted and its coastline was placed under Habsburg supervision, Montenegro's independence was formally recognized and it obtained a port on the Adriatic. In 1912 Montenegro commenced hostilities against the Ottoman Empire, beginning the First Balkan War. Allied with Serbia, Bulgaria, and Greece, it defeated the empire, permanently eliminating it from Balkan affairs. Montenegro then joined Serbia and Greece against Bulgaria in the Second Balkan War, as a result of which it gained part of the Sandžak of Novi Pazar, previously an Austrian possession, and thus acquired a common frontier with Serbia. Persistently the object of great-power interest and intrigue, Montenegro managed to maneuver among the European powers until its defeat and occupation by Austria-Hungary during World War I.

See also **Balkan Wars; Crimean War; Ottoman Empire; Russo-Turkish War; Serbia.**

BIBLIOGRAPHY

Jelavich, Barbara. *History of the Balkans.* Vols. 1 and 2. Cambridge, U.K., and New York, 1983.

Jelavich, Barbara, and Charles Jelavich. *The Establishment of the Balkan National States, 1804–1920.* Seattle, Wash., 1977.

Lampe, John R. *Yugoslavia as History: Twice There Was a Country.* Cambridge, U.K., and New York, 1996.

Palairet, Michael R. *The Balkan Economies c. 1800–1914: Evolution without Development.* Cambridge, U.K., and New York, 1997.

Stavrianos, L. S. *The Balkans since 1453.* 1958. London: Hurst, 2000.

JOVANA L. KNEŽEVIĆ

MONTESSORI, MARIA

MONTESSORI, MARIA (1870–1952), one of the most influential contributors to western educational thought.

Initially trained as a scientist and doctor, Maria Montessori is best known for developing a child-centered educational approach using instructional toys. A tough, inspired woman with irrepressible enthusiasm, and a remarkable strength of character and capacity to work, Montessori was a complex and controversial figure. For a few years before the outbreak of World War I, she was one of the most famous women in the world.

Maria, the only child of educated, middle-class parents, was born in a small Italian town and grew up in Rome. In an age when girls aspired to be wives, nuns, or teachers, she decided to become an engineer and successfully completed preparatory technical and scientific studies. By the time she enrolled at the University of Rome, Montessori switched from one male-dominated profession to another. Enthusiastically supported by her mother and grudgingly tolerated by her father, she overcame the opposition of male professors and students to study medicine. At the age of twenty-six, Montessori graduated with outstanding results to become one of the first women doctors in Italy. Over the next decade, she began private practice, held a number of part-time clinical positions, wrote specialist scientific papers, continued her own studies, and taught natural sciences in university teacher training courses.

To many contemporaries, the young woman doctor embodied the ideal of modern femininity. As a delegate to the 1896 international women's congress in Berlin and later in public lectures, Montessori argued that science had the power to liberate women from domestic drudgery and provide effective education for their children, all without robbing mothers of feminine charm. Throughout her life, she delighted in displaying competence in ladylike virtues; in the press, she was described as combining the delicacy of a talented, graceful young woman with the strength of a man.

In her early clinical work, Montessori developed an interest in the way sensory exercises with specially designed objects improved the treatment of "idiot children." By 1898 she assumed a prominent public role in the newly formed National League for the Education of Retarded Children. "Moral imbeciles," "intellectual idiots," and "congenital delinquents," she argued as the League's representative, should be removed from ordinary schools, provided with scientifically designed training, and transformed from potential burdens and parasites into productive members of society. When, in 1900, the League opened a model school, Montessori and a colleague were appointed codirectors. "I was with the children from early morning till evening as if I were a real teacher," she later recalled, "not a physician conducting an experiment." Through close observation of the children and trial and error with educational toys, Montessori became convinced that the handling of increasingly complicated objects, and sensory exercises more generally, help improve intellectual capacities; self-education through self-directed activity could transform the "unteachable" into literate children. Montessori's association with her codirector also produced an illegitimate son, who later became her closest professional associate.

In 1906 Montessori tried out her approach on "normal" toddlers in an experimental preschool in a slum district of Rome. To the disgust of her learned colleagues, the thirty-six-year-old doctor and professor became involved in the day-to-day care of fifty grubby urchins. Children, she confirmed, thrived on graduated challenges presented to them by self-correcting materials. Motivated by the enjoyment of a sense of mastery, they calmed down and taught themselves. Montessori insisted that such an instructional environment needed to be expertly guided and prepared; she did not hesitate to suppress what she saw as inappropriate behavior and rudeness. The ideal child for her was independent, self-controlled, and courteous, in turn exerting a civilizing influence on parents and, beyond them, the whole society.

Modern states, social theorists note, need self-policing, diligent workers and citizens. Montessori's system, relying on guided self-development rather than external coercion, promised to supply them. Within a year, the slum school and its successors became famous, attracting visitors, patrons, and helpers. Montessori schools and societies were established around the world. In 1910, annoyed by public distortions and commercial exploitation of her ideas, Montessori gave up all professional appointments to focus on the widening international network of schools and societies, the training of teachers, and the production and sale of instructional materials. Montessori's determined attempts to control the dissemination and application of her ideas proved controversial. In a period when children of different social groups experienced vastly different childhoods, and scientists put forward incommensurate theories about people's nature and learning, they blunted the impact of her work.

Montessori lectured, traveled, and taught to the end of her long life. Her ideas helped transform theories of human development; over time, they became part of everyday understandings and experiences of childhood.

See also **Childhood and Children; Education.**

BIBLIOGRAPHY

Kramer, Rita. *Maria Montessori: A Biography.* New York, 1976.

Martin, Jane Roland. *The Schoolhome: Rethinking Schools for Changing Families.* Cambridge, U.K., 1992.

Montessori, Maria. *Dr. Montessori's Own Handbook.* Edited by Reginald Calvert Orem. New York, 1965.

———. *The Montessori Method: The Origins of An Educational Innovation, Including an Abridged and Annotated Edition of Maria Montessori's The Montessori Method.* Edited by Gerald Lee Gutek. Lanham, Md., 2004.

Walkerdine, Valerie. "Developmental Psychology and the Child-Centered Pedagogy: The Insertion of Piaget into Early Education." In *Changing the Subject: Psychology, Social Regulation and Subjectivity,* by Julian Henriques et al. London, 1984.

———. "Progressive Pedagogy and Political Struggle." In *Feminisms and Critical Pedagogy,* edited by Carmen Luke and Jennifer Gore. New York, 1992. A shorter version of much the same argument as above.

PAVLA MILLER

MORISOT, BERTHE (1841–1895), French artist.

Berthe Morisot was one of the core members of the French art movement known as impressionism. Born in 1841 into an upper-middle-class family, she received a traditionally feminine education. Trained at home and with private tutors, her curriculum included drawing.

By the time she was in her late teens, it was clear that she and her sister Edma were exceptionally gifted and ambitious, qualities noted with some trepidation by her teachers Joseph Guichard and the famous Barbizon painter Jean-Baptiste-Camille Corot. In the mid-nineteenth century, respectable young ladies were not supposed to appear in public alone, but because Berthe and Edma Morisot painted together, they managed to work consistently for about twelve years, out-of-doors as well as in their home. Tapping into a strong amateur feminine image-making tradition that had been gaining momentum since the late eighteenth century, they painted scenes of everyday feminine life, primarily portraits, domestic interiors, and family vacation spots. As the Morisot sisters astutely understood, this imagery corresponded to a program for pioneering, avant-garde art, famously formulated by Charles Baudelaire in his *The Painter of Modern Life,* published in 1863. Baudelaire called for art to abandon academic standards of history painting in favor of modern urban subject matter.

Through their painting, Berthe and Edma came into contact with the circle of young Parisian artists and writers who were putting Baudelaire's ideas into practice. In particular, they became close friends with the brilliant leaders of a new generation, Édouard Manet and Edgar Degas. Manet painted several beautiful portraits of Berthe. Barred by bourgeois convention from participating in the café encounters during which the principles of realism and impressionism were debated and developed, the Morisot sisters nonetheless assimilated the latest trends through their personal network.

Between about 1869 and 1872, Berthe went through a crisis, initiated by the obligation felt by her sister Edma to give up art in order to marry and have children, and deepened by the military and political events shaking France, and especially Paris, during 1870 and 1871. Berthe Morisot emerged from this crisis with a decision to become, in effect though not in name, a progressive professional artist. She also decided to marry Eugène Manet, brother of the painter Édouard. Against Edouard Manet's advice, she accepted Degas's invitation to join an 1874 exhibition intended to circumvent the authority of the French Academy of Fine Arts. This exhibition, later known as the first of eight impressionist exhibitions held over the course of twelve years, launched impressionism.

Portrait of Julie Manet. Painting by Berthe Morisot, 1889. Private Collection/Bridgeman Art Library

In the first impressionist exhibition, Morisot showed a painting that epitomized her early work: *The Cradle,* painted in 1873. It shows a mother and baby, painted with light, varied, and expressive brushstrokes to render a time-honored subject in a thoroughly modern way. The image, scaled for a middle-class interior, is at once secular, tender, and analytical. Mother and baby each occupy their own areas of the image, one in full light, the other veiled, but are connected to each other compositionally, as well as by the mother's gaze and gesture.

Although critics noted the participation of a woman in the impressionist movement, their reaction was rarely negative, and indeed Morisot's colleagues seem to have never questioned her right to belong at the heart of their group. Instead, critics tended to praise Morisot's art for what they perceived as its femininity, which they saw in its subject matter, as well as in its delicate, scattered, and brightly colored style. As impressionism matured, Morisot's work evolved along with the movement. Gradually her style became more sinuous and strongly colored. She experimented with self-portraiture, and with a series of portraits of her only child, Julie, born in 1879. In these later works, Morisot explored her child's progress toward autonomy, and the melancholy of loss, especially in paintings made after the death of her husband in 1892.

Morisot also participated in the impressionist movement through her and her husband's personal, administrative, and financial support. She continued to be a close friend of the impressionist painters Degas and Pierre-Auguste Renoir for the rest of her life, and earned the admiration and friendship of the great symbolist poet Stéphane Mallarmé. Morisot died at the age of fifty-four in 1895, from influenza caught while caring for her daughter.

Many of Morisot's works remained in her family at her unforeseen death, and many others remained in private collections. This seclusion of her work, compounded by a bias in art history against women, caused Morisot's reputation to decline until textbooks no longer even included her in their account of impressionism. Morisot's reputation has also been plagued by recurrent attempts to cast her primarily as the painter Édouard Manet's muse and mistress. Beginning in the 1980s, feminist contributions to art history, together with a growing general respect for Morisot's subject matter and achievements brought about by changing attitudes to gender, have restored Morisot to the place of honor she occupied in her own lifetime. The single largest collection of her work is to be found in the Paris Musée Marmottan.

See also **Corot, Jean-Baptiste-Camille; Degas, Edgar; France; Impressionism; Manet, Édouard; Painting.**

BIBLIOGRAPHY

Berthe Morisot. Catalogue of an exhibition at the Palais des Beaux-Arts de Lille and at the Fondation Pierre Giannada à Martigny. Martigny, 2002.

Higonnet, Anne. *Berthe Morisot: A Biography.* Berkeley, Calif., 1995.

Anne Higonnet

MOROCCAN CRISES. The Moroccan Crises of 1905 and 1911 were part of a number of international incidents that threatened to embroil Europe in war before 1914. On both occasions, while the trigger for the conflict was provided by a colonial dispute, the issue was used by Germany to provoke a crisis in which its leaders hoped either to make significant territorial gains or to split up the hostile alliances that threatened to "encircle" Germany.

THE MOROCCAN CRISIS OF 1905

In April 1904, France and Britain resolved some of their long-standing differences over Morocco and Egypt. In 1904 and 1905, the Russians were losing their war against Japan, and in January 1905, internal revolution further weakened Russia. Against this background, Germany's political leaders challenged France when it tried to force the Moroccan sultan to accept pro-French reform programs in an attempt to extend its influence over Morocco in early 1905.

Although Germany provoked an international crisis over the extension of French influence in Morocco, fearing for its economic interests in the region, the concern of Germany's politicians was more about prestige than trade. They resented not having been consulted by France and Britain when they extended their influence in North Africa, and wanted to demonstrate that as a great power Germany could not simply be ignored in important colonial decisions. Friedrich von Holstein, a senior figure in the German foreign office, felt that Germany could not allow its "toes to be trodden on silently." At the heart of the crisis was Germany's desire to undermine the newly formed Entente Cordiale (March 1905) between Britain and France, to split the Entente partners before they had a chance to consolidate their bond, and to intimidate the French. Germany's leaders hoped a diplomatic victory would demonstrate the importance of the German Empire, and Kaiser William II landed in the port of Tangiers on 31 March to stake Germany's claim and to assure the sultan of Germany's support.

During the ensuing crisis, Germany insisted on the dismissal of the anti-German French foreign minister Théophile Delcassé and threatened France with war. However, their bullying tactics only led to a strengthening of the newly formed Anglo-French Entente. At the international conference at Algeciras in 1906, on which the German government had insisted in order to settle the crisis, Germany was isolated, with support only from its ally Austria-Hungary. The conference did not support Germany's request to limit the extension of French interests in Morocco.

During and following the First Moroccan Crisis Germany began to feel the full effects of its own expansionist foreign policy. British involvement in a future war was now almost certain. As a consequence Italy, allied to Germany and Austria since 1882, became a less reliable ally, for it would be unable to defend its long coastlines from Britain and might therefore opt to stay neutral in a future war. France also looked upon Germany as a likely future enemy. In 1907, Britain and Russia agreed on a military convention that effectively created a Triple Alliance against Germany, another step toward Germany's diplomatic isolation.

THE AGADIR CRISIS OF 1911

German fears of "encirclement" became even more acute as a result of the Agadir Crisis of 1911. In 1911, Berlin felt provoked by French military intervention in Morocco in the spring of that year (the "dash for Fez"). This move amounted in effect to the establishment of a French protectorate in Morocco and ran counter to the Algeciras Agreement of 1906 and to the Franco-German agreement on Morocco of 1909. Germany was again intent on asserting its status as a great power, and on ensuring adequate compensation for France's territorial gains, with an eye to weakening the Entente in the process. The public response to State Secretary for Foreign Affairs Alfred von Kiderlen-Wächter's forceful foreign policy was largely enthusiastic, and, not surprisingly, the mood among Germany's leading military men was bellicose. They advocated unleashing a war, especially in view of the then-favorable military situation. After failing to find a diplomatic solution, Germany's political leaders dispatched the gunboat *Panther* to the port of Agadir to intimidate the French, an event that marked the beginning of the Second Moroccan or Agadir Crisis.

Germany demanded the French Congo as compensation for the extension of French influence in Morocco. However, France again received support from Britain, and Germany's intervention only strengthened the links between the two Entente partners. Britain let Berlin know in no uncertain terms that it intended to support France, and David Lloyd George's famous Mansion House Speech of 21 July 1911, threatening to fight on France's side against Germany if the need arose, caused great indignation in Germany. The crisis was eventually resolved peacefully, and although Germany was given a small part of the French Congo as compensation, the outcome amounted to yet another diplomatic defeat. Moreover, Austria-Hungary's lukewarm support suggested that the ally could not necessarily be counted on, while Germany had identified itself as an aggressor to its neighbors.

In Berlin, many observers felt that only war would now hold any guarantee of changing the status quo in Germany's favor. In Germany, the crisis resulted in a bellicose and hostile anti-French and particularly anti-British mood. While Germany's political decision-makers did not actually want war in 1911, they were willing to threaten it for diplomatic gains. But in the aftermath of the crisis, demands for a preventive war became widespread, as public interest in the army became more pronounced, especially due to the propaganda work of the German Army League (Deutscher Wehrverein), founded in January 1912.

In addition, there were significant international consequences. Because Britain and Germany were being compensated for French gains in Morocco, Italy sought recompense, too, leading to Italy's annexation of Libya and Tripolitania in November 1911. The Ottoman Empire, weakened by that conflict, later became an easy target for the Serbian-led Balkan League during the Balkan Wars of 1912–1913. Italy became a more unreliable alliance partner for Germany and Austria-Hungary, while the strengthened Serbia and Montenegro posed a more serious threat to the Dual Monarchy. In France, Germany's aggressive behavior led to a revival of the *revanche* idea, a wish for seeking revenge for the lost territories following the Franco-Prussian War of 1870–1871. If the French mood had already been hostile toward Germany before Agadir, it was now distinctly anti-German. Another result of the crisis was the Anglo-French naval agreement, discussed during 1912 and signed in February 1913. The "encirclement" that Germany feared and that was to a large extent of its own making that was fast becoming an inescapable reality.

See also **France; Franco-Prussian War; Germany; Imperialism.**

BIBLIOGRAPHY

Anderson, Eugene N. *The First Moroccan Crisis, 1904–1906.* Hamden, Conn., 1966.

Barraclough, Geoffrey. *From Agadir to Armageddon: Anatomy of a Crisis.* New York and London, 1982.

Geiss, Imanuel. *German Foreign Policy 1871–1914.* London, 1976.

Rich, Norman. *Friedrich von Holstein: Politics and Diplomacy in the Era of Bismarck and Wilhelm II.* 2 vols. Cambridge, U.K., 1965.

Annika Mombauer

MOROCCO. Like most Muslim powers in North Africa and the Middle East in general, Morocco in the nineteenth century was dealing with the new international political context and grappling with the harsh economic realities that resulted from its insertion into the world economy. The country had been able to maintain political autonomy outside of Ottoman control mainly because of its geography and because successive dynasties had maintained a semblance of central authority, but it gradually succumbed to European imperial rule in the nineteenth century. Morocco faced a direct challenge from Europe and more specifically from Britain, France, and Spain. The country became the site of complex relationships that reflected in ambiguous ways both the rivalries between these European states and the intricate game of colonial politics and power relationships. In many ways the history of nineteenth-century Morocco in the context of Europe is a history characterized by defeat in a number of different ways.

POPULATION

There are no exact statistics about the Moroccan population in the nineteenth century, but some reliable estimates put their numbers at four to five million. Moroccans were made up of relatively heterogeneous tribes of Arab and Berber origins, with a numerical predominance of Berbers. The two main religious groups were the majority Sunni Muslims and the Jews. The Christians, who gradually established themselves as part of the growing colonial interest in Morocco, were very limited in numbers and were mainly of a European background. Most Moroccans were concentrated in rural areas especially in the northern Rif and western Atlas (mountain ranges); only 5 to 10 percent lived in cities. A tribal system and a complex web of tribal confederations formed the basis of social organization. Whether sedentary or nomadic, Arab or Berber, the tribe was the major unit within which an individual self-identified or was identified by others. The central power of the *makhzan,* as the Moroccan state has been called, depended on the kind of relationships that it entertained within this tribal system.

Based mainly in urban areas, successive Moroccan sultans (kings) had to maneuver between coercive and religious charismatic authority in order to maintain a political balance with the tribal confederations that were concentrated in rural areas. Up to the beginning of the nineteenth century, failure to do so meant recurrent tribal upheavals. In peaceful times, the relationship between the tribes and the cities were otherwise symbiotic. The cities were ideal markets for tribal peasants to sell their agricultural products while urban artisans and merchants could trade their different commodities with them. For centuries, trade with Europe had been an important component of the Moroccan economy, but by the beginning of the nineteenth century a major trade imbalance and a serious lack of trust characterized the Moroccan relationship with Europe.

EUROPEAN MILITARY AGGRESSION

The news that the Ottoman province of Algiers was under attack by the French in 1827 came as a warning sign for the Moroccan population that the "Christian forces" were about to conquer *dar al-islam* (Muslim house). The *makhzan* faced many internal economic problems and lacked both an effective central authority and a strong army. The first reaction of the Moroccan sultan Abd ar-Rahman ibn Hisham (r. 1822–1859) was to avoid any conflict with France; he even wrote to General Bertrand Clauzel (1772–1842), the head of the French expedition in Algeria, to congratulate him on his success. The sultan, who was aware of the structural weaknesses of his state, had no intention of facing a European power such as France. Invoking the traditional authority of the Moroccan sultan as a protector of *dar al-islam,* some merchant classes from Algeria proposed the *bay'a* (allegiance) to the sultan and pleaded for his help against the French invaders. While Abd ar-Rahman ibn Hisham initially rejected their plea on the grounds that Algerians were under the symbolic authority of the Ottoman caliph, he ultimately came to their support in 1830 by sending five hundred troops to Tlemcen. This Moroccan intervention in Algeria was doomed to failure because it was militarily weak. As a direct consequence, by January 1832 a French warship was sailing along the northern coast of Morocco forcing the Moroccan state to negotiate with France and withdraw its troops from Tlemcen. However, because of Moroccan popular support for the Algerian resistance movement, the sultan and the *ulama* (religious scholars) of Fès continued to send arms and proclaim *fatwas* (public legal opinion) that legitimated the anticolonial struggle against the French. Even though it was not very significant, the Moroccan intervention signaled that the Algerian fate and the overall colonial experience was very much interlocked with that of Morocco.

In 1844 the Moroccan state found itself once again more directly involved in Algeria when it came to the support of the emir (leader) Abdelkader

(1808–1883) in his great revolt against the French. As an astute technician of guerrilla warfare, Abdelkader was able to make use of his popularity in Morocco, cross through the eastern borders of the country, and draw the Moroccan state into direct military conflict with France. In June 1844 the French troops took over the Moroccan city Oujda. Meanwhile the French fleet launched its attacks on Essaouira in the west and Tangiers in the north of the country. In Oujda the most decisive battle took place at Isly on 14 August 1844. Within hours the Moroccan troops, commanded by the sultan's son Sidi Mohammed, had lost the battle, which resulted in total chaos and a rampage by contingents from the local tribes of Cherarda. Even though the Moroccan army outnumbered the French by thirty thousand to ten thousand, it was not technologically advanced enough to create any major challenge. If the battle of the "Three Kings" against the Portuguese forces in August 1578 was a symbol of prestige and a strong Moroccan state in the sixteenth century, the battle of Isly signaled much more clearly its gradual weakness vis-à-vis European power.

Following the battle of Isly, France did not pursue any military conquest in Morocco. For much of the nineteenth century, the country was not militarily under any European power. The principle of balance of power in Morocco guaranteed Morocco its political independence at least for a few more years. In the 1840s France was still preoccupied with the establishment of its colonial state in Algeria and was not ready yet for a new colonial venture in Morocco. More significantly, England constituted an important obstacle of French military expansion in North Africa. The British played an important role in mediating between the Moroccan sultan and the French and in strategically persuading the French to hand back Oujda. The lack of direct military expansion in nineteenth-century Morocco did not mean that the country was outside the orbit of imperial visions. European involvement in Moroccan affairs manifested itself more significantly in the economic field.

EUROPEAN ECONOMIC AGGRESSION

British mediation was clearly based on commercial interest. The defeat in the battle of Isly ushered in an era of growing economic intrusion into Morocco. The mediating role that the British were playing depended in fact on whether the Moroccan state was willing to make any concessions in terms of their commercial relations. The key British political figure in this context was John Drummond-Hay, the British consul in Tangier, who in 1848 managed to pressure the Moroccan sultan to reduce both import and export duties and to open the Moroccan market. The opening of the Moroccan markets marked the beginning of aggressive economic policies that resulted in a series of concessions to European merchants and speculators, who were gradually able to assert their rights in Morocco through the principle of extraterritoriality. On 9 December 1856 Morocco signed the General Treaty and Convention of Commerce and Navigation, which gave preferential treatment not only to British but also to all European traders. From then on the Moroccan state was unable to control its own internal economy. By 1860 the Moroccan currency, *dirham,* was much less in use because it was gradually replaced by the French *écu* and the Spanish *douro.* In addition, inflation led to a major increase in the cost of consumer goods, which had drastic effects on the different strata of the Moroccan society, especially the peasants who paid their taxes in kind. Three years after signing the treaty, Morocco faced yet another military defeat.

From the 1860s until the 1890s Morocco faced an unprecedented series of economic and political crises from which it never recovered—attempts at modernization reforms were doomed to failure. The Spanish-Moroccan War of 1859–1860 was the coup de grâce of the Moroccan state in the nineteenth century. In November 1859 the Spanish navy landed on the northern shores of Morocco without facing any significant military force from the local tribes. Instead the Spanish troops had more to fear from the spread of cholera that was threatening the city of Tétouan. Not militarily challenged, the Spanish ventured farther into Tangier only to be stopped by the British, who did not want to see Spain as a rival in the southern parts of the Straits of Gibraltar. As in the case with France in the battle of Isly, the British once again mediated a peace treaty known as the Treaty of Ouad Ras in April 1860 that guaranteed their own interest and granted Spain more territory around Ceuta and Melilla, which in 2005 were still under Spanish occupation.

The Treaty of Ouad Ras precipitated further the weakness of the *makhzan,* which internally started to lose its legitimacy as the protector of *dar al-islam* in the face of European dominance. Morocco entered the twentieth century with an economy in shambles, a weak central government, and an inability to engage in successful reforms. The Moroccan fate was now in the hands of European powers and more specifically France.

IMPERIAL RIVALRIES

By 1900 it was clear to most European states that France was going to emerge as the most important power in North Africa and Morocco more specifically. In the early-twentieth-century international context this was part of the division of Africa, Asia, and the Middle East into colonies or spheres of influence. By 1904 the French accepted the British occupation of Egypt, while the British gave their consent to French hegemony and colonial venture into Morocco. Meanwhile Italy and Spain were reassured of their control of Libya and northern Morocco respectively. But the system of balance of power and rival alliances in Europe was soon to be played out and tested in the Moroccan context.

On 31 March 1905 the German kaiser, William II (r. 1888–1918), disembarked from a German warship at Tangier in the north of Morocco and made speeches that reaffirmed German support for the independence of Morocco. Germany was clearly not genuinely interested in keeping Morocco independent but in breaking the so-called Entente Cordiale between Britain and France. As a result Germany called for an international conference, which was held in Algeciras in January 1906. With the British support for the French, the conclusions of the conference rebuffed the German government and called for more economic reforms by the Moroccan state. The "reforms" meant in reality opening further the Moroccan markets, granting more commercial and legal rights for Europeans in Morocco, and establishing, under French dominance, an international commission that ended more effectively the *makhzan's* control over the country's economy and finances. As result of the Algeciras conference, the economic and military position of France was further consolidated. As it became known in the annals of European diplomatic history, the First Moroccan Crisis of 1905 contributed more to the isolation of Germany among European states and the confirmation of France as the key imperial power in Morocco.

But Germany did not give up on using the Moroccan context to bully France. In the summer of 1911 a German gunboat, the *Panther,* arrived in the southern port of Agadir supposedly to protect German merchants from anti-European rebellions, although there was no significant threat to German interests in the south of Morocco. This became known as the Second Moroccan Crisis. British support for the French proved to be strong, and in a treaty that was signed with Germany in November 1911, France once again gained the upper hand, while Germany relinquished all claims to Morocco and received a part of the French Congo in return. On 13 March 1912 the sultan, Moulay Abd al-Hafid (r. 1908–1912), signed the Treaty of Fez, which guaranteed his religious authority but delegated all other powers to the French protectorate government.

See also **Africa; Algeria; Colonialism; France; Imperialism; Moroccan Crises; Tunisia.**

BIBLIOGRAPHY

Burke, Edmund, III. *Prelude to Protectorate in Morocco: Precolonial Protest and Resistance, 1860–1912.* Chicago, 1976.

Laroui, Abdallah. *Les origines sociales et culturelles du nationalisme marocain (1830–1912).* Paris, 1976.

Miège, Jean Louis. *Le Maroc et l'Europe, 1830–1894.* Rabat, Morocco, 1989.

Pennell, Richard. *Morocco since 1830: A History.* London, 2000.

Driss Maghraoui

MORRIS, WILLIAM (1834–1896), English poet, political thinker, and decorative artist.

William Morris was born in Walthamstow, now part of London, on 24 March 1834 and died at Kelmscott House, Hammersmith, London, on 3 October 1896. Perhaps his greatest fame in his own lifetime was as a poet. But his work as a designer with his own firm and as a politically active socialist has been more enduring. His father made a fortune as a stockbroker, allowing Morris to experiment with various careers before choosing to pursue three: poet, designer, and political thinker and activist. His early love of the Middle Ages, which helped shape all his activities, was fostered by his reading and his explorations of Epping Forest near his home and in the Savernake Forest near his boarding school, Marlborough. He went to Exeter College, Oxford, where he joined a like-minded circle of friends, most notably the future painter Edward Burne-Jones.

Morris had already come to despise what he saw as the cheap and shoddy ideas and goods of the age. At first he thought that the way of reform was to become an Anglican minister, but his interest in religion declined. Influenced by John Ruskin's *Stones of Venice* (1851–1853), particularly its fifth chapter, "On the Nature of Gothic," he determined to use art as the means of reform. He was persuaded by Ruskin's argument that workers need to have a sense of pleasure in their work and in their surroundings. Morris considered being an architect, then a painter but abandoned these careers. Moving to London he found no furniture to his liking so he designed his own. Finding no house he wished to live in, he turned to his friend Philip Webb, who designed for him, in a simplified redbrick Gothic, the influential Red House in Bexleyheath outside of London. In 1861 he formed a design firm, Morris, Marshall, Faulkner & Company, to provide for the inside of the house, and it became a commercial operation. (With some acrimony, Morris eliminated his partners in 1875 and re-formed the firm as Morris & Company.)

Morris felt that much of the design of the time was ugly and false to nature. Its purpose was not beauty but to demonstrate the wealth of its purchaser. Morris believed in talent, not genius, and felt he demonstrated this himself by working in all areas of his firm's production. Although to modern eyes many of Morris's designs appear elaborate, in their own time they represented a move toward simplicity. He designed furniture, wallpaper, stained glass, textiles, tapestries, tiles, carpets, and, toward the end of his life, books for his last enterprise, the Kelmscott Press. As the founder of the Arts and Crafts movement he had a profound effect on design and architecture not only in his own country but also in continental Europe and indeed the rest of the world. He wrote that his aim was "to combine clearness of form and firmness of structure with the mystery that comes of abundance and richness of detail" (Arts and Crafts Exhibition Society, p. 27). He wished, in his own words, "to give people pleasure in the things they must perforce *use,* that is the one great office of decoration; to give people pleasure in the things they must perforce *make,* that is the other use of it" (Morris 1882, p. 4). In his wake, various Arts and Crafts firms were formed. The movement emphasized handmade products, simplicity of form, and fitness to purpose. As such it was a reaction against Victorian objects and an extremely important influence on the look of the world in the twentieth century.

Chrysanthemum wallpaper design by William Morris, 1876. Private Collection/Bridgeman Art Library

His best-known series of poems was *The Earthly Paradise* (1868–1870), and one cartoon depicted him as "The Earthly Paradox." He was aware of being caught in a technological conundrum. He hated what he saw as the low quality of machine products, and is frequently seen as being antimachine. He certainly did not admire the machine, but he was perfectly willing to use it as a way of producing his wallpapers and chintzes at lower cost, although his firm's finer work was done by hand. He increasingly came to feel that corporate interests, to use the modern term, would demand cheaper and shoddier production. For instance, he hated the new chemical dyes and insisted on using natural ones.

Morris became more and more active in politics, as he felt that the only way that the ordinary person could make and have truly beautiful and useful objects was if socialism were introduced and the economic arrangements of society transformed. He became a convinced Marxist, but this did not lead him to change his business methods. Though his workers were well paid, he did not share the profits of his firm. To charges of hypocrisy, Morris pointed out that his one individual case would not change society and he needed his income to achieve political reform, indeed revolution, for all.

He devoted a great deal of his considerable energy to political agitation. The various political groups with which he was associated were the precursors of the British Labour Party, much as he would have disliked it given that in his view society needed to be totally transformed politically. He outlined his utopia in his most famous prose work, *News from Nowhere* (1891). Through the founding of the Society for the Protection of Ancient Buildings (1877), Morris launched the modern preservation movement. He helped create a far greater sensitivity to the need to preserve and protect the environment. Morris's legacy encompasses a belief in simplicity of form, many magnificent designs and objects, persuasive political analysis of the economic world, and a vision of socialism on a human scale.

See also **Furniture; Ruskin, John; Socialism.**

BIBLIOGRAPHY

Primary Sources

Arts and Crafts Exhibition Society. *Catalogue of the First Exhibition.* London, 1888.

Kelvin, Norman, ed. *The Collected Letters of William Morris.* 4 vols. Princeton, N.J., 1984–1996.

Morris, William. *Hopes and Fears for Art.* London, 1882.

———. *The Collected Works of William Morris.* 24 vols. Edited by May Morris. London, 1910–1915.

Secondary Sources

MacCarthy, Fiona. *William Morris: A Life for Our Time.* New York, 1995.

Stansky, Peter. *Redesigning the World: William Morris, the 1880s, and the Arts and Crafts.* Princeton, N.J., 1985.

Thompson, E. P. *William Morris: Romantic to Revolutionary.* Rev. ed. New York, 1976.

Peter Stansky

MOSCOW. Moscow, traditionally styled the other "capital" of imperial Russia along with St. Petersburg, rose from the ashes of the French invasion of 1812 to become a great cultural center by 1900. Moscow was then home to Russia's most vibrant acting company, the Moscow Art Theater, for which Anton Chekhov (1860–1904) wrote plays such as *Three Sisters* and *The Cherry Orchard.* Many of the country's most important artists, such as Mikhail Vrubel (1856–1910), worked primarily in or near Moscow. The university, founded 1755–1758, and for decades the only one in Russia, continued to be a vital locus of scholarship and social thought.

Nineteenth-century tsars were buried in St. Petersburg but crowned in Moscow, suggesting their recognition of that city as the heart of Russia. National memories of 1812 focused on Moscow because of the widespread destruction it suffered; St. Petersburg was untouched. The immense, ungainly Cathedral of Christ the Savior was erected in Moscow as the country's premier monument to the war.

Intense fighting between troops and Muscovites marked the city in 1905. Major social problems continued to 1914, further undermining support for tsarism.

LIBERALISM AND CONSERVATISM IN MOSCOW

Tension between tsarist officials and liberal Muscovites appeared by the 1790s. Alexander Radishchev, born in 1749 and a resident of the city into the early 1760s, then again in 1775–1776, managed to slip *A Journey from St. Petersburg to Moscow* past the censors and into print in 1790. The book was highly critical of serfdom and its impact on both serf owners and their peasants. Catherine II (r. 1762–1796), whose attitudes toward criticism were hardening in reaction to the French Revolution, exiled Radishchev to Siberia.

The Moscow publisher Nikolai Novikov (1744–1818) was arrested in 1792. He had helped organize learned societies, a secondary school, pharmacies, and libraries as well as a prolific publishing business. But with his arrest, due partly to his association with somewhat liberal Freemasons at the university, all unsold copies of his firm's productions were destroyed.

Ironically, the same group of Freemasons helped shape the highly conservative Nikolai Karamzin (1766–1826), Russia's first major historian. Based for most of his life in Moscow, Karamzin founded the first private literary and political journal in Russia, *Vestnik Evropy* (The European herald) in the city in 1802. It became the model for the "thick" journals that contributed immensely to the country's intellectual life in the nineteenth century. Karamzin's twelve-volume history of Russia, which glorified the monarchs' role in the country's past, began to appear in 1818. Karamzin's work launched the "statist" school of interpretation but also awakened many Russians to the fact that their nation had a history.

Alexander Pushkin (1799–1837), whose ties with Moscow were minimal, simultaneously demonstrated the marvelous creative possibilities of the Russian language. These cultural developments gratified national pride but also deepened the educated stratum's concern about Russian identity. Was the country, clearly behind the "West" technologically and otherwise, merely a poor imitation of cultured "Europe"? Or had Russians achieved anything noteworthy?

One of the most important figures to address these questions was Alexander Herzen, born into an aristocratic Moscow family in 1812. He graduated from the city's university in 1833. Moscow's distance from the political capital fostered a relatively free atmosphere in the early part of Nicholas I's reign (1825–1855), allowing students to debate the latest French and German social and philosophical ideas. From this background, Herzen identified the peasant-run village commune as the base upon which his homeland could be the first country to reach socialism. Russian radicals from the 1840s forward continued to grapple with Herzen's ideas.

If the major center of Russian literary and political life during most of the nineteenth century was St. Petersburg, Moscow remained the site of intense thought about the Russian past. Sergei Soloviev (1820–1879) taught history at the university beginning in 1845. His outlook was also statist, but he emphasized Russia's "organic" if not inevitable development. Soloviev was followed at the university by Vasily Kliuchevsky (1841–1911), who stressed the limited but vibrant political participation of the elite into the seventeenth century; then, he thought, the demands of governing a vast territory engendered the state's growing and eventually absolute domination of society. His lectures became public events that encouraged educated Russians to ponder the country's past and present political structures.

Following Kliuchevsky, Russia's leading historian was Pavel Milyukov (1859–1943), who lectured briefly at the university but taught mainly at the Moscow Pedagogical Institute. In 1895 his public criticisms of tsarism prompted the government to dismiss him and banish him from the city. Milyukov went on to become a leading liberal and to help found the Constitutional Democratic (Kadet) Party, great admirers of British political life. The Kadets' major role in protests against autocracy during the Russo-Japanese War of 1904–1905 spread discontent with the regime beyond liberal circles.

SOCIAL CONDITIONS, POLITICS, AND THE REVOLUTION OF 1905

Moscow was, and is, laid out in concentric circles around the Kremlin, a generic Russian word for citadel. The "center" was the area between the Kremlin and the boulevards, whose medians were pleasant places to stroll but also favorite sites for prostitution. Between the boulevards and the broad circular road called the Sadovoye (Garden) Ring was the "second belt," and beyond that the outskirts or "third belt." South of the Kremlin

View of the Kremlin and the Kamenny Bridge in Moscow. Painting by Fedor Yakovlevich Alekseev c. 1810. PUSHKIN MUSEUM, MOSCOW, RUSSIA/BRIDGEMAN ART LIBRARY

was a section often mentioned separately, Zamoskvoreche ("beyond the Moscow River"). Industrial workers tended to concentrate in the third belt or Zamoskvoreche; artisans, tavern and restaurant workers, and tradespeople were scattered about the city; and the wealthy lived mostly in the second belt. But some newly rich clans, for instance the Ryabushinskys and Morozovs, built luxurious and sometimes astonishing homes in the center and throughout Moscow.

The city's population in 1800 was about 250,000. By 1912 the growth rate was 4.04 percent annually, faster even than New York's, and Moscow counted 1,617,700 residents. The most rapid population increase by far was on the outskirts. Moscow remained a "big village," a sprawling hodgepodge of low structures, punctuated by the occasional mansion or posh apartment building. Immigration from the countryside prompted one observer to write in 1915 that in general Moscow was "a peasant city."

Much of the background to the upheaval of 1905 in Moscow lay in worsening social conditions. Most new arrivals were males. They often maintained ties and even some land in their home villages and returned to them after a debilitating injury or for their final years. There was no social safety net for these "peasant/workers," as the regime saw them. A 1912 census counted 165,000 workers in industry, 37 percent of all who toiled in trade and production.

In 1871 there were only 700 women for every 1,000 men in the city, a picture that encouraged drunkenness and the unfortunate Russian custom of mass fistfights as entertainment. By 1912 the female/male ratio was 839:1,000, far below the Berlin figure of 1,083:1,000, but an indication that

A view of Moscow and the Moskva River c. 1900. The St. Sophia church is on the left and the Kremlin is in the background. ©MICHAEL MASLAN HISTORIC PHOTOGRAPHS/CORBIS

Moscow's population was beginning to settle in town more permanently.

However, this trend did not mean improved conditions. In 1911, 17.6 of every 100,000 Londoners died from tuberculosis, while the rate among Muscovites was 45.6. Housing was desperately overcrowded: Berlin averaged 3.9 residents per apartment in 1899, Moscow 8.7. This picture worsened before 1905.

The average wage in the greater Moscow region in 1908 was 11 rubles 89 kopecks, while in England it was equivalent to 26.64 rubles; in North America, 56.97. But rent was high in Moscow, and in 1911 one writer estimated that the city's workers spent from 55 to 88 percent of their budgets on essentials, while in France the figure was 40 to 45 percent.

Industrial laborers' ties to the countryside and the fact that they were often unskilled textile hands, rather than St. Petersburg's more literate metal workers, retarded the militance of Moscow's workforce. But given the disastrous war with Japan, efforts by liberals to attain civil liberties, and agitation by socialists of various stripes, Moscow workers and lower-level employees became increasingly politically conscious and organized during 1905. Print workers, bakers, and railroad shop workers, for example, joined together by the fall of 1905 to press for better job conditions and political rights. Nicholas II's October Manifesto, which promised civil liberties and a legislative parliament (*duma*), split the opposition in Moscow but failed to mollify a large part of the working class and the intelligentsia.

A *soviet* (council) of workers and lower-middle-class employees formed in the city in late November. Now the police and the army, relying in part on reactionary laborers, attacked demonstrators and closed the new postal workers union. Railroad workers voted to strike in sympathy with the postal staff, and in early December the soviet supported the second general strike in three months. But the tsarist government had regrouped; soldiers fired into crowds, cleared Moscow of street barricades, and shot groups of worker-prisoners in factory courtyards. The city council (also *duma* in Russian), elected on a narrow franchise of well-to-do taxpayers, stayed on the sidelines, appalled by the army's actions but also frightened of social revolution.

THE PREWAR YEARS: TSARISM VS. LIBERALISM IN THE CITY

During the December Uprising, the soviet and its allies bitterly accused the Moscow city council of betraying the common people. After 1905 the council was dominated by Kadets and especially the more moderate Octobrists, who wished both to avoid further social unrest and to cooperate with the tsarist authorities in making Russia a constitutional monarchy. The Moscow duma adopted various programs, including building public housing and expanding municipal schools, intended to alleviate social tension and increase residents' productive capacity. But the breakdown of cooperation between the national parliament and Nicholas's government was mirrored in disputes between the Moscow and tsarist authorities over issues ranging from school curricula to limits on municipal taxation. Tsarist *gradonachalniki* (city commanders) in the large towns held far more power to regulate urban conditions than locally elected councils did. By 1912 the Moscow duma and national authorities had reached an impasse; Kadets dominated the city council, but mayors it elected from that party were barred from taking office by the state.

Tsarism remained firmly oriented toward the countryside; major "reforms" for the lower classes after 1905 involved peasants above all. Occasional benign intervention in social problems by centrally appointed officials solved little in Moscow. St. Petersburg (called Petrograd 1914–1924) led the way into the Revolutions of 1917, but Muscovites' resentment over the government's brutality in 1905 and its tepid attention to urban problems thereafter made the second capital's workers and liberals eager to see the end of the Old Regime.

See also **Cities and Towns; Russia; St. Petersburg.**

BIBLIOGRAPHY

Primary Sources

Herzen, Alexander. *My Past and Thoughts: The Memoirs of Alexander Herzen.* Translated by Constance Garnett. London, 1968.

Milyukov, Pavel Nikolaevich. *Russia and Its Crisis.* Chicago, 1905.

Secondary Sources

Bradley, Joseph. *Muzhik and Muscovite: Urbanization in Late Imperial Russia.* Berkeley, Calif., 1985.

Engelstein, Laura. *Moscow 1905: Working-Class Organization and Political Conflict.* Stanford, Calif., 1982.

Ruble, Blair A. *Second Metropolis: Pragmatic Pluralism in Gilded Age Chicago, Silver Age Moscow, and Meiji Osaka.* Washington, D.C., 2001.

Thurston, Robert W. *Liberal City, Conservative State: Moscow and Russia's Urban Crisis, 1906–1914.* New York, 1987.

ROBERT W. THURSTON

MOZZONI, ANNA MARIA (1837–1920), leader of the nineteenth-century Italian women's movement.

Anna Maria Mozzoni was a founder and the most prominent leader of the nineteenth-century Italian women's movement. Born in Milan, her lifelong commitment to democratic ideals and subsequent sympathy for socialism was shaped by her early intellectual immersion in the writings of the French philosophes, utopian socialists like Charles Fourier, and liberals like John Stuart Mill, whose book *The Subjection of Women* (1869) she translated in 1870. An opponent of Habsburg rule in her native Lombardy, she supported Giuseppe Mazzini's call for a republican solution to the Italian Risorgimento. After the unification of Italy in 1861, Mozzoni continued to agitate for women's rights, a cause that she championed until her death.

Mozzoni laid out her agenda for female emancipation in an early work, *La donna ei suoi rapporti sociali* (Woman and her relation to society; 1864). It argued for legal equality between women and men based on the liberal doctrine of natural rights and was addressed to male members of parliament who were drawing up a new code of civil law for united Italy. Her sweeping vision of a "risorgimento for women" included equality within the family, the right to own property, abolition of the sexual double standard, and access to education and the professions. Parliament ignored the demands of Mozzoni and other female emancipationists, choosing instead to perpetuate the legal control of husbands over the family and its property.

Perhaps the most radical of Mozzoni's demands at the time of unification was that of female suffrage. Mozzoni's emphasis on an issue that did not become central to the Italian women's movement until the turn of the twentieth century derived in part from her upbringing in Lombardy, where Austrian law had allowed women to participate in local "administrative" elections. In an unsuccessful campaign that lasted decades, Mozzoni sought support for female suffrage through speeches, pamphlets, and petitions to parliament (1877 and 1906).

As she tirelessly pursued equal rights for women, Mozzoni evolved from a Mazzinian democrat to a socialist. In the 1870s and early 1880s, she wrote frequently for *La donna* (Woman), an early feminist journal, and became active in the International Abolitionist Federation, an organization founded by the Englishwoman Josephine Butler to oppose state-regulated prostitution. With other democrats like Agostino Bertani and Giuseppe Nathan, she campaigned for repeal of the Italian law that required female prostitutes—but not their male customers—to register with police and undergo biweekly health examinations. The minister of education, Francesco De Sanctis, appointed her as Italy's representative to the International Women's Rights Congress held in Paris in 1878. In 1881 she founded the League for the Promotion of the Interests of Women (Lega promotrice degli interessi femminili), whose program attracted both bourgeois and working-class women with its emphasis on reform of legal codes and labor conditions. Increasingly committed to improving the lives of poor women, Mozzoni was among the founders, with Filippo Turati and Anna Kuliscioff, of the Socialist League of Milan in 1889.

Although sympathetic to socialism until her death, Mozzoni never joined the Italian Socialist Party (PSI) after its establishment in 1892. Never a Marxist, Mozzoni criticized the PSI's exclusive focus on economic issues at the expense of "bourgeois" legal reforms like female suffrage. Her most famous quarrel with the PSI, and particularly Kuliscioff, was over protectionist legislation for women workers. Promoted by Kuliscioff as necessary to protect the health of women—and especially mothers—who carried the double burden of housework and paid labor, protectionist legislation promised to limit hours, forbid night work, and offer maternity leave to working women. Mozzoni strongly opposed protectionist legislation in the name of sexual equality, arguing that such measures would make women less attractive to employers and lead to their exclusion from the workforce. Once returned to their traditional role in the home, women would lose the opportunity to organize with men on the shop floor for improvements in hours and wages for both sexes. Mozzoni's opposition did not prevent the passage of Italy's first protective legislation for women in 1902, although in a less comprehensive version than that desired by the PSI.

Studies of Mozzoni have been sparse, despite her stature in Italian historiography as "the doyenne of feminism." She was rediscovered in the 1960s by the pioneering Italian women's historian Franca Pieroni Bortolotti, who interpreted Mozzoni's unbending adherence to sexual equality, typical of nineteenth-century "female emancipationism," as more radical than early-twentieth-century "feminism," with its emphasis on women's maternal role. Annarita Buttafuoco subsequently defended this later generation of feminists against Bortolotti's imputation of conservatism, emphasizing the multiplicity and activism of bourgeois, socialist, and Catholic women's organizations after the turn of the twentieth century in the face of a cultural backlash against the women's movement. Mozzoni still awaits her biographer.

See also **Feminism; Suffragism.**

BIBLIOGRAPHY

Primary Sources

Mozzoni, Anna Maria. *La liberazione della donna.* Edited by Franca Pieroni Bortolotti. Milan, 1975.

Secondary Sources

Buttafuoco, Annarita. "Condizione delle donne e movimento di emancipazione femminile." In *Storia della società italiana.* Vol. 20: *L'Italia di Giolitti,* 145–185. Milan, 1981.

Pieroni Bortolotti, Franca. *Alle origini del movimento femminile in Italia, 1848–1892.* Turin, 1963.

———. *Socialismo e questione femminile in Italia, 1892–1922.* Milan, 1974.

Mary Gibson

MUKDEN, BATTLE OF. The Battle of Mukden was a locally decisive confrontation (19 February–10 March 1905) in northeastern China during the Russo-Japanese War of 1904–1905. It took place in the vicinity of Mukden (now called Shenyang). Both adversaries were poised to take the offensive, but General Alexei Kuropatkin's three Russian field armies were the first to give ground and then withdraw in a near rout under heavy pressure from Field Marshal Oyama Iwao's five Japanese field armies. Kuropatkin counted 300,000 troops, 1,386 field guns, and 56 machine guns against Oyama's 270,000 troops, 1,062 field guns, and 200 machine guns. Kuropatkin's initial dispositions extended east–west along a 150-kilometer (93-mile) line that was bisected by the South Manchurian Railroad just south of Mukden. His entrenched troops held these dispositions in places to a tactical depth of 15 kilometers (9.3 miles), and he backed his forward echelon with two corps in operational reserve. Oyama's dispositions initially mirrored the Russians', but were attenuated to 110 kilometers (68 miles) because he held his newly arrived Third Army (under Nogi Maresuke, victorious in the recent siege at Port Arthur) to the west and slightly to the rear, and his newly created Fifth Army (under Kawamura Kageaki) to the east and also slightly to the rear.

These "refused flanks" were part of Oyama's larger operational concept: to deceive Kuropatkin and then lock his army group in the deadly grasp of a double envelopment, thus repeating the Prussian success at Sedan in 1870. Oyama would open an offensive with Kawamura's Fifth Army in hilly terrain to the east, then add pressure with pinning attacks on Kuropatkin's center. Once Kuropatkin had risen to the bait by shifting his reserves to the east, then Oyama would launch Nogi's Third Army in a deep envelopment over open terrain to the west of Kuropatkin's right flank. The enveloping Japanese Third and Fifth Armies would link up north of Mukden, thereby trapping Kuropatkin in a battle of encirclement.

Meanwhile, Kuropatkin lacked intelligence on the Japanese order of battle. Tethered to the railroad, he expected Nogi's Third Army from Port Arthur, but Oyama's refused flanks masked both Nogi's and Kawamura's dispositions. To retain the initiative in an uncertain situation, Kuropatkin fully intended to strike first by his own right wing on 25 February against the village of Sandepu, and then develop this local attack into a general offensive. Kawamura, however, preempted him with his own attack on the night of 23–24 February, and Kuropatkin subsequently mistook steady Japanese progress against his left as Oyama's main blow with Nogi's reinforcements.

Breaking off the engagement at Sandepu, Kuropatkin reacted predictably on 25 February by dispatching the majority of his operational reserve to the east against Kawamura, only to learn two days later that Nogi's Third Army was enveloping the Russian right flank in the west. On 1 March, Kuropatkin reversed the flow of his reserves to commit them in the west, but on 2–3 March repeated Russian counterattacks failed to arrest Nogi's advance toward the South Manchurian Railroad north of Mukden. A counteroffensive by Kuropatkin's right-flank Second Army similarly failed to halt General Oku Yasutaka's supporting Japanese Second Army. As Kuropatkin shifted the Russian Second Army's dispositions to protect his right flank, General Nozu Michitsura's Fourth Army and General Kuroki Tametomo's First Army renewed general offensive operations against the entire Russian center. Under heavy pressure all along his front and with his right increasingly threatened, Kuropatkin on 6 March fell back to the Hun River. Kawamura's troops in the east scored a breakthrough, however, and with his rear now threatened from the right and left, Kuropatkin ordered a general withdrawal. In the ensuing confusion, some Russian troops fought to the last, while others simply fled. Kuropatkin lost nearly 89,000 troops, including 30,000 prisoners, and nearly all his military stores and heavy armament. With the Russian rout halted only at Xipingkai, some 175 kilometers (110 miles) north of Mukden, Kuropatkin was soon replaced by General Nikolai Petrovich Linevich. Oyama counted fewer casualties (71,000), but a battle of annihilation had eluded him.

Russian defeat did not imply Russian capitulation. Linevich still possessed the ground-force equivalent of a "fleet in being" that could be resupplied and reinforced from European Russia. Oyama, meanwhile, could not bring effective pressure to bear against Xipingkai because of manpower shortages and logistical overextension. Still, the defeat bore heavily on Russian morale and fueled the fires of domestic revolution in Russia. When combined with Admiral Togo

Heihachiro's naval battle of annihilation at Tsushima in May 1905, Mukden added up to another substantial loss in a war that the ever-weakening Russian domestic rear could not support.

Mukden presaged the age of twentieth-century world wars in several ways. It involved a half a million troops in continuous combat across vast distances over a three-week span. It also amounted to an operation on a frontal scale, with attendant requirements for assaulting entrenchments, for developing combat in depth, and for incorporating and integrating the effects of modern smokeless powder weaponry. Yet, because the force ratios were nearly equal and because neither side counted substantial advantages in mobility and firepower, the outcome did not prove strategically decisive.

See also **Armies; Japan; Russia; Russo-Japanese War.**

BIBLIOGRAPHY

Connaughton, R. M. *Rising Sun and Tumbling Bear: Russia's War with Japan.* Rev. ed. London, 2003.

Menning, Bruce W. *Bayonets before Bullets: The Imperial Russian Army, 1861–1914.* Bloomington, Ind., 1992.

Steinberg, John W., Bruce W. Menning, David Schimmelpenninck van der Oye, David Wolff, and Shinji Yokote, eds. *The Russo-Japanese War in Global Perspective: World War Zero.* Leiden, Netherlands, 2005.

Westwood, J. N. *Russia against Japan, 1904–1905: A New Look at the Russo-Japanese War.* Albany, N.Y., 1986.

BRUCE W. MENNING

MUNCH, EDVARD (1883–1944), Norwegian painter and printmaker.

Edvard Munch is recognized as a major, influential contributor to the international symbolist movement of the 1890s and, especially in his woodcuts, as a precursor of German expressionism. The paintings and prints Munch devoted to his image of *The Scream* (1893 and 1896) are his best known works and have become universally popular icons of anxiety and despair, widely reproduced in everything from posters to blow-up dolls.

Munch was born into a family that, since the eighteenth century, had been a leading contributor to Norway's religious, intellectual, and artistic life. Among his ancestors, Munch counted bishops, the historian Peter Andreas Munch (1810–1863), and the painter Jacob Munch (1776–1839), a student of Jacques-Louis David's (1748–1825). The cultural prestige did not translate into wealth, however, and Munch's own father was a military doctor whose civilian practice was located in the worker's districts of Christiania (as the city of Oslo was named until 1924). Dr. Christian Munch and his wife, Laura Cathrine Bjølstad, lived modestly, therefore, and raised their five children—Edvard was their second child and first son—according to strict pietistic Lutheran principles. Poor health, however, marked the family: Laura Munch died shortly after giving birth to her youngest child in 1868; the oldest child, Johanne Sophie, died of tuberculosis in 1877; Edvard similarly suffered from bronchitis and other respiratory diseases, nearly dying in 1878. "Sickness, insanity and death were the dark angels that stood watch at my cradle and since then have followed me throughout my life," Munch later remarked, and he traced both his personality and his art back to the stifling religious and morbid atmosphere of his childhood home.

The consensus of art historical studies concurs with Munch's assessment that a transparent symbiotic relationship exists between his art and his life. His first major work, *The Sick Child* (1884–1885), sets the paradigmatic pattern that other works later follow, as it depicts the artist's recollection of his dying sister and her grieving aunt, Karen Bjølstad, who sits at her side. Most significantly, however, the painting breaks radically with the stylistic approaches of naturalism and realism as its subjectively rendered forms, colors, and spatial organization prophetically shape a protoexpressionist art and content. In his drastic artistic innovations around 1885, Munch received the support of the Norwegian anarchist writer Hans Henrik Jæger (1854–1910) and the grouping of Norwegian students, writers, and artists known as the Christiania Bohème. Advocating anarchism, atheism, free love, and an autobiographic experimental art, the Bohème offered the young artist a conflict-laden alternative to the conservative Christian values of his home. It served as a setting, moreover, for a tumultuous love affair with a married woman, Milly Thaulow, that significantly shaped the attitudes toward women and love that became the focus of Munch's major works of the 1890s.

Melancholy. Painting by Edvard Munch c. 1890. SCALA/ART RESOURCE, NY. © 2005 THE MUNCH MUSEUM/THE MUNCH-ELLINGSEN GROUP/ARTISTS RIGHTS SOCIETY (ARS), NY.

Munch retreated from the unprecedented stylistic innovations of his *Sick Child* for several years due to the harsh criticism of his work. In 1889, however, he received a fellowship for study in Paris, where the innovations of impressionism, neoimpressionism, and synthetism asserted themselves in a new radical subjectivism in his art. He began to work on motifs such as *Death in the Sickroom, Melancholy, Madonna, The Kiss, Jealousy,* and *The Scream* that he then exhibited in 1893 in Berlin as part of a series of paintings entitled *Love.* Munch continued to work on the series throughout the 1890s and exhibited the completed frieze of twenty-two paintings in 1902 in Berlin; after selling a number of the paintings, Munch reworked many of the motifs for exhibition in 1915 as *The Frieze of Life.* A personal pictorial commentary on the nature of love, death, and the continuities of life and art, the *Frieze* motifs were also translated into prints, especially lithographs and woodcuts, beginning in 1895. Just as his paintings predicted the art of expressionism, so too his color woodcuts, such as *The Kiss,* with their broad flat forms, accentuated carving process, and visible wood graining served as prototypes for expressionist graphic art.

Munch suffered a nervous breakdown in 1908 and, after treatment in Copenhagen, returned to

Norway, where he received the commission to paint the murals for the Festival Hall of the University in Christiania, a project completed in 1915. Altered art market circumstances during World War I, moreover, brought notable changes in his work as he painted new variants on his *Frieze* paintings but also focused more on landscape, composed figure paintings, and portraits in a persistently changing, experimental style. He continued to exhibit new works assiduously throughout the 1920s and 1930s internationally, especially in Scandinavia, the United States, and Germany. Long neglected or denigrated by scholars and critics in favor of his symbolist and protoexpressionist paintings and prints, this late work is now being reevaluated and historically situated as art history moves away from modernist paradigms to accept a more pluralistic, contextual perspective of his work.

See also **Impressionism; Painting; Sweden and Norway; Van Gogh, Vincent.**

BIBLIOGRAPHY

Eggum, Arne. *Edvard Munch: Paintings, Sketches and Studies.* Translated by Ragnar Christophersen. New York, 1984.

Heller, Reinhold. *Munch: His Life and Work.* Chicago, 1984.

Tøjner, Poul Erik, ed. *Munch: In His Own Words.* New York, 2001.

Woll, Gerd. *Edvard Munch: The Complete Graphic Works.* London, 2001.

Reinhold Heller

MÜNCHENGRÄTZ, TREATY OF.

On 18 September 1833, representatives of the Russian and Austrian empires signed a convention in the Bohemian town of Münchengrätz. The treaty had resulted from a summit meeting including the emperors Francis I of Austria (r. 1804–1835) and Nicholas I of Russia (r. 1825–1855) and the Crown Prince of Prussia. The Austrian chancellor Prince Clemens von Metternich and the Russian foreign minister Count Karl Robert von Nesselrode managed further negotiations. As the treaty's preamble stated, the two empires agreed to adopt a "principle of union" in their future conduct in relation to Turkish affairs. Further, both states pledged to preserve the integrity of the Ottoman Empire. The treaty's first "patent" (that is, public) article stated the signatories' opposition to the establishment of a regency or any change of dynasty. Should either event occur, according to Article II, the two states would not recognize the change; they would also jointly determine how to prevent any harmful consequences for their respective empires, both of which bordered on Turkey. The agreement also contained two "separate and secret articles" outlining specific circumstances as the basis for future actions by Austria and Russia.

The convention constituted the Austrian and Russian response to "the recent events in Egypt." During the years 1831–1833, the Ottoman sultan Mahmud II (r. 1808–1839) had confronted a serious rebellion by his Egyptian governor Mehmet Ali. Mehmet's French-trained armies had inflicted a series of defeats on the Ottoman forces, taking Syria and advancing toward Constantinople by early 1833. In desperation, the sultan had appealed for aid to Nicholas I, at whose orders Russian troops landed in the vicinity of the Ottoman capital in April 1833. These developments led in May to a peace, according to which Mehmet Ali would retain control over Egypt, Syria, and other territories. On 8 July, Turkey and Russia concluded a treaty of alliance at Unkiar-Skelessi. The Russian contingent left Turkey shortly thereafter.

The Münchengrätz agreement represented a shared resolve by the Russian and Austrian governments to prevent any further destabilization of their Ottoman neighbor. The treaty's first secret article stated more explicitly than the public Article II that Russia and Austria would cooperate to prevent the "Pasha of Egypt" from any direct or indirect extension of authority over the Ottoman Empire's European provinces. The second secret article stipulated that, should the Ottoman Empire collapse, the two "imperial courts" would act in concert in all matters regarding the establishment of a new order. Moreover, they would collaborate to ensure that any change in the Ottoman Empire's domestic situation would not affect their own security, their existing treaty rights, or the European balance of power.

The Münchengrätz convention signaled several important developments in European diplomacy and the history of the "Eastern Question," that is, the international effects of the Ottoman Empire's ongoing decline. First, it repaired a rupture between Austria and Russia resulting from the Greek war of independence during the late 1820s. Russia had supported the Greek cause in league with France and Great Britain despite Austrian opposition. The agreement's dedication "to the name of the Most Holy and Indivisible Trinity" symbolized the restoration of the Holy Alliance, as did reference to the "conservative spirit" that guided the empires' common policy. This ideological orientation received reinforcement in the so-called Berlin convention of 15 October, which united Austria, Russia, and Prussia in a common endeavor to maintain order and the status quo in partitioned Poland. Revolutions in Belgium and France in 1830, as well as a Polish rebellion in 1830–1831 and Mehmet Ali's campaign had convinced all three rulers of the necessity to resist the forces of change.

Second, the Münchengrätz treaty served Metternich's interests by binding Russia to act in concert with Austria in Ottoman affairs, thus weakening the apparent dominance Nicholas had gained through Unkiar-Skelessi. The convention further underscored Austria's and Russia's shared interest in maintaining a weak but integral Ottoman neighbor, rather than a more dynamic state led by someone like Mehmet Ali or a set of smaller nation-states in the old empire's place.

Finally, the Münchengrätz accord sharpened suspicions elsewhere in Europe about Russia's designs on Turkey, especially since, despite Metternich's urging, its terms never became public. Russia's intervention in Turkey had already distressed statesmen in Britain and France. The British foreign secretary Henry John Temple, Lord Palmerston, believed that at Münchengrätz the two conservative empires had in fact agreed to partition the Ottoman Empire. These suspicions persisted until renewed conflict in Turkey in 1839–1841 brought about an Anglo-Russian rapprochement on Near Eastern questions.

See also **Eastern Question; Holy Alliance; Metternich, Clemens von; Ottoman Empire; Russia; Unkiar Skelessi, Treaty of.**

BIBLIOGRAPHY

Primary Sources

Martens, F. *Recueil des Traités et Conventions conclus par la Russie avec les Puissances Étrangères.* Vol. 4, part 1. pp. 445–449. St. Petersburg, 1878.

Secondary Sources

Florinsky, Michael T. *Russia: A History and an Interpretation.* 2 vols. New York, 1947, 1953.

Rich, Norman. *Great Power Diplomacy, 1814–1914.* Boston, 1992.

Schroeder, Paul. *The Transformation of European Politics, 1763–1848.* Oxford, U.K., 1994.

David M. McDonald

MUSEUMS. Museums were among the most important cultural institutions to emerge in Europe during the long nineteenth century, both reflecting and shaping the secularization, nationalization, and democratization of European culture. Earlier, churches, royalty, and their wealthy imitators had kept collections of art, treasures, and natural objects, but only after the French Revolution were these gradually transformed into the form familiar in the twenty-first century: a public institution aimed at cultural uplift for the citizenry and the preservation of cultural and natural heritage.

VARIETIES OF MUSEUMS

Early modern collections often included a wide range of objects, but by the mid-eighteenth century specialization was already occurring. Institutionally, for most of the nineteenth century, the public museum landscape featured three basic forms: state or official museums displaying art, treasures, furnishings, and antiquities, generally derived from royal collections; collections for teaching and research at state-run universities and academies, especially in natural history, comparative anatomy, and medical anatomy; and collections formed by local voluntary associations, such as patriotic clubs or natural history societies, intended primarily for the benefit of their membership but often open to the public for a few hours a week. Additionally, private, profit-oriented museums came and went; most successful among these, especially in the later nineteenth century, were the waxworks museums modeled on Madame Tussaud's in

London. (Originally a traveling show, it gained a permanent location in 1835.)

From the 1870s to 1914, museums proliferated. Specialized museums were established for ethnography, science and technology, commerce, hunting, folklife, and the celebration of cultural heroes. Additionally, hundreds of museums dedicated to local history, culture, and nature sprouted across Europe's smaller towns and provincial capitals in the same period. Rather than focusing on high art and science, these emphasized the preservation of rapidly vanishing folkways and nature. This cultivation of collective local memory through objects in museums represented a profound cultural phenomenon of the late nineteenth century.

STATE CULTURAL MUSEUMS

With their inception in the late eighteenth century, public cultural museums borrowed not only from royal models but also from sacred ones. Much art displayed in royal and civic collections had originally been intended for sacred spaces; its removal to a secular context was part of a broader assertion of the authority of secular culture characteristic of the Enlightenment. Conversely, museums, and art museums in particular, became sites for ritual revering of great art and the classical heritage as that which represented the best of European culture. The Louvre in Paris provided the leading model of a cultural museum devoted to high art.

Although the Louvre had a history as a royal residence and collection dating to the Middle Ages, when it opened as a public museum in August 1793, during the French Revolution, it represented a new kind of institution: a national museum, open free to all. Its paintings and sculptures would serve as models of taste to French citizens and sources of comparison for art students. As Napoleon's armies confiscated artwork across Europe beginning in the mid-1790s and sent it back to Paris, the new museum also symbolized the imperial power of the nation. In 1799, following trends already quietly developing in princely collections across Europe, the Louvre reorganized its Large Gallery to show the historical development of schools associated with different master artists and geographical areas (e.g., the Flemish school, the Italian school). This art-historical arrangement of paintings would become standard, and the Louvre became the leading European national art museum.

Britain offered other prominent models of cultural museums. Although a National Gallery of Art was established in 1824, it was overshadowed by the British Museum. This institution, established in 1753, retained an Enlightenment ambition to maintain a "universal" collection. As official and private adventurers donated materials from expeditions across the globe, its collections multiplied rapidly, especially its books and manuscripts (the future British Library), natural history objects, and Near Eastern and Greek antiquities. The latter included decorations looted from the Parthenon in Greece (bought from Lord Elgin in 1816), and massive statuary from ancient Egypt (the first brought back in 1819). Such exhibits both displayed Britain's imperial might and situated Britain at the apex of a long heritage of civilization.

A second approach to cultural museums developed in Britain at midcentury. Building upon the 1851 Great Exhibition, cultural reformers established a museum of arts and manufactures (opened in 1857). Rather than seeking to elevate the taste of the masses by exposing them to high art, the South Kensington Museum (renamed the Victoria and Albert Museum in 1899) emphasized the decorative arts and the importance of aesthetic surroundings and furnishings in daily life. Controlling education policy for art and design across Britain, this museum provided a leading alternative to the Louvre in its vision for shaping citizens' aesthetics.

NATURAL HISTORY MUSEUMS

If cultural museums aimed at elevating the taste of the citizenry and instructing it on its place in the civilized order, natural history museums existed primarily for research. The goal of European natural history since the late eighteenth century was to determine the true and complete classificatory order of nature, and museums supplied its essential tools. Here again, the French took the lead, nationalizing the well-supported royal collections in 1793. The new Museum of Natural History in Paris, its collections enhanced by those of departed aristocrats, swelled further from the spoils of the Napoleonic Wars. Leading naturalists such as Jean-Baptiste de Lamarck (1744–1829) and Georges Cuvier (1769–1832), Europe's foremost

Victoria and Albert Museum. Photograph c. 1909. Opened in 1857 as the South Kensington Museum and later moved to this larger building designed by architect Aston Webb, the Victoria and Albert Museum emphasized the decorative arts and the importance of surroundings and furnishings in daily life. ©HULTON-DEUTSCH COLLECTION/CORBIS

naturalist in the early nineteenth century, earned a living as professors curating the museum's different departments. Following Cuvier's theory that the true order of zoology was best revealed by comparing animals' internal anatomico-physiological organizations rather than their surface features, the natural history collections, organized taxonomically, were supplemented by a comparative anatomy collection, organized by organ system. Natural history curators around the world envied and imitated this combination.

After the publication of Charles Darwin's *Origin of Species* in 1859, evolutionary theory gave new meaning to taxonomic collections, uniting them conceptually into a tree of life, but did not change their basic organization. Natural history museums divided over whether to include humans; in Britain and France they did, but German museums were more likely to relegate humanity to separate ethnographic museums aimed at showing not the continuity of "primitive" humans with animals but the unity and diversity of humankind.

THE NEW MUSEUM IDEA

Although the official position of many state museums was that they "belonged" to the people, for most of the nineteenth century, such museums mainly served a much narrower audience of connoisseurs, offering no concessions to the ignorance of lay visitors. Most museums were open to casual visitors for only a few hours a week, typically including a Sunday afternoon, when middle-class visitors came seeking rational recreation. (Anecdotal evidence suggests that working-class visitors tended to find natural history museums more appealing than cultural museums, whereas middle-class visitors flocked to both.) As transportation networks thickened across Europe, museumgoing increased, producing pressures to make museums more accessible. In the last quarter of the century, reformers succeeded in making the museum a more truly public institution aimed at educating citizens with no specialized education in art or science.

Beginning in the late 1870s, museum directors across Europe (and America) enthusiastically adopted this new orientation. Museums expanded their opening hours, lowered their fees for at least some days, and cultivated school groups and classes of the new adult education movement. Culling overcrowded walls and cases to allow the visitor to focus undistracted on a smaller number of objects, curators removed most holdings to storage, available only to specialists upon request. This separation of "display" and "research" collections made manifest the idea that the museum served two audiences with fundamentally different needs, a principle christened the "New Museum idea" in 1893 by reformer Sir William Henry Flower (1831–1899), director of the British Museum (Natural History). Newer museums, especially local ones, often devoted themselves wholly to a general public audience.

The new public orientation encouraged museum curators to experiment with exhibit forms. Most striking is the spread in northern Europe of displays of objects recontextualized in their "natural" settings. Fin de siécle natural history museum directors led the way. Having removed their duplicates and variations to storage, the risk-takers among them supplemented their remaining classificatory exhibits with displays of animals in action, such as the dramatic exhibit of a pack of wolves attacking a small herd of elk at the Altona (Germany) City Museum, or niche-based dioramas showing animals in their native habitats, a form epitomized by the Biological Museum in Stockholm, Sweden (opened 1893). By 1914, most natural history museums had at least one such habitat display.

This shift from a classificatory goal to one setting objects in their "natural" context was not confined to natural history museums. The "period room" gained space in museums of arts and crafts; the "village kitchen" scene appeared in museums of folklore and local history; waxworks figures were used to re-create scenes from the lives of "primitives" in ethnographic museums, and from myth and history in popular waxworks museums (or "panopticons," as they were called on the Continent). Open-air museums, pioneered in Scandinavia in the 1880s, took the re-creation of a scene one step further, allowing visitors to enter an entire building landscape of a bygone era and thus step into its culture. By 1914, natural and cultural heritage had become the dominant themes of museums, simultaneously reflecting the centrality of "heritage" to the museum concept and the centrality of museums to the self-representation of European culture.

See also **Education; Leisure; Libraries; Popular and Elite Culture.**

BIBLIOGRAPHY

Primary Sources

Balcarres, Lord (David Alexander Edward Lindsay). "Museums of Art." In *Encyclopædia Britannica,* 11th ed., vol. 19, 60–64. New York, 1911.

Flower, William Henry. *Essays on Museums and Other Subjects Connected with Natural History.* Freeport, N.Y., 1972. Reprint of the 1898 edition.

Holland, William Jacob. "Museums of Science." In *Encyclopædia Britannica,* 11th ed., vol. 19, 64–69. New York, 1911.

Martin, Philipp Leopold. *Die Praxis der Naturgeschichte.* 3 vols. Stuttgart, 1870–1882.

Secondary Sources

Bennett, Tony. *The Birth of the Museum: History, Theory, Politics.* London, 1995. A provocative analysis of the social meaning of museum spaces, with an emphasis on Britain and its colonies.

Duncan, Carol, and Alan Wallach. "The Universal Survey Museum," *Art History* 3 (1980): 448–469. Analyzes the ritual functions of the museum and their origins.

Great Museums of Europe: The Dream of the Universal Museum. Introduction by Antonio Paolucci. Milan, 2002. A beautiful picture book of eight European art museums with historical essays on individual museums.

Preziosi, Donald, and Claire Farago, eds. *Grasping the World: The Idea of the Museum.* Aldershot, U.K., 2004. A comprehensive collection of essays representing the latest scholarship on museum history and theory, emphasizing art and culture.

Sandberg, Mark B. *Living Pictures, Missing Persons. Mannequins, Museums, and Modernity.* Princeton, N.J., 2003. A deeply thoughtful study of museums and modernity in Scandinavia at the turn of the twentieth century.

Sherman, Daniel J. *Worthy Monuments: Art Museums and the Politics of Culture in Nineteenth-Century France.*

Cambridge, Mass., 1989. A pioneering analysis, with emphasis on cultural and institutional politics.

LYNN K. NYHART

MUSIC. European music in the nineteenth century underwent changes in its institutions, its place in cultural life, and its compositional genres and styles, all of which retain their relevance into the present. The key institutions of musical life, so familiar today as to be taken for granted, established themselves in the course of the nineteenth century. Subscription concerts, symphony orchestras, music conservatories, and music journalism began the century in their infancy and grew to be defining features of musical production. Opera houses, already widespread in the eighteenth century, expanded their audiences and public visibility. At the same time, writing about music attested to the emergence and spread of the Romantic music aesthetic. People increasingly attributed to music the capacity to allow them to feel things more deeply and experience states of being beyond everyday hustle and bustle. Finally, shaping all these developments was the accumulation in the course of the nineteenth century of a body of musical compositions that still occupies a central place in formal musical performance and, to a lesser extent, in informal musical experience. No music of the past so dominates Western and even non-Western musical culture as does nineteenth-century European art music. The century of Beethoven, Rossini, Schubert, Bellini, Mendelssohn, Berlioz, Schumann, Chopin, Liszt, Wagner, Verdi, Brahms, Tchaikovsky, Dvořák, Bruckner, and Debussy, to name but a few people in a compositional landscape of great richness and variety, was the century in which Western tonal music explored its furthest reaches and enduringly shaped the modern listening public, whether of so-called classical or of popular music (a distinction itself a product of the nineteenth century).

MUSIC AND SOCIETY

The growing cultural confidence of the middle classes in Europe expressed itself in all aspects of the development of European music in the nineteenth century. Dramatic changes in the intellectual and political life of Europe at the end of the eighteenth century fundamentally changed the environment in which the arts, including music, flourished in the nineteenth. Except for town musicians, who had guilds like other craftsmen, musicians had for centuries composed and performed under the aegis of some kind of patronage, whether of church or court. But by 1800 the capacity of such patronage to sustain musical culture in Europe had all but collapsed, and it had become clear to forward-looking musicians that the future of European music lay with the educated, middle-class public. Aristocratic patronage still played a role, especially in maintaining expensive opera houses and a number of court orchestras, but even in such cases, patronage evolved into state support, as governments at the local and state level took over the task of maintaining musical institutions and founding new ones, especially music conservatories. The French government founded the most celebrated and ironically the most conservative of these, Paris's Conservatoire National de Musique et de Déclamation, in the middle of the revolutionary decade of the 1790s. But state support for the arts increasingly reflected the interest of expanding middle classes, not aristocrats nostalgic for court life. Educated, nonnoble elites also created new forms of musical consumption of their own. Some of these innovations remained to the side of a developing musical marketplace. Local notables organized nonprofit associations for music-lovers, like Vienna's *Gesellschaft der Musikfreunde* (Society of the Friends of Music), founded in 1812 to sponsor subscription concert series. If the community proved receptive enough, such associations could sustain a permanent orchestra, as did the London Philharmonic Society (1813), and even finance the construction of new buildings. Musical amateurs, the majority of them middle class in social position, also founded voluntary organizations for their own musical activities, the most widespread of which were amateur choral societies.

As paying customers, the European middle classes also sustained the growth of the musical marketplace, a web of commercial relations among musicians, music publishers, concert organizers, opera impresarios, and the purchasers of tickets and musical scores. This marketplace had begun to operate already in the seventeenth century: in 1637 the first public opera house opened in Venice to anyone who could buy a ticket, and in 1672 the English coal merchant Thomas Britton began to offer regular subscription concerts in his house. But the nineteenth century marked the point when commercial relations became more important than patronage in sustaining musical life. Entrepreneurs, often themselves musicians, created the business of modern concert promotion and management, renting halls and sponsoring traveling artists. The tumultuous success of the pianist Franz Liszt (1811–1886) and the violinist Niccolò Paganini (1782–1840) as traveling virtuosos in the 1820s established one type of commercial concert; the soprano Jenny Lind's American tour, organized in 1850 by P. T. Barnum, was the natural extension of this model. Also, after 1850, as the orchestra became the center of concert life and grew in size, so too did audiences become larger and commercial possibilities greater. Kings and princes had long built opera houses as imposing physical evidence of their cultural patronage. In the nineteenth century urban elites built their own cultural edifices, often not for opera but for instrumental and choral concerts. Manchester's Free Trade Hall, originally a wooden building to hold the Anti–Corn Law League's protest meeting, was rebuilt as a substantial neoclassical stone edifice in 1856, decorated with allegorical figures of free trade and filled with concerts that attested to the commercial elite's cultural aspirations.

Other aspects of musical commerce fed off concerts and contributed to their ticket sales. Music journalism grew in order to review concerts and to teach middle-class consumers how to listen to and pass judgment on music. Music critics became key figures in the development of national musical cultures, and writers like Friedrich Rochlitz (1769–1842) and Robert Schumann (1810–1856) helped to create a musically attentive public and paved the way for a later generation of concert critics, such as Eduard Hanslick in Vienna, to become cultural arbiters of the highest order. Paris, one of the busiest musical capitals of Europe, soon had fourteen music magazines with as many as two dozen music critics able to make a living writing for them. In turn, music lovers paid legions of private instructors to teach them how to sing and play the piano: Paris in 1840 had an estimated fifty thousand amateur pianists. And as increasing numbers of people had the money and the time to pursue amateur musical interests, the manufacture of musical instruments increased, especially of the piano, versatile enough to serve as solo instrument or as accompaniment to song and dance.

The nineteenth century was the century of the piano, with technological developments following one another rapidly from the 1770s on, ultimately producing by about 1860 the modern concert grand piano. More suited to the home, the upright piano, in which the strings and their casing were turned up on end, was first developed in the 1830s. The proud owners of all these pianos also bought sheet music, so publishing houses were able to underwrite a composer's livelihood, especially if the composer was willing to create two- or four-hand piano reductions of his symphonies (as was, for instance, Johannes Brahms, though anonymously). Music publishing houses also produced many dubiously helpful manuals for learning how to play an instrument or sing, and instructional charlatans proliferated, alongside sellers of cure-all tonics.

MUSICAL GENRES OF THE NINETEENTH CENTURY

If musical culture in the nineteenth century reflected the workings of new institutions as well as the lingering influence of older ones, so too did it take place along a spectrum of musical experiences from the grandly public to the intimately private. The works of nineteenth-century composers reflect this spectrum, just as do the practices of musical life. The most prestigious of nineteenth-century musical genres was the opera. Opera had established itself as the most elaborate of princely ornaments in the course of the eighteenth century in every European country, from Russia to Portugal, and where princes lost their power at the end of the century, states and cities carried on their role. In the course of the nineteenth century, the distinction between serious and comic opera, which was already blurred in the operas of Wolfgang Amadeus Mozart (1756–1791), disappeared. Instead, operas fell into national categories, albeit everywhere saturated with international influences. So, for instance, French opera from 1790 on saw the rise in popularity of the relatively small-scale *opéra comique,* which now took on more lyrical musical expression and more sober themes. The same period saw the invention, out of the declining genre of *opera seria*, of grand opera, marked by extravagant, often deliberately shocking scenic effects, enormous orchestral sound, and vast choruses of singers. Throughout the nineteenth century, Paris remained at the apogee of operatic production, with Italy providing much of the musical material. The latter half of the nineteenth century was marked in both Germany and Italy by the domination in each of a single, towering figure, Richard Wagner (1813–1883) and Giuseppe Verdi (1813–1901), each of whom transformed opera, albeit differently. As opera became increasingly large in scale, whether in the hands of French grand opera's Giacomo Meyerbeer (1791–1864) or Verdi or Wagner, the numerous eighteenth-century opera houses proved inadequate in size. The century's many new opera houses also provided a visual embodiment appropriate to the prestige and popularity of the musical spectacle inside. The Semper Opernhaus in Dresden (1841), the Royal Opera House at Convent Garden in London (1858), Wagner's Bayreuth Festspielhaus (1876), the Palais Garnier in Paris (1875), and the Teatro Costanzi (1880) in Rome were some of the most famous.

The Russian Juvenile Band. Photographed at the coronation of Tsar Nicholas II on May, 14, 1896. Marching bands became increasingly popular during the nineteenth century and, given prevailing theories of the ennobling effects of music, they were widely viewed as a healthy and moral activity for young people. ©HULTON-DEUTSCH COLLECTION/CORBIS

Just as important to public musical life in the nineteenth century was the enormous expansion in numbers of public concerts. The institutionalization of the concert involved the creation of a new ritual around the musical performance, which could actually take place in a wide range of settings, not all of them large or grand. The formal public concert had its beginnings in the urban sociability of the eighteenth century, and in the nineteenth century became the centerpiece of musical culture in Europe's many smaller cities, as well as a nearly equal partner to opera in the large and capital cities. The concert took on its now-familiar aspects in the nineteenth century: some kind of hall with seating usually arranged facing a stage; the rejection of overt theatricality in the dress of the performers or the decoration of the stage (in pointed contrast to grand opera); the applause for the arrival of the principal musicians; the conductor directing the orchestra with his back to the audience; silence during the performance, and applause afterward and only after an entire work had ended. The concert ideal was not egalitarian. It reflected a strong concept of art, which demanded of the listener high levels of training and attention and an emphasis on the musical score and its complexities as much as on the musical performance. Concert performances came to be judged as more-or-less perfect realizations of the intentions of the composer, as he had set them down on paper for posterity, and concert programs evolved from the eighteenth-century model of potpourris of musical bits and pieces, not always by identifiable composers, to major works performed in their entirety.

Central to the growth of concert life was the rise in prestige of purely instrumental music, perhaps the single most important foundation for the serious musical cultures of the nineteenth century. Complex intellectual and musical developments account for this remarkable change in the cultural value granted to instrumental music, but by the first decades of the nineteenth century, the musical public, first in Germany and England and soon across Europe, proved willing to grant an equal aesthetic value to instrumental works and operas; some, indeed, considered purely instrumental works aesthetically superior. The most important genre of instrumental music was unquestionably the symphony, with concerti, overtures, and eventually the so-called symphonic or tone poems playing a secondary role. The term *symphony* first appeared in the late sixteenth century, meaning simply "music for ensemble," and for the next two centuries it implied little more than an overture or interlude in the larger context of an opera or cantata. But with the symphonies of Joseph Haydn (1732–1809) and Mozart, the symphony became a major synthetic and cosmopolitan musical genre, marked by richness of harmony and orchestration, a strong sense of form, considerable length (typically four separate movements), and great emotional expressivity.

Ludwig van Beethoven (1770–1827) further transformed the symphony, extending its length but most importantly giving it an expressive power that led contemporaries to crown the symphony the highest of artistic creations. Writing symphonies after Beethoven became at once the most difficult and the most important of compositional tasks, and performing them proved equally challenging. The modern symphony orchestra was another direct result of the Viennese (Haydn-Mozart-Beethoven) achievement. It was larger than its predecessors and more standard in its instrumental make-up, consisting of greater numbers of string instruments than before; a woodwind section of flutes, oboes, clarinets, and bassoons; a brass section of horns, trumpets, and trombones; numerous percussionists; and often a harp as well. As the size of symphonies grew larger and orchestras grew to perform them, conducting too took on its modern guise, both in order to control the greater numbers of musicians and to guide them through a demanding musical repertoire. Among the most admired orchestras of the nineteenth century was the Gewandhaus Orchestra of Leipzig, which under the direction of Felix Mendelssohn (1809–1847) became the progenitor of the modern concert with its repertoire firmly rooted in past so-called masterworks yet still open, albeit cautiously, to new talent.

But not all musical genres or musical experiences of the nineteenth century demanded the resources needed for opera and symphony concert. The daily fare of the musical life of Paris and London, for instance, was the piano-based musicale, in which a typical program included the featured pianist and one or two other instrumentalists (violinists being the most common). Salons of the nineteenth century became important sites for concertizing and had their own quasi-formal rituals of performance and appreciation. Composers of the nineteenth century produced a great deal of music in the smaller forms appropriate to salon and recital hall. Chamber music and piano music of the nineteenth century traversed a huge range of difficulty and complexity and included forms from the solo piano etude to the octet for double string quartet. In sheer numbers, much of this music consisted of simple concoctions for the amateur, now mostly forgotten, but at the same time, the nineteenth century saw the maturation of a number of eighteenth-century genres, with Beethoven's thirty-two piano sonatas and fifteen string quartets representing for those who came after him something so great as to virtually close down the form. For whatever reason, nineteenth-century chamber and piano music is marked by immense variety, experimentation, and inventiveness, a tribute in part to the reliable audience for its composers and performers.

For women, the salon and recital hall setting could be the only available venue for musical performance. Nineteenth-century trends toward professionalization in musical careers brought about a marked decline in numbers of women performers and composers. Shut out of conservatories and excluded from professional orchestras, women musicians found professional opportunities primarily in singing and piano performance. Amateur organizations also provided a context for quasi-public performances of men and women together. Most cities had several musical associations, including amateur orchestras and chamber music groups, mixed-voice choirs, and men's glee clubs. Amateur artistry took place both in and out of the public eye and both with and without paid professionals, its relation to publicity and professionalism remaining constantly in flux. Choral performances became the most common form of public activity undertaken by amateur musicians, and the nineteenth century consequently saw the composition of much new choral music as well as a steady stream of revivals of choral works of earlier eras. In Germany and England, the outdoor regional music festival became a popular feature of musical life, centered on performances of oratorios by Handel and Haydn, as well as popular new large-scale works by composers like Mendelssohn and Johannes Brahms (1833–1897).

Mandolin chamber orchestra c. 1900. Long a fixture in folk music, the mandolin in its more modern form became a popular instrument among middle-class Europeans in the nineteenth century. © ALINARI ARCHIVES/CORBIS

COMPOSERS OF THE NINETEENTH CENTURY

The term *Romanticism* has often served as a general description for all art music of the nineteenth century, and the practice is not entirely misleading, particularly if one bears in mind that Romanticism in music refers not to uniformity of sound but rather to the cultural orientation of those who composed it and listened to it. For the music critics of the early nineteenth century, who taught educated Europeans how to listen, music itself was Romantic because its mode of expression was abstract yet capable of the most profound emotional power. Nor does the assertion that music never ceased to be Romantic in the nineteenth century, simply passing through various stages of Romanticism from early to middle to late, deny the existence of other musical trends, including historicism, exoticism, naturalism, nationalism, and even realism, each of which, when considered from a musical perspective, seems more like a current in the Romantic stream than an opposing movement. Romanticism expressed an orientation to the world that has been called "the greatest single shift in the consciousness of the West," from a belief that the world was knowable and consistent in all its parts to a belief in "the necessity of the will and the absence of a structure of things" (Berlin, p. xi). In musical life, what followed from that shift was the pursuit of originality, often through special effects and expressive extremes, created through an enriched harmonic vocabulary and the exploitation of instrumental textures and tone colors. Romanticism denoted a belief both in the importance of the arts over all other aspects of life and in the capacity of the most gifted musicians to express what is otherwise inexpressible about existence.

Musical audiences in nineteenth-century Europe listened to more than just the music of their countrymen, and composers, even minor ones, reflected international musical developments more than narrowly national traditions. Nevertheless, composers are usually identified by nationality, and the designation is neither meaningless nor merely convenient. First, in the nineteenth century Europeans consolidated their national artistic traditions—a process called canon formation. That in turn shaped how composers thought about their own creative work. Second, musicians at work in the cosmopolitan world of music, including those enjoying tremendous success outside their native land, felt the undertow of national identity, the force of which only increased over the course of the century. Third, distinctive national styles did emerge, often through the cultivation of deliberate stylistic gestures on the part of nationally conscious composers. Fourth, insofar as print culture helped to shape the meaning of music and engender a broader sense of belonging to a musical community, the different national languages of Europe consolidated a country's musical life. The consequence of all these considerations was a densely woven net of relationships and influence among composers and musicians at work in particular national cultures.

German-speaking Europe Starting with German-speaking Europe, where the boundaries of the political units never coincided with those of the category of German music, the nineteenth century established the domination of German composers in the concert halls of Europe. This reflected in part the Europe-wide acceptance of the Beethoven myth, which combined the Promethean myth of suffering and triumph with the Romantic era's extreme valorization of musical genius. The reality behind Beethoven's towering presence in the nineteenth century was his composition in the first decades of the century of the bulk of his creations, including the Third through the Ninth symphonies, most of the piano sonatas, the profoundest string quartets, and the immense *Missa Solemnis.* In these, he seemed to his successors to have explored all of human existence with an unmatchable command of musical language. In central Europe, the question quickly became how anyone could follow in his footsteps. In north Germany, Carl Maria von Weber (1786–1826) laid out an alternative path of Romantic opera but died young, with only *Der Freischütz* (1821) making a strong impression on his contemporaries. Franz Schubert (1797–1828) of Vienna approached the Beethoven problem by both following and working around him. In his short life, he wrote eight symphonies, numerous chamber works, and an unmatched corpus of over six hundred *Lieder* or art songs. He too died young, just a year after Beethoven.

Subsequent generations of German composers represented a wide range of responses to the burden of the past. Felix Mendelssohn and Robert Schumann, whose careers flourished in the early middle decades of the century, both embraced the music of the past as a living part of the music of the present. Mendelssohn, a scion of educated Germany's most famous Jewish family, drew compositional inspiration from Johann Sebastian Bach (1685–1750), Mozart, and Beethoven. He was a key figure in the nineteenth-century revival of Bach's works and integrated elements of Bach's style especially into his oratorios (*Paulus,* 1836, and *Elijah,* 1846). His instrumental compositions (including the precociously brilliant *Octet for Strings* [1825], arguably the greatest example of youthful genius in European music) showed both Mozartian grace and Beethovenian aspirations. Schumann, who founded in 1834 one of the most influential music journals of the century, the *Neue Zeitschrift für Musik,* centered his work on the smaller genres of piano music (more than thirty major works that seek to evoke mood, personality, and atmosphere) and song (more than 240). But he also wrote symphonies and welcomed, through his journalism, any sign of a new Beethoven appearing on the musical scene. This finally happened in 1854, when the twenty-year-old Johannes Brahms appeared on Schumann's doorstep with piano compositions to play for him. Schumann hailed Brahms in print as the "young eagle" swooping down from the mountains of artistic inspiration, and Brahms spent the rest of his long and fruitful life laboring under the double burden of his own and others' expectations. He did compose symphonies, string quartets, and concerti, in the tradition of Beethoven yet distinctively his own, and his *German Requiem,* as well as his contributions to the *Lieder* repertoire, reflected artistic debts to the other "giants" of the past, the tramp of whose feet he complained always to hear coming up behind him.

Richard Wagner (1813–1883), for his part, declared Beethoven's Ninth Symphony the end of the line in symphonic development, with its choral finale bursting the bonds of purely instrumental music and pointing the way forward to Wagner's own creative work—the eleven "music dramas" he composed beginning in 1842 with *Rienzi* and culminating in *Parsifal* in 1882. In between, he composed works as different as *Tristan und Isolde* (1865), the freely moving chromatic harmony of which was unprecedented in music and expressed an unrelentingly bleak story of doomed love, and *Die Meistersinger von Nürnberg* (1868), his only drama with a happy ending. He composed the great Ring cycle, consisting of four massive music dramas (*Rheingold, Die Walküre, Siegfried,* and *Götterdämmerung*) over a period of more than two decades. In 1876, it premiered in the theater he designed expressly for it, in the small Bavarian town of Bayreuth, far from what he thought of as the superficial glamor of urban theatrical display. Wagner, in turn, bequeathed a new problem to his successors, for now both opera and symphony seemed too complete for further additions. Some, like the song composer Hugo Wolf (1860–1903), turned to intense miniaturism, compressing an entire music drama into a single *Lied.* Others, like Anton Bruckner (1824–1896) and Gustav Mahler (1860–1911), turned away from opera to a kind of symphonic maximalism, which in the case of Mahler synthesized voice and instrument on a far grander, more unrestrainedly expressive scale than Beethoven had attempted.

Non-German composers, especially those to the north and east of German-speaking Europe and within the boundaries of the Vienna-centered Austro-Hungarian Empire, faced their own German problem of finding a musical voice in cultures dominated by great weight of the German musical repertoire. Franz Liszt and Frédéric Chopin (1810–1849), one born in Hungary and brought up musically in Vienna, the other the Polish-born son of a French father teaching in Warsaw, cultivated cosmopolitanism. For Chopin, this meant making his musical career in Paris, where his piano compositions, at once delicate and demanding, earned him much admiration. For Liszt, who lived longer, the route around Germany led him back through it numerous times. After retiring in 1849 from the virtuoso career that had taken him all across Europe, Liszt worked first as the court music director in Weimar then moved at the end of his life to Rome. His prolific output of piano and orchestral works represented a deliberate effort to escape Beethoven through instrumental color, extraneous poetic "programming," virtuosic elaboration, and a certain formlessness, for all of which he earned the intense admiration of some but the bitter opposition of composers like Schumann and Brahms. Others (including to some extent both Chopin and Liszt) differentiated themselves from German composition by cultivating national color in their work. Mikhail Glinka (1804–1857), who studied with German musicians in Russia as well as in Germany itself, was the first to represent a model repeated all across central and eastern Europe, of intense admiration for German musical culture combined with an equally intense desire to escape it. His musical-nationalist solution was to write Russian national operas (e.g., *A Life for the Tsar,* 1836) and orchestral works with a Russian flavor (e.g., *Kamarinskaya,* 1848). His successors in Russia consisted most prominently of the Balakirev circle of self-consciously Russian composers, known as The Five and including Alexander Borodin (1833–1887), Modest Mussorgsky (1839–1881), and Nikolai Rimsky-Korsakov (1844–1908). Peter Tchaikovsky (1840–1893) rejected the circle but nevertheless contributed to the establishment of Russian composition as a distinctive voice in European music. Antonin Dvořák (1841–1904) in Prague and Edvard Grieg (1843–1907) in Norway, both indebted to German musical culture for their training, found musical means to express the national character of their homelands by integrating folk music and its distinctive harmonies into their formal compositions. For both, their international reputations stemmed from the popular appeal both of their music and of their embodiment of a seemingly authentic national voice.

Italy and France Nineteenth century musical life can be seen to fall either under the shadow of

Beethoven or the spell of Gioacchino Rossini (1792–1868). Rossini, who liked to call himself the last of the classicists, achieved fame early with light works and comic operas, including his most famous work *Il Barbiere di Siviglia* (1816; Barber of Seville), then proceeded to write thirty-six operas in fewer than twenty years, many of them serious and all of them written under the rushed conditions of Italy's multicentered, year-round opera mania. He effectively retired from theatrical composition at age thirty-seven and spent the rest of his long life presiding genially over the musical scene in Italy and France. He not only was the architect of Italian Romanticism, in which he was followed by Vincenzo Bellini (1801–1835), Gaetano Donizetti (1797–1848), and the young Giuseppe Verdi, but he also inspired French Romanticism with his melodic vitality, formal balance, mastery of rhythm, and faultless sense of style. However the greatest of the nineteenth-century French composers, Hector Berlioz (1803–1869) and the long-lived Camille Saint-Saëns (1835–1921), brought more musical inventiveness and range to the Rossinian pleasantries. Berlioz especially was committed to the idea that instrumental music could convey as much drama and feeling as opera, without succumbing to German abstraction. Verdi added an element of seriousness to the Rossinian model, bringing politics to the opera world with works that were received by his countrymen as veiled calls for unification and freedom (e.g., *Hernani,* 1844, and *Rigoletto,* 1851). Verdi's later operas became the foundation of the grand opera repertoire of the later nineteenth century (*Il Trovatore,* 1853; *La Traviata,* 1853; *Aïda,* 1871, composed in Cairo in honor of the opening of the Suez Canal), and his choral-orchestral *Requiem* (1874) was considered in its day one of the greatest works of the century.

The grand staircase of the Paris Opera, photographed c. 1900. In the lavish interior of the Paris Opera, attending a performance became itself a form of theater. ©BETTMAN/CORBIS

The two decades before the outbreak of World War I served as a pivotal moment in musical development, both consolidating the trends of the previous century and overthrowing its musical strictures in startling, even shocking ways. This final period can be seen to begin in 1886, with the long-awaited universal recognition of an international copyright union. This finally codified the high value the previous century had placed on artistic originality and encouraged the upcoming generation to a freewheeling experimentation, now recognized by law. In France, the characteristic figure of the period was Claude Debussy (1862–1918), regarded in his time as the musical counterpart to French impressionism. His abandonment of the conventional rules of harmonic development in favor of sheer sound and texture signaled a rejection of the whole Germano-centric canon of tonal development, then reaching its most extreme form in the symphonies of Mahler. Debussy's works were generally short and evocative, as well as titled to suggest visual images like footsteps in the snow, light on the water, or moonlight. In Germany, meanwhile, the date 1908 looms large in music histories as the year when Arnold Schoenberg (1874–1951), the reluctant revolutionary, "discovered" atonality, decisively breaking with a centuries-long development of notes arranged by so-called keys, usually in the major or minor mode. Finally, 1913 marks, for both music and cultural historians, the beginning of twentieth-century turmoil with the infamously tumultuous premier in Paris of Igor Stravinsky's (1882–1971) *Rite of Spring*. This Russian composer sought to tap the primal drives of human life with percussive, irregular rhythms and clashing tones. For all these composers, something deeply Romantic persisted in their attitude toward art's special place in society, but the questions of how and even whether musical tones could express the inner life of humans or contribute to human progress had become increasingly difficult to answer.

See also **Beethoven, Ludwig van; Brahms, Johannes; Debussy, Claude; Liszt, Franz; Tchaikovsky, Peter; Wagner, Richard.**

BIBLIOGRAPHY

Primary Sources

Berlioz, Hector. *Memoirs of Hector Berlioz, from 1803 to 1865, Comprising His Travels in Germany, Italy, Russia, and England.* Translated by Rachel Holmes and Eleanor Holmes. Edited and revised translation by Ernest Newman. Reprint, New York, 1966.

Charlton, David, ed. *E. T. A. Hoffmann's Musical Writings: Kreisleriana, The Poet and the Composer, Music Criticism.* Translated by Martyn Clarke. Cambridge, U.K., 1989.

Hanslick, Eduard. *On the Musically Beautiful: A Contribution Towards the Revision of the Aesthetics of Music.* Translated by Geoffrey Payzant. Indianapolis, 1986.

Lippman, Edward, ed. *Musical Aesthetics: A Historical Reader.* Vol. 2: *The Nineteenth Century.* Stuyvesant, N.Y., 1986.

Stendhal, Richard. *Life of Rossini.* Translated by R. N. Coe. Reprint, Seattle, 1972.

Wagner, Richard. *My Life.* Translated by Andrew Gray. Edited by Mary Whittall. New York, 1983.

Secondary Sources

Abraham, Gerald. *A Hundred Years of Music.* London, 1974.

Barzun, Jacques. *Berlioz and the Romantic Century.* 3rd ed. New York, 1969.

Berlin, Isaiah. *The Roots of Romanticism.* Princeton, N.J., 1999.

Dahlhaus, Carl. *Nineteenth-Century Music.* Translated by J. Bradford Robinson. Berkeley and Los Angeles, 1989.

Daverio, John. *Nineteenth-Century Music and the German Romantic Ideology.* New York, 1993.

Dent, Edward. *The Rise of Romantic Opera.* Cambridge, U.K., 1976.

Donakowski, Conrad. *A Muse for the Masses: Ritual and Music in an Age of Democratic Revolution, 1770–1870.* Chicago, 1977.

Einstein, Alfred. *Music in the Romantic Era.* New York, 1947.

Finson, Jon W. *Nineteenth-Century Music: The Western Classical Tradition.* Upper Saddle River, N.J., 2002.

Gramit, David. *Cultivating Music: The Aspirations, Interests, and Limits of German Musical Culture, 1770–1848.* Berkeley and Los Angeles, 2002.

Holoman, D. Kern, ed. *The Nineteenth-Century Symphony.* New York, 1997.

Johnson, James. *Listening in Paris: A Cultural History.* Berkeley and Los Angeles, 1995.

Lockwood, Lewis. *Beethoven: The Music and the Life.* New York, 2003.

Metzner, Paul. *Crescendo of the Virtuoso: Spectacle, Skill, and Self-Promotion in Paris during the Age of Revolution.* Berkeley and Los Angeles, 1998.

Newman, William S. *The Sonata since Beethoven.* 3rd ed. New York, 1983.

Plantinga, Leonard G. *Romantic Music: A History of Musical Style in Nineteenth-Century Europe.* New York, 1984.

Ratner, Leonard G. *Romantic Music: Sound and Syntax.* New York, 1992.

Ringer, Alexander, ed. *The Early Romantic Era: Between Revolutions, 1789 and 1848.* Music and Society. Englewood Cliffs, N.J., 1990.

Rosen, Charles. *The Romantic Generation.* Cambridge, Mass., 1995.

Samson, Jim, ed. *The Late Romantic Era: From the Mid-19th Century to World War I.* Music and Society. Englewood Cliffs, N.J., 1991.

Spotts, Frederic. *Bayreuth: A History of the Wagner Festival.* New Haven, Conn., 1994.

Taruskin, Richard. *The Oxford History of Western Music.* Vol. 3: *The Nineteenth Century.* New York, 2005.

Weber, William. *Music and the Middle Class: The Social Structure of Concert Life in London, Paris, and Vienna.* London, 1975.

Whittall, Arnold. *Exploring Twentieth-Century Music: Tradition and Innovation.* Cambridge, U.K., 2003.

CELIA APPLEGATE

MUSIL, ROBERT (1880–1942), Austrian novelist and essayist.

Robert Musil was one of the most important minds of the twentieth century. He is best known as a German novelist from the generation of Thomas Mann, Hermann Broch, and Franz Kafka, but his intellectual significance has sometimes been overlooked, partly because he was not an academic philosopher or social scientist. Musil's great achievements as a novelist and essayist came during the interwar years—the first two volumes of his most important novel, *Der Mann ohne Eigenschaften* (*The Man without Qualities*) appeared in 1930 and 1932 respectively and most of his essays appeared after World War I—but he saw himself as representative of the experience of European intellectuals in the generation that reached maturity in the decade before the war.

Musil grew up in the smaller cities of Austria and Moravia, and he spent most of his adult life in Vienna and Berlin. He was powerfully influenced by modern physics and mathematics, but also by French aestheticism, Friedrich Nietzsche, and Ralph Waldo Emerson. His first novel, *Young Törless* (1906), was a story of adolescent crisis and conflict in an Austrian military academy, and his second volume of fiction (1911) brought together two novellas that were written from the perspectives of women. These fictional accounts of sexual experience departed from the conventions of German literature and established many of the psychological and epistemological themes of his later work. After completing his doctorate in Berlin with a dissertation on Ernst Mach, Musil turned away from an academic career in psychology and philosophy to pursue his interest in ethics as a writer. He married Martha Marcovaldi (née Heimann) in 1911 and worked as an editor for the prestigious *Neue Rundschau* (New review) in Berlin, where he experienced the internationalism of European intellectual life before 1914. Musil felt the intensity of August 1914 and went to war as an officer on the Italian front. During the last two decades of his life, his creative work was a reflection on the experience of nineteenth-century Europe and the possibilities it opened up for life in a modern, technological society.

Musil was an advocate of modern science and civilization and a critic of anti-rationalism and nationalism, but he also thought of himself as a German writer who had inherited the ethical and aesthetic concerns of Nietzsche. He drew on the tradition of the Enlightenment and modern science, but he wanted to apply these intellectual values to emotional life in new ways. He argued that Europe in the early twentieth century did not suffer from too much intellect and too little soul, as many of his contemporaries believed, but rather from too little understanding in matters of the soul (or the emotional life). His work aimed to bring thinking and feeling into more flexible relation to one another and to the demands of modern life, to contribute to the creation of a new culture and a spirituality commensurate with life in modern society. He believed that liberalism, socialism, and Christianity had all failed under the pressures of modern civilization and World War I, and he was an astute critic of the new political forms that emerged in the interwar years.

Musil spent most of his life writing a huge and never finished novel, which is set in Vienna in 1913. *The Man without Qualities* seems at first to be a historical novel about the old-fashioned problems of a multinational monarchy on the verge of disintegration. In fact, it is an intellectual adventure, an inquiry into the ideological and emotional problems of modernity, which has continued to gain in significance over the years, especially with the U.S. translations of Musil's works in the 1990s. The originality of Musil's approach to feelings and metaphor is apparent throughout the novel, but this dimension becomes more explicit in the second volume, as he concentrates on the relationship between the protagonist and his sister and their conversations about gender, ethics, and a heightened relation to experience.

Musil was one of the great clarifying minds of the twentieth century, who saw in the transformations of modernity and World War I new possibilities for living differently and creatively. He aimed at a constant refashioning of the way the world is viewed, but also wanted to recover the relation to experience, which he believed lay at the basis of world religions and ideologies.

See also **Berlin; Mann, Thomas; Modernism; Nietzsche, Friedrich; Vienna.**

BIBLIOGRAPHY

Musil, Robert von. *Young Törless.* Translated by Eithne Wilkins and Ernst Kaiser. New York, 1955.

———. *Selected Writings.* Edited by Burton Pike. New York, 1986.

———. *Precision and Soul: Essays and Addresses.* Edited and translated by Burton Pike and David S. Luft. Chicago, 1990.

———. *The Man without Qualities.* Translated by Sophie Wilkins and Burton Pike. Edited by Burton Pike. 2 vols. New York, 1995.

———. *Diaries, 1899–1941.* Translated by Philip Payne. Edited by Mark Mirsky. New York, 1998. Original German version of the diaries edited by Adolf Frisé. Offers fascinating pathways into Musil's ideas and his historical world.

Secondary Sources

Corino, Karl. *Robert Musil: Eine Biographie.* Reinbek, Germany, 2003.

Luft, David S. *Robert Musil and the Crisis of European Culture, 1880–1942,* Berkeley, Calif., 1980. Addresses Musil's intellectual development in relation to the broader context of central European intellectual and political life in the early twentieth century.

———. *Eros and Inwardness: Weininger, Musil, Doderer.* Chicago, 2003.

Rogowski, Christian. *Distinguished Outsider: Robert Musil and His Critics.* Columbia, S.C., 1994. Excellent overview.

DAVID S. LUFT

MUSSORGSKY, MODEST (1839–1881), Russian composer.

Modest Petrovich Mussorgsky was born in Karevo, Russia. He was the son of a wealthy landowner who treated his laborers extremely well and who himself had serf (peasant) ancestors. As a child, Modest was fascinated by the ancient Russian fairy tales that were read to him by his nurse. His mother was an excellent pianist and introduced her son to the basic elements of music theory at an early age. When Modest was seven, she taught him how to play several of Franz Liszt's simpler pieces on the piano. In August 1849 his father took Modest and his brother Filaret to St. Petersburg to prepare them for a military career but also arranged a meeting with a German pianist, Anton Gerke, who was scheduled to become a professor of music at the St. Petersburg Conservatory. After spending a short time at another school in 1852, Mussorgsky entered the School for Cadets of the Guard. During his first year, he composed his Porte-Enseigne Polka for piano, which his father published. His main interests (other than alcohol) were philosophy, literature, painting, science, theology (he was a devout Russian Orthodox), and music. One of his teachers was Father Krupsky, who acquainted him with the music of the Catholic, Protestant, Lutheran, and Greek Orthodox churches.

In 1856 Mussorgsky was promoted to sublieutenant in the aristocratic Preobrazhensky Guards detachment and he became acquainted with someone else who later became an important Russian composer, Alexander Borodin (1833–1837). Mussorgsky was well liked by his peers because he was never overbearing and was a fountain of information about literature, philosophy, science, art, and religion.

Later in his life, he became acquainted with the Russian composers Alexander Dargomyzhsky (1813–1869) and Mily Balakirev (1837–1910). Mussorgsky had great financial difficulties after his father died. All the money was gone, as were the serfs, who were in the process of being emancipated. He reached the high point of his musical work in the mid-1860s, despite his impoverishment. His most important operas were *Boris Godunov, Khovanshcina,* and *Soroschinsky Fair.* He also produced a large number of piano pieces, including *Pictures at an Exhibition* (orchestrated by Ravel) and *Saint John's Night on Bare Mountain.* He was a faithful adherent of the Mighty Five, an interest group that fought Westernizers such as the Rubinstein brothers and, later, Peter Tchaikovsky (1840–1893). He also wrote short pieces for the tin whistle and the recorder. His health started to deteriorate, partially because of alcoholism, and in February 1881 he suffered three heart attacks. Not one of the people he had considered close friends visited him in the hospital. He died alone on 28 March 1881 in St. Petersburg. Just before his death, Ilya Repin (1844–1930), the most important Russian painter of the time, painted Mussorgsky. This shocking portrait of his dissipation can be viewed at the State Tretyakovsky Galerie, the most important museum in Moscow.

Mussorgsky's most widely hailed work, even during the Soviet period, was the opera *Boris Godunov.* The principal role was portrayed by the greatest basso profundo of his time, Fedor Chaliapin. His other major works include *Intermezzo in Modo Classico* (1861); *Shveja: The Mistress,* both for piano, and more than sixty songs, including "The Flea," "The Hebrew Song," and "The Song of Mephistopholes."

See also **Music; Repin, Ilya; Russia; Serfs, Emancipation of; Slavophiles; Tchaikovsky, Peter; Westernizers.**

BIBLIOGRAPHY

Brook, Donald. *Six Great Russian Composers: Glinka, Borodin, Mussorgsky, Tchaikovsky, Rimsky-Korsakov, Scriabin: Their Lives and Works.* London, 1946. Contains an excellent, long chapter on Mussorgsky, with illustrations and a listing of all his works.

Brown, Malcolm Hamrick, ed. *Mussorgsky: In Memoriam, 1881–1981.* Ann Arbor, Mich., 1982. Contains sixteen annotated articles, by music historians, on the composer's life and works; an excellent index.

Leonard, Richard Anthony. *A History of Russian Music.* New York, 1957.

Seroff, Victor Ilyitch. *The Mighty Five: The Cradle of Russian National Music.* New York, 1948. A profound description of the disagreement between the Slavophiles and Westernizers.

Taruskin, Richard. *Mussorgsky: Eight Essays and an Epilogue.* Princeton, N.J., 1993. Strongly recommended; heavily annotated, scholarly, eloquent.

LEO HECHT

NADAR, FÉLIX (1820–1910), French photographer and artist.

Félix Nadar's life was one of prodigious creativity, ingenuity and he flourished as a chronicler of the bohemian and artistic elite of nineteenth century Paris. Nadar was born Gaspar-Félix Tournachon on 6 April 1820 in Paris, to Victor Tournachon, a Lyonnais printer, and Thérèse Maillet. He initially studied medicine, supported himself by writing drama criticism for newspapers, and soon became a central part of the group that was immortalized in the novel *Scènes de la Vie de Bohème* by Henri Mürger (1822–1861). Nadar straddled the societies of bohemian down-and-out artists, writers, and students and the more established circle around Charles Baudelaire (1821–1867). Nadar raised the money to publish a series of literary albums, engaging the literary lights of his acquaintance: Alexandre Dumas (1802–1870), Theophile Gautier (1811–1872), Gerard de Nerval (1808–1855), Alfred de Vigny (1797–1863), and Honoré de Balzac (1799–1850). The albums were a financial failure and were aborted before the Balzac work was even published.

By 1841, Tournachon, through a playful word game alchemy, had evolved into Nadar in his written correspondence. In this new name, he became a member of the Société des Gens de Lettres in 1842. After the political upheaval of 1848, he joined the Polish Foreign Legion, was arrested on the German border and briefly imprisoned, but Nadar promptly parlayed his experiences into an opportunity to spy for the French.

Nadar really earned renown as a caricaturist at publications such as *Le Journal pour Rire* (Newspaper for laughs), founded by his mentor and supporter, Charles Philipon (1800–1862). Although he drew hundreds of caricatures in a relatively short period of time, his lifestyle was such that he landed in debtors' prison in Clichy in 1850.

Panthéon Nadar, a singularly ambitious and ill-fated project, would mark the turning point in his life. Nadar endeavored to combine his acquaintances and drawing skill, to exploit the burgeoning cult of celebrity in Paris by creating a giant work containing the images of a thousand celebrities of arts and letters. In 1854, as his *Panthéon Nadar* was failing to result in a profit, Nadar married, moved his dependent brother into the profession of photography, and then, quite taken with medium's potential, opened up his own business. The result was a certain amount of confusion about authorship until, ultimately, Nadar had to resort to suing his brother for the sole proprietorship of his name.

Nadar's singular talents as a caricaturist and photographer were enhanced by his thorough knowledge of the art, which is evident in his prolific criticism and subtle use of light, composition, and expressiveness in his portraits. Nadar's photographic work soon gained attention, and he managed to take over the studio that Gustave Le Gray (1820–1884, who had been his brother's instructor) and the Bisson Brothers had vacated on Boulevard des Capucines in Paris. He painted the facade bright red, with his signature emblazoned

Nadar Elevating Photography to an Art. Caricature by Honoré Daumier c. 1862. ©BETTMANN/CORBIS

across it. Nadar registered a number of patents for techniques and devices that he developed to improve his practice, including a method of color photography without retouching and electrical lights with reflectors. Nadar took these lights from the studio underground to document the sewers and then the catacombs below Paris.

Nadar was a founder of an organization that was devoted to the development of flying machines heavier than air. Flights in his balloon, Le Géant, publicized the group, although their aim was to replace such devices. During the Franco-Prussian War (1870–1871), Nadar flew to 9,000 feet (above the reach of the enemy's guns) to carry communications out of Paris. Soon he organized a fleet of airmail vehicles he named after his friends, such as George Sand (1804–1876) and Victor Hugo (1802–1885). After the war, Nadar was out of money and was forced to rent out his premises and set up a more modest commercial concern, gradually transferring its management to his son, Paul. The elder Nadar now devoted himself to a series of books and memoirs.

The first Impressionist Exhibition took place in Nadar's premises on the Boulevard des Capucines. Nadar himself organized career retrospectives of two friends of his youth who had fallen into obscurity, Honoré Daumier (1808–1879) and Constantin Guys (1802–1892). At the age of seventy-seven, Nadar opened a photography studio in Marseilles. He continued to write and court publicity; in 1900, his photographs and achievements were celebrated at the Universal Exhibition. Nadar possessed curiosity, industry, warmth, optimism, entrepreneurialism, and, as such, was a prototype of the nineteenth-century Parisian.

See also **Daguerre, Louis; Daumier, Honoré; Impressionism; Photography.**

BIBLIOGRAPHY

Baldwin, Gordon, and Judith Keller. *Nadar/Warhol: Paris/New York: Photography and Fame.* Los Angeles, 1999.

Gosling, Nigel. *Nadar.* New York, 1976.

Hambourg, Maria Morris, Françoise Heilbrun and Philippe Néagu. *Nadar.* New York, 1995.

Néagu, Philippe, and Jean-Jacques Poulet-Allamagny, eds. *Nadar.* 2 vols. Paris, 1979.

DEIRDRE DONOHUE

NANKING, TREATY OF. Signed aboard the deck of the HMS *Cornwallis* on 29 August 1842 by British plenipotentiary Sir Henry Pottinger (1789–1856) and Qing dynasty (1644–1911) imperial clansman Qiying (d. 1856), the Treaty of Nanking concluded the First Opium War, the Sino-British conflict of 1839–1942. Although it was provisional in nature (the details of the pact were to be settled later), the document's twelve articles established the legal framework for the advance of British commercial interests in China under what came to be called the system of "unequal treaties." Articles Two and Five opened the five coastal cities of Canton, Amoy (Xiamen), Foochowfoo (Fuzhou), Ningpo (Ningbo), and Shanghai to British merchants and diplomats, ending the previous arrangement restricting European traders to Canton and limiting their transactions to imperially licensed Chinese merchants. Article Ten required, moreover, that tariffs and customs levied on such trade be "fair and regular." A supplementary treaty established specific rates for various articles the following year, effectively ending Chinese tariff autonomy until 1928.

Other stipulations were more directly punitive: Article Three ceded the island of Hong Kong to the British "in perpetuity," while Articles Four and Six exacted a $21 million indemnity from the Qing government to pay for British opium stocks destroyed in 1839 and the costs of the war. (Article Seven decreed that repayment take place by the end of 1845; thereafter interest would accrue at 5 percent per annum.) Conspicuously absent from the treaty were provisions regarding future trade in opium, imports of which doubled to sixty thousand chests by 1860.

Most of the remaining articles pushed China to comply with the system of international relations by which nineteenth-century European nation-states conducted their affairs. Traditional Chinese governments practiced diplomacy through a ritual hierarchy affirming the superiority of Chinese civilization in general and the universal suzerainty (dominion) of the Chinese emperor in particular. Under this formula, Beijing rewarded ritual gestures of submission with limited trading privileges. Although Asian states had long subverted the system's formal Sinocentrism by acknowledging Chinese superiority in Beijing but ignoring it elsewhere, Europeans predictably chafed at linguistic and ceremonial forms designed to suggest their inferiority and subordination. Until 1839, however, they lacked the resources necessary to force the issue. Thus, Article One made each government responsible for the property and security of the other's resident nationals, while Article Eleven stipulated the use of value-neutral language in official correspondence.

The Treaty of Nanking signaled not only China's loss of sovereignty over key aspects of political, economic, and diplomatic activity but also the dawn of a new international order in East Asia. First to dine at the table set by the British was the United States, which in 1844 secured an agreement called the Treaty of Wanghia. Although modeled on the Nanking pact, the American treaty elucidated in some detail the principle of extraterritoriality whereby Americans suspected of crimes in China could only be tried by U.S. officials under U.S. law. By October, the French had engineered a treaty of their own, the Treaty of Whampoa, that further extended the privileges secured by the British and American agreements.

The key legal precedent fueling this diplomatic feeding frenzy was contained in the 1843 supplement to the Treaty of Nanking, which granted Britain "most favored nation" status: any privileges wrested from China by another power automatically extended to London also. Thus enabled, the British seized a seemingly innocuous clause in the Treaty of Wanghia allowing for treaty revision in twelve years to demand revision of the Nanking provisions in 1854. Qing resistance resulted, ultimately, in another war and defeat by British forces. The ensuing Treaty of Tianjin (1858) expanded foreign privileges by an order of magnitude, providing for ten new treaty ports, right of travel in the Chinese hinterland, and the right of missionary proselytization throughout the country, to name but a few. Qing refusal to accept these terms spurred a resumption of hostilities culminating in the burning of the magnificent Jesuit-designed Summer Palace complex in Beijing's northwest suburbs and the imposition of the Convention of Peking (1860).

Thus, one consequence of the Treaty of Nanking was a pattern in which ostensible Chinese treaty violation resulted in punitive military action by one or more powers, which produced another treaty facilitating further foreign penetration of China. By the 1890s the treaty ports had become centers of an urban Sino-foreign culture administered under joint sovereignty. As the harbinger of European imperialism in East Asia, the Treaty of Nanking was far more significant for the process it began than the conflict it ended.

See also **China; Great Britain; Imperialism.**

BIBLIOGRAPHY

Fairbank, John King. *Trade and Diplomacy on the China Coast: The Opening of the Treaty Ports, 1842–1854.* Cambridge, Mass., 1964.

———. "The Creation of The Treaty System." In *The Cambridge History of China*, Vol. 10: *Late Ch'ing, 1800–1911*, Pt. I, edited by Denis Twitchett and John K. Fairbank, 213–263. Cambridge, U.K., 1978.

Fay, Peter Ward. *The Opium War, 1840–1842: Barbarians in the Celestine Empire in the Early Part of the Nineteenth Century and the War by Which They Forced Her Gates Apart.* Chapel Hill, N.C., 1997.

Wood, R. Derek. "The Treaty of Nanking: Form and the Foreign Office, 1842–1843." *Journal of Imperial and Commonwealth History* 24.2 (May 1996): 181–196.

JOHN WILLIAMS

NAPLES. Naples is a city burdened by powerful images and implacable stereotypes that have survived unchanged through the centuries. "A city full of thieves and tricksters," wrote the Italian natural philosopher Giambattista della Porta in 1606. A people "suddenly inflamed, suddenly moved," observed the Italian economist Ferdinando Galiani in 1779. The French traveler Augustin Creuzé de Lesser positioned the city at the frontier of civilization itself when he said in 1806, "Europe ends at Naples." It is almost impossible to find a representation that is not exaggerated and does not slip into the fraught category of exceptionalism. Naples always seems exceptional, a "paradise inhabited by devils," and a great open-air museum, a place of superstitions and enlightened humanists, of aristocracies and bootblacks.

More prosaically, the city is atypical in an Italian context above all because of the very particular association with its past. While the identity of cities such as Milan or Turin is mainly rooted in the economic and social history of the nineteenth and twentieth centuries, even in the early twenty-first century Naples reveals traces of a far more remote past that took shape in the thirteenth century during the Angevin era and was consolidated under first Aragonese and then Spanish domination in the fifteenth and sixteenth centuries. This was when the city became identified with political power, became the center of a complex government bureaucracy, was granted conspicuous financial privileges, and was provided with cheap grain from the farms of the Neapolitan kingdom. All of southern Italy, an ill-defined hinterland that stretched as far as Apulia and Sicily, already gravitated toward the capital. From these provinces, Naples imported agricultural products and artisan and manufactured goods, while its merchants busied themselves selling oil, silk, and wool from the provinces to the rest of Italy and Europe. The city became a great marketplace, but also a parasitic center. It consumed more than it produced, and as a result began to attract a continuous influx of immigrants from the countryside, and this gave the city the characteristic that is still evident in the early twenty-first century: exceptional population density. At the end of the sixteenth century, Naples was the most populous European capital, alongside Paris and London. In the first decades of the seventeenth century, it was struck by the severe demographic and political crisis that beset the kingdom, and the terrible plague of 1656 cut its population in half. But by the start of the eighteenth century, the long recession seemed to be over, heralding the prospect of better times.

On 10 May 1734, at eighteen years of age, Charles of Bourbon arrived from Spain with a splendid following of courtesans, soldiers, and knights, and twenty-four chests filled with gold. The monarch summoned to his side at Naples the cream of the southern nobility, families from Calabria, Abruzzi, and Apulia, who abandoned their own estates to their tenants and lived in their sumptuous urban residences on the revenues from their land. Meanwhile, the new dynasty launched an ambitious political program that aimed at reforming the government, including its administration, fiscal system, and commercial regulations, while at the same time seeking to emulate the style of a grand European court and endowing the capital with rich and grandiose architectural patrimony. From the theater of San Carlo to the enormous royal palace (Reggia di Caserta) with gardens that stretched out of sight, from the Capodimonte Palace to a poor house designed to house eight thousand vagrants, the 1740s and 1750s were an age of dynastic gigantism, where costs were incongruous with the city's social problems. For Naples remained seriously overpopulated, and the terrible famine of 1764 that killed thousands of citizens highlighted the grave limits of the system of production and markets. The Bourbon metropolis had become (to use the famous image of the eighteenth-century Italian jurist Gaetano Filangieri) a massive head attached to a shrunken body. The capital was politically and demographically out of proportion to its kingdom, a place that absorbed too many material and human resources and—as the Italian economist Giuseppe Maria Galanti said at the end of the eighteenth century—threatened to turn the rest of southern Italy into a desert. Yet it was a city that depended in both economic and political terms on its own territory: the Jacobin Parthenopean Republic that was created in the city in 1799 in the wake of an invading French army was drowned in blood by a monarchist uprising sprung from the provinces of the kingdom.

The city's problems were destined to worsen in the nineteenth century. With every chance of self-driven modernization gone by 1848, when its reactionary rulers betrayed the constitution and its supporters, Naples seemed to lose any sense of forward movement. In 1851 the young English politician William Gladstone denounced the Bourbon government as "the denial of God," and then at the beginning of September 1860, in the face of Giuseppe Garibaldi's advance, revolt in the provinces, and the plots of the Great Powers, the young king, Francis II, abandoned the royal palace. Naples became an ex-capital, although with its four hundred thousand inhabitants it remained by far the largest city in the new Kingdom of Italy. The city preserved many of the sociological and cultural characteristics of the period of Bourbon hegemony—numerous members of the nobility, bureaucrats, and clerics; throngs of lawyers; and fifteen thousand domestic servants, cooks, washerwomen, gardeners, and coachmen. In the context of the new nation-state, however, ancient privileges and political protections were destined to diminish. The Italian government imposed new taxes, abolished the religious orders, reduced the garrison by two-thirds, and released or pensioned off a number of city employees. Meanwhile, the city's historical domination over the rest of southern Italy began to slip as new free-trade policies removed the city's commercial privileges and ruined its important industries. The year 1861 marked the start of a period of intense deindustrialization and a sharp decline in maritime trade, and it soon became clear that the city was incapable of transforming itself from the capital of a vast state into a regional metropolis. It failed to impose an economic and cultural unity on its hinterland, as Milan was doing in Lombardy, and Turin in Piedmont, Bologna in Emilia, and Bari in Apulia. But it was also unlike those midsized cities that retained strong physical and social continuities with their rural surroundings and that became the stimulus for modernization in the nineteenth and twentieth centuries. It never became, in short, a provincial hub, and it could not find in its province the cultured and enlightened landowning bourgeoisie that in parts of central and northern Italy were promoting new forms of social and economic development.

The overcrowded Tyrrhenian metropolis was entirely different, more similar to the extreme cases of Western urbanism, the Paris lamented by Victor Hugo, the Victorian East End of London, the noisy crowd of Manhattan. Naples was marked by profound fractures. Nobles, rentiers, and professionals lived at times in the same neighborhoods with the lower classes, and indeed in the same buildings (the elites in the expensive apartments of the middle floors, and the poor in the eaves or at the bottom), but they remained "two nations," separated by a material and cultural abyss. In a city where by 1880 there was a university with 3,000 students and libraries frequented by 250,000 patrons every year, the rate of illiteracy surpassed 60 percent, and the living conditions of the populace grew ever more straitened. For their part, the elites proved reluctant to modernize. At the end of the nineteenth century, there were few of the public associations that elsewhere had wide public support. Of the few clubs that did exist, many, such as the "Whist Circle," remained closed to nonnobles. Social life took place predominantly in domestic circles. The family continued to monopolize the entire process of socialization, looking to preserve occupational continuity from father to son, regulating the matrimonial choices of the young, and preserving familial patrimonies undivided by means of testamentary practices that privileged men over women. Little wonder, then, that the liberal institutions of the new Italy struggled to take hold, that abstention from voting was extremely common, and that it became difficult even to constitute a court of assizes because of continuous resignations of the jurors. Nobles, property owners, and merchants sought to avoid every public responsibility, while the middle classes constituted only a small minority. In 1874, although the criteria for registering for the electoral rolls were far from stringent, only 3 percent of the population had the right to vote.

At the same time, the city was crisscrossed by a thick and continuous circulation of resources that

The Via Santa Lucia, Naples, c. 1900. ©ALINARI ARCHIVES/CORBIS

gave rise to many forms of material and cultural communication between the "two nations." Naples was a great marketplace, the greatest in Italy at the time. Packed, dusty, often informal, this marketplace was composed of an array of tiny shops devoted to the production and sale of merchandise and used, often, as the residence of the shopkeeper. Similar exchanges, often accompanied by lengthy negotiations over prices, also occurred on the street, in the public squares, and on the beaches. They involved not only foodstuffs and manufactured goods but also money. Networks of credit were capillary, and were often run by nonprofessionals, usually women, who in this way could make a profit on the dowries they received at marriage. This was typically a risky business, given the difficulty of recovering loans, and which, given the vertiginous increase of interest rates, easily slipped into usury. In order to survive, meanwhile, the lower classes were compelled to take on endless chains of debt. Or else they could turn to the innumerable public and private pawnshops: in the second half of the nineteenth century, Naples was the only Italian city with a pawnshop that accepted, as security for small loans, even *pannine* (domestic linens). For extreme cases, there was also the thick network of charitable institutions, which strove to alleviate poverty by offering beds, medicines for the sick, dowries for girls, soup, bread, and alms.

In the teeming urban market, however, other and less common resources were also exchanged. In 1901 a parliamentary commission found that it was impossible to obtain any service in the city from public administrators without a personal recommendation and the payment of a certain sum. The corruption of government offices was universal and gave rise to an unending cycle of illegal practices. At the same time, Neapolitans were accustomed to buying protection for their families and possessions from the all-powerful organization known as the Camorra (the local mafia), which profited from the weakness of the state by imposing, unchallenged, the rule of intimidation and violence. Great or small, extortion afflicted merchants, shopkeepers, commercial institutions, gambling parlors, coachmen, prostitutes, and even the indigent.

For many different reasons, by desire or necessity, hundreds of thousands of characters frequented the great city bazaar every day. The city had scarce resources, and lived in a condition of chronic uncertainty. It was incapable of discovering self-sustaining initiatives for economic development, but its scarce resources circulated nonetheless with intense frequency, never stopping, passing from hand to hand, fragmenting continually, and giving the impression of a multiplication of loaves and fishes. And, day after day, these operations brought into contact different social groups, upstanding citizens and criminal clans, living in aristocratic neighborhoods and slums, engaging in activities licit and illicit. It was this ceaseless circulation of people and goods that created, if such a thing existed, the culture of the city.

See also **Garibaldi, Giuseppe; Italy; Kingdom of the Two Sicilies; Rome; Sicily; Sister Republics; Trieste; Venice.**

BIBLIOGRAPHY

Acton, Harold. *The Bourbons of Naples, 1734–1825.* London, 1956.

———. *The Last Bourbons of Naples, 1825–1861.* London, 1961.

Davis, John. *Merchants, Monopolists, and Contractors: A Study of Economic Activity and Society in Bourbon Naples, 1815–1860.* New York, 1981.

De Benedetti, Augusto. "Il sistema industriale (1880–1940)." In *La Campania,* edited by Paolo Macry and Pasquale Villani, 445–605. Turin, 1990.

De Seta, Cesare. *Napoli.* Rome, 1981.

Galasso, Giuseppe. *Intervista sulla storia di Napoli.* Edited by Percy Allum. Rome, 1978.

———. *L'altra Europa: Per un'antropologia storica del Mezzogiorno d'Italia.* Rev. ed. Lecce, Italy, 1997.

Galasso, Giuseppe, ed. *Napoli.* Rome, 1987.

Gribaudi, Gabriella. *Donne, uomini, famiglie: Napoli nel Novecento.* Naples, 1999.

Lumley, Robert, and Jonathan Morris, eds. *The New History of the Italian South: The Mezzogiornio Revisited.* Exeter, Devon, U.K., 1997.

Macry, Paolo. *Ottocento: Famiglie, élites e patrimoni a Napoli.* Turin, 1988.

———. *I giochi dell'incertezza: Napoli nell'Ottocento.* Naples, 2002.

Moe, Nelson. *The View from Vesuvius: Italian Culture and the Southern Question.* Berkeley and Los Angeles, 2002.

Paolo Macry

NAPOLEON (1769–1821), French general, first consul (1799–1804), and emperor of the French (1804–1814/1815).

Perhaps only the improbable national history that gave the world Joan of Arc could also produce as outsized a figure as Napoleon Bonaparte. This height-challenged second son of an obscure Corsican family grew up to rule France and much of Europe for a decade, and he has dominated world-historical memory and imagination ever since. He remains one of the most written-about figures since Jesus Christ.

COMING OF AGE

Napoleone Buonaparte (in the original Italian spelling) was born in Ajaccio on the island of Corsica on 15 August 1769. The Corsica that produced Napoleon had been ceded to France by Genoa, the year before his birth; its culture was thus Italian, as indeed it has in many ways remained. The island was a strange and wild clime, offering an explosive combination of the primitive and promising, the reactionary and revolutionary, and its inhabitants proved most difficult of assimilation. The Buonaparte family into whose midst Napoleon arrived as the second child of five brothers and three sisters offered a most Corsican combination of the ambitious and the idealistic—Carlo, the future emperor's father, being at one and the same time frantically ambitious to improve his family's social lot, yet strongly committed to the progressive forces on the island. The latter were represented by Pasquale Paoli, the Corsican republican hero of the 1750s, who was driven (by the Genoese) into exile in England, but was hoping to return.

The paradoxes and conflicts continue. Napoleon, like his siblings, was sent to school in France. He finished his studies at the elite Royal Military School in Paris. A second lieutenant of artillery, at the tender age of sixteen (1785), he was nevertheless strongly torn between his abiding feelings of Corsican patriotism and his shrewd understanding that "making it" could likely occur only in France.

The great Revolution of 1789, which restored Paoli to power in Corsica, thus seemed to Napoleon to be a divine surprise, for it offered him the opportunity to return to his beloved native land and play a historic role. In the intervening years, however, the young officer, despite his best intentions and apparent feelings, had in fact become quite "French"; certainly his political views were strongly identified with the Revolution. Thus, when Paoli and most Corsicans gradually turned against the Revolution, Napoleon unhesitatingly chose "the French party." In 1793 he and his family were forced to flee the island for the mainland. He left without looking back. Corsica never again interested him; for better or worse, he was French.

The ensuing five years, before great military and political success crowned Napoleon, were a painful and frustrating time for the young officer, alternately thrilling and boring. Napoleon's close identification with the Jacobin party both advanced and inhibited his career. He played a critical role in winning the siege that reclaimed Toulon from the English (1793), and for this was promoted to brigadier general, at age twenty-four. But with the fall of his protector, Maximilien Robespierre, in mid-1794, the young man lost his political base; the new regime, the Directory, left him to cool his heels for a time.

Nevertheless, with France at war against much of Europe, the government badly needed this officer's unique military and strategic talents. In October 1795 (Vendémiaire Year IV, according to the Revolutionary calendar), Napoleon was given an important position in the force that suppressed a counterrevolutionary movement in Paris. For his sterling services, he was made full general and named to command the Army of the Interior. Some months later, in early 1796, he received command of the French Army of Italy.

EARLY CAMPAIGNS AND STATE-BUILDING: ITALY AND EGYPT

The wars associated with the adjective *Napoleonic* attained a degree of violence previously unknown in Europe, yet paradoxically this first campaign in Italy, which established Bonaparte's name, was more typical of the Old Regime's war of maneuver and limited engagement—typical, but speeded up. The general's compact French divisions not only floated like butterflies and stung like bees, they also darted among the foothills and plains of northern Italy with the speed and suddenness of hummingbirds. In less than a fortnight, they knocked the Kingdom of Piedmont-Sardinia out of the war. The ensuing twelve months saw them defeat several leading Austrian generals on battlefields whose names have come down to posterity (Lodi, Arcole) more thanks to paintings and myths than to the strategy deployed.

Bonaparte excelled as diplomat, as well; he played the key role in negotiating the Treaty of Campo-Formio (1797), which resulted in the French being anchored in northern Italy, while the Habsburgs were driven out, except of Venice. The "Jacobin general" put more of his imagination into state-building than into military campaigns or even diplomacy (thereby differentiating himself from Alexander the Great and Caesar, who were mainly conquerors). To be sure, all of northern Italy was heavily taxed and some of its best art was despoiled for French museums, but when Lombard patriots pressed Napoleon to overthrow their old regime and declare a republic, he did so. The resulting Cisalpine Republic saw the adoption of French constitutional models and methods, but made space, too, for Italian flourishes. Despite orders from Paris, Napoleon refused to humiliate the pope, and moreover he leaned on the oligarchical old city-state of Genoa to reform itself under a new name, the Ligurian Republic. No less a Napoleon critic than the historian Michel Vovelle finally speaks of the general's "noble ambition which in a certain sense played a positive role in the origins of Italian unity" (Vovelle, p. 184; author's translation).

The French invaded Egypt (1798) for numerous geopolitical and economic reasons, but Napoleon probably chose the assignment because the Alexandrine dimensions of it captured his imagination. The French army racked up legendary victories at the Pyramids and Mount Tabor, but military disaster struck them early on, when a British fleet under Admiral Horatio Nelson destroyed their ships in Aboukir Bay, thus marooning the French in Egypt. Like Xenophon and his Spartans in the fourth century B.C.E., Bonaparte met the challenge head on, keeping his army together and marching as far north as Syria—where the British finally bested him at Saint-Jean-d'Acre, and he returned to Egypt.

Again, it was in state-building that Napoleon flourished more than in warfare: despite local rebellion and religious conflict, he proved himself far more knowledgeable and appreciative of Islam than most modern conquerors have usually been, and he succeeded in winning over a large part of the educated and economically productive local elites to the French cause. The French remained nearly three years in Egypt, and in that time they laid many of the infrastructural and political foundations for a long-term, thoroughly "modern" colony in the nineteenth-century sense of the term. External factors alone were what drove them out: a British expeditionary force finally, barely, defeated Bonaparte's successor general, in the summer of 1801. If that officer had held out for four more months—that is, until the peace discussions between England and France got underway—the French hold on Egypt might well have survived until the twentieth century.

In any case, the expedition made one permanent important cultural achievement: the active presence of scores of French scientists, artists, and scholars, whom Napoleon had insisted on bringing (at considerable expense) in the first place, led, in the fullness of time, to the creation of the modern science of Egyptology.

With great daring (given that the Mediterranean was considered a "British lake" in 1799), Napoleon stealthily quit his army and returned to France, in late summer. The Directory, never politically stable, was in crisis—the object of machinations by numerous parties—and Bonaparte wished to play his part. Singularly famous and popular, the young general was courted by all sides, but ultimately chose to ally himself with the moderates around Emmanuel-Joseph Sieyès, a political theorist famed for his role as polemicist in 1789. Opposing both the royalists and the neo-Jacobin radicals, while skillfully conspiring with elements within the Directory itself, the Bonaparte-Sieyès group seized power—albeit, just barely—on 9 November 1799 (18 Brumaire Year VIII). The key point to note is that, technically speaking, their action was a "legal" coup d'état, because the men succeeded in getting a rump parliament to ratify their actions. This was the first use of a political ploy with a long future in world history.

POWER—THE CONSULATE

It is one thing to seize power—many parties and figures had done that in the long and tortuous decade since 1789. But it is quite another to *hold on* to power and accomplish something significant with it. This is what Bonaparte managed to do—firmly establishing himself under the Roman title of "first consul" (read: dictator) of the French Republic, while drawing into collaboration most of the great political, legal, and scientific minds of an era rich with such greatness. If he succeeded in bringing off so unprecedented an accomplishment, it was in part because Bonaparte saw to the creation of a new style of regime in the long and *rusé* (stuffed) annals of European history: a civil (not a military) dictatorship based nominally on "national sovereignty," functionally on a form of democratic mobilization (that is, on some use of the franchise and elections, notably countrywide plebiscites), and more generally on accenting an aroused and persuaded public opinion.

If Bonaparte seemed to strike out in all directions in the early years after his accession to power, the acts he performed or oversaw—from the small and symbolic to the large and material—were yet characterized by a high degree of coherence. For what he in fact managed to do was bring to port the manifold projects that the Revolution had conceived but failed to accomplish.

The "granite blocks," as these reforms may be called, by and large remained the plinth on which the French state continued to reside into the twenty-first century. They include administrative centralization (the prefectures), legal consolidation (the Napoleonic Code), a stabilized currency (the Bank of France and the franc), individual honorifics (the Legion of Honor), national education (the lycées, the University, the *grandes écoles*), and social peace (the Concordat with the Catholic Church). It is difficult to give a summary description or judgment on these measures, for many contemporaries saw them as "counterrevolutionary," while others saw them as precisely the opposite: the consolidation of 1789.

Two centuries on, the "granite blocks" may be viewed as the means by which a property-owning society of the eighteenth century, led by an Enlightenment general, strove to make a good exit from the most extravagant political ordeal of modern times (the French Revolution)—an ordeal that the general and his supporters regarded both as greatly admirable and greatly pernicious. For they had lived out Charles Dickens in advance of his writing (in *A Tale of Two Cities*): they had lived the best of times and the worst of times, and their great challenge lay in separating the two. Less than agonizing over what they had seen, they worried about what could happen if the ordeal of revolution continued. And so they stopped it while simultaneously consolidating it.

Bonaparte, in short, sought to escape "politics," as that word had come to be understood in the democratic contestation developed since 1789. Instead, the regime, to put it paradoxically, mounted a peculiarly French form of "apolitical politics": that is, government by a drummed-up "national" consensus around efficient administration, a cult of the leader, and the pursuit of military victory and French imperial glory (rather than by rival political parties, opposition newspapers, and critical parliaments).

Once again, the point is not that the Consulate *attempted* such a contradiction as an "apolitical" or "national" politics—many governments (before or since) have tried—but rather that Napoleon largely succeeded for nearly a decade at running the state without the usual checks and balances and partisan competition familiar to nearly all regimes of law. This said, however, a stubborn and dangerous counterrevolutionary opposition continued to stand against the Consulate and empire in some of France's western provinces, while from Switzerland, a small but prestigious and persistent political opposition smoldered among moderates and liberals congregated around the writer Germaine de Staël and the political theorist Benjamin Constant (and other "idéologues," as they were known).

WAR AND EMPIRE

The steep price exacted for this unprecedented experiment in "national" governance was that France largely exported its domestic conflict in these years. That is, for most of Napoleon's tenure, the nation was at war. Indeed Bonaparte justified the transformation of the dictatorial Consulate into an authoritarian empire in the failure of the Treaty of Amiens (1802) and the return of armed conflict with England and its allies. Pope Pius VII was persuaded to come to Paris for the coronation (2 December 1804) of Napoleon as the first emperor of the French—a title that emphasized the formal, if empty, role of "national sovereignty" in the eclectic, nominally democratic regime that he put together. (The empire officially remained a "republic" until 1807.)

The War of the Third Coalition (1805–1807) saw Napoleon score his greatest single victory, at the Battle of Austerlitz, where his superior strategy defeated the larger combined armies of Austria and Russia. On the other hand, the British had again destroyed the French fleet (at the Battle of Trafalgar), so that Napoleonic hegemony was confined to the European continent. Great Britain ruled the seas along with France's extensive colonial holding. Later in the war, Napoleon inflicted sharp defeats on Prussia and Russia, at Jena-Auerstedt, Eylau, and Friedland. The Treaties of Tilsit (1807) confirmed French control of western and central Europe, while reserving a degree of Russian predominance in the east. But Tsar Alexander I was obliged to defer to French policy, and this proved distasteful and difficult for him. The Austro-French war of 1809 saw the French victorious at Wagram, and Habsburg power broken at the Treaty of Schönbrunn (1809).

As Britain's allies met disaster on land, the only way left for the English and French to carry on the war was in the economic realm. Britain's order in council (1806) created a maritime blockade of the Continent by the British fleet, matched by Napoleon's Berlin and Milan Decrees (1807), with which the French cut off all European trade with the British Isles. This "trade war" severely wounded both sides, but it ultimately inflicted greater harm on Europe, for it cut the Continent off from the spices and raw materials of Africa, India, and South America.

The war and the blockade "obliged" the French, as they saw it, to take control of the entire European littoral, which their leader's and his army's military skill permitted them to do. For the first time in European history since Charlemagne, if not since Rome, one power dominated the Continent. Napoleon's writ, at one time or another, ran from Lisbon to Moscow, and Naples to Copenhagen.

Unlike earlier empires, however, the French First Empire was no homogeneous structure, geopolitically speaking. Its "inner" core included modern-day Belgium, northern Germany and the Rhineland, northern Italy, the Dalmatian coast, and even a slice of eastern Spain; these areas were outright annexed to France and run as "departments." The "outer" empire included entire kingdoms and principalities (Spain, Holland, Westphalia, etc.) that were ruled by members of Napoleon's family, all of whom paid homage to the emperor. Finally, there were the vast areas of direct French influence—subordinating alliances that were forced on the Great Powers that had lost wars to Napoleon: Prussia, Russia, and Austria. Relations between the latter and France were further "thickened" by Napoleon's marriage in 1810 to Marie-Louise, the daughter of the Austrian emperor, Francis I. (Napoleon had secured an annulment of his marriage to Josephine because she could no longer have children.) The new empress bore him a son, grandly christened the king of Rome.

The year of the imperial prince's birth (1811) proved to be the high-water mark of Napoleonic power, and is a good place to try to sum up the balance sheet of his empire. This is a field in which contemporary scholarship has taken great strides, though it must also be said that the deepening of knowledge of the interface between the French and their subordinate lands has not led to many valid generalizations. On the one hand, it is clear that French influence always entailed some measure of progressive reforms, administrative, legal, and socioeconomic—changes that essentially forced degrees of "modernization" down the throats of old regime cultures, just as the Revolution had done in France. On the other hand, it is equally sure that the empire was always regressive in its extortion from occupied lands of money, manpower, and cultural artifacts.

Where complexity arises is in giving a detailed portrait of the interface over time between the French and the myriad social strata and political parties of the occupied lands. In some regions (e.g., northern Italy, Belgium) the newcomers were welcomed, and their departure left many locals (notably liberals in sympathy with the Revolution) regretful, for the learning and profit they had received and the changes their countries had registered. In other regions (Spain, southern Italy, much of Germany), however, the natives were mostly glad to get the French the hell out, although even in the bloodiest, angriest regions, such as Spain, it must be noted that whole social sectors (e.g., bourgeois city-dwellers in liberal occupations) knew the French departure spelled the end of socioeconomic progress—and worse. (Then, too, not a few historians have commented on how comparatively little bloody revolt the French presence provoked, despite their heavy demands and governance over their empire.) At the end of the day, a number of historians, notably François Crouzet, have commented on the Napoleonic Empire's role in being a first step toward European unification, which would eventually issue in the modern-day European Union.

Yet there were problems and defeats—serious ones—beginning most obviously in 1808, when much of the Spanish population followed some of their leaders in revolt against French rule. This obliged the emperor to march an army across the Pyrenees, and bring Spain to heel. This he did, but it did not last, once he left. He was obliged to send troops desperately needed elsewhere; Spain became a hemorrhage or cancer that seriously diminished the strength of the empire.

Around the same time, relations broke down between Napoleon and the pope over the issue of French domestic and international control over the Catholic Church. Never moderate with opponents, the emperor ordered the arrest of Pius VII and his incarceration in France. This rupture with the church was less immediately debilitating than the

Spanish "ulcer," not least because it took several years for French Catholics to learn of the sorry state of relations between their emperor and their pope, but in the long run it cost Napoleon his large consensus in domestic support. French Catholics did not outright turn against him, but when the fortunes of war and diplomacy turned against the emperor, the key Catholic stratum in French public opinion, previously so grateful for the Concordat, no longer gave him unqualified support.

If Britain remained France's unrelenting foe, that nation yet had no means of militarily attacking the empire without reenlisting a major Continental ally. But after 1809, with Europe at Napoleon's feet, this proved hard to do. Franco-Russian relations, however, steadily declined after 1807, despite the apparent friendship between Tsar Alexander I and Napoleon. First, the Romanov realm was economically disobliged by its enforced participation in the Continental System (the name given the French economic blockade of England and subjugation of Europe). Then, too, Napoleon's resurrection of a Polish political entity (the Grand Duchy of Warsaw) infuriated the Russian aristocracy—a ruling class that already loathed the French for exporting elements of their Revolution.

War came in 1812, and Napoleon characteristically chose to attack his foe. He assembled the largest and most international force the world had ever seen—some five hundred thousand men—and led them across the Nieman River in June. His Grand Army inflicted bloody defeats on the Russians everywhere, including Borodino, and it even occupied the old capital of Moscow. But the tsar's government refused to sue for peace, or even negotiate, while meanwhile, the Russian populace began to harass the French. The threat of being trapped in Moscow for the winter led Napoleon to retreat, in the famous anabasis of the winter of 1812, which left his great force reduced to some ten to fifteen thousand combatants.

With France half-exsanguinated by its wars, and more especially the Russian campaign, the other great Continental powers, pressed on and bankrolled by Britain, threw off their yokes and joined Russia. The 1813 campaign in Germany saw the coalition of Russia, Austria, and Prussia defeat Napoleon and his army in several engagements, notably the great Battle of Leipzig (the Battle of the Nations). Surprisingly, the emperor retained his authority within France, and even managed to extract another army out of the exhausted realm. The final campaign—the Campaign of France, fought in and around the Champagne region—proved to be one of Napoleon's most dexterous displays of strategy in a hopeless situation.

Notwithstanding, the French capital fell, and the emperor was forced by his own marshals to abdicate, on 6 April 1814. Napoleon was exiled to the nearby island of Elba, off the northwestern Italian coast. From there, he planned his escape and return to France, no doubt further prompted by word of the plots against his life being fomented by the restored Bourbon monarchy in Paris. Napoleon's actual return—he landed in the Golfe-Juan, near Cannes, at the beginning of March 1815—came as a shock to the Great Powers gathered in Vienna. But the fact that in the next ten days, the majority of the French people, despite all the disasters of the late First Empire, welcomed the man back, who was reproclaimed emperor, struck contemporaries—as well as later observers—as nothing short of stunning.

Hardly less unpredictable was the new regime Napoleon founded. He agreed to share power with the senate and parliament, while granting far greater freedoms to the press and to individuals. The so-called Liberal Empire rallied some of Napoleon's most obdurate opponents (e.g., Lazare Carnot, Benjamin Constant); it endured a hundred days, until the emperor lost the Battle of Waterloo (18 June), and presently was shipped off into permanent exile on the distant South Atlantic island of St. Helena. However brief, this period of the Hundred Days remains one of the mysteries in modern European history—How did the French let it happen? What might the regime have become?

THE NAPOLEONIC MYTH

In his six years of confinement on St. Helena, before his death on 5 May 1821, Napoleon produced one of his most far-reaching and lasting triumphs: he dictated roughly two thousand pages of memoirs to several aides, notably Emmanuel de Las Cases, who produced a massive tome entitled *Memorial of St. Helena* (1823). Though the work is a tissue of self-delusion and contains many contradictions, misinformation, and a few outright lies, it also contains pathos, remorse, and a great deal of thoughtful (and some beautiful) writing. Coupled with the experience of the Hundred Days (the "Liberal Empire"), the St. Helena writings have succeeded in memorializing Napoleon as a sort of liberal and democratic statesman—a friend of the "little people" and a nation builder who foresaw and worked toward the spread of the Enlightenment democratic revolution into the nineteenth century, including—no minor or illegitimate claim—the consolidation of the modern nation-state (notably Italy and Germany).

These writings have done so at least in French and Continental memory. In Anglo-American history, Napoleon has often been assigned an antipodal role: that of forerunner to Adolf Hitler. Neither view is even close to accurate—though the latter one, in addition to being wrongheaded, is also insulting to the French.

The truth is, Napoleon Bonaparte's unique contribution to world history lies in two things: on the one hand, the synthesis he wrought between nominal democracy based on national sovereignty and the plebiscite, as well as on military glory and geopolitical (imperial) aggrandizement; and, on the other hand, the never-ending appeal of the individualist myth of what the "lone man" can do with enough genius, gumption, and luck.

See also **Austerlitz; Borodino; Concordat of 1801; Continental System; France; French Revolution; French Revolutionary Wars and Napoleonic Wars; Hundred Days; Jena, Battle of; Napoleonic Code; Napoleonic Empire; Peninsular War; Sister Republics; Trafalgar, Battle of; Ulm, Battle of; Waterloo.**

BIBLIOGRAPHY

Alexander, R. S. *Bonapartism and Revolutionary Tradition in France: The* Fédérés *of 1815.* Cambridge, U.K., 1991.

Bergeron, Louis. *France under Napoleon: Internal Aspects.* Translated by R. R. Palmer. Princeton, N.J., 1981.

Broers, Michael. *Europe under Napoleon, 1799–1815.* London, 1996.

Bruce, Evangeline. *Napoleon and Josephine: The Improbable Marriage.* New York, 1995.

Carrington, Dorothy. *Napoleon and His Parents: On the Threshold of History.* New York, 1990.

Chandler, David G. *The Campaigns of Napoleon.* New York, 1966.

Dwyer, Philip G., ed. *Napoleon and Europe.* New York, 2001.

Ellis, Geoffrey. *Napoleon.* London, 1996.

———. *The Napoleonic Empire.* 2nd ed. Houndmills, Basingstoke, U.K., 2003.

Englund, Steven. *Napoleon: A Political Life.* New York, 2004.

Geyl, Pieter. *Napoleon: For and Against.* Translated by Olive Renier. New Haven, Conn., 1949.

Hazareesingh, Sudhir. *The Legend of Napoleon.* London, 2004.

Herold, J. Christopher, ed. and trans. *The Mind of Napoleon: A Selection from His Written and Spoken Words.* New York, 1955.

Jones, Proctor Patterson, ed. *Napoleon: An Intimate Account of the Years of Supremacy, 1800–1814.* San Francisco, 1992. Contains selections from the memoirs of Baron Claude-François de Méneval and Louis Constant Wairy.

Kauffmann, Jean-Paul. *The Black Room at Longwood: Napoleon's Exile on Saint Helena.* Translated by Patricia Clancy. New York, 1999.

Lyons, Martyn. *Napoleon and the Legacy of the French Revolution.* Basingstoke, U.K., 1994.

Mansel, Philip. *The Eagle in Splendour: Napoleon I and His Court.* London, 1987.

Schroeder, Paul W. *The Transformation of European Politics, 1763–1848.* Oxford, U.K., 1994.

Vovelle, Michel. *Les républiques-soeurs sous le regard de la Grande Nation (1795–1803).* Paris, 2000.

Woloch, Isser. *Napoleon and His Collaborators: The Making of a Dictatorship.* New York, 2001.

Woolf, Stuart. *Napoleon's Integration of Europe.* London, 1991.

Steven Englund

NAPOLEON III (Louis-Napoleon Bonaparte, 1808–1873), emperor of France from 1852 to 1871.

In the 1869 preface to his article on *The Eighteenth Brumaire of Louis Bonaparte,* a brilliant piece of political journalism written in 1852, Karl Marx (1818–1883) described his purpose as being to "demonstrate how the *class struggle* in France created circumstances and relations that made it possible for a grotesque mediocrity to play a hero's part."

The "mediocrity" in question was Louis-Napoleon Bonaparte, born on 20 April 1808, the son of Louis Bonaparte, appointed King of Holland by his brother Napoleon I (r. 1804–1814/15), and of Hortense de Beauharnais, daughter of the emperor's first wife Josephine. As a result of the couple's separation and the exile of the Bonaparte family from France, Louis-Napoleon was brought up by his mother at the château of Arenenberg in Switzerland, surrounded by memories of empire.

In addition to childhood socialization, another formative influence on the young prince was to be the experience in the years 1830 and 1831 of joining his elder brother Napoleon-Louis in a disastrous Italian rising against Austrian occupation. The death of Napoleon-Louis and in 1832 that of Napoleon's son, the so-called Duc de Reichstadt, left Louis-Napoleon determined to assert his claim to be the great Emperor's heir. As a result of his family background and upbringing he possessed an intense sense of personal destiny. In his determination to become guardian of the Napoleonic tradition, he combined the outlook of a romantic mystic with the instincts of a political opportunist. His friend from childhood, Madame Cornu, would describe his "mission" as a "devotion first to the Napoleonic dynasty, and then to France.... His duty to his dynasty is to perpetuate it. His duty to France is to give her influence abroad and prosperity at home." To achieve these objectives he would first have to gain power.

Otherwise farcical attempts to win the support of the military garrisons at Strasbourg in 1836 and Boulogne in 1840 at least associated Louis-Napoleon with a powerful popular cult of Napoleonic glory. In a series of pamphlets enjoying a wide circulation, including *Les Réflexions politiques* (1832), *Les idées napoléoniennes* (1839), and *L'Extinction du paupérisme* (1844), Louis-Napoleon also published his own ideas. Vague and full of contradictions, these writings, reflecting the utopian optimism of the 1830s and 1840s, were to serve as his "guiding ideas." They were characterized by a determination to eliminate the "party" divisions responsible for political instability. Although sharing with conservatives a determination to safeguard social order, Louis-Napoleon was distinguished by his apparent commitment to "social reform" and to "democracy." It was assumed further that in a restored empire, the emperor would initiate policy, but periodic plebiscites would be used to approve the regime's general policies, as well as to reaffirm the almost mystical link between the emperor and "his" people. The powers of the elected assembly would be reduced to a minimum.

PRINCE-PRESIDENT OF THE REPUBLIC

Louis-Napoleon's opportunity came as a result of a severe crisis, beginning with poor harvests and a generalized economic crisis, accompanied by agitation for electoral reform, and culminating in the revolution of February 1848 that established the Second Republic and "universal" (i.e., manhood) suffrage. Continued social and political tension characterized by a renewed insurrection in Paris in June, and its brutal military repression by a republican government, ensured that as a result of disappointed expectations—or in the case of conservatives, fear of further revolution—substantial parts of the population were prepared to contemplate the election of a potential "savior." This was the strength of Bonapartism—to be able to appear as "all things to all men." Reluctantly supported by conservative politicians, Louis-Napoleon's victory in the presidential election in December 1848 was overwhelming: he gained 74.2 percent of the votes cast (5,534,520). His leading opponent, the republican General Louis Eugène Cavaignac (1802–1857) obtained only 19.5 percent (1,448,302). In Paris the successful candidate gained 58 percent of the vote, with higher proportions in the popular *quartiers* for the supposedly "socialist" author of the *Extinction du paupérisme.* However, in a still predominantly agrarian country, it was peasant support that would remain the basis of Bonaparte's electoral strength for decades to come. The Austrian diplomat Rudolf Apponyi warned conservative political leaders that, in this situation, "if they believe themselves able ... to dominate him, they are badly mistaken." This unique election of a monarchical pretender, of a man with complete faith in his historical "mission" and, once having gained power, determined to retain it, made a coup d'état almost inevitable. This was the point at which the construction of "the political system of Napoleon III" might be said to have commenced.

Initially, Louis-Napoleon sought collaboration with conservative elites in the re-establishment of social order through increasingly intense repression of the *démocrate-socialiste* left, and with the Roman Catholic Church in the inculcation of "moral order" through education. He also asserted his own independence as head of government by appointing dependent ministers and officials, while ignoring protests from deputies in the National Assembly elected in May 1849. Unable to secure the two-thirds majority in the Assembly that would have allowed him to stand for re-election in 1852, the president was well placed to employ the bureaucracy and army, in which his supporters had already been placed in key positions, to launch a carefully planned coup on 2 December 1851.

In Paris only very limited resistance occurred, due to preventive arrests and obvious military preparedness. Few workers were prepared to risk a repetition of the bloodbath of June 1848 to defend the rights of a conservative assembly against a president who presented himself as the defender of popular sovereignty and enjoyed the prestige that went with the name Bonaparte. The predominantly conservative deputies who gathered in the town hall of the tenth arrondissement refused to rally to a president who had broken his constitutional oath, but were unwilling to contemplate more than symbolic resistance to a coup d'état that promised to establish strong, authoritarian government and destroy the nightmare prospect of a socialist electoral victory in 1852. Although easily crushed, more substantial resistance in rural areas of central France, and particularly the southeast, was used both to justify the coup and a reign of terror directed at republicans.

Napoleon III. Undated photograph by Roger Fenton. Victoria & Albert Museum, London, Great Britain/Art Resource, NY

On 20 December 1851 a plebiscite was held to sanction the extension of the prince-president's authority. The electorate was asked to vote on whether "the people wish to maintain the authority of Louis-Napoleon and delegate to him the powers necessary to establish a constitution." This appeal to popular sovereignty was to be a characteristic of the new regime. Louis-Napoleon was determined to secure a large majority as a means of legitimizing his actions. It was made clear to all officials, including village mayors, that their continued employment depended on enthusiastic campaigning. The basic theme was the choice between "civilization and barbarism, society and chaos." In place of the era of disorder that had opened in 1848, a new period of order, peace, and prosperity was promised. Nationally, 7,500,000 voted "yes," 640,000 "no," and 1,500,000 abstained. Ominously, opposition was concentrated in the major cities. Coercion was widespread but primarily the result was due to the immense popularity of the prince-president. In the countryside he was perceived to be the only safeguard against renewed revolution and additionally offered protection against the restoration of the *ancien régime.* The following November, after a carefully orchestrated campaign during which Bonaparte promised peace, order, and reconciliation, and which culminated in a triumphant return to the capital where he was greeted by enthusiastic crowds and processed to the Tuileries Palace under a succession of triumphal arches, 7,824,000 voters approved the re-establishment of the hereditary empire, which was proclaimed on 2 December 1852, the anniversary of the Battle of Austerlitz.

THE SECOND EMPIRE

The new regime's origins in a coup d'état, its authoritarian and repressive character, together with its ignominious collapse in the war of 1870, subsequently ensured that it received, and indeed deserved, a bad press. By the 1930s the Second Empire was being described as a precursor of fascism. Certainly, the system of government established following the coup was constructed with the intention of strengthening the powers of the head of state at the expense of representative institutions. The emperor appointed ministers and senior officials and assumed responsibility for decision-making. The Senate was packed with supporters, the role of the elected lower house—the *Corps législatif*—with around 260 members was initially viewed as essentially consultative; although as its consent was required for legislation, it represented a potential center of opposition. For this reason its members were selected carefully and every effort was made to determine the outcome of elections through manipulation, coercion, and propaganda associating the regime with prosperity and social order. However, the decision to retain manhood suffrage clearly distinguished the Second Empire from previous monarchical regimes. This was a regime that owed its legitimacy not to divine right but to the popular will. In time, as fear of revolution declined and repression eased, the social elites that had been deprived of power by the coup were able to make use of their dominant position in the administration and *Corps législatif* to criticize the restrictions on political liberty as well as the emperor's adventurous foreign policy.

Napoleon III's objectives included revision of the treaties imposed on France in 1815 and a recasting of the map of Europe based on the principle of nationality, to involve a reconstitution of Poland, and the establishment of relatively weak confederations in Italy and Germany as well as the territorial aggrandizement of France itself. As far as possible this was to be achieved through congresses of the powers, but if necessary through engagement in limited war. The Crimean War in 1854 represented a first step, an alliance with Britain against Russia, the most reactionary of European states. Eventual military success considerably increased French prestige, although the Congress of Paris in 1856 did not result in revision of the treaties. War with the old rival Austria in 1859 brought further military successes at Magenta and Solferino in Northern Italy and a hastily concluded peace that united Lombardy to the Kingdom of Piedmont-Savoy and could not prevent Italian nationalists from seizing power in the duchies of Tuscany, Parma, and Modena, and in the Papal Romagna. As a reward, the territories of Savoy and Nice lost in 1815 were triumphantly restored to France, following plebiscites of their inhabitants. Popular images and songs, fireworks and military parades, celebrated this renewal of national glory. The dispatch of an expeditionary force to Mexico in December 1861 in pursuit of the dream of creating a French sphere of influence in the Americas while the United States was absorbed with civil war would prove to be beyond the public's comprehension, however.

The unexpected consequences of military adventure and, in particular, the collapse of the Papal States, followed in 1860 by the negotiation of a commercial treaty with Britain, ensured that both Catholics and protectionists felt betrayed. Criticism mounted. Unlike his predecessors, Napoleon III was prepared to adapt and to engage in the difficult process of regime liberalization, in spite of warnings that he risked opening the flood gates. The gradual extension of political liberties culminating in the establishment of a liberal empire in 1870 represented concessions to criticism from the social elite rather than to the growing republican movement. As well as much greater freedom of speech, the emperor accepted that ministers should be responsible to parliament as well as to himself. Nevertheless, as the elect of the people Napoleon III retained considerable personal power, including the right to dissolve parliament and appeal to the people by means of elections or plebiscites, the authority to negotiate treaties and declare war. The new constitution was approved by plebiscite on 8 May 1870 by 7,350,000 votes to 1,538,000. The future of the dynasty appeared to have been assured.

This political liberalization during the 1860s has, in a more recent "revisionist" historiography, served to excuse previous authoritarianism. Historians have also focused more on what were perceived to be the regime's positive achievements and particularly the reconstruction of Paris, the creation of a modern transportation infrastructure, the reduction of tariff protection, and, more broadly, the establishment of the conditions for rapid economic growth, for which the regime had claimed most—and deserved some—of the credit. This revisionism culminated in 1990 in the publication, by the conservative politician Philippe Séguin, of a study entitled *Louis-Napoléon le grand,* and in the inauguration of the Place Napoleon III in Paris by Séguin, flanked by Jacques Chirac (b. 1932)—then the city's mayor—and the contemporary Prince Napoleon.

CONCLUSION

"Revisionism" has probably gone too far. In a perceptive comment in his notebook, Ludovic Halévy (1834–1908), the librettist who was also responsible for preparing the minutes of the *Corps législatif,* wrote following the announcement of the plebiscite results in 1870: "Too many Yes votes. The Emperor will believe that this is still the France of 1852 and do something stupid." The decision in July 1870 to go to war against Prussia, which threatened to upset the balance of power, perfectly illustrates the danger of allowing a single individual too much power. In order to avoid loss of face, and although he realized that the army was not ready, Napoleon III chose to engage in an extremely high-risk strategy. On 28 July, this sick and prematurely aged warlord, unable to sit on his horse or to concentrate for long periods, left Paris to assume command of his armies. On 2 September, an army under his direct command was forced to capitulate at Sedan in eastern France. On 4 September, the Republic was again proclaimed in the capital. No one was prepared to defend a regime responsible for such a catastrophic failure. After Sedan, Napoleon remained a prisoner in Germany until March 1871. He subsequently established his family at Chiselhurst in England, where, planning another coup d'etat, he died on 9 January 1873.

See also **Bonapartism; Crimean War; France; Franco-Prussian War; Paris; Revolutions of 1848.**

BIBLIOGRAPHY

Agulhon, Maurice. *The Republican Experiment, 1848–52.* Cambridge, U.K, 1983.

Hazareesingh, Sudhir. *From Subject to Citizen: The Second Empire and the Emergence of Modern French Democracy.* Princeton, N.J., 1998.

McMillan, James F. *Napoleon III.* London, 1991.

Plessis, Alain. *The Rise and Fall of the Second Empire.* Translated by Jonathan Mandelbaum. Cambridge, U.K., 1985.

Price, Roger. *The French Second Republic: A Social History.* London, 1972.

———. *Napoleon III and the Second Empire.* London, 1997.

———. *The French Second Empire: An Anatomy of Political Power.* Cambridge, U.K., 2001.

———. *People and Politics in France, 1848–1870,* Cambridge, U.K., 2004.

Smith, W. H. C. *Second Empire and Commune: France 1848–1871.* London, 1985.

Zeldin, Theodore. *The Political System of Napoleon III.* London, 1958.

ROGER PRICE

NAPOLEONIC CODE. Prior to the movement for the codification of Continental law in the nineteenth century, of which the Napoleonic Code is the most prominent example, Continental legal systems were based largely on a system of law known as the *ius commune.* To the extent that it comprised a body of substantive law, the legal principles that obtained were of mixed origin. The *ius commune* could claim its roots in the Roman law of Justinian, as interpreted and expanded by the medieval Italian glossators and commentators, and as influenced by Germanic customary law. The *ius commune,* however, was not a static body of doctrine; by the nineteenth century it was imbued with humanistic principles of the fifteenth century and natural law thinking of the late seventeenth century. In form, the *ius commune* was largely nonstatutory; it was found largely in the cases, where judges sought out and applied this amalgam of doctrinal principles refined by academics and by jurists to the legal dispute before them.

In the late eighteenth century, as Enlightenment ideals spread and the *ancien régime* began to unravel, the *ius commune* came under attack as being antidemocratic. Ideologically, the *ius commune* did not comport well with emerging notions of equality. In the first place, the *ius commune* was fashioned by jurists and judges and did not necessarily reflect the popular will. Second, its principles were often class specific, creating different rules for different social classes. In its defense, as the great German jurist Friedrich Karl von Savigny (1779–1861) argued, the *ius commune* was able to reflect the spirit of the people; it was imbued with age-old custom that embodied well-ingrained legal and cultural norms. Moreover, judges and jurists, the "oracles of the law," could interpret its principles in context and add to the law in substantive areas in which the *ius commune* was incomplete.

Codification was not a novel idea in nineteenth-century continental Europe; it had been undertaken in Prussia, Italy, and Austria in the eighteenth century (though usually piecemeal) and had melded with existing law. The codification movement of the nineteenth century, however, went further. It sought to replace the *ius commune* with a comprehensive system of law based on a text to which judges could refer in resolving disputes. In theory, the code would stand alone as the source of substantive private law. Because it was complete, neither recourse to previous law nor appeal to earlier jurisprudence and its philosophical underpinnings were theoretically possible. Thus, not only were new principles of law to govern private affairs, a new role for judges was also fashioned; judges were charged to find the law rather than to make it. And law was to be discovered, indeed all of the law, in the pages of the code.

Two issues have been raised and greatly debated among legal historians of codification. First, what were the jurisprudential origins of these newly codified legal principles? Second, did the legal system constructed actually operate as theory proclaimed? The first question can be easily addressed. Codification began in France before the turn of the nineteenth century. In 1799 the National Assembly rejected two draft codes. It was only after Napoleon came to power later that year that a commission prepared an acceptable version of a civil code. The commission, however, was composed not of citizens but of lawyers steeped in existing law; two were experts in customary law, while two others were scholars of the *ius commune*. Some preparatory work on rationalizing customary law and systematizing had already been undertaken, and the commission of four built the code upon the painstaking scholarship of others. The code as it was finally promulgated in 1804 relied upon both sources, the Roman and the customary law, though most modern scholars believe that the former predominates. Perhaps the codifiers' greatest feat was that they were able to reduce complex principles of private law to language comprehensible to the nonlawyer.

Admirable though the accomplishment of the commission was, the code was arguably still incomplete. Article 7 provided that the code superseded only that law that was addressed in its chapters. Because the code thus failed to abrogate all existing law, it begged the question as to whether parts of the *ius commune* remained in force. Surviving historical evidence suggests that differences emerged in the commission as to whether existing law continued in *les matières* (the subject areas) that the code left unaddressed. A primary concern was uniformity; prior to the code, private law in France varied by region, with the south largely governed by Roman law and the north under the sway of a diffuse body of Germanic customary law. Allowing appeal to past law would continue to leave France and French law divided by geography, rather than controlled by a single body of national law, a state of affairs that likely appeared anachronistic to the nineteenth-century mind.

Linked to the question of the extent to which earlier law survived the codification is the issue of the role of judges in the new legal order. It is often difficult for lawyers to imagine a body of law that is sufficiently complete and unambiguous that it can be applied in a rote fashion by judges, particularly in complex cases. But that was indeed the code's aspiration. Judges were to be far less powerful under the emerging legal order. The position of judges would be strengthened, however, if under certain circumstances appeal could be made to earlier law. Judges would be empowered twice: first to decide whether the code resolved an issue or whether there was a lacuna that required reference to principles outside the code; and second, if a lacuna existed and it was necessary to go outside the code, the judges had to determine what law should fill the gap.

Just as there was much continuity between the substantive law redacted in the code and earlier Roman and Germanic law, there was a similar approach to judging both before and after codification. Nineteenth-century Continental civil lawyers were trained to examine a text, be it the code or the more amorphous *ius commune,* and their legal method inclined them to apply the appropriate abstract rule to the controversy. Civilian judges, unlike their common-law brethren, do not examine what has been done in the past, or indeed what ought to be done in the present; rather, they focus on the command of the lawgiver as provided in the text.

Thus there was a strong connection with the past in both the substantive law and nature of the adjudicative process after the institution of the Napoleonic Code. But there was also significant change. After all, the code was adopted shortly after France had undergone its Revolution—an upheaval in politics, society, and the law. Two important interrelated areas of law that were affected by both the Revolution and the Napoleonic Code were that of family law and inheritance. While the origins of European family law can be found in canon law, family law in France had undergone much secularization even before the Revolution. Marriage, for example, had long been considered a civil rather than a religious act. Divorce, however, was proscribed, though civil judicial separations were permitted, even if they were rarely sought.

The Revolution's focus on *égalité* (equality) produced a number of reforms of family law that were more favorable to women than preexisting law. Divorce became far more easily obtainable (even for incompatibility or by mutual consent). Child custody ceased to be patriarchal: mothers took legal custody of their daughters, fathers their sons. Alimony was granted to divorced wives, as was the possibility for divorced women to demand the return of their marriage portions. Likewise paternal authority over children was diminished.

The Napoleonic Code reversed some of the reforms of the Revolution, and it did so with a vengeance. In the first place, it restored the elements of patriarchal power that had been swept away by the Revolution. Article 213 aptly summarizes the change by proclaiming: "The husband owes protection to his wife, and the wife obedience to her husband." Legal incapacity of married women was created, resembling English law's archaic and arcane concept of coverture. While marriage remained civil, parental consent was required for male children under the age of twenty-five and females under the age of twenty-one. Given Napoleon's own tumultuous marriage, it should come as no surprise that divorce was permitted. But the grounds for divorce recognized in the code were far more limited than those sanctioned under the law fashioned by the Revolution.

Viewed in its totality, then, the code sought to restore the traditional family by bringing back at least some of its earlier legal underpinnings. The code's provisions on inheritance of property likewise reversed some of the Revolution's law. Unlike fathers under Roman law, the inheritance law of the Revolution limited the right of parents to disinherit children, permitting the parent a disposal share of only 10 percent. While the percentage was increased thereafter, the Napoleonic Code created a different balance between the disposable share that the property owner could will freely and the children's "reserved share"—a balance more favorable to the parent: those with only one surviving child could dispose freely one-half of the patrimony; those with two children, one-third; while those with three or more children could dispose of only one-quarter. Transfers of property inter vivos (that is, during the parent's life) that exceeded the disposal portion were called back to the family coffers and distributed to the children, even if the property in question had been conveyed to third parties. Some notion of Revolutionary *egalité* remained, however, because children inherited shares equally and irrespective of sex. Whether the dictates of this rather complex rule of inheritance were followed and whether property owners and their notaries were able to circumvent them through craftily drafted documents are topics of considerable historical debate. Suffice it to say that in matters of inheritance the code preserved some of both the pre- and post-Revolutionary flavors of French law.

The Napoleonic Code is a civil code and therefore did not deal with matters such as civil or criminal procedure, criminal law, and commercial law. Further codes were later adopted to deal with these matters. The code governed exclusively private law; the law of obligations, contract law, was an important component of the Napoleonic Code, and in many provisions the law reflects its Roman origins. As in Roman law, consent is the basis of a binding obligation, and obligators bind themselves and their property. But arguably the code harked back to Roman law principles because the society that the code governed was more akin to that of Rome than of the medieval France in which customary Germanic law held sway. France had undergone a transition from a society organized by family groupings to a more individualistic society. Both the law of obligations and that of ownership curiously found its modernity in the Roman rather than the Germanic heritage.

Although much amended in detail, the Napoleonic Code has survived in structure and in concept into the twenty-first century. The movement for codification that gripped France also swept across Europe in the long nineteenth century. Germany, Italy, Spain, Switzerland, and Austria among others became engaged in the process of systematizing, rationalizing, and unifying national law through codification. Like France, these emerging "nations" sought to bring together Roman and customary principles in a form intelligible to the modern educated mind. In addition, the Napoleonic Code has been transported elsewhere, most notably to the New World; the civil codes of Louisiana and Quebec adhered to today have been inspired by it, and its vestiges still govern. Indeed the survival of the Napoleonic Code in these outlying "provinces" is even more impressive given that these two enclaves are surrounded by common law jurisdictions.

See also **French Revolution; Napoleon; Napoleonic Empire.**

BIBLIOGRAPHY

Bonfield, Lloyd. "European Family Law." In *The History of the European Family,* edited by David I. Kertzer and Marzio Barbagli, vol. 2: *Family Life in the Long Nineteenth Century, 1789–1913,* 109–154. New Haven, Conn., 2002.

Lupoi, Maurizio. *The Origins of the European Legal Order.* Translated by Adrian Belton. Cambridge, U.K., 2000.

Merryman, John Henry. *The Civil Law Tradition: An Introduction to the Legal Systems of Western Europe and Latin America.* 2nd ed. Stanford, Calif., 1985.

Stein, Peter. *Roman Law in European History.* Cambridge, U.K., 1999.

van Caenegam, R. C. *An Historical Introduction to Private Law.* Translated by D. E. L. Johnston. Cambridge, U.K., 1992.

LLOYD BONFIELD

NAPOLEONIC EMPIRE.

The first Napoleonic empire was the largest, most institutionally uniform European state in modern times. Its existence preceded Napoleon Bonaparte's coronation as "emperor of the French" in 1804, and its influence on European public institutions and political culture far outlasted his fall from power in 1814/1815. Despite the transient nature and short duration of Napoleon's personal rule—as first consul of France (1799–1804) and as emperor (1804–1815)—his empire laid the foundations of modern Europe.

THE LEGACY OF THE REVOLUTIONARY WARS

When Napoleon took power in 1799, the French Republic had already been at war with most of the great European powers since 1792. Indeed, a major provocation behind the outbreak of war had been the revolutionaries' avowed "doctrine of natural frontiers." Specifically, this meant France laid claim to all territories west of the Rhine, lands hitherto within the Holy Roman Empire, comprising much of western Germany and all of present-day Belgium; the French now defined the Rhine as France's eastern frontier by right. Effectively, Revolutionary France had committed itself to a project of genuine, if limited, imperial expansion.

With the French victories of 1793 to 1795, these assertions became political realities. Between 1795 and 1799, French military advances ensured that the front lines were transformed into zones of occupation. However, French interests, unlike specific territorial claims, did not end at the nation's "natural frontiers." Ideological principles, based on the universalist claims of the Declaration of the Rights of Man and of the Citizen of 1789, served to justify the creation of "buffer states"—the "sister republics"—beyond the "natural frontiers." In 1795 the United Provinces, the modern-day Netherlands, was renamed the Batavian Republic, under a puppet government. In 1796 Napoleon created the Cispadane (later the Cisalpine) Republic in northern Italy, with himself as its president. Creation of the Helvetic Republic in present-day Switzerland followed one year later. In 1798 and 1799 in southern Italy, occupying French armies set up the Roman and Parthenopean republics over the Papal States and the mainland parts of the Kingdom of Naples, respectively. This amounted to a state system controlled by the French Republic, the resources of the system ruthlessly plundered for the war effort.

A series of military reversals in 1798 and 1799 shattered this proto-empire. By spring 1799 all of Italy and most of Germany and the Low Countries had been lost, and the French were momentarily thrown back to their own borders. Napoleon was brought to power by a clique of republican politicians in 1799, in no small part to reestablish French hegemony beyond the pre-1792 borders. Thus, Napoleon began his own career as an imperialist in the service of the French Republic and the radical ideology that had fostered expansionist ambitions.

RESTORING FRENCH HEGEMONY, 1799–1805

From the outset, Napoleon's political survival depended on the reestablishment of the republic's empire. He achieved this in a series of well-coordinated military campaigns in 1799 and 1800. By 1801, a general peace had been concluded with all the major powers, culminating in the Treaty of Amiens with Britain in March 1802. Although Britain and France were at war by 1803, Napoleon did not attack the Continental powers until 1805, allowing him to consolidate his rule not just in France itself, but in northern and central Italy and the Low Countries as well. At this stage, Napoleon did not attempt to stretch French satellite states as far afield as previous regimes. The Kingdom of Naples was returned to the Bourbons and most of the Papal States to the pope. Venice lost her independence not to the Cisalpine sister republic, but to Austria, in a piece of diplomacy that, however treacherous to the Venetians, seemed to spell a halt to French expansion driven by Revolutionary ideology.

Napoleon's ambitions lay elsewhere, however. The results of his policy of expansion by diplomacy, rather than military aggression, proved among his most seminal schemes, if also rare for their reciprocity. In a series of maneuvers, begun at the Congress of Rastatt as early as 1797, and concluded in 1803, Napoleon engineered a fundamental territorial reorganization of Germany. He achieved this in partnership with the rulers of the middle-sized states of western and southern Germany, giving French backing to their own territorial ambitions. Together, they forced Francis II, the Holy Roman emperor and ruler of Austria, to let them absorb a myriad of tiny polities into their states, whose only protection had been the emperor. In this way, Napoleon both aggrandized and bound to him the rulers of the southwestern German states of Bavaria, Baden, Würtemberg, Hesse-Darmstadt, and Nassau. This relationship was consolidated formally after his defeat of Austria and Russia in 1805, when Napoleon bound these states together into the Confederation of the Rhine, with himself as its protector.

The Napoleonic Empire was now a complex power bloc engulfing most of western and southern Europe, as much as an imperial mass, in the conventional sense. It was a hegemony, exercised through three different methods. The Revolutionary conquests were restored: the left bank of the Rhine, modern Belgium, and northwestern Italy were reannexed directly to France; satellite states were recreated in the Netherlands and north-central Italy; and western Germany east of the Rhine was now composed of the expanded, closely allied states of the Confederation of the Rhine. Beneath this complex grouping of territories, a deeper uniformity emerged, however, that belied the variegated bonds that tied them to Napoleon. All the states within the Napoleonic orbit by 1805 became deeply imbued with core French institutions, either by their direct imposition in the annexed departments, by imposed if indirect control in the newly created satellite states, or through free but conscious imitation in the Confederation of the Rhine. In the period from 1800 to 1805, all these territories saw the emergence and embedding of the key, defining institutions of the modern European state: the Napoleonic Code, which guaranteed open trials and equality before the law, and the centralized state based on prefects—civil servants appointed by the central government—and departments, the units they administered. Everywhere, local laws, weights and measures, currency, and administrative structures were replaced by those developed in France after 1789. This also entailed the abolition of the vestiges of feudalism, and of provincial and noble privileges, and the confiscation of the properties of the church. To be part of the Napoleonic hegemony meant absorbing a uniform, standardized political system; the foundations of the old order were swept away in every area the French took under their definitive control. These diversely controlled states and regions became an "inner empire," the true core of Napoleonic power. Here, French public institutions and legal and administrative practices took root; the local elites saw their advantages and found they reflected earlier, indigenous currents of reform, especially in the German states and northern Italy, those areas most influenced by the dynamic Holy Roman emperor Joseph II, in the 1780s. The importance of this process is that this political culture and its institutions endured after Napoleon's military eclipse and fall, in 1814/1815. This was a crucial phase for the future development of western Europe.

The net result of these reforms was to increase state power, the need for which became pressing when war resumed on the continent after 1805. The satellite states and those within the Confederation of the Rhine now had to pay for Napoleonic protection from the interests of the old order, which threatened to unseat the rulers of the former and undo the territorial gains of the latter. Napoleon imposed heavy conscription and taxation on all the lands of the inner empire, inside and outside France, from 1805 onward. Indeed, the contemporary test of the effectiveness of French rule, within the imperial departments, and of French-inspired reforms, in the allied states, became the ability to raise troops and revenue. If these material demands could be met, the state was viable and efficient. This process was enforced by the creation of the gendarmerie, a paramilitary police force mainly devoted to patrolling the countryside. Through it, mass conscription and heavy taxation were imposed on peasantries for whom central authority had been a mere shadow before Napoleonic rule.

Even in the more stable period of peace, 1800 to 1805, the arrival of the new state came as a traumatic shock. If institutions such as the prefectoral administrative system and the Napoleonic Code marked the importance of the new regime for the elites and propertied classes, conscription—"the blood tax"—and the presence of a police force were its clearest signs for the popular classes in the countryside. Napoleonic hegemony was punctuated by rural revolt everywhere, even in its supposed heartland, but the effectiveness of the state, its new and highly evolved coercive power, ensured that such recalcitrance remained atomized and short lived, if persistent. Northern and central Italy saw widespread, if localized, peasant revolts; rural parts of the Rhineland were plunged from very traditional forms of local justice and government, based on arbitration, for example. Independently, the German princes met similar opposition within their own borders. Some aspects of Napoleonic rule, such as the religious settlement, were never really accepted outside France, where the Concordat of 1801 was regarded as an assault upon a vibrant, popular Catholic faith. Whereas in France the Concordat was seen, initially at least, as a restoration of normalcy after the rabid anticlericalism of the 1790s, even sectors of the non-French elite saw it as an assault on their culture. The inner empire was never a popular, or populist, construct. Nor did the western European experience of the new Napoleonic state include meaningful, representative, parliamentary government. This was an aspect of the Revolution Napoleon did not export. Nevertheless, the propertied classes, which also included much of the peasantry, benefited from improved policing, particularly the extirpation of brigandage. Justice proved fair and efficient under the Napoleonic Code and was administered by an honest, professional magistracy. The equitable reparation and administration of property taxes was achieved by the compilation of accurate land registers, the cadastres, although indirect taxes soared under Napoleon. The prefects proved able and honest local administrators, all of which impressed even those politically opposed to Napoleon.

The inner empire, however, was not synonymous with the pre-Revolutionary Kingdom of France. Just as Napoleon inherited the expansionist ambitions of the Revolution, so he inherited its divisions. Although he achieved much in healing political wounds within the French elites, the demands of war ensured that his regime remained detested in those regions that had opposed the incursions of the Revolution in the 1790s. Much of southern and western France remained under virtual martial law throughout his rule. The departments that had been the theater of the great western revolt of the 1790s—known collectively as the *Vendée militaire,* after the Vendée region at its epicenter—were assigned lower conscription quotas than most of the departments of northern Italy, Belgium, or the Rhineland, while a virtual "garrison town" was built at La Roche-sur-Yon, renamed Napoleon-Vendée. Much of southwestern France virtually went over the invading British armies in 1814. Within France, the true heartland of the regime was in the more urbanized, secularized north and east. The recalcitrant traits still alive in the south and west would be magnified in the new territories acquired after the wars of 1805 to 1808.

THE "GREAT EMPIRE," 1805–1814

This round of victories altered the shape of the empire, and of Europe as a whole, in dramatic, unexpected ways. The victories of 1805 led to the seizure of the southern Italian Kingdom of Naples, where Napoleon replaced the Bourbons with his brother Joseph; the Bourbons of Parma were also deposed, and their small state annexed to France along with the sister republic of Liguria, centered on Genoa. The defeat of Prussia and Russia, in 1806 and 1807, saw territory seized from Prussia, and Hesse-Kassel in north-central Germany became a new Kingdom of Westphalia, under Napoleon's youngest brother, Jérôme. Further east, the Treaties of Tilsit, with Russia, led to the creation of a new state, the Grand Duchy of Warsaw, from Prussian Poland. In 1808 Napoleon invaded Spain and overthrew the Bourbons, transferring Joseph to Madrid, while his brother-in-law, Marshal Joachim Murat, now ruled Naples. After his defeat of Austria in 1809, Napoleon annexed Tuscany, the Papal States, and the German states bordering the North Sea in 1811. After 1805, the Napoleonic Empire was no longer a purely west European state system, but a pan-European empire. Territorially, it reached its height in 1811. There were 130 imperial departments, ruled directly from Paris, embracing forty-four million inhabitants; together with the satellite kingdoms and the Confederation of the Rhine, the "Napoleonic hegemony" contained over eighty million people.

The territories acquired in this second phase of expansion were not properly integrated into the Napoleonic legal and administrative system. They were "occupied," rather than absorbed. Spain, the largest single polity Napoleon ever tried to acquire in one step, was never properly under his control, and it became a theater of determined resistance to him. Elsewhere, resistance was less violent or overt, but equally tangible. Feudalism was widespread in northern Germany, southern Italy, and, especially, Poland, thus making the Napoleonic Code inoperable there. Westphalia and the Grand Duchy of Warsaw became important sources of conscripts, but were an "outer empire" where the "new regime" did not take root. Most of these annexations were driven by military expediency or, in the case of the Illyrian Provinces—modern Slovenia and Croatia—by diplomacy, in the hope of using them as bargaining tools with the other powers. Above all, Napoleon's annexations hugged the coastlines of Europe, as he tried to defeat Britain by a massive economic blockade. The blockade was accompanied by the Continental System, which sought to reorient European trade and industry away from British influence. The system, as distinct from the blockade, eventually denatured the imperial core. It did not mirror the empire's administrative and legal uniformity, amounting to a series of treaties protecting France, proper, from all European competition, creating a "one-way common market." Napoleon erected customs barriers that denied easy access to French markets, even to the satellite kingdoms and the departments annexed after 1797, thus alienating vast tracks of the inner empire. The system proved unworkable and instigated the catastrophic invasion of Russia, in 1812, that spelled the end of Napoleon's regime; his state system crumbled in a matter of months. Significantly, the German states deserted him only when assured that the territorial settlement of 1803 and their internal reforms would be respected. A succession of military defeats led to Napoleon's abdication in April 1814. His attempt to regain power in the "Hundred Days" of the following year was confined to France.

Napoleon's hegemony was brief, but his reforms exerted a lasting, seminal influence on western Europe. Napoleonic administrative institutions and the Napoleonic Code reemerged as the basis for civil government in the states comprising the former inner empire, the future core of the modern European Union. The centralized, culturally uniform Napoleonic model of the state shaped French overseas imperialism, first in Algeria in 1829, and then across Africa and Indochina in the late nineteenth century. The legacy of the Napoleonic Empire in European and imperial history is not Napoleon's transient military exploits, but the durability of his political reforms.

See also **Austria-Hungary; Concordat of 1801; Congress of Vienna; Continental System; French Revolution; French Revolutionary Wars and Napoleonic Wars; Great Britain; Napoleon; Napoleonic Code; Prussia; Russia; Sister Republics.**

BIBLIOGRAPHY

Broers, Michael. *Europe under Napoleon, 1799–1815.* London, 1996.

Ellis, Geoffrey. *Napoleon.* London, 1996. Destined to become the standard work in English.

———. *The Napoleonic Empire.* 2nd ed. Houndmills, Basingstoke, U.K., 2003. A good shortcut to the subject.

Lefebvre, Georges. *Napoleon.* 2 vols. Translated by Henry F. Stockhold (vol. 1) and J. E. Anderson (vol. 2). London, 1969–1974. Pathbreaking, classic Marxist account.

Lyons, Martyn. *Napoleon and the Legacy of the French Revolution.* Basingstoke, U.K., 1994. Strong on France and the early period.

Tulard, Jean. *Napoleon: The Myth of the Saviour.* Translated by Teresa Waugh. London, 1984. Seminal French biography, marred by a poor English translation.

Woloch, Isser. *The New Regime: Transformations of the French Civic Order, 1789–1820s.* New York, 1994. Essential for the internal reforms.

Woolf, Stuart. *Napoleon's Integration of Europe.* London, 1991. The classic "Euro-centered" study.

MICHAEL BROERS

NAPOLEONIC WARS. *See* **French Revolutionary and Napoleonic Wars.**

NASH, JOHN (1752–1835), English architect, developer, and city planner.

John Nash is best known for his work in creating London's Regent's Park and Regent Street. Throughout his long and prolific career Nash worked in a variety of styles, the result of two influences. The first was the classicism of Sir Robert Taylor (1714–1788), in whose offices he trained in the years before 1778. The second was the picturesque approach of landscape designer Humphry Repton (1752–1818), with whom Nash worked between 1792 and the early 1800s. For Repton, landscape design was much more than gardening, and his schemes for the estates of wealthy landowners would invariably include architectural elements designed to enhance the picturesque qualities of the landscape, in whatever style he felt best reflected the "true character" of the site. Nash provided the designs to fit, which ranged from neo-Palladian villas (Southgate Grove, Middlesex, 1797) to gothic castles (Luscombe Castle, Devon, 1800; Killymoon Castle, Ireland, c. 1803), and numerous picturesque thatched cottages (Blaise Hamlet, 1803–11). In each case considerations of a picturesque outline and the relationship of rooms to views over the landscape took precedence over classical symmetry or stylistic "correctness." To the discerning eye, Nash's gothic castles and cottages rarely appeared historically convincing, but Nash was interested in visual effects and historical associations, not in authenticity. His work with Repton played an important role in spreading and popularizing the gothic style.

In 1806 Nash was appointed architect to the Department of Woods and Forests, a post that involved the maintenance of the royal estates. In 1811 he proposed an ambitious scheme to create a park and a new residential quarter on the extensive crown lands in north London (Regent's Park, from 1812). Making a revolutionary break from the formal symmetrical squares that had been a feature of eighteenth-century London, Nash designed a romantic landscape of lakes, curving pathways, gentle slopes, and clumps of trees, with groups of houses scattered around the periphery. It was the first time the picturesque ideal of houses set within parkland had been applied at such a large scale to an urban setting, and it was

Regent Circus (detail). Engraving by Thomas Shotter Boys from his *London As It Is*, 1842. Boys's illustration shows the townhouses of Nash's Regent's Park development. PRIVATE COLLECTION/BRIDGEMAN ART LIBRARY/THE STAPLETON COLLECTION

to be Nash's most influential work. Plans to build a new palace for the Prince Regent within the park came to nothing, but Nash went ahead with his own version, surrounding the park with spectacular "palaces," which were in fact simply row houses dressed up with elaborately articulated classical facades (Cumberland Terrace, 1826–1827).

A key component of Nash's scheme was the creation of a new ceremonial and commercial route (Regent Street, from 1813) between the new park and Carlton House, the Prince Regent's London residence situated more than a mile south of the park in St. James's. The complexities of land ownership in this crowded area of the city made a straight route impractical and Nash again applied picturesque principles by designing a curving street with a number of vistas and focal points. While Nash designed many of the key buildings, individual owners and developers were encouraged to design and build their own parts of the street frontage, leading to a rich and varied streetscape. It was a sharp contrast with the officially regulated conformity of contemporary developments in Paris (*Rue de Rivoli*, Charles Percier and Pierre-Francois-Leonard Fontaine, 1802–1805) and a practical illustration of a "democratic" approach to urbanism. As with the park, Regent Street was an influential example of the application of picturesque principles in an urban context.

Through his marriage to Mary Anne Bradley in 1798, Nash entered the social circle of the future Prince Regent, and over the following years he became the prince's favored designer. Their first collaboration was the prince's country retreat in Windsor—Royal Lodge (1812–1814), a lavish palace in the guise of a thatched cottage. Then came the prince's seaside villa (Brighton Pavilion, 1815–1823), which Nash rebuilt in a fantastical oriental style complete with onion domes and elaborate chinoiserie interiors. In 1820 the prince became King George IV (r. 1820–1830) and persuaded the government he needed a new palace in London. In 1825 Parliament, envisaging minor refurbishment works, voted £200,000 for Nash to convert the old Buckingham House into Buckingham Palace. But the king had more ambitious plans and Nash was caught between the king's escalating architectural ambitions and the government's desire to economize. Unable to satisfy either, and by then in his seventies, in 1831 he was forced to retire to the gothic castle he had built on the Isle of Wight (East Cowes Castle, 1798–1821).

See also **Barry, Charles; Cities and Towns; George IV; London; Pugin, Augustus Welby.**

BIBLIOGRAPHY

Primary Sources

Repton, Humphry. *Observations on the Theory and Practice of Landscape Gardening*. London, 1803.

Secondary Sources

Davis, Terence. *John Nash, the Prince Regent's Architect.* London, 1966.

Summerson, John. *John Nash, Architect to King George IV.* London, 1935.

———. *Georgian London*. London, 1945.

MARK FOLEY

NATIONALISM. Nationalism came to dominate political and cultural life in Europe during the nineteenth century, and throughout the world in the twentieth, but defining it with any precision is far harder than recognizing its importance. The best definition is probably the least helpful: nationalism is an ideology that prioritizes the needs of the nation, making all other concerns—social justice, universal religious teachings, partisan politics, personal ambitions—subordinate to the national interest. But that just begs the question: What, exactly, is a nation? Is it defined by language, ancestry, religion, cultural affinity, geographical location, political allegiance, or some combination of all these factors? Once a nation is identified, what does it mean to pursue its interests? Does a nation have to possess an independent state? Must people of other nations be purged from that state? These questions, which have shaped the history of nationalism in Europe, have proven to be as persistent as they are irresolvable.

THE ORIGINS OF NATIONALISM

The word *nation* is based on the Latin *natio,* which referred in ancient times to a collection of people united by common ancestry. Prior to the eighteenth century, however, the term had little ideological importance. Political allegiance in medieval and early modern Europe rarely corresponded to linguistic or cultural communities, and it was perfectly normal for a variety of communities to coexist within the same town, region, or state. One's sense of "self" was neither more nor less fragmented than it is today—people would think of themselves as worshiping within this-or-that religious tradition, speaking this-or-that language, living under this-or-that monarch, having this-or-that ancestry, but no one would presume that one and only one of these categories could define a person, or that all of them should somehow come together to create a unified sense of collective belonging. The difference between premodern and modern Europe was not necessarily a change in the way people perceived themselves, but the increasingly widespread sense that the irreducible complexity of cultural diversity was a problem—one that could be and should be solved. In the worldview of the nationalist, humanity got divided into sharply defined groups and everyone inside each group was said to share an identity, in the sense of being (on some basic level) identical. The emergence of nationalism entailed the quest for (and eventual enforcement of) a homogeneity that never did and never could exist.

The ideology of nationalism does not have a clear intellectual lineage or recognized set of canonical texts—it is not even an "ideology," in the strict sense of the word, but rather a set of general attitudes about culture, community, and politics. These attitudes began to come together in the late eighteenth century, when a wide range of intellectuals (mainly in Europe, but also in the Americas) began toying with the ramifications of the idea that humanity is grouped into mutually exclusive cultural blocs, and that these blocs are coherent and cohesive enough to act as collective historical agents. Johann Gottfried von Herder (1744–1803) was one of the first European philosophers to argue that language determines the way people think. Instead of a single pattern of reasoning common to all humans, Herder posited the existence of linguistically determined modes of understanding that made communication across cultures extraordinarily difficult. This diversity was to be celebrated and protected, Herder argued, because each linguistic culture offered a distinctive contribution to humanity as a whole—he was, in other words, quite distant from any form of German chauvinism or xenophobia. But even as he praised the plurality of cultures, Herder implied a certain uniformity within each collectivity based on his assumption that the most fundamental thoughts of the people in a community were structured by the language they shared with their neighbors. It is therefore no surprise that Herder's ideas would be cited throughout the nineteenth century by nationalists who were far less cosmopolitan than he was.

Though he differed from Herder in many ways, Jean-Jacques Rousseau (1712–1778) made a similar move in the political realm, advancing the idea of an undifferentiated "general will," a sort of collective personality that took precedence over the individual personalities within it. Whereas Herder's community was defined by language, Rousseau's was marked by adherence to a "social contract" that defined subgroups within an otherwise undifferentiated humanity. Many historians of nationalism have drawn a sharp contrast between Herder and Rousseau, suggesting that the former represented a culturally defined nationalism, whereas the latter advocated a nation based on citizenship and republican liberty. Without denying the profound differences between these two thinkers, it is important to note that they were linked by a shared assumption that large-scale communities were the primary agents in history and in politics, and that those communities were bound together in ways that compelled individuals to embrace mutually exclusive identities. In this sense they were both among the first Europeans to cultivate a nationalist mode of thinking.

As intellectuals such as Herder and Rousseau were debating new ways to think about communities and politics, two developments at the end of the eighteenth century brought the concept of the nation to center stage for millions of Europeans: the French Revolution (1789) and the Partitions of Poland (1772, 1793, and 1795). The Revolution turned theories about the "general will" into a vital public issue, as the new French regime claimed to derive its authority from, and speak on behalf of, "the people." When the Revolution was threatened from abroad, a mass mobilization (the *levée en masse*) created a genuine citizen's army for the first time in European history, as hundreds of thousands of troops demonstrated their willingness to die for the nation (at least as long as the nation was coterminous with the Revolution). At almost the same time, the total destruction of the Polish Republic, previously one of the largest (albeit also one of the weakest) states in Europe, created the first significant political movement in Europe to juxtapose a call for "national liberation" with the highly charged rhetoric of the revolutionary era.

The Fenian Collar. Emblem of Irish nationalists c. 1880 bearing the portrait of Irish patriot Robert Emmet. ©CORBIS

Over the course of the coming century Poles would be joined by groups advocating the national causes of Greeks, Serbs, Croats, Bulgarians, Romanians, Hungarians, Czechs, Slovaks, Ukrainians, Lithuanians, Latvians, Estonians, Finns, Irish, Italians, and Germans—indeed, virtually every corner of Europe (and eventually the entire world) was touched in some way by some kind of national movement. These causes differed in many ways—some stressed independence, others unification, still others merely demanded recognition and respect for their languages and cultures. For all their differences, though, all these national movements spread the view that the world was divided into national communities, that every individual possessed one (and only one) national identity, and that these nations were the fundamental building blocks of history and politics.

NATIONAL IDEALISM

Johann Gottlieb Fichte (1762–1814) was already a prominent philosopher when he gave a series of lectures in 1807 and 1808 titled "Addresses to the German Nation." Like Herder, he believed that national communities were defined by language, and that those speaking different languages thought in different ways. Fichte, however, drew some specific political conclusions from these observations. At a time when most of Europe was occupied by the forces of Napoleon I, Fichte argued that all Germans should both resist foreign rule and unite within a single national state. Even more important, however, was the philosopher's justification for this political agenda: Fichte imagined a grand scheme of historical progress according to which each nation, acting through a state, contributed to the overall advancement of humanity. Each nation represented a unique principle, a specific piece of the larger puzzle that was human advancement, and the pursuit of independence and unification was the means by which this ideal would be realized.

For the first half of the nineteenth century, it was widely assumed that nationalism was a revolutionary force, tied to slogans about "liberty," "freedom," "justice," and even "democracy." At a time when Europe's ruling elites were for the most part nonnational or supranational, the claim that people of a common culture should belong to a common state was inherently disruptive. The Italian movement for national unification was almost inevitably opposed to the institutions of the Roman Catholic Church, which had an interest in sustaining the Papal States; the German national movement threatened the autonomy and authority of dozens of monarchs; the Greek independence movement challenged the Ottoman Empire; and the Polish national movement was an ever-present danger to Russia, Prussia, and Austria-Hungary. But the revolutionary reputation of mid-nineteenth-century nationalism was based on more than just this alignment of political interests. The ideology of nationalism was itself, at the time, fundamentally radical. For all the talk of language and culture, few nationalist activists in the 1830s or 1840s would go so far as to define a nation purely according to ethnographic features. Language was important, but it was not exclusively determinative. More fundamental was the "national idea" or the "national soul": an ill-defined "spiritual" communion that linked people together, imbued them with a historical mission, and positioned them within a grand scheme of historical progress. Nationalism was tied up inextricably with the romanticism and idealism that shaped European culture at the time, and this generated a sort of internationalist nationalism—an eagerness to see each national cause as part of a much broader struggle. Thus Lord Byron (1788–1824) would die while taking part in the

Greek war for independence, Poles would go into battle during a rebellion in 1830 with flags emblazoned with the slogan "For Your Freedom and Ours," and the Italian nationalist Giuseppe Mazzini (1805–1872) would found the People's International League in Britain in 1847. The flip side of the idealistic and progressive views of these early national movements was their limited social base. They could focus on the "national spirit" rather than ethnography or linguistics, because for the most part they were engaged in conspiracies rather than mass politics. Sometimes those conspiracies led to violent clashes involving thousands of people, but until at least the 1840s it was easy for national activists to place "the people" on an idealized pedestal.

A turning point in this regard were the revolutions of 1848, for it was in that year that nationalist activists from all over Europe first confronted a problem they had been carefully dodging to that point: What happens if the national liberation of one group conflicts with the national liberation of another? How can *liberty* remain a meaningful term in a nationalist framework if it cannot be universally applied, and attained equally for all? Tragically, in 1848 it became evident that the Hungarian movement's aspirations were irreconcilable with the goals of many Croats, Serbs, Slovaks, and Romanians; Czech nationalists could not achieve what they wanted without challenging the dreams of many Germans from Bohemia; any program of German unification inevitably came up against Polish hopes to restore independence; and those Polish ambitions, in turn, would have made it impossible for the Ukrainian movement to reach its objectives. None of these programs had to clash as long as everyone was talking about the "national spirit" and the ideals of freedom supposedly embodied in national liberation movements. But during the revolutions of 1848 the first stirrings of mass politics brought ethnolinguistic complexity to the forefront as never before. The Pan-Slav Congress held in Prague that year collapsed in the face of bickering among the various delegates; Germans and Poles fought over the fate of the Poznań region; and the Habsburg monarchy was able to use Croats, Romanians, Slovaks, and Serbs against rebellious Hungarians. The experiences of 1848 dealt national idealism a blow from which it never fully recovered.

NATIONAL EGOISM

In a poignant testimony to the changing shape of nationalism in the second half of the nineteenth century, Mazzini refused to participate in the political life of the newly created Italian state, even though he had fought for that cause his entire life. Italy had been built using the tools of power politics, and its government and social system failed to break from the institutions and norms of the past. It was, in other words, just another European state, and to a national idealist like Mazzini that was intolerable. A similar pattern was seen in Germany a few years later, when unification came not at the hands of revolutionaries, but under the leadership of the archconservative, Otto von Bismarck (1815–1898). Perhaps no one exemplified the new approach to nationalism better than Heinrich von Treitschke (1834–1896), a political theorist who believed that nations were bound by no universal moral restraints in their quest for independent statehood, and that the ensuing states were similarly entitled to use whatever means were necessary in pursuit of their expansionist goals. Nationalists such as Treitschke believed that nations were locked together in a struggle for survival, in which the winners would be those with the most discipline, unity, strength, and collective determination. The national interest had nothing to do with broad goals of peace, justice, or liberty—instead, the only concern for each nationalist was the welfare of his or her own nation. In this context, nationalism dovetailed with imperialism, helping to provide a justification for aggression both within Europe and in the colonial world.

Accompanying these developments in political theory came a wave of nationalization campaigns: programs (usually state-sponsored) to establish ethnolinguistic homogeneity where none had existed before. Eastern Europe provided some of the best-known examples: Hungary attempted to suppress the use of the Slovak, Romanian, Serbian, and Croatian languages; Germany tried to forcibly assimilate Poles; and the tsars attempted to spread the use of Russian to parts of the empire where it had not previously been widely spoken. While these campaigns were the most obvious, no less egregious were the much more successful programs to make France linguistically homogeneous (which it was not in the mid-nineteenth century), or to create a single Italian language for the new Italian

A young girl poses for a portrait holding an Italian flag, 1909. © ALINARI ARCHIVES/CORBIS

state. Late-nineteenth-century nationalists all over Europe came to recognize that the imagined cultural unity spoken of so glowingly earlier in the century did not, in fact, exist. Peasants in particular were notorious for their lack of "national consciousness," but the problem (for nationalists do tend to perceive cultural diversity as a problem) was not limited to isolated rural areas. In nearly all the towns of central and eastern Europe different communities lived side by side, and bilingualism was common. In these settings, national activists had to exert a great deal of energy to polarize the cultural and political atmosphere, and force people to pick the group to which they wished to belong.

The late nineteenth and early twentieth centuries, then, were marked by concerted efforts on the part of both state officials and opposition activists to "nationalize" the masses. They succeeded for a number of reasons, not least of which was the way in which competing national groups generated a climate of struggle in which each side agreed on one basic point: victory for one would mean defeat for the other. The collective hatreds that exploded during World War I and the tenuous system of "nation-states" created in Europe afterward demonstrated how successful the previous decades of "nation-building" had been. Later in the twentieth century the rhetoric of nationalism would be appropriated by anticolonial movements all over the world, appearing in a wide variety of iterations and transposing itself onto a diverse array of political conflicts. Observers have repeatedly prophesied the end of the age of nationalism, but the post–Cold War era has provided many new examples of the continued potency of national thinking, both in Europe and throughout the world.

THEORIES OF NATIONALISM

The scholarship on nationalism stood for decades in the shadow of two towering mid-twentieth-century authors: Carlton J. H. Hayes and Hans Kohn. They introduced two basic themes that persisted for many years. First, both scholars drew a distinction between a good nationalism marked by civic inclusion and a benign love of one's country, and a bad nationalism marked by aggression, cultural chauvinism, and racism. This dichotomy reproduced itself over the years in both chronological and typological schemes, even among those who claimed to eschew explicit moral assessments. Kohn himself literally mapped out these two types of nationalism, locating the good nationalism in "the West" (which for him meant France, Britain, and the United States), and the bad nationalism in "the East" (which started in Germany in his presentation). A strict spatial embodiment of nationalism's Janus face has been repeatedly debunked: the rhetoric of civil inclusion in "the West" has often been used to conceal cultural exclusion, and there are plenty of examples of "Eastern" republicanism. Nonetheless, the basic dichotomy, cast in less stark terms, persists to this day.

The second enduring element introduced by Hayes and Kohn was the way they plotted nationalism's history over time. Kohn traced the evolution of "the idea of nationalism" from the ancient Israelites to the Enlightenment, but characterized this long history as a prelude to the birth of "modern nationalism" around the time of the French Revolution. Hayes offered a slightly different narrative, but the general scheme was similar: in both cases, the emergence of national thinking was an integral part of modernity. For Hayes, Kohn, and countless historians of nationalism to follow, the nation has appeared as the primary means of organizing collectivities in the modern world, supplanting earlier forms of community and polity (first in Europe, then throughout the world).

The first historians of nationalism told this story within the genre of intellectual history, focusing on the ideologues of national and nationalist thought. Eventually this approach was challenged by social scientists who tried to explain modern nationalism by linking it to broad forces of social change. Nationalism was taken out of the realm of ideas and grounded in seemingly more concrete social dynamics (industrialization, urbanization, and the corresponding transformations of political consciousness). This approach dominated the scholarship on nationalism from the 1960s to the 1980s. Perhaps the most important moment for the historiography of nationalism came in 1983. In an extraordinary congruence of scholarly energy, three seminal texts appeared in that year: Benedict Anderson's *Imagined Communities,* Ernest Gellner's *Nations and Nationalism,* and Eric J. Hobsbawm and Terence Ranger's *The Invention of Tradition.* The English-language translation of Miroslav Hroch's *Social Preconditions of National Revival in Europe* appeared two years later, and together these four books reframed the scholarly discussion of nationalism for years to come. Gellner and Hroch spelled out theories explaining the mechanisms by which the social changes of modernization could generate new forms of self-awareness and a new politics of nationalism; Anderson, Hobsbawm, and Ranger, without actually challenging these sociological arguments, began focusing on the ways in which nationalists constructed the very nations they claimed to serve. Anderson's famous title purported to depict nations (all large-scale communities, for that matter) as "imagined," and Hobsbawm and Ranger characterized tradition as something "invented." These two loaded words alone were enough to spark debates about the degree to which nations were (or were not) grounded in enduring social formations. Anthony D. Smith, for example, responded by insisting that a nation could emerge only if an ethnic community was already in place. But as is so often the case with academic debates, the heat of the polemical exchanges obscured the broad consensus that linked most scholars of nationalism in the 1980s. Smith never questioned that modernization provided the solvents that converted ethnic groups into nations, and Anderson, Hobsbawm, and the others never really claimed that nations were as ephemeral as such terms as *invented* and *imagined* might imply. In fact, the class of 1983 grounded the process of "invention" firmly within inexorable social forces, making their nations as "real" as any social formation could possibly be. The nations described in these books are indeed created, but the agent of creation is History (with a very teleological capital *H*). They are imagined and invented only in the sense that they are rooted in a mutable historical narrative rather than an immutable natural order. Even though few serious scholars of the early twenty-first century would claim that national identity is hardwired into the human psyche, it becomes no less "real" for being historicized.

If the novelty of that batch of scholarship has been somewhat overstated, the more profound changes that came in the 1990s may have been underappreciated. Historians are still coming to terms with the much-discussed "cultural turn" that swept the discipline at that time. One unambiguously positive result has been to expand the scholarly field of vision to include aspects of the past that once escaped attention. The study of popular culture in particular has blossomed, with fascinating implications for historical understanding of national thinking. If nothing else, the focus on "culture" (indeed, the very attempt to define that elusive term) has helped to transcend the old, increasingly sterile tensions between intellectual and social history. But perhaps most profoundly, the "cultural turn" has transformed the study of nationalism by inspiring scholars to give renewed attention to the way historical narratives themselves contribute to the construction and maintenance of nations. The historiographical tradition that has been developed to understand (mainly European) nationalism has itself served the agenda of nationalism, both by naturalizing national communities and by obscuring a whole range of alternative forms of subjectivity, many of which are every bit as important in the "modern" world as national belonging. In the view of nationalists (and most of the scholars who studied them), "History" was necessarily marching forward into a world in which the nation-state was the natural, inevitable, and ultimately desirable means of structuring society and expressing popular will. Other forms of subjectivity—whether tribal or familial on the microcosmic scale, or imperial or religious on the macrocosmic scale—were relegated to subordinate positions, or scheduled for elimination altogether. A myriad of alternative ways of structuring society were silenced as being unnational, and thus unnatural, and a political framework developed under specific conditions in Europe was described as a universal historical destiny.

Nations were always said to be "emerging," "awakening," "becoming," "resurrecting," "growing," and even "dying." They are nearly always portrayed as historically dynamic, and nearly always tied to some scheme of historical progress. It is by critically focusing on nationalist historiography that one truly penetrates to the core of what it means to "be national." Adjectives such as "Italian" or "American" or "German" or "Irish" are never just sociological descriptions: they are understood to exist within a specific understanding of historical progress. Only by questioning that understanding, by revealing it as an ideological and cultural construction, can one fully perceive how national thought works. Scholars are starting to get beyond the assumption that *with time* the ideology of nationalism must necessarily move in a certain direction, and that theorists of the nation must cope in predictable ways with predictable historical developments. In fact, the study of nationalism has moved away from the macrotheorizing of sociologists and political scientists, and since the mid-1990s the historian's attention to context and contingency has returned to the forefront. Few scholars today attempt to spin grand "theories of nationalism" that claim to predict the rise and eventual fall of national thinking; instead, today's most exciting scholarship tends to employ a tighter focus on the ways specific individuals and communities use national categories to advance their own specific goals and understand their own specific circumstances.

See also **Bismarck, Otto von; Conservatism; Endecja; Franco-Prussian War; French Revolution; Leipzig, Battle of; Levée en Masse; Liberalism; Mazzini, Giuseppe; Napoleon; Republicanism; Risorgimento (Italian Unification); Socialism.**

BIBLIOGRAPHY

Primary Sources

Fichte, Johann Gottlieb. *Addresses to the German Nation.* Translated by R.F. Jones and G.H. Turnbull. Edited by George Armstrong Kelly. New York, 1968.

Herder, Johann Gottfried von. *Philosophical Writings.* Translated by Michael N. Forster. Cambridge, U.K., 2002.

Mazzini, Giuseppe. *The Duties of Man and Other Essays.* Translated by Thomas Jones. London, 1955.

Rousseau, Jean-Jacques. *The Social Contract.* Translated by G. D. H. Cole. Amherst, N.Y., 1988.

Treitschke, Heinrich von. *Politics.* Translated by Blanche Dugdale and Torben de Bille. New York, 1916.

Secondary Sources

Anderson, Benedict. *Imagined Communities: Reflections of the Origin and Spread of Nationalism.* London, 1983.

Armstrong, John A. *Nations before Nationalism.* Chapel Hill, N.C., 1982.

Breuilly, John. *Nationalism and the State.* 2nd ed. Manchester, U.K., 1993.

Brubaker, Rogers. *Nationalism Reframed: Nationhood and the National Question in the New Europe.* Cambridge, U.K., 1996.

Chatterjee, Partha. *The Nation and Its Fragments: Colonial and Postcolonial Histories.* Princeton, N.J., 1993.

Colley, Linda. *Britons: Forging the Nation, 1707–1837.* New Haven, Conn., 1992.

Duara, Prasenjit. *Rescuing History from the Nation: Questioning Narratives of Modern China.* Chicago, 1995.

Eley, Geoff, and Ronald Grigor Suny, eds. *Becoming National: A Reader.* New York, 1996.

Gellner, Ernest. *Nations and Nationalism.* Oxford, U.K., 1983.

Hayes, Carlton J. H. *The Historical Evolution of Modern Nationalism.* New York, 1931.

Hobsbawm, Eric J. *Nations and Nationalism since 1780: Programme, Myth, Reality.* Cambridge, U.K., 1990.

Hobsbawm, Eric J., and Terence Ranger, eds. *The Invention of Tradition.* Cambridge, U.K., 1983.

Hroch, Miroslav. *Social Preconditions of National Revival in Europe: A Comparative Analysis of the Social Composition of Patriotic Groups among the Smaller European Nations.* Translated by Ben Fowkes. Cambridge, U.K., 1985.

King, Jeremy. *Budweisers into Czechs and Germans: A Local History of Bohemian Politics, 1848–1948.* Princeton, N.J., 2002.

Kohn, Hans. *The Idea of Nationalism: A Study in Its Origins and Background.* New York, 1944.

Mosse, George L. *The Nationalization of the Masses: Political Symbolism and Mass Movements in Germany from the Napoleonic Wars through the Third Reich.* New York, 1975.

———. *Nationalism and Sexuality: Respectability and Abnormal Sexuality in Modern Europe.* New York, 1985.

Porter, Brian. *When Nationalism Began to Hate: Imagining Modern Politics in Nineteenth Century Poland.* New York, 2000.

Smith, Anthony D. *The Ethnic Origins of Nations.* Oxford, U.K., 1986.

Verdery, Katherine. *National Ideology under Socialism: Identity and Cultural Politics in Ceauşescu's Romania.* Berkeley, Calif., 1991.

Weber, Eugen. *Peasants into Frenchmen: The Modernization of Rural France, 1870–1914.* Stanford, Calif., 1976.

Brian Porter

NATURALISM.

See **Realism and Naturalism.**

NAVAL RIVALRY (ANGLO-GERMAN).

In 1889, the year before his retirement, German chancellor Otto von Bismarck called the British navy "the greatest factor for peace in Europe" (Beresford, vol. 2, p. 363). Just eight years later, upon his appointment as secretary of state in the Imperial Navy Office, Rear Admiral Alfred Tirpitz characterized Britain as Germany's "most dangerous enemy . . . against which we most urgently require a certain measure of naval force as a political power factor" (Steinberg, p. 126).

THE TIRPITZ PLAN

With general Anglo-German tensions rising, Tirpitz's Anglophobia appealed to Emperor William II (r. 1888–1918), who endorsed his fleet program of nineteen high-seas battleships, eight coastal battleships, twelve large cruisers, and thirty small cruisers, to be built at a cost of 58 million marks per year over seven years (1898–1905). The funding came in March 1898 when the Reichstag passed the First Navy Law by a vote of 212 to 139, with 46 abstentions; most of the Catholic Center Party joined the Conservative and National Liberal parties in the majority. Twelve of Tirpitz's nineteen battleships were existing vessels, one as small as 5,200 tons. His eight coastal battleships, 3,500 tons apiece, likewise were already in service. The twelve large cruisers included ten built or being built, some displacing just 5,700 tons. The debate over Tirpitz's first navy bill focused on the new warships it required (a 30 percent increase in the existing fleet), overlooking a provision for the automatic replacement of the warships in the plan: battleships after twenty-five years, large cruisers after twenty, and smaller cruisers after fifteen.

Further tensions stemming from the Anglo-Boer War (1899–1902) and the Boxer Rebellion (1900) helped Tirpitz secure passage of the Second Navy Law of June 1900, which increased the fleet plan to thirty-eight battleships (including the eight existing coastal battleships, counted as full-sized battleships for replacement purposes) and fourteen large and thirty-eight small cruisers. This further triumph solidified Tirpitz's reputation as Imperial Germany's most successful political figure aside from Bismarck. William II showered him with honors, including elevation to the nobility and promotion to full admiral, ignoring the negative impact of the program on Germany's international position. At the time of the First Navy Law Britain had been isolated, but in less than a decade the German naval threat had helped drive the British into the Triple Entente with France and Russia.

Tirpitz had thirty-seven of his thirty-eight battleships and all fourteen large cruisers built or under construction by 1906, when the Reichstag passed a supplementary law increasing the number of large cruisers to twenty. By this time it had become clear that the automatic replacement clauses of the navy laws would assure that a future, more left-wing Reichstag could not undo Tirpitz's grand design, a crucial factor given the long-standing trend of the Social Democratic Party (SPD) making gains in every German national election. The SPD faced a dilemma in opposing naval expansion, which provided tens of thousands of industrial jobs for its constituents, but consistently voted against every navy bill. By guaranteeing the size of the fleet, the Reichstag gave the navy the right to replace smaller old ships with larger new ships, because designs naturally had to reflect the international norm at the time the ships came due for replacement. Fortunately for Tirpitz, the oldest battleships counted in his 1898 plan reached the end of their prescribed service lives shortly after the British navy, under the direction of Admiral John Fisher (first sea lord, 1904–1910), revolutionized the construction of larger warships by building the 18,110-ton battleship HMS *Dreadnought* and a trio of hybrid battleship-cruisers, or "battle cruisers," of similar size. The German navy subsequently replaced four old 7,600-ton battleships with the four 18,900-ton dreadnoughts of the Nassau class, and their eight 3,500-ton coast defense battleships with dreadnoughts of the 22,800-ton Helgoland class and 24,700-ton Kaiser class. Eventually a cruiser of 5,700 tons was replaced by the 27,000-ton battle cruiser *Hindenburg*.

THE GREAT NAVAL RACE

The commissioning of the *Dreadnought* in December 1906 rendered all smaller and older armored warships obsolete. Fisher's dreadnought and battle cruiser designs raised the technological bar for Tirpitz's challenge but at the same time presented the Germans with an opportunity, as the British had negated their own considerable advantage in pre-dreadnought types. By the time Germany's *Nassau* entered service in October 1909, Britain already had commissioned its first five dreadnoughts and three battle cruisers. Thereafter, a supplementary navy law passed by the Reichstag in 1908 enabled Germany to close the gap under an accelerated timetable of construction of dreadnoughts and battle cruisers (or "capital ships," as the two types together became known). Meanwhile, the Liberal majority in Parliament approved just two capital ships in the naval estimates for 1908–1909, giving Britain twelve built or being built to Germany's ten. At that pace Tirpitz could achieve much better than the 3:2 ratio of inferiority that he felt would give the German fleet a chance of defeating the British in the North Sea.

The accelerated pace of German naval construction understandably alarmed the British. The same Liberal Parliament that had approved just two capital ships for 1908–1909 authorized eight for 1909–1910, four of which were to be canceled should Germany agree to negotiate an end to the naval race. As of April 1909 Britain was willing to accept a 60 percent capital ship superiority over Germany. At that time, however, Tirpitz was willing to concede only a 4:3 ratio of British superiority. By May 1910 Britain had laid down all eight new capital ships, designs that ensured a qualitative as well as quantitative advantage. The dreadnoughts of the Orion class and two Lion class battle cruisers had 13.5-inch guns rather than the 12-inch guns of the most recent British and German dreadnoughts, and the Lions would be capable of a remarkable speed of 27 knots (compared to the original *Dreadnought*'s 21 knots). In June 1910 work began on another two battle cruisers, the *Australia* and *New Zealand,* paid for by those dominions.

During the same months in 1909 and 1910 when the British laid down these ten new capital ships, the Germans started work on just three, and thus fell behind in the race by twenty-two to thirteen. Tirpitz had assumed all along that he could push the British to a point beyond which they would not or could not maintain their lead. Recognizing his grave miscalculation, in 1911 he offered to accept a 3:2 (15:10) British advantage in capital ships, close to Britain's goal of a 60 percent (16:10) advantage, as long as the British included in their total the *Australia,* the *New Zealand,* and any other ships funded by the British Empire. Meanwhile, following Tirpitz's earlier logic that a strong fleet would be a "political power factor" supporting German diplomacy, Chancellor Theobald von Bethmann Hollweg attempted to wreck the Anglo-French Entente by demanding British recognition of the territorial status quo in Europe (including a German Alsace-Lorraine) in exchange for German recognition of British naval superiority. The British found such terms unacceptable, and the race continued. In 1910–1911 and again in 1911–1912, the Germans laid down four capital ships and the British countered with five. Following an unsuccessful mission to Berlin in February 1912 by the British secretary for war, Richard Haldane, the recently appointed first lord of the admiralty, Winston Churchill, proposed a mutual one-year "naval holiday." Churchill's dismissive characterization of the German navy as a "luxury" fleet reflected his true sentiments, however, and in March 1912 the Reichstag responded by giving Tirpitz a third supplementary navy law adding three dreadnoughts to the numbers previously approved, raising the authorized strength of the German fleet to sixty-one capital ships (forty-one dreadnoughts and twenty battle cruisers).

CONCLUSION

The supplementary navy law of 1912 was Tirpitz's last triumph, as the navy had grown to consume over a third of Germany's total defense budget. While funding a dramatic expansion of the German army in 1913, the Reichstag authorized just five new capital ships for the period from 1912 to 1914. In the same two years, Parliament funded nine new dreadnoughts, and a tenth, the *Malaya,* was funded by that British colony. Five of the ten were of the 27,500-ton Queen Elizabeth class, the first British capital ships with 15-inch guns, and the first battleships fitted to burn oil only.

The increasing size, speed, and firepower of warships naturally drove up their cost. The British had built the *Dreadnought* for just under £1.73 million, but the *Queen Elizabeth,* begun seven years later, cost just over £2.68 million. On the German side, the *Nassau* had been built for just under 37 million marks, whereas the *Hindenburg,* completed eight years later, cost 59 million, 1 million more than the total cost of the sixteen new warships built in the years 1898 to 1905 under the First Navy Law. At the end of July 1914, Britain had twenty-nine capital ships in service and thirteen under construction, while Germany had eighteen in service and eight under construction. The British advantage, slightly better than 3:2, would suffice to keep the German fleet in port for most of World War I. After his naval program helped lead Germany into a war it could not win, Tirpitz contributed to the ultimate disaster by advocating unrestricted submarine warfare once the fighting began.

See also **Dreadnought; Germany; Great Britain; Imperialism.**

BIBLIOGRAPHY

Beresford, Charles William de la Poer. *The Memoirs of Admiral Lord Charles Beresford.* 2 vols. Boston, 1914.

Berghahn, Volker R. *Der Tirpitz-Plan: Genesis und Verfall einer innenpolitischen Krisenstrategie unter Wilhelm II.* Düsseldorf, 1971.

Herwig, Holger H. *"Luxury" Fleet: The Imperial German Navy, 1888–1918.* Rev. ed. London, 1987.

Lambert, Nicholas A. *Sir John Fisher's Naval Revolution.* Columbia, S.C., 1999.

Marder, Arthur J. *From the Dreadnought to Scapa Flow: The Royal Navy in the Fisher Era, 1904–1919.* 5 vols. London, 1961–1970.

Sondhaus, Lawrence. *Preparing for Weltpolitik: German Sea Power before the Tirpitz Era*. Annapolis, Md., 1997.

Steinberg, Jonathan. *Yesterday's Deterrent: Tirpitz and the Birth of the German Battle Fleet*. London, 1965.

Sumida, Jon Tetsuro. *In Defence of Naval Supremacy: Finance, Technology, and British Naval Policy, 1889–1914*. Boston, 1989.

LAWRENCE SONDHAUS

NAVARINO. The pivotal event in the Greek War of Independence (1821–1832), the Battle of Navarino was in large part the result of misunderstandings at all levels. The battle occurred alongside the island of Sphacteria, site of a famous battle during the Peloponnesian War in the fifth century B.C.E.

Greek attempts to secure independence from the Ottoman Empire had coincided with attempts of Sultan Mahmud II to reform his quasi-medieval army, abolishing the Janissary Corps. Lacking a suitable military force the sultan had been forced to request aid from his over-mighty subject Mehmet Ali, the pasha of Egypt, in 1825. Mehmet dispatched his son, Ibrahim Pasha, with a powerful naval and military force, which rapidly turned the tide of the hitherto slow moving war in favor of the Ottomans.

The interests of the great powers had been sparked by religious and historical considerations. For many in the west, Greece was the cradle of western civilization, and should not be subject to Muslim tyranny. The Russians were less concerned with cultural antecedents; the Greeks were fellow Orthodox Christians. Amid the chaos and barbarism of an insurrectionary war the British government tried to keep control of the key issues, maritime trade and the balance of power. They wanted to end a conflict that had caused a serious outbreak of piracy in the Aegean, before it could spread. A three-party agreement with France and Russia was intended to impose a cordon on the belligerents, while preventing the other two powers from exploiting the conflict for their own advantage. The tripartite naval squadron, under the overall command of Trafalgar veteran Admiral Sir Edward Codrington in HMS *Asia,* comprised eleven battleships, nine frigates, and a few smaller craft. Faced with piracy, intransigent allies, uncertain orders, and a powerful foe Codrington might have been forgiven for doing nothing. Instead he was prepared to use force to cordon off the belligerents and impose a settlement (all three admirals, "horrified by Ibrahim's atrocities" perpetrated against the local population, "stretched their neutrality in favor of the Greeks" [Woodhouse]). On 14 October his force arrived off Navarino Bay, with Admiral de Rigny commanding the French and Admiral Heiden the Russian squadrons. Inside the bay, Ibrahim's Turco-Egyptian amphibious task force included three battleships, nineteen frigates, and another forty smaller warships, along with transports for his army. Codrington and de Rigny had already interviewed Ibrahim, who agreed not to act until he had received instructions from the sultan. However, the Greek fleet under Lord Cochrane was active, and Ibrahim attempted to put to sea in pursuit. The allies escorted his ships back into the bay. Information received by the fleets suggested the Egyptian forces were using scorched earth tactics, and depopulating parts of the Morea. Unable to hover outside the bay indefinitely Codrington led the fleet into the bay around midday on 20 October. The Muslim ships were drawn up in a deep crescent formation with their flanks supported by batteries, but they allowed the British ships to anchor inside their formation. With the tension on all sides at breaking point it was inevitable that the situation would explode. When HMS *Dartmouth* sent a boat to request that a Muslim fireship be moved the Turkish crew opened fire, killing an officer and several seamen. Firing quickly became general, with the French and then Russian fleets sailing in under fire from the shore batteries, coming to support the British. After some four hours the firing died away. The firepower of the allied fleets proved decisive: three-quarters of the Turco-Egyptian fleet had been sunk or burned. The allies lost 174 killed, and 475 wounded, nearly half of whom were British. The Muslim forces lost at least four thousand. Navarino was the last naval battle fought under sail, but it was hardly a contest.

While the British government referred to the battle as "an untoward event" (anxious not to destroy the Ottoman Empire), and dismissed Codrington, Navarino broke the political impasse surrounding the Greek question. Russia declared war on Turkey in April 1828, and Egypt left the conflict in August. Hard pressed by Russia, and fearful that his vassal would break away, the sultan had to concede Greek independence, which was secured by the Treaty of London in May 1832. Mehmet Ali, dissatisfied with Cyprus as his reward for services, conquered Syria, challenging the sultan. When France exploited the chaos to invade Algiers in 1830 it seemed the region was about to collapse, but domestic instability, and the exhaustion of the other parties, soon restored order. However, the threat of a breakaway Egyptian state allied to France remained real until the British Syrian campaign in 1840 returned Mehmet Ali to his original status, and restored the balance of power in the eastern Mediterranean.

See also **Greece; Ottoman Empire.**

BIBLIOGRAPHY

Bourchier, Lady. *Memoir of the Life of Admiral Sir Edward Codrington.* London, 1873.

Woodhouse, C. M. *The Battle of Navarino.* London, 1965.

ANDREW LAMBERT

NECHAYEV, SERGEI (1847–1882), Russian revolutionary.

Sergei Gennadiyevich Nechayev, prominent Russian radical, revolutionary, and apparent sociopath, was born in the provincial city of Ivanovo in 1847 into a family of very modest means. Best remembered for his shocking amorality in the name of a political cause and nicknamed "The Jacobin" for his fanatical devotion to inspiring revolution through violence, Nechayev developed a devoted following in radical circles largely on the basis of his extraordinary personal charisma.

Nechayev was an admirer of the populist theoretician Peter Tkachev, who advocated violent social revolution, and Nikolai Chernyshevsky, the philosopher whose novel *What Is to Be Done?* (1863) created the myth of the lonely, superhuman revolutionary dedicated solely to the cause of human welfare and progress. He was also influenced by the anarchism of Mikhail Bakunin and the uncompromising dedication to revolution by means of political assassination espoused by the Land and Liberty group.

The 1860s were a period of intense government censorship and widespread arrests of activists in Russia. In 1868, at the age of twenty-one, Nechayev first came into contact with St. Petersburg conspiratorial circles, which were dominated at that time by students, and quickly gained influence among young would-be revolutionaries in the capital city. Sought by the police, he fled to Geneva in March of the following year. It was in Geneva that he met and captivated both the famous Bakunin and his compatriot, Nikolai Ogarev. Nechayev greatly exaggerated the size of his following in Russia, leading Bakunin and Ogarev to see him as a future revolutionary leader, and they helped him obtain money and make contacts with radicals around Europe. In Geneva, the three of them created the "All-Russian Revolutionary Committee," an organization that existed in name only, to give stature to Nechayev among revolutionaries in Moscow and St. Petersburg. Bakunin lent his authority to this fiction by sending Nechayev back into Russia with a stamped certificate testifying to Nechayev's importance.

Nechayev was the primary author of the famous creed "The Catechism of a Revolutionary" (1869), written with Bakunin in Geneva. The catechism urged that, in order to spark a massive peasant revolution, society must first be undermined through the most ruthless and savage methods possible. Nechayev thought of the revolution as a moral movement for which anything, including political murder and blackmail, was justifiable in the interests of future society. "The revolutionary is a doomed man," the catechism opens; he must be ready for martyrdom at any moment in the pursuit of "merciless destruction." Because the common people would not revolt (and thereby achieve happiness) until they had reached the point of absolute misery, it was in the best interests of the people to do everything possible to hasten and accentuate their desperation. In fact, Nechayev took this thinking a step further, equating himself with the revolution and beginning to think of himself as a moral force.

In September 1869 Nechayev returned to Moscow and prepared to mobilize the population and his circle for revolution. Having persuaded his colleagues in Russia that he had developed a sizable following abroad (he had not), he formed a party he called "The People's Vengeance." This organization was secret, underground, and highly centralized.

Existing memoirs indicate that Nechayev lied extravagantly, even to his closest friends and political associates, and was extraordinarily skilled at manipulating others. Knowing that students' mail was read by the censors, he sent subversive literature from abroad to moderate students through the post, hoping to use police persecution to radicalize "liberal" students. In other cases, he tricked them into breaking the law, then blackmailed them into joining his organization. He would send people he distrusted on suicidal missions.

Nechayev wasted no time acting on his "Catechism," in the process creating one of the most infamous incidents in the history of the Russian revolutionary movement. Within two months of his return to Moscow, he had personally "sentenced to death" a certain Ivan Ivanov, a comrade in his organization who expressed doubts about Nechayev's qualifications and methods. With the cooperation of (and in the presence of) several colleagues in his party, Nechayev took his vengeance in the name of the movement, first strangling, then shooting Ivanov with his own hands. Apart from atoning for personal differences, Nechayev apparently killed Ivanov as a bit of political theater, to inspire his associates that the revolutionary ends always justified the means. The result instead was the destruction of his organization, as the police arrested its surviving members while they pursued Nechayev.

Fleeing once more to Europe in January 1870, Nechayev managed again to dominate the small, insular world of Russian political émigrés through the force of his personality and his capacity for mythmaking. He was ultimately captured by Swiss authorities in August 1872 and extradited to St. Petersburg. Nechayev's 1873 trial for murder was a major event, receiving international coverage and provoking outrage both at home and abroad. One of those who attended the trial was Fyodor Dostoyevsky, who immortalized the accused by basing the evil and vengeful character of Peter Verkhovensky in his novel *The Devils* on Nechayev. For conservatives and reactionaries, the figure of Nechayev represented the dangerous moral bankruptcy of the entire revolutionary movement, though in fact he occupied only an extremist fringe. Convicted, Nechayev spent over ten years in prison, where he continued to scheme against the government and plot revenge against his personal enemies, two impulses that were intertwined in Nechayev's mind. Imprisoned, but with his personal magnetism intact, he managed to convert several of his guards to the cause during his years behind bars. In November 1882 Nechayev died in St. Petersburg's Peter and Paul Fortress prison after an illness, still only thirty-five years old.

Nechayev became a hero to the terrorist wing of the populists, which similarly embraced political violence in the name of revolution. The 1881 murder of Tsar Alexander II by the People's Will can be seen in part as the fulfillment of his legacy. In the end, Nechayev represents a prototype of the charismatic, theatrical, but wholly cynical revolutionary, the type who will undertake every unscrupulous act to achieve his or her political and personal goals, and for whom the personal and political mix in a poisonous brew of violence and revenge.

See also **Alexander II; Bakunin, Mikhail; Dostoyevsky, Fyodor; People's Will; Populists; Zasulich, Vera.**

BIBLIOGRAPHY

Pomper, Philip. *Sergei Nechaev*. New Brunswick, N.J., 1979.

Venturi, Franco. *Roots of Revolution: A History of the Populist and Socialist Movements in Nineteenth Century Russia*. New York, 1966.

JAMES HEINZEN

NELSON, HORATIO (1758–1805), the British navy's most famous leader.

Horatio Nelson held the titles Vice Admiral of the White Squadron, Knight of the Bath, Baron and Viscount of the Nile and of Burnham Thorpe, and Duke of Brontë. He was arguably the greatest naval strategist and tactician that ever paced a deck, and in significant ways a farsighted innovator, moving considerably away from eighteenth-century tradition.

Son of an impoverished clergyman, Nelson began his naval career at age twelve. By age twenty-nine he had served in a variety of positions and stations, risen to the rank of captain, commanded five ships, and was married (to Frances

Nisbet). During the period from 1787 to 1793 he was relegated to inactive status in England; in 1793 he was given another command after war broke out with France. He began considerable Mediterranean service—including a 1794 land action at Calvi, Corsica, which resulted in the blinding of his right eye.

Made a commodore in 1796, he played a decisive role in Sir John Jervis's 1797 victory over the Spanish at Cape St. Vincent. Seizing the initiative, Nelson's unorthodox action—turning out of the line-of-battle and cutting off the Spanish second division—saved the day. After the battle he received a knighthood and, due to seniority, promotion to rear admiral.

Later in 1797, leading a bold attack at Santa Cruz de Tenerife, Canary Islands, a grapeshot shattered his right arm, and the British force was defeated. By the spring of 1798 Nelson had recovered, and with a small force he entered the Mediterranean to investigate unusual French activity centered in Toulon. Reinforced by ten additional ships, he spent several stressful weeks searching the Mediterranean for an enormous enemy force that had sortied undetected. Finally catching the French near the mouth of the Nile, he aggressively attacked their squadron of warships in Aboukir Bay. Nelson sustained a severe head wound, but the night battle annihilated the French (eleven of thirteen ships), establishing British control of the Mediterranean and effectively cutting off the expeditionary army of then-general Napoleon Bonaparte.

Nelson was made a baron and returned to Naples to support Neapolitan resistance to the French. He was made a Sicilian duke in 1799, but his overinvolvement in Neapolitan politics and an affair with Emma Hamilton, the British ambassador's wife, stand as the nadir of his career.

Recalled to Britain in 1800, Nelson advanced—by seniority—to vice admiral and was appointed to the Baltic Fleet under Sir Hyde Parker (1739–1807). Early in 1801, Lady Hamilton bore him a daughter (Horatia), and he effectively broke with Lady Nelson. Soon after, the Baltic Fleet sailed to counter the Russian-instigated League of Armed Neutrality. Without declaring war, the British struck at Copenhagen with Nelson leading the attack. Although the British were hotly resisted, Nelson's planning, tactics, and determination prevailed. The Danes agreed to an armistice, and Nelson was created a viscount. He then briefly commanded in British home waters, guarding against cross-Channel invasion, before demobilizing with the Treaty of Amiens (1802).

In 1803 Nelson was appointed Mediterranean Fleet commander-in-chief as France prepared for renewed war. His task was to prevent the fleet, commanded by Pierre-Charles-Jean-Baptiste-Silvestre de Villeneuve (1763–1806), from joining French Atlantic forces for an invasion of Britain. For two years Nelson contained the enemy, continuously trying to draw them into a decisive battle. After a fruitless chase to the West Indies and back, Nelson finally brought to battle the combined French and Spanish fleets, near Cape Trafalgar, on 21 October 1805. His captains had been thoroughly indoctrinated and knew his mind; he intended to force a "pell-mell" battle by breaking the enemy line from windward—a striking abandonment of traditional line-of-battle tactics. It resulted in a spectacular victory—nearly twenty ships taken. Nelson, however, was mortally wounded by a musket shot, and died shortly after hearing of success.

Famous in his lifetime, among the public as well as the navy, Nelson remains an almost mythical hero even today. At times extraordinarily vain and egotistic, and distracted by his scandalous relationship with Lady Hamilton, Nelson was nevertheless a great innovator and strategic genius. He was both a sound and an original thinker, possessing characteristic qualities of decision, resourcefulness, unshakable perseverance, brilliant tactical insight, and swift and audacious action—all combined with an all-consuming focus on victory. Although slight of stature, frequently seasick, and often otherwise ill, he was extremely courageous and remarkably tenacious—both physically and mentally. He alternately could be quite ruthless as well as notably kind.

The foundations for Nelson's successes were his boundless imagination and limitless attention to detail. As a flag officer, he spectacularly displayed uncommon abilities for both operational readiness and logistical legerdemain. As a leader, he was particularly charismatic and consistently inspired others by example. He was unusually willing to be pleased and routinely showered compliments and praise. Unquestionably these were root causes of the popularity, cooperation, inspiration, and devotion that he always found in—and from—his subordinates.

Moreover, his habit of sharing his thoughts and intentions with his captains, and the great latitude and initiative that he allowed and encouraged among subordinates, greatly enhanced the effectiveness of his plans. He thus brought about stunning results with a minimum of direct command and control and was largely responsible for bringing about the British naval supremacy that lasted nearly a century.

See also **Congress of Vienna; French Revolutionary Wars and Napoleonic Wars; Metternich, Clemens von; Napoleonic Empire; Prussia; Restoration.**

BIBLIOGRAPHY

Forester, C. S. *Lord Nelson.* Indianapolis, Ind., 1929. Reprint, Safety Harbor, Fla., 2001.

Hayward, Joel. *For God and Glory: Lord Nelson and His Way of War.* Annapolis, Md., 2003.

Hibbert, Christopher. *Nelson: A Personal History.* Reading, Mass., 1994.

Oman, Carola. *Nelson.* New York, 1946. Reprint, Annapolis, Md., 1996.

Pocock, Tom. *Horatio Nelson.* London, 1988.

STEVEN E. MAFFEO

NETHERLANDS. In 1780 the Netherlands was still a republic. Since the Dutch revolt—the struggle for independence against Spain in the sixteenth century—the Netherlands consisted of seven almost independent provinces. The province of Holland, which covered the western part of the Netherlands, was the most prosperous and powerful. Although Holland was already urbanized to an unusual degree, Amsterdam was by far the largest city; about a tenth of the two million inhabitants of the republic lived there.

In the 1780s the republic fell into a political crisis, which was a sign of fundamental changes to come. By 1920 the population had grown to about seven million. Amsterdam was the capital and still the center of culture and colonial trade, but thanks to the German hinterland the city of Rotterdam had become the main port, and The Hague had turned into the center of government, civil servants, and diplomats. The divided republic had been replaced first by a unitary state (1798) and then by a constitutional monarchy (1813–1815 and 1848) with general male and female suffrage (1917 and 1919), and the country was developing into a modern industrialized society. Although these changes could be pictured as growth, the development was sometimes dramatic, sometimes slow, and for most of this period the Dutch felt they had to fight degeneration. The culture of the eighteenth and a large part of the nineteenth centuries was still dominated by the hope to return to the great golden age of the seventeenth century. Until the 1780s when it was surpassed by Great Britain, the republic had been the richest country in the world. It was only around 1900, when a new and rapid economic development had set in, that the intellectual elite decided that the country would perhaps never regain its former power but had instead turned into a moral guide in international relations.

1780–1848

In the 1780s the conflicts between the supporters of the Orange stadtholder, the captain of the army and the most important political figure, and the party of the Patriots developed into something resembling civil war. The Patriots used a new enlightened conception of citizenship and civil society to accuse the political establishment surrounding Prince William V of Orange, the stadtholder, of doing nothing to stop the economic and moral decay of the republic. In 1787 the Patriots were beaten, and until the advent of the French revolutionary army in 1795 the Orange Party ruled supreme. French intervention resulted in the adoption of the first constitution of the Netherlands, in 1798, the beginning of a truly unitary state. The period of first the Batavian Republic (1795–1806), then the satellite kingdom under Louis-Napoleon Bonaparte (1806–1810), and finally the annexation by Napoleon's empire (1810–1813), was one of political innovation, but also, especially at the end, economic decay and misery.

When the French departed in 1813, the Dutch looked back in horror at the turmoil they had experienced. Even people who had welcomed the political innovations with great enthusiasm were now convinced that the country needed rest. They cheered the son of William V, who became King William I of the United Kingdom of the Netherlands and Belgium (1815). This was not the end of the bewildering number of political changes. In 1830 Catholic, industrializing Belgium, with its French-speaking elite, broke away from the Netherlands with its Protestant elite, whose wealth had always been based on trade. King William I, who dominated politics and has been characterized as a competent, sober, and hard-working civil servant, wanted to hold on to the large United Kingdom. When he finally accepted the independence of Belgium (1839), this failure was probably the real reason why he abdicated in favor of his son William II in 1840.

In 1848 a revision of the constitution, inspired by the liberal leader Johan Rudolf Thorbecke, one of the most important political leaders in modern Dutch history, introduced direct suffrage for a minority and ministerial responsibility. This marked the end of a long period of unrest stimulated by international developments. It was also a sign that the enlightened civic culture, which in the first decades of the nineteenth century had turned into an inward looking and timid nationalism (Biedermeier style instead of Romanticism), was opening up. After the trauma of the period around 1800 the Dutch slowly began to get used to political conflicts again.

1848–1870

King William I had ruled with a constitution, but he dominated politics and had vigorously stimulated the economy and the digging of canals. He had not encouraged the development of modern politics or a modern, liberal economy. The Netherlands still had to cope with some problems of the past, the most famous being the slow development of a modern railway system (started in the 1830s but reaching completion only around 1870), due mainly to the system of canals and barges that had provided the republic with an efficient system of public transport. The development of industry was partly thwarted by the dominance of agriculture, which had for a long time been producing for national and international markets. It was not until the 1860s and 1870s that industrialization started to take off, and only in the 1890s did large industrial companies really begin to spread. It took some time, then, before the political changes introduced in 1848 began to influence the society.

Dutch liberalism of the third quarter of the nineteenth century presented itself as a movement of the future, but its conceptions of separation of state and society and of the well-educated citizen in fact presupposed a stable society dominated by a more or less traditional upper middle class and by a homogeneous bourgeois culture. The Netherlands was still a country of small towns with limited mobility, and it was not until the last quarter of the century that the pace of change really quickened. Until that time politics concentrated on constitutional issues, such as the role of the king and the relation between government and parliament. It was not until 1868 that the rule that the government needed the trust of a parliamentary majority was firmly established. This occurred after a series of conflicts that further reduced the role of the king. Colonial policy was one of the bones of contention. The Dutch colony of Indonesia (the Dutch East Indies) was one of the richest in the world. King William I had introduced a system of partly forced production of colonial goods by the Indonesian population, which provided the Dutch government with enormous sums of money, amounting to 50 percent of national tax revenues in the 1850s. This gave liberal governments the means to reduce taxes, but in the 1860s a conflict arose with another liberal ideal, free trade. Colonial politics had been very profitable for the government, but it allowed for only a very limited role for the private entrepreneur. Left liberals now began to push for free trade and succeeded in abolishing the forced cultivation of sugar and opening the colony for private enterprise.

The change in colonial policy in fact marked the beginning of modern Dutch imperialism. The Dutch presence in Indonesia had been mainly confined to the main island of Java but now began to spread throughout the archipelago. Entrepreneurs earned large incomes by producing tobacco, and later by exploring for petroleum. Dutch rule provoked resistance, resulting in a prolonged guerilla war (1873–1903) in fiercely independent Aceh, part of the island of Sumatra. But it also made a

A canal in Amsterdam, late nineteenth century. © MICHAEL MASLAN HISTORIC PHOTOGRAPHS/CORBIS

real impact, for instance in the fields of education and infrastructure (from 1901 this was called "ethical politics"). This was the colonial counterpart of the important changes Dutch politics and society went through around the turn of the century.

1870–1914

The liberals of 1848 had thought that progress would result in the spread of a liberal culture. In this respect the main duty of politics was to remove obstacles to future development. Around 1870 a new generation of liberals argued that the liberals had achieved a victory in constitutional matters but now had to build a new society. The most important weapon in the struggle for progress was education. In 1878 the liberal leader Johannes Kappeyne van de Coppello introduced a new law to increase the quality of primary education. By introducing new standards, but still restricting subsidies to state-funded schools, the law in fact hindered the development of privately funded denominational education. This was in line with the ideal of a liberal society, but it reinforced denominational resistance against liberal politics.

The Netherlands was a country of minorities. Although the tone of public life was Protestant, and the Dutch Reformed Church was the most important church, there was no state church and there were several varieties of Protestantism: liberal and orthodox members of the main church, a number of small dissident churches, and since 1834 a breakaway orthodox church. In addition, there was a large Catholic minority of about one-third of the population and a small Jewish minority. Religion still dominated public life to a large extent, and it was the public issue the population at large cared about the most. Once infrastructural change and the abolishing of the stamp duty on newspapers allowed leaders to reach their potential adherents by train or newspaper, orthodox Protestants in particular began to manifest themselves. The Protestant morality that still pervaded liberalism was not enough; Protestant religion had to be the basis of politics. In 1879 the charismatic clergyman, politician, and brilliant journalist Abraham Kuyper founded a Neo-Calvinist party, called the Antirevolutionaire Partij because it resented the allegedly liberal principles of the French Revolution. This was the first modern political party in the Netherlands, formed even a few years earlier than the first socialist party (the Sociaal-Democratische Bond, founded in 1882, followed in 1894 by the Sociaal-Democratische Arbeiderspartij, which accepted parliamentary politics), which elsewhere in Europe often was the first modern party. Its foundation implied that many orthodox Protestants now realized that they were a minority that had to organize itself in order to achieve its goals. Its main goal was full subsidy of orthodox Protestant primary schools. Catholics, who at first had supported the liberals in order to gain religious freedom, now became allies of the orthodox Protestants in their fight for denominational education. In 1888 this alliance won the elections, and Catholics and orthodox Protestants formed a government that introduced a new law that allowed for partial subsidy of denominational primary education (1889).

The Antirevolutionaire Partij was not only the first modern political party, but it also became the nucleus of a moral community that was much larger than the party alone. It included orthodox Protestant primary schools, a new reformed church (1886), newspapers, the Free University of Amsterdam (1880), and trade unions. At the end of this development, during the interwar period, it was possible to live in an orthodox Protestant community almost from cradle to grave. In due course this system also emerged among Catholics, who at first had not felt the need to organize because most of them lived in the almost homogeneously Catholic southern part of the country, where the orthodox Protestants were a clear minority. Socialists also partly adopted the system, and the introduction of general suffrage and proportional representation in 1917 and 1919 confirmed the existence of a number of more or less stable blocs: something over a third of the vote was Catholic, a quarter orthodox Protestant, almost the same percentage voted socialist, and the rest were either liberals of some sort (most of them also liberal Protestants) or members of small minority parties.

Although the first signs of all these changes began to appear in the 1860s, the conservative and liberal elite was particularly shaken by the developments of the 1880s. This was a decade of economic, especially agricultural, crisis, and the forceful manifestation of the minorities made the impression that the country was falling apart. This provoked nationalist sentiments. The birthday of the young queen, Wilhelmina (r. 1890–1948), developed into the national holiday Queen's Day, Indonesia was a source of national pride, and the South African Boer War (1899–1902) led to a wave of nationalism. The Boers were partly of Dutch descent and were regarded as relatives, a bit primitive perhaps, but also pure and heroic.

In the eyes of the establishment, bourgeois culture also seemed to be falling apart. Until the 1880s no bohemia had existed in the Netherlands, Romanticism was not strong, and moral and patriotic feeling were an important part of literature and the arts. In 1885 a new review was founded, the *Nieuwe Gids* (New guide). This was a reaction to the *Gids,* which had, since its founding in 1837, developed into the review of the political and cultural liberal establishment. The *Nieuwe Gids* propagated *l'art pour l'art* (art for art's sake) and was influenced by French naturalism. The bohemian Amsterdam circle of the *Nieuwe Gids* contained not only poets and novelists but also painters and other artists. Since the establishment of the *Nieuwe Gids,* the history of Dutch literature has been divided into the period before and after the Tachtigers (movement of the 1880s).

The *Nieuwe Gids* advocated radical individualism in art, and this could be regarded as the culmination of the new dynamics of Dutch society (also symbolized by the advent of the bicycle: after a slow start, already one in four inhabitants owned a bike by 1924). But these changes did not result in an individualist society. The emerging new blocs of orthodox Protestants, Catholics, and socialists all advocated emancipation, but group emancipation. A small cultural elite may have shaken off moralism in the arts, but in politics and society it was reinvented with a vengeance. The left liberal government of 1897 to 1901 was called the government of social justice and introduced social legislation on a relatively large scale for the first time. This was based on a new idea of citizenship. The liberals of 1848 had thought that only the educated independent bourgeoisie would qualify for the vote, but the left or social liberals now assumed that (almost) everybody had a right to the vote (in 1896 the suffrage was broadened) and that politics had the duty to educate the people and provide some social legislation in order to make them fit for democracy. Citizenship was a moral conception that was shared by all political blocs. Whether orthodox Protestant, Catholic, socialist, or liberal, they all thought that the individual should be educated to serve the community; modern citizens should be responsible citizens, an idea that cherished the virtue of self-restraint. The women's movement agreed and, besides a campaign for the vote, stressed the motherly qualities of women. No lax morals, no gambling, no excessive drinking—that was the message of all moral communities. The message was surprisingly successful. The percentage of extramarital births fell to about 2 percent around 1920 (compared to percentages at least four times as high in France and Germany), and the consumption of pure alcohol fell from 7 liters (7.4 quarts) per capita in the 1870s to 3 liters (3.2 quarts) in 1930. Apparently many emancipating members of the Catholic, Protestant, and socialist communities considered it their duty and also to be in their best interest to behave as responsible citizens.

See also **Amsterdam; Belgium; Colonialism; Imperialism.**

BIBLIOGRAPHY

Aerts, Remieg, Herman de Liagre Böhl, Piet de Rooy, and Henk te Velde. *Land van kleine gebaren: Een politieke geschiedenis van Nederland, 1780–1990.* Nijmegen, Netherlands, 1999.

Bank, Jan, Maarten van Buuren, Marianne Braun, and Douwe Draaisma. *Dutch Culture in a European Perspective.* Vol. 3: *1900: The Age of Bourgeois Culture.* Assen, Netherlands, 2004.

Kloek, Joost, Wijnand Mijnhardt, and Eveline Koolhaas-Grosfeld. *Dutch Culture in a European Perspective.* Vol. 2: *1800: Blueprints for a National Community.* Assen, Netherlands, 2004.

Kossmann, E. H. *The Low Countries, 1780–1940.* Oxford, U.K., 1978.

Wintle, Michael. *An Economic and Social History of the Netherlands, 1800–1920: Demographic, Economic, and Social Transition.* Cambridge, U.K., 2000.

Zanden, Jan Luiten van, and Arthur van Riel. *The Strictures of Inheritance: The Dutch Economy in the Nineteenth Century.* Translated by Ian Cressie. Princeton, N.J., 2004.

HENK TE VELDE

NEWMAN, JOHN HENRY (1801–1890),

British theologian, Victorian prose writer, Roman Catholic convert, and cardinal.

Born in London into a conventional Church of England family, John Henry Newman entered Trinity College, Oxford, in 1817, shortly after a conversion to evangelicalism. This conviction was eventually undermined by the liberal, rationalist atmosphere he encountered at Oriel College, where he was elected fellow in April 1822.

Newman took holy orders in the Church of England and in 1824 was ordained deacon. In 1825 he became a priest and was appointed curate at St. Clements, in east Oxford. Newman's religiously liberal tendencies dissipated by 1828 as his admiration attached to the works of the early church fathers. He became vicar of the university church of St. Mary's in 1828.

On 9 September 1833, Newman anonymously penned an article on the doctrine of the apostolic succession for *Tracts of the Times,* a theologically reformist periodical that he edited. His article was known as Tract 1 (*Ad clerum*), the first of twenty-four tracts he would contribute. Tractarianism, also known as the Oxford Movement, originated in 1833 under Newman's organizational and intellectual leadership as an informal High Church movement that stressed the ancient, Catholic elements in the English religious tradition and sought to return the Church of England to its seventeenth-century ideals. Newman assailed religious liberalism, defended the dogmatic authority of the church, criticized state interference in church affairs, and encouraged reticence and humility in the face of the divine mystery.

In March 1834 the first volume of Newman's *Parochial and Plain Sermons* was published. These sermons were almost as important to the Oxford Movement as the controversial Tracts, which were themselves bestsellers.

In his *Lectures on the Prophetical Office of the Church* (1837), Newman presented the English church as "reformed" but also Catholic, occupying a via media (middle way) between Protestantism and Roman Catholicism that better resembled primitive Christianity. By 1839, however, Newman began to see the Anglican via media as inconsistent and unreal.

On 27 February 1841 he published Tract 90, which aroused immediate controversy for its suggestion that the Thirty-Nine Articles of the Church of England could bear a Catholic interpretation. Richard Bagot, bishop of Oxford, requested an end to the Tracts. Newman complied, but the condemnations issued by Anglican bishops against Tract 90 alienated him further from the Anglican Church.

In the summer of 1841, while translating the Arian Controversy in the work of St. Athanasius, Newman decided that doctrinal truth historically lay with the with Roman papacy.

Newman sent parts of his uncompleted "Essay on the Development of Christian Doctrine" to the printers in late September 1845. In it, he claimed Catholicism as the only form of Christianity with a continual development guaranteed by authority. Modern Catholicism, unlike Protestantism, constituted for him the historical continuation of early Christianity.

On 9 October he was received into the Roman Catholic Church. He was ordained a Catholic priest on 30 May 1847 and in 1848 he helped to set up the Birmingham Oratory, a community of secular priests who combined pastoral duties with intellectual work.

In November 1851, Newman was appointed the president of a new Catholic university to be created in Ireland. In 1852 he delivered five of the *Discourses on the Scope and Nature of University Education,* which became the first half of *The Idea of a University* (1873). In these lectures Newman defended the idea of a liberal education in a sectarian institution and denied any inherent tensions between theology and science.

Newman opened the university on 3 November 1854 to about twenty students, but eventually found it impossible to be both provost of the Birmingham Oratory and rector of the ill-attended university. He resigned from the latter in 1857.

In 1864, Newman was challenged to defend the authenticity of his life as an Anglican. He explained his conversion to Protestants with a stirring autobiography, *Apologia pro vita sua* (A defense of his life, 1864). Its last chapter argued for the church's infallibility but was partly directed at catholic ultramontanes (exponents of centralized papal power), against whom he urged a moderate theology. The book became a bestseller, won broad critical praise, and secured Newman's financial stability for the first time since his conversion.

In 1870 he published an influential book of theology, *An Essay in Aid of a Grammar of Assent,* which argued that faith can possess certainty when it arises from evidence that is only probable.

In 1879 Newman was made a cardinal by Pope Leo XIII (r. 1878–1903). On 11 August 1890 he died at the Birmingham Oratory. He was buried in the grave of his friend Ambrose St. John at the Oratory country house at Rednal, outside Birmingham.

See also **Catholicism; Manning, Henry.**

BIBLIOGRAPHY

Chadwick, Owen. *Newman.* Oxford, U.K., 1983.

Ker, Ian T. *John Henry Newman: A Biography.* Oxford, U.K., 1988.

Martin, Brian. *John Henry Newman: His Life and Work.* London, 1982.

Newsome, David. *Convert Cardinals: John Henry Newman and Henry Edward Manning.* London, 1993.

Turner, Frank M. *John Henry Newman: The Challenge to Evangelical Religion.* New Haven, Conn., 2002.

STEPHEN VELLA

NEW ZEALAND. Possibly no country underwent greater change than did New Zealand between 1789 and 1914. A stone-age Polynesian society dependent on subsistence horticulture and hunter-gathering, inclined to ritual cannibalism of defeated enemies and long isolated from the outside world, was superseded by a society that was European in composition, culture, and aspiration, and the country's politics, economics, and appearance were transformed.

DEMOGRAPHY

Driving the transformation was demographic change. The size of the Maori population in 1789 cannot be determined precisely, but may have been around one hundred thousand. No Europeans resided among the Maori, though some soon began percolating into the country from the British penal colony established on the Australian continent the previous year. Others came in search of seals and whales, setting up rough settlements. Some of these transient occupants stayed on, joined from 1814 by small groups of missionaries primarily from the United Kingdom. Small European settlements emerged, especially in the Bay of Islands in the far north of the North Island and along the southern coasts of the South Island. Intermarriage and cohabitation of European men and Maori women was not uncommon, taking the hard edge from the racial divide.

From 1839, when there were up to 2,000 Europeans residing in the country, large numbers of permanent settlers began to arrive from Europe, colonization schemes providing impetus. By the late 1850s, the European population equaled that of Maori, and gold rushes would bring a further huge influx in the following decade. Then, from 1870, a large-scale immigration program further submerged the indigenous inhabitants. The imbalance increased as Maori, demoralized by the dislocation of their society, stricken by diseases against which they had little resistance, and increasingly marginalized economically, declined in numbers. With their population down to forty-two thousand in 1891, some were predicting their extinction; by 1914, however, a revival had begun.

In 1914, most of New Zealand's 1.1 million inhabitants had originated in the United Kingdom, mainly from England and, initially, Scotland, later Ireland. But small groups of settlers from other parts of Europe had established themselves in parts of the country—French at Akaroa, Germans in the Manawatu, Danes and Norwegians in southern Hawke's Bay, and later Dalmatians in the far north. Chinese, who arrived to work the goldfields, comprised another small minority.

POLITICS

Demographic change went hand in hand with political transformation. In 1789, Maori lived in kinship-based tribal communities (*hapu*) often in conflict with each other over land, *utu* (reciprocity), or *mana* (status) issues; no unifying sense of Maori nationalism existed. European influences exacerbated the anarchic state of the country, as the introduction of European technology, especially the musket, greatly increased the lethality of intertribal warfare in the early nineteenth century. More than twenty thousand Maori are estimated to have perished in these Musket Wars, in which small numbers of Europeans took part. Only in the 1830s did the scale of the fighting die down, as a rough balance emerged among the decimated, dislocated, and demoralized tribes.

War weariness among Maori contributed to the establishment of British authority in New Zealand, as did growing lawlessness among European residents. The influence of missionaries and a desire to preempt France helped persuade the British government to establish British sovereignty over New Zealand in 1840. In the North Island at least, an indication of Maori consent was considered necessary, and was achieved in the form of the Treaty of Waitangi, signed by some, but not all, tribal leaders on 6 February 1840 and afterward.

Initially an outlier of the Colony of New South Wales, New Zealand became a Crown Colony in its own right in 1841. Governors headed a rudimentary administration, but the settlers wasted little time in seeking self-government. They gained control of internal government in 1853. The Westminster-style system instituted in the colony had at its apex a bicameral parliament comprising an elected house of representatives and an appointed legislative council. However, with the main European settlements centered on ports separated from each other by rugged, Maori-controlled terrain, a less centralized form of government was demanded. Provincial governments in six (later ten) provinces oversaw developments in their respective areas until 1876. Elections to the house of representatives were based on manhood suffrage from 1879 (superseding a property qualification that did not exclude Maori); Maori had been accorded manhood suffrage in electing Maori representatives for four reserved seats twelve years earlier. New Zealand, in 1893, became the first state to introduce female suffrage, though not yet the right of women to sit in Parliament. From the 1890s, political parties dominated Parliament.

The growing settler domination of the incipient state did not go unchallenged by the indigenous inhabitants. Controversy over settler land acquisition fanned Maori resentment. Armed resistance to European political dominance in the far north had been overcome relatively easily by imperial troops in the years 1845 and 1846, but a more serious confrontation developed in the 1850s with the emergence of a movement to create a Maori king. Although ostensibly sparked by land issues, the fighting in the central part of the North Island in the following decade represented an attempt to reverse the process of Europeanization of the country. Imperial troops defeated the "King movement" in 1864, confining the rebels to a large informal reservation, the "King Country," in the central North Island, which eventually broke down. Later, colonial governments battled further rebellious elements, with considerable support from some Maori tribes; for many of these *kupapa* ("loyalist") Maori, the opportunity to extract *utu* for pre-1840 depredations proved more influential than any sense of pan-Maori nationalism. Confiscations of land arising from these events would leave a lasting sense of grievance.

The containment of the Maori challenge in these New Zealand wars—fighting had died away in the early 1870s—ensured the continued development of a European political community in New Zealand. Later in the century, an external challenge to settler sovereignty arose when New Zealand was invited to join the six Australian colonies in creating an Australasian federation. In eschewing this opportunity, New Zealand chose the path of continued political independence over that of subordination to the Australian-dominated federal government established in 1901. Differences in outlook based on differing historical experience, the perceived disadvantages of the 1,200-mile sea-gap, the lack of immediate economic advantages for a country with firmly established markets in the United Kingdom, and the determination of politicians, especially New Zealand Prime Minister Richard John Seddon (1845–1906, in office 1893 to 1906, and with colonial governor and later politician Sir George Grey [1812–1898] and Sir Julius Vogel [1835–1899], one of the three colossi to bestride New Zealand pre-1914 politics), not to be relegated to a secondary role—all played their part in New Zealand's decision to go it alone.

ECONOMIC TRANSFORMATION

Economic change between 1789 and 1914 matched political change. Maori had subsisted on horticulture (in the north), mainly of the *kumara* (sweet potato), supplemented by hunting and fishing. There was little intertribal trade in anything but obsidian. Early European activity in New Zealand was extractive, confined mainly to seals, whales, kauri spars (for naval vessels), and flax. Although the prospect of obtaining agricultural land drew settlers from the United Kingdom in the late 1830s—several colonization schemes were developed—it was another extractive activity, gold mining, that boosted the colony's economy in the 1860s. As the gold boom faded, farming of animals introduced from Europe (via Australia)—sheep and cows—dominated the economy. The export of wool to the United Kingdom became the main source of national income. This pastoral farming was characterized by large holdings.

Initially New Zealand's developing economy had been closely linked to those of the Australian colonies. But technological change, especially the development of steamships and refrigeration, allowed New Zealand to participate in the European economy, albeit narrowly focused on the United Kingdom. The first shipment of frozen meat from New Zealand to the United Kingdom, in 1882, opened a market for meat and, by providing an outlet for a hitherto unusable product, transformed sheep farming. The ability to sell dairy products—butter and cheese—in the British market had a similar effect on dairy farming. In making small farms more economical, these developments had important implications for the nature of landowning in the country, and contributed to the breakup of the large pastoral estates that had dominated the early economy. The proportion of New Zealand's trade going to the Australian colonies declined as New Zealand became "Britain's South Seas farm"; by 1914, 81 percent of New Zealand's exports went to the United Kingdom. The new trade in meat and dairy products led to the development of light industrial infrastructure throughout the country, especially meat processing plants and cheese factories.

Economic change went hand in hand with environmental change. Pre-1789 Maori had significantly altered New Zealand landscape with fire, but the central North Island remained heavily forested. The clearance of this area transformed New Zealand in the late nineteenth century. A pasture-based landscape emerged. At the same time, a transport infrastructure developed. A main trunk railway connected South Island cities by 1879, and Auckland and Wellington in 1908. The countryside took on a more European appearance with the planting of European flora and, detrimentally, the introduction of animals from Europe that would rapidly become economically destructive pests, especially rabbits.

In 1789, the largest concentrations of population lay in the far north. The *kainga* (village) was the primary form of settlement. With the arrival of significant numbers of Europeans, towns developed, initially at ports. Although the gold rush ensured Dunedin's preeminence between 1865 and 1881, the North Island's population exceeded that of the South Island by the end of the century; by 1914 it was drawing ahead as immigration and internal relocation altered the country's demographic profile. Auckland became the country's largest city (with 114,000 residents in 1914). It had also been the capital until 1865, when the seat of government shifted to Wellington. A third of New Zealanders in 1914 lived in the four main centers—Christchurch was the fourth—and, with those living in smaller townships, almost half the inhabitants of New Zealand were urban dwellers.

CULTURAL CHANGE

Supplanted and marginalized between 1789 and 1914, Maori tribal culture survived, minus cannibalism (which had lingered on into the 1860s), in more remote parts of the North Island. Although at first European settlers had to adapt to Maori culture, demographic change soon ensured the preeminence of European ideas, values, and mores. To differentiate themselves from Australian or British cousins, European New Zealanders acknowledged Maori culture in minor ways and called themselves "Maorilanders," but the dominant culture of the country had its roots on the other side of the globe.

Most New Zealanders in 1914 identified strongly with the British Empire. Direct kinship ties between New Zealanders and Britons played a major part, as did the lack of any strong sense of grievance against the "mother country" among the mainly British settlers. From the 1880s, self-interest reinforced sentiment. New Zealanders grew conscious of their economic dependence on the British market—and on the security of the sea-lanes to the United Kingdom. Growing challenges to British sea power, hitherto taken for granted by the settlers, awakened doubts, as did the emergence of an Asian naval power, Japan (notwithstanding the Anglo-Japanese Alliance of 1902). The South African (or Boer) War (1899–1902) tightened imperial ties: ten contingents of New Zealand troops helped defeat the Boer republics as jingoist feelings ran high at home.

In 1907, proclamation as a self-governing dominion enhanced New Zealand's status within the empire. It looked to strengthen the imperial framework, politically through some form of imperial federation, militarily by increasing the ability of the dominions to contribute to the empire's military capacity. Although the former made no headway, from 1909 New Zealand reorganized its armed forces the better to assist in imperial defense. When George V (r. 1910–1936) declared war on the German Empire on 4 August 1914, New Zealand had the means, and the desire, to participate wholeheartedly in a major European war. An 8,000-man force left Wellington in October 1914, bound for the Western Front, which it would reach in 1916 only after participating in the ill-fated Gallipoli campaign. Earlier New Zealand troops had occupied German Samoa at British request, fulfilling a long-standing but hitherto frustrated ambition.

See also **Australia; Canada; Colonialism; Colonies; Great Britain.**

BIBLIOGRAPHY

Belich, James. *Making Peoples: A History of the New Zealanders, from Polynesian Settlement to the End of the Nineteenth Century.* Auckland, New Zealand, 1996.

———. *Paradise Reforged: A History of the New Zealanders from the 1880s to the Year 2000.* Auckland, New Zealand, 2001.

King, Michael. *The Penguin History of New Zealand.* Auckland, New Zealand, 2003.

McKinnon, Malcolm, ed. *The New Zealand Historical Atlas.* Auckland, New Zealand, 1997.

Ian C. McGibbon

NICHOLAS I (1796–1855; ruled 1825–1855), emperor of Russia.

Nicholas Pavlovich Romanov ascended Russia's throne in 1825 and immediately faced revolution and danger. Confusion about the succession, combined with revolutionary sentiment fanned by the wars against Napoleon I and Alexander I's repression of dissent in the last decade of his reign, led to the Decembrist revolt upon Alexander's death. The Decembrists' purposes were confused and their revolt ill-organized and lacking substantial popular support. It occurred because Nicholas had not expected to succeed Alexander, thinking that his elder brother, Constantine, was the legal and rightful heir. He was unaware that Constantine had refused his inheritance and that Alexander had sanctioned this illegal deviation from the normal line of succession. Nicholas was as surprised as anyone when he found that he was to be Russia's next tsar.

He moved quickly to crush the Decembrists, continuing a policy that dated as far back as Catherine the Great (r. 1762–1796) of using Russian power to quell revolutions within the empire and throughout Europe. He sent many of the revolutionaries into exile and executed a handful. Nicholas was shocked by the rebellion, which had sprung from the heart of the elite young nobility, the guards regiments. He emerged from the experience with a renewed determination to fight the hydra of revolution wherever it emerged.

NEAR-CONSTANT WARFARE IN EARLY REIGN

Nicholas I spent the next five years almost constantly at war, first with Persia (1826–1828), then with Turkey (1829–1829), and finally against a massive Polish uprising (1830–1831). The struggle with Persia resulted mainly from the shah's opportunistic attempt to take advantage of obvious weakness in the Russian court in order to restore the balance in the Caucasus, tipped in Russia's favor by Alexander I's wars with Turkey and Persia. Once the shah realized that Nicholas was master in his own house and able to respond to the threat, hostilities petered out.

The Russo-Turkish War resulted from continuing Russian efforts to maintain the Russo-Turkish relationship on a desirable footing. Nicholas considered and explicitly rejected seizing the Turkish straits, but he needed to ensure that the Ottoman sultan would remain subservient to Russia in order to protect the enormous volume of Russian trade that passed through them. The sultan, for his part, felt obliged to assert his independence of his larger neighbor to the north, and he declared a jihad against Russia.

The first campaign in 1828 went poorly for the Russians. Inadequate Russian forces met unexpectedly strong Turkish resistance in the Danubian fortresses. By the following year, Nicholas and his advisors had developed a better plan that swept the Turks back to Adrianople, where they made peace. The flaws in the original planning process and the conduct of the campaign persuaded Nicholas to begin thinking about a large-scale reform of the entire Russian military administration. The experience of the Polish rebellion strengthened that impetus.

The Polish revolt of 1830 was an extension of the revolutions that wracked Europe generally in that year. In fact, it interrupted Russian preparations to send an auxiliary army to help suppress revolution in western Europe; the troops were used to suppress the Poles instead. The complexities and scale of the rebellion made its suppression difficult. Nicholas continually feared, moreover, that his problems would attract the hostile intervention of Britain or even France on behalf of the Poles, as he had feared Austrian intervention on behalf of the Turks in the previous conflict. As a result, he was more determined than ever at the end of the rebellion to reform his military, which he did in the years 1832 to 1836. This reform destroyed a nascent general staff system and replaced it with the system that still organizes the Russian military in the early twenty-first century, built around a powerful War Ministry to which even the military commanders were subordinate.

Nicholas's reforms had the same goal as his repressions: to strengthen the Russian state against the threat of revolution. The military reforms were therefore aimed as much at saving money as at improving military efficiency, for Nicholas assumed power of a state on the verge of bankruptcy. Alexander had inflated the currency and Russia's debt to pay for the wars against Napoleon and the maintenance thereafter of a vast army of more than eight hundred thousand. Nicholas added to the debt with his wars and continued to maintain a large army because he felt threatened by the rise of hostile liberalism in France and Britain and by revolution at home and abroad. The state's penury had a baleful effect on the army and navy in this period, however, as both services were starved for resources with which to train and buy equipment.

REVOLUTIONS OF 1848 AND CRIMEAN WAR

Nicholas continued to wage active war against revolution in his own states and abroad throughout his reign. When the Hungarians revolted against their Habsburg masters in 1848, Nicholas sent a contingent of 150,000 Russian soldiers to help the Austrians suppress the rebellion. He also greatly strengthened the apparatus of repression in his own lands, building the dreaded "Third Section" of His Majesty's Own Chancery into an effective organ for maintaining surveillance on the empire's intellectuals, and increasing the efficiency and severity of censorship dramatically. In 1849 his fear of domestic revolution led to the arrest, on charges of conspiracy against the state, of a number of Russian intellectuals, the so-called Petrashevsky Circle, most of whose members, in truth, probably posed no real danger to Nicholas's power. Under the doctrine of Official Nationality Nicholas attempted to maintain and increase the primacy of Orthodox Christianity, autocracy, and Russian nationalism as a way of unifying the state against the revolutionary danger.

In a sense, Nicholas had been right all along to fear revolution, for it was the Revolution of 1848 that ultimately brought to power Louis-Napoleon Bonaparte, who as French emperor Napoleon III (after 1852), eager for foreign adventure, provoked the crisis that led to the Crimean War (1853–1856). Nicholas would have preferred, as usual, to manage Turkey without attacking or destroying the Ottoman Empire, but Anglo-French support of the Turks led to conflict. The Russians would mobilize more than 2.3 million men in the course of the war—the largest army ever assembled in Europe to that date. The fear of Franco-British landings along Russia's enormous coastline, together with logistical difficulties, however, meant that only a fraction of that force ever saw action. Russia's navy, atrophied and corrupted by Nicholas's disdain for it, was unable to defend the Crimea or to support amphibious operations against the Turkish straits. Russia's penury and the vastness of its army, finally, had prevented Nicholas from purchasing the new rifled muskets for his force that the French and the British now had and from building useful railroads with which to support operations in the Crimea. Despite a far-from-brilliant military performance by the allies, therefore, the Russians were unable to hold Sevastopol or the Crimea. Nicholas died in 1855 with the war going very badly, and his successor, Alexander II, found himself obliged to make peace because of the impending bankruptcy of the state.

See also **Alexander II; Crimean War; Russia; Russo-Turkish War.**

BIBLIOGRAPHY

Kagan, Frederick W. *The Military Reforms of Nicholas I: The Origins of the Modern Russian Army.* New York, 1999.

Lincoln, W. Bruce. *Nicholas I: Emperor and Autocrat of All the Russias.* Bloomington, Ind., 1978. Reprint, DeKalb, Ill., 1989.

Riasanovsky, Nicholas V. *Nicholas I and Official Nationality in Russia, 1825–1855.* Berkeley and Los Angeles, 1959.

FREDERICK W. KAGAN

NICHOLAS II (1868–1918; ruled 1894–1917), emperor of Russia.

Nicholas II ruled the Russian Empire from November 1894 until his abdication during the February Revolution in 1917. He came to the throne at the age of twenty-six, after his father, Alexander III, died prematurely of nephritis. Nicholas's mother, Maria Fyodorovna (née Dagmar, daughter of King Christian IX of

Denmark), lived until 1928. In November 1894 Nicholas married Alexandra Fyodorovna (née Alix of Darmstadt-Hesse). She bore him four daughters—Olga, Tatiana, Maria, and Anastasia—before the birth of a male heir, Alexei, in 1904. Like many of his cousins—related through Queen Victoria's offspring—Alexei suffered from hemophilia.

Courteous and sensitive, Nicholas inherited his parents' devotion to family and a love for outdoor recreation. From his father and teachers—including the archconservative Konstantin P. Pobedonostsev—he acquired an unshakable belief in autocratic rule. Nicholas lacked, however, Alexander's imposing stature and self-assurance. Notoriously indecisive, he also proved a dogged, and sometimes devious, defender of his prerogatives.

As preparation for his future duties, Nicholas received instruction in languages, law, history, and economics from tutors, government ministers, and scholars. There followed a carefree stint as a Guards officer in the late 1880s. In 1890 and 1891 he took a grand tour of Asia and Siberia. He then served an apprenticeship as chairman of state committees dealing with the Trans-Siberian Railroad and agrarian issues. Still, his parents and advisors doubted his readiness to rule, while Nicholas himself was "terrified" when he succeeded.

Nicholas II with his wife, Alexandra, 1894. ©HISTORICAL PICTURE ARCHIVES/CORBIS

In early 1895 Nicholas dismissed liberal calls for reform as "senseless dreams." He swore instead to maintain autocracy and his father's policies: censorship, restrictions on universities, Russification, institutionalized anti-Semitism, gentry dominance in the countryside, and restraint on the zemstvos (elective local government bodies). He supported Finance Minister Sergei Witte's industrialization program, partially funded by tariffs on an overburdened rural population, while engendering a working class with its own demands. By the period between 1900 and 1902, tensions multiplied. Within government, Nicholas undermined the powerful Witte, pitting him against Vyacheslav K. Plehve, the minister of internal affairs, in economic and agrarian policies. He removed Witte as minister in August 1903. Revolutionaries assassinated Plehve in 1904, as unrest mounted among peasants, workers, and students. That summer urban and gentry constitutionalists formed the Union of Liberation; in November, a zemstvo congress called for an elective legislature to control the bureaucracy.

Revolution erupted in 1905, following "Bloody Sunday" on 22 January (9 January, old style), when troops killed over two hundred peacefully demonstrating workers in St. Petersburg. Promises of reform throughout the spring and summer provoked peasant risings and urban strikes, revolutionary terrorism, ferment among national minorities, and liberal demands for a constitution. In a manifesto published on 30 October (17 October, O.S.) Nicholas "granted" civil liberties, religious tolerance, and an elective, legislative State Duma. The new legislature convened in May 1906; Nicholas dissolved it after six contentious weeks.

The revolution had gained strength during the disastrous Russo-Japanese War (1904–1905), which also weakened the empire's international position following a period of peace inaugurated by Alexander III. Under Nicholas, the recently concluded alliance with France was balanced by correct relations with William II's Germany. Agreements with Austria-Hungary in 1897 and 1903 guaranteed the Balkan status quo. Nicholas also sponsored international talks on disarmament in The Hague in 1899. China's decline and the rise of Meiji Japan, however, brought volatility to Asian affairs. In 1897 Russia seized Port Arthur from China, creating a southern terminus for the Trans-Siberian Railroad. After the Boxer Rebellion in 1900, Russia occupied much of Manchuria, prompting the Anglo-Japanese Alliance of 1902. Nicholas wavered between the caution urged by Witte and the assertive policy advocated by the courtier A. M. Bezobrazov. Confused negotiations led to a Japanese attack on Port Arthur in early 1904, followed by Russian defeats, notably at Mukden (March 1905) and the sea battle of Tsushima (May 1905). U.S. President Theodore Roosevelt brokered a humiliating peace at Portsmouth, New Hampshire, in September 1905.

In the spring of 1906 Nicholas appointed Peter Stolypin to restore order. As prime minister and minister of internal affairs, Stolypin dominated Russian politics until his assassination in September 1911. He attacked revolutionary activists and supported Russian dominance in multiethnic areas, while instituting a land reform to cultivate peasant loyalty. On 16 June (3 June, O.S.) 1907 Stolypin invoked emergency legislation to dissolve the Second Duma, reforming the franchise to secure a more amenable legislature. The Third Duma's centrist majority partnered with Stolypin to foster military renovation and economic recovery. Nicholas chafed at the 1905 regime and his charismatic premier.

After Stolypin's death, Nicholas populated his cabinet with conservatives who shared his suspicion of the legislature. Nicholas's new assertiveness also drew on demonstrations of affection from the Russian population during the dynasty's tercentenary in 1913. Nicholas saw these displays as popular support for the monarchy against forces of reform. He took a confrontational position against the Duma and supported militant monarchists. Such gestures, as well as the anti-Semitic trial of Mendel Beilis and the increasing visibility of the "holy man" Grigory Rasputin, eroded the dynasty's mystique. Recession and the violent suppression in 1912 of a strike in Siberia provoked renewed labor unrest, culminating by July 1914 in the largest strikes since 1905.

These challenges coincided with renewed international tensions. Defeat and revolution led Nicholas to seek peace abroad until Russia recovered from the Asian debacle. In 1907 Russia reached an entente with Great Britain on Asian issues, complementing an earlier Anglo-French rapprochement, forming a new combination in European diplomacy. Continued weakness forced Russia to stand by as instability overtook the Balkans. In 1908 revolution in Turkey facilitated Austria-Hungary's annexation of Bosnia-Herzegovina, despite Russian and Serbian protests. In 1912 and 1913 Russia proved unable to defend its Slavic protégés' gains in the Balkan Wars, while German and Austrian influence grew apace. By 1914, foreign minister S. D. Sazonov and others were urging Nicholas to defend Russia's great-power status. Nicholas heeded these arguments: In July 1914 he supported Serbia's rejection of an Austrian ultimatum following the assassination of Archduke Francis Ferdinand, the Habsburg heir, in Sarajevo. In early August, Nicholas led his deeply divided empire into World War I.

See also **Alexander III; Alexandra; Revolution of 1905 (Russia); Russo-Japanese War.**

BIBLIOGRAPHY

Primary Sources

Alexander Mikhailovich. *Once a Grand Duke.* New York, 1932.

Witte, Sergei. *The Memoirs of Count Witte.* Translated and edited by Sidney Harcave. Armonk, N.Y., 1990.

Secondary Sources

Lieven, D. C. B. *Nicholas II: Emperor of All the Russias.* London, 1993.

Verner, Andrew M. *The Crisis of Russian Autocracy: Nicholas II and the 1905 Revolution.* Princeton, N.J., 1990.

Warth, Robert D. *Nicholas II: The Life and Reign of Russia's Last Monarch.* Westport, Conn., 1997.

DAVID M. MCDONALD

NIETZSCHE, FRIEDRICH (1844–1900), German philosopher.

With his declaration that "God is dead" and his ideal of the superman, which in the 1930s dominated Nazi thought in Germany but also flew into the United States as the comic-strip figure "Man of Steel," Friedrich Nietzsche is probably the most recognizable modern philosopher. He celebrated the intoxicating "Dionysian" side of life expressed in myth, dance, and music; wandered the Swiss Alps; wrote compulsively in dingy hotel rooms; and finally, in 1889, went incurably mad at the age of forty-four at the sight of a man beating a horse on the streets of Turin, Italy. He had little intellectual influence in his lifetime: his "drama was played to a finish before empty seats," wrote the critic Stefan Zweig (p. 445). Yet after his death in 1900, Nietzsche emerged as one of the most influential philosophers in Europe, his thought deeply entwined in the political projects and intellectual debates of the twentieth century.

Readers took up Nietzsche's books because they were so unfamiliar and so wicked—one Swiss critic suggested placing the warning "Danger: dynamite" on Nietzsche's work. In his fragmentary pieces, Nietzsche blasted apart the conventions that regulated social interaction and mocked the public responsibilities of government. He wrote about gods with a passion his secular age found obsolescent. At a time when the certainty that the sciences would come to know the world went virtually unquestioned, Nietzsche held all systematic knowledge to be metaphorical, thus erroneous, and ultimately a matter of fancy. If the great nineteenth-century thinkers Charles Darwin, Karl Marx, and Sigmund Freud proposed valid laws drawn from the observation of the natural world to apply to human behavior, Nietzsche imagined new worlds of the mind that might still be inhabited. He conjured up an alter-ego Zarathustra who came down from the mountains to invite people to explore endless horizons and roilsome seas. No other major philosopher wrote like this and no other was so at odds with his time. While most nineteenth-century Europeans believed themselves to be at the pinnacle of progress, Nietzsche saw a dead-end.

Nietzsche repudiated the fundamental premises of liberalism and democracy, which sought to create more fair and equal forms of collective life. He thought that European societies had turned into sick rooms, good for caring for the weak but unable to live adventurously. The nineteenth century was particularly odious to him because its inhabitants had come to believe they lived in the very best, most comfortable, and most advanced period imaginable. Nietzsche loathed the puny ambition of modern politics that was to make people even more cozy. This ferocious attack on the present condition appealed to revolutionaries. However it was not socialists who picked up Nietzsche, but dissidents of a different kind who proliferated in the unsettled decades around 1900: conservatives who rejected democracy's enfranchisement of the masses, aristocrats who despised liberalism's reforming spirit, and nationalists, who envisioned a more heroic collective history. Nietzsche's most notorious political heirs were the Nazis, who in the 1930s frequently quoted Nietzsche (with the blessing of his sister, Elizabeth Förester-Nietzsche, the keeper of Nietzsche's papers) as they constructed the Third Reich and its hierarchies of racial superiors and racial inferiors. Nietzsche remains tainted with their violence and pitilessness.

What made Nietzsche so compelling was not simply his criticism of Western civilization but also his conviction that human beings could recover what made them human if they acknowledged their ability to remake themselves. He saw people as potential masters and lamented that they remained slaves. Nietzsche's most lasting influence was on those individuals who were willing to question received wisdom. In the fin-de-siècle period, he was avidly taken up by proponents of new lifestyles: anarchists, feminists, and atheists, the prophets of religious cults and the enthusiasts of physical culture, and most of all young people anxious to find a distinctive and vital voice for their generation. For the nineteenth century, which prized maturity rather than youth, foundations over questions, Nietzsche was particularly explosive, but his thought has beckoned all those on a journey. No other philosopher can claim such a wide readership.

"GOD IS DEAD"

At the center of Nietzsche's thought is his audacious statement "God is dead." Throughout his writings, he returned repeatedly to the theme that Christianity had corrupted human beings. For the last two thousand years, he argued, Western civilization had been humiliated by a God who had made sinners out of mortals. The only way for human beings to recover their full potential was to reject God and the stifling moralities imposed in his name. These ideas were very offensive to many readers. But they are the key to Nietzsche's philosophy because Nietzsche believed that it was humans who created moral systems, who invented supernatural powers and deities, and who therefore could get rid of God as easily as they had made him up. This conviction led Nietzsche to an even more radical proposition, which was that concepts and beliefs were simply imaginative descriptions of the world. There was no real world beyond our creative rendering of it. Nietzsche believed this insight to be extraordinarily liberating because it meant that humanity was not headed toward one single authoritative or true comprehension of reality but could endlessly conjure up different places. And just as it had fashioned Christianity in one audacious step two thousand years ago, it could invent something else with another step. What Nietzsche called his perspectivism basically corresponds to the relativism of postmodernism in the early twenty-first century, which also puts forward the idea that interactions with the world depend on descriptions of it. Twentieth-century philosophy is very much the product of and a response to Nietzsche's radical perspectivism and his defiant immoralism. His contention that there is no world outside the interpretations of the world continues to attract, astonish, and anger readers.

Nietzsche also enticed readers because he wrote in an utterly new way. He used words in order to jolt readers, to dynamite them out of their preconceptions. Precisely because Nietzsche believed that language was composed of common expressions that inhibited creative thought, he experimented with different and shocking ways of saying things. His hyperbole, in which people kill God, supermen are cruel, truth is error—all this is designed to shake assumptions loose from his readers; he claims to be "writing in blood" (quoted in Solomon, p. 24). Moreover, his images and metaphors restlessly change. Sometimes Nietzsche prefers to think with mountains, altitudes, and stairs; elsewhere he is in the desert with camels or dancing around statues. Among his favorite images are eyes, which blink or remain awake, and see and resee the world anew.

Friedrich Nietzsche. Undated portrait drawing. SNARK/ART RESOURCE, NY

This emphasis on eyes is much in keeping with Nietzsche's belief that human beings can only interact with the world they have interpreted and that they move on to new experiences by redescribing the world. His poetic and figurative uses of language all signal the fabricated, changeable, and fundamentally unstable nature of meanings.

The declaration that "God is dead" is a useful entryway into Nietzsche's ideas. It introduces his condemnation of Christian morality and the modern age, his perspectival theory of knowledge, and his quest for new mythical ways of living. It also recalls Nietzsche's personal background: Nietzsche's father and maternal grandfather were German pastors in the Kingdom of Saxony and Nietzsche very much remained a preacher's son. He impresses readers as a consequential thinker, one who put great stock in his own interpretation of texts and was highly suspicious of received wisdom and traditional authority, as Luther had been of Rome. He shared with his fellow Protestants the "extravagant belief in one's ability," and also the terror of doubt and skepticism (Aschheim, p. 22).

Born in the small town of Röcken, Saxony, in 1844, Friedrich Nietzsche acquired his atheism early, while still in high school. A brilliant, if unorthodox student of Greek philology at the university in Leipzig, Nietzsche won a university post in Basel, Switzerland, at the startlingly young age of twenty-five. The conformist atmosphere of the university left him unhappy, however, and soon enough Nietzsche abandoned his professorship, set off on his journeys, and wrote with difficulty but without rest the ten or so books that make up his work before his mental collapse early in 1889 and his death in 1900. The role of the gods is a central motif in each of Nietzsche's books, from *The Birth of Tragedy* (1872), to the highly personal *Thus Spoke Zarathustra* (1883), his most well-known text, through the powerful syntheses, *Beyond Good and Evil* (1886) and *On the Genealogy of Morals* (1887), and finally to his last autobiographical fragments in *Ecce Homo* (1889); his announcement of the death of God was first detonated in *The Gay Science*, published in 1882.

What does it mean for Nietzsche to say "God is dead"? The proposition is introduced in the parable "The madman" in *The Gay Science* and it surprises readers because it is different from the more familiar insistence "There is no God." "God is dead" implies that God was once alive. Moreover, the madmen goes on to explain the death of God: "we have killed him—you and I" (sec. 125). What is important for Nietzsche is not to debate whether there is or is not a God, but for people to see themselves as the murderers of God. Nietzsche wants to expose the murderers, not the victim; the momentous act of killing, not the mute result of a dead God. He wants the people to see themselves as murderers because that would enable them to see themselves as a people who can make and destroy God and thus a people who are strong and creative and have taken control of every aspect of their lives.

Nietzsche has nothing but scorn for those atheists who took the death of God to be an unveiling of the "real" material world and thus lived on as if God had never existed. Rather, Nietzsche wants to shake contemporaries so that they see themselves as people who are able to create gods and thus are strong enough to be fully human by giving form and meaning to the world. For Nietzsche, the truthfulness of truth is not important; the audacity to make truthlike statements and live by them is. What Nietzsche often refers to as the "decadence" of his age is knowing about the death of God without knowing oneself to be the murderer of God and the creator of all concepts and ideas about the world.

Given that the God who is now dead was once alive, Nietzsche attempts to reconstruct the history of God. He does this by means of a genealogical method that looks at the historical origins of belief. There is no otherworldly or metaphysical realm. "God is dead" thus leads Nietzsche to a dramatic theory of knowledge, which can be briefly described as perspectivism. Perspectivism does not make claims about truth; it exposes new and richer ways of thinking about the world based on looking at things in a different way. In Nietzsche's view, what separates humans from other animals is collective life in a society in which members must communicate in order to survive. In order to express themselves, humans developed common languages, and these languages in turn provided humans with the tools by which they could explore and know themselves. Without language there is no knowledge, and as a result, men and women only knew themselves through the words and concepts with which they named their feelings and described the world around them.

Across time and space, each group constituted its own language and its own myths. Each was a self-contained universe. There is no common or real world "out there" because there is always the irreducible presence of different cultures and languages that enable unique interpretations. According to Nietzsche, everything humans experience is comprehended and passed on in terms of the distinct vocabularies that the groups they belong to have fashioned. "What, then, is *truth*?" Nietzsche asks: "A mobile army of metaphors, metonyms, and anthromorphisms—in short, a sum of human relations, which have been enhanced, transposed, and embellished poetically and rhetorically" (quoted in Allison, p. 78). What this means is that there is no world aside from interpretations of it—"as though there would be a world left over once we subtracted the perspectival!" (quoted in Danto, p. 76).

SYSTEMS OF MORALITY

Nietzsche is dazzled by these audacious acts of creation. The infinite capacity for creativity is what makes human beings fully human. However, Nietzsche does not just want to propose an anthropological theory of knowledge; he wants to criticize the need for certainty which kept individuals in his own time from exploring new ways of thinking about the world, and he especially wants to attack Christian morality. To do this, Nietzsche distinguishes between two systems of morality, one characterized by the distinction between good and bad, which Nietzsche identifies with the Greeks and other ancient cultures, and the other characterized by the distinction between good and evil, for which western Christianity and nineteenth-century Europe are the primary examples. That the second system succeeded the first is an extraordinary example of creative transformation, something Nietzsche cherishes in a formal way. But this particular succession Nietzsche never ceases to condemn as a crime against the potentialities of men and women because it has produced the "slave morality" of the West.

In the ancient morality of good and bad what is good is what distinguishes humans from other animals: their ability to name the universe and their desire to play in the world they have created. Anything that expands the powers of men and women to feel masterful is good. By contrast, what is bad are those things that keep people from creating and re-creating the sense of mastery, everything that is ordinary, satisfied, and comfortable. What this distinction implies is that good and bad are not judgments on the intentions of protagonists but judgments on how well the actions of protagonists have enhanced what it might mean to be human.

It is ancient Greece that for Nietzsche best expresses the enhancement of life. The Greek city-states and particularly Athens had long been cherished by Europeans as the cradle of Western civilization, but Nietzsche loves them differently. He reveres exactly what distinguished Greece from the overarching authority of Christianity that followed: the sheer variety of Greek culture; the scale of emotional registers in Greek comedy and tragedy, and the polytheistic, many-sided relations the Greeks maintained with their gods. By inventing many gods, some who celebrated exuberant passion such as Dionysius and others who honored self-discipline such as Apollo, the Greeks developed "a plurality of norms." Polytheism invited experimentation by encouraging "the free-spiriting and many-spiriting of man" and by providing examples of "the strength to create for ourselves our own new eyes—and ever again new eyes that are even more our own" (Nietzsche, *Gay Science,* sec. 143). This wonderful sentence is a clear statement of what makes people distinctively human: the will to see things from fresh perspectives. Greek culture facilitated this; Christianity did not.

If the morality of good and bad cherishes mastery and experimentation, the morality of good and evil emphasizes virtue and charity. A fascinating parable in *Thus Spoke Zarathustra* gets to the heart of the matter. Zarathustra, the prophet through whom Nietzsche preferred to speak, strolled "over the great bridge" where at once "cripples and beggars surrounded him" (pp. 137–138). A hunchback offers Zarathustra the opportunity to "heal the blind and make the lame walk." But Zarathustra refuses to do so. He rejects pity because he believes that the victims have become what he calls "inverse cripples." Zarathustra explains, telling about his encounters with cripples who identifiy themselves completely with what they do not have. Rather than remain men, they have become the leg that they do not have, the eye that no longer sees, the belly that is not filled. Nietzsche is rather cruel (and funny) in the way he makes his point: "when I . . . crossed over this bridge for the first time I did not trust my eyes and looked again and again." What he saw was "an ear as big as a man." "The tremendous ear was attached to a small, thin stalk," legs, trunk, and arms. And "if one used a magnifying glass one could even recognize a tiny envious face." These are the horrible products of the morality of pity. Across the world, Zarathustra reports, he has walked "among men as among the fragments and limbs of men." For Nietzsche, the cripples and beggars who speak to Zarathustra only in terms of what they do not have are little more than the body pieces they lack. They see themselves only in the magnified reflection of their debility and they thus walk around the world as giant eyes or tremendous ears.

The transvaluation of good and bad into good and evil is accomplished when cripples and beggars see themselves as legs and bellies and convince society to make up the losses they have suffered. What Nietzsche describes in *The Genealogy of Morals* as the morality of the "sickroom" is fueled by the resentment of the have-nots and is designed to compensate them (third essay, sec. 14). It is important to remember that Nietzsche is not separating out the weak from the strong or the poor from the rich. Rather he is condemning the centrality that suffering plays in ideas about the meaning of life.

It was the early Christians who took the biggest step in codifying the morality of good and evil and speaking in the name of the victim. While Christians could not actually undo the misfortunes of life, they created a morality that valued the meek and powerless and demeaned the strong. By inventing the concept of sin, Christianity enabled the weak to take revenge on the strong, whose freely chosen lifestyle was now regarded as a contravention of God's will. Step by step, priests reined in the nobles with the convictions of sin, and the nobles in turn developed what Nietzsche calls a "bad conscience." Nietzsche provides striking images of the former master with a guilty conscience: "this deprived creature," "this animal that rubbed itself raw against the bars of its cage" (second essay, sec. 16). Christianity also extended the promise of a glorious afterlife to compensate for a lamentable this-worldly life. Henceforth, the promise of God's rewards justified the acceptance of God's punishments, with priests serving as accountants of God's moral balance sheets. A single, all-powerful God established a single moral law that was inscribed onto the tablets of monotheism.

The morality of good and evil was the singular achievement of the great monotheistic religions. Yet it is the very break that Christianity achieved, the world-historical difference it made, that actually gave Nietzsche confidence in his view of the world as a series of utterly innovative beginnings in which men and women create for themselves their "own new eyes." "From now on," he writes in the *Genealogy of Morals,* there can be no doubt, "man is *included* among the most unexpected and exciting lucky throws in the dice game of Heraclitus' 'great child,' be he called Zeus or chance." For all the pessimism with which Nietzsche regards Christianity, it is contained in a more sweeping optimism about the "great promise" of humankind (second essay, sec. 16). This is why Nietzsche wants people to see themselves as the murderers of God—so they will continue to play the game of dice.

Nietzsche is overwhelmed by the sheer staying power of Christian morality. He lauds the scientific spirit of Renaissance inquiry, if not the certainty it places in the answers it provides, and he grudgingly notes the value the Protestant Reformation placed in the individual interpretation of sacred texts, although not its insistence on humanity's sinfulness. But the big picture is the same: the slave morality of resentment remains pervasive in the present day, even as scientists and philosophers claim that they no longer believe in God. Even the Enlightenment is fundamentally misguided because it regards its insights into the natural world and human affairs as real knowledge not just different descriptions. Thus Nietzsche cannot accept the conceit of modernity, which is its certainty of its superiority over the cultures of the past and its cleverness in understanding nature. Precisely because modern Europeans are so sure that they are at the zenith of intellectual development they are completely unwilling to imagine themselves with "new eyes." This incomprehension of anything but what *is* constitutes modernity's biggest flaw. With this critique, Nietzsche stands out as one of the few thinkers of his age to think outside of the modernity ushered in by the Enlightenment, the French Revolution, and the scientific and industrial revolutions.

SUPERMAN

If most people blink, and accept the world around them, the true hero stays completely awake in order to gain new knowledge. This hero Nietzsche named the *Übermensch,* superman (or more accurately, but clumsily, overman). What is superman? For many of Nietzsche's twentieth-century readers, superman was a frightening figure, reminiscent of everything that is cruel and ruthless in life. But the superman is a deliberately hyperbolic designation conjured up by Nietzsche to push readers to ceaselessly examine the prescriptions of their lives. The most famous account of the superman comes in Nietzsche's work of prophecy, *Thus Spoke Zarathustra,* which he published in 1883. Nietzsche chose the figure Zarathustra to be his "son" who would speak his philosophy from Zoroaster, the Persian prophet in the sixth century B.C.E. who first introduced the morality of good and evil. If Zoroaster created "this most calamitious error," it would be Nietzsche's Zarathustra who would undo it.

The superman is not so much strong as unblinking. Again and again, Nietzsche moves the the discussion away from strength toward sightfulness, as he had with the cripples and beggars at the great bridge. It is not a particular victor, or identity, or outcome that interests Nietzsche, but the willingness to move away from the triumph of the winners, from someone else's description of yourself, and away from the comforts of home. This spur to new knowledge is what characterizes the free spirits.

The first step is to assume the role of the annihilator who breaks old tablets. Nietzsche wants his readers to see the commandments of morality broken up on the ground. Do not "act 'for your neighbor'" Zarathustra urges. "Plug up your ears" when you hear moral authority demand that you do things "'for' and 'in order' and 'because'" (pp. 290–291). There is something quite belligerent about this uncompromising annihilator, but he is twinned with a more sympathetic figure who appears repeatedly in *Zarathustra*. This is the dancer who takes many steps, joyously, playfully. "Yes, I recognize Zarathustra.... Does he not walk like a dancer" (p. 11), which is to say he moves "crookedly," without purpose, and thereby evades custom and common sense. The dancer's opposite is the statue, "stiff, stupid, and stony," a "column" in the temple of moral authority (p. 294). What dancing represents for Nietzsche is the defiance of the "spirit of gravity" (p. 41), the effort to escape the frozen identities of statues. The dancer is a wonderful way to capture the unceasing, constantly turning quest for new knowledge and new ways of looking at things. The dancer is Nietzsche in his most congenial form and he is what most strongly appealed to readers in the two decades before World War I. He offered dissidents justification for alternative lifestyles and different readings of the world, and he encouraged individuals to make an endless journey of self-discovery.

Nietzsche also repeatedly introduces a third figure, the child. This is a very different image because the child does not acquire knowledge, but wakes up in a world that it sees for the first time. This fresh view is the naive belief in belief and facilitates the acquisition of new myths and new gods. For Nietzsche's readers this opened up a new realm of political and spiritual possibilities and for Nietzsche's reputation it opened a Pandora's box of troubles because it seemed he sanctioned myth-making effort of any kind.

In Zarathustra's speech "on the three metamorphoses of the spirit," the first two are pretty clear. First the camel, an animal well-adapted to take up the burdens of truth-seeking in the desert, and second the lion, whose strong spirit can oppose the "thou shalt" with "I will" and do battle with the "last god," the god of monotheism. But "to create new values—that even the lion cannot do," Nietzsche observes. The task of creation is left to the child, for "the child is innocence and forgetting, a new beginning" (pp. 26–27). Unlike the camel and the lion, the child does not leave behind or fight what is old, but wakes up to a completely new reality without the memory of having abandoned an older version. With the metamorphoses into the child, the free spirit exists inside a new myth without the self-defeating knowledge that the universe is just something made up and thus still possesses the complete confidence of living vigorously.

Many late-twentieth and early-twenty-first-century commentators are not impressed with the innocent child. The objection is that the child does not and cannot have the difficult genealogical knowledge of the origins of morality and of the fundamentally fictional nature of describing and redescribing the universe and is thus not a satisfying incarnation of Nietzsche's ideas. According to the American philosopher Richard Rorty, with the spirit's final metamorphoses, Nietzsche has "fobbed us off with the suggestion" that the child will "have all the advantages of thought with none of the disadvantages of speaking some particular language" (p. 112). Rorty repeatedly asserts that Nietzsche is good for individuals to think through in order "to make the best selves for ourselves we can" through the continual activity of redescription (p. 80), basically the business of the camel and the lion. But Nietzsche is not a useful guide to creating a good and just society, and Rorty has little patience with Nietzsche's invitation to construct new myths via the child's innocence because they undo all the genealogical work that Nietzsche has made such an effort to undertake. However, Nietzsche himself is very taken with the idea of creating new myths for society to live by and even of inventing new gods to inhabit those myths. He refers to "premature births of an as yet unproven future" (*Gay Science,* sec. 382) and to the "first-born of the twentieth century" (*Beyond Good and Evil,* sec. 214), images which suggest that Nietzsche is thinking in insistently social terms. Nietzsche's brilliant commentary, "On the Uses and Disadvantages of History for Life," published in 1874, takes as its subject the collective health of society. In it Nietzsche repeatedly attacks the nineteenth century for lacking vitality. In his view, modern men and women were not capable of imagining a future fundamentally different from the present they inhabited. For a time, Nietzsche believed that Richard Wagner, who had created a grand cycle or ring of operas that featured medieval Germanic heroes, might be able to create a new, modern myth to live by. But if Nietzsche initally believed that Wagner's art represented "the path of a German paganism . . . a specifically un-Christian way of viewing the world" (Williamson, p. 274), Nietzsche's actual exposure to Wagner's artistic circle at Bayreuth in newly unified Germany in 1876 convinced him that Wagner and his supporters simply performed an exaggerated, self-satisfied Geman nationalism. Nietzsche eventually turned his attention to uncovering the genealogy of morals, underscoring the erroneous, tendentious, and even conformist aspect to all collective interpretations. In the end, Nietzsche pursued the principle of difference. Almost everything Nietzsche wrote in the 1880s was directed against the iteration of a particular identity and against the experience of a single authentic self. Nietzsche lauds the act of creation, but does so as the premise for further movement; he values differentiation, but in order to admit the foreign and strange.

RECEPTION

Nietzsche's general celebration of the world-making ability of cultures, his criticism of the spiritual emptiness of the contemporary world, and his initial exaltation of Wagner as a source of modern myth preoccupied the reception of Nietzsche's work in the two decades after World War I. It was not the unblinking individual, but the suffering collective that was the object of attention. Moreover, in Germany, Nietzsche's contempt for the idea of global humanity reinforced the tendency to see German history as a special path from the catastrophe of military defeat to the redemption of total victory. Enthralled readers in Germany itself and curious half-alarmed readers elsewhere in Europe consistently interpreted Nietzsche's myths as national myths. Not surprisingly, the Nazis appropriated Nietzsche and elevated *Thus Spoke Zarathustra* into a canonical "Aryan text." Given Nietzsche's outspoken attack on anti-Semitism and on essential or authentic identities, Nietzsche is misplaced as a Nazi prophet. Yet his insistence on the value of creating new rules to live by, his acceptance of violent political campaigns in the case of the ancient Greeks, and his general contempt for those who cast their lives in terms of their suffering suggest how it was possible for readers in the interwar period to Nazify Nietzsche.

The main thrust of Nietzsche's thought is not the urge to kill gods or even to invent them. His emphasis is on perspective, which is why he makes so much of the state of wakefulness, condemns the weak-willed who blink, and cherishes men and women who have created for themselves their own new eyes "and ever again new eyes." It is this Nietzsche who inspired existentialist thinkers in France and Germany beginning in the 1930s and 1940s and to whom contemporary philosophers such as Michel Foucault, Jacques Derrida, and Richard Rorty return again and again. His attention to both the contingency of knowledge and the possibility of new angles of perception remain highly pertinent topics in the debates about truth, ethics, and representation. Nietzsche remains so radical because he does not operate inside the dominant rational and scientific framework of the modern era, which holds that critical thought and scientific method are actually revealing the state of the world. Rather he ascertains that all cultures and all peoples live inside the languages and perspectives and myths they have fashioned and that these forms are both life-enhancing and life-denying and are both authoritative and breakable. Moreover, the search for "the" truth is misguided, and the expectation for complete clarity is impossible. Truth is not obtainable because meaning has to be produced by human beings in their own vocabularies and these meanings will be utterly different. That superman at one point speaks in a stammer poignantly indicates the sheer effort of the individual to say something new about the world: "Then speak and stammer, 'This is *my* good; this I love.... I do not want it as divine law; I do not want it as human statue'" (*Zarathustra,* p. 36). The stammerer is a fitting image with which to conclude this entry. It recalls Nietzsche's overriding interest not in defining the world in any particular way but in telling his readers that the world we know is encompassed by ordinary language; that it is a hard struggle to think in new ways because we speak in "old tongues"; and that any such struggle is intense and highly personal and difficult to translate. The stammerer displaces superman and his strength and restores to view the individual who struggles with new sounds and new possibilities.

See also **Freud, Sigmund; Germany; Hegel, Georg Wilhelm Friedrich; Marx, Karl; Schopenhauer, Arthur; Secularization.**

BIBLIOGRAPHY

Primary Sources

Nietzsche, Friedrich. *Beyond Good and Evil.* Translated by Walter Kaufmann. New York, 1966.

———. *The Gay Science.* Translated by Walter Kaufmann. New York, 1974.

———. *On the Genealogy of Morals and Ecco Homo.* Translated by Walter Kaufmann. New York, 1967.

———. *Thus Spoke Zarathustra.* Translated by Walter Kaufmann. New York, 1966.

Secondary Sources

Allison, David B. *Reading the New Nietzsche: The Birth of Tragedy, The Gay Science, Thus Spoke Zarathustra, and On the Genealogy of Morals.* Lanham, Md., 2001.

Aschheim, Steven E. *The Nietzsche Legacy in Germany, 1980–1900.* Berkeley, Calif., 1992.

Chamberlain, Lesley. *Nietzsche in Turin: An Intimate Biography.* New York, 1996.

Danto, Arthur. *Nietzsche as Philosopher.* New York, 1965. Expanded ed. New York, 2005.

Hollingdale, R. J. *Nietzsche: The Man and His Philosophy.* Rev. ed. Cambridge, U.K., and New York, 1999.

Kaufmann, Walter. *Nietzsche: Philosopher, Psychologist, Antichrist.* 4th ed. Princeton, N.J., 1974.

Nehamas, Alexander. *Nietzsche: Life as Literature.* Cambridge, Mass., 1985.

Rorty, Richard. *Continengcy, Irony, and Solidarity.* Cambridge, U.K., 1989.

Safranski, Rüdiger. *Nietzsche: A Philosophical Biography.* Translated by Shelley Frisch. Cambridge, U.K., and New York, 2002.

Solomon, Robert C. *Living with Nietzsche: What the Great "Immoralist" Has to Teach Us.* New York, 2003.

Williamson, George S. *The Longing for Myth in Germany: Religion and Aesthetic Culture from Romanticism to Nietzsche.* Chicago, 2004.

Zweig, Stefan. *Master Builders: A Typology of the Spirit.* Translated by Eden and Cedar Paul. New York, 1939.

PETER FRITZSCHE

NIGHTINGALE, FLORENCE (1820–1910), British nurse.

Born in Florence, Italy, on 12 May 1820, Florence Nightingale would become one of the world's most recognized women during her lifetime and a cultural icon after her death. The second child of William Edward and Frances Nightingale, she was raised in the Church of England to satisfy her mother's social and political ambitions, although the family was Unitarian by descent. Educated at home by her father, Nightingale excelled at academic subjects, preferring Greek and Latin to the domestic arts encouraged for women. After much persuasion, Nightingale's father allowed her an annual maintenance of £50, enabling her financial security.

Greatly admired and expected to make a good match, Nightingale refused the marriage proposal of Richard Monckton Milnes (1809–1885) despite their shared status and social values. Her refusal illustrates the conflicts shared by many intellectual women during the Victorian era: Nightingale explained that Milnes would satisfy her intellectual and passionate nature, but that her "moral ... active nature ... requires satisfaction, and that would not find it in his life" (Woodham-Smith, p. 51).

Nightingale believed herself to be called from God to perform active service—not service through

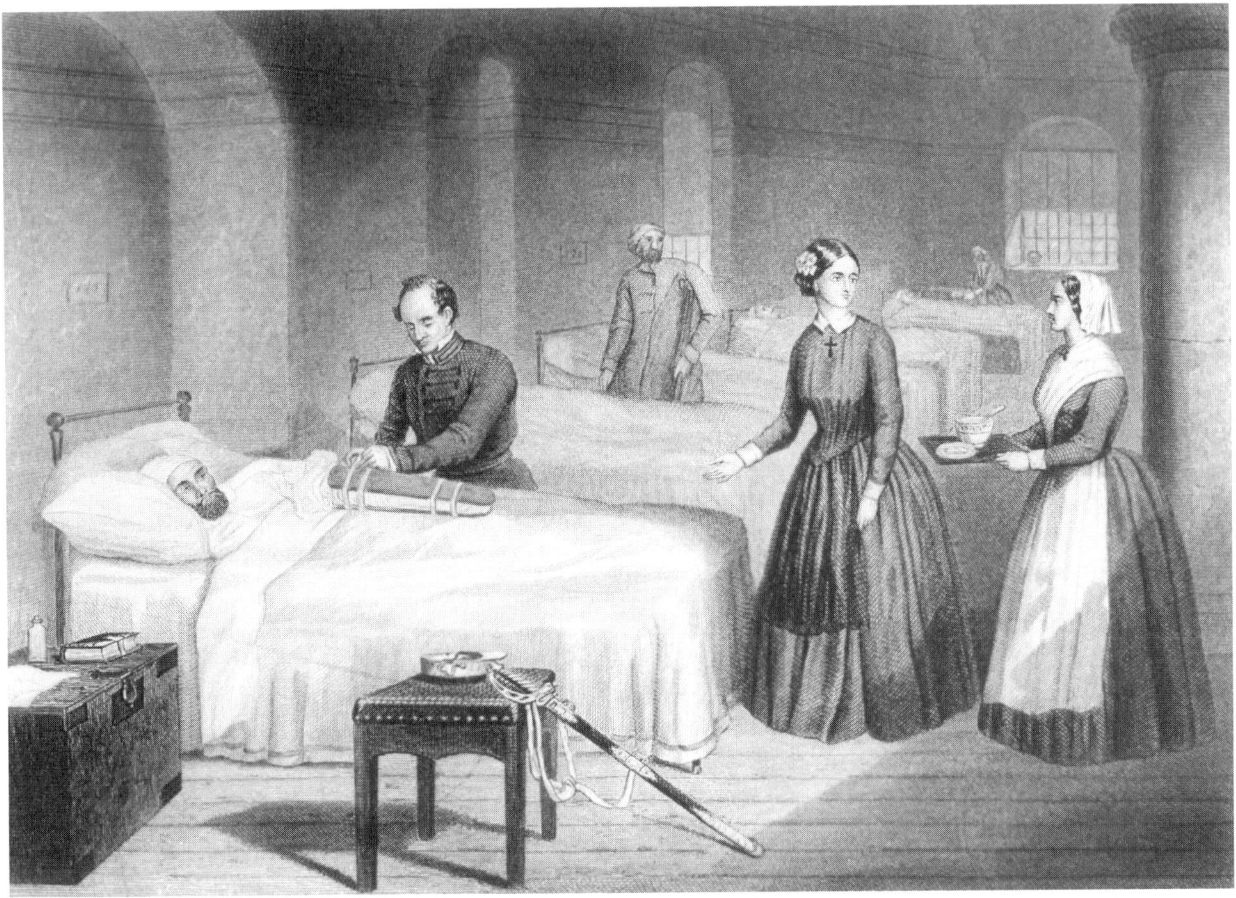

Miss Nightingale in the Hospital at Scutari. Engraving by George Greatbach after the painting by Robert Neal Hind. PRIVATE COLLECTION/BRIDGEMAN ART LIBRARY/THE STAPLETON COLLECTION

a husband. Occurring at pivotal moments in her life, Nightingale believed these experiences to be much like those of Joan of Arc (c. 1412–1431). First "called" in 1837 at seventeen, Nightingale believed God called her three subsequent times—in 1853 (prior to working at the Hospital for Gentlewomen), in 1854 (before going to the Crimea), and again in 1861 (after the death of Sidney Herbert [1810–1861]).

Visiting the hospital and school for Deaconesses at Kaiserwerth, Germany, Nightingale recognized in nursing an answer to this call to service. Because nursing was considered a low and disreputable profession, Nightingale met with resistance to her desires to study and pursue this vocation, especially from her mother. In a letter to her cousin Hilary Bonham Carter (1821–1865), she detailed her plan, "I thought something like a Protestant Sisterhood, without vows, for women of educated feeling, might be established" (Cook, vol. 1, p. 44).

During this period of depression, Nightingale wrote the three-volume *Suggestions For Thought to Searchers After Religious Truth* (privately printed, 1860), which explored what she saw as a conflict between divine and secular values. Her semi-autobiographical treatise on women's lives, "Cassandra," is included in the second volume. In 1853, Nightingale received permission to study nursing at the Kaiserwerth School for three months. Upon her return, Nightingale became the superintendent at the Establishment for Gentlewomen During Illness in London.

In 1854 Britain declared war on Russia; although England and its allies considered their Crimean engagement a military victory, the conflict exposed the appalling conditions of British military hospitals. At the request of Sidney Herbert, Minister at War, Nightingale traveled to Scutari, Turkey, with thirty-eight nurses to reform the military facilities. Nightingale quickly won the respect of the wounded soldiers, who called her "the lady with the lamp."

Returning from the Crimea, Nightingale experienced recurring bouts of a disabling illness, often preventing her from walking. Nightingale continued, however, as an advocate for health reforms.

Her statistical research influenced reforms in hospital administration and design, including the pavilion model, as well as reforms in hygiene and health care for the poor. Stressing preventative care and patient comfort, Nightingale insisted upon fresh air and water, proper drainage, cleanliness, and light for hospital wards.

In 1860, she established the Nightingale Training School for Nurses and published *Notes on Nursing*. That same year, Nightingale was the first woman elected a fellow to the Statistical Society in recognition of her statistical analyses that contributed to the reduction of the mortality rate in military hospitals. In 1883 Nightingale received the Royal Red Cross from Queen Victoria (r. 1837–1901), and in 1907 Edward VII (r. 1901–1910) honored her with the Order of Merit, making Nightingale the first woman to receive this award.

While the Crimean war may have immortalized Nightingale, Lytton Strachey, in his biographical sketch of her, describes this experience as only "the fulcrum with which she hoped to move the world. . . . For more than a generation she was to sit in secret, working her lever: her real life began at the very moment when, in the popular imagination, [it] ended" (p. 158).

On 13 August 1910, Nightingale died. In respect to her wishes, Nightingale's family declined a national funeral and interment in Westminster Abbey, burying her instead beside family.

See also **Crimean War; Nurses; Professions; Red Cross.**

BIBLIOGRAPHY

Primary Sources

Nightingale, Florence. *Notes on Nursing: What It Is, and What It Is Not.* New York, 1969.

———. *Cassandra: An Essay.* Old Westbury, N.Y., 1979.

———. *Ever Yours, Florence Nightingale: Selected Letters.* Edited by Martha Vicinus and Bea Nergaard. Cambridge, Mass., 1990.

———. *Suggestions for Thought to Searchers After Religious Truth.* Philadelphia, 1994.

———. *Collected Works of Florence Nightingale.* 6 vols. Edited by Lynn McDonald. Waterloo, Ont., 2002.

Secondary Sources

Bullough, Vern, Bonnie Bullough, and Marietta P. Stanton, eds. *Florence Nightingale and Her Era: A Collection of New Scholarship.* New York, 1990.

Cook, Sir Edward. *The Life of Florence Nightingale.* 2 vols. London, 1913.

Dossey, Barbara Montgomery. *Florence Nightingale: Mystic, Visionary, Healer.* Springhouse, Pa., 2000.

Gill, Gillian. *Nightingales: The Extraordinary Upbringing and Curious Life of Miss Florence Nightingale.* New York, 2004.

Strachey, Lytton. *Eminent Victorians: Cardinal Manning, Florence Nightingale, Dr. Arnold, and General Gordon.* New York, 1963.

Woodham-Smith, Cecil Blanche Fitz Gerald. *Florence Nightingale, 1820–1910.* New York, 1951.

Ruth Y. Jenkins

NIHILISTS. In late-nineteenth-century Europe, the term *nihilist* was often used as a synonym for Russian revolutionary. Within Russia, the term was also applied more specifically to members of a social movement associated with a subgeneration of radicals, the younger cohort of the *shestidesyatniki* (people of the [eighteen] sixties). Scholars have viewed the "nihilism" of this cohort as a symptom of disillusionment brought on by the failure of the 1861 emancipation of the serfs to transform Russia and a simultaneous shift in public opinion toward the right. This disillusionment led to subcultural activity as, for the first time, left-wing activists and intellectuals sought to distinguish themselves visibly from members of polite society. Nihilism as a movement had disappeared by the end of the 1860s. While short-lived, its influence on Russian radicalism, social thought, and literature was lasting.

BEGINNINGS IN TURGENEV

The nihilist as a cultural type was introduced to Russia on the pages of a novel. Bazarov, the eccentric young hero of Ivan Turgenev's *Fathers and Children* (1862), dresses oddly, speaks in a curt, confrontational manner, and openly expresses his contempt for ideals cherished by the "fathers," members of the author's generation. Turgenev (1818–1883) calls his hero a nihilist because of his hostility to the values and way of life of Russia's educated elite. Bazarov derides the fathers for their romanticism and, in particular, for their belief in the redeeming qualities of art and the sanctity of love and for their halfhearted commitment to improving the lot of the peasants. His pronouncements about the nature of human relations ranging from marriage to friendship and filial affection are shocking for their lack of feeling. For Bazarov, who wishes to replace the fathers' love of poetry with the pursuit of science, humans are "organisms," and their emotional needs physiological, whereas love is a function of sexual attraction rather than a reflection of an ideal of beauty.

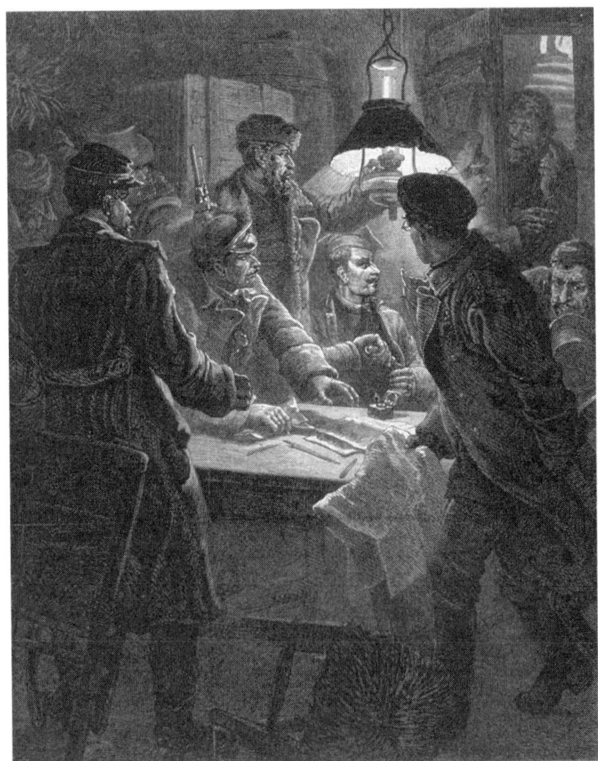

Conspiracy in Russia: A Nihilist Meeting Surprised. An 1880 illustration shows Russian police discovering a meeting of nihilists. ©CORBIS

Turgenev's novel sparked heated debate within the Left. The older *shestidesyatniki* at Nikolai Chernyshevsky's journal *Sovremennik* (The contemporary) read Bazarov as a slanderous attack on radicals perpetuated by a liberal of an older generation. They disliked the label *nihilist,* and took issue with Bazarov's rudeness, his less than gallant views on sex, his disdain for the peasantry, and his lack of a political program. In contrast, the twenty-one-year-old Dmitri Pisarev (1840–1868), a critic at *Russkoe slovo* (The Russian word), the journal favored by younger *shestidesyatniki,* accepted Turgenev's representation of a young radical as honest if incomplete. According to Pisarev, who was to become the leading spokesman of the nihilists, Turgenev meant *Fathers and Children* not as a slander but as a question. The novel asked, "Who are you young people?" In the essay "Bazarov" (1862), Pisarev formulated an answer. He described the fictional nihilist as a perfect example of a truly emancipated personality and presented him as a role model for his readers. Bazarov's negative features were portrayed in a sympathetic light. His apparent egotism and cynicism were depicted as a natural consequence of his efforts to reject all authorities and to see the world unadorned by romantic illusions. If Bazarov seemed rude, it was only because others were uncomfortable with his views. If Bazarov appeared restless, unhappy, or unpleasant in company, it was not because he wished to offend but because he understood that there was no place for him in Russian society.

CENTRAL TENDENCIES AND PRINCIPLES

In explaining Bazarov, Pisarev initiated the effort at self-definition that was to be the central tendency of nihilism. In doing so he helped his contemporaries establish a code of behavior that externalized their alienation. What had previously been an internal phenomenon was in the first years of the 1860s to become visible as the nihilists shed the forms of dress, conduct, and social relations that the intelligentsia had previously shared with the gentry. While Pisarev reluctantly accepted the label *nihilist,* he preferred to call his like-minded contemporaries "realists," "thinking proletarians," or "new people" because they were not nihilists in the classical sense of the term. They did not lack beliefs. Rather they were philosophical materialists who wanted to create a more just social order. If, unlike the men of the 1840s and the older cohort of *shestidesyatniki,* the nihilists did not actively pursue this goal, it was because they did not believe Russia was ready; they lacked their elders' optimism. For Pisarev, the first step in Russia's transformation was not revolutionary action, social reform, or overtures to the peasantry but the cultivation of a class of intellectuals that would one day assume leadership of the project of modernization.

In Pisarev's vision, the behavior of the realists was to be guided by several principles. Chief among these was the idea of the "emancipation of personality." Before realists could work to improve society, they needed to reject all authorities and thereby liberate themselves from the deadening moral constraints of the mainstream. This often required abandoning the way of life of one's parents and entering into a relationship with a member of the opposite sex based on equality and in defiance of the conventions of marriage. Another principle, "rational egoism," referred to the utilitarian calculus of pain and pleasure by which realists were to determine the best way to live their own lives. Realists were to accept only those attitudes and behaviors that could be justified by rational argument. Underlying rational egoism was a renunciation of altruism. The old intelligentsia's spirit of self-sacrifice was seen as self-defeating. Realists could pursue their own happiness and the common good simultaneously. Pisarev also preached the "destruction of aesthetics." By aesthetics he meant traditional forms of social life. Often conveyed most clearly in art, aesthetics were stifling of individuality. Their destruction, which entailed a narrowly utilitarian and often hostile attitude toward literature, was a necessary first step in the emancipation of personality. Most important for Pisarev was the formation of an informal curriculum for the education of young radicals. Through essays on a great variety of subjects, he offered them a reading list that included classics of European literature and social thought, but the central element of this curriculum was the natural sciences. Science would provide the technological foundation for Russia's future prosperity while its methods would provide realists with a means for distinguishing truth from fantasy.

In articulating nihilism's core principles, Pisarev was assisted by other writers at *Russkoe slovo,* including Nikolai Sokolov (1835–1889) and Varfolomei Zaitsev (1842–1882). While Chernyshevsky (1828–1889), the leader of the older cohort of *shestidesyatniki,* was not technically a nihilist, his novel *What Is to Be Done?* (1863) accepted the nihilists' cultural agenda and provided the most comprehensive illustration of the life of the "new people."

It is difficult to estimate with any precision whether the nihilists numbered in the hundreds or the thousands. Police reports as well as the memoirs of radicals and their opponents attest to the appearance of nihilists in cities and towns across the country. Often referred to as the *Pisarevshchina* (followers of Pisarev) or *Bazarovshchina* (followers of Bazarov), they were evident by their unusual dress. Officials were suspicious of nihilism not as a form of political subversion but as a threat to public morality because nihilist intellectuals were believed to be corrupting the children of the elite. Consequently the Moscow and St. Petersburg police were instructed by superiors in the Ministry of Internal Affairs to identify all nihilists in the capitals and to compel *nigilistki* (nihilist women), recognizable by their dark glasses, cropped hair, cigarettes, and unconventional apparel, to change their clothes or to remove themselves from the public eye. Yet, the phenomenon remained spectral, as much a product of society's deep-seated fears about modernization as a response to a social movement. The police wrote many reports but were never able to find more than a handful of nihilists. Nonetheless, they harassed the movement's leaders. *Russkoe slovo* and *Sovremennik* were both closed in 1866, and by 1870 Pisarev's collaborators were in prison or exile. Pisarev completed most of his writings from prison and died in 1868 at the age of twenty-eight, shortly after his release.

ONGOING INFLUENCE

The next intelligentsia generation, the so-called populists of the 1870s, grew up on nihilism but would come to reject it. For them, Pisarev, like Bazarov, was a hedonist, more concerned with his own pleasure than the welfare of his countrymen. The populists wished to return the emphasis of radical thought to the fate of the common people. Some scholars have suggested that the nihilists'

St. Petersburg police discovering a nihilist printing press. Engraving from *The Illustrated London News,* 6 April 1887. PRIVATE COLLECTION/BRIDGEMAN ART LIBRARY

emphasis on a revolutionary elite and personal revolt contributed to the development of anarchist and Jacobin strains within the intelligentsia. Nihilist intellectuals, however, rejected the conspiratorial politics and revolutionary violence characteristic of these movements, and Russian anarchists and Jacobins faulted the nihilists for their extreme individualism. Nonetheless, even after the 1860s, nihilist writings continued to be widely read. Memoirs from the late imperial period of leading political figures on the left (including Bolsheviks and Mensheviks) as well as members of the artistic and scientific communities testify to the importance of the works of Pisarev and other nihilists in their authors' development. Although after 1870 nihilist writings ceased to be taken seriously by leading intellectuals, they became a literature of youth, initiating several generations of high school–age progressives into the oppositional spirit of the intelligentsia and the quasi-bohemian radical counterculture that the nihilists had created and that would remain a central feature of Russian radicalism through 1917. While Russian novelists of the 1860s remained overwhelmingly hostile to nihilism, it preoccupied them. Fyodor Dostoyevsky (1821–1881), Ivan Goncharov (1812–1891), Nikolai Leskov (1831–1895), Alexei Pisemsky (1821–1881), and others all wrote antinihilist novels whose central themes, ambivalence about modernity, and fear of social disintegration were similar to those of the police reports. Indirectly, through literature, Russian nihilism was to have an impact on Western thought. For example, Friedrich Nietzsche (1844–1900), author of some of the most influential European discussions of nihilism, was influenced by Dostoyevsky's representations of Russian nihilism.

See also **Dostoyevsky, Fyodor; Goncharov, Ivan; Intelligentsia; Nechayev, Sergei; People's Will; Populists; Turgenev, Ivan.**

BIBLIOGRAPHY

Brower, Daniel R. *Training the Nihilists: Education and Radicalism in Tsarist Russia.* Ithaca, N.Y., 1975.

Coquart, Armand. *Dmitri Pisarev (1840–1868) et l'idéologie du nihilisme russe.* Paris, 1946.

Moser, Charles A. *Antinihilism in the Russian Novel of the 1860s.* The Hague, Netherlands, 1964.

Pozefsky, Peter C. *The Nihilist Imagination: Dmitrii Pisarev and the Cultural Origins of Russian Radicalism (1860–1868).* New York, 2003.

Venturi, Franco. *Roots of Revolution: A History of the Populist and Socialist Movements in Nineteenth Century Russia.* Translated by Francis Haskell. Rev. ed. London, 2001.

Walicki, Andrzej. *A History of Russian Thought from the Enlightenment to Marxism.* Translated by Hilda Andrews-Rusiecka. Stanford, Calif., 1979.

PETER C. POZEFSKY

NIJINSKY, VASLAV (1890–1950), Russian dancer.

Born in Kiev on 12 March (28 February, old style) 1890 on a tour of his dancer-parents Eleonora Bereda and Thomas Nijinsky, Vaslav Fomich Nijinsky entered the St. Petersburg Imperial Ballet School in 1898, graduating from there in 1907. That same year he joined the Maryinsky Theater, where he had already appeared as a pupil in Michel Fokine's *Acis et Galatée* (1905), in *A Midsummer Night's Dream* (1906), and with Anna Pavlova in Fokine's *Pavillon d'Armide* (1907). A sensational success, he soon became the partner of Mathilde Kschessinska, Olga Preobrajenska, and Tamara Karsavina. He was befriended by Sergei Diaghilev, who saw in the young dancer not only a potential lover but also someone to star in the Paris seasons of the Ballets Russes.

With the Ballets Russes he was idolized for his performances in the classics and in Fokine's *Les Sylphides* and *Cleopatra* (1909), *Carnaval* and *Schéhérazade* (1910), and *Le Spectre de la rose, Narcisse,* and *Petrushka* (1911). Audiences went wild for his amazing virtuosity (he had exceptional elevation, executing entrechats huit and dix); he could be savagely sexual as the Golden Slave in *Schéhérazade,* or dreamily romantic as the spirit in *Spectre de la rose.* The costume he wore for *Giselle* at the Maryinsky Theater was considered indecent, and the ensuing scandal (which some claimed Diaghilev masterminded) made him resign from the Maryinsky in 1911.

Ballets Russes program, 1912, featuring a portrait of Nijinsky by Georges Lepape. ©GIANNI DAGLI ORTI/CORBIS

Now free to devote his energies to Diaghilev full-time, Nijinsky became not only the main attraction of the Ballets Russes but also their choreographer. Diaghilev had established his company as a permanent touring ensemble for which he urged Nijinsky to create innovative works. The resulting ballets were among the most controversial in the entire history of ballet and are considered to foreshadow the many developments of later avant-garde choreography. His choreography was a revolutionary break with tradition in, for example, *L'Après-midi d'un faune* (1912), *Jeux* (1913), and *Le Sacre du Printemps* (1913). Like Fokine's, his movements were molded to reflect the different settings: in *L'Après-midi d'un faune* steps were seen in profile like Greek friezes, and in

Le Sacre du Printemps the language of the body was turned in on itself when the dance became flat-footed and convulsive. The brazen modernity of his ballets, and the overt eroticism of *Faune,* provoked strong reactions from audiences and notorious riots in the Théâtre des Champs-Elysées.

While on tour in South America in 1913, Nijinsky married the Hungarian dancer Romola de Pulszky, an act that so infuriated Diaghilev that he fired Nijinsky. The break between Nijinsky and his older impresario-lover marked the beginning of Nijinsky's decline into mental illness. He tried to establish a company of his own in 1914, but it failed after only sixteen days at the Palace Theatre in London. He went to Madrid and Vienna, where his daughter Kyra Nijinsky was born (she became a dancer and the wife of the conductor Igor Markevitch), then to Budapest, where he was interned as a Russian during World War I. Diaghilev succeeded in getting him out of Hungary for a North American tour with the Ballets Russes in 1916, for which Nijinsky choreographed Richard Strauss's *Till Eulenspiegel.* During a subsequent tour of South America he showed increasing signs of schizophrenia. He settled in St.-Moritz in Switzerland in 1918 and entered a sanatorium the following year.

Nijinsky's last public performance, a solo recital called *Marriage with God,* was given on January 1919 in a St.-Moritz hotel ballroom. Nijinsky worked on a system of dance notation, worked on plans for a ballet school, designed new ballets, and started to draw while moving from one mental hospital to another. In 1947 his family moved to London where Nijinsky died of renal failure on 8 April 1950. His body was taken to Paris and buried in the Montmartre Cemetery.

Nijinsky was one of the greatest artists ballet has ever produced, a dancer of exceptional ability and magnetism. As a choreographer he had a decisive influence on early modern dance and is now considered one of the forerunners of twentieth-century modernism. Herbert Ross made a film about his life in 1980, while Maurice Béjart choreographed a ballet about him, *Nijinsky, clown de Dieu* (Nijinsky, clown of God). *The Diary of Vaslav Nijinsky,* written over a six-week period in 1919, was published in English in 1936 in a version heavily edited by Romola Nijinsky. The unexpurgated version, edited by Joan Acocella, was published in 1999.

Vaslav Nijinsky perfoming *The Afternoon of a Faun,* 1912. ©Bettmann/Corbis

See also **Avant-Garde; Body; Diaghilev, Sergei; Homosexuality and Lesbianism; Paris; Pavlova, Anna.**

BIBLIOGRAPHY

Buckle, Richard. *Nijinsky.* New York, 1971.

Garafola, Lynn. *Diaghilev's Ballets Russes.* New York, 1989.

Kirstein, Lincoln. *Nijinsky Dancing.* New York, 1975.

Ostwald, Peter. *Vaslav Nijinsky: A Leap into Madness.* London, 1991.

Philip T. A. Johnston

NOBEL, ALFRED (1833–1896), Swedish humanitarian, chemist, and inventor.

Alfred Bernhard Nobel's early childhood was characterized by poverty and relatively difficult circumstances. His father, Immanuel Nobel (1801–1872), himself an inventor and engineer, went into bankruptcy the same year Alfred was born, due partly to a fire that destroyed much of the family's resources. Some years later, the elder Nobel decided to leave Sweden, moving first to Finland and then later to Russia. In St. Petersburg, he attempted to reestablish his business. His wife, Andrietta Nobel (née Ahlsell), Alfred's brothers, and Alfred remained in Stockholm. In 1841–1842, young Alfred spent his first and only year in school at the Jacobs Apologistic School in Stockholm. In 1842, the family was reunited in St. Petersburg. Business began to go better, and the sons were given private instruction in the home. The family's increasing wealth made it possible to send Alfred abroad for studies. In the early 1850s, he spent a couple of years in the United States, where he met the Swedish inventor John Ericsson (1803–1899). Nobel spent the following years in part on travels. He studied chemistry in Paris and journeyed to other parts of Europe.

Nobel was granted his first patent in 1857 in St. Petersburg, for a gas meter. At that time, he was becoming increasingly involved in his father's factory. Business began to decline, and Alfred was trusted with the task of seeking financial support in London and Paris. The trip was a failure, and in 1859 his father gave up and moved home to Sweden, together with Andrietta and their youngest son, Emil (1843–1864). Alfred and his two older brothers, Robert and Ludvig, continued the business in St. Petersburg for several more years. More and more, they focused their work on the development and production of explosives. In the years 1863 and 1864, Alfred Nobel was granted his first patents for the use of nitroglycerin in combination with black powder. The 1863 patent was for mixtures of nitroglycerin and black powder, and the 1864 patent described the introduction of a detonator—a very important invention in the development of effective explosives. Nobel continued to refine his detonator, or blasting cap, which consisted of a copper casing filled with a charge of mercury fulminate.

In 1863, Nobel moved back to Stockholm where he, his father, and Emil began to manufacture nitroglycerin and to market this new explosive to the mining industry. The business grew, but in 1864 catastrophe struck. The small shed in Stockholm where the nitroglycerin was prepared exploded, and Emil Nobel and four other persons were killed. Despite this, just a few months later Alfred Nobel succeeded in establishing a corporation in Stockholm named Nitroglycerin AB. This new company assumed his patents and continued the manufacture of nitroglycerin, first on a barge in the vicinity of Stockholm, and from March 1865 onward at Nobel's first true factory, at Vinterviken just outside Stockholm. Later that same year, he established another factory at Krümmel outside Hamburg. Nobel's enterprise now began to grow rapidly, but a series of accidents followed. Nobel worked hard to find a solution to these safety problems, and in 1867 he patented dynamite, a mixture of nitroglycerin and kieselghur that was much safer than pure nitroglycerin. In 1875, he further improved his invention with the patent for gelatin dynamite. In 1888–1889, Nobel patented his last truly important invention, ballastite, or smokeless powder. Of all of Nobel's more than 300 patents, ballastite became one of the most economically profitable.

Nobel established companies in several countries in Europe and in the United States. Throughout his adult life, he traveled constantly between his different places of business but maintained a permanent home in Paris. He lived there from 1873 to 1891, and had a laboratory in his home, as well as one in Sevran on the outskirts of Paris. Nobel never had a real family of his own. He was very close to his mother, and always traveled home to celebrate her birthday with extravagant presents. For eighteen years, he also had an important relationship with Sofie Hess, an Austrian woman whom he had met in 1876. Although he rented an apartment for her in Paris, they never officially appeared as a couple in public.

For Nobel, the late 1880s and early 1890s were marked by misfortune. His mother died in 1889, his brother Ludvig died in 1888, his relationship with Hess came to an end, and he was drawn into several legal proceedings, including one with the French government, which closed his laboratory. In 1891, Nobel left Paris and moved to San Remo on the Italian Riviera. There he built a new laboratory and began the last creative period of his life. During this time, he began to think about a prize for beneficial contributions to humanity. His will was kept secret until his death, known only by those who witnessed its signing in November 1895. It caused great excitement when its contents were made public following his death on 10 December 1896. Through the devoted work of one of Nobel's closest colleagues, Ragnar Sohlman (1870–1948), the Nobel Foundation was established, and the first Nobel prizes were awarded in 1901.

Nobel's posthumous letters give witness to his sense of humor. On the occasions he was asked to provide autobiographical data, his answers were brief and jocular. When his brother Ludwig was writing a biography, Alfred wrote the following about himself: "Alfred Nobel—pathetic, half alive, should have been strangled by a humanitarian doctor when he made his screeching entrance into the world. *Greatest merits:* Keeps his nails clean and is never a burden to anyone. *Greatest fault:* Lacks family, cheerful spirits and a strong stomach. *Greatest and only petition:* Not to be buried alive. *Greatest sin:* Does not worship Mammon. *Important events in his life:* None."

See also **Science and Technology.**

BIBLIOGRAPHY

Bergengren, Erik. *Alfred Nobel: The Man and His Work.* Translated by Alan Blair. London, 1962.

Fant, Kenne. *Alfred Bernhard Nobel.* Stockholm, 1991.

Lindqvist, Svante. *A Tribute to the Memory of Alfred Nobel: Inventor, Entrepreneur and Industrialist (1833–1896).* Stockholm, 2001.

Schück, Henrik, and Ragnar Solman. *Alfred Nobel och hans släkt.* Uppsala, 1926.

Solman, Ragnar. *The Legacy of Alfred Nobel: The Story Behind the Nobel Prizes.* Translated by Elspeth Harley Schubert. London, 1983.

OLOV AMELIN

NORTON, CAROLINE (1808–1877),

Anglo-Irish author and campaigner for women's rights.

Caroline Sheridan was the granddaughter of the dramatist and Whig politician Richard Brinsley Sheridan (1751–1816) and the daughter of a colonial secretary. She was a beautiful and quick-witted young woman with a good education but no dowry. She married at age nineteen, and the decision was so disastrous that it shaped the remainder of her life and led to the writings and the women's rights campaigns for which she is remembered.

Sheridan married George Norton (1800–1875), who seemed to be a good match—a barrister, a member of Parliament, and the brother of a peer. Norton turned out to be a financially irresponsible alcoholic with a violent temper who began beating his bride during the first weeks of their marriage. Caroline Norton published a startling account of this abuse (*English Laws for Women in the Nineteenth Century,* 1854), calmly relating experiences such as having a tea-kettle of boiling water set down on her hand, burning and scalding her.

Caroline Norton had few alternatives under early Victorian law. As she reminded the nation in a pamphlet, "A married woman in England has *no legal existence:* her being is absorbed in that of her husband." By law she owned no property, and any property she acquired—personal items of clothing, family inheritance, or income—belonged to her husband. She could not legally flee his home, but he had the right to pursue her into any home if she tried. Divorce was virtually impossible, requiring first the approval of the church and then of Parliament; even separation based on cruelty was not permitted if she had "condoned" his behavior by remaining with him.

Norton remained in her abusive marriage for nearly a decade, having three sons with George Norton. When he ruined the family finances, she launched a literary career, publishing successful volumes of poetry in the 1830s and 1840s. Her poetry appealed to the Victorian sense of melodrama and romance, but it also revealed a social conscience—she attacked the abuses of child labor in *Voice from the Factories* (1836) and the exploitation of the poor in *The Child of the Islands* (1845).

Norton's life changed dramatically in 1836, following an ugly dispute with her husband over their children. She returned from visiting her family to find that he had removed the children from their home and denied her the right to see them. He demanded separation under his terms—that Caroline receive no financial support and the children reside with him—threatening to seek a divorce by first suing the prime minister, Lord William Lamb Melbourne (1779–1848), for "criminal conversation" (adultery) with her. Caroline refused, and George launched his promised scandal, resulting in an 1836 trial that inspired Charles Dickens (1812–1870) to fictionalize it as *Bardell v. Pickwick.*

Although Caroline Norton was being publicly shamed as an adulteress, the law did not allow her to speak at the trial. The jury found her innocent without leaving the jury box, but by English law the failure of the adultery case meant that the Nortons could never be divorced. Laws governing infant custody provided that the children would be raised by their father, and the mother could be denied access to them. The final blow to Caroline Norton was that the law still permitted her husband to claim her royalties, as George Norton did in 1848.

Caroline Norton responded with a forceful pamphlet, *The Separation of Mother and Child* (1838), and used her political connections to press Parliament to reform the law of infant custody. Her pamphlet was intended to educate people about the law. Husbands held "despotic power" to seize children, "even should they be infants at the breast," and entrust them to anyone they wished, even a favorite prostitute. "Is this the vaunted justice—the vaunted mercy of the English code?" Norton asked. Parliament answered with the Infant Custody Act of 1839, recognizing maternal rights but stopping short of modern equality. It allowed mothers to petition the Court of Chancery for access to minor children.

When George Norton sought to seize Caroline's royalties, she had already found security through carefully crafted trusts left to her in the wills of her mother and of Lord Melbourne. She again defended herself with pamphlets about the property rights of married women and the laws of marriage. When Parliament adopted the Divorce and Matrimonial Causes Act of 1857, it was the second great advance in women's rights Norton had promoted. This law allowed a wife to obtain a divorce for the adultery of her husband if he were also guilty of cruelty, bigamy, incest, or bestiality. Her campaigns also contributed to the later adoption of the Married Women's Property Act of 1870, although she had no active role in that campaign. Despite her role in three major reforms on behalf of women, Norton never considered herself a champion of equal rights. "What I write is written in no spirit of rebellion; it puts forward no absurd claim of equality; it is simply an appeal for protection."

See also **Feminism; Marriage and Family.**

BIBLIOGRAPHY

Primary Sources

Norton, Caroline. *The Separation of Mother and Child by the Law of "Custody of Infants," Considered.* London, 1838. A lengthy excerpt is reprinted in *Women, the Family, and Freedom: the Debate in Documents,* Vol. 1, edited by Susan G. Bell and Karen M. Offen. Stanford, Calif., 1983.

———. *English Laws for Women in the Nineteenth Century.* London, 1854. Reprinted as *Caroline Norton's Defense.* Chicago, 1982.

———. *A Letter to Queen Victoria on Lord Cransorth's Marriage and Divorce Bill.* London, 1855. A lengthy excerpt is reprinted in *Victorian Women,* edited by Erna O. Hellerstein, Leslie P. Hume, and Karen M. Offen. Stanford, Calif., 1981.

Secondary Sources

Gleadle, Kathryn. *The Early Feminists: Radical Unitarians and the Emergence of the Women's Rights Movement, 1831–1851.* New York, 1995.

Shanley, Mary Lyndon. *Feminism, Marriage, and the Law in Victorian England.* Princeton, N.J., 1989.

STEVEN C. HAUSE

NORWAY. *See* **Sweden and Norway.**

NOVALIS (HARDENBERG, FRIEDRICH VON) (1772–1801), German Romantic poet and philosopher.

Friedrich Leopold von Hardenberg, known by his pen name "Novalis," is one of the best known and best loved of the early German Romantics. Born 2 May 1772 in Oberwiederstedt, Germany, he studied law in Leipzig and Wittenberg, but turned to philosophy, poetry, and the study of sciences while working in directorial posts for the Saxonian salt mines. He was a central figure in the so-called Jena Circle of early German Romanticism, a short-lived but profoundly influential group of intellectuals that included his close friend Friedrich von Schlegel, August Wilhelm von Schlegel, Caroline Schlegel (later Schelling), Friedrich Wilhelm Joseph von Schelling, Friedrich Ernst Daniel Schleiermacher, Dorothea Mendelssohn-Veit Schleiermacher, and Ludwig Tieck. He died of tuberculosis at nearly twenty-nine years of age, in March 1801.

Novalis's life was marked by personal tragedy, close intellectual friendships, and a keen interest in science and in his "practical" job for the saltworks. His love for his fiancée, Sophie von Kühn, who died in 1797 just two days short of her fifteenth birthday and two years after their engagement, has come to epitomize the poet-philosopher's life and work, along with the leitmotif of the "blue flower," the symbol of the object of poetic striving in his famous unfinished novel *Heinrich von Ofterdingen* (1802). His other well-known works include the *Geistliche Lieder* (1799; Spiritual songs), a group of "songs" that includes the *Gesangbuch* (Songbook), and *Hymnen an die Nacht* (1800; *Hymns to the Night*).

Blütenstaub (1798; Pollen), a collection of literary and philosophical reflections or "fragments" published in the Schlegels' journal *Athenäum*; *Die Lehrlinge zu Sais* (1798–1799; *The Novices of Sais*); and the essays *Glauben und Liebe* (1798; *Faith and Love*) and *Die Christenheit oder Europa* (1799; Christianity or Europe) are among his best-known writings as well. He also began an ambitious collection of material on the sciences, a "Romantic Encyclopedia" that was later given the title *Das Allgemeine Brouillon* (1798–1799).

Novalis is widely recognized and still best remembered for his literary contributions. A central figure in the early German Romantic movement, he is typically seen as a dreamy, even morbid figure, oriented toward the grave, sad and unearthly, longing to be reunited with his first fiancée. The view of Novalis as an otherwordly mystic is certainly due in part to his poetic rendering of visions of death and transcendence, captured in the remarkable poem cycle *Hymns to the Night*.

This view has been seriously challenged by recent scholarship that points out that Schlegel and Tieck, who edited the first collection of his works after his death, had much to do with creating this view of Novalis. The facts of his actual life belie the older picture of a love-struck delicate spirit pining for death. In fact, he fell in love and was engaged to be married again. Novalis had a passion for his work and enjoyed the company of a supportive and lively circle of friends. Newer interpretations focus on important aspects of his poetry that manifest a deep concern for the real world, view the universe as vital and alive in all its aspects, and in general embrace rather than reject the practical and the ordinary as well as the spiritual and enchanted aspects of life. A good example of this is the reinterpretation of his famous magical realist novel, *Heinrich von Ofterdingen* as a primarily political novel, the term Novalis himself used to describe it, as opposed to readings that see mainly a Romantic version of the bildungsroman (novel of education).

Scholarship has also begun to recognize Novalis as far more than a gifted poet. His work encompasses philosophy, the sciences, and mathematics, as well as political- and literary-theoretical views. While his fame has rested primarily on his literary works, his philosophy has come to be seen as a serious contribution and/or critical antidote to the German idealist philosophy of the early nineteenth century. In 1796 he wrote to Friedrich von Schlegel that "the study dearest to me is basically named the same as my bride: it is called philosophy—philosophy is the soul of my life and the key to my real self." It was at this time, during the illness and impending death of his first fiancée that Novalis began a serious and important study of the work of the idealist philosopher Johann Gottlieb Fichte (1762–1814). The resulting "Fichte Studies" have been the focus of philosophical reinterpretation of early German Romanticism, most notably in the work of Manfred Frank (2004), as a core text for the philosophy of that movement, and as a mouthpiece for a post-Kantian philosophical approach that is neither dogmatic nor skeptical. Indeed some scholars have seen the beginnings of a postmodern-sounding semiotic theory in certain aspects of these notes. Others have focused more attention on his later philosophical writings and writings about the sciences, arguing that these works, and especially the theory of magical idealism, are most central to his thought.

Topics that hinge on these interpretive debates include questions about the nature of what can be known, the limits of human knowledge, the possibility of genuine knowledge of the self and others, and metaphysical issues related to debates about vitalism versus mechanism, materialism versus idealism, determinism versus free will, and many others. Whether one reads Novalis as a proto-postmodernist, a critic of German idealism, or a contributor to the Romantic branch of idealism in Germany, it is clear that his philosophical work is as significant as his literary work is brilliant.

See also **Fichte, Johann Gottlieb; Germany; Romanticism; Schlegel, August Wilhelm von.**

BIBLIOGRAPHY

Frank, Manfred. *The Philosophical Foundations of Early German Romanticism.* Translated by Elizabeth Millán-Zaibert. Albany, N.Y., 2004.

Neubauer, John. *Novalis.* Boston, 1980.

O'Brien, William Arctander. *Novalis: Signs of Revolution.* Durham, N.C., 1995.

Pfefferkorn, Kristin. *Novalis: A Romantic's Theory of Language and Poetry.* New Haven, Conn., 1988.

Seyhan, Azade. *Representation and Its Discontents: The Critical Legacy of German Romanticism.* Berkeley, Calif., 1992.

Jane Kneller

NURSES. Over the course of the long nineteenth century, nursing in Europe evolved from a service performed predominantly by members of religious orders, servant-class women and men, and wives and mothers in their own homes, to a respectable career choice for middle-class women seeking to enter a modern health-care profession. The emergence of professional nursing was the direct product of several major developments in European history, including the blossoming of women's rights movements, the resurgence of religion, the rise of anticlerical politics, the rapid modernization of scientific medicine, and changing attitudes toward welfare and the poor. It is not surprising, therefore, that the history of nursing varies considerably from country to country. In Catholic countries like France, Spain, and Italy, nuns provided the majority of nursing care in hospitals until the last decades of the nineteenth century and, in some cases, into the twentieth century. Predominantly Protestant countries like England, Germany, and Sweden resorted earlier to the training of lay nurses, though religious women played an important in the development of nursing in those countries as well.

NURSING AND THE HOSPITAL

The transformation of nursing from a form of domestic or devotional service to professional occupation was in large part a consequence of changes in the institution of the hospital, especially during the second half of the nineteenth century. Until then, hospitals functioned primarily as asylums for the sick poor and the insane who had nowhere else to go. More affluent patients were cared for in their homes by servants or family members, at least until the last decades of the century. The indigent, by contrast, were brought—frequently unwillingly—to the hospitals, where they were crammed into unsanitary, overcrowded wards, often several to a bed; they could expect little if any actual medical treatment. Food was scarce and prospects for leaving the institutions alive were slim. Whatever care patients received came at the hands of members of religious nursing congregations or servant-class men and women, many of whom were former patients themselves.

While hospitals in Catholic countries relied heavily on orders like the Filles de la Charité de Saint-Vincent-de-Paul, the largest service-oriented congregation founded during the seventeenth-century, their counterparts in England and other Protestant countries were often forced to hire paupers to perform nursing duties. Long hours, unhealthy working conditions, and paltry wages discouraged all but the most desperate workers from seeking employment on the wards. Sairey Gamp, the crude, slovenly, incompetent, and ignorant nurse in Charles Dickens's novel *Martin Chuzzlewit* (1844) long stood as a symbol for unreformed lay nursing in England and elsewhere.

By the 1830s, the problem of caring for the poor had grown acute. Rapid industrialization and urbanization, first in England and within decades in Germany and France as well, brought legions of workers to cities and into workshops where harsh conditions made injury and illness likely. Poorhouses and workhouses filled to overcapacity; diseases like cholera and tuberculosis, which thrived in the overcrowded urban environment, brought renewed pressure on already inadequate health-care facilities.

Coinciding with the growing urban public health crisis was a powerful religious resurgence that swept the Continent, affecting all denominations. The numbers of active Catholic religious orders, especially for women, soared. Protestant denominations likewise turned their energies toward charitable activity. In the late 1830s, Pastor Theodore Fliedner (1800–1864) and his wife, Friederike Munster (1800–1842), established the German deaconess movement in a two hundred–bed hospital in Kaiserswerth. The deaconess movement encouraged devout Protestant women to serve as nurses in the hospital for five years after a lengthy probation period. All deaconesses received training from doctors and pharmacists. By the 1860s, the Kaiserswerth Hospital had trained approximately 1,600 deaconesses. Although work days were long (approximately sixteen hours) and the women received little pay, the establishment of the Deaconesses of Kaiserswerth was regarded by hospital reformers throughout Europe as a model for enlightened nursing practice. The influence of the deaconess movement was felt as far away as Russia and the United States. Among the many visitors who observed the nurses of Kaiserswerth Hospital were England's Elizabeth Fry (1780–1845), who subsequently founded the Institute of Nursing training facility in London in 1840, and Florence Nightingale (1820–1910), who spent three months there in 1851.

In England, the Anglican Church established several charitable orders for women including the Protestant Sisters of Charity and, in 1848, the Community of St. John's House, whose mission was explicitly to nurse the sick and poor. Members of the Community received two years of formal training before being admitted to serve in one of the hospitals run by the order.

WARTIME AND PROFESSIONALIZATION

The birth of the modern secular nursing profession is commonly associated with the endeavors of Florence Nightingale during the Crimean War (1854–1856). Faced with massive English casualties stemming from disease and infection, Secretary of War Sidney Herbert called on Nightingale, a family friend, to lead a delegation to nurse the sick and wounded at Scutari on the Bosphorus in Turkey. Gathering together a carefully screened group of thirty-eight nurses, including ten Catholic and eight Anglican religious sisters, Nightingale proceeded to institute a rigorous—critics often called it draconian—system of sanitation and care that eventually resulted in a reduction of the death rate at Scutari from 40 percent to 2 percent.

Nightingale's success quickly made her a heroine in England and throughout Europe. Her widely read *Notes on Nursing* (1859) argued that nursing was at once a vocation requiring extraordinary dedication and self-sacrifice and an honorable profession that demanded thorough training in both nursing theory and practice. In 1860 Nightingale opened a nursing school at St. Thomas Hospital, the beginning of what would soon be called the Nightingale System of nurse training. By the turn of the century, graduates of the program helped establish similar schools in Germany, Sweden, Denmark, the United States, Canada, Australia, India, and Ceylon.

In France the professionalization and secularization of nursing was caught up in the increasingly hostile politics of anticlericalism that dominated the early Third Republic. Although the Catholic nursing sisters continued to enjoy widespread popular support, many doctors and health officials in the closing decades of the century considered them premodern anachronisms in an era of enlightened, scientific medicine. Equally important, the sisters stood as reminders to anticlerical politicians of the continuing influence of the Catholic Church. Eager to secularize hospitals, the French government took the occasion of the disastrous casualty rates of the Franco-Prussian War (1870–1871) to urge municipalities to train secular nurses. Outside anticlerical Paris, however, the initiatives had limited effect. At the same time, ongoing political tensions with Britain limited the impact of Florence Nightingale's reforms in France. It was only in 1901 that the reformer and medical doctor Anna Hamilton opened the country's first "Nightingale-style" nursing school, a small, private institution in Bordeaux. Six years later, a similar school opened in Paris. On the eve of World War I, however, France still had only eight full-time secular professional nurse training schools.

But the professionalization of nursing did not always entail secularization. In early-twentieth-century Germany, more than half of the country's 75,000 nurses were religious: 26,000 were Roman Catholic sisters and 12,000 were Protestant deaconesses. The secular, professional German Nurses' Association had only 3,000 members. Similarly, the municipal government of Lyon, France's second-largest city, set up the nation's first full-time nursing school in 1899 not for ambitious, middle-class laywomen, but for the hundreds of religious sisters who staffed all the city's public hospitals. The city did not establish a lay nursing corps until the 1930s.

Despite the continuing presence of religiously based nursing, secular hospital, private, and visiting nursing made steady gains throughout most of Europe in the late nineteenth and early twentieth centuries. The rise of women's rights movements in many European countries and the simultaneous transformation of hospitals into medical research and therapeutic institutions accelerated the movement to professionalize nursing in the latter half of the nineteenth century. Alongside teaching, nursing became one of the few occupations considered acceptable for middle-class women. Although some doctors resisted rigorous theoretical training for nurses, fearing a challenge to their own professional authority, many more came to value the addition of knowledgeable assistants as long as they remained subordinate to the physicians.

The urgency of wartime medical care provided a continuing impetus to the development of professional nursing. The International Red Cross, founded by the Swiss Jean-Henri Dunant (1828–1910) at the Geneva Convention of 1864 in response to the horrors he had witnessed at the Battle of Solferino (1859), served as an institutional framework for the establishment of nurse training throughout the Continent. In many countries, Red Cross organizations were directly affiliated with the national government, giving nurses a nationalistic function that would peak during World War I when the Red Cross nurse became a popular symbol of feminine patriotic service.

By the twentieth century, nursing reform leaders, spurred on by the women's rights movement in which many of them participated, became increasingly eager to establish their professional autonomy, especially in relation to the newly powerful physicians organizations. In 1899 nurses from Great Britain, Ireland, the United States, Canada, New Zealand, Australia, Denmark, Holland, and the African Cape Colony founded the International Council of Nurses with the stated goals of encouraging self-government, establishing professional ethics, improving educational standards, and affirming minimal professional standards among participating countries. Ironically, only three countries (England, Germany, and the United States) met the ICN's standards for full national membership, though representatives of other countries were admitted as individuals.

The outbreak of World War I marked a major turning point in the development of nursing, as hundreds of thousands of volunteer and career nurses rushed to offer their services to the national cause. Never before had nurses received such public acclaim. But even before the accolades died down, some nursing leaders began to wonder if the romantic, heroic image of the wartime nurse would help or hinder the profession in the less glamorous theater of peacetime hospital wards.

See also **Nightingale, Florence; Professions; Public Health; Red Cross.**

BIBLIOGRAPHY

Bridges, Daisy Caroline. *A History of the International Council of Nurses, 1899–1964.* Philadelphia, 1967.

Bullough, Vern L., and Bonnie Bullough. *The Emergence of Modern Nursing.* 2nd ed. Toronto, 1969.

Hutchinson, John F. *Champions of Charity: War and the Rise of the Red Cross.* Boulder, Colo., 1996.

Schultheiss, Katrin. *Bodies and Souls: Politics and the Professionalization of Nursing in France, 1880–1922.* Cambridge, Mass., 2001.

Summers, Anne. *Angels and Citizens: British Women as Military Nurses, 1854–1914.* London and New York, 1988.

Vicinus, Martha. *Independent Women: Work and Community for Single Women, 1850–1920.* Chicago, 1985.

KATRIN SCHULTHEISS

OCEANIC EXPLORATION. The oceans came into focus as objects and sites of scientific study in the nineteenth century. Previously, ocean explorers sought sea routes and new lands. The aim of nineteenth-century explorers shifted from novel geographic discoveries to systematic surveys directed toward exploiting natural resources, finding new markets, and demonstrating political might. Before the invention of chronometers and the lunar-distance method solved the longitude problem, the challenge of finding longitude had drawn the attention of explorers and navigators skyward, into astronomy. With the longitude problem solved by the late eighteenth century, Captain James Cook (1728–1779) established a precedent for a scientific style of exploration that included investigation of the ocean itself. Modern science thereafter formed the basis for establishing knowledge about the ocean.

Cook's voyages demonstrated that geographic discovery was most informative when followed by detailed botanical, mineral, zoological, and geodetic investigations. This scientific style of exploration emerged in response to political and economic concerns including whaling, trading, colonial settlements, and new industrial activities. New lands and seas were surveyed for utilitarian purposes and to increase scientific knowledge. Science and empire were tightly linked by the late eighteenth century through oceanic exploration, as exemplified by the work of national botanical gardens to transport and transplant plants such as rubber for tires, cinchona with its antimalarial qualities, and the breadfruit carried by the ill-fated *Bounty.*

Control of the ocean conferred significant power on imperial nations, whose strategic and economic interests depended on trade. Knowledge of the ocean's tides, currents, storms, and seabed made possible the expansion of shipping and the inauguration of new transportation and communications technologies including the steamship and the submarine telegraph cable. An understanding of the ocean and its depths enabled European powers to dominate lands and cultures connected by its waters.

As early nineteenth-century western explorers neared completion of the discovery of the earth's landmasses and the sea routes between them, they set forth with scientific companions to the far reaches of the globe—the icy polar regions, the "dark continent" of Africa, the gigantic Himalayan mountains, and the desolate Australian outback. Oceanic exploration concentrated especially on polar regions throughout the nineteenth century, most infamously in the doomed 1845–1849 expedition led by John Franklin (1786–1847) and the numerous parties sent out in search of it. The surface and depths of the ocean also came under scrutiny at midcentury by physicists searching for laws of nature, by naturalists interested in marine organisms, and by hydrographers aiming to chart the ocean basins.

Emerging scientific interest in the sea developed in tandem with the growth of modern, professional science. Following the example of Alexander von Humboldt (1769–1859), those scientists who studied the oceans adopted his methods of collecting data over large geographic areas and mapping it to discern general laws of nature. Conceiving of the oceans as one connected whole allowed scientists to speak decisively about areas of the sea where measurements were difficult or impossible. Examples of such global synoptic studies include both the British physicist William Whewell's (1794–1866) tidal studies, especially the so-called "great tide experiment" of 1835 in which observers throughout the world took detailed tidal measurements for two weeks, and also the "Magnetic Crusade" masterminded by the British magneticist Edward Sabine (1788–1883) in the late 1830s. In the 1850s the American naval officer Matthew Fontaine Maury (1806–1873) directed a deep-sea sounding project that resulted in the first bathymetric chart of the Atlantic basin in 1853. This investigation took on importance for the emerging submarine telegraphy industry, but its origin, and the motive for tidal and magnetic studies, lay in efforts to improve navigation due to the meteoric expansion of shipping that accompanied industrialization.

In 1872 the British Admiralty dispatched HMS *Challenger* on a circumnavigation voyage to study the world's oceans. Three and a half years later, after seventy thousand nautical miles and 362 stations, *Challenger* returned with seven thousand specimens, half of them new to science, and ample evidence that life exists at all depths in the ocean. The fifty volumes of *Challenger* reports laid a solid foundation for physical, biological, chemical, and geological oceanography, but the voyage itself did not set a precedent for the practice of this new field. Instead, scientists began to study regions of the sea intensively. In 1902 eight northern European nations founded the International Council for the Exploration of the Sea. Governments supported the Council because of the economic value of fisheries combined with the recognition that marine resources were most effectively studied cooperatively. The Council served as the world's leader of marine science through the post–World War I period.

See also **Explorers; Science and Technology.**

BIBLIOGRAPHY

Brockway, Lucile H. *Science and Colonial Expansion: The Role of the British Royal Botanic Gardens.* New York, 1979.

Deacon, Margaret. *Scientists and the Sea, 1650–1900: A Study of Marine Science.* 1971. 2nd ed. Aldershot, Hampshire, U.K., and Brookfield, Vt., 1997.

Mackay, David. *In the Wake of Cook: Exploration, Science, and Empire, 1780–1801.* New York, 1985.

Reidy, Michael Sean. "The Flux and Reflux of Science: The Study of the Tides and the Organization of Early Victorian Science." Ph.D. diss., University of Minnesota, 2000.

Rozwadowski, Helen M. *Fathoming the Ocean: The Discovery and Exploration of the Deep Sea.* Cambridge, Mass., 2005.

———. *The Sea Knows No Boundaries: A Century of Marine Science Under ICES.* Copenhagen and Seattle, Wash., 2002.

HELEN M. ROZWADOWSKI

O'CONNELL, DANIEL (1775–1847),

Irish politician.

Daniel O'Connell was reared in an Irish-speaking environment. He always retained the instinctive feel of a populist politician for what ordinary people thought, and more importantly how they felt—a legacy of his childhood immersion. Never a great writer, his political philosophy was displayed through rhetoric, and he was a master at tailoring his message to suit his audience. His wit, vituperation, good humor, and energy gave him enormous command when speaking, never more so than when the crowd was large: O'Connell fed off his audiences as they fed off him, a protean figure of enormous energy and insatiable combativeness. He also carefully cultivated his self-image. A master of political theater, he blended oratorical flamboyance with meticulous organization, imposing his massive personality on every aspect of a national movement. No one more thoroughly saturated the Irish popular imagination.

UTILITARIAN PRINCIPLES

O'Connell always claimed to act on utilitarian principles—"the greatest good for the greatest number." The two leading influences on him were the English jurist and philosopher Jeremy Bentham (1748–1832) and the English philosopher and writer William Godwin (1756–1836). Bentham balanced the English tradition of rational dissent with the Continental Enlightenment, insisting that political

Daniel O'Connell speaking to a crowd. Nineteenth-century newspaper illustration. ©BETTMANN/CORBIS

rights rested fundamentally with the individual. Utilitarian politics were accordingly democratic and an instrument for social reform: "everybody to count for one, nobody for more than one." He was also profoundly influenced in his London years, 1794–1796, by William Godwin. Invoking the adage that all government rests on opinion, Godwin believed that as public opinion was progressively Enlightened, government institutions would inevitably lose their spurious authority. He diagnosed the corrupting effects of inherited property and privilege: here can be traced the origins of O'Connell's lifelong pursuit of the destruction of the unearned privilege of the Protestant ascendancy in Ireland.

O'Connell believed that that there was no incompatibility between his religious and his political ideas. He was able to create a novel blend of Catholicism and radicalism, two concepts hitherto considered incompatible. Although O'Connell maintained a strong sense of Catholic identity and acknowledged papal authority in the areas of faith and doctrine, he deplored the temporal power and possessions of the church. Throughout O'Connell's political career, he fought for freedom of religious practice and belief for all, not just Catholics, and the absolute separation of church and state.

O'Connell consistently retained a late Enlightenment belief in the power of the law to effect social and political change. The failure to incorporate Catholics fully into the new United Kingdom in 1801 convinced them that there was a close link between their political impotence and their legal isolation. O'Connell absolutely shared this conviction, informed by his daily experiences in the Irish courts. O'Connell was to be the ultimate beneficiary of this politicization of the law in the eyes of Irish Catholics.

A common thread throughout O'Connell's long career was his consistent opposition to the use of violence. O'Connell used the term *bloodless revolution* to describe his own achievement of Catholic emancipation. His capacity to harness what he called the "moral force" of mass nonviolent action became his lasting contribution to the emerging Ireland. O'Connell's innovation was to actualize the latent potential of superior Catholic numbers. The first detailed religious census in 1834 turned in Catholics at 81 percent of the total population of Ireland.

THE CATHOLIC ASSOCIATION

The Catholic Association, founded by O'Connell in 1823, flexed this newly conditioned political muscle. The democratic penny-a-month membership, astute cooption of priests, the widespread distribution of the *Catholic Register*, and the careful cultivation of a coterie of politically astute organizers created an unprecedented mobilization of Irish Catholics. The Catholic Association eventually decided to challenge landlord control of this Catholic vote. The campaign's spearhead would be the structures and personnel of the institutional church—the sole national institution available, sympathetic, and responsive to Irish Catholic needs. The 1826 general election provided an opportunity to bring this newly honed weapon to bear on O'Connell's constant target—the Irish Protestant gentry and their unearned constitutional privileges. O'Connell backed a liberal Protestant standing as a "Catholic" candidate in Waterford. His victory achieved a symbolic victory of stunning proportions for the Catholics. The transition effectively marked the end of the road for the Irish landed gentry as the dominant player in Irish politics. O'Connell conducted a further audacious coup in 1828. He personally won the Clare by-election. These sweeping victories were irresistible demonstrations of political momentum. The Catholic Emancipation Act of 1829 inevitably followed. O'Connell was instantly dubbed "The Liberator" by his grateful Irish supporters.

O'Connell insisted on the necessity for Catholics to be fully incorporated on equal terms within the public sphere of postemancipation Ireland. One of the most galling aspects of the Penal Laws was that they had consigned Catholics—the majority of the population—to a permanent status as noncitizens. After Catholic Emancipation, O'Connell led Catholics in a determined campaign to reclaim that public space; hence it was hugely important for O'Connell to make the Catholic presence felt. His "Monster Meetings," rallies, parades, and processions around the Dublin streets all staked out the public space as open to Catholics, unhindered by the previous collusion between the state and the gentry to keep them invisible and marginalized.

Just as they reclaimed public space, Catholics also sought unfettered access to the public sphere—the domain of civil society, a virtual public sphere, mediated by print culture. O'Connell's ability to orchestrate a national campaign depended on the second print revolution that gathered momentum in the 1820s. O'Connell was quick to realize the potential of the new print media to foster national opinion and hence mobilize political campaigns.

LEGACY

O'Connell's achievement was the democratization of Irish politics, an achievement that soon would generate spillover effects in Britain. In this sense, the long eighteenth century lasted from 1690 to 1829 in Irish politics, and it was O'Connell who terminated it. His victory in forcing the Irish state to shed its sectarian character was followed by the great reform act of 1832, which performed a similar function for the British state, marking the transition from an *ancien régime* to a modern parliamentary democracy.

O'Connell's long dominance of nationalist politics was finally challenged in the 1840s through the growing disenchantment of the group coalescing around the *Nation* newspaper (established 1842), which was eventually to be called Young Ireland. They formed part of a common European trend: other young movements occurred across Europe, notably in Italy, Switzerland, Austria, Greece, and Bohemia. The philosophical underpinnings of Irish nationalism shifted dramatically in the second half of the nineteenth century. O'Connell's political philosophy—essentially late Enlightenment liberalism—was eclipsed by the spread of Romanticism. This philosophical difference was the intellectual basis of O'Connell's split with Young Ireland in the 1840s. Within Irish nationalism, the emphasis on cultural nationality found little to admire in the O'Connellite approach.

O'Connell's significance should always be understood within the larger European context. He offered a role model for other European Catholic activists, because he invented an authentic relationship between tradition and modernity, and between Catholicism and democracy, salvaging positive aspects of the Enlightenment without succumbing to its irreligion. This is why O'Connell proved so inspiring to the European Catholic liberals, who sought to advance Catholicism beyond an automatic association with social conservatism, the monarchy, and a return to the *ancien régime.* O'Connell suggested that it was possible to reconcile the hierarchical world of Catholic obedience with secular democratic values of individual autonomy and equality. Other Catholic nationalist movements emerged across Europe in the first half of the nineteenth century. Poland and Belgium, closely observing the Irish example, developed a similar blend of persecuted national traditions and Catholicism, which jettisoned Enlightenment irreligion and anticlericalism while retaining its democratic principles. While he is conventionally seen as a commanding figure in Irish politics, O'Connell was arguably the most influential Catholic activist in nineteenth-century European politics. He fused Catholicism with Enlightened thinking in a potent combination that fascinated Continental Catholics. The French writer and politician Alexis de Tocqueville visited Ireland in 1835 to explore at first hand the O'Connell phenomenon of a mass-based Catholic democratic movement. In that sense, O'Connell can legitimately be claimed as an early progenitor of the European Christian democratic tradition.

See also **Catholicism; Chartism; Great Britain; Ireland; Liberalism; Nationalism.**

BIBLIOGRAPHY

Primary Sources

O'Connell, Maurice R., ed. *The Correspondence of Daniel O'Connell.* 8 vols. Dublin, 1972–1980.

Secondary Sources

Grogan, Geraldine. *The Noblest Agitator: Daniel O'Connell and the German Catholic Movement, 1830–1850.* Dublin, 1991.

Larkin, Emmet, ed. and trans. *Alexis de Tocqueville's Journey in Ireland, July–August 1835.* Washington, D.C., 1990.

MacDonagh, Oliver. *O'Connell: The Life of Daniel O'Connell, 1775–1847.* London, 1991.

Macintyre, Angus. *The Liberator: Daniel O'Connell and the Irish Party, 1830–1847.* London, 1965.

O'Faoláin, Sean. *King of the Beggars: A Life of Daniel O'Connell.* London and New York, 1938.

O'Ferrall, Fergus. *Catholic Emancipation: Daniel O'Connell and the Birth of Irish Democracy, 1820–30.* Dublin, 1985.

Reynolds, James A. *The Catholic Emancipation Crisis in Ireland, 1823–1829.* New Haven, Conn., 1954.

Uí ógáin, Ríonach. *Immortal Dan: Daniel O'Connell, in Irish Folk Tradition.* Dublin, 1995.

KEVIN WHELAN

O'CONNOR, FEARGUS (1796–1855),

Irish leader of the Chartist movement.

Feargus Edward O'Connor was born in Cork, son of Roger O'Connor, a prominent Anglo-Irish politician and pretender to the ancient throne of Ireland, and Wilhelmina Bowen. Both his father and uncle, Arthur O'Connor, were leaders of the United Irishman in the 1790s, and their views shaped his later political career. O'Connor went to school in England and Ireland before attending Trinity College, Dublin, and Gray's Inn, London, to train as a barrister. O'Connor combined the life of a gentleman farmer with a successful law practice that earned him widespread support among the poor in Cork, but he was soon drawn into politics.

In 1822, O'Connor published a scathing attack on the government of Ireland and there is evidence that he was involved in the clandestine activities of the revolutionary Whiteboys in Cork. O'Connor participated in the agitation for the Reform Bill, and in 1832 he was elected for County Cork to the reformed parliament in Westminster. He stood on a platform of repeal of the union of Ireland and England with the support of the leading Irish reformer, Daniel O'Connell (1775–1847). O'Connor's election was unexpected, a testimony to his prodigious skills as an orator and campaigner.

In Westminster, O'Connor's eagerness to press the case for repeal on the imperial Parliament led to friction with O'Connell, who sought to extract concessions from the Whig government. Despite the withdrawal of O'Connell's support, O'Connor was reelected in 1835. Within months, his parliamentary career was cut short because he lacked sufficient wealth to meet the property qualification required to be a member of Parliament (MP) at that time.

During his time in London, O'Connor had become increasingly involved in British politics; after losing his seat, he began to establish a career as a leader of British radicalism. Over the next few years, O'Connor traveled extensively (particularly in the north of England), addressing countless meeting on the evils of the Whig government's changes to the system of poor relief and lending his support to the emerging campaign for a radical reform of the political system. The program that he advocated was not new and would form the basis of the Peoples Charter (hence the name "Chartist movement") that was published in 1838. It included the demand for universal manhood suffrage, annual elections to Parliament, the secret ballot, electoral districts of equal size, payment of MPs, and the abolition of the property qualification that had denied him his seat in Parliament.

At the end of 1837, O'Connor established the newspaper, the *Northern Star,* which became the quasi-official journal of Chartism and enjoyed massive national sales and influence. He participated in the Chartists' National Convention that convened in February 1839 to present a national petition to Parliament calling for the implementation of the Charter. Although O'Connor urged delegates to adopt strong measures to force the government into submission, there is no evidence that he was involved in planning the insurrection that occurred in November 1839. In May 1840, however, he was imprisoned for eighteen months for publishing seditious speeches.

From his cell in York, O'Connor continued to the lead the movement that was reorganizing for a protracted campaign. He was released in 1841 dressed in a suit of working-class fustian cloth, a symbolic gesture that further endeared him to the laboring poor who made up the rank and file of the movement. O'Connor was again prosecuted in March 1843 and, although he was found guilty, a legal technicality meant that he was never sentenced.

After 1840, O'Connor quarreled with many Chartist leaders who sought to link the campaign for political reform to other objectives such as temperance and education, or to ally the Chartists to organizations headed by middle-class reformers. In this struggle, O'Connor retained the support of the vast majority of rank-and-file Chartists. By the end of 1843 he had changed tack, promoting the establishment of Chartist land communities. Established in 1845, the Chartist Cooperative Land Company attracted many urban workers with the prospect of life as small, independent land owners. In 1848, the Company collapsed in the face of legal obstacles and many small subscribers lost their investment. O'Connor suffered a heavy financial loss also, but this did not prevent him from continuing to hold the seat of Nottingham in the House of Commons that he had won in 1847.

His reelection to Parliament coincided with the last high point of Chartism. During 1848, as revolution spread through Europe, O'Connor promoted another national petition demanding the Charter. The campaign ended in controversy when a parliamentary committee found that it contained many bogus signatures. After 1848, O'Connor devoted his attention to forging an alliance between those he called the working Saxons and Celts. Failing health affected his final years. O'Connor was admitted to an asylum in 1852 and died there in 1855. An estimated fifty thousand people joined his funeral procession in London, a measure of the popularity of the man who personified the hopes and aspirations of a generation of working people.

See also **Chartism; Great Britain; Labor Movements; Socialism.**

BIBLIOGRAPHY

Epstein, James. *The Lion of Freedom: Feargus O'Connor and the Chartist Movement, 1832–1842.* London, 1982.

———. "Feargus Edward O'Connor." *Oxford Dictionary of National Biography,* vol. 41, edited by H. G. C. Matthew and Brian Harrison, 461–464. Oxford, U.K., 2004.

Pickering, Paul A. "The Chartist Rites of Passage: Commemorating Feargus O'Connor." In *Contested Sites: Commemoration, Memorial and Popular Politics in Nineteenth-Century Britain,* edited by Paul A. Pickering and Alex Tyrrell, 101–126. Aldershot, U.K., 2004.

Read, Donald, and Eric Glasgow. *Feargus O'Connor: Irishman and Chartist.* London, 1961.

PAUL A. PICKERING

OCTOBRISTS. The Octobrist Party, or the Union of 17 October, was for a time an important political grouping in the Russian State Duma in late imperial Russia. First organized in 1905 and 1906 around the personalities of the zemstvo activists Dmitri Shipov (1851–1920) and Mikhail Rodzianko (1859–1924) and the textile industrialist Alexander Guchkov (1862–1936), the party occupied a moderate position in a polarized political spectrum dominated by revolutionary and radical forces on the left, and extreme anti-Semitic nationalist forces on the right. It expanded to become the largest party in the Third Duma (1907–1912), and positioned itself as a staunch ally of Prime Minister Peter Stolypin (1862–1911). The party survived in fragmented form into the Fourth Duma (1912–1916), and several of its leaders played an active role in politics until the Bolshevik Revolution of 1917.

ORIGINS IN REVOLUTION OF 1905

The Octobrists took their name from the October Manifesto, the promise of reform issued by Tsar Nicholas II in the midst of the Revolution of 1905. Fearing further disorders, the Octobrists rallied to the defense of the tsarist regime against both reaction and revolution, under the condition that the tsar carry to completion his pledge to rebuild Russia "on the unshakable foundations of civil liberty." Representing moderate landowners of the Shipov wing, who emerged from the zemstvo movement of the 1890s, and elements of the nascent entrepreneurial stratum led by Guchkov, who organized themselves into the Petersburg Association of Industry and Trade in 1906, the Octobrists put forward a nationalist-monarchist platform that called for the transformation of the unlimited tsarist autocracy into a "state of laws" (*Rechtsstaat,* or *pravovoe gosudarstvo*). In the Octobrist vision, the emergence of a civil society and democracy was to occur within the firm confines of the Russian Empire, on whose "unity and indivisibility" the patriotically minded Octobrists insisted. Their aspirations toward parliamentary democracy were tempered by their fear of continued unrest, the weakness of the empire's military forces, and the international challenge posed by the rise of imperial Germany on Russia's western frontier. Thus the Octobrists offered their support to the government in the Duma during the period of the Stolypin reforms.

The fledgling political parties of the Duma period tended to form around charismatic personalities rather than programs. More than anyone else, it was Guchkov who personified the Octobrist movement. Called "a liberal with spurs" by Leon Trotsky, Guchkov embodied the vitalist and militarist spirit of the age. Descended from a family of Old Believer textile manufacturers, educated in Moscow and Berlin, Guchkov embodied the exuberance of the nascent entrepreneurial bourgeoisie in Russia. A tireless adventurer, he fought against the British in the Boer War (1899–1902), headed the Russian Red Cross during the Russo-Japanese War (1904–1905), fought numerous duels, and was an admirer of the "Blood and Iron" chancellor of Germany, Otto von Bismarck.

COLLABORATION WITH STOLYPIN

Guchkov's activist temperament embraced democratic values in theory, but nonetheless betrayed an admiration for strong political leaders who promised the restoration of order and national prestige. For the Octobrists, Stolypin was that leader. In the radicalized Second Duma (1907) the Octobrists were an inconsequential presence. But with Stolypin's "coup" of 16 June (3 June, old style) 1907, in which the prime minister illegally altered the electoral laws in favor of conservative property owners, the Octobrists emerged as the dominant party, with 154 delegates, in the Third Duma.

Though Stolypin's manipulation of the law was patently unconstitutional, Guchkov defended the action as "a sad necessity" to restore order. The Octobrists saw Stolypin as "the Russian Bismarck" who could master the chaos of revolution and move Russia toward constitutional monarchy and great-power glory. In this the Octobrists distinguished themselves from the more liberal Constitutional Democrats (Kadets), who insisted on the strict rule of law and opposed Stolypin's often high-handed tactics. The Octobrists became the bulwark of the Stolypin reforms, helping the prime minister to enact his agrarian reforms and other measures.

DECLINING INFLUENCE AND DISINTEGRATION

Octobrism represented, in Guchkov's words, "an act of faith in The Sovereign," a calculated political gamble that the tsar and his retainers were sincere in their promise to reform. It was not long, however, before the Octobrists realized that the autocracy had not changed its stripes, and that the concessions of 1905 were being reversed as the forces of order recovered the initiative. A series of political crises, beginning with the Naval General Staff debacle of 1909, soon demonstrated that the tsar and his court were unreconciled to reform. Even Prime Minister Stolypin found himself increasingly thwarted by the resurgent forces of reaction. The Octobrist compromise with the government began to fail, to the deep chagrin of Guchkov and his party. The assassination of Stolypin by a police double agent in 1911 accelerated the rightward shift of power, and by the eve of World War I the abolition of the Duma itself was being discussed at court. Guchkov admitted later that Stolypin, his erstwhile idol, had "died politically long before his physical death."

The collapse of Octobrist hopes occasioned the disintegration of the party itself. A reduced presence in the Fourth Duma (98 delegates) and growing disillusionment with the government resulted in an eventual division of the party into Left Octobrists and Zemstvo Octobrists. The leaders of the party continued to play an active role in politics during World War I. Increasingly disillusioned by the reactionary course of the regime and its failing war effort, Guchkov dabbled in schemes to overthrow and replace the tsar. When the autocracy collapsed in February (March, new style) 1917, he led the Duma delegation that secured Nicholas's abdication. He later served as minister of war in the first Provisional Government but was unable to master the forces of disintegration at work in the Russian armed forces. With the increasing radicalization of politics during the revolutionary year, moderates such as Guchkov were swept aside. After the Bolshevik seizure of power, the Octobrists served in various anti-Bolshevik governments, and most emigrated abroad after the defeat of the White armies in the civil war (1918–1920).

On his deathbed in 1936, Guchkov pronounced a final benediction on the Octobrist effort to save the Russian monarchy from its own worst instincts: "The attempt had to be made, however small the chances of success. And the chances were small, indeed."

See also **Kadets; Liberalism; Revolution of 1905 (Russia); Russia; Stolypin, Peter.**

BIBLIOGRAPHY

Hosking, Geoffrey A. *The Russian Constitutional Experiment: Government and Duma, 1907–1914.* Cambridge, U.K., 1973.

McCauley, Martin. *Octobrists to Bolsheviks: Imperial Russia, 1905–1917.* London, 1984.

Menashe, Louis. "Alexander Guchkov and the Origins of the Octobrist Party: The Russian Bourgeoisie in Politics, 1905." Ph.D. diss., New York University, 1966.

Pinchuk, Ben-Cion. *The Octobrists in the Third Duma, 1907–1912.* Seattle, Wash., 1974.

James L. West

OFFENBACH, JACQUES (1819–1880),

French composer.

Jacques Offenbach, the operetta composer who would become "King of the Second Empire" and whose music would define the character of a generation in mid-nineteenth-century Paris, was born Jakob Offenbach in Cologne, Germany. He was the seventh child of Isaac Offenbach, a music teacher and synagogue cantor. He revealed himself early as a musical prodigy on the violin and cello, and at age fourteen was accepted at the prestigious Paris Conservatoire. But the mercurial young Offenbach soon became impatient with formal lessons, and after only a year he left the Conservatoire to become a practical musician. He joined the orchestra of the Opéra-Comique, and there received an invaluable education in French light opera, whose elegance, grace, and wit inspired him throughout his life. In 1838 he began performing as a cello virtuoso in private salons. In future decades, his intimate knowledge of Paris' moneyed classes—their intrigues, brilliance, self-satisfaction, and ennui—would provide material for musical satire both scathing and affectionate.

In 1850 he returned to the theater as conductor at the Comédie-Française, but did not establish himself as a composer until the Exhibition year of 1855, when he rented a tiny theater and dubbed it the "Bouffes-Parisiens." His first work, a one-act farce called *Les deux aveugles* (The two blind beggars, 1855) was an overnight success. His license allowed him only two or three singers—a restriction he sometimes subverted by augmenting his casts with mute characters—but over time he was allowed bigger casts, and his operettas expanded. *Orphée aux enfers* (1858), with two acts, chorus, and sixteen named roles, became the model for his larger-scale operettas, including *La belle Hélène* (1864), *La vie parisienne* (1866), *La Grande-Duchesse de Gérolstein* (1867), and *La Périchole* (1868). Offenbach's satirical genius is apparent in his irreverent treatment of classical subjects (in *Orphée aux enfers* and *La belle Hélène*) and his burlesques of Second Empire society and politics (*La vie parisienne* and *La Grande-Duchesse de Gérolstein*). The Exhibition season of 1867 marked the peak of his popularity, with three Paris theaters playing his works at once.

Offenbach's comedy relies on the exaggeration and subversion of operatic conventions and clichés. A favorite trick is to quote a famous tune in an absurd situation, as when the lovers in *Ba-ta-clan* (1855) suddenly burst into the love theme from Giacomo Meyerbeer's *Les Huguenots* (1836), or Orpheus in the underworld begins to sing Christoph Willibald Gluck's "Che farò senza Euridice." A more elaborate parody is that of the patriotic trio from *Guillaume Tell* in *La belle Hélène*: where William Tell had exhorted the vacillating Arnold to save Switzerland, Agamemnon now urges Menelaus to condone his wife's infidelity. This trio also shows Offenbach's gift for letting serious statements disintegrate into wild dance rhythms. The Rossinian device of organizing musical numbers around a progression from moderate tempo to a frenzied climax became in Offenbach's hands a musical rendering of the dizzying whirl of fashionable life. Intoxication is a frequent subject, both in comic numbers for drunken men and sensuous solos for tipsy or enchanted heroines. On a few striking occasions he also depicts the melancholy "morning after," as in the courtesan Metella's rondo in Act III of *La vie parisienne*.

Offenbach's operettas circulated widely in authorized and unofficial versions. His earliest international impact was in London, where the Bouffes-Parisiens toured in 1857. His operettas inspired Sir William Schwenk Gilbert (1836–1911) and Sir Arthur Seymour Sullivan (1842–1900), who created a more respectable English form of the genre, purged of such "risque" elements as infidelity, sexual innuendo, and drunkenness. In the 1860s Offenbach frequently directed German productions of his works in Vienna; there he became friends with Johann Strauss (1804–1849) and thus influenced the development of German operetta, which by the end of the nineteenth century would outshine its Parisian forebear. In an effort to recover financially from his bankruptcy of 1874, Offenbach toured the United States during the Philadelphia Centennial Exhibition of 1876, and in his *Notes d'un musicien en voyage* he reported that American audiences were delighted to hear fully orchestrated performances, in the true Parisian style, of works that they had known only in pirated versions.

The composer's popularity declined in the 1870s after the fall of Napoleon III (r. 1852–1871). Even at the height of his success in the 1860s, he had been a target for critics of the amorality and vacuity of contemporary urban life. His status as a naturalized Frenchman and a Jewish convert to Catholicism, together with his ironic treatment of human emotions, dramatic situations, and musical materials, made him an icon of the rootless cosmopolitanism that Romantic nationalists feared and demonized. Richard Wagner (1813–1883), whose "Music of the Future" Offenbach had parodied in *Le carnaval des revues* in 1860, declared that Offenbach's music possessed "the warmth of the dung-hill; all Europe is wallowing in it." Offenbach's facetious and commercial art defied more "elevated" notions about the redemptive potential of art, theater, and music. The collapse of the Second Empire left his audience in a newly sober frame of mind, and postwar Paris, smarting after its defeat by the Prussians, had lost its taste for satires of itself served up by a native German. Offenbach's efforts to please this public produced some lovely works, such as *Fantasio* (1872) and *Le voyage dans la lune* (1875), but he could not overcome his reputation as a clown and a parodist.

After 1875, most of his creative energy was poured into his fantastical opera *Les contes d'Hoffmann*, and it was the posthumous success of *Les contes* in 1881 that redeemed Offenbach's reputation. This opera presents the German Romantic author E. T. A. Hoffmann (1776–1822) as the narrator-hero of three of his own bizarre tales. While the score bubbles with melodic and rhythmic esprit, its predominant tone is one of melancholy that progressively darkens into tragedy and neurosis. The opera's serious status was consolidated when the composer died shortly before its completion: his death from heart failure in October 1880 gave *Les contes* the prestige of a fatal work that had exacted the ultimate price from its creator. Its incomplete condition has made it a magnet for editorial and directorial interventions since its premiere at the Opera-Comique in 1881, in a version completed by Ernest Guiraud (1837–1892). The best-known version dates from Monte Carlo in 1907 and includes several beloved and utterly inauthentic numbers, including Dappertutto's aria "Scintille, diamant" and the sextet "Helas! mon coeur." Critical editions from the 1970s and the 1990s have incorporated newly discovered numbers, some unfinished and some cut during rehearsals before the premiere. Yet the opera, like its composer, remains an enigmatic synthesis of frivolity, grotesquerie, irony, and elusive yet compelling pathos.

See also **Cabarets; Debussy, Claude; Music; Napoleon III; Opera; Wagner, Richard.**

BIBLIOGRAPHY

Faris, Alexander. *Jacques Offenbach.* London, 1980.

Hadlock, Heather. *Mad Loves: Women and Music in Offenbach's* Les Contes d'Hoffmann. Princeton, N.J., 2001.

Harding, James. *Jacques Offenbach: A Biography.* London, 1980.

Kracauer, Siegfried. *Jacques Offenbach and the Paris of His Time.* Translated by Gwenda David and Eric Mosbacher. New York, 2002.

Heather Hadlock

OLD AGE. Gerontologists and some historians often point to the demographic developments of the twentieth century as so extraordinary that in comparison the history of old age in earlier centuries appears as one great continuity. Yet, already in the late nineteenth century some parts of Europe had experienced the falling fertility that brought on demographic aging, and, more than such demographic alterations, changes in the economy and workplace had an impact on the status of the aged. Moreover, the nineteenth century saw important sociocultural developments in the history of old age, and European states began providing some support for the aged.

In most of Europe, the percentage of the population over the age of sixty remained relatively stable, ranging from seven to ten percent, but regional variation was important and some aging was already visible. In France, the percentage went from 10.1 percent in 1851 to 12.3 percent in 1881 and 12.7 percent in 1911. In Sweden, those over sixty increased from 7.8 percent in 1850 to 9.3 percent in 1880 and 12 percent in 1910, but little change was evident in England (7.5 percent, 7.4 percent, and 7.9 percent) or in Germany (7.5 percent, 7.8 percent, and 7.8 percent). A fall in adult mortality had a small impact on the age pyramid, but the definitive shift to an aging population resulted from declining fertility. Birth rates fell below thirty per thousand in the 1830s in France, from 1880 to 1914 in northern and central Europe, and only after 1914 further east and south.

French aging, which preceded the general European phenomenon, occurred unevenly from region to region, with older populations emerging to the southeast of the Paris basin, in Normandy, and in the southwest. Differential fertility rates played their role, but an increasingly important factor in regional variation was migration of younger people, leaving elders in rural communities. And by the turn of the twentieth century, some urban retirees, such as civil servants, retraced their paths and pioneered twentieth-century elders' retirement to the country.

The great economic transformation of Europe in the nineteenth century set people in motion, modifying old patterns of residence. Nuclear households had long predominated in England and northwestern Europe, with a higher incidence of complex households, characterized by coresidence of aged parents and adult children, to the east and south, but great variation could be found within regions. Historians have debated whether coresidence indicated greater authority of older people but have generally concluded that, given a choice and sufficient resources, elders have usually opted for independence. Still, notarial archives in much of Europe reveal contractual relations between generations. So much food or drink, a particular room or place by the fire, or some cash allowance might be guaranteed in households that saw transmission of ownership from generation to generation. Folkloric traditions all over Europe warned against premortem transmission of property, but individual and family strategies made use of such maintenance contracts.

The dynamic economy of the nineteenth century encouraged individualism, so even when generations remained together, older and younger workers often chose different occupations, elders practicing traditional techniques, and younger workers performing newer industrial tasks. Where artisanal trades or domestic production persisted, elders maintained their position or adapted to easier jobs, but where industrialization and urbanization drove a wedge between generations, elders lost some of their workplace authority, and traditional knowledge seemed increasingly irrelevant. Workforce participation by the aged began a decline that would accelerate in the twentieth century.

Skilled workers formed friendly societies to meet the challenges of sickness and aging, and late-nineteenth- and early-twentieth-century legislation created old-age insurance schemes across Europe. They supplemented savings and charitable assistance, as workers bundled income from a variety of sources. But before examining early welfare-state arrangements, it makes sense to look at cultural representations of old age across the period, for the image of weakened, superannuated workers coexisted with a very different picture of honored, vital aged elites.

CULTURAL REPRESENTATIONS OF OLD AGE

French Revolutionary and Napoleonic-era representations of old age yielded an ambiguous legacy. A rhetoric of revolution and regeneration encouraged an association of at least some older people with an antiquated past. Elders could be viewed as holdovers from the Old Regime, and even Revolutionary and Napoleonic War veterans would come to represent a receding era. Yet, the desire to anchor and legitimize a new regime extended to the creation of a revolutionary festival honoring old age and the production of plans for old-age support.

During the period of the Directory (1795–1799), French Revolutionary festivals celebrated the stages of life, substituting generational divisions for socioeconomic ones. In the Festival of Old Age, observed annually on 10 Fructidor (the twelfth month of the French Republican calendar), local administrators honored neighborhood elders, decorating their residences, parading them through the streets, and giving them a place of honor at public ceremonies. Hymns were sung, speeches given, and dramatic performances undertaken. Public speakers and writers evoked the names of Cato the Elder (234–149 B.C.E.) and the Byzantine general Belisarius (500?–565), and plays featuring elderly characters—for example, Sophocles' *Oedipus at Colonus* and Shakespeare's *King Lear*—appeared on stage. Rhetoric that celebrated the aged appeared on other occasions as well. In the mass conscription of 23 August 1793, each cohort played its role: "Old men, taking up again the mission that they had among ancient peoples, will be carried to the public places; there they will enflame the courage of the young warriors; they will promote the hatred of kings and the unity of the Republic" (Troyansky 1989, p. 202). Honored elders in French Revolutionary culture grew out of Enlightenment precedent and anticipated nineteenth-century representations.

It may be an exaggeration to say, as did the French novelist George Sand (1804–1876), that the French Revolution invented grandparents, but rapid historical change and rising standards of living for middling and upper classes made grandparents a real presence in a culture of intimacy and sentiment between old and young. The image of the beloved grandparent represented the soft side of patriarchal or matriarchal authority. Whether in memoirs or fiction, paintings or prints, or in a new prescriptive literature, a new familial role for the aged received serious attention. Grandparents were seen as playing a major role in the education and socialization of children. Authors of memoirs affectionately recalled grandparents' roles in transmitting values, offering advice, and dominating holiday scenes.

Public life as well allowed an important role for elders. In the absence of a broad-based expectation of retirement at a particular age, business and political leaders continued to dominate European society well into advanced age. Contemporaries sometimes spoke of gerontocracy. One historian writes of gray heads triumphing in the second half of the century and evokes the names of Queen Victoria and the prime ministers Benjamin Disraeli and William Gladstone of England; Emperor William I of Germany; Prince Clemens von Metternich and Emperor Francis Joseph I of Austria; and the presidents Louis-Adolphe Thiers, Maurice MacMahon, and Jules Grévy of France. The Vatican council of 1870 revealed that two-thirds of 766 bishops and archbishops were older than sixty, including twenty-five between the ages of eighty and ninety-six.

Yet, royalty, clergy, and parliamentary leaders do not quite represent all of society, or even its elite. Privileged grandparents described in loving memoirs of the nineteenth century were often retired. We do not know how typical they were, because their withdrawal from active life depended primarily on individual investments and savings, but we glimpse some retired businessmen renovating properties and leading a life of leisure. At least they could afford to retire. That was not the case for the majority, whose plight was addressed in social thought and legislation dating back to the Revolutionary era.

EARLY WELFARE-STATE ARRANGEMENTS

In the early years of the French Revolution, the duc François de La Rochefoucauld-Liancourt (1747–1827) and the Comité de Mendicité examined the problem of poverty and the particular needs of the aged poor. Their reports favored aid at home or with an adoptive family and, for those unable to be so cared for, a system of hospices. Welfare proposals of 1793 and 1794 addressed the needs of the aged, including farmers, artisans, and dependent parents, and grandparents of defenders of the Republic. Prospectuses for old-age pensions circulated, but military needs took precedence over more general schemes for social welfare, which generally failed to be enacted. Still, the humanitarian impulses of the time would be recalled in discussions over the course of the nineteenth century, and civil servants employed by growing state bureaucracies would exercise pension rights more immediately. Individual government ministries in France established pension plans in the first half of the nineteenth century; the government combined them in 1853. The British established a unified plan for public-sector pensions in 1859, the Germans in the 1870s and 1880s.

The aged poor had to wait longer. Indeed, labor leaders expressed skepticism about benefits that workers might never live to see. But eventually they stopped conceiving of pensions as deferred wages and weighed in on public debates concerning old-age security. Prussian miners received pensions in 1854, their French counterparts in 1894. Railroad workers gained pensions throughout Europe. Social insurance was first established in Germany in 1889. While the pensions established under the German chancellor Otto von Bismarck targeted disability more than advanced age, they served as an international model in a world beginning to pay attention to old age as a social problem. Bismarck emphasized the political and social significance of his legislation:

> It is essential to generate a basic conservative conviction amongst the vast majority of unpropertied people through the feelings that come with the right to a pension. Why should the soldier of work not have a pension like the soldier of the civil service? That is state socialism, that is the legitimate operation of practical Christianity. (quoted in Scharf, p. 23)

In England, where traditions of local poor relief had been long established and undergone reform in the nineteenth century, debates over national policy occurred in the early years of the twentieth century. Changes in the labor market and a desire to discipline younger workers may have marginalized their elders. Certainly experts on social and economic questions throughout the Western world expressed ideas about the supposed obsolescence of aging workers, but the new concern for the aged poor could well have been part of a more general approach to defining particular aspects of the "social question." British old-age pensions were established in 1908 and began to be paid the following year. The majority of pensions were paid to women, and the greatest impact occurred in rural Ireland.

All across Europe at the turn of the twentieth century, politicians and social thinkers debated policies to be applied to the elderly. They evoked dreaded images of workhouses and almshouses, although entry into such institutions was always a minority experience. Policy details varied from country to country; however, ways of thinking about old age followed similar patterns. Older liberal ideas about individual thrift had encouraged the creation of optional and contributory plans, but governments increasingly turned toward ideas of mandatory and noncontributory pensions. The years leading up to World War I witnessed the creation of antecedents to the welfare-state systems that followed World War II. The initiative often came from working-class parties and labor unions, but middle-class agrarian parties in Scandinavia also lobbied effectively for social welfare institutions.

Gender was one element of the debate over aging and pensions. The image of the old worker was primarily an image of an old man, his very masculinity threatened by the weakening body. Older men experienced a kind of physical decline that the culture had already applied to women at an earlier stage of life. Ironically, women were already beginning to live significantly longer than men.

Gender differences were evident in medical discourses about aging, and the existence of separate institutions for men and women encouraged gendered research on the diseases of the aged. Despite the fact that hospitals in the nineteenth and early twentieth centuries tried to concentrate their attention on curable diseases and the young, some institutions specialized in geriatrics. Most notable were the Parisian institutions of Bicêtre and the Salpêtrière, where Maxime Durand-Fardel (1816–1899) and Jean-Martin Charcot (1825–1893) made lasting contributions to the medicalization of old age in the modern world.

See also **Childhood and Children; Demography; Welfare.**

BIBLIOGRAPHY

Baldwin, Peter. *The Politics of Social Solidarity: Class Bases of the European Welfare State, 1875–1975.* Cambridge, U.K., 1990.

Bardet, Jean-Pierre, and Jacques Dupâquier, eds. *Histoire des populations de l'Europe.* Vol. 2: *La révolution démographique, 1750–1914.* Paris, 1998.

Bois, Jean-Pierre. *Les vieux de Montaigne aux premières retraites.* Paris, 1989.

Bourdelais, Patrice. *Le nouvel âge de la vieillesse: Histoire du vieillissement de la population.* Paris, 1993.

Conrad, Christoph. *Vom Greis zum Rentner: Der Strukturwandel des Alters in Deutschland zwischen 1830 und 1930.* Göttingen, Germany, 1994.

Dumons, Bruno, and Gilles Pollet. *L'état et les retraites: Genèse d'une politique.* Paris, 1994.

Ehmer, Josef. *Sozialgeschichte des Alters.* Frankfurt, 1990.

Gourdon, Vincent. *Histoire des grands-parents.* Paris, 2001.

Johnson, Paul, and Pat Thane, eds. *Old Age from Antiquity to Post-Modernity.* London, 1998.

Kertzer, David I., and Peter Laslett, eds. *Aging in the Past: Demography, Society, and Old Age.* Berkeley, Calif., 1995.

Macnicol, John. *The Politics of Retirement in Britain, 1878–1948.* Cambridge, U.K., 1998.

Quadagno, Jill S. *Aging in Early Industrial Society: Work, Family, and Social Policy in Nineteenth-Century England.* New York, 1982.

Scharf, Thomas. *Ageing and Ageing Policy in Germany.* Oxford, U.K., 1998.

Stearns, Peter N. *Old Age in European Society: The Case of France.* New York, 1976.

Thane, Pat. *The Long History of Old Age.* London, 2005.

———. *Old Age in English History: Past Experiences, Present Issues.* Oxford, U.K., 2000.

Troyansky, David G. "Balancing Social and Cultural Approaches to the History of Old Age and Ageing in Europe: A Review and an Example from Post-Revolutionary France." In *Old Age from Antiquity to Post-Modernity,* edited by Paul Johnson and Pat Thane, 96–109. London, 1998.

———. "The Elderly." In *Encyclopedia of European Social History,* edited by Peter N. Stearns, vol. 4, 219–229. New York, 2001.

———. "Generational Discourse in the French Revolution." In *The French Revolution in Culture and Society,* edited by David G. Troyansky, Alfred Cismaru, and Norwood Andrews, Jr., 23–31. New York, 1991.

———. *Old Age in the Old Regime: Image and Experience in Eighteenth-Century France.* Ithaca, N.Y., 1989.

DAVID G. TROYANSKY

OLYMPIC GAMES. Held for the first time in the modern era in Athens, Greece, in 1896, and then every four years until the sequence was interrupted by World War I, the Games were a nineteenth-century creation inspired by ancient Greek precedents. By the 1912 Games, held in Stockholm, Sweden, the organizers of the Games had begun to invent its modern traditions, but the Games still lacked the scale and most of the symbols associated with them later in the century.

The first meeting of the International Olympic Committee, 1896. From left: Willabald Gebhardt (Germany), Pierre de Coubertin (France), Jiri Guth (Bohemia), Dimitros Vikelas (Greece), Ferenc Kemey (Hungary), Aleksei Butovsky (Russia), and Viktor Balck (Sweden). ©HULTON-DEUTSCH COLLECTION/CORBIS

The 1896 Games are often described as a continuation of the ancient Olympic Games, held from the eighth century B.C.E. (the year 776 B.C.E. is canonical) until either 393 or 424 C.E., when the pagan cults associated with the Games were suppressed by the Christianized Roman Empire. In fact, though the modern Games were inspired by the example of the ancient ones, and by the broader respect in which prewar Europe held ancient Greece, the differences between the ancient Games and those of 1896 are at least as important as their similarities.

The modern Games are, in the words of Eric Hobsbawm and Terence Ranger, an "invented tradition," one of many institutions—including sports such as baseball—that were either "refounded" or made instantly traditional in the decades before World War I. These institutions filled a social need for new civic religions, a need caused by the changes associated with economic growth, the rise of mass politics, and the decline of the aristocratic elite.

Though credit for the modern Games is often given solely to Pierre de Coubertin (1863–1937) of France, he built on and benefited from a heterogeneous array of precedents, experiments, and efforts of other enthusiasts. The Cotswold "Olympick Games" were held from 1662 to 1852 in Britain, the Greek poet Alexandros Soutsos suggested reviving the Games in 1833, and a variety of so-called Olympic competitions were either planned or held across Europe during the nineteenth century. The most important of these were the Zappas Games, held in Athens in 1859, 1870, and 1875. But, like the other competitions, the Zappas Games were not sufficiently successful to be self-sustaining.

The modern Games began in the English village of Much Wenlock. There, in 1841, Dr. William

Penny Brookes founded the Agricultural Reading Society to educate the local agricultural laborers. In 1859, the Society held the first Wenlock Olympics, which were followed by National Olympic Games in 1866. By this time, Brookes was corresponding with like-minded "founders" across Europe, including Coubertin. Inspired by Brookes, Coubertin urged the refounding of the Games at the International Athletic Congress in June 1894. This led to the formation of the International Olympic Committee (IOC), with seventy-nine delegates from twelve nations, and to a decision to hold the first Games in Athens in 1896.

For reasons that remain unclear, Coubertin then lost interest in the Games for a time. Much of the organizational work for 1896 was done by the first president of the IOC, the Greek novelist Demetrios Vikelas. But Coubertin's backing was essential to the success of the Games. Coubertin came from an aristocratic family and was educated in a classical Catholic tradition that emphasized Greek philosophy. Like many contemporaries, he was humiliated by his country's defeat in the Franco-Prussian War in 1870–1871. He believed that France had lost because it was effeminate and excessively intellectual. Prussia's Turner organizations, which combined fervent nationalism with a form of gymnastics, gave it the physical culture that France lacked. This belief was fortified by Coubertin's respect for Britain, which was expanding its already vast empire while modernizing its domestic political system. Britain was adapting to the new era; France had obviously failed to do so.

Coubertin found the secret of Britain's success in the British system of public—in American terms, private—schools. He believed that the sporting ethic taught in these schools trained Britain's leaders. The Olympics would create this kind of aristocracy in all nations. But the Olympic aristocracy would be one suitable for a democratic age. It would be open to all, with membership granted on the basis of talent and effort. This aristocracy would become modern knights: playing by the rules as an example to others, competing for the love of the game and for female applause, and inspiring healthy patriotism and mutual respect for different nations in all competitors and spectators. While Coubertin wanted to promote peace, he was not a pacifist: he believed that if the Olympic spirit prevailed, wars would not disappear, but would be less frequent and more humane.

Spectators enter the Athens stadium for the 1896 Olympic Games. ©CORBIS

The first Games were a success: three hundred athletes from thirteen nations competed in nine sports. The next two Games, in 1900, in Paris, and in 1904, in St. Louis, were near-disasters. The Paris Games were poorly organized; the St. Louis Games were so remote from Europe that most of the competitors were Americans. The Games were saved by the unofficial but professionally run Athens Games of 1906 and the London Games of 1908. In 1912, 2,500 athletes (including 57 women) from twenty-eight nations competed in thirteen sports. While medal winners continued to come primarily from the United States, Europe, and the British Empire, the future of the Games seemed assured.

While gold, silver, and bronze medals were first awarded in 1904, the 1906 and 1908 Games were—apart from those of 1896—the most important of the era. It was in 1906 that the athletes first entered the stadium in national teams; before then, they had competed as individuals. The 1908 Games, for their part, witnessed a series of nationalistic disputes between the Americans, eager to show their superiority on British soil, and the host nation, equally eager to ensure they retained pride of place. These Games thus proved that the Olympics had become a forum for competitive nationalism. This became increasingly important when the Games invented new traditions and expanded, both in scale and with the addition of the Winter Games, in the interwar years and after 1945.

See also **Athens; Philhellenic Movement; Red Cross; Sports.**

BIBLIOGRAPHY

Guttmann, Allen. *The Olympics: A History of the Modern Games.* 2nd ed. Urbana, Ill., 2002.

Hobsbawm, Eric, and Terence Ranger, eds. *The Invention of Tradition.* Cambridge, U.K., and New York, 1983. Reprint 1992.

MacAloon, John J. *This Great Symbol: Pierre de Coubertin and the Origin of the Modern Olympic Games.* Chicago, 1981.

Wallechinsky, David. *The Complete Book of the Summer Olympics: Athens 2004 Edition.* Wilmington, Del., 2004.

Young, David C. *The Modern Olympics: A Struggle for Revival.* Baltimore, Md., 1996.

TED R. BROMUND

OMDURMAN. In the intensifying European scramble for African territory from the 1880s, Britain faced threats from imperial rivals to its influential treaty position in the upper Nile, south of Egypt. Threats from Germany and Italy could be bought off diplomatically, but France was less accommodating. Indignant over its 1882 exclusion from Egypt, France declined to recognize the Sudan as a British sphere. Testing the water in the mid-1890s, Paris sent a military expedition into the Sudan to show its ambitions in the Nile valley. Confronted, Britain resolved on unequivocal conquest and occupation, and a powerful Anglo-Egyptian expeditionary force under Sir Horatio Herbert Kitchener (1850–1916) invaded the Sudan early in 1896. The country being invaded was a militant Islamic Mahdist state, ruled by the caliph Abd Allah (1846–1899), that had been resisting foreign influence and interests for over a decade. For this regime there could be no question of any negotiation with European invaders seeking to subdue caliphate power.

During the early months of their march of conquest, Kitchener's forces were able to occupy a large portion of Sudanese territory without facing much resistance, partly because of the overwhelming British rail and other technological superiority, and partly because their swift cavalry movements took their enemy by surprise. To try to block the southerly British advance, the caliph ordered total mobilization to defend what remained of his dominion. Beaten back, the Mahdist army stayed in the fight until the last months of 1898, which saw the final phase of the campaign. At Karari, north of his capital of Omdurman, Abd Allah threw his last substantial garrison against Kitchener in September 1898, meeting the enemy himself.

In the gory battle of Omdurman (or, more accurately, the battle of Karari), the Sudanese fought fiercely, deploying their handful of artillery pieces and machine guns. But across open ground they were overwhelmed by the concentrated, massed firepower of vastly superior British armaments. Nearly 11,000 Sudanese were killed and thousands more injured, for the loss of forty-nine dead and a few hundred wounded in Anglo-Egyptian ranks. To finish off warriors who lay on the ground to try to duck British firepower, Kitchener's Lancers launched one of the British army's last major cavalry charges. With some of his leading commanders either dead on the field or taken captive, Abd Allah tottered back with the remnant of his forces to a deserted Omdurman before withdrawing eastwards, where he held out despairingly for a further year. The 1898 battle had signaled the end of the Mahdist state in the Sudan.

Kitchener's virtual annihilation of the Mahdists at Omdurman strengthened his reputation for efficiency in colonial soldiering and boosted his standing as Sirdar (commander in chief) of Egypt's army. It also enabled him to face down French troops at Fashoda, Egyptian Sudan, later in 1898, clinching a bloodless victory and putting a decisive end to penetration of a British sphere. At the same time, the unsparing ruthlessness of Kitchener's campaigning in the Sudan, including the killing of wounded Mahdist soldiers (which he

The Battle of Omdurman, 2 September 1898. Illustration by Frank Dodd and W. T. Maud for the London *Graphic,* September 1898. Charging across open ground, the Mahdist army was quickly overpowered by British weaponry. GETTY IMAGES

justified on grounds of military necessity), earned him notoriety among British Liberal imperialists. At Westminster his excesses were denounced as a stain upon the morality of Britain's empire-building in Africa.

See also **Africa; Great Britain; Imperialism.**

BIBLIOGRAPHY

Daly, M. W. *Empire on the Nile: The Anglo-Egyptian Sudan, 1898–1934.* Cambridge, U.K., 1988.

Holt, P. M., and M. W. Daly. *A History of the Sudan: From the Coming of Islam to the Present Day.* 5th ed. Harlow, U.K., 2000.

Jeppie, Shamil. "Sudanese War of 1881–1898." In *Encyclopedia of Religion and War,* edited by Gabriel Palmer-Fernandez, 417–418. New York, 2004.

Magnus, Philip. *Kitchener: Portrait of an Imperialist.* London, 1958.

WILLIAM NASSON

OPERA. Opera as an art form emerged between roughly 1590 and 1610, created by composers, writers, and courtiers in Florence and Mantua who sought to revive the union of drama and music they thought characteristic of the ancient Greek theater. Outside of France, which developed its own form of musical theater after 1669 (founding of the Royal Academy of Music, or Opéra), Italian opera seria or serious opera, built around an alternation of bass-accompanied (or secco) recitative and three-part da capo arias, remained dominant across Europe down to the French Revolution, although the less prestigious opera buffa or comic opera was also spreading across the Continent during the second half of the eighteenth century. Opera seria owed its success principally to the extraordinary popularity of its star singers, both female sopranos and castrati (castrated males with soprano or alto voices). As in other areas of life, the tremendous transformation that engulfed the west after 1789 brought substantial and lasting changes to the world of opera as well.

FROM THE FRENCH REVOLUTION TO ITALIAN AND GERMAN UNIFICATION

The decades between the French Revolution and the Restoration of 1815 have been called a period of transition in Italian musical life. While the reform operas of Christoph Willibald Gluck (1714–1787) may initially have had little impact in the homeland of the art form, the less rigid opera buffa with its natural voices (no castrati), greater use of ensembles, and extended dramatic finales proved a source of renewal for the classic opera seria, still at the center of theatrical life up and down the peninsula. A synthesis of the two genres can be found in the *opere semiserie* (sentimental operas with happy endings) by Ferdinando Paër (1771–1839), *Camilla* (Vienna, 1799) and *Leonora* (Dresden, 1804), and in *Lodoïska* (Venice, 1796) and *Le due giornate* (Milan, 1801; The two days) by Johann Simon Mayr (Giovanni Simone Mayr; 1763–1845). All of these works were also inspired by French models and are examples of "rescue operas," a popular category of the time to which Beethoven's far more famous *Fidelio* (1805–1806, 1814) also belongs. Significantly, Paër was an Italian who spent much time in Germany and Mayr a German who found fame in Italy, and both incorporated into their stage works advances in orchestration and harmony inspired by German chamber and orchestral music. The staging of Gluck's Paris operas and other French works in Naples during the rulership there of Napoleon's general Joachim Murat (1808–1815) was another avenue by which inspiration from abroad reached the peninsula.

Rossini and his heirs The composer who drew on all of these influences and on his own native genius to renew both comic and serious opera in Italy was Gioacchino Antonio Rossini (1792–1868). Between 1813 and 1817 Rossini wrote four *opere buffe* that remain classics of the genre—*L'italiana in Algeri* (Venice, 1813; The Italian girl in Algiers), *Il turco in Italia* (Milan, 1814; The Turk in Italy), *Il barbiere di Siviglia* (Rome, 1816; The barber of Seville), and *La cenerentola* (Rome, 1817; Cinderella). Despite Rossini's best efforts, however, opera buffa was dying. Only three Italian comic operas written after 1819—Donizetti's *L'elisir d'amore* (1832; The elixir of love) and *Don Pasquale* (1843) and Verdi's *Falstaff* (1893)—all quite different from the classic opera buffa, have entered the repertory.

It was hence in the area of serious opera that Rossini's innovations had the more lasting impact. By applying structural features drawn from comic opera as well other changes already reflected in the works of contemporaries such as Mayr, Rossini formalized an organizational model for serious opera built around the extended, four-part scena or scene (rather than the combination secco recitative–da capo aria) consisting of an orchestral or choral introduction; a slow, lyrical aria or ensemble (cantabile); a bridging passage (tempo di mezzo); and a fast aria or ensemble (cabaletta or stretto). This "code Rossini" provided a revitalized basic framework for serious opera that Italian composers would draw on until the 1850s and beyond. Such a framework was a necessary component of an opera industry that demanded large numbers of new works every year—342 alone between the years 1838 and 1845, according to one contemporary estimate. Rossini first presented this framework in *Tancredi* (Venice, 1813), developed it further in the operas written for Naples between 1815 and 1822 such as *Otello* (1816), *Mosè in Egitto* (1818; Moses in Egypt), *La donna del lago* (1819; The lady of the lake), and *Maometto II* (1820), and perfected it in *Semiramide* (Venice, 1823), his last commission for Italy. While Rossini's serious works are less well known than his comic operas, the former can now be seen every summer at the festival held in the composer's home town of Pesaro.

Rossini's foremost heirs within Italy were the Sicilian Vincenzo Bellini (1801–1835) and the Lombard Gaetano Donizetti (1797–1848). While both adopted the new framework as a starting point, Bellini's ten and Donizetti's sixty-five stage works exhibit several significant differences when compared to those of Rossini. Thus while some of the latter's serious operas (*Ermione, Maometto II*) dispense with the happy ending typical of eighteenth-century opera seria, tragedy is the norm for his successors. Furthermore, while Rossini did set texts inspired by William Shakespeare (1564–1616; [*Otello*]) and Sir Walter Scott (1771–1832; [*La donna del lago*]), he was more attracted to classical subjects and sentiments, whereas the operas of Bellini and Donizetti are Romantic in sensibility. Bellini's masterpieces *Norma* (1831) and *I puritani* (1835), such as *Lucia di Lammermoor* (1835) and countless other works of Donizetti, all center around the theme of love thwarted by adverse social or historical circumstances, and emotions are expressed with an almost overpowering immediacy. In part, both composers achieved this effect by employing more natural voices: the hero is usually a tenor (rather than the female contralto *en travesti* still sometimes preferred by Rossini) playing opposite a soprano leading lady and a villainous baritone. Both also made use of simpler melodies and removed from the vocal line the abundant ornamentation or fioritura preferred by Rossini. The one exception is the famous mad scenes so closely identified with both composers' works and first found in Bellini's *Il pirata* (1827). In these scenes, unhappiness in love has driven the heroine insane and this state is marked by her abundant use of vocal ornamentation, in contrast to the much plainer singing style of the other characters. Despite this difference in vocal writing between Rossini on the one hand and Bellini and Donizetti on the other, all three—along with their lesser-known contemporaries Saverio Mercadante (1795–1870) and Giovanni Pacini (1796–1867)—came to be seen in the late 1800s as exponents of bel canto. This was the fine art of singing taught during the seventeenth and eighteenth centuries that stressed even tone production, exceptional breath control, agile technique, beautiful timbre, and clear articulation—a style that would be increasingly lost with the rise in the last decade of the nineteenth century of verismo opera (see below) with its stress on pure vocal power and emotive delivery.

Rossini and Paris It was not only on the future course of Italian opera that Rossini exercised a decisive influence. In 1824, having achieved everything he could in his native land, he settled in Paris and took over the directorship of the Théâtre Italien, where he assembled a top-flight company of singers and staged performances of his own works and those of his countrymen. At the same time, after writing *Il viaggio a Reims* (1825), a *pièce d'occasion* for the coronation of Charles X (r. 1824–1830), Rossini accepted the new challenge of composing for the Opéra. In 1826 he reworked *Maometto II* and presented it as *Le siège de Corinthe* (The siege of Corinth) and a year later adapted *Moisè in Egitto* as *Moïse et Pharaon* (Moses and Pharaoh). These pieces, together with the older *Fernand Cortez* (1809) of Gaspare Luigi Pacifico Spontini (1774–1851), an earlier Italian arrival in Paris, provided the inspiration for a new genre, the French "grand opera," first fully realized in *La muette de Portici* (1828; The dumb girl of Portici) of Daniel-François-Esprit Auber (1782–1871) and in Rossini's own *Guillaume Tell* (William Tell) of 1829. Such works, mounted only at the Opéra, were generally five acts long with an extended ballet in act 3. The setting was a historical one in which the conflict of two groups or peoples (Neapolitans vs. Spanish, Swiss vs. Austrians, French Catholics vs. Huguenots) serves as the backdrop for one or more love stories. Above all, grand operas presented spectacular stage effects (e.g., the eruption of Vesuvius) combined with frequent crowd scenes for mass chorus.

The great master of this genre was Giacomo Meyerbeer (1791–1864), a German-born composer who had moved to Italy at age twenty-five and written six operas in a style inspired by Rossini, who became his lifelong friend and supporter. After Rossini mounted Meyerbeer's *Il crociato in Egitto* (Venice, 1824; The crusade in Egypt) at the Théâtre Italien, the latter moved to Paris and in 1831 presented his *Robert le diable* (Robert the devil) at the Opéra. It was greeted with wild success. This was followed by *Les huguenots* (1836; The Huguenots), *Le prophète* (1849; The prophet), and *L'africaine* (1865; The african woman), all box office triumphs. The positive experiences of Rossini and Meyerbeer in the French capital soon brought Bellini and Donizetti there as well. Bellini premiered his *I puritani* at the Théâtre Italien in January 1835, just eight months before his untimely death outside Paris at age thirty-four, and

The Paris Opera House. Painting by L. Moulin c. 1875. Designed by Charles Garnier in a neo-Baroque style and constructed between 1857 and 1874, the Paris Opera House provided a magnificent setting for the works of the major composers of the day. ©Archivo Iconografico, S.A./Corbis

Donizetti wrote his *Don Pasquale* (1843) for the same theater. While his grand opera *La favorite* (1840; The favorite) eventually made its way into the repertory, neither *Les martyrs* (also 1840; The martyrs) or *Dom Sébastien* (1843), Donizetti's penultimate complete work, was well received. Indeed, aside from *La muette de Portici*, and *La favorite* only one other grand opera achieved the impact of Meyerbeer's works: *La juive* (1835; The Jewish woman) of Jacques-François-Fromental-Élie Halévy (1799–1862). By the early 1850s, the genre had passed the peak of its popularity and for the next two decades a smaller opera house, the financially embattled Théâtre Lyrique, would be the true home of artistic innovation in the French capital, specializing in works such as *Faust* (1859) and *Roméo et Juliette* (1867) by Charles-François Gounod (1818–1893), characterized by a more human scale and greater emotional directness than the typical grand opera. After 1855, the Bouffes Parisiens theater of Jacques Offenbach (1819–1880) offered serious competition to all four Parisian opera houses (the Opéra, the Opéra-Comique, the Théâtre Italien, and the Théâtre Lyrique) with its steady stream of sparkling, witty operettas.

Verdi Meanwhile, in Italy a worthy successor to Bellini and Donizetti as leader of the Italian opera school had presented himself: Giuseppe Fortunino Francesco Verdi, born in 1813 in Le Roncole north of Parma. From 1839, when his first opera (*Oberto*) appeared at La Scala, until 1850 he operated under the constraints imposed by the opera industry in Italy, producing sixteen works in little more than a decade. Verdi would later famously describe this period as his "galley years." During them, he established his reputation throughout the peninsula with a number of historical operas such as *I lombardi alla prima crociata* (Milan, 1843; The Lombards on the first crusade), *La battaglia di Legnano* (Rome, 1849; The battle of Legnano) and above all *Nabucco* (Milan, 1842). These works with their powerful choruses (*Nabucco*'s "Va pensiero" being the most famous) indirectly evoked the plight of an Italian people divided and suffering under Austrian hegemony and appealed strongly to liberals of all classes seeking unification. Verdi's most innovative opera from this epoch, however, was probably his setting of his beloved Shakespeare's *Macbeth* (1847; revised 1865).

Between 1851 and 1853, Verdi then presented three operas that within a few years had made him both world famous and wealthy—*Rigoletto* (Venice, 1851), *Il trovatore* (Rome, 1853; The troubadour), and *La traviata* (Venice, 1853; The fallen woman). While all three still honor the "code Rossini" broadly conceived, they move forward with a propulsive force and concision never before seen in the theaters of Italy. What is also striking about these operas compared to those of Bellini and Donizetti is both the relative paucity of vocal embellishments and the central role played by the duet, whether of confrontation or of love. With the money earned from these works, Verdi was able to free himself from the necessity of producing something new every year, as Donizetti had been forced to do throughout this career. Like his successful Italian predecessors before him, Verdi responded to his good fortune by moving for a time to Paris, where he took up the challenge of writing for the Opéra. Yet neither *Les vêpres siciliennes* (1855; The Sicilian vespers) nor *Don Carlos* (1867) established themselves in their French, grand opera versions. Rather, it was *Un ballo in maschera* (Rome, 1859; A masked ball), a thoroughly Italian treatment of the subject matter of an older grand opera, Auber's *Gustave III; ou, Le bal masqué* (Opéra, 1833; Gustav III; or, The masked ball) that proved to be Verdi's most fully realized work of this period.

It was during the age of Rossini, Bellini, and Verdi that the German-speaking lands finally joined Italy and France as a great home of indigenous operas. Although a German-language variant of the Italian opera seria, exemplified by the works of Reinhard Keiser (1674–1739) and Johann Mattheson (1681–1764), had emerged in Hamburg following the opening there of the Oper am Gänsemarkt in 1678, it had disappeared with that theater's closure in 1738. For the rest of the century, Germany's numerous court theaters were content for the most part to commission Italian or French operas from internationally recognized composers such as Gluck or Niccolò Jommelli (1714–1774), or to import such works from abroad and present them either in the original or in German translation. In 1776, however, Emperor Joseph II (r. 1765–1790), dissatisfied with this situation, opened the doors of the venerable Burgtheater in Vienna to a form of German musical theater known as the *Singspiel,* which, like the French opéra comique, consisted of spoken dialogue with interposed musical numbers. The next decade and a half brought forth two masterpieces in this genre, *Die Entführung aus dem Serail* (1782; The abduction from the Seraglio) and *Die Zauberflöte* (1791; The magic flute), both by Wolfgang Amadeus Mozart (1756–1791). Mozart died prematurely only a few months after the premiere of *Die Zauberflöte,* thereby depriving German opera of its great hope for the future. Instead, Revolutionary and post-Revolutionary France's growing military hegemony brought a flood of French works, mainly opéras comiques—though often quite serious ones—by composers such as André-Ernest-Modeste Grétr (1741–1813), François-Adrien Boieldieu (1775–1834), Étienne-Nicolas Méhul (1763–1817), and above all Luigi Cherubini (1760–1842). The one great German-language work of this period, *Fidelio* (1805/1806/1814) of Ludwig van Beethoven (1770–1827), employed a libretto derived from the opéra comique *Leonore; ou, L'amour conjugale* (1798; Leonore; or, Married love) by the otherwise forgotten Pierre Gaveaux (1760–1825). It was also very much inspired by Cherubini's *Les deux journées* (1800; The two days), the score of which Beethoven is said to have kept on his desk. The true turning point in the development of German opera came, however, with the premiere at the Berlin Court Theater in 1821 of *Der Freischütz* (The free shooter) by Carl Maria von Weber (1786–1826). Though heavily influenced by French works, especially those of Méhul, *Der Freischütz* quickly gained worldwide fame as the prototype of the Romantic, national opera. As such it inspired such composers as the Czech Bedřich Smetana (1824–1884), composer of *Prodaná Nevěsta* (Prague, 1866; The bartered bride), and the Pole Stanislaw Moniuszko (1819–1872), who were seeking to establish an operatic tradition in their own languages. In contrast, the father of Russian opera, Mikhail Glinka (1804–1857), was far more influenced by the music of Rossini, Bellini, and Donizetti, with which he had become acquainted during a three-year sojourn in Italy (1830–1833), when he came to write his *A Life for the Tsar* (St. Petersburg, 1836). It was left to his successor Modest Mussorgsky (1839–1881) in

A scene from *The Magic Flute*. Engraving by Joseph and Peter Schaffer, 1791. ©ARCHIVO ICONOGRAFICO, S.A./CORBIS

Boris Godunov (first version 1868–1869) to forge an operatic style that was distinctly Russian.

The long-standing goal of many of Weber's contemporaries, the creation of a truly German grand opera free from the spoken dialogue of the opéra comique and the *Singspiel*, was only achieved by Richard Wagner (1813–1883) beginning with his *Rienzi* (1842), modeled directly on the works of Meyerbeer and on Auber's *Muette de Portici*. Thereafter Wagner sought to revitalize the entire genre with his Greek-inspired ideal of the *Gesamtkunstwerk* or stage work combining music, drama, sets, and lighting on an equal footing, an ideal most fully realized in his *Tristan und Isolde* (1865; Tristan and Isolde) and in the four operas of his *Der Ring des Nibelungen* (1853–1874, premiered 1876; The ring of the Nibelung)—*Das Rheingold* (The Rhine gold), *Die Walküre* (The valkyrie), *Siegfried*, and *Götterdämmerung* (Twilight of the gods).

FROM UNIFICATION TO WORLD WAR I

Wagner was undoubtedly the opera world's most influential figure from the 1870s until the outbreak of World War I. Though by 1874 he had completed all of his thirteen operas save one (*Parsifal*, premiered 1882), it was during this period, in the wake of the inauguration of the Bayreuth Festival with performances of the complete *Ring* in 1876, that his fame spread to every corner of Europe and to the wider world. Wagner's reception focused in general on five features of the composer's work: his conception of the music drama as an equal union of words and music; his consequent rejection of the old division between recitative and musical "numbers" in favor of fully through-composed operas; the central role of "leitmotifs" or musical phrases associated with particular characters, emotions, or key events that, through modification and repetition by a greatly expanded orchestra, serve to intensify the drama independent of the vocal line; the use of an advanced, often chromatic harmonic language, especially in *Tristan* and *Parsifal*; and finally a preference for grand mythical or medieval subject matter treated at great length. In all opera-producing countries, the last decades of the nineteenth century were dominated by this reception of Wagner's music and of his theoretical writings.

Nowhere was this more true than in Germany's great rival France. Though the performance of his *Tannhäuser* at the Opéra in 1861 had been a disaster, Wagner enjoyed strong support from many French intellectuals associated with the avant-garde, most notably the poet and critic Charles Baudelaire (1821–1867). At the same time, Wagner's own outspoken German nationalism raised the ire of many French patriots in the wake of their country's devastating defeat in the Franco-Prussian War of 1870–1871. Indeed, public pressure in 1886 forced the director Léon Carvalho to cancel his plans to mount *Lohengrin* at the Opéra-Comique, and when the work was finally presented at the Opéra in 1891, a large demonstration that quickly turned into a riot occurred in front of the theater. Despite this atmosphere, many progressive composers found Wagner's influence hard to resist. Beginning in the mid-1880s, they produced a number of noteworthy operas inspired directly by both Wagner's subject matter and his musical methods: *Sigurd* (Brussels, 1884) of Ernest Reyer (1823–1909), *Gwendoline* (Brussels, 1886) of Emmanuel Chabrier (1841–1894), *Le roi d'Ys* (Opéra-Comique, 1888; The king of Ys) of Édouard Lalo (1822–1893), *Fervaal* (Brussels, 1897) of Vincent d'Indy (1851–1931), and *Le roi Arthus* (Brussels, 1903; King Arthur) of Ernest Chausson (1855–1899). Ultimately more successful than these composers were those who made judicious use of Wagner, combining some elements of his innovative musical language with subject matter and a style firmly rooted in the French *drame lyrique* of Gounod, Ambroise Thomas (1811–1896), and of course Georges Bizet (1838–1875), whose *Carmen* (Opéra-Comique 1875) Friedrich Nietzsche famously praised as the antithesis of Wagner's music dramas. Thus *Samson et Dalilah* (Weimar, 1877) of Camille Saint-Saëns (1835–1921), a good friend of Gounod, combined substantial symphonic development in the orchestra with still clearly identifiable musical numbers. This kind of synthesis was just as apparent in the work of Jules-Émile-Frédéric Massenet (1842–1912), a student of Ambroise Thomas and the most popular French opera composer of this period at the box office. In *Manon* (Opéra-Comique, 1884) and *Werther* (premiered at Vienna in 1892 after a fire had destroyed the Opéra-Comique) numbers are present, but so are leitmotifs and chromaticism, and the distinction between recitative and aria or duet has been more or less eliminated thanks to Massenet's ability to set conversation to music in an intensely lyric manner. Yet the greatest of all French operas of this period, *Pelléas et Mélisande* (Opéra-Comique, 1902) by Claude Debussy (1862–1918) achieved its effect neither by imitating Wagner nor by borrowing selectively from him, but rather by going beyond him. Through-composition is Debussy's starting point, but his brilliant orchestration ensures that Maurice Maeterlinck's enigmatic text remains far more comprehensible than is the case in Wagner's works. Furthermore, Debussy makes extensive use of the pentatonic and whole-tone scales to create an atmosphere of ambiguity and claustrophobia that is the perfect complement to the drama.

The problem of Wagner's influence was naturally even more acute in his native Germany than in France. He spawned many imitators, including August Bungert (1845–1915), who planned a nine-opera cycle—four of which he completed—based on Homer's *Iliad* and *Odyssey*. The most famous imitator was Wagner's son Siegfried (1869–1930), who inherited the genius of neither his father nor his grandfather Franz Liszt (1811–1886). One neo-Wagnerian work did, however, enter the permanent repertory: *Hänsel und Gretel* (Weimar, 1893; Hansel and Gretel) of Siegfried's student Engelbert Humperdinck (1854–1921). As in France, the most successful opera composer in Germany in this period was the one capable of employing Wagner as a starting point but then moving off in an original direction: Richard Strauss (1864–1949). In his *Elektra* (Dresden, 1909), composed to a libretto by the famous Austrian writer Hugo von Hofmannsthal (1874–1929), Strauss used a massive orchestra and a harmonic

Célestine Galli-Marié as Carmen, 1875. Galli originated the role of the gypsy in Bizet's hugely popular opera. Tchaikovsky described *Carmen* as "a masterpiece in the fullest meaning of the word." © BETTMANN/CORBIS

language on the very edge of tonality to bring to life a brutal drama of revenge. Opera was now on the verge, propelled forward by works such as *Tristan* and *Elektra,* of abandoning the tonal harmony that had always been at its core. Yet aside from one passage in *Elektra* (illustrating, appropriately, a bad dream), Strauss himself was unwilling to make this break. This was left to Arnold Schoenberg (1874–1951) in his *Erwartung* (composed 1909; Anticipation), and to his student Alban Berg (1885–1935) in *Wozzeck* (Berlin, 1925), one of the twentieth century's seminal works. Instead, Strauss turned in his next opera *Der Rosenkavalier* (Dresden, 1911; The cavalier of the rose; also to a von Hofmannsthal text) to a musically sophisticated, neo-Mozartian pastiche that, in addition to achieving lasting popularity, anticipated the neoclassicism of the interwar period and even the postmodernism of the early twenty-first century.

Italy's artists had long been in the forefront of those working for their country's unification, but the completion of the unification process with the conquest of Rome in 1870 brought with it a period of intellectual anxiety and uncertainty in the new nation. No longer a fragmented collection of provincial states, Italy now had to compare itself with mighty neighbors such as France and Germany. This situation rendered the country both more open to the latest trends in those nations, especially in the area of music, but also raised doubts about its own ability to compete despite its glorious cultural heritage. It was under these circumstances that the now fifty-seven-year-old Giuseppe Verdi took up the task of defending what he saw as the defining features of Italian opera, the centrality of the voice and of melody, against influences from abroad. Yet in his last three works, *Aida* (Cairo, 1871), *Otello* (Milan, 1887), and *Falstaff* (Milan, 1893), Verdi's style developed in a direction also found in French and German opera of the time. Thus while voice and melody still may be primary, in *Aida* Verdi moved away from traditional aria form, and in *Otello* the recitative/aria distinction has begun to blur, only to disappear altogether in *Falstaff,* which is almost numberless. There is also a brilliance of orchestration and a harmonic complexity in these last works not present in the middle-period operas. While Verdi publicly avowed his admiration for Wagner, whose compositions began to be performed in Italy in the 1870s, it would probably be wrong to attribute these changes in the late Verdi to Wagnerian or any other influence. Rather, they seem to flow from Verdi's own artistic growth—which of course involved his study of the works of other contemporaries—once freed by financial success from the constraints of the old Italian opera industry with its pressures to produce one or more new pieces per year.

From the 1880s the publishers who increasingly dominated theatrical life in Italy searched for a successor to the aging Verdi. In the early 1890s it seemed as if they had found two contenders in the persons of Pietro Mascagni (1863–1945), the composer of the wildly popular short opera *Cavalleria rusticana* (Rome, 1890; Rustic chivalry), and Ruggero Leoncavallo (1858–1919), whose *I pagliacci* (Milan, 1892; The clowns) was equally successful. While these two works, eternally yoked together, have never left the repertory, none of Mascagni or Leoncavallo's other operas made a lasting impression. The long-sought heir to the three-centuries-old Italian opera tradition turned out to be Giacomo Puccini (1858–1924), as the publisher Giulio Ricordi correctly realized. After his breakthrough with *Manon Lescaut* (Turin, 1893), Puccini next wrote three operas that have never lost their box office appeal: *La Bohème* (Turin, 1896; Bohemian life), *Tosca* (Rome, 1900) and *Madama Butterfly* (Milan, 1904). The works of all three composers are often characterized as examples of verismo (naturalism or realism) in music because of their gritty depiction of everyday life, but a more convincing common denominator is the emotionally overwrought atmosphere in all of them. Puccini developed further Massenet's techniques of expressing conversation lyrically, but his endless melody is punctuated by powerful, passionate outbursts in the form of loosely structured arias and duets. Puccini also employed a Wagner-sized orchestra to turn up the emotional volume yet further by the theatrically timed reiteration of snatches from numbers heard earlier in the work. His self-avowed goal was to produce a direct and immediate effect on the audience, and he does so by drawing on all of the tools available to a turn-of-the-century composer. This primacy of effect was in a certain sense necessary both because opera audiences were becoming less elite and because musical theater was forced increasingly to compete with other leisure time activities that demanded lower levels of concentration. Yet as the fate of opera during the interwar period across Europe would show, this art form would never be able to compete with the cinema on its own terms, despite Puccini's best efforts.

See also **Debussy, Claude; Music; Offenbach, Jacques; Rossini, Gioacchino; Verdi, Giuseppe; Wagner, Richard.**

BIBLIOGRAPHY

Primary Sources

Berlioz, Hector. *Memoirs.* Annotated and translation revised by Ernest Newman. New York, 1960.

———. *Evenings with the Orchestra.* Translated and edited by Jacques Barzun. Chicago, 1999. Translation of *Soirées de l'orchestre.*

Da Ponte, Lorenzo. *Memoirs.* Translated by Elisabeth Abbott. New York, 2000.

Stendhal. *Life of Rossini.* Translated and annotated by Richard Coe. New York, 1970.

Strunk, Oliver. *Source Readings in Western Music.* Revised edition edited by W. Oliver Strunk and Leo Treitler. New York, 1998.

Wagner, Richard. *My Life.* Translated by Andrew Gray; edited by Mary Whittall. Cambridge, U.K., 1987.

Secondary Sources

Arnold, Denis, Anthony Newcomb, Thomas Walker, Michael Talbot, Donald Grout, and Joel Sheveloff. *The New Grove Italian Baroque Masters: Monteverdi, Frescobaldi, Cavalli, Corelli, A. Scarlatti, Vivaldi, D. Scarlatti.* New York, 1984.

Bianconi, Lorenzo, and Giorgio Pestelli, eds. *Opera Production and Its Resources.* Translated by Lydia G. Cochrane. Chicago, 1998.

———. *Opera on Stage.* Translations from the Italian by Kate Singleton. Chicago, 2002.

———. *Opera in Theory and Practice, Image and Myth.* Translations from the Italian by Kenneth Chalmers and from the German by Mary Whittall. Chicago, 2003.

Fulcher, Jane. *The Nation's Image: French Grand Opera as Politics and Politicized Art.* Cambridge, U.K., 1987.

Gerhard, Anselm. *The Urbanization of Opera: Music Theater in Paris in the Nineteenth Century.* Translated by Mary Whitall. Chicago, 2000.

Gossett, Philip, William Ashbrook, Julian Budden, Friedrich Lippmann, Andrew Porter, and Mosco Carner. *The New Grove Masters of Italian Opera: Rossini, Donizetti, Bellini, Verdi, Puccini.* New York, 1983.

Grout, Donald Jay, and Hermine Weigel Williams. *A Short History of Opera.* 4th ed. New York, 2003.

Huebner, Steven. *French Opera at the Fin de Siècle: Wagnerism, Nationalism, and Style.* Oxford, U.K., 1999.

Johnson, James. *Listening in Paris: A Cultural History.* Berkeley, Calif., 1995.

Kimbell, David. *Italian Opera.* Cambridge, U.K., 1991.

Lacombe, Hervé. *The Keys to French Opera in the Nineteenth Century.* Translated from the French by Edward Schneider. Berkeley, Calif., 2001.

Orrey, Leslie. *Opera. A Concise History.* Revised and updated edition by Rodney Milnes. London, 1987.

Osborne, Charles. *The Bel Canto Operas of Rossini, Donizetti, and Bellini.* London, 1994.

Parker, Roger, ed. *The Oxford Illustrated History of Opera.* Oxford, U.K., 1994.

Sadie, Stanley, ed. *History of Opera.* New York, 1990.

Rosselli, John. *The Opera Industry in Italy from Cimarosa to Verdi: The Role of the Impresario.* Cambridge, U.K., 1984.

———. *Singers of Italian Opera: The History of a Profession.* Cambridge, U.K., 1992.

Schmierer, Elisabeth. *Kleine Geschichte der Oper.* Stuttgart, 2001.

Walsh, T. J. *Second Empire Opera: The Théâtre Lyrique, Paris, 1851–1870.* London, 1981.

Walter, Michael. *"Die Oper ist ein Irrenhaus": Sozialgeschichte der Oper im 19. Jahrhundert.* Stuttgart, 1997.

Warrack, John. *German Opera: From the Beginnings to Wagner.* Cambridge, U.K., 2001.

Weaver, William. *The Golden Century of Italian Opera from Rossini to Puccini.* New York, 1980.

THOMAS ERTMAN

OPIUM WARS. The Opium Wars is the name given to two nineteenth-century wars between China and Western countries. The military confrontations that occurred between China and Britain from 1839 to 1842 are known as the first Opium War. Historians refer to the war that transpired from 1856 to 1860 between China and joint Anglo-French forces as the second Opium War.

The goods from China carried away by your country not only supply your own consumption and use, but also can be divided up and sold to other countries, producing a triple profit. Even if you do not sell opium, you still have this threefold profit. How can you bear to go further, selling products injurious to others in order to fulfill your insatiable desire? . . . Suppose there were people from another country who carried opium for sale to England and seduced your people into buying and smoking it; certainly your honorable ruler would deeply hate it and be bitterly aroused.

Lin Zexu's Letter to Queen Victoria, 1839. In *China's Responses to the West,* edited by Ssu-yü Teng and John King Fairbanks. (Cambridge, 1954), p. 26.

FIRST OPIUM WAR (1839–1842)

Britain had established the East India Company in 1600 in part to gain access to the Chinese market. Thereafter the company enjoyed a monopoly over Britain's trade with China. Given Britain's growing demand for tea, porcelain, and silk from China, trade between China and Britain remained in China's favor down to the early nineteenth century. In order to find money to pay for these goods and cover the trade deficit, the company started to import opium to China in large quantities starting in the mid-eighteenth century. The size of these imports increased tenfold between 1800 and 1840 and provided the British with the means to pay for the tea and other goods imported from China. By the 1820s the trade balance had shifted in Britain's favor, and opium became a major commercial and diplomatic issue between China and Britain.

The opium trade was illegal in China. The Qing state had banned opium sales that were not strictly for medical purposes as early as 1729. But the law was not rigorously enforced. A century later more Chinese people had become opium smokers, which made enforcement of the ban more difficult. By the mid-1830s growing drug addiction had created such serious economic, social, financial, and political problems in China that many Chinese scholars and officials were becoming concerned about the resulting currency drain, moral decay, and diminishment of the military forces' fighting capacity. They argued that China had to ban the opium trade once and for all.

The emperor agreed and in 1838 decided that the opium trade must be stopped. He sent an official named Lin Zexu (1785–1850) to Guangzhou with a special mandate to solve the opium problem. Lin launched a comprehensive attack on the opium trade, targeting users as well as providers of the drug. In his dealing with British opium traders, he used a combination of reason, moral suasion, and coercion. He even sent a letter to Queen Victoria to argue his case. In his carefully phrased letter, Lin tried to appeal to the British queen's sense of moral responsibility and legality. When reason and moral suasion did not work, Lin blockaded the residence compound of the foreign opium traders, including the British superintendent in Guangzhou, to force them to give up more than twenty thousand chests of opium.

For the Chinese, Lin's actions were about opium. For the British, however, the drug was a key component in their trade with China. Without the profits from opium, British merchants would not be able to pay for Chinese tea and silk, and Britain was prepared even to risk war to continue the opium trade. Because the opium trade was illegal in China, Britain could not officially argue for a war to protect the opium trade. Instead, it claimed that Lin's strong action on opium insulted British national honor. In 1834 the British government abolished the East India Company's monopoly on China trade. This had serious consequences for Anglo-Chinese relations because the chief representative of British interests in China now represented his country rather than the company, so that an insult to the British trade superintendent was now a matter of state. Britain also claimed that it went to war with China to promote free trade.

On these grounds, the full British fleet under Admiral George Elliot, consisting of sixteen warships and four newly designed steamships, arrived in Guangzhou in June 1840. They blockaded Guangzhou and Ningbo and fought their way farther up the north coast, and in 1840 threatened Tianjin, a port city close to Beijing. The Qing court agreed to negotiate, and in 1842 the Treaty of Nanjing concluded the first Opium War. As a result Hong Kong was ceded to Britain, and China was forced to abolish the Guangzhou system on which Chinese trade relations had been based for over a century and agreed to allow the British to trade and reside in four coastal cities in addition to Guangzhou: Shanghai, Fuzhou, Xiamen, and Ningbo. China in addition agreed to pay an indemnity of $21 million to cover the losses claimed by the British opium traders and Britain's war expenses. A supplement to the treaty signed in 1843 extended most-favored-nation treatment (a guarantee of trading equality) to Britain, and the Qing state later granted most-favored-nation treatment to all the Great Powers. The treaty therefore symbolized the beginning of the so-called century of shame for China. Other powers immediately followed suit and forced China to sign a series of unequal treaties. The foreign powers' unequal rights in China lasted until 1943. With the Treaty of Nanjing and the unequal treaties that followed, China lost its judicial and tariff autonomy and other crucial parts of its national sovereignty. Although the nineteenth century was a century of rivalries among major European powers, because of the most-favored-nation clause they continued to be allied against China.

SECOND OPIUM WAR (1856–1860)

Despite the importance of opium in the war, the drug was not legalized by the Treaty of Nanjing. Although the British negotiators pushed the issue hard at the time, the Chinese authorities simply would not agree. British policy makers realized that as long as opium was illegal in China, their positions could be weakened. Wanting to gain more privileges in China, the British therefore looked for another pretext for war and found one in an 1856 incident involving a ship named the *Arrow*.

The *Arrow* was formerly registered in British-controlled Hong Kong but built in China and owned by a Chinese. In October 1856 the Chinese authorities arrested the *Arrow*'s Chinese crew, who were reported to have engaged in illegal activities when the ship was anchored in Guangzhou. But Britain claimed that its national flag had been insulted when the Chinese authorities boarded the ship. Although there was overwhelming evidence suggesting the British flag was unlikely to have been flying, given the British practice that no ship fly its flags while at anchor, the British government decided to use the *Arrow* incident as a pretext for military action against China. Even before the *Arrow* incident occurred, the British government had actively sought support from France and the United States for a prospective war on China. The French joined the British on the pretext of the judicial execution of a French missionary in February 1856 in the interior province of Guangxi, which was not yet opened to the West. The Anglo-French forces soon captured Guangzhou and Tianjin, where they—along with the Americans and Russians—reached a series of treaties with the Chinese in 1858. The Treaties of Tianjin contained the following provisions: the opening of ten new treaty ports, including four inland along the Chang (Yangtze) River; the establishment of permanent Western diplomatic missions in Beijing; permission for foreigners, including missionaries, to travel throughout China; the reduction of customs duties to 5 percent and of the likin tax (the internal customs dues that were levied on commodities as they moved from one locality to another) to

2.5 percent ad valorem; and the transfer of the Kowloon Peninsula, on the mainland opposite Hong Kong, from Chinese to British control. China also had to pay both Britain and France an indemnity of eight million taels (about US$ 11 million), and the treaty, by implication, legalized opium.

The Qing court, however, was strongly opposed to the idea of a permanent foreign diplomatic presence in Beijing and refused to approve the treaty. The Anglo-French troops therefore marched to Beijing and looted many Chinese treasures and burned down the Yuan Ming Yuan (the summer palace). Much of the Yuan Ming Yuan's collections later found their way into affluent homes in Europe and onto the European art market. With their troops in Beijing, Britain and France in 1860 secured the Convention of Beijing through which they were able to obtain everything they wanted and more from the Treaties of Tianjin. Tianjin became a treaty port, and France secured the right for Catholic missionaries to own properties in the interior of China.

See also **Boxer Rebellion; China; Imperialism.**

BIBLIOGRAPHY

Fay, Peter Ward. *The Opium War, 1840–1842: Barbarians in the Celestial Empire in the Early Part of the Nineteenth Century and the War by Which They Forced Her Gates Ajar.* Chapel Hill, N.C., 1975. Reprint, 1997.

Melancon, Glenn. *Britain's China Policy and the Opium War: Balancing Drugs, Violence, and National Honour, 1833–1840.* Aldershot, U.K., 2003.

Polachek, James M. *The Inner Opium War.* Cambridge, Mass., 1992.

Wong, J. Y. *Deadly Dreams: Opium, Imperialism, and the Arrow War (1856–1860) in China.* Cambridge, U.K., 1998.

XU GUOQI

OTTO, LOUISE (1819–1895), German feminist.

Louise Otto was born in Meissen in the kingdom of Saxony, which was then a state of the German confederation. The youngest daughter of a lawyer, she and her three sisters grew up in a prosperous and busy household, where women combined domestic and cultural interests. Although she attended school only until her confirmation at the age of sixteen, she continued to educate herself and developed a vocation for literature. Her parents died when she was sixteen. Her career as a writer and as a feminist was launched in 1840 with a poem entitled "Die Klöpplerinnen" (The lacemakers), in which she invoked the hardship suffered by women workers in the textile industry. Though her first novel was published under a male pseudonym, her subsequent novels—many on political themes—appeared under her own name. Her literary reputation grew steadily.

In 1844 Otto declared in a newspaper edited by the prominent left-wing politician Robert Blum that participation in politics was both a right and a duty of women. In 1848, a year when revolutions broke out in many German states, Otto gained public visibility by publishing a political statement entitled "Petition of a Girl," which urged the government of Saxony to give women workers the right to organize. Her involvement in left-wing causes brought her together with August Peters, a working-class leader to whom she became engaged. In 1849 Peters was arrested and condemned to prison for his participation in a working-class uprising in Dresden.

In 1849 Otto founded the *Frauen-Zeitung* (Women's magazine), Germany's first major feminist journal. The magazine featured articles by Otto herself and a group of like-minded women based in Leipzig. As editor, Otto distanced herself from such controversial women as the French George Sand or the German Louise Aston, whom she called "caricatures of men." She urged women to develop their distinctively feminine vocation for compassion and caring rather than to imitate men. But she affirmed gender equality as well as difference, and championed women's right to assume "a mature and independent" role in the democratic state that she hoped would result from the 1848 revolutions. Though she praised marriage and domesticity, Otto also insisted that women must also have the means to become economically independent. The journal devoted a great deal of space to vocational opportunities for women. Among these was the kindergarten, an innovative form of early childhood education developed by Friedrich Froebel, who insisted that women were best fitted to teach young children.

After the defeat of the revolutions, women journalists and political activists were among the first victims of a wave of counterrevolutionary repression. In 1850 a Saxon law aimed specifically at Otto prohibited women from editing newspapers or magazines. Though she moved her headquarters from Saxony to the Prussian town of Gera, Otto was forced to cease the publication of the *Frauen-Zeitung* in 1853. In 1851 laws were passed in Prussia and in other states that prohibited the kindergarten and forbade women to participate in political parties and associations.

In the 1850s Otto withdrew from politics, wrote novels, and married Peters after his release from prison in 1858. Thereafter she was known as Louise Otto-Peters. The couple published a newspaper, the *Mitteldeutsche Volkszeitung,* in Leipzig. Peters died in 1865. The marriage produced no children.

In 1865 Otto-Peters convened a women's conference in Leipzig. The result was the founding of Germany's first national feminist organization, the *Allgemeine Deutsche Frauenverein* (General German Women's Association), or ADF, which Otto-Peters cochaired with the teacher Auguste Schmidt. Otto-Peters edited the organization's journal, *Neue Bahnen* (New avenues) until her death. Prevented by the law against women's political participation from advocating women's suffrage, the ADF focused on educational and vocational opportunities. But Otto-Peters also raised controversial issues such as pacifism and the reform of the laws that defined the status of wives, mothers, and children. Otto-Peters died in 1895 in Leipzig.

Otto-Peters was among the most important founders of feminist movements in Germany and in other central European countries. In her long career as a politician, journalist, and author (she was the author of thirty books, including works of fiction and of feminist theory), she developed an ideology that would inspire the next generation of feminist leaders, including Helene Lange and Gertrud Bäumer. The aim of feminism, she believed, was not to make women like men but to empower women's distinctive gifts for compassion, nurture, and social responsibility. Otto-Peters combined this belief in gender difference with a strong commitment to democracy, social justice, and the right of individuals, both men and women, to live in freedom.

See also **Anneke, Mathilde-Franziska; Feminism; Germany; Revolutions of 1848.**

BIBLIOGRAPHY

Primary Sources

Gerhard, Ute, Elizabeth Hannover-Druck, and Romina Schmitter, eds. *"Dem Reich der Freiheit werb' ich Bürgerinnen": Die Frauen-Zeitung von Louise Otto.* Frankfurt am Main, 1890.

Otto-Peters, Louise. *Frauenleben im deutschen Reich: Erinnerungen aus der Vergangenheit mit Hinweis auf Gegenwart und Zukunft.* Leipzig, 1876.

———. *Das erste Vierteljahrhundert des ADF.* Leipzig, 1890.

Secondary Sources

Allen, Ann Taylor. *Feminism and Motherhood in Germany, 1800–1914.* New Brunswick, N.J., 1991.

Bäumer, Gertrud. *Gestalt im Wandel.* Berlin, 1950.

Boettcher Joeres, Ruth-Ellen. *Die Anfänge der deutschen Frauenbewegung: Louise Otto-Peters.* Frankfurt am Main, 1983.

Bussemer, Herrad-Ulrike. *Frauenemanzipation und Bildungsbürgertum: Sozialgeschichte der Frauenbewegung in der Reichsgündungszeit.* Weinheim, Germany, 1985.

Ann T. Allen

OTTOMAN EMPIRE. The last century and a half of the existence of the Ottoman Empire (1299–1922) has been subsumed under different rubrics and accorded different essences. Some see it as the expression of the Eastern Question—that is, the involvement of the European Powers in the problems of the disintegrating Ottoman state, which became the dominant concern of international relations in the nineteenth century. In this approach, the Ottoman Empire is allotted a rather passive role as, in the worst case, a Great Powers' pawn and, in the best case, a reluctantly accepted partner in the system of the international balance of power. While political and diplomatic works dominate in the treatment of the Eastern Question, it is also part and parcel of the economic and colonial expansion of the Great Powers (Russia, Great Britain, France, Austria-Hungary, Italy, and Germany). Works exploring these aspects, often within world systems theory, center-periphery relations, and colonial and postcolonial studies, emphasize the growing economic dependence of the Ottoman Empire—financial, commercial, and industrial—on the industrialized European West. Within the rubric, however, relatively little attention is accorded to internal developments.

For others, this period is characterized chiefly by the response of the Ottoman elites to the internal and external crises of the Ottoman polity. The focus is on the modernizing attempts at reform, the efforts to centralize the empire and curb the centrifugal tendencies of powerful provincial landlords (*ayans*), and adapt the state institutions to the new challenges coming from the west. Often this interpretation takes the shape of a linear teleological progression from the earliest hesitant Europeanizing endeavors in the eighteenth century, through the broad reform program and especially the constitutional movement of the nineteenth century, to the Young Turk Revolution (1908), and finally to the radical reforms of Kemal Atatürk (1881–1938) after 1923. This approach focuses mostly on the imperial center: the centralizing attempts of the sultans, the formation of a modern state bureaucracy, the elaboration of new institutions. It usually gives Balkan nationalisms and other minority movements short shrift, explaining them as mechanical exports of a western ideology or a combination between a handful of separatists buttressed by Great Power manipulation and incitement.

Another approach focuses on nationalism as the dominant ideology and practice that transformed the map of Europe and resulted in the disintegration of all European empires. As an ideology whose central goal and successful outcome was the creation of a series of independent nation-states, Balkan and Arab nationalisms are an organic element of Ottoman history. This approach is preferred in the historiographies of the secession states with their almost exclusive focus on the emergence, maturation, and victory of national-liberation struggles, a grand narrative in which the reform movement figures only as background, and the tribulations of the Eastern Question as side-effects that favored or hampered the ongoing progression of the national movements. Skewed as this approach may be, it is no less legitimate than the other two, which tend to underestimate the internal roots and power of nationalism and its effect on the reform movement.

Only by taking account of the complex dialectical interaction of all three processes can a balanced portrait of Ottoman developments in the long nineteenth century begin to appear. Several times during this period the three processes are intertwined in such a way that they produced a dramatic cumulative effect. This article attempts to link all three, and show how profoundly interrelated they all are. Still, it focuses primarily on the course and interplay between the westernizing reform movement and nationalism. The international aspect, which was instrumental for and intimately linked with the other two, will be duly invoked, but it is treated in more detail in a separate entry on the Eastern Question.

A caveat is in order about the geographical coverage of the article. The emphasis falls on developments in the European possessions of the empire (the Balkans), not only because this is an encyclopedia of Europe. With the exception of the Egyptian crises, events in the Near or Middle East became central and involved the European powers directly only at the beginning of the twentieth century, especially with the rise of Arab nationalism and the final disintegration of the empire during the First World War, the expansion of the British and French colonial empires, and the introduction of the mandate system. Otherwise, the Eastern Question of the nineteenth century was synonymous with the process of secession of the Balkan nations from the Ottoman Empire. The very name *Eastern Question* was born at the time of the Greek war for independence in the 1820s.

The Balkans had always been the demographic and economic center of the empire. In the middle of the nineteenth century, they comprised half of the Ottoman population (totaling around twenty-five million), and their population density was twice that of Anatolia, six times that of Iraq and Syria, and ten times that of the Arabian peninsula. Even on the eve of the Young Turk revolution, when the Ottomans were left with very few European possessions, the Balkan population still made up a good quarter of the total. In the nineteenth century, the Balkans continued to be the empire's agricultural, commercial, and manufacturing center, where the first factories and railroads made their appearance.

THE REFORMS OF SELIM III AND THE SERBIAN UPRISINGS

The end of the eighteenth century saw the first confluence between the three processes. The Ottoman retreat from Central Europe after the Treaty of Karlowitz (1699) dramatically deepened after the Russo-Turkish War (1768–1774), the loss of the Crimea in southern Ukraine to Russia in 1783, and thus Ottoman monopoly over the Black Sea. This reintroduced the necessity for reforms, which had been put on hold for the several peaceful decades (1739–1768). Pre-eighteenth-century reforms aimed at resuscitating the institutions of the Golden Age of the fifteenth and sixteenth centuries. The first serious rethinking of the empire's position in an international context, and a readiness to emulate foreign ways, came at the beginning of the eighteenth century. The military factor was decisive in shaping an awareness of the western challenge, and eighteenth-century reforms affected mostly the military sphere, although this period saw also the introduction of the printing press and borrowings in elite culture and fashion. The inspiration for reforms came mostly from French sources and models. At the same time, the innovations produced a strong reaction of vested conservative interests.

During the reign of Sultan Selim III (r. 1789–1807), eighteenth-century reforms reached their culmination and most sustained effort. For the first time, regular and permanent Ottoman embassies in the major European capitals were established (1792). The Russian annexation of the Crimea (1783), which gave Russia an outlet to the Black Sea, and another war with Austria and Russia (1787) provided the impetus for military reform. Selim opened military schools and set up a new infantry, the famous *nizam-i cedid* (new order), with European-style uniforms, imported rifles, and French instructors. By 1807 it numbered twenty-five thousand and was successful against Napoleon at the battle of Acre (1799). The janissary corps, the ominous infantry that had been the backbone of Ottoman success in the fifteenth and sixteenth centuries but which, by the eighteenth century, had become militarily obsolete and a major financial burden, viewed the *nizam-i cedid* as such a threat, however, that Selim was forced to disband it. He was still deposed in 1807 and killed in 1808.

Selim's reforms coincided with the outbreak of the first national rebellion in the Balkans. The First Serbian Uprising (1804), which started as a spontaneous revolt against the misrule of the *dahis* (local janissaries opposed to Selim III), was led by the charismatic Karadjordje Petrović (1760s?–1817). The insurrection received ardent support from Serb merchants living in the Habsburg empire and attracted volunteers among the different Orthodox Balkan communities. In 1805, the Sublime Porte (or Porte, the name given to the Ottoman government) proclaimed jihad (holy war) against the Serbian insurgents. The Serbian revolt is a good illustration of the complex entanglement of Balkan events in international affairs. It coincided not only with a Russo-Turkish war (1806–1812), but also with the intricate political relationships in the Napoleonic era. Trying to benefit from Great Power rivalries, Karageorge maneuvered between Paris, Vienna, and St. Petersburg. His decision to take on Russia was instrumental in transforming the initial demands for autonomy to full independence. Serbia had overthrown Ottoman control by 1807, but the deteriorating relations with Napoleon forced the Russians to conclude a peace treaty with the Ottomans, and the Porte launched a huge counteroffensive in 1813. The uprising was put down with such cruelty and vengeance that the population soon rose in a second revolt, under the leadership of Miloš Obrenović (1780–1860). While he deftly exploited the international situation after Napoleon's defeat, Miloš was careful not to pressure the Porte with unrealistic demands. His tactics paid off well: in 1830 Serbia was recognized as an autonomous hereditary principality. The subsequent decades saw the very slow transformation of the traditional system of local self-governing communities into a centralized bureaucratic state. In the economic sphere, the poor and egalitarian frontier society of Serbia began making modest strides in modernization only in the last decades of the nineteenth century, after it received full independence by the Treaty of Berlin (1878).

BALKAN ENLIGHTENMENT AND THE GREEK WAR FOR INDEPENDENCE

The Serbian revolt of 1804, unlike its Greek counterpart of 1821, has often been dismissed as a spontaneous rising in a backward agrarian region without

Galata Bridge, Istanbul, c. 1890. Completed in 1875, this pontoon bridge spanned the Golden Horn to unite newer sections of the growing metropolis with central Istanbul, where the principal govenmental and religious institutions were located. Central Istanbul is visible here in the background; the large building seen at the terminus of the bridge is the renowned Blue Mosque. ©CORBIS

a long-term national program and careful organizational preparation. Confining the Serbian revolt exclusively to the framework of the Belgrade district, however, consciously misses the point that both the Balkan Enlightenment as well as the national idea had made important strides among the Serbian elites of the adjacent Habsburg provinces who were in immediate and organic contact with their co-nationals in the Ottoman realm. What deserves stressing, however, is the combination between strong social discontent and fermenting national consciousness, even when the two were not always represented by the same social strata.

The eighteenth century saw the emergence and consolidation of an indigenous Balkan entrepreneurial merchant class. This group was made up almost exclusively of non-Muslims, for whom the military and the state bureaucracy were closed, and who were preferred partners in the expanding European trade. The "conquering Balkan Orthodox merchant" who came to dominate the imperial trade included the most diverse ethnic elements—Serbs, Vlachs, Bulgarians—but Greeks dominated, so much so that by the second half of the eighteenth century (and until the first decades of the nineteenth) Greek had become the lingua franca of Balkan commerce and, to a great extent, of education and cultural production in general. The growing wealth of this entrepreneurial class, accompanied by increased self-esteem, made the arbitrariness and lack of security of property and life in the Ottoman Empire particularly intolerable.

These merchants—well traveled, cognizant of foreign habits and manners, speaking and reading several languages—engaged or fostered others to engage in literary and educational pursuits. They provided the material support for schools, libraries, and numerous publications, and supported the secularization of school curricula. Thus (barring exceptions), one can speak of the commercial basis of the Balkan Enlightenment, as well as its strong diasporic character. In terms of expression, there was a growing interest in history, an influence coming from both the Enlightenment obsession with the classical past as well as from romanticism. Historicism, a common feature of the Balkan Enlightenment, became also one of the building blocks of the separate Balkan nationalisms.

The event that attracted the greatest contemporary attention and gave birth to the notion of the Eastern Question was the Greek War for Independence (1821–1828). Ideologically and politically, it was prepared by the whole current of ideas and events of the previous half-century: the spread of the Enlightenment and the ideas of the French revolution; the example of the Serbian uprising; the rise and strength of philhellenism in Europe. Of particular importance was the ideology of figures like Rigas Velestinlis (also known as Rigas Pheraios, 1757–1798) and Adamántios Koraïs (1748–1833). The "Society of Friends," founded in 1814 in Odessa, the center of a powerful Greek commercial diasporic community, organized the revolt. It was shaped on Masonic principles, and worked to achieve a broad Balkan Christian network with the aim of creating a Christian pan-Balkan state.

The Greek uprising came at a most inopportune moment of the international conjuncture. The principles of the Holy Alliance, announced at the Congress of Vienna (1814–1815), were strictly observed by the Great Powers and, despite pro-Christian sympathies, all denounced the Greeks as illegitimate rebels against a legal monarch. At the same time, hundreds of philhellenic volunteers from all over Europe flocked to Greece, joining the rebellious armies that at first gained considerable victories. Quite remarkable was the steady number of volunteers from other Balkan ethnic groups who fought actively on the side of the Greeks: the Bulgarians alone numbered over fourteen thousand.

In subsequent years, however, the Greek insurgents displayed an enormous degree of factionalism, and Mahmud II (1785–1839) managed to enlist the military support of Egypt. This would have provided the fatal blow against the insurgents, were it not for the intervention of Russia, Britain, and France. Following Russia's victorious war against the Ottomans (1828–1829), the London Protocol of 1830 sanctioned the formal secession of the first independent nation-state carved out of the Ottoman Empire. Created as a poor rump state, with roughly a quarter of the ethnic Greeks, in the next decades independent Greece developed as a protectorate of Russia, Britain, and France, making slow economic and social progress, and dominated by powerful irredentist feelings focused on recovering the territories inhabited by Greeks and still under foreign Ottoman rule. Its national doctrine, based on the assumption of the unbroken community of modern Greece with its classical and medieval past, and the redemption of territories inhabited by Greeks, aimed at the resurrection of the Byzantine Empire with Constantinople as its capital. It reaped slow but steady success toward the end of the century, reached its culmination during the Balkan wars, and found its fiasco with the Asia Minor invasion in the Greco-Turkish War (1919–1922).

THE REFORMS OF MAHMUD II AND THE TANZIMAT

Well into the Greek war of independence, the Ottoman Empire experienced what came to be known as the Auspicious Event: the destruction of the janissary corps by Sultan Mahmud II in 1826. Mahmud II had barely survived the conservative coup of 1808 and, while sharing his cousin Selim III's reformist views, he patiently waited for eighteen years, in the meantime building alliances and securing loyalties. The janissary corps had long lost its military significance, and its refusal to fight or poor performance against the Russians (1806–1812) and the Greek rebels in the 1820s alienated their support to the point where Mahmud II succeeded in annihilating them once and for all. The road was open for more sustained changes and, as usual, military reform was at the center. A new army along European lines was constructed, this time with Prussian instructors; a territorial militia emulating the Prussian was set up. Increased attention was devoted to education, both for military and civilian purposes. The changes in the central administration saw the gradual formation of ministries of the western type. A new stratum of bureaucrats was recruited and trained in western ways and languages (primarily French). A new postal system was set up; the first Ottoman newspaper appeared; European clothes were introduced. Mahmud II's reform reached also into the legal and agricultural systems. Most importantly, Mahmud II succeeded largely in his greatest goal: to centralize the empire by curbing the local power of the *ayans*, guilds, religious leaders, and tribes.

The big challenge came from Egypt. After Napoleon's failed invasion (1798–1799), Mehmet Ali (r. 1805–1848), an Ottoman officer of Albanian descent, became Egypt's virtual ruler. In 1824 he came to the rescue of Mahmud II against the Greeks, who were saved from destruction only by the intervention of the three Great Powers: Russia, France, and Great Britain. Muhammad Ali had implemented Europeanizing reforms with French help and built a strong army. Having most of the Arab provinces under his control, twice during his reign he challenged Mahmud II's power (1832–1833 and 1838–1839). Only Great Power involvement, seeking to keep the status quo, stripped Mehmet Ali of his gains. In the following decades Egypt moved further away from Ottoman control: a nominal possession after British occupation in 1882, Egypt was finally lost in 1914, to become a British colony.

At the height of the second Egyptian crisis, Mahmud II died and was succeeded by Abdülmecid I (r. 1839–1861). Determined to continue his father's work, alarmed by the military situation, and seeking to impress the western powers, the new sultan staked on the reformists within the bureaucracy, first and foremost Mustafa Reşid Pasha (1800–1858), and later his followers Ali Pasha (1815–1871) and Fuad Pasha (1815–1858). A proclamation of principles, the *Hatt-i Şerif of Gülhane* (1839), was promulgated, guaranteeing security of life, honor, and property, regular taxation and army recruits, and, most importantly, equality of all religions before the law. The latter was a radical breach with the ancient Islamic tradition, and proved extremely controversial. While it gave impetus to the non-Muslim communities, it strengthened the conservative Islamic opposition. The subsequent period, known as the *Tanzimat* (Reorganization, 1839–1871), continued and deepened the transformation begun in the previous years. It expanded significantly the area of state activity from its usual focus on the military and finance, into education, public works, law, administration, diplomacy, and, less successfully, the economy. It also marked the ascendancy of the bureaucracy and its emancipation from the sultan's control. During the Crimean War (1853–1856), at a time when Ottoman military weakness was exposed again, and in an attempt to mollify the Great Powers, the Porte reaffirmed its commitment to reform with the proclamation the *Hatt-i Humayun* (1856), which reiterated and developed the stance of the 1839 edict.

The Tanzimat has left a legacy of controversial assessment. Some saw it as too drastic, others as palliative and insufficient. Often, unfairly, it was accused of lack of genuine commitment, of using reforms simply to placate the Great Powers. Part of this came from the chronological coincidence between moments of international or domestic crises and reform spurs. This should be read rather as a tribute to the tactics of the reformists, who had to overcome strong opposition, and usually were able to gain the upper hand at such moments. Ultimately, it demonstrates the intimate interrelationship between all above-mentioned processes. By the 1860s, a new generation of reform-minded bureaucrats, with new perceptions of government, progress, and nation, had appeared. Impatient with the growing (especially financial) dependence on European powers, and with the autocratic tendencies of the later Tanzimat reformers, this new generation of reformers advocated democratic, constitutional ideas. They also harbored the utopia of creating a common Ottoman consciousness, something that disregarded the already advanced processes of nationalism. Known under the name of Young Ottomans, these reformers engaged passionately in literary activities, often in European exile. Their movement coincided with the intensification of another national cause in the Balkans, the Bulgarian.

THE BULGARIAN NATIONAL MOVEMENT AND THE MILLET SYSTEM

Nationalisms in the Balkans are coterminous with the gradual disintegration of two imperial formations: on the one hand, the Ottoman state; on the other hand, the Orthodox community, institutionally encompassed in the *Rum millet* (the Roman or Greek nation, that is, the Orthodox Christians conquered by Islam). It is the Bulgarian case that paradigmatically illustrates this double process. The *millet* system (i.e., the division of the population into self-governing confessional bodies beyond the Muslim community) by the middle of the nineteenth century encompassed the Jews, the Armenians or Monophysites, the Catholics, the Protestants, and the largest of them all, the Greek-Orthodox (*Rum*) community. As a largely Orthodox people, the Bulgarians belonged to the *Rum millet.* Although there had been patriotic stirrings from the second half of the eighteenth century, a sustained movement for educational and religious emancipation began in the 1820s. Until the Bulgarians began to organize their own secondary school system, the existing Greek establishments fulfilled the need for secular education among their own commercial elites. Between 1830 and 1870, a network of close to two thousand Bulgarian schools appeared, offering free education and entirely supported by the local communities. Guilds and town councils financed schools and other cultural institutions, and provided scholarships for training of teachers and students abroad. This was accompanied by the feverish publishing of textbooks, reference books, translations, and original literary works, as well as the launching of a lively periodic press. There is no doubt that this cultural revival, as well as the underlying economic progress, was directly stimulated by the favorable conditions introduced by the Tanzimat reforms.

During the 1860s and 1870s, the church struggle came to a head. It did not spring from any kind of doctrinal issues, but was essentially a political movement for a separate church. It was triggered by protests in the 1820s against the venality of the Greek clergy, in support of appointing Bulgarian high priests, and in support of the use of Bulgarian in sermons, but there were no demands for a separate church until the middle of the nineteenth century. In 1860 the Bulgarians in Constantinople virtually declared their ecclesiastical independence, and in the next decade they seceded unilaterally from the Ecumenical Patriarchate of Constantinople. This secession was not immediately recognized. The Greek Patriarchate objected strongly to losing a sizeable number of its flock after it had effectively lost the Greeks of independent Greece. The Russians, on whom Bulgarian hopes had been pinned, were averse to seeing a blow to Orthodox unity. Finally, the Porte enjoyed the opportunity to manipulate a seething dispute between two of its important communities. The conflict was finally resolved in 1870 with a sultan's *firman* (decree), which officially recognized the Bulgarian church and established a separate Bulgarian *millet.* This was an unprecedented move, effectively changing the rationale of the *millet* system, which had been conceived as the system of institutionalizing and managing religious, not ethnolinguistic groups. The Bulgarian church was instituted as an exarchate, and was promptly excommunicated by the Greek Patriarch. Of the seventy-four Orthodox dioceses, twenty-five immediately joined the exarchate, eight were divided, and, most importantly, the rest could be transferred to either jurisdiction with a vote of the flock. This started a passionate struggle exacerbating the already much deteriorated relations between Greeks and Bulgarians. In all fairness, it can be concluded that the rise of Bulgarian nationalism entailed first the process of differentiation within the Orthodox commonwealth.

One of the reasons the Porte finally supported Bulgarian church independence in 1870 after having disregarded their numerous petitions for years, if not for decades, was that in the meantime the Bulgarian political movement, which had gained momentum in the 1860s, was becoming swiftly radicalized. With the activities of Georgi Rakovski (1821–1867), Liuben Karavelov (1834–1879), Vasil Levski (1837–1873), and Khristo Botev (1848–1876), the independence movement received serious impetus and began the preparations for a national revolution.

THE EASTERN CRISIS (1875–1878) AND OTTOMAN CONSTITUTIONALISM

In the mid-1870s, the Eastern Question acquired particular relevance and reached a new stage. Not only did it create or reaffirm de facto independent Balkan states, but it also marked a new level of Great Power involvement. In 1875, the situation turned explosive when the Christian peasants in Bosnia-Herzegovina rebelled against their Muslim

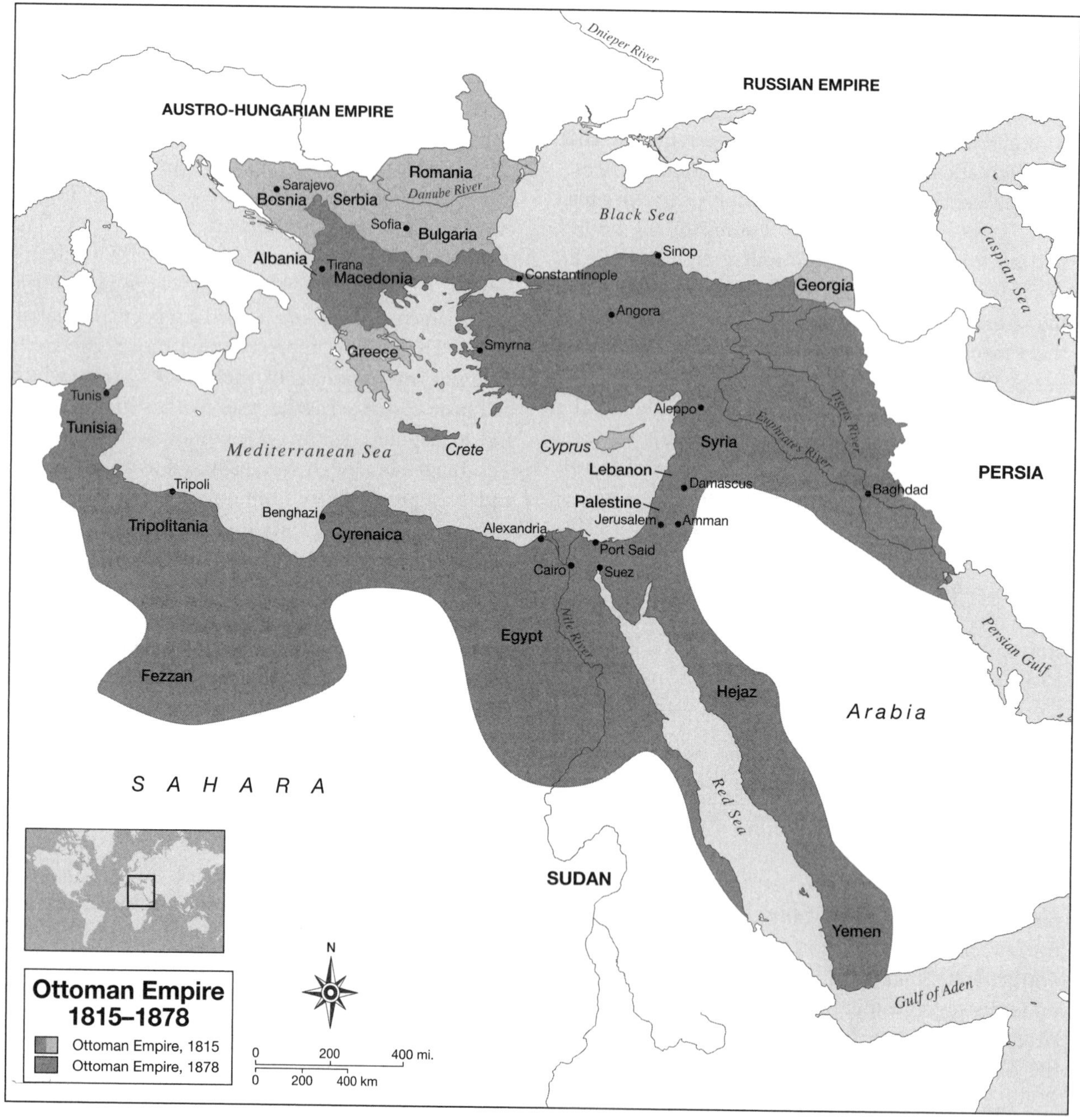

lords. While the uprising was characterized by the explosion of a social question, it was also informed to some extent by religious opposition and awareness of pan-Serb and pan-Slav national programs. It was soon followed by a more mature political revolt in Bulgaria, prepared by revolutionaries with the express purpose of Bulgarian independence. While the April Uprising of 1876 proved abortive and was crushed mercilessly, its bloody demise caused a wave of public opinion in Europe favorable to the Bulgarian cause.

It is in these circumstances that one can observe the playing out of the third symbiotic process, the Ottoman constitutional movement. In December 1876, a conference of ambassadors met in Constantinople to discuss the Eastern Crisis and propose remedies, mostly by creating autonomous districts. In a move to counter the dictate of the Great Powers, the Porte responded by promulgating the first Ottoman constitution. It was obviously motivated by Great Power pressure to placate the national movements, but also by the

Turkey's first parliament. Sultan Abdul-Hamid II sought to mollify European critics by establishing a parliament. The first meeting, held in 1876, is depicted in this contemporary engraving. © BETTMANN/CORBIS

modernizing faction, which in the constant struggles within the Ottoman elites had been pushed to the side and now used this event as an opportune moment to act. The constitution was largely the work of Midhat Pasha (1822–1883), a prominent reformer who had been governor in Bulgaria and Iraq, intermittently occupying other high positions, and who became the leader of the Young Ottoman movement. The Ottoman constitution of 1876 was limited and the first parliament short-lived. Abdul-Hamid II (r. 1876–1909) dissolved it in a year, but it became the rallying cry and program of generations of reformers to come.

The display of reform as a deterrent to European pressure also played its role. Sensing Britain's reluctance to press the Porte further, Abdul-Hamid II took an intransigent position toward the proposals of the ambassador's conference, which precipitated Russia's declaration of war (1877–1878). Russian troops eventually reached the outskirts of Constantinople and imposed the Treaty of San Stefano (March 1878). It gave full independence to Serbia, Montenegro, and Romania, which had unified the autonomous principalities of Wallachia and Moldavia in 1859. Its chief and most controversial provision was the creation of a large Bulgarian state, following the frontiers of the Bulgarian exarchate, and therefore perceived by the Bulgarians as the true and just recreation of their nation-state. This proved unacceptable to the other Great Powers, who feared that it would unduly strengthen Russia's strategic advance toward Constantinople and the straits. As a consequence, the Congress of Berlin (June–July 1878), while reaffirming Serbian, Montenegrin, and Romanian independence, divided Bulgaria in three parts, and incited future Bulgarian irredentist feelings aimed at redeeming the territories under foreign rule. The first stage of this struggle was completed when the autonomous Bulgarian Principality was unified with Eastern Rumelia (1885). Macedonia, on the other hand, remained the open wound of the Bulgarian national program. The Treaty of Berlin also endorsed the occupation of Bosnia-Herzegovina by the Habsburgs, the culmination of a trend from the end of the seventeenth century when the Ottomans, having reached Vienna, began their gradual retreat and the Habsburgs expanded eastward at their expense. The treaty also authorized the occupation of Cyprus by the British, marking the direct involvement of this power in the spoils of the empire.

The Eastern Crisis of the 1870s represents a milestone in Balkan and European history. For Europe, it marked the disintegration of the Three Emperors League of Germany, Austria-Hungary, and Russia, and the intensification of Austrian-Russian rivalry in the Balkans that had developed in the aftermath of the Crimean War. It marked the beginnings of a reversal in British policy, which heretofore had been the staunchest supporter of Ottoman integrity, and the beginnings of a German predominance in the empire. It also set the tone for the intensification of Balkan national conflicts, which culminated in the Balkan Wars.

THE RISE OF ALBANIAN AND TURKISH NATIONALISM

The three decades of Abdul-Hamid II's autocratic rule, the empire's growing economic dependence on Europe, and the continuing secessionism of its minorities triggered strong opposition among young army officers and educated Turks, especially students in the military and medical schools. In 1889, a clandestine organization, the future Committee of Union and Progress (CUP), was formed. Also known as the Young Turks, its members were by no means ideologically unified: there was a strong cleavage between Turkish nationalism (led by Ahmed Riza [1858–1930]) and Ottoman liberalism (led by Prince Sabaheddin [1877–1948]), as well as between the Paris exiles and the locally based secret revolutionary cells. This cleavage explains, on the one hand, the strong support that the CUP received at first among some minority groups—Jews, Armenians, Albanians, Kurds, Greeks, and other Christians—and their subsequent alienation when faced with the Turkifying drive of the Young Turks. They were all unified, however, in their drive to restore the constitution.

The last two decades of the nineteenth century witnessed the rise of two Muslim nationalisms: Turkish and Albanian. Coalescing somewhat later than the Christian nationalisms of the empire, they were undoubtedly reactive and preservationist and, at the same time, emulated the national movements of the Christian minorities in many ways. By the turn of the century, three ideological trends in public life served as poles of cohesion among Muslim Turks: traditional Islam, Ottomanism, and, increasingly, Turkish nationalism, whose major exponent was the sociologist Mehmet Ziya Gökalp (c. 1875–1924), a member of the CUP. While also focused on the preservation of the empire's territorial integrity, Turkish nationalism was premised on an ethnolinguistic identity, promulgating the hegemony of the Turkish element within the empire and stressing the links to other Central Asian Turkish-speaking peoples (unlike Ottomanism, which strived to create a type of Ottoman citizenship regardless of ethnic and linguistic distinctions).

Albanian nationalism was the only Balkan nationalism without a secessionist program, because its predominantly Muslim population saw its best protection under the umbrella of the retreating Sublime Porte. The Albanian cultural revival began in the 1860s among its Italian diaspora, inspired by the ideas of the Italian movement for unification, the Risorgimento. Politically, the Albanian Prizren League (1878) opposed any attempt to annex Albanian-populated territories by the newly independent Balkan Christian states and aimed at achieving cultural autonomy within the Ottoman Empire. At first tolerated and even encouraged by the Ottomans, the League made great strides in establishing a network of schools and publishing numerous books and newspapers. By 1886, however, the Porte cracked down and the use of Albanian was banned, triggering a wave of emigration. In the following decades, the activities of the Albanian diaspora intensified. At the same time, part of the remaining Albanian elites became outposts of extreme conservatism, supporting the counterrevolution against the westernizing efforts of the Young Turks, whereas others were radicalized over the Young Turks' nationalist policies.

It was around the Balkan wars that events in Albania came to a head. With the immediate danger of partition stemming from the plans of the victorious Balkan alliance, the Albanians in 1912 were forced to give up their traditional strategy of autonomy and opt for independence. More importantly, international circumstances were favorable: Albanian independence was strongly advocated by both Italy and Austria-Hungary, to prevent Serbian expansion to the Adriatic. With the Treaty of London (1913), Albania was recognized as an independent nation-state under a six-power guarantee.

FROM THE YOUNG TURK REVOLUTION TO WORLD WAR I

The decade leading to the Great War was punctuated by the Young Turk Revolution (1908) and the Balkan wars (1912–1913). The unresolved minority question in Macedonia, the activities of Greek and Bulgarian guerrillas, and especially the drastic repression of the Ilinden revolt (1903) precipitated Great Power pressure to resolve the Macedonian crisis. CUP officers argued that only a return to constitutional government could offset European intervention. By 1906 revolutionary cells had spread among serving officers in field formations, prominent among them Mustafa Kemal, the future Atatürk. These patriotic Muslim Turks were calling for the efficient defense of the empire, which could be achieved only by toppling the incompetent government. Japan's triumph over Russia (1908) was seen not only as a victory of an Oriental power against a European one, but also as the defeat of an autocrat by a constitutional regime. In July 1908, a genuine revolutionary situation forced Abdul-Hamid II to restore the constitution, and after the unsuccessful attempt at counterrevolution in 1909, he was deposed in favor of Mehmet V (r. 1909–1918). By that time, the nationalist faction among the Young Turks had taken the upper hand. It embraced repressive and centralizing policies and imposed a program of Turkification not only upon the non-Muslims, but tried to force the Turkish language upon Arabs, Albanians, and other non-Turkish Muslims. From 1913, after it had crushed all internal opposition, the Young Turks ruled through the Triumvirate of Cemal, Enver, and Talat.

The Young Turks could not stop the disintegration of the empire. In 1908 Austria-Hungary annexed Bosnia-Herzegovina, Bulgaria proclaimed full independence, and Crete, although unsuccessfully, declared union with Greece. In 1911 Tripolitania was lost to Italy. Most devastating were the Balkan wars (1912–1913), both politically and demographically, resulting in the emigration of considerable Muslim masses into Anatolia. In 1912 Serbia, Bulgaria, Greece, and Montenegro created a common front with the purpose of expelling the Ottoman Empire from its last European possessions. In this they largely succeeded, and all of Ottoman Europe, with the exception of Constantinople and its immediate hinterland, was lost. Only the Second Balkan War between the allies over their spoils allowed the Ottomans to retrieve Eastern Thrace, and the final borders coincide with the early twenty-first century's Turkish frontiers in Europe. The road to World War I and the final demise of the empire in the Middle East was set.

See also **Albania; Balkan Wars; Congress of Vienna; Crimean War; Eastern Question; Greece; Millet System; Montenegro.**

BIBLIOGRAPHY

Braude, Benjamin, and Bernard Lewis, eds. *Christians and Jews in the Ottoman Empire: The Functioning of a Plural Society,* 2 vols. New York, 1982.

Brown, L. Carl, ed. *Imperial Legacy: The Ottoman Imprint on the Balkans and the Middle East.* New York, 1996.

Clogg, Richard, ed. *Balkan Society in the Age of Greek Independence.* London, 1981.

Dakin, Douglas. *The Unification of Greece 1770–1923.* London, 1972.

Davison, Roderic. *Essays in Ottoman and Turkish History, 1774–1923: The Impact of the West.* Austin, Tex., 1990.

Deringil, Selim. *The Well-Protected Domains: Ideology and the Legitimation of Power in the Ottoman Empire, 1876–1909.* London, 1998.

Findley, Carter V. *Bureaucratic Reform in the Ottoman Empire: The Sublime Porte, 1789–1922.* Princeton, N.J., 1980.

Inalcik, Halil, and Donald Quataert, eds. *An Economic and Social History of the Ottoman Empire, 1300–1914.* Cambridge, U.K., 1994.

Jelavich, Charles and Barbara. *The Establishment of the Balkan National States, 1804–1920.* Seattle, 1977.

Karpat, Kemal. *Ottoman Population, 1830–1914: Demographic and Social Characteristics.* Madison, Wis., 1985.

Kitromilides, Paschalis. *Enlightenment, Nationalism, Orthodoxy: Studies in the Culture and Political Thought of South-eastern Europe*. Hampshire, U.K., 1994.

Lewis, Bernard. *The Emergence of Modern Turkey*. Oxford, U.K., 1961.

Mardin, Serif. *The Genesis of Young Ottoman Thought*. Princeton, N.J., 1962.

Pamuk, Sevket. *The Ottoman Empire and World Capitalism*. Cambridge, U.K., 1987.

Perry, Duncan. *The Politics of Terror: The Macedonian Liberation Movements, 1893–1903*. Durham, N.C., 1988.

Quataert, Donald. *The Ottoman Empire, 1700–1922*. New York, 2000.

Shaw, Stanford. *Between Old and New: The Ottoman Empire under Sultan Selim III, 1789–1807*. Cambridge, Mass., 1971.

Skendi, Stavro. *The Albanian National Awakening 1878–1912*. Princeton, N.J., 1967.

Stoianovich, Traian. "The Conquering Balkan Orthodox Merchant." *Journal of Economic History* 20, 1960, 234–313.

Todorov, Nikolai. *The Balkan City, 1400–1900*. Seattle, Wash., 1983.

Tunçay, Mete, and Erik Jan Zürcher, eds. *Socialism and Nationalism in the Ottoman Empire, 1876–1923*. London, 1994.

Maria Todorova

OWEN, ROBERT (1771–1858), English socialist.

The founder of British socialism, Robert Owen was born on 14 May 1771 at Newtown, Montgomeryshire, Wales. He was the son of Robert Owen (1741–1804), a sadler, ironmonger, and local postmaster, and the former Anne Williams (c. 1735–1803), a farmer's daughter. Apprenticed in 1781 to a Stamford cloth merchant, James McGuffog, Owen joined a similar London retail firm three years later. Moving to Manchester, he borrowed one hundred pounds from his brother William and commenced cotton-spinning. In 1792 he became manager of the largest local cotton mill, owned by Peter Drinkwater, and in 1800 assumed the management of the New Lanark mills on the River Clyde south of Glasgow, having first married the owner's daughter Caroline the previous year.

At New Lanark, Owen proved astonishingly successful both at refining the cotton-spinning process and improving the lot of the labor force. His profits, some 40 percent of about 12 percent return on capital per annum, brought a fortune, while his wish to experiment socially on the 1,800-strong workforce brought an increasing reputation as a reformer. Owen reduced working hours from eleven and three quarters to ten and three quarters per day, made cheaper and better goods available at the company shop, introduced infant education in the "Institute for the Formation of Character," opened in 1816, and did much to improve life in the workers' quarters. Seeking to widen the scope of his ambitions, he published *A New View of Society; or, Essays on the Principle of the Formation of the Human Character* (1813–1814), which proposed a system of national education to reduce idleness, poverty, and crime among the "lower orders," and urged the discouragement of "gin shops and pot houses" and state lottery and gambling, as well as penal reform, an end to the monopolistic position of the Church of England, and the collection of statistics on the value and demand for labor throughout the country.

Such proposals, particularly for an extension of factory reforms, fell on deaf ears, however. In the years 1815 to 1817 Owen then turned to the wider question, in the midst of a postwar depression, of solving the rapidly burgeoning problem of poverty. He now proposed, thus, to relocate the urban poor into "villages of union" motivated by a "mutual and combined interest," in the countryside, where employment would include both manufacturing and agriculture, and the proceeds would be shared in common. Increasingly hostile to the "individual system" of "buying cheap and selling dear," which he first derided at length in the *Report to the County of Lanark* (1820), Owen proposed instead the "social system" of enhanced cooperation and community life. This, by the mid-1820s, gradually came to be called "socialism" for short. Having in *Observations on the Effects of the Manufacturing System* (1815) described industrialization as likely to cause immense suffering to the working classes, Owen now sought a practical experiment to prove the worth of his principles. He acquired a ready-made community in the United States, constructed in Indiana by a German Protestant sect, the Rappites. Owen renamed it New Harmony and moved

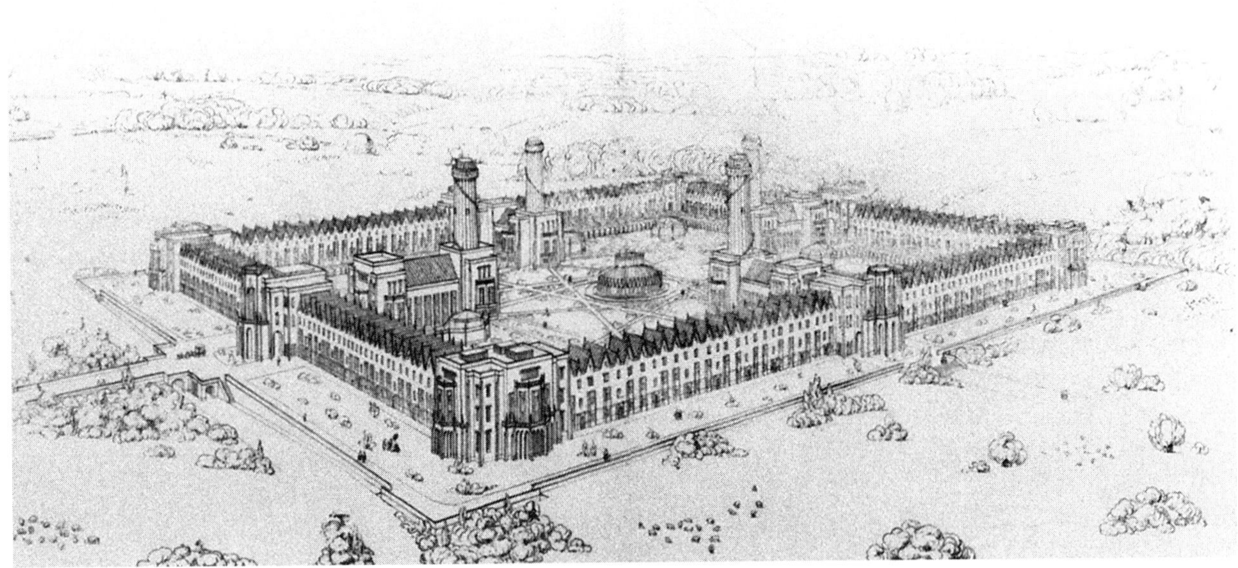

Plan for the layout of New Harmony, Indiana, c. 1825. The Utopian community was designed by architect Stedman Whitwell based on the principles espoused by Robert Owen. ©CORBIS

there in 1824. Unfortunately, insufficient attention was paid to the selection of members, and Owen tired quickly of having so many quarrelsome associates. By 1828 the community had collapsed.

Returning to Britain, Owen became briefly involved in the early 1830s in an effort to construct "exchange bazaars" in London and Birmingham, where artisans were to trade goods on the basis of labor and material costs alone, eliminating the profit of retail middlemen. In 1833 and 1834, he was also briefly involved with an effort to construct a single union of trades, the Grand National Consolidated Trades Union.

The last great phase of Owen's efforts came in the period from 1835 to 1844, when he set about publishing his mature program (*The Book of the New Moral World,* 7 parts, 1836–1844), and established a large-scale organization, with some fifty branches, to raise funds for a new community. Land was acquired at Tytherly in Hampshire, and an elaborate (and unduly expensive) central edifice constructed. But the soil was poor, and too little was invested in agriculture to ensure an adequate return. After the community failed, Owen turned to spiritualism, but was increasingly ignored in the last decade of his life.

Owen's reputation is often bifurcated into a successful capitalist phase at New Lanark and a failed socialist career thereafter. Though the writings of John Gray (1799–1883), William Thompson (1775–1833), and others were more incisive, his impact on popularizing the socialist ideal in Britain and the United States is undisputed and was extended to later generations by writers such as Fabian Frank Podmore (1856–1910), his most important biographer.

See also **Fourier, Charles; Socialism; Utopian Socialism.**

BIBLIOGRAPHY

Primary Source

Owen, Robert. *Selected Works of Robert Owen.* Edited by Gregory Claeys. 4 vols. London, 1993.

Secondary Sources

Claeys, Gregory. *Machinery, Money and the Millennium: From Moral Economy to Socialism, 1815–1860.* Princeton, N.J., 1987.

———. *Citizens and Saints: Politics and Anti-Politics in Early British Socialism.* Cambridge, U.K., 1989.

Harrison, John Fletcher Clews. *Quest for the New Moral World: Robert Owen and the Owenities in Britain and America.* New York, 1969.

Podmore, Frank. *Robert Owen: A Biography.* 2 vols. London, 1906.

GREGORY CLAEYS

30°W
20°W
10°W
0°
10°E
60°N
50°N
40°N
ICELAND
Norwegian Sea
Faroe Islands (Denmark)
Shetland Islands
Orkney Islands
NORWAY
Christiania
North Sea
Firth of Forth
Edinburgh
DENMARK
Copenhagen
Bann
Shannon
Dublin
Isle of Man
UNITED KINGDOM
Trent
Severn
Bristol
Thames
London
Amsterdam
NETHERLANDS
GERMANY
Elbe
BELGIUM
Brussels
Cologne
Rhine
Weser
Saale
Frankfurt
Main
LUXEMBOURG
Aisne
Seine
Paris
Meuse
Neckar
Danube
Munich
ATLANTIC OCEAN
Loire
FRANCE
SWITZERLAND
ALPS
Lyon
Milan
Venice
Turin
Po
Rhône
Garonne
Genoa
Arno
Tiber
Appennines
Pyrenees
ANDORRA
Marseille
Douro
Ebro
PORTUGAL
Madrid
Tagus
SPAIN
Lisbon
Barcelona
Corsica (France)
ITALY
Rome
Naples
Balearic Islands (Spain)
Minorca
Majorca
Iviza
Sardinia (Italy)
Seville
Mediterranean Sea
Sicily
Spanish Morocco
ALGERIA
MOROCCO
TUNISIA
Malta